DRAMA
CRITICISM

Guide to Gale Literary Criticism Series

For criticism on	Consult these Gale series
Authors now living or who died after December 31, 1999	*CONTEMPORARY LITERARY CRITICISM (CLC)*
Authors who died between 1900 and 1999	*TWENTIETH-CENTURY LITERARY CRITICISM (TCLC)*
Authors who died between 1800 and 1899	*NINETEENTH-CENTURY LITERATURE CRITICISM (NCLC)*
Authors who died between 1400 and 1799	*LITERATURE CRITICISM FROM 1400 TO 1800 (LC)* *SHAKESPEAREAN CRITICISM (SC)*
Authors who died before 1400	*CLASSICAL AND MEDIEVAL LITERATURE CRITICISM (CMLC)*
Authors of books for children and young adults	*CHILDREN'S LITERATURE REVIEW (CLR)*
Dramatists	*DRAMA CRITICISM (DC)*
Poets	*POETRY CRITICISM (PC)*
Short story writers	*SHORT STORY CRITICISM (SSC)*
Literary topics and movements	*HARLEM RENAISSANCE: A GALE CRITICAL COMPANION (HR)* *THE BEAT GENERATION: A GALE CRITICAL COMPANION (BG)* *FEMINISM IN LITERATURE: A GALE CRITICAL COMPANION (FL)* *GOTHIC LITERATURE: A GALE CRITICAL COMPANION (GL)*
Asian American writers of the last two hundred years	*ASIAN AMERICAN LITERATURE (AAL)*
Black writers of the past two hundred years	*BLACK LITERATURE CRITICISM (BLC-1)* *BLACK LITERATURE CRITICISM SUPPLEMENT (BLCS)* *BLACK LITERATURE CRITICISM: CLASSIC AND EMERGING AUTHORS SINCE 1950 (BLC-2)*
Hispanic writers of the late nineteenth and twentieth centuries	*HISPANIC LITERATURE CRITICISM (HLC)* *HISPANIC LITERATURE CRITICISM SUPPLEMENT (HLCS)*
Native North American writers and orators of the eighteenth, nineteenth, and twentieth centuries	*NATIVE NORTH AMERICAN LITERATURE (NNAL)*
Major authors from the Renaissance to the present	*WORLD LITERATURE CRITICISM, 1500 TO THE PRESENT (WLC)* *WORLD LITERATURE CRITICISM SUPPLEMENT (WLCS)*

ISSN 1056-4349

DRAMA CRITICISM

Criticism of the Most Significant and Widely Studied
Dramatic Works from All the World's Literatures

VOLUME 45

Marie Toft
Project Editor

GALE
CENGAGE Learning®

Detroit • New York • San Francisco • New Haven, Conn • Waterville, Maine • London

Drama Criticism, Vol. 45

Project Editor: Marie Toft

Editorial: Dana Ramel Barnes, Kathy D. Darrow, Kristen A. Dorsch, Jeffrey W. Hunter, Reed Kalso, Jelena O. Krstović, Michelle Lee, Camille Reynolds, Lawrence J. Trudeau

Content Conversion: Katrina D. Coach, Gwen Tucker

Indexing Services: Laurie Andriot

Rights and Acquisitions: Christine Myaskovsky

Composition and Electronic Capture: Gary Oudersluys

Manufacturing: Rhonda Dover

Product Manager: Mary Onorato

For product information and technology assistance, contact us at
Gale Customer Support, 1-800-877-4253.
For permission to use material from this text or product,
submit all requests online at **www.cengage.com/permissions.**
Further permissions questions can be emailed to
permissionrequest@cengage.com

While every effort has been made to ensure the reliability of the information presented in this publication, Gale, a part of Cengage Learning, does not guarantee the accuracy of the data contained herein. Gale accepts no payment for listing; and inclusion in the publication of any organization, agency, institution, publication, service, or individual does not imply endorsement of the editors or publisher. Errors brought to the attention of the publisher and verified to the satisfaction of the publisher will be corrected in future editions.

Cengage Learning, Gale
27500 Drake Rd.
Farmington Hills, MI, 48331-3535

LIBRARY OF CONGRESS CATALOG CARD NUMBER 76-46132

ISBN-13: 978-1-4144-7101-3
ISBN-10: 1-4144-7101-7

ISSN 1056-4349

Printed in Mexico
1 2 3 4 5 6 7 16 15 14 13 12

Contents

Preface vii

Acknowledgments xi

Gale Literature Product Advisory Board xiii

Preface

*D*rama Criticism (*DC*) is principally intended for beginning students of literature and theater as well as the average playgoer. The series is therefore designed to introduce readers to the most frequently studied playwrights of all time periods and nationalities and to present discerning commentary on dramatic works of enduring interest. Furthermore, *DC* seeks to acquaint the reader with the uses and functions of criticism itself. Selected from a diverse body of commentary, the essays in *DC* offer insights into the authors and their works but do not require that the reader possess a wide background in literary studies. Where appropriate, reviews of important productions of the plays discussed are also included to give students a heightened awareness of drama as a dynamic art form, one that many claim is fully realized only in performance.

DC was created in response to suggestions by the staffs of high school, college, and public libraries. These librarians observed a need for a series that assembles critical commentary on the world's most renowned dramatists in the same manner as Gale's *Short Story Criticism* (*SSC*) and *Poetry Criticism* (*PC*), which present material on writers of short fiction and poetry. Although playwrights are covered in such Gale literary criticism series as *Contemporary Literary Criticism* (*CLC*), *Twentieth-Century Literary Criticism* (*TCLC*), *Nineteenth-Century Literature Criticism* (*NCLC*), *Literature Criticism from 1400 to 1800* (*LC*), and *Classical and Medieval Literature Criticism* (*CMLC*), *DC* directs more concentrated attention on individual dramatists than is possible in the broader, survey-oriented entries in these Gale series. Commentary on the works of William Shakespeare may be found in *Shakespearean Criticism* (*SC*).

Scope of the Series

By collecting and organizing commentary on dramatists, *DC* assists students in their efforts to gain insight into literature, achieve better understanding of the texts, and formulate ideas for papers and assignments. A variety of interpretations and assessments is offered, allowing students to pursue their own interests and promoting awareness that literature is dynamic and responsive to many different opinions.

Approximately three to five authors are included in each volume, and each entry presents a historical survey of the critical response to that playwright's work. The length of an entry is intended to reflect the amount of critical attention the author has received from critics writing in English and from foreign critics in translation. Every attempt has been made to identify and include the most significant essays on each author's work. In order to provide these important critical pieces, the editors sometimes reprint essays that have appeared elsewhere in Gale's literary criticism series. Such duplication, however, never exceeds twenty percent of a *DC* volume.

Organization of the Book

A *DC* entry consists of the following elements:

- The **Author Heading** consists of the playwright's most commonly used name, followed by birth and death dates. If an author consistently wrote under a pseudonym, the pseudonym is listed in the author heading and the real name given in parentheses on the first line of the introduction. Also located at the beginning of the introduction are any name variations under which the dramatist wrote, including transliterated forms of the names of authors whose languages use nonroman alphabets.

- The **Introduction** contains background information that introduces the reader to the author and the critical debates surrounding his or her work.

- The list of **Principal Works** is divided into two sections. The first section contains the author's dramatic pieces and is organized chronologically by date of first performance. If this has not been conclusively determined, the composition or publication date is used. The second section provides information on the author's major works in other genres.

- Essays offering **overviews of the dramatist's entire literary career** give the student broad perspectives on the writer's artistic development, themes, and concerns that recur in several of his or her works, the author's place in literary history, and other wide-ranging topics.

- **Criticism** of individual plays offers the reader in-depth discussions of a select number of the author's most important works. In some cases, the criticism is divided into two sections, each arranged chronologically. When a significant performance of a play can be identified (typically, the premier of a twentieth-century work), the first section of criticism will feature **production reviews** of this staging. Most entries include sections devoted to **critical commentary** that assesses the literary merit of the selected plays. When necessary, essays are carefully excerpted to focus on the work under consideration; often, however, essays and reviews are reprinted in their entirety. Footnotes are reprinted at the end of each essay or excerpt. In the case of excerpted criticism, only those footnotes that pertain to the excerpted texts are included.

- Critical essays are prefaced by brief **Annotations** explicating each piece.

- A complete **Bibliographic Citation,** designed to help the interested reader locate the original essay or book, precedes each piece of criticism. Source citations in the Literary Criticism Series follow University of Chicago Press style, as outlined in *The Chicago Manual of Style,* 14th ed. (Chicago: The University of Chicago Press, 1993).

- An annotated bibliography of **Further Reading** appears at the end of each entry and suggests resources for additional study. In some cases, significant essays for which the editors could not obtain reprint rights are included here. Boxed material following the further reading list provides references to other biographical and critical sources on the author in series published by Gale.

Cumulative Indexes

A **Cumulative Author Index** lists all of the authors that appear in a wide variety of reference sources published by Gale, including *DC*. A complete list of these sources is found facing the first page of the Author Index. The index also includes birth and death dates and cross references between pseudonyms and actual names.

A **Cumulative Topic Index** lists the literary themes and topics treated in *DC* as well as other Literature Criticism series.

A **Cumulative Nationality Index** lists all authors featured in *DC* by nationality, followed by the number of the *DC* volume in which their entry appears.

A **Cumulative Title Index** lists in alphabetical order the individual plays discussed in the criticism contained in *DC*. Each title is followed by the author's last name and corresponding volume and page numbers where commentary on the work is located. English-language translations of original foreign-language titles are cross-referenced to the foreign titles so that all references to discussion of a work are combined in one listing.

Citing *Drama Criticism*

When citing criticism reprinted in the Literary Criticism Series, students should provide complete bibliographic information so that the cited essay can be located in the original print or electronic source. Students who quote directly from reprinted criticism may use any accepted bibliographic format, such as University of Chicago Press style or Modern Language Association (MLA) style. Both the MLA and the University of Chicago formats are acceptable and recognized as being the current standards for citations. It is important, however, to choose one format for all citations; do not mix the two formats within a list of citations.

The examples below follow recommendations for preparing a bibliography set forth in *The Chicago Manual of Style,* 14th ed. (Chicago: The University of Chicago Press, 1993); the first example pertains to material drawn from periodicals, the second to material reprinted from books:

Barker, Roberta. "The Circle Game: Gender, Time, and 'Revolution' in Tom Stoppard's *The Coast of Utopia.*" *Modern Drama* 48, no. 4 (winter 2005): 706-25. Reprinted in *Drama Criticism.* Vol. 30, edited by Thomas J. Schoenberg and Lawrence J. Trudeau, 356-66. Detroit: Gale, 2008.

Rocha, Mark William. "Black Madness in August Wilson's 'Down the Line' Cycle." In *Madness in Drama,* edited by James Redmond, 191-201. Cambridge: Cambridge University Press, 1993. Reprinted in *Drama Criticism.* Vol. 31, edited by Thomas J. Schoenberg and Lawrence J. Trudeau, 229-35. Detroit: Gale, 2008.

The examples below follow recommendations for preparing a works cited list set forth in the *MLA Handbook for Writers of Research Papers,* 5th ed. (New York: The Modern Language Association of America, 1999); the first example pertains to material drawn from periodicals, the second to material reprinted from books:

Barker, Roberta. "The Circle Game: Gender, Time, and 'Revolution' in Tom Stoppard's *The Coast of Utopia.*" *Modern Drama* 48.4 (winter 2005): 706-25. Reprinted in *Drama Criticism.* Ed. Thomas J. Schoenberg and Lawrence J. Trudeau. Vol. 30. Detroit: Gale, 2008. 356-66.

Rocha, Mark William. "Black Madness in August Wilson's 'Down the Line' Cycle." *Madness in Drama.* Ed. James Redmond. Cambridge: Cambridge University Press, 1993. 191-201. Reprinted in *Drama Criticism.* Ed. Thomas J. Schoenberg and Lawrence J. Trudeau. Vol. 31. Detroit: Gale, 2008. 229-35.

Suggestions are Welcome

Readers who wish to suggest new features, topics, or authors to appear in future volumes, or who have other suggestions or comments are cordially invited to call, write, or fax the Product Manager:

Product Manager, Literary Criticism Series
Gale
27500 Drake Road
Farmington Hills, MI 48331-3535
1-800-347-4253 (GALE)
Fax: 248-699-8884

Acknowledgments

The editors wish to thank the copyright holders of the excerpted criticism included in this volume and the permissions managers of many book and magazine publishing companies for assisting us in securing reproduction rights. We are also grateful to the staffs of the Detroit Public Library, the Library of Congress, the University of Detroit Mercy Library, Wayne State University Purdy/Kresge Library Complex, and the University of Michigan Libraries for making their resources available to us. Following is a list of the copyright holders who have granted us permission to reproduce material in this volume of *DC*. Every effort has been made to trace copyright, but if omissions have been made, please let us know.

COPYRIGHTED MATERIAL IN *DC*, VOLUME 45, WAS REPRODUCED FROM THE FOLLOWING PERIODICALS:

Anales de la literatura espanola contemporanea, v. 29, 2004; v. 34, 2009. Copyright © 2004, 2009 Society of Spanish and Spanish-American Studies. All reproduced by permission.—*Australasian Drama Studies,* v. 19, October 1991. Copyright © 1991 by *Australasian Drama Studies.* Reproduced by permission of the publisher.—*Bulletin of Hispanic Studies,* v. 77, 2000 for "Yet Another Other: Unamuno's El otro and the Anxiety for Influence" by Julia Biggane. Copyright © 2000 Taylor & Francis Group, LLC. Reproduced by permission of Taylor & Francis, Ltd., http//:www.tandf.co.uk/journals and the author.—*Commonweal,* October 28, 1925; November 21, 1941. Copyright © 1925, 1941 Commonweal Publishing Co., Inc. All reproduced by permission of Commonweal Foundation.—*Comparative Literature,* v. 31, 1979. Copyright, 1979. All rights reserved. Used by permission of the publisher.—*Cuadernos de ALDEEU,* v. 1, January 1983. Copyright © 1983 by *Cuadernos de ALDEEU.* Reproduced by permission of the publisher.—*Encounter,* v. 12, April 1959. Reproduced by permission of Curtis Brown Group Ltd., London on behalf of the Estate of Colin MacInnes. Copyright © The Estate of Colin MacInness, 1959.—*Hispania,* v. 43, September 1960. Copyright © 1960 by *Hispania.* Reproduced by permission of the publisher.—*Hispanofila,* 1980. Copyright © 1980 by *Hispanofila.* Reproduced by permission by the publisher.—*Iowa State Journal of Research,* v. 60, February 1986. Copyright © 1986 by *Iowa State Journal of Research.* Reproduced by permission of the publisher.—*Journal of Spanish Studies,* v. 7, spring, 1979. Copyright © 1979 by Society of Spanish and Spanish-American Studies, Inc. Reproduced by permission of the publisher.—*Letras Peninsulares,* v. 14, fall, 2001. Copyright © 2001 by *Letra Peninsulares.* Reproduced by permission of the publisher.—*Listener* (London), November 27, 1975 for "Method in Madness" by John Elsom. Copyright © *Listener,* 1975. Reproduced by permission of the author.—*Modern Drama,* v. 25, June, 1982; v. 51, summer, 2008. Copyright © 1982, 2008 by the University of Toronto, Graduate Centre for Study of Drama. All reproduced by permission.—*Modern Language Notes,* v. 90, March 1975. Copyright © 1975 by The Johns Hopkins University Press. Reproduced by permission of The Johns Hopkins University Press.—*New England Theatre Journal,* v. 18, 2007. Copyright © 2007 by *New England Theatre Journal.* Reproduced by permission of the publisher.—*New Statesman,* v. 36, October 11, 1930; v. 70, November 12, 1965; v. 82, October 8, 1971; v. 86, November 23, 1973; v. 90, November 28, 1975. Copyright © 1930, 1965, 1971,1973, 1975 New Statesman, Ltd. All Reproduced by permission of the publisher.—*New Yorker,* v. 34, February 7, 1959, for "Review of A Taste of Honey" by Mollie Panter-Downes. Copyright © *New Yorker,* 1959. Reproduced by permission of the Literary Estate of the author.—*Performing Arts Journal,* v. 87, 2007 for "Drama and the Human: Reflections at the Start of a Millennium" by Peter Billingham. Copyright © *Performing Arts Journal,* 2007. Reproduced by permission of the author.—*Revue des langues vivantes,* 1960. Reproduced by permission.—*South Central Review,* v. 3, summer, 1986. Copyright © 1986 by The Johns Hopkins University Press. Reproduced by permission of The Johns Hopkins University Press.—*Spectator,* v. 215, November 12, 1965; v. 227, October 9, 1971. Copyright © 1965, 1971 by *The Spectator.* All reproduced by permission of *The Spectator*—Theatre Arts, v. 43, May 1959 for "Review of A Taste of Honey" by Alan Brien. Copyright © *Theatre Arts,* 1959. Reproduced by permission of the author.—Times (London), June 9, 1925; September 25, 1930; July 3, 1941; February 2, 1959; November 4, 1965; November 15, 1973; July 22, 1981; July 27, 1985. Copyright © 1925, 1930, 1941, 1959, 1965, 1973, 1981, 1985 Times Newspapers Ltd. All reproduced by permission of the publisher.—*Times Literary Supplement,* August 7, 1981; August 9, 1985. Copyright © 1981, 1985 by The Times Supplements Limited. All reproduced from *The Times Literary Supplement* by permission—*Variety,* v. 240, November 17, 1965. Copyright © 1965 Reed Business Information, a division of Reed Elsevier, Inc. Reproduced by permission of the publisher.—*Wisconsin Studies in Contemporary Literature,* v. 7, summer, 1966. Copyright © 1966 The Board of Regents of the University of Wisconsin System. All rights reserved. Reproduced by permission.

COPYRIGHTED MATERIAL IN *DC*, VOLUME 45, WAS REPRODUCED FROM THE FOLLOWING BOOKS:

Anderson, Lindsay. From *The Encore Reader: A Chronicle of the New Drama.* Methuen & Co Ltd, 1970. Reproduced by permission of the Lindsay Anderson Archive, The University of Stirling.—Cohn, Ruby. From *Essays on Contemporary*

Gale Literature Product Advisory Board

The members of the Gale Literature Product Advisory Board—reference librarians from public and academic library systems—represent a cross-section of our customer base and offer a variety of informed perspectives on both the presentation and content of our literature products. Advisory board members assess and define such quality issues as the relevance, currency, and usefulness of the author coverage, critical content, and literary topics included in our series; evaluate the layout, presentation, and general quality of our printed volumes; provide feedback on the criteria used for selecting authors and topics covered in our series; provide suggestions for potential enhancements to our series; identify any gaps in our coverage of authors or literary topics, recommending authors or topics for inclusion; analyze the appropriateness of our content and presentation for various user audiences, such as high school students, undergraduates, graduate students, librarians, and educators; and offer feedback on any proposed changes/enhancements to our series. We wish to thank the following advisors for their advice throughout the year.

Barbara M. Bibel
Librarian
Oakland Public Library
Oakland, California

Dr. Toby Burrows
Principal Librarian
The Scholars' Centre
University of Western Australia Library
Nedlands, Western Australia

Celia C. Daniel
Associate Reference Librarian
Howard University Libraries
Washington, D.C.

David M. Durant
Reference Librarian
Joyner Library
East Carolina University
Greenville, North Carolina

Nancy T. Guidry
Librarian
Bakersfield Community College
Bakersfield, California

Heather Martin
Arts & Humanities Librarian
University of Alabama at Birmingham, Sterne Library
Birmingham, Alabama

Susan Mikula
Librarian
Indiana Free Library
Indiana, Pennsylvania

Thomas Nixon
Humanities Reference Librarian
University of North Carolina at Chapel Hill, Davis Library
Chapel Hill, North Carolina

Mark Schumacher
Jackson Library
University of North Carolina at Greensboro
Greensboro, North Carolina

Gwen Scott-Miller
Assistant Director
Sno-Isle Regional Library System
Marysville, Washington

Edward Bond
1934-

English playwright, poet, screenwriter, theorist, and translator.

INTRODUCTION

An intensely controversial and political dramatist best known for his use of graphic violence, Edward Bond has made an indelible mark on twentieth century drama. Bond's plays, especially the early works, challenged audience expectations as well as the censors of the English theater world. His provocative dramas, and the legal difficulties that followed, were instrumental in overturning the Theatre Regulation Act in 1968. Through his work, Bond has consistently approached societal problems through the lens of art and history. Whether it is in the form of social control, poverty, unemployment, or the threat of nuclear war, Bond has focused on issues related to power and justice.

BIOGRAPHICAL INFORMATION

Bond was born on July 18, 1934, to a working-class family in Holloway, North London. His parents, Gaston and Florence Bond, were farm laborers who had moved to London from East Anglia in an effort to find work during the Depression. When World War II began, Bond and his sisters, like many children in London at the time, were sent to the countryside for their safety. Unfortunately, they returned to London prior to the sustained German bombing campaign known as the London Blitz. During the Blitz, Bond was then evacuated to his grandparents' home in East Anglia. He returned to London in 1944, entering Crouch End Secondary Modern School. Not considered an exemplary student, he was nonetheless strongly influenced at fourteen by a performance of *Macbeth*. Bond left school at fifteen and worked in warehouses and factories until age nineteen, when he was called up to perform his compulsory military service—a formative experience that would shape his future views of power and privilege. Bond was stationed in Vienna as an infantryman for two years and found the military culture brutal and humiliating. After his service ended Bond began to write plays, and in 1958 he was invited to join a writers' group at the Royal Court Theatre by William Gaskill. Gaskill would later go on to direct some of Bond's best-known works. In 1962 the Royal Court staged Bond's first play *The Pope's Wedding* in a one-night performance without scenery. The pared-down production was part of the theater's special series showcasing the works of new writers without investing in a full production. In 1965 Bond was selected as a finalist to receive a Most Promising Playwright award, but the same year his play *Saved* became the subject of controversy before it was even staged. At the time, play scripts had to be officially approved for public performance by the Office of Lord Chamberlain. Lord Chamberlain denied a license to produce *Saved* unless major cuts and revisions were made, but Bond refused to make any changes. Attempting to take advantage of a loophole which allowed private clubs to stage without a license, the Royal Court went ahead with a private staging before members of the English Stage Society. But in December 1965 police surreptitiously attended a performance of the play, on orders from Lord Chamberlain's Office. In January the Royal Court Theatre was charged with producing an unlicensed play and debates on theater censorship began in the House of Lords in February. Ultimately, the Royal Court was found guilty of violating censorship laws but was not given a formal punishment. *Saved* was the last play to be officially prosecuted under the censorship laws, but Bond's next play, *Early Morning* (1968), which portrayed Queen Victoria as a lesbian in love with Florence Nightingale, earned equal scrutiny by censors and was banned. Again, the Royal Court held a private staging in March 1968, which was raided by police. No charges were filed, but further performances were prevented. Months later, a performance of Bond's *Narrow Road to the Deep North* (1968) was mounted in Coventry in defiance of the censors' demands for revisions, but no action was taken. In September 1968 the English Parliament voted to pass legislation that would end government censorship once and for all by abolishing the Theatre Regulation Act. Bond was vindicated, but public and critical response to the level of violence in his plays would continue to frustrate him. In the 1970s Bond began directing some of his own plays and demanded increased control over productions of his works. In 1985 the Royal Shakespeare Company agreed to have him codirect his seven-hour trilogy *The War Plays* (1985), but Bond found the working conditions untenable and left the production; he would later denounce the staging without him as disastrous. This caused a rift between him and members of the English theater. Although his plays continue to be produced throughout England and Europe, Bond removed to France, where he currently develops and premieres many of his plays at Le Théâtre National de Colline in Paris. Meanwhile, Bond also continues to be involved in a youth theater founded in Birmingham in 1982, Big Brum Theatre in Education Company, through which he produces plays aimed at getting children and youth involved in theater and helping them to explore the social issues specific to young people. Since the 1990s Bond has remained disillusioned with English theater and refuses to allow any of his works to be performed by the country's large national companies, but he has been involved in many other projects, including a 2003 film based on his play *In the Company of Men* (1992). In 2000 he published a major study of his dramatic theory, *The Hidden Plot.*

MAJOR DRAMATIC WORKS

Bond's most consistent themes revolve around the often subliminal rage of the working classes and the state's role in simultaneously repressing and provoking it. In the "Author's Note" to his first volume of published plays, *Plays: One* (1977), Bond explained: "Human beings are violent animals only in the way that dogs are swimming animals. We need to eat; but only when we're starving does there have to be the possibility that we will use our capacity for violence to satisfy our need for food. Violence is a means not an end." Bond's plays obliquely explore the moment when human needs have been denied and ignored by existing power structures, giving way to a violent response. His first produced play, *The Pope's Wedding,* takes place in a rural farming community in East Anglia that has been isolated and marginalized by poverty and low social status. Scopey, a farmhand, is resentful and angry about his wife Pat's commitment to care for a local elderly eccentric named Alen. He eventually murders Alen and assumes his identity. In *Saved* the violence is ostensibly brought on by stagnancy, boredom, and alienation in the lower classes and culminates in the onstage torture and murder of a baby. *Lear* (1971), considered one of Bond's greatest theatrical achievements, reimagines Shakespeare's great tragic hero as a myth and metaphor for the birth of leadership and nationhood in modern England. While Shakespeare's Lear must learn to accept suffering as a fact of human life, Bond's learns to accept responsibility for his role in creating suffering. Shakespeare figures again in Bond's play *Bingo* (1973). In the play, a retired Shakespeare becomes involved in debates over England's early enclosure laws, which removed land from public use and caused great hardship for the country's peasant class. As a land owner, Shakespeare sides with the interests of emerging capitalism and eventually commits suicide out of guilt over his decision. Bond again uses a figure from English literary history to illustrate the effects of a harsh society

on the individual in *The Fool* (1975). This time Bond rewrote the life of early-nineteenth-century poet John Clare, who rises from rural peasantry to literary fame in London, only to end up broken and mad in an asylum for lunatics. In *Restoration* (1981), Bond examines the English election of 1979 and its consequences through the lens of the Restoration era, with which he saw many parallels—specifically the lower classes' commitment to Tory ideals despite the fact that those very ideals consistently worked against their interests. With *The War Plays,* Bond returned to the present, this time with a trilogy of plays that address the threat of nuclear war at the height of the Cold War arms race. In the trilogy's first installment, *Red Black and Ignorant* (1984), the central figure, known as the Monster, is the ghost of a baby killed during a nuclear war. The play shows what kind of life the baby might have had, taking the audience forty years into a future in which he is eventually killed by his own son in another war. The second play in the series, *The Tin Can People* (1984), depicts the immediate aftermath of nuclear war, when a lone wanderer happens upon a group of survivors, with a massive supply of canned goods, who have created a military culture fueled by fear and paranoia. In *Great Peace* (1985), the trilogy's final installment, Bond focuses on a mother's experience during nuclear attack and its aftermath. Her son, a young soldier, returns home with government orders to kill a child to conserve food supplies. The soldier kills his sibling, causing his mother to go mad with grief.

CRITICAL RECEPTION

Bond's plays sparked outrage among audiences and theater critics because of their concentrated use of graphic violence, particularly Bond's depictions of violence against children. Yet, as Bond has argued in his "Author's Note" and elsewhere, his primary goal in showing violence is to make audiences understand that "Violence is not a function of human nature but of human societies." Literary critic Tony Howard noted, "The murder of children is Edward Bond's recurrent image of the social destruction of the innocent." Bond himself has said that he intends his theater to be "rational," as opposed to his contemporaries in the Theater of the Absurd movement, who portray life as essentially absurd and meaningless. Bond's humanism asserts that it is only unjust institutions that drive people to immoral behavior. According to Christopher Innes, "[A]ll social activity is presented [by Bond] as moralized violence. The sack of Troy that the authorities condone, or the anarchic murder and rape of civil war in *Lear,* the politically justified killing of the children in *Narrow Road,* or the socially condemned stoning of a baby in *Saved*—all are treated as actions of exactly the same kind and status. For Bond, violence is not an aberration but a general symptom." But while literary critics have found much to analyze in Bond's plays, theater critics have at times struggled to find value in them. In his review of a 1965 production of *Saved*, Irving Wardle wrote, "In a recent interview Mr. Bond said that his aim was to 'illuminate' violence. One would hardly have guessed this from the play itself which does nothing to lay bare the motives for violence and appeals to no emotions beyond those aroused by the act itself. According to one's proclivities these may be horror, sadistic relish, or amusement; a fair proportion of last night's audience fell into the third category." Despite Bond's statements, critics still question his motivation and beliefs regarding violence. Benedict Nightingale, for example, writes, "the emphasis on economic and social conditions seems to suggest that they alone are responsible for human suffering, and leaves us unclear whether or not Bond still thinks that mankind is also afflicted with an innate and immutable sadism."

PRINCIPAL WORKS

Plays

The Pope's Wedding 1962
Saved 1965
A Chaste Maid in Cheapside [adaptor; from the play by Thomas Middleton] 1966
The Three Sisters [with Richard Cottrell; translator; from *Tri sestry* by Anton Chekhov] 1967
Early Morning 1968
Narrow Road to the Deep North 1968
Black Mass 1970
Lear 1971
Passion 1971
Bingo: Scenes of Money and Death 1973
The Sea: A Comedy 1973
Spring Awakening [translator; from *Frühlings Erwachen* by Frank Wedekind] 1974
The Fool: Scenes of Bread and Love 1975
Grandma Faust: A Burlesque (Part One of A-A-America!) 1976
Stone 1976
The Swing: A Documentary (Part Two of A-A-America!) 1976
We Come to the River (libretto) 1976
The White Devil [adaptor; from the play by John Webster] 1976
Plays: One (Saved, Early Morning, The Pope's Wedding) 1977
The Bundle, or, New Narrow Road to the Deep North 1978
Plays: Two (Lear, The Sea, Narrow Road to the Deep North, Black Mass, Passion) 1978
The Woman: Scenes of War and Freedom 1978

The Worlds 1979
Restoration: A Pastorale 1981
Derek 1982
Summer: A European Play 1982
After the Assassinations 1983
* *The Cat* [adaptor; from the novel *Les peines de coeur d'une chatte anglaise* by Honoré de Balzac] (libretto) 1983
† *Red Black and Ignorant* 1984
† *The Tin Can People* 1984
† *Great Peace* 1985
Human Cannon 1986
Plays: Three (Bingo, The Fool, The Woman, Stone) 1987
Jackets 1989
September 1989
Jackets II 1990
* *In the Company of Men* 1992
Plays: Four (The Worlds, The Activist's Papers, Restoration, Summer) 1992
Olly's Prison (teleplay) 1993
Tuesday (teleplay) 1993
At the Inland Sea: A Play for Young People 1995
Coffee: A Tragedy 1996
Plays: Five (Human Cannon, The Bundle, In the Company of Men) 1996
Eleven Vests 1997
Plays: Six (The War Plays, Choruses from After the Assassins) 1998
* *The Crime of the Twenty-First Century* 1999
Chair (radio play) 2000
The Children 2000
Have I None 2000
Existence 2002
The Balancing Act 2003
Plays: Seven (Olly's Prison, Coffee, The Crime of the Twenty-First Century, The Swing, Derek, Fables, Stories) 2003
The Short Electra 2004
The Under Room 2005
Arcade 2006
* *Born* 2006
Plays: Eight (Born, People, Chair, Existence, The Under Room) 2006
Tune 2007
A Window 2009
There Will Be More 2010

Other Major Works

Blow-Up [with Michelangelo Antonioni and Tonino Guerra; adaptor; from the short story "Las babas del diablo" by Julio Cortázar] (screenplay) 1966
Laughter in the Dark [adaptor; from the novel by Vladimir Nabokov] (screenplay) 1969
Michael Kohlhaas [with Clement Biddle Wood and Volker Schlöndorff; adaptor; from the novella by Heinrich von Kleist] (screenplay) 1969

Nicholas and Alexandra [with James Goldman; adaptor; from the biography by Robert K. Massie] (screenplay) 1971

Walkabout [adaptor; from the novel by James Vance Marshall] (screenplay) 1971

The Swing Poems (poetry) 1976

Theatre Poems and Songs (poetry) 1978

Poems, 1978-1985 (poetry) 1987

The Hidden Plot: Notes on Theatre and the State (nonfiction) 2000

Selections from the Notebooks of Edward Bond. 2 vols. (notebooks) 2000

Edward Bond Letters. 5 vols. (letters) 1994-2001

*These works, written in English, were first performed in translation. *The Cat* was performed as *Die Englische Katze, In the Company of Men* as *La Compagnie des hommes, The Crime of the Twenty-First Century* as *Das Verbrechen des 21. Jahrhunderts* and *Born* as *Naître.*

†These plays were performed together as *The War Plays* in 1985. *Red Black and Ignorant* has also been performed under the title *The Unknown Citizen.*

AUTHOR COMMENTARY

Edward Bond and Peter Billingham (interview date November 2006)

SOURCE: Bond, Edward, and Peter Billingham. "Drama and the Human: Reflections at the Start of a Millennium." *Performing Arts Journal* 87 (2007): 1-14.

[*In the following interview conducted November 2006, Bond discusses existential and ontological issues of the twentieth century as he has examined them through his plays.*]

[*Billingham*]: *I wonder, Edward, whether first of all you could reflect upon where your writing is now and your thoughts on drama, this November 2006? We might begin by considering your play* **Born** *that is about to be produced in Paris.*

[Bond]: **Born** is the third play in what I call the Colline Tetralogy. Colline is the name of the theatre, it's one of the French national theatres based in Paris specializing in contemporary theatre. I wanted for a long time to write this play called **Coffee** and this was to do with an incident that happened in the Second World War. It's a true story. Almost always, my starting of a play is initiated by some true incident. **Coffee** was about the massacre at Babyar and one of the people who survived, a woman. It was very extraordinary because one of the reasons that she survived was that she and some others had got left in the back of a lorry in a situation where the Germans were killing thousands of people. When

these people were found, it was ordered that they must be taken back to the ravine where the others had been killed. The Germans fired across from the far edge so that the victims would fall directly into that ravine. The German soldiers who were doing the shooting were making coffee when this small number of prisoners was finally delivered for execution. They were so cross because they thought they'd done their job for the day and now it looked as if they couldn't have their coffee. One of them threw away their coffee in disgust and I thought: that's the twentieth century. It tells you everything because, for me, drama has two sides although they are the "one side": one is the kitchen table and one is the horizon of the universe. That combines the existential with the ontological and that really is what the neonate and human being is about. I thought that the coffee incident was absolutely extraordinary and I worked on that and wanted to explain: What was this? Why did the soldier do that? It was about 15 years before I wrote the play and I could understand why I had kept it in the back of my mind. I couldn't write it until I felt that I could technically handle the stage in order to write that play about that event. This led to a series of plays and whereas **Coffee** is set in the past, the following play **The Crime of the Twenty-First Century,** is set in the future.

How do that coffee incident and my reaction to it extend into the future? I discovered whilst I was doing this that what I was really dealing with is a problem that the Greeks could not deal with. This was even though they represented the origins of Western culture and of this ability to reflect upon what one is thinking and what one is doing rather than simply translating it onto the "Gods." I don't believe that this is some form of Western-centrist thinking, but I really do think that they were confronting the fundamental problems and questions that all human beings have to deal with. They therefore created this extraordinary institution of democracy. It's not what we would recognize as democracy. Nevertheless, in the end people were actually paid for their attendance in this democratic process because the farmer-participants who lived in the outlying areas couldn't afford to come into the capital city all that often. The people were required to be spectators at the theatre, which was the other main public institution alongside of the parliament and the courts of law. I think that they tried to deal with very, very profound problems.

How do you view those problems impacting our contemporary world and indeed its possible future?

They are essentially the problems of Oedipus and Orestes. Oedipus is the problem of the self and Orestes (and Antigone) is the problem of the relationship to authority and the community. Of course, both of these problems overlap but that is the basic conflict. However, they couldn't put the two together. The reason that they couldn't put the two together is that then they would have to start to ask the very fundamental questions about their own democracy. As they couldn't deal with these problems, I think they stood in the way of the development of theatre. They couldn't bring these two questions or issues together so that eventually they stopped writing plays. Greek theatre ends its radical phase with the death of Euripides and it was Euripides who had pushed these two questions very, very far. What I realized, going back to my tetralogy, was that I would have to try and put the problems of Orestes and Oedipus together. That is absolutely the expression of the problems we face.

We have technological problems—the machines we make are too powerful for us. Instead of, as they did in the past, enabling us to improve our relationship with nature, they now damage our relationship to nature. And so whereas tools were the makers of humanness now tools are becoming anti-human. We have to work out what the relationship of the individual to the community is. What is our relationship as individuals to State authority? How do human beings create themselves? I don't think that we are the products of genetic determinism. I think if that were so, we would no longer be in history but in nature. We'd be in evolution. The only way that we can create humanness is not by saying I've got a machine that enables me to till the earth: a plough. I've got a machine that enables me to go the Moon. In itself these things do not create humanness, they create new problems for humanness. The only way that you can create humanness is by dramatizing the self. We should be dramatizing the conflicts within the self and what art and drama should be doing is increasing human self-consciousness. That's not an abstract matter. Once you engage in that process you have to start asking, why am I committed to humanness? I can't say, oh, I can't decide whether or not to be human, I'll sort that out tomorrow, in the sense that one might say: I don't know whether I like classical music or not, I'll try listening to some tomorrow. If you are a human being, you are committed to it; there is an imperative to being human.

Could you develop this concept of the "human imperative" further?

You cannot simply ignore that imperative. It's not of course human solely in terms of: I've got to have clothes to wear, I've got to have sex. Because some people are prepared to give those things up for causes that they believe deeply in. In the human, therefore, there is an intellectual dimension. It's not just about the emotional or the physical; the mind has an intellectual imperative to be human. It does this because of what is already in the neonate, the newborn child. It isn't a matter of some human essence but rather of the situa-

tion—its site, and I think in modern drama site plays the role of what character did in, for example, Ibsen. The neonate seeks to be at one with the world, at home in the world, which is its site. The cause of this is biological, but the effect is what I call an "intellection," an imaginative-rational process. The ultimate effect of this is that later the post-neonatal, the child and eventually the adult in society seek justice. This is the origin of all drama. But justice is highly paradoxical. We live in unjust societies and so ultimately laws are historically "justified" but morally unjust. The law has a judge but justice has no judge. Instead it has drama, because justice is created in the site where the self touches society.

I call this the "Hamlet question": that all creativity is poised on what I call the "Hamlet-colon." This problem is furthermore very clearly posed by Nietzsche when he kills God and this gave him a problem: I've no longer got God to tell me what to do and make me do it. I no longer believe that God creates me but that I create myself, and this leads to modernist aesthetics and modern thought. What Nietzsche says in the conclusion to his *Ecce Homo* (his autobiography) is: "Have I been understood? I am Dionysus against the Crucified One." What he is saying of course is not only about himself but also poses the question: what are human beings? Having arrived at the crisis of the nineteenth century and the crisis of the Enlightenment, he then says: is it this or is it that? Am I Christ or am I Dionysus? What are human beings? That of course is really the "Hamlet-problem." Hamlet asks "To be or not to be?" Then you say, to be what? Just to say will I face the problem or will I not face the problem or can I erase the problem by killing myself? Hamlet goes around looking for accidents to save him from having to make decisions because the decisions are so momentous. What he's saying is that on one side of the colon I am the regicide who kills the King and I know who I am and I know what I do, I act. Or on the other, I do not know who I am; I think and contemplate between Dionysus and Christ.

This is something I think that Nietzsche probably gets from Hegel because Hegel has this idea of the "unhappy consciousnesses." Consequently, for example, I am a member of the universe. I can understand the universe. I am ontological in that way, but I am also this miserable worm that is absolutely nothing. Which is your identity? Nietzsche says I am Dionysus, the Beast, and the Superman. Why did Nietzsche then go mad? Well, it was because he saw a horse being viciously mistreated in Milan and he couldn't bear that, he broke down. Now, the devotees of Dionysus were encouraged by him to pull living animals to bits. So Nietzsche is lying. Nietzsche does not know whether he wants to be Dionysus or Christ. The only thing that he can be certain of is that he doesn't want to be Parsifal. Parsifal is a necrophile pretending to be interested in the light. It's a form of spiritualization of existence and that's a cop out. That was why Nietzsche quarreled so much with Wagner; initially he'd thought that Wagner was going to be the modern equivalent of Greek drama.

Is it possible to reiterate the nature of the central problem that faces us as human beings at the start of the twenty-first century?

The central problem remains: Do I understand what I am doing and if I can understand what I'm doing, how the hell can I do it? (Returning to the Hamlet-colon) I can see the consequences of what I will do, or do I act and don't take cognizance of the consequences of my action which I cannot control? You could toss a coin, except, as I said, there is intellectualization in the human mind which involves a value and the value is justice and that is ontological and that makes it much more difficult. As a human being what I have to do is to enact and enunciate justice, and that really is the colon, you see? Creativity is poised on that problem: how can I perform justice and that of course is what the theatre is about. That takes different historical forms. Different communities, societies, and cultures work out a *modus vivendi*: not just how to live, but how to live with themselves. Drama comes to a crisis it cannot solve without destabilizing society instead of freeing it from ideological rigidities. For instance, Greek drama couldn't deal with slavery as an institution, not the domestic slavery of women in *The Trojan Women*. Philosophy has to replace drama at these crises. Aristotle can say slaves should be grateful cattle; a dramatist can't say this, can't stage such slaves—their misery would have to be made comic. In fact, Greek philosophers couldn't resolve this problem either. Instead religion took it over. Religion banishes drama anyway because it wishes to reify it and monopolize it. Then religion breaks down in the Renaissance because the Reformation questions religious authority, and inevitably it seems that we need drama again to look at this problem because people no longer have an authoritative statement from philosophy. Descartes who is a contemporary of Shakespeare is saying exactly what Shakespeare is saying, but Shakespeare is much more radical. Drama has to be more radical because it is an act. Descartes can sit in front of the fire and say, "I think and therefore I am."

So you have to re-dramatize and recreate human consciousness, recreate humanness: this is what Shakespeare is about. Then he can hand over to the Enlightenment and philosophy can take over again and start speculating about this problem because drama can't take it any further at that time. Philosophy takes over and you can follow this pattern through to the end of the nineteenth century, with writers like Strindberg and Ibsen. They try to keep these two problems alive for us.

It's like Ibsen says, I want to think about this in a very rational way; I want to exclude the irrational—although he regrets this decision later on. It's very interesting: He begins by saying how do we bring water to the community but in the later plays water becomes very dangerous—it's what you're drowned in. Meanwhile Strindberg says, well this isn't really telling us what we need to know, its not dealing with the problem of Orestes and Oedipus. I call this the "Problem number 5"—it's perhaps a bit mischievous of me—yet scene five in **Born** is very critical in relation to this. Strindberg says I'm going to write the Dreamplays; he split the problem into two manageable sections but the colon is no longer there, it's no longer active. It becomes a barrier, no longer a confrontation. This will not work.

How does your understanding of Marx and his political philosophy, and its significance in terms of twentieth-century history, contribute to this critical dilemma?

The limitation of Marxism in the Victorian period was that it offered a mechanical interpretation of human nature. Marx turns Hegel upside down and says it's actually to do with material reality and not the spirit because what Hegel will finally do is to reconcile the dichotomy—the Hamlet-colon—by saying that the "World Spirit" will take care of this and resolve this for us. We are just these functions for the world spirit. Marx is absolutely true in saying that history is a product of our material relationship to the universe but I also think that imagination is material and I think it's false to make that distinction or division. It's just an ideological contrivance. Marx is right about this but he doesn't sufficiently explain how this happens, and that's why we get Stalin on one side of the colon and the Gulag on the other, because the problem has not been faced.

Human beings are not given the stages, the spaces, and the drama in which they can create a new form of humanness. One can talk about the culture of socialist man but I'm not talking about culture, I'm talking about humanness. Culture will sustain itself but humanness must be re-created. What became for me the problem of the tetralogy was exactly this: How did one resolve the challenge of the Hamlet-colon? If we can't do that, then we can't remain as human beings because this problem is not a genetic inheritance but is rather an effort of will and understanding and of submitting yourself to dramatic processes. That then takes you not necessarily to the problems of the contemporary world because people used to talk about geo-political problems but they're now chrono-political problems. This is because in the present it seems that the clock has not only two hands but six, seven, or eight—different parts of the world are living in different times. I said some years ago now that if a medieval Pope had the atom bomb, he would be obliged to use it. That would be his religious duty. He would have to use it so that the Infidels could be killed and sent off to Hell. Our problem now is a political and administrative problem in that history has fallen out of sync with itself and this creates very, very dangerous practical problems.

Those are slightly different from the problems of reconciling Oedipus and Orestes. That's necessary because if you don't do that, you cannot have a being in a new and changing world. So one is faced with trying to write a play that is going to integrate all cultures into this problem set by the Greeks. It is not a practical possibility but it is absolutely necessary for human beings that they understand themselves. This is very dangerous and this is what I am always looking to point out in my writing, which is that there is no guarantee that we will remain in history. We may return to evolution and what evolution then becomes is the way that machines administer human beings. In conclusion, what I am trying to do through the tetralogy is actually to enact what it means to be a human being.

That sense of enactment is a stimulating concept. What is provoked for me is an image from **The Pope's Wedding** *where Scopey sits in the clothes of Alen whom he has previously murdered. That sense of the enactment of paradox has been present in your work right back to those very early plays. What does that image speak to us? Has what it speaks to us changed in the intervening 40 years?*

It is a very important thing about drama is that it is visual as well as verbal. Barthes says that you don't write anything—language writes you. I often talk about the paradox and the paradox is both sides of the colon. Hegel might have argued that, if one considered *Antigone* in the context of the colon, both Antigone and Creon had equal rights. I think this is not so because Antigone is right and Creon is not. Imagination in itself is not only a humanizing ability but also a humanizing imperative. I have to describe what happens to the pre-language being, the newborn child. This will require some imagination in itself but I do think that it is absolutely important. The newborn child does not know that it is born; it does not know that there is a universe or a world—all it knows is that there is *it*. It is—I am—that's almost a religious thing. It—the neonate—develops a relationship with that world. You cannot say if I want self-consciousness to examine myself, I cannot do it—I immediately disappear, because there isn't a self. I've got a hand, I've got clothes but what is my self? I know I do certain things, I may even do a coherent series of things but the self can never look at itself. This is the origin of drama and the origin of humanness and why the two are structurally related.

When one says the neonate "is"—what is it? Come on Hamlet, be *that*! I can use my imagination to understand the rational in that situation. It has pleasure and pain.

These are two polarities. Could you then say that the self is its relationship to pleasure and pain? What those things are for us are not necessarily what they are for *it*. The infant self is not going to say, I'm going to do the crossword now as an interlude between pleasure and pain. So, in an important sense it *is* pleasure and pain. Then something happens which evolution gives us: there is pleasure and pain but they also relate to something beyond the self. It is at that point that the self is created. I do not create what is out there but what is out there defines my self. You cannot split off the self from its site. I am my relationship to my site. Then it ceases to be simply a spectrum of pleasure and pain. You create the concepts to use to define an adult world: the tragic and the comic. The pleasure becomes the comic and the pain becomes the tragic. I am a relationship to my site because that relationship is mediated through the tragic and the comic. Therefore I am a dramatic structure and I cannot abstract myself from that situation, it's just not possible. The core of drama is that problematic question: How am I existing in enduring this relationship? That is the crux of humanness; I am the site but I am also somehow responsible for it. A fish is not responsible for its sea but I am responsible in some way for the site that I am in.

In that enactment of Scopey in the clothes of Alen—is that a human imperative or a neonatal imperative that is driving Scopey? In order to locate his sense of self in terms similar to those that you have been identifying and using, does that imperative necessitate the murder of Alen?

No. Scopey is creating himself. Scopey is a fiction of course he is a device of the imagination. Being is a critical relation of the site to itself, except that it needs consciousness for that to be human. The neonate is given the existential and the ontological together and that is a highly dramatic experience that one can recreate in drama. Drama is our reality and in that reality we face the critical problem that the neonate faces between the comic and the tragic. [Like Scopey] you *are* this problem. It ultimately implicates you in all of the problems of society, of politics and culture. I am the need for justice—it is an ontological and existential imperative—not purely a desire. If I cannot solve that then I go mad.

What then are the implications for politics and political theatre that seeks to serve and express a political function?

Well, what happens when an audience comes to a play is very different from watching a screen. I think that screens criminalize their audiences, but that's another subject. When you enter a theatre what is the audience doing? Well, there is a "social self" present and at work and the "social self" is a compromise because we all live in unjust societies. If one were to say to the neonate: "You don't know how to live in society," it would say "Yes, but you don't know how to be human. You are not in a human society." When the audience faces the stage therefore, you can either lie to them or you can do something else. If Alan Bennett were to arrive at Auschwitz, he would say, as a dramatic character: "Well here we are, this is our home now, we must make the best of it. Tomorrow morning, we'll look around—there must be a tea cozy somewhere." Or they are faced with the problem that drove Nietzsche mad. You can either say, therefore, theatre is the hunt for the tea cozy or else you can say theatre is facing the problem that Nietzsche presented us with us. There is no utopia that we can go to where all of our problems will be solved and there will be no more need for the tragic and no more pain. Human beings are not like that. They are always there to be trouble—not to make trouble but to be trouble and to be troubled because its only by doing that they can get out of themselves and accept responsibility for their site and for other people. This is the only way that they can be themselves. It's not that the Greeks had answers—it's that they had questions.

Could you say some more about dramatic structure and the dramatic site?

One of the things that human beings can do is—if I tell you that you have to dramatize yourself—if you are a dramatic structure then your life is your drama, not just your story. Then we have this cultural device of being able to create fictions. Fictions are the way we relate to reality. It is not true in a certain sense. If I make a picture of a blacksmith, that picture is not going to be able to shoe horses—it's not what its function is—but it can tell me something about work and its relationship to society and so it can tell me something about myself. It can be used to pose the basic questions about humanity in order to give me a structure to reality, a grip, in order that I may enter, as opposed to merely obeying the rules of my society. In that important sense it is to make me really responsible for my society. What one does in drama is to give the audience their reality and that is done by the artifice of fiction and then I would need to talk about the logic of the imagination. We think that imagination is somehow an escape from, a relaxation from, reality. But fiction to perform its function has to have an "extra reality," an "extra device" that we don't have in real life. So Hamlet's death is nobody's death (the actor doesn't die) yet it is everyone's death. In real life I can say look, tomorrow, I'm going to win the lottery. I'm not going to win the lottery tomorrow, but I can use that ability of fiction to say yes, but come to Babyar and then I will pose you the question of what you are going to do with your coffee.

Why, in your view, is it that drama can offer such a potentially crucial and powerful instrument for the

continuation of the human in what are increasingly calamitous times?

Drama is very powerful because it can, as it were, put the universe into Scopey's coat or into a cup of coffee. If I were simply to say, massacres are terrible aren't they? Well, someone would say, no, it's necessary, you want and need to get rid of those people. Then if I say, but why did you throw your coffee away, then I'm opening up another problem and I can work at that problem. Also I can make it immediate for you because I can relate the cup of coffee to the massacre and that I think is relating the existential to the ontological or the personal to the political. I can, as it were, pose that question to the audience. Now the audience can think, I don't want to do that, I want to look for the tea cozy, and they can turn off or run out and leave the theatre because they're angry. If they were indifferent, they could just be bored. Then I say, no, you're not running away from the play. You are, in a very literal sense, running away from yourself. You have left yourself in the theatre. That I think is the power of drama and why drama is needed. The skill of drama is to set up those situations where human beings are confronted with their need to be human and it is that imperative which they can have a choice about. That is why I have this notion of accident time because when you create that on stage, the audience is in contact with their being or the being is in contact with itself. Therefore you have to create critical situations that cannot be answered by theatre; they can only be confronted by drama.

You have talked before about the irony of how capitalism came out of the Enlightenment.

When I grew up, as a young person, I was very committed to the Enlightenment because I wasn't interested in worshipping an idol or worshipping a god or submitting to class systems. I discovered that the Enlightenment enabled us to think rationally about our society. In his philosophical writings, Kant, as a response to Hume, is saying: How is it possible to know anything? What this, however, then introduces is the question of "What is value?" It's the same in Newton although, because Newton is a scientist, he knows he must be wrong. Kant doesn't know he can be wrong in quite the same way. What he is saying is there are two things that are really incompatible, but it is so and they are both true. The world is Newtonian in that we are objects in a machine that is the universe. However, he also says that we have a moral sense and that doesn't make any sense because where does it come from? The Enlightenment doesn't seem able to provide an answer. What it says is that you are that person who takes responsibility for his/her moral self. This is Kant's categorical imperative and he is very clear about this.

Could you expand slightly upon your understanding and appreciation of Kant in relation to the ideas and concerns informing your own work?

He wants to think rationally about the world and he needs to be able to define in rational terms the nature and responsibility of the moral self. What does it mean to be a moral person? What Kant is saying is that it is your duty to understand yourself. Now it's much easier to understand things than people. It's much easier to understand the table than it is to understand the carpenter. Because it's easier to understand things and because you have to administer society, you end up finding it's much easier to treat people as things and not as moral entities. Increasingly, that's what scientists do. If you treat people as things and they go wrong and you can't repair it, you get rid of it. If the leg comes off the table, you try and repair it. If you can't do that you destroy the table. If it doesn't work you get rid of it. If people are incorrigible, then you destroy them. What we call history might just be a stage in which evolution leaps over itself, leaps over humanness and replaces it with a much more efficient form of brain which has no moral problems whereby you could treat people as things. In a certain sense, you can say that Auschwitz was a great academy; it was an academy teaching a particular science of how to "solve the problems of the world." I believe that this is not something in the end that human beings can accept simply because they begin as neonates. This is what I have called Radical Innocence.

What does the concept of "Radical Innocence" signify?

In response to this concept, some people have said, "Oh you think people are born innately good." This is utter rubbish. How can I say that a child is born good? How can a child commit a crime? How can a child commit a good act? What you can say is that the child is involved in the most profound situations of humanness. Our problem at the moment is that we can increasingly treat people as things. A thing consumes without questioning and is satisfied by the act of consumption. We return once more to "To be, or not to be?" To be what? Then you can say, "To consume, or not to consume?" Consume why? Not what you consume but why.

Drama is the principal means by which such attitudes and the values informing them might be critically interrogated?

To return to your earlier question about the possibilities and purpose of drama, what you have to do is to find ways of integrating the audience very closely with their problems. I think that the Greeks had a dramatic device which enabled them to look at this very closely but which in the end stopped them from allowing drama to consume the problem. This is because they have chorus and so you have the actors—the protagonists and the antagonists—and you have the chorus. The chorus is in some sense on the outside but it also gets involved and has an opinion and it's often used to comment upon the ontological situation, especially so in Euripides. It's as if by dividing that problem in that way that you open up a gap between Orestes and Oedipus. Of course, my project is engaged in trying to bring those two elements together. If one imagines oneself as a member of the Greek audience at the theatre, what confronts one first of all is the orchestra and that's the site of the chorus and really they are the prominent characters in the situation—you see everything through them—what happens is that the protagonist has to come down into the chorus's space. Modern theatre, for example, Ibsen, turns everything the other way round. We abolish the chorus and it gets pushed out in the fjord or nature so that instead of being social, it becomes an abstract, natural force. The chorus in Greek drama was political because they could comment upon the abstract forces surrounding them. Ibsen cannot do that. The abstract forces become a danger and they don't have any relationship to the chorus. This is a problem of presentation that has to be solved and which I think *Born,* scene five, is trying to deal with.

What you have to say is that a lot of modern writing, because it's spiritually television, it gets rid of anything beyond the wall and encloses itself into the sitting room or the kitchen and doesn't allow the audience an equivalent of the chorus. If I am aware as a human being that I am involved in realities beyond the kitchen and am involved in the universe, I'm involved in the organization of society, then one has to say, but why am I? Why does this matter? Then you can see that these are also worlds in the imagination. They are still nevertheless realistic worlds. If I dream, I'm not dreaming about any other reality than this reality. In the same way the imagination must be made up of the material. If I create God, I create him materially. What one can do is to place these other worlds on stage—they are your world—you are in them. What I don't have to do is to allow ideology to control those projected worlds. If Shakespeare says, "All the world's a dream," and he puts ghosts and witches on the stage, his audiences believed in them: they could go and see witches burned. What Shakespeare did for his contemporary audience in putting witches on the stage is to put you in the stage, your being.

Always in drama you go to the stage to enter into your being, not just as a spectator. The characters on the stage present you with the problems that the neonate presents you with but of course in an adult form. If Shakespeare can do that and if the Greeks can do that, if Racine can do it, it always comes with ideological values, because ideology says heaven is up there and the witches are down there and we have to guard against witches; so ideology structures your imagination when it comes to the stage. Then you have to say that imagination is the site of ideology and so how can it be the site of freedom? However, you're not the prisoner in your time but you are the creator of your time. What I have to say, here, now in my position in 2006, is that the ideological barriers can no longer control what's inside. The ideological barriers go and so it is possible to—and you must—create not postmodern but *post-ideological* drama.

We forget what an extraordinary mind Newton was. Why is it he spent a lot of his time as an alchemist and some later critics have rebuked him for this "stupidity"? This was not stupidity. He was saying there is something missing; there is something that I don't understand. So alchemy for Newton was his extension of science—not an alterative to it. Of course you had to wait until the twentieth century to understand that light is two things and not the one thing that Newton needed it to be in order to try and map the universe. So what one has to say is, yes, I can bring all of those things upon the stage but not under an ideological license. Then they will say, but yes, look he is mad, look what Luke does in **Born**—we can't let people do something like that. My response is actually you do let people do that on stage—you object far more if it happens on the stage. What then happens is that you don't have to make the division between Strindberg and Ibsen nor do you need the ideological barriers that Shakespeare needed in order to tell the truth. Newton needed alchemy for the same reason that Einstein tells us that "God doesn't play tricks with the universe." You can then create a different dramatic structure that allows for more than one level of reality to be on the stage at the same time. The levels can then interact in a complex way. Once an aesthetic form of presenting humanness ceases to be adequate, it then starts limiting the dramatic site.

Would it in any sense act like a mutation or a straight-jacket, or both?

No, I think it's the opposite of a straightjacket. It is possible to write with great simplicity and clarity but at the same time to be able to offer other aspects of reality that enable the audience to perceive the complexities of those simplicities. I remember with my own version of **Lear** facing the problem of how do you get rid of the ghost? How do you make a ghost die? Instead of being helpful, the ghost becomes malignant. I had to find some way of enacting that, and that means making it visual. The fiction provides an enormous range of possibilities about what can go on stage. The only thing is that it has to be logical. You have to say yes, but for imagination to work, if it's not hunting for the tea cozy or winning the lottery, then there has to be a logic in it. It is the neonate's need to relate to its world—to be its site in justice.

Justice is absolutely critical and central in all that we've been discussing?

Justice only has meaning of course to later societies but its origin is there in the neonate. Once you're talking about the self in site, then you are talking about justice.

I was thinking that the neonate's imperative might be to create an order or sense of order but then one might argue that Auschwitz was the supreme example of a certain kind of order, and yet was an utter and total absence of justice?

Yes, absolutely, because it's not a question of obtaining order, because that would be like the neonate saying yes, I'll arrange things so that I am fed at six o'clock, ten o'clock, whatever, and in between times I'll twiddle my thumbs. A ship when it's in the ocean can't say well I like that wave, so I'll go with that wave but I don't like that wave and so I'm going to stay still. Well, actually being in a site isn't like that. Of course when one says site, it sounds very abstract. It is never a situation where you can just create order. It will always be problematic. You cannot even say that pain and pleasure are stable. These things have no resolution in terms of pleasure and pain but only in terms of the comic and the tragic and these are concepts.

*In your **Lear,** there is clearly a strong imperative towards order and control, which seems to be Orestean. Yet is it the case that Lear travels on a journey which takes him into the Oedipal, paradoxically, through the process of seeking to exert, establish, and maintain a state of order which is both ideological and Orestean?*

That's a very complex question! It is a hard question but it's a very good question. Can Hamlet be Lear's son? . . . The answer is no. What Shakespeare does is to use fiction to create two separate situations and there is integrity about both. If you look at Hamlet, he doesn't travel. He only travels once and then he travels—unknowingly—with his death warrant. So he returns and the only other place that Hamlet goes to is this graveyard. Once Hamlet steps outside of his castle he's in the area of death. Lear travels. He leaves the castle and travels into the wasteland as it were. What Shakespeare is doing I think is compartmentalizing the problem and that's why Hamlet depends an awful lot on accident. Hamlet says be ready for whatever comes. That's not the same as being ready to act. It is why Beckett uses the wasteland so much. He tries to put Hamlet and Lear together in *Waiting for Godot*. It is not Newton's problem. In *Godot* it's a matter of maintaining a conversation in order to pacify your other self. So it's sterile. Nobody dies in a Beckett play. What he does is to write dead characters because they're very safe. They don't have the problems of life because they're dead and that gives them a very great security.

*In **Bingo**, at the start of the play, the historical evidence tells us that Shakespeare has traveled beyond the walls of his garden (in the context of his life in London and the theatre) but has now returned to be within them: a very enclosed space. It's true isn't it that when Shakespeare goes up onto the hill in order to see the woman who has been executed on the hill, that it's not his first journey "beyond the walls"? When he goes to visit her corpse, is that a moment when those images of walking through the streets of London with heads on spikes and so on, which he talks about, is confronting the woman, confronting what he has been seeking to escape from, or not?*

Whether he's seeking to escape from it is not as clear as his obvious need to confront it, which is what he does. When he goes on to that heath, he is going onto his property. He has paid the hangman as it were. When I use space I very often tend to put a price on it. It's like at the end of *When We Dead Awaken,* Ibsen regards the mountain, which before has been the source of the trolls, etc. He now says this has the potential for great wealth and power. If you look at **Restoration,** one senses that it's an idyllic landscape. It's also, however, a very cruel landscape to the peasants. It's only Hardacre who puts a price on things. That's where the coal is and that's where money is and it's because of money that Bob will hang.

In Peter Ackroyd's biography of Shakespeare I read that Shakespeare left an ornamental sword to Combe and I thought, as a statement in highly material terms, this man with whom he had entered into discussions and agreements about the enclosure of land, it's the gift that stands out.

It's very, very strange and one wonders whether he's being ironical. He's not I don't think, but if that were the case, it's an irony that would make one weep.

From the moment when Combe enters Shakespeare's garden, he creates the conditions in which Shakespeare has to begin to make decisions about transactions, materiality and economic value in that sense. The savage death of the woman—a state sanctioned death—somehow visually, as a "theatre event" embodies the contradiction of the internalized Oedipal conflict that Shakespeare experiences, but also the Orestean conflict of land and value and money?

Yes, I think it's very important to recognize that **Bingo** is based on fact and that you can't really understand what Shakespeare was as a poet unless you realize what he did as a real estate agent. Unless you do that, you can't really write sense about Shakespeare, you can't say why he did these things. As they're not reducible to abstract descriptions but contain values, it's what Combe says to him: "I'm on the side of progress." It's

not that I want to reduce the plays to the man but that the man will give you clues to the world. He became an icon—the "sage of Stratford"—and one had to somehow get beyond that idea.

OVERVIEWS AND GENERAL STUDIES

Ruby Cohn (essay date 1981)

SOURCE: Cohen, Ruby. "The Fabulous Theater of Edward Bond." In *Essays on Contemporary British Drama,* edited by Hedwig Bock and Albert Wertheim, pp. 185-204. Munich: Max Hueber Verlag, 1981.

[*In the following essay, Cohn traces elements of fabulism throughout Bond's theatrical canon.*]

"If I had to name my theatre I would call it The Rational Theatre."[1] If I had to name Bond's theater, I would not call it rational but fabulous. Bond does not seem to me his most discerning critic, but then he has finer things to do—like write plays.[2] Although I shall not again quote Bond in order to disagree with him—and I shall quote only stingily from his essays—I realize that my view of his work diverges from his own. Bond's Fabulous Theater then, in the second and especially the third *OED* definitions: "2. Spoken of or celebrated in fable or myth; 3. Of a narrative; Of the nature of a fable or myth." Bond's plays seek rational direction through theatricalization of fable. Roaming through time and place, his ten major dramas may be grouped for convenience: surface realism of **The Pope's Wedding, Saved, The Sea**; invented or embellished history of **Early Morning, Bingo, The Fool**; war fables of **The Narrow Road to the Deep North, The Bundle, Lear,** and **The Woman.**

Author not only of these ten plays, but also five minor plays, four stories, an opera libretto, a ballet, three translations, two adaptations, several film scripts, a volume of verse, and various essays. The last rubric bristles with exposition of ideas—"Millstones round the Playwright's Neck," "Censor in Mind," "The Murder of Children." In Bond's plays, however, he *dramatizes* ideas through lapidary phrases, theatrical scenes, vivid characters, and complex fables. Living with his family in a village near Cambridge, he is politically committed to the British New Left and artistically committed to all his work, major and minor.

The drama critic may skim over the minor works, written by request, but even they show him as an irrepressible fabulist: **Black Mass** (1970), **Passion** (1971), **Stone**

(1976), *Grandma Faust* (1976), *The Swing* (1976). Blunt and funny agit-prop, they are not unrelated to Bond's opera libretto *We Come to the River* (1976). Written five years after *Lear,* the libretto depicts a comparable education of the protagonist and stages the same dramatic metaphor of insight through blinding. When the General learns that he is about to lose his sight, revulsion wells up against his profession, against the caricature figures of his country, and against the soldiers he has ordered to commit atrocities. He sees himself tainted by the destruction of two families, and, refusing to serve any longer, he is committed to an insane asylum where the mad people kill him. The opera closes on two counter-pointed choruses—the war victims (including the dead) at the river and the madmen in the asylum. Played in three areas of a vast stage, each with its own orchestra, the opera is richly textured in sound, as well as socially sophisticated in theme.[3]

Agit-prop and libretto are not of course Bond's most resonant achievements, but they mark the areas of his commitment, the liveliness of his plotting, and the deadliness of his satiric instruments—mainly dialect and parody—that cut more sparingly in his major plays, which begin with *The Pope's Wedding* (1962). Before that he submitted to the Royal Court Theatre Writer's Group "two short plays . . . one of which was rather Beckett-like, and the other rather Brecht-like in style."[4] Both masters are blended in *The Pope's Wedding,* but naturalized into Bond's theater idiom—pithy phrases, sixteen short scenes, individuals in tension with an established society. What Bond borrowed from Beckett (and perhaps from Raleigh Trevelyan's *A Hermit Disclosed*) is the hermit Alen, who fascinates the play's protagonist, Scopey. What Bond borrowed from Brecht (who learned it from Shakespeare) is the suggestion of a whole society in swift interchanges of incidental characters. What Bond borrowed from both playwrights is a nearly bare stage where the few props gain illumination. *The Pope's Wedding* sets hermit and society in an invisible English countryside (Essex) that is bankrupt economically, culturally, morally.

Bond has explained his provocative title: "The Pope's Wedding is an impossible ceremony—Scopey's asking for an invitation for something that isn't going to happen, that *can't* happen."[5] What can't happen is, however, less simple and more shocking than a pope's wedding. Scopey not only asks for an invitation to an impossible event; he commits murder when the impossible can't happen, when he cannot enter another man's skin and soul.

Twenty-two year old Scopey, whose name relates only by sound to the titular pope, strains inarticulately against the limitations of his small farm-village world: he snatches a new handbag from eighteen-year old Pat, he excels in a local cricket match, he sneaks away from the victory celebration to enjoy Pat sexually, he marries her and offers to help her care for the old hermit Alen, the charge of Pat's dead mother. Gradually replacing his wife as the old man's caretaker, Scopey leaves his cricket team, and spends so much time with the hermit that he loses his job. All in the obsession to learn: "What yoo 'ere for?" By the play's last of fifteen scenes Scopey has strangled the hermit and *become* a hermit in Alen's hut, without penetrating the phenomenon of hermitage. The pope cannot wed.

What Bond has contrived in this naturalistic play is greater sympathy for the murderer than for anyone in his environment. Like Macbeth, Scopey commits no violence onstage. Like Macbeth, Scopey defies his social order, and like Macbeth, he is unfulfilled by mere worldly comforts. Unlike Macbeth, however, Scopey has no lexicon to express his frustration, and, true to the naturalist tradition that stems from Buechner's *Woyzeck,* he vents that frustration in violence. This seldom seen theater piece provides vivid scenic fragments—a distant cricket game, a postcoitus love scene, a terrified hermit in his hut. Empty community is juxtaposed with an empty hut; the former is filled with cheap consumer goods, and the latter with piles of newspapers, cans of food, and rudimentary furnishings. Through these voids rings Bond's stripped dialogue, pleading with the audience in Pat's final line: "'Elp!"

The Pope's Wedding received a single initial performance at a Royal Court Sunday Evening, whereas *Saved* (1965) was a *succès de scandale* in the same theater. They are companion contrasts that barely hint at the variety to flow. The one is populated with rootless village youth, the other with rootless urban youth; most characters are in their early twenties. Sex sours into obsession for Scopey, and sex is displaced by concern for Len. The protagonist of *The Pope's Wedding* commits murder, and the protagonist of *Saved* watches while a baby is murdered. The protagonist of *The Pope's Wedding* chokes off his future in choking old Alen, but the protagonist of *Saved* may save or be saved by his adopted family. Bond claims: "Scopey is obviously Len in *Saved* . . ."[6]

Scopey and Len alone probe their respective worlds with questions, however monosyllabic. Early scenes in both plays reveal their sexual joy in prowess, and both protagonists wish to sustain and domesticate such joy. Len rents a room from Pam's parents, who haven't spoken to one another in some twenty-five years. After Pam bears a child, she turns against Len and takes up with Fred. Len tends Pam and the baby, and he befriends Fred, who soon tires of Pam. Quarreling with Fred in the park one evening, Pam leaves the baby in its pram. Bored, the South London youths (including Fred but lacking Len) push the pram at one another, half plaything, half weapon. When that game palls, they dare one another to pull the baby's hair, pinch it, hit it, rub its face in a soiled diaper. Egging each other on, they throw stones at the target in the pram, but leave the park when the closing bell sounds. After "A long pause" Pam returns to claim her baby; she wheels the pram away, without looking inside—at her dead infant. It is this scene that grounded Bond's reputation as a playwright of violence, when he should have received acclaim as a scenewright of skill. With flawless rhythm, abrupt gestures punctuate the Cockney banter until, unheeded by anyone on stage, a baby lies battered to death.

When Fred is imprisoned for the death of the baby, Len brings him cigarettes. Confessing that he saw the stoning from a treetop, Len blames himself: "I didn't know what t'do. Well, I should a stopped yer." Again rejected by Pam, Len has a passing flirtation with Pam's mother, and finally decides to leave the "home," but Pam's father dissuades him: "I'd like yer t'stay. If yer can see yer way to." In the final scene of *Saved* each of the four "family" members is preoccupied with his own task, the father mailing a letter, the mother straightening the living room, Pam perusing the *Radio Times,* and Len fixing a chair. The single line of dialogue is Len's request to Pam: "Fetch me 'ammer." Nobody does, but Len fixes the chair anyway—the chair broken during a fight of the older couple—and the final silence is a harmonious lull in this household where words are blows. It is an open question who is saved in this drama where no one saves a helpless infant. Searching both individuals and their societies, these naturalistic plays do not yet show Bond the fabulist.[7]

With *Early Morning* Bond takes a giant step away from naturalism and into fable, although few critics recognized it at the time—1968. In that year of historic upheaval Bond contributed his own explosive version of history, one power bloodily displacing another on earth as in heaven. If *The Pope's Wedding* shocks by its title, and *Saved* by the scene of the baby stoned, *Early Morning* offends British shibboleths of history, religion, sexual ethics, and it does so through the length of a diabolically comic fable, which ends in heaven. Before the end, however, Bond has collapsed chronology to render ridiculous the prosperous reign of Queen Victoria, that bastion of English self-satisfaction. Far from her idyllic marriage to Prince Albert, Bond has the royal couple plot one another's assassinations. The Disraeli whom Victoria liked and the Gladstone whom she disliked (both Prime Minister after the real Albert's death) join conspiratorially with him. Queen Victoria's nine children are condensed into Siamese twins, Arthur and George (the former an actual name of one of her sons, the latter otherwise rich in royal resonance). The Florence Nightingale whom Victoria decorated and the John Brown who was her favorite manservant merge into a single character who is betrothed to the Prince of Wales, raped by Queen Victoria, named the first public hangwoman, compelled by her conscience to fornicate with dying soldiers, killed while catering to Disraeli and Gladstone simultaneously; in heaven she is the only one sensitive to the unregenerate humanity of Arthur.[8]

Outrageously, Bond claims: "The events of this play are true." Very loosely, they are. Victoria stood for victory of Capitalism over Chartism, respectability over morality, family cohesion over individual creativity, and repression over freedom throughout a widespread empire. It was during her reign that British "free" trade converted England into a consumer society. Brilliantly, Bond literalizes the metaphor: law, order, and uniformity are established when human beings consume one another's humanity—the stage cannibalism. But *Early Morning* is not Gothic melodrama, in which the great are debunked and the humble ennobled; the commoners—invented characters—are as cruel as the privileged, and the only one who shrinks from horrendous deeds (bordering on Grand Guignol) is the Arthur part of the Siamese twins, who—significantly—possesses their single heart. Immoral and moral aspects of the same character, George the Crown Prince accepts the Establishment on earth and cannibalism in heaven, but Arthur demurs in both realms. The heir of Len and Scopey, he probes the basis of behavior. "Why did you kill him—" he asks repetitively of the Len of *Early Morning,* a commoner whose violence and cannibalism on earth predict that of his betters in heaven. It is Arthur who designs a tug of war to annihilate opposing inhumane armies, and it is Arthur who refuses to accede to celestial cannibalism, even if George must waste away. It is Arthur who dominates the end of the play visually in Bond's revised version of *Early Morning.* In the original last scene (of twenty-one) Victoria nails Arthur (separated from George) into his coffin with her teeth. In the revised version Arthur rises from his coffin, unseen by the others who feast on his corpse. Only Florence abstains from food as she weeps for Arthur—early mourning—and pleads dirt in her eye. With Arthur visible on high, Victoria declares: "There's no dirt in heaven. There's only peace and happiness, law and order, consent and cooperation. My life's work has borne fruit. It's settled." But closing the play, and deflating Victoria's rhetoric is Len's request: "Pass us that leg."

Sympathetic as Arthur is on his second death and ascension to an invisible heaven, it is not he who endows the play with dramatic force, but rather the inventive shock of the whole fable. The first scene surprises Albert and Disraeli plotting Victoria's murder, the third reveals Arthur and George as Siamese twins, the fifth features a pastoral picnic with moments of shoe fetishism, Lesbianism between Victoria and Florence Nightingale, poisoning of Albert by Victoria, struggles for pistol and rifle, and wounding of George Prince of Wales. By

Scene 12 George's body is decomposing, and Arthur marshalls a mammoth tug of war in which the losing army topples over a cliff, and the winners tumble to death when the cliff becomes an avalanche. Scene 16 finds the whole cast in a heaven which mirrors earth—its savagery, oppression, and pious rhetoric. Except for Arthur, all the inhabitants engage in candid cannibalism, and even he occasionally weakens into self-consumption. In the play's final scene Arthur's severed head makes love to Florence beneath her skirts, but George bites into the offending member. Arthur laughs loudly—his last sound in the play. As the whole cast picnic on Arthur's corpse, a celestial soldier pronounces his epitaph: "'E weren' a bad bloke. Juss couldn't keep 'is-self to 'is-self." This will be true of all Bond's fabulous heroes—acting in larger contexts than their mere selves.

Even today, when Bond's plays are beginning to command the attention they deserve, *Early Morning* has been less than popular. One of the few shocking plays to retain its shock power—*Look Back in Anger* is conservative; *The Blacks* is fast dating; *Godot* is already a classic—it is a Gothic farce that has tempted few directors—like Jarry's *Ubu* before recent appreciation. Arthur Arnold has acutely observed: "Shakespeare's early blunders with literal sons-in-the-pie cannibalism were never repeated, although the image is often repeated."[9] Bond does not even repeat the image, but human ferocity is often repeated—no later than his next play, the first to be set outside of England, but including English characters.

Narrow Road to the Deep North (1968), commissioned by the Canon of Coventry Cathedral for the International People and Cities Conference, was written in two and a half days, and it played to small houses in Coventry (English church plays have come a long way since T. S. Eliot produced *The Rock* for Canterbury Cathedral in 1934). Ostensibly treating the set theme of People and Cities, Bond creates Buddhists and Christians to theatricalize a plague on both their houses.

As in ***Early Morning*** Bond collapses chronology, but this goes unremarked in the unfamiliar history of Japan. The actual Basho, a seventeenth-century poet and scholar, wrote a Japanese classic *The Narrow Road to the Deep North,* at once a travel account and what his translator calls "a monument he has set up against the flow of time." Bond plunges *his* Basho right back into time while mocking it. Bond takes only the title from the poet's best-known work, and from another account an incident about an abandoned child. Subtitled "A comedy," Bond's play is set in "Japan about the seventeenth, eighteenth, or nineteenth centuries." This cavalier attitude toward time is one of the comic notes of the so-called comedy.

Bond's Basho becomes Prime Minister for a nineteenth-century British Commodore-imperialist. Before that, however, Bond's Basho behaves like the historical Basho on seeing an abandoned child: "Alas, it seems to me that this child's undeserved suffering has been caused by something far greater and more massive, what one might call the irresistible will of heaven. If it is so, child, you must raise your voice to heaven, and I must pass on, leaving you behind."[10] With few changes, Bond rhythms these words dramatically: "It hasn't done anything to *earn* this suffering—it's caused by something greater and more massive: you could call it the irresistible will of heaven. So it must cry to heaven. And I must go north." And north he goes, in search of enlightenment.

Fiction begins thirty years later, when Bond's Basho returns enlightened and again stands on his refusal—to serve as religious master to the young monk, Kiro. Basho's home city is in the grip of the warlord Shogo, who was once the child abandoned at the river. A Janus-figure, Shogo in a single scene saves Kiro from strangulation by breaking a holy pot, and a moment later condemns an innocent man to be thrown into the river. Having killed the Emperor in seizing power, he gives the infant-Emperor to Basho, to be brought up as a peasant.

Equally horrified by Shogo's sacrilege and cruelty, Basho travels north again, seeking not enlightenment but the power of an army led by an English Commodore and a Victorian Salvation Army sister Georgina. By Part II Georgina has replaced Shogo's atrocity with her efficient but even more oppressive piety. Fled on the narrow road to the deep north, Shogo and Kiro find not enlightenment but mutual interdependence, so that Kiro reluctantly follows Shogo south to conquer his city. Since the Commodore's conquest was waged in the name of the infant Emperor, Shogo kills five identically dressed children, one of whom is probably the Emperor, and Georgina goes mad. With Basho as Prime Minister, the Commodore has Shogo hacked to death. As Georgina blends a rape fantasy with a call on Jesus, Kiro disembowels himself by the very river where Basho first left the child. A man emerges from the river, scolding Kiro for not rescuing him. Kiro dies as the man dries himself. Barbarians control the city in this "comedy," but new life starts at the river and not on the narrow road to the deep north.

By 1978, a decade after ***Narrow Road*** was swiftly written, Bond revised it to ***The Bundle.*** Both plays begin and end at the river, but the adventurous mediating action diverges. The springboard is again Basho's refusal to stray from the narrow road to the deep north, to care for an abandoned child. Bond's new theater fable focuses more sharply on that child, soon grown to manhood. Like the abandoned prince in Brecht's *Caucasian*

Chalk Circle, this child thrives on the sacrifices of his adoptive parents. Like the Water-Carrier in Brecht's *Good Woman of Setzchuan* this child is named Wang, and his society resembles China on the verge of the Communist Revolution. In Bond's stage world Wang is a prime mover of that revolution; the titular bundle is a child at the play's beginning and a cargo of rifles by the end.

With **The Bundle** Edward Bond claims that he has embarked on his third cycle of plays, which dramatize an analysis instead of a story, but story is rife in **The Bundle.** What Bond does dramatize is the diametric opposition of the ethics of Basho and Wang; Basho does not shelter the abandoned baby because he pursues self-indulgence on the road north. Wang does not shelter the abandoned baby because he pursues a single-minded goal of arming the peasants to withstand their oppressors. In the first **Narrow Road** as in **Early Morning,** one tyrannical power bloodily replaces another, and the only hope on the horizon is a naked nameless man at the very end of the play. In **The Bundle** hope rests firmly on peasants armed by Wang. At play's end two major characters address the audience directly. Basho, who has served the establishment in its oppression, is still seeking a metaphysical road, whereas the revolutionary Wang is frankly didactic: "To judge rightly what is good—to choose between good and evil—that is all that it is to be human." Before that unabashed declaration, however, the play vibrates with passionate characters—the poor Ferryman and his wife who adopt the infant that Basho spurns, the competitive peasants who cooperate as soon as their oppressors are overthrown, the bandits that Wang converts into a populist army, the soldiers and merchants in unregenerate self-interest.

More than in **Narrow Road** Basho weaves his delicate poems through **The Bundle,** but Wang is a poet too, and the play abounds in imagery of water, energy, vegetation. Basho has himself become a narrow road to a perennial north.

Although **Early Morning** and **Narrow Road** brim with fabulous material, it is in **Lear** (1971) that the fabulist achieves towering mythic dimension. Bond's own summary of his play juxtaposes myth unfavorably with reality: "Act One shows a world dominated by myth. Act Two shows the clash between myth and reality, between superstitious men and the autonomous world. Act Three shows a resolution of this, in the world we prove real by dying in it." The "we" extrapolates Bond's Lear whose death closes the play. It is with a sense of "we" that I write of Bond's Fabulous Theater—theater dramatizing dynamic events about a moral giant whose fate awakens not only pity and terror but complicity.

Bond is bold to risk a **Lear** that triggers comparison with Shakespeare's tragedy, but he thereby became

England's major living dramatist. Most telling in both plays is the rechilding of the king, so that we experience the long painful fable of his education. Shakespeare's king moves from imperious rage to self-pity to contrition toward Cordelia, to compassion for the Fool, to "Poor naked wretches whereso'er you are," and, finally, to the utter humility of kneeling to Cordelia—before his variously interpreted death. Bond's Lear learns comparably: looking at the disfigured face of his daughters' victim, he confronts his own mortality. To protect his Fool-figure, the Gravedigger's Boy, he unhesitantly lies, and he later agrees to help the Ghost of the Gravedigger's Boy, to whom he did "a great wrong once, a very great wrong." After the death of Lear's daughters, he assumes responsibility for their atrocities. In the classical tradition, he sees morally after he is blinded; as Bond states it in his preface: "Lear is blind till they take his eyes away. . . . Blindness is a dramatic metaphor for insight . . ." Blind Lear offers asylum to deserters from Cordelia's wall, and he admits to her that there is no difference between his daughters and him. Finally, he learns that pastoral withdrawal is impossible within society. Failing to convince Cordelia to pull down the wall, he goes to the wall that he himself initiated, in order to undig it. In the revised end Bond has a junior officer shoot Lear, killing him instantly, but "The shovel stays upright in the earth." The wall workers are ordered to leave the scene. "The workers go quickly and orderly. One of them looks back." In that look back Bond punctuates the fabulous dimension; we should all look back on the education of his Lear; the autocrat is elevated to autodidact, wiping the slate of his mind with madness.

Bond has declared: "My plays are about the quest for freedom of one man"¹¹ Lear's quest is strongly theatrical. He has to find his way through two walls—the first cruelly visible and the second a metaphor for well-wishers and sympathetic strangers. It is only when Lear can tear down the metaphoric wall that he acquires the resolution to assault the physical wall.

Of Bond's fabulous plays **Lear** has the hardest narrative drive through eighteen scenes (with fifteen scene changes). In **Lear** Bond also achieves increased complexity of character. Lear the royal villain learns to be a victim. Warrington-Gloucester is twice dehumanized; at play's start he is the king's principal and unprincipled adviser, telling him mechanically what he wants to hear; by the end of Act I he has been tortured into a terrified dangerous animal. Although Lear's daughters are caricature termagants, even they are momentarily appealing as the ghosts of the girls they once were. In contrast, the Gravedigger's Boy—an odd designation for a man—is immediately endearing in his simplicity and tenderness, but his ghostly guise slowly alienates us before his second violent death. Cordelia is ambiguous but completely unshakespearean; a priest's daughter with small charity, a pregnant wife with an adoring lover, an ungracious hostess who reacts to rape with a single gasp and a life of hatred—she selflessly leads a revolution and is just as selflessly deaf to Lear's plea that she learn by his errors.

In Bond's Preface to *Lear* he points out that seventy odd small roles may be viewed as "one role showing the character of a society," but there is diversity in that society. The king's soldiers are as practical and shrewdly humorous as the rebel forces. Farmers, prisoners, politicians—Bond distinguishes their diction and speech rhythms. So enmeshed is Bond's social fabric that the play's first director, William Gaskill, warned his actors: "If you relate too much you'll break up the scene."[12]

Scenewright Bond works in massive contours unlocalized as to time and place. Alternating between open air and prison scenes, the play begins and ends at the wall that is both. As the river will change from enemy to friend of man in *The Bundle,* so the wall changes from defensive measure to repressive symbol for Lear, and through Lear for us. It is hard to see a stage river, but a stage wall was massive set and prop at the Royal Court Theatre.

Less ceremoniously than Shakespeare, Bond plunges us *in medias res* in his opening scene; the division of *his* kingdom happens through civil war, when Lear's daughters marry invaders. War's confusions rage through Bond's violent play, its brutalities sometime skirting Grand Guignol. To some extent Bond builds the possibility for laughter into the very horror of such scenes as the businesslike torture of Warrington while one daughter knits and the other jumps excitedly, the wisecracks of the soldiers as the blood of the Gravedigger's Boy stains the freshly laundered sheets, the corrupt comments of the judge as mad Lear looks in the mirror, the autopsy of Lear's daughter—"Then let them anatomize Regan."—and the almost clerical crown-blinding of Lear. Director Gaskill rightly enjoined the Royal Court cast: "Never play the character, always play the situation."[13]

In Bond's *Lear,* as in Shakespeare's, images of vision and maiming abound, but most striking is Bond's domestication of Shakespeare's animal imagery. As king, Bond's Lear calls his people sheep and his enemies wolves. When mad, he sees himself as a dog and a mouse. The program for the Royal Court production pictures a monkey in a cage, but Lear's plea is wider, reaching out to horse and bird, and crying: "Let that animal out of the cage!" Lear's dead daughter is to him a blend of lion, lamb, and child. He compares the subservient farmer's family unfavorably to wolf, fox, and horse, and he accuses men of behaving like jackals and wolves. Sane and admired as a saint, Lear narrates

a fable of a man's voice in a bird's body. His last fantasy wish is to be as cunning as the fox. These diverse images accumulate into a powerful illustration of Shakespeare's great line: "Unaccommodated man is no more but such a poor bare forked animal as thou art." Image and dialect, quip and anachronism, character and caricature, virtue and violence cohere theatrically in Bond's *Lear,* a fabulous drama.

Two years after this tumultous drama—in 1973—Bond completed two quieter plays, *The Sea* and *Bingo.* However, *The Sea* begins stormily, a man drowning while a paranoid coastguardsman ignores the desperate pleas of his friend who has managed to swim to shore. For the first time since *Saved* Bond returns to realism—of an East Coast English town in 1907. With the deftness acquired in sketching anachronistic societies, Bond swiftly—in eight scenes of which five take place by the sea—depicts an English village hierarchy, with Mrs. Rafi at the head, her social coterie just below her, tradesmen like the draper Hatch dependent upon her, and laborers like Hollarcut completely at her small mercy; she is a provincial Victoria—"The town is full of her cripples." Only Evens, a hermit and alcoholic, lives far from her in a beach-hut, so close to the sea that he alone ripples the realistic surface.

Although *The Sea* skirts the edge of fable, its story is more intricate than *The Pope's Wedding* or *Saved,* its society is more varied, and its characters do not precipitate into simple satire. In spite of Willy's frantic attempts at rescue, Colin drowns because Evens the wise hermit is too drunk to be helpful and Hatch the mad draper believes the coast is being invaded by extraterrestrials. Yet Evens is optimistically understanding of nature and society, and Hatch is more victim than villain. The dead man's fiancée Rose is devoted to him, and yet, on the advice of Mrs. Rafi, she joins Willy in leaving the town. Mrs. Rafi herself is at once self-pitying and self-critical.

Bond easily twists three plot-threads—the social hierarchy's daily doings, the conspiracy of the paranoid vigilantes, and the understated romance of the young lovers. Two—grotesque scenes—plays within the play—comment pointedly on the action. Mrs. Rafi is author, director, and actress in *Orpheus and Eurydice,* but she charms no one with her melodies (especially her rendition of "There's no place like home"), and, far from rescuing anyone from the underworld, she stifles everyone she touches with her well-gloved hand. She dominates the scene of Colin's funeral, theatrically set on a cliff overlooking the sea, with piano music and army guns sounding in the background, and a descant rivalry overriding any hint of grief. When Hatch interrupts the funeral with his fantasy, he seems no madder than the respectable townspeople at their service. In a harmonious final scene Evens the hermit enunciates a philosophy for the couple who will found a new society in this rightly named "Comedy": "Remember, I've told you these things so that you won't despair. But you must still change the world." The "things" Evens tells make the play resonate beyond specific realism. As loquacious a hermit as Alen of *The Pope's Wedding* was laconic, Evens comprehends the nature of the sea, and he enjoins Willy to comprehend human nature.

The protagonist of Bond's next play *Bingo* believes that he has failed to change the world, and he does despair. His name is also Willy—William Shakespeare of ***Bingo: Scenes of Money and Death.*** Bingo is a game played for money on numbered squares, and so is Bond's play. The "and" of the subtitle ties money, the goal of several characters including Shakespeare, to death, which grips several characters including Shakespeare.

Bingo belongs to the group of plays I designate as invented or embellished history, and Bond's Introduction to the published text enumerates his changes "for dramatic convenience."[14] Set in and around Shakespeare's still extant home at New Place, Stratford, in 1615-6, the play depicts a weak and bloodless bard, who is a virtual stranger in his own family and his own town, and who is confronted with the energies of nascent capitalism. Anxious about financial security, Shakespeare acquiesces to the land enclosures that starve out poor farmers and force them to migrate. The play's villain Combe—also named William—guarantees Shakespeare's holdings at the price of his silence in the protest against enclosure: "It pays to sit in a garden."

This public plot about Shakespeare, money, and death is balanced by a private plot—the whole in six scenes—about Shakespeare, money, and death, for Shakespeare's wife (never seen on stage) and daughter Judith are the money-hungry puppets he has made of them: "I loved you with money." Family love is dead, and Judith values her father's money above his life. In a parallel pattern that Bond learned from Shakespeare, he contrasts that family trio with a nameless family composed of his wise old servant, her mentally deficient husband, and their radical Puritan son. Mother loves husband and son, but son abhors the carnal appetites of his childlike father. Dispossessed by the enclosures, rebellious against such dispossession, the son accidentally shoots the father in a wintry confrontation of opposing forces.

Each half of the six-scene play pivots on an outsider's arrival in Stratford.[15] Part I presents a nameless, home-less Young Woman, soon sentenced to whipping "till the blood runs" and afterwards to hanging. She graphically binds the plot threads—given money by Shakespeare and blame by his daughter, fornicating with the feeble-minded Old Man, judged by landowner Combe in his office of magistrate. Her gibbeted body is visible

throughout Scene 3. In Part II Ben Jonson is a slimmer binding thread. Stopping in Stratford on his walk to Scotland, vigorous with lived experience, Jonson confesses his long hatred of Shakespeare, shows the dispirited Bard the poison he has no courage to swal-low, and is oblivious to the peasant-rebels at the next table of the inn.

Outsiders are gone after Scene 4, but Jonson's poison—acquisition unexplained—is in Shakespeare's posses-sion in Scenes 5 and 6. Bedridden in the final scene, Shakespeare is beset by his hysterical wife, his importunate daughter, and the Puritan son rationalizing away his guilt at his father's death. The bard intones: "Was anything done? Was anything done?" When Combe enters his sickroom, Shakespeare swallows the poison as a medicine. He falls to the floor when Judith enters. Instead of tending him, she searches frenetically for his will, crying in disappointment: "Nothing." The "emptiness and silence" at play's start lead to the death and nothing at the end.

Shakespeare is Bond's second poet-villain, following Japanese Basho in serving capitalism and failing to sup-port rebels. But Basho is virtually unknown to Western audiences, whereas Shakespeare is a culture hero. Compared to Bond's earlier shock effects, condemning Shakespeare is mild, especially since the play evokes sympathy for a man of exquisite conscience without self-pity. By unshakespearean soliloquies—pithy noun phrases, abrupt associations—Bond's stage bard is a rarity of conviction, but for few critics. Bond's portrait of old Shakespeare casts a shadow over the patina of comfort at New Place in Stratford, should one happen to visit it as I did—post-*Bingo.*

The most frequent scenic direction in *Bingo* is: "Shake-speare doesn't react," and uncannily, Patrick Stewart as Shakespeare rendered the passivity actively, silence projecting dismay at the ubiquity of suffering. In Scene 3 Puritans picnic near the gibbeted Young Woman, and they register no awareness of an abyss between such punishment and their prayers, but Shakespeare associ-ates her fate with London bear-baiting at his theater. In Scene 4 Shakespeare hears the rebellious conspiracy counterpointed against Jonson's drunken confession of hatred. Scene 6 parades the Son and Combe, social antagonists, by Shakespeare's bed. What Director Wil-liam Gaskill said of *Lear* seems just as true of *Bingo*: "I think the main moments are those when more than one thing is happening on stage at once."[16]

One might view *Bingo* (1973) and *The Fool* (1975) as Bond's classical and romantic play on the same subject—the writer's relationship with society (following facts only minimally about both the Bard and the Northamptonshire Peasant Poet). Although Bond does not obey the classical unities in *Bingo,* he approaches them, with setting in and around New Place, with time-span of a little over half a year. *Bingo* begins, like classical tragedy, close to its dénouement, driving the fable hard toward the dénouement—Shakespeare's willed death. *The Fool,* in contrast, moves back and forth geographically from Northumberland to London; the timespan is some forty years, and the plot rambles through several peripetias—John Clare seeking Mary and thus avoiding arrest, his refusal to expunge class criticism from his poems, his romanticizing of Mary while married to Patty, his commitment to an insane asylum, his brief escape from the asylum. Both Bond protagonist-poets avoid social action, but dramatic focus is more relentlessly on Shakespeare than on Clare.

The eight scenes of *The Fool* are only a slight increase over the six of *Bingo,* but they are more liberally peopled—some forty speaking parts against twelve. Digressions from the plot-line occur more often in *The Fool*—a mummer's play within the play, a London prize-fight, between a Black and an Irishman, alcoholic Charles Lamb and his mad sister Mary, Irish vagabonds (which were eliminated in the Royal Court production). These digressions are pregnant thematically, but they deflect apprehension of the narrative line. However it is language that is of almost classical limpidity in *Bingo* as compared with the variety of *The Fool*—the lugubrious piety of the parson, the gentlemen's clichés, the pseudo-lyricism of literary Mrs. Emmerson, the gambling slang of the boxer-backers, and especially the rhythmic dialect of the villagers. Never mired in unnatural diction, they express emotion through repetition of simple words, particularly "'on't" which can mean don't, won't, can't, shouldn't, wouldn't, am not. "On'y" and "'on't" pulse through John Clare's mad self-awareness before he is reduced to slavering consonants.

It would be wrong, however, to view *The Fool* as a romantic variant on *Bingo.* Martin Esslin has succinctly summarized the central difference between these two poets who have attracted Bond the playwright: "The Shakespeare of *Bingo* is a highly successful artist who becomes enmeshed in society's guilt precisely *because* he is a financial success and has to invest his money, whereas *The Fool* shows the fate of an artist who cannot support himself by his writing. . . . *The Fool* dramatizes the life story—and the bewilderment—of an individual of great talent who lacks the self-awareness which would enable him to master his personal destiny, just as he also lacks the historical and political consciousness that would allow him to make rational political decisions. . . . It is this lack of understanding which makes Bond's Clare a *fool.*"[17]

John Clare, Peasant Poet, is Bond's Fool, but capitalism—far more liberally represented than in *Bingo*—is guilty in robbing him of the Bread and Love of the subtitle—Scenes of Bread and Love. Clare the Peasant

Poet undoubtedly attracts Bond by his precise participation in the natural world, his pungent colloquial diction, his unabashed class-consciousness. For that poet in that society Bond finds two main images—the prison (the setting of Scene 4) and the madhouse (the final setting). Metaphorically, they hem Clare in in all the scenes, and yet they are the only cooperative communities in the play. Initiated by John Clare, insane laughter tears through the prison. By the final scene mad John Clare is incomprehensible, but mad Mary Lamb has no problem with his mumblings, and she imperturbably translates them into the words that magnetized him above bread or love.

Bingo and *The Fool* are Bond's first plays to carry subtitles beginning "Scenes of. . . ." The phrase misleads one to expect a drama of high points rather than the coherent structures, the theatrical fables they are. If *Bingo* coheres more deeply, *The Fool* ranges more widely. As scenes of money and death freeze *Bingo,* scenes of bread and love provide a dynamic of *The Fool.* Mary feeds Clare stolen bread; the prison warder gives bread to the prisoners; Mary Lamb has killed her mother with a breadknife. In a surrealistic scene of Clare's mad mind, Mary feeds bread to dead, blind Darkie, but he cannot swallow it. Even in his madness, Clare comes to understand the power of bread: "I am a poet an' I teach men how to eat." Durable love exists only between peasants who unite for bread—whether to present plays, steal goods, or comfort one another in prison—and their (invented) leader is pointedly named Darkie—a name that underlines Bond's scenic oppositions of light and dark. The first four scenes—Part I—are performed in darkness, and the last four—Part II—in increasingly bright light. Since no character in the play undergoes enlightenment, Bond may have intended light as a metaphor for the audience understanding. One can only hope, when the blindness of reviewers has receded into oblivion, that illumination will come.

We come finally not to a river but to a masterwork, *The Woman* (1978).[18] A play of unparalleled scale, *The Woman* is a dramatic analogue of *The Iliad* and—not *Odyssey* or *Aeneid* but *Ismeneid* or *Hecubaid.* Written before *The Bundle,* these "Scenes of War and Freedom" are viewed by Bond as the last in his second cycle of plays, whose aim is to de-mythologize the past, to reject the idea of "a golden age [in which] all the answers were known."[19] I view *The Woman* as the last to date of Bond's war fables, whose germ also lies in literature. In 1966 Bond told an interviewer that theatre could "go to the very roots of human nature. This is the sort of thing that happens in [Shakespeare's] *Lear* and *The Women of Troy.* . . . I've been inspired, I suppose, by Euripides and Shakespeare . . . and Chekhov."[20] We have seen in *Lear* and *Bingo* that Bond's inspiration is not uncritical. So too with Euripides.

The Greek playwright wrote two extant tragedies about Hecuba—*The Trojan Women* and *Hecuba*. In the one Hecuba is a national Niobe, mourning her city, and losing her only grandchild. In the other play Hecuba mourns her young son, slain by a treacherous friend. In both plays Hecuba is a raging vengeress, never seeking to comprehend her loss. Bond changes her vengeance. And if it seems academic to begin with Euripides, so did the mainly unappreciative London reviewers. More to the point, so did Bond.

Begun in 1975, Bond's early draft for **The Woman** set the first scene in Athens and the second on a nameless island. After a few months, Bond put the play aside for a year but thought about it: "I wanted to soak myself in the Mediterranean background and the place I went to a couple of years running was Malta, just to face the sun on the rocks, as it were, as simple as that. I reread all the extant Greek tragedies while I was there, and the comedies too. That was my preparation for **The Woman**."[21] Bond also admitted that he was probably influenced by what he had heard of the vast size of the Olivier stage, which opened in 1977 but has never used more than about one/third of its area; during rehearsals he wrote a poem on the Olivier, ending: "But this is a public stage / Where we speak of our times." To speak of our times Bond decided to direct his own play, insuring an epic sweep.

Structurally, **The Woman** is divided into two parts—fourteen scenes in Part I, nine in Part II. The cast is grouped as Greeks, Trojans (further divided into Bystanders, Soldiers, and Poor), Villagers, and, belonging to none of these, the Dark Man who has escaped from a silver mine. Greeks span both parts of the play, but only Hecuba of the Trojans survives to Part II, which belongs to the Villagers. In the program the scenes of Part I are indicated by their spatial setting, of Part II by their temporal setting.

Part I rewrites the *Iliad.* The Greeks attack Troy not for Helen but for a statue of the goddess of Good Fortune, and their forces are led not by Agamemnon but by Heros, who is married to Ismene. Familiar are the names (and roles) of Nestor and Ajax, but Thersites changes into a competent warrior and diplomat. In the Trojan camp Hecuba's one remaining son is simply called Son, but her daughter Cassandra, without prophetic gift, is the mother of the child Astyanax. The Villagers of Part II belong to Bond's fabulous invention. Neither Odysseus nor Aeneas wander toward the outlying island, but Heros and Nestor come seeking the statue of the goddess, which disappeared in the confusions of Greek victory. A blind Hecuba and amnesiac Ismene live among the islanders as mother and daughter.

Loosely joining these "Scenes of War and Freedom" (Part I being War, Part II Freedom) is the statue of the goddess, visible only once but verbally on many tongues. Four major characters play in both parts—the woman Hecuba, the Greek elder statesman Nestor, the handsome Greek hero Heros, and his humane wife Ismene. **The Woman** blends their stories within the societies of their ungolden age; more properly, it might be called a silver age since Athenian power rests on its far-flung silver mines.

In the fifth year of Bond's Trojan War Priam dies of old age. A Greek delegation of Thersites and Ismene try to persuade Hecuba to surrender. When the two women meet in intimacy, they do not speak in Giralducian trivialities but in deep worry about loss of life. Hecuba convinces Ismene of what she has half-realized—that the Greeks will destroy Troy with or without the statue, and therefore Ismene refuses to return to a perfidious Greece. From the walls of Troy (across the vast red battle-field of the Olivier stage) she harangues Greek soldiers to go home (as American soldiers have been urged to go home from distant lands). Ismene fails in her self-imposed mission, and Troy falls not by invasion but by Trojan rebellion of the Poor against the military clique of Hecuba's Son. Trustingly, the poor Trojans deliver the statue to the Greeks, who nevertheless sack Troy, kill its men, and raze its buildings. The Greeks sentence Ismene to death by immurement, and she refuses her husband Heros' offer of poison to curtail her suffering. In the victory momentum, Heros orders the child Astyanax flung to death from the walls of Troy, Hecuba blinds herself with the gesture of Oedipus but without his guilt; and Part I closes on the return from Troy of drunken Nestor and his looting soldiers. (It is this last scene of Part I that most closely resembles Euripides' *Women of Troy*.)

Part II takes place twelve years later in a free world, a nameless island far from Athens; visually a gray tilted disc of uneven terrain. The island Villagers work hard at their fishing and play joyously at seasonal festivals. Even events, announced in the program by "a month later," seem to partake of each season's blight. First Nestor and his men are sent to invite Hecuba to Athens, to display their great city, and to find the statue of the goddess, which will bolster Athenian power. A month later a runaway crippled slave, the Dark Man, arrives at the hut of Hecuba and Ismene, fleeing the far-off silver mines. Another month and the Dark Man has made love to the Ismene he is the first to find beautiful, undisturbed by her amnesia; he promises Hecuba to care for her daughter. Still another month and Heros arrives personally to superintend the charting of the sea into rectangles through which the fishermen will search each day until they find the statue. To ingratiate himself with Hecuba, Heros spares the life of the runaway Dark Man. Still another month and Heros, unquenchable in quest as in war, tries to jolt Ismene's memory—about himself and about the statue. Three months later, a climax as winter approaches. Nestor returns from Athens to order Heros home. Hecuba, sensing danger, claims a prophetic dream whereby the statue will be awarded to the winner of a race around the island. Heros responds to this prophecy veiled in mystery, but Hecuba and the Dark Man methodically plot his death, which alone will free them all. After they succeed, Nestor has a momentary reflex for punishment, but Hecuba persuades him not to disturb the new *status quo*. The old warrior, ever flexible, leaves for his beloved Athens. Blind Hecuba is killed in the first storm of winter. Ismene and the Dark Man, both maimed but mutually supportive, face the new day and the new season.

This summary barely hints at the narrative richness of the drama, which is intensified by character complexity. Heros is brutal, but he is a man of immense civic pride. Nestor is wily, but he too loves his city. Even Hecuba, the compassionate woman, plays the old diplomatic game to gain her worthwhile ends. Ismene comes lying to the Trojans, and the Dark Man protects her in sexist fashion. By Part II each of the women—the title might mean Ismene or Hecuba, although Hecuba took the bows—is injured, but Hecuba blinds *herself*; Ismene refuses to poison herself, and she loses her memory when she is immured *by others*. Old Hecuba finally dies alone, but young Ismene couples in the traditional ending of comedy—to start a new society, however frail in the Silver Age. Part I of *The Woman* adheres to the spirit of Euripidean tragedy, but Part II limps toward New Comedy.

The Woman has a fabulous sweep, whose dramatic conflict pulls in fundamental oppositions. Not only Greece versus Troy, but warmongering men versus peace-plotting women. Scenically, this becomes white versus dark, with dark connoting peace. In the striking scene of Ismene's treason trial, the Greek men glisten in their white togas whereas Ismene wears midnight blue, but it is she who is morally innocent, forecasting the Dark Man of Part II, who will found a new humane civilization. Subtle and significant at the Olivier Theatre was Bond's (or his designer Griffin's) deployment of geometric forms to reenforce the morality. Essentially, war was rectangular and freedom circular. Although the colossal stage of the Olivier is roughly elliptical, it is backed by a fire-curtain in rectangular steel panels. Greek uniforms consisted of copper-colored rectangles from greave to jerkin. Greek generals sat on camp-stools with rectangular seats. In contrast, Hecuba, scheming for peace, wore a vast black circular cape that bore evidence of her past through the colored rectangles in its design; the other Trojan women echoed this costume. The Greeks were often blocked parallel to the rectangular wall panels, whereas the Trojans circled the stage—Hecuba herself, the Poor after they kill the Son, the captive women after the death of Astyanax. Ismene calling for Greek desertion crosses the stage-field in a wide arc.

The omnipresent circle of Part II is the raked disc of the island on which the Villagers dance in a smaller circle. Although blocking is freer in Part II, the now silver-clad Greeks still line up, and the whole cast circles around the Dark Man when he reveals his identity as a nameless miner. Hecuba's Part II rags are tie-dyed in circles, and her eyeband circles her head; she tests the eye she thought sighted with light from a small round lamp. When the Dark Man tease-tickles Ismene, she doubles up and turns around laughing. When the Dark Man tease-tickles Hecuba, she doubles up and rolls on the ground.

Which brings me to Bond the scenewright. Even unappreciative critics cited the power of certain scenes—the regal intimacy of the first Hecuba-Ismene meeting, Ismene's mission drowned out by Greek drums, the Trojan poor moving step up step to topple the Son and their joyous manhandling of the statue as they sing out: "To the Greeks," the rigidity of Ismene's trial disintegrating into a raucous game, Greek sentinels attacked by three veiled women with plague, the dance of the Villagers, the tickling scene, a terrifying storm with the most resonant thunder I ever felt in the theater.

Verbal imagery is more sparing than visual brilliance, but there are dazzling passages. Usually, the speech is formal by this master of the colloquial. Priests and diplomats take refuge in clichés; the soldiers, the poor, and the villagers in simple syntax. Not until Ismene's trial do images flow, with Troy compared to a wounded animal. Hecuba's words rise slowly to imagery. In Scene I of Part II she explains to Ismene their presence on the island in a long lovely passage, a fable rich in water and plant recollections. But to Nestor she affirms simply: "I've no wish for revenge." Perhaps the most moving speech of the play belongs to the Dark Man, ordered to identify himself as a contestant in the race. He starts: "I don't know," then exposes the underground life of the silver miner—a fable of enslavement.

With *The Woman* Bond reaches the pinnacle of his fabulous theater. Fortunately, his fecundity continues from play to fabulous play. Mid-career he may be known through his own poem about Shakespeare:

> He is not an academic
> His written words
> Are the echoes of speech
> His learning is prefaced
> By experience
> He does not come from school
> He goes to it.[22]

Notes

1. Author's Program Note to *The Sea*.

2. Unlike Bond's reviewers, however, his critics have been discerning. I can recommend:

Tony Coult, *The Plays of Edward Bond* (London: Eyre Methuen, 1978).

Peter Iden, *Edward Bond* (Velber bei Hannover, Friedrich, 1973).

Richard Scharine, *The Plays of Edward Bond* (Lewisburg: Bucknell University Press, 1976).

Simon Trussler, *Edward Bond* (Harlow: Longman, 1976).

Anticipated is Malcolm Hay and Philip Roberts, *The Theatre of Edward Bond.*

3. I saw a German production in West Berlin, with superb blend of solos, choruses, orchestra.

4. William Gaskill quoted in Malcolm Hay and Philip Roberts, *Edward Bond, A Companion to the Plays* (London: *Theatre Quarterly Publications,* 1978), 8.

5. *Theatre Quarterly* editors, "Drama and the Dialectics of Violence," *Theatre Quarterly* 2, 5, Jan-Mar, 1972, 13.

6. *Ibid.,* 8.

7. Bond may have pondered a group of plays about Len, who, as the seventeen-year old brother of Bill, appears in *The Pope's Wedding,* and, at eighteen, in *Early Morning.* There is no cross-reference between the plays.

8. In production at the Royal Court, Bond changed some of these details. *Cf.* Hay and Roberts, 50-1.

9. Arthur Arnold, "Lines of Development in Bond's Plays," *Theatre Quarterly* 2, 5, Jan-Mar. 1972, 18.

10. Basho, tr. Nobuyuki Yuasa, *The Narrow Road to the Deep North* (Norwich: Penguin, 1966), 52.

11. Hay and Roberts, 14.

12. Gregory Dark, "Production Casebook of Edward Bond's *Lear* at the Royal Court," *Theatre Quarterly* 2, 5, Jan-March 1972, 27.

13. *Ibid.,* 31.

14. Samuel Schoenbaum discusses them in *Times Literary Supplement* (August 30, 1974).

15. This balance was reflected in Chris Dyer's panels at the 1977 Warehouse production.

16. Gregory Dark, 27.

17. Martin Esslin, "Nor yet a 'Fool' to Fame . . ." *Theatre Quarterly* 6, 21 (Spring, 1976) 44.

18. Although completed before *The Bundle, The Woman* was not published until May 1979. My analysis written prior to the publication of the text, is based on a typescript, for which I thank Cynthia Damoney of the National Theatre of Britain, and mainly on the Olivier production directed by Bond. For some helpful suggestions I thank Professor and Director Betty Osborn.

19. Hay and Roberts, 74.

20. Joseph F. McCrindle, ed. *Behind the Scenes* (New York: Holt, Rinehart and Winston, 1971), 135, 136.

21. Malcolm Hay and Philip Roberts, "Edward Bond: Stages in a Life," *Observer Magazine* (August 6, 1978), 13.

22. Edward Bond, *Theatre Poems and Songs* (London: Eyre Methuen, 1978), 56.

Jenny S. Spencer (essay date 1981)

SOURCE: Spencer, Jenny S. "Edward Bond's Dramatic Strategies." In *Contemporary English Drama,* edited by C. W. E. Bigsby, pp. 123-37. London: Edward Arnold, 1981.

[*In the following essay, Spencer examines the ways in which Bond was influenced by earlier playwrights to create a form of "rational theatre" of his own.*]

I

Edward Bond is undeniably a part of an active and innovative period in modern British theatre. The issues he is stirred by—the dehumanizing, violent effects of a class-structured, technocratic society; the alienation of the individual under capitalism; the destructive contradictions of our social and political institutions; the seeming impossibility of rational and effective political action; the need for a working-class culture—all appear in various forms in the theatre of his contemporaries. Bond's stylistic diversity testifies to the technical alternatives opened up for British playwrights by the work of Beckett, Artaud and Brecht, much of it within the experimental atmosphere of a proliferating and increasingly popular fringe theatre. The political content and didactic intention of Bond's plays link him to the broader tradition Eric Bentley has labelled 'theatre of ideas'. His controlled and realistic dialogue has been compared to both Chekhov and Pinter, his concrete and often violent imagery has precedents in both Shakespeare and the agitprop theatre of the 1960s. He writes prefaces like Shaw and theatre-poems like Brecht. Perhaps the most technically ambitious of the contemporary British playwrights, Bond has managed to create a distinctive voice in the theatre, one which resists easy definition in terms of the post-Osborne trends identified by such critics as John Russell Taylor and John Elsom.[1]

Bond calls his theatre a 'rational theatre' primarily in order to distinguish his own literary practice from that of his contemporaries. Firmly committed to humanistic values, he has little use for the avant-garde trends (catalogued by Martin Esslin in *The Theatre of the Absurd*) which assume life is meaningless and human action absurd. His protest, like that of Arden and Wesker, is strictly social and political. For Bond, playwriting is an unquestionably moral activity; his aim, he states simply, is 'to tell the truth'.[2] Few playwrights, however, have elicited responses which vary so widely from outrage to polite dismissal. He is described at times as deliberately confusing, at others as overly simplistic, as both daringly innovative and deeply conventional.[3] Sixteen years after the controversial appearance of *Saved*, Bond now commands more than a grudging respect from the critics, but he remains something of an enigma to even the most enthusiastic students of the theatre. Bond himself is quick to note that much of the resistance he encounters lies in deeply rooted cultural biases or class differences. Those who have a stake in the status quo will necessarily be discomfited by the political import of his plays and his tone of moral urgency. But Bond's literary practice presents problems for his left-wing sympathizers as well, problems which are located in how the plays work and how they should be read, rather than in the general and explicit themes with which he deals. Before we can ask whether Bond is a success or failure (or even important), we must first take a closer look at what he has set out to do, and what he has in fact accomplished.

The very breadth and range of Bond's dramatic work makes a traditional overview extremely difficult; and we cannot expect a catalogue of recurring themes, images and motifs to get us very far in the study of his unique contribution to the theatre. The most fruitful approach is one which abandons at the start certain critical assumptions: that the artist's work will retrospectively present a coherent pattern of growth and development; that the work of art must turn on the notion of unity, harmony and organic wholeness; that what can be said of the text is the same as what the text itself is saying; that the work is reducible to the literary message it encodes.[4] Bond himself has articulated some important differences between his early and later plays, and in the course of this chapter we should be able to distinguish certain distinctive techniques and recurring strategies. But while Bond's ultimate purpose remains unchanged (to create a rational society), his style and particular methods will shift in both emphasis and effect, resisting any logic of even artistic development. Also, Bond's political ideas and thematic concerns are for the most part simple and direct. They provide the subject matter for his numerous essays, prefaces and programme-notes, and on them Bond is his own best explicator. His theatrical idiom, however, is often complex, and stands in need of a more thoroughgoing analysis than has been offered to date. This is not to imply that Bond's politics can or should be separated from his aesthetic practice. One measure of his success

will depend upon the extent to which these two categories remain interdependent.

II

As the gesture of designating his theatre a rational one suggests, Bond sees himself as a realistic writer. When we think of the various kinds of exaggeration and verbal-visual poetry Bond is noted for (the caricatures of *Early Morning*, Lear's language, Shogo's mutilation in *Narrow Road to the Deep North*, Hatch's madness in *The Sea*, Clare's hallucinations in *The Fool*, Trench's party in *The Worlds*, and so on), or the number of genre types Bond has used (social comedy, Noh-play, parable, epic, history play, tragedy, etc.), such a definition must appear more than mildly inappropriate. The term 'realism' is, of course, as troublesome as the age-old problem of the relationship between art and truth. 'Realism' habitually denotes a reflection of reality which produces recognition. But just as our immediate perceptions of reality are mediated by ideology, the real in the theatre is mediated by dramatic convention. The more self-conscious theatre becomes as a self-reflective, contained, symbolic universe, the more difficult the problem for a politically conscious playwright who is still interested in 'truthful' representation onstage.

Since Brecht, however, we have at least learned to distinguish between a bourgeois realism and a critical realism. The former, presenting itself to the audience as a commodity to be consumed, can be described as integrative drama. It supports the culture's dominant ideology by posing problems too limited or easily resolved, and/or presenting reality and human nature as ahistorical, eternal and unchanging. Naive realism works like ideology to obscure the kind of dynamic contradictions which could lead to radical change. By presenting what 'is' as truth (the empirical fallacy), it tends to naturalize the very conventions on which it depends, to conceal the work's status as production. To do this, bourgeois realism depends on narrative continuity and audience identification—a readable discourse with an entirely appropriable meaning addressed to an audience fixed, unified and rendered immobile in the act of seeing. Contradictions become conflicts (static, polar categories) which are displaced to the level of psychology or resolved through the unfolding structure of the play's plot (usually linear, teleological, symmetrical).

Like Brecht, however, Bond is concerned with orienting the audience toward action rather than consumption. As he states in a letter to Tony Coult, 'Theatre is a way of judging society and helping to change it; art must interpret the world and not merely mirror it.[5] Bond is less concerned with a naturalistic surface than with the complex relationship between ideology, play and audience. His realism is of a Brechtian order: a critical-productive attitude toward the world which sees reality as historical, contradictory and subject to human intercession. Thus Bond attempts to present representations of reality (mediated by theatrical convention in the same way ideology mediates perception) which are both recognizable as our own world, and yet untenable (in need of change). Moreover, the audience must become involved (caught up but not immersed) in the play's narration of events in such a way that the analysis becomes clear. A successful reading of a Bond play will rest on the audience's ability to perceive the dynamic which arises from the dialectical interplay of its elements—between the play's objective and subjective worlds, between action and language, reason and emotion, society and individual, the historical process and the experience of the moment, judgement and description. In other words, we must actively read how the play produces, rather than simply conveys, its meaning.

Although the particular arrangement and working through of these dynamics will vary with each play, a number of Bond's strategies can be elaborated from the general premises outlined above. We might note, first of all, that the bulk of Bond's plays are historically or geographically distanced from present-day English life. According to Bond, a dramatist concerned with addressing an audience's immediate situation need not always deal directly with the present. 'The past is also an institution owned by society.'[6] Because our present social problems have a history, the way in which history is taught and understood will either help or circumscribe an individual's ability to recognize and solve those problems. While Bond's first (*The Pope's Wedding* and *Saved*) and most recent play (*The Worlds*) offer a specifically contemporary setting, the rest provide a series of 'history plays' in which Bond represents and re-interprets aspects of our historical and cultural heritage in order to create for his audience a more 'usable' past. In fact, Bond sees this activity as one of the artist's primary functions.

Since man not only makes his own history, but is situated within it, the art he creates will always have an historical dimension. Bond states in one essay, 'In literature there are no abstract statements universally true for all time—or if there are, they are trivial until given content and context.'[7] The 'truths' of art will be relativized by such things as the artist's social origins (class position) and his society's state of objective knowledge (e.g., as expressed in science and technology). Bond believes that art which has outlived its historical relevance enters into the domain of myth, and as such becomes both untrue and dangerous. He wants his audience to 'escape from a mythology of the past, which often lives on as the culture of the present'.[8] Thus *Early Morning* is a comic nightmare aimed at disturbing our comfort with Victorian history. The grotesquely caricatured figures of Queen Victoria, Glad-

stone and Disraeli are attempts to displace the history-book idealizations of such real personages, idealizations which live on to justify our present institutions and obscure the destructive contradictions on which they rest. Likewise, it is against an idealized notion of Shakespeare as a sacrosanct culture hero whose plays are true for all time, that the character of Shakespeare in *Bingo* takes shape. By imaginatively recreating Shakespeare's involvement with the Welcombe enclosures, Bond demystifies the Shakespearean myth, refusing to exempt the bard from personal responsibility for the historical developments of his own time. More importantly, Bond shows how the psychological contradictions which lead Shakespeare to suicide in *Bingo* are the result of the social contradictions of his historical moment. Shakespeare's moral failure is here inextricable from his 'bourgeois consciousness'—the class position won by economic success severely limits both his vision and his ability to act in a politically responsible manner.

Since Bond believes a society that tries to create self-consciousness in its members based on imagery, attitudes and social organizations of the past will only succeed in creating individual emotional crises,[9] he addresses the kind of art which perpetuates that past. In both *Lear* and *The Woman,* for example, we see Bond working within and against older dramatic forms. Excursions into 'theatre of quotation',[10] both plays call for the audience's recognition of a counter-text. According to Bond, Greek and Shakespearean tragedy continue to provide cultural and artistic standards for contemporary audiences, long after the plays have outlived their social usefulness. As the backbone of English dramatic tradition, Shakespeare is a figure Bond can neither ignore nor wholeheartedly accept. And, when using him as a source, Bond looks not only to the original texts, but to the modern productions which alternately offer Christian or existential interpretations of Shakespeare's plays.[11] Bond feels that Shakespeare's *King Lear* offers us an anatomy of human values which teach us how to survive in a corrupt world, rather than showing us how to act responsibly in order to change it.[12] The Shakespearean precedents which inform Bond's *Lear* are fairly easy to locate—in Lear's movement to sanity through madness, vision through blindness, and self-knowledge through suffering; in the revitalization of certain patterns of imagery; and in Lear's metaphoric language. But Bond provides wholly new social contexts for Lear's action, replete with the anachronisms which directly relate the narrative to contemporary issues. And audiences can grasp the significance of Lear's actions only by perceiving the way in which Bond reworks the Elizabethan tragic conventions. Likewise, Bond reworks the patterns of classical Greek tragedy when he rewrites the Hecuba story, replacing a psychological study in human suffering with an insight into the historical process. Bond's experiments with older dramatic forms are not limited to tragedy, however.

Behind *Narrow Road to the Deep North* stands the tradition of the Noh play, but, through the figure of Basho, Bond criticizes the Noh play's characteristically contemplative stance. While the parable as a literary form seems most appropriate for conveying universal, timeless and unchanging truths, in *The Bundle* Bond uses the parable to examine the historically relative and dialectical nature of morality itself. With Colin's death in *The Sea,* Bond injects a real note of tragedy into what might otherwise pass for a social comedy of manners. And through the figures of Willy and Evens, Bond can present and expose this world from an outsider's point of view. While reminiscent of both the well-made domestic play and Chekhovian naturalism, *The Sea* finally rejects the structure of both forms, and with them, the world-view on which they depend.

Bond claims (and rightly so) that he structures his plays 'with infinite care',[13] and we can recognize Bondian strategies in the way he handles dramatic structure. In order to articulate and represent the contradictions of the real (which are necessarily scattered and diverse), Bond cannot rely on the kind of narration which would resolve these contradictions into a specious unity or fix them into permanently irreconcilable categories. To create a literature which is consciously artistic (fictional, structured, and participating in a history of literary forms) without abandoning the project of truthful representation and political effectiveness, Bond must provide within his plays an analysis which breaks up traditional modes of narrative continuity without altogether ignoring narrative conventions. In a discussion of *The Woman,* Bond in fact states, 'We must do that highly subversive thing—tell a story with a beginning, middle and end.'[14] And indeed, Bond not only tells stories, but tells them well, using many of the elements we normally associate with traditional drama: linear chronology, the dramatic reversal, creation of suspense, highly theatrical and emotional scenes, etc. Reacting to what he sees as shortcomings in Brecht's methods, Bond insists that the analysis of an event must never swamp the recording of it. Bond may be an expert at creating discrete scenic units in a Brechtian manner, but he also provides a logical cause-effect structure which links each scene to the next. Because the issues Bond is concerned with can only be resolved in action outside the theatre, we cannot expect to find these issues resolved either within the consciousness of a character or within the structure of the plot. The incidents in Bond's plays are always clarified by other incidents, not by any general or universal principles. Thus we find in the plays a tendency toward uneven development which decentres the central problematic to various levels in order to prevent a wholly satisfactory resolution. This decentred structure affects both character development and plot construction; and with it, Bond succeeds in making his audience actively read, rather than passively receive, the message of his plays.

III

On the level of character, then, Bond will show the kind of understanding and articulation of problems that prevents meaningful action as often as showing what permits it. In the early plays, especially, Bond focuses on the characters' 'pursuit of illusions—of false solutions to personal and political problems'.[15] As a result, more questions are posed than can possibly be answered or resolved within the context set up by the play; the resolutions which are offered in the story's end do not appear as inevitable, but limited and naggingly unsatisfactory. As gestures of hope, Lear's few shovels of dirt to sabotage the wall construction, and Len's action silently mending a chair, seem painfully inadequate under the circumstances. The most obvious example is perhaps to be found in *The Sea*:

> I left the last sentence of the play unfinished because the play can have no satisfactory solution at that stage. Rose and Willy have to go away and help create a sane society—and it is for the audience to go away and complete the sentence in their own lives.[16]

The narrative of *Narrow Road* also seems to stop *in medias res,* with a stage picture which vividly juxtaposes several images—Kiro's silent suicide, Shogo's dismembered corpse, a man calling for help and pulling himself out of the river, and Basho's offstage voice making a speech, with distinctly fascist overtones, to the people. None of these characters answer the problem posed by the play—how to act in a morally responsible way. The scene is a key to Bond's use of visual-poetic images in all of his plays, however. Since the poetic image is in itself a synchronic structure, it can perform a potentially mystifying function in the theatre by obscuring specific and analytical relations within a play. Such is Bond's complaint against the 'enigmatic' verbal-visual poetry of absurdist drama. Bond's theatrical images, on the other hand, are concretizations of the very issues he presents in other ways through the characters, structure and narrative movement. In other words, he offers economy of expression which does not abstract/ condense/mystify, but represents and clarifies in a concrete and visual way complex dialectical relationships. If we examine carefully the relation of the poetic elements to the historical, time-structured elements of the plays, we find that the former represent without resolving the contradictions of the latter. Though image and event are obviously interdependent, the two aspects do not necessarily contribute to a unifying (tonal, atmospheric) effect, but rather to a kind of dialectical thinking which proceeds by leaps and disjunctions.

Finally, while the early plays present no adequate resolution, most of the later plays rely on a partial resolution accompanied by a scenic 'coda'. These endings are disturbing because they either remind us within the context of one resolution of a problem which the play has not satisfactorily addressed, or they shift the focus of the analysis to an entirely different level. With its story of a successful revolution, **The Bundle** clarifies and optimistically answers many of the questions posed earlier in **Narrow Road,** but ends on a tragic note with the accidental death of a worker. Likewise, in **The Worlds,** Terry diverts the issues of the play to an appropriately unresolved level by refusing to answer Beryl's question (will he condemn terrorist violence?) in the terms offered.

Bond's overall dramatic project is also reflected in his approach to character, and affects the structure of the plays. If the goal of realism is to embody the innate dialectics of social reality, then the truthfulness of the representation will depend, in part, on the broadness of the social picture, and on the kind of contexts offered for the characters' actions. According to Bond, we can't find out about a character's motivation by analysing his soul, and he directs his actors to avoid an understanding of character in terms of psychology. Bond also avoids the tendency of many didactic writers to present characters who are simple functions of the ideas they represent, who are derived from the conceptual in order to illustrate an argument. If art is to provide the audience with knowledge, it cannot be of a scientific nature (theories empirically verifiable), but the kind which arises from history and experience.[17] Marx's description of human consciousness is directly applicable to Bond's dramatic practice:

> We do not set out from what men say, imagine, conceive nor from men as narrated, thought of, imagined, conceived, in order to arrive at men in the flesh. We set out from real, active men and on the basis of their life-process, we demonstrate the development of the ideological reflexes and echoes of this life process. The phantoms of the human brain are also sublimates of their material life-process, which is empirically verifiable and bound to material premises. . . .[18]

Bond's characters are always determined, in the last instance, by their environment. They are shaped by the social, familial and economic relationships which Bond so carefully articulates onstage. As Bond puts it, 'I show characters in their various social roles and various social relationships (and thus achieving wholeness) rather than developing a character from its *geist.*'[19] In terms of structuring scenes, this often means setting up more than one acting centre on the stage, one situation providing a perspective or frame for another. This multiple focus forces the audience to analyse the relationship between characters and groups of characters, to see the limitations of any one character's perspective, and to avoid the kind of identification that psychological drama encourages. With voices heard from the wings, events undramatized but reacted to, characters absent but determining, Bond often suggests

an offstage reality that provides further contexts for the action occurring onstage.

In Bond's plays, an accurate representation must ultimately remain faithful in language and action to the historical situation and class position of his characters. Thus, the conflicts and relationships between characters frequently arise from, and in turn illuminate, the contradictions of a society based on class. Since these relationships are also mediated by a shared ideology (and are therefore complex), the conflicts will rarely appear as head-on, polarized confrontations, but rather as determining factors of behaviour and attitude which define and limit the characters' consciousness. Even in plays where the antagonism between classes is most forcefully presented (**The Fool, Bingo, The Bundle, The Worlds**) Bond is equally interested in exploring the relationships between characters of the same class, in examining the differing ways they react to the same situation, and why. We might note here that the materialist approach outlined above is not only relevant for the more naturalistically presented characters (Len and Pam of **Saved,** Clare and Patty of **The Fool,** etc.), but for the character whose language and actions strain credulity as well. Although he exaggerates or heightens their action for comic or emotional effects, Bond is careful to provide contexts for the violence of Shogo in **Narrow Road,** Bodice and Fontanelle in **Lear,** Fred's gang in **Saved,** and the madness of Georgiana, Hatch, Lear, Trench—contexts which prevent their actions from being read as either arbitrary or tragic (psychologically inevitable).

Just as the way in which the story is dramatized will affect the audience's ability to interpret it, so the ways in which characters perceive their situation and environment will affect their capacity for changing it. Although not really interested in psychology, Bond *is* interested in subjectivity. While history may determine the individual, and the individual alone can never alter the economic base of the capitalist state, it is individual men, engaged in action, who make history. Since the subject is the location for political practice, Bond must do more than show how subjectivity is created in his characters—he must try to create a radical subjectivity in his audience as well. This intention appears in the shift Bond sees in his own work, from plays which define a problem to plays which try to provide some kind of answer:

> We mustn't write only problem plays, we must write answer plays—or at least plays which make answers clearer and more practical. When I wrote my first plays, I was, naturally, conscious of the weight of the problems. Now I've become more conscious of the strength of human beings to provide answers. The answers aren't always light, easy or even straightforward, but the purpose—a socialist society—is clear.[20]

The change in focus manifests itself in both language and dramatic structure: we see in *The Woman, The Worlds* and *The Bundle* a tighter, more symmetrical dramatic structure which closely coheres to the argument being made, and the use (by at least some of the characters) of a more discursive, rational and consciously persuasive language. Moreover, Bond will create characters with whom the audience can more easily identify in terms of offering more plausible models of behaviour.

For Bond, 'human consciousness is class consciousness',[21] and we might distinguish here between characters who belong to a particular class, and those who become class conscious in Bond's sense of the term. It is only the latter (Darkie in *The Fool,* Wang in *The Bundle,* Hecuba in *The Woman,* Terry and the terrorists in *The Worlds,* and to some extent Lear and the Son in *Bingo*) who are able to grasp their situation in a way that allows them to act and to escape (at least temporarily or partially) being the victims of history and circumstance. These characters are not automatically endowed with an enlightened perspective, but come to it through the learning process offered by the concrete experiences and social relationships of the play. It is a practical knowledge, never a purely conceptual one, which issues in and provides a model for action. The kind of knowledge the play offers its audience will be akin to, but not identical with, the knowledge gained by the characters. But in both cases, knowledge is understood as the result of a dialectical process which moves from the realm of immediate sense perception to some kind of conceptual understanding which then issues in action. (That action then provides new sense perceptions which reinitiates the process.)[22] As we shall see, this movement is reflected in the time structure of the plays, in Bond's control over the movement and rhythm of narration. It also involves Bond's concern with the individual's relation to history, with the characters' (and our own) ability to grasp an interpretation of events in the process of history in order to understand 'the truth that life need not be an ungraspable flow of experience'.[23]

Any playwright interested in change must deal with the problem of time. And the problem of class consciousness for Marx is inseparable from the problem of the subject's capability of perceiving himself as a motive force in history, of obtaining an historical consciousness. In the early plays especially, Bond's characters are limited in their ability to learn from their experience in ways which would allow them to take meaningful (moral, politically conscious) action. This is due in part to Bond's awareness of 'the weight of the problems', one being that objective conditions change faster than subjective consciousness—that there is always a lag between external stimuli and the responses which are dictated by habit and the ideology instilled by family,

education, and religious institutions, all of which combine to make one's objective assessment of oppression more difficult. (The problem is registered in these plays in the very language used by the characters to understand and articulate their experience.) But this is also the justification for Bond's sense of urgency, an urgency written into the tempo of the plays. Thus we can identify a characteristic Bondian movement—the calm, analytical pace which builds to isolated moments that are shocking, intensely emotional or naturalistically compelling. (Look, for example, at the baby-stoning sequence in *Saved,* the velvet-cutting scene in *The Sea,* the torture scenes in *Lear,* the parson-stripping scene in *The Fool,* etc.) We are compelled by virtue of the real menace involved in these experiences—when we view a character with whom we at least partially identify, or a situation which we clearly recognize, as 'on the brink' of destruction and increasingly out of control. As opposed to Brecht's alienation-effects, Bond once referred to them as 'aggro-effects'.[24] Hallmarks of his distinctive style, these protracted moments of threatened or disturbingly explicit violence are remembered by the audience long after the performance. Commented upon at length by reviewers (both positively and negatively), they consciously provoke a reaction and play on the audience's fears. These scenes, however, are carefully choreographed by Bond, heightened often to the point of melodrama; and they usually succeed in representing the characters' own subjective experience of history—as an inexplicable concatenation of events which is increasingly overwhelming and out of control. These 'real' and traumatic experiences are determining for the characters involved, and lead to various kinds of reflective assessments (more or less adequate, depending on the play), which in turn lead to further action. The audience, of course, is always provided with a social perspective of the whole which permits a clearer understanding of the action than is allowed the characters. But the sense of urgency created by these brutally literal scenes remains—to be channelled into the activity of interpreting the play. The resulting rhythm keeps the plays from being too cerebral, from reflecting the structure of a purely logical argument.

On a more theoretical level, the problem of time and the need for an historical consciousness is registered in many of the plays by Bond's attempts to show a movement away from a symbolic and mythical world to an historical one. The relation between Acts I and II of *The Woman* demonstrates this movement most directly. In Act I, Bond continually invites the recognition of his Greek source as he presents his own version of the last three days of the Trojan War. In Act II, on the other hand, Bond tells a story entirely of his own making which bears little, if any, relation to the acknowledged source with which he began. Here Bond rewrites the consequences of a basically myth-bound action and shows the island village moving from an isolated and ideal community into a Greek-dominated historical world. Thus the annual ritual celebrations on which Act II opens must give way, due to the intrusion of the Greeks, to the future-determining deliberations of the town council on which the play ends. Bond offers a similar description of the three-part structure of *Lear*:

> Act I shows a world dominated by myth. Act II shows the clash between myth and reality, between superstitious men and the autonomous world. Act III shows a resolution of this, in the world we prove real by dying in it.[25]

Both plays begin with an accelerated tempo of events, with actions which appear to have unavoidable and fateful consequences, with a 'tragic' sense of time, only to move into a different kind of tempo—one which allows the characters to reflect on past experience, and to offer alternative models of action.

IV

One aspect of Bond's theatre which distinguishes him most clearly from the plain realism of Wesker and the 'kitchen sink' dramatists is his use of language. The dialogue of Bond's plays ranges from the naturalistic dialect of his working-class characters to the poetic reflections of Shakespeare, Lear and Trench, from the comic exaggerations of Mrs Rafi in *The Sea* and Queen Victoria in *Passion,* to the rational and persuasive discourse of Ismene, Wang and the terrorists. For Bond, language is one register of the characters' social and class position, as well as a tool for measuring their self-consciousness. Moreover, Bond is able to show through his dialogue how ideology intervenes in the consciousness of certain characters and prevents them from understanding the implications of their own actions (e.g., in the case of Mrs Rafi in *The Sea,* the gang in *Saved,* Lord Milton and the Parson in *The Fool,* and the businessmen in *The Worlds.*) In the figures of Lear, Shakespeare, Hecuba and Trench, we find evidence of a consciously imagistic and metaphoric language which does not inevitably lead to moral action (and may in fact prevent it). In the witty and concrete language of Bond's working classes, we find codes of communication which both permit survival and some measure of human group contact, though the kind of joking displacements which also prevent adequate conceptualization of experience. Katherine Worth speaks to Bond's facility with language when she claims he has created a colloquial theatre that is also visionary and poetic'.[26] The equation struck here, however, is not an easy one to maintain. In Shakespeare, for example, the colloquial and energetic language of the clowns and fools, and the visionary, poetic language of kings and heroes, are distinctly separate modes of discourse and reflect similarly distinct (often incompatible) ways of thinking. Bond's problem, and the problem of the modern realist writer, is somehow to combine these discourses without

incurring the limitations of either. He would avoid an appeal to a frankly symbolic universe, since it can ultimately have no effect in the 'real' world. And yet brute facts, situations and incidents in themselves cannot offer the kind of knowledge necessary for effective action.

In *The Fool,* Bond addresses this problem in his examination of the ambivalent position of the writer in society. Here, Bond fuses the political and the personal by presenting an analysis which seems to arise from a straightforward dramatization of particular incidents in the life of John Clare. But *The Fool* is perhaps the most carefully structured of all Bond's plays, and, for this reason, belies its own complexity. Unlike *The Bundle* or *The Worlds, The Fool* offers no individual or group of individuals who, seeking to understand the socioeconomic laws which govern their lives, clearly articulate the political thought of the play. Despite the historical distancing, its world is closer to that of *Saved* and *The Pope's Wedding.* In all three, the characters respond to situations in a distorted and painfully limited manner because their consciousnesses are so clearly shaped by material and economic forces outside their control. In those earlier plays, however, the meaning of events and their political implications not only remain outside the grasp of the characters, but tend to elude the audience as well—the initial response being that the two plays are exercises in naturalistic theatre, slices-of-life from a fragmented and alienated society. The political message of *The Fool,* on the other hand, appears to the audience by the end of the play as virtually self-evident. This clarity results from the way in which Bond structures scenes and presents relationships so that the actions and the analysis (comment upon the action) occur simultaneously.

The analysis Bond leads his audience to make falls into several distinct, though related, categories. The most obvious, and perhaps most important, is made through the central conflict of the play's plot. Using Clare's life as an historically verifiable example, Bond examines the failure of an entire society by showing the contradiction between the positive and necessary activity of writing and the social conditions which make that activity impossible (art as marketable commodity vs. art as productive activity). Secondly, Bond shows how the relation between labour and capital is reproduced in the relation between artist and patron—a relation most vividly illustrated in the boxing match of Scene 5. By making a clear connection between mental and physical labour (and connecting the fate of Darkie to Clare's own), the cause of the artist is understood as the cause of the entire working class. Finally, by showing how Clare's psychology is socially constructed, Bond demonstrates how subjectivity itself is created by social conditions. Without this vital link, the depiction of Clare's madness remains an interesting but socially irrelevant phenomenon. But because the actions of the play so clearly reveal the socioeconomic laws of Clare's world (and our own), we are able to read both the causes of Clare's failure and the political comment of the play through the very images and distortions that will serve to illustrate Clare's insanity.

As the play changes in focus from the perspective of the community (emphasized in Part I) to that of the individual (emphasized in Part II), from objective conditions to subjective consequences, the audience shares Clare's personal experience of increasing enclosure and entrapment in a world over which he has no control. By the end of the play, Clare knows freedom, and with it, health, happiness and mental stability, only through its absence, a perceived lack which he fills with the image of a lost love. Silenced and reduced to the level of a kept animal, his very condition provides the necessary comment on the attitudes expressed by the characters who survive (Patty, Lord Milton, etc.). However, Bond manages to present the 'psychological truth' of Clare's situation in a way which provokes our sympathy without demanding identification. Our learning process is not the same as Clare's own. Unlike Shakespeare in **Bingo,** Clare never gives up hope in the play; but he is, after all, the fool of the play's title. In the eyes of society, his 'madness' grants him that distinction, but he is also a fool by virtue of his limited vision and inability to understand his historical situation. As Bond writes in a theatre-poem: 'Clare, you created illusions / And they destroy poets.'[27]

Given Bond's continued fascination with Shakespeare, however, we may be able to see an even more important function for the play's title. Bond takes up the figure of the Shakespearean fool, not as a romantic myth of the outcast, but as a way of historicizing the problem of the contemporary writer; and he reworks it in order to clarify the very causes of Clare's limitations. As a poet, Clare shares the artistic function of Shakespeare's court-employed fools. We remember these characters for their biting wit, facility with language and worldly wisdom; but their criticism is emasculated by their dependent relation to their patrons. In fact, they are granted immunity from censure by virtue of their role—whatever they say is unthreatening because it is by social definition untrue. What comes from the mouth of a fool must be foolish. So the way society views the function of art invariably determines its effect.

In Clare's society, artistic activity is similarly circumscribed by the tastes and attitudes of the paying public (see Clare's discussion with Lord Radstock in Scene 5), and Clare's very role as a poet becomes a measure of his lack of freedom. Moreover, it is only the poet Lamb who, in Scene 5, is able to see the truth of the situation;

but the language he uses prevents him from being understood, and his role as an artist prevents him from being taken seriously. Hence, Mrs Emmerson's response:

> . . . I'm proud to say I didn't understand a single word. Mr Lamb, you're a poet. You have no call to go round putting ideas in people's heads . . .[28]

As the play progresses, Clare (like Lamb) comes to resemble the court-banished fools of Shakespeare's plays. Such a fool (we remember Lear's) invariably speaks the truth, despite the metaphoric and elliptical language he speaks. Patty, however, will accuse Clare of using a language totally inappropriate to their situation, with the implication that if he thought correctly he would speak differently. ('Oon't talk so daft. Talk straight so a body can hev a proper conversation. If you're on fire, you goo up in smoke . . . (etc.)').[29] Patty's reaction suggests that Clare's activity has served to isolate him from his community. But the language he speaks is also a measure of his developing self-consciousness, of a sensitivity that allows him better to understand and articulate the problems he shares with the villagers. Moreover, while the images that make their way into Clare's speech may confuse Patty, those same images, arising as they do from Clare's actual experiences in the play, make brutally literal sense to the audience.

Patty finally reads Clare's actions in terms of an individuality at odds with the general interests of the community (the same reading the upper classes offer). 'Self, allus self', is her complaint against Clare. However, within the society Bond describes in the play, only the characters sufficiently isolated from the community can come to represent the larger individual needs that the community cannot meet. In Scene 7, Mary, Darkie, the beaten boxer, the poet, and the actual experiences of hunger and physical pain become conflated in Clare's mind and lead to a vision which expresses both need and desire, real past and projected future:

> I dreamt I saw bread spat on the ground, and her say: Waste, I risk my life, (*shakes his head*) No. Birds on't waste. Thass on'y seed so you threw it on the ground. Birds hev it. Or that soak away. Bread goo from mouth t' mouth an' what it taste of: other mouths. Talkin' and laughin'. Thinkin' people. I wandered round an roun. Where to? Here. An a blind man git here before me. The blind goo in a straight line. We should hev com t'gither. She git the bread. He crack the heads when they come after us. Then she on't goo in rags. He on't blind. An' I—on't goo mad in a madhouse. . . .[30]

As isolated figures, the three are incapable of effecting the necessary changes in their society, but their very isolation impresses on us the need for change. Thus it is finally through the community's outcasts that the destructiveness of this society's social organization is presented—its inability to provide a fully human existence for any of its members.

With the elliptical, colloquial, non-symbolic poetry of Clare's speech, we return to the problem of the modern artist who, in order to 'tell the truth' and speak for a rational society that does not yet exist, must resist the conventional aesthetic discourse of his own historical moment. The problem, of course, is Bond's own; and perhaps we can see how Bond's dramatic strategies are a response to the postmodernist position of the writer, who, like Clare, would speak on behalf of his society, but finds himself in fundamental opposition to it.

Notes

1. See *The Second Wave* (Eyre Methuen, 1971) and *Post-War British Theatre* (1976).

2. Author's conversation with Bond, 1 December, 1979, Royal Court Theatre.

3. Practically any sampling of reviews of Bond's plays will substantiate this point. For a complete bibliography, see Malcolm Hay and Philip Roberts, *Edward Bond: A Companion to the Plays* (1978), pp. 79-100.

4. This approach is elaborated more fully in Pierre Macheray, *Theory of Literary Production* (1978).

5. *A Companion to the Plays,* p. 74. See also the Preface to *The Bundle* (1978).

6. Preface to *The Bundle,* p. xiv.

7. 'The Rational Theatre', *Edward Bond, Plays: Two* (1978), p. xii.

8. 'Letter to Tony Coult', *A Companion to the Plays,* p. 75.

9. Preface to *The Bundle,* p. x.

10. Shaw, Brecht, Sartre, Giraudoux, Stoppard are among the many modern playwrights who have adapted Greek and Shakespearean 'classics' for their own dramatic purposes. The practice is frequent enough in contemporary theatre to merit a label of its own.

11. A. C. Bradley has greatly influenced standard Shakespearean criticism with his Christian interpretations of *King Lear* in *Shakespearean Tragedy* (1908) while Jan Kott's existential interpretation of Lear in *Shakespeare Our Contemporary* (1967) has influenced a number of modern productions of the play.

12. See *A Companion to the Plays,* p. 53.

13. *Ibid.,* p. 56.

14. 'Green Room' discussion with Edward Bond, *Plays and Players* (November, 1978).

15. *A Companion to the Plays,* p. 56.

16. 'Letter to Tom Wild', *A Companion to the Plays,* p. 57.

17. See 'A Rational Theatre', *Plays: Two,* p. xvi.

18. Karl Marx, *The German Ideology* (1970), p. 47.

19. *Theatre Quarterly* (Vol. XIII, 1978), p. 34.

20. 'Letter to Tony Coult', *A Companion to the Plays,* p. 75.

21. *Ibid.,* p. 74.

22. Mao Tse Tung offers this definition of the learning process in 'On Practice', *Five Essays on Philosophy* (1977), pp. 1-22.

23. Preface to *The Bundle,* p. xvi.

24. *Theatre Quarterly* (Vol. XIII, 1978), p. 34.

25. Preface to *Lear* (1972), p. xiv.

26. *Revolutions in Modern English Drama* (1972), p. 168.

27. *The Fool* (New York, 1978), p. 84.

28. *Ibid.,* p. 43.

29. *Ibid.,* p. 56.

30. *Ibid.,* p. 73.

Christopher Innes (essay date June 1982)

SOURCE: Innes, Christopher. "The Political Spectrum of Edward Bond: From Rationalism to Rhapsody." *Modern Drama* 25, no. 2 (June 1982): 189-206.

[*In the following essay, Innes discusses political contradictions in Bond's plays, particularly the prefaces he writes, but finds that these are what give the plays their moral force.*]

The landmarks in contemporary English drama have been more like landmines, shattering conventional expectations, with a whole new configuration of subjects and themes emerging on the stage each time after the dust of public outrage settled. What *Look Back in Anger* had done for the fifties, **Saved** did for the sixties, and a play like *The Romans in Britain* may yet do for the eighties (though Howard Brenton's play seems to lack the qualities that might give its shock effects the same resonance). Like Osborne, Edward Bond achieved immediate prominence through the controversy surrounding his first play to be given a full production, when the Lord Chamberlain tried to throw a baby out with the bath-water. But where Osborne quickly became accepted—partly because his approach was relatively simple and consistent, partly because his plays were recognizably traditional in shape, despite his use of diatribe which shifted dramatic conflict from its conventional locus between characters within the play to a point between his protagonists and the audience— there is still little consensus about Bond.

Initially Bond was subjected to perhaps the most violent storm of protest and denigration aimed at any modern dramatist since Ibsen. Indeed, the reaction to *Saved* paralleled the original English response to *Ghosts,* even down to the vocabulary. Ibsen's "abominable play" had been condemned half a century earlier as "gross, almost putrid indecorum . . . literary carrion" (*Daily Telegraph*), with "characters either contradictory in themselves, uninteresting or abhorrent" (*Daily Chronicle*); in short, "a piece to bring the stage into disrepute and dishonour with every right-thinking man and woman" (*Lloyds*). Bond's play was attacked as being "not . . . the feeblest thing I have seen on any stage, but . . . certainly the nastiest . . ." (J. C. Trewin, *Illustrated London News,* 13 Nov. 1965), with "characters who, almost without exception are foul-mouthed, dirty-minded, illiterate and barely to be judged on any recognizable human level at all" (H. Kretzmer, *Daily Express,* 4 Nov. 1965). Meanwhile, members of the general public formed pressure groups to mobilize opinion against such pornographic, sadistic, filthy, "unfunny and obscene" plays as *Saved.*[1] At first glance this seems an unjustified over-reaction. Babies are slaughtered on stage in revered classical tragedies. Degraded dregs of society had been an accepted focus for serious plays from Gorki's *The Lower Depths* or Büchner's *Woyzeck* to Gelber's *The Connection.* The "kitchen sink" was almost a commonplace in English drama after Osborne.

Still, in contrast to the general reaction, leading theatre people and critics like Olivier, Tynan, Bryden, Esslin and Mary McCarthy recognized that *Saved* was not only strikingly original, but a deeply moral work. And with his truly impressive output of ten full-length plays, four adaptations, an opera and various short pieces in the last fifteen years, Bond is now widely accepted as the single most important contemporary British dramatist. Yet, apart perhaps from *The Sea* and *Bingo,* critical acclaim has hardly been matched by popular appreciation. In fact, the most striking thing about the stage history of even his most major work is its relative neglect by the English-speaking theatre. Up to 1977 there were only eighteen productions of *Saved* and a bare six productions of *Lear* throughout Britain, the United States, Canada, New Zealand and Australia, as compared to fifty-eight and seventeen in other countries[2]—statistics which can be put into perspective by a further comparison. Within three years of its opening, a play like Peter Shaffer's *Equus* achieved over double the number of productions, and whereas the longest

English run of *Lear* was just over one month, *Equus* was given 131 performances at the Old Vic and ran for over two years on Broadway.

Such disparity between Bond's reputation and his public exposure has created what could be called a critical credibility gap. Certainly it raises questions with which few studies of Bond have yet attempted to deal. To some extent, it might be put down to apparent obscurity, since even among those critics who established his reputation there has been little consensus about how his themes should be interpreted. To some extent, too, it is a measure of the deliberately unsettling effect of Bond's plays. But far more, it seems due to the contradictory and changing nature of his approach: his demand for objective analysis while simultaneously provoking emotion, and in particular his shift from what he labelled as "rational theatre" to "rhapsody." If we trace Bond's development from his first series of plays, ending with *The Sea,* through his second series, which runs from *Bingo* to *The Woman,* it becomes clear that this shift has radically changed the terms of his social criticism. As a result, the criteria established by early plays are totally inappropriate to his later work. However, this modulation seems to have gone generally unrecognized, because Bond himself either refuses to acknowledge the reversal of his earlier principles, or takes steps to disguise the change.

The coherence of Bond's prefaces, which repeat and elaborate a highly specific social analysis, gives his work a misleading impression of consistency. He also takes care to underline this impression by gathering all of his major plays into a double series, in each of which bleak presentations of contemporary problems and their historical roots end in a positive statement of hope, with one play from the first series being rewritten to fit into the second as *The Bundle . . . or New Narrow Road to the Deep North,* and with the imposition of formal uniformity on the second series through the use of parallel subtitles: "Scenes of Money and Death," "Scenes of Bread and Love," "Scenes of Right and Evil," "Scenes of Freedom." The apparent consistency is marked, too, by the way the same images surface in different plays—in particular, Bond's central thematic symbol, the symbiotic pairing of protagonists, which reappears from Scopey and the hermit whom he replaces by murdering in *The Pope's Wedding,* through the Siamese twins of *Early Morning,* to Hecuba and Ismene in *The Woman.* In a simple reversal of Ibsen's *Ghosts,* where society's dead haunt the living, Bond's society of "ghosts in chains" is haunted by the "pro-life" half of each pair, representing conscience. Since no one can totally escape the deadly effect of social conditioning, in Bond's earlier plays the positive qualities of these figures are indeed ghostly: "The pro-life half of the pairs . . . has been killed off like the others . . . but not completely killed." In his later plays they become dominant. Yet the scale, by which moral survival can be measured, remains constant throughout. At one extreme is active resistance to society: for instance, the assassination of Heros, the authority figure in *The Woman.* At the mid-point on the scale are symbolic acts of resistance which function as moral examples and lead to imitation: Lear's final gesture of digging up the wall he built as king, or Arthur's refusal to participate in the cannibal competitiveness of *Early Morning.* At the other extreme is Len's minimum of "restless curiosity" in *Saved,* which in one sense has to be seen as highly ambiguous—a morbid and voyeuristic fascination with murder—yet for Bond "amounts to the search for truth, and in the contexts in which . . . [Scopey and Len] find themselves it's miraculous!"[3]

On this level, Bond's social analysis has the coherence of simplicity. Social institutions, originally developed for the protection of individuals, become self-perpetuating. Law and religion, mores and morality, now have no other function but moulding individuals to serve their needs. Such repression leads to aggression, and this aggression is the driving force behind social progress. Thus, all social activity is presented as moralized violence. The sack of Troy that the authorities condone, or the anarchic murder and rape of civil war in *Lear,* the politically justified killing of the children in *Narrow Road,* or the socially condemned stoning of a baby in *Saved*—all are treated as actions of exactly the same kind and status. For Bond, violence is not an aberration but a general symptom. The infanticide for which Fred is sent to prison is no different from his beating by ordinary housewives who represent the moral outrage in the judicial system which condemns him. Indeed, the way Bond manipulates such parallels makes the point overly obvious:

FRED.

> Bloody 'eathens. Thumpin' and kickin' the van.
>
> . . . .
>
> I don't know what'll 'appen. There's bloody gangs like that roamin' everywhere. The bloody police don't do their job.[4]

Fred's criminal act is presented as a logical extension of social norms, a point also indicated by the parodistic references to disciplining children and toilet-training in the baby-killing sequence itself. But this symptom is also intended to act as a symbol ("the Massacre of the Innocents") on quite a different level, and Bond's parade of children who are stoned, put to the sword, or thrown from the battlements of an emblematic Troy is designed to image what social conditioning does to us all. For Bond,

> All our culture, education, industrial and legal organization is directed to the task of killing [people psychologically and emotionally]. . . . Education is nothing less than corruption, because it's based on institutionalizing the pupil, making him a decent citizen.[5]

Following this analysis, we are all victims; and the rulers are as repressed as those they exploit. Indeed, aggressors need to be even more strictly conditioned to function socially than those they oppress. So where Bond creates symbolic authority figures, like the monstrous imperialist Georgina, they are presented as insane.

Perhaps the clearest dramatic statement of these themes is not *Narrow Road to the Deep North,* which deals with the mechanics of oppression, but *Early Morning,* which explains its mentality. It is perhaps understandable, Bond's aim being to document the delusions of a sick society, that a critic like Esslin should have interpreted *Early Morning* as a fantasy, treating its cannibalism as an "expression of the earliest infantile sexuality, oral eroticism," the Siamese twins as "an image of childhood too: sibling rivalry . . .", and the play itself as "a dream world of infant sexuality."[6] In reaction to this kind of approach, Bond insists that *Early Morning* is "social realism." This seems a fairly arbitrary use of critical labels, but underlines that the play is intended to be a realistic demonstration of the psychology that perpetuates and justifies political power structures, an objective record of subjective illusions:

> What we perceive really isn't a straight transcription of reality, and because people do live in fantasy worlds that is part of social reality. If we could understand our problems, we wouldn't have any need of mythologies and absurd religions to close that gap. . . .
>
> . . . .
>
> I am writing about the pressures of the past that are mis-forming our present time, and that's where it received its public image and its normative values. . . .[7]

Thus, Victorian morality is seen as the legitimation of contemporary political and economic institutions, while Queen Victoria's lesbianism stands for the perversion of an individual's personality by power. The Siamese twins are the social versus the moral (and anarchist) halves of a single character. "Heaven" is the popular concept translated straight into socio-economic terms: a state in which those desires designated as "good" by the inverted morality of society can be indulged without consequence.

What the play demonstrates as well, however, is an unintentional confusion of categories that also characterizes the arguments in some of Bond's prefaces. On one level, the structure of the play is a straight-line story from Albert's palace revolution, through civil war and the deaths of all the characters, to afterlife and Arthur's "ascension." On another level, the structure corresponds to the maturing moral vision of the protagonist: Act I, childhood, where Arthur can make no sense of the self-destructive repressiveness of the establishment or its equally appalling alternatives; Act II, adolescence, where Arthur, now conditioned to accept social practices, carries them through to their logical end (the final solution, as it were, which also stands for the holocaust of nuclear war that Bond sees as the inevitable consequence if aggressive societies continue along their present lines); and Act III, adulthood, where Arthur recognizes the true nature of society and rejects it. At the same time, on a third level, the final Act is a symbolic restatement of the earlier actions—having been shown particular examples of society in action, we are then given a universalized analysis of their inner meaning. Quite apart from the overlap of conflicting perspectives, there is a serious inconsistency here. The reciprocal cannibalism of "heaven" is both an image of capitalist free enterprise and a symbol of the way "people consume each other emotionally . . . in a society where there's only taking";[8] and the first two Acts have demonstrated that there is no escape from or exception to this. Yet on this symbolic level, the very character who is totally socially conditioned and who takes the death principle of society to its logical conclusion, is able to refuse to eat. Not only that: by apparent osmosis or some undefined form of sympathetic magic, his passive example not only spreads temporary indigestion (or pangs of conscience) through the whole society, but also (rather more logically) starts a chain reaction of conversion with Florence, who is brought to question society's assumptions—"Perhaps I'm alive, perhaps we needn't be like this"—and ends by finding excuses for not eating other people.[9] This conversion is intended, of course, as a model for the future behaviour of Bond's audience. Yet all the preceding events have demonstrated nothing but the inevitability of the corruption, perversion or destruction of any instinctive moral goodness by social conditioning—so much so, that the very existence of a positive character in the context Bond has created means that the playwright must have overstated his case against society. As a result, either his social analysis is questionable, or his solution must be seen as wish-fulfilment.

It might be possible to dismiss this contradiction as simply the effect of an over-ambitious play, where the playwright has been unable to synthesize his material or provide a coherent perspective. But Bond himself sets *Early Morning* both technically and thematically above plays like either *Saved* or *Narrow Road*. In addition, exactly the same problem recurs in other plays: for example, the naked man who rescues himself at the end of *Narrow Road,* or the depiction of Len in *Saved,* which Bond has recognized as "almost irresponsibly optimistic."[10] Indeed, his attempts to resolve this paradox in his later plays make his social criticism seem more rather than less contentious; and Bond is so clearly a didactic dramatist that the validity of his message largely determines the quality of his theatre.

This statement is particularly true, since he has defined his aim in general terms as taking the audience "through the learning process of the characters' lives." In *Early Morning,* this aim conditions even the style of presentation. On yet another level, the play is written from Arthur's viewpoint: Act I is deliberately bewildering because "he is bewildered by the political set-up and his own emotional involvement in it . . ."; Act II, grotesque because he is mad; and Act III, "simple and direct . . . because . . . Arthur recovers his sanity. . . ."[11] This learning process is nowhere so literal in Bond's other plays. But whatever the merits or limitations of indoctrination through imitation, Bond's analysis of society itself calls his didactic aims into question on a much more fundamental level.

If we are all socially conditioned victims, exploiters and exploited alike, and therefore functionally insane, whom can he address? Bond implies that only those, like himself, who have managed to escape the educational process, are capable of perceiving reality. According to him, the fact that he was prevented from taking the grammar school entrance examination "was the making of me. . . . [A]fter that nobody takes you seriously. The conditioning process stops. Once you let them send you to grammar school and university, you're ruined."[12] This view leads him to highly contentious conclusions, such as the statement that "It is impossible for the upper class to create poetry now. You can only have working-class poetry; the rest is rubbish."[13] Yet, almost by definition, theatre audiences nowadays are educated. There were earlier examples of the search for a working-class audience, ranging from Joan Littlewood's establishment of a theatre in Stratford East to Arnold Wesker's Trades Union links in Centre 42, if Bond had wished to follow them. But apart from occasional pieces written for CND rallies or the Anti-Apartheid Movement, Bond's plays demand the resources and acting skills of the professional theatre with its predominantly middle-class public. And this demand is implicitly recognized within the plays. After *Saved,* very few of Bond's positive figures are proletarian. Even in *The Woman,* where an escaped slave kills the power figure responsible for setting up an unjust social structure, it is Queen Hecuba who initiates and controls this revolutionary action.

The usual problem with didactic drama is that it preaches to the converted. Bond, by contrast, seems to be addressing the inconvertible (in his terms); and this may explain certain elements in his plays that are otherwise confusing. For example, Bond labels his work "rational theatre,"[14] yet madness is one of his major themes, and his images are almost unprecedented in their visceral effect. Moreover, in *The Woman* rationalism itself seems to be dismissed, and Pericles' Athens is presented solely as a slave state.

Perhaps the best way of clarifying this paradox is to compare Bond's approach with that of Brecht, who also referred to his theatre as a "rational" one. On the surface the links are clear: Bond began at the Royal Court with exercises in Brechtian dramaturgy; he worked on updating *Roundheads and Peaked Heads*; he arranged an evening of Brecht songs (which have similarities in tone and form to his own poetry); and he admits that **Narrow Road** and **Saved** are "somewhat Brechtian in shape. . . ." But the impression that Bond is a direct follower of Brecht seems mainly due to the fact that William Gaskill directed the first productions of almost all Bond's plays up to **Bingo**; and Gaskill has described his own directorial style as being "as clinically accurate as possible . . . a legacy from the influence of Brecht. . . ."[15] Some critics indeed noted the incongruity of "Brechtian sparseness" to **Early Morning.** But their demand for "more visual fantasy"[16] proved in the event to be equally misleading. For instance, when Peter Stein produced **Early Morning** in Zürich, the setting was indeed grotesque and fantastical, with distorted perspectives and surrealistic effects. Victoria sat on an elaborate throne, like a tennis umpire's chair perched on a ladder, in a room of melting architectural shapes, with seemingly organic and sinisterly womblike walls. In the garden-party scene, the actors were dwarfed by a gigantic folding deck-chair extending up into the flies, which became successively a gallows, a mountain, a mausoleum. The effect of this hallucinatory illusion was to shift the play's viewpoint to inside the mad world, so that Arthur's insanity became its norm, with the result that Zürich critics were led to think that "Bond wants total negation," because "the only humanly possible society is one that is definitively dead. Only when there are no more men does man have a chance."[17]

Bond himself insists that "Very little scenery should be used, and in the last six scenes probably none at all," limiting even a throne-room to "*a bench, upstage, and downstage two chairs or a smaller bench. . . .*"[18] But this is the bareness of abstraction rather than Brechtian demonstration; simplification and imaginative suggestion rather than Brecht's open theatricality with the stage machinery exposed and actors stepping out of role.

In fact, what Bond shares with Brecht is not so much a theatrical form as the attitude which he has described in Brecht's work as a certain optimistic "naïvety" that "covers painful knowledge"[19] (what Brechtian critics have labelled "romanticism") and the same philosophical starting-point. For Brecht, personality is not innate, but determined by social function. The exploitive class system of capitalism imposes the strain of being evil on men, making the natural instinct to goodness a fearful temptation to be avoided because self-destructive. Bond has restated Brecht's viewpoint almost exactly:

For me people are naturally good or rather, it is natural for them to be good *or* bad. What they are depends upon their society. I believe that in a good society it is "natural" for them to be kind. If they are evil, that too has to be created.[20]

Brecht's epic techniques, however, were a response to the circumstance of a specific time and place—Germany and the rise of fascism. His ideals of objectivity, distancing and rationality were explicitly intended as what Brecht later called "a withdrawal course for emotional drug addicts":[21] an antidote to the rhetorical emotionalism and sentimentalized heroic posturing of the Nazis, who claimed Wagner as the sacred expression of the national soul. For Bond, writing for a different era and a generation who appeared to accept violence with complacent calmness, the needs of the sixties and seventies were very different. So, while acknowledging Brecht's influence, Bond sees his theatrical approach as "outdated."[22]

In this, interestingly, Bond parallels such contemporary German dramatists as Franz Xaver Kroetz or Heiner Müller. To Kroetz, the major contemporary problem is the "speechlessness" of the socially exploited who have been deprived of the verbal ability to manipulate or even recognize their situation, whereas "Brecht's figures are so fluent," having "a fund of language . . . which is not in fact conceded to them by their rulers," that "the way is open to a positive utopia, to revolution."[23] So, in contrast to Brecht's, Kroetz's characters use a truncated and brutalized dialogue very reminiscent of the speech in **Saved.** Similarly, Müller rejected Brecht's rational objectivity for violent images that would arouse immediate, emotional reactions because "the time for intervening to alter something is always less. Consequently there is really no more time for discursive dramaturgy, for a calm presentation of factual content."[24] Commenting on his version of **Lear,** Bond referred to precisely the same sense of urgency: "Shakespeare had time. He must have thought that in time certain changes would be made. But time has speeded up enormously, and for us, time is running out. . . ."[25] Not surprisingly, then, in contrast to Brecht, Bond uses short, even fragmented scenes to gain intensity, and starkly powerful images for emotional immediacy.

However, the performance values of Bond's theatre are still "rational" in the sense that his experience of staging his own plays convinced him that his scripts require a conceptual approach on the actors' part. In producing **The Woman,** for example, Bond found himself "astonished at the way the acting forced the play into the ground, buried it in irrelevant subjectivity," because the characters were being portrayed in naturalistic emotional terms. So he imposed "a new sort of acting. Put roughly and briefly, it's this. A concept, an interpretation (of the situation, not the character) must be applied to an emotion, and it is this concept or interpretation or idea that is acted. This relates the character to the social event so that he becomes its story teller."[26] This abstracting, intellectualizing quality, of course, in no way reverses Bond's earlier rejection of "anybody who imagines the answers to life are cerebral and that the problems are cerebral." It refers only to the technique of presentation. For the audience, "Theatre involves the whole person. . . . Ideas are two-dimensional . . . involvement on the stage is a three-dimensional process."[27] So the active factor in Bond's theatre is specifically the emotional third dimension—instinctive gut responses.

Even when he defines his work as the objective analysis of society, and therefore "rational," Bond's objectivity does not turn out to have its generally accepted meaning. For Bond, the primary quality that defines art *per se* is "rational objectivity, the expression of the need for interpretation, meaning, order—that is: for a justice that isn't fulfilled in the existing social order."[28] However much we may agree with Bond about the irrationality of society, his polemic creation of synonyms should give us pause. Analysed logically, his statement is a syllogism of the simplistic cats have four legs/dogs have four legs/all cats are dogs pattern. It could be laid out as follows: art is objective/attacks on society are objective/all attacks on society are art. (And conversely, no work that accepts any existing social order can qualify as art.) In other words, objectivity is not impartiality but a particular political bias, and a "rational" theatre is a theatre of political persuasion.[29] And remembering that he sees his audience as composed of spiritually dead people, we realize that Bond's function as a playwright has to be the same as Arthur's in the heaven of *Early Morning*: to cause extreme moral discomfort.

This is the effect arrived at in the way Bond uses farce, although some critics tend to treat his comedy in a traditional light as "an intellectual medium, demanding detachment. . . ."[30] But even if this conventional view has some validity for elements of *The Sea* or perhaps *Narrow Road,* the treatment of, say, the Warrington torture scene in *Lear* is much more characteristic.

FONTANELLE.

Use the boot! (SOLDIER A *kicks him.*) Jump on him!

(*She pushes* SOLDIER A.) Jump on his head!

SOLDIER A.

Lay off, lady, lay off! 'Oo's killin' 'im, me or you?

BODICE.

(*knits*) One plain, two purl, one plain.

FONTANELLE.

Throw him up and drop him. I want to hear him drop. . . .

BODICE.

(*to* SOLDIER A) Down on your knees.

SOLDIER A.

Me?

BODICE.

Down! (SOLDIER A *kneels.*) Beg for his life.

SOLDIER A.

(*confused*) 'Is? (*Aside.*) What a pair!—O spare 'im, mum.

BODICE.

(*knits*) No.

SOLDIER A.

If yer could see yer way to. 'E's a poor ol' gent, lonely ol' bugger. . . .

BODICE.

It's my duty to inform you—

SOLDIER A.

Keep still! Keep yer eyes on madam when she talks t'yer.

BODICE.

—that your pardon has been refused. . . . (*She pokes the needles into* WARRINGTON*'s ears.*) I'll just jog these in and out a little. Doodee, doodee, doodee, doo.[31]

The incongruity of juxtaposing heartless farce and human suffering is explicitly intended to be highly disturbing. As Bond has said, "the effect" of such an "inappropriate" tone "is very cruel."[32] Indeed, Bond's use of farcical comedy has to be seen as an extension of his naked images of violence. For example, on a thematic level, the baby-killing in *Saved* may be a symbol for social pressures; but in terms of dramatic function, its value is primarily that it provokes extreme reactions in an audience. As Bond commented: "everybody's reaction is different . . . people came out absolutely shaking and other people can't even watch it. So it's their reaction, I mean they must ask themselves, not ask me what I think about it."[33]

In fact, the change from graphic realism in *Saved* to the grand guignol of *Early Morning* or *Lear* is only a response to the public's capacity for accommodating themselves to violence. As Bond openly admits: "If I went on stoning babies in every play then nobody would notice it anymore. I had to find [continually new] ways of making people notice, of making those things effective. . . ." This is what he has labelled "the aggro-effect" in deliberate distinction from the Brechtian "alienation effect":

In contrast to Brecht, I think it's necessary to disturb an audience emotionally, to involve them emotionally in my plays, so I've had to find ways of making that "aggro-effect" more complete, which is in a sense to surprise them, to say "Here's a baby in a pram—you don't expect these people to stone that baby." Yet—snap—they do.[34]

By most standards, the power of the emotional reaction to either mode of presentation was all that Bond could have wished. In one of the *Lear* previews, "When the Ghost says 'People will be kind to you now, surely, you've suffered enough,' a departing gentleman in the stalls was heard to remark: 'Yes, so have we!'" With *Saved,* one critic "spent a lot of the first act shaking with claustrophobia and thinking I was going to be sick." Indeed, soon this sort of response apparently became exactly what directors of *Saved* aimed at, and the American première was described as a "complete success" almost solely on the grounds that "the walkout rate after the first half was the highest the theatre has ever had, and I have never seen an audience at a traditional play so disturbed. . . ."[35] But for any propagandist, simply provoking a rejection of his message would be obviously counter-productive. So Bond tends also to claim that his farce is designed to control the violence "by irony, so that it would become a focus to jolt the audience into thinking . . .", and he points out that, because the peak of violence is only half-way through the play, the climax is not the murder itself but the exploration of its causes and effects. These explanations seem to underestimate the power of his images of violence, which tend to produce a form of emotional overkill that makes consequential thought almost impossible. But clearly Bond sees outraging the audience emotionally as a sort of shock therapy designed to galvanize their consciences into life and provoke them into viewing society "objectively" and "rationally" (that is, from his perspective). For him, the degree of violence is nothing more than a measure of urgency, and he denies any "desire to shock."

The shock is justified by the desperation of the situation or as a way of forcing the audience to search for reasons in the rest of the play. *If* you have the effrontery to say, "I am going to use an aggressive 'aggro-effect' against an audience," if you have the impertinence to say that—and I've just said it—then it must be because you feel you have something desperately important to tell them. If they were sitting in a house on fire, you would go up to them and shake them violently. . . . And so it's only because I feel it is important to involve people in the realities of life that I sometimes use those effects.[36]

Bond's reuse of the image of "a house on fire" from an interview in 1971 (shortly after *Lear*) in an interview in 1979 (when he was working upon *The Woman*) indicates that his approach to the audience has remained fairly consistent. But beneath this there has been a radi-

cal shift in Bond's ideas, starting with his attempt to define the right relationship between writing and politics in *Bingo*; and this shift has changed the nature of his dramaturgy.

One of Bond's major themes—perhaps THE major theme after the "Violence [that] shapes and obsesses our society, . . ." which he claims to "write . . . about as naturally as Jane Austen wrote about manners"[37]—is the role and responsibility of the writer. As early as *Narrow Road,* Bond takes a writer as his protagonist, although here the traditional poet-philosopher figure is simply a contrast to his own position. Basho is an idealist who uses the abstract ideals of art as an excuse for non-involvement, then for atrocities. He provides an image of false culture, a way of attacking the academic or aesthetic approach to literature; and the fact that Basho has been singled out as the only "villain" in Bond's full-length plays perhaps indicates the strength of his conviction about the necessity for an artist to be politically committed. There is even the suggestion that if there were no injustice or oppression, then there would be no reason for art at all: "In an ideal society . . . [Basho] would have picked that baby up, gone off the stage and there would have been no necessity for a play."[38]

This concept of false culture is also implicit in *Lear,* since it was the way Shakespeare had become the epitome and justification of purely aesthetic art that provoked Bond into adapting *King Lear.*

. . . I very much object to the worshipping of that play by the academic theatre . . . because I think it is a totally dishonest experience . . . it's an invitation to be artistically lazy to say "Oh, how marvellous sensitive we are and this marvellous artistic experience we're having, understanding this play" . . . [so you] don't have to question yourself, or change your society.[39]

It should hardly be surprising, then, to find Bond starting his second sequence of plays with Shakespeare himself as a protagonist. Basho is merely a polemic figure. But because Bond has a deep admiration for Shakespeare's "intellectual strength and passionate beauty," while rejecting as dishonest his solutions and, in particular, "the reconciliation that he created on the stage . . .",[40] *Bingo* raises serious questions.

Bond presents an irreconcilable conflict between the call for sanity and justice in Shakespeare's art, and the active complicity in an unjust, irrational society in Shakespeare's life. His Shakespeare becomes the type of artist who sells out morally, invalidates everything he writes because he separates art from life. In his next play, *The Fool,* Bond examines the counter-type: John Clare as a poet who refuses to compromise. But the ending is equally bleak because moral commitment is not enough. What Bond implies is that the artist has to have an ideological programme which he can use to change political institutions. Otherwise the pressures to conform to an irrational society, together with the outrage and frustration of his moral sense, will drive him mad. Here again Bond is paralleling contemporary German drama—in this case, Peter Weiss, whose play about *Hölderlin* (written four years before *The Fool*) deals with exactly the same subject: a proto-Marxist poet without a revolution who is driven mad by the irrationality he increasingly perceives around him. The moral—explicit in Weiss, implicit in Bond—seems to be that any truly ethical poet will be forced to withdraw into a cataleptic fugue without the benefit of Marx.

These poet-protagonists are clear reflections of Bond's changing perception of his role as a playwright. In his early plays, what is important is to free the individual from social repression. Any solution in the form of a political programme is seen as simply an alternative structure of coercion, which is the reason why Arthur's apotheosis at the end of *Early Morning* is a parody of Christ's ascension. At this stage, Bond rejects leaders along with uniforms and flag-poles, and in 1969 he declared: "No, I've no Utopia, no image of the society I want to see emerge. It would simply be people being themselves."[41] For Bond, the difference between Communism and Western democracy is only that between Shogo (who socializes his citizens by naked force) and Georgina (with her subtler but more insidious psychological intimidation). In 1970, he commented that "there is *no* viable political system in existence in the world at this moment . . ." (my italics); and in *Lear,* not only the old King and his monstrous daughters with their palace revolution, but also Cordelia and her peasant revolutionaries are all equally corrupted by the necessities of power.[42] Those who overthrow the system by violence perpetuate it, and even preaching a clearly defined political vision will create precisely the oppression it is designed to avoid. "We do not need a plan of the future, we need a *method* of change."[43]

But while working through this dilemma of ends and means in *Bingo,* Bond sets Shakespeare up as the representative of his own earlier viewpoint, which was that "'you can change the world simply by being rational' . . ."—and shows that this attitude contributed to Shakespeare's suicide. As he commented: ". . . I wish that were true, but I don't think it is true. . . . [I]t is not possible to reach a rational world by wholly rational means. . . ."[44]

Of course Bond had already developed a basically irrational technique—the "aggro-effect"—though still in the hope of provoking rational thought and action outside the theatre. However, transferring this from the stage to politics is more than just a difference of degree. A therapeutic shock that jerks a deadened area of the individual's psyche back to life is one thing; a lobotomy,

or the killing of some individuals for the good of others, however surgically this is done, is quite another. And when Bond advocates political violence (as in the misleadingly undated Author's Note in *Plays: One,* which was actually written in 1976 when he was working on *The Bundle*), then he is taking a position that his earlier plays have already convincingly shown to be untenable. In fact, the ending of *The Bundle* even denies what he had earlier declared "evident moral truths . . . things that are simply wrong in themselves. For example, it's evidently wrong to kill someone."[45] This reversal may be, as Bond has claimed, a measure of the urgency of the situation. But his arguments are not logically convincing. Either his rationale is one of *poetic* justice: "Class society must be violent, but it must also create the frustration, stimulation, aggression and . . . physical violence that are the means by which it can change into a classless society"; or, when he tries to define what legitimate violence is, he falls into the end-justifies-the-means fallacy: "Right-wing political violence cannot be justified because it always serves irrationality; but left-wing political violence is justified when it helps to create a more rational society. . . ."[46]

The contradictions in Bond's political position—as outlined in prefaces and essays which, almost by definition, are secondary to the plays—could perhaps be excused, since Bond is a playwright not a political scientist, if they were not reflected so directly in his stage work. But questions of political morality aside, the dramatic implications of Bond's acceptance of the commonplace argument for terrorist violence can be clearly seen in a play like *The Woman.* Here, in Bond's most ambitious play to date, we are given a summation of all his major thematic points. War is explicitly presented as both the product of class society and that society's way of perpetuating itself. War is absurd since "even victory would cost . . . more . . . than defeat at the beginning." The Statue of Good Fortune, for which the Trojan War is being fought in Bond's symbolic version of history, stands for the myths that legitimate an unjust society and trap or destroy the oppressors who rule through them even more than those they exploit. Arthur's madness, leading him to believe that a leader who kills everyone is the greatest benefactor, recurs in Hecuba's son; Arthur's parodic ascension is repeated by Hecuba in an even more grotesque form, as she is uplifted by a waterspout that "ripped out her hair and her eyes. Her tits were sticking up like knives."[47] In addition, to Bond's image of socialization destroying the psyche in the murder of a child, we are shown the physical crippling of a slave as a symbol for the deformation of man to fit him for a biologically inappropriate role in technological society. Again a morally sane person, Ismene, who calls on the Greek soldiers to rebel because their officers are only using the war to enslave them, is driven mad by irrationality.

But here the situation is given an explicit solution: political violence and the natural life of a pastoral island. As Bond wrote in a letter to Tony Coult, "We mustn't write only problem plays, we must write answer plays. . . ."[48] The difficulty is the cliché nature of Bond's positive programme, which becomes expressed in an easiness of achievement that is dramatically unjustified. For the crippled slave to win a race against Heros, who is all that his name implies, demands a deliberate mystification of the audience. A man who is capable of transforming Athens into a tyranny with himself at the top, and who succumbs to such religious idealism that he orders his guards to throw away their weapons, is credible only on a purely symbolic level. Nothing we have seen of the Greek soldiers prepares us for an ending in which they are so dispirited by the death of their leader that they simply leave without any acts of revenge. In addition to this obvious manipulation of the dramatic action, Bond even has to stretch the logic of his symbols to make the play prove what he intends. The slave's deformed body stands explicitly for the effect of social repression which works on the mental level. In all Bond's other plays, the physical represents the psychological and emotional crippling, yet here the slave's moral sense, articulacy and kindness remain untouched by his upbringing and exploitation. Bond's source was Euripides' *Trojan Women,* and his title-change to **The Woman** is an indication of the play's thematic simplification. It is men who set up the repressive structures of a violent society, while (*pace* Victoria, Georgina, Bodice, Fontanelle, et al.) women keep their maternal instinct and so have the capacity to reject irrationality.

As Bond has put it, his first series ended with **The Sea,** which was "meant to *reassure* the audience they can cope with the problems dealt with in the series. . . ." His "second series ends with a *rhapsody,* which is in praise of human beings. In it right triumphs over bad. . . ." In structure as well as intention, it uses a contrast of "the carnage and waste of war" to "[*celebrate*] human tenacity and insight."[49] Despite a superficial similarity, there is a real difference in kind between reassurance and celebration. Similarly, "rhapsody," with its overtones of "enthusiastic extravagance," "emotionalism" and "wish-fulfilment"—qualities indeed reflected in the final positive state of **The Woman,** the Golden World of peasant innocence that is not only a somewhat impractical alternative to the modern situation, but one that had already been dismissed as illusory escapism in **Lear**—has very different connotations from the qualities of "analysis" or "social realism" which Bond stressed in his earlier plays.

If politics were indeed all, it would be comparatively easy to evaluate this development in Bond's work. When answers are so simplistic, serious doubt must be cast on the way the questions have been formulated. And since Bond's didacticism determines the shape of his drama, if his attack on society is discredited, then his message would seem to invalidate his plays. Yet, in fact, any critic dealing with Bond comes up against a conflict between means and ends similar to the dichotomy that Bond himself addresses within his work, since his plays defy easy categories. Apart from Shaw and Brecht, no other twentieth-century dramatist has deliberately measured himself against the standard of Shakespeare. The politics that make his work flawed are also what give it such moral force that it demands to be taken seriously. He is the only English-speaking dramatist who has managed to build significantly on Brecht, and his plays have had at least one tangible political effect—the abolition of censorship in the English theatre—even if the victory was an easy one by that time, since such plays as Osborne's *A Patriot for Me* had already revealed how anachronistic the Lord Chamberlain's powers were. Still, what other contemporary playwright could so legitimately claim, as Bond did in discussing **The Woman,** to have actually fulfilled the "need to set our scenes in public places, where history is formed, classes clash and whole societies move. Otherwise we're not writing about the events that most affect us and shape our future."[50]

Notes

All translations are mine.

1. Mary V. Thom, Letter on *Saved, Plays and Players,* 13, No. 5 (Feb. 1966), 6.

2. Malcolm Hay and Philip Roberts, *Edward Bond: A Companion to the Plays* (London, 1978), pp. 79-85, 90-3.

3. Edward Bond, "Letter to Irene," 7 January 1970, in Hay and Roberts, p. 43.

4. Edward Bond, *Saved,* in *Plays: One* (London, 1977), pp. 83 and 85.

5. Bond, "Letter to Irene," pp. 43-4.

6. Martin Esslin, "A Bond Honoured," *Plays and Players,* 15, No. 9 (June 1968), 26.

7. Edward Bond and Christopher Innes, "Edward Bond: From Rationalism to Rhapsody," *Canadian Theatre Review,* No. 23 (Summer 1979), 109 and 111.

8. Edward Bond and Walter Asmus, "Die Gesellschaft erzieht die Menschen zu Mördern: Interview mit Edward Bond," *Theater Heute,* 10, No. 11 (Nov. 1969).

9. Edward Bond, *Early Morning,* in *Plays: One,* pp. 211 and 223.

10. Edward Bond, Harold Hobson et al., "A Discussion with Edward Bond," *Gambit,* 5, No. 17 (1970), 32; and Bond, *Plays: One,* p. 309.

11. Edward Bond, "Letter to Ruth Leeson," 14 January 1977, and "About 'Early Morning': Letter to Michael Whitaker," 6 November 1969, in Hay and Roberts, pp. 67 and 50.

12. Bond, quoted in Hay and Roberts, p. 7.

13. Bond and Innes, 113.

14. See Bond and Innes, 112.

15. Bond and Hobson, 35; and William Gaskill and Irving Wardle, "Interview with William Gaskill," *Gambit,* 5, No. 17 (1970), 41.

16. Ronald Bryden, *Observer,* 16 March 1969, p. 26. Cf. also Esslin, "First Nights: *Early Morning,*" *Plays and Players,* 16, No. 8 (May 1969), 26.

17. Werner Wollenberger, *Zürcher Weltwoche,* 10 October 1969.

18. Bond, *Early Morning,* pp. 138 and 146.

19. Edward Bond, "Drama and the Dialectics of Violence," *Theatre Quarterly,* 2, No. 5 (1972), 13, quoted in Peter Holland, "Brecht, Bond, Gaskill, and the Practice of Political Theatre," *Theatre Quarterly,* 8, No. 30 (Summer 1978), 27.

20. Bond, quoted in Hay and Roberts, p. 26.

21. Bertolt Brecht, quoted in Manfred Wekwerth, "Berliner Ensemble 1968," *Theater Heute,* 9, No. 2 (Feb. 1968), 17.

22. John Lane, "Resounding Success," *The Times* (London), 25 September 1969, p. 8.

23. Franz Xaver Kroetz, *Süddeutscher Zeitung,* 20/21 November 1971, p. 4.

24. Heiner Müller and Horst Laube, "Drama: Die Dramatiker und die Geschichte seiner Zeit; Ein Gespräch," *Theater 1975* (*Theater Heute* Sonderheft), p. 120.

25. Bond, quoted in Hay and Roberts, p. 18.

26. Edward Bond, "Green Room: Us, Our Drama and the National Theatre," *Plays and Players,* 26, No. 1 (Oct. 1978), 8-9.

27. Bond and Hobson, 19, and Bond and Innes, 112.

28. Edward Bond, "The Rational Theatre," in *Plays: Two* (London, 1978), p. xiii.

29. This, of course, is the same definition used by Peter Weiss in *Dramen 2* (Frankfurt, 1968), pp. 468-9, and by Mao Tse-tung in "Talks at the Yenan Forum of Art and Literature" (1942), where he explained that "showing both sides of the question" meant that "every dark force which endangers the masses must be exposed, while every revolutionary struggle of the masses must be praised," and art is "good . . . if it opposes retrogression and promotes progress" (*Drama in the Modern World,* D. A. Heath [1974], pp. 560 and 558).

30. Richard Scharine, *The Plays of Edward Bond* (Lewisburg, 1976), p. 253.

31. Edward Bond, *Lear,* in *Plays: Two,* pp. 28-9.

32. Edward Bond, "Letter to Angela Praesent," 25 January 1977, in Hay and Roberts, p. 72.

33. Bond, quoted in Hay and Roberts, p. 10.

34. Bond and Innes, 112 and 113.

35. Gregory Dark, "Production Casebook No. 5: Edward Bond's 'Lear' at the Royal Court," *Theatre Quarterly,* 2, No. 5 (Jan.-March 1972), 31; Penelope Gilliatt, in *Contemporary Theatre,* ed. Geoffrey Morgan (London, 1968), p. 41; Michael Feingold, "New York 2: Ensembles," *Plays and Players,* 16, No. 8 (May 1969), 65.

36. Bond and Innes, 113.

37. Bond, *Lear,* p. 3.

38. Bond and Hobson, 9.

39. Ibid., 24. Compare Bond's comment on *Narrow Road:* "What particularly incensed me about Basho was that everybody says, oh, what a marvellous poet. I think that is absolutely phoney. I mean that is bad poetry, that's academic phoney poetry. . . . He says for instance that you get enlightenment where you are . . . and everybody says, oh, how profound. People like Basho never get enlightenment where they are, because . . . enlightenment should have come in the first scene of the play where he found the child" (Ibid., 9).

40. Bond, *Plays: Two,* pp. ix and x.

41. Bond, in *Observer,* 16 March 1969, p. 27.

42. Bond and Hobson, 8. See also Scharine, p. 147.

43. Bond, *Lear,* p. 11.

44. Edward Bond, "Conversation with Howard Davies," in Hay and Roberts, pp. 61-62.

45. Bond and Asmus.

46. Edward Bond, "On Violence," in *Plays: One,* pp. 14 and 17.

47. Edward Bond, *The Woman* (London, 1979), pp. 108, etc.

48. Edward Bond, "Letter to Tony Coult," 28 July 1977, in Hay and Roberts, p. 75.

49. Bond and Innes, 108; my italics.

50. Bond, "Green Room," 8.

David L. Hirst (essay date 1985)

SOURCE: Hirst, David L. "Diabolonian Ethics, Techniques of Subversion." In *Edward Bond*, pp. 48-86. Houndmills, England: Macmillan, 1985.

[*In the following essay, Hirst analyzes Bond's depiction of and commentary on macrocosmic and microcosmic evil, particularly in relation to events of the twentieth century.*]

> . . . I find that my work is more radical than I had thought. I began writing simply as a criticism of certain things I saw around me, and in praise of certain other things. I wanted to understand and so I had to analyze. I didn't at that time understand the implications this would have on my theatrical technique.
>
> Notebook on *Restoration*

SAVED

Saved was the play which brought Bond to the attention of the theatre-going public in 1965. Though it lacks the satiric onslaught of *Early Morning*—which was banned *in toto* by the Lord Chamberlain—and it does not advocate the cause of revolution as his later plays have done, it is in some respects an even more disturbing and challenging drama. This is because of the uncompromising presentation of the action through a sharply realistic style which exposes the more acutely the paradox at the centre of the play. We are forced to see the harsh details of the world both through the eyes of the protagonist, Len, and through those of Bond. We are presented with an accurate and minutely detailed picture of life which functions simultaneously as a savage criticism of the social and political composition of contemporary Britain. In twenty years the play has lost nothing of its immediacy; indeed growing unemployment and a shift towards more reactionary Victorian values on the part of the government have increased the truth of its criticism of social and political truths. The play forces us to see working-class people, as Len does 'at their worst and most hopeless', and yet refuses to allow us any easy or convenient moral indignation through which to vent the feelings of sympathy and anger which it provokes.

It is a long play, unfolding in thirteen independent yet inter-connected scenes a bleak prospect of contemporary life. Set in South London, it alternates between a working-class home, a prison, a cafe and a park. Beginning with an amusing scene of interrupted love-making and ending with a grim scene of social stalemate set in the same room, it portrays cruelty, violence and murder which are the more credible as they are intimately related to their recognisable, everyday setting. Bond was employing a realistic dramatic technique, familiar from the work of previous Royal Court authors, but he refines this to give his social and political satire added

force. This is evident in the first scene in which Pam has picked up Len and brought him home. Their conversation has the terseness of Pinter's dialogue, but there is absolutely no sub-text here. Indeed, the barrenness of their exchanges is a comment on the emptiness of their culture, itself a reflection of the deprivation which is characteristic of their social situation:

LEN.

This ain' the bedroom.

PAM.

Bed ain' made.

LEN.

Oo's bothered?

PAM.

It's awful. 'Ere's nice.

LEN.

Suit yourself. Yer don't mind if I take me shoes off? (*He kicks them off*). No one 'ome?

PAM.

No.

LEN.

Live on yer tod?

PAM.

No.

LEN.

O.

(*Plays: One* p. 21)

The scene is both an accurate realistic portrayal of this situation and a very funny introduction to the drama.

Bond's purpose however is not to comment on the *mores* of these working class figures—as Pinter does in *The Homecoming* or Orton in *Entertaining Mr Sloane*—but to present a life-style which is conditioned entirely by social circumstances. Pam and Len have a great deal of fun at the expense of Harry, Pam's father who interrupts them whilst preparing to leave for work. The salacious *double-entendres* which Len shouts as he is offering Pam a sweet are funny, but a firm comment on the impoverishment of his language and imagination. The social context of the scene is brought into clearer focus when we realise that Harry is about to work a night-shift. Hence he disturbs what little privacy the two lovers have. As we shall see, these issues—at first kept in the background, as Bond's initial aim is to amuse and grip his audience—assume a greater focus as the play develops and we are made to see the correlation between the cramped conditions of the home, the domestic tension this breeds, and the violence which is its inevitable expression both inside and outside the house.

When a group of my students performed *Saved* in the Allardyce Nicoll Studio of the Birmingham Department of Drama and Theatre Arts Bond sent them a 'Short Note of Violence and Culture' which included this statement:

> I know, of course, that an unhappy home might make one person a criminal and another a saint—people always respond individually. But it follows that contact with a saint might make someone else into a criminal. There is no way out of these pessimistic reflections unless we understand that, as a whole, a community takes on the characteristic of its culture—that set of ideas and culture by which the society functions. These ideas and customs are largely laid down by the owners and rulers of society. It is the individual's response to these ideas and customs that sets the character of a society. We are not creatures of instinct but of culture.

The paradox which characterises the opening of this comment is explained by the conclusion. Society unjustly deprives many of its members—specifically and literally the working people—in that they are denied economic and social conditions productive of a healthy culture. The resultant violence, bred of ignorance and frustration, is therefore the fault as much of society as of the individual. Bond's concept of culture—as we see from his other works—is not of some privileged acquisition, reserved for a select few, the icing on the cake, but rather the foundation on which society is built. A society lacking culture is a society lacking reason. Bond's firm belief in the possibility of creating a new and sane culture—one based on Marxist criteria and not on antiquated concepts of privilege—is the basis of his own continued and growing optimism.

It is important to see this so as not to fall into the trap of finding *Saved* a pessimistic play. Bond sees it as 'almost irresponsibly optimistic' precisely because he sees beyond the catalogue of violent events the play presents. These are grim indeed but Bond both examines why they occur and how they can be prevented. The scene which provoked the maximum controversy when the play was first performed and which is still profoundly disturbing is that which culminates in the murder of Pam's child. What makes the scene so theatrically effective is the psychological truth of the presentation gained through a telling observation of the attitudes of the boys: every detail is grounded in observation of social and economic fact. Pam's treatment of the baby emphasises its status as an object, moreover as an inconvenient object which has been ignored throughout scene four and has now been drugged with aspirin. It is not enough however, to dismiss Pam's attitude as oc-

casioned by apathy and viciousness; we are forced to evaluate the influence of her home life and beyond that, the economic situation which has conditioned this.

The attitude of the boys matches hers, but has an added element of macho bravado which makes it even more appalling. Barry's distortion of the nursery rhyme:

> Rock a bye baby on a tree top
> When the wind blows the cradle will rock
> When the bough breaks the cradle will fall
> And down will come baby cradle and tree
> an' bash its little brains out an' dad'll scoop
> 'em up and use 'em for bait'

is guaranteed to provoke laughter; it is he who also initiates the obscene joking with the balloon which follows. Bond is precisely pin-pointing the culture of these boys here. It is an empty and vicious one but the dramatist's condemnation reaches beyond individual psychology to wider social implications. Theirs is a culture based on contempt for life; hence the attitude to sex as obscene, the occasion for smutty jokes and physical assaults on one another. In its combination of boasting and contempt for women Mike's insistence on the availability of casual sex in the local church and late-night laundries is a further comment on this culture. The escalating violence is entirely comprehensible in terms of bravado and consideration of the child as a dirty sub-human creature with no feelings whose punishment 'is therefore justified'. There is no sadism in the attitude of the boys in this scene; their cruelty is cold, unfeeling. It is precisely because it is inexplicable in terms of straightforward emotional psychology that we are forced to consider the deeper psychological motivation which relates their action to the social and economic situation. It is for this reason that Bond's realism is essentially philosophical and political.

It is misleading to pay exclusive attention to the killing of the baby in evaluating the political purpose of Bond in this play. No less telling is the scene of domestic violence which erupts after the sexual encounter between Mary and Len. Harry, who has not spoken to his wife as long as Pam can remember, is goaded into response by Mary's advances to Len and she returns his verbal abuse with physical assault. Bond's observation of this silent battle of wills between husband and wife is one of the most accurate and emotive features of the play. It precisely defines an all-too-familiar working-class situation where incompatibility develops into hatred through an inability to communicate. The refusal to speak to one another is the ultimate expression of the barrenness of this culture: a more articulate couple might bicker, abuse one another verbally. Harry and Mary have no tools to help them; the fault is seen to be both theirs and society's. When the violence does erupt—in Mary's throwing of the bread on the floor and her hitting Harry over the head with the teapot—it is seen to be childish, pathetic. They have been reduced to animals by their way of life: Mary's dull household routine and Harry's enervating night work are inescapable realities of their economic situation, emphasised the more fully by Pamela's attitude to Len, which shows every sign of repeating the pattern established by her parents. Bond sees this as a consequence of a capitalist society which has a vested interest in exploiting the labour force and is quite unconcerned with a policy of wider cultural advancement. The solution—as he has come to see—requires a more radical re-ordering of society, though even in this play he lays down bases for a positive way forward. Len's attitude is fundamentally different from Pam's, from the other boy's and even from Harry's—who, though he reaches a new depth of understanding with Len, cannot stop nurturing his hatred for Mary. Len is the first of Bond's heroes: he learns a great deal in the play and this gives him a tenacity which he refuses to abandon. At the centre of the final scene of social stalemate he continues doggedly to mend the chair Harry broke in the row with Mary. One has only to compare Len with Beattie Bryan in Arnold Wesker's *Roots* to be fully aware of Bond's rejection of a political conversion founded essentially on personal issues and expressing itself in an attempt to convert her family to her newly acquired taste for classical music. For Bond such an acceptance of the cultural values of another class serves merely to cover over the wound; more radical surgery is needed to cure the political disease.

The precise nature of Bond's approach in *Saved* is very similar to that employed by Shaw for parallel social and economic criticism in *Mrs Warren's Profession*. Shaw declared in the Preface to this play that he wrote the drama not as an indictment of moral depravity on the part of either prostitutes or their clients, but as an exposé of the monstrous economic system which made it expedient for women to prostitute themselves rather than undertake a worse-paid, more physically arduous job. In a no less impassioned Preface Bond makes it clear that in *Saved* he is pointing a critical finger not so much at the obscenity of the gang's violence as at the iniquitous social and economic situation which gives rise to it. The basic techniques of both dramatists is the use of paradox. They both play down their condemnation of what is conventionally considered to be the ultimate in amoral behaviour so as to focus on conduct they consider to be worse. Shaw employed this strategy in many of his plays. In the Preface to *The Devil's Disciple* he explains his method in an essay entitled *On Diabolonian Ethics*: his technique is similar to that of William Blake in that he intends to confound conventional morality by exposing its hypocrisy and arguing for a more rational approach to society. In the programme for *Saved* Bond included the Blake quote: 'Bet-

ter strangle an infant in its cradle than nurse unacted desires' and he went on to expand the implications of this in his Preface to the play:

> Clearly the stoning to death of a baby in a London park is a typical English understatement. Compared to the 'strategic' bombing of German towns it is a negligible atrocity, compared to the cultural and emotional deprivation of most of our children its consequences are insignificant.

(*Plays: One,* pp. 310-11)

This is meant to be provocative. Those who are morally indignant at the killing of a child are not at first likely to connect this with the defense strategies or economic policies of the government. But Bond intends us to do so. When we recognise that public violence is a direct result of political aggression and social inequality we can stop making glib moralistic pronouncements on such conduct. As he said in his note to my students:

> Unfortunately since we live in a small world we have to think not of national society but rather of a world society. It then becomes clear that our species is threatened not by social criminals but by political ones: those who threaten us with the ultimate crime of nuclear holocaust. With the class of leaders we have we must expect to find violence on the streets. This is not because people are barbarous—but because our society is.

It is clear that Bond's drama is subversive of conventional religious and ethical values. He insists in the Preface to *Saved* that our children are morally bewildered because all the morality they are taught is grounded in religion. This religion has nothing to do with their parents' personal lives, or our economic, industrial and political life, and is contrary to the science and rationalism they are taught at other times. For them religion discredits the morality it is meant to support. He concludes that we must teach 'moral scepticism and analysis, and not faith'. (*Plays: One,* pp. 311-2). This is precisely what *Saved* is designed to encourage: through its savage central paradox—the reality of a monstrous society responsible for the ugly violence we witness—he has found a spectacularly effective technique of provoking his audience both emotionally and, beyond that, intellectually.

Apart from the moral indignation of the Lord Chamberlain who insisted on cuts which would have made a performance of the play impossible, the reaction of another contemporary critic, the writer Pamela Handsford Johnson, is worth citing at this point. In 1967 Johnson published *On Iniquity,* an examination of the motives of Myra Hindley and Ian Brady, the moors murderers. In this study she reaches the conclusion that they were both corrupted by the pornography they read, and thus anything which might be classified as likely to deprave or corrupt should be banned—not however to all, but to those whose defective education might make them susceptible to its influence. The paternalistic elitism of this approach illustrates the sort of morality Bond despises, and it is no surprise to find Johnson listing *Saved* among precisely those works that are likely to corrupt. She says:

> I do not speak of this play lightly. I have read and re-read it with the greatest care, and remain of the opinion that the scene to which I refer (scene 6) is, despite, its verbal skill, unfit for public representation. Either it sickens, or it conduces to the wrong kind of excitement. It is not conducive to social thinking, since it contains no shock of new knowledge.
>
> (*On Iniquity*, p. 49)

It is significant that she had read the play and not seen it, and she failed wholly to grasp—or to accept—the implications of Bond's 'social thinking' in the work. The title of her book is perfectly expressive of her moral approach: precisely the opposite of Bond's. She believes in moral definitions of good and bad quite unrelated to social and political conditions. For her the boys in *Saved* along with Hindley and Brady are wicked: 'iniquitous', to employ her epithet. She upholds the conservative ethical values which are the corollary of her privileged social position. She expresses the desire to put an end to what she terms 'liberal' thinking which seeks to explain crime by reference to environment; rather she holds the belief that people are born good or bad, or that at least their conduct is entirely their own responsibility. It is a recognisable attitude and one wholly at variance with Bond's whose moral stand is no less clear, but whose radical approach to ethics is dependent on a wider social and political perspective. In the 'Short Note On Violence and Culture' he states this firmly:

> In human beings the idea always takes precedent over instinct. This is a revolutionary concept because it completely changes the way in which we think of both human beings and their societies. It means that human beings act not in accordance with the emotions they bring into the world but in accordance with the ideas they are taught and acquire while they are in it. We think of emotions as motivating actions but really emotions spring from and are directed by ideas. This means that humanity is made by human beings—or rather by being human—and that ultimately when human beings are inhuman it is their interpretation of themselves and their society that is at fault. This does not mean that emotions have no importance but that they function in accordance with ideas. People become Nazis, for example, not because they have a particularly aggressive and ugly character but because their character is formed by certain ideas. These ideas then licence their emotions.

After *Saved* Bond determined to explore new theatrical techniques. Having written in a style familiar to Royal Court audiences and having, through this style, issued a more urgent political challenge, he felt the need to explore fresh dramatic forms. *Early Morning* is a radical departure from the downbeat realism of *Saved*, whilst *Narrow Road To The Deep North* saw the employment of incidents and techniques from Eastern theatre. Both *Lear* and *Bingo* employ a more subversive strategy: they respectively take a familiar Shakespearean play and details of Shakespeare's biography which they turn on their head, reaching conclusions which are at the furthest remove from received opinion and conventional interpretation. A tragedy concerned with the ethics of power is translated into a modern political morality play, and the traditional picture of the Bard retiring in peaceful fulfilment to his Stratford home is converted to a bleak examination of a failed artist's suicide. Shakespeare has exercised a large influence on Bond—who, like Shaw, has a love-hate relationship with his work. Bond, however, is not employing Shakespearean dramatic form in his re-write; *Lear* is the first exercise in his own brand of epic theatre. *The Sea, Bingo* and *The Fool* are also highly original in construction. *We Come To The River* marked a new departure: Bond was both constrained and inspired by the challenge of creating the libretto for an opera. It is after this work that he was to turn to other clearly definable examples of bourgeois theatrical form and by utilizing specific features expected by the audience, employ the dramatic medium for his own ends as a political writer. In so doing he is not deconstructing the idiom in which he is working: rather—as with *Saved* and *We Come To The River*—he is carrying to its ultimate conclusion the social and political potential inherent in the work of writers as diverse as Euripides, Farquhar and Ibsen.

THE WOMAN

The first of these plays is *The Woman*, like the opera, written in response to the challenge of a new theatrical environment: the Olivier stage at the National Theatre. Bond responded to the aspects of the space which recall the Greek amphitheatre and produced a play which in setting, scope and subject matter is strongly indebted to the drama of fifth century B.C. Athens. Between his initial conception of the play as *The Trojan Woman* early in 1974, and his completion of it (just over three years later) he spent two holidays in Malta where he soaked himself in the Mediterranean sun and re-read all the Greek tragedies. The result is a play owing a great deal to Euripides, both in respect of dramatic form and the subject matter taken from *The Trojan Woman*, but which also draws on other Greek plays such as Sophocles's *Oedipus* and *Antigone*. The scope of the drama is on the scale of *We Come To The River*. It has a large cast and narrates issues centering on two events: the fall of Troy and the arrival of the Greeks on a small Mediterranean island twelve years later. The play is in two very different parts, the first culminating in the tragic events consequent on the sack of Troy, the second leading to the liberation of the islanders from the Greeks as a result of the combined efforts and heroic action of Hecuba and the Dark Man. Hecuba is the central figure, active in both parts of the drama, moving from haughty contempt to despair in the first and from resignation to political action in the second. It is a progress which is familiar in Bond's drama. She has many affinities with Lear. Her attempt to blind herself after Troy has been taken has a parallel with the treatment he receives at the hands of his political enemies. It is also an echo of the climactic act of Sophocles's *Oedipus Rex.*

But like Oedipus—and like Bond's dramatic hero, Wang in **The Bundle**—Hecuba has more to learn. The process of her ethical and political awakening occupies the second act which is as different in style and subject matter from the first as is Sophocles's *Oedipus at Colonus* from the preceding tragedy. The significance of Ismene—a character taken from *Antigone,* the second of the Theban plays—alerts us to the importance of the entire trilogy in the overall structure of **The Woman.** In Sophocles's Theban dramas and in Aeschylus's *Orestaeia* the final note is one of hope. Oedipus learns wisdom, whilst at the conclusion of *The Eumenides* vengeance is converted to pity. In the latter Aeschylus is defending the political *status quo* through the decision of the Athenian court to temper justice with mercy. Bond's political aim is different. But it is significant that his own conclusion builds on the structure established by both these trilogies, the one dramatising enlightenment, the other attempting to put a stop to an inexorable concatenation of violent events.

That Bond wishes first to establish a recognisable dramatic context for the events of his play and, having drawn his bourgeois audience into this framework, then utilise it to teach fresh truths is borne out by the precisely similar technique he employs in a short poem published with the script of **The Woman.** This is entitled 'Pompei' and begins with a description of everyday life in the city:

> People who lived on the slope
> Went to market each day
> Met on street corners
> Saw death in the arena
> And passed by sluices that carried water to wash out
>   the blood.

The jarring of this final line makes us suddenly aware of the complacent attitude to slaughter and torture, but this is a description of the past: of cruelty which no longer exists. The first verse continues:

> Took pains to bring up their children
> Brought horses and saved against age
> While over the city the mountain smoked.

There follows a verse in which the violence and dangers hinted at in the first stanza are distanced by a liberal historical perspective:

> It's said that in those days of imperial violence
> Men lived in a dream
> Learned how to live with danger
> And energy gave way to frantic fever

This process, Bond is well aware, can easily set in whilst watching a historical play, the events of which no longer really touch us. That is why the political dramatist must make the audience aware of the relevance of the events they are witnessing to their own lives and force them to consider the implications more fully. In the poem this is effected by the shock of the sudden final line: 'How far is the missile site from your house?'

In the play the call to action also comes at the end, but throughout the audience is jolted by details which underline the contemporary relevance of the events staged. Bond's play centres on the power of a stolen statue. At the beginning of the play this has been taken to Troy; it replaces the abduction of Helen. We are on the eve of the fall of the city but the seige has continued for five years, not ten. Priam is dead, but he was not killed by Pyrrus and there is no mention of the Wooden Horse. The basic situation is the same as it is in Euripides's drama, but the details have been changed to make the modern parallel clearer. This emerges in the second part of the first scene when Greek leaders witness what is going on in Troy. This is seen entirely through the eyes of their leader, Heros, and, moreover, is acted out by the Greeks themselves: Nestor plays Hecuba, Thersites Cassandra and Ajax the Son. 'The scene', Bond informs us 'is to be imagined as occurring in Heros's head.' It presents a picture of Hecuba as a harridan refusing to listen to the advice of her family, notably over the matter of the statue:

CASSANDRA.

> Give the statue to the Greeks. Without father to guide us—

HECUBA.

> Trust the Greeks? No, I'll never do that. What would the Greeks have to lose once they'd got it? We must hold on to it—that's the only way to save our lives.

> (**The Woman** p. 17)

Here is the all-too-familiar cant of politicians supporting the arms race. It comes here with the full shock of awareness contained in the final line of 'Pompei': Hecuba's attitude calls attention to the same subject; hers is effectively a reactionary stand on disarmament. But this stand is the product of Heros's mistrust and fear of the Trojans; Hecuba is not like this at all, as we can see when we meet her. She readily falls in with Ismene's plan: to remain as a hostage in the city as a guarantee that once they have been given the statue the Greeks will go. The intuitive common sense of the women is in marked contrast to the conduct of the male leaders who refuse to act in this rational way. Hecuba's son has her imprisoned and himself fulfills the worst suspicions the Greeks had of the Trojans. He precipitates a bloody conflict which results in his own assassination, the destruction of the city, the murder of Astyanax and the enslavement of the women.

The 'Catch 22' situation exposed at the beginning of the play is seen to be entirely of the men's making. It serves to highlight the contemporary relevance of the drama but is not confined to the issue of disarmament. Bond is well aware that the real problem we are facing is the threat to the continuation of the species. Such a possibility is at the forefront in his mind and the destruction of an entire city and people is a pointed reminder of this. But the image of the statue serves to focus political issues of a different nature in the second act. By this point there are a number of survivors of the holocaust, living peacefully on an island. Hecuba's description of the waterspout that threatened to destroy them, but in fact separated them from their Greek oppressors, is another potent image of the danger from which they have escaped. But their peace is shattered by the arrival of Heros looking for them and the statue. Now his reason for taking the statue is to bolster his prestige in the new city he has established, but his chance of obtaining it is far more remote, as Hecuba informs him it has been lost at sea. The image of him fishing the seas to find it powerfully emphasises the folly of the politician desperately attempting to make his power secure, a course of action deflated by the attitude of Nestor who has little sympathy for Heros's insistence on punishing the soldier who has mistakenly allowed him through the lines:

HEROS (*TO* NESTOR).

> You think I'm unreasonable. This place is almost part of the sea. We *feel* it. All except you. Would you rush into a temple and yoo-hoo? I risk the welfare of Athens being here. It's our duty to take absolute care. We owe it to Athens. Yoo-Hooo! (*Distant roll of thunder*) It's a matter of military discipline. (*Flatly*). Now thunder.

NESTOR.

> I'm surprised I'm not accused of farting.

> (*op. cit.* p. 94)

The escalating madness of the ruler committed to maintaining an unjust society—familiar in Bond's work from **Early Morning** and **Lear** as well as **We Come To The River**—culminates in Heros's acceptance of Hecuba's challenge to a race against the Dark Man. Though the latter is crippled he wins and Heros is killed. The Dark Man and Hecuba could be accused of cheating, but Bond argues that it is the duty of the political revolutionary to bide his time and strike down his oppressor when he is thoroughly trapped in the folly of his own desperate situation.

By the end of the play Bond has taken his audience a great deal further than they may well have anticipated in the opening scene of Act 1 with its action firmly grounded in the events of the Trojan war. In so doing he has fulfilled the duty of the Marxist writer. This is pithily explained in a further appendix to the drama: 'Another Story'. Here he expresses in a brief narrative the point emphasised by Gramsci that we cannot come to terms with the future unless we understand the past. This story tells of a man, who, when lost, asked for directions from a woman and followed them. But he never reached his destination and, many years later, seeing the woman again, he asked why she had misled him. She apologised, assured him the directions had been right and that he must have misinformed her of his precise whereabouts. Bond's conclusion is:

> No one should set out on a journey till they know where they are starting. Indeed you may not know—perhaps never know—your destination: but you must know where you start. How else can you do anything or go anywhere? It follows that hope is not faith in the future but knowledge of the past. This hope is not an idle fiction but the surest of facts. It is a promise kept even before it is made.

> (*The Woman* p. 116)

This explains his interest not merely in the story of the Trojan war but also in the drama of Greek society in the fifth century B.C. 'I wanted', he has said, 'to go back and re-examine that world and how moral and rational it was, and whether or not it could be a valid example for a society like ours. I came to the conclusion that it wasn't'. (Unpublished interview with Tony Coult, August 1978. *H&RP.* p. 239) That society, however, was to provide him with a parallel with our own in another way.

The Trojan Women gave him—in Euripides's criticism of his own society—both the example of political expediency and military cruelty, and a dramatic model to use as the starting point of his own play. Euripides, the last of the three great Athenian tragic dramatists, has particular affinities with Bond. Lacking the clear-cut reactionary ethics of Aeschylus or the emphasis on individuals caught in a tragic pattern of fate which characterises the plays of Sophocles, he is a more satiric dramatist, critical of the conduct—social and political—of his contemporaries. *The Trojan Women* was inspired by his sense of outrage at a specific historical event: the savage attack on the defenceless island of Melos in 416 by the Greek forces led by Alcibiades. His play is in no sense an Aristotelian work, designed to lead the audience through a careful unity of action to identification with the central character and thus, through awareness of the reversal of his fortunes and recognition of this, effecting a purgation of the emotions of pity and terror. *The Trojan Women* is in this respect the opposite of a play like Sophocles's *Oedipus*

Rex. Though the fates of the women inspire in us pity and terror we are not allowed to experience a catharsis and leave the theatre 'calm of mind, all passion spent'. Euripides's play is episodic: we witness a series of scenes involving the fates of different characters: Hecuba, Andromache, Astyanax, Cassandra. The action is effectively over when the play begins: Troy is defeated, the women waiting to learn their fate. Euripides's technique of recalling past events (through Hecuba's narrations) and anticipating others (through Cassandra's prophecies) is appropriate to epic rather than tragedy. We are made aware of wider, bigger issues than the merely personal. The destruction of an entire city, a whole civilisation is presented to us.

Bond, too, is concerned with a wider canvas: the fates of the individuals—whether the oppressors or the liberators—are subservient to the fate of the people. That the islanders shake off the tyranny of Greece as surely as the Trojans succumbed to it through their own political folly is what matters. It is vitally important for the continuation of our own species that we learn from the lesson of their history. Bond has structured his drama in two clear parts. Having established the epic form at the start he expands its potential gradually as the play unfolds. The first act culminates in the violence as the city is destroyed. The audience has been led to expect these events from their familiarity with the story and the mode of presentation. From Euripides's drama we anticipate the sacrifice of Astyanax as the climatic act of cruelty. But the first act ends not with this, but with a far more terrible event: Hecuba's blinding.

In Bond's drama the theme of Hecuba's learning about the world and accepting her political destiny and duty is central. It is only just beginning here, but even her desperation and wish to evade reality is far more important than the sacrifice of Astyanax. She is already reacting to events and this process will continue throughout the play. Hence the killing of the child is restricted to one off-stage scream and the suffering of Cassandra is cut short by Hecuba's entry. Bond has changed here the mother of Astyanax (it was Andromache) the more to deflect our attention from the tragedy of the individual to that of the state. In his 'Notes on Acting' he further explains the importance of this shift of emotional emphasis:

> Perhaps we should say that most of the emotion occurs between the scenes and that the scenes show the consequences of these emotions. You can make a distinction between a blow and the consequences of a blow. Very few blows should be struck in the play because when they are struck they should be a knockout. So most of the blows occur before the scenes. The scene itself is the reeling effect of the blow.
>
> (*The Woman*, p. 126)

We are prepared for the second act of the play which can move freely away from the material established in the first act and in so doing bring the audience, gripped by the unfolding of a Greek epic, face to face with the consequences of the previous action both for the characters and, more importantly, for themselves.

RESTORATION

Restoration is the most cunning of Bond's plays, a witty comedy of manners written by a Marxist playwright. Of course Bond's play is much more than this: it contrasts throughout the sophisticated world of the wealthy idle aristocracy with that of the bourgeois merchant and the worker. In an influential article written in *Scrutiny* in 1937, L. C. Knights had dismissed the comedy of the post-Restoration period as trivial and dull. John Wain, applying the tyranny of left-wing dogma and critical of a drama reflective of an upper-class culture, had compared Congreve unfavourably with the author of *Charley's Aunt*. The new wave of theatre with a working-class setting which established itself at the Royal Court in the late 'fifties was suspicious of any undue concern with style. But by the mid 'sixties the fashion had altered: the age of *Hair* and Carnaby Street saw a comparable change in dramatic style as Pinter turned from comedy of menace to comedy of manners and playwrights such as Orton revealed the potential of witty social satire. Celebrated comedies of the past were revived: Noel Coward, relegated to an ignominious position in the fifties assumed the status of a classic and the dramas of the Restoration period returned to the stage. Pre-eminent in this revival of a neglected form was William Gaskill whose productions of Farquhar's *The Beaux's Stratagem* and *The Recruiting Officer* at the National and of Congreve's *The Double Dealer* at the Royal Court paved the way for a major revaluation of the genre.

Bond's decision to adapt the features of this idiom to his own ends was a very careful and shrewd one. His play is called **Restoration** but it takes place in the eighteenth century. Bond is fully aware of the difference between the plays of Wycherley and Etherege written in the reign of Charles II immediately after the Restoration of the monarchy in 1660 and those of Farquhar written in the reign of Queen Anne. Farquhar's plays—and those of his contemporary Vanbrugh—are not concerned with the savage exposé of ruthless conduct characteristic of the earlier comedies; they anticipate the good-humoured urbanity and sentimentality of Goldsmith who was writing at the end of the eighteenth century. The aristocratic playgoers of the Restoration period gradually gave way to the new class of wealthy London merchants whose tastes were very different: instead of comedies centering on the twin themes of sex and money, both of which were handled with deadly seriousness, they demanded plays which were far removed from the commercial reality of their own lives and which did not show the cleverest man winning, but the most virtuous.

The fashion-conscious beau of Bond's play, Lord Are, is a figure from Vanbrugh: he has many of the characteristics of the Lord Foppington from *The Relapse,* a character played subsequently with great success by Simon Callow who created the role of Are. In *The Relapse* the greedy and affected Lord is outwitted by his brother and Miss Hoyden, the country girl both are pursuing for her fortune. This play was particularly popular at the end of the eighteenth century as Sheridan adapted it as *A Trip To Scarborough.* But the geniality of Vanbrugh, Sheridan and Goldsmith is quite lacking in Bond's treatment. Are is a figure from earlier comedy with all the cunning and ruthlessness that is the corollary of his wit. He is more like Dorimant, Etherege's Man of Mode who outwits all his rivals to be rid of his mistress and win the hand of a wealthy heiress. The play, whilst promising a happy ending along the lines of eighteenth century romantic comedy, frustrates the audience's expectations by reverting to a dénouement in key with seventeenth-century standards of dramatic propriety. Bond's drama is in effect a comment on sentimentality and evasion of truth. Augustan sentiments such as:

> God bless the squire and his relations
> And keep us in our proper stations

he sees as falsity. He asks us to reject the sham of our present social system as surely as he rejects an improbable romantic ending to his story. If we wish in life as in the theatre to avoid reality then we must expect to pay the price.

The first scene establishes neatly the situation of the play which is firmly in the tradition of the comedy of manners. It opens with Lord Are intent on arranging his appearance to win over Ann, the wealthy heiress of Mr Hardache. Like Aimwell and Archer in *The Beaux's Stratagem* he is a fortune hunter, but as the aggressive poseur who compares the country unfavourably to the town—a theme which runs throughout Restoration comedy—he more closely resembles Vanbrugh's Lord Foppington:

ARE:

> Wha-ha! I must not laugh, it'll spoil my pose. Damn! the sketch shows a flower. 'Tis too late for the shops, I must have one from the ground.

FRANK:

> What kind sir?

ARE:

> Rip up that pesky little thing on the path. That'll teach it to grow where gentlemen walk. (FRANK *offers the flower.*) Smell it! If it smells too reprehensible throw it aside. I hate the gross odours the country gives off. 'Tis always in a sweat! Compare me to the sketch.

FRANK:

> (*checks sketch*) Leg a bit more out.

ARE:

> Lawd I shall be crippled. *Do* they stand about the country so? When I pass the boundaries of the town I lower the blinds in mourning and never go out on my estate for fear of the beasts.

(Restoration pp. 7-8)

The key to Bond's skill in this play is the way in which he is so fair and accurate in his presentation. Are is very funny, but the pastiche of this style cuts a great deal deeper. As the dramatists of the immediate post-Restoration period observed, both a witty manner and an elegant deportment were signs not only of breeding but of intelligence. Wit implies both verbal ingenuity and mental skill. It is the cleverest men who are always the winners in the plays of Wycherley and Congreve. This success is independent of conventional standards of morality: it creates its own laws. When the dramatists of the eighteenth century ignored this intransigent reality and presented the working out of financial and emotional issues dependent more on good fortune or good breeding they took the sting out of the Comedy of Manners and created a drama which was not an accurate reflection of the age. Bond recognises this: his villain is witty, clever and amoral. But what is for Are a reasoned attitude to life is not accepted by the dramatist as a rational way of organising society.

Hardache and Ann seem at first to be characters from Goldsmith. Hardache has all the geniality of Hardcastle in *She Stoops To Conquer* and Ann, though nothing like Kate Hardcastle, is very like her mother whose longing to escape from the country to London is ridiculed by the dramatist. Hardache is just such a character as Steele's Mr Sealand in *The Conscious Lovers:* an example of the rising merchant class which was taking over from the landed aristocracy at the end of the seventeenth century. At first he appears Are's dupe, unaware that his daughter is marrying a young lord who had debts to honour and is penniless. But Hardache, contemptuously dismissed by Are as 'iron founder, ship builder, mine owner and meddler and merchant in men and much else that hath money in it' proves to be as cunning as his son-in-law. He will not protect the interests of the worker, Bob; and Rose will crucially underestimate that force which we recognise in Are's description as essentially the power of capital. Ann is no less unscrupulous: she is interested solely in her husband's position, hoping he will die and leave her a wealthy young widow. But she is his inferior in appearance and in cunning. Her ridiculous scheme of pretending to be a ghost first to frighten him into taking her to London and then to scare him to death pitifully misfires as he runs his sword through her. She is no match for her husband whose style and ingenuity are the complement to his wit, as we see in his shrewd assessment of Ann:

ARE:

> Not uncomely, but the neglect is beyond redemption! Style cannot strike at any age like a conversion, its rudiments are learned in the nursery or never. That redness of cheek might be had off a coster's barrow for ha'pence. But I'll take her, as she comes with money.
>
> (*Restoration*, p. 11)

When Are later has the upper-hand in the marriage his witty refusal to keep his part of the bargain strikes a more fundamental truth in the play. Such a paradox as: 'Why, ma'am if a gentleman kept his promises society would fall apart' is an irony which conveys Bond's own message.

The marriage of Are and Ann is a union of landed aristocratic arrogance and capital. This union constitutes the oppressor of the working people who Bond, in the earlier part of the play, portrays as labourers, little better than animals. 'Treat me like an animal and I'll be one', says Frank and uses this as justification for his theft of the silver. His own rebellious conduct will lead him to the same prison and the same scaffold as the honest Bob, who is the scapegoat for Are's murder of his wife. At least Frank dies unrepentant as he had lived: in a series of powerful stage images we see him tied up like a beast when exhausted by work, caged, and then escape to live a life of drinking and whoring. Society has made him like this; nor is the honest Bob any better. Like his mother, he accepts his position, sentimentally trusting in the benevolence of the man for whom he will be sacrificed. When Bob's mother discovers Frank has stolen the spoons her cry of: 'My silver gone! I polished it for years!' has cutting satiric force. It is she who in this society is the possession, a function she accepts as completely as the parson whose pious concern for the stolen goods further emphasises the irony:

PARSON:

> This woman learns of a lifetime of wasted labour. The cherished things on which she lavished her affection are gone. How will she occupy the time she would have devoted to cleaning them?
>
> (*Restoration* p. 39)

Bond's merciless exposé of Bob's absurd servility at the end of the act when, in reply to Are's: 'Bob, throw the toast to the hens on your way to prison' he ' *weeping, picks up the toast rack and nods*' is matched by the telling image of his mother later in the play ingenuously accepting the pardons from Are and assiduously burning them at his instruction:

MOTHER:

> Kind of him. Save me fetch the kindlin'. Official pretty crown on top. Cut them out for Christmas decoration. (*Shakes her head*). Best do what yoo're towd. Bob was learning to read. (*Tears the papers*) Ont start that doo yoo ont git the work out the way.
>
> (*Restoration* p. 89)

Rose is a very different figure with a natural wit that sees straight to the heart of things. She is appalled at the complacent attitude of Bob and his mother and speaks out in his defence. She is shrewd enough to know that to defeat Are she must play by his rules. She has learnt this from her mother, a black slave, whose advice she puts to good use when she helps Frank escape. She sees further than the other servants, realising that if Are is convicted of the murder, Ann's money will go back to her father. As she expresses it tersely: 'It's not between Are and Bob. It's between two bosses.' She attempts to enlist Hardache's help; but she has underestimated—as Bond encourages the audience to do—his mercenary cunning. The benevolent father is seen in his true colours for the first time when he meets Are in prison and uses Rose's information to blackmail his son-in-law into giving him what he wants.

Here Bond craftily employs the features of Restoration comedy—in its urbanity of style and the exposure of the pecuniary motives this masks—to give us a sharply defined picture of the economic bases on which both this society and our own function:

HARDACHE:

> I don't like interfering—but she was my daughter and she'd want the right man to hang.

ARE:

> (*Calm and precise*) Why here at such a time?

HARDACHE:

> Where better? All parties to hand. If questions have to be asked they can answer them directly. And if you have to take lodgings on the prison next door—you're spared the extra journey.

ARE:

> Sir. My drinking companion the Lord Lieutenant—in whose bosom my hand lies deeper than ever the dearly beloved disciple's lay in Christ's—will not let you clap me in gaol. Tomorrow I am promised for the races, and 'twould quite spoil his party.

HARDACHE:

> Son-in-law. Your title gives you acquaintance, money gives me mine. I pay for the coach that takes your mighty friend to the races. Here's a riddle: why does a sensible man like me let his daughter marry a fop like you?

ARE:

> Fop? A fella don't boast but—

HARDACHE:

> Coal.

ARE:

> I misheard.

HARDACHE:

No. Under your land.

ARE:

I have been rooked.

HARDACHE:

Your title cost me a packet but I meant to pay for it with your coal. The marriage made it mine. Or my grandson's—I think ahead for the good of the firm. The firm'll do very nicely out of thee and me. Now this mishap upsets my grand scheme.

(pp. 74-5)

He therefore proposes another agreement which means that Bob is again sacrificed to a further alliance of authority and power. As Bob hands over his pen for the two to sign what is in effect his death warrant his comment 'Expect a pardon look like that' has a chilling theatrical irony.

It is Rose who is again compelled to take the initiative and it is her scene with Old Lady Are which draws from Bond his most sustained Restoration parody. The opening lines in which she complains of her maid having put the decanter out of her reach echo Congreve's introduction to Lady Wishfort in *The Way Of The World*. But Lady Are is every bit as selfish as her son; she has none of the folly of Lady Wishfort. What this interview exposes—through an employment of the high style of Restoration comedy—is that justice, honesty, and pathos are powerless in the face of the arrogant assurance of power and wealth. It is a fundamental theme of the Comedy of Manners which presents a character like Mrs Loveit in *The Man of Mode* entirely at the mercy of Dorilant when she is foolish enough to bare her heart to him, or delights in the confounding of a pair of criminals like Congreve's Marwould and Fainall by their more cunning rivals. When Rose kneels and says 'I beg you' Lady Are retorts with all the hauteur of Oscar Wilde's Lady Bracknell: 'Get up child. A thing is not made more impressive by being said by a dwarf.' We are made to see that justice resides in the hands of this wilful old woman, who, when Rose has left in anger, suddenly changes her mind out of spite towards her son.

Unlike Lady Are's maid Dorothea, who the old woman tells us would have waited for the guinea offered her instead of losing her temper and leaving without it, Rose is not an opportunist. She learns from her experiences and at the end of the play triumphantly emerges as an agent who will effect change. Nor is this awareness sudden or arbitrary since Bond has throughout the play employed a startlingly original technique which enriches his presentation of the *mores* of another period. The play's setting is: 'England, eighteenth century—or

another place at another time'. It is no mere irony that Lady Are should say: 'I am an old woman with an empty glass and there is nothing to think of that does not wring me with regret for the past, convulse me at the follies of the present, or make me tremble before what is to come.' Bond wastes no sympathy on her since his interpretation of history forsees her extinction and that of her class. Bond sees his characters both within the context of their own age and out of it and he matches this observation with a telling theatrical device whereby all the workers in the play are given songs in which this awareness is expressed. Though the oppressors in the play have the greatest intelligence and wit they cannot see beyond their own situation. A broader perspective is vouchsafed only to Bob, Frank, Rose and Bob's Mother, the victims of the system dramatised within the play. Though Bob and his mother are victims who will their own servitude by a passive acceptance of it, in the wider canvas of the piece—through the many interpolated songs—they share the viewpoint of Frank and Rose. This viewpoint is seen to be more accurate historically whilst its realisation in theatrical terms is more expressive. In some respects Bond learnt how to give his work this more complex texture through his collaboration with Henze: both the extensive employment of music and the complexity of vision realised in the powerful images of these songs opens up the potential of the dramatic medium.

The song: 'The Gentleman', performed by Bob and Rose immediately after Are has insisted in a perfectly reasonable way that if Bob is not hanged 'anarchy must triumph', opens up the implications of any passive acceptance of tyranny and encourages us to reject any act of kindness from an oppressor. Bond will take this up as the central theme of *Summer*; here the song functions in a very similar way to the poem 'Pompei' discussed earlier. After a series of details recounting the courtesy of a soldier: 'He steps out of the way to let her pass . . .' 'he takes the child and holds it on his shoulder' we reach the shock of: 'At the door of the gas chamber / He hands the child back to her arms'.

In the songs throughout the play Bond employs anachronisms of this sort which alert us to the contemporary relevance of his theme whilst showing us a class more conscious of its own destiny. Frank's 'Song of Learning' functions in sharp contrast to his character within the story to show us a man who is representative of this consciousness: he is no longer the individual, but a voice of the people:

For fifty thousand years I fought in their wars
I died so often I learned how to survive
For fifty thousand years I fought battles to save their
  wealth
That's how I learned to know the enemy myself.

For fifty thousand years I gave them my life
But in all that time they never learned how to live
For fifty thousand years I was governed by men of
    wealth
Now I have learned to make the laws I need for
    myself.

(p. 20)

Rose is the key link between these songs and the action of the play; she is the one character who learns through experience. In the highly poetic speech which opens the final scene she describes her vision of London. It is a horrific vision of slavery where 'men walk the streets with chains hanging from their mouths', recalling the life from which her mother escaped but equally relevant to the contemporary scene as described by Blake in his poem 'London':

> I wander through each chartered street
> Near where the chartered Thames doth flow
> And mark in every face I meet
> Marks of weakness, marks of woe.

Rose asks: 'What have I learned?' and replies 'If nothing, then *I* was hanged'. Her climactic song, before she turns and crosses the river, is significantly entitled: 'Man Is What He Knows' and concludes:

> 'Wind and rain cannot tell where
> they blow
> but we may know who we
> are and where we go.'

(p. 100)

It is Bond's assertion of hope for the future which has been powerfully realised within the complex structure of this drama.

SUMMER

In terms of dramatic form and theatrical style ***Summer***—Bond's second play for the National Theatre—is totally different from anything he had written before. It concerns four people: Xenia and her daughter, Ann who are visiting Marthe and her son, David. The setting is 'The Present'; the location 'Eastern Europe'. The opening scene edges the audience gently into the personal worlds of these four people through their inconsequential chatter: a technique of narrative exposition familiar from the plays of Ibsen, but quite new for Bond. He shows as consummate a command of this idiom as he did of the style of Greek epic or Restoration comedy: we are interested in these characters as individuals, gripped too by the element of mystery, anxious to learn for instance, the reason for the visit or the precise nature of the relationship between Ann and David. In the second scene the mystery deepens. We are very much in the theatrical world of Ibsen as Xenia informs Martha that Ann 'knows too much about the past'; we too wish to share their secrets. When we hear of the arrest

of Ann's grandfather and of his subsequent imprisonment the situation holds out all the promise of *The Wild Duck* in which we gradually discover more and more about the disgrace of Hedvig's grandfather, Ekdal, and hints at significant events in the past such as those which are gradually dragged to the surface in *Ghosts* or which live on in the gloom-laden environment of *Rosmersholm*.

When, later in this scene, David launches unprompted into his uninterrupted medical description of the symptoms of his mother's cancer the dramatic promise appears to be fulfilled, but his speech, so clinical and complex is a far cry from the veiled euphemisms of Doctor Rank in *A Doll's House* or Mrs Alving's confession to Oswald. David's apparent harshness in relating these facts not for Xenia's benefit but for his mother's, in order to force her to face reality, shifts the drama off its naturalistic axis, preparing us for the ethical discussion which is to follow. In the next scene friendly chatter between Ann and Marthe soon gives way to Marthe's discussion of one of the fundamental political issues with which the drama will deal. In response to Ann's question as to what her mother was like at her age Marthe answers: 'Very kind. All her family were. They owned half the town. That isn't a figure of speech. Factories, a bank, the local paper, the farms in the hills,' and she goes on to explain the implications of this. She expounds a fundamental thesis of Bond that kindness does not change the world and that tenderness and goodwill are irrelevent if the organisation of society is basically iniquitous:

> Your family made the people who loved and respected
> them confuse kindness with justice. That is corrupting.
> You can live without kindness, you can't live without
> justice—or fighting to get it. If you try to you're mad.
> You don't understand yourself or the world.

(***Summer,*** p. 20)

Bond's political viewpoint is more radical than Ibsen's but ethical discussions of this sort do occur in the work of the Norwegian dramatist. As Shaw pointed out, it was Ibsen who substantially changed the formula of the nineteenth century drama:

> Formerly you had in what was called a well-made play
> an exposition in the first act, a situation in the second,
> an unravelling in the third. Now you have exposition
> situation and discussion; and the discussion is the test
> of the playwright.

(Shaw: *The Quintessence of Ibsenism,* p. 87)

In ***Summer*** we have already had the exposition; now we move into a description by Marthe and Xenia of those events in their past which have shaped their lives and of which Ann is ignorant. We learn of the fact that during the war the local islands were requisitioned by the Germans who paid Xenia's father rent to use them as a concentration camp and of how Xenia used her position to save Marthe when she was about to be shot as a hostage. The situation is complicated by the fact that after the war there was a revolution in which Xenia's father was arrested and imprisoned on evidence given by Marthe whilst Xenia escaped to England. These revelations and the moral dilemma they imply disturb Ann who says: 'Let me think about what you've both told me', whilst her mother comments: 'Yes think. And learn what people do in this world.' The situation is markedly similar to that at the end of the second act of *Mrs Warren's Profession* where Vivie learns of her mother's past and is obliged to revise her opinions. Like Shaw, Bond is writing a problem play in the Ibsen mould but his techniques are more savage and his political aim more extreme.

In the next scene we shift to the islands and are brought into a closer confrontation with those events already described by Xenia and Marthe. We meet a new character, a German, who is also reliving his past and has returned for a holiday to the very place in which he served as a soldier. He is one of the most sinister characters Bond has ever created, a clever device to draw us more completely into the horrors of the extermination camps which he describes with a mixture of nostalgia and regret. He constantly protests his innocence: 'This wasn't a concentration camp. We were private soldiers: not officers, not Gestapo, not guilty'. In Bond's skilful hands his exculpatory narrative serves to incriminate him more and more. Though the German disclaims responsibility for the final horrors—'We were not criminals. We'd done everything in the open. According to the laws of war. Harsh—but war is harsh'— Bond brings home the full obscenity of the situation by a reference to the action recreated in *We Come To The River*: 'The public address system played dance music to keep spirits high. We came with marches and left with waltzes.' It is the German's justification of Nazism in that commonplace theory which is anethema to Bond—that men are by nature vile and that it is therefore vital to protect our cultural heritage—which ultimately damns him;

GERMAN:

> Men are animals. We can't be trusted with another man's wife or his money. Not even with our own daughters. No-one's safe on our streets at night. If we don't get our fodder we whine. What saves us from ourselves? Culture. The standards of our fathers. They struggled for centuries to make them strong . . . That's why we went to war.

> (*Summer*, p. 25)

More significantly this justification also incriminates Xenia for in the middle of it the German refers to 'the girl in white' who symbolised the faith of the occupying forces. This mysterious figure—a symbol in the style of Ibsen—was Xenia as a girl. In the next two scenes of the play it is the woman who will be forced to come to terms with her past in a confrontation with the implications of her conduct and life.

By bringing the subject of the Nazi death camps into a play which initially promised to be a domestic drama concerned with the tragic death of one of the characters, Bond has further applied his strategy of employing bourgeois theatrical conventions to fulfil the purposes of the political dramatist. Into the framework of this problem play he has brought the subject matter handled by Peter Weiss in *The Investigation* or Ralph Hochhuth in *The Representative*. He is much closer to Weiss than Hochhuth whose naturalistic drama set partially in Auschwitz, concentrates on the psychological and spiritual agony of a Catholic priest drawn into a sympathetic stand with the Jews. Weiss by contrast, never mentions the word 'Jew' once in his play: his rigorously austere piece of epic theatre in which a series of anonymous victims and criminals relate dispassionately the horrors of Auschwitz emphasises the culpability of the whole system: that every clerk and railway worker who assisted in the transportation of prisoners was as guilty as those in charge of the camp. Bond shares this view and relates these details not with the intention of overwhelming us with emotional horror. His aim is different from that of Peter Barnes in his more Artaudian piece *Laughter* which, like Bond's play, begins deceptively—as a situation comedy set in an office on Christmas Eve— but which moves into a description and representation of events in Auschwitz consequent on the revelation that the workers are processing orders of Cyclone B for use in the gas chambers. Bond's political point is more precise than Barnes': he sees Nazism and the inexorable extension of its logic in genocide as the inevitable consequence of capitalism and imperialism. As Marthe says in attacking what Xenia's class stood for: 'The confusion and competition led to such passion and madness that in the end there was war.' Moreover this attitude is international as Bond makes clear in a mordantly ironic poem accompanying the play:

> If Auschwitz had been in Hampshire
> There would have been Englishmen to guard it
> To administer records
> Work the gas ovens
> And keep silent
> The smoke would have drifted over these green hills.

Bond is again working out the consequences of a dramatic paradox similar to that employed in *Saved,* but here even more extreme. The ultimate horror is not the scenes of violence witnessed on the islands. What is worse is the system and philosophy which gives rise to it. And in the play it is Xenia's family who are therefore as much to blame as the Nazis whom they pretended to assist in order to betray their plans to the partisans. Xenia finds it impossible to understand how her father could have been arrested by the very partisan to whom he was betraying the Germans, but this irony is overshadowed by a greater one in that her kindness and her father's conduct were meaningless because—as Marthe points out—'the foundations of your world were crooked and so everything in it was crooked.' The play finally forces the characters to face the past as Marthe spits at Xenia, thus recalling and avenging the women imprisoned with her who when she heard who Marthe worked for said 'If I could live to spit in her face' and spat in the dirt. Xenia's response: 'You carried a dead woman's spit round in your mouth for forty years' serves the more powerfully to drive home the force of this stage image which clinches the political argument expressed through Marthe. In the next scene the German sends a bouquet of flowers to the woman he has now recognised as the 'girl in white'; his tribute fixes in a complementary image the nature of Xenia's guilt. In the two short final scenes—the last one less than a page in length—we see the naturalistic tone re-establish itself as Marthe dies and Ann prepares to leave with her mother. The last dying fall is deceptive. The responses of the characters here are in the circumstances strange, not immediately explicable. The young people admit they love each other and therefore they must part; Marthe, in saying to them: 'I die so that you might live' uses her death to show the meaning of her life. It is we, the audience, who must leave the theatre more aware of the events that they have relived and confronted, for Bond has made us realise that what we have witnessed is not only their past, but our own.

Debra A. Castillo (essay date summer 1986)

SOURCE: Castillo, Debra A. "Dehumanized or Inhuman: Doubles in Edward Bond." *South Central Review* 3, no. 2 (summer 1986): 78-89.

[*In the following essay, Castillo explores the role of doubling and dual personalities in Bond's plays to examine the two sides of the human character—as simultaneously humane and debased.*]

Much recent Bond criticism has been concerned with the difficult question of how the playwright's stated purpose of developing a "rational" theater is realized in a body of work that seems more nearly mythic than realistic. Even a superficial review of article titles confirms the centrality of this interest in reconciling the political and the poetic aspects of Bond's work.[1] Again and again, the critics return to a set of ideas and themes that are, as Jenny S. Spencer notes, quite direct and uncomplicated.[2] Their concern is not unwarranted. Bond's theater *is* political, and his focus of investigation is nothing less than the survival of all the human, humane qualities of the political animal, the dweller in a contemporary polis. Yet the discussion of these

relatively simple (in abstract formulation) ideas is rarely simple and seldom uncomplicated. Spencer herself characterizes Bond's work as an attempt "to present representations of reality (mediated by theatrical convention in the same way ideology mediates perception) which are both recognizable as our own world, and yet untenable (in need of change)."[3] The convolutions of syntax in Spencer's discussion represent difficult convolutions of thought, from the doubly metaphorical "present representations"—of reality, of convention, of ideology as filtered by perception—to the paradox of an impossibility which is immediately recognizable, her parenthetical style reflecting the difficulty of writing about rational drama in an irrational world. To use a currently fashionable term, Bond's poetic dramas "deconstruct" dominant myths of perceptions, of conventions, and of ideologies in the controlled application of a few carefully chosen images.

Ruby Cohn is quite correct in her characterization of Bond's theater as "fabulous;"[4] indeed, Bond's work develops a reasoning man's fable of our times. Where the traditional fables of Aesop use animals to demonstrate human foibles, Bond's modern fables utilize a similar, if more subtle, version of this technique by surrounding characters with images of dehumanization or metaphors connecting them to animals.

Michel Foucault's discussion of "the Other that is not only a brother but a twin, born, not of man, nor in man, but beside him and at the same time, in an identical newness, in an unavoidable duality"[5] is singularly apt in application to Bond's dramas, which are deeply involved in the examination of the self and its dehumanized other, the alienated, estranged self, an Other which is outside him (an antagonistic member of the "irrational" society), within him (a Dostoevskian dramatic projection), and beside him (a detached yet identical entity). As with Foucault, for Bond unseen power relationships determine the specific configuration of this Other (friend, enemy, alternative self) at any given moment in a complex interplay of fluid, ambiguous social forces. Bond's preface to *Lear* returns almost compulsively to this issue in his contrast of the innocent aggressiveness of the free animal to the unnatural violence of the caged one and the comparison of both free and caged animals to the panicked aggresivity of the human race.[6] Animal imagery has, in Bond, no simple identification, no simple purpose. The pure, unsocialized animal that is the double and secret self of man is thrust outside him, is perverted into beastliness, and at its limit point the "animality [that] has escaped domestication by human symbols and values . . . reveals the dark rage, the sterile madness that lie in men's hearts."[7] In his dehumanized characters, then, Bond gives voice to a painful silence and provides a fabulous, or fantastic, presence to elements which are recognized and repressed in "civilized" society:

The polis is polished
civilization is polite
            is policed.[8]

In Bond's society, the polished veneer of polite society is in unremitting tension with the raging beast, a tension which is intensified by images and metaphors that call up man's relationship to the repressed animal in both its positive and negative associations. To discuss this dehumanization in Bond's work as a whole is a project far beyond the scope of this study. Instead, I have chosen three representative early plays: *Lear,* which examines mythic and literary Britain; *Saved,* which offers Bond's metaphor of present urban society; and *Early Morning,* which simultaneously recreates the recent past and projects the future such a tradition may entail.

One of Bond's typical ploys has been to contrast the humane and the dehumanized aspects of a single personality as split into two opposing and juxtaposed dramatic characters. These characters represent real antitheses, but the difference is also, at the same time, illusory in the way a Dostoevskian double is both a real physical presence and a psychological projection. In *Lear,* the building tension and the creation of the double takes place within the play as part of its action. Before his defeat by his daughters, Lear believed himself and his country secure. The wall he was building would insure the continuance of polite society, of civilization, of a polished and perfect state that would be peaceful even if governed by fools (3). With his defeat however, the dream begins to disintegrate and the king's character splits into its human and its dehumanized halves. The king withdraws from polite society into a nostalgic green world of peace and tranquility as a pig-keeper with the Gravedigger's Boy and his wife. The assassination of the Boy and his transformation into the Ghost that accompanies Lear in his later peregrinations signals the creation of a dehumanized double, a double that is, moreover, neither ontologically stable nor complete. Katharine Worth has pointed out the fairy-tale quality of the Ghost which neatly balances the traditional uncanniness of a ghostly presence with the comforting reassurances of a familiar fable.[9] The figure of a ghost, who exists in a shadow world between life and death, is the perfect image for a double which operates on the border between reality and hallucination, partaking of both and neither. Partly an imaginative construct of Lear's nostalgic desire for a Golden Age and partly an independent being, the Ghost reflects Lear's own lack of a critical evaluation of reality. As Dostoevsky's Schedrovdarov notes in a passage that seems equally applicable to Bond's king, "before you do anything you have to make yourselves something, to assume you own shape, to become yourselves. . . . But you are abstractions, you are shadows, you are nothing. And nothing can come from nothing. You are

foreign ideas. You are a mirage. You do not stand on soil but on air. The light shines right under you. . . ."[10]

The Ghost, a dehumanized extraction of Lear's psychological immaturity, is only the first, though by far the most notable, of a series of "Others" evolved by the play. In Bond's world, even the Ghost is torn apart by new categories of opposition. Sometimes almost sinister, sometimes pathetic, the Ghost decays in death as Lear gains in wisdom and maturity in his dealings with the world. Scharine observes that "the Boy's moral maturity travels a path parallel to Lear's but in the opposite direction. By the time Lear reaches a state of only desiring to live humanely, the position of the Boy when we first met him, the Ghost of the Boy wishes only to be hidden and protected."[11] As Lear achieves insight and understanding, he returns to the world to die a politically significant death. His double, the Ghost, evolves in the opposite direction until, gored by his own pigs, he dies, ignominiously, a second time. Ultimately, the Ghost represents a regressive force that is both unfeasible and immoral in a political age, and he is quite rightly rejected even by pigs. Lear learns that human beings, who may be pig-like in many respects, are not malicious by nature, and that only through political action can his sufferings and those of his people be alleviated.

The phantasmagorical nature of the Ghost is critical to Bond's vision, since the Ghost stands for the uncanny reality/fantasy of the social pressures that give it existence. Each human being undergoes a similar dehumanizing experience under the pressures of socialization, an experience which is all the more terrifying because of its effective invisibility. The Ghost, then, not only dramatically represents a self divided, but also demonstrates an innate propensity of culture to fracture the psyche into impotent partial identities reflected in successive social masks. The Ghost of the Gravedigger's Boy, crying in fear and gored by his pigs, is one such pitiful mask, an invisible shield for the naked ego. However, as Bond notes, "the whole of civilisation is in a sense a self-mask, a self-justification,"[12] and *Early Morning*'s Arthur, who carries with him his own uncanny double in the form of his brother's disintegrating skeleton, reveals the unhappiness of the double's lot: "Who came first, the man or his shadow? The shadow, of course. I undressed a shadow once: it was white underneath and cried: it was cold" (60). Arthur's vision is deadly, for eventually the illusory comes to precede the real, the mask is perceived to be prior to the face, and, indeed, the mask is no less real in this social world than the hypothetical naked face behind it. Ironically, man thus becomes socialized by the death of all human characteristics, by his transformation into a social function, a cipher, or a shadow. "Bodies are supposed to die and souls go on living," says Arthur in a later passage: "That's not true. Souls die first and bodies live. They wander round like ghosts, they bump into each other, tread on each other, haunt each other" (101). Life in an irrational society approximates the ghostly afterlife of Bond's cannibalistic shades.

These soul-killing propensities are what make the system so devastating and so dehumanizing. The trial of Len by the lynching mob is terrifying precisely because within the dream structure of the play it retains the lineaments of realistic presentation; a trial of dehumanized puppets, of shivering shadows covered by rigid social masks. Gladstone restrains the crowd by a reference to "the book": "Yer 'ave t' 'ave yer trial t' make it legal. Yer don't wan' a act like common criminals. Trial first death after . . ." (43). Irrational man rules by the book, by the trappings of official authority divested of substance.

More frightening and more comic is Arthur's heavenly trial, where, with complete blindness to human issues, the accusers set criminal acts alongside floutings of convention as anti-social behavior of equal indefensibility. On the one hand, they accuse Arthur of serious crimes: "He rapes little girls," "He gives babies syphilis," and "He kills." But to these grave criminal acts are juxtaposed such apparently trivial accusations as "He wastes electricity," "He's a nose-picker," and "He eats dirt" (45-48). Bond's dream society carries to its logical conclusion the relative unconcern of human beings with physical violence and their overriding preoccupation with points of etiquette.

Len, the dehumanized working man kicked to death by his peers in *Early Morning,* appears in *Saved* split into his passive (Len) and active (Fred) poles. Whereas in *Early Morning* Len precipitates the first case of cannibalism by his murder of the man who broke into the queue, in *Saved* it is Fred who commits murder while Len jealously looks on from his hidden vantage point. Pam, who sleeps with both men, significantly recalls at the end of the play the earlier joke of the woman with quads (98); the submerged reference to doubles ("That'll teach 'er t'sleep with siamese twins," [p. 17]) delicately suggests a warning ignored.

As in *Early Morning,* the characters in *Saved* are almost completely dehumanized by their environment, and their possibilities for independent action are strictly limited by their implicit acceptance of what seems to them the inalterable conditions of their existence. However, where *Early Morning* emphasizes the role of social and political tradition, *Saved* stresses the function of technology and the deification of the object over the people who produce it, what Octavio Paz calls the triumph of the sign over the signified and the thing over the image.[13] A mechanical universe is substituted for a human reality in a circular process in which technology requires the negation of human values, and the disap-

pearance of these values (Paz's "images") is a necessary precondition for the development of a technological society.

For the workers in *Saved,* their jobs are a disagreeable, inevitable part of their lives, and they would prefer to forget about their work as soon as they leave the shop:

FRED:

'Lo Len. 'Ow's life.

LEN:

Usual. 'Ow's the job?

FRED:

Don't talk about it.

(33)

Later in the play, Len asks Harry a similar question: "'Ow d'yer get on at work?" and Harry replies briefly, "It's a job" (61). The reader knows very little about the specific nature of the work engaged in by these men, but the presence of the assembly line is an important underlying motif in the play. In his preface to *Lear,* Bond explains: "It does not matter how much a man doing routine work in, say, a factory or office is paid: he will still be deprived. . . . Because he is behaving in a way for which he is not designed, he is alienated from his natural self, and this will have physical and emotional consequences for him" (vi). The alienated worker evokes, in effect, the masked shadows described by Arthur.

As significance is drained from their work, and the workers are alienated from the products of their labor, a parallel drain of signification occurs in other levels of their lives. Moral institutions are as corrupt as the factory, and thus in *Saved* the church is merely the "best place for'n easy pick up" (48). By its complicity with the social order, the church becomes as impersonal as the assembly line, and inside its walls men no longer search for the meaning of life but conduct calculated, impersonal hunts for sexual gratification.

This spiritual cannibalism is made literal in the dream world of *Early Morning* for a shocking effect. Psychic, cultural, and moral hungers are intensified under the irritation and pressure of the queue, and the suppressed aggression of the socialized beast combines with these other pressures to find explosive release in Len and Joyce's murder and cannibalization of an anonymous bystander. The act of killing and eating a fellow human being parallels the more extensive rationalized murder practiced in the play's political arena. Bond makes us see that in following their instincts, Len and Joyce are acting in a manner perfectly consonant with their upbringing and that their act is no more indefensible than the equally macabre, though socially rationalized, murders committed by the ruling powers. Perhaps the most amusing aspect of this macabre scene is that although the frustrated couple murders and consumes a fellow being, they maintain to the end a perverse sense of propriety which reflects once again the absurd concern of civilized beings with etiquette; they "kep' 'is knickers on" since they "don't 'old with this rudery yer get" (23). The pornography of violence is accompanied by incongruous Victorian conventions of outward social morality. As in the post-industrial world of **Saved,** psychological unrest at the excessive rationalization of life is not turned against cultural and religious institutions, and resistance no longer takes place between labor and capital. Instead, the dehumanized object-man vents his aggression on other similarly afflicted beings.

While the nature of aggression and its amplification by the restrictions of an industrialized society are clear, the reader still echoes Arthur's question, "Why did you kill him?" (26). The apparent lack of motive is confusing, as is the sudden focusing of generalized aggressivity on this specific object. Yet while the choice of a specific object may be puzzling, for Bond the general impulse is clear. Len and Joyce's cannibalism, Fred's murder of the baby, Lear's execution, and even the Ghost's goring by his pigs respond to a common instinct; the roots of such unreasoning violence can be located in the social system that provokes it. On the one hand, the assembly-line mode of production dehumanizes man by convincing him that he is a machine and that his exertions are in no way unique. He is completely interchangeable with any other worker. At the same time, paradoxically, the loss of a sense of the sacredness of individual life derives from the Christian impulse itself. If industrialization has taught man that he has no soul, it is Christianity that teaches him to despise the body, since the body is, after all, destined for corruption. Aggression builds against the institutions which continue to aggravate man but are invulnerable to his violence. In such cases, the random murder of a scapegoat causes but little surprise: "When unappeased, violence seeks and always finds a surrogate victim. The creature that excited its fury is replaced by another, chosen only because it is vulnerable and close at hand."[14] In Bond's plays, murder is frequently, pointedly, an act of violence done to a mere body, a soul-less post-industrial entity.

The corporeal masked shadow has, in Bond's image system, its own metaphorical double, and the frightened, cowed Ghost is paired with images of healthy animals, which, when prodded, become the cornered beasts lashing out in sterile, uncomprehending rage. The animal, then, is a more ambitious, more ambiguous metaphor than the masked shadow: beautiful in its innocence; when warped by societal pressures man-as-animal reveals the traits we associate with "beastliness."

It is the beastliness which is most apparent in **Saved** where animal images consistently have an alienating effect. Harry is a "nosey ol' gander" (18) who lives in a "sty" (21). Women are called "birds" (34), "pigs" (117), or, most frequently, "cows" (23, 43, 83). Barry recalls with great relish the murder of "yellow-niggers" who were dismembered with a "pig-sticker" (29). Len and Fred's mutual courtship of Pam is discussed in a fishing boat, punctuated with graphic descriptions of how to properly bait a hook (48-49). The ultimate victim of the worker's pent-up violence, Pam's baby, is never given a human identity. His cries are confused with those of a cat stuck up a chimney (38), Pam distantly refers to him as "that" (58), and Barry sings a chilling version of a lullaby in which the baby's brains are used for bait (63). Significantly, the child is seen as an animal that can't be hurt because it is too young to have feelings (67); he "looks like a yeller-nigger," says Colin (68), and as they begin to stone the child Mike mockingly suggests calling the R.S.P.C.A. (71).

The murder of Pam's baby signals the crisis point as the enraged beastliness of the workers breaks forth in an act of violence, violence that is, as Eagleton notes, "natural because human beings are cultural."[15] Girard locates the roots of culture in an act of violence. He finds that "the primordial event must be . . . the murder of a random victim which must appear as the embodiment of the whole crisis, the sum total of all monstrous undifferentiation through a process of collective transfer made possible by the mimetic undifferentiation of the *doubles.*"[16] Pam's child, engendered by the Siamese twins Len and Fred (or Colin, or Mike, or Barry, or Pete—in the cycle of violence distinctions of biological paternity are irrelevant), comes to represent, in his lack of a clear identity, the monstrous interchangeability they support as factory workers. The child's death eases the pressure, and the images of animality and violence decrease and become less intense in the rest of the play, but Pam's unconscious recall of the story of the Siamese twins points towards another cycle of violence waiting to commence.

The recognition that the mob will be temporarily appeased by a scapegoat does not escape **Early Morning**'s Arthur. While the doctor expresses concern during the attack on Windsor castle, Arthur realizes that "they'll be all right once they've lynched someone" (42). The public hangings advocated by the Chamberlain and carried out by Victoria and Florence demonstrate a similar principle. The anger of the people is directed away from the government and focussed on relatively minor offenders. Hanging is, after all, no more than the socially approved mode of lynching, and the doctor's response to Arthur's insight is typical of the conventions he represents: "If they're lynching they'll need death certificates" (42). Even arbitrary, unmotivated violent actions can be co-opted into the social institutions, and conventions of behavior remain unshaken by the murder of a *pharmakos.*

Thus, the availability of victims does nothing to alleviate the aggression itself. Like the heavenly cannibals who must periodically appease their hunger by eating each other, so the execution of a scapegoat only temporarily appeases the hunger for freedom from society's cage. As long as man does not realize that his real enemy is the social institution that fuels his aggressivity, the cycle of violence will continue. As Chizhevsky observes, "the main trait of the ethical world is its uniformity and monotony."[17] It is no fluke that the representatives of the social system are also representatives of an eternally recurrent order. Thus, *Saved* ends with a chilling reminder of the cycle of violence; at the end of *Lear,* Cordelia takes the old king's place as a wall builder; and at the end of *Early Morning* Victoria works out her eternal roster of the order in which the inhabitants of Heaven will eat and be eaten by each other. Chizhevsky continues, "in the theory of 'eternal recurrence'—at which (in one way or another) ethical rationalism must inevitably arrive—was concentrated the whole fierceness with which the meaning of the individual concrete being was rejected."[18]

This eternal recurrence is most strikingly envisioned in *Early Morning* in Arthur's nightmare of the mill which epitomizes the blindness and futility of society's pursuit of its illusory goals. "D'you dream?" Arthur asks his Siamese twin George, now reduced to a skeleton:

> D'you dream about the mill? There are men and women and children and cattle and birds and horses pushing a mill. They're grinding other cattle and people and children: they push each other in. Some fall in. It grinds their bones, you see. The ones pushing the wheel, even the animals, look at the horizon. They stumble. Their feet get caught up in the rags and dressings that slip down from their wounds. They go round and round. At the end they go very fast. They shout. Half of them run in their sleep. Some are trampled on. They're sure they're reaching the horizon.
>
> (68)

The mill grinds and grinds, remorselessly grinding the people and animals, destroying their hopes, poisoning their dreams, negating the value of their very existences, blinding them to the approaching storm, forcing them to ignore everything but the tantalizing and inexplicably distant horizon.

The apocalyptic dust storm envisioned by Arthur is similarly foreseen by Lear, who recognizes, more clearly than *Early Morning*'s prince, that the freeing of the animal at the treadmill or the animal in the cage offers the only hope of forestalling the onrushing doom: "There's an animal in a cage. I must let it out or the earth will be destroyed. There'll be great fires and the

water will dry up. All the people will be burned and the wind will blow their ashes into huge columns of dust and they'll go round and round the earth forever! We must let it out!" (37). The caged animal is, of course, a figure for Lear himself as well as his people, and by fettering his instinctual self with artificial social and moral imperatives, Lear has goaded the animal into a violent backlash. Arthur's dream reveals the unconscious brutality and indifference to suffering of the animal who is unaware of the bars of its cage. In *Lear,* the pressures of imprisonment turn the animal into a monster that consciously and aggressively seeks to mutilate and destroy others out of a frustrated hatred of its own life. *Lear* as a whole is exceptionally rich in animal images, as many critics have noted,[19] and the animal is used in metaphor and parable as the primary representative of those natural impulses entrapped by social convention. Ruby Cohn makes this point most concisely:

> As king, Bond's Lear calls his people sheep and his enemies wolves. When mad, he sees himself as a dog and a mouse. The program for the Royal Court production pictures a monkey in a cage, but Lear's plea is wider, reaching out to horse and bird, and crying: "Let that animal out of the cage!" Lear's dead daughter is to him a blend of lion, lamb, and child. He compares the subservient farmer's family unfavorably to wolf, fox, and horse, and he accuses men of behaving like jackels and wolves. Sane and admired as a saint, Lear narrates a fable of a man's voice in a bird's body. His last fantasy wish is to be as cunning as a fox. These diverse images accumulate into a powerful illustration of Shakespeare's great line: "Unaccommodated man is no more but such a poor bare forked animal as thou art."[20]

This "poor bare forked animal," especially as depicted in Lear's metaphor of an animal in a cage, effectively describes the condition of the individual in society; however, the metaphor must be extended if it is to serve as a description of the relationship of men to each other. Clearly, each individual is divided in himself between the social mask he assumes and the remnants of instinctive life which feed his aggressivity. As each man lacks a unique center, so too does society. The conventions of social interaction are mere words covering a "moral bankruptcy" (*Saved,* 7) that becomes more and more complete since language is itself tainted by the irrational impulses of civilization. Eagleton, in his discussion of Bond's prefaces, suggests that such alienation is inevitable: "the human animal is the animal whose nature it is to overreach itself; its most distinctive mark—language—is precisely such a ceaseless distancing, transgression and transformation of the instinctual."[21] Thus, social life also rotates around an absent center, and repressed aggressivity is channelled towards the exterior, socialized masks of other humans. The superficial mask of social conventions fools the animals into a belief that something is behind it; the terrible and ironic reality is that the mask, once engendered, propagates other masks that prohibit the discovery of the lack of substance behind them.

Foucault elegantly makes a similar point. In his "Preface to Transgression," he discusses the "denatured" language of modern sexuality which has been "cast into an empty zone where it achieves whatever meager form is bestowed upon it by the establishment of its limits."[22] Just as Bond intuits the conflict between healthy animality and the masked shadow, so too Foucault distinguishes between healthy sexuality and its distancing through language. The denatured *language* of sexuality does nothing to reveal the secret of man's being. Instead, "it is that which offers itself in the superficial discourse of a solid and natural animality while obscurely addressing itself to Absence. . . ."[23] For Foucault, the circularity of sex is ineluctably bound up in the linguistic interrogation: "the universe of language has absorbed our sexuality, denatured it, placed it in a void where it established its sovereignty and where it incessantly sets up as the Law the limits it transgresses."[24] Bond would agree. Fred's sexuality is a weapon for the victimization of female bodies; his penis and the stone he throws at the child are parallel mechanisms for revenge on society. His rupture of moral conventions (seducing women in church) and his defiance of Law (the murder of the child) are equivalent gestures demonstrating the intolerable limits on human behavior and the grotesque actions that result when speech fails to voice its outrage. The sexual and industrial modes of exploitation have a common result—the reduction of man from a complex being, a healthy animal, to an interchangeable sign. Pam's house, like the factory, represents for Fred the repetition of the same, while in the churches and laundromats await the multiplicity of other bodies in which he searches for something to release himself from the eternal recurrence of the same frustrations. The irony of his erotic search and inevitable frustration is evident; even in his rebellion he cannot get off the treadmill and merely substitutes one assembly line for another. The language he hears is the repetition of the same words, the women's bodies are blank repetitions of the same body, like masks reflected in an infinite series of mirrors.

Bond recognizes the primal necessity of destroying the cage so the human animal can once again "lie in the fields, and run by the river, and groom itself in the sun, and sleep in its hole from night to morning" (*Lear,* 40), but he understands that this re-identification of man and his environment cannot occur in the context of a return to a Golden Age. Lear's withdrawal and Arthur's apotheosis essentially do nothing to change the structure of society—in their absence, the Cordelias and Victorias of the world continue their repressive reigns. The

cure, like the disease, must take place on the three levels originally infected: the personal, the social, and the linguistic.

In order to cure himself, man must recognize the nature and the source of the forces that motivate him. On the personal level, he must reunite the fragmented portions of the self and re-establish the equilibrium between his desires and the socialized tendencies that impel him towards repression. On the social and political levels, Bond envisions the creation of a democratic socialist society. He considers violence inefficient, and hopes to reach a more humane society "by rational means; that means writing plays, that means teaching, that means discussion, that means persuading, that means caring."[25] Finally, on the linguistic level, in Todorov's words, "we must break down the automatism which makes us take the word for the thing, makes us consider one as the natural product of the other."[26] Bond's plays point to the necessity, as well as the extreme difficulty, of making this revolutionary gesture, but only in this way can the dust storm be averted; only through such gestures can the animal at last enjoy the sun uncaged.

Notes

1. Important studies concerned with this issue include the following: Ruby Cohn, "The Fabulous Theater of Edward Bond," in *Essays on Contemporary British Drama* (Munich: Max Huber Verlag, 1981); Robert L. Tener, "Edward Bond's Dialectic: Irony and Dramatic Metaphors," *Modern Drama,* 25 (1982), 423-434; Christopher Innes, "Edward Bond's Political Spectrum: From Rationalism to Rhapsody," *Modern Drama,* 25 (1982), 189-206; Philip Roberts, "The Search for Epic Drama: Edward Bond's Recent Work," *Modern Drama,* 24 (1981), 458-478; Jenny S. Spencer, "Edward Bond's Dramatic Strategies," in *Contemporary English Drama,* ed. C. W. E. Bigsby (New York: Holmes and Meier, 1981); and Daniel R. Jones, "Edward Bond's 'Rational Theatre,'" *Theatre Journal,* 32 (1980), 505-517.

2. Spencer, p. 124.

3. Spencer, p. 125.

4. Cohn, p. 185.

5. Michel Foucault, *The Order of Things* (New York: Random House, 1970), p. 326.

6. Edward Bond, *Lear* (New York: Hill and Wang, 1972). See especially pages v, xi and passim throughout the preface to the play. All further references to this text and other Bond dramas will be found in the text of this paper. Editions used are as follows: *Early Morning* (London: Calder and Boyars, 1968); and *Saved* (New York: Hill and Wang, 1965).

7. Michel Foucault, *Madness and Civilization,* trans. Richard Howard (New York: Random House, 1965), p. 21.

8. Norman O. Brown, *Closing Time* (New York: Random House, 1973), p. 23.

9. Katharine J. Worth, *Revolutions in Modern English Drama* (London: G. Bell and Sons, 1972), p. 183.

10. Dimitri Chizhevsky, "The Theme of the Double in Dostoevsky," in *Dostoevsky: A Collection of Critical Essays,* ed. René Wellek (Englewood Cliffs: Prentice Hall, 1962), p. 124.

11. Richard Scharine, *The Plays of Edward Bond* (Cranbury, N.J.: Assoc. Univ. Press, 1976), p. 211.

12. "Discussion with Edward Bond," *Gambit,* 3.17 (1970), 15.

13. Octavio Paz, *Los signos en rotación y otros ensayos* (Madrid: Alianza, 1971), p. 317: "The constructions of technology are absolutely real, but they are not presences; they do not represent; they are signs of action and not images of the world. . . . The apparatuses and mechanisms of technology become insignificant as soon as they cease to function: they say nothing except that they no longer serve. Thus technology is not really a language, a system of permanent signifieds based on a vision of the world. It is a repertory of signs endowed with temporary and variable signifieds" (my translation).

14. René Girard, *Violence and the Sacred* (Baltimore: Johns Hopkins Univ. Press, 1977), p. 2.

15. Terry Eagleton, "Nature and Violence: The Prefaces of Edward Bond," *Critical Quarterly,* 26 (1984), 132.

16. Girard, pp. 78-79.

17. Chizhevsky, p. 125.

18. Chizhevsky, p. 126.

19. See for example the excellent discussions of the use of animal imagery in Bond's *Lear* in Tony Coult, *The Plays of Edward Bond* (London: Methuen, 1979), pp. 43-45; Leslie Smith, "Edward Bond's *Lear,*" *Comparative Drama,* 13 (1979), pp. 65-85 passim; and Horst Oppel and Sandra Christenson, *Edward Bond's "Lear" and Shakespeare's "Lear"* (Mainz: Akademie der Wissenschaften und der Literatur, 1974).

20. Cohn, p. 194.

21. Eagleton, p. 133.

22. Michel Foucault, *Language, Counter-Memory, Practice* (Ithaca: Cornell Univ. Press, 1977), pp. 29-30.

23. Foucault, *Language,* p. 31.

24. Foucault, *Language,* p. 50.

25. Karl-Heinz Stoll, "Interviews with Edward Bond and Arnold Wesker," *Twentieth Century Literature,* 22 (1976), 417.

26. Tzvetan Todorov, *The Poetics of Prose* (Ithaca: Cornell Univ. Press, 1977), p. 213.

SAVED (1965)

PRODUCTION REVIEWS

Irving Wardle (review date 4 November 1965)

SOURCE: Wardle, Irving. "A Question of Motives and Purpose." *Times* London (4 November 1965): 17.

[*In the following review of a 1965 production of* Saved *at London's Royal Court Theatre, directed by William Gaskill, Wardle expresses disappointment, finding the play's violence gratuitous and its tone ultimately degrading to the better instincts of humanity.*]

The hope that Edward Bond's play might live up to its title and redeem the so far disastrous new season at the Royal Court was woefully shattered last night.

The two previous productions have been distressing enough, but at least they were the work of Royal Court regulars to whom the theatre must have felt a certain loyalty. The new production raises the question of play selection in a more disturbing form. Mr. Bond, a newcomer to the theatre (with one Sunday night production to his credit), has written a work which will supply valuable ammunition to those who attack modern drama as half-baked, gratuitously violent, and squalid. Why on earth did the theatre accept it?

Saved, which concerns the liaison between a spaniel-like South London boy and a vixenish good-time girl who spends most of the evening trying to get rid of him, is a blockishly naturalistic piece, full of dead domestic langueurs and slavishly literal bawdry. It contains the ugliest scene I have ever seen on any stage—where a teenage gang daub a baby with excrement and stone it to death.

One can no longer take cover behind the phrase "bad taste" in the face of such material. But one has a right to demand what purpose it fulfils. In a recent interview

Mr. Bond said that his aim was to "illuminate" violence. One would hardly have guessed this from the play itself which does nothing to lay bare the motives for violence and appeals to no emotions beyond those aroused by the act itself. According to one's proclivities these may be horror, sadistic relish, or amusement; a fair proportion of last night's audience fell into the third category.

The most charitable interpretation of the play would be as a counterblast to theatrical fashion, stripping off the glamour to show that cruelty *is* disgusting and that domestic naturalism *is* boring. But the writing itself, with its self-admiring jokes and gloating approach to moments of brutality and erotic humiliation, does not support this view. In so far as the claustrophobically private action has any larger repercussions, it amounts to a systematic degradation of the human animal.

William Gaskill's production concentrates mercilessly on the domestic silences, but contains viciously effective performances from Tony Selby and Ronald Pickup. Barbara Ferris, an able comic actress, is miscast as the girl.

Alan Brien (review date 12 November 1965)

SOURCE: Brien, Alan. "The Monster Within." *New Statesman* 70, no. 1809 (12 November 1965): 735.

[*In the following review, Brien finds Gaskill's 1965 production of* Saved *disturbing and occasionally boring, but asserts that it successfully reveals the monstrous side of human nature.*]

It appears that British audiences and critics can stomach unlimited helpings of torture, sadism, perversion, murder and bestiality when perpetrated by foreigners upon foreigners in the past. But that was in another country, they say, like Marlowe's *Jew of Malta,* and besides the stench is dead.

The catalogue of Hunnish horrors in the Aldwych late-night reading of *The Investigation* was bravely faced and nobly endured. But when Edward Bond in *Saved* at the Royal Court shows us London youth, here and now, beating and defiling a bastard baby, spitting on its nakedness and rubbing its face in its own excrement, before stoning it to death in its pram, then the cry goes up to ban and boycott such criminal libels on our national character.

Is it thought that such things cannot happen in this gentle and civilised land? Art and life have a way of reflecting each other in an eternity of mirrors and there is nothing that can be pictured even in the most grotesque of imaginations that has not been done by somebody somewhere sometime.

When David Rudkin's *Afore Night Come* was in rehearsal at the Arts, with its ritual murder of a helpless old tramp, just such a ceremonial execution of a derelict was performed by unknown butchers in a deserted house near the Elephant and Castle.

Saved has been unfavourably compared to another play about twisted sex and casual brutality, Fred Watson's *Infanticide in the House of Fred Ginger,* where a coven of louts also destroyed a neglected infant. Mr. Watson's corner-boys had at least the thin excuse of being drunk and of putting the baby to the gin bottle as a feeble-minded boozer's joke. Mr. Bond's hooligans are presented as monsters of amorality who inflict pain simply to reassure themselves that they cannot feel another being's suffering. Yet, of the two crimes, the second is the characteristic, motiveless enormity of our age.

Mr. Bond is no more a social-realist than Dostoievsky, whose characters appear here domesticated and suburbanised in the guise of South London working people. The theme, far more carefully orchestrated than seems to have been noticed, is the uncanny, dangerous way that fantasy has of being transmuted into fact among people whose lives have no centre and no meaning.

The young Raskolnikov of the snack bars and the canals boasts of the imaginary manslaughter of a boy in a street accident—once the legend is created, it is a small step to making it true with the baby in the pram. The Prince Mishkin of the labour exchange and the back alleys, whose unfocused love weakens and corrupts all whom it touches, swears to his slippery girl that they will never become apathetic automatons like her parents—yet at the end he is chained to her family and drugged by their boredom. The chorus of street-corner roughs snigger about the sexiness of his plump, plain, middle-aged mother-in-law to be—one night in the empty house, while he mends the ladder in her stocking, the dirty joke almost becomes a dirty reality.

Mr. Bond has a fluent command of the gutter poetry of popular speech with its outrageous metaphors, its powerful cliches, its rhetorical repetitions. Even those who hate and despise his people cannot deny their physical solidity and psychological reality on stage as acted by this dedicated ensemble led by John Castle, Ronald Pickup, Tony Selby, Barbara Ferris and Gwen Nelson.

William Gaskill is an ascetic and a martinet among directors. His audiences are expected to obey his rules and he never softens the impact with an easy laugh, a sentimental gesture, a stagey flourish. His actors perform in a hard, clean, direct style which is impossible to watch except with eyes wide open and ears strained.

Saved, like Harold Pinter's *The Homecoming,* is a frontal attack on the concept of the family. The home is the centre of love, security and peace, but it can also be the centre of incest, danger and struggle. The action tests out Blake's epigram—"Sooner murder an infant in its cradle than nurse unacted desires"—by carrying it to its extreme. What if that desire is to murder an infant, or only to drop litter in the street? How does a human life weigh in the balance against egotistical satisfaction?

He gives no answers. From the general reception of his play, few people can bear even hearing the question. *Saved* makes an unsympathetic, disturbing, wearing, sometimes boring evening in the theatre. But I believe it fulfils one of the basic functions of the drama far better than *The Investigation*—that of making us remember the monster behind the mask on every one of us.

Hilary Spurling (review date 12 November 1965)

SOURCE: Spurling, Hilary. Review of *Saved,* by Edward Bond. *Spectator* 215, no. 7168 (12 November 1965): 619.

[*In the following review, Spurling excoriates Gaskill's 1965 production of* Saved, *arguing that the play is built on clichés and "self-defeating naturalism" that denies the audience even the pleasure of enjoying its prurience.*]

The Royal Court is in the dog house again. ('Just like old times,' said George Devine.) When the third new play opened last week, and belied its title according to the next morning's papers, I asked the new director how he felt. Mr. Gaskill said he firmly believed in all three plays and most of all in *Saved.* He agreed that the notices would almost certainly keep people away from the theatre. His attitude was much the same as the hero's in *Saved,* when the girl won't let him stay the night: 'You're the loser.' Mr. Gaskill found the play satisfying, profound and original: 'Have you ever seen a baby stoned to death on the stage before? Or a flabby old bag rousing sexual excitement in a young man? I think it is a triumph to have these things put on the stage.' He added that of all the modern plays he had read, Edward Bond's *Saved* reminded him most strongly of Chekhov: 'And Chekhov baffled the critics for fifty years.'

All of which puts him in a very strong position *vis-à-vis* anyone who did not like the play. I disagreed with him on almost every point; *Saved* seemed to me far from baffling. Its points of reference were transparent: four characters share a cramped South London tenement, much play is made with *Radio Times* and the hoary old ironing board, jading silence occasionally gives way to flaming rows. They would like to talk about honour and manhood, prison and the war, but their vocabulary as much as apathy lets them down. Inarticulacy is pretty much a beaten track on the stage

by now, but it still needs tactful handling. The inarticulacy of these characters is often excessively boring, and it betrays Mr. Bond into another weakness—a weakness which he shares incidentally with Noël Coward. It leads to the unspoken assumption that some things are serious (sacred used to be the word), and in turn to sentimentality, since they can't be discussed but need to be taken at face value. So, Mum and Dad lost a baby son, and we must take the hint as best we may since there is nothing more to be said about that.

Mum and Dad have not been on speaking terms for years, and by the end of the play Pam and Lenny aren't speaking either. At times Mr. Bond seems to be deliberately guying all the other plays of our times about noncommunication. I can see why the last scene is played in silence, to ram home the point that the four aren't speaking, but the play is riddled with clichés which cannot all be excused on grounds of earnestness. Pam, for instance, has an obvious reason for wearing her slip, and so has Mum when she sets up in competition. But not Dad, whose combinations are dragged in willy-nilly, and as for Lenny, it is the merest gesture to artifice when he strips off his trousers in Act 2.

The reason, Mr. Gaskill told me, why *Saved* reminded him of Chekhov, was that 'it doesn't make any moral statements. Though it is, of course, an immensely moral play.' In the few scenes where the atmosphere of conventional joylessness lifted sufficiently for the characters to emerge as real people, they did seem sympathetic. But in their joint anxiety not to condemn their characters, director and playwright seem to have overlooked that you can't suspend judgment on a vacuum. The murder of the baby, played with studious, self-defeating naturalism, failed to make even an educational point. So did Mum's attempt to seduce Lenny. One could perfectly well imagine, from seeing her in it, what Mum would look like without her dress. When she lifted her skirt, we were denied both the fascination of watching privately through a keyhole, and the pleasure of seeing it dramatised. It was altogether a very denying play. Pornography and violence effectively sterilised—which is the theatre's revenge on the documentary.

Variety (review date 17 November 1965)

SOURCE: Review of *Saved,* by Edward Bond. *Variety* 240, no. 13 (17 November 1965): 64.

[*In the following review of Gaskill's 1965 production of* Saved, *the critic finds the acting and characterization to be admirable although the play is generally "repellent."*]

To no one's surprise, the Lord Chamberlain refused to license *Saved* for public presentation and, consequently, the Royal Court Theatre had to revert to the club procedure for the Edward Bond play, and tickets are available only to members. The work is a tasteless and often repellent drama, with an unnecessary flow of crude language and gestures, which does little service to the theatre generally and will do even less to help the Royal Court in its new and disappointing repertory policy.

There are presumably louts who think it's a lark to stone a baby to death in its pram, but such brutality and horrifying incidents hardly provide satisfying theatre. There may also be sluts who think nothing of making love to a pickup in their parents' home within a few minutes of the first meeting, but it's not edifying entertainment, either. Nevertheless, that's the background of *Saved.*

Despite its generally obnoxious flavor, the play has a few redeeming qualities. The author, whose only previous stage credit is a Sunday night production at the same theatre, has a well-tuned ear for dialog, particularly of the crude and vulgar variety.

He also has a keen sense of characterization, as expressed in the strange relationship between the young girl and her family. Barbara Ferris sparkles in the frank opening scene in which she is smooching on the couch with John Castle, but there is a startling contrast to her personality after she tires of him, though he remains a lodger in the house.

There is a welcome plausibility to the role as played by Castle, while Tony Selby, who takes over as the girl's lover and the father of her child, is a typical uncouth lout. As the parents who have not spoken to each other for 20 years, Gwen Nelson and Richard Butler give impeccable portrayals.

There is one telling "tease" scene in which the mother persuades the young lodger to help her dress for a date. Dennis Waterman, Ronald Pickup, John Bull and William Stewart play the other young thugs who, with Selby, are responsible for killing the infant.

William Gaskill, who recently became artistic director for the theatre, has staged the show with considerable authority, making effective use of long sequences without dialog and little action. It would be hard to imagine more sparse sets than those designed by John Gunter, but they are more than adequate.

CRITICAL COMMENTARY

Richard Scharine (essay date 1976)

SOURCE: Scharine, Richard. *"Saved*: Sooner Murder an Infant in Its Cradle." In *The Plays of Edward Bond,* pp. 47-81. Lewisburg: Bucknell University Press, 1976.

[*In the following essay, Scharine provides a critical history of* Saved *along with a thematic overview of the play.*]

In fall 1965, William Gaskill returned from the National Theatre to succeed the late George Devine as artistic director of the English Stage Company. He immediately revived the repertory policy that Devine had abandoned early in the theater's history and used it to inaugurate three new plays, two by established Royal Court playwrights and one by a relative newcomer.[1]

The first two plays were Ann Jellicoe's *Shelley* and N. F. Simpson's *Cresta Run,* both of which received mixed and generally disappointing reviews. Nevertheless, the critics' real ire was reserved for Edward Bond, whose only previous professionally performed play, **The Pope's Wedding,** had been seen in a Royal Court Sunday-night production without decor three years earlier. His *Saved* joined the repertory on November 3.

After the Independent Theatre produced Ibsen's *Ghosts* in 1891, its manager, J. T. Grein, described himself as "the best-hated man in London." On the morning of 4 November 1965, Edward Bond must have felt that he had inherited the title. Penelope Gilliatt opened a favorable review in the London *Observer* by saying, "I spent a lot of the first act shaking with claustrophobia and thinking I was going to be sick."[2] The *unfavorable* reviews were predictably more severe. The reasons for the condemnation varied, although most critics cited several. Herbert Kretzmer began in *The* [London] *Daily Express* with the "characters who, almost without exception, are foul-mouthed, dirty-minded, illiterate, and barely to be judged on any recognizable human level at all."[3] J. C. Trewin of *The Illustrated London News* admitted:

> It may not be the feeblest thing I have seen on any stage, but it is certainly the nastiest, and contains perhaps the most horrid scene in the contemporary theatre. (Even as I write that hedging "perhaps" I delete it: nobody can hedge about *Saved.*)[4]

Irving Wardle of the London *Times* declared that "the writing itself, with its self-admiring jokes and gloating approach to moments of brutality and erotic humiliation amounts to a systematic degradation of the human animal."[5] The outcries of offended critics were followed shortly by those of aroused patrons who formed "representative organizations" in order to combat "pornographic, sadistic, filthy, unfunny, and obscene" drama.[6]

Initially, the "slaughter by the critics just emptied the theatre."[7] However, the Royal Court continued to present the play and it soon generated support among England's most influential members of the theatrical profession. Irene Worth wrote to Bond endorsing *Saved.* In the letter columns of the London *Observer,* Sir Laurence Olivier praised the play as one in which "we can experience the sacramental catharsis of a very chastening look at the sort of ground we have prepared for the next lot."[8] On 14 November, Kenneth Tynan organized a teach-in at the Royal Court at which Mary McCarthy praised *Saved* for its "remarkable delicacy" and stated that the play was concerned with "limit and decorum."[9] Bond himself responded with an open letter to the critics in the London *Observer.* In December and January the box office "picked up enormously." The opposition, however, still had a legal ace in the hole.

The English Stage Company was not unaware of the problems that might be caused by *Saved.* They had commissioned a play from Bond as a result of their pleasure with *The Pope's Wedding. Saved,* however, had come as something of a shock and it was given to the director of *The Pope's Wedding,* Keith Johnstone, for another Sunday-night production without decor.[10] At this point, Gaskill, who was planning his first season at the Royal Court, read *Saved* for the first time.

> I remember reading it straight through and being absolutely convinced that it should be done and that I should direct it myself. I had some doubts about the extremes of violence but I knew the play had to be done.[11]

On 24 June, 1965, Gaskill submitted the play to the censorship office of the Lord Chamberlain, an office that *Saved* and its successor, *Early Morning,* were to be instrumental in closing. The Lord Chamberlain's representative, the Assistant Comptroller, recommended a considerable number of cuts, including all of one scene and a major part of another. On 3 August, Gaskill and Iain Cuthbertson, a Royal Court associate director, discussed the case with the Assistant Comptroller. Gaskill promised to deliberate the proposed cuts with the author. Eight days later the Lord Chamberlain's office received a letter from the author stating that the changes would be too damaging to the play and that a decision had been made to present it to a club-audience only.[12]

The action of the Royal Court in limiting showings of *Saved* to private audiences seemed momentarily to reduce the possibilities of a legal conflict. Technically, under the Theatres Act of 1843, it was an offence to act plays anywhere "for hire" without a license from the Lord Chamberlain and the payment of anyone connected with a production defined it as a play acted "for hire." However, with some exceptions, the Lord Chamberlain had turned a blind eye to productions that were to be viewed by private groups, such as the English Stage Society, the Royal Court's private club.[13] Nevertheless, in December several performances of *Saved* were attended by police officers acting on behalf of the Lord Chamberlain's office.[14] On 14 February, eleven days after Bond had been awarded a £1,000 writer's bursary by the Arts Council and two days after a motion in the House of Lords was introduced to review the stage

censorship laws,[15] summonses were served on Gaskill and Alfred Esdaile, the Licensee of the Royal Court, for presentation of a play before it had been licensed.[16] The complaint was based on the failure of Royal Court door attendants to check for membership cards at performances of *Saved.* In actuality, the censor may have been more irritated by the fact that the play was running in repertory with licensed productions. Lord Cobbold, then Lord Chamberlain, expressed his philosophy on this practice in a 1964 interview:

> Whether or not they could strictly be brought under the Lord Chamberlain's jurisdiction—which has never actually been tested in the courts—my predecessors and I have never wished to interfere with genuine theatre clubs. Where a management uses them for a different purpose, e.g., to put on for a long run a play part of which had been refused a licence, I think rather a different position arises. The arrangement is then really being used more as an attempt to evade the law.[17]

If *Saved* was intended by the Lord Chamberlain to serve as a legal test case, it must have been a disappointing one. The English Stage Company was convicted, but the trial served as an excellent forum for both the merits of *Saved* and the censorship system. The fine was a nominal £50.[18] Nevertheless, productions of *Saved* were forbidden in England for the time being. The Royal Court had scheduled performances for 21 and 22 February, and Gaskill initially announced that these performances would take place, despite the impending legal action.[19] However, he later relented, perhaps through fear of alienating the court.

Outside of England, *Saved* received more favorable treatment. By March of 1968 Bond could legitimately claim to have "had more productions of *Saved* in Germany than I've had performances in England."[20] A production by the Cinoherni Klub of Prague intended "to illustrate the point that when personal freedom is frustrated by external authority it takes a very ugly secondary course" received Bond's personal commendation.[21] The American premiere, under the direction of Jeff Bleckner, was presented at the Yale Repertory Theater 5 December 1968. The audience's response was typical, but reviews reflect a new respect for the work itself.

> Mr. Bleckner and his cast were able to unearth the complexities of the play, and, more importantly, to sound its astonishing verbal music for us, especially in the second half. One was able to perceive that Bond's use of dialogue, seemingly the simplest realism, actually had a density and richness close to that of Chekhov. . . . The work communicated itself with complete success: the walkout rate after the first half was the highest the theatre has ever had, and I have never seen an audience at a traditional play so disturbed and stimulated.[22]

Six days later, *Saved* had its Canadian premiere at McGill University in Montreal.[23]

Meanwhile, back in England, attitudes toward Bond's work were beginning to shift. The critical success of Jane Howell's production of **Narrow Road to the Deep North** at the Belgrade Theater of Coventry in June 1968, prompted some grudging aesthetic reassessments of the earlier plays. Stressing "the legitimate points they make about political morality or class dereliction," Irving Wardle admitted to making a complete about-face in reference to **Saved** and **Early Morning.**

> Even for those who still hate his work, Bond has become one of the facts of theatrical life, no longer to be dismissed with a bored yawn or an outraged howl. And it is now time for the guilty reviewers to queue up and excuse their past arrogance and obtuseness as best they may. As one of the guiltiest, I am glad to acknowledge that my feeling toward the plays has changed, and that if I had originally responded to them as I do now I should not have applied words like "half-baked" and "untalented" to **Saved** and **Early Morning.**[24]

The retrospective "Bond season" at the Royal Court opened 7 February 1969, with **Saved.** The performers were different and a few other details had altered, but nothing was so significantly different as the reaction from the dark side of the footlights.

> After the grotesque antics in which the moral health of the nation was supposedly to be preserved by the imposition of a fine and the banning of the play, less than four years later it is staged, received with quiet respect, and recognized to be a moral tract for the times, no less. Can anyone be proved to have been depraved or corrupted by it? Has it led to sadistic orgies? Or riots in the streets of Chelsea? Where, then, are all the arguments which maintained stage censorship in being for decades? "Oh well, old boy, if you allowed that sort of thing, who knows what might happen?" Well, now we know the answer. *Nothing* except that some people emerge from the theatre with a deeper insight, a greater compassion for the sufferings of some of their fellow human beings.[25]

Finally, Peter Roberts, the editor of *Plays and Players,* called the European tour staging of **Saved** the best English production of 1969.[26]

Saved is made up of thirteen scenes: six in the living room of a South London flat; two in a bedroom of that same flat; three in a park near it; and one each in a cell and in a café. An intermission is recommended after the seventh scene. As human possibilities are reduced, the scenes become increasingly interior and restrictive. All of the park scenes occur in the first act, and four of the living-room scenes occur in the second act.

The play opens with the seduction of a South London working-class boy named Len by a girl named Pam. She brings him to the flat of her parents who haven't spoken to one another for years. There Len settles in

happily, falls in love with Pam, and even plans to marry her. She soon tires of him, however, and takes up with a young "stud" named Fred. Pam is devoted to Fred and has his baby, but Fred grows restive even before the baby is born and is anxious to break off all ties. Len, doggedly devoted, alternates between trying to reawaken Pam's interest through the tender care he takes of both her and the baby, which is otherwise ignored, and a genuine attempt to patch up affairs between her and Fred. One such attempt in the park is followed by an argument between Pam and Fred, after which she exits angrily, followed by Len, and leaves behind the baby. In the first scene banned by the Lord Chamberlain, Fred's mates, later goading Fred into taking part, begin with playing with the baby and end by smearing it with its own excrement and stoning it to death. From a distance Len sees the killing, but he does nothing. The act ends with Fred being visited in a jail cell by Len and a tearful, still-infatuated Pam.

Act Two chonicles the deteriorating relationship between Pam and Len, on whom she blames all her troubles. It is the repeat of the pattern of gradual and continuing estrangement suffered by Pam's parents, Harry and Mary. In the second scene banned by the censor, Len's sexual frustration drives him to Mary, and what begins as a simple case of stocking-mending very nearly turns into a seduction scene. It is interrupted by Harry, who leaves without comment. Fred's release from prison is the occasion for a celebration breakfast given by his friends and co-murderers. Len and Pam attend uninvited, and when she tries to force herself on Fred, she is humiliated and dismissed. Len makes one more effort to reunite himself and Pam. An argument between Mary and Harry over Len ends with the latter's being bashed by a teapot. Len, entering, tries to help but is drawn into the fight and finally agrees to leave. Harry visits Len in his room. He talks about his past with his wife and convinces Len that things would be just the same elsewhere. The play ends in a silent stalemate with all four household members in the same room. None speak with the exception of Len, who asks for a tool to help him in his attempt to fix a chair that was broken earlier in the fight. No one answers. No one helps.

Edward Bond has called **Saved** "formally a comedy" and "almost irresponsibly optimistic."[27] These two statements define simultaneously Bond's view of the universe and the cool objectivity with which he explains it. In Bond's universe, tragedy is possible because of the strict limitations placed on man, but the gods play no part—except as rationalizations for inhumane action—in defining limits and punishing the disobedient. This responsibility belongs to man himself, acting in the name of social, governmental, and religious abstractions, abstractions that man himself has created, which corrupt him and which are totally antithetical to his human needs. *Saved* is a comedy, not because its protagonist, Len, is victorious, but because he refuses to recognize defeat. It is also an Oedipal comedy. On one level, Len is in opposition to Harry, the father of Pam and the owner of the flat where Len boards. Harry is also the man whom Len will obviously become, and Harry's wife is sexually attracted to Len. Yet, despite these Freudian implications, Len and Harry do not destroy one another.

> The Oedipus outcome should be a row and death. There *is* a row and even a struggle with a knife—but Len persists in trying to help. The next scene starts with him stretched on the floor with a knife in his hand, and the old man comes in dressed as a ghost—but neither of them is dead. They talk, and for once in the play someone apart from Len is as honest and friendly as it is possible for him to be. The old man can only give a widow's mite; but in the context it is a victory—and a shared victory. It is trivial to talk of defeat in this context. The only sensible object in defeating an enemy is to make him your friend. This happens in the play, although in fact most social and personal problems are solved by alienation or killing.[28]

Saved, however, is an Oedipal comedy on yet another level. Its characters are the children of their society, sacrificed for the preservation of the industrial society Blake characterized as the "Dark Satanic Mills." Yet even the awesome restrictions of society have not destroyed Len's basic goodness. At the same time, Len has not triumphed over his society. The play remains, at final curtain, ambivalent in its attitude.

William Gaskill, Bond's chief interpreter, has said of *Saved*: "Whatever Edward may say I cannot find its ending optimistic."[29] If the synonym for optimism must be ambivalence, it is difficult to dispute him. Len has "saved" humanity from defeat, but Bond has traced the patterns of deterioration too clearly for us to believe in any kind of ultimate triumph. The path followed by Len and trod by Harry before him is that of Beckett's *Endgame,* circular and reductive as long as life lasts. Nevertheless, there is a significant difference between the philosophies of Beckett and Bond. Beckett's heroes are condemned to hope, a pain from which they would be gladly released. They continue to live because their humanity allows them no other choice. Bond's heroes cling stubbornly to their humanity, accepting even their pain as a sign of life.

The authenticity of Bond's dialogue is without question, but it is never naturalism for its own sake. In form, as much as in content, it conveys the play's motivations and themes. It is richly comic and, surprisingly, capable of carrying several levels of meaning simultaneously.

The earliest critics of *Saved* credited Edward Bond ungraciously with the power to reproduce South London speech.

> It is fluent and, so far as an outsider can tell, an accurate transcription of South London speech: but a tape recorder could reveal almost as much. . . . It strikes the audience like a handful of gravel thrown against the window (an effect I imagine Bond intended); its only departure from literal naturalism being a suspiciously conniving attitude towards the audience.[30] The author's single asset, if this is the word, is an ear for the loose lingo of vicious teenagers and the semiarticulate banalities of their elders. He reproduces the dialogue faithfully and (so it seems) without bothering to select: a recording of the slovenly, obscene horrors of everyday speech that might have been caught on tape.[31]

A few, like Mollie Panter-Downes, found *Saved*'s authenticity of language "magnificent";[32] the majority, like Hilary Spurling, found it merely "excessively boring."[33] That its authenticity might cause difficulties was admitted by the English Stage Company when it preceded its revival of *Saved* in 1969 with a neardocumentary of the same milieu, *Life Price.*[34] The publishers of the *Saved* text have supplied no fewer than twenty-seven footnotes to explain the meaning of a word or phrase, a precaution that is far from excessive and that must be unparalleled in a contemporary play being published in its own country. Beyond the words themselves is the even greater problem of accent. The first American production of *Saved* at the Yale Repertory Theater suffered from the "problem—perhaps inevitable . . . of lapsing accent or New York inflection."[35] William Gaskill was speaking in First Precepts when he discussed the casting of the revival of *Saved.*

> As a director casting Bond text, the speaking of it is almost the first essential. It's got to sound right. And certainly in *Saved* it was essential to have a high proportion of London-born people in it to speak it properly. Because it's extraordinarily inflected with a London ear. We have had Northerners in it in some of the parts, and they can get away with it, but you have to have some Cockneys in it. When you hear people read it you know that some of them will never get the sound right however good they may be as actors.[36]

The basic mode of speech in *Saved* is the attack, but it is seldom sustained and reflects no particular personal aggressiveness. It is the attack of the teased, trapped animal, striking at anything that comes too close to it out of fear or the momentary relief that comes from inflicting pain that it cannot feel itself. It jabs, then retreats with bared fangs in fear of both retaliation and, surprisingly, of the damage caused. Even when the intent does exist, that intent is hidden, possibly even from the attacker. For example, Pam's wish for Len to leave the flat before Fred is released from prison is expressed in an incessant quibbling over the location of her copy of the *Radio Times.*

To this atmosphere of pared-down communication, Bond has brought the perfect form: a pared-down line of five or six syllables that screams for verification even as it denies it to others. The people of *Saved* mistrust words, as they mistrust any human symbol or extention that might reveal them to themselves. Len stands apart from his mates in a manner that recalls Cincinnatus in Nabokov's *Invitation to a Beheading.* While Cincinnatus is condemned for obliqueness, Len is condemned for questioning obliqueness, for searching and suggesting by his questions the possibility of answers and reasons. In *Saved,* language as a tool functions only to hold others at a distance. For example, Pam, having picked up Len and brought him to her parents' flat, is willing to share her body, but avoids all other contact.

LEN.

Wass yer name?

PAM.

Yer ain' arf nosey.

LEN.

Somethin' up?

PAM.

Can't I blow me nose? (*She puts her hanky back in her bag and puts it on the table.*) Better. (*She sits on the couch.*)

LEN.

Wass yer name?

PAM.

Wass yourn?. . . .

LEN.

'Ow often yer done this?

PAM.

Don't be nosey.[37]

Bond claims to share his characters' distaste for words:

> I dislike anybody who imagines the answers to life are cerebral and that the problems are cerebral. . . . I dislike that sort of cerebral activity that imagines problems exist somewhere out *there* and don't exist *here.* One lives in the world and one must find one's way of living in the world.[38]

This attitude toward intellectualisms is illustrated by having the baby-killing Fred present the play's only plea for law and order. "I don't know what'll 'appen. There's bloody gangs like that roamin' everywhere. The bloody police don't do their job" (vii, 58).

The ironic humor of the speech is, of course, not accidental. In the gang scenes and in Len's first scene with Pam, Bond has captured the "kind of cockney badinage which is disappearing in the streets but find-

ing a loving home in the theatre, where it has always half-belonged."[39] Nevertheless, Bond's technical proficiency with language in *Saved* extends beyond a tape-recorder accuracy. An early reader of the play noted with surprised pleasure the importance of rhythm: "Edward Bond has all of the fascination of a metronome with all of those four-word speches."[40]

MARY.

. . . I could a gone t'bed, an' I will next time 'e arsts me.

HARRY.

Now 'e's caught a sniff a yer 'e'll be off with 'is tail between 'is legs! (*She hits him with the teapot. The water pours over him. Pam is too frightened to move.*) Ah!

MARY.

'Ope yer die!

HARRY.

Blood!

PAM.

Mum!. . . .

HARRY.

Doctor.

MARY.

Cracked me weddin' present. 'Im. (*Len comes in.*)

LEN.

Blimey!

HARRY.

Scalded!

PAM.

Whas's 'appenin'?. . . .

HARRY.

Yer saw 'er.

MARY.

'E went mad.

LEN.

'E's all wet.

PAM.

(*To Mary.*) Why?. . . .

HARRY.

Blood.

PAM.

(*To Mary.*) Whas's 'e done?

LEN.

'E's all wet.

MARY.

Swore at me!

PAM.

Why?

HARRY.

Doctor.

MARY.

There's nothin' wrong with 'im.

HARRY.

Scalded.

MARY.

I 'ardly touched 'im. 'E needs a good thrashin'!

LEN.

(*To Pam.*) Get a towel.

HARRY.

I ain't allowed t' touch the towels.

MARY.

I kep' this twenty-three years. Look what 'e's done to it!

PAM.

What 'appened?

LEN.

(*Looking at Harry's head.*) Yer'll 'ave t' wash that cut. It's got tea leaves in it.

(xi, 85-87)

Even as Bond's sense of rhythm enables him to generate unforced laughter from a potentially ugly domestic scene, it can also give a seemingly naturalistic speech a number of levels of meaning—a virile and nonacademic poetry. While Len and Fred are fishing in the park, Len makes an attempt to convince Fred to return to Pam. This effort is interrupted by Fred's realization that the bait is gone from his hook.

LEN.

Gone? They've 'ad it away. . . .

FRED.

More like wriggled off.

LEN.

I mounted it 'ow yer said.

FRED.

(*Winds in.*) Come 'ere. Look (*He takes a worm from the worm box*). Right, yer take yer worm. Yer roll it in yer 'and t' knock it out. Thas's first. Then yer break a bit off. Cop 'old a that. (*He gives part of the worm to Len.*) . . . Now yer thread yer 'ook, but yer leave a fair bit 'anging off like that, why, t'wiggle in the water. Then yer push yer top bit down off the gut and camer-flarge yer shank. Got it?

LEN.

Thas's 'ow I done it.

FRED.

Yeh. Main thing, keep it neat. (*He casts. The line hums.*) Lovely. (*A long silence.*) The life. (*Silence.*)

LEN.

Down the labour Monday. (*Fred grunts.*) Start somethin'. (*Silence.*) No life, broke.

FRED.

True. (*Silence. Len pokes in the worm box with a stick.*) Feed 'em on milk.

LEN.

(*Silence.*) I'll tell 'er yer ain' comin'.

(vi, 39)

The undertones are sexual and understood by the audience, if not by the characters. Fred stresses not only the superiority of his sexual technique to Len's, but the irrevocability of his break with Pam. His purely physical interests are over and he feels no moral responsibility for their consequences.

An actual physical environment plays a more important part in *Saved* than in any other Bond play. The characters are exhausted by the inhumanity of their setting. Its unchanging and unhospitable sterility is reflected in the characters' relationships with time, their world, and with one another.

> I always get the impression, whether it's true or not, that it's [South London] more industrialized. I've got a feeling, too, that it's physically flatter there—and those miles and miles of long straight streets that always look the same. I used to call it the brick desert, and this feeling of being in a desert of bricks seemed to be absolutely right for the play.[41]

The events of *Saved* must take years, but time makes no changes in the atmosphere of the play. The "desert of bricks" is as immune to change as it is barren. The men in *The Pope's Wedding* at least saw the variation of the seasons and felt some satisfaction in their work.

RON.

> I oiled that owd Ferguson this mornin'. Yoo should a seen 'er. My life!. . . .

LORRY.

> (*Wiping scythe blade.*) Beautiful owd thing, ent she. 'Ung 'er up in owd apple tree t' take the rust out on 'er.[42]

In contrast, the factory workers of *Saved* never see the end product of their labor and think of their jobs only as disagreeable but inevitable interludes.

COLIN.

> Workin'?

LEN.

> Worse luck.

> (iii, 26)

. . . .

LEN.

> 'Ow's the job?

FRED.

> Don't talk about it.

> (iv, 33)

. . . .

FRED.

> (*Shrugs, to Len.*) 'Ow's the job?

LEN.

> Stinks.

FRED.

> It don't change.

> (x, 77)

Mechanical devices exist in the world of *The Pope's Wedding,* of course, but they are personal and immediate extensions of human beings. When the wringer on his mother's washing machine breaks, Bill can—and must—fix it himself. When the television set in *Saved* doesn't work, "the man'll 'ave to come an' fix it" (iv, 29).

Sex, which in *The Pope's Wedding* is treated as a mutual and pleasurable activity, is reduced to a calculated and impersonal hunt in *Saved.*

> They opened that new church on the corner. . . . Best place out for'n easy pick up. . . . I done it before. There's little pieces all over the shop, nothin' a do. . . . The ol' bleeder shuts 'is eyes for prayers an' they're touchin' 'em up all over the place. Then the

law raided this one an' they 'ad it shut down. . . . If there's nothin' in the church, know what? . . . Do the all-night laundries. . . . Yer get all them little 'ouse-wives there.

> (vi, 48, 50-51)

Even the violence of *Saved* is impersonal and unmotivated. It is basically defensive, the sociologically verifiable effect of too many people crowded too close together.[43]

> If you cage an animal so that it can't behave in a normal way, so that it always feels threatened by the things around it, it becomes violent: And if you threaten human beings all the while, they become violent. No animal can be subjected to too much noise, for instance, because noise means danger. We have the same function in us—we don't like noise. We are living on top of motorways. Biologically we cannot function. There are H-bombs in the air all the time. The human being today is always in a state of tension and of being scared and frightened, and is therefore aggressive.[44]

To Edward Bond, industrialization is political as well as economic and social. Its society has enforced upon humans strictures that can only lead to violence. It then calls that violence an inherent part of human nature and uses it as an excuse to add still more strictures. To Edward Bond, the son of North London working-class parents and a man who left school for work at the age of fifteen, the end product of the assembly line is dehumanization.

> Well, my background is typical of 75% of the people in this country and that is that I was brought up in very much the same sort of society as *Saved.* . . . They destroy people because I mean our society could not exist unless we were destroyed. A human being was not designed to work in a factory, I mean, just as a tool. You're not made to stand at a bench day after day doing these mechanical jobs. A human being is not designed for that. Now we live in a mechanical society. We make sure if we design a machine it carries out its function absolutely right with total efficiency. The grotesque thing is that human beings are used so inefficiently, they aren't made for that sort of thing, so that nobody can be happy. Human beings are adaptable, they can survive in prisons, but at a cost.[45]

It is possible that Bond's very success in recreating a naturalistic South London environment has hampered the acceptance of *Saved* in England. Bond's play is about the corrupting effect of society upon its children—a point missed by many for whom the realistic production of *Saved* made it seem to be only a specific instance, lacking in symbolic overtones. John Russell Taylor has suggested that showing the brutal murder of the baby in the park as merely the release of similar tensions to those already on view in the flat requires a less naturalistic production, in which setting, costuming, etc., could provide parallels that would suggest the other great atrocities of our century.[46] That *Saved* has had its greatest successes in non-English speaking countries, thus doubly removing them from its original milieu, supports Taylor's assessment.

The stoning of the baby is on one level the explosive release of the aggressions created by the dehumanizing restrictions of an industrialized society. On a more poetic level, however, the stoning is a metaphor for the restrictions themselves. Whether the method be murder or unnatural conditions and control, the end result is the same: the loss of innocence and humanity.

All of Bond's characters are children of society and all are more or less battered by it. In turn, they have become the instruments of society, destroying others. They are murdered Innocents, incapable of feeling or responding, capable only of murdering others.

> Clearly the stoning to death of a baby in a London park is a typical English understatement. Compared to the "strategic" bombing of German towns it is a negligible atrocity, compared to the cultural and emotional deprivation of most of our children its consequences are insignificant.[47]

Allowing for the already discussed pressure of environmental differences, the gangs in *The Pope's Wedding* (Bill, Joe, Byo, Len, Lorry, and Ron) and in *Saved* (Fred, Barry, Pete, Colin, and Mike) seem very nearly interchangeable.

They are witty, playful, and brutal by turns. The gangs function as a chorus to the action of Bond's central characters, the matrix out of which these characters arise. The gangs supply the societal norm and it is in their context that we must see the actions of Scopey and Len. In the later plays, when the spine of the action is the development of the protagonists's understanding of his environment, the chorus will be eliminated.

Bond's handling of the chorus in *Saved* shows a marked improvement in technique over *The Pope's Wedding.* Without sacrificing its collective environmental identity, Bond has used individual gang members to illustrate the mores and values of their society. Pete, the one gang member in *Saved* who has no parallel in the earlier play, effectively epitomizes what Bond believes to be the logical end result of the enmity between society and humanity. A brutal child-killer twice over, he is not ostracized by his peers but is the recipient of their adulation and envy.

COLIN.

What a giggle, though.

MIKE.

Accidents is legal.

COLIN.

Can't touch yer.

PETE.

This coroner-twit says 'e's sorry for troublin' me.

MIKE.

The law thanks 'im for 'is 'elp.

PETE.

They paid me for comin'.

MIKE.

An' the nip's mother reckons 'e ain' got a blame 'isself.

COLIN.

She'll turn up at the funeral.

PETE.

Rraammmmmmmmm!

COLIN.

Bad for the body work.

MIKE.

Can't yer claim insurance?

(iii, 24)

Whether or not Pete is actually guilty of the manslaughter for which he was exonerated is beside the point. He seeks and receives favor for both the act and the evasion of responsibility—a measure of both the man and his society. Pete is, at the beginning, what we will see Fred become in the course of the action. The norms of his society are legal and economic rather than moral and humane. Therefore, they are essentially restrictive rather than inspiring and the human reaction is to evade their consequences. Even in rebellion, their lesson has been internalized. The success or failure of an act depends upon whether or not you get caught and whether or not "yer 'ave t' make yer time up." Therefore, Pete not only feels no remorse for his actions, he has no sympathy for Fred who, in effect, took the blame for the entire gang: "Yer made yer own decisions, didn't yer? . . . We ain' got a crawl up yer arse. . . . 'E ain' swingin' that one on me" (x, 79).

Furthermore, if Pete is considered as the model member of his society, those who would be successful can only attempt to surpass him in inhumanity. In *Saved,* Barry reacts jealously to Pete's intentionally running the boy down with his truck and because of his jealousy, he is made the focus of the gang's contempt.

MIKE.

Yer creep.

COLIN.

    Yer big creep. . . . 'E don't know nothin'.

MIKE.

    Big stingy creep.

COLIN.

    Yer wouldn't 'ave the guts. . . . What yer scratchin'?

MIKE.

    'E's got a dose.

PETE.

    Ain' surprisin'.

COLIN.

    Ain' it dropped off yet?

MIKE.

    Tied on with a ol' johnny.

COLIN.

    It's 'is girl.

MIKE.

    'Is what?

PETE.

    Gunged-up ol' boot.

(iii, 24-25)

Not surprisingly, it is Barry who first begins to tease the baby in the park. It is either he or Pete, whom he longed to emulate, who initiates each new stage in its destruction. In the end it is Barry who cannot bear to leave the scene and he is the last to cease his attack.

    Juss this one! (*He throws a stone as Peter pushes him over. It goes wide.*) Bastard! (*To Pete.*) Yer put me off! . . . I got a get it once more! (*The others have gone up left. He takes a stone from the pram and throws it at point-blank range. Hits.*) Yar! . . . Bleedin' little sod! (*He hacks into the pram. He goes up left.*)

(vi, 56)

It is a classic case of what is defined in the next chapter as social morality. Pete has learned his values from his environment and has passed them on to Barry. Barry is a successful man at last.

It is tempting to picture Fred as the villain in *Saved.* He fathered Pam's child, eventually abandoning her, and finally took a leading part in their child's death. On the other hand, there is no reason to believe that Fred's advances to Pam were unsolicited and his abandonment of her is certainly no more callous than her treatment of Len. Fred would have been perfectly willing to return

Pam to Len, but he understands why this is impossible. He is possibly even sincere when he says that he failed to recognize Len's seriousness concerning her.

    What d'yer expect? No—they're like that. Once they go off, they go right off. . . . 'Appens all the time. . . . I thought she was goin' spare. . . . I reckon it was up t' you t'say. Yer got a tongue in yer 'ead.

(vi, 40-42)

Fred's attitude toward the baby and, especially, his actions toward it are difficult to condone but not impossible to explain. As with the other characters in the play, the baby was never a human being to him. Still, he tries half-heartedly several times to halt the teasing and even refuses initially to take part in the stoning. It is not until he is convinced that "it's done now" (vi, 55) and the baby's death is inevitable, that he throws a stone. It misses, but with the act he is caught in the escalating, Oedipal frenzy of his mates. The killing happens because some kind of release from environmental pressures has to occur and this is available. Afterwards, Fred insists that the blame for the crime belongs elsewhere: to a passing gang; or to Pam for leaving the baby there, for bringing it in the first place and, ultimately, for having it.

    Blamin' me? Yer got bugger all t'blame me for, mate! Yer ruined my life, thas's all! . . . Why the bloody 'ell bring the little perisher out that time a night? . . . Yer got no right chasin' after me with a pram! Drop me right in it! . . . Never know why yer 'ad the little bleeder in the first place! Yer a bloody menace!

(vii, 57)

Through its example, society teaches its members to ignore the needs of others: "I ain' gettin' involved. Bound t'be wrong," says Harry in a response to a plea from Pam (iv, 32). "I don't wan'a get involved, mate" is Len's reaction to a question about Pam's intentions (x, 80).

In his own mind, Fred is not guilty of any crime: "It was only a kid" (vii, 59), and besides, "I wer'n the only one" (x, 82). After his release Fred explodes in anger when Len questions him as to his feeling during the killing. To admit feeling would be to admit the humanity of his victim and to admit humanity would be to admit his own culpability. Yet, the effect of his crime on Fred is central to an understanding of *Saved.*

    I wanted to show that violence and what you could call misdirected sex cannot be indulged in in an interlude from normal life and then forgotten; the agent is affected as well as the victim. These effects change the structure of his life in less obvious but more far-reaching ways than the effects of social exposure or punishment. They force compromises and give psychological wounds that often turn the remainder of his life into tragedy.[48]

For all Fred's denial of his guilt, he has subconsciously accepted both it and the definition of himself that guilt provides. He has killed, is capable of killing, and will kill again. This is evident from his own words.

> Yer're arstin' for trouble. I don't wan'a go back juss yet. . . . So I gets 'im on the landin' an' clobbers 'im. . . . Keep yer 'ands off me! So 'elp me I'll land yer so bloody 'ard they'll put me back for life!
>
> (x, 76, 78, 83)

We never see Fred again after this scene, but Len clearly predicts his future: "Yer ain' seen what it done t' 'im. 'E's like a kid. 'E'll finish up like some ol' lag, or an ol' soak. Bound to. An' soon. Yer'll see" (xii, 91). Like Pete, Fred has become socially moralized. That is, pressured by his environment (the gang) into committing a crime, he has accepted the definition of himself given by the social institutions that created his environment. He is a criminal and therefore must act as one.

It has been previously noted how Bond used contrasting scenes for structural effect and group characters as representative of environment. He also uses individual characters to show the way in which his protagonists might have developed. Seen from that viewpoint, the structural differences between the natures of Bill and Fred may well stem from the differences between Scopey and Len. Although both Scopey and Len function as thinkers and questioners of their respective societies, the former initiates action and follows it through. Dimly aware, as is Len of the shortcomings of the accepted life-style, he seeks an alternative in the hermit existence of Alen. In contrast, Bill is passive, pursued by Ol' Man Bullright's wife, ousted by Scopey from Pat's affections, and inheriting her again when Scopey drifts away from society. Len, on the other hand, initiates no action. Picked up by Pam, he loses her to Fred without protest and thereafter acts only in her behalf or in reaction to her. Unlike Scopey, who confronts his situation and ultimately is defeated by it, Len avoids confrontation and attempts, within a steadily narrowing range of opportunities, to continue existing relationships. Scopey *takes* Alen's place in society, but Len does not try to supplant Harry. He merely becomes part of Harry's household and, by his presence, keeps that household alive.

> Harry acts as the *representative* of the family when he comes to Len's room. All the members of the family need Len in some way because he's the only human being they know—the only one who's learned anything from the park killing. When Len stays, it's a moral act, though its effect is limited to one house.[49]

Other than the young man, the most obvious character similarities in the two plays lie between Alen, the hermit, and Harry, Pam's father. Both exist in an isolation that has gradually increased over the years, and both, to some extent, have that isolation penetrated by the Innocent figure (Scopey/Len). The isolation of Alen is external and obvious. His contact with others is limited to the absolute minimum required to keep him alive. Indeed, he fears anything else. This fear is not the cause of his isolation, however, but the result. Within his limits, Alen becomes friendly with Scopey, despite the fact that Scopey virtually forces his company on the old man, and his reaction to Pat's return after a long absence is touching. Under the layers of legend and time, the reason for Alen's living apart is simple: His parents always lived apart from others, which made them different. The passage of time made it increasingly difficult to bridge that difference. Ironically, Alen remains unharmed only so long as he maintains the isolation that is his curse. To be different is a singular thing and Scopey learns Alen's identity only at the cost of his own identity and Alen's life.

As Alen's isolation is external, Harry's is internal. To some extent, Harry is a functioning member of his community: he lives in a South London flat with his wife, his daughter, and a lodger; he is a war veteran; he holds a regular job; and he faithfully fills out his coupon for the football pools. Yet he has not spoken to his wife for as long as his daughter (who is twenty-five) can remember, and he breaks this silence in only one scene, which results in his being hit on the head with a teapot. He very quickly exits when he comes across his daughter bedding down with a strange young man in the living room and leaves just as quickly later in the play when he discovers the same young man in the same living room with his hand up his wife's dress. He ventures no opinions on anything but the most concrete of subjects and yet, over the years, his position within the household has become more and more tenuous.

HARRY.

> She thinks she's on top. I'll 'ave t' fall back a bit—buy a few things an' stay in me room more. I can wait. . . . I left 'er once. . . . I come back. . . . I worked it out. Why should I soil me 'ands washin' an' cookin'? Let 'er do it. She'll find out.

LEN.

> Yer do yer own washin'.

HARRY.

> Eh?

LEN.

> An' cookin.

HARRY.

> Ah, *now*.
>
> (xii, 90-93)

Harry's isolation differs from Alen's in that it is still evolving. It is similar, however, in that it prefigures the course of action for the Innocent character. At the beginning of *The Pope's Wedding,* Alen is completely alone in the shack. At its close he has been replaced literally and symbolically by Scopey. Alen's position was defined and fixed by time and circumstance; Scopey's act of murder fixes his position just as unchangeably. In the course of *Saved,* Harry makes just one more step toward a complete separation from those in his house: a reduction of his domestic privileges by Mary.

> Yer can leave my things alone for a start. All this stuff come out a my pocket. I worked for it! I ain' 'avin' you dirtyin' me kitchin. Yer can get yerself some new towels for a start! An' plates! An' knives! An' cups! Yer'll soon find a difference! . . . An' my cooker! An' my curtains! An' my sheets!

                                                      (xi, 85)

To watch the baby-stoning scene in *Saved* is horrifying, but far worse are the implications of society's condoned violence. "None of the people in *Saved* do anything they couldn't get a medal for under other circumstances."[50] Domestic restrictions dehumanize and cause violence, an excuse society uses for more restrictions. Under given circumstances, however, society licences dehumanization and violence and rewards it. When asked if he killed anyone during the war, Harry's answer shows no consciousness of any humanity among his country's political enemies.

> Must 'ave. Yer never saw the bleeders, 'ceptin' prisoners or dead. Well, I did once. I was in a room. Some bloke stood up in the door. Lost, I expect. I shot 'im. 'E fell down. Like a coat fallin' off a 'anger, I always say. Not a word. (*Pause.*) Yer never killed yer man. Yer missed that. Gives yer a sense of perspective. I was one a the lucky ones.

                                                      (xii, 92)

In his relationship with Mary, Harry has passed through the same circumstances as have Len and Pam. Furthermore, by his example, he suggests their likely future. First there was premarital sex: Harry and Mary have been married twenty-three years, and Pam is twenty-five-years old. Even earlier there was a little boy who, like Pam's child, died in the park. Second, Mary, like Pam, has been periodically unfaithful. Now they merely coexist, embodying the lifetime of implacable silence that awaits Len and Pam. At the close of the play, Harry still nurses visions of leaving, but they are as hollow as Len's stated intention to Pam not to emulate her parents: "I won't turn out like that. I wouldn't arst yer if I didn't know better'n that" (ii, 21). The fact is that Len will turn out like that and Harry will be his teacher. Presuming that he cannot continue to question without receiving answers, Len has only two other choices: he could adopt the ethic of society, become brutalized, and strike

out against individuals; or he could see society as the true villain and become revolutionary. To both these alternatives he is temperamentally and intellectually unsuited.

Yet, Len is not a saint among sinners. His motivations and his actions are sometimes ambivalent. For example, he claims parenthood and responsibility for the child primarily as an excuse to stay near Pam. Later, he returns to the park in time to have prevented the baby's death, but does not. The first is forgivable, because it results, at least, in the only interest shown in the child during its lifetime. The second is harder to understand, but the key may be found in the morbid curiosity Len exhibits about the sensations of the murderers.

LEN.

> What was it like?

FRED.

> No, talk about somethin' else.

LEN.

> No, *before.*

FRED.

> Yer 'eard the trial. . . .

LEN.

> What was it like?

FRED.

> I tol' yer.

LEN.

> No. before.

FRED.

> Before what?

LEN.

> In the park.

FRED.

> Yer saw.

LEN.

> Was's it feel like?

FRED.

> Don't know.

LEN.

> When yer was killin' it.

FRED.

Do what?

LEN.

Was's it feel like when yer killed it? . . . Whas's it like, Fred?

FRED.

(*Drinks.*) It ain't like this in there.

LEN.

Fred.

FRED.

I tol' yer.

LEN.

No, yer ain'.

FRED.

I forget.

LEN.

I thought yer'd a bin full a it. I was—

FRED.

Len!

LEN.

Curious, thas's all, 'ow it feels t'—

FRED.

No. (*He slams his fist on the table.*)

(x, 80-81)

Bond suggests that "the murder of the baby shows the Oedipus, atavistic fury fully unleashed,"[51] the destructive force released when severe restrictions and inhibitions are even momentarily removed. Society has taught men that they must be restricted or they will kill. Therefore, when the restrictions are lifted, they *do* kill. Len sees this fury and, recognizing it instinctively, is both afraid of it and fascinated by it. He is witness and accomplice, but he is not alone. The audience witnesses with him—as it witnesses a thousand worse atrocities daily—and, like Len, it does nothing.

"This sort of fury is what is kept under painful control by other people in the play, and that partly accounts for the corruption of their lives."[52] The silence between Harry and Mary is frustration and controlled rage, and its effect is felt as much by Pam as by her parents. In his theory of child and personality development, psychologist Abraham Maslow postulates that a child advances by the process of choosing between the need for safety and the delight of new experiences that lead

toward change and growth. If the child does not feel safe in the present, it will turn inward and will not feel free to contemplate change in the future.[53]

Because Len questions things as they are, he represents a threat to Pam. It is painful for Pam to admit that her family life might have been different; for to admit the possibility of love is to admit the certainty of rejection. Therefore, she responds to his constant questions about her parents' mutual silence with an equally constant series of negatives and evasions.

Never arst. . . . Never listen. It's their life. . . . Yer can't do nothin', yer know. No one'll thank yer. . . . Never know'd no difference. . . . No need. . . . Nothing t' say. . . . I never 'eard 'em. . . . *No!*

(ii, 20-21)

Pam's whole life has been a struggle to adapt to existing conditions. To question their validity at this late date is beyond her stunted emotional capacities.

For Pam, Fred is a welcome relief. Len is searching and sincere; Fred is determinedly casual and plays the game on an easily understood and undemanding physical level. However, as Bond has pointed out, the effects of misdirected sex are just as pernicious to the agent as violence. Both "force compromises and give psychological wounds that often turn the remainder of life into tragedy."[54] As Fred's life is warped by casual violence, Pam's is warped by casual sex. The depth of her feeling is as much a factor in driving away Fred as was Len's searching in frightening her. It is a modern exercise in tragic irony. Both Len and Pam have exceeded the limits of feelings as defined by the forces that shaped their world. Fittingly, it is Len that Pam blames for her loss of Fred: "'E started this. . . . Somebody's got a save me from 'im" (x, 82). To be saved within the existing society is to be stunted as an emotional being. Pam cannot be "saved" because she loves Fred. The passion cuts her off from both the emotional numbness that is the mark of her society and the one man who could appreciate her love, Len.

Pam's tragedy is traceable to Mary and Harry, but as it did not begin with them, it does not end with her. According to Maslow, one of the consequences of a child's sense of rejection is a reduction in communication. These communications and the subsequent responses to them are ultimately the foundation of self-identity. The lack of a self-identity leads to a further insecurity and defensiveness, and, finally, to the withholding of recognition and interpersonal trust from others.[55] Thus, her parents withdrawal from one another and from Pam precipitated Pam's withdrawal from Len. The pattern comes full cycle with Pam's treatment of her own baby.

Pam's baby was never recognized as a human being. In the first scene following the baby's birth, it cries incessantly and without comfort offstage while onstage, Pam,

Len, and Mary argue over the responsibility of seeing to it. Harry says nothing. The others, ultimately, do nothing. We do not even know that it is a boy until the gang takes away its diaper in the murder scene. Pam kept the baby doped with aspirin to reduce its emotional demands on her. When the doped baby fails to respond to their teasing in the park, the boys increase their violence upon it. The baby is killed because it never received what Pam lacked from her own parents—a human identity. In an obvious Bondian parallel, the baby stoned to death in the park is as much a victim of society-condoned actions as Mary's son who died in the park during wartime bombing. The program for the original production of *Saved* included a quotation from William Blake: "Sooner murder an infant in its cradle than nurse unacted desires." It is fitting epigram, but one that was widely misunderstood. For society to deny to humans their basic needs to love, create, protect, and enjoy is to murder the humanity in them as surely as if they had been stoned to death in their cribs.

What ultimately defines Len's goodness, as indeed it defines the characters in all Bond's plays, is his actions. He is sincere in his love for Pam, to the point of trying to reconcile his rival to her because that is the way she wants it. At the end of the play, he alone persists in trying to reverse the growing social malaise that infects the household. He mends the chair.

> (*Len gets off the chair and crouches beside it. His back is to the audience. He bends over the chair so that stomach or chest rest on the seat. He reaches down with his left hand and pulls the loose rear leg up into the socket. . . . Len slips his left arm round the back of the chair. His chest rests against the side edge of the seat. The fingers of his right hand touch the floor. His head lies sideways on the seat.*)

(xii, 96)

It is a powerful theatrical image, the first physical evidence of Bond's fascination with crucifixion representations. Nevertheless, for a resurrection we must wait until *Early Morning*.

Saved clearly is one of the most important English plays of the 1960s, just as John Osborne's *Look Back in Anger* was probably the most pivotal English play of the 1950s. Osborne unintentionally revolutionized the English theater. Bond intentionally aims to revolutionize English society. Written twenty years after Great Britain's socialization, *Saved* is the first great dramatic self-indictment of the welfare state. Jimmy Porter was a university man who chose to run a sweetstall in protest of a bourgeois society. Ronnie Kahn was a leftist intellectual who saw in the education of the working classes a Utopian tomorrow. The characters of *Saved* have no such spokesman, no such intellect, no such alternative, and no such vision. They are a stunted, inarticulate, dehumanized people whose very condition speaks volumes. They are rendered with accuracy and seeming clinical detachment—not because their creator lacks compassion for them, but because he detests the sentimentality that would allow his audiences to accept, without changing, the conditions that created them.

Saved established Edward Bond as more than just a documentarist with a tape recorder. If he showed an unparalleled ear for common speech, he also displayed a selective ability that allowed him to move easily from low farce to high lyricism. If his structuring seemed naturalistic and undisciplined, it included nothing unnecessary to his themes. If his characters were not always sympathetic, they were never unbelievable. More than anything else, Edward Bond is an artist who uses his art as a prosecuting attorney uses his brief: the defendant is the social order; the crime is perversion of the innocent; and the evidence is *Saved.*

Notes

1. John Russell Taylor: "Ten Years of the English Stage Company," *Tulane Drama Review* 11, no. 2 (Winter 1966): 130.

2. Penelope Gilliatt, "*Saved,*" in *Contemporary Theatre,* ed. Geoffrey Morgan (London: London Magazine Editions, 1968), p. 42.

3. Herbert Kretzmer, "*Saved,*" in *Contemporary Theatre,* ed. Geoffrey Morgan (London: Magazine Editions, 1968), p. 45.

4. J. C. Trewin, "*Saved,*" *The Illustrated London News,* 249 (13 November 1965): 32.

5. Irving Wardle, "A Question of Motives and Purposes," London *Times,* 4 November 1965, p. 17.

6. Mary V. Thom, letters on *Saved, Plays and Players* 13, no. 5 (February 1966): 8.

7. Edward Bond, quoted by Giles Gordon in "Edward Bond," *Transatlantic Review* 22 (Autumn 1966): 13.

8. Laurence Olivier, quoted on the cover of *Saved* by Edward Bond (New York: Hill and Wang, 1965).

9. London *Times,* "Critics Hold Teach-in on *Saved,*" 15 November 1965, p. 14.

10. Keith Johnstone, letter to Richard Scharine, 25 March 1971.

11. William Gaskill, letter to Richard Scharine, 19 March 1971.

12. London *Times,* "Censored Play Summonses," 15 February, 1966, p. 13.

13. Richard Findlater, *Banned!* (London: MacGibbon and McKee, Ltd., 1967), p. 150.

14. "Drama in Court—Act One," *Plays and Players* 13 no. 8 (May 1966): 66-67.

15. London *Times,* "Censorship Review may be accepted," 12 February 1966, p. 12.

16. London *Times,* "Censored Play Summonses," p. 13.

17. Lord Cobbold, as quoted in *Banned!* by Richard Findlater, p. 173.

18. Findlater, *Banned!,* p. 173.

19. London *Times,* "Saved continues next week," 16 February 1966, p. 16.

20. Alan Brien, "This Bond has not been much Honoured," London *Sunday Times,* 31 March 1968, p. 55.

21. Irving Wardle, "A Discussion with Edward Bond," *Gambit* 5, no. 17: 22.

22. Michael Feingold, "Ensembles," *Plays and Players* 16, no. 8 (May 1969): 65.

23. Toby Cole, letter to Richard Scharine, 7 June 1971.

24. Irving Wardle, "The Edward Bond View of Life," London *Times,* 15 March 1970, p. 21.

25. Martin Esslin, "Bond Unbound," *Plays and Players* 16, no. 7 (April 1969): 33.

26. Peter Roberts, "A Last Look at 1969," *Plays and Players* 17, no. 4 (January 1970): 24.

27. Edward Bond, Preface to *Saved* (New York: Hill and Wang, 1965), p. 7.

28. Bond, Preface to *Saved,* pp. 5-6.

29. Gaskill, letter, 19 March 1971.

30. Irving Wardle, "The Wrong Quarrel over the Wrong Play," *New Society* 56 (25 November 1965): 27.

31. Trewin, p. 32.

32. Mollie Panter-Downes, "Letter from London," *New Yorker* 41 (11 December 1965): 231.

33. Hilary Spurling, "A Difference of Opinion," *Spectator* 215 (12 November 1965): 619.

34. Wardle, "The Edward Bond View of Life," p. 21.

35. Feingold, "Ensembles," p. 65.

36. William Gaskill, quoted by Irving Wardle in "An Interview with William Gaskill," *Gambit* 5, no. 17: 41.

37. Edward Bond, *Saved* (New York: Hill and Wang, 1965), i, pp. 11-12. All subsequent references to *Saved* will be noted in the text.

38. Wardle, "A Discussion with Edward Bond," pp. 18-19.

39. Hugo Williams, "Theatre," *London Magazine* 6 (January 1966): 67-68.

40. Sheilah Ling, letters on *Saved, Plays and Players* 13, no. 5 (March 1966): 8.

41. Edward Bond, as quoted by Roger Hudson, Catherine Itzen, and Simon Trussler in "Drama and the Dialectics of Violence," *Theatre Quarterly* 2 (January-March 1972): 7-8.

42. Edward Bond, *The Pope's Wedding, Plays and Players* 16, no. 7 (April 1969): ii, 36 and ii, 38.

43. For example, in 1959, a French husband and wife sociology/psychology team, the Chombart de Lauwes, found that the optimum number of square meters per person was ten to fourteen per housing unit. When the space available was below ten square meters per person, social and physical pathologies doubled. Edward T. Hall, *The Hidden Dimension* (Garden City, New York: Doubleday & Company, Inc., 1966), p. 172.

44. Bond, quoted by Hudson, *et al.,* "Drama and the Dialectics of Violence," p. 9.

45. Wardle, "A Discussion with Edward Bond," pp. 17-18.

46. John Russell Taylor, *The Second Wave* (London: Methuen and Co., Ltd., 1971), pp. 82-83.

47. Bond, Preface to *Saved,* p. 7.

48. Edward Bond, "Censor in Mind," *Censorship* 4 (Autumn 1965): 9.

49. Edward Bond, letter to Richard Scharine, 2 October 1974.

50. Charles Marowitz, "If a House Is on Fire and I Cry Fire," *New York Times,* 2 January 1972, sec. 2, p. 5.

51. Bond, Preface to *Saved,* p. 6.

52. Bond, Preface to *Saved,* p. 6.

53. See Maslow's concept discussed in Kim Giffin and Mary Heider, "The Relation between Speech Anxiety and the Suppression of Communication in Childhood," in *Basic Readings in Interpersonal Communication,* eds. Kim Giffin and Bobby R. Patton (New York: Harper & Row, 1971), pp. 52-53.

54. Bond, "Censor in Mind," p. 9.

55. Giffin and Heider, p. 53.

Luc Gilleman (essay date 2007)

SOURCE: Gilleman, Luc. "'Juss Round an' Round': Edward Bond's *Saved* and the Family Machine." *New England Theatre Journal* 18 (2007): 49-76.

[*In the following essay, Gilleman examines the institution of family as intractable, stifling, and resistant to change in* Saved *and argues that Bond draws more heavily from the works of August Strindberg than of Bertolt Brecht.*]

> Why do you think they call it a nuclear family? Because they're burning alive. Because they burn and everything burns with them, till there's nothing for miles.
>
> Sid, in Anthony Neilson's *Year of the Family,* 1.7.145

INTRODUCTION

Edward Bond's **Saved** (presented on 3 November 1965, "for members only," at the Royal Court Theatre) is mainly remembered for a notorious scene in which a baby is stoned to death. Together with John Osborne's *A Patriot for Me* (1965), it featured prominently in debates leading to the abolishment of theatrical censorship in Britain. This notoriety has obscured what is most interesting about the play: its interactional complexity. Because Bond is considered a political playwright, it is tempting to approach his work thematically, as Bond does in the prefaces to his plays, and then to explain how language contributes to or illustrates ideas. This has also been the usual approach to **Saved.** Yet in a play that explores complex models of interrelatedness and features barely articulate characters, form truly is content. This article, therefore, starts with a structural analysis of the play's dialogue and stage action and ends by comparing the play's implied with its avowed political message.

SPEAKING SENSE, MAKING SENSE

The play's action is set in the South of London, in the early 1960s. A young woman, Pam, lives with her parents, Mary and Harry, who haven't spoken to each other since the death of their baby son during a London air raid. Pam introduces a lodger to the house, her lover Len. While Len makes himself at home, Pam starts an affair with a young hoodlum, Fred, with whom she soon has a child. The child is brutally killed by a gang of young men when Pam abandons it in Fred's care, in an effort to force him to acknowledge his paternity. But this is not where the play ends. We never see Pam mourning the loss of her child. And when Fred gets out of prison, Pam wants him desperately back. Since Fred has lost interest in her, she tries to tempt him with the offer of a room in her parents' house. Len, however, is not willing to leave the family. The chain of events is brutal but not implausible.

Various contexts can be made to bear on these events to argue their plausibility and contemporary relevance. *Saved* is one of many British plays that, in response to the early postwar climate of housing shortages, explore the dramatic potential of the room.[1] Only four out of **Saved**'s thirteen scenes are set in a public space; the others take place in a living room, bedroom, and prison cell. Both the living room and the bedroom are shaped in the form of a triangle "that slopes to a door back centre"—like a trap, and thus not much different from the prison cell in scene 7. These closed spaces offer no privacy: characters are constantly eavesdropping on one another or trying to catch each other in compromising situations. With its cast of bickering characters, the play exploits to both comic and tragic effect the truism that emotions flare up when people are crammed together.[2] In its scene of senseless slaughter, **Saved** demonstrates the stultification produced by modern life. While none of these characters suffers acute material poverty, their lives remain small and unfulfilling. Pam, who owns nothing and has nothing to offer, uses her child much as she uses her own body, as her only capital to spend, her only means to get what she desires: some attention to herself, for herself. In short, sociologically, psychologically, and philosophically, the play makes sense.

For a contemporary audience, the problem was not that the play did not *make* sense but that it refused to *speak* sense. Presented differently—as docudrama or melodrama, say—the same plot might have caused less offense.[3] What rankled the audience was that the mechanism (in terms of a psychological, sociological, or philosophical rationale) that generates the violence is never laid bare and discussed. Bond shows rather than tells; and he does so with pitiless accuracy and consistency, which precludes offering the audience any insight that the characters in their own befuddlement cannot possibly possess. The play's focus on the moment-to-moment, shifting realities of interaction and dialogue, and thus on the characters' inability to grasp meaning or direction of something that is constantly coming into being, is psychologically unsettling. Without proper context, the torture and death of an infant struck the audience with the force of a cosmic absurdity. Nothing of what was said or done in the play could possibly account for such a horror.

Saved, then, is Bond's experiment with a sort of purified drama—one that reneges on its commitment to narrative in its refusal to go beyond the here and now of interaction and dialogue. From that purist perspective, most plays "cheat," in that they find ways to supplement the give and take of dialogue with disguised prose narrative, speech that transcends interaction. In the past, the monologue fulfilled that function: addressed directly to the audience, it was the dramatic equivalent of "timeout." Modern plays build up the action towards emotionally charged moments, usually in confrontation scenes, when characters are allowed "set speeches," eloquent, lyrical expositions of feelings and insights, designed to add context and psychological motivation to the dialogue. But if drama is to be defined strictly as the dynamic portrayal of what happens *between* characters, then there is no place for narrative overview and insight. This is what Harold Pinter meant when he said, about *The Birthday Party,* "there is no Chorus in this play" (5): "The curtain goes up and comes down. Something has happened. Right? Cokeyed, brutish, absurd, with no comment" (2).

Dialogue deprived of narrative context can be disconcerting, as anyone knows who has eavesdropped on a conversation. And Pinter's contribution to modern theatre is the use of this to good dramatic effect. Jenny Spencer in her excellent study of Bond's work up to the early 1990s and Stephen Lacey in *British Realist Theatre* (1995) have drawn attention to the way Bond's early plays in that respect resemble those of Pinter:

> Like Pinter, Bond seems to give us all the expected ingredients of dominant forms of realism, yet produces very different effects. Both writers utilize a language that is militantly unrhetorical and elliptical, and create recognizable characters (and character types) that exist in an "everyday" reality that is nonetheless sodden with violence. There is also no authorial point of view on open display to interpret and provide a context for the action.
>
> (Lacey 146)

As is the case with a Pinter play, Bond's *Saved* depicts characters unable to soar beyond the moment in a poetic flight of felicitous prose. The difference between the two playwrights, Spencer explains, is that Bond intends not to mystify but to clarify. And she quotes Bond's assertion that "[t]he important thing is not to be intrigued or puzzled by images but always to understand them" (15). This did not happen with *Saved,* which was greeted with consternation rather than understanding.

Prose Supplements

Prominent among the many bewildered readers and spectators of *Saved* was its playwright. *Saved* ends with Len fixing a chair that has been broken during a quarrel. In his notebook, Bond wrote that his play ends where others start, meaning that he refused to offer the kind of pat closure that was expected of him. To provide the "consequential" ending, as he put it, would have amounted to "the imposition of illusion, and the glib proffering of specious explanations," whereas "[a] dramatist should describe and not impose" (73). Still, when critics "failed to do [their] job," he found it impossible to let the play speak for itself (*Notebooks* 73, 92).

Feeling his dialogue needed enlightening prose, Bond presented a critical comment on at least two separate occasions.[4] In his original author's note, Bond famously declared, "*Saved* is almost irresponsibly optimistic" (309). Convincingly arguing that point proved more difficult. In Bond's reading, *Saved* is about characters rather than relationships. It is particularly a play about Len who refuses to give in to fate: "By not playing his traditional role in the tragic Oedipus pattern of the play, Len turns it into what is formally a comedy" (310). Whereas Pam, Fred and the baby succumb to fate, he says, Len, Harry and Mary manage to escape it: "There *is* a row, and even a struggle with a knife—but Len persists in trying to help. The next scene starts with him stretched on the floor with a knife in his hand, and the old man comes in dressed as a ghost—but neither of them is dead. They talk, and for once in the play someone apart from Len is as honest and friendly as it is possible for him to be" (310).

Bond's qualification of Harry's honesty is necessary but hardly sufficient. The scene is far more complex, as becomes clear as soon as one compares what these characters are saying to what they are doing. Since in this scene, the two men are eavesdropping on Pam, trying to find out whether she's crying or making love, neither of them can be said to be "honest." Bond's explanation of a complex moment in his play is not just inadequate, it is misleading. It rather confirms what Terry Eagleton has said of Bond, that he appears in his prefaces as a "nineteenth-century rationalist" (135). His dialogue is about a century ahead of his prose.

The play's dialogue continued to vex its audience and critics. "Nobody . . . will deny that it is one of the functions of the theatre to reflect the horrific undercurrents of contemporary life," Herbert Kretzmer intoned in his review in the *Daily Express.* "But it cannot be allowed, even in the name of freedom of speech, to do so without aim, purpose, or meaning." Defenders of the play took it upon themselves to paraphrase these three into a conventional cause and effect narrative, constructing the melodrama Bond had refused to write. Martin Esslin summarized the play's events as follows:

> Pam conceived the baby irresponsibly, without love; *because* she did not want it, she does not care for it; *because* she does not care for it, the baby cries incessantly and gets on her nerves; *because* it gets on her nerves she drugs it with aspirin; and so, when, caring more for the man with whom she is infatuated than for her child, she leaves it alone in its pram, the baby does not respond to the at first casual and quite well-meant attentions of the gang; *because* it does not respond, they try to arouse it by other means, and that is how they gradually work up to greater and greater brutality, *simply* to make the mysteriously reactionless, drugged child show a sign of life. . . . The baby in the pram is neglected *because* his mother cannot picture him as a human being herself; the boys of the gang kill him *because,* having been made into an object without consciousness, they treat him like a mere object.
>
> [my emphasis][5]

As the chain of events (the baby's birth, its constant crying, its being drugged, neglected, and, murdered) is never explicitly motivated by the text, it is impossible to paraphrase the play without interpreting its action and justifying its events. Esslin does this by grounding them in a psychological theory that links lack of empathy to acts of violence, corroborated by a cultural critique of alienation.

Interpretations such as Bond and Esslin offered finally eased the play's acceptance. In revivals, the critical slant was added to the program notes or incorporated into the production. Esslin mentions a 1969 production that included a "montage of images of affluence and horror between the scenes" that "appears to suggest that an attempt is being made to link the plight of the characters in the play with the growth of television advertising and sexual titillation by pop entertainment in our age." This is rather like adding menacing music to a Pinter play. But it did have the desired effect. And now the play, Esslin says, "was received with quiet respect and recognised to be a moral tract for the times no less." "Quiet respect" and "moral tract" are deathly phrases in modern theatre. Layers of critical justifications had accrued around *Saved*'s troubling dialogues, successfully buffering their disturbing impact.

"The Noise of Language"

And yet it had not been *Saved*'s "message" but its stark dialogue that had first caught critics' attention. While drafting the play, Bond had scribbled the following in his notebook: "Why do people sit around saying nothing or talking about very trivial things? Because they have nothing to say. Because they are afraid of what they will say" (73). Esslin hailed the play as "the final step and the ultimate consummation of the linguistic revolution on the British stage": "what a distance we have come from the over-explicit clichés of the flat well-mannered banter, the dehumanised upper-class voices of an epoch which now appears positively antediluvian—although its ghost-like remnants still haunt the auditoria around Shaftesbury Avenue." Others were equally struck by the dialogue but were less enthusiastic about it. Gareth Lloyd Evans grudgingly conceded that with *Saved* Bond proves he "has a remarkable ear for the noise that language makes. Some might say that it is less the noise of language that we hear in *Saved* than that made by human animals in vain attempts to communicate with each other. But the verisimilitude he achieves is remarkable." Like other emerging playwrights of the fifties and sixties, he added, Bond was excellent at capturing speech but failed to strike a balance between mimesis and mediation. Such playwrights, he said, "drift, merely, into language" (221). Bond was a prime example of this drift, and *Saved* confused the audience because the playwright had been so keen on giving a faithful rendition of col-

loquial, regional language that he had been unable to develop a coherent overall meaning.

But while critics readily recognized the language innovations in *Saved,* none closed the gap between dramatic dialogue and critical prose by demonstrating *how* the play generates meaning. In their discussions, the vaunted "linguistic revolution" in *Saved* amounts to not much more than a stylistic innovation, a deliberate breach of the rules of decorum. At best, then, the dialogue achieves a degree of thematic relevance. So, according to David Hirst, "the barrenness of [Len and Pam's] exchanges is a comment on the emptiness of their culture, itself a reflection of the deprivation which is characteristic of their social situation" (49). This suggests that the dialogue illustrate a certain condition, much in the way costumes, props, or the set might do.

It is true that many of the verbal exchanges in *Saved* are used to create a class-typical "reality effect":

Len.

[. . . .] Yer got a fair ol'arse.

Pam.

Like your mug.

(22)

Mary.

[. . . .] Did yer put the oven out?

Len.

An' the light.

Mary.

I ain' made a money, y'know.

(48)

Mary.

Yer jealous ol' swine!

Harry.

Of a bag like you?

(119)

Phonetically reminiscent of the South London dialect and rhythms, the dialogue draws attention to itself rather than to plot or theme. Because of this idiom, combined with the lower-class thematic, dismal settings, and situations, *Saved,* like Bond's first play *The Pope's Wedding* (1962), was considered an exponent of 1950s-early 1960s "kitchen sink drama," though of an unusually gritty kind, lacking the zest and glow of more typical representatives of that genre—of John Osborne's *Look Back in Anger* (1956) or Wesker's 1960 "trilogy," for instance.[6]

Bond changed course with his next play, ***Early Morning*** (1968), a surreal farce featuring cannibalism and a lesbian affair between Queen Victoria and Florence Nightingale. His later plays, ***Narrow Road to the Deep North*** (1968), ***Lear*** (1971), or ***Bingo*** (1973), venture with similar theatrical daring into geographically and historically removed fictionalized locations. By contrast, ***Saved*** is referred to as a "blockishly naturalistic piece" and condemned or praised for its "uncompromising presentation of the action through a sharply realistic style" or its "ghastly realism."[7] The latter is a misnomer. The dialogue is laconic, even hermetic. Any attempt at identifying with the characters has to overcome linguistic opacity. This may be "realistic," in the sense of mimetic; it is certainly not "realism," a genre that requires identification with characters and transparency of language to ideas.

Thematic coherence is another expectation of realism, and it requires that ideas be clearly articulated during moments of heightened emotional intensity. In ***Saved*** however, even in situations where eloquence is traditionally expected, the dialogue consists of terse exchanges, as here in the scene portraying Len and Pam's clumsy attempts at romance:

LEN.

'Ow often yer done this?

PAM.

Don't be nosey.

LEN.

Take yer shoes off.

PAM.

In a minit.

LEN.

Can yer move yer—thass better.

PAM.

Yer d'narf fidget.

LEN.

I'm okay now.

PAM.

Ow!

LEN.

D'yer 'ave the light on?

PAM.

Suit yerself.

LEN.

I ain' fussy.

PAM.

Ow!

(22)

This is a play about people who lack the cultural capital to be effusive or conventionally coherent about their own feelings and intentions. Substituting insecure fumbling for romance and working class stichomythia for middle-class eloquence, ***Saved*** signals from the beginning that it will not play by the rules of "realism." None of this, however, explains the relationship between the dialogue's structure and meaning.

LAYERING TECHNIQUE

Far from being "noise," the language of ***Saved*** is an intricate composition. The play generates multiple meanings not by articulating them but through a complex layering of dialogue. As a result, any critical paraphrase of even a brief exchange requires a lengthy unraveling. A closer look at an excerpt from scene 9 will demonstrate this. Len is in the living room, polishing his shoes, when Mary walks in, dressed only in her slip. She is hurrying to go to the movies with Mrs. Lee, but also eager to draw Len's attention:

MARY.

'Ope yer don't mind me like this.

LEN.

You kiddin'?

(96-97)

Len offers his assistance, polishing her shoes while she pulls on her stockings. Afterwards, she asks him to stitch a run in her stockings while she has them on. The meeting is fraught with unspoken tension and sexual innuendo.

While Len is polishing her shoes, Mary complains to him about Pam's wayward character.

MARY.

She's not tellin' me 'ow t'run my 'ouse. [2]

She pulls on her stockings.

LEN.

O. [2] (*Holds up her shoes.*) Do yer? [1]

MARY.

Very nice. Juss go over the backs dear. I like t' feel nice be'ind. [1] I tol' 'er there's enough t'put up with without lookin' for trouble. [2, 3]

LEN.

Better? [1]

MARY.

Yes. [1] I 'ad enough a that pair last time. [3]

She steps into one shoe.

We're only goin' for the big film. [4] She can do what she likes outside. [2]

LEN (GIVES HER THE OTHER SHOE).

Thass yer lot. [1]

MARY.

'E wants lockin' up for life. [3] Ta, dear. [1] I don't expect yer t'understand at your age, but things don't turn out too bad. There's always someone worse off in the world. [5]

LEN (CLEARING UP THE POLISHING THINGS).

Yer can always be that one. [5]

MARY.

She's my own flesh an' blood, but she don't take after me. Not a thought in 'er 'ead. [2] She's 'ad a rough time a it. I feel sorry for 'er about the kid—[3]

LEN.

One a them things. Yer can't make too much a it. [5]

MARY.

Never 'ave 'appened if she'd a look after it right. [2, 3] Yer done a lovely job on these. [1] What yer doin' t'night? [6]

(9.98)

In the "collected plays" edition, this exchange takes about twenty-three short lines out of the thirty-four on the page. The dialogue is dense and in its layered allusiveness switches back and forth between six "levels," roughly defined as follows:

[1] Deictic references to the act of polishing the shoes.

[2] Topic discussion: Pam and What's Wrong With Her.

[3] Topic discussion: Fred and the Child Murder.

[4] Topic discussion: Mary's Planned Outing with Mrs. Lee.

[5] Topic discussion: Life and What It's All About.

[6] Topic discussion: Len's Personal Life.

By constantly returning to level [1], Mary and Len keep the other levels of their exchange implicit. Among these levels are Mary's complaints about her daughter [2]. Len acknowledges the first with a brief exclamation, "O," after which he returns to [1] without expressing an opinion. The next couple of exchanges follow a similar pattern: as the topic shifts from [2] to [3] to [4], Len and Mary keep returning to level [1], thus maintaining mutual agreement and trust.

In the next movement, level [5] plays a role similar to level [1] in that it frames the troublesome levels [2] and [3]. Mary's philosophic platitudes about "Life" are not just meant to sustain the flow of conversation; they allow Len to react generally to specific complaints. But what these complaints or accusations might be is not quite clear, since Mary unsays much of what she says, formulating her statements on levels [2] and [3] so that they cancel each other out. "She's my own flesh an' blood" is a mother's way of standing by her daughter. "[S]he don't take after me" reverses that implication. "Not a thought in 'er 'ead" similarly implies condemnation. "She's 'ad a rough time a it" and "I feel sorry for 'er about the kid" soften the blow. As it is not clear what Mary thinks of her daughter and the child's death, Len wisely keeps to level [5] with his vapid reply, "One a them things. Yer can't make too much of it." Level [5], like level [1], allows Mary and Len to gloss over the implications of what is being discussed.

This is not to say that the sum total of this brief exchange is zero—that nothing is being communicated. Level [5] is not altogether neutral; it offers a way of expressing coded opinions for which neither Len nor Mary need to take responsibility. When Mary declares, "There's always someone worse off in the world," Len answers, "yer can always be that one." This ironic rejoinder functions as a good-humored corrective on Mary's unthinking optimism. "Yer," however, is a usefully vague referent that might hide someone specific—Pam, obviously, but also others if the context for the line is extended beyond the present exchange.

Bond's layering technique involves not only line but also scene arrangement. *Saved* consists of thirteen juxtaposed scenes, not subdivided into acts. Leaving the sovereignty of each scene intact prompts extensive and complex cross-referencing not hindered or influenced by act divisions. Embedded in contexts derived from scenes 8 and 11, for instance, the quoted snippet of dialogue assumes different implications. Previous scenes show Len carrying Mary's shopping bags or Mary preparing Len's food and keeping it hot while he procrastinates. Apparently, a mutual sympathy exists between these two that need not be expressed in words. Lately, this understanding can no longer be taken for granted. Len has a chameleon-like ability to adapt himself to his immediate surroundings, sympathizing with whomever he's dealing with. With Mary, he becomes a housewife, taking on a woman's chores. With Harry, he talks manly talk, joining the battle of the sexes on the side of frustrated and humiliated men. In scene 8, he advises Harry to withhold his weekly wages from Mary. And now that Pam needs his room for Fred, he worries about his position in the household. "She said somethin' about my room?" "I ain' worried," he adds, hiding his embarrassment (97-98). Given this context, Len could well be the one "worse off" in the household, on the point of being expelled because he failed to keep his allegiances uncrossed.

Yet another context can be made to bear on the scene, offering a different view of who is the loser. Mary usually attacks Pam for strutting about in her undergarments, so when she does the same, she is being consciously provocative. But for whom is this erotic display meant? For Len, the surrogate son who, when she leaves, masturbates himself out of an Oedipal trap—or for her unseen husband? In scene 11, it appears that Mary knew her husband Harry was listening in at the door: "I'd a bet my life you'd come in!" (119). Mary's, then, was a staged performance, to trick, enrage, and humiliate a suspicious husband who refuses to sleep with her—to show he's the one "worse off." But by refusing to break the habitual silence, Harry deprives Mary of the satisfaction of knowing whether she has scored a point. If he does not understand he has been set up, he might think he has caught his wife in a pathetic attempt to seduce a man young enough to be her son. This is why in scene 11 Mary is the first to blink in her long-lasting staring contest with Harry. She breaks their long silence, and a little later also a teapot over his head, with the declaration, "some minds want boilin' in carbolic. Soap's too good for 'em" (117).

THE STRINDBERG PARADIGM

Osborne once said that, "Drama rests on the *dynamic* that is created *between* characters on the stage."[8] But for those who have to write about drama, the concreteness of interaction is hard to grasp and even harder to paraphrase. Because in *Saved* each exchange is constructed as a series of tactical moves that not only reflect upon one another, but also reverberate in multiple ways through the rest of the play, meaning remains dynamic. Theatre practitioners, trained to explore the riches of subtext in a beat-by-beat analysis, find it easier to come to grips with meaning as living gestalt than theatre critics who tend to construct summary overviews with concepts such as character, plot and theme borrowed from fictional narrative.

Critics can hardly be faulted for following Bond's lead in writing about Len and Pam individually, without considering them as mutually defining. Malcolm Hay and Philip Roberts confirm Bond's optimistic view of his protagonist, claiming, "Len does what he does against his own interest" (47). Always on the lookout for unambiguous polarities, male reviewers of the period seized upon Pam's apparently unreasonable and unprovoked attacks on Len for calling her "a blond little layabout" and a "grade-A bitch who, having got

what she wanted from the boy, turns on him with utter savagery and pours scorn and derision on his doggily devoted head" (Lambert). Since then, acquiescing into a too facile verdict, some feminist critics have neglected the power mechanism of the play and have berated it for its "gender-bias," expressed, ironically, in the portrayal of a nurturing man and a heartless woman (Wandor 61).

However, as Bond's naturalistic family play, *Saved* is influenced not so much by Brecht (who is invariably mentioned in studies of Bond) as by Strindberg—especially by the latter's handling of dramatic economy.[9] Strindberg's conviction that drama ought to be more than a Biblia Pauperum—a fable in pictures for those unable or unwilling to read—resulted in plays that favor interaction over story (Strindberg 90). In a vision only partially realized in his plays, Strindberg conceived of a theater in which each character would be inextricably tied to the others and therefore never able to fully dominate the interaction. This produced a unique vision of the relationship between character and dialogue: "I have avoided the symmetrical, mathematically constructed dialogue of the type favored in France, and have allowed [my characters'] minds to work irregularly, as people's do in real life, when, in conversation, no subject is fully exhausted, but one mind discovers in another a cog which it has a chance to engage" (Author's Preface 95). And thus arose the image of the family as a hellish piece of machinery that makes people speak and behave in ways they would never have freely chosen. As Strindberg put it, "These are my children! Each one by himself is good, but all you have to do to turn them into demons is to bring them together"[10]—an insight that anticipated Jean-Paul Sartre's "l'enfer c'est les Autres" ("hell is other people") in *No Exit* (*Huis Clos*). Accordingly, when Strindberg in his naturalistic plays described unhappy marital relationships, he did so in a way that largely absolved its participants from individual guilt.

Alternating viewpoints, Strindberg believed, are mutually defining and, together, produce a chord—that is, a sound that transcends and thus markedly differs from its individual components.[11] This dyad then communicates itself to other, initially independent, sounds, such as that, in *The Dance of Death,* of the rational Kurt who soon finds himself unable to rise above the insanity of the Captain's household. As the Captain puts it, "everyone who comes in contact with us, becomes tainted" (74). This vision correlates with theoretical speculations of the late nineteenth century—particularly those on the "folie à deux" or "folie à plusieurs," known under different names at least since the seventeenth century before Lasègue and Falret's published account of the syndrome in 1877. Enoch and Trethowan, in *Uncommon Psychiatric Syndromes,* define it as a form of insanity that communicates itself from one person to another (or to several), much as a string may vibrate with a sound emitted by another close by (184). Strindberg was much interested in the new science of electricity, which he identified as the "life force." That force could be drained or augmented through hypnosis ("animal magnetism") or, in more occult terms, through emotional vampirism. All these theories assume the primacy not of character but of energy exchange within a closed economy. For dramatic dialogue, the consequences of this assumption are considerable. If character precedes dialogue, then the latter illustrates the former. But if dialogue (and more broadly speaking, interaction) becomes the focus of the dramatic representation, then character comes into being as an evolving potential, its influence waxing and waning from moment to moment, as it is determined inter-dynamically, through relations with other characters.

Bond did not have to fall back on occult theories of the life force when he wrote *Saved.* Available to him was the vision of the family as a servo-mechanism, a homeostatic feedback machine. It was then gaining popularity in Britain, especially through the work of R. D. Laing who, in a psychiatry influenced by cybernetics, described the powerful self-regulating processes that perpetuate the "steady state" of family interactions, even if these are making individual members unhappy or insane. The family then is a system ingeniously constructed to counteract change, until it is forced to recalibrate—that is, until it settles around a new equilibrium. Political analogies made this assumption particularly meaningful, from the return of Conservatism in Britain (which demonstrated that the changes wrought by socialism after the war had not been "systemic") to the dangerous international stalemate produced by the Cold War.

Bond accordingly conceived of the family as a closed economy in which nothing is lost but everything "saved"—in which every attempt at change is absorbed back into the system until it recalibrates. The layering of dialogue, its intricate interconnectedness, conforms to this vision. Any critical paraphrase of the play should be sensitive to this inextricable interrelatedness, the strategic use of language, the reciprocal or complementary relationship between characters—and all this within a systemic vision of the family. The existential has to be made congruent with the functional, as *Saved* is a story not about people but about the system to which they belong. And whatever political implications the play may have will have to follow from that premise.

The Family System

Imagine a "family system" that, before Len's arrival, found itself in a state of equilibrium, the origin of which can be traced back to a tragic event and a violent recalibration of relationships. The death of Harry and Mary's first born has left a vacuum that threatens to swallow the family that was built around it. A perpetual violence now compensates for the drainage of signification that the child's death has provoked. For all these years, an atmosphere of constant conflict has united this family, at great cost to the individual happiness of its members. The conflict is all consuming: the outside world has become virtually irrelevant, and the family has become the only source of signification. To rage against the family while contributing indirectly towards its preservation and continuation is the pattern that marks each character's behavior.

With passing years, the conflict has become increasingly abstract, feeding mainly on itself. Two contradictory impulses perpetuate it, created by the simultaneous application of two mutually exclusive rules. One is expressed in the defiant outcry (twice repeated in the play) that "two can play at that game" (Pam, at 89; Harry, at 119) and the other, by the smug "there's always someone worse off" (Mary, at 98). When the family wheel comes to a halt, signifying a certain configuration of forces, the one who is "worse off" sets it going again by denying the other his or her victory. "It's got a stop! It ain' worth it! Juss round an' round," Pam at one moment cries in despair (93).

But how could it stop? To end the game from within would be possible only if stasis and dynamism ceased to be mutually exclusive—if, in other words, polarity of hierarchy could be established within reciprocity of behavior. By occupying the empty space at the center of that universe, a participant in this game legitimizes an increasingly abstract conflict by anchoring it in reality and (since this conflict is the only generator of significance in this system) once again puts off that moment of revelation, when, burdened with the weight of accumulated years, each will be crushed by the triviality of a wasted existence. But to be at the center is also to experience immediately the paradox of this position, that one can only be the center by virtue of the circumference. Triumph and despair, in that case, are two sides of the same coin.

Harry, for instance, has preserved a rigorous silence for many years. In a true feat of discipline, he has tried to establish a sovereign, self-sustaining existence in the house. Sitting in his chair in the darkness, eating the meals he prepares for himself, washing and ironing his own clothes, he signals his self-sufficiency and independence, especially to Mary, whom he hopes to deprive of her need to feel central in this household. Apparently in search of his football coupons, Harry silently moves in and out of rooms, catching others in compromising situations, impressing upon them his vigilant presence before disappearing. Withholding his judgment, he trusts, will add voice to his silence. And he may also hope that the skill with which he irons his shirts will not be lost on Mary. To withhold sexual attention from his wife, whom, as he tells Len, he could make squeal "like a pig," is then one more way of reminding her of his inexorable presence, his angry refusal, and her dependence (127). The message of this sexual abstention, when Harry finally puts it in words during a quarrel, is simple enough: "I can do without! Yer ain' worth it!" (119).

How others perceive him is, however, beyond Harry's control. Occupying himself with traditionally feminine occupations and preserving an image of sexual abstinence, Harry's behavior could be suspicious in the eyes of another man. So to protect his masculinity, Harry unfolds to Len the sustaining myth of army life. Shooting a man from close by in the war, Harry saw him tumble down "like a coat fallin' off a 'anger." With this act, Harry became "one a the lucky ones" whom the war has endowed with a "sense a perspective," which apparently denotes the ability to see the world strictly from your own perspective and to refuse empathy (128). It is also thanks to his army experience that Harry can take care of his own needs. Having bandaged his head after a particularly violent quarrel, Harry can proudly say: "I managed. I never arst them" (128). "Them" are Mary and Pam, or the women in general, from whose skirts a man is weaned in the army.

Like the romantic who can savor his solitude only when it is publicly recognized, Harry's self-sufficiency is a message to his family that needs to be received and understood the way it is intended. His secret fear is that his eloquent silence will fall on deaf ears, that his show of independence will be disregarded, that his self-denial will merely allow others to deny him. When he barges into rooms, who can say whether he is confronting others with the wickedness of their deeds or whether others are confronting him with the wickedness of his thoughts? Harry, in other words, is more than ever dependent on the power of the other family members to withhold or grant recognition of the self-image he proffers.

Mary depends in a similar way on the others for acceptance of her self-image of centrality and indispensability. She runs the household in an ineffectual yet conspicuous way, constantly complaining in order to draw attention to her efforts. Harry's silence and show of independence are meant to deprive her of an important source of recognition. In contrast to Harry, she reminds others of her presence by her vociferousness, calling from up or down the stairwell to people in other rooms. In accordance with the first family rule, Pam reciprocates this behavior by constantly calling out to her mother; and, in accordance with the competitive rule that enforces a polarity, both women turn a deaf ear to each other's shouting:

PAM (*CALLS*).

    Mum!—She can' 'ear.

    (*Calls.*) You 'eard!

HARRY.

    Put the wood in the 'ole.

LEN.

    I'd like t' 'ear what they're sayin' next door.

PAM.

    Let 'em say!

LEN.

    'Ole bloody neighbour'ood must know!

PAM.

    Good—let 'em know what you're like!

LEN.

    'Oo wen' on about pride?

PAM (*CALLS THROUGH DOOR.*)

    I know yer can 'ear.

MARY (*OFF*).

    You callin' Pam?

PAM (*TO* LEN).

    One thing, anythin' else goes wrong I'll know 'oo t' blame.

MARY (*OFF*).

    Pam!

PAM.

    Let 'er wait.

MARY (*OFF*).

    Pam!

(95)

In the same way as loudness is followed by loudness that is then countered with imperviousness, silence evokes silence whose message is surreptitiously denied. Mary matches Harry's silence with an equally stubborn muteness. Each of the partners then denies the other the satisfaction of monitoring how that behavior affects him or her. A curious warfare results that Bond marvelously captures in his stage directions.

The living room. Dark.

The door opens. MARY *comes in. She puts on the light.* HARRY *is sitting in the armchair. He is partly asleep.* MARY *puts sauce, salt and pepper on the table and goes out.* HARRY *gets up. He goes to the door and puts the light out. He goes back to the armchair.*

Pause.

The door opens. MARY *comes in. She puts on the light.*

(44)

The living-room.

On the table: bread, butter, breadknife, cup and saucer and milk.

MARY *sits on the couch.*

HARRY *comes in with a pot of tea. He goes to the table. He cuts and butters bread. Pause while he works.* MARY *goes out.* HARRY *goes on working.* MARY *comes back with a cup and saucer. She pours herself tea. She takes it to the couch and sits. She sips.*

HARRY *moves so that his back is to her. He puts his cup upright in his saucer. He puts milk in the cup. He reaches to pick up the teapot.*

MARY *stands, goes to the table, and moves the teapot out of his reach. She goes back to the couch. Sits. Sips.*

(117)

Such efforts to pay the other back in the same coin and then to deny each other a response strengthen the family ties into confining shackles. This is a far cry from the mutual alienation that accompanies the routine existence of partners who quietly pay tribute to the obligations of married life. The more Harry and Mary deny each other's presence, the more they are made aware of it. No presence is better recognized than by vigorous efforts to deny it recognition.

The relationship between Pam and Len is not less complex. Len has usurped Pam's position in the household. And Pam is desperate because Len's "goodness" makes her anger at him seem unreasonable. Pam felt indispensable as long as she mediated between parents who no longer acknowledge each other. She talks to both Harry and Mary but wishes not merely to mediate but to be at the center, instead of on the periphery, of the contention into which she was born. By being an object of desire at home, spied upon by her father, who, in his turn, can at any moment be caught in this act by the mother, Pam has, so far, been able to oust the dead brother from the center of this long lasting storm.

Pam's sexuality, which she displays proudly and provocatively, plays a pivotal role in the family dynamics. By conspicuously introducing her lovers into the family, she impresses her sexual powers on the others. In turn, the fact that Pam allows herself to be spied upon gives Harry the opportunity to compensate for his sexual abstention vicariously and incestuously. At the same time, however, it undermines Harry's act, allowing Mary to accuse Harry of having a "dirty mind": "Yer bin sniffin' round ever since! I ain' puttin' up with your dirt!" (119). Finally, as nobody is allowed the top

position in this household, Mary and Harry blame Pam. "That'll teach you t'bring fellas back," Mary taunts Pam, referring to Len's refusal to leave the house (49). And Harry sums up his regard for his daughter with the words, "Er sort's two a penny" (124). So, the behavior that allows Pam to imagine she is responsible for setting her parents up against each other in silent battle also keeps them together, on the one hand by compensating for Harry's sexual refusal of his wife and, on the other hand, by allowing the latter to rationalize the former's stance of self-sufficiency. And the behavior that allows Pam to imagine her centrality and superiority in this household is also what others can most easily deprecate, turning her into an object of ridicule or contempt. None of the behaviors of any of the family members will lead to change. The system, in brief, is in a state of dynamic equilibrium.

THE HOMEOSTATIC DRIVE

This family then is a perfect machine whose dynamics creates the power field that drives it. At the center of that perfect machine, at the heart of its balanced centripetal and centrifugal forces is a hollow, an absence, a space once occupied by a prime mover that now has become the absent cause of this configuration. That prime mover was the child, a "miserable creature," according to Jean-Paul Sartre, that is compelled to be "his own grandfather" because "[l]ong before our birth, even before we are conceived, parents have decided who we will be. They have called us 'he' years before we could say 'I'" (14). The newly born is an "absolute object," an empty signifier, a receptacle for each one's unfulfilled desires and thus both a generator and an absorber of significations until it assumes an identity of its own through the Oedipal struggle. When the child dies, this particular family coils upon itself, becoming an ingenious machine that through self-sustained conflict generates and reabsorbs the signification that its constituting elements crave. When a foreign factor is introduced into its system, internal forces are adjusted in a noisy process of recalibration. Once homeostasis is restored, the only sound of this self-enclosed, signifying machine is that of a violent silence.

Ambivalence of signification is the primary means by which homeostasis is preserved. Both times that Harry suddenly enters a room, he is disappointed in his expectation that he is going to witness some lurid scene. In both cases, Harry is listening at the door and enters after being seduced by what he hears. Yet in both cases, Len has a premonition that someone is listening in at the door and purposely exploits the situation. Being too nervous to continue the lovemaking after Harry has entered a first time, Len, in scene one, decides to "give 'im a thrill" and while feeding Pam "choclits" capitalizes on the double-entendres that this activity allows for.

LEN.

> Come on, there's plenty more where that come from.

> *He puts a sweet in her mouth.*

PAM (*SPLUTTERS*).

> Can't take no more!

LEN.

> Yeh—open it. Yer can do a bit more!

PAM.

> Ow!

LEN.

> Oorr lovely!

> *He tickles her. She chokes.*

> This'll put 'airs on yer chest!

(28)

Scene 9 sets up a similar situation. Len is darning a run in Mary's stocking, and Harry enters after hearing such phrases as "I'll 'ave t' get me 'and inside" and "I'll juss give it a little stretch" (102). In scene 12, Len, who is supposed to leave the house at dinnertime, is in his bedroom listening through a crack in the floor at the sounds coming from Pam's room below. With Harry, who has just entered to convince Len to stay, he discusses the meaning of the sounds. Len thinks that Pam is making love to someone she picked up from the street, whereas Harry tries to persuade him that the young woman, who in the previous scene threatened to kill herself, is, in fact, "'owlin' in bed." Action is successfully suspended by this constant insecurity as to the correct interpretation of signs, whose meaning, once decided on, seems so easily to turn into its opposite.

Ambivalent signs can be resolved when characters discuss them. But systems with a strong homeostatic drive lack effective metacommunication.[12] In this family, spying has taken the place of discussion, avoided since the child's death. So, Harry can say to Len, "we don't 'ave secrets. They make trouble" and follow this up with the warning "don't speak to 'em at all. It saved a lot of misunderstandin'" (130). This contradiction has become acceptable in the family and contributes to the preservation of the status quo. The apparent metacommunication that Harry here engages in with Len does not amount to a breaking of the rule, for it is used to prevent Len from leaving, and Harry has no intention of turning it into a habit:

LEN.

> Funny we never talked before.

HARRY.

> They listen all the time.

LEN.

> Will yer come up next Saturday night?

HARRY.

> No, no. Cause trouble. They won't stand for it.

(130)

The addition of Len as a new member in the system does not change its fundamental principles. What Bond refers to as Len's "goodness" and what may now be termed his adaptability allows his absorption into this system. Far from going against his own interests by staying in this troubled household, Len, like the other members of this family, is able to thrive vampirically on its internal tensions. Always watching and listening, he is constantly feeding his fantasy. He encourages Harry to talk about Mary's sexual performance during the early years of their marriage in the same persistent way that he wheedles stories of sexual conquests out of Fred (127). Flirting with Mary, he tells her that he can no longer be bothered with running after girls. When she leaves, he takes out his handkerchief, ready to masturbate his way out of Oedipal conflict (103). And while Fred and his gang torture and kill the baby in the park, Len stands behind a tree and watches. Later when Fred is let out of prison, Len asks him how it felt to kill the baby. Listening with Harry to the sounds coming from Pam's room, Len confides to Harry how he used to overhear her lovemaking with Fred, adding, "I'd like t'tell 'er t'jump off once more." The scene ends with the two men raptly listening.

HARRY.

> Listen!

LEN.

> What?

> HARRY *holds up his hand. Silence.*

> Still cryin'?

HARRY.

> She's gone quiet.

> *Silence.*

> There—she's movin'.

> *Silence.*

LEN.

> She's 'eard us.

HARRY.

> Best keep away, yer see. Good night.

LEN.

But—

HARRY.

Sh!

He holds up his hand again. They listen. Silence.

Pause.

HARRY.

Good night.

LEN.

'Night.

HARRY *goes.*

(130-31)

This nearly caricatured representation of eavesdropping applies not only to the men in this household but also to the whole family. "They listen all the time," says Harry in a warning that throws a different light on Mary's kind insistence, in scene 9, that Len bring up girls to his room (99). It is clear that when Len, like the other members of this family, endures, it is not out of patience but out of need.

POLITICAL IMPLICATIONS

Whereas an argument may falter, a well-chosen sound or gesture can function as a rhetorical flourish, capping off a play with a finality that one hardly dares to question. With a slamming door, Nora of Ibsen's *A Doll House* (1879) sets out on her new life. With this resounding thud, Ibsen closed the lid on that play and on questions regarding the plausibility of Nora's transformation that allows her to talk so assertively to her baffled husband. Or spectators might remember that Nora is exchanging Torvald's gentle tyranny for a far more uncertain fate. As hard as that door may have slammed behind Nora, it did not shut out the ideal of bourgeois domestic happiness. Nora leaves because she thinks marriage should be a "communion" between husband and wife, based on equality and mutual respect. So, in fact, with the slam of that door, the ideal of domesticity is given a new lease.

That lease was apparently up for renewal with Bond's *Saved,* which, in the playwright's words, is "almost irresponsibly optimistic." He too tried to press this point home not by argument, but by a striking final image, that of Len mending a chair broken in a family quarrel. Not surprisingly, spectators were more impressed by the horrifying scene in the middle of the play. It is hard to expect that the second image can outdo the emotional impact of the first, even if we learn to "clutch at straws," as Bond advises us to do ("On Violence" 309).

Bond says in his preface that people are "innately good," that they are endowed with a biological propensity for caring. Certain economic and social conditions, however, create in individuals alienation from self and others. The resulting violence is then not based on sadism but rather on insensitivity to the existential reality of others. "Violence is not an instinct we must forever repress because it threatens civilized social relationships," he says. "We are violent because we have not yet made those relationships civilized" ("Author's Note: On Violence" 12). His purpose with *Saved* is to show the violence created by capitalist relations of production and to point simultaneously to the innate human potential for goodness on which his socialist thinking depends.

As a socialist playwright, Bond does not want his audience to react fatalistically. He refers to the violence in his plays as an "aggro-effect" that is meant to shake an increasingly blasé audience into awareness. The promise of the essential goodness of human beings embodied by Len signals to the audience that the negativity evoked by the scene of extreme violence should not be born with resignation, but that it can and should be overcome. The question then is whether Len's goodness presents an alternative to the violence of the play or whether it is part of the mechanism that produces it. Here lies the problem. In this play, violence and goodness are two sides of the same coin and perpetuate the status quo. "Give me somewhere to stand, and I will move the earth," Archimedes reportedly said. Len's "goodness," however, is not sufficiently extraneous to that pernicious dynamism of violence to serve as the leverage that will finally unhinge it.

In *Saved,* Bond creates a systemic view of a family in which each member is victimized by the rules of the interaction he or she helps to create. Mary and Harry illustrate the extraordinary durability of unhappy relationships. If any of these characters thinks of imitating Nora's gesture by slamming the door and leaving, it is only as a strategic move in a neverending game of mutual contention. Alison, in *Look Back in Anger,* walks out on Jimmy, but not without leaving a letter expressing her "deep loving need" for him. And Jimmy cries out, "She couldn't say, 'You rotten bastard! I hate your guts, I'm clearing out, and I hope you rot!' No, she has to make a polite, emotional mess out of it!" (71). Harry too once left the family but returned because his exit failed to have the desired effect on Mary. The struggle, which at first is undertaken for the maintenance of the self against the forces of sociality, has become the necessary condition of that self. When Len at the end of the play reluctantly packs his suitcases, Harry advises him to stay: "Don't go. No point. . . . Yer'd come back," he tells him (128). Now sixty-eight years old,

Harry still dreams of the right moment when he will be able to leave in triumph, impressing upon the other his indispensability: "Yer'll see. If I was t'go now she'd be laughin'. She'd soon 'ave someone in my bed. She knows 'ow t' be'ave when she likes. An' cook. . . . I'll go when I'm ready. When she's on 'er pension. She won't get no one after 'er then. I'll be *out*. Then see 'ow she copes" (129).

At the end of the play, all members of this family are as deeply entrenched as ever. After a violent quarrel during which Mary and Harry have broken the silence, the "rough patch" of Len's presence in the household has been smoothed away. Len is now mending the chair. Mary and Pam are sitting on the couch. Harry is filling in his football coupon. Len, concentrating on his work, breaks the general silence by asking for a hammer. But no one pays attention, and silence resumes. The leg of the chair is back in its socket, and Len fiddles with it until the chair no longer wobbles. It is clear that nothing has changed. The family monster has merely rattled its chains; the frantic status quo will resume.

Bond's portrayal of the family corresponds with the counter culture's view of the family not as a ship tossed about violently on waves of social and moral upheaval, as in Shaw's *Heartbreak House* (1920), but as the incarnation or, according to some, the source of the fundamental paradoxes that characterize late capitalism. "Far from being the basis of the good society, the family, with its narrow privacy and tawdry secrets, is the source of all our discontents," said Edmund Leach in 1969, in a much discussed series of BBC talks on postwar society (44).[13] And in a similar series of radio talks entitled *The Politics of the Family* (1971), R. D. Laing compared the family to a homeostatic machine that quells individual, creative, or emancipating impulses. In the three decades after the war, an oppressive and malicious domesticity became a metaphor for late capitalist society that similarly thrives on mental and physical suffering thanks to an immobilizing complicity that turns each individual simultaneously into victimizer and victim.

In *Saved,* Bond offers a technically intricate and dramatically powerful representation of the workings of the family machine, based on the assumption that interactions constitute an autonomous system that thrives on individual unhappiness and acts of rebellion. When critics pointed out the fatalism of this vision, Bond accused them of lack of faith: "to the people in the play their situation appears completely without hope, but as an observer I did not give up all hope" (*Notebooks* 92). This hope for change was to be found in the prose supplements, reasoned from premises and assumptions

not shared by the play. This points to a paradox that Fredric Jameson, in a discussion of Foucault's similar vision of systemic perfection, formulates as follows:

> Insofar as the theorist wins . . . by constructing an increasingly closed and terrifying machine, to that very degree he loses, since the critical capacity of his work is thereby paralyzed, and the impulses of negation and revolt, not to speak of those of social transformation, are increasingly perceived as vain and trivial in the face of the model itself.
>
> (57)

The more sociologists and anti-psychiatrists probed into this intricately balanced complex of powers to find always more proof of the internal contradictoriness of "the system," the more they actually smoothed it out, eliminated its "rough patches" and its "wobbles," so that it became notoriously difficult for them to graft their utopian dreams on such a perfectly self-contained universe. "We can say that the rationality of the society lies in its very insanity, and that the insanity of the society is rational to the degree it is efficient," Herbert Marcuse conceded (180-81).

The richly interactive psychology of *Saved* demonstrates that Bond, like the theorists of the counter culture, assumed the interrelatedness of human behavior. Like them, he is unable to solve the problem of change within that same paradigm. Instead, he reverts in his prefaces to a subject-oriented, linear and exclusionary nineteenth-century rationalism and opts for a simplified subject psychology in whose terms Len's ambiguous behavior merely results from the richness of his existential reality (Bond, "Author's Note to *Saved*" 309). As a result, Bond's prefaces veil the mystifications his play is constantly on the point of unveiling. Perhaps this is also why the critical response to this play is often limited to remarks about how the play's language exemplifies modern society's brutalization of individuals, without dealing with the more intriguing contradiction between the family's apparent dynamic of vicious and brutal quarrels and its powerful tendency towards homeostasis.

CONCLUSION

Now more than forty years old, *Saved* shows that Bond, alongside Harold Pinter, was an early pioneer in a development that can be traced back to August Strindberg and is still being perfected today by such playwrights as Edward Albee, David Mamet, and Neil LaBute. It could be called the drama of entrapment: it presents characters as imprisoned by the rules of their relationship and links the resulting inhibition of action to seemingly irrational acts of violence.[14] Has Bond left us a straw to clutch at? At the end of the play, over and above that image of Len mending the chair, is the lasting memory of the gang of young men leering into the stroller, commenting cruelly on the child's contortions as it is spit upon, pulled by its hair, punched in its face, covered in its own excrement and vomit. As Bond explains in his preface, social conditions of alienation have reduced these men to a pre-human state of being and thus estranged them from their potential for empathy. Such an explanation, however, is nothing but a handy label stuck to a hard problem. Like the family members in this play, the young men have in fact become cogs in a larger system of which each one is both the mover and the moved. It is, as Sartre calls it, an "anxious and overzealous indifference" that unites them as they hurl stones in the stroller at close range (28). The strange humming noise they make upon leaving their victim is that of the smoothly spinning, inexorable, and all pervasive system that with equal facility has swallowed Bond's too easy rationalizations.

Notes

1. Plays featuring characters that are trying to get into a room or fear being thrown out of one are common at that time. Harold Pinter created a new theatrical idiom around this very subject, as in *The Room* (1957) and *The Caretaker* (1960), for instance.

2. As, for instance, Tennessee Williams's *A Streetcar Named Desire* (1947), John Osborne's *Look Back in Anger* (1956), Edward Albee's *Who's Afraid of Virginia Woolf* (1962), Harold Pinter's *The Homecoming* (1965), etc.

3. When the play was first produced, its portrayal of child murder was the subject of animated discussions and demonstrations. According to John Russell Taylor, "About two critics liked it, the rest hated it with quite extraordinary vehemence, and before we knew where we were it had spawned letters to the papers, television controversy, and even a Sunday-night teach-in presided over by Kenneth Tynan" (108-09). Despite having been warned about the play's graphic nature, many were unable to look beyond the violence—and often reacted violently in return. For daring to write a balanced review of the play, Penelope Gilliatt received in her mail a photograph of her child (her daughter with John Osborne) with its head cut off and painted red (16). Whatever *Saved* had to say about contemporary society, people seemed to have a hard time hearing it.

4. "Author's Note to *Saved*" (1966) and "Author's Note: On Violence" (1977), both published in the first volume of Bond's *Collected Plays*.

5. In the original text, only "treat" is italicized.

6. Arnold Wesker's *Chicken Soup with Barley, Roots*, and *I'm Talking about Jerusalem*.

7. Review of Bond's *Saved*, "Our Drama Critic," *The Times* 4 Nov. 1965 (rpt. in Lloyd Evans 136); Hirst 48; Durbach 481.

8. Osborne's preface to an excerpt of *The Entertainer* in *Writers' Theatre*, ed. Keith Waterhouse and Willis Hall (London: Heinemann, 1967), and qtd. in Alan Carter as motto to his monograph, *John Osborne*.

9. Bond continued to examine the politics of the family in many other plays (*Lear* [1971], *Bingo* [1973], *The War Plays* [1985] and *Olly's Prison* [1993] for instance), but in later plays designed less naturalistic ways of dislodging language from character that allowed more control over the plays' political message. Because of its naturalistic representation, *Olly's Prison* is often compared to *Saved*, but Bond allows its hero, Mike, a degree of insight not granted to any of the characters in *Saved*, effectively turning him into the playwright's mouthpiece: at the end of the play he identifies the "system" as "Authority" and insists that as long as people don't "see the connections," they will continue to suffer (70).

10. Qtd. by Johnson 9. See also Margret in Strindberg's *The Father*: "But, God in heaven, must two people keep tormenting the life out of each other—two people who otherwise are so kind—and so good to everyone else!" (21).

11. This musical analogy is also made by Seltzer (ix), with different implications.

12. The standard work for this kind of systemic analysis is still Watzlawick *et al.* It is based on the work of Gregory Bateson and includes an analysis of Edward Albee's *Who's Afraid of Virginia Woolf?*

13. Also qtd. in Sinfield 61.

14. An alternative theoretical model for the drama of entrapment can be found in the theories of the French researcher Henri Laborit, as for instance in his *L'Éloge de la fuite* (*In Praise of Flight*), popularized by Alain Resnais in *Mon oncle d'Amérique* (1980).

Works Cited

Bond, Edward. "Author's Note to *Saved*" (1966). *Plays: One*. 309-312.

———. "Author's Note: On Violence." *Plays: One*. 9-17.

———. *Olly's Prison*. London: Methuen, 1993.

————. *Plays: One.* London: Eyre Methuen, 1977.

————. *Saved. Plays: One.* 21-133.

————. *Selections from the Notebooks of Edward Bond.* Volume One: 1959 to 1980. Ed. Ian Stuart. London: Methuen, 2000.

Brandt, George W., ed. *Modern Theories of Drama: A Selection of Writings on Drama and Theatre 1850-1990.* Oxford: Clarendon, 1998.

Carlson, Marvin. *Theories of the Theatre: A Historical and Critical Survey from the Greeks to the Present.* Ithaca and London: Cornell UP, 1984.

Carter, Alan. *John Osborne.* Edinburgh: Oliver & Boyd, 1969.

Durbach, Errol. "Herod in the Welfare State: *Kindermord* in the Plays of Edward Bond." *Educational Theatre Journal* 27 (1975): 480-87.

Eagleton, Terry. "Nature and Violence: The Prefaces of Edward Bond." *Critical Quarterly* 26 (1984): 127-35.

Enoch, David, and William Trethowan. *Uncommon Psychiatric Syndromes.* 3rd ed. Oxford: Butterworth-Heinemann, 1991.

Esslin, Martin. "Bond Unbound." *Plays and Players* 16.7 (1969): 51.

Gilliatt, Penelope. Rev. of *Saved. The Observer.* 14 Nov. 1965. Repr. in Roberts, *Bond on File.* 16.

Hay, Malcolm, and Philip Roberts. *Bond: A Study of his Plays.* London: Eyre Methuen, 1980.

Hirst, David L. *Edward Bond.* Macmillan Modern Dramatists. London: Macmillan, 1985.

Jameson, Fredric. "Postmodernism, or, The Cultural Logic of Late Capitalism." *New Left Review* 146 (1984): 52-92.

Johnson, Walter. Introduction. *A Dream Play.* By August Strindberg. 3-15.

Kretzmer, Herbert. *Daily Express* 4 Nov. 1965. Repr. in Roberts, *Bond on File.* 16.

Laborit, Henri. *Éloge de la fuite.* Paris: Gallimard, 1976.

Lacey, Stephen. *The New Wave in Its Context 1956-1965.* London and New York: Routledge, 1995.

Laing, R. D. *The Politics of the Family, and Other Essays.* New York: Vintage Books, 1971.

Lambert, J. W. Rev. of *Saved. Sunday Times* 7 Nov. 1965. Rpt. in Gareth and Barbara Lloyd Evans. 138.

Leach, Edmund Ronald. *A Runaway World?* London: BBC, 1968.

Lloyd Evans, Gareth. *The Language of Modern Drama.* Totowa, N.J.: Rowman and Littlefield, 1977.

Lloyd Evans, Gareth, and Barbara Lloyd Evans. *Plays in Review 1956-1980: British Drama and the Critics.* London: Batsford Academic and Educational, 1985.

Marcuse, Herbert. "Liberation from the Affluent Society." *To Free a Generation: The Dialectics of Liberation.* Ed. David Cooper. New York: Macmillan, 1969.

Müller, Kurt. "Kommunikation und Gewalt: Eine kommunikationstheoretische Analyse des Cliquenverhaltens in Edward Bond's *Saved.*" *Literature in Wissenschaft und Unterricht* 28.2 (1995): 113-29.

Neilson, Anthony. *Year of the Family.* In *Plays: One.* London: Methuen, 1998. 121-194.

Osborne, John. *Look Back in Anger. Plays: One.* London: Faber, 1996.

Pinter, Harold. "A Letter to Peter Wood" (1958). *The Kenyon Review* 3.3 (1981): 2-5.

Review of Bond's *Saved.* "Our Drama Critic." *The Times* 4 Nov. 1965. Rpt. in Evans, ed., *Plays in Review 1956-1980.* 136.

Roberts, Philip, ed. *Bond on File.* Writers on File. London and New York: Methuen, 1985.

Sartre, Jean-Paul. Foreword. *The Traitor.* By André Gorz. Trans. Richard Howard. London and New York: Verso, 1989.

————. *Huis Clos. Théâtre.* Paris: Gallimard, 1947. 114-68.

————. *No Exit. No Exit and The Flies.* Trans. Stuart Gilbert. New York: Knopf, 1976. 3-61.

Seltzer, Daniel. Introduction. *The Dance of Death.* August Strindberg. Vii-xvi.

Sinfield, Alan. *Society and Literature 1945-1970: The Context of English Literature.* New York: Holmes & Meier, 1983.

Spencer, Jenny S. *Dramatic Strategies in the Plays of Edward Bond.* Cambridge: Cambridge UP, 1992.

Strindberg, August. Author's Preface to *Miss Julie* (1888). Trans. Michael Meyer. Brandt 89-98.

————. *The Dance of Death.* Trans. Arvid Paulson. New York: Norton, 1976.

————. *A Dream Play and Four Chamber Plays.* Trans. Walter Johnson. New York: Norton, 1975.

————. *The Father. Seven Plays.* Trans. Arvid Paulson. New York: Bantam, 1960. 7-56.

Taylor, John Russell. *Anger and After: A Guide to the New British Drama.* 2nd ed. London: Methuen, 1969.

Wandor, Michelene. *Look Back in Gender: Sexuality and the Family in Post-War British Drama.* London and New York: Methuen, 1987.

Waterhouse, Keith, and Willis Hall, eds. *Writers' Theatre*. London: Heinemann, 1967.

Watzlawick, Paul, Don Jackson, and Janet Beavin. *The Pragmatics of Human Communication: A Study of Interactional Patterns, Pathologies, and Paradoxes.* New York: Norton, 1967.

LEAR (1971)

PRODUCTION REVIEWS

Benedict Nightingale (review date 8 October 1971)

SOURCE: Nightingale, Benedict. "Bond in a Cage." *New Statesman* 82, no. 2116 (8 October 1971): 485.

[*In the following review of a 1971 production of* Lear *at London's Royal Court Theatre, directed by William Gaskill, Nightingale finds the play "not . . . totally dispiriting" but contradictory in message and gratuitous in its amount of violence.*]

Pick your way over the barbed wire, sneak past the wolfhounds, and you're in the grim, turreted grange that is Edward Bond's mind. A somewhat unusual butler appears, a spotty, scowling youth, casually twirling a bicycle chain, and nods brusquely in the direction of the nearest of several noises of screaming. On you go, past a few ghosts, gibbering in the approved manner, until you meet your host, who is cheerfully disembowelling his aged parents. He invites you to join in, but doesn't seem offended when you refuse—'all the more for me, eh?' The heat is oppressive, since the radiators are set for 100 degrees, and the smell of blood inescapable, since the servants carry aerosol sprays full of the stuff; and there's nowhere you can hide. The hostess is being raped in the bathroom, the children are being cooked in the kitchen, and nanny, dressed in leather, is rampaging through the bedrooms with a machine-gun. Altogether, it is an uncomfortable way to spend an evening out.

And is Bond's reworking of the *Lear* myth any easier on a visitor? On the face of it, no. It offers all his horrors except the cannibalism of *Early Morning,* and even here there's a not unworthy substitute, in the form of the mauling of a walking skeleton by excited pigs. It also reiterates the idea that people commonly regard the chance to inflict pain as a luxurious binge. Remember the thugs' whisper—'might as well enjoy ourselves,

you don't get a chance like this every day'—as they prepared to stone the baby in *Saved*? This time we get Rosemary McHale's Goneril (or 'Fontanelle', as Bond rechristens her) bobbing about in girlish glee as a tongueless captive is beaten. 'I've always wanted to sit on a man's lungs,' she shrieks, 'Let me. Give me his lungs.' That small pleasure eludes her, and us, but there's plenty to compensate. The man's hands are crushed by a soldier, and his ears put out with knitting needles by Regan, or 'Bodice', who is played by Carmel McSharry as a glum camp commandant, staring at the audience as if measuring its skin for lampshades. Later, she's bayoneted to death, and Fontanelle shot and dissected, leaving Harry Andrews's Lear to fondle her victuals before his own eyes are painstakingly extracted. All this, and more, occurs in the first two acts, and there was some speculation in the Royal Court foyer during the second interval about what Bond could possibly be holding in reserve. The body has, after all, only a limited number of members to be lopped off or mangled. The consensus was for castration; but we had, of course, reckoned without the pigs and the gored spectre.

Is it Bosch or is it bosh? Many obviously inclined to the latter conclusion; but I must admit that the more the seats around me emptied, the more the play impressed me, albeit against many of my instincts and much of my judgment. It undeniably has something, this untidy moral melodrama, with its odd mixture of the idiomatic and the rhetorical, of *Saved* and *The White Devil*; its Shakespearean ghosts, Brechtian soldiery and scurvily Bondish politicians. The old tyrant, Lear, spends his land's wealth and enslaves his population building an enormous wall which will ensure peace and safety within; the daughters marry his enemies outside, and conquer him; they're defeated by a 'popular' uprising, which seeks to secure itself by rebuilding the wall and terrorising the people in the same old way; and it's clear that this regime, too, is doomed. Nothing alters, not the paranoia of the rulers, nor the dissatisfaction of the ruled, nor the intensity of their mutual violence. So it will go on.

The play's horrors, then, have their perhaps overemphatic place in plot and theme: they also, you feel, reflect authentic pain and anger.

> How do most men live? They're hungry and no one
> feeds them, so they call for help and no one comes.
> And when their hunger's worse, they scream—and
> jackals and wolves come to tear them to pieces.

That's the voice of Bond's Lear, and the tone of amazed, affronted discovery is very characteristic of his author. Bond recreates in sweeping social terms the disgust and guilt of the small child who suddenly realises that the meat he's eating was the lamb he watched prancing with its mother. He displays that kind of innocence himself, and demands it of us too. How dare we take human evil for granted? If a Robin Redbreast in a cage puts all heaven in a rage, as one of his philosophical progenitors suggested, how much more should humanity be appalled by its own self-inflicted torments? 'Cage' is actually a recurring image in *Lear,* and the interdependence of creation a recurring idea. When one suffers, all should find his suffering intolerable. To respond otherwise is to be less than fully human. But then, as Bond also insists, very few of us are even halfway human. We are born good, but are (at best) crippled and (at worst) brutalised by circumstances. 'Society,' finally, is the enemy.

It scarcely needs pointing out that there's contradiction in his philosophy and dramatic practice alike. What's the origin of all this evil? If men are so fundamentally pure, society cannot be so impure; if society is so impure, men cannot be so pure. Again, assuming men have been so corrupted as actually to enjoy violence, isn't it dangerous to present such excesses of it onstage, and naïve to expect (as Bond evidently does) the average audience to react against them? We ought properly to be salivating and strangling one another in the stalls, with tiny cries of delight. Or is the corruption of Royal Court audiences for some reason that lesser sort, which sits back and watches, and perpetuates evil by tolerating it? Presumably. But in that case isn't it equally naïve to suppose that you can easily bludgeon so hardened an audience into fresh awareness of the reality of evil? The blunt, direct approach numbs some and makes others avert their eyes. In one way or another most of us defend ourselves against it, as we do against graphic ads for Oxfam, or television shots of dying East Pakistanis or executed Nigerians, or anything horrible and insistent. How our contemporary dramatists are to penetrate these defences, quite what form they can effectively find for the anguish many of them feel isn't for me to say. It is a formidable challenge to the imagination. But it's surely an error to presume that the multiplication of very literal horrors will do the job.

Fortunately, the quality of Bond's own anguish is more impressive than its quantity. At any rate *Lear* should put paid to the belief, held by me among others, that he's a cold writer, more actuated by rage than compassion. True, one of his objects in borrowing his raw material seems to be to accuse Shakespeare of sentimentality. His equivalents of Kent, Gloucester, Edgar and Cordelia are either non-existent or much nastier: he writes with indiscriminate dislike of those with any status or power, including his protagonist. But he does also follow Shakespeare in his handling of the beaten, humiliated Lear, as he seeks out the wretched and increasingly identifies with their lot. The words to the

Fool, 'poor boy, art cold? I am cold myself,' find their echo in a speech to Bond's odd substitute, the troubled ghost of a murdered peasant:

> Poor boy. Lie down by me. Here, I'll hold you. We'll help each other. Sing while I sleep, and I'll sing and watch you while you sleep. The sound of the human voice will comfort us.

It's a moving moment, and there are more as the blind Lear deepens in a sympathy that, you feel, his author fully shares. Suffering and madness have reduced Lear to a child, and, you'll recall, only the child is presumed by Bond to have warm, uncorrupted responses. It is a humanist's perhaps ingenuous rephrasing of Matthew 18:3: 'except ye become as little children, ye shall not build the kingdom of heaven on Earth'.

It seems unecessary to apologise for holding over my reviews of slighter plays in a week that produces one bound to cause continuing argument. Altogether, there's much in William Gaskill's production to dog the mind long afterwards, not least the ending. Andrews's rugged, ravaged patriarch, more massively dignified in his humility than in his former arrogance, stands with a spade on the wall that's come to symbolise the vanity of human effort, political oppression and the barriers between individuals, and is shot as he begins to dig it down. Yet another horror, you say; but not one that quite eradicates the impression of human nobility, briefly and precariously achieved. One could not call this journey into Bond's mind a totally dispiriting one.

Kenneth Hurren (review date 9 October 1971)

SOURCE: Hurren, Kenneth. Review of *Lear,* by Edward Bond. *Spectator* 227, no. 7476 (9 October 1971): 519-20.

[*In the following review of Gaskill's 1971 production of* Lear, *Hurren contrasts the play with Shakespeare's* King Lear, *contending that Bond interprets Lear not as a force of nature as does Shakespeare but as a product of a cruel civilization.*]

Despite the formidable solemnity of its purpose, and the free rein that is allowed throughout to the darkest and most deplorable aspects of human nature, it wouldn't be strictly accurate to say that Edward Bond's **Lear,** at the Royal Court, is nowhere to go for a laugh. There is a moment, for example, when one of Lear's dreadful daughters is chortling over the plight of some poor wretch whose tongue she has just had cut out and whose hands she is delightedly smashing to pulp. Her sister, standing by, remarks with a shrug, "She was just the same at school." There is a chuckle *there* for those who are not too preoccupied in trying to keep down their dinner, but on the whole it is a bleak business.

Just to run over the surface of the territory, the central figure, the eponymous Lear, is established at the outset as an irascible sort, obsessed with the idea of having a vast wall built around his land, shooting out of hand anyone who seems to be dragging his feet as the work progresses, and generally terrorizing his subjects. His two daughters (for Regan and Goneril, now read Bodice and Fontanelle), a treacherous pair, now betroth themselves to his enemies, with whom they would seem to have been pen-pals for some time, and promptly depose him. The new regime is even more brutal and tyrannical than the old, and it is no surprise when the girls are overthrown in a proletarian revolution—led by another young woman, by name Cordelia, wife of a young gravedigger and ostensibly a decent type but, having seen her husband shot for sheltering the fugitive Lear, and having herself been casually raped by the licentious soldiery, she is not in an especially merciful frame of mind and her own brand of totalitarianism outdoes in cruelty all that has gone before. Bodice and Fontanelle are both killed rather horribly. During the course of a kind of autopsy on Fontanelle, Lear is brought on, by now well off his trolley, and plunges his hands into her entrails searching, if I understood him correctly, for "the beast in her." Shortly thereafter it is considered necessary to remove his eyes—quite delicately and scientifically. This agony is the turning point for him. Accompanied everywhere by the ghost of the dead gravedigger (his conscience rather than his Fool), he broods penitently upon his past sins, upon the world and suffering and pity, developing a vision beyond mere sight, and is ultimately discovered trying to destroy the wall. The latest revolutionaries gun him down.

I owe this summary of the play's major events in warning to rash investors who may be looking for a gay night out after the stresses of the day; but it does not touch the heart of *Lear,* which is not to be discussed in remotely realistic terms without seeming—as in the foregoing—a grotesque parody. The same trouble might arise with some of the Greek tragedies—*Oedipus,* for instance—not to mention a work called *King Lear,* and this is the league we're batting in. The resemblances between the Bond play and the one by the late Shakespeare are not, superficially, very pronounced: there is the old man, of course, and the wicked daughters, and a character named Cordelia and another reminiscent of the Fool, but there is little similarity of plot or theme. Their affinity lies rather in the conception of Lear, in each case, as a symbolic figure.

The Shakespeare Lear is not a man at all but some towering elemental force (which is what Lamb was getting at, by the way, in his contention that he "cannot be acted," for to personify him is to diminish him), a speaker whose words are not so much addressed to the elements as they are *part* of the elements, the storm as

much within him as about him. Bond, plumbing the depths of his dismay at the ways and waywardness of man, is working the same metaphysical seam. He throws out, here and there, something more tangible—the occasional thought about the folly of isolationism and nationalism, about the dual function of walls which *do* a prison make, about violence begetting violence, about the corrosive effects of power—but these are little more than incidental embellishments with no pretensions to profundity. The core and inspiration of his play is his conception of Lear as a synoptic force emanating not from nature, as Shakespeare's, but from a sophisticated contemporary civilization, containing within himself the metaphor of man as a trapped animal in a world gone "morally insane."

Bond makes it clear in a statement handed out with the programme that he isn't writing for posterity: "I can see a continuity of technology but not of culture." I think he takes a woefully pessimistic view of the way things are going, but the hard time he has making a living from his plays is scarcely conducive to looking on the sunny side, and it probably accounts for the wild over-emphasis he is apt to apply in his arguments. Paradoxically, though, the way to prove him right would be to be unheedful of the tocsin he's ringing so dementedly. The clangour at the Court is powerfully directed by William Gaskill, who handles the episodic pattern of the piece and a large cast with minimum sprawl and maximum fluidity. The players, led by Harry Andrews as Lear (gaunt, grey, majestic and, when appropriate, turbulent), include also Carmel McSharry and Rosemary McHale as the daughters, Celestine Randall as Cordelia, and Mark McManus as the gravedigger/ghost.

BINGO (1973)

PRODUCTION REVIEWS

Irving Wardle (review date 15 November 1973)

SOURCE: Wardle, Irving. "A Time of Disillusion and Strife." *Times* London (15 November 1973): 15.

[*In the following review of a 1973 production of* Bingo *at the Northcott Theatre in Exeter, directed by Jane Howell, Wardle admires Bond's quality of writing and characterization of Shakespeare but finds elements of the staging severe and lugubrious.*]

It has stuck in many a reader's craw that practically all we know of Shakespeare's private life is his canny investment in land and his withdrawal from the theatre to finish his days as a well-to-do country gentleman.

Punishment now descends upon him in the form of a new play by Edward Bond, which presents Shakespeare's retirement as a time of disillusion, strife and suicide. There sits the poet in his spacious New Place garden with a docile retainer clipping the hedge. This rural idyll does not last long.

For one thing, the garden is his refuge from "the dark house and the detested wife", not to mention the complaints of his stupid shrewish daughter. Also he is brooding about his security ("Thank God we're not thatched"), and about the effect of enclosure on his rents. And when the landowner, William Combe, drops in Shakespeare speedily concludes his bargain with the enclosers.

As one would expect from its author, **Bingo** is not a personal drama but a public parable. Fortunately, Bond is quite indifferent to creating a "great writer" hero. His Shakespeare barely mentions poetry or the theatre. He is a man who has spent all his resources on achieving a prize which he now finds to be worthless.

Not only that: the social position he has reached also turns him into an instrument of cruelty. When a vagrant girl appears in the garden his impulse is to give her money and food. But she is on the wrong side of the law, so he is powerless to save her from being hanged. Having quit the mass cruelties of London, he finds himself conniving at the same barbarities in his place of retreat.

In short, this is another of Bond's denunciations of money and law and order. It also finds room for religious bigotry represented by a group of anti-enclosure fanatics. I do not understand their place in the scheme: but otherwise such episodes as Ben Jonson's arrival to cadge a loan, or the grasping Judith hammering frenziedly on the dying poet's bedroom door, all relate directly to the main theme.

One would say too directly were it not for the quality of the writing which shows Bond's characteristic blend of flinty dialogue and flashes of wintry comedy, periodically ascending into towering emotion. The play resembles his *Lear* as the drama of an eminent man finally learning the ways of the world. Bond succeeds partly because his writing is solid and tactile, always touching the earth, and he puts as much truth into small conflicts, like the helpless bewilderment of an intelligent man before a stupidly confident woman, as he does into the big tirades.

As Jane Howell's outgoing show at the Northcott, the production carries her stamp of selective severity. It offers a handful of details, each played to the expressive limit, whether the background fire in the Jonson scene or the isolated figure of the hanged girl in Hayden Griffin's set. Bob Peck's Shakespeare, rat-like features surmounted by a balding dome, aptly shrinks the poet to the play's dimensions, though his performance is on the lugubrious side. Rhys McConnochie swaggers sadly as the aging Jonson, and Sue Cox's spinsterish Judith projects narrow female possessiveness at its most poisonous.

Benedict Nightingale (review date 23 November 1973)

SOURCE: Nightingale, Benedict. Review of *Bingo,* by Edward Bond. *New Statesman* 86, no. 2227 (23 November 1973): 783.

[*In the following review, Nightingale finds in Howell's 1973 production of* Bingo *that Bond has matured from his earlier years of depending heavily on sensationalist violence to accomplish his thematic aims.*]

Except for some Victorians, who saw it as the face of self-help rewarded, everyone has been appalled by the stolid, pompous figure that juts out of the wall just above Shakespeare's tomb. Could this 'self-satisfied pork butcher', as Dover Wilson dubbed the monument, really be the earthly likeness of the Immortal Bard? Surely not—and yet there was a Shakespeare who, so far from conforming with the common image of poets as tousled, unworldly spendthrifts, was embarrassingly interested in acquiring property, securing his investments, pursuing debtors and their sureties in the courts, and generally achieving prosperity and status in the cabbage-patch of Stratford. The apparent dichotomy between this acquisitive burgher and the anguished author of *Timon* clearly fascinates Edward Bond; and in the bizarrely titled **Bingo,** or 'scenes of money and death', he uses it to illustrate his belief that good men must be contaminated, and may be corrupted, by a vicious economic system. Or, to put it another way: if Shakespeare was capable of cooperating in the rise of capitalism, what hope of resistance from lesser beings, like you and me?

Actually, Bob Peck's Shakespeare is less like the monster in Holy Trinity than the Droeshout engraving, and less like that than some wispy, ferrety Warwickshire poacher, the victim of too much rain and too many gamekeepers. With old age prematurely upon him, the sweet swan of Avon has shrivelled back into an ugly duckling, a bedraggled creature who sits morosely in his garden and looks with woozy, incredulous eyes at a world where men are casually murdered, beggar-girls whipped and hanged, bears baited to death, and writers seem incapable of changing anything for the better. Success has brought him no reward except money, and now money dominates and determines all his relationships: with his daughter Judith, who feels cheated of affection and thinks only of what she'll inherit; with an equally resentful and hostile Ben Jonson, in Stratford to touch his old colleague for a loan; with William Combe, who buys his tacit agreement to a plan to enclose the common land at Welcombe, notwithstanding the suffering this will cause.

He is, on the whole, a benign, sentient character, a Shakespeare that bardophiliacs won't quite be able to disown; and yet here he is, in cahoots with the wealthy oppressor and seemingly unable to do more for the poor oppressee than slip a furtive purse into his or her hand. 'Was anything done?' he repeats to himself, as he trudges through the Stratford snow, and again as he slumps into his deathbed: has he achieved anything at all? His demented wife wails and claws at the locked door; Shakespeare swallows a mickey finn slipped him by Jonson; and he dies, on the floor, while Judith tears the room apart in her anxiety to trace a new will.

It goes without saying that this Shakespeare won't be very easily reconciled with the one who rounded off *The Winter's Tale* so serenely, or, for that matter, the one who appears to rejoice at the prospect of Iago being exquisitely and endlessly tortured to death. A despairing, disgusted suicide seems scarcely less historically credible than a lesbian love-affair between Queen Victoria and Florence Nightingale. And yet, whether he's writing of the treatment of vagrants in 17th-century England or the details of Shakespeare's own dealings in Stratford, Bond consistently aims at an authenticity he never contemplates in that mad fantasy, *Early Morning*. Even the saloon-bar binge with Jonson has a basis in tradition, though Shakespeare's fatal acquisition is supposed to have been a fever, not a phial. Indeed, his account of the enclosure controversy seems rather more accurate than that of the redoubtable Rowse, who misreads a vital document in order to be able to claim that Shakespeare was opposed to the landgrabbers. Bond isn't interested in offering us a fictional archetype of suffering mankind, like his own (or Shakespeare's) Lear: he wants our attention for a specific period, an actual person. How is it (we're to ask) that a man whom we worship for his humanity could bear to live in a society we know to have been so cruel? How can we, his descendants, bear to live in a society directly derived from it?

This is the sort of question that Bond asks again and again, in play after play. All, from *Saved* to *The Sea*, may be seen as the dramatic equivalents of those insistent Oxfam ads which thrust children with sparrow-legs and pigeon-bellies under our well-nourished noses. Each insists that we face the kind of realities that make us instinctively drop our eyes and change the conversation; each consciously, perhaps presumptuously, attempts to make us more sensitive and responsible to the world's suffering.

But several things distinguish Bond's *Bingo* from, say, his *Lear*. First, the cruelties, being better documented and more unsensationally presented, are less easy to dismiss as the feverish symptoms of his pathological imagination. That is a strength. Second, the emphasis on economic and social conditions seems to suggest that they alone are responsible for human suffering, and leaves us unclear whether or not Bond still thinks that mankind is also afflicted with an innate and immutable sadism, as a bald statement of disaffection and disgust, as hard to subject to impersonal criticism as someone's suicide note.

The play's language ranges from the engagingly mundane ('you just sit there and brood all day,' the dreadful Judith tells her father, 'you must learn that people have feelings') to the self-consciously 'poetic'—but what dramatist would not become a trifle strained when called upon to write death-knell speeches for his greatest precursor? Most of the time, the dialogue is simply and unpretentiously eloquent, Jane Howell's production equally modest and straightforward—though I don't think much is gained by setting the play within what appears to be a forest of violin-strings or the beginning of some massive game of cat's cradle, Sue Cox's prim, cold Judith is a good dry run for Regan; Rhys McConnochie's Jonson, smiling venomously over his cups, might be developed into an admirably sinister Edmund; but I can, I fear, find no such grand comparison for Peck's dour angst in the main part. I wish he'd dare to be a little more like Lear, or Gloucester, or *someone* with a soul as well as a frown. But it's a fascinating play; and I'm as impressed to find it first performed in a nutshell on the Exeter campus as I was sorry to share the experience with an audience scattered into desultory twos and threes, as if to pray. When it reaches London, as it surely must, the problem will be how to prevent overcrowding in stalls and gods alike.

CRITICAL COMMENTARY

Christy L. Brown (essay date February 1986)

SOURCE: Brown, Christy L. "Edward Bond's *Bingo*: Shakespeare and the Ideology of Genius." *Iowa State Journal of Research* 60, no. 3 (February 1986): 343-54.

[*In the following essay, Brown maintains that in* Bingo *Bond explores the historical debate concerning the Welcombe enclosure from a Marxist perspective, and in particular that Bond's interpretation of Shakespeare has him siding with the bourgeois side rather than the feudal values that he typically supported in his plays.*]

As the radical British playwrights of the 1960s and '70s—Arden, Brenton, Hare, Griffiths, Churchill, and Bond—have become increasingly committed to socialism, they have viewed the artist's role in undermining ruling class ideologies as especially crucial. By challenging the dominant culture's interpretation of history, radical dramatists sought to change the consciousness of the British theatergoing public. Edward Bond has been particularly interested in shifting the audience's consciousness away from romantic and modernist concepts of art and culture toward a materialist perspective through a Marxist analysis of history.

When "uncommitted" playwrights invade the territory of the radical playwrights—history—they often use similar techniques such as discontinuous action, music, caricature, etc.—yet their underlying ideology reinforces rather than challenges the status quo. For instance, Tom Stoppard wrote *Travesties* (1971) to explain why his plays "aren't political" (Brown 243). In the play Stoppard's alter ego Henry Carr contends that Joyce's *Ulysses* "leaves the world precisely as it finds it," (Stoppard 62) thus disputing the idea that art need change society. In Peter Shaffer's *Amadeus* (1979), Salieri views Mozart's genius as derived from divine inspiration, thus reinforcing the romantic concept of the artist as creator. Mozart is depicted as composing off the top of his head, billiard cue in hand, whereas Salieri's labored efforts yield mediocre results, thus creating an antithesis between pure imagination and conscious human labor.

On the other hand, a Marxist perspective is opposed to the romantic concept of the artist as creator, as "the Godlike figure who mysteriously conjures his handiwork out of nothing" because it "severs the work from the artist's historical situation, making it appear miraculous and unmotivated." Instead, Marxism views the artist as a producer, "rooted in a particular history with particular materials at his disposal" (Eagleton 68-69). In *Bingo: Scenes of Money and Death* (1973), Edward Bond confronts the mystique of Shakespeare as the "great idol of humanist West," revered in the popular consciousness, according to Marxist Shakespearean Paul Siegal as "the detached, Godlike observer and ideologically neutral recorder of Elizabethan society who transcends any system of ideas" (2-3). Bond attempts to show that Shakespeare, both as a man and as an artist, was a product of historical circumstances and of his own particular position within the social hierarchy, and that as a product of human labor his work is subject to criticism and even revision.

To my mind, it is not so important to examine historical drama in the light of its naturalistic adherence to strict historical accuracy, an approach which has been by and large discarded by contemporary dramatists, but rather in terms of how the historical material is shaped according to the world view, the ideological preconceptions of the playwright. Thus I propose to examine how

Bond's Marxist reading of history in *Bingo* reinterprets Shakespeare's life and art from the perspective of the class conflict and changing material conditions of the period.

Bond first began to question more orthodox interpretations of Shakespeare by rewriting *King Lear* as *Lear* in 1971 in order to make the play more "relevant" to contemporary audiences. He objected to the "worshipping of that play by the academic theater" which turns it into a "purely aesthetic experience," which is nice and comfortable because "you don't have to question yourself or change your society" (Bond "Discussion" 24). Bond wanted to "refocus" the attention in the play away from Lear's relationship with the heavens toward his painful recognition that he himself is responsible for the walls he has built up to oppress other people (Hayman 23). Similarly, *Bingo* concerns the process by which Shakespeare comes to recognize that man's injustice rather than an inherently justifiable and morally sanctioned divine providence is responsible for the enclosures that oppress the peasants.

Bond's materialist reading places Shakespeare at the cutting edge of the transition from feudalism to capitalism. According to Bond, "Shakespeare lived on the edge of a political revolution, and . . . even in his own time he was in many ways out of date" (*Plays: Two* x). Shakespeare was somewhat old-fashioned in his support of a feudal ideology which was being rendered obsolete by the transformation of the economic and political structures upon which it was based. Bond's analysis would conform to that of Georg Lukàcs who contends that Shakespeare recognizes the "triumphant, humanist character of the new world, but also sees it as causing the breakdown of a patriarchal society humanly and morally better in many respects and more closely bound to the interests of the people," and that "he foresees the rule of money in this advancing new world, and the oppression and exploitation of the masses, a world of rampant egoism and ruthless greed" (Solomon 400). Such an analysis draws for example upon Shakespeare's examination in *King Lear* of the contradiction between Lear's view of the world as structured along hierarchical lines with bonds of loyalty between lord and peasant, father and children, and Goneril and Regan's Machiavellian revolt in the name of greed and self-aggrandizement which turns the world of the play "upside down,"[1] and upon Timon of Athens' revulsion against an approach to money which sees wealth not as largesse to be distributed, but as the object of competition and scrambling.

Bond sees as the major contradiction in Shakespeare's work that his essentially feudal world view of society as governed by divine providence and a just moral order conflicted with actual social conditions of the period, explaining:

His plays show this need for sanity and its political expression, justice. But how did he live? His behaviour as a property-owner made him closer to Goneril than to Lear. He supported and benefited from the Goneril-society—with its prisons, workhouses, whipping, starvation, mutilation, pulpit hysteria and all the rest of it.

(Preface to *Bingo* xii)

According to Bond, Shakespeare's tragedies inevitably questioned the viability of the ideal of "good government" posited by the history plays. By turning to the romance at the end of his career, Shakespeare provided unrealistic solutions to problems raised in the tragedies: "as Shakespeare himself knew, the peace, the reconciliation, that he created on the stage would not last an hour on the street" (*Plays: Two* ix-x). So although Shakespeare, Bond writes "spent his creative life desperately struggling to reconcile problems that obsessed him," which is the source of his "intellectual strength and passionate beauty," we should be aware of his ideological limitations rather than uncritically regarding him as a "guide to conduct" for our time (Brown 167).

Bond draws from the much overlooked record of Shakespeare's involvement in the Welcombe enclosure in 1614 to suggest that he acted as part of the "Goneril society" and thus cannot be considered a passive and ideologically neutral observer of that society. From the records of Shakespeare's other economic dealings, Bond deduces that Shakespeare was obsessed with the idea of economic security, investing in land and property with a businessman's acumen. The contradiction between the great poet dealing with questions of life, death, and the nature of human society, and the man William Shakespeare as the product of the newly acquisitive mercantilism, building his estate with the profits from the theater, forms the central issue of the play.

Enclosure of fields previously held in common by tenant farmers for the purpose of conversion to pasture for more profitable, less labor intensive sheep raising continued from the sixteenth into the nineteenth century in Britain, spurring the transition to a capitalist economy, but dispossessing thousands of peasants. The agreement Shakespeare signed with large landowners protected him against the loss of the rents he collected from his leases at Welcombe, should the enclosure take place. In *Bingo* Bond places the much neglected record of Shakespeare's signing of the agreement within the historical context of the consequences of enclosure for the peasantry, suggesting that Shakespeare was driven to commit suicide when he realized not only that the agreement implicated him in exploitation, but also that the ideology he had incorporated into his plays was inadequate to deal with the moral dilemmas of the transitional society.

By indicting Shakespeare for not acting on the side of the peasants in the matter of the enclosure, Bond echoes Brecht's contention that "private morality is not enough" (Elsom 190). A typical critical reaction to *Bingo* was that of Garry O'Connor in *Plays and Players,* who condemned Bond for the "abstract assassination of Shakespeare's reputation (a writer who lived a blameless life, happened to be gifted with genius, and probably believed in original sin)" (Brown 200). But according to Bond, Shakespeare had a choice about whether to sign the document, and "this is not a neutral document because it implies that should the people fighting the enclosers come to him for help he would refuse it" (Preface xii). When Thomas Greene approached Shakespeare on behalf of the town of Stratford and pleaded with him to oppose the proposed enclosure, Shakespeare was in fact noncommittal in his reply (Brown 172). Shakespeare historian Samuel Schoenbaum concurs that Shakespeare's "apparent detachment renders provocatively apt the large questions Mr. Bond raises about the social responsibilities of the artist in an unjust society" (Hay and Roberts 180).

To those critics who are shocked at Bond's hypothesis that Shakespeare would commit suicide, Bond perversely replies that his version "rather flatters Shakespeare" because if he "didn't end in the way shown in the play, then he was a reactionary blimp or some other fool" (Preface x). Thus Bond prefers to believe that Shakespeare would take his life out of guilt, having recognized that he has been "the hangman's assistant" (*Bingo* 48), than as, for example, Anthony Burgess argues in his biography of Shakespeare, that he "accepted the 'hangman's hands' . . . accepted that it was not his mission to change . . . the bestowals of a God who must have seemed as cruel as men" (73).

Each character in *Bingo* feels the consequences of the economic and political transition and reacts according to his or her class position. Combe is based on the historical figure of William Combe, one of a group of landowners who pursued the enclosure at Welcombe and family friend of Shakespeare. He represents the emergence of capitalism as a form of property relations; he wants to use land to make a profit from sheep rather than for subsistence farming, but the land must be emptied of peasants before this can happen. In *Bingo* Combe initiates the enclosures that will benefit the propertied class and offers Shakespeare the agreement to protect his tithes, implying that he expects no opposition to the enclosure in return. Shakespeare, curiously unresponsive in this scene, signs the agreement, rationalizing that he is "not taking sides," but simply "protecting my own interests" (7).

Combe is opposed by the Son, a fictional character introduced by Bond to represent the radical Puritan sects who fought the enclosure movement, calling for economic reforms which would have redistributed wealth. In the play he leads the group of peasants who fill in the ditches dug by Combe's men, an action which actually took place in January of 1614, but which Bond juxtaposes with the "merry meeting" between Shakespeare and Jonson recorded in John Ward's diary as the source of the fever from which Shakespeare died in 1616. History records that Combe laughed at these men and called them "Puritan knaves and underlings" (Eccles 138), illustrating the hostility of the upperclasses toward the peasantry and the link between radical religion and revolutionary social movements which Bond stresses in the character of the Son. The action, moreover, is no isolated incident, but part of a widespread anti-enclosure movement which erupted periodically up to the time of the Revolution of 1642. Anti-enclosure riots took place in 1596 and again in 1607, the year *Coriolanus* first appeared on stage, when Levellers and Diggers rose in Shakespeare's country of Warwickshire as well as in other nearby counties (Hill, *Change* 182).

In *Bingo* Combe in his historical role as Magistrate is also responsible for ordering the whipping of the Young Woman vagrant who has been hiding behind the hedges in Shakespeare's garden while the two men have been discussing the agreement. Although the Young Woman is a fictional character, Shakespeare was certainly aware of the existence of many like her. The enclosure movement spurred the transition from feudalism to capitalism by creating "masterless men" who had no place in the social hierarchy, no reciprocal relationships with lord of the manor or landowner. These "masterless men" came to be feared by the propertied classes as the "many-headed multitude" depicted in Sidney's *Arcadia* and Spenser's satire against the Levellers in *The Faerie Queen*. Many, like the Young Woman in *Bingo,* had no recourse but vagabondage and joined the "roving bands of beggars who were past the possibility of working and who terrorized their betters, continually buzzing . . . 'that the rich men have gotten all their lands and will starve the poor'" (Hill, *Change* 188). Thus historically she represents the process by which, according to Marx, "the agricultural people, first forcibly expropriated, (were) driven from their homes, turned into vagabonds, and then whipped, branded, tortured by laws grotesquely terrible, into the discipline necessary for the wage system" (Hill, *Puritanism* 224).

In *Bingo* the Young Woman becomes feeble-minded from the whipping and is subjected to starvation, homelessness, and mass rape by the youth of the town before being accused of setting fires in the neighborhood of Stratford and sentenced to hang. The play demonstrates how the propertied classes, having created her, felt threatened by her. One hundred and sixty people were hanged for vagabondage in Middlesex between 1614-15 (Hill, *Change* 188), showing that such punishment was the rule rather than the exception.

One means of escaping hanging for any crime was by pleading "benefit of clergy," the ability to read and write. In scene four of *Bingo* Jonson mentions that he used this defense to avoid being hanged for killing a man in a quarrel, which is Bond's way of emphasizing the class bias of the justice system. Since in *Henry VI, Part II*, rebel Jack Cade reverses this discriminatory law and sentences a clerk to hang for knowing how to read and write, saying "Hang him with his pen and inkhorn about his neck" (IV.ii.16-17), we can assume that Shakespeare was aware of the lower class' view of educated men as class enemies.

Scene three of *Bingo* is dominated by the Young Woman's gibbeted body, alongside which Shakespeare, unable to find the serenity he craved from New Place, sits and broods. Whereas in *King Lear* Lear begins to understand the plight of the lower classes while on the heath, it is primarily Cordelia and Gloucester, representatives of the feudal ruling class and its values, who are depicted as the victims of Goneril and Regan's greed and brutality. On the other hand, in *Bingo* it is the Young Woman vagrant's grotesque and decaying body which evokes Shakespeare's pity. Moreover, he begins to see her victimization as the responsibility of man, not God, and thus questions divine providence as the guiding principle of morality. He soliloquizes that he had "usurped the place of God, and lied . . ." (27), that "there's no higher wisdom of silence. No face brooding over the water . . . No other hand . . . no face . . . just these . . ." (26). And when in this scene Shakespeare also compares the Young Woman to the baited bear, seeing both as victims of a cruel society, Bond obviously has in mind the words of another usurper, spoken under entirely different circumstances.

One reason why it is difficult for audiences to accept Bond's premise that Shakespeare would have been driven by guilt and despair to take his own life is because in the popular imagination he is usually associated with the expansiveness of the Elizabethan Age. Historian Christopher Hill points out, however, that the spiritual and intellectual crisis that preceded the revolution in 1642 was already beginning to be felt acutely by the time of Shakespeare's death. While mercantilists and property-holders like Combe were busy transforming the mode of production, feudal ideology had fallen into confusion. According to Hill, "the Renaissance and the Reformation, the discovery of America and the new astronomy, had been far more successful in undermining old assumptions and prejudices than in substituting new truths." The ideas of Machiavelli and Giordano "must have seemed terribly wicked to timid traditionalists." Writing about the time of Shakespeare's death, Fulke Greville contrasted the brilliance of the end of Elizabeth's reign to the present "degenerate" age (*Intellectual* 8). Gloucester's words in *King Lear* anticipate the sense of the feudal world falling apart which is later to be echoed by Donne and Drayton with increasing bewilderment as the revolution drew to a head:

> Love cools, friendship falls off, brothers divide: in cities, mutinies; in countries, discord; in palaces, treason; and the bond crack'd twixt son and father. This villain of mine comes under the prediction; there's son against father: the King falls from bias of nature; there's father against child. We have seen the best of our time; machinations, hollowness, treachery, and all ruinous disorders, follow us disquietly to our graves.
>
> (I.ii.116-124)

In *Bingo* the familial strife depicted in *King Lear* is transferred to Shakespeare's own family. Judith Shakespeare, who Bond believes to have been estranged from her father (Preface ix), represents the materialism of "the Goneril society," but Bond's Shakespeare, unlike Lear, must take responsibility for having created his daughter's greed rather than attributing her unnaturalness to the gods or nature: "I started to collect for you. I loved you with money. The only thing I can afford to give you now is money . . . But money always turns to hate . . . I made you vulgar and ugly and cheap. I corrupted you" (41-42).

While Bond's depiction of Judith Shakespeare as materialistic, banal, and sexually repressed almost to the point of hysteria differs markedly from Shakespeare's self-confident, witty heroines, his version is probably closer to reality of woman's position during Shakespeare's lifetime. As Virginia Woolf in her hypothetical reconstruction of the fate of Shakespeare's "sister" Judith points out, though Shakespeare's heroines "do not seem wanting in personality and character," woman is virtually absent from the history of this period, save for G. M. Trevelyn's brief assessment of her position: "the daughter who refused to marry the gentleman of her parents' choice was liable to be locked up, beaten and flung about the room," since marriages were contracted not for "personal affection," but "family avarice." Woolf attaches particular importance to enforced chastity as operating against women's opportunity to develop creativity. She concludes that Shakespeare's sister would never have been able to develop genius because it is "not born among labouring, uneducated, servile people" (*Room* 43-50).

Bond's implication is that Judith's sexual repression and materialism stem from the same source—her role as bargaining chip in the game of property acquisition. She herself must achieve financial security and social position but can do so only through her father or husband. Like the laboring classes, then, she is condemned to historical marginality, nor does Shakespeare contribute to changing her dependence.

Shakespeare's failure in his relationship with his daughter parallels his inadequacies as a cultural father figure. In a sense the Young Woman vagrant is also Shakespeare's daughter—she is the lost daughter of the romances, the real life counterpart to his princesses disguised as prostitutes and shepardesses—but Shakespeare has done little "in care of" her.

Ironically, the most humane father-daughter relationship in the play is that which develops between the Son's father, who is Shakespeare's gardener, and the Young Woman. Like the gardener in *Richard II*, like Shakespeare's fools, the feeble-minded Old Man provides a commentary on the supposed sanity of his betters, including Shakespeare, especially in his revulsion when he hears that the Young Woman is about to be hanged. But unlike them he is given a clear class position, and his feeblemindedness a definite cause—after being forcibly impressed into the army, he suffered a head injury in the war.

The uncertainty of the new age led to an intellectual withdrawal in the form of increased unreality in literature, as the pastoral which Sydney and Spenser used to comment on society gave way to "mere escapism" (Hill *Origins* 12). In scene four of *Bingo,* Bond attributes this escapist attitude to both Shakespeare and Jonson; Shakespeare expresses the wish to escape from the violence of a society where on his way to the theatre he walks "under sixteen severed heads on a gate" (26). In the midst of casual conversation about the violence and corruption of Jacobean life, Jonson's reference to *The Winter's Tale* reminds the audience how remote the harmony Shakespeare achieved in the romances was from reality. Jonson speaks with envy of Shakespeare's "clean country limbs" (34), but as Combe and the peasants quarrel about the enclosure, he becomes absorbed in a pastoral reverie about musing with his "reflection in quiet water having the accents of philosophy" (36), oblivious that the landscape of the countryside is irrevocably transforming itself even as he speaks.

Bond thus probes what he believes are Shakespeare's limitations as a father and citizen, but also as a thinker and writer, seeing those limitations as human limitations, as stemming from the inadequacy of the world view of the period. Shakespeare and Jonson, representatives of the intellectual elite, are shown retreating from the world rather than acting to change it. Yet Bond also shows Shakespeare as beginning to recognize that he has purchased serenity dearly, and in so doing, has alienated himself from the peasant's interests, and, in Bond's words, "compromised himself in such a way that he can no longer live with himself" (Brown 197):

> I spent so much of my youth, my best energy . . . for this: New Place . . . It was all a mistake . . . I could have done so much . . . Absurd! Absurd! I howled when they suffered, but they were whipped and hanged so that I could be free. That is the right question: Not why did I sign one piece of paper?—no, no, even when I sat at my table, when I put on my clothes, I was a

hangman's assistant, a gaoler's errand boy. If children go in rags we make the wind. If the table's empty we blight the harvest. If the roof leaks we send the storm. God made the elements but we inflict them on each other. Everything can be stolen, property and qualities of the mind. But stolen things have no value. Pride and arrogance are the same when they're stolen. Even serenity.

(48)

When the financial security to be able to create *The Tempest* is achieved only at the expense of the exploitation of others, the privileged position of the artist as "seer" becomes problematic. Shakespeare can no longer avoid the terrible questions he raised in *Lear*: "I quietened the storms inside me. But the storm breaks outside" (27). Finally he comes to the realization that "every writer writes in other men's blood. The trivial, and the real. There's nothing else to write in. But only a god or a devil can write in other men's blood and not ask why they spilt it and what it cost" (43). Thus Bond proposes that the writer's special responsibility stems not from his status as the inspired voice of a God dispensing divine justice, but from his responsibility to the men whose blood is shed so that he be free to write.

Shakespeare's guilt at his own involvement in the violence and exploitation of his society freeze him into a condition of stasis symbolized by the snowstorm in scene five, and finally drive him to suicide in scene six. The Son, who represents the only possible revolutionary alternative, is also faced with living with guilt, not because he did not act, but because in the process of trying to stop the enclosure, he shot his father by mistake. He sees his action as a sign from God, and he decides rather than to continue fighting the enclosure, he will emigrate, hoping to find the New Jerusalem. Into this vaccum created by the withdrawal of the forces opposing him, Combe, who calls himself a "realist," can be expected to step. Shakespeare, the cultural hero of our time, is ironically seen to have had an inadequate understanding even of his own time. As he prepares to swallow the poison Jonson has given him, he wonders desperately if he has left a legacy for the next generation, asking himself repeatedly, "Was anything done?" Judith's frantic searching for a new will underscores this irony, as she cries, "Nothing."

Such a seemingly pessimistic ending might lead one to question whether Bond's world view indeed encompasses the possibility of radical change in the collective consciousness of the audience toward its ability to create a more just society. But in order to be true to history in a Marxist sense, Bond must not provide a false optimism about the revolutionary potential of Shakespeare's society. It could be argued from a Marxist point of view that Shakespeare's realization that "There's no higher wisdom of silence. No face brooding over the water . . . No other had . . . no face . . . just these. . . ." (26) is ahistorical, that Bond is flattering Shakespeare too much.

Ultimately *Bingo*'s major relevance may lie in its portrayal of Jacobean England as a period of acute class contradictions, violence, and upheavals not unlike those we are experiencing today, and in Bond's insistence that given such circumstances, artists are called upon to make some difficult choices about which forces they are serving—directly or indirectly—through their art.

Like Brecht, Bond is aware of the narcotic effect of empathy and catharsis in art, which can lessen the audience's ability to transform society outside the theater. While these are humanizing elements in art, under certain historical conditions they can be used as tools to pacify and suppress action (Solomon 358). The ironic ending of *Bingo* should stimulate the audience's consciousness of oppression so that the purgation takes place not in the theatre, but in the social arena. Bond implies that unless such action occurs, however, Judith's negative response to Shakespeare's question "Was anything done?" will remain the final summation of his legacy, not only to his age, but to ours as well.

Note

1. Drayton, also mentioned in John Word's diary as having been with Shakespeare when he contracted a fatal fever writes

> Certainly there's scarce one found that now
> Knows what I approve, or what to disallow;
> All arsey-varsey, nothing is its own,
> But to our proverb, all turned upside down. . . .
>
> (quoted in Hill *Intellectual* 8)

Literature Cited

Bond, Edward. *Bingo and the Sea.* New York: Hill and Wang, 1975.

———. "A Discussion with Edward Bond," *Gambit* 17 (1970), 24.

———. *Plays: Two.* London: Eyre Methuen, 1978.

Brown, Christy. "Alienation versus Commitment: The Role of the Artist Figure in Contemporary British Drama." Ph.D. dissertation. Indiana U, 1982.

Burgess, Anthony. *Shakespeare.* New York: Knopf, 1970.

Eagleton, Terry. *Marxism and Literary Criticism.* Berkeley: U of California.

Eccles, Mark. *Shakespeare in Warwickshire.* Madison: U of Wisconsin, 1961.

Elsom, John. *Post-War British Theatre.* London: Routledge and Kegan-Paul, 1976.

Hay, Malcolm, and Philip Roberts. *Bond: A Study of His Plays.* London: Eyre Methuen, 1980.

Hill, Christopher. "The Many-Headed Monster" in *Change and Continuity in 17th Century England.* London: Weidenfeld and Nicolson, 1974, pp. 181-204.

——. *Intellectual Origins of the English Revolution.* Oxford: Clarendon, 1965.

——. *Puritanism and Revolution.* New York: Schocken, 1958.

Shakespeare, William. *Complete Plays and Poems.* Cambridge: Riverside, 1942.

Siegel, Paul. *Shakespeare in His Time and Ours.* Notre Dame, Indiana: U of Notre Dame, 1968.

Solomon, Maynard, ed. *Marxism and Art: Essays Classic and Contemporary.* Detroit: Wayne State U, 1979.

Stoppard, Tom. *Travesties.* New York: Grove, 1971.

Woolf, Virginia. *A Room of One's Own.* New York: Harcourt, Brace, and World, 1957.

Lou Lappin (essay date 1986)

SOURCE: Lappin, Lou. "The Artist in Society: Bond, Shakespeare, and *Bingo.*" In *Before His Eyes: Essays in Honor of Stanley Kauffmann,* edited by Bert Cardullo, pp. 57-70. Lanham, Md.: University Press of America, 1986.

[*In the following essay, Lappin discusses the ways in which Bond depicts in* Bingo *the tension in Shakespeare's later life between the ethical ground he has explored in his art and the reality of exercising ethics in life.*]

In *Bingo,* Edward Bond does not claim to uncover any new dramatic truths. Instead, he dramatizes what is known, yet must be said—that human nature cannot exist independently of the society that formulates it. The play, he explains, reveals

> what everyone knows about the way our wishes and intentions and consciences and ideas are turned awry—by money. WS's 'crime' isn't a very bad crime—he doesn't wilfully exploit anyone, or steal wilfully from them, or punish them for criticising him . . . It is all only part of his security and prosperity . . . The play is about the compromises WS makes. But what right has he to call on the poor to make these compromises . . . Even if he shows . . . restraint he still has to make compromises with his own humanity . . . The crime relates to WS. It is brought out by his life. By his pact with society.[1]

At the end of his career Shakespeare is unable to achieve the kind of peace that a life of self-reflection might provide; instead, the opposite is true—he is res-

tive and uneasy. Through the life of art, Bond implies, the artist reproduces his own moral sanity. In *King Lear,* for instance, Shakespeare "insisted on certain moral insights, certain priorities of conduct and you did those things even if it meant your death . . . You did those things because there is no other life that's bearable. For Lear. And Shakespeare must have known that, otherwise he couldn't have written the play."[2] Yet the figure Bond creates in *Bingo* is incapable of mediating the fictive world of his plays and the actual circumstances of his life. The tension in the play is created by the dialectic between an art that is spontaneous and humanitarian and a personal experience that denies those impulses. Shakespeare, living in retirement late in his life, is not alienated from the moral propositions of his art; but he is unable to act in accordance with them. Ethical decision-making has been possible for him only through creative artifice. The disjunction between what is possible in art and what is practical in life provides the axis on which the play rests.

Art, for Bond, satisfies the need of an artist to endow reality with human significance; it provides a means for affirmation of the self as well as the world. Through art Shakespeare had created a moral imperative for action that had determined his relationship with the world; his art was a form of self-creation designed to satisfy his own moral needs. But Shakespeare no longer has the power of artistic expression, and he cannot integrate himself in the material circumstances of his world. The result is that he is unable to correct the inequities that occur around him—unable to combat the material acquisitiveness of Combe, to feel anything but pity for the displaced farmers, and unable even to treat his family with tenderness. Although he had transformed his interior world through the power of his expressiveness, Shakespeare has failed to transform the world outside through the power of action.

In the society of Stratford, having and using constitute his relations with the world. In the process, Shakespeare has altered his essence; political expediency and material concern determine his behavior. The result is exhaustion and loss. Though art should function as the most effective medium between the artist and the world, Shakespeare has lost touch with human specificity. The more he realizes the disparity between his art and his actions, the more he understands his own impoverishment. Estranged from his creative powers and guiltily recoiling from other men, he denies the spirit of his artistic achievement.

Bond's accomplishment in the play does not arise from the revelation of an individual's psychology or the sweeping portrayal of man's behavior in an irrational universe. Instead, that accomplishment rests on the following assumption: "If you are an unjust person it doesn't matter how cultured you are, how capable you are of producing wonderful sayings, wonderful characters, wonderful jokes, you will still destroy yourself."[3] Since the ethical world of Shakespeare's plays remains an implicit reflection of the artist's personality, those plays stand as indictments of his public gestures. Paradoxically, Shakespeare is separated from his own art. What he comes to realize is that he has given birth to that art at the cost of his own well-being; as symbolic extensions of his own powers, his plays are lost to him.

At the beginning of **Bingo,** Shakespeare is divided, at once the creator of the canon and the landed proprietor of New Place—a private moralist and a public materialist. The one role stands for authentic creation, the other for false needs. The result is that Shakespeare, vaguely conscious of such internal division, experiences life as fragmented. As a principal landowner, he is influenced too readily by laws governing the market. Shakespeare's alienation is an economic phenomenon that has been inculcated in him through a system of fake needs; membership in the landed gentry has forced certain pressures upon him and created false allegiances. His alienation is signified by his loss of connection with the moral truth of the plays and consequently with the formal life of art. Through his surrender to the values of Combe, the artist is separated from his product.

Shakespeare's ability to perceive reality with moral persistence remains undiminished, however. Instead of taking action, he aestheticizes reality—the artistic impulse remains intact but is cut off from its moral center, divested of commitment and practical application. It formulates itself in epiphanic, half-conscious utterances on bear-baiting, gliding swans, and clean white snow. The power of expressiveness remains but is stripped of its moral imagination. What remains are glimmerings of creativity, recalibrated fragments of the plays, broken shards of his own mental life. They concretize the gap between the "cultural hero" and the figure who signs what amounts to new poor laws to ensure his own material well-being. The attempt to aestheticize reality in images or in stylized formal address (primarily to Judith) reflects the artists's attempt to come to terms with his own disaffection, perhaps to overcome his dilemma by assimilating it artistically. In the process artistic creation ceases to be a productive and integral activity.

The inability to act has its correlative in the way Shakespeare perceives the act of writing: "Fat white fingers excreting dirty black ink. Smudges. Shadows. Shit. Silence."[4] Through art Shakespeare had created an imaginative world of human measure, yet his practical decisions deny that creation. Only by creating a humanized reality through practical measures can he lead a moral life. The dissociation of art from the artist is complicated because it is partial and incomplete. Silence and detachment have undermined Shakespeare's artistic

credentials. He has in part renounced the idea of human significance; he has silently internalized the inequity between the function of art and the role of the artist in society. This division represents a fracture in the personality of the artist and the surrender of his most essential nature: the result is his separation from other men. Shakespeare retreats into a sphere of egoism, withdraws into a solipsistic self. He is isolated from the community, preoccupied with his private interests, and haunted by images that signify his failure to act. In other men he can see only the limitation of his own freedom, and his despair at this is a measure of his separation from human values.

Bond's argument is that the root of Shakespeare's alienation lies outside his own persona and is embedded in the artificial needs that provide the basis for his social and economic relations with society. Bond asserts that, if one is to change the order of things, one must restructure the socio-economic system:

> To show that our society is irrational and therefore dangerous—and that it maintains itself by denigrating and corrupting human beings—that is what **Bingo** is about. . . . If you want to escape violence, you don't say 'violence is wrong,' you alter the conditions that create violence. . . . Society has to bear the consequences of what it is. If you want to avoid those consequences, the only way you can do it is not by applying a remedy on top but by altering the nature of the problem below. So it seems to me that **Bingo** is a demonstration of the working-out of certain truths about society which are rational and coherent and from which the audience can learn.[5]

Bond concludes that, despite Shakespeare's authority, his stature as a symbol of culture, he "is subject to the same laws as you and I or the man who drives your bus."[6] The paradox is that Shakespeare is tied to the limitations of a class system, while his art is not. He is tied to Combe's economics, yet he is socially and culturally bound to a class that doesn't share the same material relations. If the material world of the artist is denatured, the creativity of the artist is also undermined; the aesthetic cannot be divested of its social relation. If it is, the artist is split by the world he intends to create for. As capitalism gains ascendancy in **Bingo,** life becomes increasingly impersonalized and reified. Shakespeare ceases to identify with capitalistic values; he refuses to exalt an inhuman reality, but he no longer has an artistic form at his disposal in which to announce his refusal.

In the material reality of **Bingo,** art and society are opposed; Bond's interest lies in the disruption of the relationship between the artist and the community. In this context one might ask whether Shakespeare is a victim or a victimizer. Is he denied the power of artistic expression by an inhuman society, or do his actions simply reflect his own insensitivity? Capitalistic society may resist the artist as he tries to express truth in his art, but, since Shakespeare is no longer actively creative, his problem is not how to create but how to resist, how to affirm his presence in an inhuman world. Bond's premise is that the solution is not beyond Shakespeare's control; human relations need not be abstract and impersonal. Even a mythic figure like Shakespeare cannot find refuge in his creative individuality. By disavowing responsibility and by resigning himself to passivity, he creates a society that is antithetical to artistic activity. Ultimately, Shakespeare becomes rootless in a hostile world no longer designed to manifest human presence.

Bond's imaginative re-creation of Shakespeare's disillusion treats him as if he possessed the knowledge of a modern man. Rather than criticize Shakespeare, Bond condemns the segment of our contemporary culture which ignores the truth that art has practical consequences. He argues that

> cultural appreciation ignores this and is no more relevant than a game of Bingo and less honest. . . . [**Bingo** is] a sort of attack on that kind of culture which is seen as something outside life, a sort of gilding on life, or something removed from life . . . It [culture] should be about our lives and it should help us to be able to solve our problems. . . . It would be wrong to say that our problem is such and such now because of something that happened in the past. Our problem is created all the time, constantly re-created [in art as well as in life]. And it's because we don't interfere with the re-creations of our problems that we can't solve our problems.[7]

Bond passionately insists that, for our society to survive, acceptance must turn into action: "You can go quietly into your gas chambers at Auschwitz, you can sit at home and have an H bomb dropped on you."[8]

* * *

Bond's early stage directions indicate the tone of the play and implicitly suggest the path its principal figure will take. Shakespeare nods silently, reads, and in four different stage directions "doesn't react" (p. 3); he initiates no dialogue. The pattern of stasis and silence is established in the first scene. This pattern is formally resolved near the end of the play when Shakespeare mournfully asks, "How long have I been dead?" (p. 51). In between he recants a life divested of purposeful energy and meaningful action:

> I spent so much of my youth, my best energy . . . for this: New Place. Somewhere to be sane in. It was all a mistake. There's a taste of bitterness in my mouth. . . . I could have done so much. Absurd! Absurd! I howled when they suffered, but they were whipped and hanged so that I could be free. . . . I was a hangman's assistant . . . God made the elements but we inflict them on each other.

(p. 48)

Shakespeare's self-conscious silence implies an unresolved tension. His daughter Judith says what her father knows: that reflection is insufficient, that "people in this town aren't so easily impressed . . . We can all sit and think" (p. 18). Shakespeare remains either cordoned off from feeling or numbed by too much of it. Yet his first words belie his apparent detachment: he offers money to an itinerant beggar woman. That Shakespeare is capable of a solicitous gesture is crucial to Bond's argument and is hinted in the subtitle of the play: *Scenes of Money and Death.* The subtitle suggests the primacy of money in culture; it implies that Shakespeare's gesture neither has any bearing on the woman's well-being nor requires any great sacrifice on his part.

Money in capitalist society has become a means to suppress individuality. It "destroys the effect of human values in . . . society because consumer demand can't grow fast enough to maintain profits and full employment while human values are effective. . . . When livelihood and dignity depend on money, human values are replaced by money values."[9] Instead of ridding itself of poverty, a consumer society creates it by depending on its "members [to be] avaricious, ostentatious, gluttonous, envious, wasteful, selfish and inhuman."[10] In **Bingo,** Bond relates our contemporary culture—"the most irrational society that's ever existed"—to its antecedent in Shakespeare's social order, on the basis of the dependence of each on the acquisition of capital:

> We live in a closed society where you need money to live. . . . We have no natural rights, only rights granted and protected by money. Money provides . . . the ground we walk on, the air we breathe, the bed we lie on. People come to think of these things as products of money, not of the earth or human relationships, and finally as the way of getting more money to get more things. Money has its own laws and conventions, and when you live by money you must live by these.[11]

Shakespeare's avoidance of conflict at the beginning of the play and his decision to evade reality reflect a social structure in which human values are replaced by money values. When Combe, the principal landowner and magistrate, arrives, Shakespeare fails to intercede for the Young Woman. His only relation to her has been through the money he has offered her. Similarly, he takes no initiative against Combe for the enclosure of the common fields, even though he realizes that this enclosure will destroy the rural community. In the course of the play he will learn that single gestures—isolated moments of charity—have no bearing on the life of the community. When Shakespeare begins speaking, his words betray his weariness and prepare us for his complicity with Combe: "I get tired" (p. 4), "I don't know anything" (p. 3), "There's plenty of time" (p. 3). A commercial culture, Bond explains, "must finally destroy most of our moral sensitivity because the struggle for profit is much more corroding than the struggle for survival in the old pre-civilized world."[12]

Perhaps Shakespeare's need for security is not quite dramatically convincing. But Bond is not concerned with Shakespeare's psychological motivation: "What are his motives for withdrawing? I don't know . . . He's old, he's tired, he wants security . . . I'm not really interested in his motives."[13] The ideas of art and money (security) merge when Shakespeare, the aging but prosperous burgher, describes his finances: "The rents. I bought my share years ago out of money I made by writing" (p. 5). Despite the dispossession of the poor and the renters who don't have leases, he convinces Combe to guarantee his tithe income. "You'll get increased profits," Shakespeare tells Combe, "—you can afford to guarantee me against loss . . . I invested a lot of money" (p. 6). Bond comments implicitly on Shakespeare's predicament in the introduction to the play: "To get money you must behave like money. I don't mean only that money creates certain attitudes or traits in people, it *forces* certain behaviour on them."[14] Shakespeare refuses to commit his sizable political power to any group and reveals his self-interest when he claims neutrality: "I'm protecting my own interests. Not supporting you or fighting the town . . . I want security. I can't provide for the future . . . My father went bankrupt when he was old. Too easy going" (p. 7). Such specious reasoning would be less transparent if this were not the figure whose plays

> . . . show this need for sanity and its political expression, justice. How did he live? His behaviour as a property-owner made him closer to Goneril than Lear. He supported and benefited from the Goneril-society— with its prisons, workhouses, whipping, starvation, mutilation . . .[15]

Shakespeare's preeminence and moral force reside in his significance as a landowner with vested interests rather than in his artistic accomplishment. By making the arrangement with Combe, Shakespeare in effect accepts "certain laws, and a series of punishments to enforce those laws and a certain mythology to explain those laws."[16] By signing the new poor laws, he no longer functions as a symbol of culture or possesses a rational relationship with the world. By tacitly agreeing to Combe's plea—"Be noncommittal or say you think nothing will come of it. Stay in your garden" (p. 6)—he enmeshes himself in a system where capital is employed to satisfy artificial needs, foster consumption, increase profits, and promote further industrial activity. Greater unemployment and higher food prices result from the loss of corn as a marketable crop as well as from increased competition and aggressiveness. The politics of brutality and fascism are perpetuated; it is the function of the play to suggest the necessity for change:

> I think the contradictions in Shakespeare's life are similar to the contradictions in us. He was a 'corrupt seer' and we are a 'barbarous civilization'. Because of that our society could destroy itself. We believe in

certain values but our society only works by destroying them, so that our lives are a denial of our hopes. That makes our world absurd and often it makes our own species hateful to us.[17]

In a process of de-mythification, *Bingo* reveals Shakespeare's self-loathing, how any man's moral life may become lost. Shakespeare is exposed as a petit bourgeois who aligns himself with a brutal regime that is dedicated to the subjugation of the lower-class and rural community. His compromises become acts of betrayal: they condemn the Young Woman, the Son, the Old Man, and the Old Woman to a life of confinement. "A rational and free culture," Bond contends, "is based on a classless society. . . . [And] the job . . . of writers, of dramatists [is] to . . . rationally argue for a just society, to state clearly the conditions under which we live and try to make everybody understand that they must bear the consequences of the sort of life they lead."[18] The opposite view is held by the chief magistrate, who insists that the only way men have discovered of running the world depends on "the long view," a dark and fatalistic estimate of man: "Men are donkeys and they need carrots and sticks. All the other ways: they come down to bigger sticks" (p. 6). This ruthless, dehumanizing judgment is tinged with class antagonism, and provides the kind of justice that Shakespeare witnesses when the Young Woman is denied his charity because "the law says it's an offense to give alms to anyone without a licence" (p. 17). The casual insensitivity of a society depleted of human value is concealed by a rhetoric that invokes slogans about personal responsibility, payment of one's debts, and protection of the public. This is a social order that defends *injustice*. "That's why," Bond asserts, "law-and-order societies are morally responsible for the terrorism and crime they provoke."[19]

Shakespeare's inability to act undermines his instinctive good will and results in a burden that he will be unable to bear. Ultimately, he neglects culture by avoiding the action that would implement rationality. Paradoxically, as Bond has pointed out, Shakespeare's plays show the need for sanity and its political expression, justice.[20] But he himself simply watches with discomfort as the Young Woman's persecution unfolds. In his Puritan extremism, the Son envisions bestiality being visited upon her; Judith, a naive moralist, projects her own dissatisfaction with her father on the situation; the Old Man, half-maddened at the sight of an axe-handle, lurches merrily around the grounds in revelry over his debauchery of the Young Woman. Shakespeare bears witness to the meagerness and hopelessness of their positions, but says nothing. Despite his silence, his mind is alive and perceptive. When the Young Woman is finally seized by a power structure without compassion, he sighs. He allows his final offer of mediation to be brushed aside too easily. He chooses to remain, as Combe had urged, in the quiet of his garden.

Alone, ensconced in silence, he speaks only in stripped-down, practical, monosyllabic prose. There is no need for a more complex syntax because Shakespeare has nothing more complex to say. His attempts to communicate with Judith are sheerly formal: his sentences are declarative, factual, and insensate. She is not without our sympathy. She pleads with her father, "People have feelings. They suffer. Life almost breaks them" (p. 18). Hers is part of the generalized disaffection that all the characters endure. Shakespeare's ailing wife, Judith tells him, "stays in bed. She hides from you. She doesn't know who she is, or what she's supposed to do, or who she married. She's bewildered—like so many of us!" (p. 18) When Shakespeare contemptuously replies, "You speak so badly. Such banalities. So stale and ugly" (p. 18), it is her form rather than her sentiments that he coldly reproves. He is not impervious to feeling, but he has detached himself from experience in order to be able to examine it aesthetically. His remarks are leveled against Judith's means of expression, as if she were uttering lines from an inferior play and uttering them poorly at that. Shakespeare's criticism here is an extension of his art in its tendency to formulate experience abstractly. Yet, as a type of communication, such criticism impedes feeling and resists human contact.

The issue that Bond addresses through the character of Shakespeare is how the artist, or any man of conscience, assimilates moral knowledge through experience. The execution and gibbeting of the Young Woman elicit different responses from different segments of a stratified society, and Bond uses these responses to anatomize a culture that resists any sense of community or mutual responsibility and that neglects human suffering. Two farm laborers conjecture, "She die summat slow" (p. 22); they are insulated from feeling by the hardship of their own lives. The Son's Puritan extremism is framed by an Old Testament religiosity that shrilly insists on its own righteousness: at the sight of the Young Woman's body, he declares, "Lord god is wherever there's justice" (p. 22). The Son interprets experience in terms of strict moral categories: "When a soul go satan-ways lord god come to' watch an' weep" (p. 22). Judith feels complicity in the Young Woman's death; she intuitively recognizes that her action, or inaction, has somehow widened the gap between her and her father: "Are you blaming me? Is that what I've done now?" (p. 24) The Old Man recalls the grotesque, riotous atmosphere that accompanies a public execution:

> (*He starts to cry.*) O dear, I do hate a hanging. People runnin' through the streets laughin' an' sportin'. Buyin' an' sellin'. I allus enjoyed the hangings when I were a boy. Now I can't abide 'em. The conjurors with red noses takin' animals out the air an' coloured things out their pockets. The soldier lads scare us. The parson an' 'is antics.
>
> (p. 19)

Rather than become personally involved in the spectacle of the Young Woman's death, each of these witnesses detaches himself from it either morally, intellectually, or emotionally, and thus reveals his own victimization by society.

After he has regarded the gibbeted Young Woman with an expressionless face, Shakespeare literally turns his back on the sight; yet, he is the only figure to attempt to acknowledge the reality of the scene and formulate a human response: "I thought I knew the questions. Have I forgotten them?" (p. 25) This is the first time he articulates self-doubt in the play. He talks deliberately, as if to reassure himself against his own worst fears. With the first glimmer of recognition come the guilt and self-reproach that had lain in wait at the borders of his consciousness. Up to now, Bond had cast Shakespeare's inexpressiveness as a kind of emasculated potential; still, the consciousness of the artist had always been at work—selecting, observing, registering—and what finally emerges is no longer neutrality or disengagement. Shakespeare transforms the world of the hanging into one of bear-baiting, and connects the victimization of the Young Woman with that of a bear:

> The baited bear. Tied to the stake. . . . Dried mud and spume. . . . Men bringing dogs through the gate. . . . Loose them and fight. The bear wanders round the stake. It knows it can't get away. . . . Flesh and blood. Strips of skin. Teeth scrapping bone. . . . Round the stake. On and on. . . . Howls. Roars. Men baiting their beast. . . . And later the bear raises its great arm. The paw with a broken razor. And it looks as if it's making a gesture—it wasn't: only weariness or pain . . . Asking for one sign of grace . . . And the crowd roars, for more blood, more pain . . .
>
> (p. 25)

Shakespeare recites this monologue of brutal persecution in an objective, reportorial manner; the sheer horror inheres in the facts themselves—they need not be embellished by the imagination. The artist himself seems a likely surrogate for the wounded bear: impotent, staked to a circumscribed lot of ground, unable to surmount the pain and weariness.

It is Judith's assertion, "You're only interested in your ideas" (p. 26), that impels Shakespeare to utter what Bond has prepared us for by means of the monologue on bear-baiting, the Old Man's account of a public execution, and the gibbeting itself: "What does it cost to stay alive? I'm stupefied at the suffering I've seen" (p. 26). The consciousness of the artist is the consciousness of any moral man in an immoral universe. Shakespeare has begun to exchange the inactivity and silence of the early scenes for movement and action, and so succumbs to recognition and culpability: "There's no wisdom beyond your own responsibility." This is the first draft of a line from the notebooks of Leonardo Da

Vinci, the final version of which Shakespeare quotes: "There's no higher wisdom of silence" (p. 26). Bond comments:

> I thought it was very appropriate for someone like Shakespeare who has by far the most influence of any dramatist since the Greeks. And he would have said: Yes—but you see, I haven't really done anything, I haven't answered any of these problems and I haven't answered all those things that I want to, I haven't been able to set down solutions that make sense to anybody.[21]

The artist who conceived King Lear is wrenched out of his fictive self-containment and is filled with bewilderment not unlike Lear's: "I quietened the storms inside me. But the storm breaks outside" (p. 27). It is the revelation of the play that Shakespeare acknowledges the efficacy of the artist in determining culture, yet still admits that he "usurped the place of god, and lied" (p. 27). There is a dichotomy between the artist who carries on an interior life and the responsible citizen who intercedes for the spiritual health of the community: a division between contemplation and action, art and activity, imagination and reality.

By the middle of the play, Shakespeare renounces his neutrality, but his split self is not so easily united. Bond purposely refashions him as a folk hero who is beset by the same doubts as other men. He is generous, but without endangering his own interests; he would have liked to aid the Young Woman, but he did not do so. Although his intentions remain unacted upon, his position as a landowning member of the gentry at least gives him the opportunity to pose the right questions. The Old Woman servant can only lament, "I yont afford arkst questions" (p. 27). Shakespeare has always acknowledged the importance of the issues but has suppressed them for the sake of self-interest. They resurface, transformed, in his metaphoric, epiphanic utterances. In a moment of outward calm he narrates his encounter with a swan:

> A swan flew by me up the river. On a straight line just over the water. A woman in a white dress running along an empty street. Its neck was rocking like a wave. I heard its breath when it flew by. Sighing. The white swan and the dark water. Straight down the middle of the river and round a curve out of sight. I could still hear its wings. God knows where it was going. . . . (*He goes to the gibbet.*) Still perfect. Still beautiful.
>
> (pp. 27-28)

For a moment art merges with reality, just as it did during Shakespeare's monologue on bear-baiting. The scene of the hanging is transformed and aestheticized. The flight of the swan becomes a metaphor for the pure, clean life of abstract art, which is created "automatically," without interference from the imagination. Shakespeare's swan glides noiselessly, unencumbered by the life below, the lazy curve of its flight like the slow withdrawal of a spirit from reality. The gibbeted woman, disfigured by a brutal death, remains in this way aesthetically intact. Shakespeare's imagination functions as a safety valve, an escape, a means somehow to temper reality by transforming its ugliness into beauty. Yet Shakespeare's words are counterpointed and at least partly called into doubt by the choric utterance of the Old Woman, whose hardheadedness enables her to penetrate the artificiality of his speech: "Her's ugly. Her face is all a-twist. . . . She smell" (p. 28).

* * *

The artistic process rather than the life of art is the subject of the confrontation between Shakespeare and Ben Jonson at the start of Part Two of *Bingo.* Shakespeare's acknowledgement that he writes nothing because he has nothing to say, partly indicates the disjuncture between his art and his experience. Jonson, by contrast, has had a continuous series of engagements with life. He unwittingly isolates the source of Shakespeare's discomfort when he asks, "What's your life been like? Any real blood . . . ? . . . Life doesn't seem to touch you, I mean soil you. . . . You are serene" (pp. 31-32). Unsurprisingly, the artistic process seems to consume Jonson's powers without replenishing them. He shares Shakespeare's sense of impotence and articulates his more reknowned colleague's silent thoughts and hidden regrets: "I go on and on, why can't I stop? I even talk shit now. To know the seasons of life and death and walk quietly on the path between them" (p. 34). If he does not grasp Shakespeare's problem, he notices its symptoms when he adds, "Something's happening to your will. You're being sapped" (p. 32). As Shakespeare has said, he does not write because he has nothing to say. When he did have something to say, he expressed it in the context of his plays; the only thing that remains for him is to put his ideas into action and validate himself as a man of society as well as culture.

Jonson's notion of the artistic process echoes Shakespeare's vision of reality. Throughout the play, Shakespeare reflects on life like a merchant burdened by the exigencies of middle-class existence: "The garden's too big. Time goes. I'm surprised how old I've got" (p. 31). The tone is bourgeois and familiar to any middle-class household breaking apart because of internal stress. By emphasizing Shakespeare's relatedness to all men in this way, Bond suggests that any citizen should be prepared to act to change his society for the better—to bring his daily life in line with his aspirations, "the economic and political basis of society in line with our ethical propaganda."[22] Though Shakespeare and Jonson are both in despair, Bond implies that Jonson has in the past at least been passionately involved in life: he has been imprisoned four times, experienced several religious conversions, and has actually committed murder. Now he, like Shakespeare, grows desperate with thoughts of escape and solace, like any artist who has witnessed horror but stood passively aside.

Jonson's reverie, "To spend my life wandering through quiet fields. Charm fish from the water with a song. Gather simple eggs. Muse with my reflection in quiet water . . . And lie at last in some cool mossy grave . . ." (p. 36), is dramatically counterpointed by a central action in the play: the dispossession of the farm laborers. Combe confronts the rebellious peasants who refuse to be displaced by "rich thieves plunderin' the earth" (p. 35). The Son, the leader of the opposition, asks Combe, "Whose interest's that protectin'? Public or yourn?" (p. 36) As the two antithetical social classes in the play confront each other, the two writers resign themselves to positions that have no bearing on the life of the community. While Shakespeare is slumped over a table and filled with drink, Combe expounds his views of cultural evolution to the Son:

> And there can be no civilization till you've learned to live with it. I live in the real world and try to make it work. There's nothing more moral than that. But you live in a world of dreams! Well, what happens when you have to wake up? You find that real people can't live in your dreams. They don't fit, they're not good or sane or noble enough.
>
> (p. 36)

This speech supports the idea that capitalism is founded "on the proposition that men are by nature enemies and . . . works on the principle that it is natural for the strong to exploit the weak, the powerful to shape the powerless."[23] Thus the speech stands as an implied critique of Shakespeare's art, the art of an idealist who believes that men can change the shape of events, can subvert a society that prolongs itself through a distorted view of human nature. The realization that his signature endorses an exploitative political system has become impossible to endure, so Shakespeare has taken to rationalizing the system. His exhaustion in this scene intimates less his decline as an artist than his death as a force in the life of the community. The two authors, one drunk and the other unconscious, inhabit a world of blunted possibility.

Scene Five of Part Two follows the scene between Shakespeare and Ben Jonson and begins with the stage directions, "Open space. Flat white crispy empty. The fields, paths, roads, bushes and trees are covered with smooth, clean snow" (p. 39). Shakespeare idly muses over this landscape: "How clean and empty the snow is. A sea without life. An empty glass. Still smooth. No footprints. No ruts. No marks of weapons or hoes dragged through the ground. Only my footprints behind me—and they're white . . . white" (p. 39). In effect, he creates here an image of his legacy to the world, which remains "smooth" and "clean," untouched and un-

changed by his powers. Bond's notes for an earlier draft place another interpretation on these lines: "Snow = perfect ideal. When it doesn't melt, WS lives in the perfect ideal. The perfect ideal is false because it is unreal. An ideal is always a lie."[24]

When in the darkness the Son accidentally shoots his father, "Shakespeare," says Bond, "ignores the wounded figure: this is the essence of his situation. Here he is drawn into the discovery of self-knowledge, so concentrated in his self-judgement, that you could probably set fire to his coat and he wouldn't notice it."[25] For the first time, he is able to address Judith with candor on a topic of intimacy:

> When I ran away from your mother and went to London—I was so bored, she's such a silly woman, obstinate, and you take after her. Forgive me, I know that's cruel, sordid, but it's such an effort to be polite any more. . . . I loved you with money. . . . But money always turns to hate. . . . I treated you so badly. I made you vulgar and ugly and cheap. I corrupted you.
>
> (pp. 41-42)

Though he finally acknowledges complicity in the corruption of his daughter (with the same means that Combe used on him), even his contempt for her is aestheticized and detached: "Don't be angry because I hate you, Judith. My hatred isn't angry. It's cold and formal. I wouldn't harm you. . . . There's no limit to my hate. It can't be satisfied by cruelty. It's destroyed too much to be satisfied so easily. Only truth can satisfy it now" (p. 42). Judith represents to Shakespeare (however unfairly) the irrationality of life, of society; the fact that this irrationality is of no relevance to her generates her father's hatred. His hatred is more likely a self-hatred, however, generated by the gulf between his humanistic intentions and the society that has eroded them. For Shakespeare, the impasse between a creative, searching interior life and the objective, peremptory world of action results in the artist's willed demise.

Shakespeare's political as well as artistic silence resolves itself in his suicide. Each of these silences has implied and complemented the other. Although creativity satisfies an inner need for expression and is necessary to sustain culture, it cannot thrive when sealed off from practical action. The result is the dispossession of the social self in addition to the artistic one. Nobody, not even Shakespeare, can create in a void. Our final image of him is of a limp figure helplessly twitching and jerking on the floor while Judith pronounces his legacy as she ransacks the room for a new will: "Nothing. Nothing. Nothing" (pp. 51-52).

Not surprisingly, it is Combe who presides over Shakespeare's demise as he casually hands him Jonson's poison bottle. Combe emerges "as the formidable enemy he is and neither Shakespeare nor the Son can oppose him."[26] In Combe's gesture of giving Shakespeare the poison tablets, Bond crystallizes the latter's confrontation with and capitulation to the ruling class. Yet Shakespeare's taking of his own life is a refusal, finally, to be part of the capitalist system. Rather than being the disillusioned words of a sterile aesthete, his refrain, "Was anything done?" (p. 51), acknowledges his altered vision as well as a measure of self-blame. Unlike the Son, Shakespeare refuses (however belatedly) to deceive himself. He has become self-critical, enough so that he can declare, "Every writer writes in other men's blood. There's nothing else to write in. But only a god or a devil can write in other men's blood and not ask why they spilt it and at what cost" (p. 43). Implicitly, Shakespeare has come to believe, like Bond, that "morality can exist only in a culture or be forged in the quest for one."[27]

Notes

1. Malcolm Hay and Philip Roberts, *Edward Bond: A Companion to the Plays* (London: Theatre Quarterly Publications, 1978), p. 198.

2. Hay and Roberts, p. 59.

3. Karl-Heinz Stoll, "Interviews with Edward Bond and Arnold Wesker," *Twentieth Century Literature,* 22, No. 4 (Dec. 1976), p. 418.

4. Edward Bond, *Bingo* and *The Sea* (New York: Hill and Wang, 1975), p. 31. Hereafter cited by page number in the text.

5. Stoll, pp. 418, 421.

6. Stoll, p. 422.

7. Hay and Roberts, pp. 18, 21; Stoll, p. 420 (from "It would be wrong . . ." on).

8. Hay and Roberts, p. 18.

9. Bond, Intro., *Bingo,* p. xiii.

10. Bond, Intro., *Bingo,* p. xiii.

11. Bond, Intro., *Bingo,* pp. xii-xiii.

12. Hay and Roberts, p. 46.

13. Hay and Roberts, p. 62.

14. Bond, Intro., *Bingo,* p. xiii.

15. Bond, Intro., *Bingo,* p. xii.

16. Hay and Roberts, p. 60.

17. Bond, Intro., *Bingo,* p. xvi.

18. Stoll, p. 418.

19. Bond, Intro., *Bingo,* p. xv.

20. Bond, Intro., *Bingo,* p. xvi.

21. Hay and Roberts, p. 59.

22. Hay and Roberts, p. 52.

23. Hay and Roberts, p. 51.

24. Hay and Roberts, p. 195.

25. Hay and Roberts, p. 195.

26. Hay and Roberts, p. 197.

27. Edward Bond, *The Fool* and *We Come to the River* (London: Eyre Methuen, 1976), p. viii.

THE FOOL (1975)

PRODUCTION REVIEWS

John Elsom (review date 27 November 1975)

SOURCE: Elsom, John. "Method in Madness." *Listener (London)* (27 November 1975): 725-26.

[*In the following review of a 1975 production of* The Fool *at the Royal Court Theatre in London, directed by Peter Gill, Elsom finds increased maturity on Bond's part in handling of the causes and results of violence but notes that the play overall is "less moving and powerful" than Bond's earlier work,* Bingo.]

The Fool at the Royal Court is Edward Bond's latest attempt to describe the particular situation of an artist caught in the crossfire of class war. It thus follows in the direction of **Bingo** and **Narrow Road,** without quite treading on the same stones. The violent images, for which Bond is renowned, derive their force from an overall logic, about man and society, which hold them in place. The violence is not arbitrary. It is illustrative of a wider struggle, a brutalising process which goes on when there are no titbits of savagery to distract us; and the tragic inevitability, which infuses even Bond's lesser plays (of which **The Fool** is one), lies in the fact that he can see no end to the conflict. The damage has been done. The cancer of social corruption rages unchecked.

In **The Fool,** Bond hints plainly at the sort of historical perspective on which this vision is based. He even alters history a little to make the pattern more explicit, pushing the Cambridgeshire land riots further west to affect directly the youth of John Clare, the Northamptonshire 'peasant' poet who is his 'fool'. The driving of peasants from the village common land, in order to establish large 'enclosed' farms owned by the local gentry, was the first act of class deprivation; but just around the corner was the second act, the transformation of men into 'wage slaves' as the result of the Industrial Revolution. Thus, the land-deprived peasants were also forced to move from their villages in order to earn their livings in industrial towns, losing their friends, families and ways of life, as well as the acres; and this process leads to the concrete, soulless monoliths of modern society. The class war loses its human face. Men, whose livelihoods are at the mercy of exchange rates and multinationals, are not given the comfort of knowing whom precisely to hate or fear; and so their resentments do become arbitrary, picking out casual victims from the street and relieving their anger upon them.

This is Bond's perspective, as I understand it, and, of course, it can be challenged. A prime example of once fertile land which was not 'enclosed' is the Sahara desert. But just as we accept Shakespeare's feudalism, Brecht's Marxism and Claudel's Christianity, not as being theories which represent the sum total of their plays but as background philosophies which pull their various insights into shape, so with Bond we must begin where he begins, with the class war and its consequences.

Bond's artists are people who want to opt out of the class war, as, I suspect, do most of us. They see its brutalities, they have their preoccupations and they do not want to be bothered. But, of course, they cannot escape. Shakespeare, in *Bingo,* possessed a unique insight into the surrounding horrors, but with one act at the end of his life, he joined with the oppressors against the oppressed—and this drove him to suicide. John Clare's life begins and ends on the other side. He is one of the oppressed; but, for one brief spell, he is snatched up by the middle classes, fêted in London, until a homing instinct compels him to return to his cottage and his wife, Patty, where he finds himself lost, declassed and nagged.

He lives on meagre handouts from local gentry (historically, a small annuity), a generosity which he resents, although it keeps him barely breathing; and drifts into another mental world, inhabited by his first love, Mary, the daughter of a local farmer. In Bond's play, Mary is also a leader of the land rebels, sacked from her job as one of Lord Milton's servants, accepting her fate cheerfully and joining the tinkers on the road. She therefore represents something more than an old flame: rather, a defiant independence, someone who was prepared to act, count the consequences and survive, while Clare merely watched.

In his madness, Clare twists in anguish most over his impotence. In his fantasies, his true wife, Mary, disclaims him: he has not learnt how to survive with dignity. A mere wisp of bone and skin, Clare affects the reckless aggression of London prizefighters. When that

fails—for a finger could push him aside and his ranting merely embarrasses those who have to live with him— Clare subsides into silence. Lord Milton places him in a 'civilised' asylum, where he broods privately, almost unvisited, for 23 more years. That is the end of him.

If *The Fool* is a less moving and powerful play than *Bingo* (as I consider it to be), the basic problem may lie in the character of Clare. Both Shakespeare and Clare are apparently passive figures, occupying the centre of the play; but Shakespeare's passivity, so tellingly conveyed by John Gielgud, masks an internal conflict where motives pull his mind this way and that until he finally implicates himself tragically. Clare scarcely has the opportunity to choose. Clare is flotsam, whereas Shakespeare is a quiet rudder, turning his ship (and ours) on to the rocks.

This passivity, pure and simple, presents Tom Courtenay as Clare with a particularly difficult task, for his madness, unlike Shakespeare's suicide, does not derive from anything which he has exactly done, but more from being in the wrong place at the wrong time. In *The Fool,* the first onset of temporary madness comes when Clare visits his friends, the land rebels, in prison. Bond sets up a telling contrast, for Clare has just received news that his poems are to be published. During the visit, however, Clare and the prisoners hear the judicial verdict, that some rebels are to be deported, whereas one, the brother of Patty, is to be hung. Clare's horror at the thought of the hanging is thus mixed with the almost sinister elation that he personally can escape from the prison of his society; and he lapses into hysterical laughter, which seems to echo round the vaults, matching the relief of other prisoners who hear that they are not to be killed.

I found these moments at the end of the first act melodramatic, as if Bond were trying to stress and explain what was happening at the expense of ordinary credibility. A similar overtness affects other scenes, and some of them seem to have been constructed almost in memory of what Bond has done before. One such scene is where the land rebels bullyrag the local parson, stripping off his clothes and humiliating him. It dimly reminded me of the stoning scene in *Saved*; but its full power was toned down by the didacticism of the accompanying lines. 'Where yoo stole that flesh, boy? Yoor flesh is stolen goods. Yoo're covered in stolen goods when you strip!'

Another scene which seemed to miss its true impact was that in Hyde Park at the beginning of the second act, where a brutal prize-fight is going on backstage, while, in the front, Clare is being occupied in light literary chat. The fight ought to have held the horror of that scene in *Bingo* where a dead girl hangs by a pole; but, in fact, it did not. It was too stagey, and the counterpointed dialogue too obtrusive. The middle-class patrons were cartoons, and only Bill Fraser as a scribbling admiral who disapproves of radicalism made enough of his lines.

The Fool is subtitled 'Scenes of Bread and Love', and this emphasis on individual scenes means that it lacks the story flow of other Bond plays. Peter Gill, who took over from William Gaskill the rich task of directing Bond at the Court, did not, perhaps, find the factual restraint proper to his plays, thus underlining some weaknesses in this script. Where Bond explained too much, Gill gave his actors slack rope, thus encouraging them to overplay, particularly in the scenes already mentioned. But I do not wish to suggest that either the script or the production prevented *The Fool* from being anything other than an engrossing evening. It contains thought and deeply-felt emotion; rich performances from Tom Courtenay, Bridget Turner as Patty, John Normington as the clergyman whose humiliation leads to some Christian self-knowledge, Bill Fraser, and Nicholas Selby as Lord Milton; passages of tough-minded sinewy dialogue, and that capacity to open out a theme in many directions which has always been Bond's greatest asset as a dramatist.

Benedict Nightingale (review date 28 November 1975)

SOURCE: Nightingale, Benedict. "Compassionate Scribbler." *New Statesman* 90, no. 2332 (28 November 1975): 689.

[*In the following review, Nightingale offers high praise for Gill's 1975 production of* The Fool, *noting especially Bond's well-rounded depictions of the upper and lower classes.*]

'Has the world gone mad?' wails John Clare as someone drops a bagful of unsold poems beside him—and, since his chronicler is Edward Bond, the answer is hardly in doubt. In Act One his best friend is hanged for upsetting those who have been robbing the East Anglian peasantry of its land and livelihood; and in Act Two he finds himself obliged to rely on the erratic patronage of just such nobs and plunderers. Social criticism, they tell him, can't be countenanced. Nor can the celebration of free love. It is his duty to take up his pipes and be the pastoral primitive, warbling of nymphs and shepherds in bosky dells, not men and women in workhouses. As if that weren't enough, his publisher asks him to pay for the privilege of being remaindered, and his half-starved wife nags him to find a proper job and give up all that 'scribble, scribble, scribble'. And to cap even *that,* they come with a straitjacket, accusing him of getting over-excited. I was reminded of what Tom Stoppard's Rosencrantz said of another maddish victim of a disjointed world:

Your father, whom you love, dies, you are his heir, you come back to find that hardly was the corpse cold before his young brother popped onto his throne and into his sheets, thereby offending both legal and natural practice. Now why exactly are you behaving in this extraordinary manner?

This is Bond's second foray into speculative biography, and the second time he's shown us a writer floundering in the yellow sludge of British society. In *Bingo,* he postulated a suicidal Shakespeare, guilt-stricken by his collaboration with the Stratford predators: and now he takes us a few rungs down the ladder of gentility, to a perch he may well feel that he himself shares with Clare. Bond, too, is of working-class origins, writes in rural East Anglia, and has been bitterly attacked for presuming to tell the truth as he sees it. In particular, he's been accused of a morbid obsession with violence, a charge that *The Fool* should help to refute. The most obviously nasty scene has the parish parson robbed and stripped by angry labourers, who then grab at his flesh as if to rip it off. But the point is clear enough, and clearly made by one of the participants. 'You stood there two minutes, boy,' she tells the snivelling old man, 'I'm made a mock of all my life.' Which is more violent—to riot, or to provoke a riot by systematic oppression? To rob and humiliate a clergyman, or hang men for doing so? Bond doesn't wallow: he discriminates, and invites us to do so, too.

It is carefully, compassionately done: the peasants aren't idealised nor the masters glibly derided. If the play sometimes amounts to a cry of anger and pain, it is certainly a far cry from that familiar apologia for terrorist atrocity, which declares that the evil of the 'establishment' is sufficient to justify any counter-evil. Bond's own answer to institutionalised violence has never been more violence: it is, if anything, more John Clares. Certainly, *The Fool* is as much about spiritual and cultural poverty as about the literal, material sort; and it is a poverty not confined to the oppressed orders. At one point Clare's dainty patroness appears in his garden, and he impulsively hugs her and begins to weep only to remember himself and draw back: 'Sorry, mustn't.' The literate, like her, tend to dislike strong, authentic emotions and those with strong emotions, like the rampaging labourers, tend not to be literate. Poor Clare is marooned between the reading classes who do not feel and the feeling classes who do not read. And the main difference between his predicament and that of the poet nowadays—or so I suspect the author of *Saved* would maintain—is that a semi-literate rump has emerged from all that raw humanity, zonked and brutalised by a century and a half of the industrial splurge and urban clutter we see in their birth-throes in *The Fool.*

The play isn't beyond reproach, even if you accept its social analyses and cultural diagnoses, as many obviously will not. I myself thought Bond too inclined to take for granted that Clare was a writer of rare perception and potential: it's a pity that all we hear of his poetry is a couple of snatches recited, with her usual sentimentality, by the untouchable patroness. It would surely have been possible to insert rather more into the fabric of a play already unconventional enough to introduce the ghosts both of Clare's hanged friend and of Mary, the servant-girl who obsesses and distracts him in his madness. But Bond has provided enough tense, terse writing to satisfy all but the congenitally carping. There are finer scenes, perhaps; but I was most struck by the one in which four of Clare's neighbours are reprieved from the gallows. They and he laugh and laugh, like spectators at a farce, not noticing or caring that one of their number is still doomed. It is grotesque and discomforting, but also a persuasive reminder of the tenacity with which people cling on to the most wretched lives—and, of course, precisely the sort of instinctive, animal reaction that Bond's Clare is precluded from incorporating into his poetry.

Unluckily, the scene is spoiled by the laughter that sweeps onstage from other, invisible cells in the prison. It sounds dreadfully canned. But I've no more serious objection to make to Peter Gill's production, though it is mostly so stark and austere that I quite expected to see Sir Stafford Cripps stalking among the ghosts with his dispatch-case. Actually, his grey shade was probably in the office upstairs when the management was comparing the cost of the sets with its Arts Council grant. But the visual austerity suits both Bond's spare style and the uncluttered acting Mr Gill has conjured from a cast that includes Nicholas Selby as a local grandee, John Normington as a death-obsessed clergyman, Bridget Turner as Clare's harassed wife, and (of course) Tom Courtenay as the ploughman-poet himself. This is a remarkably unassuming, unactorish, unselfish performance, which is not to say it is an unperformance. We start with a sweet, responsive boy, who takes unaffected delight in everything from sex to Christmas mummery, and we end with a haggard, ravaged old corpse, glassily staring from beneath hair like stale shredded wheat. In between there are just a few moments of open anguish: a sudden, frantic twist of the body, for instance, when someone brightly suggests that Clare should sell his unwanted volumes to his fellow-villagers—'they can't read!' But such outbursts are quickly repressed, as they have to be—and here, somewhere, is the answer to anyone who finds Mr Courtenay excessively understated.

This is a picture of the artist in numb conflict with his public, his impulses and his muse, and it leaves me without breath or space for the Prospect's revived *Month in the Country* (Albery), which I propose to review next week in conjunction with its new *Room With a View*.

RESTORATION (1981)

PRODUCTION REVIEWS

Irving Wardle (review date 22 July 1981)

SOURCE: Wardle, Irving. "Triumph of Violence." *Times* London (22 July 1981): 15.

[*In the following review, Wardle offers measured praise for a 1981 production of* Restoration *at the Royal Court Theatre in London, directed by Bond, but ultimately finds it full of "bold urgent gestures in which nothing much gets said."*]

Proceeding in his mission of ripping the veil from our culture's classical sanctuaries, Edward Bond follows his exposures of Greek and Shakespearian tragedy with an unmasking of Restoration comedy. The piece is subtitled "a pastoral", but anybody who swallows that is really being led up the garden path.

Lord Are, having grabbed the title at his father's death and run through his inheritance, is now lowering himself to a union with an iron master's daughter; and when we first see the preening young fop he is arranging himself becomingly against a tree (rarely having seen one before) so as to achieve love at first sight and avoid the tedium of courtship. So far we are in a world of straight Restoration parody, for which Bond proves himself stylistically well equipped. More important than the bride, though, is the figure of young Bob, arriving from his lordship's country estate, and leading us into the below stairs society which is the play's main concern.

As I understand it **Restoration** has a clear objective combining style and statement. Up in the sunny breakfast rooms of the aristocracy of Lord Are and his grotesque old mother (affording too brief a glimpse of an aristocratically transformed Irene Handl), all is comedy; even murder and villainous betrayal. Down below, it is as dark and joyless as elsewhere in the prison house of Bond's England.

Much the most vital passages in **Restoration** are those when violence takes over, either above or below stairs.

Frank, a footman, is caught stealing a spoon, and Bob leaps at him and bolts him into a box, fully understanding that this is a hanging matter. The idea that this takes place between two *servants* introduces an element of social complexity much beyond the black and white class divisions.

Up in the breakfast room, Lord Are's disappointed young wife appears to him in the likeness of an avenging ghost, at which point he playfully drives with his sword at the spectre who drops dead with a little squeak; somewhat put out by this, the killer hands the weapon over to the guileless Bob and gets him to repeat the crime; all in a spirit of fun, for which Bob will finally pay with a hanging.

Thanks also to Simon Callow's ruthlessly ridiculously, ever beaming, Are, the social point is deftly made by bringing high comedy to tremble on the brink of farce.

There remain, alas, great snowdrifts of working-class protest drama, led by Bob's African wife (Debby Bishop), and featuring Elizabeth Bradley as a stoical housekeeper and John Barrett as a blind swineherd.

These scenes are written in Bond's folk drama style: presenting dire events in a matter-of-fact manner, and breaking off for sage parables—as if told to children but serving only to confuse the issue. Their main outlet is in the Brechtian songs, at which the actors drop out of character and period, and whose irregular lines are ingeniously, if unmemorably, contained in Nick Bicat's Eislerlike settings. Philip Davis makes something memorable from Bob, his grinning features periodically hardening into the blank stare of an Indian mask; and Hayden Griffin's set, with its menacingly mobile band, is an expressive variation on the German model. But it is an evening of bold urgent gestures in which nothing much gets said.

Peter Holland (review date 7 August 1981)

SOURCE: Holland, Peter. "Upstairs, Downstairs." *Times Literary Supplement* (7 August 1981): 906.

[*In the following review of Bond's 1981 production of* Restoration, *Holland finds the play worthy of textual revision and a better performance than it was given.*]

Restoration is set, according to the published text, in "England, eighteenth century—or another place at another time". The choice typifies a dilemma Bond has often made himself confront. He deliberately sets his desire for a precise and authentic historicity against equally strong aspirations towards a mythic, emblematic kind of writing in which historical analysis is transformed into general statement. The twin aims are rarely both satisfied in his work. In particular, the consciously "poeticized" form, drama as myth, frequently proves as emptily pretentious as the phrase here, "another place at another time". The rigour of Bond's presentation of social detail is too often befogged by the imprecision of the general lesson.

In many ways *Restoration* is closest in Bond's work to *The Fool* (1975), his last play for the Royal Court. It shares the same affectionate but unsentimentalized fascination with the East Anglian rural working class of the eighteenth century, the same horror at the identification of justice with the rights of the land-owners, the same distress at the consequences of the servants' humiliating subservience to that powerful hierarchy. *The Fool* explored the ground through the perspective offered by the life of John Clare, the peasant as poet. *Restoration* turns from the writer to a literary form, Restoration comedy.

There are two immediate problems. The social relationships embodied within the form are far less precise, here, than the direct reality of Clare's career; and the comic model is itself used by Bond in a surprisingly vague way. Bond has shown how a pre-existent form can serve as a strengthening analogue for a play—in *Lear,* and in his use of *Timon* in *The Worlds.* But where he has tried to re-insert the model into its own historical context the pull towards myth has been too strong and the historical precision has all but evaporated. *Restoration* has no precise link to any historical moment. Instead it drifts around the eighteenth century making Restoration comedy mean anything between Farquhar and Goldsmith, rather than Wycherley and Congreve.

This is not simply a pedantic complaint. The play depends on the juxtaposition of disparate styles, a series of comic conventions set beside the reality of the below-stairs life that those conventions normally submerge and ignore. In a key scene, Lord Are accidentally kills his wife and then hits on the plan of tricking his servant Bob into believing himself guilty of the murder. As a cornerstone of the contrasts and connections out of which the play is constructed, this has to be accepted by the audience as sufficient cause for the subsequent events of the play. But the scene's farcical improbability, beautifully managed in performance, forces the audience to concentrate not on the events themselves but on the social tensions inherent in the form. And when that form itself is so loosely defined, the message is seriously weakened. Lord Are has been manoeuvred into appearing as a villain but the revelation has been achieved less by the stripping away of social veneers than by the blatancy of the dramatist's manipulation.

It might seem odd, then, to find the three strengths of the play in Lord Are's comic language, in the detailed social observation and in the aggressive anachronism of the songs. It was plain in *The Sea* that Bond has a wickedly observant eye for the comedy of social ostentation, yet it is still a surprising pleasure to find in *Restoration* a style of speech that is genuinely witty. Lord Are's self-congratulatory wit is at times bedevilled by "ye" and "-eth" archaisms but it is frequently epigrammatic without being a weak imitation Wilde, and elegantly balanced without being pastiche Congreve. In itself that is quite an achievement. The low-born Lady Are, whom he marries for her money, dies in the breakfast-room while (for inordinately complicated reasons) disguised as a ghost. Lord Are is foppishly amazed: "'Tis—'twas—she. I cannot say why she is so dressed. I do not recall she mentioned a fancy-dress breakfast. Who can fathom the mind of one suddenly raised to the peerage?" Bond has given him some marvellous throwaway lines ("Bob, throw the toast to the hens on your way to prison") and Simon Callow is too intelligent an actor to miss any of the part's opportunities.

At times, too, *Restoration* has fragments of social detail that are brilliantly observed. He is particularly acute in a scene where Bob and his mother want to turn in another servant, Frank, for stealing one of Lord Are's spoons. Frank's city-bred belief in the servant's right to steal anything his master might leave lying around is set against Bob's obstinate sense of inherited duty to the Are family. His mother has for years had the job of polishing the silver cutlery, even though she will never use it: "Bad 'nough clean 'em t'let other make 'em dirty. What I want goo dirtyin' 'em meself for?" Bond refuses to treat the servants as an undifferentiated group. Instead, scenes like this establish a vast number of deep divisions: city against country, indoor servants against outdoor, black against white, old against young.

For some years now Bond has accompanied his plays by sequences of poems designed to explicate the events of the plays. For *Restoration* he has incorporated the poems into the play itself as songs with music by Nick Bicât. They have clear echoes of the Brecht-Eisler style, punctuating and commenting on the action through poetic analogues and modern parallels. Their lyrics range from Bond at his most awkwardly "poetic" ("Geese fly over the moon and do not know / That for a moment they fill the world with beauty") to a cold hardness that is more effective: "My mate was a hard case / Worked beside me on the bench for years / Hardly said a word / Talking isn't easy / When the machines run."

Restoration has an extraordinary and satisfying density, most of which is achieved without the spurious weight of flying geese. It deserves some further re-writing to make it as fully achieved a play as, say, *Bingo*. It also deserves a better performance. Not all the problems can be blamed on first-night nerves or on a cramping design that, in order to allow the band's platform to swing forward for each song, constricts and shadows movement. Nor, in spite of the bad patches, does all the blame lie with Bond's directing, though he has been better served by other directors than he serves himself. Unusually for the Royal Court, there was too much poor acting, under-powered and unimaginative. Simon

Callow, and Irene Handl in a marvellously self-indulgent cameo, were honourable exceptions.

CRITICAL COMMENTARY

Ian Stuart (essay date October 1991)

SOURCE: Stuart, Ian. "Edward Bond's *Restoration*." *Australasian Drama Studies,* no. 19 (October 1991): 51-66.

[*In the following essay, Stuart examines the relevance of* Restoration, *with its eighteenth-century setting, to the late twentieth century, and especially the relevance of a seminal 1981 production of the play.*]

Restoration was written as Bond's response to the British General Election of 1979 in which the Conservatives won a resounding victory. The play tackles the timeless issue of upper-class domination over the working class and to do this Bond finds an historical world view particularly conducive to separating out class distinctions—divorcing an individual's appearance from the reality of their class function. Bond's political dialectic is as relevant to eighteenth-century surroundings as a contemporary setting.

Despite the claims of one critic, who believes that 'any resemblance of the central characters to Restoration types is really only superficial', parallels do exist between Bond's play and the characters and techniques of late seventeenth-century English drama.[1] But despite its title, it should be emphasized that *Restoration* is set in the *eighteenth* century and therefore contains a mixture of period dramatic styles. Lord Are, for example, is a classic figure from the plays of Wycherley and Etherege whereas Hardache, for instance, is representative of the upwardly mobile, speculative classes of the eighteenth century. Bond's purpose in forcing these two historically different figures together is to show the repressive hold both lords and merchants had on the working classes. Bond has commented on the rationale behind the writing of this play:

> I wanted to write a play set in restoration themes. These are still received almost totally uncritically in the theatre. The opportunism of the characters is applauded. Humour is taken as a self-consciousness which disarms the wicked and also in a way justifies them in their exploitation of others. So their 'silliness' makes them both socially harmless and entitles them to their positions as exploiters. Tragedy is obviously excluded. Compare the simpleton in *Beaux Strategem* with Lear's fool.[2]

An examination of Bond's 1981 production and Roger Michell's Royal Shakespeare Company revival of 1988-9, in which Bond assisted during the re-rehearsal process, demonstrates the importance of Bond's work as a director in addition to the role of the play in the nineties—and beyond.[3] Among the qualities of this second production were the additions and deletions Bond made to the text. In many cases these changes give an altered perception of characters such as the Parson and Mrs Hedges.

Restoration contains thirteen characters, eight male and five female, but revolves around the actions of Lord Are, an impoverished aristocrat. As a result of his poverty, Are has decided to marry Ann, the daughter of Hardache, a wealthy industrialist. Like Mrs Pinchwife, in Wycherley's *Country Wife,* Ann is consumed with a desire to leave the country and visit London. Typifying her level of intelligence, Ann dons a white sheet and poses as the family spirit. In this outfit, she tries to persuade Are to take his wife to London on the pretext of pregnancy, claiming that to ensure the child will not carry a curse, the offspring needs to be born in town. Are is not concerned in the slightest by the presence of a 'ghost' and, once insulted, decides to be rid of it by running it through with a rapier. On discovering the spirit to be his wife, Are skilfully transfers the blame for the murder onto his servant, Bob. Rose, Lady Are's black maidservant and also Bob's wife, discovers the truth of Ann's death and tries but fails to obtain Bob's release. Protesting his innocence, Bob goes to his death.

THE UPPER CLASS

In terms of humor, Lord Are is at the centre of *Restoration*; an amusing character with wit, charm and a sardonic outlook on life. Comparisons have been made between Lord Are and Etherege's Dorimant, Vanbrugh's Lord Foppington and Congreve's Mirabell, all of which are appropriate but limit the source of Are's comedy purely to his character. Bond would prefer that humor emerged from the play's meaning. For Bond, comedy is a political device to demonstrate the seeming artificiality of an eighteenth-century world whilst, at the same time, providing an audience with the reality of how society is organized. This notion is both confirmed and complicated by the 'ghost-scene' at the end of Part One.

The episode takes place at breakfast in the Hall of Hilgay. Charged with Are's cynicism, miserliness and arrogance and Ann's persistence, the encounter gives rise to comedy:

ARE:

> My wife? What of my wife? . . . Have ye come to tell me she's to join ye? I thank ye for the good news and bid ye be gone so I may celebrate in peace.[4]

The asides, spoken directly to the audience, are also humorous and assist in breaking any sense of 'realism' which may have developed. They remind us that we are simply watching a play within the theatre. With Ann's death, which, in approach, recalls Bodice and Fontanelle's torture of Warrington in *Lear,* Bond mingles comic technique with the grotesque. Are's murder of the 'ghost' is a moment of personal insecurity—how is he to resolve the dilemma? His doubt soon passes and he recovers from the killing of 'a heavy ghost'. But what of the audience who have also witnessed the murder? Ann's death causes a momentary eclipse between the artificial world and that of reality; Are 'only' attacks a ghost but the 'reality' is that of killing his wife. This idea is to be developed further with Bob's assumption that *he* in fact has killed Ann. Moments after Ann's murder, Are continues with a witty observation: 'My wife. Stretched out on the floor. With a hole in her breast. Before breakfast. How is a man to put a good face on that?'[5] This juxtaposition of comic language and situation is a typical Bondian device forcing us to observe the source of humor and therefore question the validity of our laughter. Unrelenting, the scene continues in this manner. As with Hatch's 'innocent murder' in *The Sea,* the already dead Ann is stabbed again by Bob as she 'chases' him round the room, carried by Are. It is a grisly moment which, like Mrs Lewis's response at Brian's corpse in *Jackets II* or the actions of Dodds and Leonard from *In the Company of Men* attempting to get Oldfield's corpse to sign his will, evokes strongly mixed emotion from an audience. The moment's purpose is to confuse, and therefore question, the response of an audience. Do we laugh and, according to Bond, if so what are we laughing at? The scene's dramatic function is that of defining an audience's response to the play. It does this by confronting one of its central issues: the nature of Are and the relationship of his exploitive class towards society. Seen in an amusing but also dangerous light, the upper classes are shown as manipulators of events.

Hardache also coerces people to fit with his arrangements. For example, his only motive in arranging the marriage between Are and his daughter is his desire for the coal underneath Are's land. As a result of such a liaison, Hardache becomes a partial recipient of this wealth. Ann's death threatens this plan. In order to ensure his prosperity, Hardache blackmails Are with knowledge of Ann's real murderer. The Parson, like the Padre of *Jackets II,* protects the aristocracy. This is confirmed in discussing Lord Are with Bob at Holme Cottage:

> Lord Are is the guardian of our laws and orderer of our ways. He must stand above all taint. Topple him from his mighty seat and Beelzebub will walk the lanes of Hilgay. We cannot even contemplate it. Already the methodists rant at his lordship.[6]

This direct acknowledgment of Lord Are's position by the Parson comes in the text's new edition written for the RSC's 1988-9 production of *Restoration.* It confirms

Bond's approach, traces of which were evident in the earlier version, that religion is simply used by the Parson as a protective mask for class domination. The new text, as well as showing the Parson supporting the upper classes, exploits this dependency to satirize what Bond considers the church's moral shortcomings. Although critics of Bond's work observe that many of his characters are only one-dimensional, the Parson's character is fully developed. He understands the 'function' of the working class but is nevertheless complacent and chooses not to be involved in struggle. The theft of Are's silver, for example, causes Mrs Hedges to weep and the Parson to observe her commitment to others' wealth. Beneath the Parson's cynical observation of life bleeds an underlying Marxist (and Christian) lesson on the emptiness of material possessions. However, according to Bond, this emptiness is not to be filled by embracing God but in following the play's maxim written by Bob, spoken and taught by the Parson: 'Man is what he knows'. The Parson is happy to escape from 'truth' in alcohol but Rose, and eventually Bob, understand the meaning contained in the phrase.

THE WORKING CLASS

In **Restoration,** working-class characters are represented in four stages of development which can be seen as relative degrees of enlightenment, ranging from total ignorance to social insight. Put crudely, these are misplaced trust in the upper classes, resignation, anarchy and understanding.

Bob is the naive, unaware servant whose misplaced trust in Are costs him his life. However, Bond was very concerned that Bob should not come over as a foolish figure:

> The wider implications of Bob's misplaced fidelity, of his false consciousness, must be made clear. It mustn't be a play about a gullible boy misled by a posh crook . . . This is important. Bob isn't stupid but his intelligence is abused.[7]

As a consequence of Are's murder of Ann, Bob is blamed and imprisoned but accepts responsibility for the death. However, Bob's foolishness demonstrates the source of the problem—a society represented by Are. It is Lady Are's death that awakes in Bob a desire to 'better' himself by taking reading lessons from the Parson. In doing so, he spells out one of the play's themes: 'Man is what he knows'. Bob's realization, that his life could have been so different, only occurs towards the end of the play and, consequently, at the end of his life.

Pathetic to the extreme, but typical of how upper classes manipulate lower classes in the play, is the action of Mrs Hedges lighting a fire. At this moment, Are takes advantage of her inability to read by handing her Bob's pardon to start the fire. Mrs Hedges' regard for authority, and doing what is 'right', costs her Bob's life. Mrs Hedges is undoubtedly a victim, both of her own volition and the society which traps her. 'Wood Song' contains a spark of revolutionary fervour from Mrs Hedges with, 'All you who would resist your fate / Strike now it is already late'. And the 'Legend of Good Fortune', in which Mrs Hedges suggests Mankind has a need to defend itself against attack by outside forces. But her words and actions do not effect change. Since the initial Royal Court production of **Restoration,** the United Kingdom had fought Argentina to protect the Falkland Islands. Bond wanted to reflect the alternative feelings about the war and so wrote 'Falkland Song', replacing the 'Legend of Good Fortune', for the 1988-9 revival. This further emphasized the apathetic stand of Mrs Hedges, and our own, through a song which mirrors the war's futility whilst, at the same time, challenging an audience to consider its own injustice.

Mrs Wilson is landlady at the gaol's 'beer barrel'. Reminiscent of similar women in Bond's work, such as Mary of **Saved** and Mrs Lewis of **Jackets II,** Mrs Wilson feigns respectability to cover the inadequacy she feels as a victim of the class structure. Consequently, Mrs Wilson is obsessed with money. Everything is thought of in material terms; the door, which is broken, the beer, which is sold, and the tips given to her husband by the 'better class', although even these are not certain. As a result of being at the financial mercy of others, Mrs Wilson has a bitter streak: 'Winter coming but no one helps me with the fuel bill . . . I need a new broom. They ought to be provided by the authorities'.[8] References to 'a carpet upstairs. A few pairs of Sunday gloves' typify Mrs Wilson's illusion of a good life yet her real character emerges when she provides food for the guests: 'Help yourself. (*She pushes the plate further away.*)'[9]

Anarchy is represented by Frank. Described as the 'outdoor servant', Frank understands the way society works, shown through his 'Song of Learning', in which he tells of a working class enslaved for so long they understand 'how to blow up your hell'.[10] Frank is a radical who overturns traditional expectations. By having Frank rob Are of his silver, Bond shows him engaged in attempting to defeat society's structure: But Frank's approach, of robbing the rich, holds no future for him and, by inference, anyone who would combat the world in this way. Bond sees his revolutionary instinct as admirable but analytically believes his energies are channelled in the wrong direction, attempting to reform society piecemeal instead of replacing its total structure.

Rose, the black servant and survivor, learns society's wickedness and **Restoration** closes with her determination to effect change. Rose exhibits insight throughout the play commenting for example that Frank should not be punished for stealing: 'That lot can afford a bit of silver. Chriss the work they've got out of him, he deserves it'.[11] She releases Frank in a move which cannot be understood by the others. Unlike them, Rose recognizes the 'true' workings of human beings. This insight into the human situation is one of her characteristics.

BACKGROUND TO *RESTORATION* (1981)

For Bond, the 1981 production came at a particularly appropriate time, as Wednesday 29 July 1981 saw the wedding of Prince Charles, next in line to the British throne, to Lady Diana Spencer. This gave Bond an opportunity to draw parallels between his play and the Royal Wedding. This he did in the *Guardian* newspaper. In the article, Bond equates Are with Royalty and its manipulation of the working class:

> The wedding [of Prince Charles and Lady Diana Spencer] is a celebration of the ruling class and therefore it is a celebration of what is irrational in society. The ruling class in this country enables exploitation to be done under the guise of legality. This conceals the gangsterism that it really is.[12]

Prior to the plays' opening, street riots occurred in Brixton, South London, which ended with groups of black youths fighting the police: 279 policemen and 48 youths were injured. There were also racial riots in London (Southall), in Liverpool (Toxteth) and trouble was also reported in the cities of Birmingham, Blackburn, Bradford, Derby, Leeds, Leicester and Wolverhampton. The problems of color are addressed in the play and embodied by Rose who tries, but fails, to help Bob. For Bond, the rioting had its positive aspects: 'I thought the racist conflict was a very good and informed political confrontation—a rational response to irrationality'.[13] Bob is trapped in the middle of this conflict between the two classes. According to Bond, he represents 'the typical working class Tory voter, and the play is about his betrayal'.[14] With these insights, we can connect Bond's play to the period of political turmoil in which it was born.

REHEARSALS

The rehearsal period began in June 1981 and was, according to Philip Davis, who played Bob, too short for much experimental work.[15] Bond nevertheless had a very precise idea of what he wanted from the production and had decided that rehearsal time was to be spent exploring each character's function in great detail. Initiating such a process resulted in a great deal of bitterness between the cast and director. Eva Griffith, who played Lady Are in the production, felt that much of the difficulty lay in Bond's inability to translate his thoughts into concrete acting terms:

> All of us, especially Simon [Callow] had a great desire to know what Edward wanted and if he had been able to communicate that it would have been a great help to him as well as us. It would be marvellous to do a play the way a writer originally conceived it. With a writer that uses words as skilfully as Bond you are bound to want those words to come across in a certain way. Then it becomes difficult to put that into terms an actor can understand.[16]

Bond's apparent failure in communicating his needs to an actor is captured by Simon Callow who created Are in the first production. In his book, *Being an Actor,* Callow goes into detail about the process, both the problems he had with the role of Are and his thoughts on Bond's approach to acting.

Initially, Callow approached the role of Are 'naturalistically' as, 'a machiavel, a devil, a daemonic [sic], Olivierian figure, bestriding the stage like a colossus, eyes flashing, mouth twisted in a personal sneer.'[17] Bond gradually removed this image by informing the actor he was too 'emotional' and 'sinister'. This continued until Callow arrived at 'his new performance: . . . Eighteenth-century man, genial, agreeable, reasonable, rational, with his fixed and highly satisfactory world view'.[18] One difficulty Callow had in creating Are was his own conception of character. He describes the way in which he approaches a role:

> You're breaking down your own thought patterns and trying to reconstruct them into those of the character, pushing into emotional territory which may be strange and difficult for you, seeking the bodily centre of an alien being.[19]

Bond disagrees with this technique of constructing a character. In notes to his previous play, **The Worlds,** Bond had stated to the actors: 'Judge by the situation, not by the character or his actions. They are not to look for soul, for it's a white rabbit pulled from a hat when the truth's hard to follow.'[20] Rejecting Callow's Stanislavskian approach, which Bond might argue is only for the actor's benefit, Bond believes in situating character within a wider social context.

Callow widens his field of attack in considering Bond's concept of acting in general:

> The actor, I think, he views with distrust and suspicion. He believes that the actor's job is simple and mechanical (say the lines, do the moves) . . . and because he has no understanding of the process of acting, he's unable to understand the difficulties, and therefore, unable to solve them. He has to have recourse to giving line readings, and to running scenes over and over, in the hope that somehow they'll fall into place. They never do. All this is very frustrating, because he understands his own plays perfectly and is always right in what he says about them. But translating what he says into acting is almost impossible.[21]

Obviously this is a subjective response to a difficult situation because what Callow considers fundamental to his craft, Bond considers self-indulgent. For example, Callow was interested in establishing for himself the private life of Are as a member of the Hell-fire Club 'deeply involved with rats and dead babies'.[22] Bond was not concerned with naturalizing Are in this way. Instead he was interested in the character's dramatic and, more importantly, political function.

A characteristic style of Bond's direction is in the suggestion that poetic images must lie on the surface, not exist internally and solely for the actor. His notion of directing is turning theory into practice: an approach which means poetry can become an active vocabulary.

Davis indicates that although there was not any improvisation in rehearsals for the original production, Bond emphasized his need for the play to explore a 'non-naturalistic' approach. Bond was trying to distance Davis, and through him the audience, from a psychological reaction to the character of Bob. Irene Handl, who played Old Lady Are in the original production, represents the approach to acting Bond believes redundant. Norman Tyrrell, the Parson, remarks on her playing of the character:

> I recollect some discussion going on between Edward Bond and Irene Handl. It seemed clear to me that she was going to do her act whether he liked it or not and, in the end, he manifestly gave up. In the event, she did a solo recitation, as it were, to enormous response from the front—as near a standing ovation as can be outside of opera—almost unbalancing the play and proving, incidentally, that Edward Bond knew what he was up to.[23]

This supports Bond's notion that actors often try to make characters 'work', making it 'popular' to an audience but often being unfaithful to the demands of a script.[24] Davis adds that, in his opinion, Handl failed to appreciate the kind of play she had committed herself to:

> It occurred to some, just before we opened, that we were in a play that might cause a violent revolution or something. Irene Handl, for example, got onto it sometime on and wished she had not done it.[25]

Metaphors were just one of the techniques Bond used during the rehearsals in his short period of working with the company of *Restoration* prior to its London opening in 1989. Much of the time was spent in close textual analysis during which Bond left the first half, 'mainly Are's great comic half, almost untouched'.[26] One advantage to having Bond in rehearsals is that he is able to change an approach to his text. Roger Michell, the director of the RSC's *Restoration,* indicated Bond's solution to the difficulty they experienced with the play's penultimate scene:

The first thing he suggested was re-arranging the furniture and the scene became even more about these characters in their hermetically sealed worlds. Consequently, they found it very unnecessary to deal with each others' worlds. He took Franks' speech, about going home, and interspersed it with other bits of dialogue. So instead of being a set piece it became a splintered collection of impulses surrounded by other activities; someone crying, eating. I thought it was terrific, it really resolved that final scene for me.[27]

SETTING

Bond's stylistic interpretation of *Restoration* for the original 1981 production was, customarily, simple. One critic correctly indicates the significance of Bond's directorial choices:

> Bond is a master of stage imagery. The look of his stage—its customary bareness, its few symbolic objects—is an important means for him of moving easily between public and private worlds and of heightening and focussing our attention, to bring us further into the mental landscape inhabited by his characters . . . Lighting, groupings, spatial arrangements, function in Bond's plays as in Beckett's, with great poetic economy, for a subtle variety of dramatic purposes.[28]

Hayden Griffin's and Gemma Jackson's setting for the first production was sparse and functional. One example, according to one of the actresses, is the first scene in Lord Are's Park, defined by cut-out trees lowered from the flies.[29] No attempt was made at trying to capture a sense of reality. Griffin indicated the set was awkward not because of any deficiency, but simply difficult to 'fly' due to its peculiar angle:

> The set was a bit like a pantomime. We did a strange false perspective on it so that everything looked kind of twisted. Also we had a bridge with the musicians on it because Edward did not want them in the pit . . . We could use the musicians platform as an upper level.[30]

Griffin also designed costumes which visually assisted in dividing the upper from lower classes. Are wore resplendent period dress and his wife, 'the most beautiful costume with the most lurid colours and bows in all the wrong places'.[31] This provided a contrast to the working class; for example, Debbie Bishop, as Rose, wore a simple, plain dress and headscarf. Bond's idea about costume is that what is worn is significant and should not limit or define their character:

> When we think of clothes as being symbolic: then they impose a social posture. The suits presidents wear in office, the leisure gear they wear on a golf-course. So do your wear clothes for the place? No—the red alert may happen on the golf-course. The point in a play is that you have to choose the red alerts—and so that the character would wear 'x' isn't necessary to the situation. To dress the character—in a way which totally assumes the character as given—is a mistake.[32]

David Fielding's setting for the 1988-9 production was predominantly white with set pieces, such as the tree in the first scene, being brought on stage only for that scene. Michael Coveney makes a significant comment in his review of the play for the *Financial Times*:

> Roger Michell lays out the play cleanly on a bright white set designed by David Fielding and, as in all the best Bond productions, makes concrete the images in space.[33]

Michell has observed that in directing this play, 'You find out what each object means and you cut away until you just have those objects'.[34] The production was 'dazzlingly lit by Rick Fisher, as merciless as the impartial sun that Lord Are worships'.[35] Michell wanted the lighting to be 'as clean and as simple as possible without straying into naturalism'.[36] At Stratford-upon-Avon, Fisher introduced the idea of fluorescent tubes, lowered from the flies, for the scenes in the prison. This idea came from a company visit to a prison but, because of technical difficulties at the Pit Theatre in London, was abandoned when the production transferred. It gave the scenes an oppressive, almost surreal quality.

Music

The songs in *Restoration* aim to remove an audience from the fabricated world of fictional individuals, allowing the characters to step outside themselves and comment on their situation. There are sixteen songs: one prior to the play, ten at the end of scenes and five in the middle. For Bond, songs are 'culturally disciplined forms of weeping—or laughing—as well as stating (usually) simple philosophies: the passing of seasons and the nature of accidents.'[37] It has been observed the songs are of three 'types', and these categories make it useful in considering their function:

> Bond on occasions makes his actors come out of character for the songs themselves. On other occasions, they remain within character. Elsewhere they may begin in character but then, during the course of the song, produce views which are deliberately not compatible with the established ways of proceeding.[38]

Song is reserved exclusively for the working class in *Restoration*. According to Katherine Worth, in song 'they gain the articulacy they lack in that world'.[39] This is true of Frank's 'Song of Learning'. With greater clarity of thought and expression than he would possess in 'real' life, Frank assesses and comments on the working class situation. The song's value lies in the communication to an audience of a class position, puncturing dismissive notions that they are out of context.[40] At the end of Scene One, Bob sings to Rose in a ballad which, according to Worth, is 'not one of the most successful; on the whole, the more aggressive punchy lyrics work best.'[41] 'Roses' is designed as an outpouring of Bob's emotion and is deliberately naive in the extreme. Here,

Bond uses music to establish Bob's innocence in his understanding of the world. 'Wood Song' is an example of this third group, a song beginning in character and ends by commenting on the situation. It represents perhaps the most striking use of music in *Restoration* as the song seems to be part of the play's action and very quickly becomes a device which forces the spectators to remove themselves from the play. This connects with a statement which Bond made some years earlier, about his need to confront an audience through a different approach to music:

> I've seen good German audiences in the stalls chewing their chocolates in time to Brecht's music—and they were most certainly not seeing the world in a new way.[42]

Bond sees it as his moral responsibility as a writer to ensure that his songs produce a different response in an audience.

Nick Bicat's setting of the songs for the 1981 production were described as 'punchy and demanding', 'strident' and containing a 'unifying melody'.[43] Positioned on a scaffold at the rear of the stage, comparable to 'a Minstrel's Gallery', musicians were moved forward for each of the play's songs.[44] Philip Davis describes the music as 'modern rock and, directly or indirectly, a commentary on what was happening'.[45] Bond made his intentions with the songs clear from the beginning: 'their purpose was to cut off and pull away from the fiction of the play . . . the aristocracy have got the language and the rest of you have songs.'[46] However, the function of the play's music was questioned by some critics, unconvinced of its artistic value. Michael Billington, a firm supporter of the play, observed 'the music has the right dislocating effect, but it also makes the theatrical brew almost over-rich.'[47] It was noted by others that 'the musical impact diminishes as the evening grinds on', and that the 'raw' songs, 'dwindle into sentimentality'.[48] Despite this observation, musically, Bond seemed to achieve a cohesiveness in directing the production. This successful blending between the 'alienation' of the songs and the play was apparently lacking in the revival.

There were significant problems with music for the 1988-9 revival of *Restoration* at Stratford-upon-Avon and London. Michell wanted to form a 'consistent convention for how the audience are invited to perceive the songs'.[49] As indicated earlier, this is impossible because of the nature of the music. Michell suggested the solution was to cut the songs. Bond refused to allow this because he felt the music was being made the victim of a production that was unsuccessful in interpreting the play's two halves.

Response was quite favorable to Ilona Sekacz's new setting of the songs; comments ranging from music which 'captures the anger, the brooding lyricism and the bitter pity of Bond's lyrics' to 'the sound of Ilona Sekacz's jazz with glorious runaway trumpet makes an incongruous accompaniment to the bleak crafted words.'[50] What continued to disturb the critics, however, was both the value of the songs themselves, and their connection to the world of the play. This was made especially difficult with Bond's inclusion of the 'Falkland Song' as Malcolm Hay seems to imply:

> Roger Michell's production never quite cracks the problem of the periodic songs which point, sometimes obliquely and sometimes too heavily, at modern parallels to the situations Bond lays before us.[51]

Carl Miller, in *City Limits* observed that '*Restoration* can be recognised as one of the decade's key works'.[52] But regarding the value of the music, he conceded: 'It has flaws: the songs . . . rarely come off.'[53] Peter Kemp, writing for *The Independent,* found the songs 'crudely didactic, simplistic and devoid of dramatic or literary power.'[54] Michael Billington's difficulty lay in the songs relevance to character:

> My objection was not to the content [of the 'Falkland Song'] but to the fact that Bob's mother has previously been depicted as congenitally servile. Surely a song should have some relationship to character?[55]

Some critics proved to be totally confused, thinking the music should be linked to the eighteenth century: '[The songs' lyrics] appear to be commenting on more recent events in history than a miscarriage of justice in the early 18th century.'[56]

CRITICAL RESPONSE

Billington was one of the major critics who liked the play and its original production. He found that Bond's use of comedy, as a device to contain his political message, was a useful approach. It meant 'that he gets right away from the playing-card simplicity of agitprop and makes his point through laughter'.[57] The Breakfast Room scene, where Are kills his wife, is cited by Billington as 'one of the funniest things on the London stage'. However, many critics were concerned that *Restoration* presented the aristocracy as 'wittily resourceful and the workers as gullible bores'.[58] John Elsom, of the *Listener* magazine, even goes as far as suggesting Are's humor lies at the play's centre:

> Bond's trouble is that he likes to get a certain literary style within his sights, which he can then parody very well, up to the point where it starts to conflict with his political beliefs—and then he has to make a desperate wrench to avoid cultural corruption.[59]

Such criticisms as these fail to represent the play accurately. *Restoration* does not applaud Are for being humorous, nor come across as being a 'universally hypocritical' character. Instead, Bond goes to great lengths to show him as opportunistic, an individual who represents the abuses of the class structure. It is through his use of dramatic irony, Bond shows Are's true character.

Other press response praised Simon Callow's performance of Are, although Michael Coveney of the *Financial Times* suggested he failed to 'hit the required inflammatory style', and were unanimous in respect for Irene Handl's cameo role.[60] Few comments were made about Bond's directing style, except to allege that it allowed 'the pace to drag', and that 'many of the scenes go on far too long'.[61] In its revival, Charles Osborne declared in a national newspaper: 'Edward Bond's *Restoration,* first staged at the Royal Court Theatre a mere eight years ago, is hardly a good enough play to have been revived so soon'.[62] In a scathing review, Osborne attacked Bond for his 'crude' attempt at parodying Congreve and for writing an overlong play:

> [Bond has] a propensity to use several sentences over a joke where a phrase would suffice, to stretch out a neat little plot to breaking point by his long-windedness and his habit of introducing unnecessary characters and scenes.[63]

Kenneth Hurren referred to the play as 'Bond close to his worst' and John Gross describes the production as predictable containing 'long stretches of tedium'.[64] Alternatively, Billington referred to *Restoration* as 'one of the wittiest plays of the decade', a play he still admired in a production which was 'over-reverent and even though a work with a dozen songs cries out for more true voices'.[65] Most critics highlighted Simon Russell Beale's performance as Are with the *Independent*'s Paul Taylor mentioning his 'pudgy hands revolving like a pair of affected rotary-whisks, his eyes beady with epicene outrage . . . Simon Russell Beale's superb Are (a cross between Sir Fopling Flutter and Dorimant) is a mincing mannequin for whom surface style is the only virtue.'[66] Describing Russell Beale as 'irresistible', 'a sleek, arrogant villain', and 'impeccably monstrous', Michael Coveney remarked that Russell Beale managed to 'find even more colour and variety in the role than did Simon Callow.'[67]

Nicholas de Jongh, the *Guardian*'s theatre critic, complained that the 1988-9 production 'missed the chance of locating the play in surreal or expressionistic territory'.[68] Presumably Bond would be glad because *Restoration* fits neither group. Instead, Bond sets out to demonstrate the timelessness of class exploitation using the conventions of eighteenth-century drama for his own purposes.

Notes

All sources are unpublished unless an attribution is cited. To avoid confusion, *Restoration* and *The Cat* refers to Bond's earlier 1982 Methuen edition of the play.

1. G. E. H. Hughes, 'Edward Bond's "Restoration",' *Critical Quarterly* 25, 4 (1983), 277-8.

2. Edward Bond, letter to author, 10 February 1990.

3. Productions transfer from the Royal Shakespeare Company in Stratford-upon-Avon, to London. Edward Bond re-rehearsed sections of the play prior to its London opening at The Pit on 29 March 1989.

4. Edward Bond, *Restoration* and *The Cat,* (London: Methuen, 1982), p. 41.

5. Bond, *Restoration* and *The Cat,* p. 44.

6. Edward Bond, *Restoration* (London: Methuen, 1988), p. 28.

7. Edward Bond quoted in 'The Search for Epic Drama: Edward Bond's Recent Work', by Philip Roberts, *Modern Drama* 24, 4 (1981), 468.

8. Bond, *Restoration,* p. 28-9.

9. Bond, *Restoration,* p. 30.

10. Bond, *Restoration* and *The Cat,* p. 20.

11. Bond, *Restoration* and *The Cat,* p. 33.

12. Edward Bond quoted in the *Guardian,* 31 July 1981.

13. Edward Bond quoted in the *Guardian.*

14. Edward Bond quoted in the *Guardian.*

15. Philip Davis, personal interview, 29 January 1990.

16. Eva Griffith, personal interview, 31 January 1990.

17. Simon Callow, *Being an Actor* (New York: Grove Press, 1988), p. 165.

18. Callow, p. 165.

19. Callow, p. 135.

20. Edward Bond quoted in 'Rehearsing Optimism', *The Leveller,* 60 (July 1981), 18-19.

21. Callow, p. 133-4.

22. Callow, p. 165.

23. Norman Tyrrell, letter to author, 5 February 1990.

24. Bond stated in his 'Notes to actors of *September,*' his play produced in Canterbury Cathedral, 1989: 'You shouldn't try to make the play *work*—this is effective, this goes, I like this etc. Anything can be made to work in that way.'

25. Philip Davis, personal interview, 29 January 1990.

26. Simon Russell Beale, personal interview, 5 February 1990.

27. Roger Michell, personal interview, 4 April 1990.

28. Katherine J. Worth, 'Edward Bond' in *Essays on Contemporary British Drama* (Munich: Hueber, 1981), p. 210.

29. Eva Griffith, personal interview, 31 January 1990.

30. Hayden Griffin, personal interview, 21 February 1990.

31. Eva Griffith, personal interview, 31 January 1990.

32. Edward Bond, letter to author, 23 March 1990.

33. Michael Coveney, *Financial Times,* 14 September 1988.

34. Roger Michell, personal interview, 4 April 1990.

35. Martin Hoyle, *Financial Times,* 31 March 1989.

36. Roger Michell, personal interview, 4 April 1990.

37. Edward Bond, letter to author, 10 February 1990.

38. Roberts, 472.

39. Katherine J. Worth, 'Bond's "Restoration",' *Modern Drama* 24, 4 (1981), 483.

40. Douglas Orgill, *Daily Express,* 22 July 1981.

41. Worth, 'Bond's "Restoration",' 483.

42. Edward Bond quoted in 'On Brecht', *Theatre Quarterly* 8, 30 (1978), 34.

43. Michael Coveney, *Financial Times,* 22 July 1981; John Elsom, *The Listener,* 6 August 1981; and Lloyd Trott, *The Leveller* (63) August-September 1981, 20.

44. Philip Davis, personal interview, 29 January 1990.

45. Philip Davis, personal interview, 29 January 1990.

46. Edward Bond quoted by Philip Davis, personal interview, 29 January 1990.

47. Michael Billington, *Guardian,* 22 July 1981.

48. Coveney, 22 July 1981; Orgill and Elsom.

49. Roger Michell, personal interview, 4 April 1990.

50. Martin Hoyle, *Financial Times,* 31 March 1989; Kate Kellaway, *Observer,* 18 September 1988.

51. Malcolm Hay, *Time Out,* 5 October 1988.

52. Carl Miller, *City Limits,* 22 September 1988.

53. Miller.

54. Peter Kemp, *Independent,* 31 March 1989.

55. Michael Billington, *Guardian,* 15 September 1988.

56. Charles Osborne, *Daily Telegraph,* 1 April 1989.

57. Billington, *Guardian,* 22 July 1981.

58. Robert Cushman, *Observer,* 26 July 1981.

59. Elsom.

60. Coveney, 22 July 1981.

61. Spencer and Coveney, 22 July 1981.

62. Osborne.

63. Osborne.

64. Kenneth Hurren, *Mail on Sunday,* 2 January 1989; John Gross, *Sunday Telegraph,* 2 January 1989.

65. Billington, 15 September 1990.

66. Paul Taylor, *Independent,* 15 September 1988.

67. Schmidt, Milton Shulman, *Evening Standard* 30 March 1989; Kemp and Coveney 14 September 1988.

68. Nicholas de Jongh, *Guardian,* 31 March 1989.

THE WAR PLAYS (1985)

PRODUCTION REVIEWS

Martin Cropper (review date 27 July 1985)

SOURCE: Cropper, Martin. "Burnt Offerings after the Bomb." *Times* London (27 July 1985): 19.

[*In the following review of a 1985 Royal Shakespeare Company production of Bond's trilogy* The War Plays *at the Barbican Pit in London, directed by Nick Hamm, Cropper describes the work as "Armaggedon-porn," praising the makeup and costumes but otherwise finding the plays nearly unwatchable.*]

A notice outside the auditorium warns that this production makes use of firearms. A fairer admonition would be that it makes use of words; thousands upon thousands of them, stumbling one after the other over the course of nearly six hours of intermittently relieved tedium.

Edward Bond has discovered that war is a bad thing—specifically, nuclear war: its Darnoclean threat, the horrors of its actual occurrence, its appalling aftermath. Mr Bond's script reminds us in inertly didactic, and frequently sanctimonious, tones, that the Bomb is liable to leave its victims' skins hanging off in strips or their bodies molten amid the rubble, *Bad* war.

This Armaggedon-porn is used as a kind of fancy dress to trick out the artfully-linked stories of his trilogy. The first, **Red, Black and Ignorant,** has Ian McDiarmid as a notional citizen of the future who was born at the instant the Bomb dropped; charred from head to foot like an overdone hamburger, he introduces "scenes from the life I did not live".

An official "Buyer" offers him and his wife 20 years' subsistence in exchange for their infant son. We next see the grown young man (Gary Oldman) declining to assist a woman trapped under a collapsed wall, on the grounds that she was in competition for the same factory job as himself. We learn that exploitation truly begins with "the makers of bricks, the builders of walls", that "it isn't easy to be just in an unjust world".

Later the son returns in uniform to sing a dire Sex Pistols pastiche called "Army Song" and to carry out his mission of killing a civilian in his own street. Unable to bring himself to kill an old party in the corner house, he shoots his father instead.

The Tin Can People presents an arid grey wasteland, 17 years after the dropping of a neutron bomb. A small group of survivors has inherited the earth in the form of warehouses stacked with canned food.

Ian McDiarmid, now pink-faced and speaking in accents reminiscent of Ivor Cutler, emerges from the wilderness to join them, but joy turns to despair when first one, then another of the group collapses and dies. Suspected of carrying a deadly disease, Mr McDiarmid is killed with a home-made spear.

The third and longest play, **Great Peace,** reprises the author's twin obsessions with soldiers and babies: this time the military dictatorship has ordered each of its agents to kill a citizen under the age of five. "It's in the computer" explains Gary Oldman, eyeing up his tiny sibling and the coeval offspring of a neighbour. Once again, he baulks at the last moment and hands back the neighbour's child, only to return home and smother his mother's baby.

Wandering in the wilderness with a bundle of rags with which she communes in baby-talk, the mother (Maggie Steed) falls in with a squad of soldiers, tattered and burnt by a cataclysmic explosion, and later with a community of good guys who invite her home for a cosy candlelit dinner. She remains obdurate, however, and we last see her agonizing in the wilderness with a young man whom she takes to be her son.

Nick Hamm is notably successful in directing the group scenes of soldierly banter, but even he can make little of the gruelling monologues with their ineffably duff stabs at dramatic poetry. Christopher Tucker's make-up is excellently inventive, while the costumes (supervised by Emma Ryott) are often masterfully surreal. Maggie Steed deserves a medal, and so too does the audience.

Keith Colquhoun (review date 9 August 1985)

SOURCE: Colquhoun, Keith. "Fundamentalist Forums." *Times Literary Supplement* (9 August 1985): 878.

[*In the following review, Colquhoun observes of Hamm's 1985 Royal Shakespeare Company production of* The War Plays *that the great achievement of the trilogy is Bond's consistently depicted rage.*]

Two of the **War Plays** were first produced last year. Edward Bond has now written a third, and the trilogy is offered as a single production. You enter the Pit at the Barbican in mid-afternoon and emerge nearly eight hours and a few intervals later. During this time most of the characters who have not been killed have gone mad, although some of them were mad at the start, and you feel none too composed yourself.

To be against war is hardly a new theme in drama. What is special about Bond's treatment of this theme is his concentrated rage. He is a secular ayatollah preaching fundamentalism. You are not in his little hermitage to be entertained, but to be scourged and reminded that if you do not mend your ways the whip will bite a lot deeper. The war he writes about is in the future. After the bombs have fallen the present world will die and go to hell. There could be redemption, but don't count on it.

The strength of Bond's message is its simple conviction. In the past decade or so the likelihood of nuclear war on a world-wide scale has lessened. Although the superpowers continue to abuse each other in public they seem to have decided that they don't want to die, and have come to the conclusion that they have to make the best of the world as it is. But this is the sort of revisionism that all fundamentalists have had to counter, and it is hardly likely to deter Bond from his mission. What other playwright would have given Shakespeare a dressing down, as he did in **Bingo,** for not being more concerned about human rights in Elizabethan England, or would have rewritten *King Lear* because he considered the original Lear a bit of a compromiser?

There is no compromising in the Pit. The first play, **Red, Black and Ignorant,** opens with a monologue by a middle-aged man called Monster who, we learn, is the ghost of a baby that died in the womb when the bombs fell. We see scenes of the life he did not live. In the final scene Monster, now a father, is killed by his soldier son. In the second play, **The Tin Can People,** a stranger

arrives in a post-bomb community. A number of people die of a disease that the stranger is blamed for, and he is killed with a spear that has been re-invented for the purpose. The third play, **Great Peace,** the newest and longest, is about the mostly brutal adventures of a woman and the bundle of rags that she insists is her baby.

Most plots seem arid when they are laid out bone by bone but the three that Bond has devised are particularly unremitting in tone. Long passages of blank verse befuddle the most tolerant listener. "How can you talk about the destruction of the world and be normal?", asks one character, presumably echoing Bond's desperation. Bond's faithful congregation will recognize, perhaps with pleasure, some of his obsessions (not, one feels a pejorative word when applied to his work). The baby remains the symbol of persecuted innocence that it was in **Saved,** the play that made him famous. Bond is also concerned with the mind, or, as he sees it, the mindlessness of the soldier. Whatever the army did to him in his national service in the 1950s, he has amply repaid it since in anti-public relations.

Despite Bond's intention to harass the audience, the Royal Shakespeare Company does its best to make it comfortable. Ian McDiarmid, who wanders through the three plays, first as Monster and later in almost human forms, is a pleasure to watch. Maggie Steed, the woman in **Great Peace,** carries through a marathon part with persistence and dignity. Josette Simon is convincing as the nuclear-wise young person who could make life even more tiresome in a post bomb world. The direction, by Nick Hamm, is as coherent as the text allows.

CRITICAL COMMENTARY

Tony Howard (essay date 1996)

SOURCE: Howard, Tony. "'No One Outside These Arms': Edward Bond's *The War Plays.*" In *Acts of War: The Representation of Military Conflict on the British Stage and Television since 1945,* edited by Tony Howard and John Stokes, pp. 127-44. Aldershot, England: Scolar Press, 1996.

[*In the following essay, Howard traces the response to the Cold War in the British theater, provides an analysis of Bond's* The War Plays, *and notes that Bond's trilogy was among the last works of dramatic art to address the horrors of the Cold War.*]

> Why talk about it?
> I used to think if I did I'd be able to live normally again

How can you talk about the destruction of the world
   and be normal?
My parents talk to me in my sleep: they dont know
   they're dead: I feel guilty as if Im keeping the secret
   from them [. . .]
I tried to help the wounded—there was no medical
   knowledge or drugs
The sick came together in a few places—crawled and
   limped along the streets—followed each other's cries
When the blind touched the walls they fell on them
I shouldnt have started to speak

(THIRD WOMAN, *The Tin Can People,* p. 35)

I

In October 1979 it was announced that in order to 'modernise' its nuclear equipment and meet the challenge of Soviet developments, NATO planned to deploy 464 Cruise and 108 Pershing-2 missiles: 'Britain would take the largest number of Cruise missiles (160), followed by Italy (112), West Germany (96 plus the 108 Pershings), Holland (48), and Belgium (48)' (*Guardian,* 14 November 1979). It was less well publicised that Norway, Denmark, France and Turkey refused to have them on their soil; but the new Thatcher Government volunteered to take more than originally proposed 'because West Germany found that it did not have room'.[1] At about the same time it was agreed that Britain's 'ageing' Polaris system should be replaced by Trident submarines at the then-predicted cost of £5,000 million, although army and RAF chiefs would have preferred extra Cruise missiles under sole British control. This followed decisions taken by James Callaghan and then kept secret from most of his own Cabinet. In England, Cruise and its mobile launchers were to be based in Lakenheath, Upper Heyford and Sculthorpe and a US Air Force team toured the country choosing firing sites.

The *Daily Telegraph* (31 October 1979) reported that Cruise 'makes no noise and the only inconvenience the local population will experience is the occasional sight of the missile launchers on the road', though E. P. Thompson pointed out that this might not be good for the local population's nerves since Cruise would go 'on the road' on the eve of war. It was also disclosed that year that when a B47 crashed at Lakenheath in 1956 three nuclear bombs narrowly escaped detonation in a fire; 'It is possible', said a retired US general (in the *Omaha World-Herald*), 'that a part of eastern England would have become a desert'.[2]

A few weeks later Moscow sent troops into Afghanistan. In 1980 during the Iran hostage debacle Reagan was elected, dedicated to a massive increase in America's international standing and therefore in its arms manufacture. In 1981 Martial Law was imposed in Poland. There was a grinding sense that the Superpowers—and the Falklands reasserted Britain's right to a place in that

tiny circle—were finally gearing up for action and specifically for a 'limited' European war. The language of drama and cinema began to be used to make the thought more acceptable, with talk of battleground 'theatre' nuclear weapons and Reagan's Star Wars project against the 'evil empire', designed, like the British Civil Defence campaign 'Protect and Survive', to nurture the concept of a 'winnable' nuclear conflict. The same game was being played inside the Kremlin, where it now seems the new SS-20 missiles were also authorised by a clique in secret. In 1979 the Soviet military chief of staff Marshal Ogarkov claimed nuclear victory was 'an objective possibility' and called for increased arms spending to make it practicable.[3] In 1982, as power struggles grew around the dying Brezhnev, Ogarkov's pamphlet *Always Ready to Defend the Fatherland* insisted the Ministry of Defence must develop more 'theatre' nuclear arms and prepare for an American first-strike—which some Reagan advisors now advocated in principle. Meanwhile Ogarkov's superior and rival Marshal Ustinov was pushing to limit the increase in spending: 'To count on victory in the arms race and in nuclear war is madness.' In 1983 Thatcher and Reagan rejected the 'dual key' for Cruise which would have made a launch impossible without Whitehall agreement and she blamed the idea on a rampant 'disagreeable streak of anti-Americanism'.[4] On 22 October there were huge anti-nuclear rallies in London, Bonn, Paris and other European cities. Thatcher planned the arrival of the launchers and warheads for November: 'We were anxious to avoid very visible signs of deployment in the run-up to or during the 1983 general election campaign'.[5]

So from 1979 onwards the prospect of nuclear Armageddon was discussed openly and desperately. One function of drama is to chart the relationship between political decisions and the emotional state of individuals, and if it cannot make rulers respond it may yet focus our own fears for us—and in this case perhaps help create the language that could give them form and meaning. As Ian McEwan wrote at the time, public opinion had its roots in private fears:

> I was struck by how deeply the lives of individuals had
> been shaken by the new cold war [. . .] Those who
> were parents, or had children in their lives, seemed
> particularly affected. Love of children generates a fierce
> ambition for the world to continue [. . .]. Like others,
> I experienced the jolt of panic that wakes you before
> dawn, the daydreams of the mad rush of people and
> cars out of the city before it is destroyed, of losing a
> child in the confusion. People described the pointless-
> ness of planning ahead, a creeping sense of the ir-
> relevance of all things they valued against the threat of
> annihilation.[6]

In the UK the build-up to deployment inspired a massive growth in CND membership—and a wave of theatrical activity.

Probably the most influential attack on the 'Protect and Survive' rhetoric was Raymond Briggs' cartoon novella *When the Wind Blows* with its brilliantly simple image of a mild and ever-cheerful elderly couple improvising a fall-out shelter in their living room, confident that their fate was in safe Churchillian hands and everything would be normal by Christmas. It was adapted for the radio and filmed, and David Nielson directed a stage version which transferred in the pre-Cruise summer of 1983 from Bristol to London's Whitehall Theatre.

It was a symbolic venue because this theatre stands at the top of Whitehall—just a few hundred yards from Horse Guards, the Cenotaph, Downing Street and Parliament itself. That autumn, ironically, the Whitehall—the home of British farce under Brian Rix—housed a patriotic post-Falklands spectacle and was renamed the Theatre of War. Many early responses to the climate of uneasy debate mined the same vein of black comedy as Briggs. The credits to London Weekend Television's serial *Whoops Apocalypse* (spring 1982) featuring Peter Jones, Barry Morse and Richard Griffiths as brainless world-leaders, opened with the image of a 'modernised' poppy-seller: 'Wear your mushroom with pride'. The serial ended as grimly as the title suggests. On a different scale Harold Pinter introduced a polemical note into his playwriting for the first time with *Precisely* (1983), a short sketch featuring two urbane bureaucrats deciding what would or would not constitute 'acceptable losses' in a nuclear strike. Adrian Mitchell was a more familiar campaigner; his *King Real* for Welfare State (1983) rewrote *King Lear* with the old man offering his daughters the three keys of power to his doomsday weapon. Cloudella (Cordelia) rejects it but Raygal and Gonilla seize their chance. One is cold as ice and rides on an iceberg with a penguin as her lieutenant, the other is fiery and floats through the performance space on a one-woman tropical island with her pet monkey, Enoch. *King Real* was a typical Welfare State open-air spectacular, but it was filmed for wider dissemination and it was created for the people of Barrow. Since the Trident submarines would be built in Barrow, the local economy's dependence on the arms race made *King Real* a uniquely confrontational kind of community theatre. Cloudella is exiled, the King goes mad and the world, a giant orb with firework-cities in it, explodes beautifully. Behind all these doomsday comedies lay Milligan and Antrobus' *The Bed-Sitting Room* and it too appeared in an updated version featuring Margaret Thatcher as a parrot. The authors' ramshackle surrealism never quite hid their pain—in the sixties David Benedictus compared Spike Milligan to Lear's Fool—and the play ends with cannibalism and a woman's unnerving appeal to God to resurrect her deformed dead baby. Similarly, though Adrian Mitchell gave *King Real*'s fairy-tale characters another chance and let Cloudella save the world, the world spoke last:

When man first flew beyond the sky
He looked back into the world's blue eye.
Man said: what makes your eye so blue?
Earth said: the tears in the ocean do.
Why are the seas so full of tears?
Because I've wept so many thousand years.
Why do you weep as you dance through space?
Because I am the mother of the human race.[7]

Nuclear drama has always made the Mother the ultimate icon of moral outrage; outside black comedy, Cruise drama struck a new note and became inextricable from the social revolution in attitudes to gender that had happened since the first decade of CND.

Noel Grey's *Poppies* (1983) is set simultaneously in 1939 and 1986, when the State is trying to disperse Remembrance Day crowds and keep individuals in isolation during a looming nuclear emergency. *Poppies* first surfaced in April 1983 at a Gay CND conference which, like the play, explored the relationship between war and peace and the nature of masculinity: 'Unless men begin to relate to each other in new ways, denying the violence of the power we have been offered all our lives, we have nothing to do with peace or with new forms of social organization.'[8] This discussion went further in September and October 1983 when Howard Brenton's *The Genius* and David Edgar's *Maydays* opened at the Royal Court and the Barbican respectively. Both plays reassessed post-war history—scientific achievement in Brenton's case (*The Genius* reworks Brecht's *Galileo*) and the dreams and rude awakenings of the British Left in *Maydays*. Both plays featured disillusioned-middle-aged-intellectual male protagonists; both ended at a fictionalised version of the Greenham Common women's peace camp with the promise of new solutions.

For with the Left demoralised by Thatcher's victories, Brenton and Edgar saw Greenham as proof of Sheila Rowbotham's argument in *Beyond the Fragments* (1980)[9] that British socialism was as patriarchal as the State itself and that radically new and non-hierarchical forms of political organisation must evolve, with the women's movement as the model. Edgar's anti-hero Martin Glass campaigns against the Vietnam War in the sixties but mutates into a New Right hero of the Murdoch press who, conveniently, owns a country estate next to a Cruise base. He threatens the protesters with a court injunction:

1st Woman.

　Injunctions require names. We have no names.

Martin.

　Is this a metaphysical—

3RD WOMAN.

> Or put another way, you find our names and the court
> may order us to go. And go we will. But others will
> take over. And the same thing will keep happening.
>
> *Slight pause*
>
> We—in the sense of this—we have no names.

1ST WOMAN.

> No membership.

2ND WOMAN.

> And no committees.

3RD WOMAN.

> No printing press. No postal code. No phone.

2ND WOMAN.

> And I assure you—nobody 'in charge'.
>
> *Pause*

MARTIN.

> Well, you got it all worked out.

1ST WOMAN.

> No, not 'it all'. Just this.[10]

In *The Ploughman's Lunch* (1983) Ian McEwan accused the media of cynically misrepresenting the
women's peace movement and he developed the gender
debate more grandly the same year in his libretto for
the anti-nuclear cantata *Or Shall We Die?* where the
starting-points are a woman's experiences in Hiroshima,
the archetypal figures of a mother and child, and the
simple contrast between male and female voices.
McEwan offered Newtonian and post-Einsteinian phys-
ics as two world-views 'representing a male and female
principle, yang and yin':

> In the Newtonian universe, there is objectivity; its
> impartial observer is logical and imagines himself to be
> all-seeing and invisible; he believes that if he had ac-
> cess to all facts, then everything could be explained.
> The observer in the Einsteinian universe believes
> herself to be part of the universe she studies, part of its
> constant flux; her own consciousness and the surround-
> ing world pervade each other and are interdependent;
> [. . .] she has no illusions of her omniscience, and yet
> her power is limitless because it does not reside in her
> alone.
>
> 'Shall there be womanly times, or shall we die?' I
> believe the options to be as stark as that.[11]

During the blackout before the last scene of *The Genius*,
one feminist playwright said, 'If they end this at Greenham, I'm leaving.' They did; she did. Though male
dramatists might be paying sincere tribute to new modes
of organisation and action—and David Edgar elaborated

this throughout the decade—they were seeking symbolic
solutions and could be accused of leaving women with
the responsibility of solving the whole generation's
problems. Would male playwrights appropriate Greenham to create what Tania Modleski called 'Feminism
Without Women'?[12]

Cruise plays by women presented the peace camp far
less cosmically. Here instead of Brenton and Edgar's
anonymous Chorus (the redemptive Other) were
detailed studies of friendships and family loyalties
strained and tested as some characters committed
themselves to protest while others were left hostile or
baffled. 'Womanly times', if the phrase meant anything,
were not a romantic given but would have to be
constructed by individuals deciding where their ultimate
responsibilities lay. A group of Greenham women
formed a theatre collective, Common Ground; *The
Fence* (1984) was a semi-documentary of their experiences. Kate Phelp's *No Comment* (1984) was a monologue for a woman whose daughter is killed by troops
guarding Cruise. It was inspired by Franca Rame's *The
Mother* (where the immediate issue was Italian counter-
terrorism) and was one of several attempts to use
Rame's solo work as a model for British feminist
theatre, developing her fusion of personal stories,
tragedy, farce and political commitment. Sarah Daniels'
The Devil's Gateway (Royal Court Theatre Upstairs
1983) grew out of a Women Live theatre workshop
where the director Annie Castledine suggested Daniels
should write about Greenham. She did so indirectly,
dealing with the domestic lives of two middle-aged
women stuck in a council block in Bethnal Green. The
style crossed situation comedy with soap, but the
characters talked about Greenham in every scene and
the plot centred on a bet; a lesbian—who sees Greenham as a distraction from real gender struggles—agrees
to go there if her social-worker lover can find a single
client who sympathises with the protesters. The
prejudices are two-way and at first some of Daniels'
working-class women distrust the campaigners bitterly:
'How many bombs have we had dropped in our lives,
Betty? [. . .] Where were they when we were fighting
for our kids' lives?'[13] In the end most of the women in
The Devil's Gateway go to Greenham, shaking off
media images, and their husbands, in the process: 'Actually, Darrel was talking about the possibility of getting
a mortgage for a fall-out shelter'.[14]

After Cruise was deployed, playwrights continued to
confront the possibilities of catastrophe—and in an
unusually collective spirit. Barrie Hines's *Threads* (BBC
TV, 1984) used drama-documentary techniques borrowed from Peter Watkins' *The War Game* which was
finally broadcast in 1985, twenty years after it was
made. Hines—the author of *Kes*, here taking 'Northern
realism' in a unique direction—showed the scale of an
attack on a specific community, Sheffield. He used nar-

ration, computer graphics and actors and then showed the aftermath over the next thirteen years. Very much in tune with current CND counter-information, *Threads* took note of contingency plans to neutralise political opposition and of the growing scientific predictions of a Nuclear Winter. The final sequences develop a numbed poetry: years ahead, a nest of survivors struggle to educate children who have begun to lose the power of speech. The banal but nagging image of an ancient videotape playing to half-comprehending children is some way from the elaborate myth-making of Russell Hoban's novel *Ridley Walker,* set centuries after the Bomb, which was adapted for the stage (Manchester Royal Exchange) in February 1986, but the theme of language loss is central to both. The very end of *Threads* pinpoints the survivors' horrified discovery that radiation will attack the next generation; in a nightmare scene of childbirth, Hines too finally writes the future in women's bodies.

In 1983 the Theatre Writers' Union produced *The Peace Play Register,* a list of several hundred 'anti-war' plays from Aeschylus onwards. An autumn 1983 appendix added forty-four new titles.[15] A Peace Play Festival was planned for 1984 and in 1985 Methuen published a *Peace Plays* anthology edited by Stephen Lowe, who rephrased Ian McEwan's 'creeping sense of the irrelevance of all the things [people] valued' in more political terms:

> The fear of the holocaust permeates every thought, feeling and breath we take, like a cancer. And often like a cancer we dare not consciously face up to it, and admit its possible intrusion into our way of life. Most critically, if not faced it separates us from a creative belief in a future and increases our sense of alienation and lack of power.[16]

Such was the climate in summer 1985 when the RSC staged Edward Bond's trilogy **The War Plays** in the Pit. Bond drew on many of these trends but added a uniquely remorseless quality to the task of dramatising doomsday; whereas McEwan confessed 'I felt defeated by scale; the problem was at once so colossal and so human,' Bond accepted scale as the challenge and tried to imagine the unimaginable.

II

Bond's **War Plays** were a monumental but structurally eccentric trilogy: the first two plays, **Red Black and Ignorant** and **The Tin Can People,** each ran for around an hour, but the third, **Great Peace,** lasted three and a half. With intervals the full cycle lasted eight hours and the experience of attending it underground in the Pit felt disturbingly like being trapped in a bunker as sixteen actors came and went on a tiny bright white stage, their faces peeled by radiation burns.

Bond's trilogy is not linear. **Red Black and Ignorant,** the prologue, dramatises one temporal instant: the

audience's point of entry into the apocalypse is the moment when a missile lands and a baby is born and burned—Bond's very first focus, like the end of *Threads,* is the maternal body and a woman's preoccupation with the life she carries:

> That morning the child had moved in my womb as if
>   it wanted to run away from the world [. . .]
> Now my head was bent as I listened
> I was so intent I did not hear the explosions and passed
>   into death without knowing [. . .]
> This is the child my womb threw into the fire
>
>   (p. 5)[17]

Red Black and Ignorant shows the life it would have led in 'peacetime'. Seven Brechtian scenes from schooldays to the grave demonstrate Bond's vision of contemporary society, with the child, 'the Monster' (the 'skin, hair and clothes are charred and singed a uniform black so that he appears as if he might have been carved from a piece of coal'), played by the middle-aged Ian McDiarmid as both within and outside events.

They span two generations. At the end the Monster, whom Bond has saved from one war, is killed by his own son—a soldier in another. War has reduced parts of the city to ruins inhabited by 'freaks'; everyone else lives under martial law. There are famines and food riots and every soldier is ordered home to regulate supply and demand by killing 'one civvie-corpse':

> He chooses which
> Make the decisions hard
> Test your potential
> Know yourself
>
>   (p. 15)

The Monster notes 'The first playwrights said know yourself' and, like Tony Harrison and Howard Barker, Bond links the nuclear race to the classical heritage. There are Oedipal echoes ('When we were children we called this the corner house that stands where three roads meet', p. 17) but Bond presents the Son's murder of his father provocatively, as a sane act: 'My son learned it was better to kill what he loved | Than that one creature who is sick or lame or old or poor or a stranger should sit and stare at an empty world and find no reason why it should suffer' (p. 18). **Red Black and Ignorant** coolly assumes that, irrespective of Cruise and Trident, Western society is at best two generations away from self-destruction. Its tone is startlingly simplistic; Bond called it agit prop but it is really a Brechtian *Lehrstück* in that each scene offers the actors themselves—especially young non-professionals, with whom Bond worked increasingly after 1979—the opportunity to discuss ethical issues in rehearsal. The play lays out the principles of the whole trilogy unambiguously—so banally in fact that Bond almost seems to be challenging the audience to try to disprove them:

property is theft, the education system teaches fear, unemployment brutalizes. . . . For Bond, fears for the future are meaningless if cut off from a condemnation of the present state of Britain; the trilogy is firmly set in the Old Testament Prophetic tradition (the last play shows us Ezekiel's valley of dry bones) and he presents the immediate nuclear threat as a terminal symptom of a society which has forgotten the meaning of democracy: 'Democracy isnt the right to vote but freedom to know' (p. 19). There are almost no references throughout the trilogy to any external enemy. Whereas the Earth in *King Real* weeps, Bond's Monster describes it whistling in derision because 'There were so many rockets the world looked like a hedgehog':

> Security was so great all were suspected
> Even as they lay in their silos the rockets destroyed
>   the societies they were said to protect
>
>   (p. 15)

Red Black and Ignorant sketches a fantasy-future which is dystopian precisely because nothing has changed. Then Bond reminds the audience that it is fiction: the Monster never lived but the end of the world has already started:

> Everything before your time was the childhood of
>   humankind
> With the new weapons that age passed
> But you went on building your house with bricks that
>   were already on fire
>
>   (p. 19)

This play begins in the immediate future. It takes us some forty years into a hypothetical future which is also a cartoon history of the post-war years. Finally it curves back into the present and confronts the audience with the need to act, to rewrite tomorrow. Despite its Brechtian style, the time-paradoxes recall much millennial science-fiction: *Red Black and Ignorant* is in a way Bond's *Terminator* and the second play, *The Tin Can People,* is his equivalent to *Mad Max*. This is a richer but more conventional survival narrative describing a post-holocaust wanderer's encounter with a colony which has rebuilt society in a military complex stocked with infinite quantities of tins. *Tin Can People* is a parable play. Bond's survivors hope to create a paradise in hell's ruins and believe they have learned from the failures of the dead. They embrace the newcomer ecstatically but when an unknown sickness decimates them, he is scapegoated as a carrier. A self-appointed militaristic leader emerges from the commune and in a superb demonstration of paranoid logic he seizes a supermarket gadget used to take cans down from high shelves and frantically hammers it into a spear, then drops dead from the disease he aimed to eradicate. Another man throws the spear and skewers the intruder in a spirit of gentle curiosity: 'It was a shame not to see

if it worked'. The Tin Can People inherit our consumerism and therefore our cocktail of aggression, terror and irrationality—the newcomer must be diseased because 'Since you came seven of us have died [. . .] One of us even died before you came'—and they destroy their foodstore hysterically, gorging in the ruins till calm descends. The very last survivors accept the newcomer. They try to start again.

The Tin Can People are more than Bond's image of suicidal materialism; the play is given nauseating weight by their language, for it dwells remorselessly on the past; they are fixated with the dead and the physical horror of the catastrophe. If the first play is about showing ('Now we will show scenes from the life I did not live') *Tin Can People* is partly about speaking and the compulsion to record and articulate horror: the Third Woman quoted at the head of this essay is possessed by images and speaks on and on like the Mouth in Beckett's *Not I*: 'To tell the truth—why dont you stop me?—it was a game to watch [. . .] Please interrupt me: I cant stop speaking [. . .] So I said die die die' (pp. 35-36). The first half is packed with formal set-piece descriptions of the Bomb's effects; these are part-choric, part-messenger speeches where the whole cast have been astonished spectators at a global tragedy. Some details derive from Hiroshima but Bond pushes them into realms of baroque fantasy. Like David Nathan of the *Jewish Chronicle,* many spectators felt so oppressed that they left after this play and most reviewers dwelt on its vocabulary, whether to admire or mock or to accuse Bond of morbid self-indulgence. Yet in summer 1985 those speeches served a cathartic purpose, crystalising and sharing in public the nightmares Ian McEwan described. Bond tried to create a new Aristotelian theatre of myth, terror and pity, confronting collective fears and seeking political contexts for them. There was another factor: in the last part of the trilogy the heroine hears still more grotesque descriptions, of human beings swept by the nuclear winds ('All the bodies—livin an dead, army an civie—shot up in the sky | It was full of bodies whirlin round in circles like a painted ceilin', p. 32), but she disbelieves them:

> That dont 'appen even in this world
> Yer saw somethin yer dont like t' remember and that's
>   'ow yer forget
>
>   (p. 37)

She's right. She is talking to delirious soldiers who have massacred children, and although Bond's descriptions of horrors are meant as warnings for the audience, they are also the characters' acts of suppression and denial. They dwell on cosmic horrors to distract themselves from their own guilt. Bond suggests that the politicians' obsession with future violence represents just such a blindness to the present: 'I wanted in *The War Plays* to deal with the psychosis that exists after a nuclear bomb. But I first have to make a political analysis'.[18]

The Bomb creates a new military vocabulary where, echoing Beckett's *Endgame,* 'corpsed' replaces 'fuck' as the all-purpose obscenity and, as in Hines and Hoban, language dies through trauma and disuse. In *Tin Can People* and *Great Peace* the 'protagonists' (insofar as the word can mean anything after the Bomb) go through a phase of grotesque Beckettian isolation, wandering through a man-made (not Absurd) wasteland only one step from aphasia; they mouth their thoughts in odd images and shattered, granulated sounds. But the Tin Can People finally learn new speech-rhythms and a poised vocabulary; they come to see themselves objectively at the crossroads of history and learn how to imagine the future because they see the past as more than one moment of annihilation. When they appreciate their own crimes as well as the generals', they can articulate the trilogy's central statement:

> They'll look back at us and say we lived in prisons. They'll live in justice. Justice is a stone woman sitting in a stone room trying to make human gestures. If our children live she'll learn to make them—and then the stone will be as human as these hands which open tins.

(p. 51)

III

Disturbingly for the audience, the final and by far the longest play, *Great Peace,* turns back from this moment of hope to rewrite and reappraise the events of *Red Black and Ignorant. Great Peace* reworks several earlier scenes and themes freely, risking monotony or confusion in order to suggest that no event has pre-ordained consequences. Bond has been the most Newtonian of playwrights, preoccupied with the analysis of causes and effects, but *The War Plays* are an attempt to give post-modernism a moral purpose. So once again we start with the death of an anonymous baby. This time, though, *Great Peace* portrays a mother's painful trek through the attack and the aftermath. It is one of Bond's most massive and important works: as in *Lear* and *The Woman* we watch one individual's journey through the destruction—and just perhaps the re-birth—of a world, but this time that world is ours. Not only does Bond recapitulate themes and situations from the first two *War Plays,* he also tries to rise to his subject by making *Great Peace* both a re-examination of his own dramatic career and a meditation on European theatre.

Bond's analogies with the Athenian tragedies are important. He said they were 'all about [. . .] the ancient plague in the city, the destruction of the city: that was the destruction of the world in miniature—*The*

War Plays are about the real destruction of the whole world'.[19] *Great Peace* is actually a trilogy within the trilogy. Three sections place the anonymous protagonist (the Woman) in the *City,* a *Wilderness,* and finally a few miles away from a *New Community.* The first section is an urban family tragedy (actually known as 'the Greek play' in rehearsal). The sense of time is vague—it seems some bombs have been dropped and the soldiers think they have won a contained war—but the sense of *place* is precise. This is the working-class South London of *Saved,* revisited twenty years later.

Saved involved the killing of two babies (one onstage by a gang, the other—unseen—by a World War II bomb); so do *The War Plays.* In *Red Black and Ignorant* the child is a statistic of war, in *Great Peace* it is murdered by its own brother, himself a ruined child of the city, and in both plays the mother was played by Maggie Steed. The murder of children is Edward Bond's recurrent image of the social destruction of the innocent. The Woman in *Great Peace* is a childminder, caring for a neighbour's baby as well as her own. Her soldier son comes home: he is under Herodian orders to kill a local child to save food, and the only two children in this street are in his mother's house. Both the Woman and her son are typical Bondian victim-aggressors. They cannot imagine disobedience to an insane State, let alone coherent opposition, and Bond remorselessly shows their anguish and brutality in what they believe is an insoluble tragic dilemma. In despair the son (brilliantly played for the RSC by Gary Oldman) smothers his own sibling, tenderly. Then in the next scene, back in uniform, he refuses to pick up a cigarette packet and is shot dead as an example.

Bond served in the artillery in Vienna (1953-5) during his National Service: 'We were turned into automata,' he told Malcolm Hay and Philip Roberts. 'What really started me writing seriously was being in the army because then that presented a lot of problems that I had to sort out in some way [. . . It was] why I became the sort of dramatist I became. The army's a sort of parodied version of civil society—it's without all the face-saving rituals and without all the social excuses and just the naked barbarism.'[20] The son's death scene is a dense example of what Bond calls a Theatre Event: because he is almost totally silent and immobile, it is impossible to tell from the text whether he is in shock or whether his refusal is suicide or an act of revolt. Actors and audience alike are compelled to trace the action back, to discover causes and effects and to make informed judgements—even though the characters, locked in the systems that shaped them, cannot.

And then comes the End of the World and the death of systems. Seventeen years later Bond's Woman is discovered wandering, ragged and almost speechless, through a wasteland ravaged by radiation, chemical

warfare and a nuclear winter that he envisages as existence stripped down forever to its absolutes:

> I went through the black wind once: I turned aside but
>   it caught me
> I went through the edge: soot and dust an ash—black
> . . .
> Then I came out on the white dust—dazzled—I was
>   'alf glad t'look back at the storm
> Yer could see where it'd passed
> One 'alf of the 'ill was white an the other 'alf black
>   as if it'd bin painted along a line.

(p. 61)

She is alone in the dead landscape—'I've trod this sand
small' (p. 43)—except for a greasy bundle of rags which
she clutches to her, and only her compulsion to nurture
it drives her on. For she believes this is her child, still
alive, still a baby. The bundle is the key image of *The
War Plays*. It gives her the ghost of an identity—
'mummy'—despite the catastrophe and lets her believe
she inhabits a reality where narratives still make sense:
'I'll tell you the oldest story: the mother goes into a
burnin 'ouse t'bring out 'er child' (p. 28). As she herself
says later, 'When things are more than we can bear, we
break: that's a kindness we're given' (p. 48). The
apocalypse makes her a mythical figure, Lear and Hecuba's sister, whereas the Martial Law society cannot
survive the Bomb it hatched.

In a series of parable-like episodes, the Woman meets
other survivors: some try to give her comfort, some beg
for help. In this black and white desert, relationships
are stripped to the core and the characters must re-
invent the meaning of kinship at ground zero. A
pregnant young woman who has never seen a child
stares at the bundle: 'Is that inside me?' She is the only
survivor of the Tin Can People. She dies in childbirth,
the baby is healthy . . . and the Woman calmly
abandons it, taking its hat and shawl for her own child:
'I cant take yer with me [. . .] The world cant cope
with another mouth' (pp. 28-29). Before she leaves she
draws it a picture of a house and a happy family in the
dirt: 'I'll pay for what I took'.

The Woman is a compound of kindness, ruthlessness
and insanity here, but the scene resonates still more
because this is at least the third time Bond has staged
it—it's the moment in *Narrow Road to the Deep North*
and *The Bundle* when the poet Basho leaves a child to
die by the river and proceeds on his solipsisitic quest
for enlightenment. This time the scene is far more
complex because of the Woman's own unspeakable suffering and her self-sacrificial care of her own 'child',
but there is no doubt of her criminality; her madness is
an expression of her moral blindness, not an excuse for
it. As in a folk-tale, a human being is placed in her care
three times, once in each part of the play, and each time
she demands payment: she takes three shawls, stealing

warmth from those who have nothing else. These physical images carry the play's meaning. The rag-baby she
cares for is *literally* constructed out of the deprivations
of others. Of course the victimiser is also the victim
(her real baby was killed with a wet cloth) and Bond
makes both the Woman and the audience project changing meanings on to the cloths in wrenching acts of
imagination. Bond's post-nuclear vision is stark, but he
is more interested in responsibility than pain: in the
City, the Woman is so terrified for her baby's safety
that she presses her son to do his duty and kill the
neighbour's child. From that moment on she sees her
relationship with everything that breathes as competition and seventeen years later she is still locked in her
act: 'There's no one outside these arms' (p. 26). In
scene 11 she pushes a handcart with only her dumb
'child' for company and is revealed as Bond's rewriting
of Mother Courage.

Edward Bond's nuclear landscape is a scrapyard of
scenes from dead plays. The Woman desperately
scrabbles at her neighbour's door to seize her child, re-
enacting the end of *Bingo* where Anne Hathaway
becomes the embodiment of the marginalised, the under-
educated and the despised, scratching madly at Shakespeare's door in the futile hope that his will contains
something for her. In the Wasteland the soldiers believe
they are dead—and therefore beyond suffering—and
pound human bones into soup like Queen Victoria's
ghoulish regime in *Early Morning*'s cannibal Heaven.
When the Woman threatens their self-anaesthesia by
insisting her Bundle is alive, they rip the rags apart—
and thus, even after Doomsday, men replay the baby-
stoning scene from *Saved,* proving more clearly this
time that their violence is a form of desperation.

Great Peace also replays the central theme of *The
Woman* where, as Troy is destroyed, women comfort
one another across the borders of self-interest and madness. This time two nuclear survivors learn to sleep
holding each other like sisters. But the trilogy is
remorseless: there is no rest. As in *Lear,* Bond dismisses
the pastoral dream that any community can live in
hermetic isolation from history: the Tin Can People and
the 'dead' soldiers perish like the institutions they
grotesquely mimic, and so do compassionate individuals and delicate relationships on which the audience
pins its trust. Indeed Bond seems to ask again and again
whether suffering can absolve or reform us, only to
reply 'Not yet.'

Yet as *Great Peace* coils towards its conclusion, Bond
finally allows the Woman's psychological state to
evolve in a sequence of distinct dramatic phases:

Memory: In the City she pushed her son towards
infanticide—'We'll forget it | They make us do it, they
cant make us remember it' (p. 15)—but as she nears the

new settlement she does remember. She imagines that an old woman, her daughter, and a young man from the community are her neighbour, the neighbour's baby, and her own soldier son—cross-casting in the RSC production forced the audience to draw parallels. Actually the young man (Gary Oldman again) *becomes* her son by trying to understand her and the reasons why the soldier behaved as he did. The new community become preoccupied with the Woman as a problem and use every argument they can to persuade her to join them: they know their need for a mother. Yet she rejects love: 'So: I cut off the last of 'uman flesh' (p. 55).

Recognition: the Woman senses that the new generation has developed new values: 'Your sort can keep their word'. She breaks hers and slips away after promising to let her surrogate son stay with her: 'That was yesterday—a 'ole day's gone' (p. 62). At the close of the play the Woman is neither sentimentalised nor condemned: she is an enigma whom even the audience cannot fully understand because mercifully we have not undergone her experiences. To the new community she is a miracle, a Lazarus, but she sees herself finally as a sideshow on the outskirts of the future, a dry reed in the wind.

Inheritance: By the end of the play she and her new son reach different points of insight: he knows how to act compassionately, she knows she has no place in his world: 'They'd 'ave t' build a mad 'ouse t' keep me in!' Yet he returns again and again, walking for weeks to try to persuade her to come in. More ghosts of old scenes: . . . he is Scopey visiting the Beckettian recluse Alen in **The Pope's Wedding,** and Willy, the survivor of a boating disaster, coming to Even's hut on the sands in **The Sea.** Each time, a young man develops an extraordinary bond with a ragged 'wise fool'. The Woman has suffered too much even to begin to impart any kind of wisdom, but the young man never turns against her as Scopey turned on Alen in frustration because he had no gospel to pass on. Scopey puts on Alen's coat and takes his place in a hut piled from floor to ceiling with tins—alienation amidst plenty—but the young man in **Great Peace** brings the Woman two new 'bundles' to help her through the next savage winter: tins (this community makes its own; it has stopped scavenging off the past) and a light-blue padded coat. It is the only splash of cool colour in the whole trilogy.

Metamorphosis: At the last there is no apotheosis or even closure, only merciful release: the exhausted woman just falls dead in her tracks. Before this she accepts both that her child is dead and that the way she tried to save it long ago was 'wicked'. But what she cannot do is overcome her hatred for her son. This is actually self-hatred because she sees his 'unnatural' crime as worse than the bombers' and so she blames herself for giving birth. 'Its too close!' she cries, 'Its

out of nature!' and she sees herself—an Oedipus before Colonus—as a pariah: ''Oo can wash my 'ands? I If I used the world as a towel the grass'd die in the last fields' (p. 60).

She dreams of pressing the last breath out of the bodies of the dead to ask them the tragic sufferer's classic questions—'Tell me why I suffered an 'oo its for, an why we live on this earth an are buried in it?'—but her new son, fascinated by her tenderness towards her bundle, whistles (in derision?). He believes that if the dead could speak they would demand to know why they died and how she lived:

> Live till your own time comes t' be dead
> It'll be soon
> Till then you answer the questions
>
> (p. 61)

At the very end he returns after the winter. Her body has vanished; only her bundles—the meanings she carried—remain. The RSC covered all the scene-changes with the scream of the nuclear wind, but the trilogy ends with a silent scene, and the sound of human breath.

We have seen how Bond's trilogy, in the attempt to match its theme, weaves variations on ancient and modern classics and on Bond's own work. One last example takes us to the heart of the project. Whenever Bond's plays represent injustice as an act of violence against children, the representation of the victim is always stylised—an empty pram, a row of dolls, a bundle of cloth. In **Great Peace** Bond suddenly and startlingly deconstructs his own symbols: the soldiers unwind the bundle to try to prove the child is a fantasy. But the Woman, alone with the rags, gently puts them back together and refuses to see with 'scientific' eyes: 'Let's see the state of yer [. . .] Did that 'urt?' (p. 41).

And then the bundle speaks. It voices its fears and its compassion: 'Sh . . . I I watch you sleep I Your poor face' (p. 42).

As we should expect, Bond steers the scene back to bitterness: the Bundle relapses into silence and we next see the Woman years later, beating it in rage and frustration. The dream of hearing Truth from another's voice has failed again. But it does speak once more, when she unrolls it herself to make a pillow for the sick woman. In a sense the effect of the Trilogy depends on the way these key Theatre Events are staged. Maggie Steed spoke the child's words herself, so they offered insights into the Woman's madness and her slow evolution towards empathy. A production which gave the Bundle its own voice would make these moments visionary and Blakean. By excluding technical explanations Bond opened the scenes up for fundamental debate—for as **Red Black and Ignorant** stated, this is an enquiry into what it is to be human.

Over the next decade, no major British theatre staged a single new play by Edward Bond. He had cut himself off from the mainstream through his politics, his interest in working with young people, and his insistence on directing his own work. He was originally billed as co-director of **The War Plays** with the RSC's Nick Hamm but withdrew during rehearsals and omitted all reference to the production, even a cast-list, when the texts were republished in 1991. Coincidentally, Bond's war trilogy was succeeded at the Pit by three plays by Howard Barker including *The Castle*, his own response to Greenham Common set characteristically in a surreal and savage version of the Crusades. This production heralded Barker's acceptance as the outstanding voice of radical British drama in the late 1980s. With hindsight we may see the creation of Cruise, Pershing, Trident and Star Wars as the most expensive piece of theatre in history, a charade which challenged the audience in the Kremlin to compete till it collapsed. The wars which erupted in the ruins of the USSR and former Yugoslavia seem closer to Howard Barker's visions of perpetual catastrophe than to Bond's Olympian logic. His **War Plays** were among the last cultural expressions of the Cold War Age, of its anguished certainties.

Notes

1. *The Times*, 14 November 1979. See E. P. Thompson's analysis of press coverage in 'The Doomsday Consensus', *New Statesman*, 20 December 1979.

2. Quoted by Thompson, who used the 1956 incident to draw attention to the workings of the Official Secrets Act. The anti-nuclear plays discussed in this essay were intimately connected with the wider 'Secret State' genre of the 1980s, led for example by Troy Kennedy Martin's *Power of Darkness* (BBC TV, 1985).

3. See Martin Walker, *The Sleeping Giant* (London: Michael Joseph, 1986), pp. 128-31.

4. Margaret Thatcher, *The Downing Street Years* (London: Harper Collins, 1993), p. 267.

5. *The Downing Street Years*, p. 269.

6. Ian McEwan, Preface to *Or Shall We Die?* (London: Jonathan Cape, 1983), p. 9.

7. Adrian Mitchell, *The Tragedy of King Real*, in *Peace Plays*, ed. by Stephen Lowe (London: Methuen, 1985), p. 23.

8. Noel Greig, *Poppies* (London: Gay Men's Press, 1983), p. 5.

9. See Sheila Rowbotham, Lynne Segal and Hilary Wainwright, *Beyond the Fragments: Feminism and the Making of Socialism* (London: Merlin Press, 1979).

10. David Edgar, *Maydays* (London: Methuen, 1983), p. 69.

11. McEwan, *Or Shall We Die?*, p. 19.

12. See Tania Modleski, *Feminism Without Women: Culture and Criticism in a 'Postfeminist' Age* (London: Routledge, 1992).

13. Sarah Daniels, *The Devil's Gateway*, in *Daniels: Plays One* (London: Methuen, 1991), p. 97.

14. *The Devil's Gateway*, p. 82.

15. *The Peace Play Register*, compiled by Norman Leach, placed work in these categories: World War One; World War Two; The Development of the Bomb; Hiroshima and its Immediate Aftermath; Anti-Imperialist; Falklands; Anti-World War Three: Campaigning Plays; Anti-World War Three and Armageddon; Life in the Proximity of Air Force or Nuclear Bases; In the Bunker and Aftermath of World War Three; and Anti-War Parable Plays.

16. Lowe, Introduction to *Peace Plays*, p. 73.

17. Quotations are taken from the first edition: *The War Plays: A Trilogy* (London: Methuen, 1985), published in two volumes: *Part One: Red Black and Ignorant and Part Two: The Tin Can People* and *Part Three: Great Peace*. They were republished in a single volume in 1991 with five poems and 116 pages of commentary by Bond. The first performance of the entire trilogy was at the Barbican Pit on 25 July 1985.

18. Malcolm Hay, 'Edward Bond: British Secret Playwright', *Plays and Players*, June 1985, p. 9.

19. Malcolm Hay, p. 9.

20. Bond quoted in Malcolm Hay and Philip Roberts, *Bond: A Study of His Plays* (London: Methuen, 1980), p. 15, and in *Theatre Papers*, Second Series, No. 1: *Bingo* and *The Bundle*, Dartington College of Art, 1978, p. 2.

FURTHER READING

Criticism

Bond, Edward. "Author's Note: On Violence." In *Plays: One* (*Saved, Early Morning, The Pope's Wedding*), pp. 9-17. 1977. Reprint, London: Methuen, 1985.

   Bond discusses the evolution, causes, and role of violence in human culture.

Bond, Edward, and Giles Gordon. "Edward Bond." *Transatlantic Review,* no. 22 (autumn 1966): 7-15.

Interview that took place early in Bond's career, after the first production of *Saved,* in which he discusses his use of violence in that play as well as the need for a revival of controversial works in the English theater and his main writing influences.

Coult, Tony. "Gods." In *The Plays of Edward Bond,* pp. 26-35. London: Eyre Methuen, 1979.

Examines Bond's views on religion as a destructive force at worst and a delusion at best, particularly in *Narrow Road to the Deep North.*

Duncan, Joseph E. "The Child and the Old Man in the Plays of Edward Bond." *Modern Drama* 19, no. 1 (March 1976): 1-10.

Examines Bond's recurring juxtaposition of metaphorical figures of children and old men in his plays.

Fusco, Cassandra. "'The Wretched of the Earth': The Ethics of Political Violence and Its Ministers of Sacrifice in Edward Bond's *Jackets.*" *Études anglaises* 48, no. 3 (July-September 1995): 296-305.

Discusses the institutional power that demands the sacrifice of innocents as a means of reinforcing its power as Bond portrays it in *Jackets.*

Hay, Malcolm, and Philip Roberts. " *Lear.*" In *Bond: A Study of His Plays,* pp. 103-38. London: Eyre Methuen, 1980.

Discusses Bond's process in writing *Lear,* examining the ways in which Bond refused to look for "false optimism" or easy answers to the moral problems that arise in the play.

Holmstrom, John. Review of *Lear,* by Edward Bond. *Plays and Players* 19, no. 2 (November 1971): 42, 53.

Review of a 1971 production of *Lear* at the Royal Court Theatre in London, directed by William Gaskill; Holmstrom describes the play as "a long scream of pain and horror."

Hughes, G. E. H. "Edward Bond's *Restoration.*" *Critical Quarterly* 25, no. 4 (winter 1983): 77-81.

Argues that Bond's main premise in *Restoration*— that society is thoroughly corrupt and decaying— will not persuade an audience not already inclined to think like Bond.

Itzin, Catherine. "Edward Bond." In *Stages in the Revolution: Political Theatre in Britain Since 1968,* pp. 76-88. London: Eyre Methuen, 1980.

Discusses the evolution of Bond's political consciousness in his works following *Saved.*

Jenkins, Anthony. "Edward Bond: A Political Education." In *British and Irish Drama Since 1960,* edited by James Acheson, pp. 103-16. Houndmills, England: Macmillan, 1993.

Examines Bond's plays in the context of the political events of the times in which they were written and produced, along with the public reaction to them.

Jones, Daniel R. "Edward Bond's 'Rational Theatre.'" *Theatre Journal* 32, no. 4 (December 1980): 505-17.

Analyzes the ways in which Bond's characters come to view society as irrational and then determine to make it rational.

Lahr, John. Review of *The Fool,* by Edward Bond. *Plays and Players* 23, no. 4 (January 1976): 23-25.

Review of a 1975 production of *The Fool* at the Royal Court Theatre in London, directed by Peter Gill; Lahr praises Gill for placing a restraining hand on Bond's often excessiveness and calls the work an "astonishing spectacle."

Lamont, Rosette Clementine. "Edward Bond's Righteous Anger." *Western European Stages* 14, no. 1 (winter 2002): 27-32.

Notes the parallel events of Bond's writing of *The Crime of the Twenty-First Century* and the September 11, 2001, terrorist attacks on the United States.

Rabey, David Ian. "Bond: Blind Power." In *English Drama Since 1940,* pp. 79-86. London: Longman, 2003.

Provides an overview of Bond's portrayal of modern power structures and their effects throughout the plays in his oeuvre.

Ravenhill, Mark. "Whatever Happened to Edward Bond?" *Independent* London (2 November 2010): 20.

Brief commentary on the English theater's initial embrace and subsequent rejection of Bond, with particular mention of a retrospective of his works being produced at a pub.

Reinelt, Janelle. "Theorizing Utopia: Edward Bond's War Plays." In *The Performance of Power: Theatrical Discourse and Politics,* edited by Sue-Ellen Case and Janelle Reinelt, pp. 221-32. Iowa City: University of Iowa Press, 1991.

Examines *The War Plays* from a socialist-feminist perspective, arguing that the primacy of the gender-based family hierarchy is the foundation upon which Bond is able to build an imagined Utopian future for his characters.

Saunders, Graham. "Edward Bond and the Celebrity of Exile." *Theatre Research International* 29, no. 3 (2004): 256-66.

Discusses the effects of Bond's reputation as a "controversial" playwright on both critical and public perception of his plays and on the development of his work at La Colline Theatre in France.

Smith, Leslie. "Edward Bond's *Lear*." *Comparative Drama* 13, no. 1 (spring 1979): 65-85.

Discusses the ways in which Bond veered away from Shakespeare's *King Lear* when he wrote his own interpretation of the character in *Lear*.

Tener, Robert L. "Edward Bond's Dialectic: Irony and Dramatic Metaphors." *Modern Drama* 25, no. 3 (September 1982): 423-34.

Discusses the ways in which metaphors are used ironically in Bond's plays.

Worth, Katharine. "Bond's *Restoration*." *Modern Drama* 24, no. 4 (December 1981): 479-93.

Explores Bond's use of tragedy in *Restoration*.

Additional coverage of Bond's life and career is contained in the following sources published by Gale: *Authors and Artists for Young Adults,* **Vol. 50;** *British Writers Supplement,* **Vol. 1;** *Contemporary Authors,* **Vol. 25-28R;** *Contemporary Authors New Revision Series,* **Vols. 38, 67, 106;** *Contemporary British Dramatists;* *Contemporary Dramatists,* **Eds. 5, 6;** *Contemporary Literary Criticism,* **Vols. 4, 6, 13, 23;** *Dictionary of Literary Biography,* **Vols. 13, 310;** *DISCovering Authors Modules: Dramatists;* *Drama for Students,* **Vols. 3, 8;** *Encyclopedia of World Literature in the 20th Century,* **Ed. 3;** *Literature Resource Center;* *Major 20th-Century Writers,* **Ed. 1; and** *Modern British Literature,* **Ed. 2.**

Noël Coward
1899-1973

English playwright, screenwriter, lyricist, short story writer, novelist, autobiographer, and poet.

INTRODUCTION

One of the most enduringly admired playwrights of the twentieth century, Coward is best known for his light, sophisticated comedies that many critics have noted are deceptively complex. Centering on the leisure class, the plays tend to feature mildly scandalous characters and indirectly raise questions about morality and the validity of social codes. One of Coward's innovations was to use spontaneous, naturalistic dialogue rather than the sweeping, epigrammatic style that had been popular in early-twentieth-century theater. His early works appealed to the mood of post-World War I Jazz Age audiences, and he became widely known for the distinctive stylish sophistication of his works. Such plays as *Hay Fever* (1925), *Private Lives* (1930), and *Blithe Spirit* (1941) assured Coward theatrical success through many decades. In the late twentieth century, literary critics began examining his plays in the context of emerging queer theory and gender studies, giving them fresh relevance.

BIOGRAPHICAL INFORMATION

Coward was born in Teddington-on-Thames, a suburb of London, on December 16, 1899, to Violet Coward and Arthur Coward, a traveling musical instrument salesman. His father was often absent from home and could not provide well for the family, but Coward's mother was an ambitious and highly theatrical woman who enrolled her son in dance lessons and the Chapel Royal Choir School. Coward began performing for audiences by the age of seven and made his professional acting debut at age twelve. For the next several years he performed in plays throughout London and met many of the key figures in the English theater world and in upper-class English society. He worked and studied in the renowned acting company of Sir Charles Hawtrey, continuing to act through most of World War I until he was drafted into the Artists' Rifles regiment at age eighteen. He spent much of his nine-month service in the hospital, however, due to a concussion he had suffered. Upon recovery, he secured a medical discharge thanks to a sympathetic doctor. By this time Coward

had begun writing his own plays. Having grown up in the theater and befriended many larger-than-life personalities, Coward often modeled his characters after his friends. The newfound sexual freedom of the era, combined with the existential bitterness of the World War I generation, is reflected in his early works. His first play produced in London was *I'll Leave It to You* (1920), in which he starred as well. By 1921 he had saved enough money to buy passage on a ship to the United States, hoping to interest Broadway producers in his plays. Although he failed in that regard, Coward did absorb some of the stylistic techniques of Broadway plays during his summer living in Manhattan, and he was particularly interested in the fast pacing of American plays. Also during that summer, Coward spent much time in the company of an eccentric New York couple named Hartley Manners and Laurette Taylor, who would inspire him to write *Hay Fever*. Coward's first great success as a playwright came in 1924 with *The Vortex*, a controversial play about sex and drug addiction in which some critics saw hints of Coward's unacknowledged homosexuality. By the end of the 1920s Coward was one of the most successful and highly paid playwrights in the English-speaking world. His high-society comedies of the 1930s were equally as popular albeit shocking, with their sexual affairs among the wealthy; in fact, Coward occasionally ran up against the disapproval of the Office of Lord Chamberlain, which had the power to deny theaters the license to produce a play if it was deemed too risqué. As World War II approached, Coward was determined to take part on behalf of England. In 1938 a government official sent Coward on intelligence-gathering missions, amid performance engagements, in several European capitals. Coward was then sent to work as a secret agent in Paris and in 1940, sent to the United States. Since no one could know about this work, Coward became concerned that his apparent lack of involvement in the war effort was damaging his reputation in England, and he asked to be reassigned. He was assured that the best thing he could do for his country would be to perform for the troops to help boost morale, which he did tirelessly. In 1942 Coward wrote, produced, co-directed, and starred in the wartime film *In Which We Serve*, which earned accolades in both England and the United States. In 1943 Coward was presented with an honorary Academy Award for his work on the film, which was also nominated for Best Picture in 1944. In 1945 he fell in love with a South African actor named Graham Payn, who would remain with him until Coward's death. In the 1950s Coward's reputation suffered as critics and audiences had developed a taste for more experimental material and Coward's works were viewed as passé. Unable to afford England's high postwar taxes, he left the country and settled in Jamaica, at which point he was excoriated in the British press despite his exemplary wartime service. Nevertheless, this began a happier time in Coward's life. He saw great success with a Las Vegas cabaret show and moved to the relatively new medium of television, adapting and starring in televised versions of his plays as well as producing well-received musical specials. Also at this time he saw a revival of interest in his stage plays, especially those he wrote in the 1920s and '30s. In 1964 *Hay Fever* was the first play by a living playwright to be revived by the National Theatre. Coward was thus embraced once more in England and, in 1970, was granted a knighthood. He died of a stroke at his home in Jamaica on March 26, 1973.

MAJOR DRAMATIC WORKS

Coward's first major hit, *The Vortex,* resonated with its Lost Generation audience—the young adults who had become disillusioned by World War I—because of Coward's realistic depiction of the resentful relationship between a narcissistic middle-aged mother and her talented but cocaine-addicted son. In both London and New York Coward played the role of the son, a musical composer named Nicky Lancaster who is unable to escape his aging mother's attempts to maintain her youth and social status. Coward's next play, *Fallen Angels* (1925), established his reputation as a playwright of wide appeal. It was a lighthearted sex farce about two married women who encounter their mutual former lover. In *Hay Fever,* which he wrote in three days in 1924 and is based on the household of New York playwright Hartley Manners and his actress wife Laurette Taylor, Coward affectionately skewered the eccentric upper classes and their tendency to create mayhem with their bizarre and uncivilized behavior. The play revolves around the Bliss family—all talented, self-indulgent eccentrics who crave Bohemian credibility—each of whom invites a guest to stay the weekend without the knowledge of the others. While entertaining themselves through clever game playing, histrionics, and insouciant frankness, the Blisses alternately insult and try to seduce each of the guests, who eventually flee the home without their hosts even noticing. Coward reached the height of his success in the 1930s and 1940s. *Private Lives,* now considered one of the great light comedies of the twentieth century, opened in 1930. Despite being a comedy of manners, *Private Lives* takes a pessimistic view of love and marriage, featuring Amanda and Elyot, a divorced couple who discover they are both honeymooning at the same

hotel with their new spouses. Recalling the more radiant moments of their tumultuous marriage, they agree to elope to Paris but promptly return to their habitual quarreling. *Design for Living* (1933) was another lighthearted but risqué play, about a sprightly young sophisticate named Gilda who falls in love with two artists, Leo and Otto, but enters into a marriage of convenience with a dependable older man. When she eventually tires of her life of domesticity, however, she runs off with both Leo and Otto, suggesting that the three will live together in an unconventional arrangement. In Coward's most enduringly popular comedy, *Blithe Spirit,* a successful novelist, Charles, dabbles in spiritualism hoping to find inspiration for his latest book. He invites a well known clairvoyant named Madame Arcati to his home to hold a séance, and she unwittingly summons the ghost of his first wife, Elvira, who torments his current wife, Ruth. Hoping to bring Charles into the spirit world, Elvira tries to kill him but accidentally kills Ruth instead who, now a ghost herself, seeks revenge. At that point the hapless husband decides to exorcise himself of both wives.

CRITICAL RECEPTION

Although so many of Coward's characters were based on actual people and his plays were written during historically specific periods and in response to the predominant culture of his time, his themes have proven surprisingly relevant over the decades, and revivals of his works have been successful even into the twenty-first century. Robert F. Kiernan cited Coward's consistent use of "clean-lined structures" for the enduring popularity of his works, maintaining that while Coward had come up in the Victorian and Edwardian tradition of the well-made play, he was more essentially a modernist, eschewing any plot twists that he deemed unnecessary. Many critics have viewed Coward's willingness to create comedy out of disillusionment to be among his greatest assets as a writer. While *Blithe Spirit* was, for example, greeted with some level of shock at first because Coward appeared to be making light of death while London was being systematically bombed by the Germans during the Blitz of World War II, the playwright ultimately was correct in his assessment that British audiences needed relief from the weight of war and death, and that his lighthearted comedy was a patriotic gesture. Indeed, despite Coward's reputation for writing frothy comedies of manners, some critics always took his work seriously, comparing it favorably with the dramas of August Strindberg, Edward Albee, and Harold Pinter. According to Sos Eltis, the way Coward addresses the most serious and profound human experiences, such as death and divorce, was a pure expression of what Susan Sontag meant by "camp"—namely, "a love of the unnatural, of style and artifice" that comes from "a generous joy that mocks seriousness."

PRINCIPAL WORKS

Plays

I'll Leave It to You 1920
The Better Half 1922
The Young Idea: A Comedy of Youth 1922
London Calling! [with Ronald Jeans] 1923
The Vortex 1924
Easy Virtue 1925
Fallen Angels 1925
Hay Fever 1925
On with the Dance 1925
Three Plays: The Rat Trap, The Vortex, Fallen Angels
    1925
The Queen Was in the Parlour 1926
The Rat Trap 1926
This Was a Man 1926
Home Chat 1927
The Marquise 1927
Sirocco 1927
This Year of Grace! 1928
Bitter Sweet 1929
Private Lives: An Intimate Comedy 1930
Some Other Private Lives 1930
Cavalcade 1931
Weatherwise 1932
* *Words and Music* 1932
Design for Living 1933
Play Parade: Cavalcade, Bitter Sweet, The Vortex, Hay
    Fever, Design for Living, Private Lives, Post Mortem
    1933; revised edition, 1949
Conversation Piece 1934
† *The Astonished Heart* 1935
† *Family Album* 1935
† *Fumed Oak* 1935
† *Hands Across the Sea* 1935
Point Valaine 1935
† *Red Peppers* 1935
† *Shadow Play* 1935
† *We Were Dancing* 1935
† *Star Chamber* 1936
† *Still Life* 1936
† *Ways and Means* 1936
Operette 1938
Second Play Parade: This Year of Grace!, Words and
    Music, Operette, Conversation Piece 1939; enlarged
    edition, 1950
Post Mortem 1940
Blithe Spirit: An Improbable Farce 1941
Present Laughter 1942
This Happy Breed 1943
Sigh No More 1945
Pacific 1860: A Musical Romance 1946
Peace in Our Time 1947
Ace of Clubs 1950

Play Parade 3: The Queen Was in the Parlour, I'll
    Leave It to You, The Young Idea, Sirocco, The Rat
    Trap, This Was a Man, Home Chat, The Marquise
    1950
Relative Values: A Light Comedy 1951
Quadrille 1952
After the Ball [adaptor; from the play *Lady Winderm-*
    ere's Fan by Oscar Wilde] 1954
Play Parade 4: Tonight at 8.30, Present Laughter, This
    Happy Breed 1954
Nude with Violin 1956
South Sea Bubble 1956
Play Parade 5: Pacific 1860, Peace in Our Time, Rela-
    tive Values, Quadrille, Blithe Spirit 1958
Look after Lulu! [adaptor; from the play *Occupe-toi*
    d'Amélie by Georges Feydeau] 1959
Waiting in the Wings 1960
Sail Away 1961
Play Parade 6: Point Valaine, South Sea Bubble, Ace of
    Clubs, Nude with Violin, Waiting in the Wings 1962
The Girl Who Came to Supper [adaptor; from the play
    The Sleeping Prince by Terence Rattigan] 1963
Three Plays: Private Lives, Hay Fever, Blithe Spirit
    1965
‡ *Suite in Three Keys* 1966
Semi-Monde 1977
Long Island Sound 2002

Other Major Works

A Withered Nosegay: Imaginary Biographies (prose)
    1922
Chelsea Buns [as Hernia Whittlebot] (poems) 1925
Collected Sketches and Lyrics (sketches and lyrics) 1931
Present Indicative (autobiography) 1937
To Step Aside (short stories) 1939
Australia Visited, 1940 (broadcasts) 1941
In Which We Serve (screenplay) 1942
Middle East Diary (diary) 1944
#*Brief Encounter* [with Anthony Havelock-Allen,
    Ronald Neame, and David Lean] (screenplay) 1946
Star Quality (short stories) 1951
The Noel Coward Song Book (lyrics) 1953
Future Indefinite (autobiography) 1954
Pomp and Circumstance (novel) 1960
Collected Short Stories (short stories) 1962
Pretty Polly Barlow, and Other Stories (short stories)
    1964
The Lyrics of Noel Coward (lyrics) 1965
Bon Voyage and Other Stories (short stories) 1967
Not Yet the Dodo and Other Verses (lyrics) 1967
The Noël Coward Diaries (diaries) 1982
The Collected Short Stories. 2 vols. (short stories)
    1983-85
Noël Coward: The Complete Lyrics (lyrics) 1998

*Words and Music has also been performed under the title *Set to Music*.

†These plays were performed under the collective title *Tonight at 8.30*.

‡This performance comprised *A Song at Twilight*, *Shadows of the Evening*, and *Come into the Garden Maud*.

#Adapted from the play *Still Life* by Coward.

AUTHOR COMMENTARY

Noël Coward (introduction date 1925)

SOURCE: Coward, Noël. Introduction to *Three Plays: The Rat Trap, The Vortex, Fallen Angels*, pp. v-xii. 1925. Reprint, London: Ernest Benn Limited, 1926.

[*In the following introduction, Coward addresses numerous issues, including the degree to which his early plays remain relevant, the ways in which audiences respond to sex and violence, and the state of English theater.*]

There are contained in this volume two produced plays, **The Vortex** and **Fallen Angels,** and one unproduced, **The Rat Trap.** For years I have mourned the fact that **The Rat Trap** never saw the light of day—if a sudden exposure to the slightly resentful glare of a First Night Audience can so be named—but now the time for it is past, the sterling merits I saw in it when it was first written in 1920 have rather faded. There is an infinite sadness in looking back on early work, frightful errors of construction and painful immaturities of dialogue jump to the eye in a most depressing manner. The same thing will occur five years hence—perhaps less—when I look back upon my present work, at least I hope so, for the only consolation of going on with anything is that one feels one is progressing—even in the face of the kindly critics, both professional and amateur, who state with gentle insistence that one is not.

The Rat Trap was my first serious play, and I took a lot of trouble with it. I considered it brilliant beyond words, and filled with the most fearless and shattering truths. I can still perceive some good moments in it, particularly the very end of the play, and the scene between Keld and Sheila in the second act. The great fault of the play is a desperate desire to be witty at all costs, but when the would-be pyrotechnical frills are torn away and a few pieces of untidy but real psychology emerge it isn't so bad. I sadly fear, however, that by lying on the shelf for so long it has missed its mark, so far as being a stepping-stone in my career is concerned.

I am only just beginning to discover imperfections in **The Vortex,** as it is comparatively new (1923) and, strange as it may seem, they are not those which some of the critics pointed out. As a matter of fact, practi-cally all my notices for this play were generously adulatory, though most of them seemed concerned that I should choose such an "unpleasant" subject and such "decadent" types. I have come to the conclusion that an "unpleasant" subject is something that everybody knows about, but shrinks from the belief that other people know about it too. "Decadent" has, of course, been so enthusiastically incorporated into journalese that as a descriptive adjective it has almost ceased to mean anything at all. The minor characters in **The Vortex** drink cocktails, employ superlatives, and sometimes turn on the gramophone. Apart from these mild amusements their degeneracy is not marked. Nicky and Florence are certainly frail for the purposes of the play, but not to any hair-raising extent. Florence takes lovers occasionally and Nicky takes drugs very occasionally, despite the many exuberant phrases applied to him, such as "Crazed with dope," "Drug fiend," etc. I consider neither of these vices any more unpleasant than murder or seduction, both of which have been a standing tradition in the English theatre for many years.

Fallen Angels, which aimed no higher than to be an amusing evening's entertainment, has brought a positive hail of abuse about my ears, which is really very lucky, as, being extremely light, I fear it might not have succeeded on its own merits had it not been given the *réclame* of being "Disgusting," "Shocking," "Nauseating," "Daring," and "Outrageous." The two things in it which seem to have reduced the daily Press to such a pulp of shocked exasperation are, first, that the two wives confess to having had one love affair before marriage, and second, that they become faintly intoxicated when dining quietly together, mainly because they have spent a nervy and trying day, and feel that a little champagne will cheer them up. They have been accused variously of being "Decadent social types," "Suburban sluts" (a phrase which makes up in vituperative force for what it lacks in subtlety), and finally, with a wealth of scorn, "Modern women." This is all very peculiar and surprising, and I really am at a loss to understand it; the only possible solution of the mystery is, I think, that although the critics may be unaware of it, it is not the play they dislike at all, but my own particular attitude of mind. If this is the case, it is very unfortunate indeed, as that is the one thing that cannot be remedied either by laudatory or adverse criticism.

It would, of course, be very easy to justify the theme of **Fallen Angels** by comparing it with any of the farces and musical comedies which have for so many years sent tears of hearty laughter cascading down honest British cheeks, so easy, in fact, that I will refrain from doing so; but I do feel that the moment had come to administer a slight but austere reprimand to the critics for giving themselves away so much. Their confusion of the different strata of Society must be painfully embarrassing to the lay reader, besides being definitely bad for the "morale" of the nation at large.

I certainly deny very firmly the imputation (made by several) that I wrote **Fallen Angels** in order to be "daring" and "shocking." Neither of these exceedingly second-rate ambitions has ever occurred to me.

The English theatre is undoubtedly passing through rather a turbulent phase at the moment, owing to the ardent crusade being conducted against "Sex Plays." Here is another thing that puzzles me dreadfully: What exactly is a sex play? It is apparently a new and cancerous growth in our midst which no one seems really able to locate. Of course, all the big successes there have ever been—with one or two exceptions—have had a larger percentage of sex in them than anything else, but these can't be the cause of the trouble, otherwise surely they would have been commented upon before.

I admit there is a tendency among the modern writers to *discuss* some of the various phases of sex a little more openly than was usual a few years ago, but I fail to see where this can be harmful to the public morals. On the contrary, in many instances I should imagine it to be definitely beneficial. Rocks are infinitely more dangerous when they are submerged, and the sluggish waves of false sentiment and hypocrisy have been washing over reality far too long already in the art of this country.

Sex being the most important factor of human nature is naturally, and always will be, the fundamental root of good drama, and the well-meaning but slightly muddled zealots who are trying to banish sex from the stage will find on calmer reflection that they are bumptiously attempting a *volte face* which could only successfully be achieved by the Almighty.

One of the most disheartening difficulties for sincere dramatists to overcome is the desire of the British public to be amused and not enlightened. The problem arises: is the theatre to be a medium of expression, setting forth various aspects of reality, or merely a place of relaxation where weary business men and women can witness a pleasing spectacle bearing no relation whatsoever to the hard facts of existence and demanding no effort of concentration?

One hears on every side the petulant assertion that there is enough unpleasantness in real life without paying to be harrowed in the theatre. This attitude would be more consistent did it empty the Old Bailey during the more lurid cases, and diminish the sales of sensational Sunday newspapers. However, as a palliative to the wounded and irritated self-esteem of those teeming millions who leave the theatre untouched by our wilder intellectual flights, it is to be highly commended.

As a matter of strict fact it has been proved, over and over again, that the more violent a play is—whether the portrayed emotions be false or true—the better the public like it. Even such a commonplace occurrence as a kiss on the stage frequently has a peculiar effect on the cheaper parts of the house, unless it is handled with great tact. The least hint of reality will cause overexcited ladies and gentlemen in the gallery to make rude noises with their mouths upon the backs of their hands. I never know whether this is an expression of resentment at the possible lack of such happy salutations in their own home lives, or the sudden venting of a certain sex self-consciousness which has taken them unawares.

The great problem for the young dramatist is whether to set out from the very first writing what managers require of him, or to concentrate on creating what he requires of himself. The latter is by far the more difficult course to pursue, but in the end, providing he is backed by genuine ability, infinitely more satisfactory. Financially the first holds greater possibilities, because he can accept, without offending his artistic conscience, hack jobs, such as adaptations and re-writing the seedy farces which managers are always so eager to produce. This will provide him with a certain amount of publicity. Play agents will meet at lunch and discuss him jovially, telling each other that this young man "will write a good play one day!" They are quite wrong, because he won't unless he changes his tactics. He may, of course, write a successful farce, but by that time he will have crushed down any literary or psychological impulses he may have had at the beginning, and become lost in a maze of "situation," "technique," and "construction" from which escape is impossible.

There are, of course, hundreds of people who regard the stage purely as a commercial proposition, and shape their work accordingly along old familiar lines. These people have enormous success, and deserve it, because after all they are achieving the object for which they set out.

There will always be a public for the Cinderella story, the same as there will always be a public for Miss Ethel M. Dell and the *Girl's Companion*. In the world of amusement it is essential for someone to cater for the illiterate, mainly because at least three-quarters of the English nation must be illiterate, otherwise the yearly plethora of second-rate music, second-rate painting, second-rate plays, and second-rate literature would not be tolerated. But the fact that most people one meets would rather have a Kirchner hanging in their bedroom than a Gaugin does not depreciate the value of the Gaugin in any way, even commercially; on the contrary, it rather adds to it.

When the self-advertising denouncers of the Stage describe the English theatre as being in a "disgraceful state" they speak a bitter truth without being aware of it. It *is* in a disgraceful state, but for none of the reasons so far put forward. The actual cause of the very definite decline of our drama is that at least ninety per cent of the people at present concerned in it are mentally incapable of regarding it as art at all. I think, perhaps, that the public are still suffering from the complacent after-effects of winning the War, and have not yet regained the little discrimination they had a few years ago, otherwise they would not accept so cheerfully the somewhat tawdry efforts of our commercial managers to amuse them. One cannot, of course, blame the managers; they have their living to make and their wives and mistresses to support, but it certainly is regrettable that these noble and natural aspirations should be achieved so easily and at the cost of so little intellectual endeavour.

To assert that this age is degenerate and decadent is supremely ridiculous; it is no more degenerate and decadent than any other civilised age, the only difference is that the usual conglomeration of human vices have come to the surface a little more lately, and there is mercifully a little less hypocrisy about. Speaking for myself, I should like to say that I intend to write as honestly and sincerely as possible on any subject I choose, and if the public do not like it they need not pay to come and see it. Theatre-going, when all is said and done, is optional.

There is another very insidious blight with which the British drama has to contend, and that is that with the present democratic destruction of all social barriers "Society," like a reservoir suddenly released from its dam, has effusively swirled into the theatre and practically swamped many of our potential actors and actresses, filling them with false ambitions, and confusing the development of their talents by encouraging that most nauseating but inevitable trait latent in all of us— "snobbery." In the days when the imposing doors of the stately homes of England were austerely closed to the theatrical profession, the hard-working actor had more time to devote to his career, and achieved a good deal more in consequence. Now, of course, in the era of night clubs and cabarets, where the cream of the aristocracy enthusiastically hobnobs with the clotted cream of the profession, very little is achieved in either direction, the only tangible reward of both parties being a frequently scurrilous mass of cheap publicity which on the face of it is but a poor consolation for the loss of their respective glamour and dignity, to say nothing of the amount of time wasted in the general confusion.

The number of "Society" girls who are taking up acting at the present moment is positively frightening. They have nearly all met the leading theatrical lights at parties, and find it quite easy to insinuate themselves into various productions as understudies or the playing of

small parts for which, though they may be suitable in type, they are obviously unfitted by experience. This is, of course, grossly unfair when the stage is already filled to overflowing with quite adequately experienced people, who have endured all the usual drudgeries and hardships in order to earn their living and make careers for themselves.

I can honestly say that in all the productions with which I have been concerned so far I have never caused to be engaged anyone who was not an actor or actress by profession, and so far as it lies in my power I never shall.

It is very disheartening to reflect that England is the only country in the world where the public and Press make it possible for this inanely muddled state of affairs to exist, and it is not to be wondered at that so many of our sincere and ambitious actors and actresses have emigrated to America, where the obstacles in the path of genuine achievement are less overpowering and futile.

Probably the figure most to be pitied in connection with the English theatre to-day is the Lord Chamberlain. He has a poor time, to say the least of it, harrassed and hated by servile managers and authors, bullied by county councils and corporations waving banners of middle-class puritanism, trying sincerely to save the public morals from being corrupted, shutting his eyes fiercely to the unworthy truth that the public morals of any advanced civilisation are inevitably at a deplorably low ebb, and striving against the realisation that he is fighting a losing battle in attempting to repress eager young writers with their unpleasantly truthful problems, who, after all, are only expressing the spirit of their times and in most cases bringing coals to Newcastle.

The censorship as an institution is merely a figure-head for all those worthy British qualities most detrimental to the progress of true art, hypocrisy, sex-repression, lack of education, religious mania, respectability, and above all moral cowardice. It may be that, having as a nation achieved so much by physical courage, we have grown up in the belief that that is all that matters, which anyhow supplies a reason for our rather paltry progress in art as compared with other countries. The truth of the matter is that morally we allow ourselves to be governed too much by "fear"; fear of giving ourselves away, fear of what other people may think, fear of exposing real emotions of any sort, and a very definite fear of seeing ourselves as we really are. This being so, it is possible to realise how very necessary a Censor is to the general peace of mind—one more protecting arm of false security, one more fortification built up in order to shut out unpleasant truths, but it must be painfully uncomfortable for the wretched Buffer.

I do not wish to convey the impression that the Censor faces all his difficulties entirely alone, for he has an able staff of readers to assist him. None of them, I gather, are particularly young men, that would be too dangerous. Youth in authority is so terribly unstable and cannot be relied upon not to evolve suddenly a new conviction or be unexpectedly carried away by enthusiasm; also it lacks the matured solidity of character so revered by the middle-class mind; but it would undoubtedly be an interesting experiment to place upon the Board of Censors a few clear-thinking young men and women (morally impeccable, of course, if such a thing is possible) and watch the ultimate effect upon the national drama.

Years hence I shall probably be horrified at this reckless exposition of my youthful credo. One can, after all, be sure of nothing except that one's opinions change with the passing of time, but I have tried in this Introduction to express sincerely my views on the theatre of to-day as I see it, and although a good deal of success has come to me early in life, I definitely consider my present work to be no more than a very tentative first step towards what I hope and intend to achieve in the future.

OVERVIEWS AND GENERAL STUDIES

Robert F. Kiernan (essay date 1986)

SOURCE: Kiernan, Robert F. "The Comedies of Manners." In *Noel Coward*, pp. 25-55. New York: Ungar, 1986.

[*In the following essay, Kiernan discusses Coward's four comedies of manners in the context of the historical periods in which the genre flourished.*]

Although he professed to despise the comedy of manners,[1] Coward wrote some of the twentieth century's best examples of the genre, and almost all his plays contain its elements. It was inevitably so, for the repartee that enlivens the comedy of manners was Coward's especial talent both onstage and off, and the polished and sophisticated society that the comedy of manners satirizes was his chosen milieu. It is a conceit of the comedy of manners that the best people are the sharpest wits and the subtlest intriguers, and this amoral principle jibed almost exactly with Coward's sense of society's unwritten laws. As a homosexual, he must also have felt an affinity for the genre's disposition to regard the conventions of sexual morality as hollow.

The comedy of manners tends to flourish during periods of high style—the Restoration, the 1890s, the 1920s, the 1960s—and to fall into disrepute during periods of

temperamental sobriety. Under the aegis of romantic "sincerity" and Victorian "gloom" in the nineteenth century, the genre was generally considered immoral, a flight from conscience and commitment. Charles Lamb dared to say in its defense, "I am glad for a season to take an airing beyond the diocese of the strict conscience,"[2] but Lord Macaulay complained that the comedy of manners was a forum for "sound morality to be insulted, derided, associated with every thing mean and hateful; the unsound morality to be set off to every advantage, and inculcated by all methods, direct and indirect."[3] In his influential essay *On the Idea of Comedy and the Uses of the Comic Spirit*, George Meredith defined the genre contemptuously as "the manners of South-Sea islanders under city veneer; and, as to comic idea, vacuous as the mask without the face behind it."[4]

It is against this dark background of nineteenth-century taste that Coward's plays must be seen. His comedies of manners were successful in the gay twenties and the turbulent thirties not only because of their inherent worth as drama but because of a taste for the mannered and the artificial that was a reaction against Victorian seriousness. The same plays were scorned when World War II and the subsequent cold war encouraged more sober modes of expression, cheered again in the 1960s when a taste for high style renewed itself under the sponsorship of Carnaby Street fashions. The audience for comedy of manners seems limited, however, even when the pendulum of taste swings in its favor. The major dramatists of both the seventeenth and the twentieth centuries produced a surprisingly small number of such plays, and Coward wrote only four plays that are generally acknowledged to be comedies of manners: *Hay Fever* (1925), *Private Lives* (1930), *Design for Living* (1933), and *Relative Values* (1951).

HAY FEVER

Hay Fever was written in three days upon Coward's return from America in the autumn of 1924 and commemorates Sunday evenings he had spent in New York playing the word game "Adverbs" with the actress Laurette Taylor and her guests. The play was not originally thought well of, either by its author or by the actress Marie Tempest, to whom Coward submitted it as a possible vehicle. He knew certain scenes were good, but he feared the play as a whole was tedious. "I think the reason for this was that I was passing through a transition stage as a writer," he wrote; "my dialogue was becoming more natural and less elaborate, and I was beginning to concentrate more on the comedy values of situation rather than the comedy values of actual lines."[5]

Norman Macdermott expressed an interest in the play for his Everyman Theatre in Hampstead, but Coward persuaded him to produce *The Vortex* instead, since it offered Coward a particularly juicy role. In the wake of *The Vortex*'s success, Marie Tempest was approached again and not only found *Hay Fever* charming but insisted Coward direct her in the London production, which he did with trepidation and characteristic flair. They enjoyed a successful run despite qualified reviews. "The press naturally and inevitably described it as 'thin,' 'tenuous,' and 'trivial,'" Coward complained, "because those are their stock phrases for anything later in date and lighter in texture than *The Way of the World*." He could not refrain from pointing out that "it ran, tenuously and triumphantly, for a year."[6]

Hay Fever is a play in three acts about that most venerable of subjects, a weekend house party in a British country home. The gimmick of the play is that each member of the Bliss family has invited a guest without informing the other family members, each promising lodgings in a "Japanese" bedroom that is the best alternative to a room known as Little Hell. Each member of the family has also a vaguely romantic interest in his or her guest. Judith Bliss, a retired actress of extravagant temperament, has invited for the weekend a brawny but dim young man named Sandy Tyrell. Her husband, David, a romantic novelist, has invited a flapper named Jackie Coryton, allegedly for purposes of character study. Their son Simon is a caricaturist and has invited an older woman named Myra Arundel; his sister Sorel has invited Richard Greatham, a diplomat. It is an ill-matched group. The first act ends with the family and guests assembled for Friday afternoon tea, strained nerves all round.

In the second act, the word game "Adverbs" fails to pull the group together on Saturday evening. Bored to the point of impatience with their guests, the family members begin instinctively to improvise a substitute game in which each pretends that a small attention from some other person's guest is a declaration of undying love. This strikes panic in the guests, who find themselves unexpectedly affianced to the wrong persons—Sandy to Sorel, Myra to David, Jackie to Simon, and Richard to Judith. Richard asks if they are playing some sort of game, and Judith answers, "Yes, and a game that must be played to the finish!" Her family recognizes the line, and picking up their cue, they enact a scene from *Love's Whirlwind,* one of Judith's favorite melodramas.

Act III takes place at Sunday morning breakfast, during which the bewildered and emotionally exhausted guests vote to decamp en masse. The Blisses arrive at the table shortly after the decampment, remark upon the bad behavior of the fugitive guests, and shortly discover a new subject on which to exercise their histrionic compulsion. We understand that their behavior is a disease that afflicts vibrant people immured in the country—a kind of "hay fever."

Hay Fever is remarkable for its economy of design. Coward observed that there was no plot and remarkably little action in the play and professed surprise that it was regarded as one of his best works after it was successfully revived by the National Theatre in 1964.[7] His attitude was surely disingenuous, for *Hay Fever*'s economy of method reflects his lifelong taste for clean-lined structures. Though deeply influenced by the nineteenth-century tradition of the well-made play, Coward was in some ways a modernist. He thought unnecessary twists of plot messy, disdained visible struts and braces as vulgar, and detested long speeches as Victorian. His impulse was to temper the well-made play into an Art Deco curve.

Accordingly, *Hay Fever*'s opening scene is a swift glissade. The curtain goes up on an untidy hall, which is a visual metaphor for the untidy emotional life of the household. Simon, in a state of advanced dishevelment, is crouched on the floor sketching, while Sorel, somewhat better groomed, reads languidly. They discuss an acquaintance who wrote the book of poetry Sorel is reading, and the expositional aspect of the scene is admirably efficient. A conflict between bohemian and philistine sensibilities is established, and an indulgent cynicism with which the family treats Judith's histrionics is limned. Coward is also at pains in the scene to ease us into the play's structure of ironies. Sorel's wish that she were more "bouncing" looks forward to Judith's "bouncing" about on the sofa with Sandy; the allusion to games anticipates both the game of Adverbs and the ad hoc game of betrothals in Act II; and Judith's actressy tapping of the barometer prefigures a later tapping of the barometer that sends it crashing to the floor, a symbol of atmospheric understanding destroyed.

The scene also introduces a level of verbal and gestural stylization that borders on parody. Phrases such as "normal and bouncing" and "the Squire's lady" are invisibly in inverted commas and lead to such travesties of upper-class ellipticalness as "Awfully nice place, Cookham," and "This haddock's disgusting."[8] Simon's and Sorel's remarks about their mother prepare us to understand that all her gestures and many of the gestures she inspires in her family also border on parody. In Coward's direction of his plays, he encouraged a stylization of such ordinary actions as arranging flowers and lighting cigarettes and made them seem deliciously sly takeoffs on the fashionable world. Practicing the names of the flowers and tapping the barometer are just such takeoffs on the landed gentry.

The farcical confusion over the Japanese bedroom is so dramaturgically efficient that it cannot finally be played as farce. Although clearly a plot gimmick, the confusion provides a revealing look at Judith's artistic temperament and a first intimation that the family is deeply caught up in her sense of theater. Sorel even observes that an unwritten law of the house requires the family to play up to her mother. If Judith is disconcerted when Sorel first announces that she has promised the Japanese bedroom to Richard, she is more deeply upset when Simon adds his claim for Myra, and when David claims the room for Jackie's use, hysterics seem certain. But after an ominous pause and with a trained sense of understatement, Judith calls for music with the understanding that her family will appreciate that controlled rage needs to be soothed; requests someone—anyone—to play the piano because she has to depend on anonymous charity; asks that the music be played *to her* in order to make clear that she is the most aggrieved party; asks that the music be *very* beautiful in order to convey the ostensible depth of her anguish. She is an actress, not a fishwife.

And so it goes. As Judith glides from scene to scene, willfully exaggerating the significance of a kiss here, an embrace there, the line of action is smoothly uncluttered, a sinuous drift of her histrionic imagination. What appears to the guests to be madness is a gathering of her past performances that reaches a climax at the end of Act II, when the whole family joins her in the scene from *Love's Whirlwind.* Parody is the keynote of these scenes, and the overwrought emotions of Victorian and Edwardian melodrama are their satiric focus.

The four guests are basically foils for the stylish histrionics of the Blisses. Bromidic, unoriginal, sluggish of mind and temperament, they marshal platitudes while their hosts strike attitudes. Typically, the conversational repertoire of Jackie and Richard is nearly exhausted by observations that Italy is nice, Rome beautiful, Capri enchanting, and Dieppe dear—and as their repertoire runs dry, they speculate anxiously on whether the unconventional Blisses will serve tea at the appointed hour. Coward was always skillful in conveying the desperation of persons barely able to sustain conversation, and there is no finer demonstration of that skill than in the exchanges between Jackie and Richard.

It is Coward's fundamental joke that the Blisses are the true realists in the play despite their histrionic emotions. With evident pride in her candor, Myra confesses that she accepted Simon's invitation only in order to meet his father David, the distinguished author of romantic novels. When David suggests that she flatters him because she wants to stage an affair, Myra is conventionally outraged, but partly because David has upstaged her pretense of candor. He protests that he seems annoying only because he likes first to see things for what they are and then to affect that they are something other. "Words!" cries Myra, but she misjudges David and his family if she means that their verbal games have no foundation in reality. The Blisses can mock the conventional emotions with equanimity

and play variations up and down the emotional scale because they accept a basic truth their guests do not: that all human behavior is compounded of such imitations, consciously or unconsciously.

Even Sorel's observation that the Blisses never mean anything by what they do or say is not fair to the family, for it discounts the occasional subtext. When Judith catches her husband in Myra's arms, she elects to play the scene with dignity. But David counters her arch request to forgive the interruption by asking if there are any chocolates in the house. She continues to take a high tone, and he continues to murmur that, really, he would like nothing better than a chocolate. In the subtext of the scene, David is not just playing at comic inconsequence but telling his wife that Myra leaves him hungry and that their embrace was nothing more than a passing desire for sweets. The subtextual reassurance allows Judith to play her scene for theatrics alone, and when David joins in the scene, he is indulging her lovingly by alleging his love for Myra. Only Myra loses her sense of reality in the scene. She is too busy protesting the facts of the situation to see things as they are.

One of the most effective bits of dramaturgy in **Hay Fever** is the Blisses' ability to shift as abruptly into perfect frankness as into any other emotional key. When Simon asks Judith what they are to do about their awkward assembly of guests, Judith composes a motherly tableau, pulling him to his knees and placing his head on her right shoulder (Sorel's head on her left) and murmuring sweetly that they must be kind to everyone. But Simon is impervious to Judith's effects and objects to her performance. He even points out that she was never really beautiful on stage—which remark inspires Judith not to rage but to the dispassionate, professional observation that she managed to make audiences *think* she was. Her announcement that she will resume her career is the same sort of scene, startling not for its factual revelations but for Judith's honesty about her motive. When Sorel suggests that she retired so very finally the year before and enquires what excuse might be given for a precipitous return to the boards, Judith points unabashedly to letters from her public as the decisive factor—not to an avalanche of fan mail but to the one or two letters that *should* have been hundreds.

Such frankness is more than a parody of the family's affectation of perfect frankness, although it is that, too. David's expostulation that both his children should be in reformatories and Judith's memorable complaint that Sorel is less a good daughter to her than a critical *aunt* set the tone for Sorel's easy recognition that she is not a good hostess and for Judith's recognition that she is not and never was beautiful. What the play illumines is a paradox in which only those who play at frankness can be frank and only those who play at emotions can feel deeply. In a moment of high dudgeon, Myra says the house is a feather bed of false emotions, but her image defeats her invective. Feather beds are commodious and comfortable environments, and the family is extraordinarily at ease with true as well as with false feeling. Even Sorel forgets her wistful yearnings for a more conventional life whenever family scenes offer her a good part. Myra complains of being overwhelmed by theatrical effects in the household, but those theatrical effects betoken an animation of mind and feeling in the Blisses that makes Myra and her kind seem moribund.

Hay Fever has proven durable on the stage partly because of this mock-serious defense of the theatrical temperament, but in life Coward was less tolerant of theatrical egotists and rather disliked the 1920s cult of bad manners that *Hay Fever* did something to encourage. For those reasons, perhaps, the last act of *Hay Fever* ends with uncharacteristically heavy irony as the Blisses criticize their guests' rudeness in departing abruptly—as if they had no insight into the comedy of bad manners they themselves have staged relentlessly. There is a marked tiredness about the third act, and a whiff of déjà vu clings to comic routines dulled by repetition. Judith wants to cry when she remembers her children in their perambulators until Sorel points out she never saw them in their perambulators, to which fact Judith readily assents—but too familiarly at that point and not comically enough.

This third-act heaviness is a curious failing of a successful play, and one wonders if Coward feared that his comedy of manners had grown too tolerant of bad manners. "I had been brought up by Mother in the tradition of good manners," he once pointed out.[9] It was perhaps an enduring sense of obligation to good manners that made him withdraw a measure of sympathy from the Blisses in the last act, jeopardizing the play's tone and trivializing its fine insouciance.

PRIVATE LIVES

Private Lives was written in 1929 as a vehicle for Gertrude Lawrence. Coward had promised Lawrence the role of Sari in *Bitter Sweet,* but when the score for that operetta was complete, both she and Coward realized that her voice was not strong enough for the demanding music. As he departed on a world cruise after the New York première of *Bitter Sweet,* he promised her that his next play would be for her. The idea for *Private Lives* came to him in December 1929 in a hotel room in Tokyo: "The moment I switched out the lights, Gertie appeared in a white Molyneux dress on a terrace in the South of France and refused to go again until four a.m., by which time *Private Lives,* title and all, had constructed itself."[10] A few months later, he wrote the play in four days, and by February it was typed, revised, and ready for production. "In 1923 the play would have

been written and typed within a few days of my thinking of it," he observed, "but in 1929 I had learned the wisdom of not welcoming a new idea too ardently, so I forced it into the back of my mind, trusting to its own integrity to emerge again later on, when it had become sufficiently set and matured."[11]

Private Lives is based on elaborate coincidences. Elyot Chase and Amanda Prynne, who have been divorced from each other for five years, find themselves in adjacent hotel suites on the night each is beginning a honeymoon with a second spouse. Horrified by the situation, Elyot tells his young wife they must leave because he has a strange foreboding, while Amanda admits to her new husband that she has seen Elyot in the distance and insists they move to another hotel. Both spouses refuse to indulge what they consider hysterical nonsense, and the inevitable happens: fresh from the first quarrel of their new marriages, Elyot and Amanda fall into each other's arms and decide to run away together at once. Act I ends with the spouses, Victor and Sibyl, meeting each other and toasting absent friends.

Act II takes place a week later in a Paris flat, where Elyot and Amanda punctuate their unwedded bliss with quarrels of the headstrong sort that had destroyed their marriage years before. They have kept their quarrels in check thus far by observing five minutes of silence when either cries "sollocks," but this argument-stopping device is finally insufficient to restrain them, and they erupt into physical violence. Victor and Sibyl discover the love nest of their spouses just in time to catch them wrestling on the floor, knocking tables and lamps about in their rage.

Act III takes place the next morning and contains a number of heated exchanges, after which Elyot and Amanda agree to the divorces insisted upon by Sibyl and Victor. Their tempers cooled, Elyot and Amanda begin to charm one another anew, but their spouses become increasingly disputatious. The play ends with Sibyl and Victor trading insults and finally blows as Elyot and Amanda exit together, suitcases in hand.

Symmetry is the first and most distinctive note struck by *Private Lives.* The opening mise-en-scène is elaborately symmetrical and is usually given a mathematically precise character in production, with matching terraces, corresponding sets of French doors, identical furnishings, and a line of tubbed plants bisecting the stage as precisely as a plumb line. The dialogue and physical movement of the characters are almost as neatly balanced. Sibyl steps onto the terrace and calls to Elyot to come admire the view. Victor makes the same entrance a few minutes later, calling to Amanda in nearly the same words as Elyot from the other side of the terrace. In her newlywed's anxiety, Sibyl questions

Elyot about his marriage to Amanda. Was his first wife prettier than she? Did she dance better? Elyot's remarks about his first wife tend toward a balance that resonates with the balance of the stage settings. Rejecting Sibyl's suggestion that Amanda was to blame for the failure of their marriage, he insists that they made each *other* miserable and that they lost each *other*. Minutes later, Victor probes the happiness of Amanda's first marriage in a similar way, and Amanda strikes the same note of balance as Elyot, insisting upon a shared responsibility for their divorce.

Such neat correspondences proliferate and tend to cut across the new marriages, aligning Elyot with Amanda, Victor with Sibyl. Elyot and Amanda both want to acquire a sunburn, while both Victor and Sibyl say they hate sunburned women. Elyot and Amanda both look forward to the gambling tables, while Victor and Sibyl are surprised and vaguely scandalized that their spouses have the gaming passion. Thinking of his new marriage, Elyot hopes it will be cosy and undramatic; pressed by Victor to say that her love for him is different from her love for Elyot, Amanda says she loves him more calmly, if that's what he means. And when their respective spouses refuse to leave with them instantly, Elyot and Amanda turn ugly in identical ways. Clearly, the new marriages are mésalliances, not just because they come apart so easily, but because Amanda and Elyot are evenly matched in the play's system of balances.

A tendency of *Private Lives* to play as farce helps to explain these symmetries. From the medieval miracle plays to the Marx Brothers, farce deals with an improbable situation in which the forces of reason and convention contend with sweetly anarchic unreason. The representatives of unreason rebel in such a way as to disrupt civilized dignity but not in such a way as to make a satirical comment. The genre avoids social criticism by creating a world so artificial, so stylized and mechanical, that the everyday world is never really its subject. Indeed, the characters and values that are attacked by the forces of unreason usually resume their conventionally dominant roles when unreason's revolt is over.

Private Lives is farcical in this mode and to this degree. The extravagant symmetries of the play extenuate Elyot's and Amanda's revolts against propriety, and the clockwork mechanism of exits and entrances, timed so that one pair of characters exits as another enters, is the sort of shapeliness that suggests an ultimate order able to subsume fisticuffs as easily as a decree nisi. Victor and Sibyl represent convention until the reversal at the end of the third act.

As part of its tendency to slip into farce, *Private Lives* also tends to slip into the form of childhood games—notably hide-and-seek. Elyot recommends that he and

Amanda run from Victor and Sibyl and so they flee to free-thinking Paris, where they hide from their spouses in Amanda's flat and wait to be caught. When Sibyl and Victor succeed in finding them, Amanda plays "house," apologizing for the untidiness of the wrecked living room and ordering coffee and rolls, while Elyot plays ostrich, shutting his bedroom door and refusing to see Victor and Sibyl. Extending this game metaphor, Elyot remarks of Amanda's charade that they will shortly be playing Hunt the Slipper, apparently seeing himself both as the slipper passed from person to person and as the owner of the slipper, who must try to regain it.

This is not to say that *Private Lives* is a farce but only that it edges near to the genre. Farce is by definition unsophisticated: it is "comedy with the meaning left out,"[12] "comedy with *self-awareness* left out."[13] Elyot and Amanda are intensely self-aware and so sophisticated that they find it hard to pretend the innocence their spouses expect of them. When Victor refers to Amanda as a child, she points out that her heart is steeped in sophistication and that she has always been far too knowing. To Victor's shock, she suspects that she is abnormal deep down in her private life, and she knows she is unreliable and apt to perceive things the wrong way. Similarly, Elyot knows himself to be frivolous, and he believes in his frivolity as in a sacred trust. One mustn't be serious, he tells Amanda, for it's just what the moralists want. One must laugh and be flippant and leave the moralists to their acidic view of things.

Their amicably divorced relationship also gives Elyot and Amanda an aura of sophistication. The divorce rate increased dramatically in England after the first World War, and it increased steadily by as much as 50 percent a year through the 1920s as divorce gained acceptability. Coward's autobiography records a phenomenon of Ivor Novello's parties in the 1920s—that divorced couples were to be seen hobnobbing with each other and with each other's corespondents.[14] Such conduct was increasingly fashionable in cultivated circles but was still exceptional enough in 1930 to signal sophisticated behavior in a comedy of manners.

The farcical elements of *Private Lives* function as a point of reference for such sophistication, defining its limits and suggesting that farce lurks under the comedy of manners like trolls under a bridge. In accordance with the laws of farce, the sophistication of Elyot and Amanda takes a number of pratfalls: their suavity runs aground on old jealousies, and their glib repartee turns more than once into the squabbling of willful children. Elyot takes a notable fall when he says his flippancy is designed to bring out the acid in moralists, for we recall that Amanda has previously compared the two of them to acids in a matrimonial bottle. Does a moralist, then, lurk deep in Elyot's disdain for all that is right, decent, and traditional? Amanda catches him out when she admits to having been promiscuous during their years apart, and he protests that it doesn't suit the character of women to be promiscuous. "It doesn't suit men for women to be promiscuous," Amanda fires back.

It is because Elyot and Amanda live on the brink of farce that their verbal sophistication involves such a large measure of silliness. The most charming moments of the play transpire when they pretend to be boring and conventional, teasing the moment with banalities. A reluctance to allude in any way to the breakup of their marriage inspires them to remark with arch irrelevance upon the bigness of China and the smallness of Japan. Their pretense of religious and social sensitivities is outrageously camp, as innocent of seriousness as of consequence. Amanda affects concern that they are living in sin, and Elyot reassures her that Catholics, not believing in divorce, consider their original marriage intact in the eyes of heaven. But Amanda alleges a somewhat greater concern with the eyes of society— with which, of course, she is not really concerned at all.

Their breezy cross talk would lose a measure of its effect if Amanda and Elyot did not live on the edge of farce, where banter can turn physically aggressive at any moment. Irritated by Elyot's refusal to take seriously her affectation of a social manner, Amanda announces that she considers it unmannerly for a man to strike a woman—in response to which Elyot remarks famously that some women should be struck as regularly as gongs. The fatuity of the simile is half farcical, half self-mockery, an altogether engaging mix that positions Elyot within the comedy of manners but just barely. He has the opportunity to step into farce simply by implementing his theory of women, and that possibility is salt to the scene.

Dramaturgically, *Private Lives* is very little more than a sequence of such stylized exchanges. Yet it is an eminently theatrical play. Its dialogue is textured by an extraordinary mix of tones—disenchantment, wry humor, arrant sentimentalism, ennui, whimsy. We have *sad* statements that things are horribly funny, *dispassionate* scenes of utter rage, *cheerful* predictions of disaster. Hybrid emotions are the norm. Elyot remarks that a tune is "nasty" to prove that he is deeply moved when the orchestra plays a favorite melody he associates with Amanda and his first honeymoon. Amanda looks particularly lovely in the "damned" moonlight, he tells her, loath to trust his sentiment to such a conventional stimulant as moonlight.

Innumerable shifts in tone and this tendency of the main characters to express themselves obliquely impart to the play a sense of movement that belies its lack of dramatic action. Coward had an actor's sense of how a scene should play, and he built a scene less from ideas

and statements than from rhythms of exchange, from a counterpoint of moods, and from twists and turns of rhetoric that convey the nervous vitality of his characters. The third-act scene in which Amanda summons her most gracious manner to preside at a breakfast with Elyot, Sibyl, and Victor is typical of the play and typically masterful. Amanda's concern for passing sugar and milk pointedly omits Elyot and favors the witless Victor. A game of one-upmanship between Amanda and Sibyl is an undercurrent of the dialogue, and Victor is mindlessly ill at ease, like a dog sensitive to tension in the air without understanding its source. And yet the scene is nothing but a sharing of morning coffee—its ordinariness a counterpoint to the extraordinary array of temperaments that threatens to dissolve the ceremony of cups and saucers into open hostilities. The genius of the scene is its tempo—a retard on the cut and thrust of the dialogue that makes portentous developments wait upon the rituals of morning coffee.

The ending of the play is unexpected but somehow inevitable. Having run the course of their quarrel, Elyot and Amanda find their attraction for one another welling up again. Soon Amanda has to choke back the laughter that Elyot's irrepressibility can always induce. Victor turns on Elyot angrily as Amanda chokes on her laughter, and Sibyl springs to Elyot's defense, slapping Victor's face as he shakes her by the shoulders. Amanda and Elyot depart with smiles, presumably en route to a new love nest. This final tableau announces the triumph of frivolity: the demon of temper in Amanda and Elyot has relocated itself in Sibyl and Victor, and Elyot and Amanda take their leave as innocent of involvement in the quarrel as of concern for their spouses. It is an audacious vision—farcically symmetrical but too morally ambiguous for farce, exactly suited to a comedy of manners that proclaims contemporary manners *are* a farce. Victor's and Sibyl's quarrel actually gives us hope for them, for their bad behavior is a measure of their potential for loving one another in Coward's emotionally symmetric world.

DESIGN FOR LIVING

Design for Living was written as a showpiece for the combined talents of Coward and the Lunts. It was informally contracted for in 1921, when Alfred Lunt and Lynn Fontanne, not yet married, became fast friends with Coward while the three were living in the same theatrical boarding house in New York City's West Seventies. Full of delicatessen potato salad, dill pickles, and bravado, they sketched one evening an agenda for their nascent careers that was remarkably prophetic:

Lynn and Alfred were to be married. That was the first plan. Then they were to become definitely idols of the public. That was the second plan. Then, all this being successfully accomplished, they were to act exclusively together. This was the third plan. It remained for me to supply the fourth, which was that when all three of us had become stars of sufficient magnitude to be able to count upon an individual following irrespective of each other, then, poised serenely upon that enviable plane of achievement, we would meet and act triumphantly together.[15]

Eleven years later, the Lunts reminded Coward of the plan in a telegram that tracked him to Chile, where he was vacationing:

OUR CONTRACT WITH THEATRE GUILD UP IN JUNE WHAT ABOUT IT?[16]

Coward lost no time in setting to work. The formidable challenge of writing a play for three stars of equal magnitude was transformed into a play about three creative people functioning in off-again, on-again tandem, and the play opened in New York in January 1933 to rave notices. Reviewing the play in *The New York Times*, Brooks Atkinson recognized it for what it is: "an actors' lark" written for "an incomparable trio of high comedians."[17]

In the first act of *Design for Living,* a dealer in pictures named Ernest Friedman arrives at the Paris studio of his friend, the painter Otto Sylvus. The door is opened by Gilda, an interior decorator with whom Otto lives, and she tells Ernest that Otto is still asleep in the bedroom. Ernest mentions that a mutual friend, the playwright Leo Mercuré, has returned from America and is staying at a local hotel. When Otto bursts into the room, not from the bedroom but just back from Bordeaux, he is sent off with Ernest to visit Leo and bring him back for the day. Leo then emerges from the bedroom, where he has obviously spent the night. He and Gilda discuss their quandary—that they love each other *and* Otto, as he loves both of them. Otto returns, realizes the situation, and storms out of the studio damning them both to hell.

Act II discovers Leo and Gilda living together in Leo's London flat eighteen months later. Leo is the author of a new hit play and is sought after by hostesses and newspaper interviewers, much to his delight. Gilda finds something missing in their lives—Otto, of course—and when he arrives abruptly at their door, she falls into his arms, and he, into her bed. Otto thinks the situation of Act I has been reversed and that Leo is now the odd man out, but Gilda shocks her paramours when she abruptly leaves them both.

Act III finds Gilda two years later, ensconced as Mrs. Ernest Friedman in a luxurious New York apartment. A stage note suggests that she is more composed than before, but her vitality appears less. Otto and Leo arrive together in the middle of a small cocktail gathering and drive out the guests with their extravagantly fey conversation. Gilda insists they leave too, to avoid

scandal, but she slips them a passkey and then takes to her heels in nearly blind panic. Ernest returns from a business trip the next morning and finds Otto and Leo in his pajamas and dressing gowns, and Gilda gone. They explain quite frankly that they want Gilda back and predict that she will return to the apartment shortly. Gilda does return and confesses they are right, that she is going to leave Ernest because she cannot possibly live without them. The play ends with Ernest storming out of the room in a fury and tripping over a stack of canvases as Gilda, Otto, and Leo roar with laughter.

With its profusion of exits and entrances and its revolving door alliances, *Design for Living* owes a debt to the tradition of farce, like *Private Lives* before it. A servant named Hodge is classically farcical in her complete dishevelment, her wildly erratic *h*'s, and her understandable confusion about the sexual goings-on. When Leo and Otto are introduced to Henry and Helen Carver at Gilda's cocktail party, farce suspends the action of the play and permits a charming regression to nonsense. Leo asks if the Carvers have ever visited Chuquicamata, a copper mine in Chile, and he affects a lofty disdain when they confess they have not. Mr. Carver is made increasingly angry by Leo's supercilious manner, and his wife increasingly nervous. The situation builds explosively until Leo and Otto observe blithely that they too have never visited Chuquicamata—and the elaborate, quite unnecessary show of temperaments is suddenly rendered farcical.

But such farcical moments are less typical of *Design for Living* than moments of ideological and moral pronouncement that render the play more sober in tone than both *Private Lives* and *Hay Fever.* Ernest asks Gilda in the first act if there is any reason why she doesn't marry Otto, and she replies that there is a very good reason—that she loves him too much to bind him to her legally. Her statement is unqualified by humor or irony, with the result that it falls heavily upon the ear expecting Cowardly insouciance. Sending Otto to bring Leo back from his hotel and knowing that he will shortly have to face himself betrayed, she strikes a motherly note, cautioning him to be careful crossing roads, to look right and left and all around, and not to do anything foolish or impulsive. In another mood, she exclaims that she looks upon her own "damn" femininity with nausea. We wait in vain for a joke that will prove her feminine angst spurious. Otto and Leo are less consistently solemn than Gilda, but they too deal in profundities unrelieved by wit and argue bromidically that love is not mathematics and that principles should be adhered to.

The themes of the play are characterized by a similar drift toward solemnity. Gilda's reluctance to submerge herself in the successes of Otto and Leo is entirely serious, as is her distaste for using feminine blandishments to gain any measure of personal success. The ménage à trois projected at the last curtain promises connatural satisfactions, not indiscriminate coupling, and there is nothing comically salacious or light-minded about it, despite its reputation. Gilda's fear that commercial success will compromise Leo and Otto is not idle romanticism, any more than Leo's refusal to shut out the world and live for art alone is hedonism. All three of the protagonists are hard workers and do not lend themselves to caricature as dilettantes or adventurers. In short, life among the artists is a surprisingly solemn affair in *Design for Living*. Flippant allusions to "Love among the Artists" adorn the play but do not obscure its underlying seriousness.

A critic for *The Times* noted this mixture of seriousness and flippancy in the play and suggested, "It is not a question only of mixing conventions; it is almost a question of running away."[18] If there is something evasive about Coward's technique in the play, it is possibly because he himself dwelt comfortably in a ménage and because he believed too firmly in enjoying his own success to make fun of Otto's and Leo's pleasure in having made their fortunes. It is not clear in the play that Otto and Leo are lovers, but it is clear that they were friends before Gilda entered their lives, and when they return to her after her marriage, they project an intimacy with each other more intense than their intimacy with her. The relationship of Otto, Leo, and Gilda is too psychodynamically complex to be simply a mask, but the evident intimacy of the two men and their cultivation of Gilda may have suggested to Coward a ruse of the homosexual celebrity that he had no wish to parody.[19]

Gilda's desire to live a conventional life should have been the central joke of the play, but it is played more for drama than for laughs. Leo asks wistfully in Act II if the three of them will ever live together again, and Gilda answers vehemently that she has no wish to reconstitute the ménage à trois. But why is she so vehement? It is by no means clear that Leo implies a sexual togetherness, and it is not clear why Gilda should object to such an arrangement even if he did. Her difficulty in living first with Otto and then with Leo seems to be her feminist urge to match their commercial success as artists with a success of her own—a success she achieves while married to Ernest and which leaves her empty. A charge of running away from a biological destiny as wife and mother hangs unaccountably over Gilda as a result and explains her lapse into motherly solicitude when she is preparing to leave Otto. Indeed, her marriage to the older and distinctly paternal Ernest seems an oblique attempt both to satisfy and to evade the biological call.

But the larger question of the play is on what basis Gilda, Otto, and Leo should form an inevitable grouping. Because Gilda is in flight from one or both of her

two men until the last minutes of the play, the three are never seen to amuse each other so intensely that their unconventional relationship is justified—which is the usual logic of Coward's plays. Wit and intelligence do not distinguish the three as a unit, and so they do not rise above those around them as ineffably as Elyot, Amanda, and the Blisses. One is not even convinced that Gilda is the equal of Otto and Leo, inasmuch as she is neither successful nor particularly talented as an interior decorator. She makes her mark as a merchandiser of fine objects, but that ranks her spiritually and temperamentally with Ernest.

The laughter on which the final curtain descends underscores these equivocations of the play, inasmuch as audiences tend to be unsure whether they should join in the laughter. Coward himself recognized the difficulty:

> The three of them, after various partings and reunions and partings again, after torturing and loving and hating one another, are left together as the curtain falls, laughing. Different minds found different meanings in this laughter. Some considered it to be directed against Ernest, Gilda's husband, and the time-honoured friend of all three. If so, it was certainly cruel, and in the worst possible taste. Some saw in it a lascivious anticipation of a sort of triangular carnal frolic. Others, with less ribald imaginations, regarded it as a meaningless and slightly inept excuse to bring the curtain down. I as author, however, prefer to think that Gilda and Otto and Leo were laughing at themselves.[20]

It is not enough to say they are laughing at themselves, because Gilda, at least, has not generally found their situation humorous. Her laughter might better be played as hysterical release—a nervous, final relaxation into her fate.

Fate is important as a concept in *Design for Living,* for in the last analysis the play celebrates the irrationalism of human bonding, its victories over feminist sensitivities, the marriage contract, and heterosexual orthodoxy. Gilda, Otto, and Leo are helpless to oppose their fated union, and their jealousies and betrayals fall like ninepins before the force that draws them together. Their attraction to each other is simply ordained—a dramaturgical fate. Numerous statements in the text draw attention to that fact. Everything is glandular, Gilda opines at the beginning of the play. Chance drew the three of them together and tied their lives into a knot, says Otto in Act II. The three of them are finally of a piece, says Gilda at the end.

The best scenes in the play suggest this triumph of an irrational bond over the characters' various designs for living. The scene in which Gilda says goodbye to Otto with real affection, unhappy to leave him for Leo, is especially successful because of its stratified, irreconcilable emotions. The scene at the end of Act II in which

Leo and Otto get drunk together as their coin of tribute to anarchy is beautifully paced and inveterately a crowd pleaser. Since conventional thinking condemns the relationship of the three main characters, silliness is the idiom in which they best express their affection. Inconsequence has rarely limned affection so well as when Otto arrives to upset Leo's love nest and Gilda welcomes him nervously, but with a sense of relief.

Such scenes make *Design for Living* a comedy of linguistic manners as well as of cohabitational mores, and it is for its comedy that the play survives. In a famous line, Gilda observes that Ernest has referred to her as both a jaguar and an ox and expresses the wish that he would be less zoological. The wit is typically Coward's—brash, brittle, situational rather than epigrammatic. The American drama critic George Jean Nathan objected to the line on the basis of its vaudevillian antecedent ("So I'm a goat and a jackass, huh? You talk like you was in a zoo!"), but he failed to appreciate Coward's reworking of the joke, in which moronic aggression becomes a camp non sequitur, and the uninspired juncture of "goat," "jackass," and "zoo" becomes a play of the archly precise "zoological" against the exotic "jaguar" and the homely "ox."[21] Such honed lines are not adequate to relieve the burden of solemnity in the play, but *Design for Living* still commands British and American stages because of the sophisticated shimmer they impart.

RELATIVE VALUES

The idea for *Relative Values* came to Coward as most of the ideas for his plays, in a flash. The day of illumination was March 23, 1951—a Good Friday Coward described in his diaries as a *very* Good Friday.[22] Reviews that accused Coward of old-fashioned theatrics had prompted him to concentrate on prose fiction for several months, and he resumed playwriting with relief. "The flow is beginning," he wrote in his diary on March 26, "and oh, the bliss of writing dialogue after prose."[23] *Relative Values* began rehearsals in September with Gladys Cooper and Angela Baddeley in the leading roles, and though Cooper had only a shaky command of her lines, it opened in London on November 28, 1951, to rave reviews.

Relative Values takes place in the family living room of Marshwood House, East Kent. In the first act it is announced that Nigel, the young Earl of Marshwood, is affianced to Miranda Frayle, an American film star. Felicity, the dowager countess of Marshwood, tries to be philosophical. It is not the first marriage between an actress and a peer of the realm, she observes. The butler Crestwell is as unflappable about the coming nuptials as about all things, but Moxie, Felicity's personal maid, is deeply distressed and mutters darkly that she will walk out when Miranda walks in. Pressed by the countess to

give her real reason for leaving Marshwood House, Moxie confesses that Miranda Frayle is her sister. What to do about such a socially impossible situation? The Honorable Peter Ingleton, Felicity's nephew, suggests that Moxie be promoted to secretary-companion, but Crestwell observes that she would still be socially inferior to her sister. He suggests they pretend she has come into an inheritance and is now a resident friend of the family. With profound misgivings, Moxie agrees to the deception, since Miranda is not apt to recognize a sister she has not seen for twenty-five years.

In the second act, Nigel is all nerves upon introducing his future wife to the household. Miranda plays at being the simple, unaffected type, choosing lemonade rather than a martini, carrying needlework about with her, and gushing sentimentally about her new English home. She also affects to have had a disadvantaged childhood, a fantasy that incenses Moxie. The situation becomes melodramatic when Don Lucas arrives in pursuit of Miranda, whom he has loved notoriously both on- and offscreen. With a flash of inspiration, Felicity insists he spend the night, and in reaction Nigel announces peremptorily that he and Miranda will be married in the morning. Moxie then reveals abruptly that Miranda is her wayward sister.

Act III takes place the next morning. Both Moxie and Miranda have announced they are quitting the house, and Felicity increases Miranda's prospects of unhappiness by announcing she will be a resident mother-in-law at Marshwood and will require that Moxie remain on the staff. All this has the desired effect of throwing Miranda into Don Lucas's waiting arms—a development that suddenly suits Nigel, who has no taste for histrionics. The play ends with tranquillity reestablished, Miranda and Don Lucas fled, and Felicity hustling everyone off to church.

Like *Hay Fever, Relative Values* mixes the world of the theater and the world of the English country house. Miranda plays at being sweet and demure among chintzes in the family sitting room, while fan magazines like *Screenland* and *Photoplay* bestrew the servants' bedrooms, and girl guides seeking autographs lurk in the shrubbery. Conversely, Moxie worries about making an exhibition of herself in front of the other servants by pretending to be gentry. The mix of two such different attitudes is a durable formula for a comedic clash of manners, and Crestwell points up the antecedents of the play when he suggests that the coincidental meeting of the two sisters is in the best traditions of English High Comedy. He even invites us to consider how Somerset Maugham would have developed the situation.

With a fine sense of the outré, Coward strikes sparks from the clash of Hollywood and country-house manners. Miranda irritates everyone by affecting Goody

Two-shoes innocence and choosing lemonade over the Martini that Felicity considers a more healthy drink. Don Lucas is crassly American, addressing Felicity as "Ma'am" and Crestwell as "Fred." By some inexplicable Hollywood vulgarity, Miranda and Lucas address each other (and occasionally others) as "Pete." "Ma'am" is a vaguely royal appelation, Felicity objects, but Lucas's stumbling alternative, "Ma'am—Felicity," is worse, evoking for Felicity's ear the infelicitous "Grandma Moses" or "Mother Goddam." American speech habits are not only inelegant but confusing to the Marshwood ear, as when Lucas says he is going to play a "bum" in his next picture and Felicity tries to imagine an anatomical impersonation. Crestwell assumes his most starched manner when dealing with American syntax, and in his initial interview with Lucas he overwhelms the monosyllabic American with calculated prolixity.

Like American vulgarity, Moxie's elevation from lady's maid to friend-of-the-family tests the mettle of country-house manners. Though he has agreed to treat Moxie as a social equal, Nigel winces when she asks to be served a drink, and Felicity blanches when Lady Cynthia Hayling, who has not been told of Moxie's new status, blithely asks her to mend a torn handbag during dinner and is told in response that she will be forgetting her head next. The code of manners among the servants also has its comic turns, from Moxie's use of Crestwell's first name as a signal she is angry with him to Crestwell's habit of insulting the housemaids with such erudition that they barely understand their offenses.

But underneath such standard comedy-of-manners fare runs a serious concern with the mystique of social equality. It is amusing that servants are the first to object to Nigel's intention to marry outside his class, but allusions to villagers who reject domestic service as common and cap and apron as the garb of slavery align the Marshwood servants with a lost social order. Moxie's most ready objection to Nigel's marriage is that he is betraying his class, but because we sense deeper, more personal objections in her from the first, her notions of class seem irrelevant to real experience. Crestwell is the most eloquent of the servants in criticizing the breakdown of England's class structure, but he is so dispassionately witty and precise that his position seems more affected than considered. He defines social equality as a belief that all menial work should be done by someone else. He announces sardonically that Moxie's sudden elevation is a social experimental based on the curious notion that, as we are equal in the eyes of God, we should also be equal in the eyes of our fellow men. Utopia, he says, is a hygienic abstraction wherein everyone is hailed familiarly and there is no domestic service. Utopia sounds invidiously like the America of Don and Miranda, where everyone is "Pete."

The upper classes are predictably supportive of class distinctions but more sensitive than the servants to the republican spirit of the age. Lady Hayling acknowledges that social barriers are being swept away and that any suggestion of class distinction is de trop, but she dislikes creeping egalitarianism. Peter is a realist about social distinctions and tends toward random accommodations. He points out that Felicity might take her golf instructor to the ballet but not her butler—who, in any case, considers the ballet decadent. Nigel is willing to brave the indignity of an unseen Aunt Rose by marrying a Hollywood actress, but he worries what that standard-bearing aunt will think about Moxie being entertained in the drawing room.

Felicity is less double-minded than those around her. She tries to be receptive to her son's marriage and argues that peers of the realm have always amused themselves by marrying actresses. When Peter presses the point, she confesses that she would be happier if Nigel married someone of his own class, but she is genuinely shocked to realize that she doesn't know Moxie half as well as Moxie knows her—that only once in nineteen years of association has she ever seen Moxie in a dressing gown. Knowledge of character does not necessarily depend on seeing people in their dressing-gowns, Peter suggests lightly, but he cannot dispel Felicity's embarrassed realization that she has kept Moxie at a distance. Like Coward himself, Felicity is egocentric in a way that seems to her not morally tenable.

Felicity's wit is an effective gauge of her moral centricity. It is not Crestwell's humor—brittle, crafted, and somewhat cruel—but a humor that uses candor to undercut all codes of manners. When Felicity tells Nigel she plans to leave Marshwood to give Miranda a clear field and Nigel objects that she got along all right with Joan, his first wife, Felicity is charmingly straightforward in her observation that getting along with Joan was one of the more spectacular achievements of her life. Nigel rejoins platitudinously that Miranda is really simple and sweet, quite unlike her screen personality, and Felicity's response springs from a precise sense of her experience: she has seen her at the cinema as a hospital nurse, a gangster's moll, a nun, and Catherine the Great, she observes, so it is difficult for her to form a definite opinion. Felicity is also a master of the disingenuous riposte and refuses to be forced into false positions. She gives Miranda every benefit of the doubt, she assures Nigel—of very *grave* doubts. Miranda insists that she is not as stupid as Felicity thinks, and Felicity responds airily that she is relieved. They have nothing further to say to each other, Miranda finally explodes, and Felicity expresses fear for their long winter evenings together and proposes the purchase of a television set.

This is not to say that Felicity is herself unmannered and that *Relative Values* counterpoises natural and affected behavior. Felicity is accomplished at playing understatement against overstatement for comic effect, and she knows how to deflate grandiloquence with irrelevance, as when she squelches one of Lady Hayling's outbursts by protesting that righteous indignation should not be permitted to take freedoms with syntax. Her manipulation of Don Lucas's presence is almost too adroit, but it ensures our recognition that her candor is disingenuous, as much a manner as Nigel's amateur galumphing, Crestwell's aloofness, Miranda's needlework, and Lucas's flourish of manhood. Her moral centricity to the play is based not on being innocent of manner but on the cultivation of a manner that accommodates her kindness without compromising her intelligence and that allows the truth to be stated without equivocation.

Felicity's concern with her responsibility to the village also bears on her moral centricity. Nigel spurns all obligations to the village; Miranda sees the village only as a setting for her latest role; and the higher-ranking servants, though conscious of a need to consider the village, look down on the locals for looking down on them. Only Felicity speaks up for social obligation. She insists that old Mrs. Willis's son be given an interview for his newspaper because Mrs. Willis supports the Cottage Hospital Committee, and she argues that little Elsie Mumby can't be dismissed from the shrubbery as if she were *any* girl guide inasmuch as she enjoys local sainthood for having pulled her younger brother from a well. When Felicity insists that Don Lucas stay the night, she obviously hopes that he will steal Miranda from Nigel, but habitual consideration of social duty prompts her to add that the villagers will rise up and stone her if she lets him depart unseen. At the end of the play she waves Miranda and Don Lucas off to London and clucks the others off to the village church, that most central of country institutions, worrying because the last bell has rung and that they are already late. They must try to look as though nothing has happened, she enjoins, because, after all, nothing much has.

If nothing much has happened, it is because Felicity is felicitously triumphant. The servants are restored to their accustomed position, the Americans sent back to Hollywood, and the errant son reminded that his mother knows him through and through. The class structure is rocked in **Relative Values** but not overturned, and it is indicative of Coward's social conservatism—his fundamental disbelief in social equality—that it should be so. What is surprising in the play is that Felicity's manner succeeds not just because it mows down all other effects, like the manner of the Blisses in **Hay Fever** and of Elyot and Amanda in **Private Lives,** but because it is morally and socially sensitive. Always attuned to the changing sensibility of his audience, Coward possibly thought it tactful in 1951 to introduce a measure of social morality into the traditionally amoral comedy of manners, particularly since he

himself identified increasingly with the peerage and obviously looked to the day when he would become Sir Noel. **Relative Values** promises that Coward's adopted class would endure in an age of relative values, not just because its manners were droll, but because its mores were moral.

Notes

1. "It's no good, I simply cannot abide Restoration comedy. I am sure it was good in its time, but now its obvious, bawdy roguishness bores the hell out of me. *Love for Love* seems to me to be appallingly overwritten. It is, I suppose, kind of critics to compare me with Congreve, but I do wish they hadn't." *The Noël Coward Diaries,* ed. Graham Payn and Sheridan Morley (Boston: Little, Brown, 1982), 22 November 1964.

2. Charles Lamb, "On the Artificial Comedies of the Last Century," *The Essays of Elia,* ed. William Macdonald (London: Dent and Sons, 1914), 283.

3. Thomas Babington Macaulay, "Comic Dramatists of the Restoration," vol. 3 of *Critical and Historical Essays,* 9th ed. (London: Longman, Brown Green, Longmans, Roberts, 1858), 157.

4. George Meredith, *An Essay on Comedy and the Uses of the Comic Spirit,* ed. Lane Cooper (New York: Scribner's, 1918), 83.

5. Noel Coward, *Present Indicative: An Autobiography* (New York: Doubleday, 1947), 179.

6. Coward, Introduction to *Play Parade,* vol. 1 (Garden City, N. Y.: Doubleday, Doran, 1933), xi.

7. Coward, Introduction to *Play Parade,* vol. 1, xi.

8. "To me, the essence of good comedy writing is that perfectly ordinary phrases such as 'Just fancy!' should, by virtue of their context, achieve greater laughs than the most literate epigrams. Some of the biggest laughs in *Hay Fever* occur on such lines as 'Go on', 'No there isn't, is there?' and 'This haddock's disgusting.'" Coward, as quoted by Cole Lesley, *Remembered Laughter: The Life of Noel Coward* (New York: Knopf, 1977), 434.

9. Coward, *Present Indicative,* 204-05.

10. Coward, *Present Indicative,* 320.

11. Coward, *Present Indicative,* 320.

12. L. J. Potts, *Comedy* (London: Hutchinson's University Library, 1948), 151.

13. Jessica Milner Davis, *Farce* (London: Methuen, 1978), 88.

14. Coward, *Present Indicative,* 122.

DRAMA CRITICISM, Vol. 45

15. Coward, *Present Indicative,* 137.

16. Quoted in Lesley, *Remembered Laughter,* 150.

17. Brooks Atkinson, *The New York Times,* 25 January 1933.

18. *The Times* (London), 26 January 1939.

19. Otto's speech in Act II is a classic defense of homosexuality although that is not its ostensible subject.

20. Coward, Introduction to *Play Parade,* vol. 1, xvii.

21. George Jean Nathan, *Passing Judgments* (Rutherford, N. J.: Fairleigh Dickinson University Press, 1970), 147-48. Sean O'Casey enlarged on Nathan's argument in "Coward Codology II" in *The Green Crow* (New York: Braziller, 1956), 97-107.

22. *The Noël Coward Diaries,* 23 March 1951.

23. *The Noël Coward Diaries,* 26 March 1951.

Frances Gray (essay date 1987)

SOURCE: Gray, Frances. "Five Comedies." In *Noel Coward,* pp. 147-95. Houndmills, England: Macmillan, 1987.

[*In the following essay, Gray provides a thematic overview of Coward's major comedies.*]

> *I am no good at love*
> *My heart should be wise and free*
> *I kill the unfortunate golden goose*
> *Whoever it may be*
> *With over-articulate tenderness*
> *And too much intensity.*[1]

I. 'No Good at Love': *Private Lives* and *Design for Living*

Two people are close; they try to pass the time, get bored, quarrel, crack jokes; they encounter two other people and don't make much of them; nothing really happens; at the end of the play they are in the same state as they were at the beginning. If this sounds like *Waiting for Godot* this is not wholly coincidental. For all his dislike of the style and form employed by the Theatre of the Absurd, Coward dramatised in the story of Elyot and Amanda the sense of inhabiting a universe without meaning or controlling force; in the twenties, anticipating Beckett, he earned a label for himself in Robert Graves's summary of that decade: 'Coward was the dramatist of disillusion, as Eliot was its tragic poet, Aldous Huxley its novelist, and James Joyce its prose epic-writer.'[2]

The difference between Coward and this exalted company is not so much one of attitude as one of resonance. Beckett, or the Eliot of *The Waste Land,* or Joyce, convey with irresistible force the sense of possibilities exhausted, of convictions tested on the intellect and the nerves and found wanting; the bare conditions of the *Godot* tramps reflect their existential stripping, the one slim conviction on which they ground themselves. Coward's characters, stripped of beliefs, have egos to keep them going; they forget the outside world to live luxuriously like exotic waterflies on a surface tension composed of personal charm and the admiration it attracts. If they have a conviction amid their foggy awareness of 'cosmic thingummies', it's a belief in love: not love as a redeeming factor in existence, a goal to strive for, but as a mischievous presence that will creep up on you somehow and strip you of charm and dignity; despite all evidence to the contrary, they cannot help thinking that, this time, things might be different, that they will manage not to kill the golden goose even though they have no intention of changing themselves.

Rebecca West wrote an epitaph on Coward, a lifelong friend, that is all the more touching for its ruthless honesty:

> A sensitive man, he was also a vain man. He talked constantly about himself, thought about himself, catalogued his achievements, evaluated them, presented to listeners such conclusions as were favourable, and expected, and waited for, applause.
>
> His sensitivity knew this and was shocked, and he regularly rough-housed his own vanity by considering himself in a ridiculous light. This he did for the good of his soul. The public image of himself in top-hat and tails, the immortal spirit of the charming twenties, was merely one of his admirable inventions. It was a disguise worn by an odd and selective kind of Puritan.[3]

This 'rough-housing' is the source of comic energy in ***Private Lives***; Coward dramatises the relationship between the performer's vanity and vulnerability, allowing full rein to his own onstage charisma, and that of Lawrence, but never allowing himself, or the audience, to take it wholly seriously. Both Elyot and Amanda are accomplished mask-makers; this makes them dangerously attractive, and they duly act as honeypots to their new and uninspiring spouses. But to be loved for the sake of the mask is not satisfying to the wearer, who then becomes trapped behind it. When we first meet Amanda and Victor, it is clear that he has been captivated by her in a role she is now sick of playing, that of little girl lost:

VICTOR:

> I don't believe you're nearly as complex as you think you are.

AMANDA:

I don't think I'm particularly complex, but I know I'm unreliable.

VICTOR:

You're frightening me horribly. In what way unreliable?

AMANDA:

I'm so apt to see things the wrong way round.

VICTOR:

What sort of things?

AMANDA:

Morals. What one should do and what one shouldn't.

VICTOR FONDLY:

Darling, you're so sweet.

AMANDA:

Thank you, Victor, that's most encouraging.

The alternative, of course, is to be seen through the mask. When Elyot and Amanda meet on the balcony after five years of divorce, it is this ability to see through each other that re-creates the attraction between them; they slice through the persiflage about sacred elephants to admit clearly that the love is still there. 'You don't hold any mystery for me darling, do you mind?' says Elyot. 'There isn't a particle of you that I don't know, remember, and want.'

But once they are together, this same ability to see through the mask becomes less alluring. While they can gaily puncture the preconceptions of Sybil and Victor about sex-roles, they can't maintain the same carefree attitudes towards each other:

AMANDA:

When we were together, did you really think I was unfaithful to you?

ELYOT:

Yes, practically every day.

AMANDA:

I thought you were too; often I used to torture myself with visions of your bouncing about on divans with awful widows.

It is a critical cliché that their position is tragic: unhappy together, unhappy apart. But the reason for that position, grounded in egotism, is comic. Beckett's *Film* once showed a man in flight from the fact of being perceived, even by a dog or cat; Elyot and Amanda can't bear *not* to be seen; why else the Molyneux dress,

the carefully cultivated act at the piano? But at the same time they are deeply ambivalent about being seen *through*. They want to be simultaneously understood and retain the 'mystery' that Amanda jeers at. She sends up the idea of mask-making as a coy 'feminine' preoccupation, wielding her lipstick satirically in front of Elyot, but, at the same time, she wants to retain a certain distance. She wants to be adored but also to puncture the adoring pose of the lover if she chooses:

ELYOT *BURYING HIS FACE IN HER SHOULDER*:

I do love you so.

AMANDA:

Don't blow, dear heart, it gives me the shivers.

Elyot feels threatened by Sybil's promise to 'understand' him; his description of their relationship as 'something tremendously cosy' has a slight satirical edge; clearly he feels that she is not really equal to 'understanding' him and shows, already, a mild contempt for her; 'completely feminine little creature' is a just but not a loving epithet. On the other hand, Amanda's ability to puncture his romantic self-image with 'It's too soon after dinner' sends him into frenzies of ill-temper. Both of them despise people who take them at face value and dislike those who don't.

Private Lives never stops to analyse this paradox; it dramatises every facet of it with a quicksilver liveliness which springs from Coward's application of his craft to the abilities of his original cast. The *rapport* between Coward and Gertrude Lawrence was legendary; T. E. Lawrence, who himself understood the workings of a carefully created persona, attended a rehearsal which, as he later wrote to Coward, gave him greater pleasure than the finished production because 'I could not always tell when you were acting and when talking to one another.'[4] Gertrude Lawrence was as accomplished a mask maker as Coward. He wrote of her:

Gertie has an astounding sense of the complete reality of the moment, and her moments, dictated by the extreme variability of her moods, change so swiftly that it is frequently difficult to discover what, apart from eating, sleeping and acting, is true of her at all.[5]

Her personality informs the role of Amanda as Coward's did that of Elyot. 'It was all there,' he recalled after the first night, 'the witty, quicksilver delivery of the lines; the romantic quality, tender and alluring; the swift, brittle rages.'[6]

But the play is more than a couple of life studies or a convenient context for the magic of a particular *rapport*. It is also, as Coward pointed out, a technically demanding work, exploiting not only the personalities of the original cast but their special expertise. Both had distinguished themselves in revue; in fact Amanda was Lawrence's first dramatic role. Coward impacted revue techniques onto a full-length plot; he demanded the rapid changes in mood and pace he and Lawrence demonstrated in **London Calling!,** the same transitions from speech to song or dance, the same ability to throw away a vinegary *nonsequitur* like 'Very flat, Norfolk' with a deftness that places it as a laugh line while allowing the action to go on; and through the technical fireworks explores the emotional implications of the performer's chameleon charm. The play consists of a series of scenes which bear a close resemblance to revue sketches: newly married couples exchange awkward pleasantries at the start of the honeymoon (Coward himself wrote a sketch about wedding nights through the ages, from Victorian timidity to twenties cynicism); two lovers begin with sweet nothings and end in furious battle; two couples who have swapped partners have an excruciatingly embarrassing breakfast together; a pair of respectable strangers come to blows. Cutting across these individual episodes is the ebb and flow of the relationship between Elyot and Amanda, sometimes powerful enough to bring all action to a standstill as they contemplate their latest failure to co-exist in peace.

Superimposed over the sketches too is a very precise structure which anchors the apparently plotless story and also allows us simultaneously to admire the protagonists' energy and style and to laugh at their egotism. Bergson maintained that comedy in its most basic, slapstick form depended on the sight of a human being temporarily made to resemble a machine; the man who slips on the banana skin is suddenly reduced to a mechanical toy, controlled by something outside himself. *Private Lives* turns its characters into a very sophisticated toy indeed. Their feelings may be 'big romantic stuff' but circumstances force them into a pattern whose symmetry works against love's spontaneity. Act One opens with Sybil and Elyot on their balcony, discussing his first wife; there follows a scene with Amanda and Victor, who do exactly the same thing. Elyot and Amanda meet, and the result is two identical scenes in which they try to persuade their respective partners to leave for Paris. Both scenes end in quarrels which leave Elyot and Amanda alone on their balconies, not only in the same place for the same reason, but even carrying identical props, a pair of champagne cocktails apiece.

This ruthless symmetry is made more comic in contrast to the self-assurance of the protagonists and their apparent wealth which seems, at first, to give them total control over their own destinies. Coward's original production made use of his own talent for music; the second act, with the runaway pair alone in Paris, saw him improvising on the piano to gloss over a developing quarrel. To some of his critics this suggested padding, but it also underlined Elyot's poise. Of Lawrence

as Amanda, the choreographer Agnes de Mille wrote, 'When she walks, she streams, when she kicks, she flashes. Her speaking voice is a kind of song, quite unrealistic but lovely.'[7] In other words, Elyot and Amanda are both self-created works of art, and the relentless coincidences to which the play subjects them are an elegant equivalent of the custard pie in the face. The symmetry was stressed alongside the elegance: popping in and out onto the balconies like dolls in an Art Deco weather-house, characters frequently found themselves duplicating not just situations but even gestures; Coward and Lawrence perched on the rails in identical positions, legs crossed, arms similarly draped; they might have eyed each other belligerently but the unconscious harmony of their body-language not only made them look ridiculous but also suggested that, subconsciously, they were still close. As they stared out front, hands forming a pattern along the rails, expressions equally disgruntled, they resorted to a mixture of insult and small talk:

AMANDA:

Whose yacht is that?

ELYOT:

The Duke of Westminster's I expect. It always is.

AMANDA:

I wish I were on it.

ELYOT:

I wish you were on it too.

Adrienne Allen and Laurence Olivier fell into identical poses at the end of the first act; as the curtain fell they were uttering virtually identical lines like some idiotically irrelevant chorus. The overall effect is of a ludicrous mechanism which, time after time, knocks the carefully constructed mask of charm for six and leaves the egos of the charming face to face, naked and resentful, 'no good at love' because they are incapable of self-abandon, but too fond of attention to try and do without it.

If charm cannot preserve harmony between the charming, however, it can still provide a defence against the outside world. Elyot and Amanda may fight like panthers when they are alone together, but they also realise that they are 'figures of fun all right', and their sense of style offers a way of dealing gracefully with the situation they have irresponsibly created. Only days after their escape from Sybil and Victor they have to face them; arriving with righteous triumph in the middle of a ferocious fight between Elyot and Amanda, the cast-off spouses provide a comic version of Banquo's ghost, reproach incarnate; the response of their erring partners is to summon their play instinct to ease the tension:

SYBIL:

> It's all perfectly horrible. I feel smirched and unclean as though slimy things had been crawling all over me.

ELYOT:

> Maybe they have, that's a very old sofa.

VICTOR:

> If you don't stop your damned flippancy, I'll knock your head off.

ELYOT:

> Has it ever struck you that flippancy might cover a very real embarrassment?

Sybil and Victor may have morality on their side, but Elyot and Amanda have manners on theirs; Victor's Puritanical insistence on creating discomfort for its own sake serves to assert the primacy of charm over rectitude; as Coward once again plays symmetrical games, pairing up Elyot and Victor and Amanda and Sybil for the next quarrel, it becomes more and more apparent that Elyot and Amanda are inevitably going to be forced into an alliance against their spouses' self-satisfaction. Typically, it forms over a trivial incident. Coward brings the two couples together for a quiet interlude for the first time; and in the discomfort of breakfast and all its forced intimacy a silly joke is enough to start things off; Amanda fills in an awkward silence with a stream of persiflage about travel, 'arriving at strange places, and seeing strange people, and eating strange foods':

ELYOT:

> And making strange noises afterwards.

> *Amanda chokes violently, Victor jumps up and tries to offer assistance, but she waves him away and continues to choke.*

VICTOR *TO ELYOT*:

> That was a damned fool thing to do.

ELYOT:

> How did I know she was going to choke?

VICTOR *TO AMANDA*:

> Here, drink some coffee.

AMANDA *BREATHLESSLY GASPING*:

> Leave me alone. I'll be all right in a minute.

VICTOR *TO ELYOT*:

> You waste too much time trying to be funny.

In one last movement of his symmetrical machine, Coward sets off Victor and Sybil arguing about whether Elyot's remark was funny or not; as the strain of their enforced togetherness over the last few days finally begins to tell, they shift to personal abuse and then into violence, repeating the scene between Elyot and Amanda which they interrupted at the end of the second act. Over their screams and shouts, Elyot and Amanda wordlessly renew the bond between them; they know what they find funny and they also know that this is important, and the knowledge leads them to tiptoe away from the chaos they have caused in perfect amity. It is clearly a temporary amity; but, Coward implies, their frivolity offers them at least a chance of coping with the indignities of love.

It is not the least of Coward's achievements in the play that he convinces us, momentarily, that this *is* a happy ending. Desmond MacCarthy remarked that 'he has . . . disguised the grimness of his play . . . his conception of love is really desolating.'[8] But for some of its early critics, this very deftness betrayed the play into trivialising the issues it raised; Ivor Brown, for instance, paid tribute to the sparkle of the evening's entertainment but predicted that 'Within a few years the student of drama will be sitting in complete bewilderment . . . wondering what on earth those fellows in 1930 saw in so flimsy a trifle.'[9] The play remains a repertory staple; the reason, perhaps, is that the bravura of Elyot's attack on seriousness and the 'poor philosophers' continues to disarm; it is, after all, the business of frivolity to dodge awkward questions, and they are rarely dodged with more style than here. Coward, however, continued to explore the relationship between love and charm, between emotion and mask. In **Design For Living**, produced on Broadway only three years after the London opening of **Private Lives**, he took more risks; the result was a disappointingly short run (135 nights) and objections from the Lord Chamberlain which prevented it from opening in London until 1939.

It remains a curiously underrated play. Coward wrote of it in **Play Parade One**:

> It has been liked and disliked, and hated and admired, but never, I think, sufficiently loved by any but its three leading actors. This, perhaps, was only to be expected, as its central theme . . . must appear to be definitely anti-social. People were certainly interested and entertained and occasionally even moved by it, but it seemed, to many of them, 'unpleasant'.[10]

The difficulty lies, perhaps, not so much in that central theme itself as from a failure to read correctly the way it is treated. The story is about two men and a woman who all love one another and who exchange partners within the group several times before apparently settling down together. In 1933 this was considered 'shocking' or 'unpleasant'. When the play opened in London in 1939, with war already on the horizon, the critical response was a weary tolerance for its 'smartly silly'[11] attempt to be sensational; the *Observer* summed it up briskly as 'a hangover from the twittering twenties'.[12] John Lahr, in 1982, largely shares this view; he sees the plot as 'belaboured sensationalism' and complains that the 'issue (*sic*) of abnormal sexuality and success are never fully integrated into the action of the play'.[13] His summary of the play's ending—'The homosexual daydream of sexual abundance comes true'[14] seems to confirm that he sees the 'issue' discussed by the play as one of sexual orientation. This, I think, is the misreading of Coward's focus in *Design for Living* that has dogged it from the outset. The relationship between Leo and Otto is not the focal point of the play; still less does Coward impose upon it value-judgements like 'normal' or 'abnormal', or implicitly advocate what Ernest, the voice of orthodoxy in the play, calls 'this disgusting three-sided erotic hotch-potch' as a 'design for living' for anyone but the three protagonists. He is, rather, concerned with the interplay between the public and the private face; the private face here consists of affections and emotions and also of creative ability: Otto is a painter, Leo a writer, and Gilda an interior designer who also acts as critic and gadfly to both the men. The public face is the way these affections and talents operate in the world; all three protagonists achieve some success in their chosen *métiers* and have to evolve a relationship to their public; they also have to integrate this relationship into their personal lives; all three, too, are attractive and aware of it; this fact sometimes cuts across their affection, their mutual loyalty and also the partnerships they form at different stages in the play; it can lead them into playing conventionalised sex-roles, into manipulativeness and into jealousy.

The private faces of Leo, Otto and Gilda are thus bound up with their professional lives; talent and charm are attributes which they can market; this, in turn, means that they are also capable of standing back from their masks in a way that Elyot and Amanda, performers by instinct, cannot; within *Design for Living* there are fewer violent emotional transitions from tenderness to rage, charm to malice; instead charm is ruthlessly analysed—and we then see characters struggling to cope emotionally with what they have already understood intellectually.

The change reflects the talents of Coward's chosen cast for the play. *Design for Living* was a project conceived and written for Coward himself and his close friends Alfred Lunt and Lynn Fontanne; as he wrote in *Present Indicative,* it was a project predicated upon the eventual acquisition, by all three of them, of successful public faces—the persona of a star:

> From these shabby, uncongenial rooms we projected ourselves into future eminence. We discussed, the three of us, over potato salad and dill pickles, our most secret dreams of success. Lynn and Alfred were to be married. That was the first plan. Then they were to become definitely idols of the public. That was the second plan.

> Then, all this being successfully accomplished, they were to act exclusively together. This was the third plan. It remained for me to supply the fourth, which was than when all three of us had become stars of sufficient magnitude to be able to count upon an individual following irrespective of each other, then, poised serenely upon that enviable plane of achievement, we would meet and act triumphantly together . . .[15]

If this long-standing friendship founded on shared ambition made the play's subject—success and the public face—inevitable, the special qualities of the Lunts had a profound effect upon its style. The three of them had an onstage *rapport* as powerful as that of Coward and Lawrence—Coward and Alfred Lunt once inadvertently swapped lines for almost a whole scene and found it no great strain to carry on; but the talents of Lunt and Fontanne were very different from those of Lawrence. While she worked on instinct, their approach to acting was to treat it as a series of problems to be solved by intelligence and painstaking rehearsal. Lunt spent hours working out exactly the right way to close a door. No detail was too small. Fontanne made changes throughout the run of the play; only on the last night did she manage to develop a mechanism to create the sort of handbag that fitted Gilda's character—a small spring caused a mass of clutter to boil over like a pan of milk whenever it was opened. Highly respected stars, they worked for a long time with the Theatre Guild whose policy of high quality plays on a low budget they admired, and encouraged writers to experiment with challenging themes. *Design for Living* marked their return to Broadway.

About five years previously Lynne Fontanne had appeared as Nina Leeds in O'Neill's *Strange Interlude,* the longest role yet written for an actress. Nina is torn between two men, a situation O'Neill explores in tragic depth for more than five hours; it prompted Groucho Marx in *Animal Crackers* to leer to a pair of starlets 'We three would make an ideal couple. Pardon me while I have a strange interlude.' Coward's attitude to the play was no more reverent; Fontanne asked for his advice on the part and at her instigation he sat twice through what he described as 'the whole bloody nine acts of that bore'.[16] In fact, however, the play seems to have made some impact on him for many of the issues it raises are also examined in *Design for Living.* In both plays the woman is the emotional and intellectual centre, and in both plays she is unable to function in a conventional marriage. Both, too, demand frequent transitions from action to introspection and analysis. In *Strange Interlude* the characters speak their thoughts aloud for our benefit; Coward, less experimentally, allows his trio to confide in one another or in Ernest, their friend and butt.

But if Coward's technique is more conventional, the way in which he explores the issues raised by the triangular situation is less so; although *Design for Liv-*

ing is styled 'a comedy' it does not trivialise the questions examined by O'Neill but looks at them from a different angle.

Strange Interlude opens at a point where Nina has lost the man she really loves; she passionately regrets that they did not sleep together before his death and it soon becomes clear that neither of the two men who love her is an adequate substitute. She marries Sam, who becomes obsessed with making money, but learns that there is a streak of madness in his family and turns to Ned, her other lover, to give her a child. All three are plunged into a torment of jealousy which destroys them completely: Sam's greed reaches lunatic proportions, Ned slumps into promiscuity and allows Nina to treat him like a slave, and Nina herself becomes a jealous, even a cruel, mother. She tries to discover some system of beliefs on which to act and can only reiterate the conclusions of Sam's mother: 'Being happy, that's the nearest we can ever come to knowing what's good!'[17]

The unspoken assumption of the play is that jealousy is part and parcel of sexuality; once aroused it cannot be checked and will rage until it has destroyed everything around it like a forest fire; its seeds are planted even before Nina takes Ned as her lover; she is eternally making comparisons between Ned and Sam and her dead Gordon. This destructiveness is the dark side of love, which, O'Neill implies, is also an irresistible emotion, a passion which cannot be explained or resisted.

For Coward in *Design for Living,* both love and jealousy are problems to be faced and analysed; although he does not pretend to offer solutions he implies that it is, at least sometimes, possible for the characters who experience them to transcend them in shared understanding and perhaps laughter. Sexual attractiveness is not an uncontrollable force but part of charm's armoury, which can be used at will: both Leo and Gilda, guilty after their amorous encounter, feel that they have been playing the roles of sexual stereotype. 'There are moments in life when I look upon my own damned femininity with complete nausea', says Gilda:

> It humiliates me to the dust to think that I can go so far, clearly and intelligently, keeping faith with my own standards—which are not female standards at all— preserving a certain decent integrity, not using any tricks; then suddenly, something happens, a spark is struck and down I go into the mud! Squirming with archness, being aloof and desirable, consciously alluring, snatching and grabbing, evading and surrendering, dressed and painted for victory.

Leo similarly describes himself as 'like a mannequin. New spring model, with a few extra flounces.'

The 'extra flounces' consist of artistic success; Leo has, he admits, been showing off to Gilda, buying champagne with the takings from his latest play. 'There seemed to be something new about you', says Gilda. 'Perhaps it's having money.' Otto, when they admit that they spent the night together, also sees sexual attraction and success as intertwined. When they try to persuade him to think calmly, he rounds on Gilda with 'I expect your reason and intelligence prompted you to wear your green dress, didn't it? With the emerald earrings? And your green shoes, too, although they hurt you when you dance', and walks out after making it clear to Leo that his jealousy has more than one facet. 'Go ahead, my boy, and do great things! You've already achieved a Hotel de Luxe, a few smart suits and the woman I loved.'

As the second act begins, Coward shows the two sides of Leo's charm, success and attractiveness, pulling against each other. Gilda refuses to delude herself about the quality of his work and resents his preoccupation with what she calls 'second-hand people' who lionize him. Barbs are visible through the banter:

LEO *READING THE* DAILY MIRROR:

> *Change and Decay* is gripping throughout. The characterisation falters here and there, but the dialogue is polished and sustains a high level from first to last and is frequently witty, nay, even brilliant—

GILDA:

> I love 'nay'.

LEO:

> But—here we go, dear! But the play, on the whole, is decidedly thin.

GILDA:

> My God! They've noticed it.

LEO *JUMPING UP:*

> Thin—thin! What do they mean, 'Thin'?

GILDA:

> Just thin, darling. Thin's thin all over the world and you can't get away from it.

LEO:

> Would you call it thin?

GILDA:

> Emaciated.

When Otto turns up, also, now, a great success, it is inevitable that Gilda will fall into his arms, but the scene is not a mere re-run of the previous episode with Leo. They debate the ethics of the situation as before, they create a halo of glamour around the moment—'a moment to remember, all right,' says Otto. 'Scribble it on your heart; a flicker of ecstasy sandwiched between yesterday and tomorrow—something to be recaptured in the future without illusion, perfect in itself!' But the moment takes place nonetheless in a resolutely prosaic setting which constantly undermines it; they assemble a scratch meal of oddments rather than the glamorous trappings of Leo's night with Gilda and punctuate reflections on the nature of love with suggestions about the best sort of jam to eat with the rice pudding. Gilda realises that one element of the love she felt for both men has vanished: they do not need her any more. Otto sums up their old relationship succinctly:

> Leo and I were both struggling, a single line was in both our minds leading to success—that's what we were planning for, working like dogs for! You helped us both, jostling us on to the line again when we slipped off and warming us when we were cold in discouragement.

He rightly points out that the old days cannot be brought back but he also fails to offer more than a brief flare of desire as a new ground base for love; now that the struggles are over, what place is there for Gilda? Her own solution is to walk out on the pair of them, determined to be herself for the first time, to learn 'the lesson of paddling my own canoe . . . not just weighing down somebody else's and imagining I'm steering it.'

The plot has already begun to move with the comic symmetry of *Private Lives*. Coward now turns it into a pattern so relentlessly symmetrical that it becomes a lunatic ritual. The last possible permutation of the three lovers, Leo and Otto, open the notes that Gilda has left—identical in content, propped against the brandy-bottle like a pair of bookends—get drunk and fall weepily into each other's arms. As they work their way down the brandy bottle they recapitulate all the arguments of the play—about passion, about success, about need; as they get drunker and drunker the effect is like a record played at the wrong speed, fast and garbled and then grinding to a slurred and grating stop. They arrive at three decisions, all vaguely incompatible: they will sell themselves as hard as they can for 'More and better Success! Louder and funnier Success!' They will get away from the corruption of civilisation:

OTTO:

You'd soon be all right if you got away from all this muck.

LEO:

Yes, I know, but how?

OTTO *PUTTING HIS ARM ROUND HIS SHOULDER*:

Get on a ship, Leo—never mind where it's going! Just get on a ship—a small ship.

LEO:

How small?

OTTO:

Very small indeed; a freighter.

LEO:

Is that what you did?

OTTO:

Yes.

LEO:

Then I will. Where do very small ships sail from?

And they are, without Gilda, going to be 'awfully—awfully—lonely.'

Their alliance explodes the conventional posture of jealous lover which they both found necessary to adopt previously; now that jealousy has flown out of the window they are free to win Gilda back, and, in the final act, this is what they do. Gilda has also achieved success by selling herself: married to the conventional Ernest, she lives in a luxurious flat full of paintings and antiques—all of them for sale; she refers to it as 'my shop' and appears to be doing well. Throughout the play the sets and costumes have grown more and more expensive; Gladys Calthrop's design for the last act was almost aggressively fashionable and had a flavour of the luxury liner about it. All three have sold out their talent; the results are charming but, in the end, they have all behaved like Gilda in her green dress, making themselves attractive without a thought for integrity. But the fact that they are all three equally successful banishes the question of 'need' from their relationship. All that remains is for the tight little group anarchically to define itself against the conventional world. Otto and Leo arrive while Gilda is entertaining some rich and pompous guests; they proceed to drive them away by undermining all their small talk with devastating rudeness:

HELEN:

> It's funny how people alter; only the other day in the Colony a boy that I used to know when he was at Yale walked up to my table, and I didn't recognise him!

LEO:

Just fancy!

OTTO:

> Do you know, I have an excellent memory for names, but I cannot for the life of me remember faces. Sometimes I look at Leo suddenly and haven't the faintest idea who he is.

They stay on, popping up to greet Ernest the next morning in borrowed pyjamas like a pair of antic jack-in-the-boxes and treating him with brisk patronage as a 'dear old pet'; Gilda is finally and ineluctably drawn into the game, recognising that she is 'not different from them. We're all of a piece, the three of us'. As Ernest walks out they are united in howls of laughter—and, in Coward's first production, physically entwined in a complicated three-cornered knot, a circle impossible to break from inside or outside.

Several questions, of course, remain unanswered. In the drunk scene Coward allows the boozy expansiveness of Otto and Leo to raise some apparently incompatible ideas about commercial success and artistic integrity, and having jammed them side by side for a laugh he never re-examines them in the light of sober day. It was, indeed, a question Coward never quite answered to his own satisfaction. There remains, too, the question of whether talent and mutual attraction can hold the three together—Gilda, after all, left the group for reasons concerned precisely with that question of success. Nor have we ever seen them operating as a group of three, but always as a pair with one outsider—Otto or Leo, feeling themselves betrayed in turn, Gilda confiding to Ernest that she is leaving.

But although this is never discussed, there are visual signals that guide the audience towards acceptance of the conclusion as inevitable. As we have seen, characters find themselves moving in symmetrical patterns, like the quartet in *Private Lives*; but here the patterns are accepted and, in the case of this last tableau, chosen; the trio choose to resign themselves to the indignities love forces upon them and to create a way of life that allows for them.

After the London opening, *The Times* claimed to detect two strains at work; 'Sometimes . . . a serious play and a deeply interesting. Sometimes . . . Mr. Coward's dialogue dips and swings and glitters as though he were writing farce.'[18] The two modes, however, are united in these accepted patterns. Farce forces its characters into similar situations; frequently they become mechanical toys geared entirely to hiding in cupboards and under beds. *Design for Living* reverses this activity. The characteristic movements of Leo and Otto are not those of concealment but of self-disclosure; Gilda may hide them from Ernest with ludicrous stories ('He's had the most awful neuralgia . . . his little face is all pinched and strained') but among the three of them everything is admitted, albeit reluctantly. However callously they behave to Ernest and the rest of the world, however outrageously they strike poses, their fundamental honesty within the group gives the play moments of unusual tenderness. A production by Michael Blakemore in 1973 stressed this; the sets and costumes underlined the tendency of the three to play roles: Vanessa Redgrave as Gilda spent her time in the Paris flat in an assortment of unbecoming ethnic garments and Jeremy Brett as the departing Otto affected a shabby but dash-

ing hat and a worker's kitbag that suggested the radical chic of the Auden generation. At the same time, their stance when together was upright and frank and their eyes met as they struggled to account for their amorous comings and goings. For Sheridan Morley, Coward's friend and biographer, the production illustrated admirably the characteristic Coward attitude to love and talent: 'Live with your success, put up with its inconveniences, revel in its joys, never complain, never explain.'[19]

II. 'IMPROBABLE FARCE': *BLITHE SPIRIT*

Had a few drinks, then went to Savoy. Pretty bad blitz . . . a couple of bombs fell very near during dinner. Wall bulged a bit and door flew in. Orchestra went on playing . . . I sang . . . On the whole a very strange and amusing evening.[20]

Coward spent much of his war abroad, but in the first half of 1941 he set up the project that was to become *In Which We Serve*, wrote **Blithe Spirit** in five days and opened it within six weeks. It was to have one of the longest recorded runs in the British theatre.

If the shape of **Private Lives** looks forward to *Waiting for Godot*, **Blithe Spirit** could be seen as a forerunner of Beckett's *Play*, which shows three characters, all dead, endlessly repeating the story of their triangular relationship. The comparison is, of course, ludicrous; nothing could be further from the tone of *Play* than the anarchic flippancy of **Blithe Spirit**; but, given that Coward's play originated and entertained London in the bloodiest period of its history, it is worth noting the fact; the time and the subject matter would appear to dictate an approach closer to Beckett's.

The twenties and thirties had seen an upsurge of interest in the paranormal, in clairvoyance and spiritualism, and it was reflected in the theatre. Plays like Barrie's *Mary Rose* or Priestley's *Johnson over Jordan* provided a society that was rapidly losing its religious faith with a reassurance that death was not the end. Gareth Lloyd Evans sees in the popularity of the plays a hunger for confirmation that the sacrifices of the First World War had not been in vain, 'a passionate faith that loved ones who, in reality, had been blown to pieces in the trenches had passed on to a bourne from which they could not return but which was a place of happiness and content.'[21] Coward explodes these gentle assumptions: in **Blithe Spirit** the dead do not exist to make the lives of the living more comfortable. On the other hand, he also parodies the newer attitudes to the dead found in popular works of the late thirties and forties: one of the biggest box-office successes in the cinema in 1940 was Hitchcock's film of Daphne du Maurier's Gothic novel *Rebecca*. Here the mousey heroine has to struggle against the powerful personality of her husband's dead wife; although there is no suggestion that she has survived the grave in any form, the force of her character is strong enough to destroy the house in which she had lived and threaten the new marriage. Death here is the bringer of anarchy, danger and sexual energy.

This is also true of **Blithe Spirit.** The ordered life of the hero, Charles Condomine, is disrupted when a séance calls up the ghost of his first wife, Elvira; she hangs about the house, bringing chaos in her wake and eventually bringing about the death of his second wife Ruth—whereupon Ruth too materialises in ghostly form and the two spirits bicker over Charles until he finally manages to escape. But while du Maurier virtually equates anarchy with evil, Coward's attitude is more ambivalent: the eventually routing of the ghosts is clearly a 'happy ending', but their energy is something to be celebrated. We may pity Charles, but he is not an attractive character and the presence of Elvira is a fitting punishment for his self-satisfied and exploitative behaviour: as the play opens he is discussing his first marriage with Ruth:

RUTH:

Does it still hurt—when you think of her?

CHARLES:

No, not really—sometimes I almost wish it did—I feel rather guilty . . .

He is also planning his next book; they are expecting the medium, Madame Arcati, to dinner, so that Charles can study and use her; this appears to be his usual technique:

CHARLES:

Do you remember how I got the idea for *The Light Goes Out*?

RUTH *SUDDENLY SEEING THAT HAGGARD, RADDLED WOMAN IN THE HOTEL AT BIARRITZ*:

Of course I remember—we sat up half the night talking about it . . .

CHARLES:

She certainly came in very handy—I wonder who she was.

The new novel, *The Unseen,* is to be a monument to scepticism. Charles, in fact, is dodging two vital issues in his life—passion and personal experience; he has retreated behind a mask of smoothness, into a relationship based on 'calm', and success based on shrewd analysis of other peoples' lives. Appropriately he gets his come-uppance at the hands of two different people—the passionate Elvira and the innocent Madame Arcati.

In styling the play a 'farce', a term he rarely used, Coward is allying himself with a tradition which includes *The Comedy of Errors* and *The Importance of Being Ernest* and was to continue with the work of Joe Orton in *What the Butler Saw*—the tradition of farce as comic existential nightmare. Coward had little interest in the French farce tradition of Labiche and Feydeau which is grounded almost exclusively in the idea of sexual indiscretion in a bourgeois society: his adaptation for the Royal Court of Feydeau's *Occupe-toi d'Amélie* in 1959 contained some splendid jokes and some flashes of insight into character, but always at the expense of the manic complexity of the plot. He had still less interest in the milk-and-water British imitations grounded in *suspected* sexual indiscretions and involving a great many lost trousers and episodes in cupboards from the most innocent motives. In **Blithe Spirit,** it is not Charles's reputation which is at stake but his sanity. Like Antipholus of Ephesus and Jack Worthing, he finds that he is not the person he thought he was: at one point he is threatened with a psychiatrist and Ruth insists on treating him as 'ill'.

Endangered sanity is of course central to melodrama like *Rebecca,* and Coward parodies the idea of the vengeful dead with flippant delight: like Rebecca, Elvira is faithless but possessive; but she also has the inconsequential vagueness of Amanda; she brings the melodrama down to earth by her concern with the small change of passion:

ELVIRA:

You never suspected it but I laughed at you steadily from the altar to the grave—all your ridiculous petty jealousies and your fussings and fumings—

CHARLES:

You were feckless and irresponsible and morally unstable—I realised that before we left Budleigh Salterton.

ELVIRA:

Nobody but a monumental bore would have thought of having a honeymoon at Budleigh Salterton.

CHARLES:

What's the matter with Budleigh Salterton?

ELVIRA:

I was an eager young bride, Charles—I wanted glamour and music and romance—all I got was potted palms, seven hours a day on a damp golf course and a three-piece orchestra playing 'Merrie England.'

There is a good deal of slapstick fun with flying vases, culminating in the total destruction of the set by the now invisible ghosts of Elvira and Ruth; and the character of Madame Arcati provides a constantly funny refutation of all our pre-conceived ideas about her profession. Neither muttering hag nor Sludge-like charlatan, she radiates innocent enjoyment of life and her work, and this causes her to score off Charles again and again without realising that he is trying to make use of her. She briskly dismisses the clichés of spiritualism—'I was getting far too sedentary in London, that horrid little flat with the dim lights—they had to be dim, you know, the clients expect it.' Her childlike sensuality, taking pleasure in long bicycle rides, Nature and dry Martinis, links her firmly to the things of this world and makes her work seem ordinary, hardly worth writing novels about; and she has a good line in waspish retorts to sceptical remarks:

RUTH:

Daphne is Madame Arcati's control—she's a little girl.

DR BRADMAN:

Oh, I see—yes of course.

CHARLES:

How old is she?

MADAME ARCATI:

Rising seven when she died.

MRS BRADMAN:

And when was that?

MADAME ARCATI:

February the sixth, 1884.

MRS BRADMAN:

Poor little thing.

DR BRADMAN:

She must be a bit long in the tooth by now, I should think.

MADAME ARCATI:

You should think, Dr Bradman, but I fear you don't—at least, not profoundly enough.

As played by Margaret Rutherford in the original production (Rutherford was chosen by Coward while, oddly enough, playing Mrs Danvers in *Rebecca*) she showed the soul of an intelligent twelve-year old shining through a middle-aged body; dressed in rather childlike garments, such as an Alice band in her hair, she stood for a world of innocence that Charles could not comprehend, let alone exploit; the little maid who proves the unwitting medium through which the ghosts materialise—the bandage she wears round her head a comic version of the Red Indian costume of the cliché 'spirit guide'—adds to the impression of innocence taking its revenge upon scepticism.

But if much of the play is harmlessly comic, it also has a darker dimension. When ghosts appear in folk stories and old ballads they have demands to make, unsatisfied with the present behaviour of those they have left behind. They may call for a cessation of mourning; they may disrupt a newly formed relationship—but they always have to be placated. Keith Thomas writes of the declining belief in ghosts:

> It is now more common for people to live out their full life-span, and to die only after they have retired and withdrawn from an active role in society. This reduces the social vacuum they leave behind. The relative absence of ghosts in modern society can thus be seen as the result of a demographic change—'the disengaged social situation of the majority of the deceased'. The dead, in other words, fade away before they die. In the earlier periods, by contrast, it was commoner for men to be carried off at the prime of their life, leaving behind them a certain amount of social disturbance, which ghost-beliefs helped to dispel. The period when the soul wandered loose was that when the survivors were adapting themselves to their new pattern of social relationships.[22]

'Social disturbance' in 1941 was, of course, a common feature of the landscape once more; while audiences may not have revived the ghost-beliefs of previous generations they were in a position to understand them and to relish the 'rough-housing' of Charles Condomine's vanity in fancying himself safe behind his mask. He has settled for using his talent in writing second-rate novels and his charm in evading the passion which ought to energise it; he deftly glosses over the anxiety Ruth shows in her assertions about their marriage, assertions which she clearly hopes will be contradicted:

CHARLES:

I love you, my love.

RUTH:

I know you do—but not the wildest stretch of imagination could describe it as the first fine careless rapture.

CHARLES:

Would you like it to be?

RUTH:

Good God, no!

CHARLES:

Wasn't that a shade too vehement?

RUTH:

We're neither of us adolescent, Charles, we've neither of us led exactly prim lives, have we? And we've both been married before—careless rapture at this stage would be incongruous and embarrassing.

CHARLES:

I hope I haven't been in any way a disappointment, dear.

Charles is in many ways an early study for Hugo Latymer in his bland asexuality; and although the fact that the passions he is refusing to face were more socially acceptable to the audience of 1941 than Latymer's and hence more acceptable for comic treatment, his 'rough-housing' has its darker moments. Elvira's every entrance is accompanied by a breeze suggestive of the physical passion she represents; her conversation is full of enjoyment of earthly things—flowers, movies, cucumber sandwiches; and she revives in Charles a memory of physical desire:

ELVIRA:

That's better.

CHARLES:

What's better?

ELVIRA:

Your voice was kinder.

CHARLES:

Was I ever unkind to you when you were alive?

ELVIRA:

Often . . .

CHARLES:

Oh, how can you! I'm sure that's an exaggeration.

ELVIRA:

Not at all—you were an absolute pig that time we went to Cornwall and stayed in that awful hotel—you hit me with a billiard cue—

CHARLES:

Only very, very gently . . .

ELVIRA:

I loved you very much.

CHARLES:

I loved you too. . . .

But at the same time that passion can never find expression: it is impossible for Charles to touch Elvira and the fact that it is too late, that she is a ghost, is constantly stressed by her appearance: Coward calls for her to be completely grey, skin and clothes and even the things that she brings with her from beyond the grave, like the grey roses she carries in the second act. In the first production Kay Hammond added an unnerving note of sensuality by adding violently red lipstick to the grey make-up. By the third act Ruth too is dead and the stage often contains more grey figures than flesh-coloured ones; at the same time there is a relentless harping on the subject of physical passion:

RUTH:

You can be as rude as you like, Elvira. I don't mind a bit—as a matter of fact I should be extremely surprised if you weren't.

ELVIRA:

Why?

RUTH:

The reply to that is really too obvious.

CHARLES:

I wish you two would stop bickering for one minute.

RUTH:

This is quite definitely one of the most frustrating nights I have ever spent.

ELVIRA:

The reply to that is pretty obvious, too.

There is an edge of real frustration and anger in this picture, which the Girl-Guide earnestness of Madame Arcati does not completely dissipate. Similarly, although Coward reaps a resounding laugh at the end of the second act when Elvira is attacked by the as yet invisible ghost of Ruth, the moment at which Ruth's death is announced on the telephone is not entirely comic: we are also aware of a murderous anger and jealousy towards Charles, whose death Elvira was hoping to achieve by doctoring the car.

Constantly, the play juxtaposes conflicting responses to the situation: we are invited to enjoy the comic lines and the element of parody, but the stage picture, combining the deadly greyness of the ghosts with their often wild physical energy, has a sinister quality. Charles's dilemma, trapped between the old wife and the new, has comic echoes of Elyot Chase, but, unlike Elyot, he is not secure in his own identity: he is accused of being drunk, he imagines that he is having hallucinations, and he cannot ultimately define himself as husband, lover or widower. His final solution, to walk out on the dematerialised spirits and leave them to destroy the house, is done with a fine bravura flourish, but it is the gesture of a man who is not only 'no good at love' but content that this should be so. Charles has, traditionally, been played by actors notable for polish and easy charm—Rex Harrison, Dennis Price, and of course Coward himself; however, a 1976 revival at the National Theatre, directed by Harold Pinter, showed a Charles much more manic and scared at the situation in which he found himself, played by Richard Johnson; and this perhaps recaptured something of the play's ambivalence, its treatment of death as a joke and its simultaneous awareness of the value of life and energy and passion, originally emphasised by its context. A programme note from the first production suggests the spirit in which it was conceived:

> If an air raid warning be received during the performance the audience will be informed from the stage . . . those desiring to leave the theatre may do so but the performance will continue.

III. COMEDIES OF IMPINGEMENT: *HAY FEVER* AND *PRESENT LAUGHTER*

'Comedy of impingement' was James Agate's phrase for *The Young Idea* in a review of the 1923 production; in it he also rightly praised Coward as a new and original voice, but it seems strange that he should be the first to devise a label for a kind of comedy which, after all, was certainly not new. The arrival of an exotic stranger or strangers in a conventional community is a common and easily exploited dramatic situation. Subsequently, however, Coward was to reverse this situation to considerable effect. In these two comedies it is the conventional figures who try to impact themselves onto a world where talent rules. The result is a conflict between their conventional values and those which the talented have made for themselves.

In *Hay Fever* the arena for this clash is the country house of the Bliss family. All talented, all totally selfish, they have each invited a guest for the weekend without informing the others. They have thus unwittingly created that seed-bed of Edwardian sexual intrigue, the house-party. Instead of a series of individual encounters they have set up a temporary community; and, as the Edwardians knew, such a community needs to be bound by certain codes of etiquette: relationships may be made and broken, moral taboos preserved or violated, but good manners hold the community together in transient harmony.

The Blisses, however, see manners differently. As the play opens Sorel, who is currently attracted to a diplomat, is flirting with the idea of acquiring some conventional social graces, while Simon asserts the more usual Bliss point of view:

SOREL:

> . . . You're right about us being slap-dash, Simon. I wish we weren't.

SIMON:

> Does it matter?

SOREL:

> It must, I think—to other people.

SIMON:

> It's not our fault—it's the way we've been brought up.

SOREL:

> Well, if we're clever enough to realise that we ought to be clever enough to change ourselves.

SIMON:

> I'm not sure that I want to.

SOREL:

> We're so awfully bad-mannered.

SIMON:

> Not to people we like.

SOREL:

> The people we like put up with it because they like *us*.

SIMON:

> What do you mean, exactly, by bad manners? Lack of social tricks and small talk?

Sorel can't answer this adequately, responding vaguely with 'We've never once asked anyone if they've slept well.' Later, however, when admiring the *savoir-faire* of the diplomat, Richard, she offers a definition which has a slight double edge: 'You always say the right thing, and no one knows a bit what you're really thinking. That's what I adore.'

The Blisses are too ruthless for polite insincerities. David, for instance, has invited his guest, Jackie, to provide material for his next novel; 'she's an abject fool but a useful type', he remarks; under the strain of the unexpected invasion by four guests, he forgets Jackie completely and welcomes her with 'Who the hell are you?' Coward extracts considerable comic mileage out of the guests' attempts to remain polite at all costs. Richard and Jackie, for instance, abandoned in the hall by Simon and Judith who have borne away their own guests without bothering to introduce them, search helplessly to find some common ground:

JACKIE:

> Have you travelled a lot?

RICHARD *MODESTLY*:

> A good deal.

JACKIE:

> How lovely!

> *Richard comes down and sits on form below piano. There is a pause.*

RICHARD:

> Spain is very beautiful.

JACKIE:

Yes, I've always heard Spain was awfully nice.

Pause

RICHARD:

Except for the bull-fights. No one who ever loved horses could enjoy a bull-fight.

JACKIE:

Nor anyone who loved bulls either.

RICHARD:

Exactly.

Pause

JACKIE:

Italy's awfully nice, isn't it?

RICHARD:

Oh yes, charming.

JACKIE:

I've always wanted to go to Italy.

Pause.

At the end of the first act, the guests find themselves assembled for afternoon tea, but again the Blisses' refusal to participate in ritual politenesses makes it a devastating affair; scattered about on unsuitable seats in the hall, balancing cups and plates, they try to exchange pleasantries in the face of their hosts' indifference, but give up in discouragement; after two attempts, during which they find themselves uttering simultaneous banalities, the curtain comes down on an embarrassed pause.

The play is not simply about the Blisses' lack of conventional manners but about the manners they have made for themselves. Much of the discomfiture of the guests arises from the fact that there is a code of conduct in the house which they do not understand. Simon makes it clear at the start of the play that it is not a code for everybody. 'It's so silly of people to try and cultivate the artistic temperament', he remarks of an acquaintance. '*Au fond* she's just a normal, bouncing Englishwoman.' The Blisses are aware that they have talent and that it needs outlets for display. They adopt a variety of masks which they parade for the admiration of others. Judith, for instance, speaks of 'my Celebrated Actress glamour' as an entity which 'isn't me really'; she also recognises that certain masks are quite beyond her; despite her attempts to learn the names of the flowers and her determination in marching about with a trug and galoshes, she decides that 'I've tried terribly hard to be "landed gentry", but without any real success'. Role-play within the family provides them with a source

of endless entertainment; they can launch spontaneously and with gusto into the second act curtain scene from Judith's great stage success *Love's Whirlwind* or become totally absorbed in a reading of David's new novel; this imbues their behaviour with an enormous vitality which partly offsets their ruthlessness. Role-play is also a cohesive force for the Blisses. Although they quarrel incessantly the situation is always resolved through spontaneous improvisation. As they squabble about whose guest will get the Japanese room and who will have the boat to go on the river, Judith takes charge; she launches into a speech of tender melancholy ('A change has come over my children of late . . .'), grabs Simon and Sorel and arranges them in suitable poses which they understand only too well are cues for a scene of family togetherness:

SIMON *COMES OVER TO HIS MOTHER*:

Mother, what are we to do?

JUDITH *PULLS HIM DOWN ON HIS KNEES AND PLACES HIS HEAD ON HER RIGHT SHOULDER, SOREL'S HEAD ON HER LEFT. MAKES A CHARMING LITTLE MOTHERLY PICTURE*:

We must all be very, very kind to everyone!

SIMON:

Now then, Mother, none of that!

JUDITH *AGGRIEVED*:

I don't know what you mean, Simon.

SIMON:

You were being beautiful and sad.

JUDITH:

But I am beautiful and sad.

SIMON:

You're not particularly beautiful, darling, and you never were.

JUDITH:

Never mind; I made thousands think I was.

Judith neatly averts the quarrel and also focuses attention on herself, creating an atmosphere in which she can announce that she is returning to the stage—and does it without fooling anyone in the least. Etiquette, for the Blisses, is not to create polite and impenetrable fictions, but to create shared improvisations, fictions in which the polite guest should participate. Talented hosts need talented guests; if they end up with untalented ones, they reserve the right to show no mercy.

Coward opens the second act with a scene in which the guests' lack of role-playing talent is cruelly and comically exposed. The Blisses set up a game called

'Adverbs', allied to charades. Coward makes of this a highly entertaining comic set-piece; he explores the embarrassment of the well-mannered guest forced to assume falsely the spontaneity of a child; he doubles the embarrassment by the fact that the hosts all have some contact, through Judith, with the professional theatre and none of the guests do; and compounds it further by the Blisses' relentless criticism of their guests' performance. Judith eggs on the disintegration of the game with a piece of staggering rudeness, pronouncing 'I think, for the future, we'd better confine our efforts to social conversation and not attempt anything in the least intelligent.' This heavy irony is more than an insult, however: it is also a clear statement that the weekend is going to be played by Bliss rules whether the guests will or not. The game proves to have been a kind of initiation ceremony; for all its discomfort it is a good deal easier than the subsequent role-playing expected of the guests. In the second half of the play Coward takes a more complex look at the relationship between charm and good manners.

When *Hay Fever* opened in 1925 Coward, fresh from *The Vortex* and *Fallen Angels,* epitomised for much of his audience the 'younger generation knocking on the door of the dustbin'. With this in mind he left John Gielgud to play Nicky Lancaster in *The Vortex* on the first night of *Hay Fever* and came on at the final curtain to point out that 'this play at least, ladies and gentlemen, has been as clean as a whistle'. Clean it might be: certainly every embrace is interrupted and every burgeoning love-affair thwarted; but the second half of the play is nonetheless largely concerned with the uses that charm makes of sexual attraction and the strategies which conventional good manners employ to cope with it.

Certainly Judith's talent has no trouble in weaving a spell around Richard. She manipulates him expertly, first with a display of professional talent as she sings at the piano, then by the adoption of a carefully calculated persona:

RICHARD:

   I never realise how *dead* I am until I meet people like you. It's depressing, you know.

JUDITH:

   What nonsense! You're not a bit dead.

RICHARD:

   Do you always live here?

JUDITH:

   I'm going to, from now onwards. I intend to sink into a very beautiful old age. When the children marry, I shall wear a cap.

RICHARD *SMILING*:

   How absurd!

JUDITH:

   I don't mean a funny cap.

RICHARD:

   You're far too full of vitality to sink into anything.

JUDITH:

   It's entirely spurious vitality. If you troubled to look below the surface, you'd find a very wistful and weary spirit. I've been battling with life for a long time.

With a neat lie (she has every intention of going back to the stage) she makes herself appear to share Richard's peace-loving spirit; she also deftly calls attention to the age gap between them in order to make Richard himself deny it; and by a touch of wistfulness dissociates herself from the quarrelsome antics of 'Adverbs', instigated by her only minutes before. Richard, duly charmed, plays up as he is clearly expected to do and kisses her. It seems momentarily that host and guest have found some common territory of manners. Desire has its own set of 'good manners'; a little polite insincerity is usual.

Each of the guests makes this same mistake. Sandy Tyrrel finds himself muttering 'I believe I do love you, Sorrel'. Jackie finds Simon sympathetic, and Myra makes a deliberate attempt to captivate David, piling on the flattery with a trowel:

MYRA:

   . . . I'm a very determined woman, you know, and I made up my mind to meet you ages ago.

DAVID:

   That was charming of you. I'm not much to meet really.

MYRA:

   You see, I'd read *Broken Reeds.*

DAVID:

   Did you like it?

MYRA:

   Like it! I think it's one of the finest novels I've ever read.

DAVID:

   There now!

MYRA:

   How do you manage to know so much about women?

But for the Blisses, desire is subject to the same rules as their other kinds of behaviour. While, for the guests, flirtation involves a willing suspension of disbelief (flattery must be taken at face value, the casual kiss must have no long-term consequences while simultaneously disguising itself as a declaration of love) for the Blisses it involves *belief* in the value of the game for its own sake, in the pleasure of a cunningly constructed artifice. If the mask is to sustain its sexual glamour, it must first acknowledge itself. Sorel gently explodes Sandy's illusions: 'You kissed me because you were awfully nice and I was awfully nice and we both like kissing very much', she points out. David gives the more intelligent Myra a rougher time. He tells her firmly 'I write very bad novels . . . and you *know* I do, because you're an intelligent person.' He goes to the heart of the matter with embarrassing directness, asking 'Would you like me to make love to you?' Finally he explains the code by which he and the other Blisses live:

DAVID:

> . . . The only reason I've been so annoying is that I love to see things as they are first, and then pretend they're what they're not.

MYRA:

> Words. Masses and masses of words!

DAVID:

> They're great fun to play with.

MYRA:

> I'm glad you think so. Personally, they bore me stiff.

DAVID:

> Myra—don't be statuesque.

Judith's technique for dealing with the hypocrisies of flirtation is even more radical: pretending to accept them, she then proceeds to transmute them into a parody of the Victorian *mores* that the twenties had already begun to erode; she opens up essentially private moments into team games for the family, in which their improvisatory talents can enjoy free play. Every interrupted embrace becomes a centre for wild eddies of theatricality, Judith herself always in the major role. Thus Richard's kiss becomes the cue for her to put on the mask of erring but fundamentally noble wife. 'David must be told—everything!' she tells the terrified Richard. Confronted by Sorel and Sandy kissing in the library, she becomes the older woman who renounces her lost love à la Lady Frederick; Sorel responds with delight:

JUDITH *STARTING TO ACT*:

> It's far from easy, at my time of life, to—

SOREL *PLAYING UP*:

> Mother—Mother—say you understand and forgive!

JUDITH:

> Understand! You forget, dear, I am a woman.

SOREL:

> I know you are, Mother. That's what makes it all so poignant.

The improvisations gain momentum: the second act brings them all to a boil as Judith discovers David and Myra and plays a series of variations on the role of wronged wife. Myra becomes left behind as Judith and David top each other's melodramatic excesses; and when a puzzled Richard enters assuming that the shouting is about him, that David has indeed been 'told—everything!' he provides the Blisses with a perfect cue to unite by inadvertently quoting from *Love's Whirlwind*:

RICHARD *WITH FORCED CALM*:

> What's happened? Is this a game?
>
> *Judith's face gives a slight twitch; then, with a meaning look at Simon and Sorel, she answers him*

JUDITH *WITH SPIRIT*:

> Yes, and a game that must be played to the finish! *she flings back her arm and knocks Richard up stage.*

SIMON *GRASPING THE SITUATION*:

> Zara! What does this mean?

The curtain falls as the whole family assume their roles in the moth-eaten melodrama; Sorel raises her hand to strike Simon and is warned by a fainting Judith 'Don't strike! He is your father!!!'

The game is a way of excluding the non-talented from the Blisses' circle; but it also makes a comment on the assumptions on which they have tried to enter it; all guests, except the dim Jackie, have come for the weekend expecting to flirt, to put on the only mask in which they feel comfortable. The Pinero-like scenes they find themselves playing are a kind of nightmare in which all their masks are taken seriously, and that by people who have already demonstrated that, as Sorel puts it, 'We none of us mean anything.' Coward allows us to enjoy the comedy of masks to the full by refusing to take sides. The guests may be treated badly, but they are also capable of selfishness towards one another in their difficulties; the appalling breakfast in the third act is the stage for various attempts to secure the right to leave first and push others into staying so that their departure will seem less rude. Our last sight of the Blisses also shows their selfishness: a quarrel about the geography of Paris as described in David's novel is halted by the sound of the departing car, carrying off the people with whom they have neglected to take breakfast. Judith's comment is 'How very rude!'

Hay Fever is Coward's most exuberant play, his most unqualified celebration of the sheer fun of mask-making and the way in which the dullest phrase like 'Is this a game?' can spark off a linguistic and gestural explosion. Of all his major comedies, it is also the only one which did not contain a part for himself, and the two facts are perhaps not unconnected. Although *Hay Fever* demands exceptional ensemble playing, it centres on Judith. Coward created the part for the forceful actress Marie Tempest, who was trying in the twenties to establish herself as a capable performer of contemporary plays; she was able to exploit her rich experience of working in plays not unlike *Love's Whirlwind,* imbuing the lively parodies with affection. Since then the role has, despite Judith's vagueness, always worked best with an actress of authority—Edith Evans played in the famous National revival directed by Coward. The distancing effect of writing the major role for someone other than himself allowed Coward to portray the lethal effect of charm from the outside only, and thus, perhaps, to celebrate it in a more uninhibited fashion. In his last major comedy, however, *Present Laughter* he created a figure with a more ambivalent relationship to his mask. 'Garry Essendine', he stated in a radio talk in 1972, 'is me', and the role is a potent mixture of self-exposure and self-celebration.

As in *Hay Fever,* we see a group of relatively conventional outsiders impinging upon a circle which makes its own manners. Once again, the central figure of that circle is a performer, both on and off the stage. However, we also see, in *Present Laughter,* some of the machinery which exists to service the performer's public face. Judith calls for, and gets, the moral and histrionic support of her family as she launches into the role of loving mother or betrayed wife, but her talent appears to flow of its own accord. Garry's is a commercial proposition; the 'family' which surrounds him is his staff, a collection of secretaries, managers and domestic servants not unlike Coward's own entourage in structure. They offer affection and support but are also determined to protect their investment. They discuss his looks (including the possibility of a toupée), his appointments, his finances and his potential as an actor, stamping frequently on his desire to play Peer Gynt; they also try to control his offstage charm and the consequences of it. 'Think what fun it would be to be *un*attractive for a minute or two', urges his ex-wife and still devoted scriptwriter, Liz.

If charm depends upon businesslike support, however, it also gives back, and not only in terms of a return on the original investment. It also recognises and brings out talent in others.

GARRY:

. . . Twenty years ago Henry put all his money into *The Lost Cavalier.* And who played in it for eighteen months to capacity with extra matinees? I did. And who started his career as a producer in that play? Morris!

LIZ:

I wish you'd stop asking questions and answering them yourself, it's making me giddy.

GARRY:

Where would they have been without me? Where would Monica be now if I hadn't snatched her away from that sinister old aunt of hers and given her a job?

LIZ:

With the sinister old aunt.

GARRY:

And you! One of the most depressing melancholy actresses on the English stage. Where would you be if I hadn't forced you to give up acting and start writing?

LIZ:

Regent's Park.

GARRY:

Good God, I even had to marry you to do it.

Three outsiders attempt in different ways to fracture this delicate symbiosis. Like the guests in *Hay Fever* they fail to understand the relationship between mask and performer, but the mistake they make is different. While Richard and the others do not grasp the impact of their amorous comings and goings on the play that is running perpetually in Judith's mind, the outsiders of *Present Laughter* treat Garry's attractiveness as a function of an individual; in fact it is the property of a group. Their desires are all different. Daphne, the debutante, wants a love affair; Roland Maule, the playwright, wants Garry to stop 'prostituting himself' in boulevard comedy and commit himself to the 'theatre of tomorrow' (ie, his plays); Joanna, the wife of Garry's business partner Henry, has a more sophisticated understanding of Garry's persona; she expects him to act, offstage as well as on; while she wants casual dalliance rather than deeply felt passion, she still puts her own desire ahead of the happiness of 'the firm'. All three, in fact, hold a Romantic conception of the artist as individual, and the play happily explodes the myth while celebrating the fact that, despite its function as a business investment, charm is a magical gift to the performer at the centre of that investment.

Garry's talent, unlike Judith's, does not flow freely from the play but always works towards a goal. Constantly, he charms his way to people's affections and then tries to charm his way out of them. Daphne, for instance, has spent the night before the opening curtain watching Garry in the role of disillusioned but tender Older Man, a role that his staff know well:

DAPHNE:

We talked for hours last night. He told me all about his early struggle.

MONICA:

Did he by any chance mention that Life was passing him by?

Garry's attempts to brush off Daphne also consist largely of a display of masks. He recites Shelley, he elaborates on the fragility and beauty of illusion and the glories of what might have been. Coward's stage directions have a touch of parody about them here: Garry dismisses her view of him as too melancholy 'laughing bitterly', he asserts that he will always remember her 'with beautiful simplicity'; they are, in fact, the stage directions with which Garry is clearly directing himself in his head.

With all his hangers-on, eventually Garry resorts to the most potent mask of all—the pretence that there is no pretence, that all masks are off:

I'm always acting—watching myself go by—that's what's so horrible—I see myself all the time eating, drinking, loving, suffering—sometimes I think I'm going mad—

This technique never fails to charm. Daphne continues to haunt him, turning up incognito to an audition to recite Shelley back at him. Roland is subjected to a tirade about his play, which Garry considers 'a meaningless jumble of adolescent, pseudo intellectual poppycock', and it entrances him; drawn to Garry's energy, he too insists on hanging around.

Charm, in fact, permeates Garry's whole being. He uses it so instinctively that he cannot stop using it, for the cessation of charm becomes charming in itself. With Joanna, the most articulate and dangerous outsider, he even produces a third layer of the mask. She makes the admission that he is always acting into a springboard for a little male-female aggression:

JOANNA:

You're being conventionally odious but somehow it doesn't quite ring true. But then you never do quite ring true, do you? I expect it's because you're an actor, they're always apt to be a bit papier maché.

GARRY:

Just puppets, Joanna dear, creatures of tinsel and sawdust, how clever of you to have noticed it.

The aggression and its aftermath provokes Garry into his last and perhaps favourite pose, that of the honest voice crying in the wilderness; he rounds on Joanna's own mask:

You suddenly appear out of the night reeking with the lust of conquest, the whole atmosphere's quivering with it! You had your hair done this afternoon, didn't you? and your nails and probably your feet too! That's a new dress, isn't it? Those are new shoes! You've never worn those stockings before in your life! And your mind, even more expertly groomed to vanquish than your body. Every word, every phrase, every change of mood cunningly planned. Just the right amount of sex antagonism mixed with subtle flattery, just the right switch over, perfectly timed, from provocative implication to wistful diffidence. You want to know what I'm like, do you, under all the glittering veneer? Well this is it. This is what I'm really like—fundamentally honest!

Joanna's reply, 'Curtain!' is accurate; it also cements the basis of their subsequent love-making—they are going to play at honesty, discussing the emotional implications of a night together upon the rest of 'the firm' before dropping into free improvisation as Garry makes a love duet out of the names of London concert halls.

John Lahr sees Garry's charm as a dilemma identical with Coward's own. 'In the play Coward admits the artificiality of his persona only to make its charm triumphant. Underneath **Present Laughter**'s high spirits is a dilemma: a man who dissimulates so eagerly that he has forgotten who he is.'[23] While this description may fit Coward the playwright and actor, Garry at least has a solution. His compulsion to attract may embroil him in annoying situations: Roland, Daphne and Joanna all arrive in the final act threatening to accompany him to Africa, and Joanna vengefully insists on telling her husband that she has spent the night with Garry. He is, however, entirely capable of dealing with them all, by shutting up Roland and Daphne in the spare room and the office and by some straight talking to 'the firm' about their own love lives. There is no suggestion that he is existentially threatened by his own charm; in fact he contrasts the insecurities of the others, their attitude to sex as an anodyne or a collector's item or a security symbol, with his own awareness that attractiveness is evanescent and the peace of mind that this knowledge gives:

To me the whole business is vastly over-rated. I enjoy it for what it's worth and fully intend to go on doing so for as long as anybody's interested and when the time comes that they're not I shall be perfectly content to settle down with an apple and a good book!

The real histrionics in this scene are reserved for matters of business, for the problems of the forthcoming tour of Africa and the choice of venues for his return performance. Even *Peer Gynt* rears its head once more, and the fury of Joanna as woman scorned pales into insignificance beside Garry's tirade against the Forum theatre. As Garry tiptoes offstage with Liz as the curtain falls, we are witnessing more than a neat escape from his immediate problems. Liz is the most powerful symbol of 'the firm' who look after the Essendine mask. Garry has not lost his personality. He has, rather, handed it over to others for safe keeping.

Joanna, the outsider, is vitriolic about his dependence on his satellites. 'It's too dangerous for a little tinsel star to go twinkling off alone and unprotected,' she says sarcastically, but 'the firm' remains intact precisely because both they and Garry recognise the truth of this. The play contains episodes which come closer to French farce than anything else in Coward's *oeuvre*: but there is still a crucial difference. Garry's sense of self is never threatened, because every vicissitude prompts a therapeutic outburst, a monologue on anything from the state of the theatre to the prospect of a tour of 'what is admitted to be by everybody the most sinister continent there is': moreover, these outbursts are controlled, even fine-tuned, by the judicious comments of the firm'. 'It's a pity they're pulling down the Lyceum', says Henry acidly, and Garry switches off the *Angst* at once and has a drink. And when Joanna hides in the spare room from Henry and Morris, the action takes on the speed and energy of farce but the stakes which are being played for are different. No-one on stage has any interest in reputation or respectability; indeed the 'spare room' becomes a kind of running joke throughout the play and to 'lose a latch-key' and spend the night in it has a meaning perfectly clear to all. What is at risk, however, is the harmony of 'the firm.' Liz helps Joanna to hide while making it very clear that she will have to break with Garry:

JOANNA:

I suppose you're still in love with Garry yourself?

LIZ:

Not in the least, but even if I were it's entirely beside the point. I certainly love him. I love Henry and Morris too. We've all been devoted to one another for many years, and it would take more than you to break it up permanently. But I'm not taking any risks of you even upsetting it temporarily. You're going to do what I tell you.

JOANNA:

And what if I don't?

LIZ:

You'll be out, my dear, with all of us, for ever.

Charm may have its problems, in that it draws others into its net almost against its will; the mask may become a trap. But when charm is a business it can also create

friendship; the common task of manipulating it brings 'the firm' together. Outsiders may be hurt by it or excluded from it, but it is no longer locked in the dilemma of Elyot and Amanda, who cannot bear either to be taken at face value or to be seen through. Paradoxically, this play which celebrates stardom and egoism also celebrates comradeship and values it more highly than individual erotic passion.

Garry was also Coward's last real 'whacking good part' until the afterword of *Suite in Three Keys.* He appeared in his own plays and those of others after *Present Laughter,* but its delayed London opening in 1943 was the last occasion on which he simultaneously celebrated himself and the commercial theatre which shaped him, in a role which seems specifically designed to allow the actor's own pleasure in theatricality to have fullest play. After this the 'theatre of tomorrow', which he had incarnated in the role of the appalling Roland and shut up in a cupboard, was to become too powerful to ignore and too certain of its own intellectual strength to fear this kind of ridicule. But with his five major comedies, Coward had established his own place in the theatrical order. As Robert Bolt pointed out in a reply to Coward's strictures on the New Wave, 'We are truly sorry our first effort at a vintage of our own should taste so nasty to a cultivated palate . . . But it can't be helped. We think that other bottle is quite, quite empty. It was Mr. Coward who had the last of it.'[24]

Notes

1. *Not Yet the Dodo and Other Verses,* Heinemann 1967, p. 34.

2. Graves and Hodge, *The Long Weekend,* Four Square 1961, p. 143.

3. Sheridan Morley, *A Talent to Amuse,* Penguin 1974, p. 388.

4. Cole Lesley, *The Life of Noel Coward,* Jonathan Cape 1976, p. 139.

5. *Present Indicative,* Heinemann 1937, p. 393.

6. *Present Indicative,* p. 395.

7. Sheridan Morley, *Gertrude Lawrence,* Weidenfeld and Nicolson 1981, p. 101.

8. *New Statesman,* vol. 36, 11 December 1930.

9. *Weekend Review,* 4 October 1930.

10. *Play Parade I,* Heinemann 1934, p. xvii.

11. *Observer,* 29 January 1939.

12. *Observer,* 29 January 1939.

13. John Lahr, *Coward the Playwright,* Methuen 1982, p. 85.

14. John Lahr, *Coward the Playwright,* p. 82.

15. *Present Indicative,* pp. 158-9.

16. Maurice Zolotow, *Stagestruck,* Heinemann 1965, p. 132.

17. O'Neill, *Strange Interlude,* Jonathan Cape 1928, p. 112.

18. *The Times,* 26 January 1939.

19. Sheridan Morley, *Review Copies,* Robson 1974, p. 220.

20. *The Noel Coward Diaries,* Payn and Morley, Weidenfeld and Nicolson 1982, p. 6, April 1941.

21. Gareth Lloyd Evans, *The Language of Modern Drama,* Dent 1977, p. 29.

22. Keith Thomas, *Religion and the Decline of Magic,* Penguin 1973, p. 717.

23. Lahr, *Coward the Playwright,* p. 32.

24. *Sunday Times,* 29 January 1961.

Milton Levin (essay date 1989)

SOURCE: Levin, Milton. "'Just the Echo of a Sigh.'" In *Noël Coward, Updated Edition,* pp. 21-59. Boston: Twayne Publishers, 1989.

[*In the following essay, Levin explores Coward's serious plays, maintaining that while they are worth consideration, their shortcomings have prevented them from being as well regarded as his comedies.*]

There is a photograph of Noël Coward by Mark Swain[1] that comes about as close as any single item could to capturing the most popular image of the man. Dressed in a dinner jacket (the photograph almost whispers "impeccably dressed"), Coward stands in a fashionable slouch, left hand in jacket pocket, the thumb outside the pocket, a king-sized cigarette in a long, silver-trimmed holder in the raised right hand, and his head is tilted back. There is a carnation in the lapel buttonhole and an impressive triangle of handkerchief above the breast pocket. The smile is not quite there. Sophistication, aplomb, polish, and a touch of insolence—all these, and more, seem embodied here. How gratifying that the author of *Private Lives,* of *Design for Living,* and of *Present Laughter* should really look the part. When he appeared on the stage in a Las Vegas night club dressed like this, who would mistake him for anybody else? In any final evaluation of Coward's work, this suave figure must take first place, but there are other Noël Cowards, at least one of whom is a far more serious, although hardly somber, figure.

Coward as composer, as performer, and, pre-eminently, as the writer of comedy has overshadowed the writer of serious plays. He wrote over a dozen such works, many of which were very successful in production and some of which must be rated equally successful artistically within the narrow limits of their intentions. It is, however, that very narrowness of intention and of subject matter that makes the serious plays less important than the comedies and makes a consideration of the serious plays a logical prelude to a discussion of the comedies. The comedies are not only superior as a whole, but they often show Coward's limitations as a serious dramatist converted into assets. But "less important" does not mean "unimportant." Coward's skills are as evident and as impressive in *Cavalcade* as in *Blithe Spirit,* and *Still Life* is a beautifully constructed one-act play. Yet, while skill can itself be a major source of delight in a comedy, it is expected to serve some larger purpose if a serious play is to demand attention beyond the moment of reading or performance. Coward rarely attempted to deal with such larger purposes, and it is this more than anything that gives his serious work, for all its polish and theatrical power, a secondary but very respectable place.

Coward's serious plays range from the already mentioned Ruritanian melodrama in *The Queen Was in the Parlour* to the quiet, realistic vignettes of *Still Life*; from the psychological drama of *The Vortex,* almost classical in maintaining the unities, to the panorama of *Cavalcade.* What they have in common is best explained in negative terms. Although many end unhappily, they have nothing of the tragic about them either in intent or in execution; few of them aim at eliciting more than a quiet sob or, as Coward put it in the song "I'll See You Again," "just the echo of a sigh." Although some deal with situations that an Ibsen or a Shaw might have used to demonstrate or argue questions of public morality or political philosophy, only *Post-Mortem* (significantly the only one of Coward's published plays never to have been performed) can be said to have a thesis. And, although all these plays are realistic in the sense of accepting the conventions of the fourth wall, of representational scenery, of careful attention to the passage of time, and of the logical, plausible plot, Coward rarely comes to terms on a deeper level with his characters in the way of the realistic playwright like Ibsen, Chekov, or Arthur Miller—instead, each character is conceived in comic terms; that is, two-dimensionally, more as an embodiment of certain premises than as an individual with individual motivation.

THE VORTEX

Quite different conclusions were forecast when *The Vortex* appeared in 1924. Although it was not the first Coward play to be produced, it was the first to capture both public and critical acclaim; the history of its first production is almost the prototype of the story of the new, serious playwright. Norman Macdermott had, in 1920, converted "an old drill hall in Hampstead into what was, by 1924, the flourishing try-out and repertory theatre, the Everyman." Coward submitted some plays to him and, although Macdermott tended to prefer *Hay Fever,* "as there was no good part for me in that, I managed to sheer him over to *The Vortex.*"[2]

The road to opening night was strewn with obstacles. Initial casting was difficult because the rule at the Everyman was that all actors appeared at a fixed salary of five pounds a week; the theater depended, therefore, on actors who were willing to take a chance on appearing in a success that could be moved to the West End where salaries would revert to normal. And this unpleasant play by a virtually unknown playwright looked to many suspiciously like a failure. Once casting was finally completed, Macdermott revealed that the play would have to be abandoned unless an additional two hundred pounds were raised, but Coward turned to Michael Arlen, whose *The Green Hat* had just become a bestseller, and raised the money. Then one of the leading actresses developed diphtheria and had to be replaced; and, even more serious, Kate Cutler, for whom Coward had written the role of the mother, became incensed about the way Coward had enlarged his own part, that of Nicky, in rewriting the last act, and resigned from the cast a week before the opening. In desperation, Coward turned to Lilian Braithwaite, an actress he greatly admired but who seemed to most people, especially to Macdermott, completely wrong for the role. Nonetheless, she was engaged. Coward wrote:

> Meanwhile, I was having a spirited duel with the Lord Chamberlain (Lord Cromer) in his office in St. James's. He had at first refused point-blank to grant a licence for the play because of the unpleasantness of its theme, and it was only after a long-drawn-out argument, during which, I must say, he was charming and sympathetic, that I persuaded him that the play was little more than a moral tract. With a whimsical and rather weary smile he finally granted the licence. . . .[3]

The licence was granted only a few hours before the opening on 25 November 1924, and the favorable response of the audience proved that all the agony and confusion had been well worth it. *The Vortex* played at the Everyman for twelve performances, and then moved to the West End for another two hundred and twenty-four. The next fall Coward appeared in the play in New York, where it was received with equal enthusiasm.

The Vortex, a mixture of Ibsen and Maugham, has also a strong suggestion of *Hamlet* in the play's ancestry. Florence Lancaster, who is probably in her fifties, is motivated by a desire to remain young-looking, physically desirable, and adored by all. She is having an affair with Tom Veryan, the latest of the young men who

have helped her retain illusions about her youth and beauty. Her husband, David, has long since retreated into the background, manages his farm and closes his eyes to his wife's behavior. Their son, Nicky, twenty-four, returns from a year of music study in Paris and announces that he is tentatively engaged to Bunty Mainwaring. Florence conceals her concern and invites Bunty to a weekend house party.

There Bunty and Tom, who had known each other before, fall in love; Florence discovers them kissing, and against a background of wild jazz played by Nicky at the piano, she hysterically orders the two young people out of her house. In the last act, mother and son confront each other. He gets her to confess that her young men have been more to her than handsome escorts, and he confesses that he has been taking dope. The play ends with both promising to try to be different, but the future looks bleak. Nicky says early in the last act: "To-morrow morning I shall see things quite differently. That's true—that's the tragedy of it, and you won't see. To-morrow morning I *shall* see things quite differently. All this will seem unreal—a nightmare—the machinery of our lives will go on again and gloss over the truth as it always does—and our chance will be gone forever."[4] The chance is *not* lost; nonetheless, the character of the mother makes the possibility of profound reform unlikely.

The form of the play is that of *Ghosts*; indeed, the final moments of *The Vortex,* where mother and son are alone on the stage and all illusions are shattered, are more than just an echo of Ibsen's play. Florence Lancaster's plight is not so desperate as Mrs. Alving's, but there is clearly the same sense of the abyss open before the heroine's feet: "She sits quite still, staring in front of her—the tears rolling down her cheeks, and she is stroking Nicky's hair mechanically in an effort to calm him."

The style, however, is more like Maugham's. Especially in the first act, the tone is witty and flippant. Most of the exposition is carried by Helen and Pauncefort (called "Pawnie"), two of Florence's most sophisticated friends, and they introduce the two central characters and suggest the nature of the theme:

PAWNIE:

> I expect Florence will just go on and on, then suddenly become quite beautifully old, and go on and on still more.

HELEN:

> It's too late now for her to become beautifully old, I'm afraid. She'll have to be young indefinitely.

PAWNIE:

> I don't suppose she'll mind that, but it's trying for David.

HELEN:

And fiendish for Nicky.

PAWNIE:

Oh, no, my dear; you're quite wrong there. I'm sure Nicky doesn't care a damn.

HELEN:

He only takes things seriously in spurts, but still he's very young.

PAWNIE:

Do you really think that's a good excuse?

HELEN:

No, I'm afraid not, especially when so much depends on it.

PAWNIE:

What does depend on it?

HELEN:

Everything—his life's happiness.

PAWNIE:

Don't be so terribly intense, dear. . . .

. . . . .

HELEN:

He may have had everything he wanted, but he's had none of the things he really needs.

PAWNIE:

Are you talking socially or spiritually?

HELEN:

You're quite right, Pawnie, you wouldn't be so beautifully preserved if you'd wasted any of your valuable time on sincerity.

(99-100)

Compared with Maugham's *The Constant Wife,* for example, Coward's characters are drawn more broadly, and the insults are more obvious and cruel. The question is just how successfully Coward can modulate from such a brittle tone into one more suitable for the revelations and recognitions of the last act.

Pawnie's comment, "Don't be so terribly intense," reveals his callous dilettantism but is also a justifiable deflation of Helen's oracular, but trite comment. Something similar can be said for much of the third act; while the son is intent on lacerating his mother's conscience, the language lags behind:

NICKY:

You ran after him up the stairs because your vanity wouldn't let you lose him. It isn't that you love him—that would be easier—you never love anyone, you only love them loving you—all your so-called passion and temperament is false—your whole existence has degenerated into an endless empty craving for admiration and flattery—and then you say you've done no harm to anybody. Father used to be a clever man, with a strong will and a capacity for enjoying everything—I can remember him like that—and now he's nothing—a complete nonentity because his spirit's crushed. How could it be otherwise? You've let him down consistently for years—and God knows I'm nothing for him to look forward to—but I might have been if it hadn't been for you—

FLORENCE:

Don't talk like that. Don't—don't. It can't be such a crime being loved—it can't be such a crime being happy—

NICKY:

You're not happy—you're never happy—you're fighting—fighting all the time to keep your youth and your looks—because you can't bear the thought of living without them—as though they mattered in the end.

FLORENCE [*HYSTERICALLY*]:

What does anything matter—ever?

(171)

The weakness of these speeches is apparent: they are impressive but full of empty abstractions. Too much sounds like the author's résumé rather than the passionate outcry of a son who has, in the course of an hour, been jilted by his fiancée, discovered his mother's adultery, and realized the true nature of his mother's character and the disastrous effect it has had on both his father and himself.

Of course, language alone is not at fault, for an author's style is inseparable from his whole approach to character and situation. Coward said, "My original motive in *The Vortex* was to write a good play with a whacking good part in it for myself, and I am thankful to say, with a few modest reservations, that I succeeded."[5] Certainly the role of Nicky has a great deal to offer a performer, particularly a young one who cares little for subtleties and much for powerful effects. Nicky is the equal of any character in his ability to trade witty insults, yet he has an anguished soul beneath; he is a competent pianist; he is a dope addict; he is in love; he is a doting son; and finally, he must face the painful, but ever-so-theatrical task of castigating his own beloved mother.

All is not equally clear or convincing. What, for example, is the nature of the relationship between Nicky and Bunty? Coward keeps the action moving fast, shifts masks quickly; and somehow the impression of a complex character is created. The mother's role is almost as tempting to an actress, but, like Nicky's, it is only a "whacking good part." They are not convincing, full-drawn characters; and some of the others—the father, for example—are hardly characters at all, and exist only because tangible actors are on stage.

Nonetheless, considering the author's age and the general situation of the English theater in 1924, *The Vortex* deserved its success, as well as the hope that Coward was a new playwright from whom much could be expected. Aside from Shaw, there were few British playwrights whose work went beyond fairly conventional melodrama and light comedy, and none of these was so young, so clever, and so shocking as Coward. None of the new plays had the immediacy and nervous energy of *The Vortex* which seemed to go to the very heart of modern decadence and corruption (and decadence among the upper classes always seems more shocking than elsewhere); nor had anyone before Coward had the audacity to make such a sympathetic display of dope addiction, gigolos, and mother-baiting. And none of the new plays came from such an impressive young man—author, actor, director, composer, and, thanks to the machinery of publicity, bon vivant.

Following *The Vortex* Coward produced, in rapid succession, a new revue, *On with the Dance* (1925); two new comedies, *Fallen Angels* and *Hay Fever* (both 1925); a Ruritanian melodrama, *The Queen Was in the Parlour* (1926); and another serious play, *Easy Virtue* (New York, 1925; London, 1926). Most of these, except for the revue, are works that were substantially completed before *The Vortex* was produced. All were not greeted with equal enthusiasm, but Coward's stock remained high. His ability to extract a maximum of theatrical power from meager materials was undeniable.

EASY VIRTUE

In the opening scene of *Easy Virtue* (1925), the Whittakers—the Colonel, Mrs. Whittaker, and their two daughters, Marion and Hilda—await the arrival of John, the only son, who has recently married a woman they have never met. When John arrives, his wife, Larita, proves to be an extremely elegant woman, older than John, and, to the Whittakers' dismay, divorced. Although Colonel Whittaker treats Larita kindly, the other members of the family are cold. Larita is dreadfully bored; John's hearty dedication to tennis and other outdoor sports revolts her; and the hatred emanating from the other women grows more intense daily. The situation comes to a head three months later, and the climax is precipitated by Hilda's discovery of a newspaper account of a suicide fifteen years earlier in which Larita seems to have had some responsibility.

Hilda's revelation of this story causes a quarrel in which Larita charges Marion with prudery and repressed desires, and Mrs. Whittaker orders Larita to spend the

evening in her room, although this is the evening when the Whittakers are giving a dance. At the height of the dance, Larita appears, extravagantly dressed and bejeweled. She explains to Sarah Hurst, John's childhood sweetheart, that she is going away and asks Sarah to take care of John, implying that Sarah and John should soon be able to marry. Then, telling no one about her intentions, she walks out to her waiting car, and the curtain falls.

Coward's own comments on the play deserve to be quoted almost in full:

> From the 'eighties onwards until the outbreak of the 1914-18 War the London theatre was enriched by a series of plays, notably by Somerset Maugham or Arthur Pinero, which were described as "drawing-room dramas." I suppose that the apotheosis of these was *The Second Mrs. Tanqueray,* but there were many others. . . . All of these "drawing-room dramas" dealt with the psychological and social problems of the upper middle classes. The characters in them were, as a general rule, wealthy, well-bred, articulate and motivated by the exigencies of the world to which they belonged. This world was snobbish, conventional, polite, and limited by its own codes and rules of behavior, and it was the contravention of these codes and rules—to our eyes so foolish and old-fashioned—that supplied the dramatic content of most of the plays I have mentioned. The heroine of *His House in Order* [Pinero] rebelled against the narrow pomposities of the family into which she had married. Lady Frederick [in Maugham's play of the same name], by gallantly and daringly exposing the secrets of her dressing-table, deflected the attentions of a young man who was infatuated by her into a more suitable alliance. In a recent revival of the play, this scene still proved to be dramatically impeccable. The unhappy Paula Tanqueray tried valiantly to live down her earlier moral turpitude, but ultimately gave up the struggle and perished offstage in an aura of righteous atonement, just before the final curtain. It is easy nowadays to laugh at these vanished moral attitudes, but they were poignant enough in their time because they were true. Those high-toned drawing-room histrionics are over and done with. Women with pasts to-day receive far more enthusiastic social recognition than women without pasts. The narrow-mindedness, the moral righteousness, and the over-rigid social codes have disappeared, but with them have gone much that was graceful, well-behaved, and endearing. It was in a mood of nostalgic regret at the decline of such conventions that I wrote *Easy Virtue.* When it was produced, several critics triumphantly pounced on the fact that the play was similar in form and tone and plot to the plays of Pinero. I myself was unimpressed by their perception, for the form and tone and plot of a Pinero play was exactly what I had tried to achieve.[6]

This passage is very curious indeed. What is said about the prewar "drawing-room dramas" is well and sympathetically said and is another sign of how thoroughly Coward was himself a product of those years although most of his plays present an up-to-date mask to the world. However, the relevance of the last few sentences to *Easy Virtue* is a bit difficult to find, for what conventions are viewed nostalgically? Certainly what little there is in the play of the "graceful, the well-behaved and the endearing" belongs to the woman with a past, not to the narrow-minded society in which she feels herself trapped. Anyway, "the narrow-mindedness, the moral righteousness, and the over-rigid social codes" have certainly not disappeared, if the Whittaker household is in any way representative; in fact, with the aid of some simple Freudian formulations, Coward demonstrates that these attitudes have not only remained but have grown more sinister since they take their origins in twisted psyches rather than in "the exigencies of the world" to which the characters belong. Could this, perhaps, have been his point, that what was once acceptable because it had social approval has become ugly when it is the manifestation of the dark subconscious? If this is the source of "nostalgic regret," the play is a rather oblique way of presenting it. Only one thing is quite accurate; "the form and tone and plot" are certainly those of a Pinero play.

Easy Virtue is "*The Second Mrs. Tanqueray* brought down to date,"[7] and *The Vortex* turned upside down. Except for Colonel Whittaker who, like the father in *The Vortex,* represents solid sensibleness, and Sarah Hurst, a well-balanced young woman, all the positive values lie with Larita and her world. Yet how does it differ from Florence Lancaster's world? Larita is presented as generous and broad-minded, well-read, and well-informed, and as having as her only illusion the belief that she could find contentment with John, but the Whittaker women are presented as provincial, narrow-minded, repressed, and emasculating.

But Mrs. Whittaker and Marion are caricatures, and Larita's depth must be taken too much on faith. Larita's conversations with Charles Burleigh, the only person who "talks her language," are trivial and gossipy, and her past, presented in veiled terms justifies James Agate's statement that in this play Coward "has attained to that pure idealism which prompts the schoolboy who has been taken to see La Dame aux Camelias to believe for the next ten years that a cocotte is the noblest work of man if not of God."[8]

Coward charged that Jane Cowl, who played Larita both in New York and London, distorted the play by stressing its tragic rather than its comic overtones and by responding to the Whittakers with deep emotion rather than with exasperation. To the reader, however, these distinctions do not alter the basic nature of the play. What Coward most regretted about the passing of the Pinero-type play, it would seem, was not the actual world it may have mirrored, but the opportunity for striking black and white contrasts and for more "whacking good" parts.

THE QUEEN WAS IN THE PARLOUR

The Queen Was in the Parlour (1926) exploits yet another source of theatrical excitement, pure hokum. Nadya, the widow of the Archduke Alexander of Krayia, as an expatriate in Paris has found true love with Sabien Pastal, whom she plans to marry. Her peace is shattered by the arrival of General Krish who brings the news of the assassination of the king of Krayia, for Nadya must return to be their queen. Reluctantly, she writes a letter of farewell to Sabien and leaves for Krayia. A year later, on the eve of Nadya's marriage to Prince Keri of Zalgar, Sabien finds his way to her, asks to spend one last night, and Nadya agrees. Unfortunately, it is also the night chosen by dissident forces in Krayia to begin a revolution. General Krish and Prince Keri try to get Nadya to escape, but she, *en negligée,* faces the crowd from her balcony, tells them to shoot her—if they have the courage—and, with Prince Keri beside her, recaptures the people's loyalty. There is a shot in Nadya's bedroom, and General Krish enters, saying "Your Majesty, a man has been shot trying to get in at your window." Thus, both the peace of Krayia and Nadya's honor are preserved; somehow, adultery before the coronation and a wedding doesn't count.

Despite some moments of comedy and some clever, tongue-in-cheek allusions to the fountainhead of Ruritanian romance, Anthony Hope's *The Prisoner of Zenda,* Coward's play is meant to be taken seriously. This effect may still be possible for a certain audience for whom royal figures exist in a rarefied atmosphere, but *The Queen Was in the Parlour* must now seem dated and inane to most people.

SIROCCO

In *Sirocco*—originally written in 1921, but considerably rewritten before if was produced in 1927—the heroine is Lucy, a goodlooking, naturally quiet Englishwoman still in her early twenties. She has been married for three years to Stephen Griffin, an unimaginative, thoroughly conventional executive in an oil company. As the play opens, he is leaving for some weeks in Tunis, but he stolidly refuses to let Lucy go with him, insisting that she will be much better off with his mother and the rest of the English colony in Bellagualia, an Italian Riviera resort. His inability to comprehend Lucy's boredom with the smug, parochial English group not only intensifies her irritation and despair but leaves her open to the suave advances of Sirio Marson, a painter of mixed Italian and English ancestry, and a polished philanderer.

At a local *festa,* where the English behave more fatuously than ever, Lucy succumbs to Sirio's advances, and they go off to his studio in Florence. A week later, Lucy finds that most of the glamour has evaporated; she is appalled by Sirio's slovenly habits, his amorality, his refusal to think beyond the pleasures of the moment. While Sirio is out, Lucy has a visit from her husband and mother-in-law. Stephen "magnanimously" offers Lucy the chance to return to him, but his motives are transparently selfish. Lucy sends the Griffins away, but, when Sirio returns, she finds his hedonism as repulsive as her husband's respectability. They quarrel and come to blows, Sirio storms out, and Lucy, just before the curtain "[*suddenly lifts her arms above her head. With exultance*]" and says, "I'm free—free for the first time in my life. [*Her face changes.*] God help me! [*She leans on the table and buries her head in her arms*]."⁹

Sirocco was possibly the most thorough failure of Coward's career. On the opening night, the audience received the first act dully, but in the middle of the second act "the storm broke" during the love scene: "The gallery shrieked with mirth and made sucking sounds when he kissed her, and from then onwards proceeded to punctuate every line with catcalls and various other animal noises. The last act was chaos from beginning to end. The gallery, upper circle, and pit hooted and yelled, while the stalls, boxes, and dress circle whispered and shushed. Most of the lines weren't heard at all. . . . The curtain finally fell amid a bedlam of sound. . . ."¹⁰

Coward suspected that the demonstration had been organized by enemies, and he may well have been right since it is difficult now to understand what in the play could have created such a response. Although the execution falters, the basic outline has a good deal to recommend it. Indeed, St. John Ervine found the moral substance of the play impressive:

> Mr. Coward has, in short, written a tract. *This,* he says in effect, is what all this cinema romance amounts to, something foul and sluttish and finally impossible. Routine affection may be, and no doubt is, devastatingly dull, but vamp-love, movie-passion—these are duller still, and those who mistake Hollywood for heaven are likely to land in hell. I protest against the assumption, now too commonly made, that Mr. Coward is a flippant youth who delights in the pretence that vice is virtue. The faults in this play are numerous . . . but all these faults are the faults of a young mind, made excessively indignant by what it conceives to be wrongs and injustices. His sincerity is transparent, and his motives . . . are generous.¹¹

In 1927, just a year after Rudolph Valentino's death, the comments about movie passion were surely more apropos than they seem to be now; Ivor Novello, who played Sirio, looks, in the photographs of the production, as if a resemblance to Valentino might well have been intended. The fact that Novello was already a popular movie actor also may have influenced Ervine to see the play as a commentary on the movies, but to the reader today this limits the play unnecessarily. Ervine is

right, however, in seeing that the basic nature of the play is moral and realistic. In fact, the audience's outrage is surely traceable in part to its refusal to accept the possibility of such things being true of a proper young Englishwoman.

The difficulty with *Sirocco* lies, as it does in *The Vortex* and in *Easy Virtue,* in the basically theatrical nature of the characters and the situation. Neither Lucy nor Sirio is clearly defined except insofar as conventional and abstract labels can be affixed. Lucy is young, beautiful, romantic, and, in the language of the sentimental novel, ready to be swept off her feet (but what has her life with her husband been like for the last three years? And why three years, except that for Coward this seems always to represent the outer limits of passion?). Sirio is the passionate Latin, magnetic and amoral.

These labels are hardly different in kind from those applicable to the minor characters, who are more reasonably stereotypes: Stephen is the stolid oaf; his mother, the dignified, but narrowminded dowager; Francine Trott, the hearty, overgrown schoolgirl; the Reverend Crutch, the complacent minister. Appropriate enough for comedy, and perhaps not altogether as stereotyped in 1927 as novelists and playwrights were to make them before that decade was over, these characters are hardly enough to carry the weight of a serious analysis of love and passion.

The same criticism applies to the situations. The *festa* in the second act is drawn in primary colors; the cold English are prudish and patronizing, and the hot-blooded Italians are uninhibited and "natural." With the aid of liberal servings of Asti, Sirio draws Lucy into his world, but not before Coward has invoked the deus ex machina. Sirio bravely stops a violent fight, is himself stabbed in the hand, and his bravery and injury combine to destroy Lucy's defenses. In the last act, another deus appears: a letter from Sirio's mother. Sirio's stepfather has run off with *his* mistress, and the mother wants Sirio home. Coming when it does, this letter conveniently serves to reinforce Lucy's disgust with the world into which she has wandered, helps to illuminate her finer moral character, and quickly gets Sirio off the stage and out of Lucy's life. In short, the plot progresses through coincidence rather than character.

Finally, the dialogue does not have the nervous energy, the mixture of wit and brutality, that keeps *The Vortex* afloat. Since the characters are quite outside the milieu with which Coward usually deals, the dialogue, both comic and serious, must also be on a much less sophisticated level. This play is fine so long as it concerns itself with pictures of the self-satisfied English abroad; but when Coward is faced by the problem of presenting his Latin lover, he oscillates between making Sirio impressively fluent and comically inept. For example, when Sirio's seductive powers are approaching their peak, he speaks like this: "You are like a deep pool in the rocks—nothing moving—very cool and still—but there is a little channel you know nothing about, and one day you will be taken by surprise. The great sea will come swirling in froth and foam and coloured bubbles, and you will be stirred to your depths—strange forces you never realized will be dragged to the surface. I am warning you" (55).

A week later, after passion has run its course and disillusion has set in, his fluency has diminished: "You are being capable—I hate you when you are capable. You are making the better of a bad job, eh? Rising to an occasion. For God's sake stop and let us both sit and scream." As for Lucy, in climactic moments she, like Nicky in **The Vortex,** resorts to speeches of analysis where something more powerful is called for:

> [*To her husband when he asks her to return with him*]: No, no—don't go—I must make you see—I want to make you understand that I'm sorry, really sorry for having upset you and made things difficult, but it's not as serious and important as you think it is—really and truly it isn't, because you don't love me, Stephen; you never have really, and I don't love you. We were silly to marry, and it's been a failure; it's no life for either of us just existing on and on without warmth until we're old—we're miles apart and always have been. Don't look like that, I'm not talking nonsense—it's from my heart all this—I want you to see—I want you to see—. . . . Let me speak—you must, this is probably the last time we shall ever see each other, and you must listen to me. If you had loved me, really loved me, this could never have happened—that's not an excuse, it's the truth.
>
> (74)

Perhaps in real life a Lucy might talk like this, but on the stage how very stale, flat and unprofitable her words sound.

Post-Mortem

Sirocco opened in London on 24 November 1927 and created for the moment a pause in Coward's mounting success and reputation. However, the next two years saw his career move forward with astonishing vigor. In January 1928 he appeared in the leading role of the London production of S. N. Behrman's *The Second Man*; in March of that year his revue, **This Year of Grace,** opened in London; in October **This Year of Grace** opened in New York, with Coward in the cast; in July 1929 **Bitter-Sweet** opened in London; in November the American company of **Bitter-Sweet** opened in New York. All of these were, in the press agent's word, "triumphs." When, on 29 November 1929, Coward set sail from San Francisco for a leisurely holiday in the Orient, the disaster of **Sirocco** was ancient history. On his return to England some months later, he had three

interesting items in his luggage: an unfinished and soon to be discarded novel, *Julian Kane*; the completed script for **Private Lives**; and "an angry little vilification of war called **Post-Mortem.**"

The genesis of **Post-Mortem** (1933) is outlined in *Present Indicative*. In Singapore, Coward had appeared as Stanhope in *Journey's End* as "an amusing experiment" and to help out a touring company called "The Quaints." On the boat from Ceylon to Marseilles, he wrote, "my mind was strongly affected by *Journey's End* and I had read several current war novels one after the other." Coward does not mention which war novels he had been reading: those like *A Farewell to Arms* and *All Quiet on the Western Front*—both published in 1929 and, along with *Journey's End,* part of a strong and fashionable movement to debunk war—or more sentimental work. In either case, Coward is concerned in his play with stressing two points: first, that life twelve years after the war is more empty, mindless and corrupt than ever; second, the chief proof of this state is that very few can face the truth about the war itself.

The play is cast in a mold of semi-fantasy. The first scene takes place in "a company headquarters in a quiet section of the Front Line in the spring of 1917." Discussion is stimulated by a particularly offensive item in the *Mercury,* a tabloid published by John Cavan's father; the item is an open letter to England, "I Gave My Son," by Lady Stagg-Mortimer. Cavan, as disgusted as the rest, is hopeful that after the war is over the public will eventually know the truth. Perry Lomas, a poet, is pessimistic: "Never, never, never! They'll never know whichever way it goes, victory or defeat. They'll smarm it all over with memorials and Rolls of Honour and Angels of Mons, and it'll look so noble and glorious in retrospect that they'll all start itching for another war, egged on by deaf old gentlemen in clubs who wish they were twenty years younger, and newspaper owners and oily financiers, and the splendid women of England happy and proud to give their sons and husbands and lovers, and even their photographs."[12]

John Cavan, who refuses to accept such a dark view, insists that "something will come out of it" and that he's "treading water, waiting to see": "I have a feeling that one might see the whole business just for a second before one dies. Like going under an anaesthetic, everything becomes blurred and enormous and then suddenly clears, just for the fraction of a fraction of a moment. Perhaps that infinitesimal moment is what we're all waiting for, really" (288). That "fraction of a fraction of a moment" occupies most of the rest of the play. A few minutes after making this speech, John goes out on a patrol. He is hit and carried back to the shelter; in his last moments of life, he finds himself projected forward into 1930.

Six scenes are devoted to John Cavan's visit to 1930. In the first and last he is with his mother; between these two scenes he calls on Monica, his former fiancée; then on Perry Lomas, who has recently published a book on the war that has caused considerable dismay; then goes to the offices of the *Mercury*, where his father has assembled a group of distinguished citizens who call for having Perry's book burned; and finally attends a dinner party with three of the officers who were with Cavan in France. His mother warns John at their first meeting that "There's nothing, nothing worth finding out," and the other scenes become increasingly painful as John realizes how true Perry's prophecy was. In the last scene, back at John's deathbed, he opens his eyes and says, "You were right, Perry—a poor joke!"

In *Post-Mortem* Coward *has* written a tract in which Perry Lomas, the poet, has the key speech:

> Nothing's happening, really. There are strides being made forward in science and equal sized strides being made backwards in hypocrisy. People are just the same: individually pleasant and collectively idiotic. Machinery is growing magnificently, people paint pictures of it and compose ballets about it, the artists are cottoning on to that very quickly because they're scared that soon there won't be any other sort of beauty left, and they'll be stranded with nothing to paint and nothing to write. Religion is doing very well. The Catholic Church still tops the bill as far as finance and general efficiency go. The Church of England is still staggering along without much conviction. . . . Christian Science is coming up smiling, a slightly superior smile, but always a smile. God is Love, there is no pain, Pain is error. Everything that isn't Love is error; like hell it is. Politically all is confusion, but that's nothing new. There's still poverty, unemployment, pain, greed, cruelty, passion, and crime. There's still meanness, jealousy, money, and disease. The competitive sporting spirit is being admirably fostered, particularly as regards the Olympic Games. A superb preparation for the next war, fully realized by everyone but the public that will be involved. The newspapers still lie over anything of importance, and the majority still believes them implicitly. The only real difference in post-war conditions is that there are so many women whose heartache will never heal. The rest is the same, only faster and more meretricious. The war is fashionable now, like a pleasantly harrowing film. . . . Go back to your mother for the time that's left, say good-bye to her, be sweet to her as you're sweet to everybody and just a little sweeter; that may be worth something, although it passes in a flash. . . . Hold close to your own love wherever it lies, don't leave it lonely while you wander about aimlessly in chaos searching for some half-formulated ideal. An ideal of what? Fundamental good in human nature! Bunk! Spiritual understanding? Bunk! God in some compassionate dream waiting to open your eyes to truth? Bunk! Bunk! Bunk! It's all a joke with nobody to laugh at it.
>
> (328-29)

Perry ends the scene by killing himself.

The despair is close to complete, and *Post-Mortem* goes far beyond being merely "an angry little vilification of war." If anything, it is the peace which is vilified; war is seen as having some value in itself:

JOHN:

> Have you completely forgotten that strange feeling we had in the war? Have you found anything in your lives to equal it in strength? A sort of splendid carelessness it was, holding us together. Cut off from everything we were used to, but somehow not lonely, except when we were on leave, or when letters came. Depending only upon the immediate moment. No past, no future, and no conviction of God. God died early in the war, for most of us. Can you remember our small delights? How exciting they were? Sleep, warmth, food, drink, unexpected comforts snatched out of turmoil, so simple in enjoyment, and so incredibly satisfying.
>
> (354)

Coward's own comments on *Post-Mortem* strike a note of humility:

> I wrote *Post-Mortem* with the utmost sincerity; this, I think, must be fairly obvious to anyone who reads it. In fact, I tore my emotions to shreds over it. The result was similar to my performance as Stanhope: confused, underrehearsed, and hysterical. Unlike my performance as Stanhope, however, it had some very fine moments. There is, I believe, some of the best writing I have ever done in it, also some of the worst. I have no deep regrets over it, as I know my intentions to have been of the purest. I passionately believed in the truth of what I was writing: too passionately. . . . Through lack of detachment and lack of real experience of my subject, I muddled the issues of the play. I might have done better had I given more time to it and less vehemence. However, it helped to purge my system of certain accumulated acids.[13]

Certainly those speeches that praise the glories and exaltation of brotherhood in battle reflect a lack of experience. Lack of detachment is evident in the scenes with the mother, for these scenes are virtually a parody of the maudlin stiff-upper-lip tradition. But, when Coward attacks postwar hypocrisy, he achieves a high level of satire.

By far the best scene in the play is that in the *Mercury* office. This scene, which at first suggests a revue sketch, soon goes far beyond this suggestion into a surrealistic, expressionistic sequence of considerable force, but it is quite out of keeping with the style of the rest of the play. The guiding genius of the scene is Alfred Borrow, city editor, who sees everything in journalistic clichés and distortions. Shortly after meeting John, Borrow begins to turn the moment into a newspaper story: "Return of Sir James Cavan's only son after thirteen years! His mother, a white-haired patrician lady, smiled at our special representative with shining eyes. 'My son,' she said simply. Just that, but in those two words the meed of mother love was welling over" (333). This last device, ascribing volumes of meaning to simple phrases, becomes a dominant motif, virtually a refrain:

BORROW:

"We're out to win," said Sir James Cavan's son smilingly. Just that, but in those simple words what wealth of feeling, what brave, brimming enthusiasm.

(334)

BORROW:

"Dad's right," he said. Just two simple words, but, somehow, somehow, one understood.

(344)

A technique used persistently in the scene, one reminiscent of the German expressionists, is that of making all the characters—except John, of course—utterly mechanical. They fail to hear a word John addresses to them; instead, each remains fixed in his own pattern of thought and statement. The climax is reached when Lady Stagg-Mortimer rises to speak; the secretary produces a typewritten sheet, and *Borrow reads the speech, while Lady Stagg-Mortimer gesticulates and opens and shuts her mouth silently.*" The scene ends with John's speech praising death, destruction, and despair; and it is set to a background of "God and Country" being chanted *in a monotone, quite softly*" by Sir James Cavan, Alfred Borrow, Lady Stagg-Mortimer, Miss Beaver and the Bishop of Ketchworth (347). Only in this scene is there a successful blending of message and dramatic form. Most of the other scenes—the one with Perry is a partial exception—are static, discursive, and too often extended far beyond the demands of the point being illustrated.

Post-Mortem is an anomaly in the canon of Coward's work. Although its most forceful moments are theatrical in the best sense of the word, Coward insists that it "was not actually written for the theatre," and there is no record that it has ever been produced. It appeared in *Play Parade*, volume 1, published in 1933, as one of "the most representative of my works," but there are certainly no other Coward plays at all like it in fact, other works of his dealing with war take quite a different view. Are its dark pessimism and despair "representative"? If such moods played any significant part in Coward's personality, he did a successful job of keeping them out of his work.

Although one would think at first glance that *Post-Mortem*, presented as a work in which he "had a lot to say," would be a key in discussing Coward's work, the play turns out to be more a sport than a revelation. True, some of the attitudes appear in other places, and the overall tone might be taken as a deeper, darker version of the disillusionment that lightly shadows the

edges of most of Coward's plays. However, *Post-Mortem* makes most sense as a transient phenomenon that is not inconsistent with the main body of his work but is not representative of it.

CAVALCADE

Whatever prevented *Post-Mortem* from being produced, it was certainly not any technical difficulty; few plays call for more elaborate mechanical ingenuity and production finesse than Coward's next play. *Cavalcade* (1931) was quite consciously conceived of as a spectacle for London's Coliseum: "I felt an urge to test my producing powers on a large scale. My mind's eyes visualized a series of tremendous mob scenes—the storming of the Bastille—the massacre of the Huguenots—I believe even the Decline and Fall of the Roman Empire flirted with me for a little."[14] After dismissing many such subjects—the Second Empire lingered longest—Coward came across a bound volume of the *Illustrated London News,* and the first pictures he saw in it were of a troopship leaving for the Boer War. This stimulated his imagination. Starting with that scene, Coward wrote a series of scenes covering the period between New Year's Eve, 1899, and an evening in 1930. The period is almost exactly that of Coward's own life (he was born a little more than a week before Christmas of 1899); and at least one episode in the play, the seaside "concert party," is autobiographical.

The play consists of two interwoven stories, that of the Marryots, an upper-class family (Robert Marryot is knighted about half way through the play), and that of the Bridges, originally servants to the Marryots, later owners of a pub. Significant moments in their lives are entwined with important moments of English history: both Robert Marryot and Alfred Bridges fight in the Boer War; Robert Marryot has a place in the funeral procession for Queen Victoria; Edward Marryot and his bride are lost on the *Titanic*; Joey Marryot, who has been having an affair with Fanny Bridges, is lost in World War I. Other scenes take place against backgrounds reflecting current tastes and activities.

Cavalcade invites a purely statistical discussion: there are twenty-two scenes, using a total of sixteen settings; the original program lists forty roles, plus "crowds, soldiers, sailors, guests, etc."; Coward claims the production required three thousand, seven hundred costumes; the Drury Lane Theatre, where the play was eventually presented, needed two new hydraulic lifts to handle the production (the unavailability of the Coliseum made Coward dispense with a revolving stage); and, following four hundred and five performances, *Cavalcade* was made with very little revision into a highly successful film.

The dramatic scenes occupy only a part of the play, and much of the impact depends on music: "The emotional basis of *Cavalcade* was undoubtedly music. The whole story was threaded onto a string of popular melodies. This ultimately was a big contributing factor to its success. Popular tunes probe the memory more swiftly than anything else."[15] There was also Coward's original music, especially the music for "Mirabelle" (Coward's version of the popular operetta) and the "Twentieth-Century Blues" for the final night-club scene.

Other devices, many drawn from the films, were used successfully. In the course of many scenes, and frequently in the darkness between them, voices of newsboys shouted headlines. Over the proscenium, the date of each scene appeared in lights. There were also a number of scenes that depended on a combination of visual effects and sounds but had little or no dialogue. Part 1, scene 6 is in Kensington Gardens, 27 January 1901; there is no dialogue: *"everyone is in black and they walk slowly as though perpetually conscious of the country's mourning. Even the children are in black and one woman leading a large brown dog has tied an enormous black crepe bow on to his collar."* Part 2, scene 7, one of the most effective in production, follows in its entirety:

> Above the proscenium 1914 glows in lights. It changes to 1915, 1916, 1917 and 1918. Meanwhile, soldiers march uphill endlessly. Out of darkness into darkness. Sometimes they sing gay songs, sometimes they whistle, sometimes they march silently, but the sound of their tramping feet is unceasing. Below the vision of them brightly-dressed, energetic women appear in pools of light, singing stirring recruiting songs—"Sunday I walk out with a soldier," "We don't want to lose you," etc., etc. With 1918 they fade away, as also does the vision of the soldiers, although the soldiers can still be heard far off, marching and singing their songs.[16]

Clearly, then, *Cavalcade* is a spectacle of which the sense can only partially be recaptured by reading the text or by looking at pictures of the production. *Cavalcade* was in part an attempt to adapt cinematic techniques to the stage, and it was certainly one of the last attempts to compete with the camera on these grounds. Now that the films have proved, even in the case of *Cavalcade* itself, that they can do such things much better, it is doubtful whether the play could ever again be produced on stage. Not even Coward's most elaborate revues and operettes can compare in complexity.

Nonetheless, the text has a great deal of interest. Some of the bitterness of *Post-Mortem* finds its way into the play, albeit in a muted form. Jane Marryot, like John Cavan's mother, represents the strongest antiwar position, and one of her speeches (when the beginning of World War I is announced) echoes the sentiments of the earlier play: "Drink to the war, then, if you want to. I'm not going to. I can't! Rule Britannia! Send us victorious, happy and glorious! Drink, Joey, you're only a baby still, but you're old enough for war. Drink like the Germans are drinking, to Victory and Defeat, and stupid, tragic sorrow. But leave me out of it, please!" (183). Furthermore, the last scene, "Evening—1930," begins with Fanny's singing the "Twentieth-Century Blues," a song of disillusion, boredom and near-despair:

> When the song is finished, people rise from table and dance without apparently any particular enjoyment; it is the dull dancing of habit. The lights fade away from everything but the dancers, who appear to be rising in the air. They disappear and down stage left six "incurables" in blue hospital uniform are sitting making baskets. They disappear and Fanny is seen singing her song for a moment, then far away up stage a jazz band is seen playing wildly. Then down stage Jane and Robert standing with glasses of champagne held aloft, then Ellen sitting in front of a radio loud speaker; then Margaret dancing with a young man. The visions are repeated quicker and quicker, while across the darkness runs a Riley light sign spelling out news. Noise grows louder and louder. Steam rivets, loud speakers, jazz bands, aeroplane propellers, etc., until the general effect is complete chaos.

> (198-99)

Neither attitude is, however, left to remain as a final statement. Jane's earlier bitterness is balanced by her toast of New Year's Eve, 1929, a toast that became the best-remembered and most honored speech in the play: "Now, then, let's couple the Future of England with the past of England. The glories and victories and triumphs that are over, and the sorrows that are over, too. Let's drink to our sons who made part of the pattern and to our hearts that died with them. Let's drink to the spirit of gallantry and courage, that made a strange heaven out of unbelievable Hell, and let's drink to the hope that one day this country of ours, which we love so much, will find dignity and greatness and peace again" (197).

As for the final scene, after achieving chaos, "Suddenly it all fades into darkness and silence and away at the back a Union Jack glows through the blackness. The lights slowly come up and the whole stage is composed of massive tiers, upon which stand the entire Company. The Union Jack flies over their heads as they sing 'God Save the King'" (199).

When Coward appeared for the curtain speech he said, "It was one of the few occasions of my life that I have ever walked on to a stage not knowing what I was going to say." He delivered "a rather incoherent little speech which finished with the phrase: 'I hope that this play has made you feel that, in spite of the troublous time we are living in, it is still pretty exciting to be English.'"[17] It was certainly a most appropriate curtain line, and a good deal truer to Coward's usual feelings than the despair of *Post-Mortem*.

Cavalcade, a theatrical triumph on a large scale, dazzlingly displayed all of Coward's theatrical talents except his acting, and demonstrated his command of the whole range of popular theater. Examination of one scene, that of Queen Victoria's funeral, reveals how very adept Coward had become. The scene is set in the Marryot drawing-room, a large room with two small balconies overlooking the street. The scene begins quietly and domestically with Jane's serving cocoa and trying to keep the children in line. At first, references to the queen are muted. Then the cortege is sighted, and the servants are called in. The Marryots and their guests stand on one balcony, the servants on another. Joe must be reprimanded for throwing cake, and Jane worries about Bridges' catching cold, but finally there is silence for a moment. As the music of the death march nears, the children grow more excited and must again be reminded to stand at attention. Persons in the cortege are pointed out. Then, again, there are no words, as everyone stands stiffly; the music is at its loudest. When the music begins to die away, Cook bursts into tears, and then only two lines are spoken before the lights fade:

JANE:

Five kings riding behind her.

JOE:

Mum, she must have been a very little lady.

(158)

The scene is a model of economy and interwoven themes. There is the grief of the adults counterpointed against the innocent exuberance of the children. However, even the children begin to comprehend; Joe's last line is a masterpiece of sentimental compression and still has the power to moisten eyes when the scene is done as a one-act sketch. There is the sense of ordinary life going forward in a well-to-do but in no way extraordinary household against a background of national mourning that affects all. All is beautifully calculated, balanced and smooth.

If the play seems trite and obvious today, much of that is no doubt due to its very success and to the pattern it helped to set: as a sentimental chronicle, it antedates such works as Laurence Houseman's *Victoria Regina* (1935), Marcel Achard's *Auprès de ma blonde* (1945; adapted by S. N. Behrman in 1949 as *I Know My Love*), Jan de Hartog's *The Four-Poster* (1951), and countless films. Coward himself was to return to a variant of the form in **This Happy Breed,** both as a play and a film.

POINT VALAINE

In typical Coward fashion, **Cavalcade** was followed by **Words and Music,** a work of quite a different type, and one of his most successful revues. This was followed in turn by **Design for Living,** in which the Lunts as actors,

and Coward as both writer and actor, displayed their skill in a high comedy. Then came **Conversation Piece,** "a romantic comedy with music," set in Brighton in 1811, in which Coward played a French aristocrat. As if this were not enough variety, and as if he were anxious to repay the Lunts by providing them with a piece that would demonstrate their versatility, Coward wrote **Point Valaine** (1935).

The play is dedicated to William Somerset Maugham, and so it should be. It takes place in Maugham country, a small, semi-tropical island, during the rainy season; the specific locale is a hotel that was once a mission building. The emotional climate is as overheated as the geographical one, and, as if to make the dedication doubly appropriate, Coward clearly used Maugham as the model for one of his characters. Mortimer Quinn is a novelist who has come to Point Valaine to rest and, if inspiration strikes him, to write; a character of cool detachment, Quinn says of himself: "I always affect to despise human nature. My role in life is clearly marked. Cynical, detached, unscrupulous, an ironic observer and recorder of other people's passions. It is a nice facade to sit behind, but a little bleak."[18]

As a result, he can comment on the action dispassionately and wittily, but, when it serves the plot, he can be marvelously understanding or even sinister. He is also useful for handling the pointer to indicate the tone of the drama: "I prefer more subtle drama, strange little twists in psychology—small unaccountable happenings in people's minds" (23). And twists in psychology are the focus. Linda Valaine, in her early forties, owns the hotel. Helping Linda run the hotel is the Russian refugee Stefan, a brutish, brooding man. A new guest is Martin Welford, a young pilot who is taking a rest cure after two harrowing weeks in the jungle following a plane crash. Martin and Linda are drawn together, although the audience learns fairly early that Linda is Stefan's mistress. Finally, on a night when Stefan is stranded on a neighboring island because the launch is out of commission, Linda allows Martin to come to her room. Stefan manages to get back, discovers what is happening, hysterically plays his accordion outside Linda's door, and, when she comes out, viciously and loudly sneers at her present lover. After Martin leaves, Stefan becomes abject; he pleads with Linda to remain true to him. She refuses and tells Stefan that she wishes he were dead. In despair, Stefan leaps into the sea. The next morning one of the servants discovers Stefan's shark-torn body at the shore. Linda can only say, in a harsh, cold voice, "I must see about engaging a new head waiter."

The play was unsuccessful both in England and in America. Coward attributed this to the weakness of theme and character: "It was neither big enough for tragedy nor light enough for comedy; the characters were well drawn, but not one of them was either interesting or kind. The young man, the only one with any claim to sympathy from the audience . . . struck me on closer analysis as silly, overidealistic, and a prig."[19]

The characters are interesting enough to support the needs of a melodrama, which is all the play can claim to be; but, even as such, it fails most seriously. The trouble lies in the slow tempo of the play, particularly the first two acts, and in the sporadic and somewhat artificial manner in which the plot emerges. Furthermore, the peripheral material—comic pictures of vacationers, Quinn's problems with a young magazine writer, details of hotel management—is by no means as amusing as it is meant to be and is constantly interfering with the main tale. Act 1 is almost pure exposition of an extremely mechanical type. The scene of Stefan's rage, which begins act 3, is by far the best scene in the play and is one of Coward's rare and most successful attempts at putting raw feelings on the stage. However, by then it is too late to save the play which has been waiting desperately for this moment.

Coward often built a successful three-act play out of material that might seem thin for a fifteen-minute sketch—*Private Lives* is the best example—yet in *Point Valaine,* where the basic outline is more than adequate for a full-length work, much of the play is padding. As it happens, Coward's next venture was into the realm of the one-act play where he was to be far more successful in dealing with "twists in psychology—small unaccountable happenings in people's minds."

One Acts

For that delightful and eminently successful potpourri entitled *Tonight at 8:30,* Coward provided two serious plays, *The Astonished Heart* and *Still Life,* both of which are among the best things he did. Perhaps, as Terence Rattigan remarks, "it is difficult . . . for him to sustain a serious mood for long."[20]

The title of *The Astonished Heart* is explained in the play itself when Christian Faber, the protagonist, decides to check a biblical quotation for a speech he is preparing. The quotation, Deut. 28:28, states that, as a punishment for disobedience, "The Lord shall smite thee with madness, and blindness, and astonishment of the heart." Such is the fate of Faber, although the madness and blindness are metaphorical. An eminent psychiatrist, Faber finds himself suddenly "submerged" in a passionate affair with Leonora Vail, a former schoolmate of his wife, Barbara. Barbara recommends that Christian and Leonora enjoy an extended holiday until passion cools and Christian is able to return to her and his work with a clear head; but her remedy fails. While Leonora's ardor wanes, Christian grows even

more irrational, jealousy now adding to his frenzy. Finally, Leonora breaks the bond; Christian throws himself from the window. On his deathbed, he calls for Leonora, but after she sees him, moments before his death, she can only report, "He didn't know me, he thought I was you, he said—'Baba—I'm not submerged any more'—and then he said 'Baba' again—and then—then he died."

Perhaps largely because of the compression of the one-act play, *The Astonished Heart* is one of Coward's most successful serious works. The characteristically too easily defined personality who is so frequent in many of Coward's plays would in any case be more readily acceptable in a play lasting less than an hour, but Christian and Barbara Faber are actually better developed characters than Lucy in *Sirocco.* Christian's three scenes of progressively greater irrationality are concisely yet convincingly executed, and there is no sense of the arbitrary or of the manipulated in his suicide. Barbara is even a better written character: her strength, her common sense, and her poise are solid. In the scene in which she suggests that her husband and his mistress take a holiday together, no readjustment of perceptions is needed. Of the three main characters, only Leonora remains somewhat ill-defined. Is she really not much more than a philanderer, or was she serious before Christian's jealousy destroyed their love? The mystery is not, however, terribly important since she does not occupy the center of attention for any great length of time.

When *The Astonished Heart* was first performed in London, Ivor Brown found the acting unsatisfactory: "Mr. Coward and Miss Lawrence play the desperate lovers in the tight-lipped, back-to-the-audience, self-suppressive, word-swallowing style of emotional acting which is fashionable today. Of this style they offer a first-rate example, but it is not a good style of acting for a play the paramount interest of which lies in the violence of erotic passion and in the virtuosity with which this demonic possession is portrayed. I should define *The Astonished Heart* as a piece for 'ham' actors presented by vegetarians of the first lustre."[21]

Although Brown surely underestimated the amount of self-suppressive behavior inherent in the play, his comment is a valuable one. Not only does it provide a concise picture of Coward as an actor in serious roles, but it points to a basic weakness in Coward's whole treatment of serious situations. In many of Coward's plays the most promising scenes—in the sense of being emotionally climactic—are weakened by the characters' tendency to analyze and summarize rather than to explode in a truly passionate manner. The last scenes of *The Vortex* and of *Sirocco* are particularly weak. Christian Faber's speeches indicate how far Coward had come in refining, but not actually overcoming this characteristic procedure, and Brown's comment calls attention to the way this approach is underlined in production. Again the one-act structure, with its insistent demand for compression, is a decisive factor; developed as a full-length play, **The Astonished Heart** would hardly have been as successful if the level of emotional expression had remained the same.

It is more than the one-act form that creates success in **Still Life.** In it, the setting and circumstances not only compel just such tight-lipped utterance but also create a sense of explosive emotions in the very process of negating any opportunity for them to be vented. **Still Life** is, like **The Astonished Heart,** a multiscened play tracing the course of illicit love from beginning to end. The setting throughout is the refreshment room of the Milford Junction railroad station. In the background are some railway employees. Mrs. Bagot, manager of the refreshment room and a very "refined" widow, is being jocularly courted by Albert Godby, a ticket inspector. Mrs. Bagot's assistant, Beryl Waters, a young girl, is much admired by Stanley, a candy seller. This group forms a comic genre picture that is almost a play in itself. In the foreground are Alec Harvey and Laura Jesson. He is a general practitioner who comes into Milford once a week to work at the hospital on his special interest, preventive medicine. She is a housewife who comes in almost every week for shopping and a movie. The play follows the course of their romance from an accidental meeting, when Alec takes a cinder out of Laura's eye, to their parting.

The crisis in the relationship occurs when Laura finally agrees to meet Alec at the apartment of a friend who is always out until late. On this day, unfortunately, the friend returns early and discovers the lovers. Terribly humiliated, Laura decides that they must stop seeing each other; reluctantly Alec agrees and decides to accept a job in public health in Johannesburg. Their last meeting, some weeks later, is interrupted by Dolly Messiter, one of Laura's friends, who joins the two at their table and gossips until Alec has left for his train. Laura rushes out to the platform—she may be contemplating suicide—but then returns, and the play ends.

Coward thought **Still Life** the "most mature play" of all the more or less serious plays in **Tonight at 8:30.** Its maturity is one both of form and content. The counterpoint between foreground and background is brilliantly established. In almost every way the story of Mrs. Bagot and her circle contributes directly to the total effect. First, the realistic setting, with its stir of activity, underlines the painful control needed by the two protagonists, as well as their isolation. Second, Mrs. Bagot's scolding, nagging, and general uppishness are both funny in themselves (her concern about the symmetry of her arrangement of cakes is a good example), and these characteristics make an ironic contrast to the

concealment, the furtiveness, and most of all the deep passion of Alec and Laura. There is a sense of class distinction here, for middle-class nuances of feeling contrast with the coarser, more superficial responses of the Cockney, but diversity is only stressed enough to throw the central story into higher relief.

In addition, there are the changes in the relationships between Mrs. Bagot and Albert and between Beryl and Stanley that show how time is passing and how these people are free to delay and skirmish, to play at courtship almost indefinitely. However, none of this contrast is stressed. On the contrary, the total effect is that of the thoroughly achieved realistic play, where nothing seems planned but all is natural, fluid, almost accidental. The same quality appears in the dialogues between Alec and Laura. Coward presents the fragments of a continuing conversation, but we are always informed of what is happening. We are able to pick up immediately the story line and the emotional tone in each scene despite the fact that Alec's and Laura's appearances in the room are only the tag ends of the days they spend together.

So successful is the whole presentation that it comes as a surprise to realize how very slight the story itself is. The three major steps in the plot—the cinder in the eye, the apartment owner's unexpected return, and the gossipy friend's frustration of the final meeting—are well-worn coincidences. The theme that basic decency wins out is hardly a novel idea. Yet, both characters and their situation are endowed with a weight and substance that are rare for Coward. In large part the solidity of the refreshment room gives such reality to the lovers, but they are also very carefully observed individuals. Finally, and perhaps most significantly, the whole play is given life and its fullest pathos by the restrained dialogue, in which little is said but much implied.

Excellent proof of the value of the form of **Still Life** can be found in the film version that Coward wrote, **Brief Encounter.** Although he needed to expand the story considerably in order to make a full-length film, and although he introduced a wide range of locales to supplement the railroad refreshment room, Coward wisely adhered to the same basic pattern: the fragile love of Laura and Alec constantly hampered and always threatened by the essentially public nature of their meetings. Thanks to the sensitive performances of Celia Johnson and Trevor Howard and the fine direction of David Lean, **Brief Encounter** has become a film classic, a beautiful preservation of Coward's writing at its most tender and sympathetic.

This Happy Breed

Coward's fullest examination of the simple annals of simple people was his next serious play, **This Happy Breed,** written in 1939 but not produced until late in

1942. Although Coward called the play "a suburban middle-class family comedy," it surely belongs in this chapter rather than the next. It does have a happy ending, a good many comic moments, and few moments of pathos or pain. The overall tone, however, is one of gentle reminiscence, and the mood at the end of the play is quiet, even meditative.

Covering the period between June 1919 and June 1939, *This Happy Breed* chronicles the life of the Gibbons family from the time they move into a house at No. 17 Sycamore Road, Clapham Common, to the day they move out. The play begins as Frank Gibbons, recently demobilized from the army, moves into No. 17 with his family: his wife, Ethel; his sister, Sylvia; his mother-in-law, Mrs. Flint; and three children, Vi, Queenie, and Reg. On the first day, they discover that their next-door neighbors are the Mitchells; Bob Mitchell and Frank Gibbons had known each other in the army. In this first scene most of the thematic lines are established. Mrs. Flint and Sylvia are eternally quarreling. Ethel and Frank are very much in love, but of rather different natures: she is religious, prudish and conventional, even slightly shrewish; he is agnostic, tolerant, and sensible. How they will all act in a crisis is predictable, but this is no weakness, suspense not being a major ingredient of the play. Indeed, the plot is essentially unsensational. Reg comes under the influence of Sam Leadbitter, a Communist, and has a falling out with the family during the General Strike of 1926. Soon afterwards, however, both give up their radicalism; Sam marries Vi Gibbons and settles down, and Reg marries Phyllis Blake, a girl very much like his sister Vi. Less than a year later, both Reg and Phyllis are killed in an automobile accident.

The most important dramatic focus of the play is Queenie. Although in love with Billy Mitchell, Queenie resents the limitations of middle-class life and runs away with a married man. Frank is sympathetic and would like to keep track of his daughter, but Ethel tries her best to forget Queenie and will not have her name mentioned in the house. Five years later, Billy returns home on leave from the navy married to Queenie. He has found her in France where she has spent the last four years at various jobs since being deserted by her lover. After only a moment's hesitation, Ethel welcomes her back. The play ends a few years later: Queenie has gone to Singapore to join Billy, leaving her child in her parents' charge. Bob Mitchell, whose wife had died a few years before, has moved out of the house next door; Sam and Vi are busy with their children; Mrs. Flint is dead; and Sylvia has become Mrs. Wilmot's assistant at the Christian Science "reading and rest room in Baker Street." Frank and Ethel are preparing to move out of No. 17 into a small flat where Frank will learn to do without a garden and a cat. As Ethel works in another room, Frank talks to Queenie's baby. It is June 1939:

There's not much to worry about really, so long as you remember one or two things always. The first is that life isn't all jam for anybody, and you've got to have trouble of some kind or another, whoever you are. But if you don't let it get you down, however bad it is, you won't go far wrong. . . . We're human beings, we are—all of us—and that's what people are liable to forget. Human beings don't like peace and good will and everybody loving everybody else. However much they may think they do, they don't because they're not made like that. Human beings like eating and drinking and loving and hating. They also like showing off, grabbing all they can, fighting for their rights, and bossing anybody who'll give 'em half a chance. You belong to a race that's been bossy for years and the reason it's held on as long as it has is that nine times out of ten it's behaved decently and treated people right. Just lately, I'll admit, we've been giving at the knees a bit and letting people down who trusted us and allowing noisy little men to bully us with a lot of guns and bombs and aeroplanes. But don't worry—that won't last—the people themselves, the ordinary people like you and me know something better than all the fussy old politicians put together—we know what we belong to, where we come from, and where we're going. We may not know it with our brains, but we know it with our roots. And we know another thing, too, and it's this. We 'aven't lived and died and struggled all these hundreds of years to get decency and justice and freedom for ourselves without being prepared to fight fifty wars if need be—to keep 'em.[22]

The play is a sort of *Cavalcade* seen through the wrong end of the telescope: instead of epic or pageant, there are nine scenes all set in the Gibbons' dining room; instead of hundreds, a cast of twelve; instead of wars, royal balls and royal funerals, the General Strike, the abdication of Edward VIII, and Chamberlain's visit to Munich. Even these matters are pushed into the background, the concern being much more with a realistic picture of family change. Only the faith in English staunchness has remained undimmed since Coward's curtain speech for *Cavalcade.*

The difference between *Cavalcade* and *This Happy Breed* reflects a real and profound change in English life. Although written less than ten years earlier, *Cavalcade* has a basically aristocratic outlook. The Marryots are members of the ruling class while the Bridges are servants and pubkeepers, and between them stretches a void. There are indications toward the end of the play that this situation is changing, but these indications are brief and almost perfunctory. The focus in *Cavalcade* is always on Jane Marryot, a lady in far more than title. A tribute to England and English virtues, *Cavalcade* is a far cry from *This Happy Breed,* Coward's tribute to the ordinary Englishman. The imminence of war hangs over the play, and it is the middle-class soldier, sailor, and civilian whom Coward recognizes now as the object of concern. Alfred Bridges went proudly off to the Boer War as Robert Marryot's bat man, the master-servant relationship undisturbed; but forty years later, Frank

Gibbons, who could well be Alfred Bridges' son, would hardly see himself or his children in such a position.

The work as a whole does not contain much obvious patriotic appeal, or much preaching of any sort. Its real strength lies, as with *Still Life,* in the solidity and weight of the characters, no matter how trivial the moment. As might be expected, the comic moments are major contributions to the play's success, and Mrs. Flint and Sylvia, as Dickensian a pair of characters as Coward ever drew, carry most of the comic burden.

The body of the play consists of genre pictures. There is, naturally enough with the dining-room setting, much serving of tea and meals. There the family gathers around the radio listening to the abdication speech. There is a Christmas party; some mild carousing when Frank and Bob Mitchell return drunk from a gathering of veterans; and, at the beginning and the end of the play, scenes of moving—boxes and hampers, pictures off the walls, bare windows. In its less spectacular way, *This Happy Breed* depends almost as much on visual effects as does *Cavalcade,* for, unless the realistic passage of time can be convincingly presented, all else fails.

PEACE IN OUR TIME

This Happy Breed, completed just before the outbreak of World War II, is one of Coward's gentlest plays; *Peace In Our Time,* written in 1947, is the most violent and melodramatic. *This Happy Breed* celebrates the English doggedness Coward hoped would see England through the worst that might come. *Peace in Our Time* pictures the English undergoing the very worst: occupation by the Germans. The stimulus for the play came from Coward's visit to Paris soon after the Liberation:

> Almost immediately upon my arrival in Paris I found myself in a delicate and embarrassing position regarding many of my French theatrical colleagues. There was unease and tension in the atmosphere and a great deal of gossip and argument on all sides about who had collaborated and who hadn't; who had been passive; who had been active; who had been concerned with the Resistance; who had been moderate; who had been pro-British and who had been anti, etc. . . .
>
> A little later, when I returned to England, I started a private game with a few of my intimate friends. This game was a hypothetical discussion of what would have happened to the English theatre and our associates in it if, in the autumn of 1940, the Battle of Britain had been lost instead of won and our country had been invaded and occupied by the Germans. It was a cruel little game . . . but it did serve a purpose because it gave me the idea of writing a play about the occupation of England. I chose the setting of a London public house because it seemed to me that only in such a deep-rooted institution as a British "pub" could I assemble together enough varied and representative types to illustrate my theme.[23]

As his proprietor of the pub The Shy Gazelle, Coward used Fred Shattuck, very much the same solid, sensible and profoundly, if quietly, patriotic Englishman as Frank Gibbons.

Peace in Our Time takes its title from Prime Minister Chamberlain's statement of reassurance upon his return, in 1938, from signing the Munich Pact, which opened the door for Hitler's takeover of Czechoslovakia. This phrase grew ever more infamous as World War II ran its ugly course, and its use as a title for a play dealing with an England in defeat, a fate Chamberlain's policies brought close to reality, was a brilliant one.

The play is in two acts of four scenes each. The first scene is in November 1940, shortly after the Germans have occupied England; the last takes place in May 1945, as the Resistance comes to full life with the Allied armies approaching London. In the other scenes the course of the Occupation is traced. At first resentful but unsure, most of the English gradually became involved in underground activities; some continue with their regular lives, like Phyllis, the barmaid, whose chief interest is the cinema; and a few, especially Gladys Mott, a prostitute, and Chorley Bannister, editor of an intellectual magazine, become collaborators.

At first, the Germans are confident that the sensible English will succumb to the "inevitable," but slowly the invaders become oppressive. The climax is Doris Shattuck's death after torture. The final scene provides an emotional catharsis. As the street-fighting grows more intense, George Bourne brings to The Shy Gazelle a Nazi functionary, Albrecht Richter. The Resistance forces are going to kill him in retaliation for Doris's death, but they decide to let the German troops do the job for them. They tie him to a chair, gag him, face him toward the locked door, put a Resistance armband on his arm and a Resistance cap over his face, turn on the forbidden radio station, and leave by the back door. A moment later, the Germans arrive; and, finding the door locked, they fire round after round of machine gun bullets through the door. Richter topples to the floor as the curtain falls.

The methods of *Still Life* and *This Happy Breed* are applied once more with great success. The setting, simple and ordinary, provides a strong counterpoint between the unsensational and unheroic setting and actions on stage and the violent, dangerous, and heroic actions that occur mainly off stage. The importance of the solidly realistic picture to be created on-stage is indicated in Coward's remarks on the difficulty of producing the play in America:

> In the English production we rehearsed from the first day in the actual set. The bar and the bar stools, the glasses, bottles, cigarettes, ash trays, etc. were all in

place so that the actors, by the time we reached our opening night . . . knew exactly how to co-ordinate their dialogue with their props and business.

In the American theatre this kind of production would be out of the question. . . . None of the actual furniture or properties can be used without the employment of a full staff, and the cost of this would naturally be so crippling to a production that no management could be expected to pay it.

(15-16)

In addition to the setting, the major factors contributing to the realistic effect are the characters and the construction of the episodes. The location of the pub, "somewhere between Knightsbridge and Sloane Square," allows for a vivid assortment of customers ranging from some theater people, like Lyia Vivian, and writers, like Chorley Bannister and Janet Braid, to some rather ordinary folk, nondescript like the Graingers or drunkenly argumentative like the Blakes. None, however, is terribly important in public life as far as the usual hierarchies of importance are concerned, although late in the play George Bourne does turn out to be "the Boss" of the Resistance. Much the same is true of the enemy; aside from occasional soldiers who appear to check identification cards or come with Gladys Mott, the only Nazi is Richter, a sincere adherent to his country's policies and goals, but not a particularly important member of the German forces. The stress is, therefore, on the routine rather than the unusual; the Resistance activities themselves enter the picture gradually, almost automatically, paralleling as it were the decline in both the quantity and the quality of the spirits available at the bar.

Each scene follows a basic pattern. Beginning with a loose and apparently undynamic picture of the saloon bar with an assorted group of characters talking in random fashion, each gradually grows to some sort of climax, which adds to the developing plot and tension. This basic method of *Still Life* and of *This Happy Breed* was first developed by Coward in some of the key scenes of *Cavalcade.*

The first scene of *Peace in Our Time* establishes the pattern. The regulars in the bar talk together, asking about trips they have taken, word from their families, etc. There are some oblique and caustic references to "them," otherwise not identified. About halfway through the scene, Janet Braid and Chorley Bannister begin to argue about Bannister's editorial adaptability, but on the surface there is no particular reason to interpret this in political terms. Shortly thereafter, when Richter enters, all conversation stops when he buys a drink. He tries, not very successfully, to make conversation, then leaves. Still, nothing is clear, though the air has grown thicker and more ominous. Richter's nationality is not discussed—he speaks English perfectly—and although his appearance adds new fuel to the quarrel between Chorley and Janet, the lines of disagreement remain abstract.

Then, Nora Shattuck turns on the radio to get the news. The announcer is a standard British Broadcasting Company type who gives some ambiguous war news before discussing plans for the next day's opening of Parliament. There is nothing particularly unusual about these plans until the last seconds of the scene when the announcer presents the order of the procession: "In the first open landau will be seated the Fuehrer. The carriages following will contain Air Chief Marshal Goering, Dr. Goebbels, and high-ranking Army, Navy and Air Force officers. . . ." And " *The lights fade.*" No other scene attempts quite so shattering a surprise, but the outline remains the same for the rest of the play. Even in that last scene, with the sound of grenades and guns in the background, the opening minutes still have an air of nonchalance.

In the foreword to the American edition, Coward attempted to forestall criticism of the play's "unabashed patriotism" by asking his readers to imagine how they might feel were America in the same situation. In truth, the patriotism of *Peace in Our Time* is much more penetrating than that in *Cavalcade* or *This Happy Breed.* Not only do the circumstances of the play do much to justify the patriotic appeals, but Coward has succeeded in making his tirades dramatically dynamic. Janet Braid, witty and articulate, lashing out at Bannister, sets the adrenalin flowing in both actress and audience:

As these are the last words I ever intend to address to you, Chorley, I want you to remember them. First of all, I despise you from the bottom of my soul. You and your kind pride yourselves on being intellectuals, don't you? You babble a lot of snobbish nonsense about art and letters and beauty. You consider yourselves to be far above such primitive emotions as love and hate and devotion to a cause. You run your little high-brow magazines and change your politics with every wind that blows. . . . In the years before the war you were squealing for disarmament at a moment when to be fully armed was vitally necessary for our survival. You were all pacifists then. . . . Later, a very little later, having listened obediently to a few foreign agitators, you were launching virulent attacks on British imperialism. That was when you were all bright little Communists. Now of course your intellectual ardours are devoted exclusively to Fascism—an easy transition. Where are you going next—you clever ones? What will your attitude be when England is free again, when your German friends are blasted to hell and driven into oblivion? You had better make your plans quickly—there is hardly any time to be lost. Get ready for a lightning change of views, Chorley. Make it snappy, you drivelling little rat. . . . And when you are arranging with your friends to have me put into a concentration camp, remember to tell them exactly what I said. I said, "Down with Hitler!" And I hope he rots in hell with all the strutting, yelping jackals round him! Down with the Third Bloody Reich and down into the lowest depths with every Englishman who gave our enemies lip service and fawned on them and by so doing flung his country's pride into the dust!

[*Janet gives Chorley two ringing slaps on the face which send him staggering against the bar, and walks out.*]

(152)

Oversimplified, sophomoric, melodramatic? Of course. But how very satisfying this speech is because it comes when it does.

WAITING IN THE WINGS

In *Still Life, This Happy Breed,* and *Peace in Our Time,* Coward achieved great poignancy and force by embedding each firmly in a matrix of scrupulously observed and vividly and wittily presented routine life. Even the melodrama of *Peace in Our Time* is familiar enough, and the fact that this action occurs in England would be at best only an ingenious variation on a standard pattern without the solidity of The Shy Gazelle. In each case, the background has served to heighten the force of the story by underlining its verisimilitude and by providing a channel for Coward's powers of restrained understatement. Furthermore, in each case the setting and background have their own interest in the details of ordinary life. In Coward's *Waiting in the Wings* (1960), this method has been carried one step further, for in this play setting and background are virtually all there is since the story hardly exists.

Waiting in the Wings is set in a "small charity home for retired actresses." Those who live there have all been leading ladies; none is under sixty, and all are very much aware that they have little to look forward to except death. The play is held together by a few unifying strands: the problem of getting the Committee to build a solarium; the problem of reconciling May Davenport and Lotta Bainbridge, who are now daily confronted with each other after thirty years of enmity; the problem of Sarita Myrtle, who grows more and more senile and loves to play with matches. A newspaper's article on The Wings (the name of the home) results, after considerable squabbling and difficulties, in the publisher's providing the money for the solarium; at the end of the play the old ladies who most bitterly complained of the cold wind on the terrace are beginning to complain that the solarium is too hot, a typically Cowardian touch of ironic symmetry. May and Lotta are reconciled on the night Sarita sets fire to the curtains in her room. Sarita is taken away to an asylum, but makes a superb exit.

In addition, Deirdre O'Malley, sharp-tongued and overpious, dies of a heart attack. Lotta receives a visit from her son, who had gone to Canada thirty-three years before with her husband and from whom she had heard almost nothing since. She gently and painfully refuses to go to live with him and his family. Perry Lascoe, secretary to the Committee and much beloved by all the ladies, is fired for his part in arranging for a reporter to visit The Wings; he is reinstated thanks to May's influence. Osgood Meeker, seventy, continues to come every Sunday to visit Martha Carrington, ninety-five, with whom he has been in love since he was seventeen. And Miss Archie, the resident superintendent, continues to cope in her military way. All of this activity is of importance or interest only insofar as it provides opportunities for observing the ladies in action.

Such a structure allows not only for a large number of elderly actresses to demonstrate their versatility, but for Coward to demonstrate his as well. Here his interest in and his nostalgia for the old songs and old musical shows are seen. The ladies often reminisce about their early years and sing some of the old songs; the play ends with almost everybody on stage singing "Oh Mr. Kaiser" to welcome a new arrival, Topsy Baskerville, who had once made the song famous. Coward's talent for writing scenes of restrained pathos is shown particularly in Lotta's meeting with her son. Of character comedy, there is Deirdre O'Malley. Of wild, fantastic comedy, we have Sarita's ramblings, mingling lines from old plays, backstage jargon, details of her past life and occasional moments of clarity. The witty, slightly bad-tempered badinage of the characteristic Coward type is present throughout, but appears particularly in the scenes involving Lotta and May.

Despite its versatility and other charms, *Waiting in the Wings* is not a success. A meaningful sense of loss, of waste, of imminent death does not develop, although Coward is careful to have these themes frequently mentioned. Not only the retired ladies but even the younger people involved are all such "characters" that they can only sporadically engage the audience's sympathies. Of the three crucial moments of the play, only Lotta's dismissal of her son really carries much weight. Deirdre's death and Sarita's departure for the asylum are ironic and striking but they remain theatrical clichés—they do not touch the audience.

SUITE IN THREE KEYS

First produced in London in April and May of 1966, *Suite in Three Keys* consists of three works: *A Song at Twilight,* a full-length play, and two one-acts, *Shadows of the Evening* and *Come into the Garden Maud.* The first two are serious plays, the last a light comedy. All three use the same setting, a suite in a Swiss hotel. The central figure in each play is an elderly man—in *A Song at Twilight,* a novelist in many ways similar to Somerset Maugham; in *Come into the Garden Maud,* an American millionaire; and in *Shadows of the Evening,* a publisher—and in each play he is in conflict with his wife and mistress. All three plays are, like *Waiting in the Wings,* and some of Coward's late stories, preoccupied with age, illness, and death; they end with a reassertion of love and stoic agnosticism.

These three plays provided another demonstration of Coward's versatility both as an author and an actor (he played all three leading male roles), but they are little more than mechanically skillful reworkings of familiar material. In *Come into the Garden Maud,* a good-hearted, hen-pecked American leaves his social-climbing wife for a warm-hearted woman of the world. In *Shadows of the Evening,* after the doctor diagnoses the hero's illness as incurable, husband, wife, and mistress agree to live as happily and fully as possible for the few remaining months. *A Song at Twilight* has slightly more substance and caused a brief stir in London because in it the author argued against the British law making homosexual acts a crime. However, the law was already being rewritten at the time the play was produced, and Coward's frankness and outrage, limited to this single legal problem in an otherwise thin and predictable story, are out of date.

COWARD'S DEVELOPMENT

Terence Rattigan has aptly stated that "development" is too often taken to mean attempting more and more serious subjects, or striving to emulate some critic's standard that may have little to do with the writer's interests and abilities. Coward, he says, developed as "we all develop . . . by the simple process of growing and gathering experience" and by improving his craft.[24] By setting *Waiting in the Wings* next to *The Vortex* we may indicate how accurate this statement is. The subject matter of *The Vortex* is, if anything, more serious and certainly more sensational and more forcefully presented, but how much better the playwright knows and understands the ladies of The Wings.

Coward's serious plays show a clear line of change, one moving from harrowing and lurid subjects—dope addiction, gigoloism, and torrid seduction—to more ordinary topics—old age, family loyalty, and bereavement—and from exotic characters and settings more and more into the boundaries of middle-class life. The alarms and excursions of *Peace in Our Time* are in the long run only temporary, if painful, interruptions in the even and healthy tenor of solid English life; and in *Waiting in the Wings* it is ultimately more important that the characters are old ladies preparing for death than that they are all former stars.

Coward's development in play construction parallels his changes in subject matter. The success of *The Vortex* depends in large part on a sequence of strenuously witty and explosively emotional scenes tied together any which way, but *Waiting in the Wings* shows a well-trained and assured, as opposed to a cocksure, hand at work. We could hardly imagine the twenty-five-year-old Coward attempting to maintain interest for long without relying on melodramatic, "strong" situations, complete with applause-sparking curtain lines.

It would be a mistake, however, to overemphasize differences while ignoring how the later plays reflect many of the same premises and limitations of the earlier ones. At the heart of almost every play is the concept of the "whacking good part," although the stress has changed from ranting to subtle delineation. But, although an actor's enthusiasm can grow out of an author's profound concern with a character—Shakespeare's Hamlet, for example, or Ibsen's Hedda Gabler—the reverse is rarely, if ever, true: a playwright's determination to provide himself or some other character with a striking part is not enough—and this fault has generally been Coward's. Frank Gibbons is a far cry from Nicky Lancaster, but they are brothers under the skin, both collections of bits and pieces, neither a fully created character. Frank comes closer; it is possible to imagine him in various situations, but Nicky exists only in the play, perhaps only when an actor lends him some of his own reality. Even at his most serious, Coward remained a comic writer, writing plays with basically two-dimensional characters. They are, in the older sense of the word, "humorous" characters—embodiments of a few distinctive traits.

The level of significance in Coward's serious plays has also not changed much over the decades. Bothered since the early 1930s by certain weaknesses in English society, Coward dramatized his concerns in a number of plays, primarily in *Post-Mortem, Cavalcade, This Happy Breed,* and *Peace in Our Time,* but the analysis never penetrated far beyond the level of the popular magazine. Despite the pessimism of *Post-Mortem,* Coward usually found solace in the enduring value of sound English character, and he defined such value in platitudes. In his nonpolitical plays—*The Astonished Heart, Still Life,* and *Waiting in the Wings,* for example—the same is true on a psychological level; there is pathos but not tragedy, and English stoicism is the chief virtue. This characteristic of the plays is unobjectionable certainly, but thin.

The Vortex may have struck a large part of the audience as a vehement denunciation of vice and as an exposé of the silver cord as a garotte. In the early 1930s it may still have seemed reasonable to think of Coward as "fundamentally a Savonarola."[25] In retrospect, however, it appears that Coward was always more concerned with theatrical effectiveness than with finding forms in which to present ideas or denunciations that demanded expression. Such themes as are presented were Coward's reflections on matters that were in the air, and while his presentation is usually intelligent and sincere, even briefly startling in novelty or outspokenness, it rarely goes beyond the superficial.

In conclusion, to Coward's work in serious dramas (as is true with minor variations about all his work except several of the best comedies) time brought a considerable increase in skill and some changes in subject matter but little change in the level of perception and significance. As a writer of serious plays, Coward remained an artist of skill, sensibleness, and charm. The serious tone he could best create and maintain was one of a gentle, restrained pathos; but Coward's effects grew far less out of depths of character or a philosophical view of society than from an awareness of theatrical effect. So long as the theater remains wedded to realism, at least some of these works—**Still Life, This Happy Breed,** perhaps even **The Vortex**—are certain to be performed, while others less likely to be produced—**Cavalcade, Peace in Our Time,** and **Post-Mortem**—should find readers for some time to come.

Notes

1. See, for example, the cover of *Short Stories, Short Plays and Songs by Noel Coward* (New York: 1955).

2. *Present Indicative,* 187.

3. Ibid., 194.

4. *The Vortex,* in *Plays: One* (London: Methuen, 1979), 169; hereafter cited by page number in the text.

5. Introduction to *Play Parade,* vol. 1 (Garden City, N.Y.: Doubleday, 1933), x.

6. Introduction to *Play Parade,* vol. 2 (London: Heinemann, 1950), viii-x.

7. Review of *Easy Virtue, New York Times,* 8 December 1925; quoted in *Theatrical Companion to Coward,* 81.

8. James Agate, review of *Easy Virtue,* London *Sunday Times,* 13 June 1926; quoted in *Theatrical Companion to Coward,* 83.

9. *Sirocco,* in *The Plays of Noel Coward* (Garden City, N.Y.: Doubleday, Doran & Co., 1928), 88; hereafter cited by page number in the text.

10. *Present Indicative,* 270-71.

11. St. John Ervine, review of *Sirocco,* London *Observer,* 27 November 1927; quoted in *Theatrical Companion to Coward,* 26-27.

12. *Post-Mortem,* in *Plays: Two* (London: Methuen, 1979), 285; hereafter cited by page number in the text.

13. *Present Indicative,* 334-35.

14. Ibid., 340.

15. Ibid., 341.

16. *Cavalcade,* in *Plays: Three* (London: Methuen, 1979), 183-84; hereafter cited by page number in the text.

17. Ibid., 351.

18. *Point Valaine* (London: Heinemann, 1935), 97; hereafter cited by page number in the text.

19. *Future Indefinite* (Garden City, N.Y.: Doubleday, 1954), 326-27.

20. Terence Rattigan, "Noel Coward," *Theatrical Companion to Coward,* 4.

21. Ivor Brown, review of "The Astonished Heart," London *Observer,* 12 January 1936; quoted in *Theatrical Companion to Coward,* 238.

22. *This Happy Breed,* in *Plays: Four* (London: Methuen, 1979), 371-72.

23. Foreword to *Peace in Our Time* (Garden City, N.Y.: Doubleday, 1948), 13-14; hereafter cited by page number in the text.

24. Rattigan, "Noel Coward," in *Theatrical Companion to Coward,* 3.

25. G. B. Stern, quoted in Braybrooke, *Amazing Mr. Noel Coward* [1933], as being from a "recent magazine article," 162.

Sean O'Connor (essay date 1998)

SOURCE: O'Connor, Sean. "Public Lives, Private Faces." In *Straight Acting: Popular Gay Drama from Wilde to Rattigan,* pp. 95-126. London: Cassell, 1998.

[*In the following essay, O'Connor explores the ways in which Coward created his own public persona, which he then consistently incorporated into and explored in his plays.*]

NOËL COWARD'S PERFORMANCE OF A LIFETIME

When an all-male version of **Private Lives** was proposed, it didn't take long to reach a decision. No! Ditto **Fallen Angels.** Remembering the posters which advertised the fact that *The Boys in the Band* is not a musical! I shudder to think what they'd have done to us!

Graham Payn[1]

It was absolutely preposterous, the notion that gays were writing about gays, but disguising them as straights. Tennessee Williams knew the difference between men and women as well as I do. If you're writing about men, you're writing about men, and if you're writing about women, you're writing about women. But then rumour began that *Who's Afraid of Virginia Woolf?* was really about four men, which led to attempts at all-male productions of the play, which led me to close them down. For the same reason I don't allow all-female versions of *The Zoo Story.* Because they're incorrect. But somehow the sniping has never gone away.

Edward Albee[2]

To say that only a woman can portray the passions of a woman . . . is to rob the art of acting of all claim to objectivity, and to assign to the mere accident of sex what properly belongs to imaginative insight and creative energy.

Oscar Wilde[3]

As we slip into the next century, one wonders which of Noël Coward's seemingly slight creations will survive in the popular cultural imagination; the balcony scene from *Private Lives,* perhaps? 'Mad Dogs and Englishmen'? *Brief Encounter*? Madam Arcati? Perhaps his most complex creation and surely one of the iconographic figures of the twentieth century is 'Noël Coward' himself. As early as 1953, Kenneth Tynan recognized that 'Even the youngest of us will know in fifty years time exactly what we mean by a "very Noël Coward sort of person".'[4] Forty-four years later, Tynan's prediction seems to have been fulfilled; Diet Coke's Wimbledon '97 TV campaign had a Coward sound-alike trilling his way through a jingle which parodied 'Mad Dogs and Englishmen'. We don't need to see the dressing-gown or the cigarette-holder; we instantly know that the advertisement refers to Noël.

From the very beginnings of his theatrical career, Coward the performer was inextricably linked with Coward the author. He consciously fashioned and exploited this symbiotic relationship between his theatrical image and his public persona. Coward's were unashamedly commercial plays with starring roles intended for himself. In 1924, the then comparatively unknown Coward refused to compromise when the Everyman Theatre balked at the idea of his playing the lead in *The Vortex*; ultimately he had his own way and the play was a controversial success. He continued to promote himself through his work, from *Private Lives* in the 1930s and *Present Laughter* during the war years through to his final stage appearance in *A Song at Twilight* in 1965. As he matured, so too did the age range of his characters; their preoccupations developed from the ambitious and aspiring to the milieu of the successful and the famous. Coward's life infused his art and vice versa; consequently the autobiographical strain running through his work is very strong.

Though posterity will inevitably record Coward as a playwright of the 1930s, his first full-length play was completed at the end of the First World War. In *The Rat Trap* (1918) we are introduced to a bohemian couple, both writers, struggling to balance fluctuating fame and success whilst retaining the equilibrium of their relationship. The aspiring novelist Sheila Brandreth is warned by a friend on the eve of her wedding to aspiring playwright Keld Maxwell that one of them will have to make sacrifices if the relationship is to succeed: 'either you or Keld will have to sacrifice a certain amount of personality'.[5] Sheila relinquishes her writing

in order to become a housewife, but leaves the now successful Keld when she discovers he has been having an affair with an actress. Ultimately Sheila returns to her writing and Keld returns to Sheila. But though pregnant and willing to take Keld back for the child's sake, Sheila declares that she no longer loves him. The theme of warring bohemian egos is further explored in *Design for Living* where Otto and Leo, an artist and a playwright, compete for Gilda as their fortunes prosper. When both have become successful, Gilda, feeling used up by her two lovers, marries the humourless Ernest, leaving Otto and Leo to find solace in each other. Eventually Gilda herself becomes a successful interior designer in New York and when Otto and Leo visit her, the three realize that they cannot live apart. Now that all three are successful, they settle for a *ménage à trois.* *Present Laughter* was written when Coward was forty, and examines the burdens of power and fame in the orbit of a star actor, his retinue and fans. It is a rather world-weary portrayal of the artist. The unproduced *Long Island Sound* is based on the satirical short story, 'What Mad Pursuit?' It concerns a British playwright invited for a quiet weekend to escape the flurry of New York. But the protagonist finds himself relentlessly pursued by fans and well-meaning guests, who drive him to distraction. In a desperate effort to find peace and quiet he leaps out of the window, preferring the peace of death or injury; it's a classic Cowardian exit from chaos.

Coward's stage roles provide intermittent snapshots of himself in prose at various ages in his life. He observed later in his career: 'I've been a "personality" actor all my life. I've established in my early years the sophisticated, urbane type, which is in tune with my own personality.'[6] Even *Blithe Spirit,* though not originally performed by Coward, was written with himself in mind. Charles Condomine is a successful, sophisticated middle-aged writer with a talent for mixing cocktails as 'dry as a bone'. In tune, indeed.

Just as the caricatured visage of George Bernard Shaw as God-Author manipulates the puppet strings of Julie Andrews and Rex Harrison in the publicity for the original production of *My Fair Lady,* Coward played God in his own universe. He created the inner lives and motivations of his characters on the page and then went on to give them a physical, public reality as a performer on the stage. Consequently some of those roles, particularly Elyot Chase in *Private Lives* and Garry Essendine in *Present Laughter,* continue to resonate with shadows of Coward's performance, his inflections and mannerisms. Keith Baxter who played Elyot opposite Joan Collins in the 1990 West End revival of *Private Lives* remembers how difficult it was to get away from Coward's speech rhythms, which seem to be ingrained in the dialogue. Excerpts from the play were recorded on vinyl, an exceptional indication of success even in the 1930s, with Coward and Lawrence repeating their famous stage relationship for posterity. This recording continues to haunt subsequent productions with its definitive performances. Rather territorially, Coward formulated such definitive characterizations by establishing aspects of himself as elements of his stage characters. Well aware of the public's perception of him, Coward actually exploited it in self-mockery, as when the aspiring writer in **Present Laughter** accuses Essendine: 'All you do is to wear dressing-gowns and make witty remarks'. David Lean's film version of **Blithe Spirit** (1945) begins with a nursery rhyme, accompanied by a tune from a musical box:

> When we are young
> We read and believe
> The most fantastic things.
> When we grow older and wiser
> We learn, with perhaps a little regret
> That these things can never be.[7]

The screen then goes to black and we hear a familiar voice add: 'We are quite, quite wrrr-ong!' The inimitable trills and clipped consonants were Coward's trademarks. Even as early as 1945, before the proliferation of the media, Coward was sure that his celebrity was such that even without introduction or billing his vocal mannerisms would be immediately recognizable.

Coward surrounded himself, both privately and professionally, with a stock of trusted friends and colleagues. He wrote plays and parts not only for himself, but with particular actor friends in mind. **Design for Living** and **Quadrille** were written for Alfred Lunt and Lynne Fontanne, the golden couple of Broadway. He frequently claimed that he wrote a part in each of his plays for his close friend, Joyce Carey. Carey was the daughter of Lilian Braithwaite, who had created the role of the mother in **The Vortex.** Joyce Carey herself memorably played Mrs Bagot, the 'refained' refreshment-room manageress in *Brief Encounter,* and is particularly moving as the doomed working-class wife in *In Which We Serve.* Most famously, Coward wrote **Private Lives** and **Tonight at 8.30** as vehicles for himself (of course) and Gertrude Lawrence. In writing for known quantities, Coward was able to tailor-make roles. In creating his plays, he had no pretensions about textual 'sanctity', for text and personality were intertwined. Consequently, Coward was able to control other actors/characters' responses to his own performance. Coward's principal designer, Gladys Calthrop, was also a great personal friend and collaborated with Coward from 1922 onwards. His early financial affairs were taken over by his lover, Jock Wilson, who continued to look after them even when their relationship had ended. And who should replace Coward and play opposite Gertrude Lawrence in the 1948 American revival of **Tonight at 8.30,** that series of demanding vehicles written specifically for Noël and Gertie? It would be impossible to

repeat the Coward/Lawrence magic and anybody stepping into Coward's shoes opposite Lawrence would have a legendary partnership to live up to. Coward's roles were taken over by a young, little-known song-and-dance man called Graham Payn. He also happened to be Coward's lover; the revival was an unmitigated disaster.

The Coward circle seems close, perhaps even a little closed. But with his increasing popularity, particularly between the wars, it would have been necessary for Coward to rely on his friends' and associates' discretion in protecting and promoting his reputation. This warm, incestuous closeness is examined in detail in **Present Laughter**:

GARRY.

> You and Henry and Monica and Liz and I share something of inestimable importance to all of us, and that is mutual respect and trust. God knows it's been hard won. We can look back on years and years of bloody conflict with ourselves and each other. But now we're all middle-aged we can admit, with a certain mellow tranquillity, that it's been well worth it. Here we are, five people closely woven together by affection and work and intimate knowledge of each other.[8]

In his memoir, Graham Payn observes that 'A troupe of characters parades through the diaries like the cast of one of Noël's plays. He referred to them as the "Family".' Payn compares the ambience and characters of **Present Laughter** with the frenetic milieu at Coward's studio in Gerald Road, 'anytime from the early 1930's to the mid-50's'.[9]

Before the rise of the director in the postwar theatre of the kitchen sink movement, plays were often directed by the leading actor. Before the war, writers certainly didn't have the say in casting and rehearsal which they were to acquire in the 1960s. Coward's position as writer/performer made him very powerful in the production of his own work and much of it he originally directed himself. With the current fashion of writer-directors like Terry Johnson, David Mamet and David Hare, it no longer seems so unusual, but in some ways Coward paved the way for them; he was the first living playwright to direct his own work at the National Theatre when he staged **Hay Fever** there in 1964. Script, design, casting, performance, direction: Coward had almost total control over the artistic presentation of his work from an early stage in his career, which he continued to exert until the end of it. Does such control imply a reluctance, or even a resistance, to interpretation by other theatrical practitioners? It was Kenneth Tynan who suggested that the National Theatre revive one of Coward's early works, and even in 1964 Coward was still regarded as the best interpreter of his own writing. It is only comparatively recently that Coward's work has been explored, examined and interpreted by other directors and designers and that performers have felt released from the traditional paraphernalia of a Coward play with its vowels, trills and cigarette-holders, a style very much associated with Coward himself.

Present Laughter examines the sexual intrigues surrounding Garry Essendine, a leading 'romantic comedian'. Essendine himself is rather promiscuous and his promiscuity is regarded very much as a matter of course by his servants and secretary. The action of the play is cyclical, opening with the young debutante, Daphne Stillington, who is Essendine's most recent conquest. She had lost her latchkey the previous evening and spent the night in the spare room. The loss of one's latchkey is adopted as a euphemistic excuse to stay overnight in Garry's bed. The key has a rather obvious sexual symbolism and the spare room is used by guests in the morning as a nod to convention. It also, very conveniently, would have countered any objections to the play by the Lord Chamberlain on grounds of immorality. Essendine's 'family' has been infiltrated by the vampish Joanna Lypiatt, who has married Essendine's business manager, Henry. She has also been conducting an affair with Essendine's accountant, Morris. In the course of the play, she reveals that these two relationships were calculated ways of getting to know Essendine better and that it is Garry she really wants; he willingly succumbs to her charms. Joanna is also consigned to the spare room after she eventually spends the night with Garry. The recurrent use of the spare room in the action underlines its symbolic function. The two off-stage areas continually used and referred to are the spare bedroom and the office, the arenas of private and public life, sex and stage. The play examines Essendine's self-imposed division between his sex life and his business life, a division under which Coward himself lived. The spare room is Coward's closet. In this world of bed-hopping between friends, and the lies and performances that follow, Garry claims to be the only character who is honest about his philandering. When Joanna propositions Essendine, he responds with lines from a play, a ploy which she duly recognizes. Such a tactic, she feels, is a proof of his emotional tepidness:

JOANNA.

> It proved that you are no more sincere emotionally than I am, that you no longer need or desire the pangs of love, but are perfectly willing to settle for the fun of love. It's an adult point of view and I salute it.[10]

Joanna's argument has little to do with love. She proposes an honest, purely sexual relationship, unhindered by the responsibilities of marriage or the trappings of romance. But Garry is appalled by the ease with which Joanna dupes her husband and her long-term lover. In his denunciation of Joanna, Morris and

Henry's mutual and complicated sexual deceptions, Essendine observes that his own attitude to sex is comparatively straightforward:

> To me the whole business is vastly over-rated. I enjoy it for what it's worth and fully intend to go on doing so for as long as anybody's interested and when the time comes that they're not I shall be perfectly content to settle down with an apple and a good book![11]

Coward sets up Essendine from the very beginning of the play as a heterosexual philanderer but with a homosexual's self-conscious anxiety about the maintenance of his public persona and reputation.[12] But Coward complicates the possibility of Essendine's sexuality by the introduction of a young writer, Roland Maule. Maule has sent Essendine a play that he has written. It is a raw effort, rather serious and very uncommercial. Maule disparages Essendine's style of West End theatre and Essendine himself. Essendine tires of Maule's idealistic but naive views on theatre. He loses his temper and advises Maule to go and work in a repertory theatre where he might 'Learn from the ground up how plays are constructed and what is actable and what isn't.' Maule is overwhelmed by Essendine's vehemence and his attitude; he is quite hypnotized:

ROLAND.

> You've been a sort of obsession with me. . . . I felt somehow that I wasn't at peace with myself and gradually, bit by bit, I began to realise that you signified something to me.

GARRY.

> What sort of something?

ROLAND.

> I don't quite know—not yet.[13]

Maule's devotion to Essendine is certainly that of the pupil for his guru. But Coward's calculatedly ambiguous way of exploring this devotion leaves sufficient room for speculation about Maule's erotic interest in that direction. Coward implies that Maule finally identifies his own sexuality and recognizes in Garry a similar sexual orientation. In a recent production of the play on Broadway,[14] Maule turns up at Essendine's flat naked under a raincoat and offers his body quite overtly to strains of 'Mad About The Boy'. That might well be taking dramatic licence over the hills and far away, but ***Present Laughter*** certainly dramatizes a theatrical environment where anything goes. Daphne doesn't believe that 'real love should be bound by Church or Law'; Joanna flippantly disregards her marriage vows and Liz and Garry 'never quite got round' to getting a divorce. The Essendine set are fashionably amoral and pay little heed to convention. It comes as no surprise that Essendine receives fan mail from young men he has only briefly encountered:

MONICA.

Here's one signed 'Joe'. . . . He seems to have met you in the South of France.

GARRY.

I do get about, don't I? (*looking at the letter*) Oh, it's Joe.

MONICA.

(*patiently*) That's what I said.

GARRY.

Joe was wonderful. I met him in a bar in Marseilles. He's dark green and comes from Madras.[15]

Essendine also makes enthusiastic observations about the attractiveness of a young naval officer he had met who has a hankering for the stage, but it's neither the boy's nautical knowledge nor his thespian skill that Garry is interested in:

LIZ.

What does he look like?

GARRY.

Absolutely marvellous, if it's the one I think it is, vast strapping shoulders and tiny, tiny hips like a wasp . . .[16]

In the same way, Coward later implies Hugo Latymer's homosexuality by having him dwell on the physical attributes of his manservant, Felix, in *A Song at Twilight*: 'You look as though you should be a good swimmer yourself, with those shoulders.'[17]

Roland Maule visits the flat a second time the evening before Essendine is to leave for Africa. He recognizes that they both have been acting in real life (perhaps straight acting?):

GARRY.

Listen, what exactly do you want, really?

ROLAND.

To be with you.[18]

Maule tries to seduce Essendine with the same intensity that Daphne has pursued him. Both want to accompany him to Africa. Their pursuit of Essendine is couched in exactly the same terms in two different scenes:

DAPHNE.

You needn't be frightened—I won't make any demands on you whatever. I don't want you to marry me or anything like that.[19]

and

ROLAND.

You needn't be frightened that I shall get in your way or make demands on you.

To which Essendine responds comically 'You mean you don't expect me to marry you!'[20] At this point Garry has already pushed Daphne into his office and now Maule has locked himself in the spare room that has been the haven for all of Essendine's female conquests; Maule thereby identifies himself as one of them.

Garry Essendine lives a life of opportunistic promiscuity. Women, men, best friends' wives: all are fair game. Fidelity means very little. In order to resolve the confusion before his trip to Africa, Liz Essendine decides to take Garry back. Not out of love, but for 'the good of the firm', a real marriage of convenience. Essendine creeps out of the flat with Liz, leaving Maule locked in the bedroom and Daphne in the office (an indication that Garry can't fully compartmentalize the different aspects of his life and that sometimes the emotional takes over both bedroom and office?). *Present Laughter* is a cynical, unromantic study of human egotism, with Garry, the great individualist, continually in pursuit of personal pleasure, 'for as long as anybody's interested'.

Though obviously very aware of the attempts to reform the laws affecting homosexuals in the 1950s and 1960s, as his diaries indicate, Coward never 'came out' in public. Sheridan Morley was refused permission to discuss Coward's private life in his 1969 biography, *A Talent to Amuse*. When Coward was sent the proofs of Morley's book, he observed, 'I'm afraid Sherry has to do a bit more work [of expurgation]. There are still a few old ladies in Worthing who don't know . . .'.[21] Coward, like Maugham, staunchly believed that 'One's real inside self is a private place and should always stay like that. It is no one else's business.'[22] Coward had actually written stories with homosexual protagonists, such as 'Star Quality' and 'Me and the Girls', the latter of which is written in the first person by a sickly camp queen who manages a female dance troupe. He had also written the poem, 'Not Yet the Dodo', which is peopled by explicitly homosexual characters, but he seemed reluctant to discuss homosexuality directly in 'his' medium, the stage, until *A Song at Twilight* in 1966. Coward played the central character, an ageing writer with a homosexual past, but he did not expect audiences to interpret the piece as autobiography. Indeed, he went out of his way to imply that the character of Hugo Latymer was based on Somerset Maugham: *The Times* believed that the identification of Latymer as Maugham was 'beyond question'. As long as Latymer was regarded as a cipher for Maugham, audiences would not take the play as a thinly disguised confessional by Coward himself. In the 1920s and early 1930s Coward had 'joined Maugham in destroying the reputation of the well-born, the well-to-do and the well-educated'.[23] The two men became friends and Coward had often visited Maugham at his villa on Cap Ferrat, but after Maugham's attack on Syrie in 1962 and with the decline of his mental state, Coward's friendship with Maugham cooled: 'There's such a thing as *too* old', Coward observed. There was talk of libel suits against Coward over the similarity of Hugo Latymer to Maugham, but in 1965 Maugham conveniently died before the production opened.

A Song at Twilight examines Coward's own dilemma about the moulding and maintenance of his public reputation. Hugo Latymer is blackmailed by an old lover, Carlotta Gray, who has possession of a series of love letters Latymer had written to a former male lover, Perry Sheldon. Carlotta issues Latymer with a threat: 'Owing to your ceaseless vigilance your "bubble reputation" must be as solid as a football by now. You mustn't be surprised that certain people should wish to kick it about a bit.'[24] She claims that she isn't motivated by self-interest and that her intention is to make Latymer face up to himself: Carlotta is Latymer's self-appointed Nemesis. Latymer's love letters to Sheldon are genuine and passionate, written 'before your mind had become corrupted by fame and your heart by caution'.[25] But Latymer feels that the caution he has exercised in his life and work has been necessitated by the prejudices of the establishment and the reading public: 'It takes more than a few outspoken books and plays and speeches in Parliament to uproot moral prejudice from the Anglo-Saxon mind.'[26] Carlotta's most stinging sally is one which haunted Coward as well as Maugham and Rattigan: 'You might have been a great writer instead of merely a successful one, and you might also have been a far happier man.'[27]

Coward had spent over half a century developing his persona as the archetypal heterosexual dandy and was loathe to dispel the myth because of a change in social fashion or a modification in the law, for he had 'taken a lot of trouble with [his] public face'. The two most indelible images of Coward are aimed at promoting the same carefully constructed image of 'The Master': successful, suave, single but straight. Photographic images were very important in constructing the Coward myth. There is the image of the precocious young man about town of the 1920s, complete with cigarette-holder and silk dressing-gown. And there is the older Coward, promoting his postwar cabaret shows in Las Vegas: drinking a cup of tea now, but still debonair, standing in a dinner-jacket out in the sun-baked Californian desert. The former image depicts the bard of the new bohemianism of the jazz age. The latter embodies the triumph of the sophisticate. Here is the older Coward, survivor of the changing fashions of the twentieth century, nonchalantly drinking the Englishman's drink, whilst the land dries up around him for lack of rain.

Coward had realized the importance of presenting the public with the image they expected to see. At the height of his fame, he met the aspiring Cecil Beaton on a transatlantic crossing and advised discretion in the public display of one's tastes and behaviour. Beaton recalls Coward's advice:

> 'It is important not to let the public have a loophole to lampoon you.' That, he explained, was why he studied his own 'facade'. Now take his voice; it was definite, harsh, rugged. He moved firmly, dressed quietly . . . 'You should appraise yourself,' he went on. 'Your sleeves are too tight, your voice too high and too precise. You mustn't do it. It closes so many doors. It limits you unnecessarily, and young men with half your intelligence will laugh at you.' He shook his head, wrinkled his forehead and added disarmingly, 'It's hard I know. One would like to indulge one's own tastes. I myself dearly love a good match, yet I know it is overdoing it to wear tie, socks and handkerchief of the same colour. I take ruthless stock of myself in the mirror before going out. A polo jumper or unfortunate tie exposes one to danger.'[28]

The anxiety of 'indulging one's own tastes' in bed, whilst conveying a veneer of public 'respectability' is a tension which informed Coward's private life and provided a theme which he explored throughout his work. Whilst retaining a huge popular following, Coward was adept at manipulating his appeal to different audiences. For the ladies of Worthing, younger then, Coward presented a naughty, stylish, often hilarious exposé of the leisured, arty classes. But Coward's work was also littered with subtextual resonances for those who found the prevailing moral code difficult to live within or just plain wrong. The ambiguity of Coward's texts and performances, both on and off-stage, characterizes a style which he maintained to the very end of his career.

In two of his final film appearances Coward exploited the ambiguities of his own reputation. In both *Boom!* (1968, dir. Joseph Losey) and *The Italian Job* (1969, dir. Peter Collinson) Coward's contribution is very camp. *Boom!* is a version of Tennessee Williams's drama of sex, death and middle age under the Mediterranean midday sun, *The Milk Train Doesn't Stop Here Any More*. Supporting Elizabeth Taylor and Richard Burton, Coward plays the waspish Witch of Capri. But this character is female in the stage version. Was Coward exploiting the fact that the audience had guessed by now that he was gay and had tacitly accepted it? Or was he exploiting the knowledge of *some* members of the audience, attuned to reading ciphers and signals, in a private cinematic joke for those 'in the know'? Coward's final appearance on film was opposite Michael Caine in *The Italian Job,* a jaunty example of late 1960s Euro-froth. Coward plays Mr Bridger, a crime lord who runs his empire from a British prison cell. Despite his residence at Her Majesty's Pleasure,

Mr Bridger is an impeccably turned-out gentleman awarded great privileges by the warders and Governor (John Le Mesurier) whom he treats with the courtesy of a duchess. Devoted to the British Royal family, he has covered the walls of his cell with pictures of them, particularly the Queen and the Queen Mother, and is singularly displeased when he notices that 'some of that mob in E block are not standing to attention when the National Anthem is played at the end of the nightly TV'. Coward himself was well acquainted with the Royal family and enjoyed a particular friendship with the Queen Mother. With his upper lip ever stiff and his manners ever polished, Mr Bridger is the epitome of the polite, deferential middle-class English gentleman, and not unlike the persona that Coward had been presenting in both his literary and public life since the 1920s. But Mr Bridger, the apparent personification of good manners, is also a criminal. The movie places Bridger at the centre of a successful criminal organization which he governs at arm's length. It seems unlikely that he would ever have made himself vulnerable enough to get caught, which begs the question *why* is he in prison at all?

Coward's presentation of the character defines Bridger as sovereign of the prison, more specifically, 'Queen' of the place. Throughout the film, Bridger gives 'the royal wave' to lesser mortals. When he is interviewing the Governor about Michael Caine breaking into his private lavatory for a chat, Bridger sits directly under a portrait of the Queen. (There is also the give-away lampshade in Bridger's cell: frilly and pink!) Bridger's sexuality, even for an audience unused to reading the symbols which a gay audience takes for granted, seems pretty obvious. He is continually accompanied by his fawningly camp companion, Keats. Keats is played by Coward's real-life lover, Graham Payn, who has had a long history of playing in Coward's work. Payn recalls in his memoirs, 'I found myself acting as film counterpart to my real-life role'.[29] Coward was playing a counterpoint to his real-life role as well: that of establishment icon harbouring a sexuality which had only recently been decriminalized and still provoked popular antipathy. In his presentation of Bridger, Coward suggests the character's homosexuality without explicitly stating it. It is a trick he had been turning in his writing for years: suggestive, sly, naughty, but never direct.

Such a style also depends on the collaboration of certain sections of the audience, as well as the relative ignorance (or innocence) of the rest. Alan Sinfield argues that Coward plays a dextrous balancing act in his work, exploiting a 'knowing subculture of privileged insiders in defiance of the respectable playgoers whose exclusion was both a necessary defensive manoeuvre and part of the joke'.[30] Sinfield observes that Coward reflected and promoted a very particular style, one that

we now recognize as the twentieth-century gay/queer identity. Oscar Wilde had manipulated the figure of the dandy into the aesthete: effete, aristocratic and of independent means. It was only after the Wilde trials that effeminacy, an interest in the arts, leisure and wealth were for the first time equated with homosexuality. Wilde got away with it for as long as he did because his ambiguous public persona was simply carrying on a particular tradition within the leisured classes.

This is the homosexual culture that Coward inherited after his birth in 1899, just a year before Wilde's death. Coward had sprung from the genteel villas of Teddington and eschewed the iconography of 1890s aestheticism, which retained its Wilde-sullied reputation until the 1920s. Coward developed a new style of aestheticism for the 1920s: a world of silk dressing-gowns, chrome and white drawing-rooms *à la* Syrie Maugham. In the same way that Wilde found a mode of expression in dandyism or the aesthetic creed, Coward attached himself to the post-Great War movement: cynical, young bohemianism. Robert Graves observed in his remembrances of the inter-war years, *The Long Weekend* (1940), that bohemianism in the 1920s stood for a 'gay disorderliness of life, cheerful bad manners and no fixed hours or sexual standards'.[31] The 1920s were the decade of the 'bright young things', who railed against the Edwardian culture which had culminated in the First World War. Women lost the costumes which emphasized their hips and busts and had their hair bobbed; an androgynous, 'boyish' look was in fashion. Cecil Beaton later recalled how this ambiguous, androgynous world evolved into a sensibility of camp:

> All sorts of men enjoyed imitating the exaggerated, clipped manner of certain leading actors and adopted the confident manner of those who were aware of their charms . . . Noël Coward's influence spread even to the outposts of Rickmansworth and Poona. Hearty naval commanders or jolly colonels acquired the 'camp' manners of calling everything from Joan of Arc to Merlin 'lots of fun' and the adjective 'terribly' peppered every sentence. All sorts of men suddenly wanted to look like Noël Coward—sleek, shiny and well-groomed with a cigarette, telephone or cocktail at hand.[32]

Both Alan Sinfield and Philip Hoare examine Coward's use of the word 'gay' in his work of the 1920s and 1930s and how his manipulation of it has contributed to the word's popular usage in the late twentieth century. It is most prevalent in Coward's revue songs. Revue had a reputation for the risqué and tended to be allowed a greater licence than 'proper' plays. Coward's rather outrageous 'Green Carnation' song from *Bitter Sweet* seems pretty blatant today, overtly conjuring the world of the dangerous Oscar Wilde:

> Faded boys, jaded boys, come what may,
> Art is our inspiration,
> And as we are the reason for the Nineties being gay,
> We all wear a green carnation.[33]

In the sketch from **Words and Music** (1932) which introduced 'Mad About The Boy', a series of women—a society hostess, a schoolgirl, a cockney and finally a tart—sing about the object of their desire, a hero of the silver screen. The schoolgirl knows that 'Houseman really / Wrote *The Shropshire Lad* about the boy'. The tart nudges the subtext even further:

> He has a gay appeal
> That makes me feel
> There's maybe something sad about the boy.[34]

Are the women aware that their devotion can never be reciprocated, not only because their beloved is a Hollywood fantasy but also because, like many screen stars from Valentino to Rock Hudson, they are gay? According to Graham Payn a 'lost' verse was to have been added to the 1938 New York production, called **Set to Music.** A business man is discovered in a 'smart office setting':

> Mad about the boy,
> I know it's silly,
> But I'm mad about the boy,
> And even Doctor Freud cannot explain
> Those vexing dreams
> I've had about the boy.
> When I told my wife,
> She said:
> 'I've never heard such nonsense in my life!'
> Her lack of sympathy
> Embarrassed me
> And made me frankly *glad* about the boy.
> My doctor can't advise me,
> He'd help me if he could;
> Three times he's tried to psychoanalyse me
> But it's just no good.
> People I employ
> Have the impertinence
> To call me Myrna Loy.
> I rise above it,
> Frankly love it,
> 'Cos I'm absolutely
> MAD ABOUT THE BOY![35]

The 'lost' verse was never included, but it provides a fascinating analogue to Coward's study of psychoanalysis and sex in **The Astonished Heart,** particularly the film version, in which a besuited writer consults his analyst about an obsessive homosexual relationship he is attempting to juggle alongside his marriage.

The word 'gay' certainly seems to have acquired its contemporary use relating to homosexual behaviour or manners in America, and Coward's transatlantic lifestyle in the 1920s and 1930s would surely have exposed him to the slang of theatrical circles over there. 'Gay' was used in its modern sense by British gay men at least during the Second World War, as the *Carry On* comedian Kenneth Williams's wartime diaries reveal. Coward's **Design for Living** was premiered on Broad-

way in 1933 with a scandalous reputation following the production's provincial tour. In *We Can Always Call Them Bulgarians,* an American study of gay plays on Broadway, Kaier Curtin notes that the adjective 'gay' was used in almost every review of the US production. Did it simply indicate that this dangerous play was a light comedy? Or were the reviewers using shorthand to describe the presentation on stage of a subversive sexual agenda? Studying the success of Coward's plays and songs on both sides of the Atlantic in this period as well as the development of the use of the word 'gay' in homosexual circles outside the theatre, Alan Sinfield concludes that the specialized usage of 'gay' as an adjective to describe homosexual behaviour 'gained currency through Coward's plays and the milieu that they helped to constitute'.[36]

COWARD'S WAY

PRIVATE LIVES

> Thank God I'm normal.
>
> John Osborne[37]

VICTOR.

> I'm glad I'm normal.

AMANDA.

> What an odd thing to be glad about.
>
> Noël Coward, *Private Lives*[38]

The epitome of Coward's style and apex of his achievement is **Private Lives.** The structure of the play skilfully reflects its thesis: the world of Elyot and Amanda is a cyclical one. Once unhappily married to each other the two are now unhappily divorced, each spending their honeymoon with their respective new spouses, Sibyl and Victor. They meet on their terrace, as fate has decreed that they have honeymoon suites next door to each other. Realizing that they are still in love with each other, they run away to Amanda's flat in Paris, leaving Sibyl and Victor behind. After a brief period of bliss, Elyot and Amanda begin to get on each other's nerves as petty past jealousies and character traits exhibit themselves once more. They fall back into their old habits of bickering and fighting and are eventually discovered in a particularly violent scrap by the arrival of the bewildered Victor and Sibyl. The next morning Sibyl and Victor reconcile themselves to their respective spouses and in so doing begin to bicker with each other. Elyot and Amanda creep out of the flat in collusive silence, leaving Sibyl and Victor to their well-matched squabbling.

Private Lives is a pure distillation of one of Coward's favourite themes: the tension between restraint and its corrosive opposite, chaos. Coward explores a particular type of reticence and awkwardness, an embarrassment over emotional/sexual issues which is very English. When they first meet again, Elyot and Amanda attempt to communicate in the polite language of restraint in order not to reveal their true feelings:

AMANDA.

What have you been doing lately? During these last years?

ELYOT.

Travelling about. I went round the world you know after . . .

AMANDA.

(*hurriedly*) Yes, yes, I know. How was it?

ELYOT.

The world?

AMANDA.

Yes.

ELYOT.

Oh, highly enjoyable.

AMANDA.

China must be very interesting.

ELYOT.

Very big, China.

AMANDA.

And Japan . . .

ELYOT.

Very small.[39]

Such social chatter deflects, but doesn't disguise, their deep-rooted attraction to each other, which exhibits itself both in moments of desire (ELYOT. There isn't a particle of you that I don't know, remember and want . . .) and in moments of discord. They can neither live with nor without each other. Having got back together, they attempt to control and regulate their behaviour by imposing an invented phrase when arguments seem to be brewing, 'Soloman Isaacs'. But even this they corrupt to the vaguely indecent sounding 'Sollocks!' Amanda realizes that they must control themselves, restrain their natural impulse to argue, because 'it's the bickering that always starts it'. Coward had explored a prototype version of the Amanda/Elyot relationship in **The Rat Trap** as early as 1918. Like Elyot and Amanda, Keld and Sheila are caught in a cycle of arguments and reconciliation, where the bickering is regarded as a necessary part of the relationship:

KELD.

I love every word you write I—

SHEILA.

(*slowly*) You said all that last week when we'd just made up a quarrel, don't you remember?

KELD.

Yes, perhaps I did, more or less, but really I can't see—

SHEILA.

You'll say it again next week, and we shall kiss and be frightfully in love until the next time after that.[40]

Keld and Sheila, like Elyot and Amanda, are trapped in each other. Sheila realizes that the only way to break the cycle is to marry somebody who won't compete either professionally or emotionally, somebody without ambition: 'We're like two rats in a trap, fighting, fighting fighting. You need a commonplace, dull, domesticated wife with no brain and boundless, open-mouthed enthusiasm for every mortal thing you do.'[41]

Elyot and Amanda have acted on Sheila's advice, but find themselves married to completely unsuitable partners. When forced to compare their present relationships with their own in the past, the new ones are found wanting. In Sibyl, Elyot has found the perfect 'dull, domesticated wife with no brain'. Sibyl doesn't threaten Elyot and, consequently, he claims to have found contentment: 'Love is no use unless it's wise and kind and undramatic. Something steady and sweet, to smooth out your nerves when you're tired. Something tremendously cosy; and unflurried by scenes and jealousies. That's what I want.'[42] It sounds as if Elyot wants a cup of tea rather than a relationship. Love that's 'kind and undramatic' and 'steady and sweet' might be Earl Grey, but it certainly isn't passion. Elyot, like Amanda, really prefers storms in his teacup. Amanda admits to Victor that she loves him 'more calmly' than she had loved Elyot. The passion and violence of Elyot and Amanda's relationship is constantly compared to their cooler relationships with Victor and Sibyl in a series of contrasts that emphasize their natural compatibility and the unsuitability, even perversity, of their present matches. Elyot is described as a violent, passionate man who has struck Amanda 'More than once . . . in several places' and would like to cut off the irritating Sibyl's head 'with a meat axe'. Amanda has been correspondingly violent to Elyot, having broken 'four gramophone records over his head'. Elyot and Amanda exchange their desire for each other in passionate exhibitions of temper and bickering. They provoke and stimulate each other. Victor and Sibyl are straightforward, simple and unprovocative:

SIBYL.

I hate these half masculine women who go banging about . . . I should think you needed a little quiet womanliness after Amanda.[43]

Coward undervalued his achievement in the creation of Victor and Sibyl, dismissing them as 'puppets thrown in to assist the plot and to provide contrast'.[44] But they are an important touchstone of normality, good manners and ordinariness which offsets Elyot and Amanda's idiosyncrasies. They also complete the intricate cyclical pattern of the play: infected by Elyot and Amanda's standards they eventually begin to adopt their behaviour. At the beginning of the play, even the smallest details express their difference from Elyot and Amanda. They refer to their spouses with diminutives straight out of the nursery, 'Elli' and 'Mandy', further emphasizing the childlike and passionless nature of these new relationships:

VICTOR.

You know I feel rather scared of you at close quarters.

AMANDA.

That promises to be very embarrassing.[45]

Embarrassing and inappropriate to the honeymoon spirit. Neither Victor nor Sibyl likes sunburned women, not thinking it 'awfully suitable'. Amanda, however, is determined to turn a 'nice, crisp brown'. Coward and Gertrude Lawrence were part of the Riviera social set who made sunburn fashionable for the first time in the 1920s. Elyot and Amanda's love of sunburn is ultra-fashionable and also indicates a sense of gender equality which is alien to the rather pompous and old-fashioned notions about feminine beauty which Victor expresses and to which Sibyl is quite happy to conform. Neither do Amanda and Elyot care for 'heartiness' in men, rejecting the conventional gender roles which society would have them play:

ELYOT.

If you think you'd like me to smoke a pipe, I shall try and master it.[46]

Elyot is quite content to be thought unmanly and effete, just as Amanda is happy to be thought 'half-masculine': conventional notions of gender really don't bother them. In contrast Sibyl is a 'completely feminine little creature' who 'likes a man to be a man'. In Act III Victor challenges Elyot to 'behave like a man', which Elyot finds 'very right and proper and highly traditional, but . . . won't get us very far'.[47] The contrast between Victor and Elyot, Sibyl and Amanda is the contrast of the uninitiated with those who are 'jagged with sophistication'. Sibyl and Victor are innocents in the complex emotional tangle of Elyot and Amanda's relationship. Unknowingly, they become drawn into the cycle of Elyot and Amanda's life. When Amanda wonders whose yacht she spies, Elyot can make a socially educated guess: 'the Duke of Westminster's I expect. It usually is.' When Sibyl sees the yacht, Victor

can only 'wonder who it belongs to'. Elyot and Amanda share a social and emotional hinterland which is completely alien to their new spouses. These superficial contrasts serve to underline the differences of personal morality between Elyot/Amanda and Victor/Sibyl. When both Elyot and Amanda admit a compulsion to gamble in the casino on their respective honeymoon nights, their new spouses become rather alarmed: is this an indication of the tenor of their lives together, that their new partners prefer gambling to honeymoon romance? Elyot and Amanda reveal that they are resigned to the fact that chance rather than custom rules their lives.

Ultimately, the ability of Elyot and Amanda to control themselves and succumb to the vagaries of good manners fails and Act II ends famously with the pair of them writhing on the floor, *'rolling over and over in paroxysms of rage'* with Amanda screaming 'Beast, brute, swine, cad, beast, beast, brute, devil.'[48] It is a savage parody of sexual coupling, with the confused Victor and Sibyl looking on voyeuristically; for, despite the cocktails and Molyneux dresses, sex is the motivating force of **Private Lives,** with the repartée and violent arguments only the tip of Coward's iceberg. Cecil Beaton remembered Gertrude Lawrence's ability to ooze sexuality as Amanda:

> Though not a great beauty, she used her gifts to heighten her attractiveness and possessed the flavour and personality of the age to a high degree. She was a combination of remarkable contrasts. Her mellifluous voice was yet rather curdled. Her somewhat simian features were sunburnt. The long, loose-fitting dresses she wore suggested more than an indication of the vital, well-shaped figure beneath them; she could look remarkably provocative in a dress that covered her body almost completely. She smoked cigarettes with a nuance that implied having just come out of bed and wanting to get back into it.[49]

That 'just fucked' look characterizes the tone of the play, more so than the art deco paraphernalia which so often suffocates productions of it. The play advocates the supremacy of the sex instinct over all other considerations: legal, moral or religious. 'I'm apt to see [morals] the wrong way round',[50] Amanda admits to the uncomprehending Victor. Elyot and Amanda aren't complicated by familial responsibilities, neither by keeping up a family name nor by having to consider children of their own. They live for pleasure, for the experience of life. In many ways they are typical inhabitants of the hedonistic 1920s. Their lives are not conditioned by the desire or necessity to procreate and both have been sexually promiscuous. In 1930, it was only thirty years since the publication of Freud's *Interpretation of Dreams,* and his notion of the natural practice of non-procreational sex was in the process of becoming popularized. Like George and Martha in *Who's Afraid of Virginia Woolf* (1962), Elyot and

Amanda will live in this dance of union and parting for ever. When they run off to Paris together, Amanda observes that they're now living in sin:

ELYOT.

> Not according to the Catholics, Catholics don't recognise divorce. We're married as ever we were.

AMANDA.

> Yes, dear, but we're not Catholics.

ELYOT.

> Never mind, it's nice to think they'd sort of back us up. We were married in the eyes of Heaven, and we still are.

AMANDA.

> We may be alright in the eyes of Heaven, but we look like being in the hell of a mess socially.[51]

Religion is manipulated by Elyot and Amanda to suit their social convenience and marriage is flippantly regarded as a social ceremony rather than a sacrament or spiritual commitment. The housekeeper in *The Rat Trap,* speaking from her own experience and from her observation of the deteriorating relationship between Sheila and Keld, sees marriage as only a 'snare', an unhappy convention that doesn't solve the problems of sharing a life with somebody: 'The one thing love never teaches you is how to manage each other.'[52] This is Amanda and Elyot's problem, but rather than seek the solution to their erratic relationship within themselves, Amanda blames the institution of marriage itself for destabilizing her relationship with Elyot: 'I believe it was just the fact of our being married and clamped together publicly that wrecked us before.'[53] Now that their renewed relationship will be a private one and necessarily lived outside society, they will have no such excuses to fall back on. When they dance to the gramophone they satirize the society they have now placed themselves beyond:

AMANDA.

> Is that the Grand Duchess Olga lying under the piano?

ELYOT.

> Yes, her husband died a few weeks ago, you know, on his way back from Pulborough. So sad.

AMANDA.

> What on earth was he doing in Pulborough?

ELYOT.

> Nobody knows exactly, but there have been the usual stories.[54]

They are funny and camp and apparently happy, but when they stop dancing they find that they are alone in their fantasy ballroom. Elyot and Amanda are a breed apart, the same sophisticated species. They have a shared culture, a shared language and a shared sense of humour. When they first meet, Amanda finishes the song Elyot is humming, a moment of their shared past revisited. Coward noted in *Present Indicative* that 'We [i.e. he and Gertrude Lawrence] had the parts, or rather, the part, as "Elyot" and "Amanda" are practically synonymous'.[55] Their relationship lasts as long as it lasts. It changes, they split, they re-form. This symbiotic relationship echoes Aristophanes's speech in Plato's *Symposium*: two halves of the same divided soul searching for fulfilment in each other.[56] In many ways, Elyot and Amanda's relationship dramatizes the Platonic theory of love: a search for truth and beauty by two people of the same sex, inspired by mutual affection for each other. It is telling that the song that brings the two back together is 'Someday I'll Find You'. They find each other again because they are 'soul-mates'. Each of them recognizes that they are mutually to blame for the state of their relationship and both accept that blame. In Act I, Elyot admits, 'We made each other miserable' and that 'We lost each other'. Elyot and Amanda are not only synonymous but also inevitable.

In Coward's universe control, decency and manners are the antithesis of passion and individualism, and works as superficially different as *Private Lives* and *Brief Encounter* uphold the same agenda. Coward explores this thesis throughout the 1920s and 1930s in some of his most celebrated works—*Hay Fever, The Vortex, Design for Living*—all of which present characters who attempt to control their behaviour and capitulate to 'good manners', but who ultimately fail. Each of these works also explores some sort of unorthodox sexuality. In *Hay Fever* the Blisses respond outrageously melodramatically to the smallest declaration of affection, sending up the very idea of heterosexual relationships and romantic love as a game. *The Vortex* explores the world of drug dependency and Oedipal love. Coward's design for living in the play of that name is a bisexual threesome. As part of their rejection of the prevailing social and moral codes, Elyot and Amanda are typical of Coward's 1930s characters in their refusal to capitulate to the dictates of any religion:

ELYOT.

> You have no faith, that's what's wrong with you.

AMANDA.

> Absolutely none.

ELYOT.

> Don't you believe in—? (*He nods upwards.*)

AMANDA.

> No, do you?

ELYOT.

No. What about—? (*He points downwards.*)

AMANDA.

Oh dear, no.[57]

Elyot and Amanda inhabit the modernist universe of Conrad, Eliot and Forster. They share the bleak apprehension of human existence that Forster explored in *A Passage to India,* but laugh at the abyss that terrifies Miss Quested and Mrs Moore. In the Marabar Caves 'Everything exists, nothing has value'. Mrs Moore despises 'poor little talkative Christianity, and she knew that all its divine words from "Let there be light" to "It is finished" only amounted to "boum"',[58] the cave's terrible, empty echo:

ELYOT.

Let's be superficial and pity the poor philosophers. Let's blow trumpets and squeakers and enjoy the party as much as we can like small quite idiotic schoolchildren. Let's savour the delight of the moment. Come and kiss me darling before your body rots and worms pop in and out of your eye sockets.[59]

Like Forster, Coward concludes that there is no solution to the dilemma of mortality: 'Death's very laughable. . . . All done with mirrors.' The only option is to love, to live in the present. It is the pessimism that distinguishes Modernist literature; life for Elyot and Amanda is simply a cycle of 'Birth and copulation and death'.[60] Their separate travels around the world, their affairs and marriages are mere distractions in the dark and empty twentieth-century universe. As soon as they see each other again their fates are sealed. Elyot's attraction to Amanda expresses a simple, deep human need: 'You don't hold any mystery for me, do you mind? There isn't a particle of you that I don't know, remember, and want'.[61]

Private Lives differs from most of Coward's other comedies because it does actually explore the protagonists' lives as lived in private rather than the burden of fame and the adoption of a public persona. From *The Rat Trap, Design for Living* and *Present Laughter* to his final stage work *A Song at Twilight,* Coward explores how the public face complicates the private, and the uneasy relationship that exists between the two. Elyot and Amanda on the other hand don't care about their public face. They don't care about society and if they are exposed they will 'behave exquisitely'. Recognizing that their attitudes and behaviour aren't the norm, they cherish their ambivalence:

VICTOR.

I'm glad I'm normal.

AMANDA.

What an odd thing to be glad about. Why?

VICTOR.

Well, aren't you?

AMANDA.

I'm not so sure I'm normal.[62]

Leo, Otto and Gilda, in **Design for Living,** travel from Paris to London to New York in order to fit their 'abnormal' relationship into an established society. They try to reconcile themselves with the society of the major metropolitan centres of Western civilization. They, like Elyot and Amanda, discover that the only way to live outside society's conventions is to live without it. Amanda's knowledge of her own difference enables her to see just how different we all are and how absurd, therefore, are the plastic conventions of society:

I think very few people are completely normal really, deep down in their private lives. It all depends on a combination of circumstances. If all the various cosmic thingummys fuse at the same moment, and the right spark is struck, there's no knowing what one mightn't do.[63]

Amanda admits the possibility of everything. There are no hard and fast rules. Such an all-embracing philosophy is full of opportunity and novelty. But it is also a philosophy of risk. In rejecting the safe tracks of convention, Amanda also rejects their security. But the acceptance of the mutability of relationships is regarded as par for the course, the price of liberty. Elyot and Amanda's acceptance of change and loss as part of life, particularly the death of love, is rather sad:

ELYOT.

Things that ought to matter dreadfully, don't matter at all when one's happy, do they?

AMANDA.

What is so horrible is that one can't stay happy.

ELYOT.

Darling don't say that.

AMANDA.

It's true, the whole business is a very poor joke.

ELYOT.

Meaning that sacred and beautiful thing, Love?

AMANDA.

Yes, meaning just that.

ELYOT.

(*striding up and down the room melodramatically*)
What does it all mean, that's what I ask myself in my
ceaseless quest for ultimate truth. Dear God, what does
it all mean?

AMANDA.

Don't laugh at me, I'm serious.[64]

In the 1960s, Coward observed that the theme of *Private
Lives* was 'two people who love each other too much. I
wouldn't say it's a tragedy, but there's a certain sadness
below it . . .'. Elyot and Amanda are aware that things
will never remain constant and that love, trust and
dependency necessarily incur pain, mistrust and disappointment. It is no coincidence that Leo, the Coward-
figure in *Design for Living,* scores his first success with
a play called *Change and Decay.* It could be a subtitle
for *Private Lives.* Like *The Importance of Being Earnest,* when first reviewed, *Private Lives* was dismissed
as a triviality, a piece of fluff. Nearly seventy years later
it reveals itself to be a superb black comedy of sexual
manners masquerading as a light comedy. Marriage is
discussed flippantly and fidelity within it is trivialized.
The play is Coward's rallying cry in support of
unorthodox ways of living. In the world of *Private Lives*
there are no certainties other than death; and it is death
alone that puts an end to physical pleasure, not laws,
not morals and certainly not the inconstant conventions
of society.

BLITHE SPIRIT

Sometimes in the corridors, I fancy I hear her just
behind me. That quick, light footstep . . . I've fancied
I hear her . . . calling to Mr de Winter the way she
used to. Do you think she can see us now? Do you
think the dead come back and watch the living?[65]

So asks the wonderfully obsessive housekeeper, Mrs
Danvers, in Daphne du Maurier's hugely popular stage
adaptation of her even more successful novel, *Rebecca.*
Du Maurier's biographer, Margaret Forster, observes
that the author was disappointed by early criticism of
the novel in 1938 which focused on its gothic Brontë-
like qualities. Du Maurier had intended the novel as a
psychological examination of the second Mrs de
Winter's jealous obsession with her husband's dead
wife, Rebecca. Du Maurier's stage version opened in
the West End in April 1940. Celia Johnson played the
second Mrs de Winter and Margaret Rutherford played
Mrs Danvers. Coward's *Blithe Spirit* opened at the Piccadilly Theatre in July 1941, with Rutherford playing
Madam Arcati. The two plays were amongst the most
successful of the war, and *Blithe Spirit*'s run of 1,997
performances was only surpassed by that of *The Mouse-
trap.* Though both *Blithe Spirit* and *Rebecca* were written, as well as produced, during a major world conflict,

neither directly mentions the war. However, both plays
examine narratives in which people in their prime have
unexpectedly died and in so doing are able to discuss
death and the operation of grief. Margaret Rutherford,
who created the role of Madam Arcati, genuinely
believed in spiritualism and only took on the part when
she had been assured that it was not to be a send-up: 'I
regard this as a very serious play, almost a tragedy. I
don't see it as a comedy at all.'[66] Coward and du Maurier do explore wartime anxieties about death, but do so
in the English way, with discretion. Though Rebecca
remains unseen throughout the drama, she forms the
same sort of *ménage à trois* that Charles, Ruth and
Elvira do in *Blithe Spirit.* Rebecca is not a ghost, but
rather a psychological manifestation in the mind of the
second Mrs de Winter. Elvira, on the other hand, does
come back and 'watch the living', haunting both Charles
and his second wife, Ruth.

Elvira's appearance as a ghost and the ensuing supernatural pranks are wonderfully theatrical. But like
Rebecca, Blithe Spirit is as much a play about sexual
jealousy as it is about mortality. The title quotes Shelley's 'To a Skylark':

Hail to thee, blithe Spirit!
Bird thou never wert,
That from Heaven, or near it,
Pourest thy full heart
In profuse strains of unpremeditated art.

Shelley's poem provides more than just a sexy title,
though, as it actually reflects the darkly humorous tone
of the play:

Our sincerest laughter
With some pain is fraught;
Our sweetest songs are those that tell of saddest
thought.

Coward had gone to the Welsh village of Portmeirion
with Joyce Carey in order to write the play. Portmeirion
is Clough Williams-Ellis's bizarre fantasy version of a
Mediterranean village, a mass Italianate folly, and
perhaps the absurdity of the surroundings contributed to
the strange tragi-comic humour of the play. Carey was
intending to write a play about the young Romantic
poet, John Keats, and his beloved Fanny Brawne, and
the discussion of the work of the Romantics between
the two friends seems to have been absorbed into
Coward's play. Shelley's contemporary and fellow
champion of Romanticism, William Wordsworth, had
written a companion poem, 'To the Cuckoo', which
also reflects Coward's title:

O blithe New-comer! I have heard,
I hear thee and rejoice.
O Cuckoo! shall I call thee Bird,
Or but a wandering Voice;

Cuckoos, of course, are traditionally believed to steal other birds' nests. When Madam Arcati opens the windows to take some air before the seance, it is not the skylark she hears but a cuckoo: 'That cuckoo is very angry'.[67] Ruth has stolen Elvira's 'nest' as well as her mate. Charles and Ruth Condomine have both been married before and each of their respective spouses has died. Like the second marriages of Elyot and Amanda in *Private Lives,* the Condomines' relationship is much calmer than their first marriages. Both have experienced a certain promiscuity and have now settled into a comfortable, not particularly passionate, relationship:

RUTH.

> We've neither of us led exactly prim lives, have we? . . . Careless rapture at this stage would be incongruous and embarrassing.[68]

Even before the arrival of Madam Arcati for the seance, Ruth asks, 'Was she more physically attractive than I am?' The fact is that Elvira *was* more attractive than Ruth. Just as Elyot and Amanda talk about their former spouses just a little too much for comfort on their second honeymoons, Ruth insists on comparing herself to Elvira. It seems that Charles is no more happy with Ruth's cool, comfortable love than Elyot is with a love that's 'wise and kind and undramatic'. After Elvira's arrival, Ruth becomes 'glacial' and 'increasingly domineering'. Charles talks of her 'gentle comradely hand'. With Elvira to compare her to, Ruth is 'granite . . . sheer, unyielding granite'. Elvira is simply the catalyst who reveals Charles's dissatisfaction with Ruth to himself.

Charles is a writer who is keen to gather material for his new book, *The Unseen,* which is to be about a charlatan spiritualist. He wants to pick up some tricks of the trade first hand and has consequently invited a local medium to dinner, Madam Arcati. After dinner Madam Arcati, the Condomines and their guests, the sceptical Dr Bradman and his wife, settle down to a seance. After the seance, Madam Arcati senses that there has been some sort of psychic happening, and indeed Charles's first wife has materialized but only Charles can see and hear her. The deceased Elvira enters the Condomines' living-room as if she has just left a cocktail party, albeit one that is attended by Joan of Arc, Merlin and Ghenghis Khan. Manners and breeding still count: 'It's considered vulgar to say "dead" where I come from.' The other world doesn't seem so very different from the one Elvira has left. In order to revisit Charles, Elvira has had to 'fill in all those forms and wait about in draughty passages for hours', as if she were applying for a wartime travel permit. Like the American troop song popular during the war, Elvira's new 'home' is referred to as 'over there' or 'on the other side' as if she had recently returned from a cruise on the *Queen Mary*. When asked where she actually

comes from Elvira replies that she has 'forgotten'. As in *Private Lives* death is 'laughable, such a cunning little mystery. All done with mirrors.' There is little metaphysical speculation in *Blithe Spirit.* Heaven and Hell are only mentioned as expletives. The ease with which Charles and Elvira talk to each other on their first supernatural meeting reflects the same sort of comfortable familiarity that Elyot and Amanda displayed on their first meeting since the divorce. Though she can neither drink nor eat, Elvira can, of course, smoke. Much of the comedy of Elvira is that she is so ordinary and familiar—so lively, in fact.

Madam Arcati implies that Elvira's materialization must have been inspired by Charles's wishful thinking. For Charles, there isn't a particle of Elvira that he doesn't 'know, remember and want'. Even before she appears, Charles has been haunted by her memory. When she challenges him, Charles says that 'I shall always love the memory of you'. He yearns to touch her, as their previous relationship had been physical and passionate, even violent: 'you hit me with a billiard cue'. Charles is haunted by the memory of desire. In Elvira's return, like Leontes in *The Winter's Tale,* Charles has been offered the fulfilment of a fantasy, the resurrection of a loved one, the opportunity for a second chance. Charles asks Elvira, 'Is it cold—being a ghost?', just as Leontes touches the statue of Hermione and finds that 'she's warm'. A touching frustration exists between Charles and Elvira, as they can both see and hear their object of desire, but cannot fulfil their yearning to touch each other:

ELVIRA.

> I loved you very much.

CHARLES.

> I loved you too. . . . No I can't touch you—isn't that horrible?[69]

The return of Elvira from beyond the grave initiates a bizarre 'astral' *ménage à trois*. The triangular relationship is a favourite Cowardian device in which he challenges the apparent security of conventional relationships. Charles's relationship with Ruth is passionless in contrast with the very physical relations he had enjoyed with Elvira. His relationship with Ruth now cold, and unable to physically consummate his relationship with his dead wife, Charles is in a peculiar state of sexual stasis, a sort of erotic limbo.

The structure and much of the comedy of *Blithe Spirit,* like *Private Lives* and *Design for Living,* is cyclical. When Ruth becomes exasperated by Charles's insistence that Elvira has materialized, she shouts, 'To Hell with Elvira!' But Elvira has only recently arrived from wherever she is resident 'over there'. When Elvira soothingly seduces Charles she dismisses Ruth in Ruth's own language: 'To Hell with Ruth.' Like Mrs Arbuthnot in *A Woman of No Importance,* Elvira dismisses her rival with the language of the enemy. Her understanding of Ruth and her language, the language of the living, is part of her danger. She is both familiar and 'other'.

Cowardian comedy is like a formal dance, a never-ending game of exchanging partners. These characters live for the moment and pay little heed to mortality. Without children to occupy them or oblige them to stay together, and with little serious regard for marriage vows, these relationships last as long as desire lasts. Structurally and thematically the characters are caught in cycles of their own making—of bickering and making up and bickering again. When Ruth and Elvira are finally being dematerialized, Elvira venomously admits that she had slept with Captain Bracegirdle whilst on her honeymoon with Charles adding that she 'couldn't have enjoyed it more . . .'. Like Rattigan's Alan Howard in *French Without Tears* and Maugham's dual heroes in *Home and Beauty,* Charles Condomine now frees himself of the tenacious grasp of the female sex. Charles realizes that he has been 'hag-ridden' all his life, first by his mother and then by Elvira, Ruth and the voracious Mrs Winthrop Llewelyn. He now delights in his new-found, woman-free liberty and though he knows that the three are bound to meet again one day, vows 'to enjoy myself as I've never enjoyed myself before'. Charles, like Elvira, is talking about sexual enjoyment. Having rid himself of the two women in his life once and for all, we wonder just who he is going to enjoy himself with? Perhaps Charles thinks he'll be lucky with women third time round? Or perhaps his new freedom will involve the boys this time?

The final scene in the 1945 film version has Charles leaving the house, with the unseen poltergeist spirits of Ruth and Elvira rather too helpfully sending him on his way. Charles drives off in his car. Elvira and Ruth stand on the bridge where Ruth had died and wait for Charles's booby-trapped car to crash. Charles's ghost drops between the two female spirits. Theirs will be a supernatural *ménage à trois,* where they can bicker and reconcile their differences for eternity. Like George and Martha and Elyot and Amanda, the three ghosts are trapped with each other in a compulsive and never-ending cycle. The ending of the play offers Charles a temporary freedom as the two female ghosts destroy the house between them and he exits from the ensuing chaos, sarcastically quoting from *Romeo and Juliet,* the archetypal tragic romance: 'parting is such *sweet* sorrow!' Romeo and Juliet are united in death because of their devotion for each other, and eventually Charles will be reunited for eternity and in enmity with both Ruth and Elvira. But the last line is also an ironic reference back to Shelley's 'To a Skylark', further stressing

the bitter-sweet tone of the play.[70] The ending of the film speeds up the whole process and we catch a glimpse of Charles's eternal fate. Anticipating Sartre's conclusion to his black comedy, *Huis Clos,* Charles discovers that hell really is other people, or, reading both Coward (and Sartre) less sympathetically, that hell is an eternity trapped by women:

INEZ.

So here we are, for ever. (*laughs*)

ESTELLE.

(*with a peal of laughter*) For ever. My God, how funny! For ever.

GARCIN.

(*looks at the two women and joins in the laughter*) For ever and ever, and ever.

(*They slump on to their respective sofas. A long silence. Their laughter dies away, and they gaze at each other.*)

GARCIN.

Well, well, let's get on with it . . .[71]

Notes

1. Graham Payn (with Barry Day), *My Life with Noël Coward* (London: Applause, 1994), p. 278.

2. Edward Albee, article in *New York Times,* quoted in *Evening Standard* (London), undated cutting.

3. Oscar Wilde in Richard Ellman (ed.), *The Artist as Critic* (London: W. H. Allen, 1970), p. 192.

4. Kenneth Tynan, 'A tribute to Mr Coward (1953)', in *A View of the English Stage 1944-65* (London: Methuen, 1984), p. 137.

5. Noël Coward, *The Rat Trap,* in *Play Parade,* Vol. III (London: Heinemann, 1950), p. 370.

6. Graham Payn, *My Life with Noël Coward,* p. 297.

7. *Blithe Spirit* (1945), director, David Lean; screenplay by Anthony Havelock-Allan, David Lean and Ronald Neame from Coward's play.

8. Noël Coward, *Present Laughter,* in *Plays: Four* (London: Methuen, 1983), p. 182.

9. Payn, *My Life with Noël Coward,* p. 209.

10. Coward, *Present Laughter,* p. 236.

11. *Ibid.,* p. 242.

12. Garry.

I'm always acting—watching myself go by—that's what's so horrible—I see myself all the time, drinking, loving, suffering—sometimes I think I'm going mad—

(*Present Laughter,* Act 1, p. 148)

13. *Ibid.,* p. 174.

14. Directed by Scott Elliott and featuring Frank Langella as Essendine. See John Lahr, 'Mr Producer, I'm talkin' to you, Sir', *New Yorker,* 25 November 1996, pp. 123-25.

15. *Ibid.,* p. 222.

16. *Ibid.,* p. 224.

17. Noël Coward, *A Song at Twilight,* in *Plays: Five* (London: Methuen, 1983), p. 371.

18. Coward, *Present Laughter,* p. 233.

19. *Ibid.,* p. 231.

20. *Ibid.,* p. 234.

21. Philip Hoare, *Noël Coward: A Biography* (London: Sinclair-Stevenson, 1995), p. 509.

22. Payn, *My Life with Noël Coward,* p. 138.

23. *Ibid.,* p. 139.

24. Coward, *A Song at Twilight,* p. 409.

25. *Ibid.,* p. 406.

26. *Ibid.,* p. 418.

27. *Ibid.,* p. 424.

28. Cecil Beaton, *Self-portrait with Friends,* edited by Richard Buckle (London: Weidenfeld & Nicolson, 1979), pp. 11-12.

29. Payn, *My Life with Noël Coward,* p. 238.

30. Alan Sinfield, 'Private lives/public theatre: Noël Coward and the politics of homosexual representation', *Representations,* 36 (Fall 1991), pp. 43-63.

31. Robert Graves and Alan Hodge, *The Long Weekend* (London: Faber, 1940), p. 12.

32. Cecil Beaton, *The Glass of Fashion* (London: Cassell, 1954), p. 153 (reprinted 1989).

33. Noël Coward, *Bitter Sweet,* in *Plays: Two* (London: Methuen, 1979), p. 171.

34. Noël Coward, *The Lyrics of Noël Coward* (New York: Tusk/Overlook, 1983).

35. Payn, *My Life With Noël Coward,* p. 4.

36. Sinfield, 'Private lives/public theatre'.

37. John Osborne, *The Entertainer* (London: Faber & Faber, 1957), p. 60.

38. Noël Coward, *Private Lives,* in *Plays: Two* (London: Methuen, 1985), p. 16.

39. *Ibid.,* pp. 33-4.

40. Coward, *The Rat Trap,* p. 395.

41. *Ibid.,* p. 401.

42. Coward, *Private Lives,* p. 7.

43. *Ibid.,* p. 8.

44. Noël Coward, Introduction, *Plays: Two,* p. xiv.

45. Coward, *Private Lives,* p. 15.

46. *Ibid.,* p. 7.

47. *Ibid.,* p. 73.

48. *Ibid.,* p. 64.

49. Cecil Beaton, *The Glass of Fashion* (London: Cassell, 1954), pp. 153-4.

50. Coward, *Private Lives,* p. 17.

51. *Ibid.,* pp. 42-3.

52. Coward, *The Rat Trap,* p. 433.

53. Coward, *Private Lives,* p. 43.

54. *Ibid.,* p. 46.

55. Noël Coward, *Present Indicative: The Autobiography of Noël Coward* (London: Methuen, 1986), p. 229.

56. In this period, classical writing which discussed 'the unspeakable vice of the Greeks' was important in the construction of homosexual identity. The *Symposium* was particularly important as a way for homosexual (usually educated) men to identify their sexuality. It was also often used by homosexual men as a relatively safe way of proclaiming their sexuality to others. Being ancient Greek, classical and therefore 'educational', the *Symposium* was almost absolved of its radical agenda and therefore a safe shared frame of reference. In *Maurice,* Clive repeatedly asks Maurice to read the *Symposium* in the vacation, as a way of making it clear what sort of relationship he would like to have with him. As well as discussing the position of various types of homosexual relationship in Athenian democracy, the *Symposium* also examines the cultural status of different forms of heterosexual relationships. In Diotima's speech on the nature of sexual love, Plato places procreation as the lowest form that Eros can take.

57. Coward, *Private Lives,* p. 50.

58. E. M. Forster, *A Passage to India* (London: Arnold, 1971), p. 157.

59. Coward, *Private Lives,* p. 57.

60. T. S. Eliot, 'Sweeney Agonistes', in *Collected Poems and Plays* (London: Faber & Faber, 1969), p. 122.

61. Coward, *Private Lives,* p. 35.

62. *Ibid.,* p. 16.

63. *Ibid.*

64. *Ibid.,* p. 56.

65. Daphne du Maurier, Stage version of *Rebecca* (London: Samuel French, 1939), p. 37.

66. Hoare, *Noël Coward,* p. 321.

67. Noël Coward, *Blithe Spirit,* in *Plays: Four,* p. 24.

68. *Ibid.,* p. 9.

69. *Ibid.,* p. 48.

70. Shelley, 'To a Skylark', 'Our sweetest songs are those that tell of saddest thought.'

71. Jean-Paul Sartre, *Huis Clos,* translated by Stuart Gilbert as *In Camera,* in *Three European Plays* (London: Penguin, 1965), p. 191.

Sos Eltis (essay date summer 2008)

SOURCE: Eltis, Sos. "Bringing Out the Acid: Noël Coward, Harold Pinter, Ivy Compton-Burnett and the Uses of Camp."[1] *Modern Drama* 51, no. 2 (summer 2008): 211-32.

[*In the following essay, Eltis describes the essence of "camp" as outlined by Susan Sontag in her famous essay "Camp" and relates the ways in which Coward's plays illustrate Sontag's premise.*]

"These notes are for Oscar Wilde," wrote Susan Sontag in her famous essay on "Camp" (277). Wildean epigrams intersperse her observations, both as illustrations of the workings and mindset of the sensibility she defines as camp, and as an indication that camp can be seen not merely as a matter of taste, but as a mode of operating and a philosophy of life. Noël Coward dismissed Wilde as "a tiresome, affected sod," "silly, conceited, inadequate" and, worst of all, "a 'beauty-lover',", his distaste hardly suggesting a close affinity between the author of *Private Lives* and Sontag's camp aesthetic of artifice and frivolity, of which Wilde is for her the epitome.[2] Coward's plays receive glancing mention in Sontag's "Notes" as an example of intentional camp, that which means to be funny, as opposed to "Genuine Camp," which is always naïve and takes itself entirely seriously (282). Yet Sontag's "Notes on 'Camp'" repeatedly evoke an ethos and style that lies at the heart of Coward's theatrical technique.

The essence of camp sensibility, Sontag declares, is a love of the unnatural, of style and artifice. Rooted in passion, it is the glorification of character: "Character," she writes, "is understood as a state of continual incandescence—a person being one, very intense thing" (286). Urban not rural, closely related to boredom, playful, witty and frivolous, Sontag's camp describes the essence of so many of Coward's characters, inhabiting the Riviera and the cocktail hour with careful insouciance, raising a finely-shaped eyebrow at the obtuseness of others and themselves (275-292). Camp captures both the mode of his plays and their mood; it "incarnates a victory of 'style' over 'content,' 'aesthetics' over 'morality,' of irony over tragedy" (287), which springs, not from the sterility and emotional aloofness that such priorities could suggest, but from a generous joy that mocks seriousness and lightly reveals the brutality that underlies moral strictures. "Camp taste is, above all, a mode of enjoyment, of appreciation—not judgement," according to Sontag, and it offers a comic vision of the world, "not a bitter or polemical comedy," but comedy as "an experience of under-involvement, of detachment" (291, 288).

From the early works— *I'll Leave it to You* (1919), *The Young Idea* (1921), and *This Was a Man* (1926)— through to his most celebrated comedies— *Hay Fever* (1924), *Private Lives* (1929), *Design for Living* (1932), *Present Laughter* (1939), *Blithe Spirit* (1941)—and encompassing numerous revue sketches along the way, frivolity, irony, and poise are at the heart of Coward's writing.[3] The sensibility that Sontag celebrates breathes through them, not just as the element they inhabit but as a technique they very deliberately employ. Many of Coward's plays, of course, eschew this sensibility and style, all those, in particular, that were written with deliberately "serious" intent—*Post Mortem* (1930), *Cavalcade* (1931), *This Happy Breed* (1939), and *Peace in Our Time* (1947), for example. But the absent-minded insouciance of plays like *Blithe Spirit* and *Present Laughter,* disdaining to ask the audience's love or approval for their protagonists, is unmistakably camp. In *Hay Fever,* for example, no curtain speeches expound the superiority of the Bliss family's values; audiences are left to be entertained or irritated by them and their ability to run rings round the staid and self-important. The plays' comic resolutions are incomplete: *Blithe Spirit*'s Charles Condomine fleeing the furious ghosts of his dead wives; Elyot and Amanda at the end of *Private Lives,* escaping hand-in-hand to an uncertain future of passion and intense irritation; the Bliss family self-centredly oblivious to the discomfiture of their surreptitiously departing guests. This is the ironic disengagement of camp, operating outside the conventional borders of comedy and tragedy, lacking the emotional and social commitment that gives them meaning.

Sontag identifies two kinds of camp: naïve or pure camp is unintentional, innocently vulgar, "good because it's awful" (292); conscious camp, on the other hand, is intentionally funny, a self-performance she describes as

"Being-as-Playing-a-Role . . . the farthest extension, in sensibility, of the metaphor of life as theatre" (280).[4] Sontag cites Coward as an example of this self-conscious "camping," and his characters are, indeed, knowing self-performers, commenting on the success or otherwise of their effects (282).

Present Laughter is Coward's comic critique of self-performance as a *modus vivendi*. Garry Essendine's existence is an unceasing theatrical performance, his matinee idol persona leading him to seduce women as an almost Pavlovian reflex. He is trapped by the mechanism of his own charm—a charm and persona that, the play reveals, are constructed and maintained with considerable expertise not only by Garry himself but by a team of friends and employees, who guard his sleep, answer his mail, and prevent him from playing Peer Gynt. Having spent so much of the play delivering theatrical set pieces as his own spontaneous thoughts, Garry tries to dismiss a string of unwanted admirers with tirades of declarative emotion, only to have each of them reject the bits that don't suit their purposes as insincere acting and select the bits that do as "truth." Yet the question of where performance ceases and interiority begins is never answered. The play breaks down such simple binaries. In keeping with Harold Pinter's famous declaration that "there can be no hard distinctions between . . . what is true and what is false . . . it can be both true and false," so Garry Essendine's instincts, emotions, and needs lie in uneasy but not necessarily contradictory relation to his hyper-articulacy, self-awareness and self-construction ("Writing for the Theatre" 11). The play is a comic analysis of theatricality and identity, which challenges both performers and audience to determine the relation between sincerity and style, "essential self" and performance.[5]

Present Laughter is itself an exercise in Being-as-Playing-a-Role, for just as Garry's self-performance defies any simple division between life and theatre, so the play as a whole hovers provocatively between dramatic reality and metatheatricality. Challenged to identify the note of "truth" or "sincerity" in Garry's utterances, the audience is further baffled in struggling to determine on what level of "reality" to receive the play itself. When Joanna, another would-be lover offering her services to Garry, is interrupted by the doorbell and wonders who it is, Garry exclaims, "With any luck it's the Lord Chamberlain," as if calling on the theatrical censor to rescue him from this excess of sexual opportunity (237). When Garry informs Morris that provincial audiences have often proved to be more intelligent than London ones, Morris warns him to "Be careful! Someone might hear!"—a line which plays equally well inside or outside the capital (243). Thus when Garry tiptoes out with his ex-wife Liz, leaving his aspiring lovers to argue it out between themselves, the echo of Elyot and

Amanda's exit in ***Private Lives*** offers a further challenge to the search for authenticity and truth. In this sense, Coward's play is not just an exercise in life-as-theatre but an examination of it, not just knowingly camp but self-questioningly so.

Sontag notes the vulgar use of the verb, "to camp," and defines it as "a mode of seduction—one which employs flamboyant mannerisms susceptible of a double interpretation; gestures full of duplicity, with a witty meaning for cognoscenti and another, more impersonal, for outsiders" (281). Coward's dialogue could thus be identified as verbal camp. The Bliss family in ***Hay Fever*** constantly use language in a way that is entirely comprehensible to them but leaves their guests high and dry; Elyot and Amanda leave their legal spouses floundering in their inability to master the acquired layers of meaning beyond the literal level of their exchanges. This mastery of subtext is the aspect of Coward's writing that Kenneth Tynan sums up in a quote from Coward's one-act ***Shadow Play***: "Small talk, . . . a lot of small talk, with other thoughts going on beneath" (qtd. in Tynan 59). The original context of this line is a broken marriage, where a painful irony derives from the inability of each partner to read the other's subtext. But when Coward's characters camp verbally, it is a collusion that serves to isolate and disable the forces of moral seriousness and disapproval. "The whole point of camp," according to Sontag, is "to dethrone the serious," and its power is to reveal sincerity as "simple philistinism, intellectual narrowness" (288). Or, as Elyot in ***Private Lives*** puts it, "Be flippant. Laugh at everything, all their sacred shibboleths. Flippancy brings out the acid in their damned sweetness and light" (56). Elyot spends the last act of ***Private Lives*** doing precisely that, using humour, flippancy, and irony to reveal the boorishness and bullying that underpin Victor and Sibyl's insistence on social and sexual conformity.

Coward's humour, irony, frivolity, theatricality, and artifice thus place him centrally in Sontag's outline of the camp sensibility, and later theorists have generally accepted these attributes as vital markers of camp. But, having shot camp into the critical and popular limelight, Sontag's 1964 essay has been widely criticized on a variety of grounds: she was quickly accused of appropriating an exclusively homosexual discourse and rendering it anodyne and palatable for the heterosexual mainstream, and numerous critics have since offered alternative and multiple definitions of camp as a mode of performance, reception, style, cultural sensibility, aesthetic, or discourse or as a combination of these (see, e.g., Booth; Core; Cleto). Perhaps most importantly, Sontag has been challenged on her assumption that "[t]o emphasise style is to slight content, or to introduce an attitude which is neutral with respect to content. It goes without saying that the Camp sensibility is disengaged, depoliticised—or at least apolitical" (277).[6] Coward may seem a perfect example of this airy detachment, but his use of style and aesthetic surface was often deceptively complex, making him an interesting test case for the power and limitations of camp.

Looking back from the 1960s at the rise of fascism in 1930s Europe, Coward's autobiographical writings eschew political analysis for aesthetics. The root of Germany's problem, he averred, was the absence of a Teutonic sense of humour, as evidenced by their ability to take Hitler seriously, when "[h]is physical appearance alone should have been sufficient for a belly laugh," with his "stumpy female little legs, those rounded hips and that comedic moustache" (*Past Conditional* 278). Lest this frivolity should seem accidental, Coward quickly follows it up with a description of his own attendance at a fascist rally in Italy in 1938. He hears cries from the stadium of "Duce—Duce—Duce" and prepares to be discreetly amused, but "I was not prepared for the actual close-up of the hero when he appeared. He had, most unwisely, squeezed his squat little figure into a dazzling white uniform; his face, bursting out of the top of it looked like an enormous, purple-red Victoria plum surmounted by a black and gold tasselled foragecap several sizes too small." Add Mussolini's expression, his fascist salute "like a clockwork doll," and his pomposity and self-importance reduce Coward to "uncontrollable laughter" (279). Coward then narrates his dash from the stadium to release his *"fou rire* [hysterical laughter]" in the safety of a taxi, reflecting on his good fortune that the Italians are not as quick on the draw as the Germans, or he would have been in serious trouble. Writing with full knowledge of the reality behind these supposedly comedic figures and of the full consequences paid by humanity, Coward offers a fit of the giggles as his life-endangering contribution to the war. He leaves his own self-image deliberately uncertain: is he parodying his own frivolity? is he irredeemably superficial? or is this refusal to engage with fascism on any level beyond comic aesthetics the most absolute and unanswerably final dismissal?

Coward can inject the destabilizing aesthetics of style with just one word. As he does in his novel, *Pomp and Circumstance* (1960), set on the mythical colonial island of Samolo. The British heroine muses on her own *laissez-faire* attitude to the sexual morality of the Samolan islanders, and their relative innocence compared to morally disapproving and corrupt Americans and Europeans: "There are no dope addicts or nymphomaniacs or dypsomaniacs or pathological sex murderers in Samolo. There is a great deal of sex which goes on all the time with a winsome disregard of gender, but there are very few sex crimes." (16). "Winsome" is a

masterstroke. Implying harmlessness together with style and charm, the adjective imperceptibly shifts the terms of judgement to the aesthetic and entirely personal, while implicitly challenging any automatic link between heterosexuality and communally agreed moral norms.

Coward is finely attuned to the subtle links between terms of judgement and the value schemes attached to them, and his sudden switching of terms can offer sly challenges to assumed standards of assessment. His diary comments on John Osborne's *Look Back in Anger*, the play at the vanguard of a theatre movement set on proving Coward and his contemporaries obsolete, serve as a neat example of such destabilizing tactics:

> I have just read *Look Back in Anger* by John Osborne and it is full of talent and fairly well constructed, but I wish I knew why the hero is so dreadfully cross and what about? I should also like to know how, where and why he and his friend run a sweet-stall and if, considering the hero's unparalleled capacity for invective, they ever manage to sell any sweets?
>
> (17 Feb. 1957, *Diaries* 349)

Starting with the mild tone of carefully fair but faintly bewildered appreciation, Coward's appeal to standards of good manners and practical realities subtly and humorously challenges the coherence and sufficiency of Osborne's creation.

In a 1978 essay, "For Interpretation: Notes against Camp," which condemns camp on the same grounds on which Sontag embraced it, Andrew Britton dismisses camp as a stylistic vacuum: "Camp is chronically averse to value judgements . . . : the obsession with 'style' entails both an astonishing irresponsiveness to tone and a refusal to acknowledge that styles are necessarily the bearers of attitudes, judgements, values, assumptions of which it's necessary to be aware, and between which it's necessary to discriminate" (141-42). Coward, however, has an acute awareness of precisely the way in which value systems are embedded in language, and sudden shifts in register are a vital element in his dramatic technique. His is not a homogeneous, content-less emphasis on surface but a very precise and deliberate deployment of style to challenge assumed values and judgements. The terms *flippant* and *frivolous,* so often applied to Coward's protagonists, both inside and outside the plays, denote a lack of consonance between the issue under discussion and the manner in which it is discussed, an inappropriate juxtaposition of style and subject matter. Such dissonance implies the absence of a proper harmony between linguistic register and moral judgement, between tone and vocabulary and the value scheme they imply, and this disjunction is a deliberate and significant technique.

Coward's dialogue is, perhaps, most renowned for its subtext, for the moments when words and meaning are at greatest remove from one another, and display his precise control of a dramatic medium where communication happens not wordlessly but in a complex and tangential relation to the words: Elyot and Amanda on the balcony in the first act of *Private Lives,* admiring the Duke of Westminster's yacht and discussing the Taj Mahal, or Garry Essendine drawing inexorably closer to Joanna in *Present Laughter,* until they sink passionately back onto the sofa while discussing the relative merits of the Albert and Queen's Halls. In a wonderfully suggestive article, Frances Gray likens these moments (where the characters consciously deliver their lines until a tiny erotic pause leads them into unity and explicitly passionate declarations) to the dancing of Fred Astaire in his film pairings with Ginger Rogers, Astaire always visibly thinking as he dances, until, with a tiny magical pause, the two dancers unmistakeably come together in the dance ("Moving"). These are the moments when the dialogue most overtly "camps," at a height of style over substance, coded meanings shared by the lovers, with the audience as privileged interpreters. Coward's central protagonists are virtuoso dancers in this sense, but their virtuosity lies not only in the grace and artistry of their dance but in their ability to switch with lightning speed from one dance step to another; split-second moves are performed almost invisibly from jazz to ballet to fox-trot to waltz. Camp is one mode of linguistic dance that Coward deploys with deliberate and precise effect, but it is married with a remarkable ability to change the pace, tempo, and style of dance almost imperceptibly at any moment. These changes highlight the artificiality of every dance step, making the audience aware of the formality of the rules that underlie the apparently free-flowing movement. The artistry of the protagonists' performance is not just their command of the moves but also their skilful evading of the fixity of form.[7]

In *A Private Life,* a 1983 BBC documentary, Pinter speaks of his admiration for Coward's "objectivity of the stage" (qtd. in Hoare 458), his refusing to take sides or to validate any one character; and Coward's exploitation of camp and other linguistic registers, his refusal to allow one language to become the norm, is crucial in this. Coward took time to develop this technique. In his early play *The Young Idea,* Eustace Dabbit, a county hunting type, condemns the unseen Beryl: "She's got no go in her, that girl. She borrowed the top of my Thermos, and never returned it. Shallow, very shallow" (92). Here the juxtaposition of values works as a sign of the character's muddled thinking, the upper-middle class's lack of emotional depth or self-awareness. The mercurial twins, Gerda and Sholto, are the heroes of the piece, invading the county set to rescue their father from its stultifying hypocrisy. Their self-mocking performances as dutiful children infuriate the landed gentry, but the play demands that the audience be as charmed by their mischief as their father is. Later plays like *Hay Fever, Private Lives,* and *Blithe Spirit* do not invite approval or admiration for their central protagonists—irritation and exasperation, they imply, are an entirely reasonable response to the atrocious hospitality of *Hay Fever*'s Bliss family or the murderous antics of the ghostly Elvira in *Blithe Spirit.* It is judgement and condemnation that are problematic. The sudden switches in linguistic register, the ever-shifting pattern of language, disarm the language of normative values and moral disapproval both onstage and off. Crucially, Coward eschews the "coded, ironic wink" of complicity with the audience, the shared superiority that invites the audience alongside the playwright or characters in their ability to read and appreciate the campness of the performance (Piggford 298). Instead, the plays preserve their neutrality: eschewing complicity, they disdain to solicit audience approval, destabilizing normative language and judgements without endorsing an alternative.

Design for Living is the clearest example of this technique in operation. The play charts the progress of a socially and sexually unconventional relationship: Gilda lives with Otto, sleeps with Leo, leaves Otto for Leo, sleeps with Otto, leaves Leo and marries Ernest, leaves Ernest for Otto and Leo. John Lahr rejected Tynan's characterization of Coward's language as "small talk, with other thoughts going on behind" (Tynan 59) and asserted instead that "Coward's characters live nervily on the surface of life, and say pretty much what they mean" (8-9). Certainly Gilda, the emotional centre of *Design for Living,* spends most of the play searching for a language in which to express her feelings accurately, and reproves others for a lack of such rigour. Her language is often wonderfully baroque as she struggles to articulate the emotional and physical intensity of her post-coital self-awareness (and most of the play is post-coital, like Arthur Schnitzler's *La Ronde* (1897), which Coward referenced when suggesting that *Design for Living* could be staged in a gigantic bed) (qtd. in Morley). With a vivid injection of Websterian macabre Gilda presents herself to Ernest, their serious art-dealing friend, as the "[p]ortrait of a woman in three cardinal colours . . . of a too loving spirit tied down to a predatory female carcass" and invites him to "Walk up! Walk up and see the Fat Lady and the Monkey Man and the Living Skeleton and the Three Famous Hermaphrodites!" (15). When Ernest lapses into clichés and dead turns of phrase, she rapidly picks him up on it: "There you go again! 'Strong as an ox!' 'Obstinate as a mule!' Just a pack of Animal Grab—that's what I am! Bring out all the other cards. 'Gentle as a dove!' 'Playful as a kitten!'" (1.9). What is the "absolute deep-down truth" of their feelings, she demands of Leo, because, until they know that, they "can only sit here flicking words about" (1.21). Similarly enraged by their articulacy, Otto exclaims with sudden fury, "That's what's wrong with us! So many words—too many words, masses and masses of words, spewed about till we're choked with them" (2.3.83).

All three ruthlessly puncture false rhetoric and verbal posturing. When Otto banishes Leo from his sight with an ironic cry of "old, old Loyal friend," Leo mockingly applauds, "Bravo, Deathless Drama!" (32). Assumptions of martyrdom, "wisdom," or "philosophy" are bitterly rejected; when Gilda attempts to maintain her social poise, Leo mocks her serene small-talk: "How lonely are you in your little box so high above the arena? Don't you ever feel that you want to come down in the cheap seats again, nearer to the blood and the sand and the warm smells, nearer to Life and Death?" (3.1.105). That Leo's appeal to Gilda to acknowledge physical reality and immediate feeling should be phrased in terms of seats at a theatrical spectacle is significant. The three lovers are unremittingly self-conscious, assessing each other's performances and aware of their own. Like Amanda and Elyot in *Private Lives,* they are finely aware of their expected gender roles and comment ironically on how their performances measure up to them. Thus Gilda analyses her turn in the role of seductive woman: "Squirming with archness, being aloof and desirable, consciously alluring, snatching and grabbing, evading and surrendering, dressed and painted for victory. An object of strange contempt!" (1.1.14).[8] They adopt the language of romantic convention, only to unsettle it and its associated implications:

OTTO.

You look so terribly sweet when you're angry.

GILDA.

Another illusion. I'm not sweet.

OTTO.

Those were only love words. You mustn't be so crushing. How are we to conduct this revivalist meeting without love words?

(2.2.63)

Romantic rhetoric belongs to a different kind of theatre, which they can wittily perform but whose roles are too confining, denying the complexity and immediacy of their desires. When Gilda and Leo contemplate a grand marriage and thrilling honeymoon, they slip seamlessly into a performance of high romance, only to have Gilda interrupt it with comic brutality:

GILDA.

Just you and me, alone, finding out about each other.

LEO.

I'd be very gentle with you, very tender.

GILDA.

You'd get a sock in the jaw, if you were!

(2.2.37)

They can play the roles and speak the language of traditional lovers, but its idealistic rhetoric falsifies the carnal realities of their relationship.

The trio of lovers switches from one mode of speech to another at lightning speed, moving seamlessly among rhetorical styles and leaving those unable to perform this linguistic quick-step speechless and gasping:

OTTO.

One can't be too careful, you know—people are so deceptive.

LEO (*GRANDILOQUENTLY.*)

It's all a question of masks, really; brittle, painted masks.

We all wear them as a form of protection; modern life forces us to. We must have some means of shielding our timid, shrinking souls from the glare of civilization.

OTTO.

Be careful, Leo. Remember how you upset yourself in Mombasa!

LEO.

That was fish.

(*Helen and Henry exchange startled glances.*)

(3.3.101-02)

The guests, however used to social performance, only know how to play one fixed role and are outplayed by Otto and Leo's mercurial transformations. But judgement itself is unsettled, as the grounds of engagement are constantly shifted. Dancing from one register to the next, the lovers move from polite travelogue, to practical necessity, to extravagant metaphor, to theatrical self-assessment:

GRACE (*SINKING INTO A CHAIR.*)

Where did you come from on your freight boat, Mr. Mercuré?

Leo.

Manila.

Otto.

It was very hot in Manila.

Leo.

It was also very hot in Singapore.

Gilda (*drily.*)

It always is, I believe.

Otto.

It was cooler in Hong Kong; and in Vladivostock it was downright cold!

Leo.

We had to wear mittens.

Helen.

Was all this a pleasure trip?

Leo.

Life is a pleasure trip, Mrs Carver; a Cheap Excursion.

Otto.

That was very beautifully put, Leo. I shall always remember it.

(3.1103)

The duo's breathtaking linguistic switches, skipping effortlessly from dogged literalness to philosophical musing while sending up each mode with the very ease with which they perform it, leave the guests unable to respond at all. To engage in conversation, some shared ground is needed, some assumption about what language is to be exchanged, but Otto and Leo's mercurial changes deny their interlocutors any stable linguistic ground.

The play as a whole operates in a similar way, switching key so often from flippancy to seriousness, from one rhetorical style to another, that the very terms and language of judgement are unsettled. Ernest's final outraged condemnation of the trio, as they accept a *ménage à trois* as their only viable and honest relationship, is an attempt to assert heterosexual conformity as normative and natural. Dismissing them and their "disgusting three-sided erotic hotch-potch!" as "unscrupulous, worthless," "shifty and irresponsible and abominable," Ernest is further enraged by their "ill-timed flippancy" (3.2.123). His frenzy of adjectives as he spits out judgements in moral outrage becomes ludicrous and uncontrolled. In the context of the trio's disruptive linguistic playfulness, Ernest's crescendo of condemnations is a poorly choreographed overplaying in one mode.

The play ends as Leo, Otto, and Gilda "*break down utterly and roar with laughter*" (124). Having revealed the inadequacy of language to express or encompass their feelings for each other, they abandon it altogether. Deliberately ambiguous, they could be laughing at Ernest, at themselves, at the preceding action, or (as Coward noted some saw it) in "lascivious anticipation of some sort of carnal frolic" (qtd. in Morley, Introduction). The instability is crucial. The audience is not asked to approve or disapprove of the trio; in fact, they are not asked to judge at all. The language of moral and sexual strictures, and along with it the naturalized norm of heterosexual monogamy, have been disabled, and Coward simply offers their relationship as fact—though exactly what the facts of their relationship are remains for each reader or viewer to determine.[9] The trio does not desire social approval and neither does Coward's play. It does not present the trio's relationship or their sexuality as tolerable, admirable, natural or satisfactory—to do so would be to admit the validity of any such judgements or the audience or society's right to make them. Instead, it disrupts and renders painfully self-conscious the very use of such terms.

Contemporary reviewers were puzzled by precisely this combination of unstable language and by the problem it posed as to the level on which to receive and judge the play. As one reviewer wrote in the *New York Times,* musing on the playwright's "way of his own":

It is a decadent way if you feel obliged to pull a long, moral face over his breezy fandango. It is an audacious and hilarious way if you relish the attack and retreat of artificial comedy that bristles with wit. Occasionally Mr. Coward appears to be asking you to look upon the volatile emotions of his characters as real, and that—if it is true—would be a pity. For he is the master of impudence and tart whimsy, of plain words that leap out of the dialogue like shafts of laughter.

(Atkinson 178)

The reviewer insists on fixing the play in the mode of light comedy, while being forced to acknowledge its instability, the problem of determining how to take it. Reviewing the London opening several years later, a critic in the London *Times* was similarly challenged by dialogue that "dips and swings and glitters," noting uneasily that "[b]oth moods, the serious and the flippant, are good, each in its kind, but they are dangerously joined" (179). Unable to dance gracefully from one level to another like Coward's trio, the critics were left painfully aware of the inadequacy of any one mode of judgement to encompass the play. George Piggford neatly sums up the relation between a camp performance and its audience:

Camp celebrates alienation and distance because it moves beyond the boundaries outlined by dominant ways of understanding identity, gender and sexuality.

Those who cannot read the camp in a performance (whether framed by a text or not) are bound to become disoriented, mystified, frustrated. . . . Those who can read the camp will also be disoriented; the difference is that they will revel in and celebrate the sensation.

(297)

Contemporary reviewers certainly displayed little inclination to enjoy this disorientation.

Verbal indirection, the ability to work by implication and nuance, was a quality that Coward also admired in other writers. In a 1957 diary entry, he counterpoises the freedom and formlessness of contemporary writing with the constraints and style of the past, while gently sending up the conservatism of his own taste:

I have just finished the first volume of *The Portrait of a Lady* and have been entirely charmed by it. Mr James's urbanity, taste and sense of behaviour are so consoling in these jagged *Look Back in Anger* years. . . . I know that all those rigid social codes and snobbishness of the immediate past were frequently frustrating and hypocritical, but compared with the *un*-reticence and hurly-burly of today, they have a delicious nostalgia. How agreeable it is to grow older.

(12 May 1957, *Diaries* 353; emphasis in original)

His dislike of the work of "new wave" playwrights such as Beckett, Wesker, and Osborne is well known, and he gave it full expression in a series of articles for the *Sunday Times* in 1961. More interesting are the precise terms in which he expressed his dislike and the values he propounded. Musing in his diary on the mixed reviews and muted success of his new musical **Sail Away,** later in 1961, Coward devoted an unusually long entry to analysing the strengths and weaknesses of the play and production and exploring the extent to which his tastes matched those of public and critics:

I don't care for the present trends either in literature or the theatre. Pornography bores me. Squalor disgusts me. Garishness, vulgarity and commonness of mind offend me, and problems of social significance on the stage, unless superbly well presented, to me are the negation of entertainment. Subtlety, discretion, restraint, finesse, charm, intelligence, good manners, talent and glamour still enchant me.

(29 Oct. 1961, *Diaries* 484)

There is a recurrent emphasis here on control, on style rooted in restriction and indirection. Significantly, Dan Rebellato, in his revisionist *1956 and All That* (1999), has argued that playwrights like Osborne and Wesker were celebrated for their direct and overt (or as Coward would put it, "*un*reticent") declarations of heterosexual emotion and desire. Rebellato redefines the "new wave" as an attempt to reclaim the theatre from a covert homosexual domination, manifested in the "prolifera-

tion of meanings, the apparently secret coding, the hidden audiences, the self-conscious fictionality of the stage discourse" (223). Coward's interest in precisely such writing, which operated within social and stylistic constraints—playing the game perfectly while revealing the narrowness, prejudice, and power underlying the game—can thus be located as resisting this reassertion of a supposedly transparent and normative heterosexuality.

Coward picked out one new writer as an exception to his disdain for new-wave writing. In one of his *Sunday Times* articles, after railing against the "bigoted" assumption that "reasonably educated people who behave with restraint in emotional crises are necessarily 'clipped,' 'arid,' 'bloodless,' and 'unreal,'" he singled out Pinter as the one writer who, despite repetitiousness and obscurity, displayed "an unmistakeable sense of theatre" (qtd. in Russell 91). Coward saw *The Room* and *The Dumb Waiter* in March 1960 and found them "completely incomprehensible and insultingly boring," but when he saw *The Caretaker* two months later he revised his opinion entirely, writing that, "after seeing this I'd like to see them again because I think I'm on to Pinter's wavelength. He is at least a genuine original. . . . The writing is at moments brilliant and quite unlike anyone else's."[10] He was again "immensely impressed" by *The Collection* and expressed his admiration in material terms by providing financial backing for a film of *The Caretaker* in 1962 (29 July 1962, *Diaries* 510).[11] Four years later, Coward again picked out Pinter's use of language: "Pinter is a very curious, strange element. He uses language marvellously well. He is what I would call a genuine original. Some of his plays are a little obscure, a little difficult, but he's a superb craftsman, creating atmosphere with words that sometimes are violently unexpected" (qtd. in Esslin 24). Tynan recognized an affinity between the two writers when he noted that Pinter's "spare, allusive dialogue owes a great deal to Coward's sense of verbal tact," and other critics have linked their comic use of place names like Sidcup and Budleigh Salterton (59). But the vast majority of critics writing on Pinter either fail to mention Coward at all or place him in contrast, embodying the distance between old-school, well-heeled privilege and the well-made play, on the one hand, and the new-wave *avant garde,* on the other, who rejected the constrictions of form, injecting a tougher realism and wider social relevance into their drama.[12] But actors and directors, working closely with the texture of Coward and Pinter's language, have noted much deeper affinities in the styles and patterns of their dialogue. David Jones, directing Pinter himself as Deeley in *Old Times,* noted that "Harold played it very fast and light and inconsequential and what I heard was Noël

Coward" (qtd. in Billington 214). Similarly, Douglas Hodge, who has acted in numerous Pinter productions, insists that there are "striking similarities in the experience of performing Coward and Pinter" because Pinter has "an ear for old-fashioned, proscenium-arch, stand-up Noël Coward drama," together with "an incredible theatrical sense of both comic and dramatic timing, like Noël Coward and the Marx Brothers combined!" (qtd. in Smith 202).

The "old-fashioned, proscenium-arch, stand-up," for which Pinter has such an ear could conversely be described as linguistic camp, an exercise in style, a flawless surface that stands in problematic relation to its content. Pinter, just like Coward, uses style as a lever: his characters can reproduce perfectly the surface patterns of social exchange, only to render them suddenly strange and artificial; they switch from one linguistic mode to another in a split second, disarming those who cannot follow their moves and undermining the values and assumptions that underpin their language.

In *The Caretaker,* Mick is the master of such techniques. In Act Three, when he finally turns on Davies, he does so by cutting the ground from under his every statement, switching linguistic registers to leave Davies stuttering and uncharacteristically speechless. When Davies says that Mick has "got sense," not like his brother Aston, Mick picks him up on it: "You saying my brother hasn't got any sense?" (68). Mick refuses to let Davies's comment remain careless or off-hand, instead pinning it down as a reference to Aston's history of mental illness. He then progressively disables Davies's capacity to engage in conversation at all, constantly shifting the linguistic coinage of their exchanges:

MICK.

> What did he say then, when you told him I'd offered you the job as caretaker?

DAVIES.

> He . . . he said . . . he said . . . something about . . . he lived here.

MICK.

> Yes, he's got a point, en he?

DAVIES.

> A point! This is your house, en't? You let him live here!

MICK.

> I could tell him to go, I suppose.

DAVIES.

> That's what I'm saying.

MICK.

> Yes. I could tell him to go. I mean, I'm the landlord. On the other hand, he's the sitting tenant. Giving him notice, you see, what it is, it's a technical matter, that's what it is. It depends how you regard this room. I mean it depends whether you regard this room as furnished or unfurnished. See what I mean?

> (68-69)

Left silent by the shift to legal language, Davies tries to bring the exchange back to basics:

DAVIES.

> I tell you he should go back where he come from!

MICK (*TURNING TO LOOK AT HIM.*)

> Come from?

DAVIES.

> Yes.

MICK.

> Where did he come from?

DAVIES.

> Well . . . he . . . he . . .

MICK.

> You get a bit out of your depth sometimes, don't you?

> (69)

Again, Davies is not allowed to get away with vague colloquialism. Mick pushes him for a literal meaning, challenging him to make explicit any reference to Aston's time in hospital. He then shifts Davies's vague assertions of competence into the threateningly definite claim that he is an interior decorator. Davies attempts to return the conversation to a more casual level, but Mick deflates his vague claim to "turn my hand to most things" by bombarding him with the baroque and comically ornate language of interior design: "You wouldn't be able to decorate out a table in afromosia teak veneer, an armchair in oatmeal tweed and a beech frame settee with a woven sea-grass seat?" (70). When Davies protests that "I never said nothing about that . . . you start calling me names—," Mick takes "names" literally rather than figuratively and re-starts the argument about Davies's also being known as Jenkins. Increasingly bewildered and frustrated, Davies tries to redirect Mick's anger at Aston, whom he inadvisably calls "nutty":

MICK.

> Nutty? Who's nutty?

> *Pause.*

> Did you call my brother nutty? My brother? That's a bit of . . . that's a bit of an impertinent thing to say, isn't it?

> (71)

Mick's unexpected use of "impertinent" is another neat move, giving Davies the status of an ill-disciplined child and invoking the standards of polite social intercourse. Silently circling Davies, Mick then polishes his opponent off with a tirade accusing him of violence, deceit, unpredictability, and savagery, delivered in a hilariously disconcerting amalgam of linguistic styles, from the casually colloquial ("Ever since you come into this house there's been nothing but trouble"), and the comically obscene ("And to put the old tin lid on it, you stink from arse-hole to breakfast time"), to a cool reassertion of calmly measured civility ("It's all most regrettable but it looks as though I'm compelled to pay you off for your caretaking work") (71-72). This is the "old-fashioned, proscenium-arch stand up" described by Douglas Hodge, a bravura performance in which Mick switches seamlessly from one style of speech to another, supposedly losing his temper but always perfectly in control. His use of the demotic is as stylized and calculated as his use of technical jargon. Pinter's characters are deliberate and precise in their use of the obscene—a trait they share with Coward's private writings and conversations, in which expletives were often used with careful calculation. Tynan described panning Coward's latest show and then dining alone in a smart New York restaurant, only to be spotted by the playwright: "With eyebrows quizzically arched and upper lip raised to unveil his teeth, he leaned towards me. 'Mr T.,' he said crisply, 'you are a cunt. Come and have dinner with me'" (58).

Pinter's characters, like Coward's, are able to play the social game perfectly, but they also render it strange, performing polite language with ironic self-consciousness. After Mick delivers his lengthy monologue on how Davies reminds him of his uncle's brother, who had a penchant for nuts, his "I hope you slept well last night" comes as a mocking assault rather than a conventionally courteous inquiry (29). The complex power games played by James and Bill over a bunch of grapes in *The Collection* (129) or between Ruth and Lenny over a glass of water in *The Homecoming* (1.33-35) are similar examples of the skilful performance of polite interchange that renders it curiously unsettling and bizarre. Pinter's characters, like Coward's, can be divided into those who can and those who can't play this game, those who can and those who can't manipulate linguistic styles and registers to suit their purpose, disarming and disabling less skilled participants. Coward's comment that the play's "basic premise is victory rather than defeat" suggests that he identified with Mick as the emotional focus (qtd. in Esslin, 24). Mick's verbal dexterity and the subtlety and humour of his manoeuvrings could be described as a more brutal extension of the techniques deployed by Coward's protagonists; this is camp with the gloves off.

Camp prioritizes style over substance, aesthetics over morality; both Coward and Pinter exploit this disjunction, moving from one perfectly formed verbal style to another in order to dislocate assumptions and unsettle judgement. There is a continuity between Goldberg and McCann's interrogation of Stanley in *The Birthday Party*, disconcerting and paralysing him with a bewildering mixture of literal, metaphorical, philosophical, sanitary, historical, and rhetorical questions, and Ruth's enigmatic farewell to Teddy in *The Homecoming*—"Don't become a stranger"—whose conventionality leaves it hovering between literal request and mockingly polite emptiness (*Birthday* 2.56-63; *Homecoming* 2.80). The disjunction between style and substance and the disorienting switches of register disable and disarm, as the addressee is unable to decide on what level to interpret or respond to their words.

The Homecoming is a verbal battleground. Teddy, Ruth, Lenny, and Max are all adept self-performers with an ability to maintain surface niceties while acutely aware of the implications of verbal patterns and phrases. Always conscious of their own performances, they are masters of the camp aesthetic of life-as-playing-a-role. And, as with Coward's arch-performers, it is often impossible to know where performance begins or ends. Ruth uses erotic undertones to assert and protect herself, meeting the implied threat of Lenny's sexualized monologues and clearing ground between herself and her husband. Her success in out-negotiating Max and Lenny as prospective pimps leaves them painfully uncertain how to take her words, unsure whether she is acting out a purely verbal power-struggle or has agreed to a binding contract. The impossibility of locating her real intentions or feelings leaves the balance of power in her hands as the curtain falls. Pinter makes his audience unprivileged witnesses to this performance, as disoriented and bewildered as its protagonists, with no access to motives, intentions, or meanings. Just as Coward's comic disruptions included the audience's own judgements and assumptions, so the uncertainty and threat of Pinter's plays extends offstage. No wink of complicity hints at the border between reality and artifice; the performance is so seamless that these very terms become dangerously redundant.

On seeing *The Homecoming* in 1965, Coward greeted it as "an extraordinary play," describing Pinter admiringly as "[a] sort of Cockney Ivy Compton-Burnett" (3 Aug. 1965, *Diaries* 605). It is a surprising analogy but an acute one. Compton-Burnett's novels centre repeatedly on the late-Victorian or Edwardian family as a site of power-struggles, covert aggression, and manipulation. In a 1960 radio interview, the novelist John Bowen commented, "You write of the family as being a destructive unit." To which she replied, "I write of power being destructive and parents had absolute power over children in those days. One or the other had" (qtd. in Spurling 418). Under a surface of polite conformity, the older generation stifles their offspring, arbitrarily wielding power or imposing unceasing emotional demands, while siblings, cousins, and lovers are equally capable of destructive egotism and uncompromising ruthlessness. Incest, infanticide, stolen inheritances and lovers, suicide, and betrayal, all participate in a narrative of calm detachment, almost entirely handed over to dialogue, without narrative interpolations or judgements. Motives, thoughts, and intentions remain opaque, while the reader is left to interpret and negotiate the possible meanings and impulses behind each speech.

There is an undeniable campness running through Compton-Burnett's novels. The inhabitants are knowing self-performers, prone to commenting on their own artistry and the impression created. In *A Family and a Fortune* (1939), Dudley discusses his image as man of property—benefactor or miser as he dispenses or retains his newly inherited wealth according to the demands of circumstance, staging himself ironically as he assesses the nuances of his offers and retractions and the impression they create (see esp. chs. 4, 6, 7). Less benignly, in *A House and Its Head* (1935), Duncan drags his frail wife from her deathbed in order that the proper family unity may be preserved at the breakfast table and then assuages the feeling of guilt that follows by framing himself retrospectively as a perfect husband, while his daughters and nephew assess his performance with humorous irony:

> "Mother is not here to console him for her death," said Nance to Grant. "It will be his last grievance against her. Or I cannot imagine a later one."
>
> "If his married happiness goes on increasing, I don't know what we are to do. The contrast must also increase."
>
> (87)

Everyone is, to some degree, creating, projecting, or preserving a role for him- or herself; the crucial difference is between those who do so knowingly and those who are dangerously unaware and who believe in their own creations. Not even children are exempt: Julius and Dora, two adolescents whose mother has just died, pray to their invented god for freedom from their imposed performance of childish naïveté:

> "As we have not yet put away childish things, grant that real childhood may content our father, and that he may not require of us the strange—strange pretence of it—"
>
> "Travesty," supplied Reuben, in a rapid undertone.
>
> "Strange travesty of it that his heart desires."
>
> (235)

Indeed, a belief in the reality of one's self-creation is dangerous; the most destructive characters in many of the novels are those who fail to understand life-as-playing-a-role, becoming absorbed instead in the idea of their emotional sincerity and the inevitability of their feelings, like self-congratulating Aunt Matty in *A Family and a Fortune* or the inconsolable and smothering widow Sophia in *Brothers and Sisters* (1929). The inscrutability of the narrative means that the reader can only speculate as to the real feelings or thoughts that underlie these performances—Anna in *Elders and Betters* (1944) burns a will in order to inherit her dying aunt's money and drives the rightful beneficiary to suicide by ruthlessly destroying her sense of self (a particularly Pinteresque form of violence), while, at the same time, she presents herself as plain-dealing and straight-talking. The discrepancy is painfully clear, but where one version of her self blends into the other is indecipherable, as is the degree of self-deception or deliberate manipulation involved. Aware, like Coward's Elyot Chase, that flippancy is a highly effective form of defence, Compton-Burnett's characters repeatedly respond to the enormity of events with an apparent carelessness, evading and disarming explicit moral judgement. The dislocating disjunction between the style of their speech and the weightiness of the subject matter—their deliberate frivolity and humour—calls into question the adequacy of any language to encompass their experiences. Their dialogue sets style over content, aesthetics over morality, and serves to emphasize the inadequacy of the available moral templates. In *Brothers and Sisters* (1929), the three siblings learn that their parents were actually half-brother and sister, sharing the same father, and announce the news to their friends with characteristic humour:

> "You simply have to tell us who your other grandfather was."
>
> "Simply that," said Dinah. "It is too simple. The lack of variety is the trouble." They all began to laugh.
>
> (218)

Duncan, the overbearing *pater familias* of *A House and Its Head,* is a match for the younger generation, switching subtly from the figurative to the literal, ignoring or picking up nuances with assured force, as his daughters and nephew use flippancy and irony in an attempt to side-step his authority:

> "What is that book, Grant?"
>
> Grant uttered the title of a scientific work, inimical to the faith of the day.
>
> "Did you remember that I refused to give it to you?"
>
> "Yes, Uncle. That is why I asked somebody else."

"Did you say I had forbidden it in the house?"

"No, or I should not have been given it."

Duncan took the book, and walking to the fire, placed it upon the flames.

"Oh, Father, really!" said Nance.

"Really? Yes, really, Nance. I shall do my best to guide you—to force you, it must be, into the way you must go. I would not face the consequences of doing otherwise."

"Would not the consequences be more widely distributed?"

"I shall really do what I can to achieve it," went on Duncan, as if he had not heard, "and I trust it will not be impossible. I do not do it in my own strength."

"How untrue!" murmured Grant. "As if more strength than he has, is possible!"

(17)

Duncan declares he consigned his own copy to the flames, having found that "on every page there is poison"—a hypocrisy that the children can only respond to with humour, as Grant observes, "It keeps the home fires burning" (22). When his uncle takes him publicly to task over making an exhibition of himself with a maid-servant behind the house, they once again fight a duel through linguistic nuance and subtle shifts of meaning:

"Surely you have enough decency and dignity, enough respect for your aunt and cousins, for womanhood in general, to hold you from such a depth? I am unable to think my training has brought you to it."

"I am glad, Uncle."

"It will go hard with me, if I have to believe it. But do not stoop to deceit. If that is of any good, you have stooped far enough."

"Well, what am I to do?" said Grant.

"I should have been able to repudiate such a rumour. But in the face of what I have known of you, I could not. I found myself in that humbling place. I cannot discuss such a matter before my daughters."

"I am very glad," said Grant. "I feel a great respect for womanhood. More than you do, perhaps. I was beginning to think you could discuss the matter before them."

(20)[13]

Grant evades his uncle's authority by responding with careful literalness to selected sections of his speech, avoiding the hammer blows of meaning by spinning out alternative nuances.

Like *Private Lives, Design for Living,* and *Present Laughter, The Collection,* and *The Homecoming,* Compton-Burnett's novels leave judgement suspended.

No poetic justice shapes their ends, no tragic closure is offered, nor is there even measured discussion or recognition of what has passed. All three writers offer power games played out in dialogue, from ruthless verbal duels to playful skirmishes, their characters depending on an ability to shift register, to switch seamlessly between styles, to disarm judgement and deflect and destabilize antipathetic sets of values. Readers and audiences are unprivileged witnesses, left to negotiate meanings, motives, and deceptions with as little certainty or security as the protagonists.

Susan Sontag made Coward her prime example of conscious camp, and her list of "[r]andom examples of items which are part of the canon of Camp" included "Tiffany lamps," "old Flash Gordon comics," and "the novels of Ronald Firbank and Ivy Compton-Burnett" (277-78). It took Coward's expert eye to detect Pinter's unlikely place in such company. Yet their camp is not, as Sontag would have it "disengaged, depoliticised," but is a means of evading and challenging hostile ideologies—most significantly heterosexual social conformity and the suffocating demands of the family. Coward's is closest to the playful camp described by Sontag, "a mode of enjoyment, of appreciation—not judgment" (291); but his apparent insouciance covers a skilful and deliberate unsettling of moral and sexual judgement. Pinter's and Compton-Burnett's characters similarly deploy camp in their more desperate fight for emotional survival against bludgeoning and stifling forces whose threat resonates beyond the personal and emotional; as Edward Sackville-West wrote of Compton-Burnett after the war, "Apart from physical violence and starvation, there is no feature of the totalitarian régime which has not its counterpart in the atrocious families depicted in these books" (qtd. in Spurling 419). The evanescent, boundary blurring of camp makes it a powerful means of disrupting and denaturalizing imposed ideologies, be they sexual, social, or political. Camp, as deployed by Coward, Pinter, and Compton-Burnett, is a vital defensive strategy.

Camp in their hands can become a potent ideological weapon. The verbal acrobatics of Coward and Compton-Burnett undermine orthodoxy's claim to normality, unsettling assumptions and disabling judgements. But Pinter chillingly demonstrates that camp's power is not inherently tied to any political allegiance; it can be used aggressively or defensively, to resist conformity or to deprive the individual of any sense of value or fundamental truth. The sinister Goldberg and McCann use verbal camp in the interrogation that reduces Stanley to the gibbering wreck carried away at the end of *The Birthday Party.* Most disturbingly, in *One for the Road* (1984), the state torturer Nicholas uses the lightning switches, irony, slippery theatricality, and disarming stylistic detachment of camp as part of his armoury of techniques, alongside physical torture, rape, and murder. Pouring occasional glasses of whisky, Nicholas addresses the bruised and helpless Victor:

NICHOLAS.

> I've heard so much about you. I'm terribly pleased to meet you. Well, I'm not sure that pleased is the right word. One has to be so scrupulous about language. Intrigued. I'm intrigued. Firstly because I've heard so much about you. Secondly because if you don't respect me you're unique. Everyone else knows the voice of God speaks through me. You're not a religious man, I take it?
>
> *Pause.*
>
> You don't believe in a guiding light?
>
> *Pause.*
>
> What then?
>
> *Pause.*
>
> So . . . morally . . . you flounder in wet shit. You know . . . like when you've eaten a rancid omelette.
>
> *Pause.*
>
> I think I deserve one for the road.

(376-77)

With a terrifying combination of wit, obscenity, brutality, banality, cruelty, and empty platitude, Nicholas systematically disorients and humiliates his victim. In the hands of a ruthless and oppressive state, camp's potential for disrupting any sense of the "self-evident" becomes a means of depriving the individual of any instinctive sense of human decency, justice, or rights. The camp disengagement of Coward, Pinter, and Compton-Burnett refuses to offer the audience a safe and stable platform from which to view the action. In *One for the Road* this camp detachment is taken to its extreme; to share Nicholas's knowing wink of complicity is to glance into a moral abyss.

Notes

1. With thanks to the Noël Coward Society and to the English Society of St Hugh's College, Oxford.

2. Diary entries, 14 July 1946, 11 Nov. 1949, *Diaries* 60, 135.

3. Dates given for Coward's works denote year in which composition was completed.

4. Frances Gray notes that the unfortunate consequences of misinterpreting the element of camp in Coward's work are self-parodying performances of the plays, where lines are delivered with detached condescension (*Noël* 120-22).

5. Though not discussed in Jonathan Dollimore's *Sexual Dissidence,* Coward's work relates closely to Dollimore's analysis of Oscar Wilde's and Joe Orton's use of performance to challenge a depth-model of identity.

6. See, e.g., Newton; Butler, *Gender Trouble; Bodies That Matter*; Sedgwick, on camp and drag as subversion of gender norms.

7. The metaphor of musical rhythm also recurs frequently in actors' and directors' descriptions of Coward's language. Corin Redgrave, Christopher Newton, Malcolm Sinclair, and Juliet Stevenson all talk of the "musical score" of his lines, where every syllable is crucial to the effect. Newton notes also that "[h]is characters think in quarter seconds"; see "Practitioners" 186-87, 188, 190, 212-15.

8. Their knowing performance of gender roles fits closely with same-sex camp, theorized by Pamela Robertson as a camp critique of normalized gender roles that avoids the potential misogyny of drag.

9. Exactly what those relationships are remains deliberately ambiguous especially in the possibility that the sexual triangle is completed by Otto and Leo. So, for example, Sean Mathias's 1994 production at the Donmar Warehouse ended Act Two with Otto and Leo in a passionate kiss, whereas Alan Sinfield describes the lovers as being allowed to be charming in their heterosexuality, while Ernest is a humourless "queen." (58).

10. Diary entries, 27 Mar. 1960, 2 May 1960, *Diaries* 431, 436.

11. Other backers included Richard Burton, Elizabeth Taylor, Peter Sellars, and Peter Hall; see Billington 142.

12. No mention of Coward in, e.g., Merritt; Batty; Begley. Brief mention of Coward as part of middle-class theatre of manners in, e.g., Thompson; Peacock.

13. For a detailed analysis of similar verbal manoeuvrings in *Elders and Betters,* see Pittock.

Works Cited

Atkinson, Brooks. Rev. of *Design for Living. New York Times* 25 Jan. 1933. Mander and Mitchenson. 178-79.

Batty, Mark. *Harold Pinter.* Tavistock: Northcote House, 2001.

Begley, Varun. *Harold Pinter and the Twilight of Modernism.* Toronto: U of Toronto P, 2005.

Billington, Michael. *The Life and Work of Harold Pinter.* London: Faber, 1996.

Booth, Mark. *Camp.* London: Quartet, 1983.

Britton, Andrew. "For Interpretation: Notes against Camp." 1978-79. Cleto 136-42.

Butler, Judith. *Bodies That Matter: On the Discursive Limits of "Sex."* London: Routledge, 1993.

———. *Gender Trouble: Feminism and the Subversion of Identity.* London: Routledge, 1989.

Cleto, Fabio, ed. *Camp—Queer Aesthetics and the Performing Subject: A Reader.* Edinburgh: Edinburgh UP, 1999.

Compton-Burnett, Ivy. *Brothers and Sisters.* London: Gollancz, 1967.

———. *Elders and Betters.* 1944. London: Gollancz, 1970.

———. *A Family and a Fortune.* London: Gollancz, 1939.

———. *A House and Its Head.* London: Eyre and Spottiswoode, 1951.

Core, Philip. *Camp: The Lie That Tells the Truth.* London: Plexus, 1984.

Coward, Noël. *Blithe Spirit. Plays: Four.* London: Methuen, 1993. 1-131.

———. *Design for Living. Plays: Three.* London: Methuen, 1994. 1-124.

Coward, Noël. *Hay Fever. Plays: One.* 1-94.

———. *The Noël Coward Diaries.* Ed. Graham Payn and Sheridan Morley. London: Macmillan, 1982.

———. *Past Conditional: 1931-1933. Autobiography, Consisting of Present Indicative, Future Indefinite and the Uncompleted Past Conditional.* Intro. Sheridan Morley. London: Methuen, 1986. 245-290.

———. *Pomp and Circumstance.* London: Methuen, 1984.

———. *Present Laughter. Plays: Four.* London: Methuen, 1993. 133-247.

———. *Private Lives. Plays: Two.* London: Methuen, 1982. 1-90.

———. *The Young Idea. Plays: Eight.* London: Methuen, 2000. 74-143.

Rev. of *Design for Living. Times* [London] 26 Jan. 1939. Mander and Mitchenson. 179-80.

Dollimore, Jonathan. *Sexual Dissidence: Augustine to Wilde, Freud to Foucault.* Oxford: Clarendon, 1991.

Esslin, Martin. *Pinter: A Study of his Plays.* New York: Norton, 1976.

Gray, Frances. "Moving with Coward." *Look Back in Pleasure: Noël Coward Reconsidered.* Ed. Joel Kaplan and Sheila Stowell. London: Methuen, 2000. 91-102.

———. *Noël Coward.* Basingstoke, UK: Macmillan, 1987.

Hoare, Philip. *Noël Coward: A Biography.* London: Mandarin, 1996.

Lahr, John. *Coward the Playwright.* London: Methuen, 1982.

Mander, Raymond, and Joe Mitchenson, eds. *Theatrical Companion to Coward: A Pictorial Record of the First Performances of the Theatrical Works of Noël Coward.* London: Rockliffe, 1957.

Merritt, Susan Hollis. *Pinter in Play: Critical Strategies and the Plays of Harold Pinter.* Durham, NC: Duke UP, 1990.

Morley, Introduction. Coward, *Design for Living.* vii-xv.

Newton, Esther. *Mother Camp: Female Impersonators in America.* Chicago: U of Chicago P, 1979.

Peacock, D. Keith. *Harold Pinter and the New British Theatre.* London: Greenwood Press, 1997.

Piggford, George. "'Who's that Girl?' Annie Lennox, Woolf's *Orlando* and Female Camp Androgyny." Cleto 283-99.

Pinter, Harold. *The Birthday Party.* 1958. *Plays: One.* London: Methuen, 1987. 17-98.

———. *The Collection. Plays: Two.* London: Faber, 1991. 119-57.

———. *The Caretaker.* 1960. *Plays: Two.* London: Faber, 1991. 1-76.

———. *The Homecoming.* London: Methuen, 1975.

———. *One for the Road. Plays: Four.* London: Faber, 1993. 371-95.

———. "Writing for the Theatre." 1962. *Plays: One.* London: 9-16.

Pittock, Malcolm. "Ivy Compton-Burnett's Use of Dialogue." *English Studies* 51.1 (1970): 43-46.

"Practitioners on Coward." *Look Back in Pleasure.* Ed. Joel Kaplan and Sheila Stowell. London: Methuen, 2000. 181-216.

Rebellato, Dan. *1956 and All That.* London: Routledge, 1999.

Robertson, Pamela. *Guilty Pleasures: Feminist Camp from Mae West to Madonna.* Durham, NC: Duke UP, 1996.

Russell, Jacqui, ed. *File on Coward.* London: Methuen, 1987.

Sedgwick, Eve Kosofsky. *The Epistemology of the Closet.* Berkeley: U of California P, 1990.

Sinfield, Alan. "Private Lives / Public Theater: Noel Coward and the Politics of Homosexual Representation." *Representations* 36 (1991): 43-63.

Smith, Ian, ed. *Pinter in the Theatre.* London: Hern, 2005.

Spurling, Hilary. *Ivy: The Life of I. Compton-Burnett.* London: Cohen, 1995.

Sontag, Susan. "Notes on 'Camp.'" 1964. *Against Interpretation and Other Essays.* London: André Deutsch, 1987. 275-92.

Thompson, David T. *Pinter: The Player's Playwright.* Basingstoke, UK: Macmillan, 1985.

Tynan, Kenneth. "In Memory of Mr Coward." *The Sound of Two Hands Clapping.* London: Cape, 1975.

Design for Living. By Noël Coward. Prod. Sean Mathias. Donmar Warehouse, London. Sept.-Nov., 1994.

HAY FEVER (1925)

PRODUCTION REVIEWS

Times London (review date 9 June 1925)

SOURCE: Review of *Hay Fever,* by Noël Coward. *Times* London (9 June 1925): 14.

[*In the following review of a 1925 production of* Hay Fever *at the Ambassadors Theatre in London, directed by Coward, the critic praises his "wit" and "madcap humour" as well as the performances.*]

Everybody will remember the queer Bohemian household in *The Constant Nymph.* The Bliss family in *Hay Fever* is just such another, only a little more so. Father is a romantic novelist, mother an ex-actress, while the youngsters, Sorel and Simon, are just a pair of those precocious, quarrelsome, impudent children that Mr. Noel Coward is so fond of portraying. Each of the four invites a week-end guest, independently of the others, and then leaves the guest to arrive unwelcomed, abashed, and bewildered. They all pair off, however, and begin flirting furiously, until mother, the chief offender—for she ogles not one swain, but two—discovers father embracing one of the guests, to whom she promptly and magnanimously "gives" him. And did she

not catch Sorel being kissed by another visitor in the billiard-room, and as promptly "give" her to that visitor? Simon, too, got "engaged" to someone else in the shrubbery, and duly received the maternal blessing. And, to crown all, mother was so emotionally stirred that she dashed into a recital of one of her old parts, with the "support" of Sorel and Simon.

Next morning the four guests, supposing the family (not without reason) to be mad, silently stole away with their luggage behind the backs of the family, all quarrelling furiously about a mistake in Parisian topography in father's new novel (does the Rue St. Honoré run into the Place de la Concorde, or do you have to go down the Rue Boissy d'Anglas?), and mother said, "How rude!" Curtain.

It will be seen that it is all, as usual, Mr. Coward's fun. All the better fun, be it added, for being punctuated, as usual, with Mr. Coward's wit. Its main purpose, however, is to serve as a vehicle for Miss Marie Tempest's brilliantly comic acting. She takes it gaily as an opportunity for displaying her virtuosity (including her old musicianship in the warbling of a French ballad), and is altogether at her brightest and best. Miss Helen Spencer's Sorel is a dainty piece of girlish impudence, and the rest of the cast all enter with gusto into the madcap humour of the evening. The audience were delighted, and insisted on a speech of thanks from Mr. Coward, who claimed that his play, whether it pleased or wearied, was, at any rate, "as clean as a whistle." Be that as it may, it certainly did not weary.

R. Dana Skinner (review date 28 October 1925)

SOURCE: Skinner, R. Dana. Review of *Hay Fever,* by Noël Coward. *Commonweal* 2, no. 25 (28 October 1925): 624.

[*In the following review, Skinner finds Coward's 1925 production of* Hay Fever *uninspiring though "meticulous" but notes that the actors manage to carry it regardless of its flaws.*]

This latest play by Noel Coward, the author of *The Vortex,* is a good example of mechanical skill minus inspiration. Whatever its defects and whatever the futility of the theme of *The Vortex,* it at least showed unmistakably the theatrical vitality which comes from strong feeling at the time of writing. *Hay Fever,* by contrast, is a meticulous little comedy of English character written, one might imagine, as an amusing stunt and dependent entirely upon rapid dialogue and the invincible humor of human nature laid bare.

It is nothing more than the story of a week-end in the country home of an English actress who can never resist the temptation of dramatizing every situation in her life.

Her husband, a novelist, her son, an artist, and her daughter, a frank and energetic young person are quite accustomed to the business of playing up to their mother on every occasion and entering into her innocent scheme of home-made dramatics. But the various week-end guests who find themselves casually assembled on this occasion are less adept and have in consequence about as uncomfortable a time as four human beings could crowd into twenty-four hours. It is rather typical of the whole play that the four guests make their escape from the house during the height of a family squabble and that their departure is only noticed when it has become a fact of history. Miss Laura Hope Crews, Mr. Gavin Muir, and Mr. Harry Davenport carry the burden of this thin comedy by some very clever work as the actress, her son and her husband, respectively. But the play sags heavily at times, due chiefly, I think, to poor direction. *Hay Fever* is only slightly more stimulating than its name.

PRIVATE LIVES (1930)

PRODUCTION REVIEWS

Times London (review date 25 September 1930)

SOURCE: Review of *Private Lives,* by Noël Coward. *Times* London (25 September 1930): 10.

[*In the following review of a 1930 production of* Private Lives *at the Phoenix Theatre in London, directed by Coward, the critic finds the play superficial and light but nonetheless entertaining and worth seeing.*]

On the adjoining balconies of a French hotel are two couples married this morning—Amanda with Victor, Sybil with Elyot. Now, it happens that five years ago Elyot and Amanda were divorced because they loved each other so much that they were for ever quarrelling. They meet on the balcony; they discuss two champagne cocktails and the spouses to whom they were this morning linked; they dither, embrace, and flee. That is the first act, an omelette relatively rich in eggs. In Paris they quarrel, and that is the second act. Next morning Sybil and Victor, having breakfasted, quarrel likewise, and that is the third. And yet what an entertaining play it is! Mr. Coward has an unsurpassed gift for combining entertainment with nothingness.

And he does it with two characters, though there appear to be four; for he depends scarcely at all on Victor and Sybil, and has, indeed, spent so little of his wit on them

that, until at last they sit down to an irresistibly droll breakfast party, Mr. Olivier and Miss Allen have their work cut out to prevent two people, intended to be dull in life, from being dull on the stage. The evening thus consists in three scenes—a love-scene on the balcony; a bicker and a free fight on a sofa; and another fight (breakfast included) among the *débris* of the previous engagement. Marvellously, they are enough. Amanda and Elyot are the fine, flippant flower of Mr. Coward's talent. What would happen if the parts were indifferently well played we tremble to think, but Miss Gertrude Lawrence has a brilliant sparkle and an extraordinary skill in embellishing speech with silence, Mr. Coward's wayward mannerisms have here their most fitting background, and the dialogue which might seem in print a trickle of inanities becomes in the theatre a perfectly timed and directed interplay of nonsense.

There are moments when even Mr. Coward falters. Before the quarrel reaches its climax the play, because there is nothing else to happen and the author's patter is exhausted, is temporarily converted into a concert party; and again, before breakfast, the patter nearly peters out. But Mr. Coward can pad as no one else can pad; he has made of dramatic upholstery an art and provides a delightful support for our utmost laziness. Some day, perhaps, he will invite us to more austere pleasure; we must be content to await the passing of his determination to be defiantly young. "Let's be superficial and pity the poor Philosophers," says Elyot in a moment of solemnity. "Let's blow trumpets and squeakers and enjoy the party as much as we can. . . . Come and kiss me darling, before your body rots, and worms pop in and out of your eye sockets." If there were people who spoke like that about the time of the Peace of Versailles, have they not since grown up?

Desmond MacCarthy (review date 11 October 1930)

SOURCE: MacCarthy, Desmond. "Two Comedies." *New Statesman* 36, no. 911 (11 October 1930): 14-15.

[*In the following excerpted review of Coward's 1930 production of* Private Lives *(and a production of Somerset Maugham's* The Breadwinner*), MacCarthy contrasts the views of love and marriage held by Coward with those held by the Russian novelist Leo Tolstoy, finding that* Private Lives *actually is a serious examination of the subject despite its comic form.*]

Mr. Somerset Maugham is not an Ibsen, and Mr. Noel Coward's resemblance to Tolstoy is not striking, but the themes of *The Breadwinner* and **Private Lives** resemble respectively those of *A Doll's House* and *The Kreutzer Sonata*; only they are brought up to date and turned topsy-turvy. In *The Breadwinner* a husband, not a wife, leaves a "doll's house" to live and learn, and in **Private**

Lives we are invited (most successfully) to laugh over—yes, and to envy—the violent alternations from tenderness to exasperation and back again, which between man and woman, husband and wife, Tolstoy felt to be so loathsomely hideous and humiliating that he saw no cure for them but to stamp sex out of life altogether. Hopeless remedy, of course—quite hopeless.

These two comedies now running in London, and with every prospect of continuing to please, are symptomatic of the times. It is not the Noras who now excite the sympathy of dramatists and audiences but the Helmers—the predicament of "breadwinners," not of wives. Isn't the slavery, we now ask ourselves, of the breadwinner to his job often as humiliating as that of woman to "the home"? If she kicks, why should not he? And when "Norval," as I shall continue to think of him, slips into freedom from a home in which he has been for years a mere breadwinner, slips away, after exposing the selfishness of his wife and children, the sympathies of the modern audience appeared to go with him, as they once went with Nora when she slammed behind her the door of the "doll's house."

This shift of sympathy is significant. But the comparison between *The Kreutzer Sonata* and *Private Lives* is still more significant. To do Tolstoy's contemporaries justice, they never thought that story one of his good books. There was a fanaticism in it far from admirable, and the deduction of a sweeping conclusion from a particular case shocked common sense. What is interesting is that Mr. Noel Coward and Tolstoy agree about the nature of passion, only while the old prophet says, "Look, isn't it ignoble and the very opposite of love?", the young comic dramatist, who does not pretend to be a thinker but, as a matter of fact, has a clearer view of life than many who pretend to teach, says, "Isn't it exciting and amusing?"

In *Private Lives* two honeymoons are entertainingly contrasted. The relation between Amanda Prynne and Elyot Chase is based upon the kind of attraction which alone, according to the dramatist, matters between man and woman, while their respective relations to their lawful spouses are unreal and conventional. A moment's reflection shows the weakness of both *The Kreutzer Sonata* and of *Private Lives* as pictures of life. The former is based on blind fear of lust, and in *Private Lives* we only see the beginning of the story. The worst is to come. We hear what chapter one of the lives of Amanda and Elyot was like. Their marriage ended after exasperated quarrels in divorce and remarriage to others. Though we only watch the first three days of their lives after they have bilked their just-wedded partners and come together again, these show that chapter two will probably repeat chapter one. We watch scenes of rapturous tenderness modulate into the exchange of such sentiments between them as "You damned sadistic bully!" "You loose-living wicked little beast!" and

finally into a scrimmage on the floor. True, the curtain falls on reconcilement and thus the audience is sent smiling away. *That* shindy has not mattered. Why should it? It is not the first or the second or the fifth that does. But anyone who has watched human nature knows that soon, and often very soon, shindies destroy the beautiful and tender overtones of passion and that mutual confidence which makes even its momentary satisfaction satisfying. So, although the play apparently ends happily, and the story is so deftly and amusingly conducted that the audience envies Mr. Coward's lovers, no one, if he or she reflects, can agree with Amanda's pronouncement upon her lover and herself: "We may be all right in the eyes of heaven, but we look like being in a hell of a mess socially." No: they are in a hell of a mess all round. It is not the least of Mr. Coward's achievements that he has thus disguised the grimness of his play and that his conception of love is really desolating.

I wonder, if these lines catch his eye, what he will think of this analysis of his airy, quick little play? That I am dissecting a butterfly which was just meant to amuse us with its flutterings, and have rubbed off its bloom? Perhaps. Let me assure him that I enjoyed its flutterings and bright changing colours very much.

The interpretation of character and scene throughout was admirable. What a talent Miss Gertrude Lawrence has! If you want unflagging vivacity in an actor or actress look for him or her among Variety Artists. They have "go" and sparkling finish. They must have them, also the faculty of making much out of mere hints. They have to hold attention, often alone on the stage, by making the best of comic and sentimental hints often of the barest good as Miss Lawrence (what praise!) and Miss Adrienne Allen and Mr. Olivier played their parts as they should have been played. They understood and showed it. Mr. Coward's great gift as a dramatist, as I have occasion to repeat whenever I write about him, is that his dialogue has the rhythm of life, and the rhythm of modern life is more broken and much quicker than that of twenty years ago. He understands, too, that it is more important that a joke on the stage should be spontaneous than perfect. If it is a brilliant piece of wit so much the better, but it must be first exactly in the right key. Mr. Maugham is not nearly so deft at catching that life-rhythm, and his wit is deliberate rather than quick. Consequently when it is not first-rate, it disappoints. On the other hand he has a firmer grip of what he is writing about, and all the implications of his subject. He always knows where he is. He is adept in making his characters betray themselves in typical lines. Sometimes he abuses this power, and you think, "But if that person could say *that,* he or she would know more about themselves than the dramatist intends them to." But at others he puts into their mouths a line which illuminates the character naturally, as well as the situation from beginning to end. He has a firmer grasp of ultimate futilities.

BLITHE SPIRIT (1941)

PRODUCTION REVIEWS

Times London (review date 3 July 1941)

SOURCE: Review of *Blithe Spirit,* by Noël Coward. *Times* London (3 July 1941): 2.

[*In the following review of a 1941 production of* Blithe Spirit *at the Piccadilly Theatre in London, directed by Coward, the critic finds the play deceptively rich despite the lightness of its tone toward the subject matter.*]

An improbable farce, Mr. Coward calls it, and one or two dissatisfied gallery voices seemed to agree, but that is just what it is not. Without a single lapse into improbability it achieves the impossible, as Barrie used to do, though he was never satisfied merely to ask for laughter. The cow may jump over the moon, but only as a cow would if a cow could jump so high.

In other words, the author's light, easy, amusing way with ectoplasm, poltergeists, hypnotic trances and the like is so adroitly sustained, so much a matter of cause and effect on the comic plane, that we are surprised only as we are meant to be surprised when, at the bidding of the briskly fantastic, madly sincere Mme. Arcati the first Mrs. Condoman returns after death and makes herself scandalously at home in her husband's pleasant Kentish country house. She is a minx, though an engaging minx. Since her departure her husband has married a woman whose sympathetic dignity entitles her to respect. Needless to say, she gets no respect from the minx, and in due course the husband has two reembodied spirits on his hands. So has the dramatist; but he is until the penultimate scene infinitely the less embarrassed of the two.

What one pert woman will do to her successor when she has the unhallowed freedom of the spirit world, how dire may be the fate of a wife whose husband is always apt to be conversing with an invisible rival, and the reaction of a husband afflicted by two ghostly wives—these are the strands of our entertainment. It is by no means an easy dramatic knot to untie, and the dénouement carries the possibly ungallant and certainly facile implication that wives present only one serious problem to the well regulated masculine mind: how are they to be got rid of?

But why in these days of low diet should we bother about implications, gallant or otherwise, when we are presented with a piece of fooling as delicious in its way as *Hay Fever. Blithe Spirit* has not perhaps the same

rare freedom from emotional alloy, for one of the wives comes perilously near to our sense of pity, but for whole scenes on end Mr. Coward is displaying that alertness of humour and impudence of attack which put the purely nonsensical *Hay Fever* into the class of *The Importance of Being Earnest.* He is served by acting as purely comic as the text will allow. The minx, as Miss Kay Hammond plays her, is "a most individual and bewildering ghost" whom we can well imagine "tossing her head amusedly among the ancient dead." Miss Fay Compton's performance is flawless. Mr. Cecil Parker contributes another humorous study of a defective sense of humour, of an intelligence which just falls short of wisdom, and Miss Margaret Rutherford is a delight.

Grenville Vernon (review date 21 November 1941)

SOURCE: Vernon, Grenville. Review of *Blithe Spirit,* by Noël Coward. *Commonweal* 35, no. 5 (21 November 1941): 123-24.

[*In the following review of a 1941 production of* Blithe Spirit *at the Morosco Theater in New York, Vernon is amused but ultimately frustrated by Coward's attempts to deal with death and the afterlife, finding the tone of the play not serious enough for the subject matter.*]

Whatever you may *not* find in a Noel Coward comedy, you will always find skilful acting and impeccable workmanship. This is the case in his latest offering. You have Mildred Natwick as a comic medium, who proves herself again one of the most vital and, when she wants to be, most amusing of our actresses; Peggy Wood, always charming; Clifton Webb, who from a dancer has turned into one of the most expert of light comedians; Jacqueline Clark, a comic maid *par excellence*; and a young English actress, Leonora Corbett, who though for three acts a ghost, is so delightfully humorous, so good looking and so ingratiating that you don't wonder that Mr. Webb had not forgotten her. All these players play in the true Noel Coward vein, which means with grace, certitude and well bred impudence. In fact the only possible criticism is that Miss Wood and Mr. Webb are not always as distinct in their enunciation as might be wished. So much for the performance. I felt the play itself less satisfying. This doesn't mean that it is not enjoyable; it distinctly is. But despite its dialogue, which is fully up to Mr. Coward's standard, I came away with a feeling of frustration.

It would be useless at this late date to object to Mr. Coward's basic frivolity. It is a part of him, or at least of the society of which he usually writes. Once or twice he has taken a bigger canvas, and in one play, *Cavalcade,* he has painted it successfully. But as a rule he has as a dramatist been a sort of later Oscar Wilde, giving amusing voice to the foibles of a frivolous and decadent world. In *Blithe Spirit* he writes of this world with his usual wit and his usual light-heartedness. The trouble is that this time he brings in the world beyond the grave, in the shape first of one ghost and then another. He does make the ghosts amusing, even, for an act or so, fascinating. But after a while we begin to ask for something more. To make death a joke doesn't bear extended treatment. A full length play dealing with death, even a three act comedy, must have in it more meat than Mr. Coward gives us. Before we are through with *Blithe Spirit,* the ghosts of the two wives become so evanescent that they no longer interest. Frivolity is all very well as long as it is kept this side of the grave.

FURTHER READING

Criticism

Albee, Edward. "Noël Coward." In *Stretching My Mind,* pp. 37-41. New York: Carroll & Graf Publishers, 2005.

  Originally published in 1965 as the introduction to a volume of plays by Coward. Asserts that Coward is one of the most memorable playwrights of the twentieth century.

DiGaetani, John Louis. "Noel Coward: Narcissism." In *Stages of Struggle: Modern Playwrights and Their Psychological Inspirations,* pp. 37-50. Jefferson, N.C.: McFarland & Company, 2008.

  Examines the ways in which the psychological profile of narcissism influenced Coward as a child and later affected the kinds of plays he wrote as well as the company he chose to keep as an adult.

Farfan, Penny. "Noël Coward and Sexual Modernism: *Private Lives* as Queer Comedy." *Modern Drama* 48, no. 4 (winter 2005): 677-88.

  Reads *Private Lives* in the context of Aristophanes's theory of mythic gender union and argues that although the play appears to address a heterosexual love interest, it in fact subverts gender norms upon which conventional comedy relies.

Holland, Peter. "Noël Coward and Comic Geometry." In *English Comedy,* edited by Michael Cordner, Peter Holland, and John Kerrigan, pp. 267-87. Cambridge: Cambridge University Press, 1994.

  Explores Coward's application of Renaissance and Jacobean comic structure.

Kaplan, Joel, and Sheila Stowell, eds. *Look Back in Pleasure: Noël Coward Reconsidered.* London: Methuen, 2000, 238 p.

  Book-length examination of Coward's theatrical legacy at the time of his centenary.

Lahr, John. "Ghosts in the Fun Machine." In *Coward the Playwright,* pp. 114-36. London: Methuen, 1982.

  Examines Coward's ongoing fascination with death and the way he used ghosts in his plays as a means of accessing both humor and sadness.

Loss, Archie K. "Waiting for Amanda: Noël Coward as Comedian of the Absurd." *Journal of Modern Literature* 11, no. 2 (July 1984): 299-306.

  Finds that after the first act *Private Lives* develops into an absurdist examination of language and props.

Plunka, G. A. "A Source for Eugène Ionesco's *La Cantatrice chauve*: Noël Coward's *Blithe Spirit.*" *Neophilologus* 89 (2005): 539-47.

  Presents evidence that Ionesco's first play was intended to be a parody of *Blithe Spirit.*

Rattigan, Terence. "Noël Coward—An Appreciation of His Work in the Theatre." In *Theatrical Companion to Coward: A Pictorial Record of the First Performances of the Theatrical Works of Noël Coward,* by Raymond Mander and Joe Mitchenson, pp. 1-6. London: Rockliff, 1957.

  Presents a brief explanation of why Coward's plays continue to interest both audiences and critics.

Additional coverage of Coward's life and career is contained in the following sources published by Gale: *Authors in the News,* Vol. 1; *British Writers Supplement,* Vol. 2; *Concise Dictionary of British Literary Biography, 1914-1945; Contemporary Authors,* Vols. 17-18; *Contemporary Authors New Revision Series,* Vols. 35, 132, 190; *Contemporary Authors Permanent Series,* Vol. 2; *Contemporary British Dramatists; Contemporary Literary Criticism,* Vols. 1, 9, 29, 51; *Dictionary of Literary Biography,* Vols. 10, 245; *DISCovering Authors, 3.0; DISCovering Authors Modules: Dramatists; Drama for Students,* Vols. 3, 6; *Encyclopedia of World Literature in the 20th Century,* Ed. 3; *The International Dictionary of Films and Filmmakers: Writers and Production Artists,* Eds. 3, 4; *Literature Resource Center; Major 20th-Century Writers,* Eds. 1, 2; *Major 21st-Century Writers; Modern British Literature,* Ed. 2; *Reference Guide to English Literature,* Ed. 2; and *Twayne's English Authors.*

Shelagh Delaney
1939-2011

English playwright, screenwriter, and short story writer.

INTRODUCTION

Delaney's reputation as a dramatist rests largely upon her first play, *A Taste of Honey* (1958), which drew heavily from her working-class upbringing in Salford, an industrial inland port city near Manchester. Sometimes classified alongside the "Angry Young Man" plays that were credited with bringing a new life and urgency to British theater in the 1950s, *A Taste of Honey* also contains elements of the literary and dramatic traditions of northern England as well as characteristics that would become common in the feminist literature of the 1960s and 1970s.

BIOGRAPHICAL INFORMATION

Delaney was born in Salford on November 25, 1939, to Elsie Delaney and Joseph Delaney, a bus ticket inspector. An unremarkable student, she attended three different primary schools and failed the examination to qualify for grammar school, going instead to Broughton Secondary School. Although she later moved on to the grammar school, she found formal education uninspiring and left before graduating. She took a series of low skill jobs and, pursuing an ambition to become an author, began writing *A Taste of Honey,* as a novel. At age eighteen, she began revising her novel-in-progress into a play immediately after seeing a production of Terence Rattigan's *Variation on a Theme.* Dissatisfied with Rattigan's play, especially the way it portrayed homosexuality—a very difficult subject for playwrights at the time, because plays that even hinted at it were usually officially censored—she was convinced she could write a better, more sensitive play. Two weeks later Delaney had completed her script and sent it to Joan Littlewood's Theatre Workshop in London's East End for a professional opinion. Two weeks after that the play went into rehearsal. Successful runs in London and New York resulted in a Charles Henry Foyle Award for best new drama of 1958 and a New York Drama Critics' Circle Award for best foreign play of 1961. Delaney's next play, *The Lion in Love* (1960), did not live up to the standard set by *A Taste of Honey* and failed commercially. Delaney co-wrote with director Tony Richardson the screenplay for the film adaptation of *A Taste of Honey,* which won a British Academy Film Award for best British screenplay in 1961. Delaney published a collection of short stories in 1963 and has since written screenplays, teleplays, and radio plays. She was inducted into the Royal Society of Literature in 1985. On November 20, 2011, Delaney died from cancer and heart failure, at her daughter's home in Suffolk.

MAJOR DRAMATIC WORKS

The plot of *A Taste of Honey* revolves around the relationship of a mother and daughter in working-class northern England. The mother, Helen, is described as a "semi-whore" who runs off with a former paramour, Peter, in the first act. Jo, her teenaged daughter, is left alone in their rented room. Jo spends Christmas with Jimmie, a black sailor from Cardiff with whom she has a brief relationship. He disappears, presumably to return to the Navy, unknowingly leaving Jo pregnant and alone. She befriends a struggling gay art student named Geof, who has been thrown out of his home. He moves in and becomes a kind of surrogate parent-spouse figure for Jo, and the two live together happily for a time. Helen returns, having been secretly called by Geof, who is then caught between the two women as they quarrel. Helen offers Jo money that she has gotten from Peter, as well as a home with them, but at this point Peter enters, snatches away the money, and storms out, with Helen following him. Geof and Jo return to their happy domesticity, preparing for the birth of the baby. Helen, however, returns once more—this time permanently as Peter has thrown her out. The strength of her personality overwhelms Geof, who leaves while Jo is asleep. When she awakens, Helen tells her that he has just gone out shopping. At this point Jo tells Helen that the baby's father is black, and Helen, unable to handle this information, runs out to drink just as Jo is going into labor. *A Taste of Honey* addresses generational misconceptions, social ills such as alcoholism and poverty, racism, and prescribed gender roles all in the context of a mother-daughter relationship that is by turns brutal and tender.

CRITICAL RECEPTION

Delaney's frankness about social taboos and the ease with which she depicted difficult subject matter belied her age and astonished critics at the time. A fairly large number of commentators wondered if the play had undergone major revisions in the hands of theater director Joan Littlewood, claiming that Littlewood most likely had rewritten large portions of the play to make it more polished than the version she was given by Delaney. Cynicism also set in among drama critics, who waited anxiously for Delaney's next play with the expectation that she could not possibly live up to the success of her debut. Indeed, when *The Lion in Love* did premier, critics and audiences were disappointed despite the fact that some observers agreed that the play was a more mature and well-rounded exploration of themes similar to those Delaney had explored in *A Taste of Honey*. The most striking characteristics of *A Taste of Honey*, according to critics, are Delaney's proto-feminist depiction of ambivalence toward pregnancy, her use of naturalistic, northern English dialogue peppered with popular-theatre-style wisecracks and insults, and the overall authenticity of her portrayal of life as experienced by its central character, Jo, which critics have described as exuberantly real yet also dreamlike.

PRINCIPAL WORKS

Plays

A Taste of Honey 1958
The Lion in Love 1960
Did Your Nanny Come from Bergen? (teleplay) 1970
St. Martin's Summer (teleplay) 1974
Find Me First (teleplay) 1979
*The House That Jack Built 1979
So Does the Nightingale (radio play) 1980
Don't Worry about Matilda (radio play) 1981
Country Life (radio play) 2006
Whoopi Goldberg's Country Life (radio play) 2010

Other Major Works

†*A Taste of Honey* [with Tony Richardson] (screenplay) 1961
Sweetly Sings the Donkey (short stories) 1963
Charlie Bubbles (screenplay) 1967
‡*The White Bus* (screenplay) 1967
Dance with a Stranger (screenplay) 1985

*Adapted from a series of six television playlets, written by Delaney, that was broadcast in 1977.

†Adapted from the play by Delaney.

‡Adapted from the short story by Delaney.

AUTHOR COMMENTARY

Shelagh Delaney and Laurence Kitchin (interview date 2 February 1959)

SOURCE: Delaney, Shelagh, and Laurence Kitchin. "Meeting Shelagh Delaney." *Times* London (2 February 1959): 12.

[*In the following interview, Delaney explains her early schooling and how she began to write.*]

The wildest of fiction could offer few parallels to the success of Miss Shelagh Delaney whose play *A Taste of Honey* (nursed by Miss Joan Littlewood) will be transferred to Wyndham's Theatre on February 10 after its second run at Theatre Workshop. In the eyes of the law this author is an infant too young to enter into valid contracts, other than for necessaries, or to marry without parental consent. Yet her play has already aroused serious critical attention, brought her a small fortune in film rights and put her name at the head of the list of contemporary dramatists in a new series of paper-backed plays. A conversation with Miss Delaney last week left one convinced that here is a case of logical precocity more relevant to the arts than that of the Regency "Infant Roscius," William Betty.

Without any retinue of chaperons or advisers Miss Delaney came into the deserted coffee-room of Theatre Workshop and introduced herself. She is 6ft. tall, with the poised, rangy figure of a dancer or Californian tennis player, has hazel eyes and dark hair, worn in a style she cannot classify, though it could be Italian. Consoled by a cigarette and her raincoat for the desolation to be felt in all theatres outside performance hours, she patiently tried to isolate events and people one takes for granted at 20 with eyes on the road ahead.

"My grandparents were Irish," said Miss Delaney, "and my father half Irish. He was a bus inspector and a very great reader and story teller. Yes, true stories about his war experiences in the Lancashire Fusiliers—North Africa, Monte Cassino. He was badly wounded at Medjez el Bab and two Germans helped him. An officer handed his gun over to them and they let him be taken back to hospital. They said something which meant, 'War is no good.' He used to tell me it in German, but I can't remember the words." There seems to be no rhetoric or sentimentality in Miss Delaney's nature, and none in her distinct but not in the least broad Lancashire intonation. The relationship with her father, who died last July, leads back to a Socialist grandfather of the Keir Hardie tradition and forward to the welfare state, which provided her education, in a uniquely British social pattern. In Salford, where she was born, there were many slum houses with outside lavatories and no bathroom, in fact the detritus of the Industrial Revolution; there was also a Radical solution for it. Thirdly there was a tradition of popular culture: the music-hall and the "penny crush," a ritual Saturday cinema show.

"That's what it used to be called," said Miss Delaney. "It was the week's climax for us, too, and we had a roaring time. We used to take part in it, laugh and shout. I remember in the Kit Carson serial there were masked men, dressed in black. We used to sort of traipse round the streets singing their song. Of course, there was pantomime. The first I saw was *Goldilocks and the Three Bears*. It was a habit to go the Salford Hippodrome and the cinema, often three times a week.

"I was at three different primary schools—confusing? No, I enjoyed the change. My father rang them up after I took the 11-plus, but they said there were not enough places in the high school. At 15 I was transferred there and got five passes in G.C.E. I left at 17 and, instead of training to be a teacher, I took jobs as a shop assistant, a clerk in a milk depot, and usherette, and in the research photography department of Metro-Vickers, who employ 23,000 people. That was my longest job. There was a great variety of people to get to know. All the time I intended to write. I knew I could, by comparing my essays with the ones the other girls wrote."

IMPRESSED BY *OTHELLO*

"Straight plays? They took us to see Sir Laurence Olivier in *Caesar and Cleopatra* when we were doing Egypt at school." Suddenly Miss Delaney remembered the first play she had even seen. "I'd been kept in after school at Broughton Secondary. I had done something. I was in the headmistresses's study and had just finished some lines. Miss Leek said to me: 'I'm going upstairs to watch a performance of *Othello*. Do you want to see it?'"

It was by some school amateur group. "I said to myself: 'Anything for a laugh'" Miss Delaney remembers. "But I enjoyed *Othello*. It made a great impression on me. I was 12 at the time. I already realized I could write and I am grateful to Miss Leek. What I wrote she understood, and she didn't harp so much as others on rigid English. I write as people talk.

"I began *A Taste of Honey* as a novel, but I was too busy enjoying myself, going out dancing. I wasn't getting very far with the novel and I suddenly realized I could do a play better. I had strong ideas about what I wanted to see in the theatre. We used to object to plays where factory workers come cap in hand and call the boss 'Sir'. Usually North Country people are shown as gormless, whereas in actual fact they are very alive and cynical.

A PROMPT REPLY

"Then I saw *Variation on a Theme*. It seemed a sort of parade ground for the star to traipse about in Mr. Norman Hartnell's creations. The thing that did get me was this: I think Miss Margaret Leighton is a great actress and I felt she was wasting her time. I just went home and started work."

"In the evenings"?

"No," said Miss Delaney, obstinately evasive as if still under the scrutiny of a Salford schoolteacher or employer, "I was 'off' for a fortnight."

Soon afterwards a newspaper report of conflict between the Lord Chamberlain and Theatre Workshop caught her eye. Miss Delaney sent off her manuscript to Stratford, E., and had a favourable reply within a week. A promising dramatist and an organization ready to help her development, by admitting her into its artistic routine, had made contact. Miss Delaney's inflexible sense of vocation has taken her from Salford to London, but without too marked a change of environment. Theatre Workshop began as the idea of a group of Radicals in Manchester.

OVERVIEWS AND GENERAL STUDIES

John Russell Taylor (essay date 1962)

SOURCE: Taylor, John Russell. "Shelagh Delaney." In *Anger and After: A Guide to the New British Drama*, pp. 109-18. 1962. Reprint, London: Methuen and Co Ltd, 1963.

[*In the following essay, Taylor offers a comparative reading between* A Taste of Honey *in its original manuscript form and the version that eventually appeared on stage.*]

Surely no dramatist can ever have got farther on a smaller body of work than Shelagh Delaney. She is one of the three or four names in the new drama that everyone has heard of, she has achieved a considerable reputation with the critics and the theatre-going public, high sales with published texts and in one case a prompt film adaptation right on the heels of long and successful runs in the West End and on Broadway. And yet she is now just 23, and she has written only two plays, the second a commercial and for the most part a critical flop. Her future career remains the big question-mark in the English theatrical scene; it is quite possible that she will never again live up to the achievement of her first play, *A Taste of Honey,* and after her second, ***The Lion in Love,*** a number of commentators were quite ready to write this off as a freak success. Too ready, perhaps, for despite its obvious weaknesses and overall inferiority to ***A Taste of Honey, The Lion in Love*** does show in certain respects an advance on the first, and may well prove to be a transitional work. Anyway, with an author of 23 it is early days to make any sweeping judgement.

Shelagh Delaney was born and brought up in the industrial town of Salford, Lancashire. A late developer, she failed her 11-plus and went to a local secondary modern school. Later, there was talk of transferring her to a grammar school, but by that time she had lost any academic ambitions she might have had and left school at 16. With no special qualifications, she took what jobs offered, working for a while in an engineering factory, and at the age of 17 began work on *A Taste of Honey.* Why a drama, rather than a novel or poetry? Because, according to her own account, she saw Rattigan's *Variation on a Theme* on tour and thought that if this was drama, she could do better herself. Unlike many other people who have thought the same, however, she set about doing something practical to find out whether she could or not, and the result was *A Taste of Honey.*

Judgment of the play as it originally left its 18-year-old author's hands has been complicated, of course, by the fact that it was accepted for production at Theatre Workshop and went through the process of adaptation and elaboration which is usual there. Shelagh Delaney was not present until nearly the final run-through (when, it is recorded, she noticed no differences until they were pointed out to her), and by then most of the major alterations had been made, though further modifications continued to be made right up to the West End opening (including a new, softened conclusion insisted on by the West End manager). Since the play as acted and published is, after all, our prime concern here, I shall write mainly about that version, but I have been able, through the kindness of Joan Littlewood, to read the original script, and I shall give some account of it, for interest's sake and, incidentally, because it helps to clarify the answers to some puzzling questions about Joan Littlewood's production methods and Shelagh Delaney's potential staying-power.

The Stratford production as it finally emerged was in Joan Littlewood's characteristic manner, a sort of magnified realism in which everything is like life but somehow larger than life. This method kept intact the realistic core of the play—the important relationships between mother and daughter and between daughter and homosexual art student—and also helped to carry one over doubts about the two other characters, the ne-gro sailor and the mother's new husband. The plot is simple enough. Helen, a feckless prostitute (or nearly)

and her schoolgirl daughter Josephine, move into a comfortless attic flat in a slum, but Helen soon decides to marry her latest friend Peter and leaves; Josephine falls into the arms of a negro sailor. When we next meet her she is pregnant, and being looked after by Geoffrey, a motherly art student who bustles round keeping the place tidy and making little garments for the baby, but this idyll is interrupted by the return of Helen, whose marriage is not working out, and who has consequently decided that her place is with her daughter. Geoffrey leaves.

Told thus baldly there sounds to be little to the play, and indeed in conventional terms there is little: it has no 'ideas' which can be isolated and considered as such apart from their dramatic context, and if one tries to read the play away from the theatre, without attributing to its characters the *personae* of the actors who originally played them, it is virtually non-existent. One does not even notice the improbabilities of the men, Peter in particular (is he a serious George Sanders-style world-weary charmer or merely a phony with a shaky accent and a shady past?), because all the characters seem equally shadowy. And yet in the theatre the whole thing works, and works almost infallibly—it has the unique power of holding us simply as a tale that is told, and the words the characters are given to speak take on, when spoken, a strange independent life of their own. A lot of it, admittedly, is in any case very funny: one thinks of Helen gazing thoughtfully at her unpromising urchin of a daughter and wondering if she could turn her into 'a mountain of voluptuous temptation', or Jo, remarking wrily of Peter's suggestion that she should give Helen an engagement ring 'I should have thought their courtship had passed the stage of symbolism' (it is humour in the music-hall style, of course, and therefore particularly sympathetic to the Theatre Workshop atmosphere).

But more than that, it has—such of it as concerns Jo and Helen at least—the disturbing ring of truth about it: the two characters individually, and the relationship between them, are completely believable, though their situation must surely be exceptional to the point of uniqueness, even if it is not completely impossible. There is more than first meets the eye in Jo's assertion that she is contemporary—'I really do live at the same time as myself, don't I?' She accepts life, as it is, without looking for a loophole in time or place: even when she takes an exotic lover it is for here and now, not as a way out (and anyway he proves to come from Cardiff); she makes no attempt to move away from the squalid flat in its squalid area when her mother has gone, and does not even want to go to hospital to have her baby. Her only moments of rebellion, when she an-nounces that she does not want to be a woman, or have the child, are over almost before they have begun. Helen, too, is in her way a realist: she will try various means of escape, but never with any great conviction that they will work, and when things go wrong, as with her marriage, she is not really surprised.

They accept their life and go on living, without making any too serious complaint about their lot; unlike Jimmy Porter and his followers, Jo is not angry, nor does she rail savagely and ineffectually against the others—authority, the Establishment, fate. In practice, she recognizes that her fate is in her own hands, and takes responsibility for the running of her own life without a second's thought—indeed, in almost every way the action might be taking place before the Welfare State was invented. And this is perhaps a clue to the almost dreamlike effect the play has in performance. None of the characters looks outward at life beyond the closed circle of the stage world; they all live for and in each other, and finally all the rest, even Helen, seem to exist only as incidentals in Jo's world, entering momentarily into her dream of life and vanishing when they have no further usefulness for it.

(It may be remarked, parenthetically, that this effect, along with much else, is lost in the 1961 film version, scripted by Shelagh Delaney in collaboration with the director, Tony Richardson. Here the treatment is uncompromisingly realistic and exterior, and consequently the script-writers find themselves trapped into devoting an excessive amount of time to useless illustration and explanation. Not only do we see Jo in the real world outside—at school; working, surprisingly efficiently, in the shoe shop—but we have to be present at her first encounter with Peter and see how, exactly, she falls out with him (during a trip to Blackpool), to be shown in detail how she gets involved with the coloured sailor and, later, her first meetings with Geoffrey and the circumstances in which he comes to share her flat. In the process, the special quality the play has of just letting things happen, one after another (like in a dream) disappears and modifications clearly intended to strengthen the material succeed, paradoxically enough, only in making it seem thinner and more contrived.)

The big question which has puzzled critics, of course, is how much of all this was present in the play as originally written by Shelagh Delaney. Well, interestingly enough, the author's original typescript turns out, on inspection, to be not so radically different from the version finally performed as most published comment on the subject would lead one to believe. The dialogue throughout has been pruned and tightened—rather more, evidently, than is usual in rehearsal—but most of the most celebrated lines are already there (except, oddly, Jo's famous definition of contemporaneity, 'I really do live at the same time as myself, don't I?') and the character of Jo, the play's *raison d'être* is already completely created and unmistakably the same. The principal differences there are concern the character of

Peter and the ending, though there is some reshuffling of scenes in Act I (in which, originally, the second scene between Jo and the coloured sailor came after Helen's departure) and Act II, where the present single visit of Helen and Peter to Jo and Geof was originally two separate visits, one by Helen alone and the other by Helen and Peter.

There are also one or two significant deletions. In the first act Helen tells Peter as well as Jo the story of her brief romance with the idiot who fathered Jo, and he takes it quite seriously (nor does Geof later pour cold water on it). She also has one or two elaborate flights of rhetoric about Life and Death which have subsequently been suppressed, in the interests, presumably, of consistent characterization. Geof, too, has his big speech of self-revelation at the beginning of the second act, explaining how he took to men because he wanted a girl so much but was too unattractive for them to take any notice of him, which has later disappeared in the general toning-down of references to his homosexuality.

But the most far-reaching changes are those concerning Peter's character and the end of the play. Peter originally is a complete 17-year-old's dream figure of cosmopolitan sophistication, speaking throughout in a style of intricately throwaway cynicism. In the second act, however (in which, incidentally, his marriage to Helen seems to be working out quite satisfactorily), he reveals a child-loving heart of gold beneath the cynical exterior when, in an extraordinary scene just before he and Helen visit Jo, he suggests that they should take on the baby, and Jo, too, if she will come!

And this, ultimately, is what looks like happening. Where in the final version Geof just reminds Jo lightly of his earlier proposal of marriage, in the original he has a long and impassioned declaration and is rejected, after which Helen comes, ready to see to everything and take Jo back to her and Peter's home after the baby is born. Jo is carried off to hospital while Geof is out and when he returns he has a longish exchange with Helen, which ends with his resigning himself to the fact that Jo will go back to her mother once the baby is born, and being left alone in the flat holding the doll, the nearest he will ever get to having a child of his own, as the curtain falls.

The play is obviously much superior in its final version, but it is not *so* different, and the only modifications which one might find out of keeping are very minor: the introduction of a few lines addressed, music-hall style, straight at the audience, and the slight fantastication involved in having the characters dance on and off to music. But essentially the process of communal revision has served (and here the true genius of Joan Littlewood as a director emerges) to bring out the best in the author's work while staying completely true to its spirit.

Even in its final form, the play is still intensely introspective, still very much the acting out in dramatic terms of a young girl's fantasies, and extraordinary achievement as it remains, the perceptive critic of the day might be pardoned for wondering what would happen when its author, like her own central character, opted for adult life and moved out from her own world of fantasy into the real world about her. In the circumstances **The Lion in Love,** though by no means totally successful, or even as successful as **A Taste of Honey,** is a remarkably encouraging sign. Its scope is much wider than that of the earlier play; it has more characters, a more diffuse action, and the central character is now a mature woman, instead of a girl just emerging from childhood. For though the relationship between Peg and her drunken mother Kit is in some ways similar to that between Jo and Helen, there is no doubt this time that the mother is the centre of interest, and the world outside Peg's own private world breaks in with a vengeance instead of being kept discreetly at a distance. The plot, such as it is, concerns a number of possibilities, some of which are resolved in action while others are left hanging. Peg decides to marry her Glaswegian dress-designer boy friend, her brother Banner decides to go to Australia, their father nearly, but not quite, decides to leave Kit for the prosperous and eager Cross-Lane Nora, but cannot finally resolve himself to it, and Andy, part-time pimp and friend of the family, plans to go into show business again, but gives up the idea.

While in **A Taste of Honey** the essence of the piece lies primarily in what happens to Jo, here the action counts for virtually nothing: rather do the fragments of plot serve as an excuse for us to examine these people, to see how they live together and to try and understand why they are as they are as we follow them through a few inconclusive weeks of their life. For the first time the author tries to offer some explanation: where **A Taste of Honey** really gave us little chance to speculate on the reasons for what we saw, **The Lion in Love** proclaims even by its title that its intentions are more far-reaching and ambitious. For the reference is to the fable of Aesop in which a lion falls in love with a forester's daughter and allows the forester to remove all his defences as a condition of the marriage—after which, of course, he has his brains beaten out for his pains, the moral being 'Nothing can be more fatal to peace than the ill-assorted marriages into which rash love may lead'.

The ill-assorted marriage here is that of Frank and Kit, which is tearing them both apart but keeps them trapped together in a bond of pity and desperation. Kit drinks in her misery and once unsuccessfully attempted suicide, but feels in general 'What good does regretting do? We've just got to make the best of a bad job, haven't we?' Frank, who tells Kit at one point that he has regret-ted marrying her every day of his life, and believes that if 'it was a pretty poor bargain all round, I got the worst of it, didn't I?' (he married her when they discovered she was pregnant) dreams of escape with Nora, but finds that he cannot make the clean break he wants with Kit whatever he does and returns home at the last.

The relationship between them rings completely true and the character of Frank in particular is perhaps the first really believable man Shelagh Delaney has created. The other principal male, however, the ebullient dress-designer Loll, is not at all convincing, and his romance with the thoroughly real and down-to-earth Peg is consequently one of the weakest elements in the piece. Its chief weakness, however, is not in either the characterization or the plotting, but in the quality of the dialogue the characters are given to speak. One would not question Shelagh Delaney's ear, which seems, as far as a non-Salfordian can judge, impeccable, nor her skill in noting down precisely what she hears, but in this play her critical sense and her ability to select seem at times to have deserted her. A lot of the writing here not only seems like the small change of unintelligent everyday conversation, but actually is just that, virtually untouched by the dramatist's art. It needs thickening in some way—the close-ups of television would help, or the sort of elucidatory narration in which a novel would embed it—but as it stands it makes quite unfair demands on the actors. Take the character of the old grandfather Jesse, with his seemingly endless fund of worn and featureless traditional sayings: if he is meant to be lovable and 'real' the actor must work overtime to make him so, with virtually no aid from the dramatist, who has simply made him as boring as such a person would be in real life to someone with whom he did not share a history of affectionate regard. Or again, take the character of Kit herself. She is believable, completely believable, and Patricia Burke's playing of her in the Royal Court production was emotionally dead on centre, and yet somehow she failed to come over from the stage as a living character simply because the actress's accent was wrong—a small enough thing in the ordinary way and one which one learns to disregard after an initial adjustment (the television production of Alun Owen's *After the Funeral* afforded a perfect example of the process). But here the accent proved crucial, and it seems reasonable to suppose that a characterization which depends for its success or failure entirely on so tenuous a consideration must have something wrong with it.

What can we expect next from Shelagh Delaney? If she can combine the skill in handling dialogue and the compact construction finally achieved in her first play with the wider field of reference and the new penetration of character revealed in her second, the result should be pretty remarkable. But in what mode will it be? Rumour has it that she is working on a play set in fifteenth-century Derby, which would be an interesting deviation from the modern world and the kitchen sink. In any case, a move away from realism seems on the cards for her. Elements of dream and song were already present in *A Taste of Honey*: there is Jo's dream ('I was standing in a garden and there were some policemen digging and guess what they found planted under a rosebush—you!'), Helen's dreamlike recollection of Shining Clough, and the strangely moving scene in which Jo and Geof, two children forced to grow up before their time, exchange nursery rhymes. In *The Lion in Love* the elements are even more prominent: Jesse's song 'Winter's coming in, my lass,' closely precedes the final curtain, and even more significantly, Peg's long fairy tale brings down the curtain of act two on a totally unexpected note of poetry. This last is an interesting document altogether:

> It happened a long time ago. The weather was fine and there was plenty of food and good beer to drink. There was a country and like all good countries it had a King. He wasn't a bad old stick either, as Kings go, and his Queen was a good-looking woman. So, he did his King-ing in the daytime and his Queening in the night and everything passed off very pleasant for everyone concerned. But like all good things it had to come to an end, and soon the King went off to war and the Queen was left on her own for years. And naturally enough she got a bit fed up with it, and one night when she was in bed she heard the West Wind knocking on her bedroom door. Well, she knew what he was after all right, but she let him in all the same, and soon after he'd whispered a few sweet nothings in her ear she succumbed to his passion and one thing led to another and when she woke up next morning she found she was pregnant. So—the West Wind carried her off to his palace and when her husband came back from the wars and found out that she'd buzzed off he was very upset. Anyway, after a bit he got angry and he snatched a thunderbolt out of the sky and threw it and he followed it to the place where it had landed, but his wife wasn't there. So he did the same thing again and again until he arrived at the palace. Well, by this time the West Wind had got a bit fed up with the Queen and he'd left her flat, her and her baby, and when the Queen realized that her husband the King had caught up with her she felt so ashamed of herself that she ran away with her child and jumped off the edge of the world, straight into the sea. And as soon as she touched the water she was changed into a great rock.

The elements of the situation in the play (an illegitimate baby, an ill-matched coupling, a desertion) recur here confused and transformed as though in a dream, and the result is a completely adult fairy story in which, as in life, there is no simple happy ending. The ability to transmute reality into this sort of myth, powerful even if only half-apprehended, is not one we would have necessarily expected to find in the author of *A Taste of Honey,* and apart from this instance it is not enough used in *The Lion in Love.* But if Shelagh Delaney were ever to give it free rein, putting the qualities we already

know she possesses to work in the creation of the new piece, what a play we might have then! Time alone will show whether she can do this, or indeed whether she will ever want to. But then at 23 one has all the time in the world.

Helene Keyssar (essay date 1984)

SOURCE: Keyssar, Helene. "Foothills: Precursors of Feminist Drama." In *Feminist Theatre: An Introduction to Plays of Contemporary British and American Women,* pp. 22-52. 1984. Reprint, New York: Grove Press, 1985.

[*In the following excerpt, Keyssar provides an overview of the feminist elements in* A Taste of Honey.]

Reared in a working-class industrial environment in Salford, in the north of England, Delaney had dropped out of school at sixteen and written *A Taste of Honey,* the play she brought to the Theatre Workshop, because she was convinced she could write more convincing drama than she had seen on stage.[1] The Theatre Workshop revised and tightened the play in rehearsal; later, it moved to the West End and Broadway, was made into a film, and brought its author instant acclaim as a major new figure in British drama.

A Taste of Honey is a play about women; its greatest weakness is in its conception of the male characters who, with one exception, function to forward the plot but are incidental to the lives of the women. Like many subsequent feminist dramas, the two central characters are a mother and daughter. *A Taste of Honey* neither assumes nor sentimentalises this bond. Helen, the mother, is described in the opening stage direction as a 'semi-whore'. Her daughter, Jo, at seventeen, has a caustic wit, an untrained talent for drawing, and neither desire nor ability to imagine the world beyond the moment and the 'comfortless' flat where she lives. Near the end of the play, Jo poignantly summarises to her friend, Geof, her relationship with her mother: 'You know, I used to try to hold my mother's hands, but she always used to pull them away from me. So silly really. She had so much love for everyone else, but none for me.'[2]

The mutual acknowledgement that defines genuine love occurs between Helen and Jo, but each resists and conceals her affection, and Helen does her best to deny responsibility to and for her daughter. Early in the play, Helen decides to marry her latest lover, a heavy-drinking man with money in his pocket who sees women only as objects of his desire. She marries Peter for fun and to escape the squalor of her life with Jo. Literally deserted, Jo takes up with a black sailor who seals his proposal of marriage with a cheap ring and takes off for his next voyage, unknowingly leaving Jo pregnant. Jo's friend Geof, an art student whose only prior sexual experience has been with other men, moves in with Jo to nurture her through pregnancy.

As Michelene Wandor has commented, *A Taste of Honey* is 'rooted in domestic, female-centred experience', and thus presents a very different world from that usually seen on stage, at least before the 1970s.³ More precisely, the play's activities are those of the daily life of ordinary working-class people, and central to that life is the struggle involved in every aspect of the 'domestic'. Interaction between the characters is mediated by food, clothes, cleaning, sleeping, health—the most mundane and elemental necessities of daily life, but also those aspects of life usually dismissed simultaneously as trivial and as the unique concerns of women.

In contrast to some more recent feminist work that dwells on the menial and repetitive qualities of such activity, Delaney exploits this context to reveal her characters' strength, ingenuity and vulnerability. Helen and Jo each make a series of decisions that clarify what decision-making is about for many people and especially for women. Knowing that her mother will be off with one man or another for Christmas, Jo invites her first 'boyfriend', a black sailor (whose transitory role is underlined by the absence of any name for him in the script) to spend the holiday with her. Her invitation is in part motivated by loneliness but there is also a simple desire identical to that in her mother to enjoy the moment when it presents a possibility of pleasure. 'I may as well be naughty while I've got the chance', she declares to the sailor. Neither Jo nor her mother are presented as hedonists or 'bad' women. The paradox in the play's strategy is that while much of what these women say and do is outside the bounds of assumed social mores for women, the consistency of their behaviour and their lack of surprise at each other's acts normalise their world even for the middle-class spectator.

As much as Jo and Helen defy stereotypes of women, Jo's friend Geof challenges conventional images of men. Although Helen is repulsed by his nurturance of Jo and his assumption of housekeeping tasks, we are not allowed to do so. Geof's role resists assumptions that effeminancy equals weakness and thus explodes a male stereotype. What we see of him is a young man who is able to be responsible to another without demanding anything in return, who loves Jo and would like to be loved in return but does not expect any payment for his caring. His desire to marry Jo is neither inauthentic nor pathetic; he obviously likes her wit and lack of affectation, the same qualities that draw the audience to her. Helen's rejection of Geof as a 'cretin' and Jo's inability to love him in a 'marrying' way reveal more about the inadequacies of their points of view than about Geof.

The importance of context and point of view to this play is apparent when one compares Littlewood's initial production with more recent renderings. The Theatre Workshop production of *A Taste of Honey* persistently undermined the naturalistic inclination of the dialogue, setting and plot. A live jazz trio played intermittently throughout the show, and was acknowledged by the actors-as-characters. Moments of passion, confusion and sadness were extended and articulated through bits of songs sung by the characters. The interplay between music and words, musicians and actors provided a context in which the barrier between actors and characters, stage world and audience could be penetrated.

At one moment in the Theatre Workshop production, Jo came fully downstage and addressed her 'character's' lines to the audience, not as a Hamlet-like soliloquy, but as the words of the actress that momentarily coincided with those of the character. The effect was at once to hypnotise and perplex the audience, but it also set up a context in which the actress playing Helen could address her near-final lines 'I ask you, what would you do?' to the audience. Early in the play, Helen had told Jo that she didn't go to the cinema or the theatre because 'it's all mauling and muttering, can't hear what they're saying half the time and when you do it's not worth listening to'. Littlewood's production was an attempt to make a theatre that would address Helen and those in the audience who shared her alienation from conventional theatre. Theatre was becoming personal and political.

Perhaps in the wake of too many such gestures towards audiences, and hesitations, including my own, about the breaking of the wall between performers and spectators, recent productions of *A Taste of Honey* have rigorously maintained the 'fourth wall'.⁴ There is a potentially destructive ambiguity in the spectator's role when confronted with a challenge from someone who bears neither the responsibility of character nor of a 'real-world' person. Yet in presenting *A Taste of Honey* as a conventional realistic drama as was done in the film and more recently in the New York Roundabout Theater production (so successful that it was moved to Broadway), many of its most striking challenges to sexual politics are lost. The play becomes a poignant story of a hapless young girl, her brief-lived love affair with a black man, her separation and reunion with her mother. Helen's dismissal of Geof is not necessarily a sign of progress, but it is difficult to call this act into question in a straight, realistic production. The importance of *A Taste of Honey* lies in the degree to which the audience feels the weight of Helen's last question: 'what would you do?' This can be, as it was for Littlewood, a political act that shifts responsibility from the stage to the audience.

Delaney's only other produced theatre piece, *The Lion in Love,* was a commercial failure. First produced in 1960, and rarely re-produced, *The Lion in Love* is none the less a confirmation of Delaney's ability to transform both the structure and the point of view of contemporary drama. The play is a vivid example of theatrical naturalism, and as such rearticulates the differences between realism and naturalism. Realism most frequently is set in a living room, is concerned with psychological revelations about a small group of middle-class characters, and is tightly bound to plot. Naturalism tends towards more public spaces where larger groups of working-class people and social 'outlaws' divide focus. It is the behaviour rather than the hidden motivations of these people that is at issue, the community interacting with social and physical environment that is displayed and examined.

The working-class street-market setting of *The Lion in Love* is not, then, a setting without precedent, nor is the dispersion of focus among a number of characters a unique theatrical convention. But the particular attention paid to women in this world and to the texture of relationships between women and men does reinform the naturalistic mode and foreshadows a number of feminist plays of the seventies. As in *A Taste of Honey,* Delaney again is concerned with a mother and daughter, Kit and Peg, but in *The Lion in Love* the eccentric, alcoholic mother, Kit, is the main source of energy, both constructive and destructive, for the community she inhabits.

Kit's daughter, Peg, acknowledges the complexity of her mother's role in an extraordinary tale she tells to her grandfather near the end of the play. At the beginning of Peg's tale, a King and Queen play their conventional gender roles. The King does his 'Kinging in the daytime and his Queening in the night', and then goes off to war. Unlike the virtuous Queens of old, however, this Queen becomes frustrated waiting around for her husband and goes off with the 'West Wind' for a fling. The story ends with provocative ambiguity: bored with his conquest, the West Wind dumps the Queen and the child he has fathered, and:

> when the Queen realized that her husband the King had caught up with her she felt so ashamed of herself that she ran away with her child and jumped off the edge of the world, straight into the sea. And as soon as she touched the water she was changed into a great rock.[5]

Peg's tale expresses a wish that her mother feel shame, but it also visualises her mother—the barely disguised Queen—as a 'great rock'.

This resistance to the reduction of male and female roles to either old paradigms or new clichés is the driving force of *The Lion in Love.* Kit embodies a wonderfully feminist version of dramatic irony: she knows, as the men in the play repeatedly avow, that men find women to be 'funny things' and obstacles to their pleasure, and she knows that therein lies not weakness but strength—for herself, her daughter, and all of her 'daughters' in the audience.

Notes

1. John Russell Taylor, *Anger and After* (London: Eyre Methuen, 1962) p. 131.

2. Shelagh Delaney, *A Taste of Honey* (New York: Grove Press, 1959) p. 72.

3. Michelene Wandor, *Understudies* (London: Eyre Methuen, 1981) p. 75.

4. Helene Keyssar, 'I Love You, Who Are You: the Strategy of Drama in Recognition Scenes', *PMLA,* March 1977, pp. 297-306.

5. Shelagh Delaney, *The Lion in Love* (London: Eyre Methuen, 1961) p. 85.

A TASTE OF HONEY (1958)

PRODUCTION REVIEWS

Lindsay Anderson (review date July 1958)

SOURCE: Anderson, Lindsay. Review of *A Taste of Honey,* by Shelagh Delaney. In *The Encore Reader: A Chronicle of the New Drama,* edited by Charles Marowitz, Tom Milne, and Owen Hale, pp. 78-80. 1965. Reprint, London: Methuen & Co Ltd, 1970.

[*In the following review, originally published in* Encore *in July 1958, Anderson considers a production of* A Taste of Honey *at the Theatre Royal in London, directed by Joan Littlewood, to be surprisingly mature and authentic.*]

To talk as we do about popular theatre, about new working-class audiences, about plays that will interpret the common experiences of today—all this is one thing, and a good thing too. But how much better even, how much more exciting, to find such theatre suddenly here, suddenly sprung up under our feet! This was the first joyful thing about Theatre Workshop's performance of *A Taste of Honey.*

A work of complete, exhilarating originality, it has all the strength, and none of the weaknesses, of a pronounced, authentic local accent. Going north in Britain is always like a trip into another country, and *A Taste of Honey* is a real escape from the middlebrow, middle-class vacuum of the West End. It is real, contemporary poetry, in the sense that its world is both the one we know and read about every Sunday in the *News of the World*—and at the same time the world seen through the eyes and imagination of a courageous, sensitive and outspoken person.

Just how far Josephine, the plump, untidy schoolgirl who moves into a Salford attic with her flighty Mum, just how far she is Shelagh Delaney, we cannot, of course, say. But the play belongs to her just as unmistakably as *The Catcher in the Rye* belongs to Holden Caulfield. She learns about life the hard way. Her mother goes off again, this time to marry a peculiar, drunken upper-class boy with one eye and a weakness for older women. She spends Christmas with a charming Negro sailor, and ends up pregnant. She shares her room with a brisk, affectionate, vulnerable, queer art student, who knows pretty well how to manage her and likes the idea of babies more than she does. Pretty well anything could have been made of this material, which is written in vivid, salty language and presented without regard for conventions of dramatic shape. In fact, so truthful is Miss Delaney, so buoyant in spirit, and so keenly alive to what is preposterous, vulgar and ruthless in human beings (as well as to what is generous, creative and warm), that she makes us forget about judging. We simply respond, as to the experience itself.

The world has always been a corrupt and disappointing place; but the total commercialization, the deadening over-organization of the big societies of today make us prize more than ever the naïve, spontaneous, honest visions of youth. This is where this play compares interestingly with *The Catcher in the Rye*. Like Holden, Josephine is a sophisticated innocent. Precious little surprises her; but her reactions are pure and direct, her intuitions are acute, and her eye is very sharp. The little kid she watches, out in the yard, with hair so dirty it looks as though it's going to walk away—"He doesn't do anything, he just sits on the front doorstep. He never goes to school. . . ." Holden would have noticed him; and he would have made the same right moral and social comment. Mothers like that shouldn't be allowed to have children. But Josephine is luckier than Holden in some ways: she is tougher, with a common-sense, Lancashire working-class resilience that will always pull her through. And this makes her different too from the middle-class angry young man, the egocentric rebel. Josephine is not a rebel; she is a revolutionary.

One of the most extraordinary things about this play is its lack of bitterness, its instinctive maturity. This quality was emphasized by Joan Littlewood's production, which seemed to me quite brilliant. Driving the play along at break-neck pace, stuffing it with wry and

humorous invention, she made sentimentalism impossible. The abandoning of the fourth wall, the sudden patches of pure music hall, panto-style, were daring, but completely justified by their success. No soppy "identification" here; just the ludicrous, bitter-sweet truth, a shared story. And so, when the lyrical moments did come, we could credit them, knowing the reality from which they sprang.

Grateful (as actors always seem to be) for first-rate material and production, the company played together splendidly, with the complete rightness of tone that alone could bring off the most startling and difficult transitions. Frances Cuka, as Josephine, had exactly the right, adolescent fitfulness, the abrupt rages and tendernesses, the concealed longing for affection, and the inner, unshakeable optimism. As her mother, Avis Bunnage managed most skilfully to combine the broadest, eye-on-the-gallery caricature, with straightforward, detailed naturalism. Surely this was real Brechtian playing. John Bay made a most exotic grotesque out of the seedy boy friend; and as the art student, Murray Melvin gave a performance that was a miracle of tact and sincerity. John Bury's set was bold, simple and effective as usual; and the jazz interludes by the Apex trio gave the whole evening a friendly, contemporary and hopeful air. The movement continues.

Mollie Panter-Downes (review date 7 February 1959)

SOURCE: Panter-Downes, Mollie. Review of *A Taste of Honey,* by Shelagh Delaney. *New Yorker* 34, no. 51 (7 February 1959): 97-8.

[*In the following review, Panter-Downes calls Delaney an "original, exuberant writer" and her play nearly perfectly staged by the Theatre Workshop, directed by Littlewood.*]

A Remarkable new play is coming to Wyndham's Theatre on February 10th, after having a three-week refresher return run at the Theatre Royal, Stratford (the East End Stratford-atte-Bowe, not Shakespeare's home), where it was first put on, with resounding success, last May. The play is the Theatre Workshop production of *A Taste of Honey,* by a tall, good-looking nineteen-year-old Lancashire girl, Shelagh Delaney. Stratford has been for the last six years the permanent home of the Theatre Workshop, and, like the Lyric, in Hammersmith, and the Royal Court, in Sloane Square, is the London equivalent of Off Broadway. It is farther off Shaftesbury Avenue than either of the others, but, like them, it is the home of consistently intelligent theatre, and has a highly individual producer, Joan Littlewood. Miss Delaney, who used to work in a Lancashire factory before she started writing, knocked off *A Taste* in two weeks flat. It has won her, to date, an Arts Council bursary of a hundred pounds and the Charles Henry Foyle New Play Award for 1958, besides rounds of applause from the critics. She is an original, exuberant writer, with a wonderful ear for a theatrical line. Her play takes place entirely in a scruffy bed-sitting room in her known Lancashire world, inhabited by a middle-aged tart called Helen and her daughter Jo, and later (after the mother has gone off with a well-heeled admirer) by the girl and a homeless art student, who live in a sort of pathetic, platonic babes-in-the-wood relationship after he has drifted in to anchor on her sofa. Jo is now pregnant by a colored sailor, who never makes good his promise to come back for her, and the second and best half of the play is the touching, funny, often bitingly frank domestic dialogue between her and the sofa's lodger, who maternally shoulders the cooking and scrubbing, insists on her drinking milk and reading a baby-care manual, soothes her out of her nightmare fears of inherited insanity, and is himself helped to escape from homosexuality. The play ends tragically, as might be expected. In the roles of the daughter and the boy, Frances Cuka and a thin, pale young actor named Murray Melvin are perfect.

Colin MacInnes (review date April 1959)

SOURCE: MacInnes, Colin. "A Taste of Reality." *Encounter* 12, no. 4 (April 1959): 70-1.

[*In the following review of a 1959 production of* A Taste of Honey, *directed by Littlewood at Wyndham's Theatre, MacInnes praises the authenticity of Delaney's play and laments the self-imposed insulation of the educated classes against the kinds of experiences depicted in the play.*]

Shelagh Delaney's *A Taste of Honey* [at Wyndham's, in London] is the first English play I've seen in which a coloured man, and a queer boy, are presented as natural characters, factually, without a nudge or shudder. It is also the first play I can remember about working-class people that entirely escapes being a "working-class play": no patronage, no dogma—just the thing as it is, taken straight. In general hilarious and sardonic, the play has authentic lyrical moments arising naturally from the very situations that created the hilarity; and however tart and ludicrous, it gives a final overwhelming impression of good health—of a feeling for life that is positive, sensible, and generous.

With a small chosen range of five persons, remarkable variations are played. The mother and daughter are firmly fixed and held as absolutely central figures: their drama is the eternal struggle of the generations, and

what binds them together (in spite of the irrelevancies of the three men) is their instinct for continuing life, whatever its conditions. With the men, the choice of the mother's lounge-bar lover, and of the coloured and queer boys referred to, enables the author to introduce the subsidiary themes of faded commercial love, of compulsive young animal love, and of tender but sterile love, all with assurance, tact, and skill. And because the relationships between all the five characters have been completely worked out (in so far as they appear on stage together), we even have such sub-sub-themes as the reaction of the "normal" mother to the queer boy, and of the daughter's attraction-repulsion to her mother's H-certificate Lothario.

It is, of course, wonderful that a woman of nineteen has written this play, but I must make it clear I think no note of condescension is permissible on account of Shelagh Delaney's age. The play lives in its own right entirely. It is true it is so very good one feels that the author could, at certain moments, have gone even deeper—but perhaps not without upsetting the structure, which at present exactly holds the weight of the dramatic situations. Greater depth, if necessary, will doubtless come with the next play, and the next. The only defects I could see were that the girl's mental-spiritual-physical age seemed to fluctuate a bit disturbingly (especially between scenes 1 and 2), and that the mother's solo piece on the wonder of first love verged (for an agonised moment) on the purple aria.

The play gives a great thirst for more authentic portraits of the mid-20th century English world. As one skips through contemporary novels, or scans the acreage of fish-and-chip dailies and the very square footage of the very predictable weeklies, as one blinks unbelievingly at "British" films and stares boss-eyed at the frantic race against time that constitutes the telly, it is amazing—it really is—how very little one can learn about life in England here and now. Consider only some themes suggested in *A Taste of Honey*: what have we learned, elsewhere, about working-class child-mothers, ageing semi-professional whores, the authentic agonies of homosexual love, and the new race of English-born coloured boys? Or, to consider other contemporary themes, what really revealing things have we had about the millions of teenagers, about the Teds, or about the multitudinous Commonwealth minorities in our midst—the Cypriots, the Maltese, and the several hundred thousand Pakistanis? What do we know about the new men of the 1950s—the advertising intermediaries, the television witch-doctors, and the show-business buccaneers? Has there been anything good about emblematic figures like the house-property dealers, the upstart travel agents, and the men behind the chain-stores that sell separates to the girls and Italian suitings to the boys? And most of all—most, most of all—what do we know about "uneducated" people, their daily lives, and their vast pop culture? The answer is nothing much. This last decade will be remembered as the one in which the biggest social changes happened, and the very least was discovered about them by "the arts."

I think there are two causes for this, for the rareness of Delaneys. The first is that divine curiosity seems to have deserted our writers altogether. The second and deeper reason (it probably determines the first) is that the "educated" public—the chief absorbers of "culture" above the pop level—are themselves prodigiously self-insulated against experience. In the popular phrase, they just "don't want to know." Around them seethes a great flux of bizarre new social groupings, through which they proceed, like tourists traversing the casbah, unseeing and unaware. Economic conditions are still such that it is possible for the "educated" to lead worthy and quite well-remunerated lives without having the remotest notion of what is really happening in England—let alone outside it, in its name. And the instinct not to want to know is powerfully reinforced by that blind universal faith so many educated English men and women have to-day—that if you don't look closely at what the world, near and far, is growing to be like, it somehow won't be like that at all.

"The arts" thus become, not a mirror held to nature, but a mirror that reflects simply these "arts" themselves. We have novels about books, newspapers about the press, plays about actors, films about the cinema (no, about nothing), and telly programmes that disclose only the internal confusions of the corporations and companies that project them. Then down from Salford comes this splendid young prophetess who, with typical good sense, calls at the right address among the conspirators in Stratford, E. 15, who then carry her voice into "the heart of Theatreland." At Wyndham's, we have been looking back with that Boy Friend for years, and the question now is whether we can see that the 1950s are so much more peculiar and disturbing than the 1920s ever weren't. As Helen and Josephine walk on to John Bury's bleak, poetic set, one glances round the stalls and holds one's breath. Are they slumming, or are they listening at last?

Alan Brien (review date May 1959)

SOURCE: Brien, Alan. Review of *A Taste of Honey,* by Shelagh Delaney. *Theatre Arts* 43, no. 5 (May 1959): 9-10.

[*In the following review of Littlewood's production of* A Taste of Honey, *Brien provides an uncertain assessment of the play, asserting that while the cast and directing are largely responsible for its success, the play itself is "not so much dramaturgy as anthropology."*]

Let us assume that the current season began last June. It was then that a play called *A Taste of Honey* opened in the slummy, chummy East End of London—a twenty-minute subway ride away from Piccadilly Circus. The place was the Theatre Royal, Stratford East, which is a creaky old vaudeville house in a back street. The producers were an enthusiastic, leftish group of braw, Brechtian paupers called Theatre Workshop. The author was a nineteen-year-old, a gawky provincial giantess of a photographer's assistant from smoggy Manchester. Her name was Shelagh Delaney and she had only been inside a theatre twice in her life. It would be almost impossible to imagine a less hopeful collection of omens for success. But the production was a minor triumph that split the critics into two camps. On one side the posh Sundays and the literary weeklies frothed and lathered with excitement. On the other, the mass-circulation dailies reacted with baffled, suspicious shrugs. The controversy jerked open the cautious, worldly eyes of West End managements, and *A Taste of Honey* (with only one change of cast) can now be seen at a small, cozy theatre in the heart of town.

A Taste of Honey is perhaps more portent than achievement. It is a comet that will loom larger in British eyes than in American ones, flaring as it does across a dead and darkling theatrical sky. The play resembles a film script in which the author shows an adolescent contempt for logic or realism or shape or practicability on a stage. It is a woozy, wandering, late-night anecdote that staggers from farce to tragedy and weaves between fact and fantasy. It is an unguided tour round the inside of one young woman's skull. We meet a pregnant schoolgirl with a music-hall tart of a mother, a Negro lover out of a nightmare, a comic-strip cad of a stepfather, and a homosexual art student of a best friend. They are all realised in different styles, but all the time, I felt that Miss Delaney was living in the today of Britain, growing up in a world that can be seen in any suburb, though it is seldom seen on the stage. It is not so much dramaturgy as anthropology—tribal rites interpreted by a genuine cannibal.

The production owes a great deal of its success to Joan Littlewood, the indefatigable Mother Courage of Theatre Workshop, who directed. She has given it the full Berliner Ensemble treatment. There is a jazz trio jamming away from a stage box; characters chat confidentially to the audience; entrances and exits are choreographed rather than staged in a regular manner. Her young cast, all of whom were unknown in the West End a year ago, will have their names in lights for years to come. There is Avis Bunnage (even the name is defiantly uncommercial), the mother, who bangs her personality across the footlights and could get us to sing a chorus of "Tipperary" at the wave of an arm. There is Murray Melvin as a skinny, wet fribble of a working-class homosexual, a figure few famous actors would dare prance upon the stage with such finicking accuracy. But most memorable is Frances Cuka, the schoolgirl, who has one of those rare, real, unactorlike faces. Her theatrical aunts are Gracie Fields and Anna Magnani—though with her bird's-nest hair, her blunt comic nose and her star-spangled eyes, she is an original in her own right.

CRITICAL COMMENTARY

Jacques Noël (essay date 1960)

SOURCE: Noël, Jacques. "Some Aspects of Shelagh Delaney's Use of Language in *A Taste of Honey.*" *Revue des langues vivantes / Tijdschrift voor levende talen,* no. 26 (1960): 284-90.

[*In the following essay, Noël discusses the ways in which Delaney's characters use words and patterns of speech to delineate their evolving worldviews as the play progresses.*]

Shelagh Delaney was 19 years old when she wrote *A Taste of Honey.* The daughter of a bus driver, she was working in an engineering factory. *A Taste of Honey* is her first attempt at a play. It was first performed at the Theatre Royal, Stratford, London, on May 27th 1958, by Theatre Workshop. Shortly after, Graham Greene described it as having «all the freshness of Mr. Osborne's *Look Back in Anger* and a greater maturity». On February 10th 1959, it was first produced in the West End, at Wyndham's Theatre, where it met with great success. Before trying to show that the success is that of a promising young author, and is not due only to Joan Littlewood's excellent production, let us say briefly what the play is about.

Jo is living, far from willingly, in a squalid flat in a squalid district with HELEN, her mother, a «semi-whore». Helen marries a rake, PETER, and leaves her daughter to shift for herself. Jo meets her first BOY FRIEND, a coloured young man: but the boy goes away to the Army and never comes back. Jo is left pregnant. Fortunately, another boy, GEOF, puts up in her flat and helps her. Helen will eventually return to the flat for good, after having been kicked out by Peter. She expels Geof, whose presence, however, is no longer necessary, for Jo is now ready to accept the child she is bearing, the flat she is living in, and even her mother's presence in the flat.

What strikes us most in this play is the meaningless life all the characters lead, except Jo. Helen likes whisky and «never thinks» (P. 9). Peter is a perfect rake and, when Peter and Helen marry, they only think of 'having

a good time'. Jo's taste of honey, in spite of its tangible consequence, is presented as a dream, and her boy friend merely as the instrument of this dream. As to Geof, he has no home, and he is a pansy, so that his love for Jo is bound to remain a dream . . .

In short, the theme of the play is Jo's conquest of moral values. We are shown that love as lust and love as dream are bound to issue in failure, because they make life meaningless and chaotic; yet life is finally given order and meaning because of Geof's devotion to Jo and especially because Jo takes an active part in her own transformation.

The purpose of this article is to show how the change from topsy-turvy agitation, which Jo shares with the world around her, to life worth living is expressed by the way the characters, and especially Jo, talk of themselves, of each other, of the people (and things) around them.

1. THE CORRUPTION OF HUMAN RELATIONSHIPS. LIFE SEEN AS DEATH-LIKE.

Several aspects of human relationships are perverted or belittled by all sorts of comparisons and cynical references.

Jo calls her friend Geof, who is a pansy, «big sister» (P. 54, P. 55) or «an old woman» (P. 72). This is affectionate, and yet it reminds us of Geof's peculiarity. With a different intention, but with the same effect, Helen calls Geof «Nursemaid» (P. 61) and Peter, more viciously, calls him «Mary» (P. 65) and «Jezebel» (P. 66). The irony is all the more pungent when we bear in mind that Jo can only reckon on 'his' devotion and help to break with her moral aimlessness: «I hate babies»—«(. . .) Motherhood is supposed to come natural to women.»—«It comes natural to you, Geoffrey Ingram. You'd make somebody a wonderful wife.» (P. 55).

In one of the nursery rhymes (!) Geof recites for Jo, he refers to the Oedipus story (P. 51), and, later on, Peter refers to himself as Oedipus (P. 65, P. 66), with an obvious hint at his marriage with Helen:

HELEN:

Listen, love, I'm old enough to be your mother.

PETER (*PETTING HER*):

Now you know I like this mother and son relationship.

(. . .)

HELEN:

Well, you certainly liberate something in me. And I don't think it's maternal instincts either.

(P. 18)

This reply of Helen's suggests that she will disregard her duty as a mother[1] and abandon her daughter. As Jo puts it: «She had so much love for everyone else, but none for me.» (P. 72).

If we are to believe Helen, the world is mere chaos, and, as such, appeals to her: «We're all at the steering wheel of our own destiny. Careering along like drunken drivers. I'm going to get married.» (P. 29).[2] Like her, we cannot help associating her marriage with drunkenness,[3] almost with criminal folly;[4] and the comparison implies that she does not care who gets destroyed in the process, i.e. her daughter.

Jo tells her mother (P. 13, P. 14) that she dreamt of her getting buried.[5] Further on, they speak about the bed:

Jo:

(. . .) What's the bed like?

Helen:

Like a coffin only not half as comfortable.

Jo:

Have you ever tried a coffin?

Helen:

I dare say I will one day.

(P. 21)

But in the following extracts, death and meaninglessness are associated with Helen's marriage and lust, and with her daughter. Referring to her mother's marriage, Jo says: «I'd sooner go to my own funeral.» (P. 37). Helen's wedding happens to be on a sunny day and when she exclaims: «happy the bride the sun shines on» (P. 39), Jo replies «Yeah, and happy the corpse the rain rains on.»[6]

After her love affair, Jo tells Geof «I'm sick of love» (P. 53);[7] according to her and to her mother, Jo looks like «a ghost» (P. 50), «a ghost warmed up» (P. 63).[8] The flower bulbs Jo had tried to grow (P. 11, P. 12), much to Helen's displeasure, «never grew» (P. 71). These associations with death are all the more ominous because we know Jo is pregnant. They all lead to a critical moment in the play which I shall quote later.

When Geof had mentioned abortion, Jo had replied: «I know, but I think that's terrible.» (P. 49); yet when speaking of herself, she tells her mother, partly to spite her it is true: «I wish you had done (i.e. got rid of her before she was born). You did with plenty of others, I know.» To which Helen replies: «I'll kill her. (. . .)» (P. 62). Some time after Geof has compared her «housecoat» to «a badly tailored shroud» (P. 70) Jo, in a fit of dejection, flings Geof's present, «a life-sized doll» (P. 74) to the ground.

Chaos and death are inseparable from both forms of love: Helen's lust and Jo's romance.

2. PEOPLE AS THINGS AND AS ANIMALS.

Human relationships are distorted and death is associated with the perversion of human relationships. Human beings are presented as belonging to an inferior order, as things or as animals. This 'diminishing' of human life, which reveals the nature of both the characters speaking and the characters referred to, is found mainly in Peter's and Helen's words. Jo sometimes speaks in the same way, but even when she does not, Peter's and Helen's attitude to life has some bearing upon her, because we fear lest she should adopt the same attitude as her mother, and ruin both herself and her child.[9]

Being a rake, Peter best represents moral disorder. He tells Helen: «You can't afford to lose a man like me (. . .). This is the old firm. (. . .)» (P. 17; P. 18). As Jo rightly remarks, he marries not Helen, but her figure («it») (P. 30).

Before her love affair, Jo shows signs of disorder. She eagerly asks Peter all sorts of questions, as though she felt some kind of interest in the way he lives: (about a photograph) «I bet you've had thousands of girl friends. What was this one with the long legs called?» (P. 32); to which Peter replies: «Ah! Yes, number thirty-eight. A charming little thing.» Jo's remark to her mother «Have you got the monopoly?» (of marriage or sex) (P. 41) and Helen's reference to «the market value» (P. 42) of her soul, are in the same vein and show that Helen and even Jo tend to share Peter's moral depravation.

Peter's cynical indecency and coarseness are however unrivalled, as when obviously referring to Jo's pregnancy he sings: «Who's got a bun in the oven? Who's got a cake in the stove?» (P. 65). Or when speaking of Oedipus: «the old bag turned out to be his mother . . . » (P. 65). Even Helen is shocked by this, and she will be still more so when Peter (rightly) compares her to «a bloody unrestored oil painting» (P. 65). Peter's coarseness is further revealed when he speaks of somebody picking up «a couple of grapefruit on a thirty-two bust.»

Peter speaks of Geof as «the lily» (P. 65), as «that little fruitcake parcel» (P. 68) and this enhances our feeling that Jo is in a bad mess: the only one capable of helping her is a pansy.

Peter's and the other characters' moral depravation might appeal to us because it gives birth to, if not witty, at least stimulating and unexpected repartees. But the extracts which follow mostly present people or things as filthy, so that they make moral chaos unattractive.

Both Peter and Helen seem to feel perfectly comfortable in their dirty world: Helen «I've always said we should be used for manure when we're gone.» (P. 14);[10]

or Peter «The world is littered with women I've rejected.» (P. 19). Jo complains: «I feel like throwing myself in the river.»

GEOF:

I wouldn't do that. It's full of rubbish.

JO:

Well that's all I am, isn't it?

(P. 55, P. 56)

She once talks of babies as «scrappy things», «covered in rolls of fat», which can be «dumped» on a doorstep (P. 55).

Helen's preference goes, it seems, to comparisons involving animals. She calls Jo «a silly cat» (P. 10), «(. . .) a bloody termite (. . .)» (P. 17), her former husband «a rat» (P. 28), Geof «a monkey» (P. 61), Jo «a little bloodsucker» (P. 61); Jo and Geof are living «like pigs in a pigsty» (P. 81, P. 83); she speaks of a cheap local cinema as «a proper little flea pit» (P. 27), of the flat as «this chicken run» (P. 60). When, at the end of the play, she feels ready to accept her grandchild and decides she will «call it Blackbird», we get a sense that, even if her attitude is more human, since the comparison is almost affectionate and not disgusting, she herself has changed very little: she once more compares a person to an animal.

Jo takes after her mother, but on the whole, her comparisons are less derogatory,[11] more complex. Geof is breathing «like a horse» (P. 58): the comparison is merely unpleasant, but not disgusting. When she tells Geof she is «not having a little animal nibbling away» at her, the image merely shows that she has not yet overcome the crisis in her, that, as Geof puts it, she is again «trying to be inhuman.» (P. 56).

3. LIFE MAKING SENSE.

From what we have just noted about the perversion of human values it appears that Jo never yields completely to disorder. She may be young, she is earnest: that is probably what prompts the black boy to say how much she puzzles him: «Women never have young minds. They are born three thousand years old» (P. 25). Here, women—i.e. Jo—are almost compared to gods; compare with Peter's remark on page 19 «The world is littered with women I've rejected.»

Even in «this black hole of Calcutta» (P. 35), children are heard in the street (see stage directions on P. 54 and 57). Almost at the same moment, we share Geof's and Jo's amazement when the baby moves and «kicks» her.

At times, Helen shows in her own way genuine concern for her daughter's situation: «Don't get trapped. Marriage can be hell for a kid.» (P. 41) (cp. the boy's cyni-cal reference to «Matrimony»: «I'm trapped into a barbaric cult . . .» on page 25), «He certainly left you a nice Christmas box. It did happen at Christmas, I suppose?» (P. 61) (cp. Peter's indecent song on P. 65: «Who's got a bun in the oven?»).

Still, Geof more than anyone else encourages Jo to return to moral order. Given Jo's disgust for sex, the fact that Geof is a pansy can only be a good thing: he is not dangerous. Besides, his devotion is constant. Although his attitude towards sex is not any healthier than Peter's, we tend to forget Geof's personal oddity, because Peter is vicious, aggressive and coarse, whereas Geof, once he realizes that his suit can lead nowhere, concentrates on helping Jo and succeeds in curing her (e.g. P. 56, Geof: «Stop pitying yourself»). This is why Jo acknowledges their spiritual marriage[12] and expresses her thankfulness for his loyalty when she calls him «an old watchdog» (P. 85). Though he puts it in a conceited way, Geof realizes the part he played in Jo's return to life making sense: «You need somebody to love you while you're looking for someone to love.» (P. 76). That «someone to love» which Jo is looking for and which, once found, restores her moral order, is . . . *herself* with the child she is bearing.[13]

Other admirable passages, of which I can only quote short extracts throw light on Jo's humanism:

(P. 50) Jo to Geof: «I'm an extraordinary person. There's only one of me like there's only one of you.»

(P. 25) When her boy tells her «you've got to stop eating (. . .) we're saving up to get married» or when he suggests, on page 38, «Let me be your Othello and you my Desdemona», Jo simply doesn't understand the point.

(P. 70) She struggles to «be contemporary», i.e. to «live at the same time as» herself.

Her love for the coloured boy was love for «only a dream» (P. 75), it was a form of escapism. She long pretended that he was a «Prince, son of a chieftain» (P. 53), but eventually she realizes that «We're all *princes* in our own *little* kingdom.» (P. 79).[14]

In the progress from topsy-turvy life to the restoration of moral order, Jo plays a central part. Even the repartees which best illustrate moral disorder, and which are mostly spoken by Peter and Helen, have some bearing on the young girl: e.g. the association of death and filth with love refer directly or indirectly to Jo; she is the victim.

To make us visualize moral chaos in Peter and Helen, and partly in Geof and Jo, Shelagh Delaney makes us see human beings as in a dream in which human relationships are distorted, life is seen as death, people as things and as animals. The stage directions aim at the same dreamlike impression: after the scenes there is a («Fade out») (P. 22).

If moral chaos leads nowhere, this very failure is itself a positive element: it leads to Jo's rejection of life as a dream and to her becoming aware of the banal, and even banally expressed, but nevertheless fundamental truth, that what makes life important, i.e. worth living, is just to respect and accept life, not as a dream but as it is, by feeling «really important» (P. 81) as an individual, no matter who you live with, where you live, what happens or who you are. We are deeply moved by Jo's acceptance of her destiny, especially as a mother; all the more so, because this choice implies her saying no to distorted forms of life which threaten us all.

Notes

1. The idea of marriage is further distorted by the coloured boy's reference to it as «a barbaric cult» (P. 25).

2. Later on, Helen facetiously introduces her drunken husband as the «President of the local Temperance Society» (P. 65).

3. Drunkenness being a kind of escapism, it is worth noting Helen's and Jo's attitude to 'darkness': (P. 22).

    (*Scene One*) Helen:

    > Everything is seen at its best in the dark—including me. I love it. Can't understand why you're so scared of it.

    Jo:

    > I'm not frightened of the darkness outside. It's the darkness inside houses I don't like.

    [. . .]

    (*Scene Two*) *They stop by the door.* (. . .) Jo:

    > Doesn't it go dark early? I like winter. I like it better than all the other seasons.

    Boy:

    > I like it too. When it goes dark early it gives me more time for—(*He kisses her.*)

4. Though the sense of danger is not explicit, love is also spoken of in terms of war: Helen calls herself «a free lance» (P. 18) when Peter visits her «new headquarters» (P. 16). Peter, who has lost one of his eyes, is described as a «Pirate King» (P. 36).

5. We have been told that Jo's father is dead.

6. Similar instances: Jo: (. . .) You make me sick. (P. 8); Jo: I'm sick of you. (P. 15).

7. On another occasion Helen says of her daughter: «You make me sick.»

8. The allusions to death are not all gloomy. «Helen to Jo: I would never have dared talk to my mother like that when I was *her* age. She'd have knocked me into the middle of next week.» (P. 12) By the way, this use of the third person to address somebody who is present is one of the dramatist's favourite tricks to emphasize the disorder in human relationships.

9. For brevity's sake we shall not deal with the influence of the sordid surroundings the characters live in. One example will suffice: Peter calls Jo and Helen's flat «this black hole of Calcutta» (P. 35). This sets the play in a social perspective by referring to an episode of Anglo-Indian history.

10. Helen's attitude is more complex later on when, speaking of Peter's new house, she says: «At the moment, it's like my face, unblemished! Oh look at that, every line tells a dirty story, hey?» (P. 42) Peter never chooses himself as his own target; he is aggressive towards other people, and does not consider himself part of his filthy world.

11. Her mother barges «around just like a bull in a china shop» (P. 78); Helen's «flu bugs» (P. 15) are bound to be filthy; as to Geof, he calls Jo's boy friend «that black beast of a prince of yours» . . . (P. 58).

12. «It's a bit daft talking about getting married, isn't it? We've been married for a thousand years.» (P. 76) Note the contrast between this presentation of friendship as something eternal and the presentation of love as something deathlike.

13. At this point, it is worth noting that Jo and her mother always hold an honest (I do not mean to say a true) view on religion:

    Helen:

    > (. . .) Heaven must be the hell of a place. Nothing but repentant sinners up there, isn't it? All the pimps, prostitutes and politicians in creation trying to cash in on eternity and their little tin gods. Where's my hat?

    > (P. 42)

    Jo:

    > people (. . .) like to pray to the Almighty just in case he turns out to exist when they snuff it, they like to take out an insurance policy.

    > (P. 71)

14. This is Jo's reply to Helen who, after returning for good to the flat with all sorts of more or less useless things for the baby, exclaims «The baby's going to be dressed like a *prince*», which shows that she is still living in a dream.

Arthur K. Oberg (essay date summer 1966)

SOURCE: Oberg, Arthur K. "*A Taste of Honey* and the Popular Play." *Wisconsin Studies in Contemporary Literature* 7, no. 2 (summer 1966): 160-67.

[*In the following essay, Oberg traces the success of the original production of* A Taste of Honey *to its early-twentieth-century music-hall style.*]

Shelagh Delaney's *A Taste of Honey* remains so consistently associated with Joan Littlewood and her Theatre Workshop that it has become legendary as a modern popular play. What the text originally contained is as much disputed as are the merits and shortcomings of Miss Littlewood's 1958 production of the piece.[1] What we can discern is the particular status that this production of *A Taste of Honey* achieved as an effort and symbol of creative collaboration. Although *A Taste of Honey* is never prescriptively social or political in the way that other Joan Littlewood presentations were, the text and the kind of production it received earmark *A Taste of Honey* for importance in the history of the revival of the grass-roots, popular play. It is to the popular features of group production and of music-hall and vernacular humor and style that we may first turn.

Whether we trace Joan Littlewood's Theatre Workshop ideals to the practices of Brecht or *commedia dell'arte* or music-hall routines, our attention finally focuses upon the sophisticated and conscious use that Miss Littlewood made of what could be realized within the constantly evolving, at times improvised play.[2] The success of this workshop presentation of *A Taste of Honey* derived from the play's distinctively theatrical nature, suited to the production's "humour in the music-hall style."[3] While some of the jazz exits and entrances have been deplored as Joan Littlewood's stock-in-trade, there is an appropriateness in the improvisation, routines, and out-of-character speeches in the play. One of the first things an audience notices about *A Taste of Honey* is the quickness and naturalness of its pace. Helen and Jo, mother and daughter and the two central characters, are instinctively theatrical. Expert at taking up a line and twisting a word or phrase, they enjoy the routines or performances into which they lapse. Behind their words we hear speech that attempts to evade, depersonalize, and disguise feelings and genuine concern for one another. When Helen and her daughter joke and indulge in a "steady patter of insult jokes"[4] in the music-hall style, decorum is satisfied; Helen once played and sang in a little pub, and Jo, at several points in the play, aspires to a similar job. As in John Osborne's *The Entertainer,* technique is justified by the material at hand. Both plays extend the technical interest of Eliot or Auden and Isherwood in the music-hall style[5] to situations for which it is unmistakably decorous as a style.

Combining Lancashire vernacular with the "bounce" of the music-hall line, Shelagh Delaney secures her play in a popular soil. She joins the energy of the once vital music-hall to the energy of speech—vocabulary, idiom, and syntax—that is freshly colloquial in ways that middle and upper-class English speech is not. One hears in the play a conscious selection taken from the speech Shelagh Delaney spoke and heard from childhood. And one sees routines familiar to the playwright from popular entertainment.[6]

In joining Lancashire speech to music-hall routines, Shelagh Delaney employs a vernacular which sounds poetic because it is both similar to and different from the speech we are accustomed to hear.[7] Like Synge's Anglo-Irish or Jack Gelber's cool talk or Arthur Miller's cliché-riddled language, Miss Delaney's vernacular brings into the theatre another "kind of talk" based on popular speech.

Much of the style of *A Taste of Honey* admittedly is accounted for by this vernacular—repetitive tags ("isn't it," "don't you," "you know"), ungrammatical and syntactically curious expression, colloquial metaphor:

HELEN:

> Don't snatch. Have you no manners? What's these?[8]

HELEN:

> She can't do a thing for herself, that girl.
>
> (p. 10)

HELEN:

> I would never have dared talk to my mother like that when I was her age. She'd have knocked me into the middle of next week.
>
> (p. 12)

Style also derives from Miss Delaney's ear for the humor in isolating phrases that have crept into our speech from the commercial or popular media; the newspaper headline, the advertising slogan, and the capsule movie comment wind in and out of the characters' talk. But it is finally the music-hall tradition that most distinctively contributes to what emerges as the style of *A Taste of Honey.* There are not only the direct addresses to the audience in Joan Littlewood's fashion, but also the use of the extended tale or the dirty joke ("Did I ever tell you about the . . ."), and the detached and beyond-character remark. Helen and Jo are as able a team as Eliot's Klip and Krum from *Sweeney Agonistes.* They alternately throw out and answer lines. Helen and Jo are virtuoso performers, and the other characters acquire their own inventive repertoires in the course of the play. *A Taste of Honey* keeps breaking into little acts or dramas. We see and hear mock-heroics, mock-homily, mock-melodrama:

HELEN:

> What a damn silly place to put a window. This place is cold enough, isn't it, without giving shelter to the four winds.
>
> (p. 11)

Jo:

Well, here endeth the third lesson.

(p. 69)

Helen:

All right, you thought you knew it all before, didn't you? But you came a cropper. Now it's "poor little Josephine, the tragedy queen, hasn't life been hard on her."

(p. 63)

As mother and daughter encounter one another there are scenes out of stylized, Victorian melodrama where stereotyped responses to virtue and vice grow out of situations that demand courage and grace. However much Helen and Jo's remarks to one another are intended to inflict pain, they more often are hypocritical or an indication of mixed antagonism and love. As Jo calls her mother by her Christian name we are alerted less to formality or informality than to strain. When Helen and Jo suddenly begin talking *of*, instead of *to*, one another, Shelagh Delaney adapts a primarily aesthetic device of distancing—common to so much of popular art, whether music-hall or *commedia dell'arte* or Brecht—in order to reveal a state of personal relationships:

Jo:

You can afford something better than this old ruin.

Helen:

When you start earning you can start moaning.

Jo:

Can't be soon enough for me. I'm cold and my shoes let water . . . what a place . . . and we're supposed to be living off *her* immoral earnings.

(p. 7)

Helen:

Pass me a glass, Jo.

Jo:

Where are they?

Helen:

I don't know.

Jo:

You packed 'em. *She'd* lose her head if it was loose.

(p. 7; my italics.)

Here Helen and Jo resort to language, a potentially communicative art, for disguising how deeply they feel. A social and economic matter may also be involved in their frequent third person address.[9] Helen and Jo's

world is one of cemeteries, tenements, and slaughterhouses. In response to such overcrowded surroundings where privacy and identity are difficult to maintain, they have come to view themselves as detached and ultimately alone. Thus, what might have seemed at first but a linguistic habit of lower-class speech in the end is seen to have more complex origins. When Jimmy Porter in *Look Back in Anger* talks of his wife Alison in the third person, we discover a similar situation. Beginning as a normal and possible use of the third person when three people are one on stage, it soon becomes indicative of Jimmy's response to a world of attic dwellings and estranged people. It is only after Alison burns herself on the iron that Jimmy sees her again as a person and returns momentarily to more personal address.

Detachment, evident in the third person address and in the routines of the characters in *A Taste of Honey,* evidences serious disparities that the music-hall humor never adequately heals or hides.[10] Helen and Jo's succession of quick lines occasionally snaps or develops into revealing monologues, and there is the consciousness of routines that cannot always be kept up and of humor that cannot remain funny. However many occasions may be created for the coming of a good line, awkward moments occur which neither the counterpointing of the music nor the sense of timing of the characters can offset. And this is intentionally done. Words and phrases penetrate the brash music-hall patter to indicate painful relationships and an overwhelmingly sober play.

If Shelagh Delaney's use of a popular frame—Lancashire vernacular, workshop production, and a detached music-hall humor and style—at times risks masking the feelings of the characters too well, it also risks making the text of the play seem "virtually non-existent."[11] How precarious the text has to be is evident in a consideration of its subject; Helen, a semi-whore, decides to marry a man (Peter) who has deceived her into thinking he will make her an honest and happy woman; before their brief marriage breaks up Helen's sixteen-year-old daughter (Jo), in response to Helen's marriage and to growing up, has two interludes—the first, with a Negro sailor (Jimmie) who leaves her pregnant; the second, with a homosexual art student (Geof) who shares her mixed feelings toward babies, men, womanhood, sex. By the end of the play mother and daughter are again together, the illegitimate daughter now awaiting her own illegitimate child, a black one. In order to delineate these delicate relationships, Shelagh Delaney is faced with the difficulty of supplying speech for characters who are uncertain of role and whose lower-class suspicion of overt emotion strives against its verbal expression. Jo, neither adult nor child, has been brought up by a part-time mother and whore. In presenting their characters, Miss Delaney succeeds to the extent that she fails to place them in full light. While she artfully suggests by the popular elements of Lancashire speech and music-hall routine the evasion that typifies their lives, at the same time she is forced to undercut whatever emotion or poetry threatens to break the play apart. As a result, the play fiercely balances between fact and fantasy, reality and the timeless world of play-acting and nursery rhyme. *A Taste of Honey* could be performed successfully as a straightforward, realistic play. But this only pays the play a compliment at the expense of ignoring a "magnified realism"[12] arising from the same stylized, popular music-hall tradition that we saw preventing too expressive a text. That *A Taste of Honey* is strictly neither realistic nor stylized is not its weakness, as John Arden has argued,[13] but its defining genius.

Problems of text are less easily put aside, and they are concerned with what might be called the impasse of the popular play. In partaking of the vigor of a grass-roots, popular tradition, Shelagh Delaney accepts the limitations of the medium as well. Partly these limitations relate to the myth of the popular play with its preference for the unlettered and the concretely representational. Partly they are the faults of Miss Delaney's particular play whose stylized detachment, based on popular materials, ends in inhibiting other forms of stylization within the work. What once might have passed for sensitive delineation of character or for unsure craft becomes complicated by considerations of imposed artistic arrest. In evolving structure, themes, and text Shelagh Delaney cannot press too hard without disastrous results, or in other words, without destroying the popular idea of the popular play. As the performer-characters in *A Taste of Honey* mock expressive language, they succeed less in preparing an audience for whatever emotion or symbolic, poetic speech might occur than in working against a conscious, literary style. Shelagh Delaney has to settle for half-formed effects, and we are not surprised when her characters stop to query their own and other characters' remarks. Although parts of the play share the directness of dream sequences, things are more often defined by what they are not ("not marrying love" [p. 76]) or by what they uncertainly are:

Jo:

> Get back to your fancy man or your husband, or whatever you like to call him.
>
> (p. 62)

HELEN:

> What do you call this set up?
>
> (p. 80)

Uncertain effects or intentions also occur in Miss Delaney's use of imagistic language. Images of beds and coffins, brides and corpses, and housecoats and shrouds are abandoned before being adequately con-

nected in our minds by the playwright, and we never know to what extent she explicitly wishes an audience to associate marriage, madness, and death. Similarly, although Jo's interludes with Jimmie and Geof or Helen and Jo's relationships with men present contrasted parallels, more complex interlockings fail to receive the emphases they demand.

Ironically, the popular materials that are responsible for the vitality of the play conclude by making *A Taste of Honey* an abortive major work. Something built into the nature of the popular play is at cross-purposes with a more complex and extensive development of language and character, structure and theme. Shelagh Delaney's humorous "All About and To a Female Artist," in her *Sweetly Sings the Donkey,* reveals both an awareness that *A Taste of Honey* remains an unfully realized work and an acknowledgement that it aspires to serious dramatic stature.[14] Although unaware of it, Miss Delaney here attests to the impasse of the popular play. In becoming too realized it may have to abandon those qualities (e.g., detached humor, improvisation) that originally made it a popular work of art.

As the music-hall routines run down and recur, Shelagh Delaney lays out the movement that *A Taste of Honey* is to take. The play ends as it began, with Helen and Jo together. Although it is now to *Jo's* apartment that Helen returns, the indication of this return is finally too slight to assure our seeing that Jo, like Christy Mahon at the conclusion of *The Playboy of the Western World,* has assumed the controlling role. But what is even more disturbing is the lack of development that extends to what the play is about, a radical family situation. First, there are so many allusions sacrificed to humor that the playwright forfeits having important references to Ibsen's *Ghosts* or to a "blasted family reunion" bear their required weight. Secondly, the undercutting and detachment evident in the Lancashire idiom and in the music-hall routines too ably contribute to disguising Jo's agony of being a real stepdaughter to Peter after having spent sixteen years as virtual stepdaughter to Helen. That *A Taste of Honey* is Shelagh Delaney's attempt to write her own *The Family Reunion* is likely to escape our regard. Not enough prominence is afforded Jo's desire and need to speak about her mother or to her question, "What was my father like?" (p. 42) Although Jo desperately and relentlessly inquires of her father from each character, her searchings tend to be obscured in a way that Harry's question to Agatha, "Tell me now, who were my parents?"[15] is not. Jo's question, undercut and half explored, becomes barely distinguishable from any number of surrounding and ordinary lines in the play.

Shelagh Delaney's failure to enlighten her own family reunion is not an isolated example of what is left unrealized in *A Taste of Honey.* When the gas knobs are all turned on near the end of the play, their relation to an earlier occurrence seems random rather than intentional. And when one of the nursery rhymes rehearses the tale of the man who scratched out both his eyes, a connection with Helen's fancy man and with Oedipus is inadequately underlined. As *A Taste of Honey* presses toward fuller language, elaborately patterned structure, and thematic expansion, the vernacular and "humour in the music-hall style" repeatedly work toward dissolving that ultimate seriousness with which only the unpopular play can be innocently concerned.

Notes

1. John Russell Taylor, *The Angry British Theatre: New British Drama* (New York, 1962), pp. 97-100, 109-14. Taylor, having seen the original text, claims that the Theatre Workshop version is actually less different than has often been surmised.

2. For Brecht's sophistication in his use of popular materials, blending them with traditional and unpopular ones, see Martin Esslin, *Brecht: the Man and His Work* (Garden City, N. Y., 1961), p. 139. For the alertness to "nuance" of *European* vaudeville or music-hall performers see Douglas Gilbert, *American Vaudeville: Its Life and Times* (New York, 1940), p. 135.

3. Taylor, *The Angry British Theatre*, p. 111.

4. Henry Popkin, Introduction, *The New British Drama*, ed. Popkin (New York, 1964), p. 19.

5. Eliot's *Sweeney Agonistes* and Auden and Isherwood's *The Dog Beneath the Skin* reveal this interest. For some considerations on "the music-hall comedian" see T. S. Eliot, "The Possibility of a Poetic Drama," *The Sacred Wood* (London, 1920), p. 70.

6. Shelagh Delaney Interview, *The Times*, February 2, 1959, reprinted in Laurence Kitchin, *Mid-Century Drama* (London, 1960), pp. 175-77.

7. For the "great creative principle of similarity in dissimilarity" as applied to Synge's rhythms see Alan Price, *Synge and Anglo-Irish Drama* (London, 1961), p. 46; in this connection see Ronald Peacock on Synge in *The Poet in the Theatre* (New York, 1946), pp. 111, 115. On "vernacular poetry" in contemporary drama see Kitchin, *Mid-Century Drama*, p. 107.

8. Shelagh Delaney, *A Taste of Honey* (New York, 1959), p. 14. Quotations hereafter are given in the text and taken from this edition of the play.

9. I am indebted for this suggestion to William Alfred.

10. For the *assumed* detachment of the vaudeville or music-hall performer see Bernard Sobel, *A Pictorial History of Vaudeville* (New York, 1961), p. 195; see also Esslin, *Brecht*, p. 111.

11. Taylor, *The Angry British Theatre*, p. 111.

12. *Ibid.*, p. 110.

13. John Arden, "Verse in the Theatre," *New Theatre Magazine*, II (1961), 15-17.

14. Shelagh Delaney, "All About and To a Female Artist," *Sweetly Sings the Donkey* (London, 1964), pp. 91-100.

15. T. S. Eliot, *The Family Reunion, The Complete Poems and Plays: 1909-1950* (New York, 1952), p. 273.

Edward J. Esche (essay date 1992)

SOURCE: Esche, Edward J. "Shelagh Delaney's *A Taste of Honey* as Serious Text: A Semiotic Reading." In *The Death of the Playwright?: Modern British Drama and Literary Theory*, edited by Adrian Page, pp. 67-81. Houndmills, England: Macmillan, 1992.

[*In the following essay, Esche reinterprets the classical and Elizabethan understanding of tragedy and applies his definition to* A Taste of Honey.]

A Taste of Honey has a rich stage and publishing history. It was a success when first performed by Theatre Workshop, in the Theatre Royal at Stratford, London on 27 May 1958; and soon became a 'smash hit' when it transferred to Wyndham's Theatre, London on 10 February 1959. In the same year, the play made the transatlantic cultural leap to New York; it has since never left the theatre as a performance text and continues to receive professional revivals.[1] The play is still in print as a script on both sides of the Atlantic,[2] but it has undoubtedly gained its widest popular dissemination through an adapted film version.[3] American financiers initially offered to back the film if Audrey Hepburn played the leading role of Jo,[4] which is an indication of what a hot cultural property the film was perceived to be. The play text achieved true canonical status in the early eighties with widespread school syllabus selection. The two decade time-lag here is hard for me to explain beyond the obvious observation that the eighties brought us back to problems of mass unemployment and homelessness. Perhaps detailed work on which examination boards selected the play and when might net some more precise answers, but whatever the explanation the canonisation was completed in the eighties with the publication of student texts and accompanying study notes volumes.[5] The play has, however, not caught the attention of academe: we are now over thirty years away from the first appearance of *A Taste of Honey,* and as far as I can discover, only one article has been written which was devoted entirely to the play.[6] There have, of course, been numerous 'mentions' of it in book studies and articles on modern British drama, but it has not been given the serious academic attention as a cultural product in its own right which is usually accorded to similar works of such initial and sustained success. This chapter begins to redress that imbalance by providing an approach to the play through a limited (and sometimes questioning) application of the soft semiotics recently articulated by Martin Esslin.[7] It concludes by claiming the stature of tragedy for the reading that emerges, not because the play fits a mould in a Greco-Elizabethan tradition, but because the term 'tragedy' has been hijacked to that tradition for far too long; I want it back, and with it the status of seriousness accorded its object.

CRITICAL BACKGROUND

The following is a typical example of comment on *A Taste of Honey*:

> [The play] feels spontaneous but it is also ingenuous and inconclusive, with some dreadfully artificial lines. However, it is very haunting, in parts beautifully written, and with a deceptive structural toughness that goes beyond the use of music-hall technique, the direct address to the audience, and the episodic form of a variety act. It is easy to see why the play has become one of the staples of secondary-school English classes; engaging and easy to read, it remains exactly what it was—a play written by a young person about a world in which adults are suspicious and grasping and the young are self-absorbed and looking for independence. The cult of youth was in the ascendant as well as the cult of working-class style.[8]

This is damning with faint praise indeed, and a model of most of the criticism the play has received since its creation. It is fraught with traditional impressionistic responses. The vague generalities of praise ('spontaneous', 'haunting', containing 'structural toughness') are more than countered by the equally vague citings of limitation ('dreadfully artificial lines', 'in *parts* beautifully written'), and the final judgement is conclusively dismissal: the play remains fodder worthy only of the secondary-school syllabus, which is understandable because, after all, it was written by a '*young* person' and continually reveals the limitations of the 'cult of *youth*'. The phrase 'it remains exactly what it was' authoritatively places the work as little more than an historical document unworthy of resonances accorded to (it is implied) 'better' writing—the ability to move somehow outside of its time. So much for *A Taste of Honey*. The curious thing about this thumbnail response is its tone of received opinion: we all know this to be self-evident—but do we? Where are the original arguments which might have established or even proved these conclusions?

A search through the critical history, even as scarce as it is, reveals that early comment was lively and varied. Lindsay Anderson, one of the leading theatre and film directors of the day, noted the Brechtian playing of Avis Bunnage which 'managed most skilfully to combine the broadest, eye-on-the-gallery caricature, with straightforward, detailed naturalism',[9] while Colin MacInnes, that fine sociological recorder of the fifties, remarked that 'The play gives a great thirst for more authentic portraits of the mid-twentieth-century English world'.[10] Raymond Williams, Britain's most influential literary critic, actually singled out *A Taste of Honey* as the most effective example of the general characteristic of all the new British drama in the fifties, which he described as a new sound or new wave of feeling, 'that of a general restlessness, disorganization and frustration'.[11] Clearly, the play engaged some of the leading minds of the time, but for whatever reasons, and one may well be that most theatrical revivals have stressed (in my view quite inappropriately) the naturalistic possibilities of performance,[12] the variety of critical response has simply not survived. What has come through to us is something much more limited, another strain of criticism which existed beside, sometimes even within the same critical writings as the ones just cited. In this argument the play is first and foremost about characters in relation to their world. Jo, for instance, is often described as having a 'working-class resilience that will always pull her through';[13] more generally, life goes on 'with a boisterous appetite for tomorrow'.[14] Delaney herself seems to support such a view when she refers to the characters' ability to 'take in their stride whatever happens to them and remain cheerful'.[15] So, the 'feel' or 'impression' of the play becomes comfortable: it had 'a feeling for life that [was] positive';[16] 'It deals joyfully with what might in other hands, have been a tragic situation'.[17] There is an overwhelming consensus in the critical writing that the play is an example of cheery chaps, or rather chapesses, muddling through a difficult world, and, by extension, cheering us spectators with their resilience. But I teach *A Taste of Honey* to third-year degree students of all ages and backgrounds at Anglia College, and their fascination with the play rests in other, less centrally-addressed areas of interest. Not a single student in my experience comes away from the play thinking that they have seen or read a cheery or cheering text, and neither do I. The following is an attempt to offer a critical reading (and it is only one) which somehow accounts for personal responses so vastly different from received critical opinion.

SOFT SEMIOTICS

Martin Esslin is humble about the claims of a semiotic critical theory: 'this *semiotic* approach is, basically, extremely simple and practical'.[18] He is fairly distrustful of the extreme claims of semiotics as a critical tool, but highly supportive of it as a way of explaining precisely how drama achieves its effects.[19] He offers a general compilation of various theories for use, stressing what is similar; thus the idea of *which* semiotic theory we need to address does not really arise. Esslin's approach, his soft semiotics, can be applied to *A Taste of Honey* to clear away broadly impressionistic responses to the play and replace them with explanations of specific responses which will in turn accumulate to an interpretation based on a reasoned argument. But we should approach the exercise with caution, because as we break the 'total image down into the separate items of information that have been present, and convert the multidimensional instant impression into a linear sequence of separate ingredients', we should remember that 'for each member of the audience this impact of the image, at any given moment, will be different, simply because different people notice different things in a different sequence' (Esslin, pp. 36-8). In other words, the reception given to separate bits of information will vary from spectator (or reader) to spectator. Of course, there is a question begged here: how are we receiving the bits of information? The text that we address in most cases is a script, but with a play it could well be a workshop version,[20] a professional production or even a film adaptation. It is a curious fact that most criticism written on a play of many years' popularity is usually based upon a script with a remembered or projected view of professional performance. That is what I am about to do in this chapter, but I wish to stress that such an approach is *not* the only one, and certainly not a privileged one. Finally, the 'script' in the case of *A Taste of Honey* masquerades as stable, but we know that it was not when first presented for performance: we know that it underwent considerable collective revision,[21] the precise amount of which will remain a mystery until further research. And even as we look at the printed text today, it may appear to be stable, but it is not. What, for instance, is the precise meaning of 'Music'? The choice a director (cerebral or professional) makes determines the reading of the action, but we shall come to that later.

Esslin divides the signs of drama into six different groupings for purposes of his discussion: icon, index, symbol; the frame; the actor; visuals and design; the words; music and sound. The first of these is a set of basic signs first articulated by Pierce as early semiotic theory.[22] An icon is a sign that represents exactly what it signifies: a table on a stage is an icon of a table in reality. An index is a type of sign which derives its meaning from a relationship of contiguity to the object it depicts (Esslin, p. 44): a frightened look is a gesture that could be described as an index because it points to something causing the fright. A symbol is a sign which derives meaning entirely from convention: the colour of white, for instance, is a Western symbol of purity or happiness, whereas it is an Oriental colour symbol of mourning. I will return to the notion of the frame later. The next four areas are what will concern us for most of what follows. We will be applying each of the four groups of signs which Esslin notes to *A Taste of Honey*.

Incidentally, he claims that the order in which these groupings are presented corresponds precisely to the weight each has in the dramatic spectacle; so, for instance, the visuals are always of more weight than words in the decoding or communicative process of interpretation.

THE ACTOR

'The actor is the iconic sign *par excellence*' (Esslin, p. 56) which we read on at least three levels. First, s/he is a 'real person'; second, s/he is a transformation made up and trained to appear to be the fictional character that s/he is playing; third, s/he is the 'fiction' itself, for which s/he stands as a representation. So Jo is, on this first level, the real actress Caroline Milmore (in the case of the recent Royal Exchange Theatre Company revival). On the second level, Jo is the fictional character of that name in *A Taste of Honey* being played by Caroline Milmore, who has been made up to appear an adolescent and who uses her acting expertise to interpret the character. On the third level, Jo becomes the fiction for which she stands; the job of critic is to identify precisely what that is and how its meaning is established. On this level the sign Jo is a blending of everything in the script and everything in the actress that contributes to the portrayal on the stage. There may also be a further category of signification: Jo may become a representative of a class of individuals for which she stands (adolescent working-class girls, buoyant female spirits, etc.), but this level, although a corollary of the third, seems to me a limitation of meaning to merely one of many interpretations, though of course class typicality is a strength which has appealed to critics such as Piscator, Brecht and Lukàcs.

The actor has at her/his disposal a wide range of techniques and, for lack of a better word, accidentals to create her/his fiction. Among the techniques Esslin lists vocal interpretation, facial expression, gesture and movement, make-up and costume (pp. 63-4). Accidentals would include various uncontrollable things, such as involuntary responses (blushing, a twitch of the eye), unintentional suggestiveness (voice timbre may suggest hardness to a member of the audience). Most of this is very difficult to address as I am mainly reacting to and writing about the published script, but we should always be aware of the possibilities available to us. Esslin probably underestimates the role of accidentals in semiotic encoding because the line between what is controlled and what is uncontrollable is a blurred one: it becomes absolutely broken when we consider suggestiveness associated with accidentals such as skin pigmentation (an Asian Jo), mobility (a handicapped Jo) or accent (an Irish Jo). Again, I make my choice and try not to pay any attention to accidentals here; I apply theory severely and comment only upon the technical aspects that are embedded in the script. One of those is certainly movement, and in particular, entrances and exits. Quite often the characters dance on and off stage. This can be read iconically as simple dance movement; it can be read also as an index pointing to its own noteworthiness because it is an unusual form of entering or leaving most spaces; finally, it can be read as a symbol indicating that we are not in the realm of naturalistic drama, but rather in something much more akin to an eclectic style somewhere between Brechtian technique and naturalism.

One of the aspects of the actor-as-sign that Esslin does not address fully is that of the body. He does mention that as a fiction Juliet is supposed to be beautiful; it does not matter if the actress who might play her is not beautiful—the spectator will understand her as beautiful nevertheless (p. 58). But he does not attempt further explanation of sexual signification. For instance, take the example of one actor slapping another in the face. If a male strikes a male, or a female strikes a male, or even a female strikes a female, we may have (broadly speaking) a similar response, but if a male strikes a female, the action probably registers more violently to us than the other three combinations. Why? Because of the sexual codings of the bodies administering and receiving the blows: the sex of each makes a large difference to our reactions. Similarly, the sex of the body, in this case that of Jo, is charged with meaning, the most important of which in the play may well be its procreative function, because, during the play that body changes before our eyes as it swells through pregnancy; by the final curtain, the body is in labour and about to give birth. In feminist criticism, this particular sign of the actor's sex is probably of more importance than any other. One feminist critic, Michelene Wandor, notes that 'the gender bias in this play is reversed from that of most other plays', and concludes, rather lamely, that 'the family of women appears to be the one constant factor, but even that is fraught . . .'.[23] It is clearly much more than fraught, as we shall see, but we should recognise that here again, possibilities of interpretation exist. Feminist critics rarely address this play, but when they do it is with the understanding that the central mother-daughter relationship is at worst 'problematic' and at best 'loving'.[24] As we shall see, this strain of feminist reading wilfully neglects some of the social concerns which are at the heart of the play and directly *determined* by that central female relationship, but such is criticism: ours is a wilful practice.

Wandor reiterates an important point originally made by MacInnes about character grouping. She notes that the female characters carry our main interest in this play; the male characters seem to come and go, attaching or disengaging themselves from the central pair.[25] The play opens with the entrance of a mother and daughter, which is a pairing that is highly charged, if only because of the absences it might suggest. The grouping points to a

family, but the father is missing. The absent male coupled with the squalor of the set might indicate a single-parent family. As we follow this particular sign-system of character-grouping through the play, we watch it disintegrate (as Helen leaves Jo for Peter), re-form near the end of the play (when Helen comes back to the flat after she has been thrown out of Peter's house) and then disintegrate again at the very end of the play (when she leaves Jo in the first pangs of labour to get a drink). The mother and daughter grouping thus breaks twice, and the second time it occurs at a weighted, some would maintain the most weighted moment of the play—at the end. The fact that the moment is also one that is heavily charged for the female body (when it begins labour for the first time) is crucially important. I have never directly experienced this moment, but most (not all) women I have spoken to about it describe this time as a moment when they need support. In the play script (and we cannot fantasise here about what may or may not happen afterwards), Jo gets no support: she is abandoned.[26] The simple charting of the sign-system of character grouping defines the female relationship between Jo and Helen as one of abandonment, and we can only conclude at those final moments that Jo is left isolated because there are no other alternative character groupings possible, such as those we saw earlier in the play between Jo and Jimmie or between Jo and Geoff.

VISUALS AND DESIGN

The most important visual aspect of *A Taste of Honey* is its set. Throughout the entire play we are in a cheap, rundown flat in Salford in the 'today' of 1958. In semiotic terms, what is a realistic set is of course not the thing itself, but a sign for *what may be* a realistic type of flat in Lancashire, and that type of flat must be read as squalid. The set in turn codes the bodies on it; if it is squalid, then those on it are probably too poor to be anywhere else, or at the very least, must have a definite reason for inhabiting that space. One other thing that we can say with certainty is that this set clearly defines itself as other than the comfortable space we inhabit in the theatre as we view the play. The set does change throughout the performance, from the filthy squalor of the opening, to the inhabitable organisation after the arrival of Jo and Helen, to the comfortable, almost homely atmosphere created by Jo alone and afterwards with Geoff.

Another important set of visual signs in the play is the properties. Two of them deserve specific attention: the drawings and the flower bulbs. Jo's drawings are mentioned twice, and both times they function as indices pointing to the character as interested in art; considering the setting, such activity might be thought out-of-the-ordinary. But the props also function as symbols indicating both times that they are mentioned that Jo has a potential for creative work, even if it needs to be developed, as Geoff says. Of course, one of the points of the drawings is that they remain static: they are not added to or developed, and thus the potential that they indicate is never realised. The flower bulbs are another set of properties in the play, probably the most conspicuous. Jo brings them to the flat to plant because she likes flower boxes. As icons, they are simply flowers, but they are also indices pointing to a major difference between Jo and Helen, that of aesthetic taste. Jo would rather try to decorate her environment with varieties of pleasing colour. (The shading of the light bulb can be read in exactly the same way.) The bulbs also take on further meanings of symbol when they are discovered by Geoff much later in the play, hidden under the sofa in the flat. At that point, they are dead. Quite clearly, they are symbols of, again, the potentiality of growth, and through growth, of the potentiality of beauty. The two properties work as reinforcements of each other, and both indicate processes that end in exactly the same way: in failure and loss—the bulbs die and the drawings are relics of an activity that we never see taken up again.

Words

Words and articulation are the privileged areas of the literary critic, but they are often far less powerful as signs in drama than either actors, actions or properties. Esslin consistently emphasises the 'principle of the primacy of the actor and action' (p. 75), and he is absolutely correct to do so. There is nothing controversial about this. Jimmie *says* that he will come back to Jo, but he does not; we then read his behaviour, not by what he said but by what he did, by the action, not the words of the play. But many (one might even say most) critics have been reluctant to read the fiction that is 'Jo' in the same way; her words and words about her are regularly given primacy over the other signs of the play. She *says* she is independent, but the signs of the play point in exactly the opposite direction.

Again, Esslin's simplicity is admirable in stating a position for the examination of words in plays: 'in drama the meaning of the words ultimately derives from the *situation* from which they spring' (pp. 86-7). So, language is never straight; it must be read in a variety of contexts. In *A Taste of Honey* Delaney seems to be using the technique of paralleling similar phrases and thoughts to generate meanings. Peter's arrogant assertion to Helen when proposing marriage is, 'You can't afford to lose a man like me' (p. 17), which parallels Jimmie's assertion to Jo later in the play: 'There isn't another man like me anywhere. I'm one on his own' (p. 36). And both men abandon the women to whom they pledge allegiance, thereby proving that the positive value that they seem to be claiming for themselves is entirely spurious. Jo too asserts her own uniqueness immediately after Jimmie's lines quoted above and later

when she is with Geoff: 'There's only one of me like there's only one of you', and Geoff agrees, 'We're unique!' (p. 50). But are the confident assertions that these two attractive characters in the play make any more creditable than those made by the two unattractive male characters? In Geoff's case it is hard to be sure, but Jo proves to be one in a pattern. Again, we have to look to parallels for meaning.

Jo is clearly frightened of becoming like her mother, and is pleased when Jimmie tells that she is not at all like her (pp. 37-8), but in the first scene of the play when we see them both together, there is a parallel of action: shortly after we hear Helen reminisce about her first job 'in a tatty little pub' (p. 12) we hear Jo say that *she* wants to get a job in a pub, which will be her first job. Much later in the play, Geoff warns Jo that she may turn out exactly like her mother, which Jo denies (p. 72), but the action of the scene underscores Geoff's observation that she already is similar in many ways. Just before the exchange between the two characters, Jo has become frightened and has asked Geoff to hold her hand. She reminisces about her earlier life when she 'used to try and hold my mother's hands, but she always used to pull them away from me' (pp. 71-2). Then when Geoff tells her that she and her mother are similar, '*She pushes his hand away*' (p. 72). Jo's action is a direct parallel to that of Helen. And there are larger parallels of action, the most important probably is that of the two pregnancies. We are told that Helen became pregnant with Jo after her first sexual experience (pp. 43-4); similarly, we see that Jo has become pregnant with her child after her first sexual experience. Clearly, Jo's claim for uniqueness cannot be proven on the level of these parallel actions of behaviour.

Music and Sound

There is no musical notation in any of the published scripts of *A Taste of Honey* currently available. Stage directions in the scripts simply refer to '*Music*', which can obviously be quite versatile and entertaining, but which also remains as vacant of meaning as those in most Shakespearian texts. Clearly, a director has a range of options as to how the music works in any given performance, and since this area of the script is utterly malleable, I do not propose to discuss it at length. Sounds are a slightly different matter. There are plenty in the script, ranging from standard situations of farce, such as offstage business of exploding a gas cooker or tumbling through pots and pans, to something altogether more resonant. At the end of the play Jo goes into labour, and as she does she screams in pain. After the scream, a stage direction tells us that '*Children sing outside.*' Again, the actual words or rhyme being sung would encode this stage direction in a variety of ways, but since that information is not specified, we can only, in fact, concentrate on the stage direction itself. It is a sound quote from earlier in the play, where we heard it twice in the same scene between Geoff and Jo. In the first instance (p. 54), it triggered a general discussion about child neglect, and in the second instance (p. 57), it forms an ironic background to Geoff's attempt to 'start something' with Jo. In both cases the children's singing underscores Jo's pregnancy and the future it will bring, a future which combines the fact of the physical presence of the child and also the possibility that it may join the crowd of 'filthy children' making the sound. Thus the final image, of the female body in labour and deserted quite literally as Helen flees the flat for a drink, must be read against these sounds.

THE FRAME

We can now challenge several of the interpretations offered for *A Taste of Honey* by considering the idea of the frame. Framing devices exist in a variety of forms, and they all place the play in a context which generates expectancy in us as spectators/readers. The performance space itself is often a potent frame: going out to a West End theatre creates a different set of expectations from going out to a town hall in Lancashire. The acting company is another important frame: we would expect that a play done by The Women's Theatre Group would emphasise women's concerns, while we would not necessarily make that assumption if the same play was being presented by, for instance, The Royal Shakespeare Company. Reviews also function as powerful frames: raves create the expectation of 'good' theatre, while slatings do just the opposite. And there are probably many more frames which set various contexts for us (including that created by publishing a play in a student edition), but one of the most important frames in literary criticism remains that of genre. Unlike many critics, I think that such labels are important. The 'biggest' and most 'important' label has traditionally been that of 'tragedy', and with it the inference that the tragic play contains highly serious matter. We saw that Kenneth Tynan's impression was characteristic of the received reading of the play: 'It deals joyfully with what might in other hands have been a tragic situation.'[27] But in the reading that is outlined above, the notion of joy and cheeriness has no place, mainly because I avoided discussing the element of the jokes. The jokes are often very funny, but most of them are verbal signs, and are, according to Esslin, not necessarily as heavily weighted in their meaning as some of the other signs I have been discussing. Now Tynan, more clearly than any other critic, articulates avoidance of an issue I want to address: he tells us that he has chosen to avoid using the term tragedy for the play. He begs a huge question: what would a tragic situation look like in this play? I believe it looks like the situation in which Jo finds herself at end of the play.

Arthur Miller defines the tragic figure, and by extension her/his situation, as one who 'engages . . . questions

. . . whose answers define humanity and the right way to live so that the world is a home, instead of a battle-ground or a fog in which disembodied spirits pass each other in an endless night'.[28] Those kinds of questions are raised directly at the end of *A Taste of Honey*. The limited semiotic reading of the play that I have offered exposes a pattern of overall action that could be described as cyclical,[29] accompanied by a downward movement—Jo repeats the pattern of her mother and various symbols of growth end in ruin. The tragic experience is not necessarily just of Jo as class typicality (although that aspect is included), but it is, again, of the fiction that she represents, and that fiction is of an individual *young* woman trapped in a downward spiral of social and economic decay. The most chilling feature of this tragedy is that it is repetitive, and, again, not simply for Jo. As she screams in the pain of labour, the process, the cycle of single mother trapped in poverty with its inherent possibility of neglect, may be starting all over again for the child about to be born. Such action is a clear and powerful articulation of abuse breeding abuse; the jokes simply serve the function of papering over or disguising a pattern of social fracture, and thereby deepening rather than negating the tragic experience. There is resilience and humour throughout, but there is no solution offered to the cycle of decay.

WAYS FORWARD

This article has only scratched the surface of an extremely rich and complex play worthy of detailed and extended study. Let us hope that we will cease to read comments such as that the play has no 'ideas', or that it has 'no clear-cut message';[30] but much more needs to be done. In particular, the historical context needs to be more fully charted; I suspect that Jo's claim for unique-ness could be justified on the grounds of her choice of a black sailor and a gay art student as male companions. What criteria (or opportunisms?) were at work in Joan Littlewood's choice of Delaney's script for performance by the Theatre Royal? The Brechtian influences also deserve much further examination; a study of the first musical score would be of major importance here. And as we all watch the intoxicating events in East Europe, notion(s) of class typicality will engage our thought. The question of speech prefixes is fascinating: 'Helen' is one which wears a dubious weight of history; 'Jo' is sexually indeterminate; 'Boy' is extraordinary when ap-plied, as it is in the play, to a black man. More work needs to be done on performance generally with such a rich revival history. Finally, why has the play 'resided' on school syllabuses and not been addressed in any substantial way by the higher establishments of educa-tion and academe?

Notes

1. Including those by The Royal Exchange Theatre Company, Manchester, first performance 2 March

1989, director Ian Hastings, and by the Nottingham Playhouse, first performance 25 January 1989.

2. Shelagh Delaney, *A Taste of Honey* (London: Methuen, first published January 1959, new edition April 1959) and Shelagh Delaney, *A Taste of Honey* (New York: Grove, 1959).

3. *A Taste of Honey*, screenplay by Shelagh Delaney and Tony Richardson, directed by Tony Richardson (1961).

4. Pam Cook (ed.) *The Cinema Book* (London: British Film Institute: 1985), p. 49.

5. Shelagh Delaney, *A Taste of Honey* (With a Commentary and Notes by Glenda Leeming), Methuen Student Editions (London: Methuen, 1982); Shelagh Delaney, *A Taste of Honey,* ed. Ray Speakman (London: Heinemann, Methuen, 1989) in The Hereford Plays series: Susan Quilliam, *A Taste of Honey* by Shelagh Delaney (Harmondsworth: Penguin, 1987) in Penguin Passnotes; John Jenkins, *A Taste of Honey* by Shelagh Delaney (London: Pan Books, 1988) in Brodie's Notes.

6. Arthur K. Oberg, 'A Taste of Honey and the Popular Play', *Wisconsin Studies in Popular Literature* (now *Contemporary Literature*) 7, 1966, 160-67.

7. Martin Esslin, *The Field of Drama: How the Signs of Drama Create Meaning on Stage and Screen* (London: Methuen, 1987).

8. Colin Chambers and Mike Prior, *Playwrights' Progress: Patterns of Postwar British Drama* (London: Amber Lane Press, 1987), pp. 37-8.

9. Lindsay Anderson, *A Taste of Honey,* Review in Charles Marowitz, Tom Milne, Owen Hale (eds), *New Theatre Voices of the Fifties and Sixties: Selections from* Encore *Magazine 1956-1963* (London: Eyre Methuen reissue, 1981), p. 80; reprinted from *Encore,* 1958.

10. Colin MacInnes, 'A Taste of Reality' in *England, Half England* (London: MacGibbon & Kee, 1961), p. 206; reprinted from *Encounter,* April 1959: for new cultural mappings of the fifties see also Rick Rylance (ed.), *Ideas and Production: A Journal in the History of Ideas,* 'Culture and Experience in the 1950s', Vols IX-X.

11. Raymond Williams, 'New English Drama' in John Russell Brown (ed.), *Modern British Dramatists: A Collection of Critical Essays* (Englewood Cliffs, New Jersey: Prentice-Hall, 1968), pp. 32-3; reprinted from *Twentieth Century,* CLXX, no. 1011 (1961), 169-80.

12. See Helene Keyssar, *Feminist Theatre* (London: Macmillan, 1984), p. 42.

13. Anderson, p. 79.

14. Kenneth Tynan, *A Taste of Honey,* review in Gareth and Barbara Lloyd Evans (eds), *Plays in Review 1956-1980: British Drama and Its Critics* (London: Batsford Academic and Educational, 1985), p. 66; reprinted from *The Observer,* 1 June 1958.

15. Methuen Student Edition, p. xvii.

16. MacInnes, p. 205.

17. Kenneth Tynan, in *A Taste of Honey,* Royal Exchange Theatre Company Programme (Manchester, 1989), unpaginated; reprinted from *A View of the English Stage 1944-1956* (London: Methuen, 1984).

18. Esslin, p. 10.

19. See Keir Elam, *The Semiotics of Theatre and Drama* (London and New York: Methuen, 1980) for such extreme claims.

20. For an excellent discussion about workshop practice, see Simon Shepherd, 'Acting Against Boredom: Some Utopian Thoughts on Workshops' in Lesley Aers and Nigel Wheale (eds), *Shakespeare in the Changing Curriculum* (London: Routledge, forthcoming).

21. See John Russell Taylor, *Anger and After: A Guide to the New British Drama* (London: Methuen, 1962; revised 1969), pp. 131-2 and Howard Goorney, *The Theatre Workshop Story* (London: Eyre Methuen, 1981), pp. 109 and 112.

22. One of the best introductions to semiotic theory is Kaja Silverman, *The Subject of Semiotics* (Oxford and New York: Oxford University Press, 1983), which includes explanations of these terms based on Pierce's own *Collected Papers,* pp. 19-25.

23. Michelene Wandor, *Look Back in Gender: Sexuality and the Family in Post-War British Drama* (London and New York: Methuen, 1987), pp. 41-2.

24. For instance, see Wandor, pp. 39-43 and Keyssar, pp. 38-43.

25. MacInnes, p. 205; Wandor, p. 40; Keyssar, p. 39.

26. For readings that do not view the ending as despair see Williams, Wandor and Keyssar.

27. See note 14 above.

28. Arthur Miller, 'Introduction' to *Collected Plays* (New York: The Viking Press, 1957), p. 32.

29. See Oberg, p. 164 for the hint of repetition that has led me to note this pattern.

30. Taylor, p. 132 and Leeming, Methuen Student Edition, p. xvi, respectively.

Michelene Wandor (essay date 2001)

SOURCE: Wandor, Michelene. "Voices from the Distaff Side: Mother and Daughter." In *Post-War British Drama: Looking Back in Gender,* pp. 60-3. London: Routledge, 2001.

[*In the following essay, Wandor examines Delaney's depiction of gender roles in* A Taste of Honey *as a reflection of the wider time and culture and within the framework of the notion of "family."*]

The post-war theme of domestic displacement here takes on a new gendered turn. Recently moved into 'a comfortless flat in Manchester', Helen ('a semi-whore') and her daughter Jo establish their love-hate relationship in a home where familial roles are raw and unconventional. There is no father around, and Jo and Helen share the ironic intimacy of a double bed—ironic since their intimacy is fraught, painful and based on a closeness which at the same time is undermined by the needs of each woman to establish her separate identity.

This 'family', then, has no man to head it, no secure, long-term home to house it. The expected norms are reversed: Jo is the more responsible of the two (shades of *Absolutely Fabulous* . . .), Helen more interested in how she looks and in going out to have a good time. Marking the generational changes, Helen comments:

> You bring them up and they turn round and talk to you like that. I would never have dared talk to my mother like that when I was her age. She'd have knocked me into the middle of next week.

Jo wants to leave school, and to get away from Helen. The two are clearly used to their nomadic existence, and Helen's succession of boyfriends. She may be cynical about men, but she cannot do without one. Expectations are reversed and taboos broken. Helen refuses to be defined as only a mother. She is an older woman who likes drinking, sex and going out. However, there are painful consequences to this:

Jo:

> You should prepare my meals like a proper mother.

Helen:

> Have I ever laid claim to being a proper mother?

A further and striking theatrical taboo is also broken: here is a play, in a domestic setting, which follows the fortunes of the women at its centre. Male characters come and go according to the needs of the female gender-driven story, and we do not follow the men's emotions or dilemmas. This familial 'outsider' paring—single mum and daughter—is joined by the further outsider figure of Jo's boyfriend, described as 'a coloured naval rating', doing his National Service. Unlike Pinter's McCann, this man carries none of the immediately sinister overtones of a feared racial Other, although he is depersonalised in the cast list as 'Boy', his name, Jimmy, only spoken much later on in the play.

When Peter and Helen decide to get married and go on honeymoon, Boy stays with Jo over Christmas. Helen is a woman who seems very sure of her sexuality; by contrast, Jo, still very young, is less sure. On Helen's wedding day, Jo questions her about her father, to learn that she was the outcome of a one-night stand. Helen, despite her insistence on living her life exactly as she wants, still hankers after conventions, challenging Jo: 'Why don't you learn from my mistakes?'

In Act 2, Boy has gone and Jo is pregnant—from another one-night stand. Geof, a gay man, moves in with Jo, the two of them just good friends. Here the subversion of conventional gender roles goes even further. Jo is deeply ambiguous about her pregnancy, unsure about motherhood: 'I hate babies.' When she talks about breastfeeding, she is even more fearful: 'I'm not having a little animal nibbling away at me, it's cannibalistic. Like being eaten alive.'

When Geof buys her a doll on which to practise, she bursts out: 'I'll bash its brains out. I'll kill it. I don't want his baby, Geof. I don't want to be a mother. I don't want to be a woman.'

Geof, on the other hand, becomes a dual substitute mother, looking after Jo, and preparing cot and clothes for the baby. He has all the feelings which, according to conventional gender expectation, Jo should have. She says: 'It comes natural to you . . . you'd make someone a wonderful wife.'

Despite a bit of effort, both Jo and Geof appear to be primarily asexual. Geof admits that he has never kissed a girl, and when they try, Jo reacts angrily, saying she does not 'enjoy all this panting and grunting'. The struggle to make sense of the complexities of sex, affection and love lead Jo to come down on the side of an undemanding friendship and affection: 'I always want to have you with me because I know you'll never ask anything from me.'

Jo is afraid of becoming a mother because she has not herself been properly mothered: 'I used to try and hold my mother's hands, but she always used to pull them away from me. . . . She had so much love for everyone else, but none for me.' However, the prospect of an unconventional alternative family—single mother, gay father-figure and illegitimate baby—is diverted when Helen comes back, her marriage having broken down. Traditional motherhood imperatives return, and Helen behaves so appallingly towards Geof that he leaves. As soon as he has gone, Helen and Jo revert to their old sniping love-hate relationship, exacerbated when Jo tells Helen that the baby may be black. There is a moment when it appears that Helen might be too shocked to stay—indeed, she is impelled to go out to get a drink—but it is clear from the very end that she is coming back, that Jo wants her to come back. The play concludes with Jo reciting an old-fashioned folk rhyme—a reference, perhaps, to the possible friendship with Geof which, on the basis of everything we have seen, has to be impossible now that Helen is back.

In this shifting family combination, Geof is a good, kind 'brother' throughout, concerned for Jo's best interests, even when he has been thrown out. Imaginatively, this seems to be made possible by the fact that although everything in his manner and speech tells us he is gay, we know nothing about his history, and he has no sexual relationships within the world of the play. Thus, like Cliff, he is an asexual male, who is therefore available for friendship with a woman.

The emotional language of the play is raw and vibrant— these characters have no problems expressing real, nitty-gritty feelings and conflicts about fundamental emotional issues; perhaps this is because of their working-class roots, although each is socially displaced from the conventional norms: single mother and part-time whore, illegitimate teenage mother, gay white man, black sailor boy; a series of 'outsiders' to British culture (of whatever class), in which the hierarchy descends from the biological mother-daughter relationship which wins out over all others, however abrasive it is.

Sexuality is problematic for everyone—even for Helen, whose relationship breaks down. Interestingly, although all kinds of socially unconventional bondings look possible, in the end the biological, socially validated triumphs: the mother and daughter relationship overrides all the taboos. The issues and dilemmas are radical: motherhood is thrust on many women; nurturing is not necessarily an automatic maternal instinct, whereas a man may well feel 'maternal', yet be prevented from being able to express himself. The values of the mother-daughter blood relationship prevail as the strongest, and thus the women, while they may not be in total control of their emotional relationships, do manage the domestic space, and the gender dynamic of the plot is (unusually) female. Motherhood—even though in two kinds of crisis—takes centre stage, by implication raising questions about what kinds of families audiences of the time live in, and what kinds of alternative families they might set up.

FURTHER READING

Criticism

Boles, William C. "'Have I Ever Laid Claims to Being a Proper Mother?': The Stigma of Maternity in Shelagh Delaney's *A Taste of Honey.*" *Text & Presentation* 17 (1996): 1-5.

> Contrasts the sociocultural and scientific view of pregnancy and motherhood during the 1950s as the natural role for women with the ambivalent view presented in *A Taste of Honey.*

Winterson, Jeanette. "My Hero, Shelagh Delaney." *Guardian (London)* (18 September 2010): 5.

> Asserts that reviews of *A Taste of Honey* and *The Lion in Love* "read like a depressing essay in sexism" and suggests that because Delaney was written off as a "flash in the pan" and lacked sufficient support in the theater world, her playwriting career was stifled.

Additional coverage of Delaney's life and career is contained in the following sources published by Gale: *Concise Dictionary of British Literary Biography, 1960 to Present*; *Contemporary Authors,* **Vols. 17-20R;** *Contemporary Authors New Revision Series,* **Vols. 30, 67;** *Contemporary British Dramatists*; *Contemporary Dramatists,* **Eds. 5, 6;** *Contemporary Literary Criticism,* **Vol. 29;** *Contemporary Women Dramatists*; *Dictionary of Literary Biography,* **Vol. 13;** *Discovering Authors Modules: Dramatists*; *Drama for Students,* **Vol. 7;** *Literature Resource Center*; **and** *Major 20th-Century Writers,* **Ed. 1.**

Miguel de Unamuno
1864-1936

(Full name Miguel de Unamuno y Jugo) Spanish playwright, novelist, poet, essayist, journalist, short story writer, autobiographer, and translator.

INTRODUCTION

Unamuno was an important figure in the Spanish cultural movement known as the Generation of 1898—a group of literary figures and intellectuals who came of age during the Spanish-American War and objected to the conservative restoration period that followed Spain's defeat. In his writings he dealt with existential problems related to the tension between reason and faith, religion and free thought, and the inevitable tragedy of death. Renowned as a poet, fiction writer, and essayist, in general his plays lacked, ironically, the dramatic intensity of his fiction. Nevertheless his dramatic theory is considered to have profoundly influenced the development of Spanish theater in the twentieth century.

BIOGRAPHICAL INFORMATION

Unamuno was born on September 29, 1864, in the Basque city of Bilbao, to Félix de Unamuno, a baker, and his wife, who was also his niece, Salomé Jugo. When Unamuno was six years old his father died, and Unamuno was then raised by his mother and an uncle in a devout Catholic household. As a child, Unamuno witnessed civil war violence during the Carlist siege of Bilbao. Unamuno studied philosophy and letters at the University of Madrid, writing a doctoral thesis on the origins of the Basque people and language, which had been subjects of strong interest to him since he was a young student. When he received his doctoral degree in 1884, he returned to Bilbao and for six years he studied in preparation for the *oposiciones,* highly competitive national examinations for teaching posts, while tutoring to support himself. He secured a professorship at the University of Salamanca and, in 1891, married Concepción (Concha) Lizárraga Encénnarro, with whom he eventually had nine children, and moved to Salamanca to begin his scholarly duties. He developed an interest in socialist thought and from 1894 to 1897 he regularly contributed articles to a socialist weekly journal based in Bilbao, *La Lucha de Clases.* Unamuno's infant son, Raimundo, contracted meningitis in 1896 and his deteriorating health, which eventually resulted in his death at age six, triggered a spiritual crisis in Unamuno

in 1897. He found himself unable to find comfort in either his intellectual convictions or the Catholic tradition in which he was raised. That year, his first novel, *Paz en la guerra* (*Peace in War*), was published. He then wrote his first play, completed in 1898 and first performed in 1909, *La esfinge*; like all of his plays, it struggled to reach the stage. Unamuno gradually came to play an important role in Spanish intellectual life as part of the Generation of 1898, along with other such Spanish intellectuals as Ramón del Valle-Inclán, Antonio Machado, and Joaquín Costa. Unamuno served as rector of the University of Salamanca, while continuing to teach there, from 1900 to 1914, a time of great upheaval as Spain adjusted to the aftermath of the Spanish-American War. Although the war lasted only ten weeks, it resulted in Spain's loss of Cuba, Puerto Rico, Guam, and the Philippines. The humiliating loss caused a crisis of confidence in the Spanish public and the Spanish monarchy became increasingly autocratic under King Alonso XIII. In 1912 Unamuno published his well-known treatise *Del sentimiento trágico de la vida en los hombres y en los pueblos* (*The Tragic Sense of Life in Men and Peoples*). In 1914 Unamuno was dismissed from his rector post after criticizing the King's policies, but he remained at the university in other roles. The aristocratic General Primo de Rivera assumed control of the country and installed himself as dictator in 1923. Unamuno campaigned against the dictatorship and was exiled to the island of Fuerteventura in the Canaries in 1924. After a few months, he escaped to Paris, where he and his cause became well known among intellectuals. He lived in exile in France for five years, mostly in the French Basque town of Hendaye. After Rivera fell from power in 1930, Unamuno returned to Spain and resumed his rectorship at the University of Salamanca. In 1936 civil war erupted in Spain when Generalissimo Francisco Franco came to power. Unamuno publicly denounced Franco and subsequently was dismissed from the University and placed under house arrest, where he died from a stroke on December 31, 1936.

MAJOR DRAMATIC WORKS

Unamuno's works explore the anxiety and alienation derived from conflict between reason and faith, the tragic nature of life, and the inevitability of death. Unamuno's contemplation of these themes led him to philosophical conclusions that precursed Existentialism. Like the *modernista* authors of his time, Unamuno cre-

ated works that were abstract and symbolic; for Unamuno, some of his most highly metaphorical works
appeared following the period of despair he suffered
when his child became gravely ill. Like many members
of his generation, Unamuno found Catholicism unhelp-
ful, but was unable to place his faith in anything else
his culture could offer either. In plays such as *La venda*
(1921), Unamuno questions the nature of human existence itself when María, a young woman who has been
blind since birth, undergoes surgery to restore her
eyesight. Shortly afterward she is called to her dying
father's bedside, but she is overwhelmed and disoriented
by having vision and ties a blindfold around her eyes,
making her way through the city to her father using just
a cane and her intuition. Once she arrives, her father
insists that she remove the blindfold and look at him
for the first time, but she refuses, believing that he will
no longer be the father she knows if she sees him. When
her sister tears the blindfold away, the shock of being
seen by his daughter for the first time kills the father.
At that point María puts the blindfold back and insists
she never wants to see again. María cannot reconcile
her father's need to be seen with her own need to follow her own inner vision. Plays such as *La esfinge* and
Soledad (1953) are similarly defined more by their
symbolism than by their action or dramatic impact. In
La esfinge the protagonist, Angel, is a political activist
and intellectual beset by spiritual doubt and skepticism.
He despairs of the futility of introducing Spain's
masses, who have been shaped by centuries of Catholicism and monarchism, to the principles of political and
intellectual libertarianism. He refuses to accept the role
of revolutionary leader and is subsequently shot and
killed. Despite the political nature of the play, however,
Angel's struggle is primarily expressed through imagery
of music and water, which symbolize Angel's desire for
spiritual purity both within himself and in his country.
In *Soledad* Unamuno also used symbols, including
water and music, as a means through which to express
the ambivalence and skepticism of his protagonist,
Agustín, who, following the death of his young son,
tries to decide between a career in literature or one in
politics while doubting the significance of any endeavor.
Unamuno's interest in the divided self took a more
literal turn in his play *El otro* (1932; *The Other*), in
which identical twins Cosme and Damián are both in
love with the same woman, Laura, who cannot tell them
apart. Ultimately, Cosme marries Laura, Damián marries Damiana, and there is peace between them for a
time. But when hostilities erupt again, one brother kills
the other, but no one knows which one is which, possibly including the surviving brother, who eventually
commits suicide. The nursemaid who tended the brothers as children is believed to know which is which, but
in the end she refuses to say, insisting that no one can
really know who anyone is. In *El hermano Juan*
(published in 1934) Unamuno, who is known to have
detested the myth of Don Juan, has the famous Spanish

seducer undergo a crisis of conscience and, ultimately,
act as a conduit through which the ideal of love and
marriage occurs for others.

CRITICAL RECEPTION

In terms of his fiction, Unamuno is widely considered
to have been the greatest Spanish writer since Miguel
de Cervantes. His novels and stories are marked by
psychological depth and intense drama. Critics have
found with regret that, ironically, Unamuno overall
never was able to transfer that dramatic quality to his
plays and was, in fact, rather impatient with the
demands of writing for the theater. D. L. Shaw has
noted that, while Unamuno infused the characters in his
plays with great psychological complexity with his use
of imagery and symbolism, he failed to weave this successfully into the dramatic structure of his plays. Derek
Gagen summarized that, "With few exceptions [literary
critics] note a failure to adapt to the traditional demands
of the genre and of the audience and they accordingly
concentrate on thematic and biographical considerations." Gagen insisted, however, that, with the publication of his influential early essay "La regeneración del
teatro español" in 1896, Unamuno's place in the
"reform" of Spanish theater was assured. However,
Gagen noted, Unamuno quickly lost favor with
politically-oriented critics who celebrated his early
dramatic principles, as he drifted away from socialism
toward liberalism. The most distinguishing aspect of his
dramatic theory is its concern with the interior struggle
of the protagonist. Stephen J. Summerhill has summarized Unamuno's dramaturgy thusly: "Eschewing the
complicated plots, realistic settings and romantic themes
of the era's bourgeois theater, don Miguel sought a
stripped down representation of the 'agonía' or interior
conflicts of the self as it endures the mysteries of existence and death."

PRINCIPAL WORKS

Plays

La esfinge 1909
La difunta 1910
El pasado que vuelve 1910
Fedra 1918
*La venda 1921
Raquel encadenada 1926
†*Sombras de sueño* 1930
El otro [*The Other*] 1932
Medea [translator; from *Medea* by Lucius Anneas
    Seneca] 1933
‡*El hermano Juan* 1934

Soledad 1953

Teatro: Fedra, Soledad, Raquel encadenada, Medea 1954

Teatro completo 1959

La princesa doña Lambra 1964

Obras completas. 9 vols. (novels, essays, poetry, plays, and novellas) 1966-71

Other Major Works

En torno al casticismo (essay) 1895

La regeneración del teatro español (essay) 1896

Paz en la guerra [Peace in War] (novel) 1897

De la enseñanza superior en España (essay) 1899

Nicodemo el fariseo (essay) 1899

Tres ensayos (essays) 1900

Amor y pedagogía [Love and Pedagogy] (novel) 1902

Paisajes (essay) 1902

De mi país (essay) 1903

Vida de Don Quijote y Sancho [The Life of Don Quixote and Sancho] (essay) 1905

Poesías (poetry) 1907

Recuerdos de niñez y de mocedad (autobiography) 1908

Mi religión y otros ensayos breves [Perplexities and Paradoxes] (essays) 1910

Por tierras de Portugal y de España (essay) 1911

Rosario de sonetos líricos (poetry) 1911

Soliloquios y conversaciones (essays) 1911

Contra esto y aquello (essay) 1912

Del sentimiento trágico de la vida en los hombres y en los pueblos [The Tragic Sense of Life in Men and Peoples] (essay) 1912

El espejo de la muerte (short stories) 1913

Niebla [Mist] (novel) 1914

Abel Sánchez: Una historia de pasíon [Abel Sánchez] (novel) 1917

Ensayos. 7 vols. *[Essays and Soliloquies]* (essays) 1916-18

El Cristo de Velázquez [The Christ of Velázquez] (poetry) 1920

Tres novelas ejemplares y un prólogo (Dos madres, El marqués de Lumbría, Nada menos que todo un hombre) [Three Exemplary Novels and a Prologue (Two Mothers, The Marquis of Lumbria, A He Man)] (novellas) 1920

Tulio Montalbán y Julio Macedo (novella) 1920

La tía Tula (novella) 1921

Andanzas y visiones españolas (essay) 1922

Sensaciones de Bilbao (essay) 1922

Rimas de dentro (poetry) 1923

Teresa: Rimas de un poeta desconocido presentadas y presentado por Miguel de Unamuno (poetry) 1923

La agonía del cristianismo [The Agony of Christianity] (essay) 1925

De Fuerteventura a París: Diario íntimo de confinamiento y destierro vertido en sonetos (poetry and prose) 1925

Cómo se hace una novela (essay) 1927

Romancero del destierro (poetry) 1928

Dos artículos y dos discursos (essays) 1930

#*San Manuel Bueno, mártir, y tres historias más [Saint Emmanuel the Good, Martyr]* (novellas) 1933

La ciudad de Henoc, comentario, 1933 (essay) 1941

Antología poética (poetry) 1942

Cuatro narraciones (short stories) 1943

Cuenca Ibérica (lenguaje y paisaje) (essay) 1943

Temas argentinos (essay) 1943

Almas de jóvenes (prose) 1944

El caballero de la triste figura (prose) 1944

La dignidad humana (essay) 1944

Viejos y jóvenes (prose) 1944

La enormidad de España (prose) 1945

Algunas consideraciones sobre la literatura hispan-oamericana (essays) 1947

Visiones y comentarios (essays) 1949

Madrid (essay) 1950

Mi Salamanca (essay) 1950

Vida literaria (essays) 1951

Poems (poetry) 1952

Cancionero: Diario poético (poetry) 1953

España y los españoles (essays) 1955

Inquietudes y meditaciones (essays) 1957

Cincuenta poesías inéditas (poetry) 1958

Mi vida y otros recuerdos personales (autobiography) 1959

Cuentos. 2 vols. (short stories) 1961

Del diario poético (poetry) 1961

El gaucho Martín Fierro (essay) 1967

Diario íntimo [The Private World] (autobiography) 1970

Cartas 1903-1933 (letters) 1972

Ver con los ojos y otros relatos novelescos (short stories) 1973

The Last Poems of Miguel de Unamuno (poetry) 1974

Artículos olvidados sobre España y la primera Guerra mundial (journalism) 1976

Escritos socialistas: Artículos inéditos sobre el socialismo, 1894-1922 (journalism) 1976

El torno a las artes: Del teatro, el cine, las bellas artes, la política y las letras (journalism) 1976

Crónica política española (1915-1923) (journalism) 1977

De mi vida (autobiography) 1979

República española y España republicana (1931-1936) (journalism) 1979

Unamuno: Artículos y discursos sobre canarias (journalism) 1980

Ensueño de una patria: Periodismo republicano, 1931-36 (journalism) 1984

Miguel de Unamuno's Political Writings (1918-1924). 3 vols. (journalism) 1996

Unamuno y el socialismo: Artículos recuperados (1886-1928) (journalism) 1997

*Adapted from the short story by Unamuno.

†Adapted from the novella *Tulio Montalbán y Julio Macedo* by Unamuno.

‡Date reflects first publication.

#Comprises *San Manuel Bueno, mártir, La novela de Don Sandalio, jugador de ajedrez, Un pobre hombre rico,* and *Una historia de amor.*

OVERVIEWS AND GENERAL STUDIES

Frank Sedwick (essay date September 1960)

SOURCE: Sedwick, Frank. "Unamuno and Woman-hood: His Theater." *Hispania* 43, no. 3 (September 1960): 309-13.

[*In the following essay, Sedwick examines Unamuno's premise in most of his plays that women chiefly experience true love and fulfillment through maternity.*]

It is the present purpose to add a few thoughts to R. L. Predmore's article entitled "Flesh and Spirit in the Works of Unamuno,"[1] a part of which emphasizes Unamuno's motherhood complex. Indeed one of Unamuno's obsessions was his reverence for women, based on woman's will and her yearning for maternity. Consequently many of his feminine characters have a preoccupation with motherhood as their basic motivation in most matters: a woman is either a mother or a potential mother, as distinguished from female, *hembra,* a term which Unamuno seldom uses without disdain.

Unamuno repeatedly asserts that woman's love is simply compassion, that her surrender to the lover is through sympathy or self-identification with his suffering.[2] This is intended to apply as well to conjugal love. Woman is capable chiefly of maternal love, and physical passion itself is to a large extent a kind of maternal instinct to proffer asylum. Unamuno says even of nuns that ". . . las pobres monjitas en su celda rinden culto al Niño Jesús, más que al Esposo,"[3] an idea that he develops more fully in *Una historia de amor* when he describes life in a convent.[4] Owing to her ability to "suffer with" (Lat. *patior, compassio* > Span. *compasión*: identical to the concept inherent in the Greek derivative *sympathy*), woman contributed her share toward making Don Juan what he is. This is part of Unamuno's proposition in **El hermano Juan,** in which the reader is even provided with a list of sometimes-inadvertent seductresses, some of whom are Eve, Helen of Troy, Dido, Desdemona, Melibea, Isolde, Emma Bovary, Juliet, Carmen, Marguerite, and Manon.[5] "¡Pobres! ¡pobres! ¡pobres! . . . Os engañó un pobre diablo que hizo de serpiente . . . vuestra víctima . . ."[6] Why "¡pobres!"? Because all were real women, not *hembras,* each responsive to her instinct for motherhood, her urge to offer sanctuary. If like Carmen she can master and withdraw her sympathy, her reason is to extend it to another. Life is love; love is procreation; therefore life is procreation. "¡Vivir es criar!"[7] With this definition of life, Unamuno the writer, so acutely sensitive to the mysteries of creation, may have felt compelled to write of woman, birth, and motherhood. As he says in the essay *El resorte moral,* "la mujer es el verdadero principio de continuidad de un pueblo, el arca de sus más preciadas y más profundas tradiciones."[8]

Unamuno's readers become familiar with his predilection for intense, agonistic, struggling characters and his defense of them as creatures of fiction (see the *Prólogo* to his *Tres novelas ejemplares*). Yet many of Unamuno's female literary creations seem artificially drawn, because in his insistence on their "realidad íntima" he often overintensifies them to the extent that they lack some of the other complexities of the feminine point of view. He appears even to be ill at ease with them and to join his reader in studying them. Many become stereotyped in their obsessive aspiration to motherhood, or if that state is unattainable, to a simulation of motherhood or a substitute for it, like tía Tula, two of the three female characters in **El otro,** the women in **El hermano Juan,** the aunt of the Marqués de Lumbría, Liduvina in *Una historia de amor,* and—the extreme example of woman's necessity for having children, even vicariously—Raquel in *Dos madres.* When motherhood is achieved, however, Unamuno's women sometimes acquire a bovine complacency that makes them unexciting as literary characters. Two such mothers are Antonia in *Abel Sánchez* and Marina in *Amor y pedagogía.*

In 1954 four little-known Unamuno plays became available in a volume called **Teatro,** printed in Barcelona. Manuel García Blanco, who little by little has been publishing Unamuno's complete works as well as the separate series *Cuadernos de la cátedra Miguel de Unamuno,* enriched the edition with a prologue and bibliographical notes. Previously only a few Hispanists had known where to seek the original texts of these four plays, **Fedra, Medea, Soledad,** and **Raquel encadenada,** the last two of which had never before been published. Each of these four plays belongs to the womanhood-motherhood theme. For this reason they invite analysis, even though admittedly the theater of Unamuno is not a key but a complement to the main currents of thought found in his more solid works.

In this volume of **Teatro,** Raquel is *encadenada* because she is childless. Soledad too is childless after the death of her first baby. Fedra falls in love with her stepson, owing not a little to the fact that she has no children of her own. All three plays present the problem of the childless wife. Medea, of course, in the translation from Seneca, kills her children as a woman's superlative sacrifice in revenge for a wife's greatest injury. Because the plot of *Medea* is well known and because Unamuno's **Medea** is not original, being a rendition of Latin verse into Spanish prose, it will be omitted from the present discussion.

In a prologue Unamuno tells the reader that the generative argument of his **Fedra** is the same as that of Euripides' *Hippolytus* and of Racine's *Phèdre,* but that the dénouement is wholly different from that of both tragedies.[9] Fedra falls in love with her stepson, Hipólito, and in order to force him to become her lover, she threatens to inform the husband and father, Pedro, that it is Hipólito who is soliciting her. She is forced to carry out her threat, but tragedy for anyone other than Fedra is averted when she dies of love, remorse, and a physically weak heart. The childless Fedra loved Hipólito as both paramour and mother. The curious psychological ingredients of Fedra's love are seen in I,4:

FEDRA.

¡Quiero ser tuya, toda tuya!

HIPÓLITO.

¡No, lo que tú quieres es que sea tuyo yo!

FEDRA.

¡Sí, mío, mío, mío y sólo mío!

HIPÓLITO.

Tu hijo . . .

FEDRA.

Pues bien, hijo, ¡ven a mis brazos!

The play is a neatly constructed drama, polished and reduced to an absolute minimum of necessary dialogue and description as Unamuno is accustomed to do.

On the contrary, **Soledad** is a weak play. The idealistic dramatist Agustín is married to Soledad, a practical woman but one obsessed with the tragic death of their young son. Agustín is distraught at not being able to work out his ideas for a new play. Friends arrive and urge Agustín to abandon his writing and run for political office. Finally he accedes to their wishes, but later when his political idealism is misinterpreted and his friends do not have the courage to defend him publicly, he refuses to elude the police and is imprisoned. While he is in jail his mother, Sofía, dies. Upon his release, Agustín, in mental torment, seeks refuge from the world in his faithful wife, whose words of a mother "hijo mío . . . duerme . . . duerme . . ."[10] bring the action to an end. The play lacks a clear argument or purpose. All the characters are weak, and frequently the action lags. Unamuno did not achieve here the drama of bared souls in conflict, the "cerebral" type of drama without setting or stage effects to which he would educate the public.[11]

The recurring notion that the husband is loved maternally can be found in the words of Agustín (III,1) when he says to Soledad: "Pero la tierra no es patria, la tierra es *matria*, matria como tú, Soledad de mi vida, matria . . . madre . . . madre . . ." In the continuing conversation, the symbolism of the name Soledad is apparent as *sol*, the mother from which comes all light, the source of life and the universal curative. After Sofía dies, Soledad is more than ever both mother and wife to

Agustín. In reply to Agustín's "¿Me quieres?" Soledad says, "¡Agustín, hijo!" Then a few speeches later in the same scene (III, 4):

AGUSTÍN.

¡Tu mano, Sol, tu mano . . . , mi ancla! Mano de madre. . . .

SOLEDAD.

Lo fué. . . .

AGUSTÍN.

Lo es, Sol, lo es. Toda mano de mujer es mano de madre. . . . Y eres mi madre, mujer. Tu hijo no murió, Soledad. . . . Trae su caballo . . . , mi caballo. . . .

In the final scene, Soledad again addresses Agustín as "my son," after which she sings a nursery rhyme to him at his request: "Cántame, Soledad, acúname. . . ." During the slow final curtain Soledad is heard to repeat: ". . . sleep, my son, sleep, sleep, my son, sleep, sleep. . . ."

The significance of this "hijo mío," which Unamuno causes his women to exclaim again and again in his works,[12] has been well covered by Antonio Sánchez Barbudo; it was what Concha said to her husband, Miguel de Unamuno, on a most significant occasion—his religious crisis of 1897.[13] A newly-available article by Unamuno, "Carta a mujeres," yields an interesting veiled affirmation of the event:

Y sé de un hombre que no acabó de descubrir la intensidad y la profundidad toda con que su mujer le quería hasta una vez en que, presa de una sofocante congoja espiritual, le abrió aquélla sus brazos al verle llorar exclamando: ¡hijo mío! En este grito es donde descubrió, dice él, toda la profundidad del amor.[14]

In the same article, Unamuno says also that "la mujer, sea madre, novia, esposa, hermana o hija nuestra, es siempre nuestra madre, es un espíritu serenador que apacigua nuestras tormentas,"[15] and that ". . . toda mujer es para todo hombre madre."[16] It is certain, therefore, (1) that Unamuno's concept of wifehood was identical to that of motherhood, that all woman's love is mother love, and (2) that this notion either arose in, or was reinforced by, his own marital relationship.

Raquel encadenada is another drama which continues in the same vein. Raquel is a violin virtuosa; Simón is both her husband and her business manager; Aurelio is Raquel's first love. The opening conversation reveals the obstacles of the plot: Raquel's extreme frustration because she is childless; Aurelio's continuing affection for Raquel; and Simón's coldness, parsimoniousness, and his antipathy toward Aurelio, especially because the pleasure-seeker Aurelio has just inherited a fortune. Without blaming Simón for her childless state, Raquel does beg that they take a vacation together. Simón, most miserly of misers, refuses to sacrifice Raquel's theatrical engagements, nor will he agree to her plan to adopt a homeless nephew. Aurelio arrives at their home unexpectedly to plead with Raquel that she come to care for his sick son, who is illegitimate but "reconocido." (The mother had died in childbirth back in the days before Raquel's marriage to Simón.) Raquel accedes, against Simón's wishes. In her longed-for role of the mother, Raquel becomes so fond of the boy that she refuses to play the violin except for him. Finally Raquel deserts Simón, her home, her property, and her profession in order that she may go to live with Aurelio and her "son."[17]

Of the three plays, **Raquel encadenada** is the one which best conveys Unamuno's message of woman's torture when she is childless. It is also a play with a most skillfully drawn character—Simón, the perfect Scrooge, whose heart, unlike Scrooge's, was never finally penetrated. The Raquel who is chained is not so intense as some of Unamuno's other women like Raquel of *Dos madres,* whose impulsion to a state of maternity is truly dynamic. Fedra herself seems too unsubtle and forward, even daring, in her revelation of passion to Hipólito. She pursues him openly. One cannot fail to observe a certain tenacity of the woman in love or the one desirous of children, like Fedra and the chained Raquel, but the studied flaunting of convention in some of Unamuno's women (like that of their creator) is hardly characteristic of the female sex. On the contrary, others like Antonia in *Abel Sánchez,* tía Tula, Soledad, Marina in *Amor y pedagogía,* and Elvira of **Sombras de sueño** are only submissive shades. Many of Unamuno's women act chiefly on instinct, with the result that they are frequently too simple as either black or white, right or wrong, happy or unhappy, too bold or too timid. They lack tenderness. Marriage or sexual love in his plays and novels is seldom a matter of strong emotional attraction or compatibility; rather it is for one or both of the mates the possible means for some desired result, usually parenthood. In the process, Unamuno thus tends to overemphasize his premise (that all woman's love is *compasión,* and as such, maternal love) to such a degree that he eliminates, as unimportant to the "realidad íntima," other related motivating influences and emotions.

In his essays Unamuno said that women are what must change most in Spain, and that the role of woman is what has made the United States great. He insists that women have more common sense than men even when they have less intelligence. These are valid and intelligent observations. Unamuno the scholar indeed knew woman in the abstract. But Unamuno the man of flesh and blood knew only one woman of flesh and blood— his wife Concha. He never knew any other woman intimately. The Salamancan professor was not a bohemian. He did not even drink or smoke. He almost never went to the theater or even indulged in social calls. Concha, a most simple, unintellectual, pious, and homespun woman, behaved as a Spanish woman should, while her learned spouse with his head in the clouds wrote of how the Spanish woman must change. There were eight children. Concha was only a mother, a refuge. She was *woman* to her husband: *woman,* the symbol of motherhood. Was not Concha the model for all of her husband's literary portraits of women?

It should be recognized that Unamuno himself perceived his inadequacy for portraying feminine roles. "Confieso que estas pobres mujeres que pasan por el tablado de mi *El hermano Juan* están apenas delineadas."[18] In *Amor y pedagogía,* Unamuno confesses quite candidly that ". . . el autor no sabe hacer mujeres, no lo ha sabido nunca."[19] Yet all the plays in **Teatro** have to do with the womanhood-motherhood topic; and both **El otro** and **El hermano Juan** are variations of the same theme, as are also some of Unamuno's non-dramatic works. So it is that the master of paradox leaves unwritten another paradox for his readers to decipher: if I cannot write of women, it is because I know only one woman, though in this manner I know all women.

Notes

1. *PMLA,* LXX, No. 4, Part 1 (Sept., 1955), 587-605.

2. Two examples of such statements would be: "La mujer se rinde al amante porque le siente sufrir con el deseo," from *Del sentimiento trágico de la vida* (Buenos Aires, 1950), p. 113; and "Parece que el amor es en la mujer compasión," from *Soliloquios y conversaciones* (Buenos Aires, 1944), p. 149.

3. Miguel de Unamuno, *El otro y El hermano Juan* (Buenos Aires, 1946), prologue to *El hermano Juan,* p. 69.

4. Miguel de Unamuno, *San Manuel Bueno, mártir, y tres historias más* (Buenos Aires, 1942), pp. 161-162 (*Una historia de amor*).

   Here is the significant passage:

   > Tenía cada una en su celda su niñito Jesús, un lindo muñeco al que vestía y desnudaba y adoraba. Poníanle flores, le besaban, sobre todo a hurtadillas; alguna lo brezaba sobre sus rodillas como a un niño de verdad. Rodeábanles de flores. Una vez que un fotógrafo entró, con permiso del obispo, a sacar la vista de un arco románico que daba sobre el jardín, acudieron las monjas, cada una con su niño Jesús, para que les sacase el retrato.

   > "¡Quítate ahí," decía una a otra; "el mío es más lindo, mira qué ojos tiene!"

   > Liduvina miraba en silencio y con el corazón oprimido aquella rivalidad ingenua de madres marradas.

Another relevant passage is in Unamuno's *La agonía del cristianismo* (Buenos Aires, 1944), p. 25:

> El sufrimiento de los monjes y de las monjas, de los solitarios de ambos sexos, no es un sufrimiento de sexualidad, sino de maternidad y paternidad, es decir, de finalidad.

5. *El otro y El hermano Juan,* p. 147.

6. Ibid.

7. Ibid., p. 140.

8. Miguel de Unamuno, *Mi religión y otros ensayos breves* (Buenos Aires, 1945), p. 40.

9. Miguel de Unamuno, *Teatro* (Barcelona, 1954), p. 50.

10. Ibid., p. 145.

11. Ibid., p. 46.

12. A few examples, in addition to those of the plays at hand are: *El otro,* p. 21, said by the *ama,* "¡Pobre hijo mío!" and also p. 47 "¡Hijo mío! ¡Hijo mío!" In *El hermano Juan,* p. 83, Inés says to Don Juan: "Pero ¿qué te pasa, Juan?, ¿qué tienes, hijo?" Juan replies: "Hijo . . . , hijo . . . ¿Ahora me llamas hijo? ¡Mujer! Madre. . . ." At the tragic end of *Amor y pedagogía* (Buenos Aires, 1940), p. 126, Marina says "¡Hijo mío!" first to her dead son and immediately afterward to her distraught husband. Then the husband, Fulgencio, moans "¡Madre!" and faints in her arms. Further similar examples, but not with the words *hijo mío,* emphasize Unamuno's insistence that woman feels only maternal love for man: On p. 93 of *El hermano Juan,* Elvira calls Don Juan "niño"; on p. 102 Don Juan reminds Elvira how when they used to play house as children he was always "tu niño." On p. 149 of the same work:

Juan.

    Me aguarda mi madre . . . , la tiniebla madre. . . .

Elvira.

    ¿Madre, o esposa?

Juan.

    Igual me da.

13. Antonio Sánchez Barbudo, "La formación del pensamiento de Unamuno, Una experiencia decisiva: la crisis de 1897," *Hispanic Review,* XVIII (July, 1950), 218-243.

14. *De esto y de aquello,* III (Buenos Aires, 1953), 234-235. Besides this version, and the ones which Sánchez Barbudo cites, Unamuno wrote of this event on at least two more occasions. He referred to it as "heart trouble" in a letter to Juan Maragall dated February 15, 1907: "Un día hace años,

cuando me preocupaba lo cardíaco, al verme llorar presa de congoja, lanzó un ¡hijo mío! que aun me repercute." This passage can be found on p. 56 of *Unamuno y Maragall. Epistolario y escritos complementarios* (Barcelona, 1951). Then in *Cómo se hace una novela* (Buenos Aires, 1927, pp. 102-103), Unamuno wrote: "¿Pero . . . me quiere más que mi Concha, la madre de mis ocho hijos y mi verdadera madre? Mi verdadera madre, sí. En un momento de suprema, de abismática congoja, cuando me vió en las garras del Angel de la Nada, llorar con un llanto sobre-humano, me gritó desde, el fondo de sus entrañas maternales, sobre-humanas, divinas, arrojándose en mis brazos: '¡hijo mío!' Entonces descubrí todo lo que Dios hizo para mí en esta mujer, la madre de mis hijos, mi virgen madre, que no tiene otra novela que mi novela, ella, mi espejo de santa inconciencia divina, de eternidad."

15. *De esto y de aquello,* III, 234.

16. Ibid., p. 231.

17. I have already noted the more than vague resemblance of plot between *Raquel encadenada* and the original version of Luigi Pirandello's little-known early novel, *Suo marito,* later revised and called *Giustino Roncella nato Boggiòlo.* See "Unamuno and Pirandello Revisited," *Italica,* XXXIII (March, 1956), p. 49.

18. *El otro y El hermano Juan,* p. 73.

19. *Amor y pedagogía,* p. 11.

Lucille V. Braun (essay date March 1975)

SOURCE: Braun, Lucille V. "'Ver que me ves': Eyes and Looks in Unamuno's Works." *Modern Language Notes* 90, no. 2 (March 1975): 212-30.

[*In the following essay, Braun discusses the metaphorical significance of eyes and the act of looking in Unamuno's works.*]

References to eyes and looks occur repeatedly in Unamuno's writings and serve to dramatize all his major preoccupations.[1] It is not unusual for Unamuno—or one of his characters—to recoil as a pair of eyes seems to question or negate all hope of immortality.[2] Sometimes the warmth of a glance may envelop an individual and give him greater self-assurance. At other times a look symbolizes the subjugation of one personality to another. There is a practical reason why an author intimately concerned with the problem of personality and averse to realistic detail and leisurely development of character should resort to the "shorthand" of the eye.

It is an excellent device for giving a personality dramatic presence, since there the self appears as if concentrated. However, both the frequency and the often strange intensity of the imagery suggest that for Unamuno eyes and looks carried deep personal as well as fictional significance.

What may well be his first use of eye imagery comes in the short story "Ver con los ojos" (1886) about a young man who returns home from the university, depressed, taciturn, and without faith. The local doctor offers unsolicited advice: "¡Tristezas teóricas, Juanito!, tristezas teóricas . . . , ¡ojos . . . ! ¡ooooojos!, te faltan ojos para mirar al cielo!" (II, 764). Soon the student falls in love and in effect acquires new vision through the eyes of his sweetheart. Unamuno was to use essentially the same image when he wrote in 1934, after the death of his wife: "Dentro de tus ojos de saber sereno / vi al conocerte que el mundo era bueno" (VI, 1405).

The most striking formulations, however, appear after Don Miguel's spiritual crisis of 1897. *La venda* (1899) merits special attention, for in this play the language of the eye acquires greater complexity and anticipates the most characteristic meanings found in later works. The heroine of the piece, blind since birth and still convalescent from the operation that gave her sight, learns that her father is dying and hurries to his bedside. In order to find her way through the city, she must cover her eyes and borrow a cane, since visually the streets are unfamiliar to her. On the level of obvious symbolism she represents blind faith which has no need of reason or science (the doctors who gave her sight) to reach, know, and love her father. To repeat Iris Zavala's question, "¿Sería muy aventurado decir que el padre es Dios, antropomorfizado . . . ?"[3] The work becomes interesting for our purposes, however, exactly at the point where the symbolic line seems to falter and Unamuno's own preoccupations intrude. The father, not content with María's intuitive vision, insists with great agitation that she remove her blindfold and look at him: "Por lo menos que te vea los ojos, . . . esos ojos en los que tantas veces me vi mientras tú no me veías con ellos. Cuántas veces me quedé extasiado contemplándotelos, mirándome dolorosamente en ellos y diciendo: '¿Para qué tan hermosos si no ven?'" (V, 242). And again: "Pero tú ábrelos . . . , quítate eso . . . , mírame . . . ; . . . Tú me ves acaso, pero yo no veo que me ves, y quiero ver que me ves . . ." (V, 243).

María, however, wishes in these last moments to be with the father she has always known, not with the strange new person her eyes would see. Finally her sister snatches away the blindfold and father and daughter look at each other for the first time. The powerful emotion proves fatal for the elderly man—although, using a less rational criterion, one might speak of a look that kills. The major point for us, though, is the intense need to see that one is seen. In the father's case, this desired confirmation of his existence becomes particularly acute with the imminence of death, the ultimate dissolution of self. The father repeats his plea several times and, so heartfelt is it, that María's insistence on retaining her own concept of him seems almost selfish. Once she answers that her sightless eyes had served her father well as an "espejo vivo," "para que tú, padre, te vieras en ellos." Yet even this reflection has not satisfied him. Here a second important theme—that of the eye as a living mirror—emerges. (Unamuno found actual mirrors frightening, for they reflect an identical image, but with no reciprocating consciousness looking back.) So far as María was concerned, there was less danger that her visionless eyes could give rise to the alienating experience of the mirror, for her whole loving personality had always responded to her father. Yet none of this is enough. Apparently the reciprocal look is the factor prized above all.

At the end of the play, Unamuno attempts to reassert the main ideological thrust by having María replace her blindfold and declare she never wants to see again. Nonetheless, the father's anguished need to be seen—a version of Unamuno's own, I feel—remains an unassimilated element.

Despite shifting meanings and a fundamental ambivalence—the longing to be seen is paralleled by a dread of it—most of Unamuno's eye images fit into the three categories already implicit in *La venda*: beneficent eyes that confirm one's sense of self; destructive looks that annihilate one's innermost being; and eyes that serve as "espejos vivos," often creating for the viewer the strange illusion that as he sees himself in miniature in the other's pupils, he is transmitting his personality, engendering himself anew, or even returning to infancy. The first two categories function with equal force to express the problems of individual personality and that of immortality, concerns which ultimately are manifestations of the same basic ontological insecurity. This article will review examples of the three major types of images and, where appropriate, introduce recent psychological and psychoanalytic theories (Lacan, Sartre, Fenichel, R. D. Laing) which cast light on Unamuno's sense of self.

BENEFICENT EYES

In the midst of a rather curious account of how the eye evolved from a pigmented spot with tropic function to an organ of vision ("La ideocracia," 1900), there is a passage which epitomizes the primary life-sustaining effect the eye can have for Unamuno: "Sí, el ojo es para algo más hondo que para ver; es para alegrar el alma; el ojo bebe luz, y la luz vivifica las entrañas del *oculado* . . ." (I, 960). Here the light floods in to bathe the inner self. A variation on this concept gives us eyes like those of the first wife of Ramiro (*La tía Tula*) which serve to "beber y atesorar luz . . . y derramarla luego convertida en paz" (II, 1063). Similarly, the protagonist of *Niebla,* when at Eugenia's side, found himself "absorto en la misteriosa luz espiritual que de aquellos ojos irradiaba" (II, 580).⁴ A whole complex of Unamunian images is formed by combining words like "luz," "alegría," "irradiar," "derramar," and "atesorar."

The eyes of Unamuno's wife were just such eyes. His verse, especially, is full of tributes to them and scarcely any period fails to provide examples. In 1907, he writes: "La alegría que hinche tu corazón rebasa / de tus ojos, se vierte, y me inunda la casa" (VI, 831). Again in 1912: "Llueve desde tus ojos alegría / sobre mi casa. / De no haber anudado nuestras vidas, / ¿es que yo hoy viviría?" (VI, 899). One of my favorites is a short poem from 1928: "Cállate, que ya sé lo que quieres decirme; / mírame a que te mire que me miras clara," (VI, 1013). The second line is perhaps the most beautiful realization of the "Ver que me ves" motif, which we encountered incomplete in the case of the father in *La venda*.⁵

Why are friendly eyes so crucial in Unamuno's world? On the level of positive contributions, they enable the self to flourish, create the emotional climate for dialogue—"No sé hablar si no veo unos ojos que me miran y no siento tras de ellos un espíritu que me atiende" (V, 951)—, and may even carry much of the burden of communication between two people: "Cuando las dos almas niñas se miraban por las ventanas serenas de los ojos, sonreían al verse . . . la una porque veía la otra y las dos porque se sentían una" (II, 775). However, they also avert dangers that are psychologically very real. We have just heard Unamuno ask if, without his wife's eyes, he would still be alive. In *Niebla* exaggerated epithets for Eugenia's eyes—endless variations on the phrase "místicas estrellas gemelas"—fill the text, but suddenly Augusto's existential anguish is laid bare. "Son tus ojos cual clavos encendidos / que mi cuerpo a mi espíritu sujetan, / . . . / ¡Si esa luz de mi vida se apagara, / desuncidos espíritu y materia, / perderíame en brumas celestiales / y del profundo en la voraz tiniebla!" (II, 653). Evidently Augusto is threatened by a dangerous split between spirit and matter (not unlike the mind body dichotomy of some schizoid states) and actually needs her gaze to hold himself together.

Yet to be desirable a look need not be benevolent, need not offer the possibility of understanding. For the Unamuno who sought earthly fame just being looked at and admired was enough. The prologue (1934) to *El hermano Juan* gives us his definitive evaluation of Don Juan: ". . . se dignaba ser mirado—y admirado—,

darse a las miradas de los demás." He then adds a concluding line which stands all alone: "Ser mirado, ser admirado y dejar nombre. ¡Dejar nombre!" (V, 716). Condensed in this formula is all of Unamuno's longing for earthly fame and the importance of "ser mirado" in the sequence is far more than a play on words. Similarly, in Unamuno's version, Cain kills Abel because God "ve con buenos ojos al uno y no al otro." It was not a question of whose fortunes would prosper, but of "la [necesidad] de ser recibido en la mente, en la memoria, del Creador de cielo y tierra, de que este Señor le mire" (V, 715). It is of the utmost importance that God see man, for only thus will he retain him in his memory and give him eternal life. Taken together, the two forms of "representation"—before God and man—are a major element in Don Miguel's concern with being seen.

EYES AS MIRRORS

A second function of the eye depends on Unamuno's theories of self-knowledge. Despairing of ever finding himself through direct intuition, he asserts: ". . . nuestro mejor espejo es cada uno de nuestros prójimos" (VII, 861). The term "espejo" is best read, of course, as a range of interpersonal relations. Even so, Unamuno frequently veers toward a surprisingly literal use of eyes as mirrors, not of their owner's reality, but of his own. Linked with this tendency is a deep need to see himself from without: "¡Poderse ver desde fuera!, ¡poderse ver desde fuera! Esto he deseado muchas veces" (VIII, 821. From *Diario íntimo*). The ideal, forever impossible, would be to see himself from without as *another would see him.* The concept of eyes as "espejos vivos" was a specious solution, for it permitted the illusion that when he saw himself reflected in the other's eyes, he was actually seeing himself *through* the other's eyes, escaping from himself into the other consciousness, and giving himself objective reality. Although the words he quotes in the following statement are those of his tiny son, they express an idea dear to the father: ". . . he pasado lo mejor de la vida, chapuzándome en mí mismo, en mi propio pozo. . . . Y por eso necesito salir de mí y verme desde fuera . . . Ayer, mi hijo menor, Ramoncito, de cinco años, me decía: 'Si nos miramos a los ojos, yo estoy en tus ojos y tú en los míos, y si no nos miramos, tú estás en tus ojos y yo en los míos'" (VII, 585).

A highly unusual subgroup of images derives from the smallness of one's reflection in another's pupils. "Nos vemos por primera vez en las niñas de los ojos de la que nos amamanta, así como la madre se descubre madre, o sea inmortal y eterna, en el par de retratos propios que viven en los ojos de su hijo. Parecen muy pequeñitos . . . pero son el núcleo de toda su visión del mundo" (VII, 892). Some kind of mother-child relationship almost always obtains when the "verse pequeño" formula is used, although the spiritual mother is not necessarily the biological one.[6] In *Dos madres* Raquel, who was sterile, decided that her lover Juan must give her a child by marrying Berta. When in time he brought her the happy news that he was to be a father, Raquel kissed him, "mirándole a los ojos, mirándose en las niñas de ellos, pequeñita, y luego volvía a besarle. Miraba con ahinco su propio retrato minúsculo, en los ojos de él, y luego como loca, murmurando con voz ronca: '¡Déjame que me bese!' le cubrió los ojos de besos . . ." (II, 991). We see vividly how her will has supplanted his; his eyes, rather than mirroring his inner reality, now reflect hers. That she sees herself as "pequeñita" is a way of saying that her image is her child, somehow transmitted through the actual father in a unique variation on the notion that the child is the image of the parent. As the novel progresses, Raquel effectively displaces all the blood relatives and makes the little girl hers.[7]

At other times the tiny reflection induces the fantasy that the viewer is again a child. Unamuno's preference for the word "niña" over "pupila" facilitates the process, for he is deliberately playing with the primary meaning of "niño" as "child," as in "en sus niñas / se acurrucan las montañas, / aniñándose" (VI, 1059). Augusto Pérez implores Rosario not to close her eyes: "Déjame que me vea en ellos como en un espejo, que me vea tan chiquitito . . . Sólo así llegaré a conocerme . . . Viéndome en ojos de mujer . . ." (II, 645-646). The desire to return to the womb is even clearer in Apolodoro's musings about Clarita: "¡Hoy me ha visto . . . con esos ojos sin mancha; hoy he estado en ellos, chiquitito, patas arriba, acurrucadito en las redonditas niñas de sus ojos virginales!" (II, 369). This is obviously a fetal position.

For Unamuno and his characters seeing one's image in the eyes of another is a satisfying experience. Jacques Lacan's theory of *le stade du miroir* presents the matter in a different light and provides a psychoanalytic basis for giving Unamuno's fascination with mirrors—and eye-mirrors—the full importance that critics have long felt it possessed.[8] Since Lacan's theory is complex and has undergone several modifications, a general summary, like that of Anthony Wilden, is a good starting point:

> The "mirror phase" derives its name from the importance of mirror relationships in childhood. The significance of children's attempts to appropriate or control their own image in a mirror . . . is that their actions are symptomatic of . . . deeper relationships. Through his perception of the image of another human being, the child discovers a form (*Gestalt*), a corporeal unity, which is lacking to him at this particular stage of his development. Noting the physiological evidence for the maturing of the cortex after birth . . . Lacan interprets the child's fascination with the other's image

as an anticipation of his maturing to a future point of corporeal unity by identifying himself with this image. . . . this primordial experience is symptomatic of what makes the *moi* an Imaginary construct. The ego is an *Idealich*, another self, and the *stade du miroir* is the source of all later identifications.[9]

Although in early formulations Lacan stresses the genetic aspects of the *stade du miroir*, considering it a phase in children's development, he later interprets it in a structural sense, incorporating it into the schemata he uses to illustrate the dialectic of intersubjectivity.[10] The very heart of his theory, however, remains the idea that the *moi* or ego so constituted is an "alienated self," for "'the human individual fastens himself to an image which alienates him from himself,' so that 'man's ego is for ever irreducible to his lived identity.'"[11]

If Lacan is correct, the self to be found in mirrors is imaginary—always a lure or trap.[12] Nor does substituting an eye for the mirror basically change matters. To the degree the subject sees only himself, the other person is not an effective presence. Unamuno cannot have been totally unaware of some of these implications, at least in the case of weak characters like Apolodoro and Augusto Pérez. In his own experiences of *desdoblamiento*, he found his likeness in a mirror frighteningly alien. But he seems totally caught up in the attempt of strong individuals like Raquel and Tula to project their image in the eyes of those who serve as their instruments.

Finally, following Lacan even further, we glimpse the underlying cause of all of Unamuno's preoccupations. Again the explication is provided by Wilden:

> If the child does not escape the attraction of this alienated self, he is potentially embroiled in the pathological search for the lost object of which Freud spoke in his earliest works. Since the discovery of the lack of object is for Lacan the condition and the cause of desire, the adult quest for transcendence, lost time, lost paradises, lost plenitude, or any of the myriad forms the lack of object may take . . . can be reduced, if one wishes, to the question asked by Oedipus: "Who (or what) am I?" . . . To pose the question at all is the subject's way of recognizing that he is neither who he thinks he is nor what he wants to be, since at the level of the *parole vide* he will always find that he is another.[13]

As if by way of illustration, there is Unamuno's intense desire for immortality, his longing for the lost faith of childhood, and, as shown in his article "¡Plenitud de plenitudes y todo plenitud!" (1904), the need to be intimately convinced of his own substantiality. Yet the customary order has been reversed. The question of identity, usually subordinated to his desperate grasping for eternity, stands revealed as the most basic concern of all.

Reference to Sartre is almost obligatory when one talks of eyes and looks, for his theories stimulated much of the current interest in the topic. In Sartrian terms, the eye cannot simultaneously be perceived as an eye—nor as a mirror—and as a look. ". . . mon appréhension d'un regard tourné vers moi paraît sur fond de destruction des yeux qui 'me regardent.'"[14] Conversely, insofar as they are an object I look at or see myself in, I cannot experience them as *another* looking at me. Being seen transforms the person seen into an "*ego* pour l'autre au milieu d'un monde qui s'écoule vers l'autre"[15] or more simply, he becomes an object, a transcendence transcended, a defenseless being for a freedom that is not his freedom. There are many similarities between Sartre's theory of the look and Don Miguel's position, since both writers are concerned with how the self comes to know itself and with the role of the other in this process. Yet even when they appear to be making the same distinction, the meaning may be quite different. Consider the following verses, where Unamuno too differentiates between the eye and the look. "No me mires a los ojos, / sino a la mirada, mira / que quien se queda en la carne / no llega nunca a la vida. / Mírame como a un espejo / que te mira, que quien mira / no más que a ojos de la carne / según va mirando olvida" (VI, 951). First of all, what for Sartre would be a logical impossibility, "un espejo que te mira," is perfectly possible for Unamuno. Then too, the entire concept of the look changes. For Sartre one can be only an *être-regardé* or an *être-regardant*.[16] Unamuno accepts half of this. If the other looks only at the surface (my eyes), he views me as an indifferent object, but if I am a *mirada* for him, he does not thereby become an object. Instead he perceives my *vida,* penetrates to the essence of my being, and understands me in the deepest possible sense. In another passage, we read: "No apartes tus ojos de los míos . . . Deja en directa communión las almas . . . ¡Mírame a la mirada y no a mí!" (V, 161). The fact that the look can be the vehicle for true communion of souls is a very significant difference between Unamuno and the French thinker.[17]

DESTRUCTIVE EYES

Like the look of the legendary Medusa, which turned men to stone, those in Unamuno's world can be deadly. For almost every kind of confirming glance there is a destructive variety. Life-giving eyes have their opposite in lethal eyes like those to which the hapless Juan of *Dos madres* succumbed.[18] Eyes which admire may instead see one as ridiculous or simply not notice at all. Eyes that penetrate to the depths of one's being may represent true understanding, but may also steal the self. And Unamuno, who used others as his mirror, trembled at the prospect that they would do the same to him.[19] Certainly the degree of menace varies. The "magic" look which kills shades down to a look which causes loss of self—a look not unlike the Sartrian gaze—and, further weakened, merely makes one feel ridiculous or insignificant. However, a potential for death always seems to underlie the milder versions.

As symbolic representations of death, Unamuno uses three main figures: the Coco (bogeyman), the Sphinx, and Death personified. All possess terrifying eyes in his private mythology.

The bogeyman is a fear figure from childhood and, judging from the frequency with which the adult Unamuno mentions him, must have loomed large in his young imagination.[20] In *Niebla* reference to the creature comes right after the death of little Augusto's father. The mother clutches the boy to her crying "¡hijo mío!" "Y él . . . sin atreverse a volver la cara ni a apartarla de la dulce oscuridad de aquel regazo palpitante, por miedo a encontrarse con los ojos devoradores del Coco" (II, 571).[21] If this scene incorporated memories of Unamuno's own early loss, as seems likely, it is easy to understand how a child might link the terrifying event with the most fearful creature he could imagine. In "El Coco caballero" (1900) the monster is simply death, come to carry off the poet's firstborn. His eyes are mere sockets: "no veía . . . sus ojos horribles / vacíos . . . dos cuencas . . . / dos nidos de sombra . . ." (VI, 305). Thus the Coco, whose features are usually vague in keeping with the undefined menace he represents, is for Unamuno a bringer of death and has eyes especially to be avoided.

The Sphinx in what is probably her first appearance in Don Miguel's works (1899) poses a suitably Unamunian riddle, "¿cuál es el fin de la vida? . . . ¡adivíname o te devoro!" (I, 765). By 1905 her glance suggests a truth capable of inducing madness: "¡La perspectiva del no ser! Tal es la mirada enloquecedora de la Esfinge" (III, 1101). In contrast to the Coco, the Sphinx symbol accompanies a more conceptualized approach to the problem of death. In the first case there is an irrational hope that the threat will disappear if one takes refuge in the arms of mother or wife. However, the mature Unamuno recommends that man look the Sphinx straight in the eye and avoid ignoble evasions. He criticizes Menéndez y Pelayo for losing himself in scholarship: "No se atrevió a mirarle ojos a ojos humanos a la Esfinge, y se puso a examinarle las garras leoninas y las alas aguileñas, hasta a contrale las cerdas de la cola bovina . . . Le aterraba el misterio" (III, 1232). Obviously well informed about the various human and animal portions of the Sphinx, Unamuno still stresses the death-giving look—"la mirada / que les cortaba el respiro" (VI, 992)—which, to the best of my knowledge, is not part of traditional representations of the beast.[22]

In the play *La esfinge* (1898) there is no actual Sphinx. Instead the fatal question about the meaning of life is posed by the eyes that look out at Angel from the portrait of his dead mother: "Parece que me mira mi madre desde más allá de la tumba, desde el misterio silencioso . . . ¿Qué hay allí? Es una obsesión . . . que no me deja. Esa nada, esa nada terrible que se me presenta en cuanto cierro los ojos . . ."²³ Later he remarks: "Esa mirada me persigue; es la mirada del misterio" (V, 182 and 184).

The third major figure is Death herself whose look is felt to be more deadly than she is. "Apriétanos a oscuras a tu seno," the poet begs, and the phrase simultaneously evokes the embraces of a loving mother and the wild dream that from the darkness of this womb man could be reborn to eternal life. Her eyes, however, belie that hope. Their empty sockets have seen "la verdad desnuda"—the nothingness beyond—as if only one "vacío" could fully perceive another. "Cuando nos lleves, Muerte, / vuelve atrás la cabeza, / ¡no nos mires, por Dios, oh, no nos mires, / . . . / Apriétanos a oscuras a tu seno / mas sin mirarnos; / ¡tu seno es dulce, tu mirada horrible! / ¡Engáñanos, oh Muerte! / Aparta de nostros esos ojos, / sólo el vacío tinieblas, / esos que han visto la verdad desnuda /—sólo el vacío puede verla pura—, / ¡engáñanos, oh Muerte!" (VI, 862. See also "La intrusa," VI, 392).²⁴

Sphinx, Coco, Death—all are intermediate degrees of the ultimate anguish foreseen by San Manuel Bueno: ". . . dice la Escritura que el que le ve la cara a Dios, que el que le ve al sueño los ojos de la cara con que nos mira, se muere sin remedio y para siempre" (II, 1148). For man to have his look returned by a deity who is pure "sueño" is to feel his own reality irremediably dissolve.²⁵

It is when Unamuno turns to the problem of personality, however, that the most subtle and pathological reactions surface. In "Robleda, el actor" (1920), the performer, whose fear of being seen dates back to childhood, states that he chose his profession "buscando borrarme, desaparecer en los personajes que representara y que nadie me viera ni me mirara sino a ellos." Accused of pride, he replies: "¿Soberbio yo? . . . Por timidez me aventuro a las tablas. Es el horror a que se me vea, a que reparen en mí, a que me miren a la mirada y me roben así el secreto de mi soledad, es eso lo que me hace meterme en los personajes que represento" (II, 881-2). In many ways the fears of the fictional Robleda are those of Unamuno. The crucial statement, "que me roben el secreto de mi soledad,"²⁶ echoes the famous cry from *Del sentimiento trágico*: "¡Mi yo, que me arrebatan mi yo!" (VII, 136) and Robleda's need to hide in his roles has a counterpart in Unamuno's horror of being comprehended: "Pero tú deja que te busquen y que no te encuentren, porque el día en que te encontrasen no eres ya tú" (V, 991). Might this not be the motivation for his role playing, the constant mystification as to which of his "yos" is the real one? The self can hardly be stolen if it cannot be identified.

In *Niebla* Augusto and Eugenia live in a world where looks have almost physical consistency: "Y siguieron los dos . . . cortando con sus almas la enmarañada telaraña espiritual de la calle. Porque la calle forma un tejido en que se entrecruzan miradas de deseo, de envidia, de desdén, de compasión, de amor, de odio . . ." (II, 562). On one fateful day, no one noticed Augusto— with disastrous results for his sense of self: ". . . no se fijaban en él, involuntariamente por supuesto, ni le hacían caso, por no conocerle sin duda, sintió que su yo, aquel yo del '¡yo soy yo!', se le iba achicando, achicando y se le replegaba en el cuerpo y aun dentro de éste buscaba un rinconcito en que acurrucarse y que no se le viera" (II, 623). One notes a strange ambivalence. The self becomes smaller and smaller as a result of *not* being seen. Presumably it longs to be seen. Then, in a surprising reversal, the diminished self hides to avoid being seen. What better example of what Laing considers the two sides of the coin: the need to be seen and the fear of being seen.²⁷

Finally, we come to the experience of "desdoblamiento," induced either by staring at oneself in the mirror or, fictionally, by the entrance of a double. The self feels itself dissolve, for the normal boundaries between it and the other no longer hold. The other has the appearance of the self, yet looks at the self with the indifference of a stranger. Unamuno has, in fact, described moments in which his own alienated image struck terror in his heart and it is this autobiographical aspect which most critics have emphasized.²⁸ What has not been brought out fully, however, is the role of the eye in triggering the reaction. In the slightly fictionalized version found in *Cómo se hace una novela,* an exchange of looks is crucial: "Y he aquí por qué no puedo mirarme un rato al espejo, porque al punto se me van los ojos tras de mis ojos, tras su retrato, y desde que miro a mi mirada me siento vaciarme de mí mismo, perder mi historia, mi leyenda, mi novela, volver a la inconciencia, al pasado, a la nada" (VIII, 734. See also *El otro,* V, 662).

Related to the whole question of destructive eyes— especially those that become weapons in a battle of wills²⁹—is Unamuno's tendency to describe the look as something felt physically. This is difficult ground because so many images of this kind have become part of everyday language (e.g. *mirada penetrante, clavar los ojos, devorar con los ojos,* etc.) and lost most of their intensity in the process. However, he uses combinations that are just strange enough to restore the primary meaning. When Raquel looks at Juan with "una mirada de taladro" (II, 987) or when Augusto Pérez fixes his creator "con una de esas miradas perforadoras que parecen atravesar la mira e ir más allá . . ." (II, 666), the effect goes beyond that of a common adjective like *penetrante.* Other strikingly tactile examples are the following: "¡Todo se me volvía apartar mis ojos de ella por no cortarme; pero nada, ella tirando de los míos!" (II, 1047); "Tengo la sensación del toque de unos ojos . . ." (II, 559); and the use of *lamer* in "¡No mirarla como la miraban otros hombres! ¡No devorarla con los ojos, o más bien lamerle con ellos los de ella, y la boca y la cara toda!" (II, 594).[30]

It is extremely interesting to review the examples just cited—and previous mentions of "ojos devoradores"—in the light of psychoanalytical findings. Freud early pointed out the phallic symbolism of the eye, but this intuition is only a beginning.[31] Fenichel goes on to posit the equation "to look at = to devour"[32] and adds that sadistic oral incorporation can exist even "when the phallic significance of the eye is unmistakable."[33] Summarizing the major possibilities, he declares: "In the unconscious, to look at an object may mean various things, the most noteworthy of which are as follows: to devour the object looked at, to grow like it (be forced to imitate it), or conversely, to force it to grow like oneself."[34] One discovers, moreover, a surprising overlap between other manifestations of scoptophilia and Unamuno's obsessions. The psychoanalyst explains the prohibition of looking at God in this way: ". . . looking implies identification. If man looks upon God face to face, something of the glory of God passes into him. It is this impious act, the likening of oneself to God, which is forbidden when man is forbidden to look at God."[35] In **La esfinge** Angel has the portrait of his dead mother removed because her eyes are so upsetting. His uneasiness is illuminated by Fenichel's words: "Again the eyes of the dead must be closed, because otherwise they would slay with their look those who still live; . . . the sadism of the eyes is once more displaced from the person looking to the object looked at."[36] Fenichel also discusses fantasies of "eye impregnation" and ocular introjection, citing the case of a patient who "as a little boy was convinced that children could grow inside a mother's head, because, whenever he looked closely into his mother's eyes, he could see there the image of a child."[37] Here we are close to the obsession of Raquel (*Dos madres*) and to Unamuno's own experiences. Finally, according to our source, the unconscious provides a "punishment" for the scoptophiliac. The obverse of his own sadistic, destructive look is the fear that such a power will be turned against him.[38]

Regardless of one's opinions about the validity of Freudian theory, there can be little doubt that the kind of eye imagery occuring in Unamuno's writings is the same Fenichel found worthy of study.

Perhaps more congenial to the literary critic are the ideas of R. D. Laing.[39] No one familiar with Unamuno's works can read *The Divided Self* without a shock of recognition. Don Miguel's record of his experiences and anxieties is very similar to the clinical pattern of primary ontological insecurity, typical of the schizoid personality.[40] One of the Scottish psychiatrist's main points is that a securely established sense of identity is not easily lost, but that those individuals who have never acquired it engage in a ceaseless struggle to preserve the self. His patients, like Unamuno, look into mirrors trying to convince themselves that they really exist. One of them, James, usually prey to feelings of inner emptiness and worthlessness, experienced an exhilarating sense of union with nature, but "was terrified at the threatened loss of identity involved in this merging and fusion of his self with the whole world. He knew of no half-way stage between radical isolation in self-absorption or complete absorption into all there was. He was afraid of being absorbed into Nature . . . with irrevocable loss of his self, yet what he dreaded that also he most longed for."[41] What James felt is much like the semi-autobiographical account of Pachico's ecstasy in *Paz en la guerra*: "Desvanécesele la sensación del contacto corpóreo con la tierra y la del peso del cuerpo se le disipa. Esponjado en el ámbito y el aire, enajenado de sí, le gana una resignación honda . . . Despiértasele entonces la comunión entre el mundo que le rodea y el que encierra en su propio seno" (II, 300). Individuals unsure of their own existence also fear anything which makes them lose their self-awareness.[42] Such is the danger Unamuno found in music: "Esto . . . nos derrite. La música disuelve la individualidad" (V, 995-6). Laing also speaks of the risk of engulfment in "being understood (thus grasped, comprehended), in being loved or even simply in being seen."[43] The schizoid person "must remain always ungraspable, elusive, transcendent." Is this not Unamuno in the guise of Robleda? Lastly, his *monodiálogos* and inner conversation with shadow friends that he preferred to the give-and-take of real dialogue (III, 378) sound much like "trying to be omnipotent by enclosing within his own being, without recourse to a creative relationship to others, modes of relationship that require the effective presence to him of other people and of the outer world . . ."[44]

Against a background of primary ontological insecurity, Unamuno's preoccupation with being seen falls into place. Laing finds in such cases the "frequently preeminent importance to the person of being seen."[45] Yet the counter impulse—to be invisible, unnoticed—is always there. "In a world full of danger, to be a potentially seeable object is to be constantly exposed to danger. Self-consciousness, then, may be the apprehensive awareness of oneself as potentially exposed to danger by the simple fact of being visible to others. . . . Quite often, in fact, the balance swings right over so that the individual feels that his greatest risk is to be the object of another person's awareness. The myth of Perseus and the Medusa's head, the 'evil eye,' delusions of death rays and so on are I believe referable to this dread."[46]

Thus eye imagery in Unamuno arises from the very ground of his being and, more often than not, goes beyond conventional usage to state some essential reaction of the self. It can be a vehicle for extremely powerful statements, especially in its destructive forms. We now know why he found the benign look of some eyes enormously reassuring and why other looks were literally felt as destroying his innermost being. We understand too why eyes and looks are a dominant motif throughout his literary production. In terms of understanding Unamuno's personality, this aspect is fully as important—though less dramatic, perhaps—than the oft cited experiences of *desdoblamiento* and Pachico's trance. Like them, it is, of course, still secondary and only acquires its full significance when viewed as one additional manifestation of his basic ontological insecurity. Yet it is very close to the heart of the problem, for seeing and being seen are prime modes of becoming aware of the other and of satisfying the need to be perceived.

Notes

1. Critics who have mentioned eyes and looks have usually done so in the context of given works, without indicating how central they are to Unamuno's world. Angel R. Fernández y González, however, singles out "El subtema de la mirada a los ojos como causa de la muerte . . ." in his "Unamuno: Diario inédito y vivencia poética de la muerte," *BBMP* [*Boletín de la Biblioteca Menéndez Pelayo*], 43 (1967), 276. And Carlos Blanco Aguinaga has commented very perceptively on what Doña Concha's eyes meant to her husband: "Rara es la vez que nos habla Unamuno de doña Concepción sin que . . . se detenga en la contemplación de sus ojos, de la paz interior que para él significaban. . . . De los ojos de su mujer brotaba, en efecto, la paz a que volvía siempre, como a la idea de la niñez, el Unamuno cansado de sus guerras." *El Unamuno contemplativo* (Mexico, 1959), pp. 116-117.

2. Two fine examples are the poems "Cruzando un lugar," (VI, 183-184) and "Al Perro Remo," (VI, 1030). As here, all parenthetical references in the text are to the *Obras completas de Miguel de Unamuno,* ed. Manuel García Blanco (Madrid: Escelicer, 1966-) and include volume number and page.

3. Iris M. Zavala, *Unamuno y su teatro de conciencia,* Acta Salamanticensia, XVII: 1 (Salamanca, 1963), p. 31.

4. Poem XX of *El Cristo de Velázquez,* representing Christ as an eagle, is a magnificent expression of the longing for eternity in terms of light: ". . . Aguila blanca / que a raudales bebiendo viva lumbre / del Sol eterno con divinos ojos / nos la das en tu sangre derretida, / llévanos a abrevar del Sol eterno / con nuestros ojos luz, a que veamos / la cara a la Verdad . . ." (VI, 436).

5. It comes as no surprise to learn that Unamuno told his daughter Felisa that, when his wife was dying, "the hardest thing for him was to see her eyes as they followed his every movement until he went out of the room—and the memory of those eyes!" Quoted by Margaret Thomas Rudd in *The Lone Heretic: A Biography of Miguel de Unamuno y Jugo* (Austin: Univ. of Texas Press, 1963), pp. 285-286.

6. In *La tía Tula,* Gertrudis loved Ramiro, but her sister Rosa was the one who married him. After Rosa's death, he marries again and a daughter is born of the second marriage. Although there is no possible biological inheritance, this child has the eyes of Gertrudis, the dominant figure in the household. The latter acknowledges the similarity: "Puede ser . . . , puede ser . . . Al menos le he enseñado a mirar . . ." (II, 1099-1100). It becomes progressively clearer that Tula is the real mother of all Ramiro's children, although she left the task of reproduction to others.

7. In the final pages of the book, when Juan is dead, a probable suicide, the complicity of the two women in his destruction is evident in the line, "¡Qué mirada la que Raquel y Berta se cruzaron sobre el cuerpo blanco y quieto de su Juan!" (II, 997).

8. Jacques Lacan, "Le Stade du miroir comme formateur de la fonction du Je, telle qu'elle nous est révélée dans l'expérience psychanalytique," *Revue Française de Psychanalyse,* 13 (1949), 449-455; rpt. in *Ecrits I* (Paris: Editions du Seuil, 1970), pp. 89-97.

9. Anthony Wilden, *The Language of the Self* (Baltimore: The Johns Hopkins Press, 1968), p. 160.

10. Wilden, p. 162.

11. This is why Lacan speaks of "paranoic human knowledge," of a "formal stagnation" which "constitutes the *ego* and objects under attributes of permanence, identity and substantiality, in short, as entities or 'things' which are quite different from those *Gestalten* which we can in experience isolate within the shifting fields of force of animal desire." Quote in text and those in this note from Jacques Lacan, "L'aggresivité en psychanalyse," in *Ecrits* (Paris: Editions du Seuil, 1966), pp. 104 and 111, as quoted by Jean Roussel, "Introduction to Jacques Lacan," *New Left Review,* 51 (1968), 65.

12. Wilden, p. 175.

13. Wilden, pp. 165-166.

14. Jean-Paul Sartre, *L'être et le néant* (Paris: Gallimard, 1943), p. 316.

15. Sartre, p. 319.

16. "Selon qu'autrui est pour moi objet ou moi-même objet-pour-autrui." Sartre, p. 339.

17. In effect, what Unamuno said in 1898 is not very different from Merleau-Ponty's objection to the Sartrian theory: "En réalité le regard d'autrui ne me transforme en objet, et mon regard ne le transforme en objet, que si l'un et l'autre nous nous retirons dans le fond de notre nature pensante, si nous nous faisons l'un et l'autre regard inhumain, si chacun sent ses actions, non pas reprises et comprises, mais observées comme celles d'un insecte. C'est par example ce qui arrive quand je subis le regard d'un inconnu. Mais, même alors, l'objectivation de chacun par le regard de l'autre n'est ressentie comme pénible que parce qu'elle prend la place d'une communication possible." M. Merleau-Ponty, *Phénoménologie de la perception* (Paris: Gallimard, 1945), p. 414.

18. "Los ojos azules y claros de Berta, la doncella, como un mar sin fondo y sin orillas, le llamaban al abismo, y detrás de él, o mejor en torno de él, envolviéndole, los ojos negros y tenebrosos de Raquel, la viuda, como una noche sin fondo y sin estrellas, empujábanle al mismo abismo" (II, 983).

19. The fears of the earth giant in "¡Pobre gigante!" are a thinly disguised version of his own: ". . . temblaba de que al hombre se le ocurriese . . . ir a mirarse como en el espejo de un pozo en las niñas de sus ojos soñadores" (VII, 674).

20. Snatches of the lullaby, "Duerme, niño chiquito / que viene el Coco / a llevarse a los niños / que duermen poco," appear often in his works, particularly in *Amor y pedagogía*. Blanco Aguinaga, pp. 145-149 studies cradle songs more deeply.

21. See *Abel Sánchez* (II, 702) for a comparable description in which the Coco stands for hate.

22. Several psychoanalytic explanations of the Sphinx have been proposed. For Otto Rank in *The Trauma of Birth* (New York: Robert Brunner, 1957), pp. 144-145, ". . . the mixed figure of the Sphinx representing the anxiety experience as such has been recognized by Psychoanalysis as a mother symbol, and her character as 'strangler' makes the reference to the birth anxiety unambiguous. . . . But the Sphinx, conforming to its character as strangler, represents not only in its latent content the wish to return into the mother, as the danger of being swallowed, but it also represents in its manifest form parturition itself and the struggle against it, in that the human upper body grows out of the animal-like (maternal) lower body without finally being able to free itself from it." C. G. Jung declares: "The Sphinx is a semi-theriomorphic representation of that 'mother image' which may be designated as the 'terrible mother,' of whom many traces are found in mythology. . . . The libido which was represented theriomorphically is the 'animal' sexuality which is in a repressed state. . . . In as far as the repressed libido manifests itself under certain conditions, as anxiety, these animals are generally of a horrible nature. In consciousness we are attached by all sacred bonds to the mother; in the dream she pursues us as a terrible animal." *Psychology of the Unconscious,* trans. Beatrice M. Hinkle (1916; rpt. New York: Dodd Mead, 1952), pp. 202-203. Carlos París in *Unamuno: Estructura de su mundo intelectual* (Barcelona, 1968), p. 352, gives a distinctly psychoanalytical reading of Unamuno's use of the Sphinx: "Meyer, en su exploración de la ontología unamuniana nos habla de una 'avidez ontológica', expresión que no puede menos que recordarnos a la 'avidez oral' de la terminología psicoanalítica ya aludida. También el temor de la muerte, que Freud conecta con esta etapa. Y el tema obsesionante en Unamuno del suicidio vinculado a la insatisfacción oral según ciertos autores destacan. Desde esta posición básica de la libido oral se ilumina parcialmente el tema de la madre mala—y su simbolismo la esfinge—, tan importante en Unamuno, sobre el cual nos veremos obligados a volver. Así como inversamente la búsqueda perenne de la madre buena, protectora, compasiva." París has opened up a promising line of investigation, for Unamuno was unusually interested in the Sphinx.

23. Unamuno repeatedly uses the eyes of the dead and dying for dramatic effect. At times they merely question, like those of Rosa in *La tía Tula*: "Y parecía aquella mirada una pregunta desesperada y suprema, como si a punto de partírse para nunca más volver a tierra, preguntase por el oculto sentido de la vida" (II, 1065). At other times they have the power to discover the ultimate truth (or horror): "Hamlet, tendido en tierra . . . con los abiertos ojos ya sin vida, miraba al cielo, como queriendo oír el silencio de Dios, oír con los ojos" (V, 1168).

24. Another example links the eyes of the Sphinx with the pools of quiet water that always whispered of suicide to Unamuno. Writing in 1908 of José Asunción Silva, he aks: "¿Encontró la llave del misterio? ¿Leyó el sino en el fondo de las pupilas inmóviles de la eterna Esfinge?" and concludes ". . . quedará Silva, que clavó sus ojos en los ojos de la eterna Esfinge y bañó su corazón en el lago—lago de terrible quietud y calma de sobrehaz—de las perdurables e imperecederas inquietudes" (VIII, 964 and 968). The dangers of the eye as a pool in which the self sinks and dissolves

go, to be sure, far beyond the Sphinx context. See Blanco Aguinaga, pp. 121-122 and also San Manuel Bueno's discussion of quiet waters and suicide (II, 1144).

25. Aurora de Albornoz in *La presencia de Miguel de Unamuno en Antonio Machado* (Madrid: Gredos, 1968), pp. 333-336, dedicates a section of her chapter "Formulaciones comunes" to the phrase "Ver la cara de Dios." As she indicates (p. 334), Unamuno had been struck by the appearance of the Biblical warning "quien ve a Dios se muere" in Ibsen's *Brand* and in Kierkegaard (III, 290). The Bible, however, mentions only God's face and our author, for purely subjective reasons, often localizes the threat in the eyes. Typical examples are Nos. 20 and 1713 of the *Cancionero* (VI, 955 and 1410). At times of greater belief—or greater need to believe—Unamuno uses the symbol of God's eyes with exactly the opposite value. Envisioning a decidedly maternal God, Angel declares in *La esfinge*: "¡Sólo quiero que el Padre invisible me coja en su regazo, sentir el calor de su inmenso pecho, el ritmo de su respiración, mirarme en su mirada, en ese cielo limpio y puro, y dormir en paz!" (V, 208).

26. To bring this statement into perspective, allow me to quote from R. D. Laing's fine study, *The Divided Self* (1960; rpt. Baltimore: Penguin, 1965), p. 106: "The schizoid individual is frequently tormented by . . . the equally compulsive nature of his sense of his body as an object in the world of others. The heightened sense of being always seen, or at any rate of being always potentially seeable, may be principally referable to the body, but the preoccupation with being seeable may be condensed with the idea of the mental self being penetrable, and vulnerable, as when the individual feels that one can look right through him into his 'mind' or 'soul.' Such 'plate-glass' feelings are usually spoken about in terms of metaphor or simile, but in psychotic conditions the gaze or scrutiny of the other can be experienced as an actual penetration into the core of the 'inner' self." He also describes as a common schizophrenic complaint the feeling that the self has been stolen (p. 92).

27. Laing, p. 113: "The compulsive preoccupation with being seen or simply with being visible, suggests that we must be dealing with underlying phantasies of being invisible. If, as we saw, being visible can be both in itself persecutory and a reassurance that one is still alive, then being invisible will have equally ambiguous meanings."

28. There is an interesting discussion of these matters in Paul Ilie's chapter "The Splitting of the Self" in his *Unamuno: An Existentialist View of the Self and Society* (Madison: Univ. of Wisconsin Press, 1967), pp. 28-48.

29. The best examples are in *Dos madres* and *La tía Tula*.

30. We might add as a biographical footnote that Unamuno's own children experienced his gaze as something to be escaped. Rudd tells us (p. 84): ". . . Unamuno would seek to penetrate his innermost being until the child's one wish was to be released from the grip of his piercing eyes."

31. Sigmund Freud, *The Interpretation of Dreams,* trans. A. A. Brill (1913; rpt. New York: Random House, 1950), p. 270, n. 72.

32. This quotation is from p. 373 of Fenichel's "The Scoptophilic Instinct and Identification," in *The Collected Papers of Otto Fenichel: First Series* (New York: Norton, 1953), pp. 373-397. The study originally appeared in the *Int. Z. Psa.* [*Internationale Zeitschrift für Psychoanalyse*] 21 (1935), 561-583.

33. Fenichel, p. 374. He justifies this interpretation on p. 390: "We begin to realize what is the idea which in the unconscious is the link between the penis and the mouth. It is that of the vagina, which is seen but not comprehended and about which the child is uncertain whether it conceals within it a penis or is a kind of devouring mouth. In the unconscious, contradictions can exist side by side. To be turned into rigid stone symbolizes not only erection but also castration, just as the eye symbolizes not only a penis but a vagina (and a mouth)."

34. Fenichel, p. 376.

35. Fenichel, pp. 390-391.

36. Fenichel, p. 391.

37. Fenichel, p. 378.

38. Fenichel, pp. 387 and 396.

39. The applicability of Laing's concepts to Unamuno has previously been indicated by Andrés Franco in *El teatro de Unamuno* (Madrid: Insula, 1971), p. 76 and by Frances W. Weber in "Unamuno's *Niebla*: From Novel to Dream" *PMLA,* 88 (1973), 217, n. 8.

40. A. R. Fernández y González, "Unamuno en su espejo," *BBMP,* 42 (1966), 250 considers him "un tipo esquizotímico, no exagerado, pues encontró su compensación en la agresividad instintiva."

41. Laing, p. 91. See also p. 111. François Meyer, *La ontología de Miguel de Unamuno* (Madrid: Gredos, 1962), pp. 59-66 describes a similar situation.

42. Laing, pp. 109 and 113.

43. Laing, p. 44.

44. Laing, p. 75.

45. Laing, p. 109.

46. Laing, pp. 109-110.

D. L. Shaw (essay date spring 1979)

SOURCE: Shaw, D. L. "Imagery and Symbolism in the Theatre of Unamuno: *La esfinge* and *Soledad*." *Journal of Spanish Studies* 7, no. 1 (spring 1979): 87-104.

[*In the following essay, Shaw explores the significance of water and music imagery in Unamuno's plays* La esfinge *and* Soledad, *especially in regards to Unamuno's persistent interest in politics in both his works and his life.*]

D. G. Turner in his recent book *Unamuno's Webs of Fatality*[1] draws attention afresh to «highly developed use of imagery and symbolism» as «the most polished aspect of *Amor y pedagogía*.» He goes on to emphasise that it was «a technique which had already reached an advanced stage in the stylistically very different *Paz en la guerra*.» There are several studies of this technique both on a broad scale (e. g. Carlos Blanco Aguinaga's *El Unamuno contemplativo* [Mexico, 1959]) and in respect of individual works (e. g. Ricardo Gullón's analysis of metaphors of hatred in *Autobiografías de Unamuno* [Madrid, 1964], pp. 123-59). But similar studies relating to Unamuno's theatre are almost wholly lacking.[2] In what follows it is proposed to pay special attention to two works in which it is especially prominent: *La esfinge* (1898) and *Soledad* (1921).

LA ESFINGE

I have attempted to indicate elsewhere[3] some of the more serious structural shortcomings of Unamuno's first major play. The extreme density of imagery in the dialogue and the heavy stress which Unamuno lays on symbolism would certainly prove an additional problem in actual performance. We can see this clearly by examining the three basic areas of imagery which are outstanding in the play. These are connected with childhood, water and music. The first reference to music occurs in the opening scene at the end of bitterly ironic speech by the hero, Angel, which announces a prominent theme of *La esfinge*: the futility of libertarian endeavour on behalf of the masses. When the end of the world comes, Angel declares, «entonces cartarán las esferas celestiales el himno a nuestra libertad tan soñada» (*Obras completas* [Madrid, 1958], XII, 219).[4] His own hymn, in contrast, is according to his wife Eufemia «un himno a la sencillez» (p. 235). It is related to a «Mundo de pura armonía, de sonidos sin ideas, de libertad abso-

luta» (p. 237) and through this in turn to childhood and the simple faith with which Unamuno associated the maternal cradle-song. Angel's deepest longing is thus appropriately symbolized by the music of the piano which is heard in Acts I and II. Since it expresses no ideas, it liberates the hearer from the faith-eroding intellectualism which was one of Unamuno's chief afflictions, especially at this time. In consequence it is both «pura» and «adormecedora.» Angel's frustration in his relationship with his wife is similarly conveyed by his reproach to her that she is not «una nota pura, purísima, adormecedora» (p. 237), that she has no cradle-song to sing him (p. 240).

We perceive afresh before the end of Act I that this song, when sung by a woman to a man and not to a child, is sung expressly to soothe his fears of «el último sueño, el sueño sin despertar» (p. 246) by providing loving spiritual support. In *Soledad, El hermano Juan* and some of Unamuno's novels, notably *Abel Sánchez,* it is this provision of spiritual support which reemerges as the supreme function of women and especially of wives who, as Unamuno was himself to point out, using a characteristic water-image, in 1934 «Pasan por mis obras, casi siempre en silencio, o lo más susurrando, rezando, callándose al oído—al oído del corazón—de sus hombres. ungiéndolos con el rocío de su entrañable humanidad» (p. 879). Finally in Act I Angel's decision to abandon the political struggle in order to cleanse and re-temper his spirit is again expressed by means of a musical image, as the will to «entonar mi corazón y después, cuando le hiera el Espíritu . . . me arrancará limpia y pura mi nota, la mía propia, para que vaya a perderse en la infinita sinfonía, en el cántico universal al amor del Padre» (p. 249).

In Act II the music imagery reemerges in two symbolic scenes. Throughout the play Angel's attitude to the mass of the common people, reflecting that of Unamuno, is markedly ambivalent. Despite his role as a popular agitator, he inwardly distrusts progressive political action aimed at a concept of liberty which is designed exclusively to «libertar a todos los hombres de la miseria corporal» (p. 300). At the same time he deeply envies the spiritual simplicity of the unsophisticated. This last is now symbolized in Martina, the maid-servant, by whose inarticulate piety Angel is momentarily attracted. Reproached by his wife, he excuses himself with the words «Su aspecto, su mirada, que es pura música . . . ; toda ella me envuelve en atmósfera de paz» (p. 268). When, shortly afterwards, Eufemia leaves him, he is on the verge of suicide, but is restrained from shooting himself by hearing Stradella's *Pietà Signore* which his neighbour happens to be playing. The basic melodrama of the scene is attenuated for the alert reader (though one suspects not perhaps for a possible spectator) by his recognition of the emphasis laid on the music's symbolic meaning. This meaning—a spiritual peace too deep for expression in words—is underlined afresh in scene III of the last act. Here Angel explicitly associates music, that of the clavichord belonging to the parish priest of his childhood and that of the organ in the cathedral which he frequented during his adolescence, with «el sueño de mi niñez.» So it is right that the whole pattern of music imagery in the play should culminate in Angel's dying request to Eufemia: «Cántame el canto de cuna para el sueño que no acaba . . . ; arrulla mi agonía . . . » (p. 311).

One of the links between the music and the water imagery in *La esfinge* is the idea of purity. The words *puro, pura, pureza, purificar* occur more than twenty times in the text of the play, associated especially with music. What Unamuno clearly has in mind is a state of grace purified once and for all of the logical, verbal concepts and analytic arguments which had led to his state of malaise. In a similar way water is visualized as having the same refreshing function, washing away doubt and *congoja*. The opening image is that of Act I, scene IV, which contrasts the salt sea of earthly endeavour «que cuanto más de él se bebe, da más sed» and the «aguas mansas y silenciosas del regato oculto» (p. 225) which slake all thirst. The key aspect of the image is the sentence «Es preciso que las aguas del mar soberbio suban al cielo y que allí en nube se purifiquen.» Only the water that falls from heaven, purged of all bitterness, can cleanse the soul.

Felipe, who stands for spirituality in the play, develops the original image in the next scene. The «regato oculto» becomes «la fuente de la vida íntima» which Angel's earthly preoccupations with progress for others or glory for himself will dry up. What is needed is not social engineering but «un consuelo que bañe en adelante las almas de los que sufren» (p. 227) associated with «pureza de intención.» In contrast Eufemia calls on Angel to «bañarte en gente» and is rewarded with the angry suggestion: «quieres que tu nombre sobrenade al olvido enlazado en las aguas de la historia al mío» (p. 238).

The water imagery of Angel's curtain speech at the end of Act I reveals a deeper aspiration beneath his political activism. Already in scene V he had explained to Felipe that «la causa de la libertad del pueblo» was for him merely a means of escape from «ese monstruoso egoismo . . . que a todas horas me pone ante los ojos del espíritu el espectro de la muerte y tras ella el inmenso vacío eterno» (p. 229). To lose himself in the crowd was to escape from himself and his anguishing insight. But in the next speech «quiero serlo todo. Serlo todo para gozar de la paz del todo,» the idea is broadened. In *En torno al casticismo* Unamuno had introduced the idea of something analogous to a mystical process by which peoples and individuals, through a special kind of self-purifying examination of conscience, can arrive

at a state in which «se anegan en la humanidad entera» (***O.C.*** [***Obras completas***] III [Madrid 1958], 193). Clearly this is behind what Angel longs for here and suggests the real meaning of Eufemia's invitation to him to «bathe himself in the people.»

At the climax of the act the idea reemerges more ambiguously as Angel addresses his fiercely beating heart «Quieres latir en todo y con todo: palpitar con el universo entero, . . . ¡Y con tanto anhelar derramarte me ahogas!» (p. 250). But this extension of the original notion of fusing oneself with humanity until it brings fusion with the entire universe is suddenly modified as Angel symbolically drains a glass of water with the cry «¡Quien pudiera sorberse así el Espíritu Universal!» No less symbolically he then sprinkles a few drops of water on his forehead in a gesture of rebaptism of himself. It portends his new life after renouncing the material progress, the glory and the «destiny» which had drawn him into politics. These are the equivalents in Act I of the world, the flesh and the devil. Instead of pouring out the whole of himself into the world, he now longs for the opposite: absorption into the bosom of God «¡Dios mío! ¡Anégame, ahógame ¡Que sienta mi vida derretirse en tu seno!» So the two outward influences: that of Eufemia, drawing Angel towards progress, fame and «history» via positive involvement, and that of his friend Felipe, drawing him towards spirituality and peaceful «intrahistoric» life in the countryside via retreat, are both expressed in similar figurative language, a *derramarse* and a *derretirse*, neither of which Angel can fully accept.

Underlying this struggle is Angel's more private and inner struggle between faith and doubt. Both of these inner forces are once more expressed in Act II by water imagery. Late in the act, in scene IX, during a discussion with his political associates who, like Eufemia, are attempting to bring him back into the political arena, Angel uses almost the exact opposite of the image with which Act I had reached its climax. To drain the cup «apurar de un trago el cáliz para consumir las heces» (p. 278) is now converted into an image of suicide. It is to be followed not by the semi-mystical idea of drowning in God's bosom, but instead by submersion in «el misterio.» Unamuno's use of the same figure of speech both in respect of the water of life and in respect of the water of annihilation, is highly significant.

Earlier in the same scene Angel had returned to a variant of the *regato oculto/fuente íntima* image. In this case the reference is to the «brocal del alma» and implicitly to the hidden water beneath. This is further developed in Angel's assertion of his need to «escarbar sin descanso en el fondo del alma hasta descubrir el manantial de frescura que la riegue, el arroyo de mi niñez» (p. 273). With this the play's basic pattern of imagery is complete. Music, symbolising beatific serene faith unassailable by verbal *lógica,* and water, symbolising the water of life which washes away fear of death and annihilation, are each directly associated with childhood's purity and simplicity. One of the more ironic pieces of dialogue in Act I occurs in fact in scene XII when, during an attempt to dissuade Angel from abandoning politics, Joaquín repeatedly uses the words *niño* and *niñerías.* For as we previously saw in scene IX Angel's aspiration is precisely that of recovering his ability to «rezar como de niño» (p. 241). Hence he begs God in his longest soliloquy «Dame fuerzas para que . . . brote de mis labios la plegaria de la infancia» (p. 241) and early in Act II calls on Eufemia to join him in the countryside «allí me mimarás como a un niño, a ver si logras devolverme la infacia» (p. 241). The idea of returning to childhood is developed insistently throughout the play, reaching a climax in the last act when, after the exit of Felipe's children, Angel refers to «el aroma vivificante de mi niñez» and hears Felipe confirm his longing with the assertion «El niño que en nosotros todos duerme es la sal de nuestro espíritu, el justo que nos justifica» (p. 290). So in the last scene of the play the reconciliation of Angel and Eufemia is accompanied almost inevitably by the latter's repeated «¡hijo mío!,» the cry that was to reecho through Unamuno's work right down to *San Manuel Bueno, mártir.* As Angel dies the theme of childhood reaches its apotheosis when his desire to become Eufemia's «hijo espiritual» (p. 281) is in his mind fulfilled by her cry, and he can at last say to her «¡Así . . . así . . . , Eufemia . . . , así . . . hijo . . . , hijo tuyo! ¿No querías ser madre? Y me tenías a mí, al niño de siempre . . . , a tu hijo . . . » (p. 309).

We can advance certain tentative conclusions. The most cursory study of the imagery and symbolism of *La esfinge* underline its importance among the early works of Unamuno. Since the publication by Gallego Morell of Unamuno's letter to Ganivet of November 20, 1898,[5] the play's close reflection of the author's deep crisis of the previous year has been clearly established. But of greater importance is Blanco Aguinaga's *El Unamuno contemplativo.* At the time the book was written the play was available only in typescript and Blanco mentions it only in passing. In retrospect, however, it can be seen to illustrate and confirm as early as 1898, practically all his major conclusions. In Angel's struggle between action/*agonismo* on the one hand and the contemplative life of spiritual self-revelation in the countryside, the division between the two Unamunos of Blanco's concluding chapter is already clear. Unamuno's attraction to music, and especially to the preferably wordless crooning of cradle-songs «una de las querencias claves de su personalidad no agónica» (Blanco, p. 83), the themes of childhood, the *mujer-madre,* her associations with dreaming and with water imagery, nature as a refuge, the longing to *anegarse,* these are all present. More especially we can see in *La esfinge* the clearest possible prefiguration of that rejec-

tion of progressive ideology which Ribbans dates from 1899[6] and which according to Blanco Aguinaga was so tragically intensified after 1930. In fact the more we read again Blanco's fundamental book, the greater seems the importance of *La esfinge,* its imagery and symbolism, for the understanding of Unamuno's early development.

It is also noteworthy that the pattern of imagery and symbolism briefly here explored, which was to reemerge insistently in much of Unamuno's later work, rests on a substructure of more familiar and conventional expression derived ultimately from romanticism. This is no way surprising. The combination, visible in Angel, of a strong impulse towards libertarian endeavour and a haunting conviction of the futility of all endeavour in a life of pure contingency and in a world without purpose, goes right back to Espronceda and Larra. Unamuno's description of Angel to Ganivet as «un tribuno popular, jefe presunto de una revolución» but who is an «obsesionado por la nada de ultratumba, a quien persigue de continuo el espectro de la muerte»[7] has unmistakably romantic overtones. Hence the language in which Angel's inner conflict and aspiration are expressed becomes an amalgam of references to «glory» as the answer to his «vacío del alma» (p. 221), to action as a distraction for «Esa nada, esa nada terrible que se me presenta en cuanto cierro los ojos» (p. 265), to goodness, beauty and truth as «nombres sonoros con que encubrir el vacío» (p. 277)—all romantic topoi—and the more original pattern of images and symbols just described.

No less romantic in origin is Angel's sense of being the victim of an arbitrarily adverse fate. His reference to «una desgracia del Destino» (p. 238) underlying his plunge into politics, and more unexpectedly his exclamation «estoy expiando algún crimen de antes de que naciera» (p. 264) are early expressions of an aspect of Unamuno's thought which has only recently been systematically studied. D. G. Turner has shown how throughout his work after 1897 Unamuno can be seen to have persistently and confusingly juxtaposed the concepts of «a superior fatal force» against which his characters struggle in vain, and «a fundamentally beneficial cosmic movement» which is sometimes equated with divine Providence.[8] The Unamuno of *La esfinge* is no exception. For Angel's sense of a cruelly unjust fatality determining his actions is counterbalanced by his recognition of Felipe as «un providencial mensajero, un enviado del Espíritu, un ángel» (p. 230). The fact is that the conflict to which Angel is subjected in the play is irreconcilable with the theory of inevitable and spontaneous regeneration which J. W. Butt has argued convincingly Unamuno had evolved in 1896-7.[9] It illustrates his shift away from an optimistic determinism derived from Taine and Herbert Spencer towards the characteristic ambivalence about the roles of God,

Fate and Chance which Turner has investigated and which has its roots deep in romantic sensibility. It is hardly too much to say that *La esfinge* occupies a key position in Unamuno's early creative work, coming as it does just after the crisis of 1897 and *Nicodemo el fariseo* which was written at the end of the same year.[10] In it we see clearly the break up of that general confidence in a «conprensión viva de lo necesario» (*O.C.* III [Madrid 1958], 198) which had sustained the harmonious tone of *Paz en la guerra*. It marks its autor's sudden relapse into the struggle against that invading scepticism which Ganivet had diagnosed nine years before in *España filosófica contemporánea* as the chief source of intellectual malaise and a major legacy of the romantics.

Finally, at the technical level, it is hard to avoid the conclusion that Unamuno was systematically using in *La esfinge* a type of language which would have been more appropriate in a verse-drama of a non-realist kind than in a domestic conflict with a political setting. Possibly Unamuno himself became aware of this. For in *La venda*, *Fedra* and *El pasado que vuelve* we notice a definite change of style. What survive are certain themes. That of the divided personality, for example, which reappears on Fedra's «¡Es que no soy yo, ama, no soy yo!» and her reference to «alguna otra que llevo dentro» (p. 410). These words, followed by the Nurse's «¡Como su madre!» recall Angel's sense of carrying within himself a guilt inherited from the past. Similarly the theme of fatality looms large in *Fedra* and reappears at the end of *El pasado que vuelve*. The symbol of the sphynx occurs in *Fedra* and that of the mirror figures prominently in *La venda*. But in general the language of these plays, stark in *Fedra,* a little banal in *El pasado que vuelve* and *La venda,* is markedly less figurative than in Unamuno's first major play.

SOLEDAD

Soledad is very different. It is arguable that the content of the three intervening plays did not touch Unamuno closely. *La venda* is in any case only a brief development of a single idea. *Fedra*'s theme of passionate incestuous love and the emphasis on money of *El pasado que vuelve* hardly strike one as typically unamunesque. But in *Soledad* the plot centers around literary creativeness and the lure of political activism, with both of which Unamuno was always deeply involved personally. The combination seems to have stimulated a sudden return to the densely figurative style of *La esfinge.* Nor is this the only point of comparison between the two plays; for, as we have just seen, politics once more play a decisive part in the plot. In the opinion of Andrés Franco indeed the similarity is so great that he can speak of a *refundición,*[11] though this seems an overstatement. Certainly Franco is correct, however, in his assertion «Si los argumentos se parecen, es porque

los problemas planteados en *La esfinge* no se habían resuelto en la conciencia de Unamuno.»[12] If anything they had become more acute. What is also of great interest is the fact that only in his theatre and principally in these two plays does Unamuno's constant attraction by the political arena (an attraction which dominated a large sector of his nonliterary life) manifest itself clearly. It is curiously absent from his fiction.

The real survival, however, is the theme of authenticity. Eufemia in *La esfinge* had no doubts in this respect. For her the cause of liberty and progress was «una causa grande y noble» and Angel's freedom from family ties a «providential» factor enabling him to fulfil a «verdadera misión» (p. 221). Angel was far less sure. He was haunted by a sense of insincerity which is inextricably connected with the scepticism he feels about his own autonomy and the worth of human endeavour. It seems probably that this scepticism, which Unamuno appears instinctively to have associated with sinfulness, is the source of the aspiration to purity which, as noted earlier, connects the water and music imagery in the play. In the same way the essence of childhood, the third of *La esfinge*'s basic areas of imagery, was for Unamuno also its purity (i. e. lack of intellectual insight). Hence his reference in a poem to the sleep of a child containing «la más alta verdad»

> porque él duerme de Dios en el regazo
> en abrazo con todo lo que es puro,
> con todo lo que vive sin saberlo

(*O.C.* XIII [Madrid 1958], 877)

Scepticism also gives rise to two other symbolic images which appear again in Unamuno's later work: those connected with chess and with the theatre. Behind the game of chess in Act I, scene VIII of *La esfinge* lies the familiar idea that we, mankind, are but pawns in the hand of God, with only the illusion of autonomous behaviour. It is significant that the chief musical symbol, the playing of *Pietà Signore*, breaks in on the game of chess between Angel and Eufemia, that same game which provokes in the former the «impure» suspicion that his behaviour is inescapably determined. In total contrast the music interposes its own implication of a «Mundo de pura armonía . . . de libertad absoluta» (p. 237). This is one of the central symbolic scenes of the play. The analogy between life and the theatre is even more central to Unamuno's conception or reality. Already in *La esfinge* it is being used to express the idea which was to reach its peak of development in *Cómo se hace una novela,* the idea of the inauthenticity of the public personality. «No hago más que representar un papel, Felipe,» Angel confesses to his friend, «me paso la vida contemplándome, hecho teatro de mí mismo» (p. 228). The connection with the water imagery is plain. Angel is not sure whether devoting himself to the people is a way not only of annihilating his egotism and «torturas de lujo» but also of pouring himself out so as to mingle himself in the people's intrahistoricity and through it to unify himself with the Spirit of the Universe. Equally he is in doubt whether he ought instead to withdraw from the people into Nature and seek to drown in the bosom of God. The same language: *derramarse, derretirse, sumergirse, anegarse,* is applied to both impulses. But at the same time both are feared to be mere play-acting.

This is the anxiety which reappears in *Soledad.* Unamuno, as Andrés Franco has pointed out, had just been an unsuccessful candidate in the elections of 1920. As with *La esfinge,* the play bears the impress of his recent experience; it is, as the hero, Agustín, indicates, «El drama de un drama» (p. 653). In appearance Agustín makes his choice between continuing to write for the theatre and embracing the active life of politics. But once more there is the suspicion in his mind that both sides of the alternative are in some respect false and futile. The great difference between *Soledad* and *La esfinge,* however, is that whereas in the latter the choice is between two possible roads to authenticity, in the former the choice is between two modes of inauthenticity. *La esfinge* ends with Angel's death, but *Soledad* *begins* with references to death, that of Agustín's son. Visually represented in every scene by his toy horse, the child's death dominates Agustín's thinking throughout the play, mocking his efforts to convince himself that human activity in any form is valid.

The imagery associated with the theatre in *Soledad* operates at three levels. The first of these is concerned with play-writing itself, Agustín's main occupation prior to the opening of the play. It carries with it a very clear restatement of Unamuno's conception of the relationship between art and the artist's lived experience. At the same time it expresses his awareness of the shortcomings of that very conception. The Generation of 1898, as is well known, differed fundamentally from the *modernistas* on the question of the relationship of art to life. For them art arose directly from the artist's own human experience, preoccupations, and especially from his inner tragic vision, to all of which his creative imagination was in the end subordinate. As early as 1899 Unamuno had announced this essentially romantic standpoint when he wrote «Tengamos, primero, que decir algo jugoso, fuerte, hondo y universalmente humano, y luego, del fondo, brotará la forma.»[13] He never moved from this subsequently to any significant extent. It is the essence of Agustín's position in *Soledad.* Of his audience he declares «Es menester que sientan mis torturas, que mis criaturas palpiten de vida» (p. 592), and this is confirmed by his wife's comment «Yo sé los muertos que le están labrando el espíritu . . . ¡El muerto!» (p. 592). She refers to their dead son.

Agustín's theatre, then, reflecting Unamuno's, draws its inspiration directly from his private suffering; his plays are «criaturas del dolor» (p. 599).

There are two disadvantages. The first concerns the audience's reaction. Unable to perceive or to identify themselves with the playwright's tragic insight they respond with incomprehension, boredom, or even laughter. Unamuno uses two images to convey this idea. The first, borrowed from Browning, is that of a statue of Laocöon who, though tormented by invisible serpents, seems merely to be yawning. The other is that of the lobster boiled alive in seawater, whose desperate contortions are a source of amusement to the onlookers. Both images vividly express Unamuno's deep-seated frustration and dissatisfaction with reactions to his work, especially to his theatre. Unfortunately the use he makes of the Laocöon image shows that his response was to emphasise more stubbornly than ever the original idea. Agustín insists that «hay que dar carne a las serpientes» (p. 597). The solution, that is, is to intensify the relationship between his plays and his own suffering, rather than refining his techniques of expression. This is one of the clues to Unamuno's failure as a dramatist.

The second disadvantage concerns the author. For paradoxically the more the creative writer succeeds in converting his private sorrows into works of art which may convey consolation to others, the more these sorrows become «literature» in his own eyes. Contrasting himself with his wife, Agustín confesses «tengo vergüenza de que mi dolor no es como el suyo, de que el arte me acorche, de que hago con mis dolores . . . ¡literatura! . . . Y me avergüenza que mientras ella va allá [to the cemetery] a . . . vivir, yo voy por el camino recogiendo semillas de dramas» (p. 607). This awareness of an invading inauthenticity in all aspects of behaviour and feelings, even those most related to inner *congoja,* Agustín shares with Angel of *La esfinge.* It runs closely parallel to the notion of lack of individual autonomy of action. The two ideas converge to produce a sense of total ultimate futility.

From this Agustín attempts to escape into the life of political action. It is of course an illusion which at the conscious intellectual level Unamuno had already rejected before the turn of the century. He was to reject it afresh five years after *Soledad* in *Sombras de sueño.* Yet the desire to intervene in Spanish politics haunted him to the end of his life. Agustín's question in Act I, scene V «¿No puedo esculpir pueblo . . . forjar ciudadanía desde el teatro y con el arte?» contains a curious survival of the pre-1900 *noventayochista* idea of the need for political commitment on the part of writers, which Azorín, for example, had affirmed stridently in *Notas sociales.* It was to reemerge concretely in the early poetry of Unamuno's exile. For the moment, however, Agustín determines to try instead the «más alta dramaturgía» of political action. But even as he decides to do so he is assailed by the same sense of inauthenticity which he suffers from as a writer. «No creo a mí mismo, me lanzo al tablado . . . político y me represento. ¿Y cuál soy yo?» (p. 615).

His failure is a foregone conclusion. Predictably therefore the second and more banal level of theatre imagery in *Soledad* is that which presents politics as simple play-acting, a mere «hediondo retablo de títeres, de muñecos de palo, más ficción que el otro» (p. 622). This image in turn suggests the ironic one of Agustín as Don Quixote in the Maese Pedro episode mounted on his dead son's toy horse. As was the case when he was playing his earlier role as a playwright, the outcome is a split in his personality: «empezaba a no conocerme . . . , a no serme» (p. 631).

The symbol of the child's toy horse introduces the third level of theatre imagery in *Soledad,* the abstract level. Behind the connection which Soledad, Agustín's wife, establishes between the death of their son Ramoncín and the inspiration for a play on the biblical subject of Hagar, lies the idea that Agustín is consciously trying to replace his dead son with «hijos de ensueño, de niebla.» They are in a sense the child's «brothers» (p. 622), since Soledad herself also participates in their conception and birth. Unlike Ramoncín, however, they have some possibility, if Agustín's plays stand the test of time, of achieving a certain immortality and even of conferring it on him. Hence the symbolic names of the two women in his life, Gloria and Soledad. He is trapped between his desire for that shadow of immortality, as a mere name, which literary glory can bring, and the solitude which accompanies his recognition that his «obras de política» and his «obras de teatro» alike will in the end, like his son, die and be forgotten. Only the toy horse is specifically declared to be immortal, by analogy with Don Quixote's Clavileño. It seems to represent not only the ever-presence of death, but also mankind's unconquerable—chimerical—longing for transcendence. Hence the suggestion that Agustín was riding on it when he sought glory in politics (p. 627) and the stage direction referring to it in Act II, scene IV. Unamuno could hardly have chosen a more ironical symbol for «este hambre, esta sed, este sueño, este ahogo de vida eterna» (p. 634) than the cardboard plaything of a dead child.

As Act II progresses this more abstract dimension of the play gradually predominates over the opening theme of Agustín's choice between public and private creative activity. *Soledad,* that is, becomes increasingly «El drama del sueño de cada uno» (p. 653). As it does so the imagery and symbolism undergo a slow alteration. Once more a feature of the change is that more traditionally romantic aspects come to the fore. Agustín is in fact the most complex of the three central figures

of Unamuno's later theatre who have much in common with the romantic hero-type: himself, Macedo, the mysterious suicidal stranger of *Sombras de sueño* and Juan of *El hermano Juan* in whom there are echoes of Zorrilla's Tenorio.

Already at the end of Act I the romantic scenario combining the revolutionary ideal and *vacío del alma* is in being. Indeed the curtain scene of the act culminates with a double reference to the inner emptiness of both Agustín and Soledad. In Act II references to prison make their appearance. Though they are not so clearly connected with the romantics' use of prison as a symbol of man's unhappy existential situation[14] as those of *La novela de don Sandalio* are, the role of imprisonment in *Soledad* is still that of intensifying the hero's despair. Not wholly unconnected is the complex symbolism of Soledad herself and the imagery associated with it. Traditionally the romantic hero was a solitary, cut off by his insight from the frenzied crowd but consoled by love. Here the formula is still basically the same. As Luis González-del-Valle points out in his compact and incisive chapter on Unamuno as a tragic dramatist (*La tragedia en el teatro de Unamuno, Valle-Inclán y García Lorca* [New York, 1975], pp. 37-64):

> Agustín trata de llenar su vacío personal, de garantizar la procreación de su «yo» en el futuro, a través de la inmortalidad de su fama. A esta inmortalidad se aproximará Agustín por dos vías: el teatro y la política. Su fracaso en ambas esferas lo llevará más tarde a buscar un escape en su esposa Soledad.
>
> (p. 54)

To be sure Soledad's role of *mujer-madre* is closely (even too closely) similar to Eufemia's in *La esfinge.* The familiar vocabulary (*achicarse, aniñarse, hacerse niño, cunar, acunar, brezar*), together with the exclamation «¡hijo mío!», reappear, and the final scene of the play contains an actual cradlesong. But Soledad also has the symbolic role which her name emphasises. In part she stands for solitude itself, that solitude which is the natural refuge of men like Agustín, to which he naturally returns when his foray into the world of the collectivity, the world of politics, has collapsed. It was the solitude which the creative writer especially feels which had originally impelled Agustín outwards into active participation in the social struggle. Now on his return to solitude after the play-acting of politics, he finds his authenticity again, the ability to «ser más mío, ser más yo» (p. 623).

From here on, however, the task of interpretation becomes hazardous. Agustín's return from the political arena is a return to the embrace of Soledad in both the literal and symbolic senses, but it is also a return to the toils of the invisible serpents of tragic insight. This is what explains the very obvious and rather confusing dualities which characterise the imagery of the latter part of the play. Soledad is both *refugio* and *cárcel/ tumba, tierra* and *carne.* Although she herself believes that after Ramoncín's death her heart is «oscuro y frío como la tierra que le arropa» (p. 616), that is to say, she associates herself figuratively with the idea of «tierra muerta» (p. 646), Agustín associates her with «luz y calor, Sol» (p. 646), and with «Sol de carne que enciende y alumbra» (p. 656) and so with «tierra viva» (p. 646) and «mi última tierra» (p. 648). González-del-Valle, in his perceptive analysis of Soledad as the second tragic figure in the play, is the only critic to have emphasised the contrast between her own tragic role: «Esta incapacidad de Soledad a no poder apreciar el valor de los sueños, de lo espiritual, es lo que la convierte, en la obra, en el símbolo de la infecundidad, del fracaso y de la muerte . . . » (González-del-Valle, p. 60) and the fact that at the same time Agustín insists on seeing her as a positive force, an «anchor», as well as «sunlight» and «living earth». This contrast remains unresolved at the end of the play despite the shift of symbolism in the final scene.

Even before his imprisonment Agustín reveals that the collapse of his dream of action had rendered more acute the anguish he already felt at the beginning of the play. Punctually the yearning to return to childhood makes its appearance (p. 634). But this time Agustín longs to be «menos que niño,» to return to the womb and sleep there forever the sleep of the unborn. When the sleep image returns in Act III, scene I, it prefaces the long quotation from the poem 'El Cristo yacente de Santa Clara, de Palencia' which Agustín recites. Its emphasis is heavily on the word *tierra,* which Unamuno connects with intranscendence and hence with annihilation:

. . . este Cristo de mi tierra es tierra . . .
. . . todo no es más que tierra
todo no es más que nada . . . nada . . . nada . . .

Hence the invisible serpent of tragic insight is now called «La serpiente de tierra» (p. 642). It provokes Agustín's desire to «dormir para siempre,» to accept annihilation. This is the lowest point in his spiritual trajectory, brought about by his imprisonment and the strengthened sense of life's inescapable oppression which it symbolises.

But immediately the idea of sleep stimulates reference to dreaming as a positive creative act. As in *Niebla* and *La novela de don Sandalio,* the proof of existence is to exist in the minds of others «El sueño de dos es ya la realidad.» At this point Soledad becomes the guarantor of Agustín's «substantial» existence. His political associates, formerly described as «gusanos . . . lumacos . . . lombrices . . . comiendo tierra» (pp. 627-8), are now dismissed as mere shadows and the glory Agustín hoped to achieve as a playwright as a mere dream. But

the mutual love of the husband and wife signifies existential reality. Hence Agustín's anxious question «¿Me quieres, Soledad, me quieres? ¿Me sueñas, di Sol, Soledad, me sueñas?» (p. 642) and in turn her «¡Pues suéñame a mí, Agustín» (p. 644). This link with real existence becomes at once a link with immortality, for being that is truly substantial is immortal. Thus Agustín is able to declare «tu regazo, Sol, Soledad, no es tierra, es carne . . . sí . . . carne, carne palpitante de vida» (p. 644), in fact, «carne inmortal.» As childhood faith had been associated with the mother image in *La esfinge,* so now immortality is associated with the return to Soledad's *regazo.* Her «luz» triumphs over «este escenario de locos» [the world of *tierra*] where «todo es tan oscuro» (p. 654). Ramming home the technique Agustín adds «Simbolismos . . . , ¡a saber . . . !»

Well he may. For in the final scene of the play the symbolism of Soledad is built up to a climax and brought together at last specifically with that of the toy horse. Her hand, «mano de tierra,» becomes at last «mano de Dios.» By loving and «dreaming» him, Soledad has secured Agustín's reality and hence his survival beyond the grave. We now recognize the meaning of the *estribillo* repeated by Agustín's mother Sofía «¿Le arropasteis bien?,» which is later related to Christ by Soledad in Act III, scene I. The idea is that by keeping the child warm in her memory, by continuing to «dream» him, she is keeping him alive, just as the collective dreaming of mankind keeps the dead Christ alive to secure their immortality. So Agustín affirms «Tu hijo no murió, Soledad . . . Trae su caballo . . . , mi caballo . . . » (p. 658). And now finally Agustín can face death («viene la tierra») confident that it will not be the end. Andrés Franco's chapter title «El amor como camino de eternización»[15] is no less applicable to *Soledad* than to *Fedra.*

In *Soledad,* then, we see once more Unamuno's tendency to adapt a romantic scenario to express his inner vision and aspiration. A feature of his technique which we have recognized is to embroider on to the inherited figurative vocabulary, which remains halfhidden, a complex pattern of new symbols and metaphors, intended to lay bare the recesses of personality in the major characters, to «crear almas» as Agustín says, which will produce «escalofrío de alma» (p. 611) in the audience.

Iris Zavala in her pioneering book on Unamuno's theatre asserts, in my view correctly, that *Soledad* «es representativa de su segunda gran crisis, que culminará en *Cómo se hace una novela.*»[16] At the same time, that is, that this play looks back to *La esfinge,* it also looks forward to what is perhaps the dominant theme of Unamuno's later work; what is *serse*?, what constitutes the authenticity of the individual personality? In it we begin to see clearly how the problem of the survival of the personality became further complicated by the mystery of the personality itself. The imagery and symbolism of **Soledad** are suggested by this evolution.

In the foregoing essay an attempt has been made to explore the relationship between themes, imagery and symbolism in two closely related plays of Unamuno. Two conclusions may be tentatively advanced. The first is that Unamuno uses figurative language and symbolism almost exclusively to deepen the meaning of his plays or the psychological and spiritual complexity of the character in them. Rarely if ever is it successfully knitted into the actual dramatic structure of the plays themselves, as it is so often, for example, in Lorca. This is a further example of Unamuno's impatience with the technicalities of theatre craftsmanship. The second conclusion relates to his work as a whole, in which one of the few remaining central areas which still awaits a fully systematic and comprehensive study is that of his imagery and symbolism. I hope to have shown that in this connection an analysis of the relevant aspects of his theatre is an indispensible preliminary to any more general work.

Notes

1. (London, 1974), p. 36.

2. But see Iris Zavala, *Unamuno y su teatro de conciencia* (Salamanca, 1963), pp. 189-90 on mirror symbolism generally and Gilbert Smith, «Unamuno, Ortega and the 'Otro',» *Revista de Estudios Hispánicos,* VI, No. 3 (1972), esp. pp. 376-77 on the mirror and the key in *El otro.* Fragmentary references to the symbolism of soledad and the toy horse in the play *Soledad* are to be found in F. Sedwick, «Unamuno and Womanhood,» *Hispania,* XLIII, No. 3 (1960), 311 and M. García Blanco, «A propósito del drama *Soledad,* de Unamuno,» *Revista «Gran Via» de Actualidades, Artes y Letras,* 85 (1953), 11. Similarly E. García Luengo, «Teatro, *Soledad* de Unamuno. Drama inédito,» *Indice de Artes y Letras,* 68/9 (1953), 27 alludes to theatre imagery in the play, but without distinguishing among its different levels.

3. See my article «Three Plays of Unamuno: A Survey of his Dramatic Technique,» *Forum for Modern Language Studies,* XIII (1977), 253-63.

4. All bracketed page references to the plays are to this volume.

5. A. Gallego Morell, «Tres cartas inéditas de Unamuno a Ganivet,» *Insula,* 35 (1948), 1-2 & 7.

6. G. Ribbans, «Unamuno en 1899: su separación definitiva de la ideología progresista,» *Cuadernos de la Cátedra Miguel de Unamuno,* XII (1962), 15-30.

7. Cit. A. García Blanco in the prologue to *Obras Completas* (Madrid, 1958), XII, 11.

8. D. G. Turner, *op. cit.,* p. 151.

9. J. W. Butt, «Determinism and the Inadequacies of Unamuno's Radicalism, 1886-97,» *Bulletin of Hispanic Studies,* XLVI (1969), 226-40.

10. Cf. especially Unamuno's remark to Clarín in his letter to him of May 9, 1900: «en mi drama me he confesado más aún que en el *Nicodemo,*» cit. A. Franco, *El teatro de Unamuno* (Madrid, 1971), p. 63.

11. A. Franco, *op. cit.,* p. 159.

12. A. Franco, *op. cit.,* p. 160.

13. 'Los cerebrales', *La Ilustración Española y Americana,* October 22, 1899 (uncollected).

14. See my *Historia de la literatura española, el siglo XIX,* 3rd ed. (Barcelona, 1976), V, p. 37.

15. A. Franco, *op. cit.,* p. 139.

16. I. Zavala, *op. cit.,* p. 67.

Derek Gagen (essay date 1989)

SOURCE: Gagen, Derek. "Unamuno and the Regeneration of the Spanish Theatre." In *Re-Reading Unamuno,* edited by Nicholas G. Round, pp. 53-79. Glasgow: University of Glasgow Department of Hispanic Studies, 1989.

[*In the following essay, Gagen discusses the paradoxical nature of Unamuno's dramatic output, noting that although the writer experienced little critical or popular success with his plays during his lifetime, he nonetheless played an essential role in establishing pre-Civil War Spanish drama.*]

In his book of memoirs, *La arboleda perdida,* Rafael Alberti recalls how in 1931 he and María Teresa León invited Unamuno to their flat in Madrid and were surprised at his response when they urged him to read some of his latest work. They had expected Unamuno to recite some verse but instead he read them a play:

—¡Hombre, no! Verá usted—me atajó—. Preferiría leerles mi última obra de teatro, aún en borrador: *El hermano Juan.* Va a interesarles.[1]

Of course Unamuno knew that Alberti was the dramatist of the moment: *Fermín Galán* was in rehearsal and Unamuno had sent a telegram of support on the tumultuous first night of *El hombre deshabitado* a few months previously.[2] Alberti, writing twenty years later, had forgotten the content of the play and recalled only the effect that Unamuno made on them and on César Vallejo, who was also present. The anecdote bears repetition, however, for it illustrates the importance that Unamuno accorded to his drama.

Long before 1931 Unamuno had made clear that, for him, writing for the theatre was essential, not for the additional income it might provide,[3] but because he had things to say:

> Es un escándalo eso del teatro. Pero si me he metido en él no es por codicia, sino porque tengo cosas que decir que sólo por el teatro pueden llegar: cosas muy crudas y tal vez cínicas.[4]

Reading or sending his plays to friends was in practice the most frequent form in which Unamuno found an audience. The Albertis and César Vallejo were receptors just as Juan Barco and Jiménez Ilundain had been for the first redaction of *La esfinge* in 1899.[5] Unamuno was well aware that plays were designed for the stage and not for the printed word: 'Me resisto a imprimir obras de teatro, escritas para ser oídas y vistas, no para ser leídas.'[6] This declaration, uttered early in his career as a dramatist, leads Unamuno to establish a distinction between drama and theatre, echoed in 1918 in the 'Exordio' to *Fedra* and in the interview with Julio Romano at the premiere of *El otro* in 1932:

> *El otro* no es literatura dramática, sino teatro. No es para leído, sino para ser representado.[7]

Yet only late in his lifetime were any of his plays given professional productions in the mainstream of Spanish theatre. Unamuno felt that his plays expressed something important, uniquely capable of being communicated theatrically; yet they were spurned then, and even today few Unamuno specialists regard them as successful in theatrical terms. Paradoxically, however, the picture is not complete unless we add two further observations. First, in some sectors of the theatrical world Unamuno was highly regarded during his lifetime and, since his death, no consideration of the Spanish drama of the early twentieth century could be written without paying attention to his role and position, however negative the judgment of that role and position might ultimately be. And second, no account of the modern Spanish theatre could fail to devote some consideration to the essay 'La regeneración del teatro español' which was published in *La España Moderna*, 8, no. 91 (July, 1896). As a statement of the nature and purpose of the theatre, it takes its place in a line stretching from Jovellanos, through Böhl de Faber, Durán and others in the early nineteenth century, down to Grau, Araquistáin, Sastre and the many analysts of *la crisis teatral* who so proliferate in the Franco period.

It was this perception of a paradox, that a (commercially) unsuccessful playwright should have written an essay that is so influential, which led me to investigate in the present paper the relationship between Unamuno and the theatre of his time. I propose to consider briefly the more representative views of Unamuno's theatre, and to confront these with the responses of Unamuno's contemporaries, before proceeding to consider the circumstances in which Unamuno wrote his celebrated essay and began writing for the theatre. This will enable us to consider Unamuno's development within the framework of pre-Civil War drama and at least to ask whether his *drumas,* while as different from *dramas* as *nivolas* are from *novelas,* may not be just as worthy of attention.

The central paradox of Unamuno as a dramatist has been neatly conveyed by Edward Friedman who points out that Unamuno's novels have strong dramatic quality 'while his theatre has been considered anti-dramatic or lacking in dramatic technique'.[8] The *locus classicus* of negative assessments is Guillermo de Torre's essay 'Triedro de Unamuno'.[9] For Torre, Unamuno was consistently unaware of the technical restrictions imposed by each genre and, in the specific case of the theatre, ignored the demands and reactions of the audience. Here Torre used to considerable effect the reaction of Unamuno's correspondent Jiménez Ilundain to reading the first draft of *La esfinge*: 'Teatralmente es obra de quien jamás ha visto el teatro y apenas lo ha leído',[10] and the technical backwardness is emphasized in the consideration of each of the individual plays.[11]

Such a perception informs the work of most critics who have devoted themselves to Unamuno's theatre. With few exceptions they note a failure to adapt to the traditional demands of the genre and of the audience and they accordingly concentrate on thematic and biographical considerations. The full-length studies of Zavala and Franco offer rich examples of this approach.[12] Indeed, Andrés Franco's chapter on dramatic technique largely follows the strictures of Unamuno's contemporary correspondents on his lack of technical apprenticeship and merely develops arguments put forward by Lázaro Carreter in 1955.[13]

Lázaro's pioneering study was important mainly because it adopted a minimally analytic approach to the critical clichés regarding Unamuno's dramatic craftsmanship. His example was followed by Ruiz Ramón who, in his highly influential *Historia del teatro español,* vol. 2 (Madrid, 1971), emphasized 'el fracaso de la dramaturgia unamuniana en el plano de la realización estrictamente dramática. El teatro de Unamuno se queda, por así decirlo, en conato de teatro, por exceso de reducción formal' (p. 83). This emphasis on the schematic nature of the plays has been echoed by several critics recently. Donald Shaw has led the way in undertaking a detailed analysis of what are perceived as defects in dramatic craftsmanship. First examining the dramatic structure of *La esfinge* (1898), *Fedra* (1910) and *El otro* (1926), he identified two main areas of difficulty: Unamuno's habit of concentrating on conflicts within an individual rather than conflict between the individual and external pressures; and secondly the refusal on Unamuno's part to construct dramatic climaxes at the end of each act.[14] Shaw's article raises many questions—not least whether the standard naturalistic framework of exposition plus crisis is the only viable form theatrically—but it was the first to address with any degree of specificity the *idée reçue* of Unamuno's lack of craftsmanship. The critic's reliance on traditional criteria of *carpintería teatral* is a matter which leads him to conclusions that diverge from some commentators, such as Friedman and José Javier Granja, who feel that account should be taken of Unamuno's intention. Granja argues that the theatrical form employed by Unamuno derives from the central subject area,[15] while for Friedman too a structural analysis 'must necessarily comprehend the entire thematic framework implicit in the play rather than the finite bounds of onstage action'.[16]

Donald Shaw has further developed his analysis in a study of imagery and symbolism in *La esfinge* and *Soledad,*[17] this being, as we shall see, an important element in Unamuno's understanding of the theatre as discussed in 'La regeneración del teatro español'. (Indeed Shaw emphasizes that Unamuno's use of symbolism throughout his work still awaits analysis.) Here again, however, Shaw finds Unamuno's technique to be wanting: only rarely are figurative language and symbolism 'successfully knitted into the actual dramatic structure of the plays themselves'.

Now it may be that Shaw has chosen to seek dramatically effective use of symbols in the wrong plays. I have recently sought to suggest, for example, that in *La venda* Unamuno uses the symbol of blindness in a polysemic manner that is both fully theatrical and cognate with its use by a whole range of playwrights from Maeterlinck to Buero Vallejo.[18] In doing so, I have merely followed a distinguished band of commentators who have taken a far more positive view of Unamuno's contribution to the Spanish theatre and have moreover in some cases, like Donald Shaw, concerned themselves with the sign-systems of his theatrical discourse.

The main thrust of the 'new view' of Unamuno's theatre lies, however, in exposing his role in the reform or regeneration of the Spanish drama. In the highly influential series of essays originally published in *Triunfo* (January-March 1970) and collected as *Treinta años de teatro de la derecha* (Barcelona, 1971) José Monleón accorded very considerable importance to the role played by Unamuno in the technically innovative development of a new theatre in the early twentieth century. Following the avant-garde theorists such as Meyerhold, Monleón links the *pièce bien faite* and

criteria such as *carpintería teatral* with a paternalistic well-ordered world view. This mould is broken by Unamuno, Valle-Inclán and García Lorca. 'Los tres se negaron a aceptar el concepto de "teatralidad" acuñado por el público y la crítica tradicionales' (p. 142). In the case of Unamuno, Monleón discerns a refusal to bend to the dictatorship of a system which he criticizes in works such as 'La regeneración del teatro español'. Thus, to attack Unamuno's technique as nontheatrical is simply to accuse it of failing to conform to one sort of theatricality (p. 144). Monleón's thesis is developed more coherently in *El teatro del 98 frente a la sociedad española* (Madrid, 1975) where he probes the concept of theatricality, defined here as 'una visión y vivencia dramática de la realidad' and even more insistently sees a social context to Unamuno's drama:

> En esta gran lista de dramaturgos de la crisis social del viejo Occidente, donde figuran los Strindberg, Ibsen, Lenormand o Pirandello, Unamuno es el nombre español.

(p. 27)

The social context proposed by Monleón leads him—presumably because the collapse of the bourgeoisie in the nineteenth century is a broad phenomenon—to see Unamuno in European terms. In this he reaches conclusions closely similar to those of Ruiz Ramón in his *Estudios de teatro español clásico y contemporáneo* (Madrid, 1978). Whereas in his *Historia del teatro español* he had repeated the standard accusation against Unamuno's craftsmanship, while granting him pride of place in the chapter on 'Innovadores y disidentes', Ruiz Ramón now situates Unamuno in a line of reforming zealots. Indeed the revolutionary tradition is seen as stretching from Unamuno's essay of 1896 to Lorca's first tour with La Barraca in 1932 and, more significantly for our purpose, Unamuno's dramatic *depuración,* the suppression of theatrical ornament, is given a European context. Unamuno is seen as aspiring to what Jacques Copeau achieved at the Vieux Colombier from 1913. Yet, given the restrictions within which any innovator operated in the Spanish theatre at that time, Unamuno suffered from the *invisibilidad* which, for Ruiz Ramón, characterizes the situation of a number of leading playwrights.

On the other hand Gwynne Edwards in a stimulating survey of contemporary Spanish theatre, while relating Unamuno's drama to the work of other European playwrights of the twentieth century—Eliot, Beckett, Giraudoux, Cocteau—follows Shaw, Ribbans and Robertson in pinpointing the lack of 'genuine theatrical effectiveness'.[19] Indeed it may seem characteristic that a British Hispanist, essentially developing Ruiz Ramón's argument that the true perspective against which to view such dramatists is European, should nevertheless not accord major status to Unamuno.

The positive assessments of Unamuno's role associated with Monleón and Ruiz Ramón have been complemented by a pair of studies by María del Pilar Palomo which look at the semiotics of his theatre. The interest of her approach is that she is ultimately concerned with the same questions as Donald Shaw. Thus in her study of *La esfinge* she examines the process of communication—above all, symbol, gesture and other paraverbal elements—and suggests cogent reasons why Unamuno mistrusted the actors and directors on whom he needed to rely.[20] She sees this as a problem of reception, recognizing that this raises issues that are sociological rather than semiological; that is, the audience did not fail to understand (as Torre, Shaw, *et alii* seem to imply) but rejected the message or signal which they comprehended perfectly (as Monleón and Ruiz Ramón imply). Pilar Palomo clearly rejects the arguments of Torre. No less clearly by examining, as Donald Shaw has done, the use of symbol and myth, she reminds us that in this respect Unamuno was employing what were for Spain innovative strategies on stage.[21]

By establishing that there exists a duality of critical response to Unamuno's theatre, we have only served to confirm a picture already clear in his own lifetime. From the negative reaction to early redactions of *La esfinge,* to the rejection of his plays by Thuillier, Fernando Díaz de Mendoza and others, Unamuno received rebuff after rebuff from the theatrical establishment. But there is another side. By the end of his life Unamuno seemed to have entered the charmed circle of accepted habitués of the green room and dress rehearsal.

Two incidents involving Lorca illustrate this in telling manner. When Lorca arrived in Buenos Aires in October 1933, the name of Unamuno was raised by Pablo Suero in an interview published in *Noticias Gráficas*:[22]

—¿Y Unamuno qué dice?

—Pues verá usted, Unamuno no dice nada porque cuando uno le pregunta no contesta . . .

Y a poco de esto que puede parecer un modo de salir del paso, García Lorca habla con admiración del *Don Juan* de Unamuno, de *El otro,* de la enormidad de esta figura tan española y genial del viejo rector de Salamanca . . .

Here we have evidence that by the 1930s Unamuno had been accepted as part of the new literary world. This is seen most clearly in the press reports of the final dress rehearsal of *Yerma* in 1935. At that time the opening of a play in Madrid was attended by much press publicity. The evening newspapers carried accounts of the work for days before the first performance and, for the more important theatrical occasions, sent reporters to dress rehearsals and premiere so as to interview distinguished members of the audience. Thus Benavente or the Quinteros or some politician with literary interests

would express an instant opinion. By December 1935 Lorca was an established figure in the commercial theatre: the triumphs of 1933 in Madrid and Buenos Aires had ensured that. At the dress rehearsal we find not only La Argentinita and various actors but, as José Luis Salado reported in *La Voz,* 'también han venido las más ilustres barbas españolas: la de Unamuno, la de Valle-Inclán, la de don Jacinto'. Benavente left after the first Act, Valle chatted to an actress, and Unamuno characteristically, after praising *Yerma,* took the opportunity to plug *Raquel encadenada*.[23]

This anecdote seems exemplary. Unamuno was by now sufficiently in the swim of the *mundillo teatral* to visit the dress rehearsal at the Teatro Español, yet still felt the need to draw public attention to his own work. We must not forget, however, that Unamuno's importance had been asserted long before this by some of the most influential figures in the Spanish literary and theatrical world. When Monleón and Ruiz Ramón seek to establish the crucial nature of Unamuno's role they are indeed only following in the footsteps of figures as important as Diez-Canedo and Rivas Cherif.

The most influential statement of Unamuno's importance is found in Diez-Canedo's essay 'Panorama del teatro español desde 1914 hasta 1936', published in *Theatre in a Changing Europe* (New York, 1937) and later in *Hora de España.* After noting the importance of the role of Benavente in the sweeping changes of the 1890s, Díez-Canedo argued that the most effective efforts at renewal had come from writers such as Valle and Unamuno:

> Grandes escritores, no dedicados especialmente al teatro, han compuesto para él obras que nos dan las mejores novedades o los más vivos gérmenes de renovación a la hora actual. Así las de Miguel de Unamuno y las de Ramón del Valle-Inclán, hayan sido representadas o no. Es probable que, cuando se haga en lo futuro la historia del teatro español de estos tiempos, las tragedias y farsas de ambos escritores marquen sus valores más altos.[24]

Díez-Canedo had been making this point in reviews since the 1920s, while at the same time noting how productions of Unamuno's plays often disregarded the dramatist's intention. Thus the 'escenario vulgar' provided for the 1924 production of *Fedra* clashed with Unamuno's stage directions.[25] A cluttered set rendered ineffective the *tragedia desnuda.*

The significant point for our present discussion is, however, that this production 'por una compañía de tan buena voluntad como triste recordación' was part of an attempt to set up at the Teatro Martín, an Arts Theatre of the sort that Martínez Sierra had established at the Eslava from 1917.[26]

Indeed it becomes clear that Unamuno was widely regarded in the 1920s as an avant-garde dramatist working in the same non-naturalist mode as figures such as

Valle and Jacinto Grau. Thus we find that the most innovative director of the time, Cipriano Rivas Cherif, was responsible for a number of productions. On Unamuno's return from exile in February 1930, Rivas Cherif performed *Sombras de sueño* in Segovia, Salamanca and at the Español in Madrid.[27] He used some of Unamuno's plays with the students of the Teatro Escuela and they presented *La venda* in Salamanca in 1933.[28]

It is hardly surprising, then, that the most prestigious theatrical company in Spain, that of Margarita Xirgu, should have undertaken the first performance of *El otro* in December 1932. From the moment that the Xirgu-Borrás company had taken over the Español, they had produced a variety of classical and contemporary plays in the non-naturalistic mode, ranging from Calderón's *El gran teatro del mundo* to Alberti's *Fermín Galán* and using the stage in an invigoratingly original manner.[29]

By the 1930s, indeed, Unamuno had achieved a degree of acceptance within progressive literary circles undreamt of in the early years of the century when he so often complained of the cliques and cabals of the theatre world.[30] Unfortunately, by that time, his political stance and his move away from *engagement* had alienated him from the sort of politically committed literary figures who had applauded 'La regeneración del teatro español' in 1896. How this came about is the subject of the rest of this paper.

* * *

It is clear that the 1890s provide the key to an understanding of the development of Unamuno's thought and literary technique. Those few critics who have attempted to set 'La regeneración del teatro español' within the context of Unamuno's evolution have all emphasized the circumstances of that decade, although none—so far as I am aware—have linked the essay to an important debate in the Madrid press on the subject of a Spanish equivalent to Antoine's *Théâtre Libre*.

Of course it is twenty years since Pérez de la Dehesa, discussing Unamuno's period of active Socialism, emphasized what he termed the 'estética sociológica de Unamuno' which he traced in the essay on the drama, published in July 1896, and the lecture 'Sobre el cultivo de la demótica', delivered at Seville in December of the same year.[31] Clearly the same awareness of Volksgeist informed these statements as had imbued *En torno al casticismò*, published the previous year like 'La regeneración del teatro español' in *La España Moderna*. Herbert Ramsden's study of *En torno al casticismo* raised doubts regarding the sea change that Blanco Aguinaga, Pérez de la Dehesa and others saw as taking place in

Unamuno's thought: the shift from a Socialist stance to agonizing existential Christian thought might not be as clear-cut as was at first claimed.[32] However, Demetrios Basdekis in his study of 'El populismo del primer Unamuno' continued to emphasize the Utopian Socialist basis of the writings of the 1890s.[33]

Indeed Unamuno's concern with the social purpose of art at this stage of his career is demonstrated beyond doubt. Thus in the review of Joaquín Dicenta's *Juan José* published in *La Lucha de clases* in December 1895, he treats the play as if it were an accurate reflection of class reality. '¿Que si tiene tesis socialista?', he asks and in reply asserts that a Socialist message lies within any phenomenon:

> Tesis lo tiene todo en rigor; el movimiento de los astros tiene tesis astronómica, el movimiento de una máquina tiene tesis mecánica, el funcionamiento de un órgano animal tiene tesis fisiológica. Y en este sentido todo fenómeno social tiene hoy tesis socialista.

Thus, he concluded:

> El drama del señor Dicenta es bueno artísticamente por revelar la esencia de la vida social de hoy en uno de sus aspectos, por ser resplandor de la verdad, por revelamos la honda significación de un mundo. No es bueno por tener tesis socialista, sino que tiene tesis socialista por ser bueno.[34]

Yet this Socialism cohabited with a spiritual awareness even before the crisis in 1897. It comes as no surprise to read of Unamuno's appalled reaction when he attended the dress rehearsal of Dicenta's *El señor feudal*, four days before delivering the lecture 'Sobre el cultivo de la demótica':

> Ayer tarde me di el primer baño de charco. Estuve al ensayo general de la obra de Dicenta que se estrenará mañana, *El señor feudal*. Teatro teatral, y lo que es peor inmoral e irreligioso. Todo lo peor de la burguesía trasladado al pueblo, y en vez de elevado ideal cristiano tono de odio, de rencor, de envidia. Llaman por ahí socialismo a una de las cosas más repugnantes que conozco.[35]

The correspondence with Mugica shows clearly the tensions between Unamuno's Socialist materialism and the idealistic side to his temperament. Thus in a letter written in May 1895 he wrote:

> Soy socialista convencido, pero, amigo, los que aquí figuran como tales son intratables; fanáticos necios de Marx, ignorantes, ordenancistas, intolerantes, llenos de prejuicios de origen burgués, ciegos a las virtudes y a los servicios de la clase media, desconocedores del proceso evolutivo, en fin, que de todo tienen menos de sentido social. A mí empiezan a llamarme místico, idealista y qué sé yo cuántas cosas más. Me incomodé cuando les oí la enorme barbaridad de que para ser socialista hay que abrazar el materialismo.[36]

The materialism of scientific Socialism had never appealed to Unamuno. As he had asserted to Mugica in May 1893, Socialism is a matter of moral and religious reform. Thus he is far from surprised that Tolstoy, Ibsen, Amicis, are attracted to Socialism:

> Nos vamos a él todos los que tenemos abierta el alma a la verdadera realidad. Y adelantará más según se vaya borrando el rastro del pedantesco e insufrible Carlos Marx y se vayan disipando las garrulerías de Bebel. El socialismo es ante todo una gran reforma *moral y religiosa*, más que económica.[37]

It is this tension between the deterministic materialism (be it Socialism or evolutionary determinism) and the idealism within Unamuno's mental framework that will account for the nature of his plea for regeneration in the theatre of Spain.

Given his concern to understand the people and circumstances of Spain it was natural that Unamuno should turn his attention to the theatre. Indeed in the third article in the series *En torno al casticismo* he had discussed Calderón at some length. In a note to 'La regeneración del teatro español' he reminded his readers of this:

> En esta misma Revista, en el número de Abril de 1895, tomo LXXVI, hice reflexiones acerca de Calderón en este respecto, en el tercero de los cinco artículos que bajo el título común de 'En torno al casticismo'. me hizo la Revista la gracia de publicar. El presente ensayo es en esencia consecuencia y secuela de aquéllos.[38]

Nothing could be more clear: the logic of 'En torno al casticismo' urged him to consider Spain's theatre.

Unamuno was turning his gaze on that theatre at a particularly interesting moment in its development and, as it happens, at a period about which we are unusually well informed. In his *Le Théâtre en Espagne,* published in 1897, Henry Lyonnet provided a detailed account of the theatrical life of Madrid. It is a surprising picture, with only the Teatro Real, the Español and the Comedia not devoted entirely to *género chico*; and a gloomy account is given of Emilio Mario leaving the Comedia after twenty-two years:

> Seul, au milieu de difficultés sans nombre, perdant tour à tour ses meilleurs éléments de succès qui passaient en Amérique, en province ou à l'*Espagnol,* il a tenu tête à l'orage pendant vingt-deux ans dans ce théâtre de la *Comedia* qu'il avait inauguré en 1875, et dont il se voit forcé de fermer les portes à Pâques 1897, en quête d'un local pour la saison prochaine, ce dernier refuge de la comédie sérieuse étant livré à son tour à la *zarzuela*! Signe des temps.[39]

This was the company which had produced the first performance of Dicenta's *Juan José,* with Thuillier (who was to turn down **La esfinge**), and of *Doña Per-* *fecta.* Its travails amply demonstrate why Unamuno found it so hard to break into the world of the Spanish theatre. At the same time Lyonnet reports that the *género chico* and *zarzuela* such as *La marcha de Cádiz* gave three hundred performances in the 1896-97 season at the Eslava.[40]

There was, however, something more positive for Lyonnet to report. He had noted slightly that in France the Comédie Française was at least the home of Molière, whereas the Madrid theatre had almost forgotten the classics of the Spanish Golden Age. Indeed the Teatro Español had been blacked out until January 1895 when María Guerrero had taken it over for ten years. La Guerrero's mixture of classic and modern plays is seen to be a genuinely innovating element in the world of Spanish theatre, and Lyonnet describes in some detail the production of Lope's *El castigo sin venganza* with María Guerrero and her husband Fernando Díaz de Mendoza as the incestuous lovers.

Lyonnet's account offers an important context for Unamuno's essay published the previous year. However, although the French critic describes the work of Galdós, Benavente, and Dicenta, he does not refer to the important debates about theatre which were going on in literary reviews and the press.

In recent years scholars have uncovered a mass of evidence to show how, in Barcelona and in Madrid (often in that order), an awareness of naturalism and symbolism was built up. Following Anna Balakian, Rubio Jiménez argues that these two were but facets of the same philosophical fatalism, Zola and Maeterlinck representing different technical solutions to an identical intellectual problem perhaps.[41] Ibsen and the Scandinavians, anarchists and Socialists, all were grist to the mill of writers on the theatre in the little magazines of the 1890s. And plays such as Cano's *La Pasionaria, El pan del pobre* (the adaptation of Hauptmann's *Weavers* by González Llana and Francos Rodríguez), and Galdós' *La de San Quintín*—all mentioned by Unamuno in his essay—had evoked praise and commentary among progressive writers.

Nothing demonstrates more remarkably the degree to which Spanish intellectual circles were open to theatrical debates and issues from across the Pyrenees than the polemic on the *Théâtre Libre* which filled the pages of *Los Lunes del Imparcial* in July and August 1896.

Commentators such as Clarín had long been aware of the significance of André Antoine's *Théâtre Libre,* founded in 1887, as had the Catalan modernists.[42] By 1896 the idea of a *Teatro libre* had developed a long way from Antoine's conception, at least in Madrid, to judge from the question posed to a number of distinguished writers in the issue of *Los Lunes del Imparcial* on 6th July 1896:

¿Cree usted conveniente la fundación de ese teatro para los fines del arte?

¿Entiende usted que cabe en el género dramático más amplitud de la que existe y que es posible admitir en nuestro tiempo la libertad de fondo y forma propia del Teatro Clásico Español?

Since Echegaray, Pereda, Eusebio Blanco and Clarín responded to the question in that same number, I deduce that the enquiry was not conceived overnight. It seems more than likely that Unamuno had wind of the *encuesta* when writing 'La regeneración del teatro español', also published in July 1896.

The responses to the questions are, with the exception of those of Clarín, uniformly depressing in their obsession with questions of public morality and decency, and their failure to see the need for reform. A characteristic response was that of Pardo Bazán who attacked *Juan José,* expressing surprise at its being performed in 'un teatro correctísimo', and censured the crudity of María Guerrero's production of *El castigo sin venganza.* When Gómez de Baquero reported upon the debate in the August number of *La España moderna,*[43] he tartly observed that 'no se trata de un teatro libre, sino de un teatro *más libre* que el actual'. Moreover, he observed that the concern with the morality of art is a red herring: art, he affirms, is neither moral nor immoral, but amoral. With considerable perception he emphasized the commercial structure of theatre, the cult of popularity:

En el teatro tal como hoy se halla establecido o sea en el teatro de empresa, influirá siempre de un modo decisivo el gusto del público, tanto por ser aquél un negocio industrial cuanto por la naturaleza de la representación, que es, como se ha dicho, un verdadero juicio oral y público. Por reformar el teatro hay que empezar por reformar el público.

(pp. 117-18)

It would seem, then, that July 1896 was an appropriate time for Unamuno to have published his essay. It may have been 'en esencia consecuencia y secuela' to the five articles in the series *En torno al casticismo,* but it also added an extra element to a wide-ranging debate on the role and nature of the theatre in Spain. Furthermore, in his essay Unamuno was to take into account numerous features later described by Lyonnet—the influences of the musical theatre; the commercial nature of the theatre industry; the role of actors; the revival of Golden Age theatre—and to contrast most of these with the breath of renewal that could also be discerned.

It might be asked what experience Unamuno had of the theatre. His correspondence shows familiarity with Ibsen as early as 1893,[44] and in 1892 he began his reading of Sudermann whose name constantly surfaces in the correspondence with Mugica. Unamuno translated *Die*

Ehre, published in *El Nervión* as *La honra*—or 'El honor' as Unamuno entitled it when writing to Mugica in May 1895 announcing that Fernández Villegas (i.e. 'Zeda') was to adapt it for the stage.[45] Unamuno was clearly aware of the problems that this might involve for later in 1895, with reference to a play that Mugica hoped to have produced, he wrote:

Me dijo Rafael Rochelt que pensaba usted venir por el otoño y yo asocié esto a la obra teatral que tiene usted presentado. Me parece que se hace ilusiones, pues según mis informes no hay cosa más pesada que el hacer que le pongan a uno en escena; como en todo rige la recomendación y el favoritismo.[46]

Unamuno's prejudices were soon to be confirmed. As we noted above, in December 1896 he visited the dress rehearsal of Dicenta's *El señor feudal,* and although flattered by the deference shown him by critics and playwrights alike, he felt depressed by them:

No se salen de su pequeño círculo, no ven más allá de Madrid, no sienten, no oyen, no razonan.[47]

They seemed to Unamuno to lack culture and vision. The fiasco of Zeda's version of Unamuno's Sudermann translation doubtless confirmed his pessimism. It was in rehearsal by February 1897 and proved a success. But, as Unamuno reported:

Ha obtenido éxito franco el desarreglo que Villegas ha hecho de mi traducción de 'La honra', a la que ha puesto por nombre 'El bajo y el principal'. Se empeñó en hacer mangas y capirotes por miedo, no sé a qué . . .[48]

Within a few months of the publication of his plea for the regeneration of the theatre, then, Unamuno was to have his diagnosis of its ills confirmed. A serious play had been distorted to suit the tastes of the public.

* * *

The essay itself took pride of place in the July issue of *La España Moderna* and despite the loose format—Unamuno refers to them as 'deshilvanadas notas'—the argument is clear enough.

His initial observation is simple, namely that critical attention had of late been concentrating both on the drama of Spain's Golden Age and on that being produced elsewhere in Europe in the late nineteenth century. Unamuno proposed to recall the history of Spanish drama and leave the reader in a position to:

fijarse en los males que hoy éste [el teatro] sufre, y examinar luego las tendencias nuevas, *forma* de la regeneración, y la vida dramática del pueblo español actual, *fondo* de ella.

(6; *OC* [*Obras completas*], I, 890)

The close link between *pueblo*—which he will clearly distinguish from *público,* the theatre audiences of the time—and reform or renewal is thus established from the opening of the essay.

The section 'Algo, muy breve, de historia' follows the method familiar from *En torno al casticismo.* Unamuno's account of the history of Spanish drama emphasizes the importance of the *pueblo,* even while bringing out the religious nature of the mystery plays alongside the farces and pantomimes of profane tradition. (He was of course to produce in **El otro** his own updated mystery play.) But he sees no clash between sacred and profane: the tension rather lies between popular and learned (*erudito*) tradition. Here will lie the nucleus of his findings and of his prescription for an end to the theatre's ills:

> Cuando las dos tendencias se unen y el proceso docto informa al vulgar tomando de él materia y alma, el drama sube en excelencia, pero siempre que los doctos se apartan del pueblo, caen ellos en el cultivo de vaciedades muertas y el pueblo en recrearse con truculentos disparates.

> (8; *OC,* I, 892)

Such at the end of the essay will be his view of contemporary Spanish theatre. It is clear that for Unamuno at this stage of his development as a thinker the role of the *pueblo* is paramount. That is why here (8; *OC,* I, 892n) and in the essay 'Sobre el cultivo de la demótica'[49] he emphasized the value of folklore studies. But 'la expresión más genuina de la conciencia colectiva del pueblo' lies in the theatre (10; *OC,* I, 893) for it is a collective activity involving interaction between audience and creator:

> El teatro es algo colectivo, es donde el público interviene más y el poeta menos.

> (11; *OC,* I, 894)

For Unamuno this relationship reaches its height in Lope, a genuinely popular dramatist, whereas Calderón was national—or perhaps *castizo,* in the terms of the third article of *En torno al casticismo.*

Having placed these cards on the table Unamuno now addresses himself to the ills of the contemporary Spanish stage. He calls as witness 'Zeda', that same Fernández Villegas who was so to pervert Unamuno's Sudermann translation, but who had published a caustic commentary on the state of the theatre in *El imparcial* the previous year. Zeda had castigated the formula-ridden comic diversion that filled the theatres. However, Unamuno adds a note of caution. Some popular theatre, the *género chico,* was 'lo que queda de más vivo y más real' (14; *OC,* I, 896). What was wrong with the theatre was its reliance on formulae:

> Conviene en ocasiones tales la irrupción en escena de algún *bárbaro* que ahuyente al público no pueblo, un azote de todo convencionalismo. No importe que fracase; ha abierto vereda por donde pueden pasar los dramas no teatrales. Sí, dramas no teatrales.

> (15; *OC,* I 896)

For the first time Unamuno was to suggest the possibility of there being another way of going about writing drama. The way that he rejected was easily described. Dramatists lived in a self-enclosed world that fed upon itself. They did not come from the people; they went to the people for a good story from time to time. But the audience of most theatres were *público* not *pueblo.* Only in genuinely popular halls such as the *Novedades* (where *El pan del pueblo* had been played) did the audience have 'aglo de pueblo' (16; *OC,* I, 897).

Not until this stage does Unamuno begin to discuss new trends in the theatre, returning to his initial observation: the Spanish classics and the European moderns. 'Por un lado Ibsen, por otro Calderón; lo sensato juntarlos' (17; *OC,* I, 898). Thus he praises the *lunes clásicos* which María Guerrero had put on at the Español, at which Lyonnet had seen the performance of *El castigo sin venganza.*[50] But it was also necessary to 'abrir el pecho a lo moderno' (18; *OC,* I, 898). By this he understood three main tendencies—realism, thesis drama, and symbolism—and to these he now devoted lengthy discussions. Recent studies by critics such as Rubio Jiménez have clearly established that each of these areas of theatrical activity had received publicity in Spanish intellectual circles. However, Unamuno does not necessarily take what might seem the party line of *La España Moderna, La Lucha de Clases,* and other radical journals to which he contributed. His well-known horror of pedantry no doubt led him to berate the detailed photographic accuracy of realists and naturalists. 'El teatro vivo sale del pueblo' (20; *OC,* I, 900) and theatrical convention, itself a response to 'la visión popular', suggests that naturalistic acting styles are unlikely to be successful.

This important passage suggests that Unamuno was rather more aware of questions of technique than is generally accounted to be the case. Naturalistic staging and verisimilitude had begun to replace the conventions of Romantic acting tradition. I have referred elsewhere to the significance of Benavente's stage direction early in Act I of *El nido ajeno* when the actor playing Manuel, about to deliver a speech on the human condition, is instructed to avoid 'el tono solemne y declamatorio'.[51] Yet for Unamuno traditional acting conventions, based on what the *pueblo* will accept, are vital. In a note he criticizes 'cierta engañosa naturalidad en el diálogo que se logra a costa de que no lo oigan en el paraíso los que para oírlo pagan'. The shouts of 'más alto' from the gods are, in Unamuno's eyes, a sufficient condemnation of naturalistic acting (21; *OC,* I, 900n).

This awareness of the semiotics of acting also led Unamuno to a critique of the piling up of naturalistic detail
and the slanted plots of thesis plays. It is the audience
that draws the moral or message, for the artist, whether
he seeks to or not, cannot but express his *Weltanscha-
uung*: 'el artista es moral por fuerza, y su moralidad,
buena o mala, tiñe su visión y empapa su obra' (22;
OC, I, 901). But this is not the sort of moral-majority
stance exemplified in the responses of Pereda and Pardo
Bazán to the *Imparcial* questionnaire on 'Teatro ¿libre?'.
The cathartic purpose of theatre, which serves as a 'lib-
erador de pasiones' is sufficient morality. Unamuno
points to the paradox of a *bien pensant* audience which
'se asusta de ver en escena *El castigo sin venganza,* y
se precipita a presenciar vistas de causas públicas desnudas de todo velo público' (23; *OC,* I, 902).

For Unamuno, then, traditional theatre conventions and
subjects are justified. He is far from extolling all
European importations or fashions even at this early
stage of his career. Zola is attacked for clinical detail:
he is at his best 'cuando habla en necio' (24; *OC,* I,
903n). It is absurd to seek to employ scientific determinism in art (25; *OC,* I, 903n). On the other hand, Unamuno welcomes the interest in psychological probing.
Here again we find evidence of concerns that will be
central to his own drama:

> Naturalísimo es que en el teatro se tire a mostrar la re-
> alidad total y el interior de las almas.

(24; *OC,* I, 902)

Thus, monologues are so important, he declares, and
other non-naturalistic devices such as the appearance of
ghosts and 'todo lo maravilloso' on the stage. We see,
therefore, that here too the essentially fictive—rather
than mimetic—devices that are so much a feature of
Unamuno's dramaturgy are justified in this early essay.
The dramatist who used asides, as Franco notes,[52] when
others had long since abandoned the technique, or
produced the *monodiálogos* throughout his career, was
self-consciously aware of the effects they would
produce. Monologue allowed the psychological depth
that Unamuno sought in drama and which brought back
to the theatre 'remozado y vigorizado en baño de mayor
realidad, el espíritu que informó nuestros autos sacramentales y los dramas alegóricos' (25; *OC,* I, 903). For
Unamuno, symbolist theatre meant a return to a theatre
of ideas. Calderón and Tirso had used allegorical
representation to communicate popular religious belief:
modern dramatists must seek the vital symbols of the
faith that the *pueblo* held in 1896 (26; *OC,* I, 904).

What Unamuno meant by this is clarified in the section
'El teatro popular y el nacional'. Here again he
emphasizes the importance of responding to the *pueblo*
of contemporary Spain as Lope had done to the *pueblo*
of his day. As before he distinguishes between the

national dramatist Calderón and the popular Lope. Of
course Unamuno's concept of Lope is hardly one that
today's scholars would recognize, but the message is
clear:

> Todas las tendencias apuntadas concurrían a la reforma
> del teatro, pero su verdadera regeneración está en que
> vuelva a ser lo que fue, en que se sumerja en su primi-
> tiva e íntima esencia, sofocada en el ámbito histórico.

(26; *OC,* I, 904)

The essence of Spain's theatrical had, therefore, been
choked in the historical circumstances of Restoration
Spain. The conservative bourgeoisie[53] were stifling the
popular spirit in the theatre and so the theatre would
presumably need to look elsewhere. Unamuno now
proceeds to suggest that the historical process must be
understood: the break-up of old style patriotism, leading
divergently to regionalism and internationalism, suggests that the new theatre will need to take cognisance
of these new realities. The way forward has been shown
by Galdós. If only he had applied to *Realidad* the
original idea of *La de San Quintín;* if only he would
dramatize *Doña Perfecta*—as, of course, he did later in
that year. Moreover, Unamuno can point to genuinely
popular successes: Cano's *La Pasionaria; El pan del
pobre,* the adaptation of Hauptmann's *Weavers.* Such
plays reflect the change in popular consciousness that
Unamuno discerns for they were applauded by the
pueblo, not the fashionable 'todo Madrid' (32; *OC,* I,
907).[54]

Were this Unamuno's only conclusion, we might well
be tempted to argue that he had manifestly failed both
to discern all the dramatic currents present in the 1890s
and to obey his own advice when he came to write for
the stage. Yet we have seen that earlier in the essay he
pointed the way precisely to the drama of interior
struggle that was to be his distinctive contribution.
Moreover, these final pages of the essay show a much
greater breadth of vision than applause for Galdós and
Hauptmann might indicate. Thus, having discussed the
role of a collective protagonist as a kind of modern
chorus in Hauptmann, Unamuno also draws attention to
the Wagnerian synthesis of theatre arts:

> el teatro mismo que tomado en amplísimo sentido rep-
> resenta el fondo primero de donde brotaron diferen-
> ciándose las artes, y en la literaria la épica y la lírica,
> volverá a reunirlas en poderosa síntesis como tal vez
> fundirá de nuevo lo profano con lo religioso.

In a note, Unamuno emphasizes the role of Wagner in
such a synthesis and adds: 'Aún no ha influído Wagner
lo que debiera fuera de la música' (29; *OC,* I, 906).

Such a synthesis, characteristic of the symbolist, non-
naturalistic tradition that we associate with Maeterlinck,
may seem foreign to Unamuno's dramatic technique,

which tends to a bare essentialism. But the final pages of the essay only serve to corroborate the importance of idealistic—rather than realistic—elements in Unamuno's conception of the stage.

Unamuno's plea for religious theatre sets out as an attack on the capitalist framework of the Spanish stage. For Unamuno:

> En el fondo de todo problema literario y aún estético, se halla, como en el fondo de todo lo humano, una base económica y un alma religiosa.
>
> (32; *OC,* I, 908)

It is absurd, then, for critics and scholars, well fed and warmly wrapped, to ignore the economics of literary productions. The trouble lies in the box-office:

> En contaduría es donde puede ahondarse los elementos de nuestra dramaturgia y estética teatral.
>
> (33; *OC,* I 909)

Yet in the days of Spain's theatrical Golden Age laws of supply and demand did not decide such matters. To Unamuno it is appalling that a poet such as Burns should have ended his days in the Excise Division checking the specific gravity of beer. And so the essay concludes with the dream of an age when machines will leave men free for artistic endeavour. That will be the age of the Nietzschean superman, not the most brutish but the most human.

The vision is of a theatre that is religious. On a Sunday afternoon the masses crowd to see it:

> La muchedumbre se agolpa al aire libre, bajo el ancho cielo común a todos, de donde sobre todos llueve luz de vida, de visión y de alegría; va a celebrar el pueblo un *misterio* comulgando en espíritu en el altar del Sobre-Arte.

This passage, as Rubio Jiménez remarks,[55] might have found its place in an anarchist journal of the times. Unamuno ends with a fantasy more akin to Robespierre's *Fête de l' Etre Suprême* than to the products of André Antoine's *Théâtre Libre.*

In the context of *En torno al casticismo* and 'Sobre el cultivo de la demótica', Unamuno's essay may well have the significance accorded to it by Pérez de la Dehesa and Basdekis. Yet in the year before the great religious crisis which was to lead to the first two plays *La esfinge* and *La venda,* Unamuno showed considerable awareness of the problems besetting the Spanish theatre and proposed solutions that could only be termed Socialist, within the idiosyncratic model of Socialism that characterized his political beliefs in the 1890s. His analysis reflects the same mixture of naturalism and symbolism as has been discerned in the theatre of that

decade by recent commentators and the influence of symbolism, already greatly emphasized in the essay, came to assume an even greater significance and even at one stage seemed likely to divert him from the theatre. In February 1897 he wrote to Mugica after the publication of *Paz en la guerra:*

> Nada de teatro, por Dios, nada de teatro. Nadie debe salirse de su terreno, y yo voy de la novela no al teatro, sino a las meditaciones filosófico religiosas, a las *rêveries* al modo de Maeterlinck o de Schleiermacher. Acabaré escribiendo sermones laicos y libros de meditaciones. El teatro es muy cortante.[56]

The reference to Maeterlinck is clearly to *Le Trésor des humbles,* praised as 'de lo que más me gusta moderno francés' in a letter dated 28th July 1898.[57] When he did turn to the theatre, later in that year,[58] it was in order to write *La esfinge,* in which a politically active character turns from revolution to a concern with the inner life, a work whose naturalistic staging may seem to clash with its symbolist message, other than in the celebrated scene with the mirror that closes Act I.[59]

Yet it is surely the scene with the mirror, or the chilling final scene of *La venda,* with María—her eyes bandaged—holding her dead father's cold hand, which pointed the way for Unamuno. It is multilayered symbolism of action and attitude which provided a new grammar for the theatre and in later years made critics such as Diez-Canedo show respect for Unamuno as an innovator. In the essay of 1896 Unamuno had evinced enough concern with non-naturalistic acting, with symbolist drama, with the revelation of a character's soul, to suggest that he was not likely to work within the naturalistic genre which, under Benavente's influence, was to dominate the stage for decades after 1896.

We should perhaps recall that Diez-Canedo linked Unamuno with Valle-Inclán as the truly interesting playwrights of the 1920s. Bearing in mind the argument of John Lyon in *The Theatre of Valle-Inclán,* namely that Valle's divergence from the ground-rules of the stage in the early twentieth century derived from his underlying philosophy,[60] perhaps it is time for critics to ask what effects are produced by such divergence in the case of Unamuno.

After all, Unamuno's well-documented impatience with contemporary theatre practice was no less considerable than Valle's. When he added to the cast-list of *Soledad* 'la criada inevitable', he was making a valuable point, no less valuable than those he made in the 'Exordio' to *Fedra* or the 'Autocrítica' to *El otro.* Can we really criticize him for rejecting the advice, vouchsafed by Jiménez Ilundain, to study Sardou and Echegaray?[61] What he sought to achieve was not the sort of dramatic craftsmanship or *carpintería teatral* beloved by Benavente and his band.

The scope of the present paper does not allow me to pursue this point further other than to sketch out the issues that are raised. Shaw's analysis seems here to offer a fruitful basis for future investigation. He has noted the changes made in the Phaedra plot by Unamuno when compared with the dramatic structures employed by Euripides and Racine. A useful comparison might be established between Unamuno's *Fedra* of 1910 (rejected by María Guerrero) and Benavente's *La malquerida* of 1913 (in which La Guerrero triumphed). Shaw's study highlights the diminished role of the nurse in *Fedra,* and the very early placing by Unamuno of the declaration in Act I. In Benavente's play, the roles are reversed: Acacia is a bewildered Hippolytus and Esteban a latter-day Phaedra. There *is* a climax at the end of each act but, true to this sort of dramatic exposition—it is the grammar of the detective story—the effect is a step-by-step revelation. Esteban's longings are revealed and, slowly, Acacia comes to realize that she shares them. The method is different in the two plays—and so is the dramatic purpose.

Where such a comparison might most clearly reveal Unamuno's methodology is in his mystery play *El otro.* The latter-day Calderonian mode of plays such as Alberti's *El hombre deshabitado,* in the rich vein of Margarita Xirgu's revival of *El gran teatro del mundo,* contrasts with the spare sobriety of staging in *El otro.* This suggests that Unamuno ultimately sought a 'poor theatre' solution rather than the 'total theatre' of Valle, Alberti, and the avant-garde. In eliminating the complex naturalistic or expressionistic sets so characteristic of the early twentieth-century drama, Unamuno seems to anticipate the 'poor theatre' of Jerzy Grotowski. In the 'Exordio' to *Fedra* he made clear that the tragedy was to be played before a white sheet as backcloth, with the actors in simple modern dress:

> No quiere necesitar esta tragedia del concurso de pintor escenógrafo, ni de sastre y modisto, ni de peluquero. Aspiro a que cuanto diga y exprese Fedra, por ejemplo, sea de tal intensidad trágica, que los espectadores—y sobre todo las espectadoras—no tengan que distraerse mirando cómo va vestida la actriz que la representa.[62]

Similarly, in the 'Autocrítica' to *El otro,* Unamuno rejected 'Esas minucias del arte realista de justificar las entradas y las salidas de los sujetos y hacer coherentes otros detalles'.[63]

The style of playing demanded by such a text is that described by Grotowski in *Towards a Poor Theatre* as a 'via negativa':

> In terms of formal technique, we do not work by proliferation of signs, or by accumulation of signs (as in the formal repetition of oriental theatre). Rather, we subtract, seeking *distillation* of sign by eliminating those elements of 'natural' behaviour which obscure pure impulse.[64]

Grotowski speaks of 'gradually eliminating whatever proved superfluous', such as make-up, costume, lighting, as well as the division between audience and actors. It is this actor-spectator relationship—in some ways less close in Unamuno's theatre than is that of character and reader in the fictions—which Unamuno stops short of developing. His dramas never break through the proscenium arch as do those of Pirandello. Yet it remains the case that Unamuno's plays need the services of what Grotowski terms the 'holy actor':

> The technique of the 'holy actor' is an *inductive technique* (i.e. a technique of elimination), whereas that of the 'courtesan actor' is a *deductive technique* (i.e. an accumulation of skills).[65]

Despite Grotowski's emphasis on physical training, on the basic exercises that prepare the body, the decisive factor is 'the actor's technique of psychic penetration'.[66] Similarly, the audience is not there to be entertained, or to have 'cultural needs' satisfied:

> We are concerned with the spectator who has genuine spiritual needs and who really wishes, through confrontation with the performance, to analyse himself.[67]

Reading these words we recall Unamuno's declaration in the 'Autocrítica' to *El otro*:

> no he escrito esta obra no más que para que los espectadores y las espectadoras pasen el rato, mascullando acaso chocolatinas.[68]

In this, of course, Unamuno was at one with that other avant-garde of Valle-Inclán, Alberti, Lorca, Aub, *et alii* and it is understandable that he should by 1932 at last have achieved *entrée* into the green room of the Español.

If, however, Unamuno had been accepted by some critics and fellow playwrights, other more radical commentators were by the 1930s turning against him. Their judgment, most damning in view of what he had proclaimed in the essay of 1896, was that he had betrayed the *pueblo*.

The tone of the new committed criticism had been set by Luis Araquistáin in *La batalla teatral* (Madrid, 1930), a study which reads at times like an updated version of 'La regeneración del teatro español'. Unamuno's distinction between *pueblo* and *público* is still the basis of the argument, and still a *renovación* from abroad is being called for. But Araquistáin's Socialist stance, with its paradoxical call for a *teatro de minorías,* soon gave way before more radical onslaughts. The sharpest of the radical commentators of the 1930s was Ramón Sender. In an essay on Pabst's film version of *The Threepenny Opera,* Sender compared it with the bourgeois dross that was on offer elsewhere:

No se concibe que después de aplaudir una película como ésa se puede tolerar *Una hora contigo o El beso fatal,* pornografía fácil en el cine. O *Santa Rusia o El otro,* novedosismo despistado o testarudez frente al espejo, en el teatro. Benavente, el elegante y el *artístico,* o Unamuno, el tozudo y el beodo del espíritu, no pueden comprender ya nada de eso.[69]

The Moscow periodical *International Literature* saw *El otro,* like *San Manuel Bueno, mártir,* as 'a serious menace at the present stage of the revolutionary movement among the Spanish intelligentsia'. For the Russian commentator, 'the collective principle and its expression—the masses—are altogether absent in Unamuno's work'.[70] Perhaps the theatre was still in need of regeneration: Unamuno has apparently been left behind.

And yet there was still the old enemy, the formula-laden theatre of the easy joke and sniggering innuendo. In the month that saw the premiere of *El otro* at the Español, the playgoer could see *Crime and punishment, El gran galeoto,* and a couple of classics; but the Madrid stage also offered *El milionario y la bailarina* of Pilar Millán Astray; *El orgullo de Albacete* of Paso y Abati, and *En la pantalla las prefieren rubias* of Serrano Anguita.

Notes

1. Rafael Alberti, *La arboleda perdida* (Buenos Aires: Compañía General Fabril, 1959).

2. ibid, p. 310.

3. Andrés Franco, *El teatro de Unamuno* (Madrid: Insula, 1971), p. 38.

4. Letter to Juan Arzadún (24th November 1909), quoted in *OC,* V, *Teatro completo y monodiálogos,* 39.

5. Cf. *OC,* V, 15-30.

6. *OC,* V, 7.

7. *OC,* V, 88.

8. E. H. Friedman, 'From Concept to Drama; the Other Unamuno', *Hispanófila,* 23, no. 68 (1980), 29.

9. Guillermo de Torre, *La difícil universalidad española* (Madrid: Gredos, 1965), pp. 200-56.

10. *OC,* V, 15.

11. Torre, p. 206. It is unfortunate that Torre failed to make use of other available materials which, as we shall see, make clear that Unamuno was familiar with a good deal of late nineteenth-century drama.

12. Franco, *El teatro de Unamuno,* passim; Iris M. Zavala, *Unamuno y su teatro de conciencia* (Salamanca: Universidad, 1963).

13. F. Lázaro Carreter, 'El teatro de Unamuno', *CCMU* [*Cuadernos de la Cátedra Miguel de Unamuno*], 7 (1956), 5-29.

14. D. L. Shaw, 'Three Plays of Unamuno: a Survey of his Dramatic Technique', *FMLS* [*Forum for Modern Language Studies*], 13 (1977), 253-64.

15. José Javier Granja, 'El problema de la personalidad a través del teatro de Unamuno', *LetD* [*Letras de Deusto*], 14 (1977), 105-27.

16. Friedman, p. 36.

17. D. L. Shaw, 'Imagery and Symbolism in the theatre of Unamuno: *La esfinge* and *Soledad*', *JSS* [*Journal of Spanish Studies*], 7 (1979), 87-104.

18. D. H. Gagen, '"Veo mejor desde que he cegado." Blindness as a Dramatic Symbol in the Plays of Buero Vallejo', *MLR* [*Modern Language Review*], 81 (1986), 637.

19. Gwynne Edwards, *Dramatists in Perspective: Spanish Theatre in the Twentieth Century* (Cardiff: University of Wales Press, 1985); Geoffrey Ribbans, 'La obra de Unamuno en la perspectiva de hoy', *CCMU,* 27-29 (1983), 7-24; David Robertson, 'Unas notas sobre el teatro de Unamuno', *CCMU,* 27-29 (1983), 175-80.

20. María del Pilar Palomo, 'El proceso comunicativo de *La esfinge*' in *Semiología del teatro,* ed. L. García Lorenzo and J. M. Diez Borque (Barcelona: Planeta, 1975), pp. 147-67.

21. María del Pilar Palomo, 'Símbolo y mito en el teatro de Unamuno' in *El teatro y su crítica. Reunión de Málaga de 1973* (Málaga: Inst. de Cultura de la Diputación Provincial, 1975), pp. 277-43.

22. Federico García Lorca, *Bodas de sangre,* ed. Mario Hernández (Madrid: Alianza, 1984), p. 200.

23. José Luis Salado, 'Antes del estreno. Diálogo con tres barbas ilustres', *La Voz,* 29th December 1934 in *Federico García Lorca (El escritor y la crítica),* ed. Ildefonso Manuel Gil (Madrid: Taurus, 1973), pp. 473-5.

24. Enrique Diez-Canedo, *Artículos de crítica teatral* (Mexico: Mortiz, 1968), I, 44.

25. ibid, IV, 9.

26. ibid, IV, 14.

27. *OC,* V, 83-4. Given the subject matter of *Sombras de sueño* it could on the other hand be argued that the political circumstances as much as Unamuno's distinctive contribution to theatrical development would account for Rivas Cherif's choice of play and playwright. Primo de Rivera's fall from power

in January 1930 had allowed for Unamuno's return from exile, which had become a major political event. In *Sombras de sueño* Tulio Montalbán is portrayed as one 'luchando en pro de la libertad de su pueblo' (*OC,* V, 618), who had fought against oppression. The heart of the play is of course not political at all but rather the tension between the 'real' Macedo and the 'fictive' Montalbán, but Rivas Cherif was a political radical and there were precedents in the Spain of the Dictatorship for granting plays an undue political emphasis. The example of Lorca's *Mariana Pineda* comes readily to mind.

28. Franco, p. 17.

29. Antonia Rodrigo, *Margarita Xirgu y su teatro* (Barcelona: Planeta, 1974).

30. Rodrigo, pp. 193-4 recounts the circumstances which led to Unamuno's translating in a fortnight the *Medea* of Seneca, which Xirgu performed at Mérida in June 1933. The whole undertaking was the result of a chance remark by Fernando de los Ríos during a visit to the Español.

31. Rafael Pérez de la Dehesa, *Política y sociedad en el primer Unamuno* (Madrid: Ciencia Nueva, 1966), p. 162.

32. Herbert Ramsden, *The 1898 Movement in Spain* (Manchester: UP, 1974).

33. Demetrios Basdekis, 'El populismo del primer Unamuno' in *La crisis de fin de siglo: ideología y literatura. Estudios en memoria de R. Pérez de la Dehesa* (Barcelona: Ariel, 1975), pp. 242-9.

34. *OC,* IX, 550-1.

35. *Cartas inéditas de Miguel de Unamuno,* ed. Sergio Fernández Larraín (Santiago de Chile: Zig-Zag, 1965), p. 246 (cited here as *CI*). A more positive assessment is offered by Eduardo Bustillo, *Campañas teatrales* (Madrid: Sucesores de Rivadeneyra, 1901), pp. 217-21.

36. *CI,* pp. 228-9.

37. *CI,* p. 196.

38. 'La regeneración del teatro español', *La España Moderna,* 8, 91 (July 1896), 5-36; also *OC,* I, 890-910. All further references to this article are included in the text. Citations follow the original but page-references to *OC* are also given.

39. Henry Lyonnet, *Le Théâtre en Espagne* (Paris: Ollendorff, 1897), p. 60.

40. ibid, p. 160. We may note that only twenty years later the Eslava was the home of Martínez Sierra's 'Teatro de Arte', a striking example of the change that was to come over Madrid's theatre and that was to make possible the eventual breakthrough of dramatists such as Valle, Unamuno, and Lorca.

41. Jesús Rubio Jiménez, *Ideología teatro en España* (Zaragoza: Universidad, 1982), p. 41. The position is akin to that which holds that Spanish *modernismo* and the 1898 Generation are not to be differentiated.

42. Sergio Beser, *Leopoldo Alas, crítico literario* (Madrid: Gredos, 1968). My account of the debate is taken from Rubio Jiménez, pp. 102-6.

43. 'Teatro ¿libre?', *La España Moderna,* 8, 92 (August 1896), 113-18.

44. *CI,* p. 196.

45. *CI,* pp. 227-8.

46. *CI,* p. 234.

47. *CI,* p. 247.

48. *CI,* p. 252. Rubio Jiménez, pp. 72-3 notes the importance of Sudermann whose merits had been extolled by José Yxart, *El arte escénico en España,* I (Barcelona: 'La Vanguardia', 1894). The reviews of the piece to which Rubio Jiménez refers confirm Unamuno's view.

49. *OC,* IX, 47-59. The lecture was delivered at Seville where in the previous decade Machado y Alvarez and Rodríguez Marín had established the first serious research centre in Spain to concern itself with folklore studies.

50. Bustillo, pp. 167-9 took a rather different view of the Monday night performances at the Español. Earlier actors such as Romea had revived the classics 'por amor al arte'; la Guerrero did so 'por exigencia de la moda'.

51. D. H. Gagen, 'Traditional Imagery and Avant-garde Staging. Rafael Alberti's *El hombre deshabitado*' in *Staging in the Spanish Theatre,* ed. Margaret A. Rees (Leeds: Trinity and All Saints College, 1984), 51-86.

52. Franco, p. 292. As with the use of the *confidant,* as Franco notes, so also with the aside, Unamuno employed a device which was to return to favour. Lorca uses the aside, for example, in *La casa de Bernarda Alba.*

53. I adopt the term used by Miguel Martínez Cuadrado, *La burguesía conservadora 1874-1931* (Madrid: Alianza, 1973).

54. Bustillo, p. 128 gives details of the opposition to *El pan del pobre.* See also David George, '*Poor Man's Bread*: a Spanish Version of Hauptmann's *The Weavers*', *TRI* [*Theatre Research International*], 12 (1987), 23-38.

55. Rubio Jiménez, p. 88.

56. *CI*, p. 251.

57. *CI*, p. 270.

58. The first reference comes in a letter to Ganivet dated 20th November 1898 (*OC*, V, 8).

59. *OC*, V, 170. For the significance of the mirror as a dramatic symbol see Zavala, *Unamuno y su teatro de conciencia.*

60. John Lyon, *The Theatre of Valle-Inclán* (Cambridge: UP, 1985), p. 10.

61. *OC*, V, 18.

62. *OC*, V, 302.

63. *OC*, V, 653-4.

64. Jerzy Grotowski, *Towards a Poor Theatre* (Holstebro: Odin Teatret, 1968), p. 18.

65. ibid, p. 35.

66. ibid, p. 37.

67. ibid, p. 40.

68. *OC*, V, 654.

69. R. J. Sender, *Proclamación de la sonrisa* (Madrid: Pueyo, 1934), p. 55.

70. *International Literature: Organ of the International Union of Revolutionary Writers,* 6 (December 1934), 96.

LA ESFINGE (1909)

CRITICAL COMMENTARY

Stephen J. Summerhill (essay date fall 2001)

SOURCE: Summerhill, Stephen J. "Freedom, the Invisible and the Sublime in Unamuno's *La Esfinge*." *Letras Peninsulares* 14, no. 2 (fall 2001): 227-42.

[*In the following essay, Summerhill analyzes the non-autobiographical elements of* La esfinge *and suggests that the play is underappreciated.*]

La esfinge (1898) was Unamuno's first work for the theater and therefore his first attempt to create that peculiar kind of drama focused on passionate inner struggle that Iris Zavala has called his "teatro de con-

ciencia." Eschewing the complicated plots, realistic settings and romantic themes of the era's bourgeois theater, don Miguel sought a stripped down representation of the "agonía" or interior conflicts of the self as it endures the mysteries of existence and death. In such works, external action tends to be replaced by an intense concentration on a passionate main character whose struggle points to a kind of ancient or primitive experience laden with poetry and myth. Unamuno was seeking what he called a "desnudo de alma," a baring of the soul or spirit—both his own and of his characters—, so that we as readers or spectators would be touched in our souls by the deep, hidden truth of what he wrote.

While such an approach creates a theater of great intensity, don Miguel's plays have never been well received by public or critics, most of whom find them static and overwrought, with too much emphasis on concept and not enough on technique. Such criticisms are generally accurate but they should not prevent us from acknowledging that Unamuno's mytho-poetical dramas constitute an important example of the difficult struggle to create an independent or alternative theater in modern Spain. Almost alone at the dawn of the twentieth century, don Miguel's "teatro de conciencia" fought to break down the closed theatrical world of the period and thereby anticipated the later flowering of modern theater during the 1920s and 1930s under such authors as Valle-Inclán, Jacinto Grau, García Lorca, and others.[1]

In the case of *La esfinge,* the usual negatives about Unamuno's theater are made stronger by the fact that criticism has focused almost exclusively on the autobiographical dimension of the play while tending to overlook other aspects that make it a work of dramatic fiction and that may be important for understanding larger issues in don Miguel's thought. To be sure, much in the play echoes Unamuno's crisis of 1897 and many statements of the main character, Angel, virtually repeat passages found in don Miguel's other writings of the period such as the *Diario íntimo* or his letters to Jiménez Ilundain.[2] At the same time, however, there is more to *La esfinge* than this.

Previous criticism seems not to have noticed, for example, that the action of the play hinges on a basic conflict among the characters about how to achieve freedom, a fact that provides a strong sense of dramatic tension within a plot development that is independent of the author. At the same time, throughout *La esfinge* we find frequent allusions to the need for characters to acquire a capacity to see and hear experiences that are linked to an essential reality which is also a kind of freedom. The connection between these different domains—freedom on the one hand and sight/hearing on the other—is not readily apparent in the play and gives the whole an air of mystery or enigma, especially because the ultimate objectives of sight and hearing seem to lie beyond the realm of normal experience, that is, they are invisible and silent. What is meant by this? How does one represent what cannot be seen or heard, and what form do the invisible and the silent take? These are questions I would like to explore in the following pages by looking closely at *La esfinge* and then framing what we find within the larger context of Unamuno's work. When we recall that in don Miguel's next play, *La venda* (1899), the main character María puts on a blindfold in order to be able to see, it becomes clear that seeing the invisible is not limited to *La esfinge* but stands as a recurring preoccupation of Unamuno's work during this period of his life. Later, I will suggest that the idea points to an important aesthetic issue we have yet to understand thoroughly in don Miguel's writing, the sublime, a point that will require a brief comparison with *La venda* as well as reference to contemporary aesthetic thought. Eventually, then, we will come back to the author, though only after studying *La esfinge* without emphasizing autobiographical allusions. Ultimately, my objective is not to disregard Unamuno but to increase our understanding of his thought at the same time as we seek a more adequate appreciation of *La esfinge*. Let us begin by turning directly to the play.

The basic situation of *La esfinge* is that the main character, Angel, is the leader of a revolutionary movement that seeks to throw off the shackles of authority in order to liberate the people. We never learn much about the forces of authority Angel opposes nor the principles of the revolutionary movement he leads but simply that the two sides exist. This means, however, that from the beginning, freedom, understood as the struggle for social emancipation, stands as a main theme of the work, and is defended by most of the characters, including Angel, his followers, and no less importantly, his wife Eufemia, who insists that she and Angel are better off without children so that they can be free to help others: "Hasta esta soledad en que vivimos y que acaso más de uno nos compadezca, nos deja libres, libres para obra más grande que la de fundar una familia . . ." (Unamuno, *Obras completas* 5: 150-51).

At the outset, however, Angel is also suffering a spiritual crisis that has led him to ask if freedom in the social sense of the word is sufficient. A non-revolutionary friend, Felipe, argues that social emancipation only leads to new forms of slavery: "una falsa libertad que convertirán en esclavitud muy pronto" (153). Influenced by such notions, Angel has begun to follow an individualistic, politically disengaged path of seeking a different kind of freedom focused on feeling and the inner self: "¡Libertad! Es lo que quiero: libertad de ser como por dentro me siento . . . ¡Libertad! ¡Verdadera libertad!" (169). He wants to be what he feels he must be rather than what others want of him: "¡Sí, libertad, libertad!

¡Santa libertad de ser como Dios me hizo y no como me quiere el mundo . . . ; libertad!" (207). By the end of the first act, such sentiments lead him to withdraw from revolutionary action and to turn inward in search of more personal answers. His followers, however, do not disappear from the play, but on the contrary keep coming back to plead for him to rejoin the movement. He typically responds with insults that lead to hostility and separation, including from Eufemia, who by the end of the second act has become tired of his disregard for her and decides to leave him.

Because Angel abandons the revolution, it ends up lacking a strong leader and eventually is defeated in the third and last act of the play. Angered at what they believe was Angel's betrayal of the cause, his followers form into a mob and come looking for vengeance against him. At the end, he speaks to them one last time but insults them again by declaring that they do not know what real freedom is: "¡Viva la libertad!, que es la vida. Os lo digo también yo . . . , la santa libertad . . . , el alma del mundo . . . el espíritu de la idea . . . Pero cuán pocos, hijos míos, [. . .] llegan al seno de la libertad misma . . . Pedís libertad y venís a quitármela; no queréis que sea como soy . . . ¡Libertad!" (214). Suddenly an anonymous bullet is shot from the crowd and Angel is mortally wounded. In the end, he may have thought that he possessed a more authentic idea of freedom, but he remained chained to a revolutionary past that made him pay for abandoning his comrades.

At its most basic level, then, the action of *La esfinge* centers on a conflict between individual and collective freedom. Angel's wish to be free to pursue his inner truth clashes with, and is ultimately defeated by the collective goal of social liberation. This includes a related conflict in which members of revolutionary groups are expected to sacrifice their personal freedom by conforming to the larger goals of the movement. In the first act, for example, Angel complains that his comrades say they are seeking a new society of freedom and tolerance but they refuse to accept that one of their own might think differently than they: "Mucho de predicar tolerancia, sinceridad, libertad; pero cuando alguien quiere ser de veras sincero y libre, ¡contra él todos!" (169).

In a similar vein, Angel's desire for the freedom to seek inner peace is interpreted by others as the selfish pride of one who puts his own wishes ahead of the freedom of others. As Eusebio says to him: "Tú has sido siempre un hombre débil, sin voluntad ni valor, sin más que inteligencia pelada: un cobarde. Y ahora adoptas ese aire de extravagancia para vomitar cuanto se te pudría dentro. Estás muy enfermo, sí, pero de orgullo . . . Es una enfermedad muy triste . . ." (178). Even Angel seems eventually to agree that he is too proud. In the third act he accuses himself of "satánica soberbia" (207) in his desire to appear different from others; and at the end he concedes that true freedom is the humility of sacrificing personal goals in order to defend the cause of the people: "Libertad . . . ; la libertad está en ser humilde . . ." (218).

But if individual freedom is defeated in the play, so is collective freedom. The revolutionary movement is torn apart by rivalries among factions, and some of the revolutionaries themselves have a questionable commitment to the cause. Such is the case of the aesthete Teodoro, for example, who is only interested in the revolution as a source of art, whether in the form of Angel's beautiful speeches or his tormented confessions of failure. And of course, the revolution itself is not successful in breaking the chains of oppression. In fact, it makes them worse by suppressing Angel's individual freedom through mob violence. In the end, then, freedom as an individual or collective ideal is not achieved in the play.

Beyond this conflict over social freedom, *La esfinge* also points to a different level of the problem that is proposed as more important, the freedom Angel seeks in response to his crisis and search for inner truth. Here is where seeing and hearing become significant as symbols of the issues at stake. As early as Act I, scene 2, the play draws attention to the idea of seeing by presenting an argument between Eusebio and Eufemia over which of the two understands Angel better. Eusebio used to be Eufemia's lover until she left him for Angel, so he is motivated by a certain resentment that makes him want to diminish Angel in her eyes. He is now Angel's doctor and says that his patient suffers an inner emptiness that Eufemia is trying to hide by filling him with delusions of becoming a revolutionary leader. With great irony, he comments that he knows she sees Angel clearly, meaning that he believes she does not:

EUSEBIO.

Mira, Eufemia: seamos sinceros siempre; es la eterna cantinela de tu gran hombre. Sé que empiezas a ver claro.

Catching his irony, she responds, and then so does he:

EUFEMIA.

Ves visiones

EUSEBIO.

Veo realidades y las veo por dentro.

(148)

Each believes he or she sees the real Angel and that the other sees only a delusion based on what he or she wants to believe. Which one is correct or are they both wrong? Can anyone see the real Angel? What is meant by *seeing* another and how is this tied to freedom? From early in the play, questions such as these focus our attention on the importance and the difficulty of seeing beyond the deceptive surface of life.

Shortly afterwards, seeing and hearing are mentioned in the presence of Angel. Felipe tells him that if he wants to find inner truth, he must "purify" his sight and hearing: "Purifica tu vista y purificarás el mundo a tus ojos. Si tus oídos son castos, castigarán cuanto oigan" (153). Angel responds with anguish that he feels as if he were deaf and blind because he cannot grasp the truth: "Mi corazón no tiene ojos, Felipe; está ciego porque está sordo . . . , dormido . . ." (154). Later on, he declares to Eufemia that his goal is to acquire an "ojo espiritual" (162) or visionary capacity that would permit him to strip away the surface and see the hidden reality underneath. We might think he is achieving such power when, during the same conversation, he hears a neighbor playing the piano and comments that music speaks "absolute freedom:" "¡Mundo de pura armonía, de sonidos sin ideas, de libertad absoluta! Palpita en él desligada el alma de las cosas" (160). Though he feels deaf and blind, hearing music suddenly puts Angel in touch with freedom through a deeper awareness of "el alma de las cosas."

During the course of his conversation with Eufemia, Angel says that she too is blind because she sees only what is before her eyes, "lo visible," an accusation to which she responds that he, Angel, has become fixated on what he cannot see, "lo invisible" (162). If Eusebio had earlier commented that Eufemia sees visions and now Angel says that she only sees the visible, there is no real contradiction in these statements. Eufemia is presented in contrast to Angel as a character who lacks an "ojo espiritual" or real ability to see because her gaze is not motivated by a search for a deeper understanding of life. The fact that she only cares about Angel becoming famous suggests to him that ". . . tienes acorchada el alma y presa de la obsesión de la gloria" (162). The deeper understanding he means would be an awareness that fame is unimportant because one day neither of them will see or hear what others are saying about them: "Nuestros oídos taponados por la tierra, y vueltos tierra ellos mismos, no oirán lo que de nosotros se diga; esos tus ojos que se me agarraron al corazón se liquidarán al cabo . . ." (161). If Eufemia could recognize how the threat of death makes every moment of life fragile and precious, perhaps she would get in touch with her soul and acquire a spiritual rather than an illusion-oriented vision. This does not happen until the end of the play when, as Angel lies dying, Eufemia desperately calls out to him like a mother caring for a son. This is the maternal urge she had always suppressed and that is now awakened out of compassion toward Angel's suffering. However, it is ineffective, and as he dies she can only cry: "¡Hijo de mi alma!" (220).

Suffering and death finally put her in touch with the soul, though it is too late. At the end, Eufemia is left in futile anguish.

In contrast to Eufemia, throughout the play Angel is conscious of death and nothingness, "esa nada terrible que se me presenta en cuanto cierro los ojos" (182), and this drives him to search for that deeper reality of the soul: "Si nos viésemos todos desnudas las almas, fundiríase en amor una inmensa compasión mutua . . ." (149). Or: "¡Ah, si pudiésemos asomarnos al brocal del alma del prójimo!" (189). Indeed, during a conversation with Eufemia, he tries to wake her up to real sight by insisting that she look into his eyes and communicate with him "soul to soul:" "No apartes tus ojos de los míos . . . Deja en directa comunión las almas . . . ¡Mírame a la mirada no a mí!" (161).[3]

This "soul" that Angel seeks is a principle of transcendent subjectivity tied to a religious experience of the divine. In the first act, he says: "¡Dame fuerzas, Dios mío, para que crea en Ti! ¡Dame fuerzas para que renunciando a mí mismo me encuentre al cabo en paz! Dame fuerzas para que humillándome doble mis rodillas y brote de mis labios la plegaria de la infancia" (163). It is God whom Angel seeks by defeating worldly ambition and recovering the innocence of childhood, "la plegaria de la infancia," when he believed in prayer and the supreme being. If he could return to childhood, it would be equivalent to uncovering the soul and finding true freedom, life within the divine. Thus, God, childhood, music, and freedom come together as the object of a new visionary or spiritual sight that would give authentic meaning to Angel's life by permitting him to overcome his consciousness of death and find inner wholeness.

But just as Angel is unable to free himself from the revolutionary movement, so too he remains blind or sightless, unable to see the invisible world of God and the soul. At the end of the first act, just after sending his letter of withdrawal to the revolutionaries, Angel is alone in his room and suddenly sees himself in a mirror. The stage directions note: *En los paseos por la estancia pasa frente al espejo, y ahora, al aproximarse a él cabizbajo, vislumbra de pronto su propia imagen como una sombra extraña y se detiene ante ella sobrecojido* (170). Here, sight reveals not a soul but the world of the visible, an image of Angel's external appearance. It is a portrait of alienation, a moment when Angel sees himself as others see him from the outside. And the implication is that this *other* in the mirror is more real than the self who is looking at it.

In the second act, another version of the same experience is presented when Angel is haunted by a picture on the wall of his dead mother looking at him. Her gaze seems to carry an accusation that is linked to self-loss and original sin:

No, no tengo alma pura . . . ; estoy expiando algún crimen de antes de que naciera . . . (*Fijándose en el retrato de su madre.*) ¿Ves ese cuadro? Parece que me mira mi madre desde más allá de la tumba, desde el misterio silencioso . . . ¿Qué hay allí? Es una obsesión, que no me deja. Esa nada, esa nada terrible que se me presenta en cuanto cierro los ojos.

(182)

Once again, Angel sees himself as *other,* a person being watched by someone whose gaze tells him he is insubstantial. He then closes his eyes but sees nothingness. In both cases, he is unable to conjure up that "spiritual eye" or visionary capacity he so much wants, and he ends up seeing not a soul but its absence.

In the same way, Angel is unable to "see" or re-discover the lost paradise of childhood. In the third act, he overhears Felipe tell the story of Adam and Eve to his children, and immediately evokes his own childhood as a kind of paradise when he was raised in a village close to nature and far from history. At that time, school was mostly listening to legends and myths, that is, experiences based on visions of the imagination. The young Angel received guidance from a simple parish priest whose fundamental lesson was that each person should cultivate goodness: "'¡Conque a ser bueno, Angel!'" (205). This priest played the clavichord in such a way that the echoes of the music "me hacían ver en aquel hogar casto la concentración viva de los tranquilos siglos de mi aldea . . ." (205).[4] When Angel evokes this music, Felipe comments: "¡Qué cuadro de libertad, Angel, de verdadera libertad . . . , de libertad cristiana!" (205). The freedom alluded to is that of the child who remains integrated into, and fulfilled by the timeless past of his village, "los tranquilos siglos de mi aldea." In the same way, Angel hopes to overcome the alienating gaze of otherness by seeing himself in the eyes of God: "¡Sólo quiero que el Padre invisible me coja en su regazo, sentir el calor de su inmenso pecho, el ritmo de su respiración, *mirarme en su mirada,* en ese cielo limpio y puro, y dormir en paz!" (208. Emphasis mine). This "mirarme en su mirada" would be the ideal form of sight in the play because the self would see itself through the non-alienating or fulfilling gaze of the divine.

And yet, it is all impossible. As the accusatory look from the picture of his mother suggested, Angel has been separated from childhood and now wanders lost and without direction. Until the end, Eufemia refuses to treat him as the child he wishes he could be; and not only is he unable to "desnudar el alma," but his repeated insults of others show that he is by no means the good person the priest told him to be. The divine remains invisible, beyond his grasp, and freedom is an unreachable ideal. When the mob kills him at the end, his fate is definitively reduced to being the soul-less object of the gaze of others. *Otherness* is all there is.

Overall, then, the action and development of *La esfinge* present the story of one man's failed search to see the invisible world of freedom in both the material sense of social emancipation, and also in the religious sense of finding God and personal identity. At the end, the audience is left to ask if this failure could have been avoided, if it expresses a flaw in the way the search was conducted, or if perhaps the ultimate objective—freedom, the soul and God—never existed in the first place. The choice is important because on it hinges the problem of seeing the invisible that plays so much of a role in the work. What finally is meant by the invisible? Is it something real that remains beyond comprehension, or is it simply a delusion, something non-existent? I would argue that the play itself does not provide an answer to this question and ends up thoroughly ambiguous, though at the same time, it insists that, even if the invisible is illusory, it is an essential aspect of life. Angel wants to believe that the invisible exists and that those who don't believe in it are deluded, but the course of events in the play leaves us wondering if Angel isn't really the deluded one. Throughout the play, he defends the idea of finding the soul, of resting within the gaze of the divine, and of achieving the ultimate dream of freedom; but the reality of his experience is otherness, the absence of God, and a failure to be free. Are the objects of Angel's search mere fallacies, or do they really exist? In the end, all we can say is that, even if they are fallacies, Angel considers them essential to his life.

The same ambiguity prevails when we consider the Edenic myth in the play because the situation depends on whether we believe that myths are true or not. Did an original paradise really exist or is such an idea but a rationalization intended to explain present suffering? A religious consciousness would say that it was real, in which case God and freedom do exist but simply remain beyond our present grasp. It would then be legitimate to believe that one need only return to that Edenic past or discover a sublimation of it in the present in order to see the invisible and restore lost wholeness. This clearly is Angel's wish, but if the myth was never more than a rationalization, then nothing was lost nor can it be restored because it never existed in the first place.

Ultimately, then, we never really progress beyond the situation presented at the outset of *La esfinge* in the unresolved debate between Eusebio and Eufemia. "Ves visiones," she says. "Veo realidades y las veo por dentro," he answers (148). Just what does anyone see? No one can know for certain if freedom, the soul and God are real or illusory because they remain definitively unpresentable.

This final ambiguity no doubt coincides with Unamuno's own thinking, which was never certain that the invisible exists but could not live without trying to find

it. We know for example, that he eventually developed the idea that the soul is not a pre-existing principle of human life but a project each person must create. "Hacerse un alma" was don Miguel's way of stating this, and it meant that the soul is not already given but is a function of desire, what he called "querer ser." The soul must be created through the effort to achieve a life that is worthy of eternity although one can never know for sure if one achieves it. By the same token, God is not a given in the universe but an imaginary being created from mankind's wish that a creator could exist. If one has faith in imagination, God will exist as creator, in which case the invisible will be true. Theoretically, then, one should be able to see the invisible by an act of will, though like Angel, Unamuno never actually seems to accomplish it and is always burdened by doubt.

Given these philosophical issues and as anticipated at the outset, I would suggest that the idea of seeing the invisible in *La Esfinge* points to an aesthetic problem of great importance in contemporary art theory, the sublime. By the sublime, I do not mean the rhetorical idea of eloquence as posed in Longinus, nor am I thinking strictly of romantic theory as developed by Burke and Kant, although Kant's acceptance of the supersensible does seem relevant to Unamuno's search for the divine.[5] Mostly, however, I am referring to the reformulation of Kant first proposed by Lyotard and subsequently expanded throughout contemporary aesthetic theory. According to the French philosopher, the sublime is "perhaps the only mode of artistic sensibility to characterize the modern" (Avant-garde, 200) and can be defined as the attempt "to present the fact that the unpresentable exists. To make visible the fact that there is something which can be conceived and which can neither be seen nor made visible" (Postmodern, 78). In direct terms, then, the modern sublime is the attempt to present the unpresentable or to speak the unspeakable. Appearing toward the end of the nineteenth century, it was a reaction against realism and the depiction of the ordinary by posing the fundamental importance in all human life of the extraordinary and unlimited. This inevitably included a fascination for mystery, the strange, and the distorted, in short: all that did not fit patterns of the typical. In this sense, as Jean-Luc Nancy observes, the sublime is opposed to beauty: "Form or contour is limitation, which is the concern of the beautiful: the *unlimited*, to the contrary, is the concern of the sublime" (35). And as the Unamuno of *La esfinge* well knew, it is also the domain of freedom: "In the sublime, the imagination qua free play of presentation comes into contact with its limit—which is freedom" (Nancy 49). It is also important to note that, as Lyotard observes, the sublime points to the incommensurability between concept and reality, for one can conceive of the infinite but can only present it by saying that it cannot be presented: "At the edge of the break, infinity, or the absoluteness of the Idea can be revealed in what Kant calls a negative presentation or even a non-presentation" (Avant-garde, 204).[6]

It is important to insist that the issue of the sublime is not to give visibility to the invisible or to put the unspeakable into words, for in that case, they would no longer be sublime. Rather, it is to capture the invisible *as invisible* and the unspeakable *as unspeakable*. In the words of Lacoue-Labarthe, the sublime is "the presentation of the non-presentable, or more rigorously, to take up the formula of Lyotard, the presentation (of this:) that there is the nonpresentable" (74). This makes indeterminacy a key aspect of the sublime because its essence lies in what it does not present or speak. In the same way, Lacoue-Labarthe stresses the importance of paradox and contradiction as integral to the sublime (86-88).

Lyotard describes two modes of the modern sublime.[7] First, there is a nostalgic kind in which the writer seeks to present a lost absolute along with a certain melancholy at the inability to recover it (Postmodern, 79). This kind of vision seems more closely attached to romanticism's interest in the supersensible world, except that it is understood as lost. Then there is a sublime that Lyotard calls "novatio" and that is focused on the future. It explores the infinite openness of art as a process of relentless experimentation and is best exemplified by the avant-garde (Unpresentable, 68). An additional characteristic of both forms is that they often strive "to make seen what makes one see, and not what is visible" (Avant-garde, 207). That is, rather than presenting a specific theme or issue of the unpresentable, the sublime often explores the very conditions of representation, most of which are overlooked or taken for granted in traditional art, especially realism. In this sense, a common form of the modern sublime is metafiction or art about art.

I would suggest that in *La esfinge,* Unamuno expresses Lyotard's first or nostalgic version of the sublime. He was trying to depict a search for a spiritual realm of God, immortal souls and freedom that he believed had once been visible, but that historically had disappeared or become hidden. It had been a paradise of innocence associated with nature that had been displaced by the rise of modernity, that is, revolutionary violence, science, and the concern for fame and wealth, all of which appear in *La esfinge* as characteristics of the modern world. But though the spiritual was no longer visible, existence was meaningless without it. Therefore, the objective of Angel in the play is to recover it for himself and the world. The fact that he could not find it but could not accept that it does not exist captures exactly that condition of seeking the invisible *as invisible* which is the sublime. The situation was profoundly contradictory because the very thing that was most needed was

precisely what would always remain out of reach. And since it once was visible, it is difficult to avoid a sense of melancholy for what used to be there but can no longer be found. Here too is where we see Unamuno's distance from romanticism, which would be closer to a sense of ravishment or rapture at the presence of the unpresentable. Don Miguel is distinctly modern in his sense of separation from what is definitively unreachable. That one might even go so far as to doubt the very existence of the invisible only intensified the indeterminacy that characterized Unamuno's sublime by adding to it an element of desperation.

It is important to note that in *La esfinge,* Unamuno chose an essentially realistic or verisimilar mode of representation in which the sublime is conveyed symbolically, through a metaphorical play on words embodied in the actions of the characters. That is, the characters live within a contemporary world governed by the laws of verisimilitude, while the sublime is conveyed figuratively by the metaphor of seeing/not seeing. Characters like Eufemia who see only the visible world are presented as metaphorically "blind," while Angel, the character who seeks the invisible is presented as the only one who really "sees," even though ultimately he too fails to glimpse the invisible. In this sense, real sight is the wish to see the invisible even if one is unable, while blindness is the state of not caring about the invisible or accepting that the visible is all there is.

Compare this to Unamuno's next play, *La venda,* which also depends on the image of seeing/not seeing but does so by taking the metaphor literally. In the work, the main character María, needs a blindfold in order to find her way to her father's house. In context, we realize that blindness represents the spiritual sight of faith and María's father is understood as God. Evidently, then, the situation and characters represent ideas, and the incommensurability between concept and reality on which the sublime depends has disappeared. Indeed, the goal is no longer to present the invisible *as invisible,* but on the contrary to make it visible. This can only be done allegorically because the very condition of invisibility means that any attempt to give it a concrete appearance must be inadequate and arbitrary. Allegory thus replaces the sublime as a representational mode intended to overcome invisibility. Not content to leave the riddle of the sphinx unsolved, Unamuno actually peers into the abyss and offers his answer to its mystery, which in this case is the idea that with faith we will find God. Of course, the message is conveyed in such an artificial manner that it fails to provide a convincing solution and can stand only as an opinion. María's father, for example, does not adequately convey the idea of God, who exceeds representation. In the end, the only way to speak the unspeakable is to say that it cannot be spoken.

The shift to allegory that we see in *La venda* occurs everywhere in Unamuno as a result of the crisis of 1897,[8] and stands as a fundamental characteristic of his work. Not content to wallow in lamentations about the inability to speak, don Miguel dedicated himself to pushing through the barrier and touching that "desnudo de alma" he so desperately wanted to see. It would take us too far afield to detail the several methods he developed in order to accomplish this, but from the point of view of representation and literature, all roads led to allegory because uncovering the invisible can only be achieved by means of allegorical figuration. Over and over again, don Miguel moved from the sublime to the allegorical in his effort to overcome silence and speak what he believed was the hidden essence of being. Ironically, the absence of form that is implied by the idea of "desnudar" actually led Unamuno to one of the most artificial of literary forms.[9]

The importance of *La esfinge* is that it does not yet turn to allegory. That is, it is one of Unamuno's few post-1897 works to stay within the sublime and give us a direct apprehension of the frustration it imposes. Angel never sees behind the curtain of mystery and he is left without answers, in a state of blockage from God, freedom and the soul. The mystery of the sphinx remains intact and the Unamunian sublime is shown in its pure state, so to speak, as a true inability to see, a seeing of the invisible *as invisible* without ever being able to make it visible. This makes *La esfinge* quite unique in Unamuno's work: still realistic like *Paz en la guerra,* but unlike that novel, now directly confronted by the mystery of being to which Unamuno would dedicate the rest of his life. Subsequently, realism would be countered by allegory as don Miguel entered his maturity and developed works such as *Amor y pedagogía* (1902), his first novel with a distinctly allegorical foundation. *La esfinge* stands at the threshold of this later phase as one of those special moments when the radical paradox of the sublime is there, before our eyes, letting us see only its absence and refusal to be seen.

This brief overview of the sublime was not intended to capture the full importance and reach of the unpresentable in Unamuno, but it should be enough to show that the issue was significant as a foundation of his approach to representation. It also helps us confirm our sense of his historical place between romanticism and the avant-garde: separated from the ravishment or rapture that romanticism felt toward the sublime, looking back nostalgically on those lost days of plenitude, yet in his way, also anticipating that more formal concentration on the invisible that would constitute the avant-garde.

Turning more specifically to *La esfinge,* we can also suggest that detecting the problem of the sublime in the play may help explain why it has been so poorly accepted as theater. The idea of representing the invisible focuses attention on what by definition is unpresentable and absent. In the era, this was simply too radical a concept because it seemed almost to defy the very nature of actors, action and stage performance, which required concrete, visible things on stage. When one adds to this the overtly religious idea of seeking God, even the revolutionary theme of freedom cannot bring the play back to normal or typical themes for its era. In the end, *La esfinge* defied too many norms of the period's theater and ended up too "personal" or idiosyncratic to be accepted.

As drama, however,—and we readily acknowledge that plays must be both drama and theater—*La esfinge* continues to deserve more attention than it has received. The theme of freedom is developed effectively through a conflict that is presented on several levels, both internally in Angel, and externally in his relationship with the world. The metaphor of seeing/not seeing adds metaphorical depth and increases the possibilities of meaning in the play. By addressing the question of presenting the unpresentable, don Miguel increases the dramatic tension while announcing significant issues in modern aesthetics and in his own work. *La esfinge* stands as an important example of Unamuno's deepest concerns and is an interesting drama about the search for freedom and God.

Notes

1. Ruiz Ramón, *Historia* 77-93, presents a balanced view of the achievements and failures of Unamuno's theater. His later 1992 article does not mention Unamuno but clearly shows the difficulties faced by innovative dramatists in the early part of the century.

2. In the introduction to his edition of *La esfinge,* 37-46, Paulino provides an extensive review of the many autobiographical allusions noted by Franco, Zavala, and Palomo.

3. Of course, such statements remind us of Unamuno's goal of "desnudar el alma" mentioned at the outset: to strip the soul bare in order to reach the deepest reality of human experience. However, as in the case with other details here—for example, the wife as mother—we need to stay focused on the action of the play without resorting to autobiographical explanations. We will come back to the soul and the author at the end.

4. This priest is very similar to the one who appears in *Nuevo mundo* (44-47).

5. Though the bibliography on the sublime is immense, excellent summaries can be found in Lacoue-Labarthe and Crowther. Concerning

Longinus, Michel Deguy has suggested that "the speech of exalted discourse" (6) can be understood as seeking the divine, in which case, the classical author would involve more than rhetorical eloquence and would also be relevant to Unamuno. I have studied the sublime in Unamuno's *Nuevo mundo* and the *Diario intimo*.

6. Unamuno made a similar statement in *Del sentimiento trágico de la vida*: "No, lo absoluta, lo irrevocablemente irracional es inexpresable, es intransmisible. Pero lo contra-racional, no. Acaso no hay modo de racionalizar lo irracional; pero le hay de racionalizar lo contra-racional, y es tratando de exponerlo. Como sólo es inteligible, de veras inteligible, lo racional, como lo absurdo está condenado, careciendo como carece de sentido, a ser intransmisible, veréis que cuando algo que parece irracional o absurdo logra uno expresarlo y que se lo entiendan, se resuelve con algo racional siempre, aunque sea en la negación de lo que se afirma" (7: 184). That is, a "negación de lo que se afirma" would be a statement to the effect that "X" cannot be stated.

7. Crowther offers an excellent discussion of Lyotard's two forms of the modern sublime on 153-161.

8. In an important deconstructive reading of Unamuno, Francisco La Rubia Prado has perceptively shown how don Miguel's romantic organicism inevitably led to allegory.

9. By no means am I suggesting that allegory is deficient or inferior to some other kind of representation such as, for example, symbolism or realism. Ultimately, we need to learn to read allegory differently. See my counter-interpretation of *Dos madres* for an example of one attempt to approach allegory in a whole new way.

Works Cited

Benítez, Hernán. *El drama religioso de Unamuno [y cartas a J. Ilundain]*. Buenos Aires: Universidad de Buenos Aires, 1949.

Crowther, Paul. *Critical Aesthetics and Postmodernism*. Oxford: Oxford U P, 1993.

Deguy, Michel. "The Discourse of Exaltation (Meyahzyopeiv): Contribution to a Re-reading of Pseudo-Longinus," *Of the Sublime: Presence in Question; Essays by Jean-François Courtine, et al*. Trans. Jeffrey S. Librett. Albany: State University of New York Press, 1993. 5-24.

Franco, Andrés. *El teatro de Unamuno*. Madrid: Insula, 1971.

Lacoue-Labarthe, Philippe, "Sublime Truth," *Of the Sublime: Presence in Question; Essays by Jean-François Courtine, et al*. Trans. Jeffrey S. Librett. Albany: State University of New York Press, 1993. 71-108.

La Rubia Prado, Francisco. *Alegorías de la voluntad; Pensamiento orgánico, retórica y deconstrucción en la obra de Miguel de Unamuno*. Madrid: Libertarias/Prodhufi, 1996.

Lyotard, Jean-François. *The Postmodern Condition; A Report on Knowledge*. Trans. Geoff Bennington and Brian Massumi. Minneapolis: U of Minnesota P, 1984.

———. "Presenting the Unpresentable: The Sublime," *Art Forum,* April, 1982. 64-69.

———. "The Sublime and the Avant-Garde," *The Lyotard Reader*. Ed. Andrew Benjamin. Oxford: Blackwell, 1989. 196-211.

Palomo, María del Pilar. "El proceso comunicativo de *La esfinge,*" *Semiología del teatro*. Eds. José María Díez Borque y Luciano García Lorenzo. Barcelona: Planeta, 1975. 145-66.

———. "Símbolo y mito en el teatro de Unamuno," *El teatro y su crítica; Reunión de Málaga de 1973*. Ed. Manuel Alvar. Málaga: Instituto de Cultura de la Diputación Provincial de Málaga, 1975. 225-43.

Paulino, José. "Introducción," *Miguel de Unamuno; La esfinge, La venda, Fedra; Teatro*. Madrid: Castalia, 1987. Pp. 7-77.

Ruiz Ramón, Francisco. *Historia del teatro español; Siglo XX*. 2ª ed. Madrid: Cátedra, 1975.

———. "El drama del teatro español contemporáneo," *ALEC [Anales de la literatura española contemporánea]*, 17, 1-2 (1992), 11-36.

Summerhill, Stephen J. "The Autobiographical Subject as Allegorical Construct in Unamuno's *Diario íntimo,*" *Nuevas Perspectivas Sobre el 98*. Ed. John P. Gabriele. Frankfurt am Main/Madrid: Iberoamericana, 1999. 33-42.

———. "Narrar el alma: *Nuevo mundo* y la alegoría en Unamuno," *Salamanca en el Siglo XX*. Ed. Conrad Kent. Salamanca: Librería Cervantes/Ohio Wesleyan Univ., 1997. 99-114.

———. "Theory and Practice of the Novel in Unamuno: The Case of *Dos madres,*" *Revista Hispánica Moderna*, 45, 1 (Junio, 1992), 15-34.

Unamuno, Miguel de. *Nuevo mundo*. Ed. Laureano Robles. Madrid: Trotta, 1994.

———. *Obras completas*. Ed. Manuel García Blanco. Vols. 5, 7. Madrid: Escelicer, 1967-68.

Zavala, Iris M. *Unamuno y su teatro de conciencia*. Salamanca: Acta Salmanticensia, 1963.

Katrina M. Heil (essay date 2009)

SOURCE: Heil, Katrina M. "*La Esfinge:*[1] Unamuno's Tragic Sense on the Stage." *Anales de la literatura española contemporánea* 34, no. 2 (2009): 93-118.

[In the following essay, Heil examines the tragic vision that Unamuno projects in La esfinge, *maintaining that the writer's plays had a striking effect on the development of twentieth-century Spanish tragedy.]*

Ricardo Doménech claims that Miguel de Unamuno "ocupa un lugar de excepción en el camino de la tragedia española moderna, no por ser autor de grandes tragedias, sino por ser el más trágico de nuestros escritores contemporáneos" (115). Unamuno is considered Spain's most tragic author for his tragic view of life, expressed repeatedly throughout his prolific literary career and most clearly in *Del sentimiento trágico de la vida* (1911-12). The goal of the present study is to bring to light Unamuno's invaluable contributions in the trajectory of twentieth-century Spanish tragedy through an analysis of his first tragic drama, *La Esfinge* (1898). This drama marks an important milestone in Unamuno's literary production; it expresses a remarkably well-developed version of his tragic sense of life some fourteen years before writing *Del sentimiento* and at least two before discovering the philosophies of Kierkegaard.[2] In 1996, Doménech concludes the following about the state of modern tragedy: "Hoy con mayor razón, cuando tantos castillos en el aire se han venido abajo, advertimos con claridad que la visión trágica—a menudo ligada al simbolismo y al existencialismo—es la forma de arte y de pensamiento que se mantiene en pie, con toda su vigencia, en este atardecer del siglo" (112).[3] Unamuno can be credited for introducing this modern, existential and tragic view of the world into the mainstream of Spanish thought in the twentieth century. Unamuno's tragic sense of life represented on the stage stands as a counter-example to the claims of George Steiner and others that tragedy is dead in the modern world. It is for this reason that Unamuno, while not an acclaimed tragedian himself, remains a central figure in the perseverance of tragedy as a viable literary and artistic genre.

In order to establish the critical role of *La Esfinge* in the development of twentieth-century Spanish tragedy, I will first consider how Unamuno's existentialist philosophy both answers the claim that tragedy is dead in the modern world and contrasts with the world-view most often expressed in the Theater of the Absurd,[4] and follow with an examination of Unamuno's views about the particular suitability of drama for expressing his tragic view of human existence. Subsequently, I will explore at greater length several tragic themes developed in *La Esfinge* that reappear in *Del sentimiento,* taking into consideration the progression of Unamuno's tragic

sense of life during the fourteen years that separate these two works, and conclude with an analysis of *La Esfinge*'s merits and weaknesses as an example of modern tragedy.

Unamuno was not the only playwright interested in reviving tragedy in the early part of the twentieth century. Ramón del Valle-Inclán, Jacinto Grau and later, Federico García Lorca all wrote dramas that they called tragedies or that critics have found representative of this genre. Unamuno, however, developed and introduced into Spanish thought a Kierkegaardian existentialism founded in the conflict between faith and doubt, which he sought to represent on the stage through tragedy. This philosophy is characterized by its unwillingness to abandon hope in the face of the apparent absurdity of human existence. The tragedies of Valle-Inclán, Grau and Lorca also represent struggles between hope and doubt and in 1958, Antonio Buero Vallejo developed a theory of tragedy based upon this struggle, which he found present in all tragedy since its inception in Ancient Greece.[5] What is unique to twentieth-century Spanish tragedy is the undercurrent of an existentialist philosophy that seems to come ever closer to the conclusion that life is meaningless and that there is no higher meaning or order to the universe. The preservation of hope in the face of this looming conclusion, however, is essential to tragedy in the twentieth century and it also distinguishes this Unamunian form of existential tragedy from the Theater of the Absurd. In the second half of the twentieth century, the works of Buero Vallejo and Alfonso Sastre are testament to the continued interest in the genre of tragedy, and we have reason to believe this interest will continue into the twenty-first. As recently as 1998, for example, the new and very promising playwright Paloma Pedrero calls her play, *Una estrella,* a "tragedia burlada" because its protagonist is able to find hope in the midst of her misfortune and therefore the means to confront and overcome her own personal tragedy (238).[6]

In his arguments about the death of tragedy, Steiner claims that the modern age, beginning with the Enlightenment, has been governed by two exceedingly optimistic views of the world: faith in progress through reason and scientific discovery and faith in the Judeo-Christian God, who promises immortality of the soul and final justice (8). Steiner considers both of these views anti-tragic because:

> [t]ragic drama tells us that the spheres of reason, order, and justice are terribly limited and that no progress in our science or technical resources will enlarge their relevance. Outside and within man is *l'autre,* the "otherness" of the world. Call it what you will: a hidden or malevolent god, blind fate, the solicitations of hell, or the brute fury of our animal blood. It waits for us in ambush at the crossroads. It mocks us and destroys us.
>
> (8-9)

Steiner fails to recognize, however, a modern tragic theme created by the confrontation of these beliefs, which Unamuno describes in *Del sentimiento*: the existential crisis created in the attempt—which inevitably fails—to reconcile faith with reason. The Unamunian tragic sense of life at once shatters both faith in the Judeo-Christian God as well as in scientific progress. Unamuno argues that our modern age of reason is the most tragic of all because it is reason that destroys faith: "es una verdadera enfermedad, y trágica, la que nos da el apetito de conocer por gusto del conocimiento mismo" (*Del sentimiento* 122).[7] If reason tells us that we are mortal and that human existence lacks higher meaning, any scientific or social progress is also meaningless: "Progresar, ¿para qué?" (475). The hollowness of progress leads Unamuno to conclude that, "acaso la enfermedad misma sea la condición esencial de lo que llamamos progreso, y el progreso mismo una enfermedad" (119). In this way, one type of anti-tragic faith described by Steiner, faith in progress, destroys the other and more important type of anti-tragic faith described by Steiner, faith in immortality, thus revealing the futility of faith in progress as well. Unamuno's tragic sense of life, therefore, describes a view of human existence within which, following Steiner's own standards, tragedy is indeed possible.

In contrast to Steiner's view, Walter Kaufmann states that, "[w]e have been told that tragedy is dead, that it died of optimism, faith in reason, confidence in progress. Tragedy is not dead, but what estranges us from it is just the opposite: despair" (xviii). Kaufmann claims that despair does not make tragedy impossible, but that it makes us unable to access it. The emotion of despair, provoked by the apparent meaninglessness of the universe, is often linked to the Theater of the Absurd. According to Unamuno, however, despair is not the ultimate emotion derived from the tragic sense of life. For the purpose of clarification between Unamunian tragedy and Theater of the Absurd, it is necessary to recognize a distinction between Kierkegaard's philosophy, which Unamuno embraces, and later French existentialism. Kierkegaard, often referred to as the father of existentialism, recognizes the rational absurdity of religious faith but, unlike later philosophers such as Sartre and Camus, nevertheless claims that such faith adds positive value to human existence. The hero of Kierkegaard's *Fear and Trembling*, the Knight of Faith, is defined by his ability to make the leap into the absurd. In this essay, under the pseudonym Johannes de Silentio, Kierkegaard confesses that "I cannot close my eyes and throw myself trustingly into the absurd, for me it is impossible, but I do not praise myself on that account" (63). For Unamuno as well, such faith, which promises immortality, is the foundation of a meaningful existence but it is similarly unattainable.

Later existentialists such as Sartre and Camus treat the meaninglessness of existence as given and therefore abandon the pursuit of faith. Plays belonging to the tradition of Theater of the Absurd operate under the assumption that there is no higher meaning to human existence. Tragedy, however, cannot operate under such an assumption. Donald Shaw, for example, asks and then asserts the following: "What are the implications for tragedy of scepticism about ultimate values and of doubts about a ruling cosmic order? It does not seem to negate tragic vision entirely, as George Steiner seems to argue in *The Death of Tragedy*, for tragedy has always questioned the harmony of the universe" ("Lorca's Late Plays" 204). As Shaw correctly recognizes, since its beginning in the Ancient world, tragedy has concerned itself with questions about the order of the universe or, in more modern terms, about the ultimate meaning of existence. In his essay, "La tragedia," Buero Vallejo argues the same about the role of tragedy: "El absurdo del mundo tiene muy poco que ver con la tragedia como último contenido a deducir, aunque tenga mucho que ver con ella como apariencia a investigar" (71). In *Del sentimiento*, Unamuno is unwilling to accept what reason tells him: that nothingness awaits him after death. Instead, he leaves the question of the afterlife open: "El '¿y si hay?' y el '¿y si no hay?' son las bases de nuestra vida íntima" (256). By leaving the question open in tragedy, there is room for the opposite emotion of despair: hope.

Shaw argues that if a play asserts the non-existence of "some over-arching order [. . .] the playwright can only succeed in conveying misery or despair, not tragic emotion" (203). For this reason, Shaw continues, "in the absence of an accepted pattern of values, tragedy gives way to Theatre of the Absurd" (203). Yet Unamuno's tragic sense of life does not reach the extreme doubt that accepts unquestioningly the absurdity of existence. Unamuno advocates maintaining the struggle between the heart, which wants to believe, and the head, which finds overwhelming reasons to doubt. From this struggle, "nace la santa, la dulce, la salvadora incertidumbre, nuestro supremo consuelo" (*Del sentimiento* 255). Unamuno claims time and again that this uncertainty, which is tragic, "ha de fundar su esperanza" (242). This rebirth of hope in the midst of the struggle between faith and doubt is what prevents tragedy from being an affirmation of an absurd view of the world. However, it must be emphasized again that existential tragedy is not an affirmation of the Christian view of the world either, for an authentic existence requires recognition of the rational shortcomings of faith. The cycle of hope and doubt inherent in the philosophies of thinkers such as Unamuno and Kierkegaard lies between the two poles of absolute faith and despair. It is here that tragedy is indeed possible in our times, as Unamuno first reveals on the stage with **La Esfinge**.

Given the immense amount of literary criticism dedicated to defining the genre of tragedy, some final comments about this subject are needed. In the *Poetics,* Aristotle delineates a substantive definition of tragedy, based upon his observations of the characteristics of existing tragedies. While many modern critics proclaim the impossibility of meeting the Aristotelian requirements listed in the *Poetics,* the most important elements of tragedy described by Aristotle can be—and indeed are—met on the stage today. Aristotle's definition of tragedy hinges upon the arousal of fear and pity in the spectator.[8] In the *Poetics,* a tragic plot that will produce these emotions is treated as the most important element of tragedy to which all others are secondary.[9] Following Oscar Mandel, Luis González-del-Valle also prefers a substantive definition of tragedy, which "begin[s] with the work of art itself" (18).[10] González-del-Valle argues against those critics who claim that tragedy is dead in the modern world, explaining that, "[u]na visión filosófica de lo que la tragedia debe ser y no la realidad de existentes obras determina su negación de lo trágico en la realidad" (17). González-del-Valle's adaptation of Mandel's definition of tragedy is a nicely simplified and very appropriate modernization of Aristotle's preferred tragic plot: "un protagonista por quien sentimos buena voluntad es impulsado, en un mundo determinado, a tomar una acción de cierta magnitud, y como resultado de esta acción, siguiendo las leyes que rigen a este mundo en que todo sucede, inevitablemente termina con un sufrimiento espiritual o físico" (169).

Defining tragedy has never been an exact science in part because a definition based upon the spectator's response is highly subjective, given that many spectators are apt to respond somewhat differently to the same events represented on the stage. For this reason, González-del-Valle avoids any mention of the arousal of fear and pity.[11] However, his definition does insist that the spectator feel goodwill towards the protagonist; the downfall of a protagonist towards whom the spectator feels ill will is not tragic. Indeed, it is hard to come up with an adequate definition of tragedy that completely ignores the response of the spectator. The most enduring Greek tragedies, for example *Oedipus Rex* and *Medea,* have provoked a similar response throughout history and in widely different cultures. Patricide followed by an incestuous relationship with the mother, much like a mother killing her own children, seems to be universally fearful and—assuming goodwill towards the protagonist—pitiable. Seeing as the spectator's response is central to Aristotle's definition, in this study I will consider what it is fair to assume would be the emotional response of *most* spectators, keeping in mind that there will always be varied responses that can be attributed to the historical moment when the play is represented, the cultural background of the audience and differences in personal disposition.

Unamuno, trained in philology at the University of Madrid, was a professor of both Latin and Greek at the University of Salamanca, where he served as rector intermittently from 1901 until his death in 1936. He was certainly familiar with Greek tragedy. In fact, he made use of classic tragedy twice in his career as a playwright: with his own version of *Fedra* (1910) and with his translation of Seneca's *Medea* (1933), which was staged in the renovated Roman theater in Mérida with Margarita Xirgu and Enrique Borrás in the leading roles (*O.C.* V, 103). Unamuno's own attempts at writing tragedy, however, are widely viewed as failures and are therefore given relatively little critical attention.[12] In spite of his continuous struggle with getting his works staged in Spain,[13] Unamuno continued to write plays for more than thirty years. Clearly, he viewed drama as an appropriate medium for artistic expression of his ideas. It is therefore worthwhile to consider briefly what motivated Unamuno to express his tragic sense of life through the genre of tragedy.

Jesús María Lasagabaster argues that, "son sobre todo razones más profundas, existenciales, en última instancia, las que hacen que Unamuno, ensayista, novelista, poeta, tenga que escribir también teatro" (9). Cirilio Flórez tells us that, "al defender una mitologización de la razón [Unamuno] aspira a hacer hueco dentro de la filosofía a la conciencia creyente" (294). Unamuno's existential philosophy of the tragic sense of life transfers itself quite easily to prose fiction. In her study on the relationship between existential thought and the fictional technique of Kierkegaard, Sartre and Beckett, Edith Kern argues that "[f]rom its inception, existential thought has felt itself at home in fiction" (vii). She cites Unamuno's view that the philosophy of the man of flesh and blood is closer to poetry than to a science and concludes that "the paradox and absurdity of life can be more readily deduced from fundamental human situations portrayed in fiction than described in the logical language of philosophy" (vii). In addition, the self of existential philosophy is best expressed subjectively in the first person. In drama, each character is given a first-person voice and consequently, a presence as subjectivity. For this reason, it seems that drama is in many ways the ideal genre to portray a philosophy concerned with subjective existence, as well as relationships with others who, in turn, also exist subjectively.

Unamuno is drawn to drama as a means to expose the struggles of the soul that he feels have been neglected: "No he querido callar lo que callan los otros; he querido poner al desnudo, no ya mi alma, sino el alma humana" (*O.C.* VII, 173).[14] Unamuno expresses this desire to portray the human soul through drama in a later play, **Soledad** (1921), through the words of its autobiographical protagonist—a playwright—Agustín: "Voy a crear almas, a poner almas ante las almas" (*O.C.* V, 483). In his introduction to *Del sentimiento,* Antonio Sánchez-

Barbudo sees another, more personal motivation for Unamuno's writing: "Muchas veces se tiene la impresión de que con su pelea y con sus gritos lo que hace, conscientemente o no, es acallar su más íntima pena, el vacío de su corazón" (28). Writing, then, affords Unamuno the same catharsis that he hopes his readers will get reading or watching his plays. Sánchez-Barbudo also suggests that drama, perhaps more so than other genres, serves as a confessional for Unamuno, pointing to a letter written to Clarín on May 9, 1900, in which he admits "en mi drama me he confesado" (10). It is also quite easy to imagine that Unamuno views the theater as a sort of religious temple where the spectators recognize and lament together what he perceives to be the tragic sense of life. "Lo más santo de un templo es que es el lugar a que se va a llorar en común. Un *Miserere* cantado en común por una muchedumbre, azotada del destino, vale tanto como una filosofía. No basta curar la peste, hay que saber llorarla. ¡Sí, hay que saber llorar!" (*Del sentimiento* 116).

Unamuno's thoughts about the suitability of drama to express his views on the tragic sense of life were clearly already taking form when he wrote his first drama, **La Esfinge.** Unamuno considered calling this drama *Gloria o paz,* or *La muerte es paz,* but in the end settled on **La Esfinge** (*O.C.* V, 8). The Sphinx, a mythical monster that devours those who cannot answer his riddles, represents Unamuno's own torment at his inability to find an answer to the great existential riddle of what lies beyond the grave. The titles that Unamuno considered for this play reveal the central theme of this work to which all others are related: the struggle between glory, which represents the attempt to give a mortal life meaning, and peace, which comes from faith in immortality. From this basic struggle, which lies at the heart of **La Esfinge,** many related themes worthy of discussion in themselves emerge, such as the futility of existence, the conflicting pursuits of glory and of peace, the idealization of blind faith, the question of authenticity and the relationship of the self with the other. All are central to Unamuno's views about the tragic sense of life and will therefore be considered as represented in **La Esfinge,** in relation to *Del sentimiento.*

Given that **La Esfinge** was written just one year after Unamuno's religious crisis of 1897, Ricardo Gullón argues that, "resultaba casi inevitable que en el tono y en el acento del actante resonaran los de quien, al crearlo, buscaba espejo para reconocerse y analizarse" (231). In this play, Ángel, the leader of a revolutionary movement about which we know little, becomes so concerned with the question of immortality that he abandons the cause and in doing so manifests a suspicion Unamuno would express later in *Del sentimiento* about the actions of heroes: "Creo [. . .] que muchos de los más grandes héroes, acaso los mayores,

han sido desesperados, y que por desesperación acabaron sus hazañas" (268). In Andrés Franco's study on this play, he argues, "Don Miguel siempre está presente en sus dramas, pero en esta pieza ocupa él, claramente visible detrás del artificio literario, el centro del tablado" (59). Ángel, much like Unamuno himself, is obsessed with the idea of the nothingness that reason tells him follows death and the resultant loss of religious faith. Rationally concluding that the afterlife doesn't exist, Ángel develops the idea that faith creates its object: "la fe crea su objeto . . . En fuerza de desear algo logramos sacarlo de la nada" (182). Unamuno expresses the same thought twelve years later in *Del sentimiento*: "La fe crea, en cierto modo, su objeto. Y la fe en Dios consiste en crear a Dios" (234). As a result of his loss of faith, Ángel becomes obsessed with thoughts of his own mortality. Speaking to his wife he confesses his affliction: "Es una obsesión, Eufemia, que no me deja. Esa nada, esa nada terrible que se me presenta en cuanto cierro los ojos . . ." (*O.C.* V, 182).[15]

The seemingly inevitable absorption into nothingness at death leads Ángel to conclude that all human endeavors in life are futile. "Día llegará en que a esta vieja tierra le tocará su turno y, hecha también polvo, se esparcirá por los espacios llevándose nuestra ciencia, nuestro arte, nuestra civilización toda reducida a aerolitos pelados" (146). In this play, the game of chess serves as a symbol of the futility of life and the revolutionary struggle in a similar fashion that Sisyphus' condemnation to push a rock up a hill every day, only to watch it roll back down, would later symbolize the futility of life for Camus. As Ángel idly plays the game, he argues to Eufemia that it doesn't matter who wins, "blancos o negros, [. . .] irán luego confundidos a la misma caja para recomenzar otra vez, y otra. ¿Y la utilidad final? ¡Divertirnos, matar el tiempo!" (160). Franco notes that "la alegoría del ajedrez está arraigada en la tradición de las letras hispánicas" (74), recalling chapter XII of the second book of the *Quijote,* and concludes that the symbolism of chess in **La Esfinge** is "una prefiguración del concepto unamuniano de la vida como representación" (74). The idea that the world is a stage and the meaninglessness of existence go hand in hand.

In concurrence with the later claims of *Del sentimiento,* Ángel argues in **La Esfinge** that, given the apparent futility of existence, the glory of continuing the revolutionary cause of which he is an admired leader would not provide his life with any final meaning. In an argument with his wife immediately following the chess game, he claims "¡Gloria, gloria! Nuestros oídos taponados de la tierra, y vueltos tierra ellos mismos, no oirán lo que de nosotros se diga" (161). Later, Ángel asks his friends, who have come to dissuade him from abandoning the cause, "¿Cómo puede ser mía la gloria cuando yo no exista? ¡Sin mí no hay mío!" (192). In the face of mortality, Ángel describes worldly fame as, "¡Indestructible aspiración a la eternidad! ¡Sombra de eternidad!" (192). Eufemia pushes Ángel to continue leading the revolution and establish his name in history for his sake and, it seems, in order to achieve her own fame as well. But Ángel's doctor—as well as Eufemia's former suitor—Eusebio, warns her that, "[q]uieres llenar el vacío de su alma tupiéndolo de gloria. Ese vacío no se llena así" (148). Only moments later, Ángel argues the same thing:

EUFEMIA.

Sólo con una causa grande y noble llenarás el vacío que sientes.

ÁNGEL.

¡Crecerá más!

EUFEMIA.

¡No!

ÁNGEL.

Es eso como el mar, que cuánto más de él se bebe, da más sed.

(248)

Their marriage is infertile, and it is implied that Eufemia desires Ángel's renown as a replacement for the fulfillment that children would bring her.[16] Having children and the quest for glory are linked in *La Esfinge*; both represent an attempt to achieve immortality. Eufemia tries to convince Ángel that they are better off without children; "nos deja libres para obra más grande que la de fundar una familia" (151). Not long after, when the couple is speaking "de alma a alma" as Ángel suggests, he almost cruelly—forcing her to sit down and listen to him—argues that she is pursuing his success only because he was unable to give her children. "Sé que ya que no te perpetúes en hijos de la carne, quieres dejar tu nombre unido a un nombre imperecedero [. . .] ¡Como no te he dado hijos, me pides gloria!" (162). Ángel's claim shares a striking similarity, in language and in theme, with Unamuno's later claim in *Del sentimiento*: "Cuando las dudas invaden y nublan la fe en la inmortalidad del alma, cobra brío y doloroso empuje el ansia de perpetuar el nombre y la fama" (164). In both works, Unamuno makes it clear that worldly fame is no substitute for immortality in the afterlife.

Turning now to the characteristics of the peace that Unamuno envisioned in the disjunctive of the contemplated title, *Gloria o paz,* as presented in *La Esfinge,* there appears to be a shift in Unamuno's thinking on this subject sometime after writing this play, before writing *Del sentimiento*. In 1912, Unamuno claims, "no quiero poner paz entre mi corazón y mi cabeza, entre mi fe y mi razón" (*Del sentimiento* 256). In even sharper

contrast with this play, Unamuno's closing line of *Del sentimiento* is: "¡Y Dios no te dé paz y sí gloria!" (515).[17] The assumption is that the glory Unamuno speaks of at the end of *Del sentimiento* does not refer to the worldly fame that *La Esfinge* rejects as a substitute for immortality, for he makes the same argument in *Del sentimiento* (164). Presumably, the glory referred to here is one derived from the authenticity of not abandoning the struggle between faith and doubt, connected to his claim that the individual's job in life is to become irreplaceable (*Del sentimiento* 444) and thereby call attention to the injustice inherent in the possibility that nothingness awaits after death (428). What is clear from Unamuno's closing line of *Del sentimiento* is that he does not advocate the pursuit of inner peace; instead he prefers the vital struggle between the heart and the head.

Nelson Orringer argues that Unamuno first develops this concept of glory, which is "la esencia del quijotismo" (44), in *Vida de Don Quijote* in 1904, where Unamuno makes it clear that "la fe en el ideal de la gloria, como toda forma de fe religiosa conocida a Unamuno, cuesta esfuerzo para mantener" (44-45).[18] The Unamuno of 1898, however, has not yet developed this argument so clearly, and Ángel expresses several times the desire for peace. His last dying words are "¡Paz! . . . ¡Paz! . . . ¡Paz! . . . ," and the final words of the play come from the faithfully religious Felipe, Ángel's most loyal friend, "¡Dios le dé paz!" (220). However, since the existence of God is palpably in question, such peace is far from assured, all of which bears consistency with the arguments of *Del sentimiento*. The peace of death could just as easily come from nothingness, which is portrayed in this drama and in his later essays as terrible. Therefore, while *La Esfinge* does not spell out as clearly the argument that the most vital existence is one that maintains the struggle between faith and doubt, Unamuno's early ruminations on this subject are clear. Franco interprets Ángel's death as symbolizing a rebirth; "[e]s, para el autor, un morir simbólico para renacer a la esperanza de la fe" (69). However, as Unamuno shows in this work and elsewhere, a rebirth into the hope of faith is far from peaceful. For this reason, Ángel's death leads to the same cycle of hope and doubt as seen in *Del sentimiento*: the hope that death will bring an immortal peace and the doubt that there is anything after death.

Peace is also linked in this play to simple faith. Ángel wishes to return to the simplicity and blind faith of his youth: "Quiero humillarme, ser como los sencillos, rezar como de niño, maquinalmente, por rutina" (163). Ángel also admires the simplicity of his servant, Martina:

ÁNGEL.

¿Tienes miedo a morirte?

MARTINA.

Pero ¡si no estoy enferma . . . !

ÁNGEL.

¿Y si te mueres?

MARTINA.

Algún día será . . . [. . .] Cuando Dios quiera . . . , ¿qué remedio?

(164-65)

In the final act, Ángel seeks refuge in the house of Felipe. At this point, Unamuno creates a substantial pause in the action of the play with a long conversation between the two friends, which seems primarily devoted to creating images of peace and nostalgia for blind faith. Felipe's children, who provoke in Ángel a flood of memories, represent the lost innocence of youth. Ángel remembers his upbringing in the country, and in particular, his teacher, don Pascual: "Su recuerdo encarna para mí el ámbito maternal de la pobre aldea en que meció mi niñez de mi alma. Su casa me inspiraba el mismo respeto que la iglesia; es más, me parecía una iglesia más íntima y más recogida" (204). Unamuno evokes sensual imagery in this scene, which is associated with the peace of blind faith; Ángel recalls the smell of incense "con que don Pascual sahumaba su hogar" (204) as well as the music of his clavichord. "[E]n aquellos ecos que parecían purificar el ámbito y que, casados al perfume del incienso, me hacían ver en aquel hogar casto la concentración viva de los tranquilos siglos de mi aldea . . ." (204-5). In "Imagery and Symbolism in the Theater of Unamuno," Shaw shows the extensive use of music, water, and childhood imagery as symbols of peace and simple faith in this play. For example, one of the most important uses of music occurs when, after learning that his wife has left him, Ángel is about to shoot himself and he hears his neighbor play *Pietà Signore* on the piano, which stops him (197). Shaw argues that "[t]he basic melodrama of the scene is attenuated for the alert reader (though one suspects not perhaps for a possible spectator) by his recognition of the emphasis laid on the music's symbolic meaning [. . .]—a spiritual peace too deep for expression in words" (89). The final use of music as a symbol of peace in this play is the *canto de cuna* that Ángel requests his wife sing to him as he dies, mimicking Unamuno's real life experience during his crisis of 1897 when his wife awoke to his sobs and shouted "¡Hijo mío!," taking him in her arms as a mother would a child (*Del sentimiento,* Intro. Sánchez-Barbudo, 12).

Unamuno argues that any rational thinker must conclude that nothingness awaits after death: "Y así como antes de nacer no fuimos ni tenemos recuerdo alguno personal de entonces, así después de morir no seremos. Esto es lo racional" (*Del sentimiento* 206). Yet, as witnessed in his treatment of the faithful characters Martina and Felipe, Unamuno maintains an almost reverent attitude towards those who have not lost their simple faith.[19] He does not accuse them of existential inauthenticity. Instead, he seems to regard the greatest example of inauthenticity in *La Esfinge* as indifference to mortality or claiming that a mortal existence can still have meaning. Teodoro, a revolutionary comrade, is represented as the aesthete of the group who is interested in the revolution and in Ángel for his eloquent speeches. When Ángel laments that, in the end, everything they work for will be reduced to "aerolitos pelados," Teodoro exclaims, "¡Hermosa evocación! ¡Trágico de verdad!" (146). However, the stage directions tell us that he does not feel the weight of Ángel's words, because he has been listening and commenting distractedly: "*mientras hablaba* Ángel *estaba arreglándose la corbata al espejo*" (146). Unamuno would reveal his scorn for such indifference again in *Del sentimiento*: "Y a todos nos falta algo; sólo que unos lo sienten y otros no. O hacen que no lo sienten, y entonces son unos hipócritas" (115). Unamuno also portrays the pursuit of worldly meaning as insufficient for existential authenticity through Ángel's arguments. Another revolutionary comrade, Nicolás, tries to convince Ángel to fight, "¡[p]or la verdad; por la belleza; por el bien!" (192), to which Ángel responds: "¡Verdad! . . . ¿Verdad de qué? ¿Qué belleza? ¿El bien de quien? Nunca os faltan nombres sonoros con que encubrir el vacío . . ." (193). Similarly, in *Del sentimiento,* Unamuno argues that the greatest example of hypocrisy is found in the fact that "[los racionalistas] se empeñan en convencer al hombre que hay motivos para vivir y hay consuelo de haber nacido" (227-28).

The idea of existential authenticity in *La Esfinge* is also connected to the problem of the self: the conflict between who one really is and how one is perceived, by others as well as by oneself. When Joaquín, another comrade in the revolution, accuses Ángel of being a traitor, Ángel responds that, "¡[n]o quiero serlo a mi conciencia!" (193). Shortly thereafter, he asks "¿por qué he de ser como me queréis vosotros y no como yo me quiero?" (195). Ángel's former pursuit of glory is clearly one example in which Ángel's authentic self has differed from his perception of himself. Ángel reveals to Felipe another example of this betrayal of the self when he admits that he has pretended to be crazy. "¿Por qué crees que lo hacía, Felipe? Por intrigar al prójimo; por hacerme el interesante; por aquello de que la locura y el genio . . . , ¡qué sé yo por qué!" (207). The confrontation between one's genuine self and the perception of oneself—that is, the "other" within—is dramatized best in the much discussed mirror scene, which will be echoed later in *El otro* (1926), and which Franco calls "uno de los momentos más logrados de todo el teatro unamuniano" (74). In his introduction to Unamuno's *Obras completas,* Manuel García Blanco links this scene to an experience that Unamuno describes in an article written for *La Nación* of Buenos Aires on November 24, 1913, titled "Días de limpieza": "La sensación, sensación que puede llegar a ser pavorosa, que yo he experimentado alguna vez, es la de quedarme un rato a solas mirándome a un espejo y acabar por verme como otro, como un extraño" (12). In the first act of the play, Ángel passes in front of a mirror and "*vislumbra de pronto su propia imagen como una sombra extraña y se detiene ante ella sobrecogido*" (170). He asks himself, "¿Sombra? . . . ¡No! . . . ¡No! . . . ¡Vivo!" and then, "[*d*]*e pronto, sintiendo una violenta palpitación, lanza un gemido y se lleva la mano al pecho*" (170). In this scene, we must imagine that Ángel has felt the Unamunian fear at viewing himself as an other, a stranger that does not represent who he feels himself to be.

Related to the conflict between the self and the other is the selfishness that results from Ángel's obsession with his own mortality. Much as González-del-Valle will argue that Fedra's main fault is egoism (43), Ángel is also plagued by his self-centeredness. This view is widely shared. Franco argues that Ángel, above all, suffers "una radical egolatría" (66). Stephen Summerhill makes the same argument (230). Unamuno certainly intended for Ángel's arrogance and lack of consideration for others to be seen as his main fault; Ángel himself recognizes this on several occasions. For example, as he dies, he admits to his friends, "[h]e querido hacer de vosotros, mis amigos, un comentario a mí: vosotros satélites, y el astro yo . . . ; no he querido que os manifestarais . . . Y también vosotros tenéis vuestra alma, tan alma como la mía" (218). He undergoes a similar recognition earlier, when Eufemia leaves him: "¡Su problema! Luego ella también lo tiene . . . ¡Sí, tiene su alma como yo!" (195). However, it takes her leaving for him to recognize this. Eufemia exposes his inability to recognize her as an equal long before she abandons him. After their heated discussion following the aforementioned chess game, she shouts at him as she walks out, "¡Eufemia no es una pieza de ajedrez!" (163), and later, she even more clearly confesses in a Kantian tone: "Hace tiempo que me he convencido de que me tomas no de fin, sino de medio, como tú dirías. Para ti no hay más fin que tú mismo [. . .] todo lo que sufres es un inmenso orgullo masculino, un egoísmo monstruoso" (174). As he is dying, Ángel concludes that his death is deserved, "es el pago merecido a mi soberbia" (220). In the previous scene, as Ángel confronts the crowd, he shouts, "no debo callarme porque soy palabra" (214), echoing the Biblical idea that God is the Word. Franco, analyzing Ángel's reference to his own "satánica soberbia" (207), suggests that Unamuno chose the name Ángel for its correlation with Satan as the angel fallen for having tried to equal God (66). This indeed seems corroborated by the text, where references to Ángel's pride and selfishness abound.[20]

Clearly, Unamuno's first drama portrays rich and well-developed tragic themes ignored by Steiner when he claimed in 1961 that tragedy is dead in the modern world. One cannot ignore, however, that Unamuno's dramas—with the possible exceptions of *Fedra* and *El otro*—are not heralded as successful tragedies. For this reason, I will close this study with a brief consideration of some of the technical shortcomings of *La Esfinge.* In response to the predominance of realism and naturalism in the bourgeois theater of the time, Unamuno writes in "Teatro de teatro" (1899), "¡Todo es inverosímil! Tal debe ser nuestro lema" (Elizalde 64). Unamuno's rejection of verisimilitude, however, does not stem solely from his rejection of the theater of his day, nor is it something that ought to be linked to his earlier plays alone; it also reflects the subordination of what he considers unnecessary and inconsequential details to the "drama of the soul" with which he is primarily concerned, as he explains in 1932 in his *Autocrítica* to *El otro* (1926), published six years after he completed the play itself: "Claro está que como en este "misterio" lo que importa es la verdad íntima, profunda, del drama del alma, no me anduve en esas minucias del arte realista de justificar entradas y salidas de los sujetos y hacer coherentes otros detalles. Eso está bien cuando se trata de fantoches, marionetas o muñecos" (*O.C.* V, 654). Unamuno's inattention to "esas minucias del arte realista" is apparent in *La Esfinge* as well. In the introduction to volume V of Unamuno's *Obras completas,* García Blanco reproduces one of the first critiques of *La Esfinge* from a letter written to Unamuno in January of 1899 by his friend Jiménez Ilundain, who finds the lack of verisimilitude in this tragedy to create enormous barriers between the audience and Unamuno's characters. Ilundain first points to the lack of humanity in the characters that results from Unamuno's focus on ideas: "Quiere usted pintar un estado de alma y se pinta a sí mismo con toda exactitud. Supone con esto que ha hecho una obra real y humana, y es todo lo contrario. No hay en ella nada humano en el protagonista y menos en su mujer" (15). For this reason, Ilundain also warns that the focus on abstract concepts in *La Esfinge* "hará que sólo la comprendan los genios, que deben abundar poco y que generalmente son algo envidiosos" (16).

Summerhill argues that, "Unamuno chose an essentially realistic or verisimilar mode of representation in which the sublime is conveyed symbolically" (237-8). However, there are repeated moments when the language is so symbolic and abstract that the reader/spectator could start to see the action as unrealistic. For example, as Ángel dies, he asks "¿Qué quiere decir la muerte?" and Joaquín replies, "¡Vida!" (217). Similarly, to Ángel's following question, "¿Qué quiere decir la vida?," Felipe answers, "¡Muerte!" (217). Here Unamuno's focus is clearly on abstract concepts, which results in a somewhat implausible death scene. In general, the characters in this play use a high and philosophical language uncommon in everyday discourse. It is this fact that provokes Ilundain's sharpest criticism of this play: the unrealistic figure of Eufemia. "La mujer de Ángel, ¿dónde diablos ha visto usted semejante mujer? [. . .] Aclare ese personaje, porque no se le entiende; y hágale hablar como una mujer y no como un filósofo" (17).²¹ In addition to the unrealistic language used by the characters, at times their actions fail to appear justified. For example, Eufemia's drastic and sudden change of heart at the end of the play is, if not improbable, poorly explained. The lack of verisimilitude in *La Esfinge* is at the very least distracting and it therefore presents an obstacle in conveying the tragic themes Unamuno wished to share with his community.

Perhaps an even larger obstacle is created by Ángel's selfishness. In the *Poetics,* Aristotle insists that the protagonist be admirable (1454b8-13). But Ángel, who exhibits a growing awareness of his self-centeredness and inability to look at other people as ends in themselves, does not change his actions as a result. Tía Ramona, Eufemia's aunt, seems to summarize the problem of Ángel's personality best. Eufemia tells her that Ángel, "[e]s brusco, pero, en el fondo, cariñoso," to which she responds, "[t]an en el fondo que es como si no lo fuese . . . En el fondo todos somos buenos" (171). Ángel argues at the beginning of the play that absolute honesty would allow people to understand and therefore genuinely love one another (149). However Ángel, throughout the play, seems concerned only with other people understanding *him.* After he abandons the revolution, Nicolás expresses a legitimate concern: "Y así nos dejas, a tus amigos; en la estacada . . . , a merced de Moreno [the opposition leader about whom we know very little] y de su gente . . ." (194). But Ángel concludes that his friends simply want to use him for their own protection, failing to recognize that his actions put his friends in this position. He responds to Nicolás: "Tengo que atender a mi salud. ¡Buscaos la vida!" (194).

Aristotle insists that the protagonist be admirable because the audience is likely to feel the most fear and pity for a character that they can relate to and esteem. While in modern tragedy the hero need not be a king or a member of the upper class, the hero must at least provoke sympathy. Due to Ángel's self-centeredness and arrogance, as well as the questionable sincerity of his recognition of these faults, the reader may not experience feelings of fear and pity throughout the play, and therefore, may not undergo a catharsis of these emotions. Seeing as this is the ultimate goal of tragedy according to Aristotle, the compromising of the tragic emotions by Ángel's less-than-admirable personality makes *La Esfinge* a weaker tragedy.

Doménech offers great insight as to why Unamuno's theater, while greatly appreciated by few, is misunderstood by most: "Quienes comparten ese sentimiento trágico, suelen gustar del teatro unamuniano [. . .] Quienes son insensibles a esa cosmovisión trágica, reparan sólo en su forma teatral poca elaborada" (115). This claim is perfectly applicable to *La Esfinge.* Someone deeply and personally burdened by the problem of immortality and of the futility of existence would more easily explain and therefore forgive Ángel's self-centeredness. But to those who do not understand or feel with similar intensity his crisis, his behavior might seem more like cruel indifference towards his wife, friends and followers in the revolution, making his death less pitiable and fearful—in short, less tragic. These shortcomings, however, do not undermine the importance of Unamuno in the development of a new model for Spanish tragedy in the twentieth century, which stands as a counter-example to George Steiner's claims about the impossibility of tragedy in the modern world. In *Del sentimiento,* Unamuno describes a modern tragic conflict, which lies between the absolute optimism of faith and the absolute pessimism of extreme doubt, which denies the capacities of modern progress and of religious faith, yet still maintains a rebellious hope that refuses to abandon the most troubling and often unanswerable questions that concern the genre of tragedy. *La Esfinge,* predating Unamuno's philosophical *magnus opus* by some twelve years, provides us with the first example of this movement in twentieth-century Spanish tragedy.

Notes

1. This title appears in literary criticism both capitalized, *La Esfinge,* and left in the lower-case, *La esfinge.* In Volume V of Unamuno's *Obras completas,* Manuel García Blanco has opted for the capitalized version, and I have followed his lead.

2. Donald Palmer shows, through a letter Unamuno wrote to Clarín on April 3, 1900, that at this time Unamuno was planning to read Kierkegaard (308). What cannot be proven is if and when Unamuno read *Fear and Trembling,* the essay that deals most directly with the problem of faith. However, Palmer argues, and I agree with him, that Unamuno must have read this essay at least in part before writing *Vida de Don Quijote y Sancho* in 1904. He finds evidence for this in the change in tone between this book and his 1898 essay "¡Muera Don Quijote!," as well as in Unamuno's use of the expression "knight of faith," which only appears in *Fear and Trembling* (308-10). Seven years after he wrote *Vida,* in *Del sentimiento,* Unamuno also makes reference to the Kierkegaardian leap (109), a central concept of *Fear and Trem-*

bling. It is important to consider whether or not Unamuno read this particular essay because it bears directly on the arguments of *Del sentimiento,* which in turn gives us a picture of a modern theme that is truly tragic. For the purposes of this study, however, I do not wish to go any further into the specific arguments about exactly how much influence Kierkegaard had on Unamuno, and to what extent Unamuno's thinking was original. It is clear that, to a certain extent, Unamuno was original; he developed many "Kierkegaardian" views before ever having read him, as a result of his crisis of 1897. At the same time, a strong influence by Kierkegaard is also clear, particularly in his later writings, where some of his earlier concepts seem to be refined as a result of having read Kierkegaard. Deszo Csejtei reminds us that, regardless of the exact level of Kierkegaardian influence in his writings, Unamuno played a crucial role in being one of the first to introduce Kierkegaard to the mainstream of European thought and that "[w]ith the spiritual association of the Danish and Spanish-Basque thinkers, the entire European culture has become richer" (721).

3. Doménech made this claim in 1996 at a conference celebrating Antonio Buero Vallejo's eightieth birthday, held at the Universidad Complutense (Madrid). In 1998, the proceedings from this conference were published in *Antonio Buero Vallejo literatura y filosofía.*

4. Theater of the Absurd is a term applied to works that are seen to concretize Camus' philosophy of the absurd as explained in *The Myth of Sisyphus* (1942). The paradigm examples of plays grouped under this heading are Samuel Beckett's *Waiting for Godot* (1948-49) and Eugène Ionesco's *The Bald Soprano* (1948) and *The Rhinoceros* (1959). The center of this movement is in Paris in the 1940s-1960s. Naturally affiliated with this movement, therefore, are plays written by France's most prominent existentialist philosophers, particularly Camus' *Caligula* (1938) and *Cross Purpose* (1944) and Sartre's *The Flies* (1942) and *No Exit* (1948). There are examples of plays considered representative of Theater of the Absurd from throughout Europe and Latin America: in Spain, Fernando Arrabal's *El cementerio de automóviles* (1958); in Cuba, Virgilio Piñera's *Electra Garrigó* (1959); in Great Britain, Harold Pinter's *The Caretaker* (1960) and in Poland, Slawomir Mrozek's *The Police* (1958).

5. In comparison with other twentieth-century tragedians, Unamuno and Buero Vallejo more pointedly insist upon the rebirth of hope in the face of tragic circumstances. The influence of Unamuno's philosophy on later Spanish tragedians seems greatest in the very successful tragedies of Buero Vallejo. Doménech is not overstating the fact that, "[e]l unamuniano 'sentimiento trágico de la vida' late en todas las creaciones dramáticas de Buero, desde su primer estreno hasta los más recientes. No hablo de coincidencias externas . . . sino de una compartida visión trágica del mundo." (116).

6. In her introduction to Pedrero's *Juego de noches,* Virtudes Serrano argues that Buero Vallejo's tragedies of hope are one of Pedrero's most prominent influences (32).

7. All quotes from *Del sentimiento* are from Nelson Orringer's edition (Tecnos 2005) unless otherwise noted.

8. "Tragedy is a representation of a serious, complete action which has magnitude, in embellished speech, with each of its elements [used] separately in the various parts [of the play]; [represented] by people acting and not by narration; accomplishing by means of pity and terror the catharsis of such emotions" (*Poetics* VI, 1449b22-28).

9. Aristotle takes the arousal of fear and pity into consideration in his discussion of all elements of tragedy. The importance of a compelling plot, with reversals, error and recognition, about an admirable, albeit flawed, protagonist, is directly linked to the importance of a tragedy provoking fear and pity in the spectator. It is true that there are other formal conditions set forth in the *Poetics* that are not always met today, such as the play being written in verse, and the use of a chorus and music. We must remember, however, that Aristotle's emphasis is on the *mythos,* the story or the plot of the tragedy, which he calls the "soul" of tragedy, and ranks first in the order of importance. Second most important in a tragedy, according to Aristotle, are the characters, and third, reasoning of the characters, portrayed in the play through speeches and the like. Aristotle gives fourth place to diction, about which he says, "I mean, as we said earlier, communication by means of language, which has the same potential in the case of both verse and [prose] speeches" (VI, 1450b13-14). Given Aristotle's own description of diction, it is hard to imagine that a play's being in prose instead of verse would cause Aristotle to refuse it as a tragedy. We must also remember that tragedy in verse was the only example of tragedy in Ancient Greece. The use of verse or prose seems very much related to what an audience expects and is

used to. As for the remaining parts of tragedy, Aristotle says this: "[S]ong is the most important of the embellishments. Spectacle is something enthralling, but it is very artless and least particular to the art of poetic composition. The potential of tragedy exists even without a performance and actors" (6, 1450b15-19). The ranking of importance that Aristotle gives the various parts of tragedy, in addition to the fact that he thinks tragedy is possible even when it is not performed, make it clear that for Aristotle the tragedy lies in the story, first and foremost, and how that story is told. The story must be told in a way that most effectively arouses fear and pity. Put in the simplest and most general terms possible, this is Aristotle's most basic requisite for tragedy. For a far more detailed analysis of the relevance of Aristotle's *Poetics* to twentieth-century tragedy, see the first chapter of my dissertation, "Modern Tragedy in the Absence of God: An Analysis of Unamuno and Buero Vallejo", presented at The University of Texas at Austin in 2006.

10. González-del-Valle bases his definition on the one given by Oscar Mandel in *A Definition of Tragedy*. New York: New York University Press, 1961. This quote is taken from p. 10 of this book.

11. González-del-Valle prefers Mandel's definition of tragedy because "está tratando de evitar el subjetivismo que ha caracterizado a otras visiones de este mismo género, anteriores a la suya, ya que aquí no se exigen tales reacciones, como terror o miedo, que en mucho dependen del temperamento de cada individuo" (19).

12. In addition to Manuel García Blanco's, Andrés Franco's and Iris M. Zavala's comprehensive studies, we have a collection of essays on Unamuno's theater put together by Jesús María Lasagabaster, Luis González-del-Valle's comparative study on the tragedy of Unamuno, Valle-Inclán and García Lorca, and a handful of smaller studies on particular works.

13. For a complete summary of Unamuno's attempts to have his plays represented as well as many examples of criticism from his friends and critics, see Manuel García Blanco's introduction to volume V of Unamuno's *Obras Completas,* and Andrés Franco's *El teatro de Unamuno.*

14. Nelson Orringer's edition of *Del sentimiento* contains a typographical error of this quote, which alters its meaning. In his version, this quote reads, "No [missing text] he querido poner al desnudo, no ya mi alma, sino el alma humana" (262), leaving out "he querido callar lo que callan otros;" where indicated. In Unamuno's *Obras completas* (VII, 183), as well as in Sánchez-Barbudo's edition (173) the quote appears in the form I have cited it in this study.

15. All quotes from *La Esfinge* are from *Obras completas* V.

16. Frustrated maternal aspirations in women are a recurring theme in Unamuno's drama and other works of prose fiction, appearing in six of his eleven dramas; we see examples of it here and in *La venda, Fedra, Soledad, Raquel encadenada* and *El otro.*

17. Orringer claims that Unamuno is influenced here by his reading of Auguste Sebatier, a nineteenth-century French theologian. Orringer finds similarities between this line and Sebatier's interpretation of Matthew 10:34—"Think not I am come to send peace on earth: I came not to send peace, but a sword"—which, according to Sabatier, reveals that "para el principio cristiano, en efecto, la guerra es la vida. Dejar de luchar [. . .] es morir" (515).

18. Orringer also argues that Unamuno's views developed in *Vida de Don Quijote y Sancho* are heavily influenced by his repeated readings of *Des Réputations littéraires* (1893), written by Paul Stapfer, a nineteenth-century historian of world literature and philosopher of religion (43).

19. This idealization of those with blind faith seems stronger in Unamuno's earlier works when we compare his treatment of blind faith in this play as well as in his next, *La venda* (1899), with the treatment of it in *San Manuel Bueno, Mártir* (1931) where the representative of blind faith, Blasillo el bobo, is portrayed as an idiot.

20. A few more examples of references to Ángel's self-absorption in the text include the following: Ángel recognizes the self-centeredness inherent in his obsession with his own death: "Es ese monstruoso egoísmo lo que a todas horas me pone ante los ojos del espíritu el espectro de la muerte" (154). Eufemia agrees that Ángel's obsession with death entails a certain amount of narcissism when she tells him that "[c]omo vives lleno de ti mismo, crees que en muriéndote tú se acaba el mundo" (174). She reminds Ángel that his behavior affects those around him when, in response to his complaint that "[t]ú no sabes lo que sufro," she reminds him: "¡Y lo que haces sufrir!" (163). Tía Ramona also complains that Ángel's abstract preoccupations do not forgive his mistreatment of others: "Está bien pensar en cosas muy altas, muy altas, pero los demás también somos personas" (172). And finally, Joaquín also tells Ángel directly that what he suffers from more than anything is his own self-centeredness: "Sé una vez siquiera

hombre natural . . . , humano . . . Arroja de ti esa egoísta voluptuosidad de la tristeza . . ." (211).

21. García Blanco also reproduces Unamuno's response to Ilundain, written on May 24, 1899. Answering to Ilundain's many criticisms, Unamuno argues that, "conste que no aspiro a un éxito teatral, si para conseguirlo he de sacrificar lo, a mi juicio, insacrificable. Me importa poco que no lo entiendan. [. . .] Más que hacer dramas para el público, quiero hacer púbilco para los dramas" (29).

Works Cited

Aristotle. *Poetics*. Trans. Richard Janko. Indianapolis: Hackett, 1987.

Buero Vallejo, Antonio. "La tragedia." *El teatro: enciclopedia del arte escénico*. Ed. Guillermo Díaz-Plaja. Barcelona: Noguer, 1958. 63-87.

Csejtei, Deszo. "The Knight of Faith on Spanish Land: Kierkegaard and Unamuno." *Letras Peninsulares* 13.2-3 (2000-01): 707-23.

Doménech, Ricardo. "Buero Vallejo y el camino de la tragedia." *Antonio Buero Vallejo literatura y filosofía: Homenaje de la Universidad Complutense al dramaturgo en su 80 aniversario*. Ed. Ana María Leyra. Madrid: Ed. Complutense, 1998. 109-118.

Elizalde, Ignacio. "Características del teatro de Unamuno." *El teatro de Miguel de Unamuno*. Ed. Jesús María Lasagabaster. San Sebastián: Univ. de Deusto, 1988. 47-66.

Flórez Miguel, Cirilio. "La crisis de 1898: Interpretación filosófica." *Anuario Filosófico* 31.1 (1998): 289-303.

Franco, Andrés. *El teatro de Unamuno*. Madrid: Ínsula, 1971.

González-del-Valle, Luis. *La tragedia en el teatro de Unamuno, Valle-Inclán y García Lorca*. New York: Eliseo Torres, 1975.

Gullón, Ricardo. "Unamuno en su teatro." *El teatro de Miguel de Unamuno*. Ed. Jesús María Lasagabaster. San Sebastián: Univ. de Deusto, 1988. 227-41.

Kaufmann, Walter. *Tragedy and Philosophy*. New York: Anchor Books, 1969.

Kern, Edith. *Existential Thought and Fictional Technique: Kierkegaard, Sartre, Beckett*. New Haven: Yale UP, 1970.

Kierkegaard, Søren. *Fear and Trembling*. Trans. Alastair Hannay. London: Penguin, 1985.

Lasagabaster, Jesús María. "Introducción." *El teatro de Miguel de Unamuno*. Ed. Jesús María Lasagabaster. San Sebastián: Univ. de Deusto, 1988. 8-10.

Palmer, Donald D. "Unamuno's Don Quijote and Kierkegaard's Abraham." *Revista de Estudios Hispánicos* 3 (1969): 295-312.

Pedrero, Paloma. *Juego de noches. Nueve obras en un acto*. Intro. and Ed. Virtudes Serrano. Madrid: Cátedra, 2005.

Shaw, D. L. "Imagery and Symbolism in the Theater of Unamuno: *La Esfinge* and *Soledad*." *Journal of Spanish Studies: Twentieth Century* 7.1 (1979): 87-104.

———. "Lorca's Late Plays and the Idea of Tragedy." *Essays on Hispanic themes in Honour of Edward C. Riley*. Eds. Jennifer Lowe and Philip Swanson. Edinburgh: University of Edinburgh, 1989. 200-08.

Steiner, George. *The Death of Tragedy*. New York: Alfred A. Knopf, 1961.

Summerhill, Stephen J. "Freedom, the Invisible and the Sublime in Unamuno's *La esfinge*." *Letras Peninsulares* 14.2 (2001): 227-42.

Unamuno, Miguel de. *Del sentimiento trágico de la vida* y *La agonía del cristianismo*. Ed. Antonio Sánchez-Barbudo. Madrid: Akal, 1983.

———. *Del sentimiento trágico de la vida en los hombres y en los pueblos* y *El tratado del amor de Dios*. Intro. and Ed. Nelson Orringer. Madrid: Tecnos, 2005.

———. *Obras completas por Miguel de Unamuno*. Vols. V and VII. Intro. Manuel García Blanco. Madrid: Escelicer, 1968. 9 vols.

———. *Vida de Don Quijote y Sancho*. Madrid: Austral, 1964.

Zavala, Iris M. "La dialogía del teatro unamuniano: Género interno." *El teatro de Miguel de Unamuno*. Ed. Jesús María Lasagabaster. San Sebastián: Univ. de Deusto, 1988. 13-26.

———. *Unamuno y su teatro de conciencia*. Salamanca: U de Salamanca, 1963.

EL OTRO (1932; *THE OTHER*)

CRITICAL COMMENTARY

Robert B. Heilman (essay date 1979)

SOURCE: Heilman, Robert B. "Farce Transformed: Plautus, Shakespeare, and Unamuno." *Comparative Literature* 31 (1979): 113-23.

[*In the following essay, Heilman traces the trajectory of farce as a theatrical genre and finds ties among the Roman comic playwright Plautus, William Shakespeare, and Unamuno.*]

Farce is neither the fetus nor the corpse of comedy.

Farce is a generator of materials that can be utilized and even transformed by other modes—by comedy, of course, but even by romantic and tragic styles.

In the next-to-last of his dozen dramas—*El Otro (The Other)*, 1932—Miguel de Unamuno (1864-1936) accomplishes a remarkable metamorphosis of certain raw materials of farce. He brings them into the realms of fundamental human melodrama and of tragedy. Here, as in other plays, he explores the themes of his best known work, *The Tragic Sense of Life* (1913). A still more significant point for dramatic criticism: if one read *The Other* without knowing who wrote it, one might suppose it to be by Pirandello. A characteristic Pirandellian procedure is the translation of a basically farcical situation into an epistemological problem.

These diverse points can be boldly juxtaposed because the working out of their relationships canvasses each issue better than would an independent treatment of it.

To say that farce is neither the fetus nor the corpse of comedy is to say that farce is neither a temporary primitive stage which necessarily grows into full comedy, nor the residue when comedy goes into a decline. Nevertheless cultural history, rather than some organic rise and fall, may make farce seem like the earliest, or the dilapidated latest, stage of comic form. We can see a development in time from early Greek phallic rites—fertility farce, as it were—to the sophisticated comedy of Aristophanes; from the farce of the miracle plays and sixteenth-century drama to Shakespearean high comedy; from the *commedia dell' arte* of the Italian Renaissance, Molière's first instrument, to the brilliant comedy which Molière evolved from it. But while culture makes possible the emergence of more mature forms, it does not wipe out the more primitive ones; farce is never rejected but continues a healthy independent life alongside more advanced comedies. This is not what fetuses do. The opposite movement, the decline from mature to more primitive forms, also occurs in history: there is a backsliding from Aristophanes to Menander, Plautus, and Terence; from Molière to Labiche and Feydeau. But again this is a cultural phenomenon: a change in society's values or taste causes the stage to give more of its time to less mature and demanding forms. The farce that may take over after a period of comic achievement or even brilliance (e.g., as in the English theater in the decades after Wilde, Shaw, Synge, and O'Casey) is not a dying ember, an organic deterioration, or a skeleton of what went before. It is a perfectly healthy form that, for reasons which may be very complex and which are not our business here, occupies for a time the theatrical energies of a culture. So, if in any given historical stretch we can see the comic stage—the stage that is concerned with the skirmishings

in society rather than with the war in the soul—going through phases dominated first by farce, then by comedy of character, and then again by farce, we cannot interpret these events by the analogy of natural or organic growth and decline.

But let us eliminate the downhill movement, which I have so far included only for theoretical completeness, and stick to the uphill movement. In this, there is a way to use farce as a base for a kind of evolutionary development. This hypothetical evolution is not chronological (although it can take place in time), but logical: out of farce come elements which, added to or altered by the dramatist, lead into the structure or tone of other genres. Farce provides building blocks for different kinds of constructions. That is, we can make a schematic diagram of evolutionary relationships between farcical and less primitive forms.

Farce is primarily physical. It is strenuous and tireless; all resources go into bodily activity. This is because no energy goes into real thought. No energy goes into real feeling, though stereotyped emotional responses may be screamed at us. No energy goes into moral concern, though moral fervor is often simulated. A good deal of the time, no energy goes into acts of will; action is then an automatic result of banana-peel incidents. Things happen to people more often than people make things happen. In sum, farce elects to depict the human being at a stage where he has not yet taken on the burdens of mind, feeling, conscience, and will. When people lack intelligence, feelings, moral concern, and will, there is nothing to linger over, and action has to be speedy. The chase is a key event in farce. Fast pace is not a primary quality in farce, but is an inevitable by-product of the primary qualities we have listed. Besides, what is fast is generally automatic, and automatism is of the farcical essence. Likewise mechanicalness, responsiveness to stimuli.

This ideal account of farce is not always matched by farcical practice, which tends to let some touch of mind, feeling, conscience, or will appear in some characters. Will is the first element to assert itself; through it, some characters try to make things happen instead of reacting to things that happen to them. Will causes the quick mad plans, the ingenious extemporizations, the opportunistic about-faces that make farce a medley of scurry, scramble, and chase. We see this in all kinds of farcical confusions, including the specialized form of bedroom farce. We can learn something about farce by distinguishing bedroom farce and porn. In farce, sexual entrepreneurs lack feeling, try rather than succeed, and hurry rather than linger. But porn depends on intensity, success, and the long-held writing scene: the recipe is so standardized that the result is porn corn. In farce, eroticism is dehydrated into a quick formality needed to get or keep things going.

Here we may seem a long distance from Unamuno's *The Other.* We are and we aren't. I want to move from the preceding abstractions to Unamuno's singular plot by three brief intermediate stops—one in Plautus and two in Shakespeare. Ties will emerge: strange patterns of confusion.

Plautus' *Menaechmi* is an almost flawless archetype of farcical procedure: up confusion and down probability (and it's not really so much down probability as that probability is irrelevant). Here we first see the twins that introduce the perennial dramatic issue of who's who, farcical and otherwise. Plautus' pair are both named Menaechmus; though brought up from infancy in different towns, Syracuse and Epidamnus, they can be distinguished by nobody. Menaechmus Syracuse, on a six-year hunt for his lost twin, lands in Epidamnus. He is immediately called "Menaechmus" by various people whom he has never seen before. Does it ever occur to him that he has reached the end of his six-year hunt? Never, never in the slightest. Such headwork is excluded by convention. So misunderstandings, arguments, and fights break out; everyone is angry, but no one is really hurt. True feelings are excluded by convention. The home-town Menaechmus is carrying on with a whore who lives next door (the Roman stage made things more convenient than modern zoning does); he steals a dress and jewels from his wife for the girl, and then the immigrant Menaechmus steals them from the girl. The only problem is whether the thief gets caught and if caught, can lie out of it. Moral concern is excluded by convention. Finally, most of the action results from accidental meetings; things happen to people rather than being brought about by action of the will, which is excluded by convention (though here it does act occasionally).

Now when Shakespeare remakes *Menaechmi* as *The Comedy of Errors,* he moves in two different directions which illustrate two of the possible treatments of the materials generated by farce. One direction is obvious: Shakespeare doubles the ante. Each Menaechmus becomes an Antipholus, and each Antipholus has as slave a twin named Dromio. The possibilities of confusion are vastly multiplied. Shakespeare does other multiplications: he increases Plautus' one physical beating to five, with others promised or threatened, and the physical objects that cause misunderstandings and fights from three to five. Just for the fun of it, Shakespeare adds as well as multiplies: he contributes the grotesque kitchen wench who amorously pursues one Dromio, and he extends the characteristic three-liner jokes of Plautus into larger verbal games such as the description of the wench by an elaborate geographical metaphor.

With such a reckless hyperbole of farcical basics, it is amazing that Shakespeare also moves in a sharply different direction, or really in two different directions.

His first sharp move away from Plautus is to juxtapose the who's-who farce with materials that are not farcical at all, are, indeed, those of melodrama and romance. Aegeon, the twins' father, also on a family search, lands in Ephesus, where, by a legal technicality, he can be executed. His danger is real, and what is more he even gets some sympathy from the local Duke: here are incursions of the genuine feeling excluded by farce. Aegeon is not only saved but recovers a long-lost wife, and his unmarried son falls in love with his sister-in-law; these are the materials of romance. But still more interesting than this annexing of the nonfarcical to basically farcical territory is the transforming of the basically farcical into something else. Take the lockout scene borrowed from Plautus' *Amphitruo*: the native Antipholus, shut out of his house while his twin dines inside, roars around, exchanges insults with the servants, and threatens to break down the door. This is sheer farce. But then Shakespeare modifies the tone when Balthazar urges the raging husband to have "patience," to guard his "reputation," to recall the "honour" of his wife and his "long experience of her wisdom, . . . virtue, . . . and modesty," and to wait for a later explanation instead of increasing an uproar that will arouse "vulgar comment" (III.i.86, 89-91, 101). Patience, reasonableness, decorum belong to a fuller humanity than farce admits, as does Antipholus' partial acquiescence in sensible proposals. There is still greater augmentation of humanity in Shakespeare's treatment of Antipholus' wife Adriana, who comes out of the farcical mold of the ranting jealous wife. But Adriana has ideas: she and her sister Luciana argue about the subordination of wives to husbands (II.i.10-41). She can reproach her supposedly faithless husband soberly, and can even speak in paradox: if he is licentious, she herself is "possessed with an adulterous blot" since "we two be one" (II.ii.138, 140). Though she can rage about her husband, she can also assert, "Ah but I think him better than I say," and "My heart prays for him, though my tongue do curse" (IV.ii.25, 28). Here is feeling beyond farce. Still more significant: at the end Adriana, trapped by the Abbess' clever interrogation, acknowledges that she has been a nagging wife. With this anagnorisis, unimaginable in farce, the action is that of comedy of character.

This amplification of humanity in a farcical staple, the actual or potential shrew, is managed differently in *The Taming of the Shrew.* Adriana is humanized by traits that take her beyond mechanical responses into thoughts and feelings; Kate is subjected to a discipline which admits nothing but mechanical automatic responses. With Adriana, the *donnée* is farcical, but the author imagines a character who spontaneously enlarges the *donnée*; with Kate the *donnée* and the altering of it are both farcical. The changing of Kate is imaged as the training of an animal; the automatic and conditioned responses to stimuli are an ultimate of farcical action.

In this there is the essence of psychological farce. Yet it moves toward comedy of character: the trainer is ultimately a loving man, and the trainee, far from being a depersonalized victim of a system, is really freed from a curse and delivered into a freer, more imaginative, happier life. Ironically, a farcical method turns a farcical character into an amiable participant in comic life. Conversely, Charles Marowitz' *The Shrew* (London, 1975) transforms a farcical *donnée* into bitter satire by making Petruchio a destructive sadist, and Kate's younger sister Bianca into a female sadist who annihilates her man by a diabolically ingenious alternation of tantrums, tears, and titillations.

The Lucentio-Bianca action, secondary though it is in Shakespeare's play, is critically interesting because it takes the confused-identity business of *The Comedy of Errors* into a less primitive phase: some people don't know who's who because other people assume false identities. Instead of the genetic accident of identical twinship (a biological banana-peel episode, as it were), we have voluntary actions: the will is activated by a romantic quest. Here is a basic pattern of action that we have seen, with numerous variations, in scores of dramas during and since the Renaissance—from perennial physical disguises of all kinds to psychological and moral disguises such as those of Wycherley's Horner and Molière's Tartuffe. Traditionally the audiences of such plays know who's who, while some or most of the surrounding cast do not. Then in a new twentieth-century twist the audience is made to share in the cast's ignorance of a key identity, a method used ingeniously in Anthony Shaffer's *Sleuth* (here a farcical form is transmogrified into a melodramatic structure).

A subtler refinement of the who's-who motif originates earlier; it is best exemplified in Molière's *The Misanthrope*, where the protagonist's sense of his own identity is unreliable, and where we must deal with ambiguity but not yet mystery. Alceste does not quite take the next step from this erroneous certainty of self-identity to a puzzled uncertainty about self-identity. When the issue changes from "Who's who?" to "What is he?" the inquiry is a more demanding one, but when the question becomes "Who am I?" the pursuit of mystery may seem to have got out of hand. "Who am I?" (or, "I want to know who I am") can lead to tedious narcissistic lucubrations outside the theater and on stage. Though the dramatist may sympathize with such research-by-mirror, another kind of reflection game is likely to take over: in this, every man may be sure who he is, but others can never agree who he is. Each reading of a problematic identity reflects the observer's angle of vision, and no two angles are alike. The identity that all seek, or think they can pin down, floats away in a misty sea of irreconcilable subjectivities. Having said this, we need hardly add, "the Pirandello way." By now the simple problem of identity that originates in a pair of look-alikes has been gradually reworked until it has issued in an epistemological or even metaphysical mystery. Temporary misunderstandings have given way to a permanent enigma. Once A looked like B; now A looks only like any observer's image of him, and all observers are immutably different. Besides, A may even have found himself capable of enough roles to have become a puzzle to himself.

Now when confusion of the who's-who mode has progressed as if evolutionarily to the point at which the problem is psychological and possibly metaphysical, we might expect that a playwright would not again turn to so apparently simple a source of drama as twinship. Yet that is just what Unamuno does in *The Other: A Mystery in Three Acts and an Epilogue* (written in 1926, produced and published in 1932).[1] Like Shakespeare moving on from Plautus, he is impelled to multiply twinship. But unlike Shakespeare, who garnishes a central farcical dish with nonfarcical additions, Unamuno transforms the farcical center into an intense imaging of melodramatic passions and even tragic feeling. Identicality, though even here it may involve indistinguishability, spurs competitiveness and destructiveness.

The twins Cosme and Damián make passionate love to Laura, who (like the wife in Plautus and in Shakespeare) cannot tell them apart. In her account of it, "their rivalry was ferocious," they "terrified" her, and "they won me over, or won over me, with their violence" (II.ii, p. 264). They agreed that whoever did not marry her would go away; one left, and she married the other, Cosme. Later Damián married Damiana. Damián visited Cosme, who murdered him and put the body in the cellar. Damiana comes to demand what they did with her husband, though in one speech she addresses Cosme as "Damián." Each of the women appears to believe that the surviving twin is her husband, and both approach him enticingly. He rages at both of them as "furies." Their rivalry exacerbates his distraught state, which we take to be caused by guilt, self-hatred, a sense of lost identity, and a conviction of deadness that identifies him with the corpse. He commits suicide, Damiana sneers triumphantly at Laura, and three observers comment on the "mad" quartet and their imbroglio to which, à la Pirandello, there is said to be no "public solution" (Epilogue, p. 296).

There is no "public solution" because Unamuno has so ingeniously managed things—uncertainties and riddling speeches in the two pairs—that while we do take Cosme to be both homicide and suicide, it just could be the other way around. Cosme calls himself "the other" and "The Other"; this duality of identity, which becomes a set verbalized matter after the murder, looms large in the attitudes of all agonists (and is important enough to provide Unamuno with his title). Thus the twinship that comes out of farce symbolizes profound problems of kinship. The survivor, we assume, speaks for both brothers. A twin, he says, is a mirror; this mirror becomes unbearably painful. For one thing, it makes a visible object for the self-hatred that Unamuno appears to postulate as a given (thus the homicidal act is also suicidal). Further, self-hatred is a product of jealousy, and jealousy is inevitable when one "does not feel that he is different, obviously different, distinguishably different" (III.ii, p. 277). Though twinship is thus generalized as a symbol of nondistinctiveness or nonuniqueness, Unamuno is more intent on analyzing what lies under kinship—the love/hate ambiguity and the sibling rivalry of which the ultimate form is fratricide.

Unamuno thus remarkably deepens the materials that traditionally belonged to farce. At the same time he makes an extraordinary fusion of this transmuted farce with a Biblical myth—the Cain-and-Abel story that has caught the imagination of various modern dramatists.[2] "Cain! Cain! I call myself that name every night," cries The Other (II.iv, p. 268), and from now on, in the imagination and speech of both himself and others, he is regularly Cain (for convenience I shall call him that). Now in this one sense the twins are distinguished: the dead man is Abel, and the survivor is Cain, and Cain and Abel, we suppose, have to be different souls as they are different bodies. Yet almost immediately Unamuno makes astonishing moves toward the restoration of indistinguishability. The idea of the identity of Cain and Abel has to be articulated by the survivor, but Unamuno makes no move to counter dramatically the line taken by this Cain: "Who is the assassin? Who the assassinated? . . . Which one is Cain? And which one Abel? . . . Hate your brother as you hate yourself! . . . Who is the dead one? Who is the more dead? . . . And I tell myself that if Cain had not killed Abel, Abel would have killed Cain. . . . In any case, does one become Cain for having killed one's brother, or does one kill one's brother because one is Cain? . . . I? One and the other, Cain and Abel, hangman and hanged!" (II.iv, pp. 267-69). And he goes on paradoxically to impute a Cain-like nature to Abel: "He's killing me . . . Abel is implacable. Abel never forgives. Abel is evil! Yes, yes, if Cain hadn't killed him, Abel would have killed Cain . . . Abel is killing me. Abel! What hast thou done with thy brother? Whoever gets himself executed is as evil as whoever acts as executioner. To let oneself become a victim is a diabolic vengeance" (II.vi, p. 271). Cain may, of course, be warding off guilt by outrageous accusation, but everything he says is consistent with the direction of Unamuno's dramatic thought: if we take twinship deeper than the level of visual indistinguishability (the old stage game), it means psychological and moral indistinguishability. Unamuno carries this out by departing from the myth: the original Cain lived on, but

this one commits suicide—the final proof of a twinship in which the two poles of fratricide are suicide-by-getting-murdered and suicide-by-murdering.

Yet this is by no means the end of the doubleness that fascinates the dramatist. Cain goes on, in a series of misogynic thrusts, to interpret the two wives, Laura and Damiana, as doubles, that is, as identical in nature and motive. He thinks that, just as each brother desired "the other" woman, so each woman desired "the other" brother: "One always desires what one doesn't have." He becomes more distraught. "Between the two of you you're destroying me. . . . The two of you killed the one . . . and the two of you will kill the other. . . . You're both the same . . . There's no difference between you. . . . The same fury . . . And both of us feared your fury" (III.iii, pp. 280-82). "And now I'm in the hands . . . of the two furies" (III.iv, p. 284). His speech before his final exit includes these words: "I'm leaving . . . It's horrible to be saddled with these furies . . . Two women on the back of one dead man" (III.vi, p. 288).

In effect Unamuno is doing what Shakespeare did—adding another pair of twins to the inherited story, though these are metaphorical rather than literal. Both "furies" want to claim Cain—as an actual or spiritual husband/lover. Each insists that she is his loved one. Each believes that Cain killed "for my sake." Each demands that he make a choice now, ratifying a choice made earlier by marital or adulterous or desired embrace. Each makes amorous gestures. Shakespearean confusions are translated into the idiom of rapacious rivalry; Unamuno seeks out the dark underside of moral twinship, the nexus of sex and violence before this had become a commonplace of man-in-the-street wisdom. But once again the astonishing turnabout: the separation of the twins, like that which turned the brothers into Cain and Abel. Yet with a difference that prevents bland repetition; while that earlier distinction was promptly blurred by the introduction of a new mode of identity between the men, the one between the women gradually becomes more marked. Damiana is the more aggressive of the two—bolder, more brazen, more fierce and relentless. Let Laura be the widow, she demands; "you were both," she avers to Cain, "in love with me" (III.iii, p. 281). She gets into a screaming match with Laura and demands that Cain kill her. Here is where the dramatic break comes. Laura says she'll go away so that there will be "no more killing"; she tells Damiana, "We can't divide him up. . . . I'll leave him for you" (III.v, pp. 285-86). Damiana sneers at this "judgment of Solomon" (which, of course, implies that Cain is actually Laura's Cosme) and tears on in a manic vociferation of superiority, possession, domination. While Unamuno has made Cain and Abel into identical twins, he has made these female "twins" into a clearly differentiable Cain and Abel. He makes this metaphorical transformation explicit through some key phrases spoken by Damiana in a rancorous diatribe against Laura: "Poor little victim! . . . Poor little barren Abela! . . . Poor meek lamb! Poor little Abela!" (III.ix, p. 291).

This clear distinguishing of Damiana and "Abela" after the dramatic insistence that Cain and Abel are indistinguishable might let us suspect, in Unamuno, a fear lest an excess of twinship fuse all individualities in a common human mass. But just when he dissolves the second pair of "twins," he suddenly brings in what is in effect a third pair (and thus outdistances the hyperboles of farce). Damiana has called Laura "barren Abela." This is an especial triumph: Damiana has already declared that she is pregnant, bearing the offspring, she claims, "of both [brothers]" (III.iii, p. 283). What is more—this is her climactic shock—she is carrying two, "like Jacob and Esau" (whose fighting "in their mother's womb" Cain has already likened to the "fraternal hatred" of Cosme and Damián; II.iv, p. 267). Damiana goes on, savagely satisfied, "I can feel the struggle going on in my womb. Each one trying to come into the world first so as to be the first to get the other one out of the world" (III.ix, p. 292). Except for an Epilogue in which three noncombatants declare the two love/hate pairs "mad" and, probing for the actualities, hardly go beyond ambiguities and "mystery," the play ends with Damiana's pride in a womb where "the eternal warfare between brothers is reborn."

This rather ample description (which still neglects various intricacies of the plot and thought) should reveal something of the subtlety and paradox of Unamuno's employment of an ancient motif. Insofar as twinship is an affair of simultaneity, farce uses likeness for temporary confusions, Unamuno to symbolize moral resemblance and even identity in areas where we might ordinarily take differentiation for granted. Then to simultaneity Unamuno adds succession in time: an innovation that declares the unquenchability of the emotions, inherent in or imaged by kinship, that we might expect time to assuage. The tenacity of the feud seems unlikely to be relaxed by the charity, with its offspring forgetfulness, proposed in the Epilogue as the requisite solvent. But however Unamuno's complexities are to be defined—and they elude reduction to propositions—his method reveals an extraordinary "evolutionary" development not only of the primitive general stuff of farce, but of a particular stuff that might seem least open to modifications of its primal simplicity. Perhaps in this we learn something about modal power to transform, as well as about diverse generic potentialities in apparently unmalleable materials.

Once we have traced twins from Plautus to Shakespeare (there are historical connections between them) and from both of them to Unamuno (as far as I know, there

are no historical connections here), we may seem to have outlined a cultural advance which means that "we have put childish things behind us." We may want to lament that the trivialities of farce remain on the stage, that evolution has not freed the world from lower things and made it safe for higher. Not so, not so. Farce has a function which is to be understood; hence it does not deserve the disparagement which the person of culture is likely to think its only due. Nor on the other hand need a defender puff it up into a grander status than it can have, as some recent figures in drama, swinging on the inevitable pendulum of changing attitudes, tend to do. For instance, such dramatists as Ionesco and Dürrenmatt apply the term "tragic farce" to some of their plays. They may, of course, only be speaking very modestly, but I suspect that they are ascribing to farce a depth or range that custom has not perceived. This is just what certain critics do. They consider farce to be not only a central element in comedy but also an expression of the revolutionary spirit in man, the voice of all his resentment against the system, even a symptom of anarchic longings and a deep-lying addiction to chaos. This carries rehabilitation too far. One can make a case for farce without magnifying it into an escape hatch for the eternal rebel and Yahoo in man. If we accept farce as technically the presentation of man at a level of mechanical, physical existence—that is, with little, if any, thought, feeling, moral concern, or will—then its function in the general human scene is clear enough. It provides a brief holiday from responsibility, a vacation from both the vulnerability that can never be eliminated and the obligations that may never be rejected, in human existence. Farce is an hour's respite from order and from the absolute necessity of seeking it. It symbolizes not a wish to tear down, but a temporary release from the Atlantean labor of holding up. It is a momentary truancy, finally, not from external pressures and systems, but from the heavy, the lasting burdens of being fully human.

The social critic would have grounds for action only if farce took sole possession of the stage. A theatergoer could not survive on an exclusive diet of farce. Nor could he live only on the grave conundrums of Unamuno.

Notes

1. References are to the text in Miguel de Unamuno, *Ficciones: Four Stories and a Play,* trans. Anthony Kerrigan, with an Introduction and Notes by Martin Nozick, Bollingen Series 85, No. 7 (Princeton, N.J., 1976). References are to act, scene, and page in this edition.

2. Since Byron's *Cain: A Mystery* (1821) the subject has been used repeatedly. There is some sympathy with Cain, or the rebellious spirit in Eden, in W. V. Moody's *The Death of Eve* (1912, unfinished)

and in *Caín* (1928) by the Chilean dramatist Antonio Acevedo Hernández (1928). The story is retold picturesquely in Marc Connelly's *Green Pastures* (1930) and allegorically as a comment on life in Russian-occupied Lithuania by Antanas Škėma in *Žvakidė* (1957). The theme appears in a number of plays in German: Anten Wildgans, *Kain* (1920); Alfred Neumann, *Abel* (1948); and Erich Nossack, *Die Rotte Kain* (*The Cain Tribe,* 1948). The Viennese Wildgans' interpretation of Cain as a hostile and aggressive type provides the general pattern for three plays, two English and one American. In Shaw's *Back to Methusaleh* (1921) Cain appears first as a jaunty defender of the fight-and-conquer mode of life and scorner of Adam's agricultural drudgery; next as Cain Adamson Napoleon, confident conquistador; then finally as a ghost uttering a Shavian lament that the strong have killed each other off and only the weak survive. In Thornton Wilder's *The Skin of Our Teeth* (1942) Henry Antrobus, a modern Cain (called by the name "Cain" only in crises), is resentful, quarrelsome, paranoid, an embodiment of the spirit of war. There is a similar reading in Christopher Fry's *A Sleep of Prisoners* (1951), in which a tense World War II officer is identified, in dreams, with Cain and other quick-to-anger-and-attack Old Testament characters. He is balanced off against an Abel type who also appears in different mythical *personae.* Unamuno anticipated Wilder and Fry in using modern characters who embody mythical archetypes, went beyond them in probing the characters, and departed from them in specializing his *personae* as bearers of the fratricidal impulse.

Edward H. Friedman (essay date 1980)

SOURCE: Friedman, Edward H. "From Concept to Drama: The Other Unamuno." *Hispanofila,* no. 68 (1980): 29-38.

[*In the following essay, Friedman examines Unamuno's preoccupation with the problem of the "ambivalence of the self" in all of his plays, but particularly in* El otro.]

> . . . no he escrito esta obra no más que para que los espectadores y las espectadoras pasen el rato, mascullando acaso chocolatinas.
>
> Miguel de Unamuno, Autocrítica, *El otro.*

One of the numerous Unamunian paradoxes is the fact that the author's novels have a strongly dramatic quality—in the use of interior dialogue and a sustained high emotional level—, while his theater has been considered anti-dramatic or lacking in dramatic technique. Un-amuno himself admitted that his plays were not for the critics, nor for the actors, but for the individual soul. The works are *drumas,* a word used by the protagonist of **Soledad,** and are to drama what the *nivolas* are to the novel: ideological plays presented on unadorned stages by actors who portray not man as a concept but man of flesh and blood. Fernando Lázaro denotes as one of the thematic divisions of Unamuno's drama the problem of the reality of literary characters (*entes de ficción*) with no distinction between historical existence and fictional existence.[1] The intimate reality of a fictional character is identical to that of man, since both are products of a development or transformation—*un hacerse*—, and therefore, Unamuno creates *personas* rather than *personajes.*[2]

Unamuno's theater is a literary theater in the sense that all visual elements and movement are subordinated to the dialogue. He conceived a theater to be heard rather than to be seen: "Prefiero un público ciego a un público sordo," he remarked. The primary aim of drama, according to the theory of Unamuno, is to show total reality and the interior of the soul, to reveal to the audience (*los oyentes*) the profundity of the conscience.

Iris Zavala in *Unamuno y su teatro de conciencia* notes two fundamental aspects of Unamuno's dramatic theory: the religious and the popular. Even more than religious, Unamuno's theater is mystical—full of mystery, of myth, of unreality. Man is the scenification of a dream of God, and the theater is then a microcosmic representation of the world as a stage. The author's attempts to reach the essence of the individual lead him also to search for the primary sources of the Spanish spirit. If self-examination leads to personal unity, the acceptance of the intrahistoric past leads to collective unity, to a knowledge of man and of men. The predominance of intrahistory over history in Unamuno recalls Aristotle's classification of tragedy before history, a juxtaposition based on inner continuity and universal application as superior to factual happenings (*Poetics,* ix).

In his article "Acción y pasión dramáticas" (1922). Un-amuno states that the depiction of the personality is more essential to drama than the logical succession of events. The material stage, as well as the psychical, must be a manifestation of the different types of *yos* that each man carries within himself. Paul Ilie, in *Unamuno: An Existential View of Self and Society,* examines these divisions of the self into separate entities, or *yos,* "in which various ego fragments distinguish themselves and sometimes claim autonomy."[3] The objectification and consequent alienation of the self results in the creation of the Other—detachment from one's own being, the antithesis of which is total unawareness of the self. Man's effort to know himself causes him to objectify part of himself. The alienated self loses identity with its subject and can no longer feel consciousness through its former self. Depersonal-ization is the tragic outcome of an excessive dependence upon the world's view of the self, which, though not an accurate view, attains dominance over the subjective self. The Other is therefore both "a psychological product of alienation and the social alter-ego which the individual uses to participate in the world" (p. 94). The process of *desdoblamiento,* physical or mental redupli-cation, probably finds its archetype in the story of Narcissus, and the multiple self has been a frequent literary convention from the mythological Proteus and Plautine comedy (*Amphitruo, Menaechmi*) onward.

The ambivalence of the self represented a major problem for Unamuno the man and a major literary device of Unamuno the writer. According to Ilie, "Un-amuno could feel a self he could not see, and see a self that could not be felt" (p. 33), and the doubt as to which was the authentic self was a source of metaphysical anguish. Unamuno's common symbol of the external self was the mirror image, "material proof that man existed in the world as integrally as any other visual object" (p. 29). The supreme example of *desdo-blamiento* was to watch himself in the mirror while listening to a recording of his own voice, at least in part an allusion to the Narcissus-Echo myth. Seeing and hearing oneself as others do and realizing that the self which society recognizes is not the innermost self results in a desperate sense of terror. Unamuno's confrontation with *el otro*—the idea of his living the problems of his fictional characters—in Ilie's judgment qualifies him "as an existentialist philosopher in the deepest sense possible" (p. 31).

In *El otro* (1926), Unamuno put into dramatic form the concept of the Other, which had marked many of his earlier works and which may be seen in the novels beginning with *Amor y pedagogía* (1902). *Abel Sánchez* (1917) deals with Joaquín Monegro's struggle with the physical *otro,* Abel, at times indistinguishable from the *otro* of Joaquín's own consciousness. The short story "Artemio, heautontimoroumenos" (1918) presents Arte-mio A. Silva, a self-tormentor, whose dichotomous existence includes what Armando Zubizarreta calls "los dos yos clásicos, el religioso y el mundano."[4] The reduplication here is neither physical nor mental, but ethical. One *yo* is essentially theistic, hypocritical, of moral scruples; the other egotistic, cynical, external. Both selves are ultimately judged cowards, and their battle between ambition and pride finally resolves in mutual destruction. *Tulio Montalbán y Julio Macedo* (1920), a short novel which Unamuno later converted into the drama *Sombras de sueño,* centers on a man who tries to shed his former self, but instead is condemned to carry a dead spirit within himself. The most striking antecedent of *El otro* is the short story "El que se enterró" (1908), in which Emilio explains to a friend a strange suffering and fear of death which culminated in his murder by a mysterious visitor, his double. As the life went out of Emilio, his conscious-ness was transformed into that of his counterpart, his "yo de fuera." The new—or other—Emilio then buried his dead self and assumed his new *yo* until his death from pneumonia, a form of death as conventional as his other was rare.

Historically, **El otro** is a product of Unamuno's stay in Hendaya, a time when the author was obsessed with his *yos ex-futuros,* the *yos* he had hoped to become but did not. Zubizarreta calls the dead body of the work the child that Unamuno was trying to reconquer—his lost childhood—and the assassin Unamuno the atheist.[5] Dur-ing this period, Unamuno reread *Abel Sánchez* for a second edition, which evidently led to further consider-ation of the Cain-Abel myth. The argument of **El otro** is as follows: The identical twins Cosme and Damián fall in love with the same woman, Laura. Since she cannot distinguish between them and consequently loves them both, she allows the brothers to choose between themselves which one will marry her. Cosme wins, and according to a prior agreement, Damián leaves and later marries Damiana. Cosme attends the wedding, and thus meets his sister-in-law. After a period of tranquility, Damián visits his brother and the two renew their former hostilities. One kills the other and from this erupts the mystery: Which is the dead twin and which the survivor? The killer himself does not know and insists that he be referred to as *el otro, el uno* being the corpse which he has deposited in the cellar. Laura's brother Ernesto and the doctor Don Juan unsuccessfully attempt to solve the mystery. The Ama has known both of the twins all their lives—she had nursed one of the infants but interchanged with the mother. She does not concern herself with the search for identity, but seems to be intent upon saving the spiritual son who remains within reach. Each of the two wives believes she knows who the survivor is, confronting and ultimately torment-ing *el Otro.* The exterior struggle of *el Otro* now reaches a final desperation, and he commits suicide. In the epilogue, Ernesto and the doctor interrogate the Ama, still trying to discover the identities of the brothers. The Ama answers that the mystery is insoluble, since no one truly knows who he is.

The scene of **El otro** is the often-used Renada, the reduplication of nothingness. The choice of names seems consistently ironic: *Damián* suggests Damon of the Damon and Pythias legend, the epitome of true friendship and the antithesis of fratricide. *Cosme* brings to mind *cosmos,* an orderly, harmonious universe, far removed from the chaotic world of the play. *Damiana* is the feminine form of Damián, and has the same con-notation, that of self-interest rather than compassion. *Damián* also recalls Saint Peter Damian (Pietro Damiani), an Italian cardinal and doctor of the Church, influential in the eleventh-century reform movement;

and *Cosme,* an eighth-century bishop in Palestine and later a saint. The most obvious and direct allusion, however, is to the saints Damian and Cosme of the third century, brothers martyred during the reign of Diocletian. Both were doctors and have become the patron saints of physicians and surgeons. Cosme and Damián of *El otro* symbolize the martyrdom of the spirit, and in spirit they die simultaneously. In the play, Unamuno traces the course from psychical to corporeal death. The name *Laura* recalls the object of many of Petrarch's love poems. Petrarch's systematic world of Renaissance humanism corresponds to the undisturbed world of the twins before meeting Laura. Laura, because she is desired by both brothers, complicates their lives, just as her fourteenth-century counterpart does to the life of Petrarch, because his beloved is married to someone else. The names of the other two men, *Juan* and *Ernesto,* when compared with the names of the brothers, provide the variation *culto-vulgar* seen in the full names of some of Unamuno's characters, among them Augusto Pérez (in *Niebla*) and Alejandro Gómez (in *Nada menos que todo un hombre*). Ricardo Gullón compares the names of the twins to Castor and Pollux.[6] The mythological sons of Leda had separate fathers: Castor was the son of the king of Sparta and Pollux the son of Jupiter in the form of a swan. Conversely, the twins in *El otro* have two mothers, the mother who bore them and *el Ama,* their spiritual mother.

The basic motif of the play is the mystery, and the primary image, the mirror. Unamuno calls *El otro* a mystery in three acts and an epilogue. The word *misterio* appears twice in the first speech and at least twenty-four times within the play. Unamuno immediately provides the information that one twin has killed the other, and the mystery is the identity of the survivor. The killer himself does not know who he is, and the Ama, the only person who could identify the remaining twin, cannot or will not do so. The indistinguishable twins seem to represent physical and mental *desdoblamiento,* with the character *el Otro* as the exterior being, as form seeking substance. The interior being is dead, however, and the mystery becomes the pervasive mystery of the human personality.

Gullón considers the mirror a means of expressing the self-hatred of *el Otro:* ". . . este angustiado que no sabe quién es, se niega a reconocerse y ni siquiera quiere ver su imagen en el espejo revelador, es la antítesis del Don Quijote declarando enfáticamente: 'Yo sé quién soy.'"[7] *El Otro* has all the mirrors in the house covered; he is searching for the inner self, and the mirror can provide only another external image, another social view of the type which so frightened Unamuno. The cellar, the depths of the house, contains the body of the inner or most profound self. This cadaver is not buried as is that of Emilio in "El que se enterró," and while it is within reach physically, no spiritual encounter is possible, and *el Otro* is doomed to incompleteness. This partial existence is a primary cause of his anguish, together with the knowledge that he himself is responsible for the death of his brother, for he is the victim and executioner of the self. The characters in the drama are dealing with the external self, and although the emotions they feel are at times strong, they are of a basically shallow nature. Laura and Damiana are motivated by external forces, and if they seek penetration, it is penetration in its most blatantly physical sense.

In *El otro,* Unamuno's recurrent preoccupation with the Cain-Abel myth reaches its paradoxical apex, for the unnamed Cain figure could just as easily be Abel, in form or spirit. The Ama says in the epilogue: "El castigo de Caín es sentirse Abel, y el de Abel sentirse Caín. . . ." Because the other characters sympathize with *el Otro,* the ostensible Cain figure, he himself says: ". . . yo os digo que también merece compasión Abel, ¡pobrecito Abel!" (III, iii). Unamuno clearly differentiates the two wives: Laura is the seduced; Damiana, the seductress. Ironically, perhaps perceptively, *el Otro* does not see the distinction. For him, "Las dos sois la otra," "la misma furia." Damiana, as the dominant female character and an expectant mother, refers to her adversary as Abela, and Laura in turn calls her Caína. Damiana is sure that she will have twins, for she can feel a struggle within her womb, reminiscent of Rebecca's pregnancy with Jacob and Esau. Each of Damiana's twins is fighting to come out into the world first, to receive the birthright of being *el uno* rather than *el otro.* Consistent with her role as the seductress, Damiana represents the continuity of the tragic conflict, for as a mother, she will keep the battle alive by providing combatants. Significantly, the birth—or rebirth—will take place in Renada, which suggests the Latin *renata* (reborn).

When Damiana arrives at Cosme's house, she tells Laura that she has come because Cosme has not answered her inquiries about her husband's whereabouts. Right before the death of *el Otro,* she says that she was summoned by Caín. In the epilogue, Ernesto notes this discrepancy. Ernesto, however, fails to comprehend an even greater contradiction: the two ways in which *el Otro* explains the death. In Act I, Scene IV, *el Otro* describes the entrance of his double, who stared at him as he was being drained of life and whose form he took after death. In Act II, Scene IV, he recounts the hatred which led to fratricide. The first explanation is an almost exact duplication of the description of death in "El que se enterró." Gullón considers this technique a result of the "ambiente modernista" in which the story was written.[8] Accordingly, for the critic, its incorporation into the play is merely a literary device. However, the second account of the death is consistent with the Cain-Abel theme. The use of two versions seems to amplify the ambiguity presented by Damiana's two stories, and obviously conforms with the general ambiguity of the play. The first "death" represents mental *desdoblamiento* and the figurative or symbolic level of the work; the second, physical *desdoblamiento* and the literal level.

Modern tragedy tends to relegate physical nature to human nature, and its protagonists are rarely gods or demigods. If Willie Loman in *Death of a Salesman* symbolizes the little man as a tragic hero, *el Otro* represents Everyman in an ineludible regression from incomplete existence. His universality results not from a resolution of the individual conflict, but from the conflict itself: man's struggle to maintain a sense of compatibility between his internal and external selves. In **El otro,** Unamuno presents a figure in isolation—surrounded by characters as undefined and empty as the stage on which the play is presented. The lost twin, the personification of the exterior being, has killed his spiritual self—figuratively the interiority of the self; literally, the other twin—and now cannot live with a partial identity. Both wives try to win *el Otro,* whom each considers the unattainable brother, the one she did not marry. The Ama has never tried to separate interiority and exteriority, and saw the twins as a collective unit. With a mother's art of pardoning and forgetting, she wishes to save the identity of the surviving twin, whichever he may be. The doctor and Ernesto represent cold rationality; they attempt to solve the mystery, not to discover the man, and are quick to diagnose *el Otro* as crazy. In Pirandellian terms, we have six characters in search of identity and at the same time an identity in search of characters. Unamuno has provided skeletal forms with the key to penetration, the interior self as a vital force, paradoxically dead before the play begins. Therefore, the only climax—or anti-climax—is the death of the exterior self, or *el Otro.*

Cosme and Damián's struggle for priority results in the death of one of them. The play outwardly concerns itself with the mysterious identity of *el Otro* and the attempts to solve the enigma. Just as earlier the contention for superiority had led to fratricide, the inadequacies of a partial existence result in suicide, or death of the last remaining *yo.* The imminent childbirth of Damiana, with its promise of a recurrence of the conflict, produces a cyclical effect, for the unborn twins will prolong the antagonistic relationship of the fragmented components of the self.

From a substantive, as opposed to conceptual, standpoint, the principal emphasis belongs to direct treatment of the material, to the means of arriving at the intimate truth ("verdad íntima") rather than this truth itself. The play focuses on *el Otro*'s moral disintegration following the fratricide. Unamuno depicts Cain after the murder, Cain discovering that he is his brother's keeper because his brother's existence is ultimately linked with his

own. The literary persona becomes a *persona non grata* in his own mind. The other characters seek in vain to discover the identity of the assassin, until their persistence and his mental torment drive *el Otro* to suicide, leaving the external mystery unsolved.

A structural approach to **El otro**—a conventional structural approach, at any rate—must necessarily comprehend the entire thematic framework implicit in the play, rather than the finite bounds of the onstage action. The dramatic process is not introduced through exposition, but may be seen as effected *a priori.* Unamuno's mystery is unlike the riddle of Laius' murder in *Oedipus Rex,* culminating in the *cognitio* scene in which Oedipus discovers that he is the killer. In **El otro,** the death of the vitalizing force of human existence (*el uno*) initiates a repulsion towards life in the surviving *yo* (*el otro*), and the *misterio* does not involve identification as much as duplication of the self; the mystery does not lie in the immediate confusion of the fratricide, but in the impenetrable mystery of the conscience and the separation of the individual psyches. Northrop Frye sees the hero of tragedy as disturbing a balance in nature,[9] and here Unamuno represents this balance as a co-existence of the antithetical selves. The protagonist disrupts the equilibrium by destroying the threat to his autonomy and, in an ironic reversal, unconsciously eliminates the possibility of self-survival.

In these terms, the conflict emerges from the hostility of Cosme and Damián in life. The work, then, begins—in a manner of speaking—*in extremas res,* as a complement to the tragic consequences of *yoísmo.* **El otro** is a post-tragedy in the sense that the primary threads of the tragic order of events are completed before the opening of the play. Frye speaks of the violation of a moral law as a catalyst of the tragic development.[10] Here, the sin of fratricide, whose archetype can be found in the Cain-Abel myth, both instigates and defines the dramatic scheme. The *Angst,* or feeling of anxiety or dread, may be seen in the first account of death, that corresponding to the death scene of "El que se enterró." The *Augenblick,* or crucial moment, comes with the second form of death, the actual murder of one twin by the other, determining the subsequent suicide of *el Otro.* The self-destruction does not result from the solving of the mystery as in Sophocles, but from a final desperation. The initial realization of the situation, which could be considered the anagnorisis, has taken place as soon as the protagonist views himself as the Other. The suicide of Act III is the culminating point of the physical play, and the logical and unavoidable eventuation of the thematic scope of the work, Unamuno's "drama del alma." Nevertheless, *el Otro* is not only doomed before the opening scene, but he recognizes the ultimate implications of his crime, and therefore the suicide as a dramatic recourse should have a minimal shock value. In Poe's "William Wilson," the harassed title figure cannot kill his counterpart without killing himself; death is both the climax and the conclusion. Unamuno's analogous climax is not represented on stage, and *El otro* extends from post-climax to conclusion or anti-climax.

Unamuno's consistently prevalent tragic sense pervades the work, be it tragedy, post-tragedy, or tragic epilogue. The beginning, middle, and even the end of its tragic construction are to be felt rather than seen, as Unamuno portrays the psychological deterioration from end to extinction. Robert B. Heilman states, "The pathological extreme of the tragic condition is schizophrenia—where normal dividedness is magnified into the split that is illness. The pathological extreme of the melodramatic condition is paranoia—in one phase, the sense of a hostile 'they' who will make one their victim. . . ."[11] In *El otro,* the killing off of the schizoid self makes the surviving self a victim not of a destructive "they" but of a psychotic "I." If co-existence is difficult, partial existence is impossible.

Unamuno's tendency toward transcendental preoccupations and the lack of movement in *El otro* directly violate the Aristotelian view of action as the primary element of tragedy. Language is the predominant tool of Unamuno's dramaturgy; words convey ideas, and actions indicate reactions to words and ideas. The abstractions which Unamuno attempts to express can only be clarified in the dialogue. The resulting play is a static work, but intrinsically dramatic because its root is the dramaticism of the human mind—a human mind, that of the author himself. If Pirandello in *Sei Personaggi* is conspicuous by his absence, Unamuno is conspicuous by his presence. His final stroke of subjectivity is found in the epilogue when the Ama, discussing the *misterio,* says: "Unamuno no sabe quién es."

Unamuno the dramatist aims for revelation rather than amusement, for introspection rather than spectacle. On the basis of *El otro,* we must conclude with Iris Zavala that Unamuno's theater—a metaphysical theater with ultra-scenic interests—perhaps "resulta demasiado dramático para ser teatral."[12] The author himself saw the need for an audience unsatisfied with complacence—"el otro público . . . de los que conmigo se arriman alguna vez al brocal del pozo sin fondo de nuestra conciencia humana personal, y de bruces sobre él tratan de descubrir su propia verdad, la verdad de sí mismos."[13] The dramatic material thus serves both as a source of tension and as an agent of self-discovery on the part of this "other audience."

Notes

1. "El teatro de Unamuno", *Cuadernos de la Cátedra Miguel de Unamuno,* 7 (Salamanca: Facultad de Filosofía y Letras, Universidad de Salamanca, 1956), 18.

2. In discussing Unamuno's dramatic theory, I follow closely the concepts presented by Iris M. Zavala in *Unamuno y su teatro de conciencia* (Salamanca: Universidad de Salamanca, Filosofía y Letras, 1963), Chapter IV, "Teoría dramática unamuniana: Un teatro en función del hombre", pp. 113-38.

3. (Madison: The University of Wisconsin Press, 1967), p. 91. This discussion of *el otro* is based on Ilie's examination of the concept in Chapters II ("The Splitting of the Self"), pp. 28-47; and VI ("The Structure of the Self"), pp. 91-116.

4. *Unamuno en su "nivola"* (Madrid: Taurus, 1960), p. 307.

5. *Ibid.,* p. 304.

6. *Autobiografías de Unamuno* (Madrid: Editorial Gredos, 1964), p. 166.

7. *Ibid.,* p. 170.

8. *Ibid.,* p. 174.

9. *Anatomy of Criticism: Four Essays* (New York: Atheneum, 1969), p. 209.

10. *Ibid.,* p. 210.

11. "Tragedy and Melodrama: Speculations on Generic Form," *Perspectives on Drama,* ed. James L. Calderwood and Harold E. Toliver (New York: Oxford University Press, 1968), p. 161.

12. Zavala, p. 7.

13. Unamuno, Autocrítica, *El otro, Obras completas* (Madrid: Escelicer 1966), V, 654.

Norman C. Miller (essay date January 1983)

SOURCE: Miller, Norman C. "Miguel de Unamuno's *El Otro*: Anti-Realism and Realism." *Cuadernos de ALDEEU* 1, no. 1 (January 1983): 37-44.

[*In the following essay, Miller argues that Unamuno relied upon psychological realism in* El otro *despite the fact that in the play he was reacting to the realism of the Spanish theater of the time with anti-realism.*]

Miguel de Unamuno's 1926 drama *El Otro* has long been recognized as an outstanding example of his *teatro esquemático* in which the dramatist reduces the plot, setting, dramatic language, and characterization to an essential minimum in order to focus on certain ideas or human problems with which he was preoccupied.[1] In fact, the themes of sibling rivalry, the *personalidad escindida* or the "double" are found in many earlier works such as his novel *Abel Sánchez* (1917), the short stories "El que se enterró" (1908), "Tulio Montalbán y Julio Mancedo" (1920), and the plays *La Esfinge* (1898) and *Sombras de sueño* (1926). What has not been so clearly understood, however, is that in spite of his conscious rejection of virtually all the norms of conventional realism—norms that were still adhered to in the theater of Benavente and others against whom Unamuno was reacting,—this play is extremely realistic in its psychological portrayal of the protagonist. It is my intention to mention briefly the more obvious anti-realistic qualities of this drama and then to explore its contrasting psychological realism.

My analysis of the play's psychological aspects differs from Carlos Feal Deibe's in that I regard Cosme and Damián, the identical twins, as two separate entities, whereas Deibe and other critics believe that Unamuno intended them to be one and the same person. Deibe states, ". . . nos enfrentamos con el tema de la doble personalidad y no con el de una dualidad de personas."[2] For him the drama is a Freudian Oedipal fantasy; the dead brother is actually the interiorized image of the father whom the protagonist, El Otro, has symbolically killed in his desire to regain the mother figures, Laura, Damiana, and Ama. Hence there is no act of fratricide, or patricide either for that matter, since the twin brother (the imaginary father) does not exist in reality. The entire psychological drama is thus reduced to a symbolic metaphor: ". . . no hay en el drama una duplicación de personas, sino que éstas son simplemente proyecciones de seres que viven en el interior de una persona única: la de su creador, reflejado en El Otro. El muerto es, entonces, el padre (o, secundariamente, hermano) interiorizado. Es decir, que el drama representa . . . una fantasía infantil edípica."[3] I believe that if we accept as a basic premise that the play is literally about a conflict between identical twin brothers, it can be dealt with less as an abstract philosophical or poetic fantasy and more as a realistic study of human psychology in which the emotional conflicts of the protagonist are viewed as the result of specific, readily identifiable, psychological factors.

Unamuno's deliberate rejection of realism is evident from the start. The plot, in terms of what actually develops on stage, is minimal and skeletonized because, just as in classical Greek tragedy, the main events have already occurred before the play begins. The drama is based on a series of implausible events which quickly acquire an aura of unreality. In addition, the action seems to take place in a timeless, abstract locale. The mise-en-scène consists of a mirror, from which El Otro recoils, a door dividing the stage into two rooms, and a table with two or three chairs. At no point is there an attempt to let the scenery suggest a contemporary, realistic setting, for although the play ostensibly takes place in Cosme's home, the house is also a symbolic jail, insane asylum, or cemetery according to the ever-changing perspective of El Otro and the other characters in the play.

Even the dramatic language contributes to an illusion of unreality, for the dialogue frequently avoids imitating everyday speech and tends to be highly concentrated, to contain no superfluous words. Nearly every statement is significant. At times there is a deliberate use of poetic language in order to create an almost legendary aura, as in this description of El Otro's fatal encounter with his brother:

> Los dos mellizos, los que como Esaú y Jacob se peleaban ya desde el vientre de su madre, con odio fraternal, con odio que era demoníaco, los dos hermanos se encontraron . . . Era al caer de la tarde, recién muerto el sol, cuando se funden las sombras y el verde del campo se hace negro . . . ¡Odia a tu hermano como te odias a ti mismo! Y llenos de odio a sí mismos, dispuestos a suicidarse mutuamente, por una mujer . . . , por otra mujer . . . , pelearon . . . Y el uno sintió que en sus manos, heladas por el terror, se le helaba el cuello del otro . . . Y miró a los ojos muertos del hermano por si se veía muerto en ellos . . . Las sombras de la noche que llegaba envolvieron el dolor del otro . . . Y Dios se callaba . . . ¡Y sigue callándose todavía![4]

Although the cast contains a total of six characters, the entire play is centered around one, El Otro, to whom the dramatist devotes his full attention. The others serve basically two functions: they cause El Otro to reveal his inner struggle and torments, and they act as interpreters of this struggle, who, by seeking to explain it to themselves, interpret it for the audience. All the minor characters are symbols for human types, and as such they are one-sided and lack verisimilitude. They remain underdeveloped in comparison to El Otro whose complexity overshadows them to such an extent that the drama might properly be said to have only one character. But even the protagonist is a symbol, for he represents man's eternal quest for personal identity and spiritual integrity. In fact, Unamuno speaks of his drama as basically a study of the human personality: "Trato en él de uno de esos temas eternos, más interesante aún que el del amor: el de la personalidad."[5]

Because of the evident wish to minimize the use of realism and to utilize his protagonist as a universal symbol, it is surprising to discover the extent to which Unamuno has employed psychological realism in portraying El Otro's mental processes. The protagonist's psyche, including his bizarre symptoms, can be explained logically by modern psychoanalytic theories, and his complex personality is seen to be the inevitable outcome of certain circumstantial factors in his life. The fact that the two brothers were identical twins made it difficult for either to conceive of himself as more than a mirrored reflection of the other. For each, the other was like a projection of himself, a duplicate copy, an extension of his own being, or a fragmented, splintered part of himself that he could never reintegrate with his own ego.

Consequently, each brother was a threat to the other, a constant reminder that he was somehow incomplete, that he lacked a unified, separate personality and soul uniquely his own. At one point El Otro remarks, "¡Ah, terrible tortura la de nacer doble! ¡De no ser siempre uno y el mismo!"[6]

Mutual hatred, whether on a conscious or an unconscious level, as well as difficulty in establishing a separate identity and an adequate self-image are universal problems with nearly all identical twins, who frequently consider themselves as only "half persons," due to the existence of "the other."[7] This situation, referred to in psychoanalytic literature as the "twinning reaction," is characterized by: "a fusion of object and self-representations in which the two merge, leading to a loss of ego boundary between the two individuals and a loss of identity."[8] The confusion about self and object representation accounts for an excessive use of identification and projection.[9] The fact that the individual regards his twin as a partial extension of himself produces the former situation, which, in turn, causes him to project or ascribe his own thoughts, including murderous thoughts and wishes, to the twin with whom he has identified. As a result, twins frequently conceive of their own aggressiveness as a threat directed back at themselves, since they assume that their feelings are those of their twin as well.[10] El Otro graphically illustrates this particular facet of his psychology at the beginning of Act III. Confronting his own image in the mirror, he extends his hands towards it as if to seize it by the throat, but upon seeing these hands coming towards him, he grasps his own throat as though to strangle himself. In other words, his aggression towards the hated twin turns on himself and he becomes his own victim.

Because the two are one, it follows that to hate one's twin is to hate oneself as well. In the case of Cosme and Damián, each hated himself for being unable to distinguish his own ego from that of his brother. El Otro admits, "Se odia a sí mismo el que no se siente distinguido."[11] Each brother eventually realized that he could be free only through the death of the other, but since each had identified with the other, the necessary murder would be psychologically equivalent to suicide. One brother could not destroy his twin without destroying himself. This reluctance to pursue their conflict to its inevitable conclusion is explained by Laura as: ". . . llegaron a temer que se mataran el uno al otro, algo así como un suicidio mutuo."[12] Therefore the killing was prevented for years until the two women, Laura and Damiana, provided the catalytic agent that finally

precipitated it. When the murder did occur, however, the implications of self-destruction were so strong that afterwards El Otro exclaimed, "Y no sé si fui homicida o suicida."[13]

To understand El Otro's act of murder, we must again refer to basic psychoanalytic concepts. El Otro recounts that during his final confrontation with his brother, he experienced a sensation of regressing into the past, to the time when he was born: "Empecé a vivir hacia atrás."[14] When he arrived at the moment of his birth, he seemed to die: "Me morí al llegar a cuando nací, a cuando nacimos."[15] This psychic regression represents a return to the more primal, id instincts and to primary process functioning, as well as a return to the source of his anxiety. He possibly makes a Freudian slip of the tongue in saying "a cuando nací," and he immediately corrects it to "a cuando nacimos." His own ego is incapable of conceptualizing itself in any other terms than "we." At the moment when he and his brother were born, he died in the sense that the presence of his twin negated, from the beginning, his chance to have a unique, individual self. During this return to the origin of the identity anxiety, he acted upon his id impulse to destroy the threat to his ego and killed his brother. Since this impulse could not have gained supremacy under normal conditions, it was necessary for him to suffer a lapse of consciousness during which time the restrictive force of the superego was sufficiently weakened to allow the id to gain temporary control of the ego. When he recovered from this lapse, he discovered that his brother was dead: "Al rato me fue retornando la conciencia, resucité; pero sentado ahí, donde tú estás, y aquí, donde estoy, estaba mi cadáver."[16]

All of these events occurred before the play begins, and what we actually witness on the stage is the aftermath, El Otro's struggle to achieve self-identity after committing fratricide. But this struggle is doomed to failure because the protagonist is overwhelmed by grief and remorse. His guilt at having killed his twin has made the purpose of the crime unattainable, and it is precisely this feeling of guilt that helps explain many of the symptoms of El Otro's apparent madness. For example, he refuses to allow anyone to enter his room while he is asleep in order to prevent others from overhearing his self-accusations: "¡Caín! ¡Caín! ¡Caín! Me lo digo yo a mí mismo todas las noches, en sueños, y por eso duermo solo, encerrado y lejos de todos. ¡Para que no me oiga . . . ., para que no me oiga yo a mí mismo!"[17] El Otro's insistence that all mirrors be covered is understandable when we realize that for him, to look into a mirror is to see his dead brother and to be reminded of his crime and guilt. In Act II El Otro confides to Ama that his sense of guilt is destroying him. He feels that he is carrying his brother inside himself and that his dead twin, which is to say his own guilt, is destroying him from within: "Le llevo dentro, muerto, Ama. Me está matando . . . Acabará conmigo."[18] In the epilogue Ama attempts to explain the main symptom of his insanity—his confusion about his identity—in terms of a simple guilt reaction: "¡Pobrecito hijo mío! ¡A él, al matador, el remordimiento le hacía creer que era la víctima, que era el muerto! El verdugo se cree la víctima; lleva dentro de sí el cadáver de la víctima, y aquí está su dolor. El castigo de Caín es sentirse Abel, y el de Abel sentirse Caín . . ."[19] She comments that his inability to distinguish himself from his dead brother was a means of punishing himself, of becoming "dead" also.

This explanation, however, overlooks other possibilities. El Otro's identification with the murdered twin may well be an example of denial, a defense mechanism whose purpose is to negate the fact of his brother's death and thereby save himself from the guilt of having killed him. In other words, because El Otro is alive, his twin must be at least partially alive as well since they are now one.[20] However, it is also possible that his inability to know who he is may represent an attempt to disassociate himself from himself as the surviving brother. By denying his own identity, he is attempting to deny his connection with himself as his brother's murderer. When Ernesto accuses him of having killed his twin, El Otro remarks: "¿Yo? ¿Asesino yo? Pero ¿Quién soy yo? ¿Quién es el asesino? ¿Quién el asesinado? ¿Quién el verdugo? ¿Quién la víctima? ¿Quién Caín? ¿Quién Abel? ¿Quién soy yo, Cosme o Damián?"[21] Ironically, the act of fratricide, which disposed of the external presence of the twin, also assured that El Otro would internalize his image to such a degree that he could never free himself from him. He was condemned to carry his brother within him for the rest of his life—a burden so intolerable that suicide became the only solution.

Finally, there were other psychological factors that also contributed to his decision to commit suicide. According to current psychoanalytic theory, a frequently encountered problem among identical twins is the "strong tendency to picture the world as full of twins."[22] That is to say, they project their preoccupation with their twin upon the world at large and tend to view all other situations in terms of a struggle between conflicting dualities. This from of projection, often referred to in psychoanalysis as displacement, is the result of transferring, usually during early childhood, original feelings from the twin to others in the immediate environment. In the case of El Otro, the preoccupation with his twin brother caused him to regard the world as consisting of a series of terrible and insoluble dualities. Not only did the existence of an identical twin force him to have two egoes or selves, but even as a child he was faced with the inherent confusion of being raised by two equally strong mother figures, for his real mother shared her maternal role with Ama. Later, both Laura and Damiana claimed him as a husband, thus giving

him two wives who were warring with one another. Even God was an insoluble duality, for he was not only God in the Christian sense of the word, but also Destiny. El Otro remarks, "Todo doble . . . , todo doble . . . ¡Dios también doble! . . . ¡Su otro nombre es el Destino! . . . ¡Dios es también otro!"[23] The uncertainties and terrible inner struggle that resulted from El Otro's being constantly suspended between and tormented by these many sets of perplexing and frequently hostile dualities contributed to his decision to renounce life altogether.

In conclusion, this play offers an interesting combination of elements that point to both the abandonment of realistic theater with respect to plot, setting, language, and characterization, and to an adherence to psychological realism with regard to the psyche of the protagonist. The play was no doubt intended to be an experimental drama, and the playwright rejected verisimilitude in the conventional sense of the word. The plot is reduced to a schematic minimum, and the protagonist and other supporting characters are little more than symbolic incarnations of certain ideas or human types that Unamuno was interested in exploring. But within this generally anti-realistic framework, the personality and psychological problems of the protagonist are accurately drawn in that they are entirely consistent with modern psychoanalytic theories. Hence, *El Otro* seems to be yet another example of Unamuno's tendency to use paradox, to combine opposing concepts, in this case anti-realism and realism, within the same work.

Notes

1. Francisco Ruiz Ramón, *Historia del teatro español, siglo XX* (Madrid: Alianza Editorial, 1971), pp. 82-83 and Andrés Franco, *El teatro de Unamuno* (Madrid: Insula, 1971), pp. 209-26.

2. *Unamuno: "El otro" y don Juan* (Madrid: Cupsa Editorial, 1976), p. 30.

3. Deibe, p. 26.

4. Miguel de Unamuno, *Obras completas* (New York: Las Américas Publ. Co., 1968), V, 674-75.

5. Unamuno, p. 87.

6. Unamuno, p. 686.

7. Jules Glenn, "Opposite Sex Twins," *Journal of American Psychoanalytic Association,* 14 (1966), 737.

8. Edward D. Joseph and Jack H. Tabor, "The Simultaneous Analysis of a pair of Identical Twins and the Twinning Reaction," *The Psychoanalytic Study of the Child,* 16 (1961), 295.

9. Glenn, pp. 737-57.

10. Dorothy Burlingham, "A Study of Identical Twins," *The Psychoanalytic Study of the Child,* 18 (1963), 386-87, 398.

11. Unamuno, p. 686.

12. Unamuno, p. 670.

13. Unamuno, p. 683.

14. Unamuno, p. 662.

15. Unamuno, p. 662.

16. Unamuno, p. 662.

17. Unamuno, p. 675.

18. Unamuno, p. 678.

19. Unamuno, p. 707.

20. The use of precisely this ego defense mechanism is reported in "The Psychology of Twins" by Edward D. Joseph in the *Journal of American Psychoanalytic Association,* 9 (1961), 158: "He conceived the fantasy of having taken his brother inside himself. Thus his twin was not dead, but remained alive within him."

21. Unamuno, p. 674.

22. Glenn, p. 737.

23. Unamuno, pp. 679-80.

Julia Biggane (essay date 2000)

SOURCE: Biggane, Julia. "Yet Another Other: Unamuno's *El otro* and the Anxiety for Influence." *Bulletin of Hispanic Studies* 77 (2000): 479-91.

[*In the following essay, Biggane attempts to explain why other critics have so often made efforts to find literary sources and parallels between Unamuno's* El otro *and earlier works by other authors.*]

El otro (1926) has traditionally been seen as shot through with other textual ghosts, and criticism is notable for its eagerness to identify the play's relations to other novels, plays and short stories. Apart from examining the explicit references to the biblical myth of Cain and Abel in the play, critics have identified an extraordinarily diverse network of other supposed influences and commonalities. Ricardo Gullón claims important parallels between *El otro* and both Dostoyevsky's *The Double* and Henry James' *The Jolly Corner*.[1] Andrés Franco claims *The Jolly Corner*'s influence on *El otro,* and notes the play's similarities with Pirandello's *Così'e (si vi pare)* and *Come me vuoi;* Donald Shaw notes parallels with Pirandello's *Enrico IV*.[2] Derek Gagen calls *El otro* Unamuno's 'updated mystery play', an opinion shared by Francisco Ruiz Ramón, who likens the play to 'los mejores autos sacramentales de Calderón'.[3] Gilbert Smith examines the play's complex relations with Ortega's *El hombre y la gente,* whereas Edward Friedman is not only keen to trace *El otro*'s use of the Cain-Abel and Cosme-Damian stories, but also claims important links with Unamuno's own previous texts.[4] Norman Miller and Ángel Valbuena Prat also claim links between *El otro* and, variously, *Abel Sánchez* (1920), 'El que se enterró' (1908), *Tulio Montalbán y Julio Macedo* (1920) and the play *Sombras del Sueño* (1926).[5] Examining myths and archetypes in *El otro,* Roberta Johnson links the play to a wider turn-of-the-century preoccupation with the double, which appears also in Dostoevsky's *The Double,* Maupassant's *The Horla,* Wilde's *The Picture of Dorian Gray,* Henry James' *The Jolly Corner,* Rappaport's *The Dybbuk* and Max Aub's *El desconfiado* and *Narcissus.*[6]

Some of the studies are content to identify supposed influences or pinpoint precedents for *El otro;* others posit a more complex set of relations between the play and other texts. All, though, take an instrumental view of these relations, whereby the play adapts, mirrors or incorporates myths, tropes and figures from other specific novels, plays and short stories in making its own statement about subjectivity and identity. This article aims to problematize *El otro*'s relations with other texts, seeking to turn the strategies of source criticism and comparative readings of *El otro* back on themselves, and then to suggest some 'sources' for source-based or comparative readings of the play by speculating about critical motives or drives behind such approaches to it. Such a reversal in critical approach attempts to illustrate some of the limitations and problems involved in source-based approaches to the play, and then to allow for a discussion of alternative ways of theorizing *El otro*'s relations with its supposed sources, or other texts, while acknowledging that such readings bring their own irresolvable questions and problems.

One possible motivation for readings of *El otro* that are keen to see sources for or parallels with other texts, may be the critic's desire to add to the authority or legitimacy of Unamuno's theatre, which is commonly felt to be his weakest genre, by claiming relations with substantive and canonical texts and writers on its behalf. Ricardo Gullón, for example, dismisses facile designations of Unamuno as idiosyncratic genius, or as simply 'un fenómeno de la literatura o el pensamiento universal', claiming that 'genial fue, pero genialidad no quiere decir desvinculación de la tradición y la cultura. [. . .] Olvidar, como tantas veces se olvida, que don Miguel, si no hombre libresco, fue lector voraz, de vastísima cultura, es error indispensable [*sic*]'.[7] Gullón then reads Unamuno in the light of Dostoevski, Kierkegaard and Henry James, thus inserting his theatre and prose fiction into a canonized tradition of writers and thinkers. Francisco Ruiz Ramón claims that 'Unamuno tiene derecho a ser situado en la corriente del teatro europeo [. . .] de Claudel, Eliot, Anderson, Cocteau, Giraudoux, parte de Anouilh etc.'.[8] At times, there is an assumption that the play itself intentionally invites comparison with other texts in order to universalize its thesis. Norman C. Miller, for instance, refers to Unamuno's 'evident wish to minimise the use of realism and to utilize his protagonist as a universal symbol'; and Edward Friedman, having compared *El otro* to *Death of a Salesman* (on the grounds that both are modern tragedies with very mortal protagonists) and the plays of Pirandello, claims that El Otro 'represents Everyman'.[9] According to such readings, the play is thus deliberately set in an unspecified place and time, the characters and situations are given little explicit cultural specificity, and are not conventionally mimetic, substantial or coherent. El Ama is not even named, while the twins' names, Cosme and Damian (after the fourth-century Cilician martyrs), and the biblical references to Cain and Abel, and Esau and Jacob, give the twins a generalized, mythic, rather than conventionally realist, particularized status. The minimalist scenography might be seen as a further resistance to concrete particularization or specificity. With the exception of the entirely-mimed first scene of Act III, only skeletal, highly terse stage directions and set descriptions are given, principally limiting themselves to the movement of characters on stage, or to listing the furniture and props that are to appear in each scene. There is little expository description, and little detail about characters' appearance or emotions is given.

El Otro's refusal to name himself, or claim for himself any stable or complete identity, may also be seen as undermining his individualized particularity, forcing him into a vaguely-defined, and therefore generalized existential position. A universalizing reading may also take its cue from Unamuno's own 'Autocrítica'—some brief comments on *El otro,* and its audience, that Unamuno published in response to the play's poor opening notices on the Madrid stage in 1932. It states:

> *El otro* [. . .] me ha brotado de la obsesión [. . .] del misterio—no problema—de la personalidad, del sentimiento congojoso de nuestra identidad y continuidad individual y personal [. . .]. Claro está que como en este 'misterio' lo que importa es la verdad íntima, profunda, del drama del alma, no me anduve en esas minucias del arte realista de justificar las entradas y las salidas de los sujetos y hacer coherentes otros detalles.[10]

Unamuno goes on to note that such an approach may lose him the sympathy of some of the audience, but that 'no he escrito esta obra no más que para que los espectadores y las espectadoras pasen el rato, mascullando acaso chocolatinas'. He places his faith instead in

> el otro público. El de los que conmigo se arriman alguna vez al brocal del pozo sin fondo de nuestra conciencia humana personal, y de bruces sobre él tratan de descubrir su propia verdad, la verdad de sí mismos.[11]

If the text concerns itself primarily with such general, major issues ('la personalidad', 'nuestra identidad', 'el drama del alma'), refusing to become mired in distract-

ing particularization or socio-historical contextualization, it allows easier comparison with a variety of other texts (which may cross linguistic, cultural and generic boundaries) that are substantive enough to tackle similar issues of universal import. The play's stated ultimate aim, to allow the reader to discover 'la verdad íntima, profunda', of the human soul, may also be read as signalling a contribution to a canonized existential tradition in literature and drama, adding further legitimacy and authority to the work. It is interesting to note in passing that, in a metaphorical doubling, while such universalizing readings may add legitimacy and value to *El otro,* they may also coincidentally bestow legitimacy and value to the critic, whose *modus operandi* demonstrates wide reading as well as fine perception.

A second possible motivation for source-based or comparative readings of *El otro* might be the critic's anxiety to compensate for the apparent lack and absence in the play. Ruiz Ramón refers to the 'exceso de reducción formal' in Unamuno's theatre, claiming that 'tanto las pasiones como los caracteres, la acción y la palabra son esquemáticos, sin suficiente encarnadura dramática, y, por ende, sin bastante instalación en la realidad plenamente carnal [. . .]. He aquí el problema del teatro unamuniano: no [. . .] consiguió sino crear puros dramas esquemáticos, es decir dramas no realizados suficientemente como tales dramas'.[12] Donald Shaw also sees lack and absence in the plays in terms of 'failure', and refers to *El otro*'s and other plays' lack of suspense, lack of 'autonomous dramatic movement' built into individual acts and their tendency towards anti-climax.[13] Lázaro Carreter calls the plays 'dramas esqueléticos, puras líneas que definen y desarrollan el problema, sin que jamás se preocupe de vestirlos de carne para hacerlos familiares al espectador, para captar su confianza, para darles, en suma, verosimilitud existencial'.[14] It is notable that such absences and or lacks are seen as defects or problems in *El otro* and other plays; as such, perhaps critics feel a need to provide a solution. Absence is certainly easily read into the skeletal scenography, and lack may be seen as constitutive of the thematic level of *El otro* too. Explaining to El Ama why he hated his twin, El Otro describes the pain caused by his perceived absence from himself:

> Desde pequeñitos sufrí al verme fuera de mí mismo . . ., no podía soportar aquel espejo . . ., no podía verme fuera de mí.
>
> (Act II, Scene 6)[15]

Here, the presence of the identical other, either in the mirror, or as a twin, underlines the absence and incompleteness of the self. Absence can also be read into several other episodes and features of the play. Following their struggle over Laura, both twins agree to absent themselves physically from one another, as Laura explains in Act II, Scene 2. After her speech, El Otro then accuses Laura of always having desired the other, absent twin: 'siempre al que no tenías delante, al ausente, al otro' (II, 2). The twins' origins may be seen symbolically as an absence: their birthplace is Renada, and the audience is told very little about their early life or their parentage. And just before the twins' final confrontation, El Otro tells Ernesto that he wanted to be alone to 'revisar papeles, quemar recuerdos, hacer abono de ceniza en la memoria' (I, 4). El Otro makes it clear that his own identity is irretrievably absent from the beginning of the play. He no longer exists as either twin following the final confrontation:

> Se me quedó mirando a los ojos y mirándose en mis ojos y entonces sentí que se me derretía la conciencia, el alma; que empezaba a vivir, o mejor a desvivir, hacia atrás, retro-tiempo, como en una película que se haga correr al revés [. . .] y desfiló mi vida y volví a tener veinte años, y diez, y cinco, y me hice niño [. . .] desnací . . . me morí. Me morí al llegar a cuando nací, a cuando nacimos.
>
> (I, 4)

El Otro, now occupying a psychological lacuna between his self and his brother ('Yo no soy Cosme, yo no soy Damian'), is both empty (having been 'unborn'), and yet still doubled as he remains inseparable from the other ('Le llevo dentro, muerto'). This complex sense of both existential absence and doubling, which only increases El Otro's sense of self-lack or self-absence seems to be irresolvable. Even El Otro's own physical self-annihilation cannot definitively solve the problem, as Damiana suggests that she is pregnant, and will give birth to feuding twins whom she can already feel fighting in the womb (III, 3). Nor is this double absence confined to El Otro, as Laura and Damiana reduplicate El Otro's fight with his brother. Laura was not able to distinguish between the twins while they were wooing her; now El Otro refuses to say which of the two women is his wife, condemning them first to a futile fight over possession of El Otro because neither can bear the thought that it is her husband that is absent (dead), and then absenting himself by suicide and condemning them to an even more devastating absence. A more general self-absence is also suggested by El Ama in the closing lines of the play, when she states 'Yo no sé quien soy, vosotros no sabéis quiénes sois, el historiador no sabe quien es [. . .] no sabe quién es ninguno de los que nos oyen. Todo hombre se muere, cuando el Destino le traza la muerte, sin haberse conocido, y toda muerte es un suicidio, el de Caín'. The stage directions further note that 'Donde dice "el historiador no sabe quién es", puede decirse "Unamuno no sabe quién es"' (Epílogo). El Otro's situation can be generalized even further, by noting that his fight with his br(other) mirrors traditional psychoanalytical theories of the subject, who is always already split, cloven by an unresolvable constant conflict between the conscious and the unconscious, and so

constituted by a radical absence of unity, completeness or autonomy. To return to the possible sources for a source-based reading of *El otro,* it may be tempting to speculate that, in an identificatory move, critics might recognize El Otro's cleft self as corresponding to the split in their own self, and seek to heal the split in text and self by shoring up *El otro* and filling it with other plays, novels, short stories. The temptation becomes even stronger when one notes that so many of the imputed sources or parallels for *El otro* are not alien others but internal others, as they are part of the author's own textual corpus (*Abel Sánchez,* 'El que se enterró',*Tulio Montalbán y Julio Macedo,* *La esfinge* and *Sombras del sueño*), and might be considered a form of ideal other self which would reinforce, but not this time conflict with or usurp, the lacking self of *El Otro.* In any case, irrespective of tempting psychoanalytic speculations, what seems to emerge is a critical urge to account for or fill in the incompleteness on which the Unamunian text is based.

A third possible origin of source-based, associative or comparative readings of *El otro* may be critical anxieties about originality in the text. The reader's attention is commonly drawn to the play's extensive similarities with other works by Unamuno. Gilbert Smith, for example, claims that *El otro* 'is a synthesis of the many facets of 'el otro' present in previous works by Unamuno'.[16] Edward Friedman notes that 'in *El otro,* Unamuno put into dramatic form the concept of the Other, which had marked many of his earlier works. [. . .] The most striking antecedent of *El otro* is the short story "El que se enterró"'. Friedman also describes Unamuno's 'recurrent preocupation with the Cain-Abel myth' in relation to *El otro.*[17] And part of El Otro's suffering within the play may be read as stemming from his sense of unoriginality, his lack of uniqueness. He is an exact reproduction of his twin, and he explains the torture of being unindividuated to El Ama in Act II, Scene 6:

> El camino para odiarse es [. . .] verse doble [. . .] distinguirnos por el nombre, por una cinta, una prenda . . . ¡Ser un nombre! [. . .] Cuando uno no es siempre uno se hace malo . . . Para volverse malo no hay como tener de continuo un espejo delante, y más un espejo vivo, que respira.

Shortly afterwards, El Otro reveals that even those with whom he is most intimate—El Ama, and both Laura and Damiana—cannot tell him apart from his twin. Challenging Laura to say which twin she fell in love with, he claims plaintively: 'Es que el amor debe distinguir'. El Otro's lack of individuation is not solved by his murdering his twin, because not only do the other characters still not know which twin he is, but he himself claims still to be carrying around his identical dead twin inside himself. The possibility that Damiana will give birth to another set of feuding twins might be seen as further underlining El Otro's sense of unoriginality:

OTRO:

> Dios no puede, no debe condenarme a tener hijos, a volver a ser otra vez . . . otro

DAMIANA:

> Pues lo serás. Que te voy a dar . . . otro, otro tú.

OTRO:

> ¿Otra vez? ¿Otra vez a nacer? ¿Otra vez a morir? ¡Oh no, no, no!

DAMIANA:

> ¿De quién el hijo?, di.

OTRO:

> Yo no puedo tener hijos. Dios no puede condenarme a tener hijos . . . a volver a ser otra vez otro.

(III, 3)

El Otro's verbal repetitiveness in this passage could be seen as further underlining the chain of reproduction or repetition that seems to be facing him, and frustrating his attempts to assert a singular, unique identity. His ultimate failure to individuate himself is neatly illustrated after his death, when Ernesto casually declares in the epilogue:

> sea quien fuera el que fue muerto por el otro y el que se suicidó, la situación de las dos viudas queda asegurada y no hay por qué ahondar en el crimen de un loco.

The repeated references to Cain and Abel in relation to El Otro's killing of his twin, first by El Otro himself (I, 4; II, 4,5,6; III, 2, 4), then by Damiana and Laura (III, 5, 7, 8 and 9) and finally by El Ama in the epilogue, may further be read as undermining El Otro's sense of unique, original selfhood. Even the very act with which he might have expected to liberate himself from his double ('un espejo que respira') only invokes another double and seems to affirm his status as mere simulacrum. That it is not only El Otro who invokes his derivativeness in relation to Cain and Abel might be construed as further undermining the notion of original individuality in the play: in Scene 9 of Act II, Laura accuses Damiana of driving El Otro to suicide and calls her 'Caína'; shortly before, Damiana has sarcastically addressed Laura as 'pobrecita Abela'. Do El Otro's anxieties about his own originality and uniqueness trigger the critic into conflating character and text (both of which, after all, have the same name) and to attend to questions about the uniqueness and originality of the play itself? This is not, of course, to claim that any

critic accuses *El otro* of lack of originality, but the number of studies concerned with relating the play to other texts might indicate an unconscious feeling of uneasiness about the play's autonomy or individuality (particularly, perhaps, in relation to other texts by Unamuno).

All my above source-based readings of the source-derived or comparative criticism of *El otro* allow coherent readings of the play. They are, however, open to the charge of being reductive in their representation of the links between the text and the critic, and are dependent on a simplistically speculative economy of cause, effect and intention, and perhaps, too, misread parallels as links or meaningful relations. On the other hand, it is not clear that these readings are any less reductive than some of source criticism's or associative readings' own attempts to trace stable origins for *El otro,* to posit a transhistorical or decontextualized link between other texts and *El otro,* or an unproblematic transformation of the former into the latter. I am thinking here of three readings of the play in particular: firstly, Ricardo Gullón's assertions that

> Unamuno leyó bien a Dostoevski [. . .] y lo menciona con relativa frecuencia [. . .]. Apenas se ha rozado la idea de una posible conexión entre *El doble* [. . .] y *El otro* [. . .]. Los sentimientos de Goliadkin y el hermano gemelo [. . .] son análogos. [. . .] La analogía es natural; los personajes sufren idéntica amenaza: la sombra es el posesivo antagonista de ambos.
>
> En 1909 escribió Henry James un extraño cuento titulado *The Jolly Corner,* al que me he referido a propósito de *El otro,* de Unamuno. Las coincidencias entre la invención de James y la de don Miguel son notables y arrancan, creo yo, de una común preocupación por los problemas de la identidad y la complejidad del ser;[18]

secondly, Edward Friedman's claim that

> Modern tragedy tends to relegate physical nature to human nature [. . .]. If Willie Loman in *Death of a Salesman* symbolises the little man as a tragic hero, el Otro represents Everyman in an eludible regression from incomplete existence. His universality results not from a resolution of the individual conflict, but from the conflict itself;[19]

thirdly, Roberta Lee Johnson's proposition that

> We discover in *El otro* certain universal psychological motifs brought to light by Otto Rank and Carl Jung and certain universal literary patterns detected by Northrup Frye and Harry Slowchower.[20]

This is not, of course, to devalue the work of Gullón, Friedman or Johnson, who have produced interesting readings of *El otro*; it is merely to point out that their (and others') articles raise questions and problems about the play's relations to other texts that they do not address or answer. And *any* reading which seeks to present

El otro, to whatever extent, as a reworking of or response to other specific texts or origins will, to some degree, fall into the same traps, however circumspect its language or tentative its conclusions.

Once the attempt to identify influences, meaningful parallels or inspirations from or reworking of other specific texts is put aside though, *El otro*'s relations with other texts can be re-theorized as intertextual, and the possible sources for the play reconceptualized. Julia Kristeva, reading Bakhtin, says that 'any text is constructed as a mosaic of quotations; any text is the absorption and transformation of another'.[21] Roland Barthes agrees, and is keen to stress that intertextuality is not confined to relations between literary texts: 'Bits of code, formulae, rhythmic models, fragments of social languages etc. pass into the text and are redistributed within it, for there is always language before and around the text'.[22] Barthes also clearly distinguishes intertextuality from source criticism, claiming that 'the intertext is a general field of anonymous formulae whose origins can scarcely ever be located; of unconscious or automatic quotation'.[23] Clearly, some quotations may be less unconscious and anonymous than others, but if we admit that intertextuality 'is the condition of any text whatever', it is pointless to try and posit a single or finite series of stable intertextual sources for a piece of writing.[24] Intertextuality is a continually changing network, whose connections shift, re-align themselves, appear and disappear according to each reading subject's history and interpretative strategies. Intertextuality, then, contests the autonomy and originality of any given text. The text becomes an exposed and protean 'tissue of past', unable to create a barrier allowing a complete or unique identity around itself.[25] Freeing *El otro* in this way from a supposed debt of influence to, or from other dialogic relations with, other specific texts, and seeing it instead as a 'general field of anonymous [not necessarily literary] formulae' allows readings of the play that do not seek to reify its relation to other texts. Moreover, opening the field of its relations with other texts so radically also allows the critic to attend more specifically to *El otro* itself, because if it is no longer yoked to named other texts that cross cultural, historical and linguistic boundaries, it no longer needs to be read as a timeless or dehistoricized universal tragedy.

The historical, political and cultural circumstances of its composition and performance can, in fact, be added to the heterogeneous mass of *El otro*'s intertexts. The critic need not hierarchize their possible relations to the play and can instead concentrate on the new readings that they offer. It is well known that *El otro* was written while Unamuno was in exile in Hendaye, having escaped imprisonment in Fuerteventura for his political speeches and writings. Less attention is paid to the fact that the projected premiere of the play in San Sebastián

was officially suppressed, and that it was to be another six years before *El otro* was performed for the first time (in the Teatro Español in Madrid in December 1932). The play was not published until 1930. By 1926, suppression and censorship were not, of course, new to Unamuno: in the same year, he mentions in a letter to Jean Cassou that circulation of *L'agonie du Christianisme* (translated into French by Cassou from Unamuno's unpublished Spanish manuscript) had been prohibited in Spain.[26] In the same year, he sends some unpublished verses to Cassou, and writes:

> Estos intermedios son para usted y le ruego que no dé la tentación de hacerlos publicar en España. Mientras siga la censura ejercida por esos bárbaros no quiero que pase bajo ella ni lo más inocente mío . . .[27]

It is probably fair to infer that *El otro* was written in the knowledge that it might well not be performed or published in Spain in the near future (in 1926, Unamuno was not optimistic about the possibilities of an end to his exile).[28] In fact, a year after it was written, Unamuno states in a letter to Wenceslao Roces: 'espero que mi drama *El otro* se represente en Buenos Aires, en Berlín y acaso en Varsovia antes que en España'.[29]

Considering the play in this light can produce at least two different politicized readings. At its crudest, one of these readings might simply see the protagonist El Otro as an allegory of Spain, a national self and body politic split into two opposed halves, each half unable either to affirm a separate complete identity independent of the other, or to destroy the other half and break free from its internecine struggle. The lack of conventionally realist concrete particularization in the characterization, temporal-spatial location and scenography of the play might be seen as supporting a generalizing or allegorical reading. Another politicized reading might view *El otro* as a play that, in part, articulates the problematic nature of its own performative and textual identity. Written by an exiled and censored Spanish author, the play had little apparent chance of initial performance or publication in Spain, seemingly destined instead to be premiered and circulated first either in translation or clandestinely. As a literary and dramatic construct, then, *El otro* can be read as having a fragile and split or divided identity, just as its protagonist can.

A reading that sees *El otro* as a play that articulates its own fragile or thwarted textual or performative identity need not be political. During his lifetime, Unamuno's theatre was not considered to be an important part of his literary output, and many of his plays faced a struggle to be performed. His first, *La esfinge,* written in 1898, was not performed until 1908 and not published until 1934. *La venda,* written in 1899, did not premiere until 1921, eight years after it had been published in *El libro popular. Soledad* (1921) and Unamuno's 1933 translation of Seneca's *Medea* were neither performed nor published until after Unamuno's death, and even the relatively well-known *Fedra* (1910) and *El hermano Juan* (1929) were not published until 1924 and 1934 respectively. By 1927, the year after he finished *El otro,* Unamuno claimed to have eight plays as yet unpublished. In part, his plays were not better known because, as Unamuno explained, 'Me resisto a imprimir obras de teatro, escritas para ser oídas y vistas, no para ser leídas'.[30] But as García Blanco demonstrates in his prologue to the collected plays, it was not always easy for Unamuno to find an audience either in Spain or abroad, and he left more than two dozen unpublished or unperformed manuscripts or notes for dramatic projects.[31] And Unamuno did not always convince critics that his plays were theatrical, rather than prose-fiction projects. Fernando Lázaro Carreter refers to two principal difficulties facing the audience of Unamuno's austere 'drama del alma':

> Una [dificultad] [. . .] la inherente a un tema siempre al vivo, y al que el alma ha de dedicar todas sus potencias, sin ningún alivio sensorial. Y otra dificultad superior: la de dar por buena la estética dramática de don Miguel, lo cual supone la renuncia a los hábitos de espectador o de lector de teatro.[32]

Donald Shaw comments:

> We [. . .] have to refer to Unamuno's *narrative* concept of drama. Unhappily, the qualities which made him a distinguished innovator in fiction played him false on the stage.[33]

El otro's representation of a troubled and ultimately doomed search for a separate and complete identity may be read in part as a metatextual comment on its own literary and performative identity as theatre, or on Unamuno's dramatic enterprise as a whole.

While intertextual or metatextual readings of *El otro* can at least acknowledge its status as a literary artefact produced at a specific historical, political or cultural juncture, they cannot solve the problem of how, as Claire Colebrook puts it, 'the text relates to its outside'.[34] Indeed, if history, politics and biography are themselves intertexts, is it even possible to talk about an extra-textual outside? Trying to link *El otro* with any sort of outside (or 'other') remains highly problematic and always culminates in a dissolving or fatal compromising of its own textual self: according to a source-critical reading, the play is, in part, an assimilation, adaptation or reworking of another text, whereby *El otro* carries around its 'other' text(s) within it just as El Otro claims to carry around his dead brother within him; according to an intertextual reading, *El otro* is but part of a limitless mosaic of quotations and fragments of other texts and textualities, and can never even begin to delimit a separate identity for itself.

The uncertainties and complexities of *El otro*'s textual self may well leave the critic yearning for the shockingly bold simplicity of Emilio Salcedo's biography of Unamuno. Salcedo's particular account of *El otro*'s source and its relation to an 'outside' is beguilingly straightforward. He alleges that while Unamuno was in exile in Hendaye

> De Bilbao le llegan noticias de que su hermano Félix está harto de preguntas y se ha puesto en la solapa un cartelito con un 'no me hablen de mi hermano' que hiere a don Miguel, y de esta herida nacerá su tragedia *El otro*.[35]

Ultimately though, it is as hard to posit or delimit an outside for *El otro* as it is as hard for El Otro to delimit his own outside or other. As a result, despite our instinctive critical anxiety for source, influence, cause and 'outsides', it is difficult to read *El otro* as anything other than a simple radical performative utterance, enacting its own dissolution of self as it bespeaks it.

Notes

1. Ricardo Gullón, 'Imágenes del otro', *Revista Hispánica Moderna,* XXXI (1965), 210-21 (pp. 220-21); 'Imágenes de *El otro*', in *Spanish Thought and Letters in the Twentieth Century,* ed E. I. Fox and G. Bleiberg (Nashville: Univ. of Vanderbilt Press, 1966), 257-69 (p. 260).

2. Andrés Franco, *El teatro de Unamuno* (Madrid: Ínsula, 1971), 225; Donald Shaw, 'Three Plays of Unamuno: A Survey of his Dramatic Technique', *Forum for Modern Language Studies,* XIII (1977), 253-63 (p. 260).

3. Derek Gagen, 'Unamuno and the Regeneration of the Spanish Theatre', in *Re-reading Unamuno,* ed. Nicholas Round (Glasgow: Dept of Hispanic Studies, Univ. of Glasgow, 1989), 53-79 (p. 67); Francisco Ruiz Ramón, *Historia del teatro español: siglo XX* (Madrid: Cátedra, 1977), 90.

4. Gilbert Smith, 'Unamuno, Ortega and the *Otro*' *Revista de Estudios Hispánicos,* VI (1972), 373-85; Edward Friedman, 'From Concept to Drama: the Other Unamuno', *Hispanófila,* XXIII (1980), 29-39.

5. Norman Miller, 'Miguel de Unamuno's *El otro*: Anti-Realism and Realism', *Cuadernos de Aldeeu,* I (1983), 37-44; Ángel Valbuena Prat, *Historia del teatro español* (Barcelona: Noguer, 1956), 594-95.

6. Roberta Lee Johnson, 'Archetypes, Structures and Myths in Unamuno's *El otro*', in *Analysis of Hispanic Texts: Current Trends in Methodology. Second York College Colloquium,* ed. L. Davies and I. Taran (Jamaica: Bilingual Press, York College, undated), 32-47.

7. Gullón, 'Imágenes del otro', 210.

8. Ruiz Ramón, *Historia del teatro español: siglo XX,* 79.

9. Miller '*El otro*: Anti-Realism and Realism', 39; Friedman, 'From Concept to Drama', 35.

10. Miguel de Unamuno, *Obras completas,* ed. Manuel García Blanco (Madrid: Afrodisio Aguado, 1958), 12 vols; XII, 653.

11. Unamuno, *Obras completas,* XII, 653.

12. Ruiz Ramón, *Historia del teatro español: siglo XX,* 80-81.

13. Shaw, 'Three Plays of Unamuno', 263.

14. Fernando Lázaro Carreter, 'El teatro de Unamuno', *Cuadernos de la Cátedra Miguel de Unamuno,* VII (1956), 5-29 (p. 10).

15. The text used is that of the 1958 *Obras completas.* However, rather than page numbers, I give act and scene numbers in parentheses after all quotations and citations.

16. Smith, 'Unamuno, Ortega and the *Otro*', 374.

17. Friedman, 'From Concept to Drama', 31-34.

18. Gullón, 'Imágenes del otro', 217, 220; 'Imágenes de *El otro*', 260.

19. Friedman, 'From Concept to Drama', 35.

20. Johnson, 'Archetypes, Structures and Myths in Unamuno's *El otro*', 32.

21. Julia Kristeva, 'Word, Dialogue and Novel', in *A Kristeva Reader,* ed. Toril Moi (Oxford: Blackwell, 1986), 34-61 (p. 37).

22. Roland Barthes, 'The Theory of the Text', in *Untying the Text: A Post-Structuralist Reader,* ed. Robert Young (Boston: Routledge, 1981), 31-47 (p. 39).

23. *Ibid.*

24. *Ibid.*

25. Barthes, 'The Theory of the Text', 39.

26. Miguel de Unamuno, *Epistolario inédito,* ed. Laureano Robles (Madrid: Espasa-Calpe, 1991), 2 vols; II, 185.

27. *Epistolario inédito,* II, 237.

28. In a letter to Jean Cassou in January 1926, Unamuno had written: '[. . .] me temo que, contra las profecías de mis amigos de España, este mi destierro se prolongue' (*Epistolario inédito,* II, 184-85).

29. *Epistolario inédito,* II, 227.

30. *Obras completas,* XII, 10.

31. *Ibid.,* 9-189.

32. Fernando Lázaro Carreter, 'El teatro de Unamuno', *Cuadernos de la Cátedra Miguel de Unamuno,* VII (1956), 5-29 (p. 12).

33. Shaw, 'Three Plays of Unamuno', 263.

34. Claire Colebrook, *New Literary Histories: New Historicism and Contemporary Criticism* (Manchester: Manchester U. P., 1997), vii.

35. Emilio Salcedo, *Vida de don Manuel: Unamuno en su tiempo, en su España, en su Salamanca: un hombre en lucha con su leyenda* (Salamanca: Anaya, 1964), 291.

EL HERMANO JUAN (1934)

CRITICAL COMMENTARY

Sarah Wright (essay date 2004)

SOURCE: Wright, Sarah. "Ethical Seductions: A Comparative Reading of Unamuno's *El hermano Juan* and Kierkegaard's *Either/Or.*" *Anales de la literatura española contemporánea* 29, no. 2 (2004): 119-34.

[*In the following essay, Wright examines Unamuno's* El hermano Juan *alongside Søren Kierkegaard's* Either/Or, *with particular regard to Unamuno's "antipathy" for the myth of Don Juan and his simultaneous attraction to Kierkegaard's work, which deals with the myth.*]

The antipathy felt by Miguel de Unamuno (1864-1936) towards the infamous Spanish seducer, "aquel estúpido fanfarrón" Don Juan, has been extensively documented (Dominicis). His play **El hermano Juan** of 1929 was the culmination of years of (mainly negative) reflection on the myth (Franco 227-33). At the same time, Unamuno's attraction to the ideas of Danish theologian Søren Kierkegaard (1813-1855) is legendary within Unamuno criticism: his interest in Kierkegaard's works was so strong that he famously learned Danish so as to read them in the original language.[1] Kierkegaard was fascinated by the Don Juan type and its variations: his *Either/Or* (1843) features not only a portrait of a cold, manipulative seducer (in the character of Johannes), but also contains a pseudonymously-written essay on the joyous "musical-erotic," a daemonical principle encapsulated in Mozart's score for *Don Giovanni*.

In this article, I aim to read Unamuno's *El hermano Juan* through the prism of Kierkegaard's *Either/Or,* to draw out the coalescence of ideas in the two works connected with the figure of Don Juan. This is an approach which I believe to be unprecedented. Previous studies on Unamuno's dramatic work have stressed the play's meta-theatrical aspects (Fajardo; Franco; Zavala; Zubizarreta), its theatrical technique (Shaw), viewed it as an illustration of some of Unamuno's main ideas (Krzynowek) or else have attempted a psychoanalytic reading of the play's protagonist (Feal Deibe). At the same time, major studies which compare Unamunian and Kierkegaardian thought have avoided reference to *El hermano Juan* (Collado, Evans, Roberts) whilst focus-articles concentrate on Kierkegaardian influences on his major works (Webber; Sinclair). A comparative reading of Unamuno's *El hermano Juan* with Kierkegaard's *Either/Or* will draw out themes common to both: forms of love and the amatory cure; free-will (represented by the choice); the angst of human finitude and the quest for immortality; the tensions between binary oppositions and triadic dialectical discourses; religion as a "leap of faith."

Kierkegaard's *Either/Or* is a meditation on seduction. A large part of the work is given over to a description of Johannes's seduction of the innocent Cordelia in the so-called "Diary of a Seducer" (alongside less salacious works such as an academic essay on the importance of the spirit in music and the letters of Judge William, a rather crusty old killjoy who preaches the ethical significance of marriage). But there is another seduction enacted: that of the reader. The reader is like the work's editor, Victor Eremita, who claims that he found a pile of papers inside an antique writing desk that he had bought after glimpsing its "fatal beauty" in a second-hand dealer's window and immediately fell under its spell. The pile of papers, located in a concealed drawer which springs open one day revealing its secret treasures (the illicitly copied diary as well as the other papers), immediately sets in motion the desire to know more, on the part of Eremita, and Kierkegaard's reader. Thus A's hint that we should doubt that "the outward is the inward, the inward the outward" (Kierkegaard, *Either/Or* 27) offers a challenge to the reader to discover the inner secrets of this text amongst its outwardly coherent exterior. But if seduction etymologically means "to lead astray," then this work is an "ethical seduction" (Saez Tajafuerce), for in its bewildering play of personae embodied in its pseudonymously-written components, the work attempts to deceive the (wayward) reader into a more honest, direct relationship with God (Holmes Hartshorne 1990).

Critics of Kierkegaard's *Either/Or* have discerned three stages of existence which the individual must pass through on the way to religious truth: the aesthetic, the ethical and the religious. Clear resonances of these stages can, I believe, be found in Unamuno's *El hermano Juan,* and it is to this aspect that I shall now turn.

The pseudonymous and fictitious editor of *Either/Or,* Victor Eremita, decides to divide his cache of papers into two groups. On the one hand, there are a series of letters written on legal foolscap: a series of musings of an ethical nature which he attributes to "B" (the retired Judge William). Whilst the writer of the other papers swears that he found "The Seducer's Diary" and copied it down, in a supremely ironic stroke Kierkegaard has Eremita reject this tale as a subterfuge, claiming that we are all familiar with the "old literary device" by which "one author" is enclosed inside another like the boxes in a Chinese puzzle. Eremita muses that the rest of the papers (with the exception of a sermon sent to Judge William) can be attributed to one writer: A. Critics concur that A comes to represent the aesthetic view of life, (whilst Judge Williams portrays the ethical). A is the aesthete *par excellence*: he revels in the sensuality presented variously through the aestheticism of *Don Giovanni* as the highest incarnation of the immediacy of the musical erotic, and in the more reflective but equally hedonistic pleasure-seeking of the sybarite Johannes. Aestheticism runs the gamut from a coarse, instinct-driven pursuit of physical pleasure in the sexual relationship, to a refined aestheticism enjoyed by cultured individuals who enjoy intellectual and artistic forms of pleasure: both cases are marked by their pursuit of pleasure. Both, too, lack constancy, commitment, when they see an attractive alternative, they simply change direction (Watts 192).

Aestheticism is expressed in Unamuno's *El hermano Juan* in the shape of the past life of its protagonist, Don Juan. In Unamuno's dramatic piece, Don Juan's past has been characterised by womanising and by a lack of commitment: he is the embodiment of the Don Juan type. In fact, we learn that he is none other than Zorrilla's romantic Don Juan (from *Don Juan Tenorio* of 1844): his literary origin is symbolised by his nineteenth century clothing which clashes with the modern dress of his fellow characters. As he spouts phrases lifted straight from Zorrilla's verse, he is a theatrical type ("¡Sí representándome. En este teatro del mundo, cada cual nace condenado a un papel" [Unamuno, *El hermano Juan* 133]). Thus at once he is the embodiment of immediate sensuality in his dealings with women, and pure, unmediated aesthetic theatricality—he is all surface, a series of boastings and braggings about his sexual performance, of ruthless acts without thought to the consequences ("pero mira, Inés, dejémonos de cavilaciones, y a lo del momento" [133])—he is pure aesthetic show.

When we meet Unamuno's Don Juan, he appears to be undergoing a crisis of conscience. At the start of the play he is confronted with his past lovers, Elvira and

Inés, as well as the mother of one of his ex-lovers who has committed suicide. Yet whilst he attempts to shrug off the consequences of his past actions, he soon begins to be filled with doubts: "no puedo quererte . . . no sé querer . . . no quiero querer . . . no quiero a nadie y no debo seguir engañándote" (134). Thus although when he first meets Inés's betrothed Benito his first reaction is to try to strangle him, in a typical restaging of the Don Juan type who becomes "the more aroused as another man sidles close to his coveted mistress" (Kristeva 193), nevertheless this Don Juan stops himself just in time. He convinces the virginal Inés that she should marry Benito for "él sabrá hacerte mujer, y yo no; nací condenado a no poder hacer mujer a mujer alguna, ni a mí hombre" in spite of Inés's professions of love for him (Unamuno, *El hermano Juan* 132). Later, he will similarly encourage his childhood sweetheart Elvira (with whom he slept, as a baby, in the same cradle) to marry the doctor Antonio. Elvira provocatively asks Antonio, "¿te conformarías con lo que él te dejara de desecho, con mis escurrajas?" (163) to which Antonio replies "Yo sé mejor que tú, Elvira, lo que tú buscas. Acabarías queriéndome" (163). Juan steps aside, removing himself from the scenario to allow the marriage to take place.

Choosing marriage to a life partner over a string of futile seductions may remind us of Judge William's exposition (a series of letters to A) on living an ethical life in Kierkegaard's *Either/Or*. According to Judge William, the aesthete's ephemeral pleasures must be countermanded by the ethical pursuit of resolute duty. A person living in the ethical sphere of consciousness has realised that "all attempts to live a meaningful existence by satisfying sensual or intellectual desires are doomed to failure" (Watts 200). Instead he strives to embody universal values such as freedom, justice and peace. The ethical life finds its supreme form in the Christian marriage. It is love which makes the marriage so transforming: take away love and "a shared life is either just a satisfaction of sensual desire or an association, a partnership in the interests of some goal. But love has in itself precisely the quality of eternity, whether the love is of the superstitious, romantic, chivalrous kind or the deeper moral and religious love which is filled with an energetic and vital assurance" (Kierkegaard, *Either/Or* 399). "So let Don Juan keep his leafy bower, the knight the dark heaven and its stars if he cannot see above it; marriage has its heaven even higher" (299). Can we see Unamuno's Don Juan, in his attempts to strive for the union of the two couples in his life, Elvira and Antonio; Inés and Benito, as the attempt to create ethical forms of life? If life, like the *either*/or of Kierkegaard's title, is a choice, or series of choices, is Don Juan's joining of two other couples an attempt to sacrifice his pleasures so that the others may "make [their] humble propagation of the human race upon the earth" (Kierkegaard, *Either/Or* 417), as he is aware that

he himself can never bear children?[2] Is he turning away from the aesthete's life of his youth into a new ethical engagement with life?

The paradoxical factor which emerges from Kierkegaard's schemata (this binary between the aesthetic and the ethical, in which the latter is the favoured term) is the alienating effect of the pomposity of Judge William's words: he is dry and boring (compared with the *ennui* expressed by the aesthete), which may lead us to wonder whether Kierkegaard's method with this work was simply to lure the reader into the text with the frothy "Seducer's Diary," before presenting the dry passages on ethical marriages in an attempt to offer variation to stave off boredom (much in the manner of the description of "Crop Rotation" contained within the same volume). Yet Judge William's examples of the ethical marriage, aside from their dryness, often verge on the absurd. Such is the example of the "orientalist scholar" from Holland who was puzzling over a "diacritic" on a page of his Dutch edition. His wife, who has called him for dinner, blows on the page and the dot reveals itself to be a grain of snuff: "the scholar hastens happily to the dinner-table, happy that the vowel point had disappeared, even happier in his wife" (Kierkegaard, *Either/Or* 575). Hall shows how Judge William is every bit as deceiving as his aesthetical antithesis. For as Judge William writes to persuade the aesthete against certain kinds of marriage (the marriage of convenience, the scenarios of over comfortable domestic life), he fails to recognise those elements in his own marriage, thereby performing a deconstruction of his own text (117). But most of all, Judge William, in his pompous comparison of his marriage to a church wherein he may be "simultaneously priest and congregation" and suggesting that "when a person has reached a certain age he ought to be able to be his own pastor" (Hall 118), he is eschewing the truly humble position before God that a true relation with God demands. Thus, "his unwarranted confidence in his own ability to summon forth and interpret God's presence precludes a truly humbling encounter with his creator" (118). Hence, "the happily, dutifully married Christian is thus as much of the irreligious puzzle as the seducer" (110).

In reading the works of B, then, when set against A, we are reminded of how similar the two apparently disparate spheres may be—each works dialectically to expose the fallacies of the other. If *Either/Or* offers the choice of two disparate realms, then the suggestion suddenly emerges that neither one can offer an ideal. Kierkegaard's aim, in this work, is maieutic (elsewhere he refers to "my maieutic carefulness" (Kierkegaard, *Works* ix). Maieutic, from the Greek *maia* for midwife, refers to the Socratic method of allowing the listener/reader to come to his/her own conclusions from a myriad of different points of view.[3] Kierkegaard repeatedly makes the point that he believes that the reader should come to his own conclusions, thereby removing the authority of the author (in a stroke which may remind us of Unamuno's own version of the "death of the author" in, for example, *Niebla*).[4] In *Works of Love,* Kierkegaard writes that "the highest one human being can do for another is to make him free, help him to stand by himself—[. . .] if this is to be done the helper must make himself anonymous, must magnanimously will to annihilate himself. In the spiritual sense he was, as he called himself, a midwife" (276). It is from the understanding of these two separate worlds that the reader may engage in the text. Thus rather than the nihilism suggested by A's provocative assertion that "marry and you will regret it, don't marry and you will regret it," Kierkegaard hopes that what will be gained from an understanding of the dialectic of these two terms is that the individual must appeal to a higher sphere. The move towards this higher sphere demands understanding (self-knowledge) as well as a "leap of faith"—for this is the sphere of God.[5]

Kierkegaard's invocation of the "midwife" may remind us of Unamuno's Don Juan, who claims that he wants to become a "nodrizo." Speaking to the couples he has brought together, Brother Juan paraphrases Genesis 3, 16 and 19 to declare that his aim is for them to have children:

>   Y si es varón el primero, llamadle Juan, en memoria
>   mía, al pobrecito desterrado hijo de Eva . . .

ANTONIO:

>   Así serás su padrino . . .

JUAN:

>   Sí, apadrinar es mi sino . . . Aunque más que padrino
>   me siento . . . *madrino*; mejor, ¡*nodrizo*!

>   (190)

Bretz (488-89) has noted the "role of go-between or the transgendered self-designation of *nodrizo,* appropriating the Spanish word for wet-nurse in a previously inconceivable masculine form."[6] I suggest that the "nodrizo" is Unamuno's invocation of Kierkegaard's "midwife," who in turn relates to Socratic teaching. In Unamuno's text, does Don Juan therefore ethically arrange marriages for the two couples, rather than entering into marriage himself, as part of an attempt to remove intermediaries between himself and God? In his invocation of the midwife, Don Juan gives birth to a new version of himself ostensibly to pass into the religious sphere: sinner becomes saint, Don Juan renames himself Brother Juan.[7]

What Unamuno appears to have grasped from Kierkegaard's texts, is the close relationship between the aesthete and the ethical deviser, and the importance of the dialectic between these two for the emergence of

religion. He finds elements of all three of these spheres embodied in the figure of Don Juan (who remarks that, "los antiguos [. . .] me llamaron Cupido" [195]). Love in its many forms, to my mind, is the element that links all of these elements, and it is this that I would now like to explore in the context of Kierkegaard's work and Unamuno's Don Juan.

As Hannay has written, Kierkegaard's *Either/Or* can be read as covering "the spectrum of arbitrary self-love, erotic love, and marital love, and Judge William ends with a borrowed sermon from the Jylland pastor on the love of God" (Kierkegaard, *Works* x). Even the essay on "The Rotation of Crops" could be read as a variation of the theme of avoiding boredom in marriage by an analogy with rotating crops within the same soil. In *Works of Love* (1847), Kierkegaard presents an extended thesis on these various forms of love. In a discussion in that work under the heading "You Shall love the neighbour," Kierkegaard considers the notion that "anyone who insightfully and earnestly reflects on this matter will readily see that the issue must be posed in this way: shall erotic love [*Elskov*] and friendship be the highest love [*Kjerlighed*] or shall love be dethroned?" (*Works* 44). Kierkegaard's musings on the hierarchies between "one who loves the neighbour" and the "selfishness of preferential love" which must be "rooted out" for the "equality of the eternal" to be preserved (44) finds a clear resonance in Unamuno's play. For who better to incarnate preferential, self-interested love than Don Juan, (Salinas draws parallels between Unamuno's Don Juan and Narcissus). Don Juan is the supreme icon of erotic love, messenger of Eros. Yet in Unamuno's play, erotic love in Don Juan is displaced by brotherly love, by love of one's neighbour. Don Juan renames himself Brother Juan; *eros* is replaced by *agape.* This idea is illustrated most clearly in Juan's relations with the women in his life: when Inés arrives, desperate to enter into (erotic) union with him, he suggests that she marry Benito instead. In the case of Elvira, who reminds him that they were childhood sweethearts, he prefers to remain a brother. The play on the word "brother" is clear: "brother" refers to familial relations as well as the religious order.[8] In Brother Juan's final scene with the women, he asks them to kneel before him and fondly strokes their heads. If, as Céline Léon and Sylvia Walsh (1997: 3) suggest, "the first, or aesthetic, sphere is that of seduction, where a single man seduces many women, or concentrates his negative attentions on a single one. The second (ethical) has to do with marriage, namely, the committed relationship to one woman. The third, or religious sphere, is that of 'the exception,' namely that in which man abstains from commerce with women," then Brother Juan appears to have entered the religious. His erotic love has turned to brotherly love, his misogynistic devilment turns to abstention from sex, in fact to a withdrawal from erotic relationships altogether: the pleasures of the flesh turn to the power of the spirit. There is a quality of the "amatory cure" about this love. It has a transformative power. It is as if Brother Juan believes that he can atone for the crimes of Don Juan as he brings together the other couples in marriage and in committed relationships, whilst he practices only brotherly, neighbourly and religious love. Sylvia Walsh Utterback finds in Kierkegaard's Don Juan the potential for a "spiritual sensuousness" which can express an aesthetic religiousness. Drawing on Da Ponte's lyrical "thousand and three," she suggests that this be seen as a metaphor for "loving all": she sees the Don Juan as paradigmatic for the "basic human desire for communion with others" (635). "Love is religious when it is explicitly or implicitly grounded in God to the ultimate as embracing all." In Unamuno's play, Brother Juan claims that he has readied the women for love, preparing them for their later commitment to other men. Yet I am not wholly convinced by Walsh Utterback's argument: it seems to me that the seducer's erotic misogyny is far removed from the ideals of Christian love even at the most abstract of levels. But Walsh Utterback does point up love as an important link between Don Juan and Christianity. I submit that Unamuno uses Don Juan, the erotic icon, to contrast love in the spectrum from erotic desire to Christian love, which spin endlessly within the same figure.⁹

If Unamuno's Brother Juan encapsulates the extremes of erotic and brotherly love, of *eros* and *agape,* then in the world of binary opposites within which he operates, other oppositions are highlighted in this binary universe too. Thus where Don Juan was distinguished by his outwardliness, his care for appearances and show, Brother Juan is preoccupied with the inner life, with reflection and inwardliness. Where the relationships he formed earlier with women were fleeting and transient, now he aims for lasting friendships. Where earlier he had dealt in mendacity, now he angles at the truth. His female lovers have now become his sisters. In a reworking of the Zorrilla tale, the Commendatore who comes to take his revenge on Don Juan for seducing his daughter is here rendered as Doña Petra, who arrives to take her revenge when her daughter commits suicide but whom Don Juan remonstrates for her part in her daughter's death (there are suggestions that Doña Petra herself may have fallen for Don Juan's charms). In this economy, inner is substituted for outer, sister for lover, female for male, thereby revealing the binary oppositions which fill Don Juan's world. Yet just as Hall shows that there are similarities between the aesthete's form of love and that of Judge William's ethical union, so now binaries appear to collapse into one another in Unamuno's play. For the assertion of each term (female, inner, truth, sister) carries within it the trace or memory of its opposite (male, outer, lies, lover). Kierkegaard's writing shows that when binaries collapse (as in, for example, the either/or of the choice between aesthete and ethical)

a third term can be envisioned, encapsulated in the religious. Brother Juan attempts to find a third term, a Hegelian "mediation," a way out of these binaries, in his reincarnation of a gender neutral ("nodrizo"), celibate go-between. Yet he finds that he is unable to escape from the binary system. As a figure who tests the limits of society, Don Juan can only emerge out of a religious universe, but similarly, Brother Juan threatens constantly to revert to Don Juan. Brother Juan is not-Don Juan and vice versa.¹⁰

Life, in Unamuno's conception in this play, is posed as a series of choices (the either/or), a series of ethical questions as to how one ought to behave. In turning against his past, embodied in the form of Don Juan, Brother Juan shows that he is fighting schizophrenically in a constant war against himself. Metaphorically, election of a choice incurs the death of the other option. Yet Don Juan refuses to be laid to rest. However much he tries to change himself, to make ethical choices, Brother Juan is reminded of his past lives. In a sense Brother Juan encapsulates the notion of the choice, either this route or that, this choice or that choice (Franco equates him with Shakespeare's Hamlet "su obsession con el ser y el no ser" [253]). But free will is here also posited as warring against the "leap of faith." The unknown consequences of our choices imply the exercising of a "leap of faith" into the future. For Don Juan, the final choice is always whether to be redeemed (in the Zorrilla version) or to descend into the depths of Hell (in Tirso de Molina). In his conversion to Brother Juan, Unamuno's protagonist appears to attempt to safeguard his reception in Heaven. But much like Kierkegaard's pompous Judge William, Unamuno's Brother Juan is rather less than humble in his attitude towards God. His demonstration of brotherly love appears to be a desire to be remembered well by the other characters. Meanwhile, his meddling into the lives of others could be seen as a desire on the part of the protagonist to write the script of those around him as well as his own. Finally, he announces his forthcoming death—presumably a suicide (the exercise of his free will). But this death is also conceptualised as a marriage with "ella."¹¹ In a brilliant revision on the psychoanalytic notions of Don Juan as a man who is constantly searching for his mother (in the work of Otto Rank, amongst others), this Brother Juan will enter into a marriage with his mother (which is death). Unamuno offers a provocative warning to those psychoanalysts who would try to understand his protagonist (as he has Juan disparagingly refer to the work of the doctor Antonio to find a cure in Act Two Scene 5), yet in this play on the terms brother and mother, we cannot fail to see this desire to seduce the mother as other than a failed Oedipal complex (Feal Deibe). As such, it represents a desire for omnipotence, representing as it does, a desire to supplant the father, which, given the play on the word "brother," which for Brother Juan stresses his position in the family of God, represents an omnipotent desire to supplant God.[12]

In *Del sentimiento trágico de la vida,* Unamuno wrote that he saw his mission thus:

> quebrantar la fe de unos y de otros y de los terceros. La fe en la afirmación, la fe en la negación y la fe en la abstención y esto por fe en la fe misma: es combatir a todos que se resignan, sea el catolicismo, sea el racionalismo, sea el agnosticismo; es hacer que todos vivan inquietos y anhelantes.
>
> (297-98)

Unamuno's play offers an ambiguous end to the Don Juan tale and as such, offers no easy solutions to the question of faith. For if Brother Juan, in his "leap of faith" into death ensures that he will discover the truth about God, nevertheless the audience/reader is left to ponder the unknowability of the afterlife. If God does exist, Brother Juan's attempt for union with the mother, thereby supplanting the father, must surely incur his wrath. If, on the other hand, all that is waiting for Brother Juan is a Godless void, then his leap of faith will have been in vain.

Notes

This research was made possible by a grant under the Research Leave Scheme of the Arts and Humanities Research Board. I gratefully acknowledge the support offered by the AHRB as well as that of the colleagues who supported me in my application. The Arts and Humanities Research Board (AHRB) funds postgraduate and advanced research within the UK's higher education institutions. All AHRB awards are made on the basis of academic excellence. The AHRB is not responsible for the views or research outcomes expressed by its award holders.

1. Valdés and Valdés write that Unamuno bought Kierkegaard's complete works published by Drachman and Heiberg between 1901 and 1906.

2. The inability of Don Juan to produce progeny is a common theme in Don Juan versions, as for example, in Gregorio Marañón's 1924 essay, "Notas para una biología de Don Juan."

3. In Plato's dialogues Socrates states, "my art of midwifery is in general like theirs [that of the midwife at a birth]; the only difference is that my patients are men, not women, and my concern is not with the body, but with the soul that is in travail of birth" (Plato 855).

4. For a fascinating discussion of the theme of the "death of the author" in Unamuno's work, see Wyers.

5. Kierkegaard never uses the term "leap of faith," but his work has come to be conceptualised in these terms (Ferreira).

6. Cf. Franco (246), who draws on the theories of Gregorio Marañón to suggest that Unamuno's play debates the question of virility.

7. Brother Juan follows a list of converts who had formerly lived the lives of sinners such as, for example, St. Augustine (354-430 AD), whose *Confessions* charted the passage from his previous life in sin to his conversion. I thank Guillermo Martínez-Correcher for drawing my attention to the similarities between Don Juan and St. Augustine. This theme is underscored in the play as Don Juan recognises that in a previous life Padre Teófilo had been Mephistopheles to Don Juan's Faust.

8. There is much game-playing with words in this play, such as the play on the word "Don" from Don Juan, which can also mean "gift": "Don de mujeres" (Unamuno 148). The play is also full of different registers, from the religious to the medical. Bretz even finds the language of advertising.

9. Perhaps Unamuno, like the postmodern critics of Kierkegaard, finds that A and B may be the same person and thus encapsulate the extremes of aesthetic and ethical living.

10. In Derridean terms we could speak of the word in terms of its "erasure." In Hegel's discussions of the contradiction, "one concept is, for instance, called *blue* . . . the other *not-blue,* so that this other would not be an affirmative (like, for instance, yellow), but is just the abstractly negative that has to be held fast . . ." As Jon Stewart writes, "the first concept is determined by the second in so far as it is conceived *as an opposite.* Thus, concepts are complementary, and any given concept, insofar as it is an opposite, stands in a necessary relation to another concept" (196). Hegel introduces the "law of the excluded middle," according to which, "a concept is determined both by what it is and what it is not. For example, north is what it is (i.e. self-identity), but it is also determined by what it is not, namely, as the opposite of south. Thus north is both north and not north at the same time" (197). Whilst Hegel is traditionally "conceived as the philosopher of mediation, Kierkegaard is thought to be the philosopher of the either/or." Yet Stewart finds traces of the Hegelian appeal to a "triadic dialectic" even within the tome which bears the dichotomous title "either/or" (232). He notes, for example, that in Kierkegaard "there is a sense in which a third category, 'the religious,' comes to complement the first two" (231). For an excellent analysis of Kierkegaard's debt to Hegel, see Jon Stewart. I

am very grateful to Jon Stewart for allowing me to view his study prior to its publication.

11. It is perhaps no more than an interesting coincidence that the father of St. Francis of Assisi was named Don Pietro, that Francis's mother had wanted to call her son Giovanni but was overruled by her husband, and that St. Francis spoke often of going to meet "sister death."

12. As he goes to his death, Brother Juan cries out "¿Y que [Dios] me perdone? . . . Soy yo quien tengo que perdonarle . . . [. . .] que me haya hecho como me está haciendo . . ." (Unamuno 196).

Works Cited

Bretz, Mary Lee. *Encounters Across Borders: The Changing Visions of Spanish Modernism, 1890-1930*. Lewisburg: Bucknell UP. London: Associated UP, 2001.

Collado, Jesús-Antonio. *Kierkegaard y Unamuno: La existencia religiosa*. Madrid: Gredos, 1962.

Dominicis, María C. *Don Juan en el teatro español del siglo XX*. Miami: Ediciones Universal, 1978.

Evans, Jan. "The Formation of the Self in the Novels of Miguel de Unamuno: A Kierkegaardian Reading." Diss., Michigan State U, 2001.

Fajardo, Diógenes. "El Don Juan de Unamuno: 'El hermano Juan o el mundo es teatro.'" *Thesaurus* 42.2 (May-Aug. 1987): 370-79.

Feal Deibe, Carlos. *Unamuno: "El otro" y Don Juan*. Madrid: Cursa Editorial, 1976.

Ferreira, M. Jaime. "Faith and the Kierkegaardian Leap." *The Cambridge Companion to Kierkegaard*. Ed. Alastair Hannay and Gordon D. Marino. Cambridge: Cambridge UP, 1998. 207-34.

Franco, Andrés. *El teatro de Unamuno*. Madrid: Ínsula, 1971.

Hall, Amy Laura. *Kierkegaard and the Treachery of Love*. Cambridge: Cambridge UP, 2002.

Holmes Hartshorne, M. *Kierkegaard, Godly Deceiver. The Nature and Meaning of His Pseudonymous Writings*. New York: Columbia UP, 1990.

Kierkegaard, Søren. *Either/Or: A Fragment of Life*. Ed. Alastair Hannay. London: Penguin. 1992.

———. *Works of Love*. Ed. Howard V. Hong and Edna H. Hong. Princeton, New Jersey: Princeton UP, 1995.

Kristeva, Julia. *Tales of Love*. Trans. Leon S. Roudiez. New York: Columbia UP, 1987.

Krzynowek, Gloria Domeque. "El hermano Juan: Unamuno y Don Juan." *Crítica Hispánica* 18.1 (1996): 149-58.

Léon, Céline and Sylvia Walsh, eds. *Feminist Interpretations of Søren Kierkegaard*. Pennsylvania: Pennsylvania State UP, 1997.

Marañón, Gregorio. "Notas para una biología de Don Juan." *Revista de occidente* 3 (1924): 15-53.

Plato. *The Collected Dialogues of Plato*. Ed. Edith Hamilton and Huntingdon Cairns. Princeton: Princeton UP, 1963.

Roberts, Gemma. *Unamuno: afinidades y coincidencias kierkegaardianas*. Boulder, Colorado: Society of Spanish and Spanish-American Studies, 1986.

Salinas, Pedro. "Don Juan Tenorio Frente a Miguel de Unamuno." 1934. *Literatura Española Siglo XX*. Mexico: Antigua Librería, 1949.

Saez Tajafuerce, Begonya. "Kierkegaardian Seduction, or the Aesthetic Actio(nes) in distans." *Diacritics* 30.1 (2000): 78-88.

Shaw, Donald. "Acerca de la técnica dramática de *El hermano Juan*." *El teatro de Miguel de Unamuno*. Ed. Jesús María Lasagabaster. San Sebastián: Universidad de Deusto, 1986. 213-26.

Sinclair, Alison. "Concepts of Tragedy in Unamuno and Kierkegaard." *Re-reading Unamuno*. Ed. Nicholas Round. Glasgow: U of Glasgow P, 1989. 121-32.

Stewart, Jon. *Kierkegaard's Relations to Hegel Reconsidered*. Cambridge: Cambridge UP, 2003.

Unamuno y Jugo, Miguel de. *El otro. El hermano Juan*. Ed. José Paulino. Madrid: Espasa Calpe, 1946.

———. *Del sentimiento trágico de la vida en los hombres y en los pueblos*. 1913. *Obras Completas*. Ed. M. García Blanco. Vol. 7. Madrid: Escelicer, 1967. 106-302.

Valdés, Mario and Elena Valdés. *An Unamuno Source Book*. Toronto: U of Toronto P, 1973.

Walsh Utterback, Sylvia. "Don Juan and the Representation of Spiritual Sensuousness." *Journal of the American Academy of Religion* 47.4 (1979): 627-44.

Watts, Michael. *Kierkegaard*. Oxford: Oneworld Publications, 2003.

Webber, Ruth House. "Kierkegaard and the Elaboration of Unamuno's *Niebla*." *Hispanic Review* 32 (1964): 118-34.

Wyers, Francis. "Unamuno and 'The Death of the Author.'" *Hispanic Review* 58 (1990): 325-46.

Zavala, Iris. *Unamuno y su teatro de conciencia*. Salamanca: Acta Salmanticensia, 1963.

Zubizarreta, Armando F. *Unamuno en su nivola*. Madrid: Taurus, 1960.

FURTHER READING

Criticism

Ketz, Victoria. "Avian Motifs, Apiarian Images and Adulterous Women in the Theater of Valle Inclán and Unamuno." *Monographic Review* 20 (2004): 85-102.

Explores the use of imagery of birds and bees to represent women who break out of the traditional bonds of marriage in Spanish literature, including *Raquel encadenada*.

Orringer, Nelson R. "Philosophy and Tragedy in Two Newly Discovered *Fedras* by Unamuno." *Anales de la literatura española contemporánea* 22, no. 3 (1997): 549-64.

Explores Unamuno's fascination with the ancient Phaedra myth and his interpretation of it in *Fedra*.

Pauker, Eleanor K. "Unamuno's *La venda*: Short Story and Drama." *Hispania* 39, no. 3 (September 1956): 309-12.

Discusses similarities and differences between Unamuno's short story "La venda" and his adaptation of it into a play.

Sedwick, Frank. "Unamuno and Pirandello Revisited." *Italica* 33, no. 1 (March 1956): 40-51.

Discusses links between Unamuno and Italian dramatist Luigi Pirandello.

Additional coverage of Unamuno's life and career is contained in the following sources published by Gale: *Contemporary Authors*, Vols. 104, 131; *Contemporary Authors New Revision Series*, Vol. 81; *Gale Contextual Encyclopedia of World Literature*; *Dictionary of Literary Biography*, Vols. 108, 322; *DISCovering Authors Modules: Multicultural Authors* and *Novelists*; *Encyclopedia of World Literature in the 20th Century*, Ed. 3; *European Writers*, Vol. 8; *Hispanic Literature Criticism*, Ed. 2; *Hispanic Writers*, Eds. 1, 2; *Literature Resource Center*; *Major 20th-Century Writers*, Eds. 1, 2; *Major 21st-Century Writers*; *Reference Guide to Short Fiction*, Ed. 2; *Reference Guide to World Literature*, Eds. 2, 3; *Short Stories for Students*, Vol. 20; *Short Story Criticism*, Vols. 11, 69; *Twayne's World Authors*; and *Twentieth-Century Literary Criticism*, Vols. 2, 9, 148, 237.

How to Use This Index

CDALBS = *Concise Dictionary of American Literary Biography Supplement*
CDBLB = *Concise Dictionary of British Literary Biography*
CMW = *St. James Guide to Crime & Mystery Writers*
CN = *Contemporary Novelists*
CP = *Contemporary Poets*
CPW = *Contemporary Popular Writers*
CSW = *Contemporary Southern Writers*
CWD = *Contemporary Women Dramatists*
CWP = *Contemporary Women Poets*
CWRI = *St. James Guide to Children's Writers*
CWW = *Contemporary World Writers*
DA = *DISCovering Authors*
DA3 = *DISCovering Authors 3.0*
DAB = *DISCovering Authors: British Edition*
DAC = *DISCovering Authors: Canadian Edition*
DAM = *DISCovering Authors: Modules*
   DRAM: *Dramatists Module;* **MST:** *Most-studied Authors Module;*
   MULT: *Multicultural Authors Module;* **NOV:** *Novelists Module;*
   POET: *Poets Module;* **POP:** *Popular Fiction and Genre Authors Module*
DFS = *Drama for Students*
DLB = *Dictionary of Literary Biography*
DLBD = *Dictionary of Literary Biography Documentary Series*
DLBY = *Dictionary of Literary Biography Yearbook*
DNFS = *Literature of Developing Nations for Students*
EFS = *Epics for Students*
EW = *European Writers*
EWL = *Encyclopedia of World Literature in the 20th Century*
EXPN = *Exploring Novels*
EXPP = *Exploring Poetry*
EXPS = *Exploring Short Stories*
FANT = *St. James Guide to Fantasy Writers*
FW = *Feminist Writers*
GFL = *Guide to French Literature,* Beginnings to 1789, 1798 to the Present
GLL = *Gay and Lesbian Literature*
HGG = *St. James Guide to Horror, Ghost & Gothic Writers*
HW = *Hispanic Writers*
IDFW = *International Dictionary of Films and Filmmakers: Writers and Production Artists*
IDTP = *International Dictionary of Theatre: Playwrights*
LAIT = *Literature and Its Times*
LAW = *Latin American Writers*
JRDA = *Junior DISCovering Authors*
MAICYA = *Major Authors and Illustrators for Children and Young Adults*
MAICYAS = *Major Authors and Illustrators for Children and Young Adults Supplement*
MAWW = *Modern American Women Writers*
MJW = *Modern Japanese Writers*
MTCW = *Major 20th-Century Writers*
NCFS = *Nonfiction Classics for Students*
NFS = *Novels for Students*
PAB = *Poets: American and British*
PFS = *Poetry for Students*
RGAL = *Reference Guide to American Literature*
RGEL = *Reference Guide to English Literature*
RGSF = *Reference Guide to Short Fiction*
RGWL = *Reference Guide to World Literature*
RHW = *Twentieth-Century Romance and Historical Writers*
SAAS = *Something about the Author Autobiography Series*
SATA = *Something about the Author*
SFW = *St. James Guide to Science Fiction Writers*
SSFS = *Short Stories for Students*
TCWW = *Twentieth-Century Western Writers*
WLIT = *World Literature and Its Times*
WP = *World Poets*
YABC = *Yesterday's Authors of Books for Children*
YAW = *St. James Guide to Young Adult Writers*

Literary Criticism Series
Cumulative Author Index

Adler, Carole Schwerdtfeger
See Adler, C. S.
Adler, Renata 1938- .... **CLC 8, 31**
See also CA 49-52; CANR 95; CN 4, 5, 6;
MTCW 1
Adorno, Theodor W(iesengrund)
1903-1969 .... **TCLC 111**
See also CA 89-92; 25-28R; CANR 89;
DLB 242; EWL 3
Ady, Endre 1877-1919 .... **TCLC 11, 253**
See also CA 107; CDWLB 4; DLB 215;
EW 9; EWL 3
A.E.
See Russell, George William
Aelfric c. 955-c. 1010 .... **CMLC 46, 128**
See also DLB 146
Aelred of Rievaulx 1110-1167 .... **CMLC 123**
Aeschines c. 390B.C.-c. 320B.C. .. **CMLC 47**
See also DLB 176
Aeschylus 525(?)B.C.-456(?)B.C. . **CMLC 11,**
51, 94; DC 8; WLCS
See also AW 1; CDWLB 1; DA; DAB;
DAC; DAM DRAM, MST; DFS 5, 10,
26; DLB 176; LMFS 1; RGWL 2, 3;
TWA; WLIT 8
Aesop 620(?)B.C.-560(?)B.C. .... **CMLC 24;**
SSC 164
See also CLR 14; MAICYA 1, 2; SATA 64
Affable Hawk
See MacCarthy, Sir (Charles Otto) Desmond
Africa, Ben
See Bosman, Herman Charles
Afrika, Jan
See Breytenbach, Breyten
Afton, Effie
See Harper, Frances Ellen Watkins
Agapida, Fray Antonio
See Irving, Washington
Agar, Emile
See Kacew, Romain
Agee, James 1909-1955 ..... **TCLC 1, 19, 180**
See also AAYA 44; AITN 1; AMW; CA 108;
148; CANR 131; CDALB 1941-1968;
DAM NOV; DLB 2, 26, 152; DLBY
1989; EWL 3; LAIT 3; LATS 1:2; MAL
5; MTCW 2; MTFW 2005; NFS 22;
RGAL 4; TUS
Agee, James Rufus
See Agee, James
A Gentlewoman in New England
See Bradstreet, Anne
A Gentlewoman in Those Parts
See Bradstreet, Anne
Aghill, Gordon
See Silverberg, Robert
Agnon, S. Y. 1888-1970 . **CLC 4, 8, 14; SSC**
30, 120; TCLC 151
See also CA 17-18; 25-28R; CANR 60, 102,
211; CAP 2; DLB 329; EWL 3; MTCW
1, 2; RGHL; RGSF 2; RGWL 2, 3; WLIT
6
Agnon, Shmuel Yosef Halevi
See Agnon, S. Y.
Agrippa von Nettesheim, Henry Cornelius
1486-1535 .... **LC 27**
Aguilera Malta, Demetrio 1909-1981 . **HLCS**
1
See also CA 111; 124; CANR 87; DAM
MULT, NOV; DLB 145; EWL 3; HW 1;
RGWL 3
Agustini, Delmira 1886-1914 .... **HLCS 1**
See also CA 166; DLB 290; HW 1, 2; LAW
Aherne, Owen
See Cassill, R(onald) V(erlin)
Ai 1947-2010 .... **CLC 4, 14, 69; PC 72**
See also CA 85-88; CAAS 13; CANR 70;
CP 6, 7; DLB 120; PFS 16

Aickman, Robert (Fordyce) 1914-1981 . **CLC**
57
See also CA 5-8R; CANR 3, 72, 100; DLB
261; HGG; SUFW 1, 2
Aidoo, (Christina) Ama Ata 1942- .... **BLCS;**
CLC 177, 314
See also AFW; BRWS 15; BW 1; CA 101;
CANR 62, 144; CD 5, 6; CDWLB 3; CN
6, 7; CWD; CWP; DLB 117; DNFS 1, 2;
EWL 3; FW; WLIT 2
Aiken, Conrad 1889-1973 .. **CLC 1, 3, 5, 10,**
52; PC 26; SSC 9
See also AMW; CA 5-8R; 45-48; CANR 4,
60; CDALB 1929-1941; CN 1; CP 1;
DAM NOV, POET; DLB 9, 45, 102; EWL
3; EXPS; HGG; MAL 5; MTCW 1, 2;
MTFW 2005; PFS 24; RGAL 4; RGSF 2;
SATA 3, 30; SSFS 8, 34; TUS
Aiken, Conrad Potter
See Aiken, Conrad
Aiken, Joan (Delano) 1924-2004 ..... **CLC 35**
See also AAYA 1, 25; CA 9-12R, 182; 223;
CAAE 182; CANR 4, 23, 34, 64, 121;
CLR 1, 19, 90; DLB 161; FANT; HGG;
JRDA; MAICYA 1, 2; MTCW 1; RHW;
SAAS 1; SATA 2, 30, 73; SATA-Essay
109; SATA-Obit 152; SSFS 33; SUFW 2;
WYA; YAW
Ainsworth, William Harrison 1805-1882 .....
NCLC 13
See also DLB 21; HGG; RGEL 2; SATA
24; SUFW 1
Aitmatov, Chingiz 1928-2008 . **CLC 71; SSC**
131
See also CA 103; CANR 38; CWW 2; DLB
302; EWL 3; MTCW 1; RGSF 2; SATA
56
Aitmatov, Chingiz Torekulovich
See Aitmatov, Chingiz
Ajar, Emile
See Kacew, Romain
Akers, Floyd
See Baum, L. Frank
Akhmadulina, Bella 1937-2010 ...... **CLC 53;**
PC 43
See also CA 65-68; CWP; CWW 2; DAM
POET; DLB 359; EWL 3
Akhmadulina, Bella Akhatovna
See Akhmadulina, Bella
Akhmatova, Anna 1888-1966 ... **CLC 11, 25,**
64, 126; PC 2, 55
See also CA 19-20; 25-28R; CANR 35;
CAP 1; DA3; DAM POET; DLB 295; EW
10; EWL 3; FL 1:5; MTCW 1, 2; PFS 18,
27, 32, 36; RGWL 2, 3
Aksakov, Sergei Timofeevich 1791-1859 ......
NCLC 2, 181
See also DLB 198
Aksenov, Vasilii
See Aksyonov, Vassily
Aksenov, Vasilii Pavlovich
See Aksyonov, Vassily
Aksenov, Vassily
See Aksyonov, Vassily
Akst, Daniel 1956- .... **CLC 109**
See also CA 161; CANR 110
Aksyonov, Vassily 1932-2009 .... **CLC 22, 37,**
101
See also CA 53-56; CANR 12, 48, 77;
CWW 2; DLB 302; EWL 3
Aksyonov, Vassily Pavlovich
See Aksyonov, Vassily
Akutagawa Ryunosuke 1892-1927 .. **SSC 44;**
TCLC 16, 259
See also CA 117; 154; DLB 180; EWL 3;
MJW; RGSF 2; RGWL 2, 3; SSFS 35
Alabaster, William 1568-1640 .... **LC 90**
See also DLB 132; RGEL 2

Alain 1868-1951 .... **TCLC 41**
See also CA 163; EWL 3; GFL 1789 to the
Present
Alain de Lille c. 1116-c. 1203 ..... **CMLC 53,**
138
See also DLB 208
Alain-Fournier
See Fournier, Henri-Alban
Al-Amin, Jamil Abdullah 1943- ..... **BLC 1:1**
See also BW 1, 3; CA 112; 125; CANR 82;
DAM MULT
Alan of Lille
See Alain de Lille
Alanus de Insluis
See Alain de Lille
Alarcon, Pedro Antonio de 1833-1891 ....
NCLC 1, 219; SSC 64
Alas (y Urena), Leopoldo (Enrique Garcia)
1852-1901 .... **TCLC 29**
See also CA 113; 131; HW 1; RGSF 2
Albee, Edward (III) 1928- ... **CLC 1, 2, 3, 5,**
9, 11, 13, 25, 53, 86, 113; DC 11; WLC
1
See also AAYA 51; AITN 1; AMW; CA
5-8R; CABS 3; CAD; CANR 8, 54, 74,
124; CD 5, 6; CDALB 1941-1968; DA;
DA3; DAB; DAC; DAM DRAM, MST;
DFS 25; DLB 7, 266; EWL 3; INT
CANR-8; LAIT 4; LMFS 2; MAL 5;
MTCW 1, 2; MTFW 2005; RGAL 4; TUS
Albee, Edward Franklin
See Albee, Edward (III)
Alberti, Leon Battista 1404-1472 ..... **LC 173**
Alberti, Rafael 1902-1999 .... **CLC 7**
See also CA 85-88; 185; CANR 81; CWW
2; DLB 108; EWL 3; HW 2; RGWL 2, 3
Alberti Merello, Rafael
See Alberti, Rafael
Albert of Saxony c. 1316-1390 ... **CMLC 110**
Albert the Great 1193(?)-1280 ..... **CMLC 16**
See also DLB 115
Alcaeus c. 620B.C.- .... **CMLC 65**
See also DLB 176
Alcala-Galiano, Juan Valera y
See Valera y Alcala-Galiano, Juan
Alcayaga, Lucila Godoy
See Mistral, Gabriela
Alciato, Andrea 1492-1550 .... **LC 116**
Alcott, Amos Bronson 1799-1888 .. **NCLC 1,**
167
See also DLB 1, 223
Alcott, Louisa May 1832-1888 . **NCLC 6, 58,**
83, 218; SSC 27, 98, 164; WLC 1
See also AAYA 20; AMWS 1; BPFB 1;
BYA 2; CDALB 1865-1917; CLR 1, 38,
109; DA; DA3; DAB; DAC; DAM MST,
NOV; DLB 1, 42, 79, 223, 239, 242;
DLBD 14; FL 1:2; FW; JRDA; LAIT 2;
MAICYA 1, 2; NFS 12; RGAL 4; SATA
100; TUS; WCH; WYA; YABC 1; YAW
Alcuin c. 730-804 .... **CMLC 69, 139**
See also DLB 148
Aldanov, M. A.
See Aldanov, Mark (Alexandrovich)
Aldanov, Mark (Alexandrovich)
1886-1957 .... **TCLC 23**
See also CA 118; 181; DLB 317
Aldhelm c. 639-709 .... **CMLC 90**
Aldington, Richard 1892-1962 .... **CLC 49**
See also CA 85-88; CANR 45; DLB 20, 36,
100, 149; LMFS 2; RGEL 2
Aldiss, Brian W. 1925- . **CLC 5, 14, 40, 290;**
SSC 36
See also AAYA 42; CA 5-8R, 190; CAAE
190; CAAS 2; CANR 5, 28, 64, 121, 168;
CN 1, 2, 3, 4, 5, 6, 7; DAM NOV; DLB
14, 261, 271; MTCW 1, 2; MTFW 2005;
SATA 34; SCFW 1, 2; SFW 4

Anouilh, Jean 1910-1987 .... **CLC 1, 3, 8, 13, 40, 50; DC 8, 21; TCLC 195**
See also AAYA 67; CA 17-20R; 123; CANR 32; DAM DRAM; DFS 9, 10, 19; DLB 321; EW 13; EWL 3; GFL 1789 to the Present; MTCW 1, 2; MTFW 2005; RGWL 2, 3; TWA

Anouilh, Jean Marie Lucien Pierre
See Anouilh, Jean

Ansa, Tina McElroy 1949- .... **BLC 2:1**
See also BW 2; CA 142; CANR 143; CSW

Anselm of Canterbury 1033(?)-1109 . **CMLC 67**
See also DLB 115

Anthony, Florence
See Ai

Anthony, John
See Ciardi, John (Anthony)

Anthony, Peter
See Shaffer, Anthony; Shaffer, Peter

Anthony, Piers 1934- .... **CLC 35**
See also AAYA 11, 48; BYA 7; CA 200; CAAE 200; CANR 28, 56, 73, 102, 133, 202; CLR 118; CPW; DAM POP; DLB 8; FANT; MAICYA 2; MAICYAS 1; MTCW 1, 2; MTFW 2005; SAAS 22; SATA 84, 129; SATA-Essay 129; SFW 4; SUFW 1, 2; YAW

Anthony, Susan B(rownell) 1820-1906 .... **TCLC 84**
See also CA 211; FW

Antin, David 1932- .... **PC 124**
See also CA 73-76; CP 1, 3, 4, 5, 6, 7; DLB 169

Antin, Mary 1881-1949 .... **TCLC 247**
See also AMWS 20; CA 118; 181; DLB 221; DLBY 1984

Antiphon c. 480B.C.-c. 411B.C. ... **CMLC 55**

Antoine, Marc
See Proust, Marcel

Antoninus, Brother
See Everson, William

Antonioni, Michelangelo 1912-2007 ..... **CLC 20, 144, 259**
See also CA 73-76; 262; CANR 45, 77

Antschel, Paul
See Celan, Paul

Anwar, Chairil 1922-1949 .... **TCLC 22**
See also CA 121; 219; EWL 3; RGWL 3

Anyidoho, Kofi 1947- .... **BLC 2:1**
See also BW 3; CA 178; CP 5, 6, 7; DLB 157; EWL 3

Anzaldua, Gloria (Evanjelina) 1942-2004 ... **CLC 200; HLCS 1**
See also CA 175; 227; CSW; CWP; DLB 122; FW; LLW; RGAL 4; SATA-Obit 154

Apess, William 1798-1839(?) .... **NCLC 73; NNAL**
See also DAM MULT; DLB 175, 243

Apollinaire, Guillaume 1880-1918 ...... **PC 7; TCLC 3, 8, 51**
See also CA 104; 152; DAM POET; DLB 258, 321; EW 9; EWL 3; GFL 1789 to the Present; MTCW 2; PFS 24; RGWL 2, 3; TWA; WP

Apollonius of Rhodes
See Apollonius Rhodius

Apollonius Rhodius c. 300B.C.-c. 220B.C. ... **CMLC 28**
See also AW 1; DLB 176; RGWL 2, 3

Appelfeld, Aharon 1932- .. **CLC 23, 47, 317; SSC 42**
See also CA 112; 133; CANR 86, 160, 207; CWW 2; DLB 299; EWL 3; RGHL; RGSF 2; WLIT 6

Appelfeld, Aron
See Appelfeld, Aharon

Apple, Max 1941- .... **CLC 9, 33; SSC 50**
See also AMWS 17; CA 81-84; CANR 19, 54, 214; DLB 130

Apple, Max Isaac
See Apple, Max

Appleman, Philip (Dean) 1926- .... **CLC 51**
See also CA 13-16R; CAAS 18; CANR 6, 29, 56

Appleton, Lawrence
See Lovecraft, H. P.

Apteryx
See Eliot, T. S.

Apuleius, (Lucius Madaurensis) c. 125-c. 164 .... **CMLC 1, 84**
See also AW 2; CDWLB 1; DLB 211; RGWL 2, 3; SUFW; WLIT 8

Aquin, Hubert 1929-1977 .... **CLC 15**
See also CA 105; DLB 53; EWL 3

Aquinas, Thomas 1224(?)-1274 .. **CMLC 33, 137**
See also DLB 115; EW 1; TWA

Aragon, Louis 1897-1982 . **CLC 3, 22; TCLC 123**
See also CA 69-72; 108; CANR 28, 71; DAM NOV, POET; DLB 72, 258; EW 11; EWL 3; GFL 1789 to the Present; GLL 2; LMFS 2; MTCW 1, 2; RGWL 2, 3

Arany, Janos 1817-1882 .... **NCLC 34**

Aranyos, Kakay 1847-1910 ....
See Mikszath, Kalman

Aratus of Soli c. 315B.C.-c. 240B.C. . **CMLC 64, 114**
See also DLB 176

Arbuthnot, John 1667-1735 .... **LC 1**
See also BRWS 16; DLB 101

Archer, Herbert Winslow
See Mencken, H. L.

Archer, Jeffrey 1940- .... **CLC 28**
See also AAYA 16; BEST 89:3; BPFB 1; CA 77-80; CANR 22, 52, 95, 136, 209; CPW; DA3; DAM POP; INT CANR-22; MTFW 2005

Archer, Jeffrey Howard
See Archer, Jeffrey

Archer, Jules 1915- .... **CLC 12**
See also CA 9-12R; CANR 6, 69; SAAS 5; SATA 4, 85

Archer, Lee
See Ellison, Harlan

Archilochus c. 7th cent. B.C.- ...... **CMLC 44**
See also DLB 176

Ard, William
See Jakes, John

Arden, John 1930- .... **CLC 6, 13, 15**
See also BRWS 2; CA 13-16R; CAAS 4; CANR 31, 65, 67, 124; CBD; CD 5, 6; DAM DRAM; DFS 9; DLB 13, 245; EWL 3; MTCW 1

Arenas, Reinaldo 1943-1990 . **CLC 41; HLC 1; TCLC 191**
See also CA 124; 128; 133; CANR 73, 106; DAM MULT; DLB 145; EWL 3; GLL 2; HW 1; LAW; LAWS 1; MTCW 2; MTFW 2005; RGSF 2; RGWL 3; WLIT 1

Arendt, Hannah 1906-1975 ...... **CLC 66, 98; TCLC 193**
See also CA 17-20R; 61-64; CANR 26, 60, 172; DLB 242; MTCW 1, 2

Aretino, Pietro 1492-1556 .... **LC 12, 165**
See also RGWL 2, 3

Arghezi, Tudor
See Theodorescu, Ion N.

Arguedas, Jose Maria 1911-1969 ... **CLC 10, 18; HLCS 1; TCLC 147**
See also CA 89-92; CANR 73; DLB 113; EWL 3; HW 1; LAW; RGWL 2, 3; WLIT 1

Argueta, Manlio 1936- .... **CLC 31**
See also CA 131; CANR 73; CWW 2; DLB 145; EWL 3; HW 1; RGWL 3

Arias, Ron 1941- .... **HLC 1**
See also CA 131; CANR 81, 136; DAM MULT; DLB 82; HW 1, 2; MTCW 2; MTFW 2005

Ariosto, Lodovico
See Ariosto, Ludovico

Ariosto, Ludovico 1474-1533 . **LC 6, 87; PC 42**
See also EW 2; RGWL 2, 3; WLIT 7

Aristides
See Epstein, Joseph

Aristides Quintilianus fl. c. 100-fl. c. 400 .... **CMLC 122**

Aristophanes 450B.C.-385B.C. ...... **CMLC 4, 51, 138; DC 2; WLCS**
See also AW 1; CDWLB 1; DA; DA3; DAB; DAC; DAM DRAM, MST; DFS 10; DLB 176; LMFS 1; RGWL 2, 3; TWA; WLIT 8

Aristotle 384B.C.-322B.C. ... **CMLC 31, 123; WLCS**
See also AW 1; CDWLB 1; DA; DA3; DAB; DAC; DAM MST; DLB 176; RGWL 2, 3; TWA; WLIT 8

Arlt, Roberto 1900-1942 . **HLC 1; TCLC 29, 255**
See also CA 123; 131; CANR 67; DAM MULT; DLB 305; EWL 3; HW 1, 2; IDTP; LAW

Arlt, Roberto Godofredo Christophersen
See Arlt, Roberto

Armah, Ayi Kwei 1939- . **BLC 1:1, 2:1; CLC 5, 33, 136**
See also AFW; BRWS 10; BW 1; CA 61-64; CANR 21, 64; CDWLB 3; CN 1, 2, 3, 4, 5, 6, 7; DAM MULT, POET; DLB 117; EWL 3; MTCW 1; WLIT 2

Armatrading, Joan 1950- .... **CLC 17**
See also CA 114; 186

Armin, Robert 1568(?)-1615(?) .... **LC 120**

Armitage, Frank
See Carpenter, John

Armstrong, Jeannette (C.) 1948- .... **NNAL**
See also CA 149; CCA 1; CN 6, 7; DAC; DLB 334; SATA 102

Armytage, R.
See Watson, Rosamund Marriott

Arnauld, Antoine 1612-1694 .... **LC 169**
See also DLB 268

Arnette, Robert
See Silverberg, Robert

Arnim, Achim von (Ludwig Joachim von Arnim) 1781-1831 . **NCLC 5, 159; SSC 29**
See also DLB 90

Arnim, Bettina von 1785-1859 .... **NCLC 38, 123**
See also DLB 90; RGWL 2, 3

Arnold, Matthew 1822-1888 .... **NCLC 6, 29, 89, 126, 218; PC 5, 94; WLC 1**
See also BRW 5; CDBLB 1832-1890; DA; DAC; DAM MST, POET; DLB 32, 57; EXPP; PAB; PFS 2; TEA; WP

Arnold, Thomas 1795-1842 .... **NCLC 18**
See also DLB 55

Arnow, Harriette (Louisa) Simpson 1908-1986 .... **CLC 2, 7, 18; TCLC 196**
See also BPFB 1; CA 9-12R; 118; CANR 14; CN 2, 3, 4; DLB 6; FW; MTCW 1, 2; RHW; SATA 42; SATA-Obit 47

Arouet, Francois-Marie
See Voltaire

Arp, Hans
See Arp, Jean

Arp, Jean 1887-1966 ...... **CLC 5; TCLC 115**
See also CA 81-84; 25-28R; CANR 42, 77; EW 10

Arrabal
See Arrabal, Fernando

1980, 1989; EWL 3; FANT; LMFS 2; MAL 5; MTCW 1, 2; MTFW 2005; RGAL 4; RGSF 2; SATA 7; SATA-Obit 62; SSFS 17

Barthelme, Frederick 1943- .... **CLC 36, 117**
See also AMWS 11; CA 114; 122; CANR 77, 209; CN 4, 5, 6, 7; CSW; DLB 244; DLBY 1985; EWL 3; INT CA-122

Barthes, Roland (Gerard) 1915-1980 .. **CLC 24, 83; TCLC 135**
See also CA 130; 97-100; CANR 66; DLB 296; EW 13; EWL 3; GFL 1789 to the Present; MTCW 1, 2; TWA

Bartram, William 1739-1823 ...... **NCLC 145**
See also ANW; DLB 37

Barzun, Jacques 1907- .... **CLC 51, 145**
See also CA 61-64; CANR 22, 95

Barzun, Jacques Martin
See Barzun, Jacques

Bashevis, Isaac
See Singer, Isaac Bashevis

Bashevis, Yitskhok
See Singer, Isaac Bashevis

Bashkirtseff, Marie 1859-1884 ..... **NCLC 27**

Basho, Matsuo
See Matsuo Basho

Basil of Caesaria c. 330-379 .... **CMLC 35**

Basket, Raney
See Edgerton, Clyde

Bass, Kingsley B., Jr.
See Bullins, Ed

Bass, Rick 1958- . **CLC 79, 143, 286; SSC 60**
See also AMWS 16; ANW; CA 126; CANR 53, 93, 145, 183; CSW; DLB 212, 275

Bassani, Giorgio 1916-2000 .... **CLC 9**
See also CA 65-68; 190; CANR 33; CWW 2; DLB 128, 177, 299; EWL 3; MTCW 1; RGHL; RGWL 2, 3

Bassine, Helen
See Yglesias, Helen

Bastian, Ann CLC 70

Bastos, Augusto Roa
See Roa Bastos, Augusto

Bataille, Georges 1897-1962 .... **CLC 29; TCLC 155**
See also CA 101; 89-92; EWL 3

Bates, H(erbert) E(rnest) 1905-1974 .... **CLC 46; SSC 10**
See also CA 93-96; 45-48; CANR 34; CN 1; DA3; DAB; DAM POP; DLB 162, 191; EWL 3; EXPS; MTCW 1, 2; RGSF 2; SSFS 7

Batiushkov, Konstantin Nikolaevich 1787-1855 .... **NCLC 254**
See also DLB 205

Bauchart
See Camus, Albert

Baudelaire, Charles 1821-1867 ...... **NCLC 6, 29, 55, 155; PC 1, 106; SSC 18; WLC 1**
See also DA; DA3; DAB; DAC; DAM MST, POET; DLB 217; EW 7; GFL 1789 to the Present; LMFS 2; PFS 21, 38; RGWL 2, 3; TWA

Baudouin, Marcel
See Peguy, Charles (Pierre)

Baudouin, Pierre
See Peguy, Charles (Pierre)

Baudrillard, Jean 1929-2007 .... **CLC 60**
See also CA 252; 258; DLB 296

Baum, L. Frank 1856-1919 ..... **TCLC 7, 132**
See also AAYA 46; BYA 16; CA 108; 133; CLR 15, 107; CWRI 5; DLB 22; FANT; JRDA; MAICYA 1, 2; MTCW 1, 2; NFS 13; RGAL 4; SATA 18, 100; WCH

Baum, Louis F.
See Baum, L. Frank

Baum, Lyman Frank
See Baum, L. Frank

Bauman, Zygmunt 1925- .... **CLC 314**
See also CA 127; CANR 205

Baumbach, Jonathan 1933- .... **CLC 6, 23**
See also CA 13-16R, 284; CAAE 284; CAAS 5; CANR 12, 66, 140; CN 3, 4, 5, 6, 7; DLBY 1980; INT CANR-12; MTCW 1

Baumgarten, Alexander Gottlieb 1714-1762 .... **LC 199**

Bausch, Richard 1945- .... **CLC 51**
See also AMWS 7; CA 101; CAAS 14; CANR 43, 61, 87, 164, 200; CN 7; CSW; DLB 130; MAL 5

Bausch, Richard Carl
See Bausch, Richard

Baxter, Charles 1947- .... **CLC 45, 78**
See also AMWS 17; CA 57-60; CANR 40, 64, 104, 133, 188; CPW; DAM POP; DLB 130; MAL 5; MTCW 2; MTFW 2005; TCLE 1:1

Baxter, Charles Morley
See Baxter, Charles

Baxter, George Owen
See Faust, Frederick

Baxter, James K(eir) 1926-1972 .... **CLC 14; TCLC 249**
See also CA 77-80; CP 1; EWL 3

Baxter, John
See Hunt, E. Howard

Bayer, Sylvia
See Glassco, John

Bayle, Pierre 1647-1706 .... **LC 126**
See also DLB 268, 313; GFL Beginnings to 1789

Baynton, Barbara 1857-1929 . **TCLC 57, 211**
See also DLB 230; RGSF 2

Beagle, Peter S. 1939- .... **CLC 7, 104**
See also AAYA 47; BPFB 1; BYA 9, 10, 16; CA 9-12R; CANR 4, 51, 73, 110, 213; DA3; DLBY 1980; FANT; INT CANR-4; MTCW 2; MTFW 2005; SATA 60, 130; SUFW 1, 2; YAW

Beagle, Peter Soyer
See Beagle, Peter S.

Bean, Normal
See Burroughs, Edgar Rice

Beard, Charles A(ustin) 1874-1948 ... **TCLC 15**
See also CA 115; 189; DLB 17; SATA 18

Beardsley, Aubrey 1872-1898 .... **NCLC 6**

Beatrice of Nazareth 1200-1268 . **CMLC 124**

Beattie, Ann 1947- .... **CLC 8, 13, 18, 40, 63, 146, 293; SSC 11, 130**
See also AMWS 5; BEST 90:2; BPFB 1; CA 81-84; CANR 53, 73, 128, 225; CN 4, 5, 6, 7; CPW; DA3; DAM NOV, POP; DLB 218, 278; DLBY 1982; EWL 3; MAL 5; MTCW 1, 2; MTFW 2005; RGAL 4; RGSF 2; SSFS 9; TUS

Beattie, James 1735-1803 .... **NCLC 25**
See also DLB 109

Beauchamp, Katherine Mansfield
See Mansfield, Katherine

Beaumarchais, Pierre-Augustin Caron de 1732-1799 .... **DC 4; LC 61, 192**
See also DAM DRAM; DFS 14, 16; DLB 313; EW 4; GFL Beginnings to 1789; RGWL 2, 3

Beaumont, Francis 1584(?)-1616 . **DC 6; LC 33**
See also BRW 2; CDBLB Before 1660; DLB 58; TEA

Beauvoir, Simone de 1908-1986 ... **CLC 1, 2, 4, 8, 14, 31, 44, 50, 71, 124; SSC 35; TCLC 221; WLC 1**
See also BPFB 1; CA 9-12R; 118; CANR 28, 61; DA; DA3; DAB; DAC; DAM MST, NOV; DLB 72; DLBY 1986; EW 12; EWL 3; FL 1:5; FW; GFL 1789 to the Present; LMFS 2; MTCW 1, 2; MTFW 2005; RGSF 2; RGWL 2, 3; TWA

Beauvoir, Simone Lucie Ernestine Marie Bertrand de
See Beauvoir, Simone de

Becker, Carl (Lotus) 1873-1945 .... **TCLC 63**
See also CA 157; DLB 17

Becker, Jurek 1937-1997 .... **CLC 7, 19**
See also CA 85-88; 157; CANR 60, 117; CWW 2; DLB 75, 299; EWL 3; RGHL

Becker, Walter 1950- .... **CLC 26**

Becket, Thomas a 1118(?)-1170 ... **CMLC 83**

Beckett, Samuel 1906-1989 .. **CLC 1, 2, 3, 4, 6, 9, 10, 11, 14, 18, 29, 57, 59, 83; DC 22; SSC 16, 74, 161; TCLC 145; WLC 1**
See also BRWC 2; BRWR 1; BRWS 1; CA 5-8R; 130; CANR 33, 61; CBD; CDBLB 1945-1960; CN 1, 2, 3, 4; CP 1, 2, 3, 4; DA; DA3; DAB; DAC; DAM DRAM, MST, NOV; DFS 2, 7, 18; DLB 13, 15, 233, 319, 321, 329; DLBY 1990; EWL 3; GFL 1789 to the Present; LATS 1:2; LMFS 2; MTCW 1, 2; MTFW 2005; RGSF 2; RGWL 2, 3; SSFS 15; TEA; WLIT 4

Beckett, Samuel Barclay
See Beckett, Samuel

Beckford, William 1760-1844 ...... **NCLC 16, 214**
See also BRW 3; DLB 39, 213; GL 2; HGG; LMFS 1; SUFW

Beckham, Barry 1944- .... **BLC 1:1**
See also BW 1; CA 29-32R; CANR 26, 62; CN 1, 2, 3, 4, 5, 6; DAM MULT; DLB 33

Beckman, Gunnel 1910- .... **CLC 26**
See also CA 33-36R; CANR 15, 114; CLR 25; MAICYA 1, 2; SAAS 9; SATA 6

Becque, Henri 1837-1899 .. **DC 21; NCLC 3**
See also DLB 192; GFL 1789 to the Present

Becquer, Gustavo Adolfo 1836-1870 .. **HLCS 1; NCLC 106; PC 113**
See also DAM MULT

Beddoes, Thomas Lovell 1803-1849 . **DC 15; NCLC 3, 154**
See also BRWS 11; DLB 96

Bede c. 673-735 .... **CMLC 20, 130**
See also DLB 146; TEA

Bedford, Denton R. 1907-(?) .... **NNAL**

Bedford, Donald F.
See Fearing, Kenneth

Beecher, Catharine Esther 1800-1878 .... **NCLC 30**
See also DLB 1, 243

Beecher, John 1904-1980 .... **CLC 6**
See also AITN 1; CA 5-8R; 105; CANR 8; CP 1, 2, 3

Beer, Johann 1655-1700 .... **LC 5**
See also DLB 168

Beer, Patricia 1924- .... **CLC 58**
See also BRWS 14; CA 61-64; 183; CANR 13, 46; CP 1, 2, 3, 4, 5, 6; CWP; DLB 40; FW

Beerbohm, Max
See Beerbohm, (Henry) Max(imilian)

Beerbohm, (Henry) Max(imilian) 1872-1956 .... **TCLC 1, 24**
See also BRWS 2; CA 104; 154; CANR 79; DLB 34, 100; FANT; MTCW 2

Beer-Hofmann, Richard 1866-1945 ... **TCLC 60**
See also CA 160; DLB 81

Beethoven, Ludwig van 1770(?)-1827 .... **NCLC 227**

Beg, Shemus
See Stephens, James

Begiebing, Robert J(ohn) 1946- ...... **CLC 70**
See also CA 122; CANR 40, 88

Benoit de Sainte-Maure fl. 12th cent. - ....
CMLC 90
Benson, A. C. 1862-1925 .... **TCLC 123**
See also DLB 98
Benson, E(dward) F(rederic) 1867-1940 ......
TCLC 27
See also CA 114; 157; DLB 135, 153;
HGG; SUFW 1
Benson, Jackson J. 1930- .... **CLC 34**
See also CA 25-28R; CANR 214; DLB 111
Benson, Sally 1900-1972 .... **CLC 17**
See also CA 19-20; 37-40R; CAP 1; SATA
1, 35; SATA-Obit 27
Benson, Stella 1892-1933 .... **TCLC 17**
See also CA 117; 154, 155; DLB 36, 162;
FANT; TEA
Bentham, Jeremy 1748-1832 . **NCLC 38, 237**
See also DLB 107, 158, 252
Bentley, E(dmund) C(lerihew) 1875-1956 ...
TCLC 12
See also CA 108; 232; DLB 70; MSW
Bentley, Eric 1916- .... **CLC 24**
See also CA 5-8R; CAD; CANR 6, 67;
CBD; CD 5, 6; INT CANR-6
Bentley, Eric Russell
See Bentley, Eric
ben Uzair, Salem
See Horne, Richard Henry Hengist
Beolco, Angelo 1496-1542 .... **LC 139**
Beranger, Pierre Jean de 1780-1857 . **NCLC
34; PC 112**
Berdyaev, Nicolas
See Berdyaev, Nikolai (Aleksandrovich)
Berdyaev, Nikolai (Aleksandrovich)
1874-1948 .... **TCLC 67**
See also CA 120; 157
Berdyayev, Nikolai (Aleksandrovich)
See Berdyaev, Nikolai (Aleksandrovich)
Berendt, John 1939- .... **CLC 86**
See also CA 146; CANR 75, 83, 151
Berendt, John Lawrence
See Berendt, John
Berengar of Tours c. 1000-1088 . **CMLC 124**
Beresford, J(ohn) D(avys) 1873-1947 . **TCLC
81**
See also CA 112; 155; DLB 162, 178, 197;
SFW 4; SUFW 1
Bergelson, David (Rafailovich) 1884-1952 ...
TCLC 81
See also CA 220; DLB 333; EWL 3
Bergelson, Dovid
See Bergelson, David (Rafailovich)
Berger, Colonel
See Malraux, Andre
Berger, John 1926- .... **CLC 2, 19**
See also BRWS 4; CA 81-84; CANR 51,
78, 117, 163, 200; CN 1, 2, 3, 4, 5, 6, 7;
DLB 14, 207, 319, 326
Berger, John Peter
See Berger, John
Berger, Melvin H. 1927- .... **CLC 12**
See also CA 5-8R; CANR 4, 142; CLR 32;
SAAS 2; SATA 5, 88, 158; SATA-Essay
124
Berger, Thomas 1924- .. **CLC 3, 5, 8, 11, 18,
38, 259**
See also BPFB 1; CA 1-4R; CANR 5, 28,
51, 128; CN 1, 2, 3, 4, 5, 6, 7; DAM
NOV; DLB 2; DLBY 1980; EWL 3;
FANT; INT CANR-28; MAL 5; MTCW
1, 2; MTFW 2005; RHW; TCLE 1:1;
TCWW 1, 2
Bergman, Ernst Ingmar
See Bergman, Ingmar
Bergman, Ingmar 1918-2007 ... **CLC 16, 72,
210**
See also AAYA 61; CA 81-84; 262; CANR
33, 70; CWW 2; DLB 257; MTCW 2;
MTFW 2005

Bergson, Henri(-Louis) 1859-1941 ..... **TCLC
32**
See also CA 164; DLB 329; EW 8; EWL 3;
GFL 1789 to the Present
Bergstein, Eleanor 1938- .... **CLC 4**
See also CA 53-56; CANR 5
Berkeley, George 1685-1753 .... **LC 65**
See also DLB 31, 101, 252
Berkoff, Steven 1937- .... **CLC 56**
See also CA 104; CANR 72; CBD; CD 5, 6
Berlin, Isaiah 1909-1997 .... **TCLC 105**
See also CA 85-88; 162
Bermant, Chaim (Icyk) 1929-1998 . **CLC 40**
See also CA 57-60; CANR 6, 31, 57, 105;
CN 2, 3, 4, 5, 6
Bern, Victoria
See Fisher, M(ary) F(rances) K(ennedy)
Bernanos, (Paul Louis) Georges
1888-1948 .... **TCLC 3**
See also CA 104; 130; CANR 94; DLB 72;
EWL 3; GFL 1789 to the Present; RGWL
2, 3
Bernard, April 1956- .... **CLC 59**
See also CA 131; CANR 144, 230
Bernard, Mary Ann
See Soderbergh, Steven
Bernard of Clairvaux 1090-1153 . **CMLC 71**
See also DLB 208
Bernard Silvestris fl. c. 1130-fl. c. 1160 ....
CMLC 87
See also DLB 208
Bernart de Ventadorn c. 1130-c. 1190 ....
CMLC 98
Berne, Victoria
See Fisher, M(ary) F(rances) K(ennedy)
Bernhard, Thomas 1931-1989 .... **CLC 3, 32,
61; DC 14; TCLC 165**
See also CA 85-88; 127; CANR 32, 57; CD-
WLB 2; DLB 85, 124; EWL 3; MTCW 1;
RGHL; RGWL 2, 3
Bernhardt, Sarah (Henriette Rosine)
1844-1923 .... **TCLC 75**
See also CA 157
Bernstein, Charles 1950- .... **CLC 142**
See also CA 129; CAAS 24; CANR 90; CP
4, 5, 6, 7; DLB 169
Bernstein, Ingrid
See Kirsch, Sarah
Beroul fl. c. 12th cent. - .... **CMLC 75**
Berriault, Gina 1926-1999 ...... **CLC 54, 109;
SSC 30**
See also CA 116; 129; 185; CANR 66; DLB
130; SSFS 7,11
Berrigan, Daniel 1921- .... **CLC 4**
See also CA 33-36R, 187; CAAE 187;
CAAS 1; CANR 11, 43, 78, 219; CP 1, 2,
3, 4, 5, 6, 7; DLB 5
Berrigan, Edmund Joseph Michael, Jr.
1934-1983 .... **CLC 37; PC 103**
See also CA 61-64; 110; CANR 14, 102;
CP 1, 2, 3; DLB 5, 169; WP
Berrigan, Ted
See Berrigan, Edmund Joseph Michael, Jr.
Berry, Charles Edward Anderson 1931- .....
CLC 17
See also CA 115
Berry, Chuck
See Berry, Charles Edward Anderson
Berry, Jonas
See Ashbery, John
Berry, Wendell 1934- ... **CLC 4, 6, 8, 27, 46,
279; PC 28**
See also AITN 1; AMWS 10; ANW; CA
73-76; CANR 50, 73, 101, 132, 174, 228;
CP 1, 2, 3, 4, 5, 6, 7; CSW; DAM POET;
DLB 5, 6, 234, 275, 342; MTCW 2;
MTFW 2005; PFS 30; TCLE 1:1
Berry, Wendell Erdman
See Berry, Wendell

Berryman, John 1914-1972 . **CLC 1, 2, 3, 4,
6, 8, 10, 13, 25, 62; PC 64**
See also AMW; CA 13-16; 33-36R; CABS
2; CANR 35; CAP 1; CDALB 1941-1968;
CP 1; DAM POET; DLB 48; EWL 3;
MAL 5; MTCW 1, 2; MTFW 2005; PAB;
PFS 27; RGAL 4; WP
Berssenbrugge, Mei-mei 1947- .... **PC 115**
See also CA 104; DLB 312
Bertolucci, Bernardo 1940- ..... **CLC 16, 157**
See also CA 106; CANR 125
Berton, Pierre (Francis de Marigny)
1920-2004 .... **CLC 104**
See also CA 1-4R; 233; CANR 2, 56, 144;
CPW; DLB 68; SATA 99; SATA-Obit 158
Bertrand, Aloysius 1807-1841 .... **NCLC 31**
See also DLB 217
Bertrand, Louis oAloysiusc
See Bertrand, Aloysius
Bertran de Born c. 1140-1215 .... **CMLC 5**
Besant, Annie (Wood) 1847-1933 ... **TCLC 9**
See also CA 105; 185
Bessie, Alvah 1904-1985 .... **CLC 23**
See also CA 5-8R; 116; CANR 2, 80; DLB
26
Bestuzhev, Aleksandr Aleksandrovich
1797-1837 .... **NCLC 131**
See also DLB 198
Bethlen, T.D.
See Silverberg, Robert
Beti, Mongo 1932-2001 ... **BLC 1:1; CLC 27**
See also AFW; BW 1, 3; CA 114; 124;
CANR 81; DA3; DAM MULT; DLB 360;
EWL 3; MTCW 1, 2
Betjeman, John 1906-1984 ..... **CLC 2, 6, 10,
34, 43; PC 75**
See also BRW 7; CA 9-12R; 112; CANR
33, 56; CDBLB 1945-1960; CP 1, 2, 3;
DA3; DAB; DAM MST, POET; DLB 20;
DLBY 1984; EWL 3; MTCW 1, 2
Bettelheim, Bruno 1903-1990 .... **CLC 79;
TCLC 143**
See also CA 81-84; 131; CANR 23, 61;
DA3; MTCW 1, 2; RGHL
Betti, Ugo 1892-1953 .... **TCLC 5**
See also CA 104; 155; EWL 3; RGWL 2, 3
Betts, Doris (Waugh) 1932- .... **CLC 3, 6, 28,
275; SSC 45**
See also CA 13-16R; CANR 9, 66, 77; CN
6, 7; CSW; DLB 218; DLBY 1982; INT
CANR-9; RGAL 4
Bevan, Alistair
See Roberts, Keith (John Kingston)
Bey, Pilaff
See Douglas, (George) Norman
Beyala, Calixthe 1961- .... **BLC 2:1**
See also EWL 3
Beynon, John
See Harris, John (Wyndham Parkes Lucas)
Beynon
Bhabha, Homi K. 1949- .... **CLC 285**
Bialik, Chaim Nachman 1873-1934 ... **TCLC
25, 201**
See also CA 170; EWL 3; WLIT 6
Bialik, Hayyim Nahman
See Bialik, Chaim Nachman
Bickerstaff, Isaac
See Swift, Jonathan
Bidart, Frank 1939- .... **CLC 33**
See also AMWS 15; CA 140; CANR 106,
215; CP 5, 6, 7; PFS 26
Bienek, Horst 1930- .... **CLC 7, 11**
See also CA 73-76; DLB 75
Bierce, Ambrose 1842-1914(?) ..... **SSC 9, 72,
124; TCLC 1, 7, 44; WLC 1**
See also AAYA 55; AMW; BYA 11; CA
104; 139; CANR 78; CDALB 1865-1917;
DA; DA3; DAC; DAM MST; DLB 11,

Blue Cloud, Peter (Aroniawenrate) 1933- ... NNAL
See also CA 117; CANR 40; DAM MULT; DLB 342

Bluggage, Oranthy
See Alcott, Louisa May

Blume, Judy 1938- .... **CLC 12, 30**
See also AAYA 3, 26; BYA 1, 8, 12; CA 29-32R; CANR 13, 37, 66, 124, 186; CLR 2, 15, 69; CPW; DA3; DAM NOV, POP; DLB 52; JRDA; MAICYA 1, 2; MAICYAS 1; MTCW 1, 2; MTFW 2005; NFS 24; SATA 2, 31, 79, 142, 195; WYA; YAW

Blume, Judy Sussman
See Blume, Judy

Blunden, Edmund (Charles) 1896-1974 ....
CLC 2, 56; PC 66
See also BRW 6; BRWS 11; CA 17-18; 45-48; CANR 54; CAP 2; CP 1, 2; DLB 20, 100, 155; MTCW 1; PAB

Bly, Robert 1926- ... **CLC 1, 2, 5, 10, 15, 38, 128; PC 39**
See also AMWS 4; CA 5-8R; CANR 41, 73, 125; CP 1, 2, 3, 4, 5, 6, 7; DA3; DAM POET; DLB 5, 342; EWL 3; MAL 5; MTCW 1, 2; MTFW 2005; PFS 6, 17; RGAL 4

Bly, Robert Elwood
See Bly, Robert

Boas, Franz 1858-1942 .... **TCLC 56**
See also CA 115; 181

Bobette
See Simenon, Georges

Boccaccio, Giovanni 1313-1375 .. **CMLC 13, 57; SSC 10, 87**
See also EW 2; RGSF 2; RGWL 2, 3; SSFS 28; TWA; WLIT 7

Bochco, Steven 1943- .... **CLC 35**
See also AAYA 11, 71; CA 124; 138

Bock, Charles 1970- .... **CLC 299**
See also CA 274

Bode, Sigmund
See O'Doherty, Brian

Bodel, Jean 1167(?)-1210 .... **CMLC 28**

Bodenheim, Maxwell 1892-1954 ... **TCLC 44**
See also CA 110; 187; DLB 9, 45; MAL 5; RGAL 4

Bodenheimer, Maxwell
See Bodenheim, Maxwell

Bodker, Cecil
See Bodker, Cecil

Bodker, Cecil 1927- .... **CLC 21**
See also CA 73-76; CANR 13, 44, 111; CLR 23; MAICYA 1, 2; SATA 14, 133

Boell, Heinrich 1917-1985 .... **CLC 2, 3, 6, 9, 11, 15, 27, 32, 72; SSC 23; TCLC 185; WLC 1**
See also BPFB 1; CA 21-24R; 116; CANR 24; CDWLB 2; DA; DA3; DAB; DAC; DAM MST, NOV; DLB 69, 329; DLBY 1985; EW 13; EWL 3; MTCW 1, 2; MTFW 2005; RGHL; RGSF 2; RGWL 2, 3; SSFS 20; TWA

Boell, Heinrich Theodor
See Boell, Heinrich

Boerne, Alfred
See Doeblin, Alfred

Boethius c. 480-c. 524 .... **CMLC 15, 136**
See also DLB 115; RGWL 2, 3; WLIT 8

Boff, Leonardo (Genezio Darci) 1938- . **CLC 70; HLC 1**
See also CA 150; DAM MULT; HW 2

Bogan, Louise 1897-1970 ...... **CLC 4, 39, 46, 93; PC 12**
See also AMWS 3; CA 73-76; 25-28R; CANR 33, 82; CP 1; DAM POET; DLB 45, 169; EWL 3; MAL 5; MBL; MTCW 1, 2; PFS 21, 39; RGAL 4

Bogarde, Dirk
See Van Den Bogarde, Derek Jules Gaspard Ulric Niven

Bogat, Shatan
See Kacew, Romain

Bogomolny, Robert L. 1938- .... **SSC 41; TCLC 11**
See also CA 121, 164; DLB 182; EWL 3; MJW; RGSF 2; RGWL 2, 3; TWA

Bogomolny, Robert Lee
See Bogomolny, Robert L.

Bogosian, Eric 1953- .... **CLC 45, 141**
See also CA 138; CAD; CANR 102, 148, 217; CD 5, 6; DLB 341

Bograd, Larry 1953- .... **CLC 35**
See also CA 93-96; CANR 57; SAAS 21; SATA 33, 89; WYA

Bohme, Jakob 1575-1624 .... **LC 178**
See also DLB 164

Boiardo, Matteo Maria 1441-1494 ..... **LC 6, 168**

Boileau-Despreaux, Nicolas 1636-1711 ... **LC 3, 164**
See also DLB 268; EW 3; GFL Beginnings to 1789; RGWL 2, 3

Boissard, Maurice
See Leautaud, Paul

Bojer, Johan 1872-1959 .... **TCLC 64**
See also CA 189; EWL 3

Bok, Edward W(illiam) 1863-1930 .... **TCLC 101**
See also CA 217; DLB 91; DLBD 16

Boker, George Henry 1823-1890 . **NCLC 125**
See also RGAL 4

Boland, Eavan 1944- .. **CLC 40, 67, 113; PC 58**
See also BRWS 5; CA 143, 207; CAAE 207; CANR 61, 180; CP 1, 6, 7; CWP; DAM POET; DLB 40; FW; MTCW 2; MTFW 2005; PFS 12, 22, 31, 39

Boland, Eavan Aisling
See Boland, Eavan

Bolano, Roberto 1953-2003 .... **CLC 294**
See also CA 229; CANR 175

Bolingbroke, Viscount
See St. John, Henry

Boll, Heinrich
See Boell, Heinrich

Bolt, Lee
See Faust, Frederick

Bolt, Robert (Oxton) 1924-1995 .... **CLC 14; TCLC 175**
See also CA 17-20R; 147; CANR 35, 67; CBD; DAM DRAM; DFS 2; DLB 13, 233; EWL 3; LAIT 1; MTCW 1

Bombal, Maria Luisa 1910-1980 ... **HLCS 1; SSC 37**
See also CA 127; CANR 72; EWL 3; HW 1; LAW; RGSF 2

Bombet, Louis-Alexandre-Cesar
See Stendhal

Bomkauf
See Kaufman, Bob (Garnell)

Bonaventura **NCLC 35, 252**
See also DLB 90

Bonaventure 1217(?)-1274 .... **CMLC 79**
See also DLB 115; LMFS 1

Bond, Edward 1934- . **CLC 4, 6, 13, 23; DC 45**
See also AAYA 50; BRWS 1; CA 25-28R; CANR 38, 67, 106; CBD; CD 5, 6; DAM DRAM; DFS 3, 8; DLB 13, 310; EWL 3; MTCW 1

Bonham, Frank 1914-1989 .... **CLC 12**
See also AAYA 1, 70; BYA 1, 3; CA 9-12R; CANR 4, 36; JRDA; MAICYA 1, 2; SAAS 3; SATA 1, 49; SATA-Obit 62; TCWW 1, 2; YAW

Bonnefoy, Yves 1923- . **CLC 9, 15, 58; PC 58**
See also CA 85-88; CANR 33, 75, 97, 136; CWW 2; DAM MST, POET; DLB 258; EWL 3; GFL 1789 to the Present; MTCW 1, 2; MTFW 2005

Bonner, Marita
See Occomy, Marita (Odette) Bonner

Bonnin, Gertrude 1876-1938 .... **NNAL**
See also CA 150; DAM MULT; DLB 175

Bontemps, Arna 1902-1973 . **BLC 1:1; CLC 1, 18; HR 1:2**
See also BW 1; CA 1-4R; 41-44R; CANR 4, 35; CLR 6; CP 1; CWRI 5; DA3; DAM MULT, NOV, POET; DLB 48, 51; JRDA; MAICYA 1, 2; MAL 5; MTCW 1, 2; PFS 32; SATA 2, 44; SATA-Obit 24; WCH; WP

Bontemps, Arnaud Wendell
See Bontemps, Arna

Boot, William
See Stoppard, Tom

Booth, Irwin
See Hoch, Edward D.

Booth, Martin 1944-2004 .... **CLC 13**
See also CA 93-96; 188; 223; CAAE 188; CAAS 2; CANR 92; CP 1, 2, 3, 4

Booth, Philip 1925-2007 .... **CLC 23**
See also CA 5-8R; 262; CANR 5, 88; CP 1, 2, 3, 4, 5, 6, 7; DLBY 1982

Booth, Philip Edmund
See Booth, Philip

Booth, Wayne C. 1921-2005 .... **CLC 24**
See also CA 1-4R; 244; CAAS 5; CANR 3, 43, 117; DLB 67

Booth, Wayne Clayson
See Booth, Wayne C.

Borchert, Wolfgang 1921-1947 .... **DC 42; TCLC 5**
See also CA 104; 188; DLB 69, 124; EWL 3

Borel, Petrus 1809-1859 .... **NCLC 41**
See also DLB 119; GFL 1789 to the Present

Borges, Jorge Luis 1899-1986 .. **CLC 1, 2, 3, 4, 6, 8, 9, 10, 13, 19, 44, 48, 83; HLC 1; PC 22, 32; SSC 4, 41, 100, 159; TCLC 109; WLC 1**
See also AAYA 26; BPFB 1; CA 21-24R; CANR 19, 33, 75, 105, 133; CDWLB 3; DA; DA3; DAB; DAC; DAM MST, MULT; DLB 113, 283; DLBY 1986; DNFS 1, 2; EWL 3; HW 1, 2; LAW; LMFS 2; MSW; MTCW 1, 2; MTFW 2005; PFS 27; RGHL; RGSF 2; RGWL 2, 3; SFW 4; SSFS 17; TWA; WLIT 1

Borne, Ludwig 1786-1837 .... **NCLC 193**
See also DLB 90

Borowski, Tadeusz 1922-1951 .... **SSC 48; TCLC 9**
See also CA 106; 154; CDWLB 4; DLB 215; EWL 3; RGHL; RGSF 2; RGWL 3; SSFS 13

Borrow, George (Henry) 1803-1881 .. **NCLC 9**
See also BRWS 12; DLB 21, 55, 166

Bosch (Gavino), Juan 1909-2001 .... **HLCS 1**
See also CA 151; 204; DAM MST, MULT; DLB 145; HW 1, 2

Bosman, Herman Charles 1905-1951 . **TCLC 49**
See also CA 160; DLB 225; RGSF 2

Bosschere, Jean de 1878(?)-1953 .. **TCLC 19**
See also CA 115; 186

Boswell, James 1740-1795 ..... **LC 4, 50, 182; WLC 1**
See also BRW 3; CDBLB 1660-1789; DA; DAB; DAC; DAM MST; DLB 104, 142; TEA; WLIT 3

Brandys, Kazimierz 1916-2000 .... **CLC 62**
See also CA 239; EWL 3

Branley, Franklyn M(ansfield) 1915-2002 ...
CLC 21
See also CA 33-36R; 207; CANR 14, 39;
CLR 13; MAICYA 1, 2; SAAS 16; SATA
4, 68, 136

Brant, Beth (E.) 1941- .... **NNAL**
See also CA 144; FW

Brant, Sebastian 1457-1521 .... **LC 112**
See also DLB 179; RGWL 2, 3

Brathwaite, Edward Kamau 1930- ...... **BLC
2:1; BLCS; CLC 11, 305; PC 56**
See also BRWS 12; BW 2, 3; CA 25-28R;
CANR 11, 26, 47, 107; CDWLB 3; CP 1,
2, 3, 4, 5, 6, 7; DAM POET; DLB 125;
EWL 3

Brathwaite, Kamau
See Brathwaite, Edward Kamau

Brautigan, Richard 1935-1984 . **CLC 1, 3, 5,
9, 12, 34, 42; PC 94; TCLC 133**
See also BPFB 1; CA 53-56; 113; CANR
34; CN 1, 2, 3; CP 1, 2, 3, 4; DA3; DAM
NOV; DLB 2, 5, 206; DLBY 1980, 1984;
FANT; MAL 5; MTCW 1; RGAL 4;
SATA 56

Brautigan, Richard Gary
See Brautigan, Richard

Brave Bird, Mary
See Crow Dog, Mary

Braverman, Kate 1950- .... **CLC 67**
See also CA 89-92; CANR 141; DLB 335

Brecht, Bertolt 1898-1956 ... **DC 3; TCLC 1,
6, 13, 35, 169; WLC 1**
See also CA 104; 133; CANR 62; CDWLB
2; DA; DA3; DAB; DAC; DAM DRAM,
MST; DFS 4, 5, 9; DLB 56, 124; EW 11;
EWL 3; IDTP; MTCW 1, 2; MTFW 2005;
RGHL; RGWL 2, 3; TWA

Brecht, Eugen Berthold Friedrich
See Brecht, Bertolt

Brecht, Eugen Bertolt Friedrich
See Brecht, Bertolt

Bremer, Fredrika 1801-1865 .... **NCLC 11**
See also DLB 254

Brennan, Christopher John 1870-1932 ....
TCLC 17
See also CA 117; 188; DLB 230; EWL 3

Brennan, Maeve 1917-1993 .. **CLC 5; TCLC
124**
See also CA 81-84; CANR 72, 100

Brenner, Jozef 1887-1919 .... **TCLC 13**
See also CA 111; 240

Brent, Linda
See Jacobs, Harriet A.

Brentano, Clemens (Maria) 1778-1842 ....
NCLC 1, 191; SSC 115
See also DLB 90; RGWL 2, 3

Brent of Bin Bin
See Franklin, (Stella Maria Sarah) Miles
(Lampe)

Brenton, Howard 1942- .... **CLC 31**
See also CA 69-72; CANR 33, 67; CBD;
CD 5, 6; DLB 13; MTCW 1

Breslin, James
See Breslin, Jimmy

Breslin, Jimmy 1930- .... **CLC 4, 43**
See also CA 73-76; CANR 31, 75, 139, 187;
DAM NOV; DLB 185; MTCW 2; MTFW
2005

Bresson, Robert 1901(?)-1999 .... **CLC 16**
See also CA 110; 187; CANR 49

Breton, Andre 1896-1966 . **CLC 2, 9, 15, 54;
PC 15; TCLC 247**
See also CA 19-20; 25-28R; CANR 40, 60;
CAP 2; DLB 65, 258; EW 11; EWL 3;
GFL 1789 to the Present; LMFS 2;
MTCW 1, 2; MTFW 2005; RGWL 2, 3;
TWA; WP

Breton, Nicholas c. 1554-c. 1626 ...... **LC 133**
See also DLB 136

Breytenbach, Breyten 1939(?)- . **CLC 23, 37,
126**
See also CA 113; 129; CANR 61, 122, 202;
CWW 2; DAM POET; DLB 225; EWL 3

Bridgers, Sue Ellen 1942- .... **CLC 26**
See also AAYA 8, 49; BYA 7, 8; CA 65-68;
CANR 11, 36; CLR 18; DLB 52; JRDA;
MAICYA 1, 2; SAAS 1; SATA 22, 90;
SATA-Essay 109; WYA; YAW

Bridges, Robert (Seymour) 1844-1930 ... **PC
28; TCLC 1**
See also BRW 6; CA 104; 152; CDBLB
1890-1914; DAM POET; DLB 19, 98

Bridie, James
See Mavor, Osborne Henry

Brin, David 1950- .... **CLC 34**
See also AAYA 21; CA 102; CANR 24, 70,
125, 127; INT CANR-24; SATA 65;
SCFW 2; SFW 4

Brink, Andre 1935- .... **CLC 18, 36, 106**
See also AFW; BRWS 6; CA 104; CANR
39, 62, 109, 133, 182; CN 4, 5, 6, 7; DLB
225; EWL 3; INT CA-103; LATS 1:2;
MTCW 1, 2; MTFW 2005; WLIT 2

Brink, Andre Philippus
See Brink, Andre

Brinsmead, H. F(ay)
See Brinsmead, H(esba) F(ay)

Brinsmead, H. F.
See Brinsmead, H(esba) F(ay)

Brinsmead, H(esba) F(ay) 1922- ..... **CLC 21**
See also CA 21-24R; CANR 10; CLR 47;
CWRI 5; MAICYA 1, 2; SAAS 5; SATA
18, 78

Brittain, Vera (Mary) 1893(?)-1970 ..... **CLC
23; TCLC 228**
See also BRWS 10; CA 13-16; 25-28R;
CANR 58; CAP 1; DLB 191; FW; MTCW
1, 2

Broch, Hermann 1886-1951 .. **TCLC 20, 204**
See also CA 117; 211; CDWLB 2; DLB 85,
124; EW 10; EWL 3; RGWL 2, 3

Brock, Rose
See Hansen, Joseph

Brod, Max 1884-1968 .... **TCLC 115**
See also CA 5-8R; 25-28R; CANR 7; DLB
81; EWL 3

Brodkey, Harold (Roy) 1930-1996 . **CLC 56;
TCLC 123**
See also CA 111; 151; CANR 71; CN 4, 5,
6; DLB 130

Brodskii, Iosif
See Brodsky, Joseph

Brodskii, Iosif Alexandrovich
See Brodsky, Joseph

Brodsky, Iosif Alexandrovich
See Brodsky, Joseph

Brodsky, Joseph 1940-1996 .... **CLC 4, 6, 13,
36, 100; PC 9; TCLC 219**
See also AAYA 71; AITN 1; AMWS 8; CA
41-44R; 151; CANR 37, 106; CWW 2;
DA3; DAM POET; DLB 285, 329; EWL
3; MTCW 1, 2; MTFW 2005; PFS 35;
RGWL 2, 3

Brodsky, Michael 1948- .... **CLC 19**
See also CA 102; CANR 18, 41, 58, 147;
DLB 244

Brodsky, Michael Mark
See Brodsky, Michael

Brodzki, Bella CLC 65

Brome, Richard 1590(?)-1652 .... **LC 61**
See also BRWS 10; DLB 58

Bromell, Henry 1947- .... **CLC 5**
See also CA 53-56; CANR 9, 115, 116

Bromfield, Louis (Brucker) 1896-1956 ....
TCLC 11
See also CA 107; 155; DLB 4, 9, 86; RGAL
4; RHW

Broner, E. M. 1930-2011 .... **CLC 19**
See also CA 17-20R; CANR 8, 25, 72, 216;
CN 4, 5, 6; DLB 28

Broner, Esther Masserman
See Broner, E. M.

Bronk, William 1918-1999 .... **CLC 10**
See also AMWS 21; CA 89-92; 177; CANR
23; CP 3, 4, 5, 6, 7; DLB 165

Bronstein, Lev Davidovich
See Trotsky, Leon

Bronte, Anne 1820-1849 .. **NCLC 4, 71, 102,
235**
See also BRW 5; BRWR 1; DA3; DLB 21,
199, 340; NFS 26; TEA

Bronte, (Patrick) Branwell 1817-1848 ....
NCLC 109
See also DLB 340

Bronte, Charlotte 1816-1855 ..... **NCLC 3, 8,
33, 58, 105, 155, 217, 229; WLC 1**
See also AAYA 17; BRW 5; BRWC 2;
BRWR 1; BYA 2; CDBLB 1832-1890;
DA; DA3; DAB; DAC; DAM MST, NOV;
DLB 21, 159, 199, 340; EXPN; FL 1:2;
GL 2; LAIT 2; NFS 4, 36; TEA; WLIT 4

Bronte, Emily 1818-1848 . **NCLC 16, 35, 165,
244; PC 8; WLC 1**
See also AAYA 17; BPFB 1; BRW 5;
BRWC 1; BRWR 1; BYA 3; CDBLB
1832-1890; DA; DA3; DAB; DAC; DAM
MST, NOV, POET; DLB 21, 32, 199, 340;
EXPN; FL 1:2; GL 2; LAIT 1; NFS 2;
PFS 33; TEA; WLIT 3

Bronte, Emily Jane
See Bronte, Emily

Brontes
See Bronte, Anne; Bronte, (Patrick) Branwell; Bronte, Charlotte; Bronte, Emily

Brooke, Frances 1724-1789 .... **LC 6, 48**
See also DLB 39, 99

Brooke, Henry 1703(?)-1783 .... **LC 1**
See also DLB 39

Brooke, Rupert 1887-1915 . **PC 24; TCLC 2,
7; WLC 1**
See also BRWS 3; CA 104; 132; CANR 61;
CDBLB 1914-1945; DA; DAB; DAC;
DAM MST, POET; DLB 19, 216; EXPP;
GLL 2; MTCW 1, 2; MTFW 2005; PFS
7; TEA

Brooke, Rupert Chawner
See Brooke, Rupert

Brooke-Haven, P.
See Wodehouse, P. G.

Brooke-Rose, Christine 1923(?)- .... **CLC 40,
184**
See also BRWS 4; CA 13-16R; CANR 58,
118, 183; CN 1, 2, 3, 4, 5, 6, 7; DLB 14,
231; EWL 3; SFW 4

Brookner, Anita 1928- . **CLC 32, 34, 51, 136,
237**
See also BRWS 4; CA 114; 120; CANR 37,
56, 87, 130, 212; CN 4, 5, 6, 7; CPW;
DA3; DAB; DAM POP; DLB 194, 326;
DLBY 1987; EWL 3; MTCW 1, 2; MTFW
2005; NFS 23; TEA

Brooks, Cleanth 1906-1994 ...... **CLC 24, 86,
110**
See also AMWS 14; CA 17-20R; 145;
CANR 33, 35; CSW; DLB 63; DLBY
1994; EWL 3; INT CANR-35; MAL 5;
MTCW 1, 2; MTFW 2005

Brooks, George
See Baum, L. Frank

POP; DLB 173, 335; INT CA-112; MAL 5; MTCW 2; MTFW 2005; SSFS 11, 22

Butler, Samuel 1612-1680 ... **LC 16, 43, 173; PC 94**
See also DLB 101, 126; RGEL 2

Butler, Samuel 1835-1902 .... **TCLC 1, 33; WLC 1**
See also BRWS 2; CA 143; CDBLB 1890-1914; DA; DA3; DAB; DAC; DAM MST, NOV; DLB 18, 57, 174; RGEL 2; SFW 4; TEA

Butler, Walter C.
See Faust, Frederick

Butor, Michel (Marie Francois) 1926- . **CLC 1, 3, 8, 11, 15, 161**
See also CA 9-12R; CANR 33, 66; CWW 2; DLB 83; EW 13; EWL 3; GFL 1789 to the Present; MTCW 1, 2; MTFW 2005

Butts, Mary 1890(?)-1937 .. **SSC 124; TCLC 77**
See also CA 148; DLB 240

Buxton, Ralph
See Silverstein, Alvin; Silverstein, Virginia B.

Buzo, Alex
See Buzo, Alex

Buzo, Alex 1944- .... **CLC 61**
See also CA 97-100; CANR 17, 39, 69; CD 5, 6; DLB 289

Buzo, Alexander John
See Buzo, Alex

Buzzati, Dino 1906-1972 .... **CLC 36**
See also CA 160; 33-36R; DLB 177; RGWL 2, 3; SFW 4

Byars, Betsy 1928- .... **CLC 35**
See also AAYA 19; BYA 3; CA 33-36R, 183; CAAE 183; CANR 18, 36, 57, 102, 148; CLR 1, 16, 72; DLB 52; INT CANR-18; JRDA; MAICYA 1, 2; MAICYAS 1; MTCW 1; SAAS 1; SATA 4, 46, 80, 163, 223; SATA-Essay 108; WYA; YAW

Byars, Betsy Cromer
See Byars, Betsy

Byatt, A. S. 1936- ...... **CLC 19, 65, 136, 223, 312; SSC 91**
See also BPFB 1; BRWC 2; BRWS 4; CA 13-16R; CANR 13, 33, 50, 75, 96, 133, 205; CN 1, 2, 3, 4, 5, 6; DA3; DAM NOV, POP; DLB 14, 194, 319, 326; EWL 3; MTCW 1, 2; MTFW 2005; RGSF 2; RHW; SSFS 26; TEA

Byatt, Antonia Susan Drabble
See Byatt, A. S.

Byrd, William II 1674-1744 .... **LC 112**
See also DLB 24, 140; RGAL 4

Byrne, David 1952- .... **CLC 26**
See also CA 127; CANR 215

Byrne, John Joseph
See Leonard, Hugh

Byrne, John Keyes
See Leonard, Hugh

Byron, George Gordon
See Lord Byron

Byron, George Gordon Noel
See Lord Byron

Byron, Robert 1905-1941 .... **TCLC 67**
See also CA 160; DLB 195

C. 3. 3.
See Wilde, Oscar

Caballero, Fernan 1796-1877 .... **NCLC 10**

Cabell, Branch
See Cabell, James Branch

Cabell, James Branch 1879-1958 ... **TCLC 6**
See also CA 105; 152; DLB 9, 78; FANT; MAL 5; MTCW 2; RGAL 4; SUFW 1

Cabeza de Vaca, Alvar Nunez 1490-1557(?) .... **LC 61**

Cable, George Washington 1844-1925 .. **SSC 4, 155; TCLC 4**
See also CA 104; 155; DLB 12, 74; DLBD 13; RGAL 4; TUS

Cabral de Melo Neto, Joao 1920-1999 . **CLC 76**
See also CA 151; CWW 2; DAM MULT; DLB 307; EWL 3; LAW; LAWS 1

Cabrera, Lydia 1900-1991 .... **TCLC 223**
See also CA 178; DLB 145; EWL 3; HW 1; LAWS 1

Cabrera Infante, G. 1929-2005 .. **CLC 5, 25, 45, 120, 291; HLC 1; SSC 39**
See also CA 85-88; 236; CANR 29, 65, 110; CDWLB 3; CWW 2; DA3; DAM MULT; DLB 113; EWL 3; HW 1, 2; LAW; LAWS 1; MTCW 1, 2; MTFW 2005; RGSF 2; WLIT 1

Cabrera Infante, Guillermo
See Cabrera Infante, G.

Cade, Toni
See Bambara, Toni Cade

Cadmus and Harmonia
See Buchan, John

Caedmon fl. 658-680 .... **CMLC 7, 133**
See also DLB 146

Caeiro, Alberto
See Pessoa, Fernando

Caesar, Julius
See Julius Caesar

Cage, John (Milton), (Jr.) 1912-1992 ... **CLC 41; PC 58**
See also CA 13-16R; 169; CANR 9, 78; DLB 193; INT CANR-9; TCLE 1:1

Cahan, Abraham 1860-1951 .... **TCLC 71**
See also CA 108; 154; DLB 9, 25, 28; MAL 5; RGAL 4

Cain, Christopher
See Fleming, Thomas

Cain, G.
See Cabrera Infante, G.

Cain, Guillermo
See Cabrera Infante, G.

Cain, James M(allahan) 1892-1977 . **CLC 3, 11, 28**
See also AITN 1; BPFB 1; CA 17-20R; 73-76; CANR 8, 34, 61; CMW 4; CN 1, 2; DLB 226; EWL 3; MAL 5; MSW; MTCW 1; RGAL 4

Caine, Hall 1853-1931 .... **TCLC 97**
See also RHW

Caine, Mark
See Raphael, Frederic

Calasso, Roberto 1941- .... **CLC 81**
See also CA 143; CANR 89, 223

Calderon de la Barca, Pedro 1600-1681 . **DC 3; HLCS 1; LC 23, 136**
See also DFS 23; EW 2; RGWL 2, 3; TWA

Caldwell, Erskine 1903-1987 . **CLC 1, 8, 14, 50, 60; SSC 19, 147; TCLC 117**
See also AITN 1; AMW; BPFB 1; CA 1-4R; 121; CAAS 1; CANR 2, 33; CN 1, 2, 3, 4; DA3; DAM NOV; DLB 9, 86; EWL 3; MAL 5; MTCW 1, 2; MTFW 2005; RGAL 4; RGSF 2; TUS

Caldwell, Gail 1951- .... **CLC 309**
See also CA 313

Caldwell, (Janet Miriam) Taylor (Holland) 1900-1985 .... **CLC 2, 28, 39**
See also BPFB 1; CA 5-8R; 116; CANR 5; DA3; DAM NOV, POP; DLBD 17; MTCW 2; RHW

Calhoun, John Caldwell 1782-1850 .. **NCLC 15**
See also DLB 3, 248

Calisher, Hortense 1911-2009 .. **CLC 2, 4, 8, 38, 134; SSC 15**
See also CA 1-4R; 282; CANR 1, 22, 117; CN 1, 2, 3, 4, 5, 6, 7; DA3; DAM NOV;

DLB 2, 218; INT CANR-22; MAL 5; MTCW 1, 2; MTFW 2005; RGAL 4; RGSF 2

Callaghan, Morley 1903-1990 .... **CLC 3, 14, 41, 65; TCLC 145**
See also CA 9-12R; 132; CANR 33, 73; CN 1, 2, 3, 4; DAC; DAM MST; DLB 68; EWL 3; MTCW 1, 2; MTFW 2005; RGEL 2; RGSF 2; SSFS 19

Callaghan, Morley Edward
See Callaghan, Morley

Callimachus c. 305B.C.-c. 240B.C. ... **CMLC 18**
See also AW 1; DLB 176; RGWL 2, 3

Calvin, Jean
See Calvin, John

Calvin, John 1509-1564 .... **LC 37**
See also DLB 327; GFL Beginnings to 1789

Calvino, Italo 1923-1985 .. **CLC 5, 8, 11, 22, 33, 39, 73; SSC 3, 48; TCLC 183**
See also AAYA 58; CA 85-88; 116; CANR 23, 61, 132; DAM NOV; DLB 196; EW 13; EWL 3; MTCW 1, 2; MTFW 2005; RGHL; RGSF 2; RGWL 2, 3; SFW 4; SSFS 12, 31; WLIT 7

Camara Laye
See Laye, Camara

Cambridge, A Gentleman of the University of
See Crowley, Edward Alexander

Camden, William 1551-1623 .... **LC 77**
See also DLB 172

Cameron, Carey 1952- .... **CLC 59**
See also CA 135

Cameron, Peter 1959- .... **CLC 44**
See also AMWS 12; CA 125; CANR 50, 117, 188; DLB 234; GLL 2

Camoens, Luis Vaz de 1524(?)-1580 ....
See Camoes, Luis de

Camoes, Luis de 1524(?)-1580 . **HLCS 1; LC 62, 191; PC 31**
See also DLB 287; EW 2; RGWL 2, 3

Camp, Madeleine L'Engle
See L'Engle, Madeleine

Campana, Dino 1885-1932 .... **TCLC 20**
See also CA 117; 246; DLB 114; EWL 3

Campanella, Tommaso 1568-1639 ..... **LC 32**
See also RGWL 2, 3

Campbell, Bebe Moore 1950-2006 . **BLC 2:1; CLC 246**
See also AAYA 26; BW 2, 3; CA 139; 254; CANR 81, 134; DLB 227; MTCW 2; MTFW 2005

Campbell, John Ramsey
See Campbell, Ramsey

Campbell, John W. 1910-1971 .... **CLC 32**
See also CA 21-22; 29-32R; CANR 34; CAP 2; DLB 8; MTCW 1; SCFW 1, 2; SFW 4

Campbell, John Wood, Jr.
See Campbell, John W.

Campbell, Joseph 1904-1987 .... **CLC 69; TCLC 140**
See also AAYA 3, 66; BEST 89:2; CA 1-4R; 124; CANR 3, 28, 61, 107; DA3; MTCW 1, 2

Campbell, Maria 1940- ...... **CLC 85; NNAL**
See also CA 102; CANR 54; CCA 1; DAC

Campbell, Ramsey 1946- .. **CLC 42; SSC 19**
See also AAYA 51; CA 57-60, 228; CAAE 228; CANR 7, 102, 171; DLB 261; HGG; INT CANR-7; SUFW 1, 2

Campbell, (Ignatius) Roy (Dunnachie) 1901-1957 .... **TCLC 5**
See also AFW; CA 104; 155; DLB 20, 225; EWL 3; MTCW 2; RGEL 2

Campbell, Thomas 1777-1844 ...... **NCLC 19**
See also DLB 93, 144; RGEL 2

EW 7; EWL 3; EXPS; LAIT 3; LATS 1:1; RGSF 2; RGWL 2, 3; SATA 90; SSFS 5, 13, 14, 26, 29, 33; TWA

Chekhov, Anton Pavlovich
See Chekhov, Anton

Cheney, Lynne V. 1941- .... **CLC 70**
See also CA 89-92; CANR 58, 117, 193; SATA 152

Cheney, Lynne Vincent
See Cheney, Lynne V.

Chenier, Andre-Marie de 1762-1794 . **LC 174**
See also EW 4; GFL Beginnings to 1789; TWA

Chernyshevsky, Nikolai Gavrilovich
See Chernyshevsky, Nikolay Gavrilovich

Chernyshevsky, Nikolay Gavrilovich
1828-1889 .... **NCLC 1**
See also DLB 238

Cherry, Carolyn Janice
See Cherryh, C.J.

Cherryh, C.J. 1942- .... **CLC 35**
See also AAYA 24; BPFB 1; CA 65-68; CANR 10, 147, 179; DLBY 1980; FANT; SATA 93, 172; SCFW 2; YAW

Chesler, Phyllis 1940- .... **CLC 247**
See also CA 49-52; CANR 4, 59, 140, 189; FW

Chesnut, Mary 1823-1886 .... **NCLC 250**
See also DLB 239

Chesnut, Mary Boykin
See Chesnut, Mary

Chesnutt, Charles W(addell) 1858-1932 ......
BLC 1; SSC 7, 54, 139; TCLC 5, 39
See also AFAW 1, 2; AMWS 14; BW 1, 3; CA 106; 125; CANR 76; DAM MULT; DLB 12, 50, 78; EWL 3; MAL 5; MTCW 1, 2; MTFW 2005; RGAL 4; RGSF 2; SSFS 11, 26

Chester, Alfred 1929(?)-1971 .... **CLC 49**
See also CA 196; 33-36R; DLB 130; MAL 5

Chesterton, G. K. 1874-1936 . **PC 28; SSC 1, 46, 148; TCLC 1, 6, 64**
See also AAYA 57; BRW 6; CA 104; 132; CANR 73, 131; CDBLB 1914-1945; CMW 4; DAM NOV, POET; DLB 10, 19, 34, 70, 98, 149, 178; EWL 3; FANT; MSW; MTCW 1, 2; MTFW 2005; RGEL 2; RGSF 2; SATA 27; SUFW 1

Chesterton, Gilbert Keith
See Chesterton, G. K.

Chettle, Henry 1560-1607(?) .... **LC 112**
See also DLB 136; RGEL 2

Chiang, Pin-chin 1904-1986 .... **CLC 68**
See also CA 118; DLB 328; EWL 3; RGWL 3

Chiang Ping-chih
See Chiang, Pin-chin

Chief Joseph 1840-1904 .... **NNAL**
See also CA 152; DA3; DAM MULT

Chief Seattle 1786(?)-1866 .... **NNAL**
See also DA3; DAM MULT

Ch'ien, Chung-shu
See Qian, Zhongshu

Chikamatsu Monzaemon 1653-1724 . **LC 66**
See also RGWL 2, 3

Child, Francis James 1825-1896 . **NCLC 173**
See also DLB 1, 64, 235

Child, L. Maria
See Child, Lydia Maria

Child, Lydia Maria 1802-1880 . **NCLC 6, 73**
See also DLB 1, 74, 243; RGAL 4; SATA 67

Child, Mrs.
See Child, Lydia Maria

Child, Philip 1898-1978 .... **CLC 19, 68**
See also CA 13-14; CAP 1; CP 1; DLB 68; RHW; SATA 47

Childers, Erskine 1870-1922 .... **TCLC 65**
See also BRWS 17; CA 113; 153; DLB 70

Childress, Alice 1920-1994 ... **BLC 1:1; CLC 12, 15, 86, 96; DC 4; TCLC 116**
See also AAYA 8; BW 2, 3; BYA 2; CA 45-48; 146; CAD; CANR 3, 27, 50, 74; CLR 14; CWD; DA3; DAM DRAM, MULT, NOV; DFS 2, 8, 14, 26; DLB 7, 38, 249; JRDA; LAIT 5; MAICYA 1, 2; MAIC-YAS 1; MAL 5; MTCW 1, 2; MTFW 2005; RGAL 4; SATA 7, 48, 81; TUS; WYA; YAW

Chin, Frank 1940- ... **AAL; CLC 135; DC 7**
See also CA 33-36R; CAD; CANR 71; CD 5, 6; DAM MULT; DLB 206, 312; LAIT 5; RGAL 4

Chin, Frank Chew, Jr.
See Chin, Frank

Chin, Marilyn 1955- .... **PC 40**
See also CA 129; CANR 70, 113, 218; CWP; DLB 312; PFS 28, 41

Chin, Marilyn Mei Ling
See Chin, Marilyn

Chislett, (Margaret) Anne 1943- ..... **CLC 34**
See also CA 151

Chitty, Thomas Willes
See Hinde, Thomas

Chivers, Thomas Holley 1809-1858 .. **NCLC 49**
See also DLB 3, 248; RGAL 4

Chlamyda, Jehudil
See Gorky, Maxim

Ch'o, Chou
See Shu-Jen, Chou

Choi, Susan 1969- .... **CLC 119**
See also CA 223; CANR 188

Chomette, Rene Lucien 1898-1981 . **CLC 20**
See also CA 103

Chomsky, Avram Noam
See Chomsky, Noam

Chomsky, Noam 1928- .... **CLC 132**
See also CA 17-20R; CANR 28, 62, 110, 132, 179; DA3; DLB 246; MTCW 1, 2; MTFW 2005

Chona, Maria 1845(?)-1936 .... **NNAL**
See also CA 144

Chopin, Kate 1851-1904 ...... **SSC 8, 68, 110; TCLC 127; WLCS**
See also AAYA 33; AMWR 2; BYA 11, 15; CA 104; 122; CDALB 1865-1917; DA3; DAB; DAC; DAM MST, NOV; DLB 12, 78; EXPN; EXPS; FL 1:3; FW; LAIT 3; MAL 5; MBL; NFS 3; RGAL 4; RGSF 2; SSFS 2, 13, 17, 26, 35; TUS

Chopin, Katherine
See Chopin, Kate

Chretien de Troyes c. 12th cent. - ..... **CMLC 10, 135**
See also DLB 208; EW 1; RGWL 2, 3; TWA

Christie
See Ichikawa, Kon

Christie, Agatha 1890-1976 ...... **CLC 1, 6, 8, 12, 39, 48, 110; DC 39**
See also AAYA 9; AITN 1, 2; BPFB 1; BRWS 2; CA 17-20R; 61-64; CANR 10, 37, 108; CBD; CDBLB 1914-1945; CMW 4; CN 1, 2; CPW; CWD; DA3; DAB; DAC; DAM NOV; DFS 2; DLB 13, 77, 245; MSW; MTCW 1, 2; MTFW 2005; NFS 8, 30, 33; RGEL 2; RHW; SATA 36; SSFS 31, 34; TEA; YAW

Christie, Agatha Mary Clarissa
See Christie, Agatha

Christie, Ann Philippa
See Pearce, Philippa

Christie, Philippa
See Pearce, Philippa

Christine de Pisan
See Christine de Pizan

Christine de Pizan 1365(?)-1431(?) ..... **LC 9, 130; PC 68**
See also DLB 208; FL 1:1; FW; RGWL 2, 3

Chuang-Tzu c. 369B.C.-c. 286B.C. ... **CMLC 57**

Chubb, Elmer
See Masters, Edgar Lee

Chulkov, Mikhail Dmitrievich 1743-1792 ... **LC 2**
See also DLB 150

Chung, Sonya CLC 318
See also CA 307

Churchill, Caryl 1938- ..... **CLC 31, 55, 157; DC 5**
See also BRWS 4; CA 102; CANR 22, 46, 108; CBD; CD 5, 6; CWD; DFS 25; DLB 13, 310; EWL 3; FW; MTCW 1; RGEL 2

Churchill, Charles 1731-1764 .... **LC 3**
See also DLB 109; RGEL 2

Churchill, Chick
See Churchill, Caryl

Churchill, Sir Winston 1874-1965 ..... **TCLC 113**
See also BRW 6; CA 97-100; CDBLB 1890-1914; DA3; DLB 100, 329; DLBD 16; LAIT 4; MTCW 1, 2

Churchill, Sir Winston Leonard Spencer
See Churchill, Sir Winston

Churchyard, Thomas 1520(?)-1604 . **LC 187**
See also DLB 132; RGEL 2

Chute, Carolyn 1947- .... **CLC 39**
See also CA 123; CANR 135, 213; CN 7; DLB 350

Ciardi, John (Anthony) 1916-1986 . **CLC 10, 40, 44, 129; PC 69**
See also CA 5-8R; 118; CAAS 2; CANR 5, 33; CLR 19; CP 1, 2, 3, 4; CWRI 5; DAM POET; DLB 5; DLBY 1986; INT CANR-5; MAICYA 1, 2; MAL 5; MTCW 1, 2; MTFW 2005; RGAL 4; SAAS 26; SATA 1, 65; SATA-Obit 46

Cibber, Colley 1671-1757 .... **LC 66**
See also DLB 84; RGEL 2

Cicero, Marcus Tullius 106B.C.-43B.C. .... **CMLC 121**
See also AW 1; CDWLB 1; DLB 211; RGWL 2, 3; WLIT 8

Cimino, Michael 1943- .... **CLC 16**
See also CA 105

Cioran, E(mil) M. 1911-1995 .... **CLC 64**
See also CA 25-28R; 149; CANR 91; DLB 220; EWL 3

Circus, Anthony
See Hoch, Edward D.

Cisneros, Sandra 1954- ... **CLC 69, 118, 193, 305; HLC 1; PC 52; SSC 32, 72, 143**
See also AAYA 9, 53; AMWS 7; CA 131; CANR 64, 118; CLR 123; CN 7; CWP; DA3; DAM MULT; DLB 122, 152; EWL 3; EXPN; FL 1:5; FW; HW 1, 2; LAIT 5; LATS 1:2; LLW; MAICYA 2; MAL 5; MTCW 2; MTFW 2005; NFS 2; PFS 19; RGAL 4; RGSF 2; SSFS 3, 13, 27, 32; WLIT 1; YAW

Cixous, Helene 1937- .... **CLC 92, 253**
See also CA 126; CANR 55, 123; CWW 2; DLB 83, 242; EWL 3; FL 1:5; FW; GLL 2; MTCW 1, 2; MTFW 2005; TWA

Clair, Rene
See Chomette, Rene Lucien

Clampitt, Amy 1920-1994 ... **CLC 32; PC 19**
See also AMWS 9; CA 110; 146; CANR 29, 79; CP 4, 5; DLB 105; MAL 5; PFS 27, 39

Clancy, Thomas L., Jr.
See Clancy, Tom

Clancy, Tom 1947- .... **CLC 45, 112**
See also AAYA 9, 51; BEST 89:1, 90:1; BPFB 1; BYA 10, 11; CA 125; 131; CANR 62, 105, 132; CMW 4; CPW; DA3; DAM NOV, POP; DLB 227; INT CA-131; MTCW 1, 2; MTFW 2005

Clare, John 1793-1864 . **NCLC 9, 86; PC 23**
See also BRWS 11; DAB; DAM POET; DLB 55, 96; RGEL 2

Clarin
See Alas (y Urena), Leopoldo (Enrique Garcia)

Clark, Al C.
See Goines, Donald

Clark, Brian (Robert)
See Clark, (Robert) Brian

Clark, (Robert) Brian 1932- .... **CLC 29**
See also CA 41-44R; CANR 67; CBD; CD 5, 6

Clark, Curt
See Westlake, Donald E.

Clark, Eleanor 1913-1996 .... **CLC 5, 19**
See also CA 9-12R; 151; CANR 41; CN 1, 2, 3, 4, 5, 6; DLB 6

Clark, J. P.
See Clark-Bekederemo, J. P.

Clark, John Pepper
See Clark-Bekederemo, J. P.

Clark, Kenneth (Mackenzie) 1903-1983 ......
TCLC 147
See also CA 93-96; 109; CANR 36; MTCW 1, 2; MTFW 2005

Clark, M. R.
See Clark, Mavis Thorpe

Clark, Mavis Thorpe 1909-1999 ..... **CLC 12**
See also CA 57-60; CANR 8, 37, 107; CLR 30; CWRI 5; MAICYA 1, 2; SAAS 5; SATA 8, 74

Clark, Walter Van Tilburg 1909-1971 . **CLC 28**
See also CA 9-12R; 33-36R; CANR 63, 113; CN 1; DLB 9, 206; LAIT 2; MAL 5; NFS 40; RGAL 4; SATA 8; TCWW 1, 2

Clark-Bekederemo, J. P. 1935- ..... **BLC 1:1; CLC 38; DC 5**
See also AAYA 79; AFW; BW 1; CA 65-68; CANR 16, 72; CD 5, 6; CDWLB 3; CP 1, 2, 3, 4, 5, 6, 7; DAM DRAM, MULT; DFS 13; DLB 117; EWL 3; MTCW 2; MTFW 2005; RGEL 2

Clark-Bekederemo, John Pepper
See Clark-Bekederemo, J. P.

Clark Bekederemo, Johnson Pepper
See Clark-Bekederemo, J. P.

Clarke, Arthur
See Clarke, Arthur C.

Clarke, Arthur C. 1917-2008 . **CLC 1, 4, 13, 18, 35, 136; SSC 3**
See also AAYA 4, 33; BPFB 1; BYA 13; CA 1-4R; 270; CANR 2, 28, 55, 74, 130, 196; CLR 119; CN 1, 2, 3, 4, 5, 6, 7; CPW; DA3; DAM POP; DLB 261; JRDA; LAIT 5; MAICYA 1, 2; MTCW 1, 2; MTFW 2005; SATA 13, 70, 115; SATA-Obit 191; SCFW 1, 2; SFW 4; SSFS 4, 18, 29; TCLE 1:1; YAW

Clarke, Arthur Charles
See Clarke, Arthur C.

Clarke, Austin 1896-1974 ...... **CLC 6, 9; PC 112**
See also BRWS 15; CA 29-32; 49-52; CAP 2; CP 1, 2; DAM POET; DLB 10, 20; EWL 3; RGEL 2

Clarke, Austin 1934- . **BLC 1:1; CLC 8, 53; SSC 45, 116**
See also BW 1; CA 25-28R; CAAS 16; CANR 14, 32, 68, 140, 220; CN 1, 2, 3,

4, 5, 6, 7; DAC; DAM MULT; DLB 53, 125; DNFS 2; MTCW 2; MTFW 2005; RGSF 2

Clarke, Gillian 1937- .... **CLC 61**
See also CA 106; CP 3, 4, 5, 6, 7; CWP; DLB 40

Clarke, Marcus (Andrew Hislop)
1846-1881 .... **NCLC 19; SSC 94**
See also DLB 230; RGEL 2; RGSF 2

Clarke, Shirley 1925-1997 .... **CLC 16**
See also CA 189

Clash, The
See Headon, (Nicky) Topper; Jones, Mick; Simonon, Paul; Strummer, Joe

Claudel, Paul (Louis Charles Marie)
1868-1955 .... **TCLC 2, 10**
See also CA 104; 165; DLB 192, 258, 321; EW 8; EWL 3; GFL 1789 to the Present; RGWL 2, 3; TWA

Claudian 370(?)-404(?) .... **CMLC 46**
See also RGWL 2, 3

Claudius, Matthias 1740-1815 ...... **NCLC 75**
See also DLB 97

Clavell, James 1925-1994 ...... **CLC 6, 25, 87**
See also BPFB 1; CA 25-28R; 146; CANR 26, 48; CN 5; CPW; DA3; DAM NOV, POP; MTCW 1, 2; MTFW 2005; NFS 10; RHW

Clayman, Gregory CLC 65

Cleage, Pearl 1948- .... **DC 32**
See also BW 2; CA 41-44R; CANR 27, 148, 177, 226; DFS 14, 16; DLB 228; NFS 17

Cleage, Pearl Michelle
See Cleage, Pearl

Cleaver, (Leroy) Eldridge 1935-1998 ... **BLC 1:1; CLC 30, 119**
See also BW 1, 3; CA 21-24R; 167; CANR 16, 75; DA3; DAM MULT; MTCW 2; YAW

Cleese, John (Marwood) 1939- .... **CLC 21**
See also CA 112; 116; CANR 35; MTCW 1

Cleishbotham, Jebediah
See Scott, Sir Walter

Cleland, John 1710-1789 .... **LC 2, 48**
See also DLB 39; RGEL 2

Clemens, Samuel
See Twain, Mark

Clemens, Samuel Langhorne
See Twain, Mark

Clement of Alexandria 150(?)-215(?) ....
CMLC 41

Cleophil
See Congreve, William

Clerihew, E.
See Bentley, E(dmund) C(lerihew)

Clerk, N. W.
See Lewis, C. S.

Cleveland, John 1613-1658 .... **LC 106**
See also DLB 126; RGEL 2

Cliff, Jimmy
See Chambers, James

Cliff, Michelle 1946- .... **BLCS; CLC 120**
See also BW 2; CA 116; CANR 39, 72; CD-WLB 3; DLB 157; FW; GLL 2

Clifford, Lady Anne 1590-1676 .... **LC 76**
See also DLB 151

Clifton, Lucille 1936-2010 ...... **BLC 1:1, 2:1; CLC 19, 66, 162, 283; PC 17**
See also AFAW 2; BW 2, 3; CA 49-52; CANR 2, 24, 42, 76, 97, 138; CLR 5; CP 2, 3, 4, 5, 6, 7; CSW; CWP; CWRI 5; DA3; DAM MULT, POET; DLB 5, 41; EXPP; MAICYA 1, 2; MTCW 1, 2; MTFW 2005; PFS 1, 14, 29, 41; SATA 20, 69, 128; SSFS 34; WP

Clifton, Thelma Lucille
See Clifton, Lucille

Clinton, Dirk
See Silverberg, Robert

Clough, Arthur Hugh 1819-1861 . **NCLC 27, 163; PC 103**
See also BRW 5; DLB 32; RGEL 2

Clutha, Janet
See Frame, Janet

Clutha, Janet Paterson Frame
See Frame, Janet

Clyne, Terence
See Blatty, William Peter

Cobalt, Martin
See Mayne, William

Cobb, Irvin S(hrewsbury) 1876-1944 . **TCLC 77**
See also CA 175; DLB 11, 25, 86

Cobbett, William 1763-1835 .... **NCLC 49**
See also DLB 43, 107, 158; RGEL 2

Coben, Harlan 1962- .... **CLC 269**
See also AAYA 83; CA 164; CANR 162, 199

Coburn, D(onald) L(ee) 1938- .... **CLC 10**
See also CA 89-92; DFS 23

Cockburn, Catharine Trotter
See Trotter, Catharine

Cocteau, Jean 1889-1963 . **CLC 1, 8, 15, 16, 43; DC 17; TCLC 119; WLC 2**
See also AAYA 74; CA 25-28; CANR 40; CAP 2; DA; DA3; DAB; DAC; DAM DRAM, MST, NOV; DFS 24; DLB 65, 258, 321; EW 10; EWL 3; GFL 1789 to the Present; MTCW 1, 2; RGWL 2, 3; TWA

Cocteau, Jean Maurice Eugene Clement
See Cocteau, Jean

Codrescu, Andrei 1946- .... **CLC 46, 121**
See also CA 33-36R; CAAS 19; CANR 13, 34, 53, 76, 125, 223; CN 7; DA3; DAM POET; MAL 5; MTCW 2; MTFW 2005

Coe, Max
See Bourne, Randolph S(illiman)

Coe, Tucker
See Westlake, Donald E.

Coelho, Paulo 1947- .... **CLC 258**
See also CA 152; CANR 80, 93, 155, 194; NFS 29

Coen, Ethan 1957- .... **CLC 108, 267**
See also AAYA 54; CA 126; CANR 85

Coen, Joel 1954- .... **CLC 108, 267**
See also AAYA 54; CA 126; CANR 119

The Coen Brothers
See Coen, Ethan; Coen, Joel

Coetzee, J. M. 1940- ... **CLC 23, 33, 66, 117, 161, 162, 305**
See also AAYA 37; AFW; BRWS 6; CA 77-80; CANR 41, 54, 74, 114, 133, 180; CN 4, 5, 6, 7; DA3; DAM NOV; DLB 225, 326, 329; EWL 3; LMFS 2; MTCW 1, 2; MTFW 2005; NFS 21; WLIT 2; WWE 1

Coetzee, John Maxwell
See Coetzee, J. M.

Coffey, Brian
See Koontz, Dean

Coffin, Robert P. Tristram 1892-1955 ....
TCLC 95
See also CA 123; 169; DLB 45

Coffin, Robert Peter Tristram
See Coffin, Robert P. Tristram

Cohan, George M. 1878-1942 .... **TCLC 60**
See also CA 157; DLB 249; RGAL 4

Cohan, George Michael
See Cohan, George M.

Cohen, Arthur A(llen) 1928-1986 .... **CLC 7, 31**
See also CA 1-4R; 120; CANR 1, 17, 42; DLB 28; RGHL

Cohen, Leonard 1934- . **CLC 3, 38, 260; PC 109**
See also CA 21-24R; CANR 14, 69; CN 1, 2, 3, 4, 5, 6; CP 1, 2, 3, 4, 5, 6, 7; DAC; DAM MST; DLB 53; EWL 3; MTCW 1

Cohen, Leonard Norman
See Cohen, Leonard

Cohen, Matt(hew) 1942-1999 .... **CLC 19**
See also CA 61-64; 187; CAAS 18; CANR 40; CN 1, 2, 3, 4, 5, 6; DAC; DLB 53

Cohen-Solal, Annie 1948- .... **CLC 50**
See also CA 239

Colegate, Isabel 1931- .... **CLC 36**
See also CA 17-20R; CANR 8, 22, 74; CN 4, 5, 6, 7; DLB 14, 231; INT CANR-22; MTCW 1

Coleman, Emmett
See Reed, Ishmael

Coleridge, Hartley 1796-1849 .... **NCLC 90**
See also DLB 96

Coleridge, M. E.
See Coleridge, Mary E(lizabeth)

Coleridge, Mary E(lizabeth) 1861-1907 ....
TCLC 73
See also CA 116; 166; DLB 19, 98

Coleridge, Samuel Taylor 1772-1834 . **NCLC 9, 54, 99, 111, 177, 197, 231; PC 11, 39, 67, 100; WLC 2**
See also AAYA 66; BRW 4; BRWR 2; BYA 4; CDBLB 1789-1832; DA; DA3; DAB; DAC; DAM MST, POET; DLB 93, 107; EXPP; LATS 1:1; LMFS 1; PAB; PFS 4, 5, 39; RGEL 2; TEA; WLIT 3; WP

Coleridge, Sara 1802-1852 .... **NCLC 31**
See also DLB 199

Coles, Don 1928- .... **CLC 46**
See also CA 115; CANR 38; CP 5, 6, 7

Coles, Robert 1929- .... **CLC 108**
See also CA 45-48; CANR 3, 32, 66, 70, 135, 225; INT CANR-32; SATA 23

Coles, Robert Martin
See Coles, Robert

Colette 1873-1954 .. **SSC 10, 93; TCLC 1, 5, 16**
See also CA 104; 131; DA3; DAM NOV; DLB 65; EW 9; EWL 3; GFL 1789 to the Present; GLL 1; MTCW 1, 2; MTFW 2005; RGWL 2, 3; TWA

Colette, Sidonie-Gabrielle
See Colette

Collett, (Jacobine) Camilla (Wergeland) 1813-1895 .... **NCLC 22**
See also DLB 354

Collier, Christopher 1930- .... **CLC 30**
See also AAYA 13; BYA 2; CA 33-36R; CANR 13, 33, 102; CLR 126; JRDA; MAICYA 1, 2; NFS 38; SATA 16, 70; WYA; YAW 1

Collier, James Lincoln 1928- .... **CLC 30**
See also AAYA 13; BYA 2; CA 9-12R; CANR 4, 33, 60, 102, 208; CLR 3, 126; DAM POP; JRDA; MAICYA 1, 2; NFS 38; SAAS 21; SATA 8, 70, 166; WYA; YAW 1

Collier, Jeremy 1650-1726 .... **LC 6, 157**
See also DLB 336

Collier, John 1901-1980 . **SSC 19; TCLC 127**
See also CA 65-68; 97-100; CANR 10; CN 1, 2; DLB 77, 255; FANT; SUFW 1

Collier, Mary 1690-1762 .... **LC 86**
See also DLB 95

Collingwood, R(obin) G(eorge) 1889(?)-1943 .... **TCLC 67**
See also CA 117; 155; DLB 262

Collins, Billy 1941- .... **PC 68**
See also AAYA 64; AMWS 21; CA 151; CANR 92, 211; CP 7; MTFW 2005; PFS 18

Collins, Hunt
See Hunter, Evan

Collins, Linda 1931- .... **CLC 44**
See also CA 125

Collins, Merle 1950- .... **BLC 2:1**
See also BW 3; CA 175; DLB 157

Collins, Tom
See Furphy, Joseph

Collins, Wilkie 1824-1889 .. **NCLC 1, 18, 93, 255; SSC 93**
See also BRWS 6; CDBLB 1832-1890; CMW 4; DFS 28; DLB 18, 70, 159; GL 2; MSW; NFS 39; RGEL 2; RGSF 2; SUFW 1; WLIT 4

Collins, William 1721-1759 .... **LC 4, 40; PC 72**
See also BRW 3; DAM POET; DLB 109; RGEL 2

Collins, William Wilkie
See Collins, Wilkie

Collodi, Carlo 1826-1890 .... **NCLC 54**
See also CLR 5, 120; MAICYA 1,2; SATA 29, 100; WCH; WLIT 7

Colman, George
See Glassco, John

Colman, George, the Elder 1732-1794 ... **LC 98**
See also RGEL 2

Colonna, Vittoria 1492-1547 .... **LC 71**
See also RGWL 2, 3

Colt, Winchester Remington
See Hubbard, L. Ron

Colter, Cyrus J. 1910-2002 .... **CLC 58**
See also BW 1; CA 65-68; 205; CANR 10, 66; CN 2, 3, 4, 5, 6; DLB 33

Colton, James
See Hansen, Joseph

Colum, Padraic 1881-1972 .... **CLC 28**
See also BYA 4; CA 73-76; 33-36R; CANR 35; CLR 36; CP 1; CWRI 5; DLB 19; MAICYA 1, 2; MTCW 1; RGEL 2; SATA 15; WCH

Colvin, James
See Moorcock, Michael

Colwin, Laurie (E.) 1944-1992 ... **CLC 5, 13, 23, 84**
See also CA 89-92; 139; CANR 20, 46; DLB 218; DLBY 1980; MTCW 1

Comfort, Alex(ander) 1920-2000 .... **CLC 7**
See also CA 1-4R; 190; CANR 1, 45; CN 1, 2, 3, 4; CP 1, 2, 3, 4, 5, 6, 7; DAM POP; MTCW 2

Comfort, Montgomery
See Campbell, Ramsey

Compton-Burnett, I. 1892(?)-1969 ... **CLC 1, 3, 10, 15, 34; TCLC 180**
See also BRW 7; CA 1-4R; 25-28R; CANR 4; DAM NOV; DLB 36; EWL 3; MTCW 1, 2; RGEL 2

Compton-Burnett, Ivy
See Compton-Burnett, I.

Comstock, Anthony 1844-1915 ..... **TCLC 13**
See also CA 110; 169

Comte, Auguste 1798-1857 .... **NCLC 54**

Conan Doyle, Arthur
See Doyle, Sir Arthur Conan

Conde (Abellan), Carmen 1901-1996 . **HLCS 1**
See also CA 177; CWW 2; DLB 108; EWL 3; HW 2

Conde, Maryse 1937- .... **BLC 2:1; BLCS; CLC 52, 92, 247**
See also BW 2, 3; CA 110, 190; CAAE 190; CANR 30, 53, 76, 171; CWW 2; DAM MULT; EWL 3; MTCW 2; MTFW 2005

Condillac, Etienne Bonnot de 1714-1780 ..... **LC 26**
See also DLB 313

Condon, Richard 1915-1996 .... **CLC 4, 6, 8, 10, 45, 100**
See also BEST 90:3; BPFB 1; CA 1-4R; 151; CAAS 1; CANR 2, 23, 164; CMW 4; CN 1, 2, 3, 4, 5, 6; DAM NOV; INT CANR-23; MAL 5; MTCW 1, 2

Condon, Richard Thomas
See Condon, Richard

Condorcet
See Condorcet, marquis de Marie-Jean-Antoine-Nicolas Caritat

Condorcet, marquis de Marie-Jean-Antoine-Nicolas Caritat 1743-1794 .... **LC 104**
See also DLB 313; GFL Beginnings to 1789

Confucius 551B.C.-479B.C. .. **CMLC 19, 65; WLCS**
See also DA; DA3; DAB; DAC; DAM MST

Congreve, William 1670-1729 .. **DC 2; LC 5, 21, 170; WLC 2**
See also BRW 2; CDBLB 1660-1789; DA; DAB; DAC; DAM DRAM, MST, POET; DFS 15; DLB 39, 84; RGEL 2; WLIT 3

Conley, Robert J. 1940- .... **NNAL**
See also CA 41-44R; 295; CAAE 295; CANR 15, 34, 45, 96, 186; DAM MULT; TCWW 2

Connell, Evan S. 1924- .... **CLC 4, 6, 45**
See also AAYA 7; AMWS 14; CA 1-4R; CAAS 2; CANR 2, 39, 76, 97, 140, 195; CN 1, 2, 3, 4, 5, 6; DAM NOV; DLB 2, 335; DLBY 1981; MAL 5; MTCW 1, 2; MTFW 2005

Connell, Evan Shelby, Jr.
See Connell, Evan S.

Connelly, Marc(us Cook) 1890-1980 . **CLC 7**
See also CA 85-88; 102; CAD; CANR 30; DFS 12; DLB 7; DLBY 1980; MAL 5; RGAL 4; SATA-Obit 25

Connelly, Michael 1956- .... **CLC 293**
See also AMWS 21; CA 158; CANR 91, 180; CMW 4; LNFS 2

Connolly, Paul
See Wicker, Tom

Connor, Ralph
See Gordon, Charles William

Conrad, Joseph 1857-1924 .... **SSC 9, 67, 69, 71, 153; TCLC 1, 6, 13, 25, 43, 57; WLC 2**
See also AAYA 26; BPFB 1; BRW 6; BRWC 1; BRWR 2; BYA 2; CA 104; 131; CANR 60; CDBLB 1890-1914; DA; DA3; DAB; DAC; DAM MST, NOV; DLB 10, 34, 98, 156; EWL 3; EXPN; EXPS; LAIT 2; LATS 1:1; LMFS 1; MTCW 1, 2; MTFW 2005; NFS 2, 16; RGEL 2; RGSF 2; SATA 27; SSFS 1, 12, 31; TEA; WLIT 4

Conrad, Robert Arnold
See Hart, Moss

Conroy, Donald Patrick
See Conroy, Pat

Conroy, Pat 1945- .... **CLC 30, 74**
See also AAYA 8, 52; AITN 1; BPFB 1; CA 85-88; CANR 24, 53, 129; CN 7; CPW; CSW; DA3; DAM NOV, POP; DLB 6; LAIT 5; MAL 5; MTCW 1, 2; MTFW 2005

Constant (de Rebecque), (Henri) Benjamin 1767-1830 .... **NCLC 6, 182**
See also DLB 119; EW 4; GFL 1789 to the Present

Conway, Jill K. 1934- .... **CLC 152**
See also CA 130; CANR 94

Conway, Jill Ker
See Conway, Jill K.

Conybeare, Charles Augustus
See Eliot, T. S.

Cook, Michael 1933-1994 .... **CLC 58**
See also CA 93-96; CANR 68; DLB 53

Cook, Robin 1940- .... **CLC 14**
See also AAYA 32; BEST 90:2; BPFB 1; CA 108; 111; CANR 41, 90, 109, 181, 219; CPW; DA3; DAM POP; HGG; INT CA-111

Cook, Roy
See Silverberg, Robert
Cooke, Elizabeth 1948- .... **CLC 55**
See also CA 129
Cooke, John Esten 1830-1886 .... **NCLC 5**
See also DLB 3, 248; RGAL 4
Cooke, John Estes
See Baum, L. Frank
Cooke, M. E.
See Creasey, John
Cooke, Margaret
See Creasey, John
Cooke, Rose Terry 1827-1892 ... **NCLC 110; SSC 149**
See also DLB 12, 74
Cook-Lynn, Elizabeth 1930- .... **CLC 93; NNAL**
See also CA 133; DAM MULT; DLB 175
Cooney, Ray CLC 62
See also CBD
Cooper, Anthony Ashley 1671-1713 . **LC 107**
See also DLB 101, 336
Cooper, Dennis 1953- .... **CLC 203**
See also CA 133; CANR 72, 86, 204; GLL 1; HGG
Cooper, Douglas 1960- .... **CLC 86**
Cooper, Henry St. John
See Creasey, John
Cooper, J. California (?)- .... **CLC 56**
See also AAYA 12; BW 1; CA 125; CANR 55, 207; DAM MULT; DLB 212
Cooper, James Fenimore 1789-1851 . **NCLC 1, 27, 54, 203**
See also AAYA 22; AMW; BPFB 1; CDALB 1640-1865; CLR 105; DA3; DLB 3, 183, 250, 254; LAIT 1; NFS 25; RGAL 4; SATA 19; TUS; WCH
Cooper, Joan California
See Cooper, J. California
Cooper, Susan Fenimore 1813-1894 .. **NCLC 129**
See also ANW; DLB 239, 254
Coover, Robert 1932- . **CLC 3, 7, 15, 32, 46, 87, 161, 306; SSC 15, 101**
See also AMWS 5; BPFB 1; CA 45-48; CANR 3, 37, 58, 115, 228; CN 1, 2, 3, 4, 5, 6, 7; DAM NOV; DLB 2, 227; DLBY 1981; EWL 3; MAL 5; MTCW 1, 2; MTFW 2005; RGAL 4; RGSF 2
Copeland, Stewart 1952- .... **CLC 26**
See also CA 305
Copeland, Stewart Armstrong
See Copeland, Stewart
Copernicus, Nicolaus 1473-1543 .... **LC 45**
Coppard, A(lfred) E(dgar) 1878-1957 .. **SSC 21; TCLC 5**
See also BRWS 8; CA 114; 167; DLB 162; EWL 3; HGG; RGEL 2; RGSF 2; SUFW 1; YABC 1
Coppee, Francois 1842-1908 .... **TCLC 25**
See also CA 170; DLB 217
Coppola, Francis Ford 1939- .. **CLC 16, 126**
See also AAYA 39; CA 77-80; CANR 40, 78; DLB 44
Copway, George 1818-1869 .... **NNAL**
See also DAM MULT; DLB 175, 183
Corbiere, Tristan 1845-1875 .... **NCLC 43**
See also DLB 217; GFL 1789 to the Present
Corcoran, Barbara (Asenath) 1911-2003 ..... **CLC 17**
See also AAYA 14; CA 21-24R, 191; CAAE 191; CAAS 2; CANR 11, 28, 48; CLR 50; DLB 52; JRDA; MAICYA 2; MAIC-YAS 1; RHW; SAAS 20; SATA 3, 77; SATA-Essay 125
Cordelier, Maurice
See Giraudoux, Jean
Cordier, Gilbert
See Rohmer, Eric

Corelli, Marie
See Mackay, Mary
Corinna c. 225B.C.-c. 305B.C. ..... **CMLC 72**
Corman, Cid 1924-2004 .... **CLC 9**
See also CA 85-88; 225; CAAS 2; CANR 44; CP 1, 2, 3, 4, 5, 6, 7; DAM POET; DLB 5, 193
Corman, Sidney
See Corman, Cid
Cormier, Robert 1925-2000 .... **CLC 12, 30**
See also AAYA 3, 19; BYA 1, 2, 6, 8, 9; CA 1-4R; CANR 5, 23, 76, 93; CDALB 1968-1988; CLR 12, 55, 167; DA; DAB; DAC; DAM MST, NOV; DLB 52; EXPN; INT CANR-23; JRDA; LAIT 5; MAICYA 1, 2; MTCW 1, 2; MTFW 2005; NFS 2, 18; SATA 10, 45, 83; SATA-Obit 122; WYA; YAW
Cormier, Robert Edmund
See Cormier, Robert
Corn, Alfred (DeWitt III) 1943- ..... **CLC 33**
See also CA 179; CAAE 179; CAAS 25; CANR 44; CP 3, 4, 5, 6, 7; CSW; DLB 120, 282; DLBY 1980
Corneille, Pierre 1606-1684 . **DC 21; LC 28, 135**
See also DAB; DAM MST; DFS 21; DLB 268; EW 3; GFL Beginnings to 1789; RGWL 2, 3; TWA
Cornwell, David
See le Carre, John
Cornwell, David John Moore
See le Carre, John
Cornwell, Patricia 1956- .... **CLC 155**
See also AAYA 16, 56; BPFB 1; CA 134; CANR 53, 131, 195; CMW 4; CPW; CSW; DAM POP; DLB 306; MSW; MTCW 2; MTFW 2005
Cornwell, Patricia Daniels
See Cornwell, Patricia
Cornwell, Smith
See Smith, David (Jeddie)
Corso, Gregory 1930-2001 ... **CLC 1, 11; PC 33, 108**
See also AMWS 12; BG 1:2; CA 5-8R; 193; CANR 41, 76, 132; CP 1, 2, 3, 4, 5, 6, 7; DA3; DLB 5, 16, 237; LMFS 2; MAL 5; MTCW 1, 2; MTFW 2005; WP
Cortazar, Julio 1914-1984 .. **CLC 2, 3, 5, 10, 13, 15, 33, 34, 92; HLC 1; SSC 7, 76, 156; TCLC 252**
See also AAYA 85; BPFB 1; CA 21-24R; CANR 12, 32, 81; CDWLB 3; DA3; DAM MULT, NOV; DLB 113; EWL 3; EXPS; HW 1, 2; LAW; MTCW 1, 2; MTFW 2005; RGSF 2; RGWL 2, 3; SSFS 3, 20, 28, 31, 34; TWA; WLIT 1
Cortes, Hernan 1485-1547 .... **LC 31**
Cortez, Jayne 1936- .... **BLC 2:1**
See also BW 2, 3; CA 73-76; CANR 13, 31, 68, 126; CWP; DLB 41; EWL 3
Corvinus, Jakob
See Raabe, Wilhelm (Karl)
Corwin, Cecil
See Kornbluth, C(yril) M.
Cosic, Dobrica 1921- .... **CLC 14**
See also CA 122; 138; CDWLB 4; CWW 2; DLB 181; EWL 3
Costain, Thomas B(ertram) 1885-1965 . **CLC 30**
See also BYA 3; CA 5-8R; 25-28R; DLB 9; RHW
Costantini, Humberto 1924(?)-1987 ..... **CLC 49**
See also CA 131; 122; EWL 3; HW 1
Costello, Elvis 1954(?)- .... **CLC 21**
See also CA 204
Costenoble, Philostene
See Ghelderode, Michel de

Cotes, Cecil V.
See Duncan, Sara Jeannette
Cotter, Joseph Seamon Sr. 1861-1949 .. **BLC 1:1; TCLC 28**
See also BW 1; CA 124; DAM MULT; DLB 50
Cotton, John 1584-1652 .... **LC 176**
See also DLB 24; TUS
Couch, Arthur Thomas Quiller
See Quiller-Couch, Sir Arthur (Thomas)
Coulton, James
See Hansen, Joseph
Couperus, Louis (Marie Anne) 1863-1923 .. **TCLC 15**
See also CA 115; EWL 3; RGWL 2, 3
Coupland, Douglas 1961- .... **CLC 85, 133**
See also AAYA 34; CA 142; CANR 57, 90, 130, 172, 213; CCA 1; CN 7; CPW; DAC; DAM POP; DLB 334
Coupland, Douglas Campbell
See Coupland, Douglas
Court, Wesli
See Turco, Lewis
Courtenay, Bryce 1933- .... **CLC 59**
See also CA 138; CPW; NFS 32
Courtney, Robert
See Ellison, Harlan
Cousteau, Jacques 1910-1997 .... **CLC 30**
See also CA 65-68; 159; CANR 15, 67, 201; MTCW 1; SATA 38, 98
Cousteau, Jacques-Yves
See Cousteau, Jacques
Coventry, Francis 1725-1754 .... **LC 46**
See also DLB 39
Coverdale, Miles c. 1487-1569 .... **LC 77**
See also DLB 167
Cowan, Peter (Walkinshaw) 1914-2002 . **SSC 28**
See also CA 21-24R; CANR 9, 25, 50, 83; CN 1, 2, 3, 4, 5, 6, 7; DLB 260; RGSF 2
Coward, Noel 1899-1973 .. **CLC 1, 9, 29, 51; DC 45**
See also AITN 1; BRWS 2; CA 17-18; 41-44R; CANR 35, 132, 190; CAP 2; CBD; CDBLB 1914-1945; DA3; DAM DRAM; DFS 3, 6; DLB 10, 245; EWL 3; IDFW 3, 4; MTCW 1, 2; MTFW 2005; RGEL 2; TEA
Coward, Noel Peirce
See Coward, Noel
Cowley, Abraham 1618-1667 . **LC 43; PC 90**
See also BRW 2; DLB 131, 151; PAB; RGEL 2
Cowley, Malcolm 1898-1989 .... **CLC 39**
See also AMWS 2; CA 5-8R; 128; CANR 3, 55; CP 1, 2, 3, 4; DLB 4, 48; DLBY 1981, 1989; EWL 3; MAL 5; MTCW 1, 2; MTFW 2005
Cowper, William 1731-1800 .... **NCLC 8, 94; PC 40**
See also BRW 3; BRWR 3; DA3; DAM POET; DLB 104, 109; RGEL 2
Cox, William Trevor
See Trevor, William
Coyle, William
See Keneally, Thomas
Coyne, P. J.
See Masters, Hilary
Cozzens, James Gould 1903-1978 .... **CLC 1, 4, 11, 92**
See also AMW; BPFB 1; CA 9-12R; 81-84; CANR 19; CDALB 1941-1968; CN 1, 2; DLB 9, 294; DLBD 2; DLBY 1984, 1997; EWL 3; MAL 5; MTCW 1, 2; MTFW 2005; RGAL 4
Crabbe, George 1754-1832 .. **NCLC 26, 121; PC 97**
See also BRW 3; DLB 93; RGEL 2

Cummins, Maria Susanna 1827-1866 .... NCLC **139**
See also DLB 42; YABC 1

Cunha, Euclides (Rodrigues Pimenta) da 1866-1909 .... TCLC **24**
See also CA 123; 219; DLB 307; LAW; WLIT 1

Cunningham, E. V.
See Fast, Howard

Cunningham, J. Morgan
See Westlake, Donald E.

Cunningham, J(ames) V(incent) 1911-1985 .... CLC **3, 31;** PC **92**
See also CA 1-4R; 115; CANR 1, 72; CP 1, 2, 3, 4; DLB 5

Cunningham, Julia (Woolfolk) 1916- .. CLC **12**
See also CA 9-12R; CANR 4, 19, 36; CWRI 5; JRDA; MAICYA 1, 2; SAAS 2; SATA 1, 26, 132

Cunningham, Michael 1952- ... CLC **34, 243**
See also AMWS 15; CA 136; CANR 96, 160, 227; CN 7; DLB 292; GLL 2; MTFW 2005; NFS 23

Cunningham Graham, R. B.
See Cunninghame Graham, Robert Bontine

Cunninghame Graham, Robert Bontine 1852-1936 .... TCLC **19**
See also CA 119; 184; DLB 98, 135, 174; RGEL 2; RGSF 2

Cunninghame Graham, Robert Gallnigad Bontine
See Cunninghame Graham, Robert Bontine

Curnow, (Thomas) Allen (Monro) 1911-2001 .... PC **48**
See also CA 69-72; 202; CANR 48, 99; CP 1, 2, 3, 4, 5, 6, 7; EWL 3; RGEL 2

Currie, Ellen 19(?)- .... CLC **44**

Curtin, Philip
See Lowndes, Marie Adelaide (Belloc)

Curtin, Phillip
See Lowndes, Marie Adelaide (Belloc)

Curtis, Price
See Ellison, Harlan

Cusanus, Nicolaus 1401-1464 ....
See Nicholas of Cusa

Cutrate, Joe
See Spiegelman, Art

Cynewulf fl. 9th cent. - .... CMLC **23, 117**
See also DLB 146; RGEL 2

Cyprian, St. c. 200-258 .... CMLC **127**

Cyrano de Bergerac, Savinien de 1619-1655 .... LC **65**
See also DLB 268; GFL Beginnings to 1789; RGWL 2, 3

Cyril of Alexandria c. 375-c. 430 . CMLC **59**

Czaczkes, Shmuel Yosef Halevi
See Agnon, S. Y.

Dabrowska, Maria (Szumska) 1889-1965 .... CLC **15**
See also CA 106; CDWLB 4; DLB 215; EWL 3

Dabydeen, David 1955- .... CLC **34**
See also BW 1; CA 125; CANR 56, 92; CN 6, 7; CP 5, 6, 7; DLB 347

Dacey, Philip 1939- .... CLC **51**
See also CA 37-40R; 231; CAAE 231; CAAS 17; CANR 14, 32, 64; CP 4, 5, 6, 7; DLB 105

Dacre, Charlotte c. 1772-1825(?) . NCLC **151**

Dafydd ap Gwilym c. 1320-c. 1380 .... PC **56**

Dagerman, Stig (Halvard) 1923-1954 . TCLC **17**
See also CA 117; 155; DLB 259; EWL 3

D'Aguiar, Fred 1960- .... BLC **2:1;** CLC **145**
See also CA 148; CANR 83, 101; CN 7; CP 5, 6, 7; DLB 157; EWL 3

Dahl, Roald 1916-1990 ..... CLC **1, 6, 18, 79;** TCLC **173**
See also AAYA 15; BPFB 1; BRWS 4; BYA 5; CA 1-4R; 133; CANR 6, 32, 37, 62; CLR 1, 7, 41, 111; CN 1, 2, 3, 4; CPW; DA3; DAB; DAC; DAM MST, NOV, POP; DLB 139, 255; HGG; JRDA; MAICYA 1, 2; MTCW 1, 2; MTFW 2005; RGSF 2; SATA 1, 26, 73; SATA-Obit 65; SSFS 4, 30; TEA; YAW

Dahlberg, Edward 1900-1977 ...... CLC **1, 7, 14;** TCLC **208**
See also CA 9-12R; 69-72; CANR 31, 62; CN 1, 2; DLB 48; MAL 5; MTCW 1; RGAL 4

Dahlie, Michael 1970(?)- .... CLC **299**
See also CA 283

Daitch, Susan 1954- .... CLC **103**
See also CA 161

Dale, Colin
See Lawrence, T. E.

Dale, George E.
See Asimov, Isaac

d'Alembert, Jean Le Rond 1717-1783 ... LC **126**

Dalton, Roque 1935-1975(?) .... HLCS **1;** PC **36**
See also CA 176; DLB 283; HW 2

Daly, Elizabeth 1878-1967 .... CLC **52**
See also CA 23-24; 25-28R; CANR 60; CAP 2; CMW 4

Daly, Mary 1928-2010 .... CLC **173**
See also CA 25-28R; CANR 30, 62, 166; FW; GLL 1; MTCW 1

Daly, Maureen 1921-2006 .... CLC **17**
See also AAYA 5, 58; BYA 6; CA 253; CANR 37, 83, 108; CLR 96; JRDA; MAICYA 1, 2; SAAS 1; SATA 2, 129; SATA-Obit 176; WYA; YAW

Damas, Leon-Gontran 1912-1978 .. CLC **84;** TCLC **204**
See also BW 1; CA 125; 73-76; EWL 3

Damocles
See Benedetti, Mario

Dana, Richard Henry Sr. 1787-1879 . NCLC **53**

Dangarembga, Tsitsi 1959- .... BLC **2:1**
See also BW 3; CA 163; DLB 360; NFS 28; WLIT 2

Daniel, Samuel 1562(?)-1619 ...... LC **24, 171**
See also DLB 62; RGEL 2

Daniels, Brett
See Adler, Renata

Dannay, Frederic 1905-1982 .... CLC **3, 11**
See also BPFB 3; CA 1-4R; 107; CANR 1, 39; CMW 4; DAM POP; DLB 137; MSW; MTCW 1; RGAL 4

D'Annunzio, Gabriele 1863-1938 .. TCLC **6, 40, 215**
See also CA 104; 155; EW 8; EWL 3; RGWL 2, 3; TWA; WLIT 7

Danois, N. le
See Gourmont, Remy(-Marie-Charles) de

Dante 1265-1321 ... CMLC **3, 18, 39, 70;** PC **21, 108;** WLCS
See also DA; DA3; DAB; DAC; DAM MST, POET; EFS 1:1, 2:1; EW 1; LAIT 1; RGWL 2, 3; TWA; WLIT 7; WP

d'Antibes, Germain
See Simenon, Georges

Danticat, Edwidge 1969- ...... BLC **2:1;** CLC **94, 139, 228;** SSC **100**
See also AAYA 29, 85; CA 152, 192; CAAE 192; CANR 73, 129, 179; CN 7; DLB 350; DNFS 1; EXPS; LATS 1:2; LNFS 3; MTCW 2; MTFW 2005; NFS 28, 37; SSFS 1, 25; YAW

Danvers, Dennis 1947- .... CLC **70**

Danziger, Paula 1944-2004 .... CLC **21**
See also AAYA 4, 36; BYA 6, 7, 14; CA 112; 115; 229; CANR 37, 132; CLR 20; JRDA; MAICYA 1, 2; MTFW 2005; SATA 36, 63, 102, 149; SATA-Brief 30; SATA-Obit 155; WYA; YAW

Da Ponte, Lorenzo 1749-1838 ...... NCLC **50**

d'Aragona, Tullia 1510(?)-1556 .... LC **121**

Dario, Ruben 1867-1916 ..... HLC **1;** PC **15;** TCLC **4, 265**
See also CA 131; CANR 81; DAM MULT; DLB 290; EWL 3; HW 1, 2; LAW; MTCW 1, 2; MTFW 2005; RGWL 2, 3

Darko, Amma 1956- .... BLC **2:1**

Darley, George 1795-1846 . NCLC **2;** PC **125**
See also DLB 96; RGEL 2

Darrow, Clarence (Seward) 1857-1938 .... TCLC **81**
See also CA 164; DLB 303

Darwin, Charles 1809-1882 .... NCLC **57**
See also BRWS 7; DLB 57, 166; LATS 1:1; RGEL 2; TEA; WLIT 4

Darwin, Erasmus 1731-1802 .... NCLC **106**
See also BRWS 16; DLB 93; RGEL 2

Darwish, Mahmoud 1941-2008 .... PC **86**
See also CA 164; CANR 133; CWW 2; EWL 3; MTCW 2; MTFW 2005

Darwish, Mahmud -2008 ....
See Darwish, Mahmoud

Daryush, Elizabeth 1887-1977 .... CLC **6, 19**
See also CA 49-52; CANR 3, 81; DLB 20

Das, Kamala 1934-2009 .... CLC **191;** PC **43**
See also CA 101; 287; CANR 27, 59; CP 1, 2, 3, 4, 5, 6, 7; CWP; DLB 323; FW

Dasgupta, Surendranath 1887-1952 .. TCLC **81**
See also CA 157

Dashwood, Edmee Elizabeth Monica de la Pasture 1890-1943 .... TCLC **61**
See also CA 119; 154; DLB 34; RHW

da Silva, Antonio Jose 1705-1739 ...... NCLC **114**

Daudet, (Louis Marie) Alphonse 1840-1897 .... NCLC **1**
See also DLB 123; GFL 1789 to the Present; RGSF 2

Daudet, Alphonse Marie Leon 1867-1942 ... SSC **94**
See also CA 217

d'Aulnoy, Marie-Catherine c. 1650-1705 .... LC **100**

Daumal, Rene 1908-1944 .... TCLC **14**
See also CA 114; 247; EWL 3

Davenant, William 1606-1668 ... LC **13, 166;** PC **99**
See also DLB 58, 126; RGEL 2

Davenport, Guy (Mattison, Jr.) 1927-2005 .. CLC **6, 14, 38, 241;** SSC **16**
See also CA 33-36R; 235; CANR 23, 73; CN 3, 4, 5, 6; CSW; DLB 130

David, Robert
See Nezval, Vitezslav

Davidson, Donald (Grady) 1893-1968 . CLC **2, 13, 19**
See also CA 5-8R; 25-28R; CANR 4, 84; DLB 45

Davidson, Hugh
See Hamilton, Edmond

Davidson, John 1857-1909 .... TCLC **24**
See also CA 118; 217; DLB 19; RGEL 2

Davidson, Sara 1943- .... CLC **9**
See also CA 81-84; CANR 44, 68; DLB 185

Davie, Donald (Alfred) 1922-1995 ... CLC **5, 8, 10, 31;** PC **29**
See also BRWS 6; CA 1-4R; 149; CAAS 3; CANR 1, 44; CP 1, 2, 3, 4, 5, 6; DLB 27; MTCW 1; RGEL 2

Diamano, Silmang
See Senghor, Leopold Sedar
Diamant, Anita 1951- .... **CLC 239**
See also CA 145; CANR 126, 219; NFS 36
Diamond, Neil 1941- .... **CLC 30**
See also CA 108
Diaz, Junot 1968- .... **CLC 258; SSC 144**
See also AAYA 83; BYA 12; CA 161;
CANR 119, 183; LLW; NFS 36; SSFS 20
Diaz del Castillo, Bernal c. 1496-1584 ....
HLCS 1; LC 31
See also DLB 318; LAW
di Bassetto, Corno
See Shaw, George Bernard
Dick, Philip K. 1928-1982 .. **CLC 10, 30, 72;**
SSC 57
See also AAYA 24; BPFB 1; BYA 11; CA
49-52; 106; CANR 2, 16, 132; CN 2, 3;
CPW; DA3; DAM NOV, POP; DLB 8;
MTCW 1, 2; MTFW 2005; NFS 5, 26;
SCFW 1, 2; SFW 4
Dick, Philip Kindred
See Dick, Philip K.
Dickens, Charles 1812-1870 . **NCLC 3, 8, 18,**
26, 37, 50, 86, 105, 113, 161, 187, 203,
206, 211, 217, 219, 230, 231, 239; SSC
17, 49, 88; WLC 2
See also AAYA 23; BRW 5; BRWC 1, 2;
BYA 1, 2, 3, 13, 14; CDBLB 1832-1890;
CLR 95, 162; CMW 4; DA; DA3; DAB;
DAC; DAM MST, NOV; DLB 21, 55, 70,
159, 166; EXPN; GL 2; HGG; JRDA;
LAIT 1, 2; LATS 1:1; LMFS 1; MAICYA
1, 2; NFS 4, 5, 10, 14, 20, 25, 30, 33;
RGEL 2; RGSF 2; SATA 15; SUFW 1;
TEA; WCH; WLIT 4; WYA
Dickens, Charles John Huffam
See Dickens, Charles
Dickey, James 1923-1997 ..... **CLC 1, 2, 4, 7,**
10, 15, 47, 109; PC 40; TCLC 151
See also AAYA 50; AITN 1, 2; AMWS 4;
BPFB 1; CA 9-12R; 156; CABS 2; CANR
10, 48, 61, 105; CDALB 1968-1988; CP
1, 2, 3, 4, 5, 6; CPW; CSW; DA3; DAM
NOV, POET, POP; DLB 5, 193, 342;
DLBD 7; DLBY 1982, 1994, 1996, 1997,
1998; EWL 3; INT CANR-10; MAL 5;
MTCW 1, 2; NFS 9; PFS 6, 11; RGAL 4;
TUS
Dickey, James Lafayette
See Dickey, James
Dickey, William 1928-1994 .... **CLC 3, 28**
See also CA 9-12R; 145; CANR 24, 79; CP
1, 2, 3, 4; DLB 5
Dickinson, Charles 1951- .... **CLC 49**
See also CA 128; CANR 141
Dickinson, Emily 1830-1886 .. **NCLC 21, 77,**
171; PC 1; WLC 2
See also AAYA 22; AMW; AMWR 1;
CDALB 1865-1917; DA; DA3; DAB;
DAC; DAM MST, POET; DLB 1, 243;
EXPP; FL 1:3; MBL; PAB; PFS 1, 2, 3,
4, 5, 6, 8, 10, 11, 13, 16, 28, 32, 35;
RGAL 4; SATA 29; TUS; WP; WYA
Dickinson, Emily Elizabeth
See Dickinson, Emily
Dickinson, Mrs. Herbert Ward
See Phelps, Elizabeth Stuart
Dickinson, Peter 1927- .... **CLC 12, 35**
See also AAYA 9, 49; BYA 5; CA 41-44R;
CANR 31, 58, 88, 134, 195; CLR 29, 125;
CMW 4; DLB 87, 161, 276; JRDA; MAI-
CYA 1, 2; SATA 5, 62, 95, 150, 229; SFW
4; WYA; YAW
Dickinson, Peter Malcolm de Brissac
See Dickinson, Peter
Dickson, Carr
See Carr, John Dickson

Dickson, Carter
See Carr, John Dickson
Diderot, Denis 1713-1784 .... **LC 26, 126**
See also DLB 313; EW 4; GFL Beginnings
to 1789; LMFS 1; RGWL 2, 3
Didion, Joan 1934- . **CLC 1, 3, 8, 14, 32, 129**
See also AITN 1; AMWS 4; CA 5-8R;
CANR 14, 52, 76, 125, 174; CDALB
1968-1988; CN 2, 3, 4, 5, 6, 7; DA3;
DAM NOV; DLB 2, 173, 185; DLBY
1981, 1986; EWL 3; MAL 5; MBL;
MTCW 1, 2; MTFW 2005; NFS 3; RGAL
4; TCLE 1:1; TCWW 2; TUS
di Donato, Pietro 1911-1992 .... **TCLC 159**
See also AMWS 20; CA 101; 136; DLB 9
Dietrich, Robert
See Hunt, E. Howard
Difusa, Pati
See Almodovar, Pedro
di Lampedusa, Giuseppe Tomasi
See Lampedusa, Giuseppe di
Dillard, Annie 1945- .... **CLC 9, 60, 115, 216**
See also AAYA 6, 43; AMWS 6; ANW; CA
49-52; CANR 3, 43, 62, 90, 125, 214;
DA3; DAM NOV; DLB 275, 278; DLBY
1980; LAIT 4, 5; MAL 5; MTCW 1, 2;
MTFW 2005; NCFS 1; RGAL 4; SATA
10, 140; TCLE 1:1; TUS
Dillard, R(ichard) H(enry) W(ilde) 1937- ...
CLC 5
See also CA 21-24R; CAAS 7; CANR 10;
CP 2, 3, 4, 5, 6, 7; CSW; DLB 5, 244
Dillon, Eilis 1920-1994 .... **CLC 17**
See also CA 9-12R; 182; 147; CAAE 182;
CAAS 3; CANR 4, 38, 78; CLR 26; MAI-
CYA 1, 2; MAICYAS 1; SATA 2, 74;
SATA-Essay 105; SATA-Obit 83; YAW
Dimont, Penelope
See Mortimer, Penelope (Ruth)
Dinesen, Isak
See Blixen, Karen
Ding Ling
See Chiang, Pin-chin
Diodorus Siculus c. 90B.C.-c. 31B.C. . **CMLC**
88
Dionysius of Halicarnassus c. 60B.C.-c.
7B.C. .... **CMLC 126**
Diphusa, Patty
See Almodovar, Pedro
Disch, Thomas M. 1940-2008 ...... **CLC 7, 36**
See also AAYA 17; BPFB 1; CA 21-24R;
274; CAAS 4; CANR 17, 36, 54, 89; CLR
18; CP 5, 6, 7; DA3; DLB 8, 282; HGG;
MAICYA 1, 2; MTCW 1, 2; MTFW 2005;
SAAS 15; SATA 92; SATA-Obit 195;
SCFW 1, 2; SFW 4; SUFW 2
Disch, Thomas Michael
See Disch, Thomas M.
Disch, Tom
See Disch, Thomas M.
d'Isly, Georges
See Simenon, Georges
Disraeli, Benjamin 1804-1881 . **NCLC 2, 39,**
79
See also BRW 4; DLB 21, 55; RGEL 2
D'Israeli, Isaac 1766-1848 .... **NCLC 217**
See also DLB 107
Ditcum, Steve
See Crumb, R.
Divakaruni, Chitra Banerjee 1956- ..... **CLC**
316
See also CA 182; CANR 127, 189, 226; CN
7; DLB 323; NFS 38; PFS 34; SATA 160,
222; SSFS 18, 24
Dixon, Paige
See Corcoran, Barbara (Asenath)
Dixon, Stephen 1936- .... **CLC 52; SSC 16**
See also AMWS 12; CA 89-92; CANR 17,
40, 54, 91, 175; CN 4, 5, 6, 7; DLB 130;
MAL 5

Dixon, Thomas, Jr. 1864-1946 .... **TCLC 163**
See also RHW
Djebar, Assia 1936- ...... **BLC 2:1; CLC 182,**
296; SSC 114
See also CA 188; CANR 169; DLB 346;
EWL 3; RGWL 3; WLIT 2
Doak, Annie
See Dillard, Annie
Dobell, Sydney Thompson 1824-1874 ....
NCLC 43; PC 100
See also DLB 32; RGEL 2
Doblin, Alfred
See Doeblin, Alfred
Dobroliubov, Nikolai Aleksandrovich
See Dobrolyubov, Nikolai Alexandrovich
Dobrolyubov, Nikolai Alexandrovich
1836-1861 .... **NCLC 5**
See also DLB 277
Dobson, Austin 1840-1921 .... **TCLC 79**
See also DLB 35, 144
Dobyns, Stephen 1941- .... **CLC 37, 233**
See also AMWS 13; CA 45-48; CANR 2,
18, 99; CMW 4; CP 4, 5, 6, 7; PFS 23
Doctorow, Cory 1971- .... **CLC 273**
See also AAYA 84; CA 221; CANR 203
Doctorow, E. L. 1931- ..... **CLC 6, 11, 15, 18,**
37, 44, 65, 113, 214
See also AAYA 22; AITN 2; AMWS 4;
BEST 89:3; BPFB 1; CA 45-48; CANR
2, 33, 51, 76, 97, 133, 170, 218; CDALB
1968-1988; CN 3, 4, 5, 6, 7; CPW; DA3;
DAM NOV, POP; DLB 2, 28, 173; DLBY
1980; EWL 3; LAIT 3; MAL 5; MTCW
1, 2; MTFW 2005; NFS 6; RGAL 4;
RGHL; RHW; SSFS 27; TCLE 1:1;
TCWW 1, 2; TUS
Doctorow, Edgar Lawrence
See Doctorow, E. L.
Dodgson, Charles Lutwidge
See Carroll, Lewis
Dodsley, Robert 1703-1764 .... **LC 97**
See also DLB 95, 154; RGEL 2
Dodson, Owen (Vincent) 1914-1983 ..... **BLC**
1:1; CLC 79
See also BW 1; CA 65-68; 110; CANR 24;
DAM MULT; DLB 76
Doeblin, Alfred 1878-1957 .... **TCLC 13**
See also CA 110; 141; CDWLB 2; DLB 66;
EWL 3; RGWL 2, 3
Doerr, Harriet 1910-2002 .... **CLC 34**
See also CA 117; 122; 213; CANR 47; INT
CA-122; LATS 1:2
Domecq, Honorio Bustos
See Bioy Casares, Adolfo; Borges, Jorge
Luis
Domini, Rey
See Lorde, Audre
Dominic, R. B.
See Hennissart, Martha
Dominique
See Proust, Marcel
Don, A
See Stephen, Sir Leslie
Donaldson, Stephen R. 1947- .. **CLC 46, 138**
See also AAYA 36; BPFB 1; CA 89-92;
CANR 13, 55, 99, 228; CPW; DAM POP;
FANT; INT CANR-13; SATA 121; SFW
4; SUFW 1, 2
Donleavy, J(ames) P(atrick) 1926- ... **CLC 1,**
4, 6, 10, 45
See also AITN 2; BPFB 1; CA 9-12R;
CANR 24, 49, 62, 80, 124; CBD; CD 5,
6; CN 1, 2, 3, 4, 5, 6, 7; DLB 6, 173; INT
CANR-24; MAL 5; MTCW 1, 2; MTFW
2005; RGAL 4
Donnadieu, Marguerite
See Duras, Marguerite

Donne, John 1572-1631 .. **LC 10, 24, 91; PC 1, 43; WLC 2**
See also AAYA 67; BRW 1; BRWC 1; BRWR 2; CDBLB Before 1660; DA; DAB; DAC; DAM MST, POET; DLB 121, 151; EXPP; PAB; PFS 2, 11, 35, 41; RGEL 3; TEA; WLIT 3; WP

Donnell, David 1939(?)- .... **CLC 34**
See also CA 197

Donoghue, Denis 1928- .... **CLC 209**
See also CA 17-20R; CANR 16, 102, 206

Donoghue, Emma 1969- .... **CLC 239**
See also CA 155; CANR 103, 152, 196; DLB 267; GLL 2; SATA 101

Donoghue, P.S.
See Hunt, E. Howard

Donoso, Jose 1924-1996 .... **CLC 4, 8, 11, 32, 99; HLC 1; SSC 34; TCLC 133**
See also CA 81-84; 155; CANR 32, 73; CD-WLB 3; CWW 2; DAM MULT; DLB 113; EWL 3; HW 1, 2; LAW; LAWS 1; MTCW 1, 2; MTFW 2005; RGSF 2; WLIT 1

Donoso Yanez, Jose
See Donoso, Jose

Donovan, John 1928-1992 .... **CLC 35**
See also AAYA 20; CA 97-100; 137; CLR 3; MAICYA 1, 2; SATA 72; SATA-Brief 29; YAW

Don Roberto
See Cunninghame Graham, Robert Bontine

Doolittle, Hilda 1886-1961 ...... **CLC 3, 8, 14, 31, 34, 73; PC 5, 127; WLC 3**
See also AAYA 66; AMWS 1; CA 97-100; CANR 35, 131; DA; DAC; DAM MST, POET; DLB 4, 45; EWL 3; FL 1:5; FW; GLL 1; LMFS 2; MAL 5; MBL; MTCW 1, 2; MTFW 2005; PFS 6, 28; RGAL 4

Doppo
See Kunikida Doppo

Doppo, Kunikida
See Kunikida Doppo

Dorfman, Ariel 1942- .... **CLC 48, 77, 189; HLC 1**
See also CA 124; 130; CANR 67, 70, 135; CWW 2; DAM MULT; DFS 4; EWL 3; HW 1, 2; INT CA-130; WLIT 1

Dorn, Edward 1929-1999 .. **CLC 10, 18; PC 115**
See also CA 93-96; 187; CANR 42, 79; CP 1, 2, 3, 4, 5, 6, 7; DLB 5; INT CA-93-96; WP

Dorn, Edward Merton
See Dorn, Edward

Dor-Ner, Zvi CLC 70

Dorris, Michael 1945-1997 .... **CLC 109; NNAL**
See also AAYA 20; BEST 90:1; BYA 12; CA 102; 157; CANR 19, 46, 75; CLR 58; DA3; DAM MULT, NOV; DLB 175; LAIT 5; MTCW 2; MTFW 2005; NFS 3; RGAL 4; SATA 75; SATA-Obit 94; TCWW 2; YAW

Dorris, Michael A.
See Dorris, Michael

Dorris, Michael Anthony
See Dorris, Michael

Dorsan, Luc
See Simenon, Georges

Dorsange, Jean
See Simenon, Georges

Dorset
See Sackville, Thomas

Dos Passos, John 1896-1970 .... **CLC 1, 4, 8, 11, 15, 25, 34, 82; WLC 2**
See also AMW; BPFB 1; CA 1-4R; 29-32R; CANR 3; CDALB 1929-1941; DA; DA3; DAB; DAC; DAM MST, NOV; DLB 4,

9, 274, 316; DLBD 1, 15; DLBY 1996; EWL 3; MAL 5; MTCW 1, 2; MTFW 2005; NFS 14; RGAL 4; TUS

Dos Passos, John Roderigo
See Dos Passos, John

Dossage, Jean
See Simenon, Georges

Dostoevsky, Fedor
See Dostoevsky, Fyodor

Dostoevsky, Fedor Mikhailovich
See Dostoevsky, Fyodor

Dostoevsky, Fyodor 1821-1881 .. **NCLC 2, 7, 21, 33, 43, 119, 167, 202, 238; SSC 2, 33, 44, 134; WLC 2**
See also AAYA 40; DA; DA3; DAB; DAC; DAM MST, NOV; DLB 238; EW 7; EXPN; LATS 1:1; LMFS 1, 2; NFS 28; RGSF 2; RGWL 2, 3; SSFS 8, 30; TWA

Doty, Mark 1953(?)- .... **CLC 176; PC 53**
See also AMWS 11; CA 161, 183; CAAE 183; CANR 110, 173; CP 7; PFS 28, 40

Doty, Mark A.
See Doty, Mark

Doty, Mark Alan
See Doty, Mark

Doty, M.R.
See Doty, Mark

Doughty, Charles M(ontagu) 1843-1926 ...... **TCLC 27**
See also CA 115; 178; DLB 19, 57, 174

Douglas, Ellen 1921- .... **CLC 73**
See also CA 115; CANR 41, 83; CN 5, 6, 7; CSW; DLB 292

Douglas, Gavin 1475(?)-1522 .... **LC 20**
See also DLB 132; RGEL 2

Douglas, George
See Brown, George Douglas

Douglas, Keith (Castellain) 1920-1944 ... **PC 106; TCLC 40**
See also BRW 7; CA 160; DLB 27; EWL 3; PAB; RGEL 2

Douglas, Leonard
See Bradbury, Ray

Douglas, Michael
See Crichton, Michael

Douglas, (George) Norman 1868-1952 .... **TCLC 68**
See also BRW 6; CA 119; 157; DLB 34, 195; RGEL 2

Douglas, William
See Brown, George Douglas

Douglass, Frederick 1817(?)-1895 . **BLC 1:1; NCLC 7, 55, 141, 235; WLC 2**
See also AAYA 48; AFAW 1, 2; AMWC 1; AMWS 3; CDALB 1640-1865; DA; DA3; DAC; DAM MST, MULT; DLB 1, 43, 50, 79, 243; FW; LAIT 2; NCFS 2; RGAL 4; SATA 29

Dourado, (Waldomiro Freitas) Autran 1926- .... **CLC 23, 60**
See also CA 25-28R; 179; CANR 34, 81; DLB 145, 307; HW 2

Dourado, Waldomiro Freitas Autran
See Dourado, (Waldomiro Freitas) Autran

Dove, Rita 1952- . **BLC 2:1; BLCS; CLC 50, 81; PC 6**
See also AAYA 46; AMWS 4; BW 2; CA 109; CAAS 19; CANR 27, 42, 68, 76, 97, 132, 217; CDALBS; CP 5, 6, 7; CSW; CWP; DA3; DAM MULT, POET; DLB 120; EWL 3; EXPP; MAL 5; MTCW 2; MTFW 2005; PFS 1, 15, 37; RGAL 4

Dove, Rita Frances
See Dove, Rita

Doveglion
See Villa, Jose Garcia

Dowell, Coleman 1925-1985 .... **CLC 60**
See also CA 25-28R; 117; CANR 10; DLB 130; GLL 2

Downing, Major Jack
See Smith, Seba

Dowson, Ernest (Christopher) 1867-1900 ... **TCLC 4**
See also CA 105; 150; DLB 19, 135; RGEL 2

Doyle, A. Conan
See Doyle, Sir Arthur Conan

Doyle, Sir Arthur Conan 1859-1930 ..... **SSC 12, 83, 95; TCLC 7; WLC 2**
See also AAYA 14; BPFB 1; BRWS 2; BYA 4, 5, 11; CA 104; 122; CANR 131; CD-BLB 1890-1914; CLR 106; CMW 4; DA; DA3; DAB; DAC; DAM MST, NOV; DLB 18, 70, 156, 178; EXPS; HGG; LAIT 2; MSW; MTCW 1, 2; MTFW 2005; NFS 28; RGEL 2; RGSF 2; RHW; SATA 24; SCFW 1, 2; SFW 4; SSFS 2; TEA; WCH; WLIT 4; WYA; YAW

Doyle, Conan
See Doyle, Sir Arthur Conan

Doyle, John
See Graves, Robert

Doyle, Roddy 1958- .... **CLC 81, 178**
See also AAYA 14; BRWS 5; CA 143; CANR 73, 128, 168, 200; CN 6, 7; DA3; DLB 194, 326; MTCW 2; MTFW 2005

Doyle, Sir A. Conan
See Doyle, Sir Arthur Conan

Dr. A
See Asimov, Isaac; Silverstein, Alvin; Silverstein, Virginia B.

Drabble, Margaret 1939- ..... **CLC 2, 3, 5, 8, 10, 22, 53, 129**
See also BRWS 4; CA 13-16R; CANR 18, 35, 63, 112, 131, 174, 218; CDBLB 1960 to Present; CN 1, 2, 3, 4, 5, 6, 7; CPW; DA3; DAB; DAC; DAM MST, NOV, POP; DLB 14, 155, 231; EWL 3; FW; MTCW 1, 2; MTFW 2005; RGEL 2; SATA 48; TEA

Drakulic, Slavenka
See Drakulic, Slavenka

Drakulic, Slavenka 1949- .... **CLC 173**
See also CA 144; CANR 92, 198, 229; DLB 353

Drakulic-Ilic, Slavenka
See Drakulic, Slavenka

Drakulic-Ilic, Slavenka
See Drakulic, Slavenka

Drapier, M. B.
See Swift, Jonathan

Drayham, James
See Mencken, H. L.

Drayton, Michael 1563-1631 . **LC 8, 161; PC 98**
See also DAM POET; DLB 121; RGEL 2

Dreadstone, Carl
See Campbell, Ramsey

Dreiser, Theodore 1871-1945 ... **SSC 30, 114; TCLC 10, 18, 35, 83; WLC 2**
See also AMW; AMWC 2; AMWR 2; BYA 15, 16; CA 106; 132; CDALB 1865-1917; DA; DA3; DAC; DAM MST, NOV; DLB 9, 12, 102, 137, 361; DLBD 1; EWL 3; LAIT 2; LMFS 2; MAL 5; MTCW 1, 2; MTFW 2005; NFS 8, 17; RGAL 4; TUS

Dreiser, Theodore Herman Albert
See Dreiser, Theodore

Drexler, Rosalyn 1926- .... **CLC 2, 6**
See also CA 81-84; CAD; CANR 68, 124; CD 5, 6; CWD; MAL 5

Dreyer, Carl Theodor 1889-1968 .... **CLC 16**
See also CA 116

Drieu la Rochelle, Pierre 1893-1945 . **TCLC 21**
See also CA 117; 250; DLB 72; EWL 3; GFL 1789 to the Present

270, 351; EXPP; LAIT 2; LMFS 1; NCFS 3; PFS 4, 17, 34; RGAL 4; TUS; WP

Eminem 1972- .... **CLC 226**
See also CA 245

Eminescu, Mihail 1850-1889 . **NCLC 33, 131**

Empedocles 5th cent. B.C.- .... **CMLC 50**
See also DLB 176

Empson, William 1906-1984 .. **CLC 3, 8, 19, 33, 34; PC 104**
See also BRWS 2; CA 17-20R; 112; CANR 31, 61; CP 1, 2, 3; DLB 20; EWL 3; MTCW 1, 2; RGEL 2

Enchi, Fumiko 1905-1986 .... **CLC 31**
See also CA 129; 121; DLB 182; EWL 3; FW; MJW

Enchi, Fumiko Ueda
See Enchi, Fumiko

Enchi Fumiko
See Enchi, Fumiko

Ende, Michael (Andreas Helmuth) 1929-1995 .... **CLC 31**
See also BYA 5; CA 118; 124; 149; CANR 36, 110; CLR 14, 138; DLB 75; MAICYA 1, 2; MAICYAS 1; SATA 61, 130; SATA-Brief 42; SATA-Obit 86

Endo, Shusaku 1923-1996 .... **CLC 7, 14, 19, 54, 99; SSC 48; TCLC 152**
See also CA 29-32R; 153; CANR 21, 54, 131; CWW 2; DA3; DAM NOV; DLB 182; EWL 3; MTCW 1, 2; MTFW 2005; RGSF 2; RGWL 2, 3

Endo Shusaku
See Endo, Shusaku

Engel, Marian 1933-1985 ... **CLC 36; TCLC 137**
See also CA 25-28R; CANR 12; CN 2, 3; DLB 53; FW; INT CANR-12

Engelhardt, Frederick
See Hubbard, L. Ron

Engels, Friedrich 1820-1895 . **NCLC 85, 114**
See also DLB 129; LATS 1:1

Enquist, Per Olov 1934- .... **CLC 257**
See also CA 109; 193; CANR 155; CWW 2; DLB 257; EWL 3

Enright, D(ennis) J(oseph) 1920-2002 . **CLC 4, 8, 31; PC 93**
See also CA 1-4R; 211; CANR 1, 42, 83; CN 1, 2; CP 1, 2, 3, 4, 5, 6, 7; DLB 27; EWL 3; SATA 25; SATA-Obit 140

Ensler, Eve 1953- .... **CLC 212**
See also CA 172; CANR 126, 163; DFS 23

Enzensberger, Hans Magnus 1929- ...... **CLC 43; PC 28**
See also CA 116; 119; CANR 103; CWW 2; EWL 3

Ephron, Nora 1941- .... **CLC 17, 31**
See also AAYA 35; AITN 2; CA 65-68; CANR 12, 39, 83, 161; DFS 22

Epictetus c. 55-c. 135 .... **CMLC 126**
See also AW 2; DLB 176

Epicurus 341B.C.-270B.C. .... **CMLC 21**
See also DLB 176

Epinay, Louise d' 1726-1783 .... **LC 138**
See also DLB 313

Epsilon
See Betjeman, John

Epstein, Daniel Mark 1948- .... **CLC 7**
See also CA 49-52; CANR 2, 53, 90, 193

Epstein, Jacob 1956- .... **CLC 19**
See also CA 114

Epstein, Jean 1897-1953 .... **TCLC 92**

Epstein, Joseph 1937- .... **CLC 39, 204**
See also AMWS 14; CA 112; 119; CANR 50, 65, 117, 164, 190, 225

Epstein, Leslie 1938- .... **CLC 27**
See also AMWS 12; CA 73-76, 215; CAAE 215; CAAS 12; CANR 23, 69, 162; DLB 299; RGHL

Equiano, Olaudah 1745(?)-1797 ... **BLC 1:2; LC 16, 143**
See also AFAW 1, 2; AMWS 17; CDWLB 3; DAM MULT; DLB 37, 50; WLIT 2

Erasmus, Desiderius 1469(?)-1536 .... **LC 16, 93**
See also DLB 136; EW 2; LMFS 1; RGWL 2, 3; TWA

Ercilla y Zuniga, Don Alonso de 1533-1594 .... **LC 190**
See also LAW

Erdman, Paul E. 1932-2007 .... **CLC 25**
See also AITN 1; CA 61-64; 259; CANR 13, 43, 84

Erdman, Paul Emil
See Erdman, Paul E.

Erdrich, Karen Louise
See Erdrich, Louise

Erdrich, Louise 1954- .... **CLC 39, 54, 120, 176; NNAL; PC 52; SSC 121**
See also AAYA 10, 47; AMWS 4; BEST 89:1; BPFB 1; CA 114; CANR 41, 62, 118, 138, 190; CDALBS; CN 5, 6, 7; CP 6, 7; CPW; CWP; DA3; DAM MULT, NOV, POP; DLB 152, 175, 206; EWL 3; EXPP; FL 1:5; LAIT 5; LATS 1:2; MAL 5; MTCW 1, 2; MTFW 2005; NFS 5, 37, 40; PFS 14; RGAL 4; SATA 94, 141; SSFS 14, 22, 30; TCWW 2

Erenburg, Ilya
See Ehrenburg, Ilya

Erenburg, Ilya Grigoryevich
See Ehrenburg, Ilya

Erickson, Stephen Michael
See Erickson, Steve

Erickson, Steve 1950- .... **CLC 64**
See also CA 129; CANR 60, 68, 136, 195; MTFW 2005; SFW 4; SUFW 2

Erickson, Walter
See Fast, Howard

Ericson, Walter
See Fast, Howard

Eriksson, Buntel
See Bergman, Ingmar

Eriugena, John Scottus c. 810-877 ... **CMLC 65**
See also DLB 115

Ernaux, Annie 1940- .... **CLC 88, 184**
See also CA 147; CANR 93, 208; MTFW 2005; NCFS 3, 5

Erskine, John 1879-1951 .... **TCLC 84**
See also CA 112; 159; DLB 9, 102; FANT

Erwin, Will
See Eisner, Will

Eschenbach, Wolfram von
See von Eschenbach, Wolfram

Eseki, Bruno
See Mphahlele, Es'kia

Esekie, Bruno
See Mphahlele, Es'kia

Esenin, S.A.
See Esenin, Sergei

Esenin, Sergei 1895-1925 .... **TCLC 4**
See also CA 104; EWL 3; RGWL 2, 3

Esenin, Sergei Aleksandrovich
See Esenin, Sergei

Eshleman, Clayton 1935- .... **CLC 7**
See also CA 33-36R, 212; CAAE 212; CAAS 6; CANR 93; CP 1, 2, 3, 4, 5, 6, 7; DLB 5

Espada, Martin 1957- .... **PC 74**
See also CA 159; CANR 80; CP 7; EXPP; LLW; MAL 5; PFS 13, 16

Espriella, Don Manuel Alvarez
See Southey, Robert

Espriu, Salvador 1913-1985 .... **CLC 9**
See also CA 154; 115; DLB 134; EWL 3

Espronceda, Jose de 1808-1842 .... **NCLC 39**

Esquivel, Laura 1950- ... **CLC 141; HLCS 1**
See also AAYA 29; CA 143; CANR 68, 113, 161; DA3; DNFS 2; LAIT 3; LMFS 2; MTCW 2; MTFW 2005; NFS 5; WLIT 1

Esse, James
See Stephens, James

Esterbrook, Tom
See Hubbard, L. Ron

Esterhazy, Peter 1950- .... **CLC 251**
See also CA 140; CANR 137, 223; CDWLB 4; CWW 2; DLB 232; EWL 3; RGWL 3

Estleman, Loren D. 1952- .... **CLC 48**
See also AAYA 27; CA 85-88; CANR 27, 74, 139, 177; CMW 4; CPW; DA3; DAM NOV, POP; DLB 226; INT CANR-27; MTCW 1, 2; MTFW 2005; TCWW 1, 2

Etherege, Sir George 1636-1692 . **DC 23; LC 78**
See also BRW 2; DAM DRAM; DLB 80; PAB; RGEL 2

Euclid 306B.C.-283B.C. .... **CMLC 25**

Eugenides, Jeffrey 1960- .. **CLC 81, 212, 312**
See also AAYA 51; CA 144; CANR 120; DLB 350; MTFW 2005; NFS 24

Euripides c. 484B.C.-406B.C. ...... **CMLC 23, 51; DC 4; WLCS**
See also AW 1; CDWLB 1; DA; DA3; DAB; DAC; DAM DRAM, MST; DFS 1, 4, 6, 25, 27; DLB 176; LAIT 1; LMFS 1; RGWL 2, 3; WLIT 8

Eusebius c. 263-c. 339 .... **CMLC 103**

Evan, Evin
See Faust, Frederick

Evans, Caradoc 1878-1945 .. **SSC 43; TCLC 85**
See also DLB 162

Evans, Evan
See Faust, Frederick

Evans, Marian
See Eliot, George

Evans, Mary Ann
See Eliot, George

Evarts, Esther
See Benson, Sally

Evelyn, John 1620-1706 .... **LC 144**
See also BRW 2; RGEL 2

Everett, Percival 1956- .... **CLC 57, 304**
See also AMWS 18; BW 2; CA 129; CANR 94, 134, 179, 219; CN 7; CSW; DLB 350; MTFW 2005

Everett, Percival L.
See Everett, Percival

Everson, R(onald) G(ilmour) 1903-1992 ..... **CLC 27**
See also CA 17-20R; CP 1, 2, 3, 4; DLB 88

Everson, William 1912-1994 ... **CLC 1, 5, 14**
See also BG 1:2; CA 9-12R; 145; CANR 20; CP 1; DLB 5, 16, 212; MTCW 1

Everson, William Oliver
See Everson, William

Evtushenko, Evgenii Aleksandrovich
See Yevtushenko, Yevgenyn

Ewart, Gavin (Buchanan) 1916-1995 .. **CLC 13, 46**
See also BRWS 7; CA 89-92; 150; CANR 17, 46; CP 1, 2, 3, 4, 5, 6; DLB 40; MTCW 1

Ewers, Hanns Heinz 1871-1943 .... **TCLC 12**
See also CA 109; 149

Ewing, Frederick R.
See Sturgeon, Theodore (Hamilton)

Exley, Frederick (Earl) 1929-1992 ... **CLC 6, 11**
See also AITN 2; BPFB 1; CA 81-84; 138; CANR 117; DLB 143; DLBY 1981

Eynhardt, Guillermo
  See Quiroga, Horacio (Sylvestre)
Ezekiel, Nissim (Moses) 1924-2004 . **CLC 61**
  See also CA 61-64; 223; CP 1, 2, 3, 4, 5, 6, 7; DLB 323; EWL 3
Ezekiel, Tish O'Dowd 1943- .... **CLC 34**
  See also CA 129
Fadeev, Aleksandr Aleksandrovich
  See Bulgya, Alexander Alexandrovich
Fadeev, Alexandr Alexandrovich
  See Bulgya, Alexander Alexandrovich
Fadeyev, A.
  See Bulgya, Alexander Alexandrovich
Fadeyev, Alexander
  See Bulgya, Alexander Alexandrovich
Fagen, Donald 1948- .... **CLC 26**
Fainzil'berg, Il'ia Arnol'dovich
  See Fainzilberg, Ilya Arnoldovich
Fainzilberg, Ilya Arnoldovich 1897-1937 .....
    TCLC 21
  See also CA 120; 165; DLB 272; EWL 3
Fair, Ronald L. 1932- .... **CLC 18**
  See also BW 1; CA 69-72; CANR 25; DLB 33
Fairbairn, Roger
  See Carr, John Dickson
Fairbairns, Zoe (Ann) 1948- .... **CLC 32**
  See also CA 103; CANR 21, 85; CN 4, 5, 6, 7
Fairfield, Flora
  See Alcott, Louisa May
Falco, Gian
  See Papini, Giovanni
Falconer, James
  See Kirkup, James
Falconer, Kenneth
  See Kornbluth, C(yril) M.
Falkland, Samuel
  See Heijermans, Herman
Fallaci, Oriana 1930-2006 .... **CLC 11, 110**
  See also CA 77-80; 253; CANR 15, 58, 134; FW; MTCW 1
Faludi, Susan 1959- .... **CLC 140**
  See also CA 138; CANR 126, 194; FW; MTCW 2; MTFW 2005; NCFS 3
Faludy, George 1913- .... **CLC 42**
  See also CA 21-24R
Faludy, Gyoergy
  See Faludy, George
Fanon, Frantz 1925-1961 ..... **BLC 1:2; CLC 74; TCLC 188**
  See also BW 1; CA 116; 89-92; DAM MULT; DLB 296; LMFS 2; WLIT 2
Fanshawe, Ann 1625-1680 .... **LC 11**
Fante, John (Thomas) 1911-1983 .. **CLC 60; SSC 65**
  See also AMWS 11; CA 69-72; 109; CANR 23, 104; DLB 130; DLBY 1983
Farah, Nuruddin 1945- . **BLC 1:2, 2:2; CLC 53, 137**
  See also AFW; BW 2, 3; CA 106; CANR 81, 148; CDWLB 3; CN 4, 5, 6, 7; DAM MULT; DLB 125; EWL 3; WLIT 2
Fardusi
  See Ferdowsi, Abu'l Qasem
Fargue, Leon-Paul 1876(?)-1947 ... **TCLC 11**
  See also CA 109; CANR 107; DLB 258; EWL 3
Farigoule, Louis
  See Romains, Jules
Farina, Richard 1936(?)-1966 .... **CLC 9**
  See also CA 81-84; 25-28R
Farley, Walter (Lorimer) 1915-1989 .... **CLC 17**
  See also AAYA 58; BYA 14; CA 17-20R; CANR 8, 29, 84; DLB 22; JRDA; MAI-CYA 1, 2; SATA 2, 43, 132; YAW

Farmer, Philip Jose
  See Farmer, Philip Jose
Farmer, Philip Jose 1918-2009 .. **CLC 1, 19, 299**
  See also AAYA 28; BPFB 1; CA 1-4R; 283; CANR 4, 35, 111, 220; DLB 8; MTCW 1; SATA 93; SATA-Obit 201; SCFW 1, 2; SFW 4
Farmer, Philipe Jos
  See Farmer, Philip Jose
Farquhar, George 1677-1707 . **DC 38; LC 21**
  See also BRW 2; DAM DRAM; DLB 84; RGEL 2
Farrell, James Gordon
  See Farrell, J.G.
Farrell, James T(homas) 1904-1979 . **CLC 1, 4, 8, 11, 66; SSC 28; TCLC 228**
  See also AMW; BPFB 1; CA 5-8R; 89-92; CANR 9, 61; CN 1, 2; DLB 4, 9, 86; DLBD 2; EWL 3; MAL 5; MTCW 1, 2; MTFW 2005; RGAL 4
Farrell, J.G. 1935-1979 .... **CLC 6**
  See also CA 73-76; 89-92; CANR 36; CN 1, 2; DLB 14, 271, 326; MTCW 1; RGEL 2; RHW; WLIT 4
Farrell, M. J.
  See Keane, Mary Nesta
Farrell, Warren (Thomas) 1943- ..... **CLC 70**
  See also CA 146; CANR 120
Farren, Richard J.
  See Betjeman, John
Farren, Richard M.
  See Betjeman, John
Farrugia, Mario Benedetti
  See Bentley, Eric
Farrugia, Mario Orlando Hardy Hamlet Brenno Benedetti
  See Benedetti, Mario
Fassbinder, Rainer Werner 1946-1982 . **CLC 20**
  See also CA 93-96; 106; CANR 31
Fast, Howard 1914-2003 .... **CLC 23, 131**
  See also AAYA 16; BPFB 1; CA 1-4R, 181; 214; CAAE 181; CAAS 18; CANR 1, 33, 54, 75, 98, 140; CMW 4; CN 1, 2, 3, 4, 5, 6, 7; CPW; DAM NOV; DLB 9; INT CANR-33; LATS 1:1; MAL 5; MTCW 2; MTFW 2005; NFS 35; RHW; SATA 7; SATA-Essay 107; TCWW 1, 2; YAW
Faulcon, Robert
  See Holdstock, Robert
Faulkner, William 1897-1962 ... **CLC 1, 3, 6, 8, 9, 11, 14, 18, 28, 52, 68; SSC 1, 35, 42, 92, 97; TCLC 141; WLC 2**
  See also AAYA 7; AMW; AMWR 1; BPFB 1; BYA 5, 15; CA 81-84; CANR 33; CDALB 1929-1941; DA; DA3; DAB; DAC; DAM MST, NOV; DLB 9, 11, 44, 102, 316, 330; DLBD 2; DLBY 1986, 1997; EWL 3; EXPN; EXPS; GL 2; LAIT 2; LATS 1:1; LMFS 2; MAL 5; MTCW 1, 2; MTFW 2005; NFS 4, 8, 13, 24, 33, 38; RGAL 4; RGSF 2; SSFS 2, 5, 6, 12, 27; TUS
Faulkner, William Cuthbert
  See Faulkner, William
Fauset, Jessie Redmon 1882(?)-1961 .... **BLC 1:2; CLC 19, 54; HR 1:2**
  See also AFAW 2; BW 1; CA 109; CANR 83; DAM MULT; DLB 51; FW; LMFS 2; MAL 5; MBL
Faust, Frederick 1892-1944 .... **TCLC 49**
  See also BPFB 1; CA 108; 152; CANR 143; DAM POP; DLB 256; TCWW 1, 2; TUS
Faust, Frederick Schiller
  See Faust, Frederick
Faust, Irvin 1924- .... **CLC 8**
  See also CA 33-36R; CANR 28, 67; CN 1, 2, 3, 4, 5, 6, 7; DLB 2, 28, 218, 278; DLBY 1980

Fawkes, Guy
  See Benchley, Robert (Charles)
Fearing, Kenneth 1902-1961 .... **CLC 51**
  See also CA 93-96; CANR 59; CMW 4; DLB 9; MAL 5; RGAL 4
Fearing, Kenneth Flexner
  See Fearing, Kenneth
Fecamps, Elise
  See Creasey, John
Federman, Raymond 1928-2009 . **CLC 6, 47**
  See also CA 17-20R, 208; 292; CAAE 208; CAAS 8; CANR 10, 43, 83, 108; CN 3, 4, 5, 6; DLBY 1980
Federspiel, J.F. 1931-2007 .... **CLC 42**
  See also CA 146; 257
Federspiel, Juerg F.
  See Federspiel, J.F.
Federspiel, Jurg F.
  See Federspiel, J.F.
Feiffer, Jules 1929- .... **CLC 2, 8, 64**
  See also AAYA 3, 62; CA 17-20R; CAD; CANR 30, 59, 129, 161, 192; CD 5, 6; DAM DRAM; DLB 7, 44; INT CANR-30; MTCW 1; SATA 8, 61, 111, 157, 201
Feiffer, Jules Ralph
  See Feiffer, Jules
Feige, Hermann Albert Otto Maximilian
  See Traven, B.
Fei-Kan, Li
  See Jin, Ba
Feinberg, David B. 1956-1994 .... **CLC 59**
  See also CA 135; 147
Feinstein, Elaine 1930- .... **CLC 36**
  See also CA 69-72; CAAS 1; CANR 31, 68, 121, 162; CN 3, 4, 5, 6, 7; CP 2, 3, 4, 5, 6, 7; CWP; DLB 14, 40; MTCW 1
Feke, Gilbert David CLC 65
Feldman, Irving (Mordecai) 1928- ... **CLC 7**
  See also CA 1-4R; CANR 1; CP 1, 2, 3, 4, 5, 6, 7; DLB 169; TCLE 1:1
Felix-Tchicaya, Gerald
  See Tchicaya, Gerald Felix
Fellini, Federico 1920-1993 .... **CLC 16, 85**
  See also CA 65-68; 143; CANR 33
Felltham, Owen 1602(?)-1668 .... **LC 92**
  See also DLB 126, 151
Felsen, Henry Gregor 1916-1995 .... **CLC 17**
  See also CA 1-4R; 180; CANR 1; SAAS 2; SATA 1
Felski, Rita CLC 65
Fenelon, Francois de Pons de Salignac de la Mothe- 1651-1715 .... **LC 134**
  See also DLB 268; EW 3; GFL Beginnings to 1789
Fenno, Jack
  See Calisher, Hortense
Fenollosa, Ernest (Francisco) 1853-1908 .....
    TCLC 91
Fenton, James 1949- .... **CLC 32, 209**
  See also CA 102; DLB 108, 160; CP 2, 3, 4, 5, 6, 7; DLB 40; PFS 11
Fenton, James Martin
  See Fenton, James
Ferber, Edna 1887-1968 .... **CLC 18, 93**
  See also AITN 1; CA 5-8R; 25-28R; CANR 68, 105; DLB 9, 28, 86, 266; MAL 5; MTCW 1, 2; MTFW 2005; RGAL 4; RHW; SATA 7; TCWW 1, 2
Ferdousi
  See Ferdowsi, Abu'l Qasem
Ferdovsi
  See Ferdowsi, Abu'l Qasem
Ferdowsi
  See Ferdowsi, Abu'l Qasem
Ferdowsi, Abolghasem Mansour
  See Ferdowsi, Abu'l Qasem
Ferdowsi, Abol-Qasem
  See Ferdowsi, Abu'l Qasem

Ferdowsi, Abolqasem
    See Ferdowsi, Abu'l Qasem
Ferdowsi, Abu'l Qasem 940-1020(?) . **CMLC 43**
    See also CA 276; RGWL 2, 3; WLIT 6
Ferdowsi, A.M.
    See Ferdowsi, Abu'l Qasem
Ferdowsi, Hakim Abolghasem
    See Ferdowsi, Abu'l Qasem
Ferguson, Helen
    See Kavan, Anna
Ferguson, Niall 1964- .... **CLC 134, 250**
    See also CA 190; CANR 154, 200
Ferguson, Niall Campbell
    See Ferguson, Niall
Ferguson, Samuel 1810-1886 .... **NCLC 33**
    See also DLB 32; RGEL 2
Fergusson, Robert 1750-1774 .... **LC 29**
    See also DLB 109; RGEL 2
Ferling, Lawrence
    See Ferlinghetti, Lawrence
Ferlinghetti, Lawrence 1919(?)- ... **CLC 2, 6, 10, 27, 111; PC 1**
    See also AAYA 74; BG 1:2; CA 5-8R; CAD; CANR 3, 41, 73, 125, 172; CDALB 1941-1968; CP 1, 2, 3, 4, 5, 6, 7; DA3; DAM POET; DLB 5, 16; MAL 5; MTCW 1, 2; MTFW 2005; PFS 28, 41; RGAL 4; WP
Ferlinghetti, Lawrence Monsanto
    See Ferlinghetti, Lawrence
Fern, Fanny
    See Parton, Sara Payson Willis
Fernandez, Vicente Garcia Huidobro
    See Huidobro Fernandez, Vicente Garcia
Fernandez-Armesto, Felipe 1950- ... **CLC 70**
    See also CA 142; CANR 93, 153, 189
Fernandez-Armesto, Felipe Fermin Ricardo
    See Fernandez-Armesto, Felipe
Fernandez de Lizardi, Jose Joaquin
    See Lizardi, Jose Joaquin Fernandez de
Ferre, Rosario 1938- .... **CLC 139; HLCS 1; SSC 36, 106**
    See also CA 131; CANR 55, 81, 134; CWW 2; DLB 145; EWL 3; HW 1, 2; LAWS 1; MTCW 2; MTFW 2005; WLIT 1
Ferrer, Gabriel (Francisco Victor) Miro
    See Miro (Ferrer), Gabriel (Francisco Victor)
Ferrier, Susan (Edmonstone) 1782-1854 ...... **NCLC 8**
    See also DLB 116; RGEL 2
Ferrigno, Robert 1947- .... **CLC 65**
    See also CA 140; CANR 125, 161
Ferris, Joshua 1974- .... **CLC 280**
    See also CA 262
Ferron, Jacques 1921-1985 .... **CLC 94**
    See also CA 117; 129; CCA 1; DAC; DLB 60; EWL 3
Feuchtwanger, Lion 1884-1958 .... **TCLC 3**
    See also CA 104; 187; DLB 66; EWL 3; RGHL
Feuerbach, Ludwig 1804-1872 ... **NCLC 139**
    See also DLB 133
Feuillet, Octave 1821-1890 .... **NCLC 45**
    See also DLB 192
Feydeau, Georges 1862-1921 .... **TCLC 22**
    See also CA 113; 152; CANR 84; DAM DRAM; DLB 192; EWL 3; GFL 1789 to the Present; RGWL 2, 3
Feydeau, Georges Leon JulesMarie
    See Feydeau, Georges
Fichte, Johann Gottlieb 1762-1814 ... **NCLC 62**
    See also DLB 90
Ficino, Marsilio 1433-1499 .... **LC 12, 152**
    See also LMFS 1
Fiedeler, Hans
    See Doeblin, Alfred

Fiedler, Leslie A(aron) 1917-2003 .... **CLC 4, 13, 24**
    See also AMWS 13; CA 9-12R; 212; CANR 7, 63; CN 1, 2, 3, 4, 5, 6; DLB 28, 67; EWL 3; MAL 5; MTCW 1, 2; RGAL 4; TUS
Field, Andrew 1938- .... **CLC 44**
    See also CA 97-100; CANR 25
Field, Eugene 1850-1895 .... **NCLC 3**
    See also DLB 23, 42, 140; DLBD 13; MAI-CYA 1, 2; RGAL 4; SATA 16
Field, Gans T.
    See Wellman, Manly Wade
Field, Michael 1915-1971 .... **TCLC 43**
    See also CA 29-32R
Fielding, Helen 1958- .... **CLC 146, 217**
    See also AAYA 65; CA 172; CANR 127; DLB 231; MTFW 2005
Fielding, Henry 1707-1754 ...... **LC 1, 46, 85, 151, 154; WLC 2**
    See also BRW 3; BRWR 1; CDBLB 1660-1789; DA; DA3; DAB; DAC; DAM DRAM, MST, NOV; DFS 28; DLB 39, 84, 101; NFS 18, 32; RGEL 2; TEA; WLIT 3
Fielding, Sarah 1710-1768 .... **LC 1, 44**
    See also DLB 39; RGEL 2; TEA
Fields, W. C. 1880-1946 .... **TCLC 80**
    See also DLB 44
Fierstein, Harvey 1954- .... **CLC 33**
    See also CA 123; 129; CAD; CD 5, 6; CPW; DA3; DAM DRAM, POP; DFS 6; DLB 266; GLL; MAL 5
Fierstein, Harvey Forbes
    See Fierstein, Harvey
Figes, Eva 1932- .... **CLC 31**
    See also CA 53-56; CANR 4, 44, 83, 207; CN 2, 3, 4, 5, 6, 7; DLB 14, 271; FW; RGHL
Filippo, Eduardo de
    See de Filippo, Eduardo
Finch, Anne 1661-1720 .... **LC 3, 137; PC 21**
    See also BRWS 9; DLB 95; PFS 30; RGEL 2
Finch, Robert (Duer Claydon) 1900-1995 ... **CLC 18**
    See also CA 57-60; CANR 9, 24, 49; CP 1, 2, 3, 4, 5, 6; DLB 88
Findley, Timothy 1930-2002 ... **CLC 27, 102; SSC 145**
    See also AMWS 20; CA 25-28R; 206; CANR 12, 42, 69, 109; CCA 1; CN 4, 5, 6, 7; DAC; DAM MST; DLB 53; FANT; RHW
Fink, William
    See Mencken, H. L.
Firbank, Louis 1942- .... **CLC 21**
    See also CA 117
Firbank, (Arthur Annesley) Ronald 1886-1926 .... **TCLC 1**
    See also BRWS 2; CA 104; 177; DLB 36; EWL 3; RGEL 2
Firdaosi
    See Ferdowsi, Abu'l Qasem
Firdausi
    See Ferdowsi, Abu'l Qasem
Firdavsi, Abulqosimi
    See Ferdowsi, Abu'l Qasem
Firdavsii, Abulqosim
    See Ferdowsi, Abu'l Qasem
Firdawsi, Abu al-Qasim
    See Ferdowsi, Abu'l Qasem
Firdosi
    See Ferdowsi, Abu'l Qasem
Firdousi
    See Ferdowsi, Abu'l Qasem
Firdousi, Abu'l-Qasim
    See Ferdowsi, Abu'l Qasem

Firdovsi, A.
    See Ferdowsi, Abu'l Qasem
Firdovsi, Abulgasim
    See Ferdowsi, Abu'l Qasem
Firdusi
    See Ferdowsi, Abu'l Qasem
Fish, Stanley 1938- .... **CLC 142**
    See also CA 112; 132; CANR 90; DLB 67
Fish, Stanley E.
    See Fish, Stanley
Fish, Stanley Eugene
    See Fish, Stanley
Fisher, Dorothy (Frances) Canfield 1879-1958 .... **TCLC 87**
    See also CA 114; 136; CANR 80; CLR 71; CWRI 5; DLB 9, 102, 284; MAICYA 1, 2; MAL 5; YABC 1
Fisher, M(ary) F(rances) K(ennedy) 1908-1992 .... **CLC 76, 87**
    See also AMWS 17; CA 77-80; 138; CANR 44; MTCW 2
Fisher, Roy 1930- .... **CLC 25; PC 121**
    See also CA 81-84; CAAS 10; CANR 16; CP 1, 2, 3, 4, 5, 6, 7; DLB 40
Fisher, Rudolph 1897-1934 .... **BLC 1:2; HR 1:2; SSC 25; TCLC 11, 255**
    See also BW 1, 3; CA 107; 124; CANR 80; DAM MULT; DLB 51, 102
Fisher, Vardis (Alvero) 1895-1968 ... **CLC 7; TCLC 140**
    See also CA 5-8R; 25-28R; CANR 68; DLB 9, 206; MAL 5; RGAL 4; TCWW 1, 2
Fiske, Tarleton
    See Bloch, Robert (Albert)
Fitch, Clarke
    See Sinclair, Upton
Fitch, John IV
    See Cormier, Robert
Fitzgerald, Captain Hugh
    See Baum, L. Frank
FitzGerald, Edward 1809-1883 ..... **NCLC 9, 153; PC 79**
    See also BRW 4; DLB 32; RGEL 2
Fitzgerald, F. Scott 1896-1940 ..... **SSC 6, 31, 75, 143; TCLC 1, 6, 14, 28, 55, 157; WLC 2**
    See also AAYA 24; AITN 1; AMW; AMWC 2; AMWR 1; BPFB 1; CA 110; 123; CDALB 1917-1929; DA; DA3; DAB; DAC; DAM MST, NOV; DLB 4, 9, 86, 219, 273; DLBD 1, 15, 16; DLBY 1981, 1996; EWL 3; EXPN; EXPS; LAIT 3; MAL 5; MTCW 1, 2; MTFW 2005; NFS 2, 19, 20; RGAL 4; RGSF 2; SSFS 4, 15, 21, 25; TUS
Fitzgerald, Francis Scott Key
    See Fitzgerald, F. Scott
Fitzgerald, Penelope 1916-2000 ...... **CLC 19, 51, 61, 143**
    See also BRWS 5; CA 85-88; 190; CAAS 10; CANR 56, 86, 131; CN 3, 4, 5, 6, 7; DLB 14, 194, 326; EWL 3; MTCW 2; MTFW 2005
Fitzgerald, Robert (Stuart) 1910-1985 . **CLC 39**
    See also CA 1-4R; 114; CANR 1; CP 1, 2, 3, 4; DLBY 1980; MAL 5
FitzGerald, Robert D(avid) 1902-1987 . **CLC 19**
    See also CA 17-20R; CP 1, 2, 3, 4; DLB 260; RGEL 2
Fitzgerald, Zelda (Sayre) 1900-1948 . **TCLC 52**
    See also AMWS 9; CA 117; 126; DLBY 1984
Flagg, Fannie 1941- .... **CLC 297**
    See also CA 111; CANR 40; CPW; CSW; DA3; DAM POP; NFS 7

Frost, Frederick
See Faust, Frederick

Frost, Robert 1874-1963 . CLC 1, 3, 4, 9, 10, 13, 15, 26, 34, 44; PC 1, 39, 71; TCLC 236; WLC 2
See also AAYA 21; AMW; AMWR 1; CA 89-92; CANR 33; CDALB 1917-1929; CLR 67; DA; DA3; DAB; DAC; DAM MST, POET; DLB 54, 284, 342; DLBD 7; EWL 3; EXPP; MAL 5; MTCW 1, 2; MTFW 2005; PAB; PFS 1, 2, 3, 4, 5, 6, 7, 10, 13, 32, 35, 41; RGAL 4; SATA 14; TUS; WP; WYA

Frost, Robert Lee
See Frost, Robert

Froude, James Anthony 1818-1894 ... NCLC 43
See also DLB 18, 57, 144

Froy, Herald
See Waterhouse, Keith

Fry, Christopher 1907-2005 . CLC 2, 10, 14; DC 36
See also BRWS 3; CA 17-20R; 240; CAAS 23; CANR 9, 30, 74, 132; CBD; CD 5, 6; CP 1, 2, 3, 4, 5, 6, 7; DAM DRAM; DLB 13; EWL 3; MTCW 1, 2; MTFW 2005; RGEL 2; SATA 66; TEA

Frye, (Herman) Northrop 1912-1991 .. CLC 24, 70; TCLC 165
See also CA 5-8R; 133; CANR 8, 37; DLB 67, 68, 246; EWL 3; MTCW 1, 2; MTFW 2005; RGAL 4; TWA

Fuchs, Daniel 1909-1993 .... CLC 8, 22
See also CA 81-84; 142; CAAS 5; CANR 40; CN 1, 2, 3, 4, 5; DLB 9, 26, 28; DLBY 1993; MAL 5

Fuchs, Daniel 1934- .... CLC 34
See also CA 37-40R; CANR 14, 48

Fuentes, Carlos 1928- . CLC 3, 8, 10, 13, 22, 41, 60, 113, 288; HLC 1; SSC 24, 125; WLC 2
See also AAYA 4, 45; AITN 2; BPFB 1; CA 69-72; CANR 10, 32, 68, 104, 138, 197; CDWLB 3; CWW 2; DA; DA3; DAB; DAC; DAM MST, MULT, NOV; DLB 113; DNFS 2; EWL 3; HW 1, 2; LAIT 3; LATS 1:2; LAW; LAWS 1; LMFS 2; MTCW 1, 2; MTFW 2005; NFS 8; RGSF 2; RGWL 2, 3; TWA; WLIT 1

Fuentes, Gregorio Lopez y
See Lopez y Fuentes, Gregorio

Fuentes Macias, Carlos Manuel
See Fuentes, Carlos

Fuertes, Gloria 1918-1998 .... PC 27
See also CA 178, 180; DLB 108; HW 2; SATA 115

Fugard, Athol 1932- ... CLC 5, 9, 14, 25, 40, 80, 211; DC 3
See also AAYA 17; AFW; BRWS 15; CA 85-88; CANR 32, 54, 118; CD 5, 6; DAM DRAM; DFS 3, 6, 10, 24; DLB 225; DNFS 1, 2; EWL 3; LATS 1:2; MTCW 1; MTFW 2005; RGEL 2; WLIT 2

Fugard, Harold Athol
See Fugard, Athol

Fugard, Sheila 1932- .... CLC 48
See also CA 125

Fuguet, Alberto 1964- .... CLC 308
See also CA 170; CANR 144

Fujiwara no Teika 1162-1241 ...... CMLC 73
See also DLB 203

Fukuyama, Francis 1952- ...... CLC 131, 320
See also CA 140; CANR 72, 125, 170

Fuller, Charles (H.), (Jr.) 1939- .... BLC 1:2; CLC 25; DC 1
See also BW 2; CA 108; 112; CAD; CANR 87; CD 5, 6; DAM DRAM, MULT; DFS 8; DLB 38, 266; EWL 3; INT CA-112; MAL 5; MTCW 1

Fuller, Henry Blake 1857-1929 ... TCLC 103
See also CA 108; 177; DLB 12; RGAL 4

Fuller, John (Leopold) 1937- .... CLC 62
See also CA 21-24R; CANR 9, 44; CP 1, 2, 3, 4, 5, 6, 7; DLB 40

Fuller, Margaret 1810-1850 ..... NCLC 5, 50, 211
See also AMWS 2; CDALB 1640-1865; DLB 1, 59, 73, 183, 223, 239; FW; LMFS 1; SATA 25

Fuller, Roy (Broadbent) 1912-1991 . CLC 4, 28
See also BRWS 7; CA 5-8R; 135; CAAS 10; CANR 53, 83; CN 1, 2, 3, 4, 5; CP 1, 2, 3, 4, 5; CWRI 5; DLB 15, 20; EWL 3; RGEL 2; SATA 87

Fuller, Sarah Margaret
See Fuller, Margaret

Fuller, Thomas 1608-1661 .... LC 111
See also DLB 151

Fulton, Alice 1952- .... CLC 52
See also CA 116; CANR 57, 88, 200; CP 5, 6, 7; CWP; DLB 193; PFS 25

Fundi
See Baraka, Amiri

Furey, Michael
See Ward, Arthur Henry Sarsfield

Furphy, Joseph 1843-1912 .... TCLC 25
See also CA 163; DLB 230; EWL 3; RGEL 2

Furst, Alan 1941- .... CLC 255
See also CA 69-72; CANR 12, 34, 59, 102, 159, 193; DLB 350; DLBY 01

Fuson, Robert H(enderson) 1927- .. CLC 70
See also CA 89-92; CANR 103

Fussell, Paul 1924- .... CLC 74
See also BEST 90:1; CA 17-20R; CANR 8, 21, 35, 69, 135; INT CANR-21; MTCW 1, 2; MTFW 2005

Futabatei, Shimei 1864-1909 .... TCLC 44
See also CA 162; DLB 180; EWL 3; MJW

Futabatei Shimei
See Futabatei, Shimei

Futrelle, Jacques 1875-1912 .... TCLC 19
See also CA 113; 155; CMW 4

GAB
See Russell, George William

Gaberman, Judie Angell
See Angell, Judie

Gaboriau, Emile 1835-1873 .... NCLC 14
See also CMW 4; MSW

Gadda, Carlo Emilio 1893-1973 .... CLC 11; TCLC 144
See also CA 89-92; DLB 177; EWL 3; WLIT 7

Gaddis, William 1922-1998 .. CLC 1, 3, 6, 8, 10, 19, 43, 86
See also AMWS 4; BPFB 1; CA 17-20R; 172; CANR 21, 48, 148; CN 1, 2, 3, 4, 5, 6; DLB 2, 278; EWL 3; MAL 5; MTCW 1, 2; MTFW 2005; RGAL 4

Gage, Walter
See Inge, William (Motter)

Gaiman, Neil 1960- .... CLC 319
See also AAYA 19, 42, 82; CA 133; CANR 81, 129, 188; CLR 109; DLB 261; HGG; MTFW 2005; SATA 85, 146, 197, 228; SFW 2; SUFW 2

Gaiman, Neil Richard
See Gaiman, Neil

Gaines, Ernest J. 1933- ... BLC 1:2; CLC 3, 11, 18, 86, 181, 300; SSC 68, 137
See also AAYA 18; AFAW 1, 2; AITN 1; BPFB 1; BW 2, 3; BYA 6; CA 9-12R; CANR 6, 24, 42, 75, 126; CDALB 1968-1988; CLR 62; CN 1, 2, 3, 4, 5, 6, 7; CSW; DA3; DAM MULT; DLB 2, 33, 152; DLBY 1980; EWL 3; EXPN; LAIT

5; LATS 1:2; MAL 5; MTCW 1, 2; MTFW 2005; NFS 5, 7, 16; RGAL 4; RGSF 2; RHW; SATA 86; SSFS 5; YAW

Gaines, Ernest James
See Gaines, Ernest J.

Gaitskill, Mary 1954- .... CLC 69, 300
See also CA 128; CANR 61, 152, 208; DLB 244; TCLE 1:1

Gaitskill, Mary Lawrence
See Gaitskill, Mary

Gaius Suetonius Tranquillus
See Suetonius

Galdos, Benito Perez
See Perez Galdos, Benito

Gale, Zona 1874-1938 .... DC 30; SSC 159; TCLC 7
See also CA 105; 153; CANR 84; DAM DRAM; DFS 17; DLB 9, 78, 228; RGAL 4

Galeano, Eduardo 1940- . CLC 72; HLCS 1
See also CA 29-32R; CANR 13, 32, 100, 163, 211; HW 1

Galeano, Eduardo Hughes
See Galeano, Eduardo

Galiano, Juan Valera y Alcala
See Valera y Alcala-Galiano, Juan

Galilei, Galileo 1564-1642 .... LC 45, 188

Gallagher, Tess 1943- ...... CLC 18, 63; PC 9
See also CA 106; CP 3, 4, 5, 6, 7; CWP; DAM POET; DLB 120, 212, 244; PFS 16

Gallant, Mavis 1922- .... CLC 7, 18, 38, 172, 288; SSC 5, 78
See also CA 69-72; CANR 29, 69, 117; CCA 1; CN 1, 2, 3, 4, 5, 6, 7; DAC; DAM MST; DLB 53; EWL 3; MTCW 1, 2; MTFW 2005; RGEL 2; RGSF 2

Gallant, Roy A(rthur) 1924- .... CLC 17
See also CA 5-8R; CANR 4, 29, 54, 117; CLR 30; MAICYA 1, 2; SATA 4, 68, 110

Gallico, Paul 1897-1976 .... CLC 2
See also AITN 1; CA 5-8R; 69-72; CANR 23; CN 1, 2; DLB 9, 171; FANT; MAICYA 1, 2; SATA 13

Gallico, Paul William
See Gallico, Paul

Gallo, Max Louis 1932- .... CLC 95
See also CA 85-88

Gallois, Lucien
See Desnos, Robert

Gallup, Ralph
See Whitemore, Hugh (John)

Galsworthy, John 1867-1933 .... SSC 22; TCLC 1, 45; WLC 2
See also BRW 6; CA 104; 141; CANR 75; CDBLB 1890-1914; DA; DA3; DAB; DAC; DAM DRAM, MST, NOV; DLB 10, 34, 98, 162, 330; DLBD 16; EWL 3; MTCW 2; RGEL 2; SSFS 3; TEA

Galt, John 1779-1839 .... NCLC 1, 110
See also DLB 99, 116, 159; RGEL 2; RGSF 2

Galvin, James 1951- .... CLC 38
See also CA 108; CANR 26

Gamboa, Federico 1864-1939 .... TCLC 36
See also CA 167; HW 2; LAW

Gandhi, M. K.
See Gandhi, Mohandas Karamchand

Gandhi, Mahatma
See Gandhi, Mohandas Karamchand

Gandhi, Mohandas Karamchand 1869-1948 .... TCLC 59
See also CA 121; 132; DA3; DAM MULT; DLB 323; MTCW 1, 2

Gann, Ernest Kellogg 1910-1991 .... CLC 23
See also AITN 1; BPFB 2; CA 1-4R; 136; CANR 1, 83; RHW

Gao Xingjian
See Xingjian, Gao

Garber, Eric
See Holleran, Andrew

Garber, Esther
See Lee, Tanith

Garcia, Cristina 1958- .... **CLC 76**
See also AMWS 11; CA 141; CANR 73, 130, 172; CN 7; DLB 292; DNFS 1; EWL 3; HW 2; LLW; MTFW 2005; NFS 38; SATA 208

Garcia Lorca, Federico 1898-1936 ..... **DC 2; HLC 2; PC 3; TCLC 1, 7, 49, 181, 197; WLC 2**
See also AAYA 46; CA 104; 131; CANR 81; DA; DA3; DAB; DAC; DAM DRAM, MST, MULT, POET; DFS 4; DLB 108; EW 11; EWL 3; HW 1, 2; LATS 1:2; MTCW 1, 2; MTFW 2005; PFS 20, 31, 38; RGWL 2, 3; TWA; WP

Garcia Marquez, Gabriel 1928- .. **CLC 2, 3, 8, 10, 15, 27, 47, 55, 68, 170, 254; HLC 1; SSC 8, 83, 162; WLC 3**
See also AAYA 3, 33; BEST 89:1, 90:4; BPFB 2; BYA 12, 16; CA 33-36R; CANR 10, 28, 50, 75, 82, 128, 204; CDWLB 3; CPW; CWW 2; DA; DA3; DAB; DAC; DAM MST, MULT, NOV, POP; DLB 113, 330; DNFS 1, 2; EWL 3; EXPN; EXPS; HW 1, 2; LAIT 2; LATS 1:2; LAW; LAWS 1; LMFS 2; MTCW 1, 2; MTFW 2005; NCFS 3; NFS 1, 5, 10; RGSF 2; RGWL 2, 3; SSFS 1, 6, 16, 21; TWA; WLIT 1

Garcia Marquez, Gabriel Jose
See Garcia Marquez, Gabriel

Garcia Marquez, Gabriel Jose
See Garcia Marquez, Gabriel

Garcilaso de la Vega, El Inca 1539-1616 ..... **HLCS 1; LC 127**
See also DLB 318; LAW

Gard, Janice
See Latham, Jean Lee

Gard, Roger Martin du
See Martin du Gard, Roger

Gardam, Jane 1928- .... **CLC 43**
See also CA 49-52; CANR 2, 18, 33, 54, 106, 167, 206; CLR 12; DLB 14, 161, 231; MAICYA 1, 2; MTCW 1; SAAS 9; SATA 39, 76, 130; SATA-Brief 28; YAW

Gardam, Jane Mary
See Gardam, Jane

Gardens, S. S.
See Snodgrass, W. D.

Gardner, Herb(ert George) 1934-2003 . **CLC 44**
See also CA 149; 220; CAD; CANR 119; CD 5, 6; DFS 18, 20

Gardner, John, Jr. 1933-1982 .. **CLC 2, 3, 5, 7, 8, 10, 18, 28, 34; SSC 7; TCLC 195**
See also AAYA 45; AITN 1; AMWS 6; BPFB 2; CA 65-68; 107; CANR 33, 73; CDALBS; CN 2, 3; CPW; DA3; DAM NOV, POP; DLB 2; DLBY 1982; EWL 3; FANT; LATS 1:2; MAL 5; MTCW 1, 2; MTFW 2005; NFS 3; RGAL 4; RGSF 2; SATA 40; SATA-Obit 31; SSFS 8

Gardner, John 1926-2007 .... **CLC 30**
See also CA 103; 263; CANR 15, 69, 127, 183; CMW 4; CPW; DAM POP; MTCW 1

Gardner, John Champlin, Jr.
See Gardner, John, Jr.

Gardner, John Edmund
See Gardner, John

Gardner, Miriam
See Bradley, Marion Zimmer

Gardner, Noel
See Kuttner, Henry

Gardons, S.S.
See Snodgrass, W. D.

Garfield, Leon 1921-1996 .... **CLC 12**
See also AAYA 8, 69; BYA 1, 3; CA 17-20R; 152; CANR 38, 41, 78; CLR 21, 166; DLB 161; JRDA; MAICYA 1, 2; MAICYAS 1; SATA 1, 32, 76; SATA-Obit 90; TEA; WYA; YAW

Garland, (Hannibal) Hamlin 1860-1940 ...... **SSC 18, 117; TCLC 3, 256**
See also CA 104; DLB 12, 71, 78, 186; MAL 5; RGAL 4; RGSF 2; TCWW 1, 2

Garneau, (Hector de) Saint-Denys 1912-1943 .... **TCLC 13**
See also CA 111; DLB 88

Garner, Alan 1934- .... **CLC 17**
See also AAYA 18; BYA 3, 5; CA 73-76, 178; CAAE 178; CANR 15, 64, 134; CLR 20, 130; CPW; DAB; DAM POP; DLB 161, 261; FANT; MAICYA 1, 2; MTCW 1, 2; MTFW 2005; SATA 18, 69; SATA-Essay 108; SUFW 1, 2; YAW

Garner, Helen 1942- .... **SSC 135**
See also CA 124; 127; CANR 71, 206; CN 4, 5, 6, 7; DLB 325; GLL 2; RGSF 2

Garner, Hugh 1913-1979 .... **CLC 13**
See also CA 69-72; CANR 31; CCA 1; CN 1, 2; DLB 68

Garnett, David 1892-1981 .... **CLC 3**
See also CA 5-8R; 103; CANR 17, 79; CN 1, 2; DLB 34; FANT; MTCW 2; RGEL 2; SFW 4; SUFW 1

Garnier, Robert c. 1545-1590 .... **LC 119**
See also DLB 327; GFL Beginnings to 1789

Garrett, George 1929-2008 .. **CLC 3, 11, 51; SSC 30**
See also AMWS 7; BPFB 2; CA 1-4R, 202; 272; CAAE 202; CAAS 5; CANR 1, 42, 67, 109, 199; CN 1, 2, 3, 4, 5, 6, 7; CP 1, 2, 3, 4, 5, 6, 7; CSW; DLB 2, 5, 130, 152; DLBY 1983

Garrett, George P.
See Garrett, George

Garrett, George Palmer
See Garrett, George

Garrett, George Palmer, Jr.
See Garrett, George

Garrick, David 1717-1779 .... **LC 15, 156**
See also DAM DRAM; DLB 84, 213; RGEL 2

Garrigue, Jean 1914-1972 .... **CLC 2, 8**
See also CA 5-8R; 37-40R; CANR 20; CP 1; MAL 5

Garrison, Frederick
See Sinclair, Upton

Garrison, William Lloyd 1805-1879 . **NCLC 149**
See also CDALB 1640-1865; DLB 1, 43, 235

Garro, Elena 1920(?)-1998 . **HLCS 1; TCLC 153**
See also CA 131; 169; CWW 2; DLB 145; EWL 3; HW 1; LAWS 1; WLIT 1

Garth, Will
See Hamilton, Edmond; Kuttner, Henry

Garvey, Marcus (Moziah, Jr.) 1887-1940 .... **BLC 1:2; HR 1:2; TCLC 41**
See also BW 1; CA 120; 124; CANR 79; DAM MULT; DLB 345

Gary, Romain
See Kacew, Romain

Gascar, Pierre
See Fournier, Pierre

Gascoigne, George 1539-1577 .... **LC 108**
See also DLB 136; RGEL 2

Gascoyne, David (Emery) 1916-2001 ... **CLC 45**
See also CA 65-68; 200; CANR 10, 28, 54; CP 1, 2, 3, 4, 5, 6, 7; DLB 20; MTCW 1; RGEL 2

Gaskell, Elizabeth 1810-1865 .. **NCLC 5, 70, 97, 137, 214; SSC 25, 97**
See also AAYA 80; BRW 5; BRWR 3; CD-BLB 1832-1890; DAB; DAM MST; DLB 21, 144, 159; RGEL 2; RGSF 2; TEA

Gass, William H. 1924- . **CLC 1, 2, 8, 11, 15, 39, 132; SSC 12**
See also AMWS 6; CA 17-20R; CANR 30, 71, 100; CN 1, 2, 3, 4, 5, 6, 7; DLB 2, 227; EWL 3; MAL 5; MTCW 1, 2; MTFW 2005; RGAL 4

Gassendi, Pierre 1592-1655 .... **LC 54**
See also GFL Beginnings to 1789

Gasset, Jose Ortega y
See Ortega y Gasset, Jose

Gates, Henry Louis, Jr. 1950- . **BLCS; CLC 65**
See also AMWS 20; BW 2, 3; CA 109; CANR 25, 53, 75, 125, 203; CSW; DA3; DAM MULT; DLB 67; EWL 3; MAL 5; MTCW 2; MTFW 2005; RGAL 4

Gatos, Stephanie
See Katz, Steve

Gautier, Theophile 1811-1872 . **NCLC 1, 59, 243; PC 18; SSC 20**
See also DAM POET; DLB 119; EW 6; GFL 1789 to the Present; RGWL 2, 3; SUFW; TWA

Gautreaux, Tim 1947- ... **CLC 270; SSC 125**
See also CA 187; CANR 207; CSW; DLB 292

Gautreaux, Tim Martin
See Gautreaux, Tim

Gay, John 1685-1732 ..... **DC 39; LC 49, 176**
See also BRW 3; DAM DRAM; DLB 84, 95; RGEL 2; WLIT 3

Gay, Oliver
See Gogarty, Oliver St. John

Gay, Peter 1923- .... **CLC 158**
See also CA 13-16R; CANR 18, 41, 77, 147, 196; INT CANR-18; RGHL

Gay, Peter Jack
See Gay, Peter

Gaye, Marvin (Pentz, Jr.) 1939-1984 ... **CLC 26**
See also CA 195; 112

Gebler, Carlo 1954- .... **CLC 39**
See also CA 119; 133; CANR 96, 186; DLB 271

Gebler, Carlo Ernest
See Gebler, Carlo

Gee, Maggie 1948- .... **CLC 57**
See also CA 130; CANR 125; CN 4, 5, 6, 7; DLB 207; MTFW 2005

Gee, Maurice 1931- .... **CLC 29**
See also AAYA 42; CA 97-100; CANR 67, 123, 204; CLR 56; CN 2, 3, 4, 5, 6, 7; CWRI 5; EWL 3; MAICYA 2; RGSF 2; SATA 46, 101, 227

Gee, Maurice Gough
See Gee, Maurice

Geiogamah, Hanay 1945- .... **NNAL**
See also CA 153; DAM MULT; DLB 175

Gelbart, Larry 1928-2009 .... **CLC 21, 61**
See also CA 73-76; 290; CAD; CANR 45, 94; CD 5, 6

Gelbart, Larry Simon
See Gelbart, Larry

Gelber, Jack 1932-2003 ..... **CLC 1, 6, 14, 79**
See also CA 1-4R; 216; CAD; CANR 2; DLB 7, 228; MAL 5

Gellhorn, Martha 1908-1998 ..... **CLC 14, 60**
See also Gellhorn, Martha Ellis
See also CA 77-80; 164; CANR 44; CN 1, 2, 3, 4, 5, 6 7; DLB 364; DLBY 1982, 1998

Gellhorn, Martha Ellis
See Gellhorn, Martha

Genet, Jean 1910-1986 . **CLC 1, 2, 5, 10, 14, 44, 46; DC 25; TCLC 128**
  See also CA 13-16R; CANR 18; DA3; DAM DRAM; DFS 10; DLB 72, 321; DLBY 1986; EW 13; EWL 3; GFL 1789 to the Present; GLL 1; LMFS 2; MTCW 1, 2; MTFW 2005; RGWL 2, 3; TWA

Genlis, Stephanie-Felicite Ducrest 1746-1830 .... **NCLC 166**
  See also DLB 313

Gent, Peter 1942-2011 .... **CLC 29**
  See also AITN 1; CA 89-92; DLBY 1982

Gentile, Giovanni 1875-1944 .... **TCLC 96**
  See also CA 119

Geoffrey of Monmouth c. 1100-1155 . **CMLC 44**
  See also DLB 146; TEA

Geoffrey of Vinsauf fl. c. 12th cent. - . **CMLC 129**

George, Jean
  See George, Jean Craighead

George, Jean C.
  See George, Jean Craighead

George, Jean Craighead 1919- .... **CLC 35**
  See also AAYA 8, 69; BYA 2, 4; CA 5-8R; CANR 25, 198; CLR 1, 80, 136; DLB 52; JRDA; MAICYA 1, 2; SATA 2, 68, 124, 170, 226; WYA; YAW

George, Stefan (Anton) 1868-1933 .... **TCLC 2, 14**
  See also CA 104; 193; EW 8; EWL 3

Georges, Georges Martin
  See Simenon, Georges

Gerald of Wales c. 1146-c. 1223 .. **CMLC 60**

Gerhardi, William Alexander
  See Gerhardie, William Alexander

Gerhardie, William Alexander 1895-1977 ... **CLC 5**
  See also CA 25-28R; 73-76; CANR 18; CN 1, 2; DLB 36; RGEL 2

Germain, Sylvie 1954- .... **CLC 283**
  See also CA 191

Gerome
  See France, Anatole

Gerson, Jean 1363-1429 .... **LC 77**
  See also DLB 208

Gersonides 1288-1344 .... **CMLC 49**
  See also DLB 115

Gerstler, Amy 1956- .... **CLC 70**
  See also CA 146; CANR 99

Gertler, T. CLC 34
  See also CA 116; 121

Gertrude of Helfta c. 1256-c. 1301 .. **CMLC 105**

Gertsen, Aleksandr Ivanovich
  See Herzen, Aleksandr Ivanovich

Gervase of Melkley c. 1185-c. 1216 . **CMLC 121**

Ghalib
  See Ghalib, Asadullah Khan

Ghalib, Asadullah Khan 1797-1869 .. **NCLC 39, 78**
  See also DAM POET; RGWL 2, 3

Ghelderode, Michel de 1898-1962 ... **CLC 6, 11; DC 15; TCLC 187**
  See also CA 85-88; CANR 40, 77; DAM DRAM; DLB 321; EW 11; EWL 3; TWA

Ghiselin, Brewster 1903-2001 .... **CLC 23**
  See also CA 13-16R; CAAS 10; CANR 13; CP 1, 2, 3, 4, 5, 6, 7

Ghose, Aurabinda 1872-1950 .... **TCLC 63**
  See also CA 163; EWL 3

Ghose, Aurobindo
  See Ghose, Aurabinda

Ghose, Zulfikar 1935- .... **CLC 42, 200**
  See also CA 65-68; CANR 67; CN 1, 2, 3, 4, 5, 6, 7; CP 1, 2, 3, 4, 5, 6, 7; DLB 323; EWL 3

Ghosh, Amitav 1956- .... **CLC 44, 153, 300**
  See also CA 147; CANR 80, 158, 205; CN 6, 7; DLB 323; WWE 1

Giacosa, Giuseppe 1847-1906 .... **TCLC 7**
  See also CA 104

Gibb, Lee
  See Waterhouse, Keith

Gibbon, Edward 1737-1794 .... **LC 97**
  See also BRW 3; DLB 104, 336; RGEL 2

Gibbon, Lewis Grassic
  See Mitchell, James Leslie

Gibbons, Kaye 1960- .... **CLC 50, 88, 145**
  See also AAYA 34; AMWS 10; CA 151; CANR 75, 127; CN 7; CSW; DA3; DAM POP; DLB 292; MTCW 2; MTFW 2005; NFS 3; RGAL 4; SATA 117

Gibran, Kahlil 1883-1931 ... **PC 9; TCLC 1, 9, 205**
  See also AMWS 20; CA 104; 150; DA3; DAM POET, POP; DLB 346; EWL 3; MTCW 2; WLIT 6

Gibran, Khalil
  See Gibran, Kahlil

Gibson, Mel 1956- .... **CLC 215**
  See also AAYA 80

Gibson, William 1914-2008 .... **CLC 23**
  See also CA 9-12R; 279; CAD; CANR 9, 42, 75, 125; CD 5, 6; DA; DAB; DAC; DAM DRAM, MST; DFS 2, 28; DLB 7; LAIT 2; MAL 5; MTCW 2; MTFW 2005; SATA 66; SATA-Obit 199; YAW

Gibson, William 1948- ...... **CLC 39, 63, 186, 192; SSC 52**
  See also AAYA 12, 59; AMWS 16; BPFB 2; CA 126; 133; CANR 52, 90, 106, 172, 229; CN 6, 7; CPW; DA3; DAM POP; DLB 251; MTCW 2; MTFW 2005; NFS 38; SCFW 2; SFW 4; SSFS 26

Gibson, William Ford
  See Gibson, William

Gide, Andre 1869-1951 .... **SSC 13; TCLC 5, 12, 36, 177; WLC 3**
  See also CA 104; 124; DA; DA3; DAB; DAC; DAM MST, NOV; DLB 65, 321; 330; EW 8; EWL 3; GFL 1789 to the Present; MTCW 1, 2; MTFW 2005; NFS 21; RGSF 2; RGWL 2, 3; TWA

Gide, Andre Paul Guillaume
  See Gide, Andre

Gifford, Barry 1946- .... **CLC 34**
  See also CA 65-68; CANR 9, 30, 40, 90, 180

Gifford, Barry Colby
  See Gifford, Barry

Gilbert, Frank
  See De Voto, Bernard (Augustine)

Gilbert, W(illiam) S(chwenck) 1836-1911 ... **TCLC 3**
  See also CA 104; 173; DAM DRAM, POET; DLB 344; RGEL 2; SATA 36

Gilbert of Poitiers c. 1085-1154 .. **CMLC 85**

Gilbreth, Frank B., Jr. 1911-2001 ... **CLC 17**
  See also CA 9-12R; SATA 2

Gilbreth, Frank Bunker
  See Gilbreth, Frank B., Jr.

Gilchrist, Ellen 1935- . **CLC 34, 48, 143, 264; SSC 14, 63**
  See also BPFB 2; CA 113; 116; CANR 41, 61, 104, 191; CN 4, 5, 6, 7; CPW; CSW; DAM POP; DLB 130; EWL 3; EXPS; MTCW 1, 2; MTFW 2005; RGAL 4; RGSF 2; SSFS 9

Gilchrist, Ellen Louise
  See Gilchrist, Ellen

Gildas fl. 6th cent. - .... **CMLC 99**

Giles, Molly 1942- .... **CLC 39**
  See also CA 126; CANR 98

Gill, Arthur Eric Rowton Peter Joseph
  See Gill, Eric

Gill, Eric 1882-1940 .... **TCLC 85**
  See Gill, Arthur Eric Rowton Peter Joseph
  See also CA 120; DLB 98

Gill, Patrick
  See Creasey, John

Gillette, Douglas CLC 70

Gilliam, Terry 1940- .... **CLC 21, 141**
  See also AAYA 19, 59; CA 108; 113; CANR 35; INT CA-113

Gilliam, Terry Vance
  See Gilliam, Terry

Gillian, Jerry
  See Gilliam, Terry

Gilliatt, Penelope (Ann Douglass) 1932-1993 .... **CLC 2, 10, 13, 53**
  See also AITN 2; CA 13-16R; 141; CANR 49; CN 1, 2, 3, 4, 5; DLB 14

Gilligan, Carol 1936- .... **CLC 208**
  See also CA 142; CANR 121, 187; FW

Gilman, Charlotte Anna Perkins Stetson
  See Gilman, Charlotte Perkins

Gilman, Charlotte Perkins 1860-1935 .. **SSC 13, 62; TCLC 9, 37, 117, 201**
  See also AAYA 75; AMWS 11; BYA 11; CA 106; 150; DLB 221; EXPS; FL 1:5; FW; HGG; LAIT 2; MBL; MTCW 2; MTFW 2005; NFS 36; RGAL 4; RGSF 2; SFW 4; SSFS 1, 18

Gilmore, Mary (Jean Cameron) 1865-1962 .... **PC 87**
  See also CA 114; DLB 260; RGEL 2; SATA 49

Gilmour, David 1946- .... **CLC 35**

Gilpin, William 1724-1804 .... **NCLC 30**

Gilray, J. D.
  See Mencken, H. L.

Gilroy, Frank D(aniel) 1925- .... **CLC 2**
  See also CA 81-84; CAD; CANR 32, 64, 86; CD 5, 6; DFS 17; DLB 7

Gilstrap, John 1957(?)- .... **CLC 99**
  See also AAYA 67; CA 160; CANR 101, 229

Ginsberg, Allen 1926-1997 ... **CLC 1, 2, 3, 4, 6, 13, 36, 69, 109; PC 4, 47; TCLC 120; WLC 3**
  See also AAYA 33; AITN 1; AMWC 1; AMWS 2; BG 1:2; CA 1-4R; 157; CANR 2, 41, 63, 95; CDALB 1941-1968; CP 1, 2, 3, 4, 5, 6; DA; DA3; DAB; DAC; DAM MST, POET; DLB 5, 16, 169, 237; EWL 3; GLL 1; LMFS 2; MAL 5; MTCW 1, 2; MTFW 2005; PAB; PFS 29; RGAL 4; TUS; WP

Ginzburg, Eugenia
  See Ginzburg, Evgeniia

Ginzburg, Evgeniia 1904-1977 .... **CLC 59**
  See also DLB 302

Ginzburg, Natalia 1916-1991 ..... **CLC 5, 11, 54, 70; SSC 65; TCLC 156**
  See also CA 85-88; 135; CANR 33; DFS 14; DLB 177; EW 13; EWL 3; MTCW 1, 2; MTFW 2005; RGHL; RGWL 2, 3

Gioia, (Michael) Dana 1950- .... **CLC 251**
  See also AMWS 15; CA 130; CANR 70, 88; CP 6, 7; DLB 120, 282; PFS 24

Giono, Jean 1895-1970 ... **CLC 4, 11; TCLC 124**
  See also CA 45-48; 29-32R; CANR 2, 35; DLB 72, 321; EWL 3; GFL 1789 to the Present; MTCW 1; RGWL 2, 3

Giovanni, Nikki 1943- . **BLC 1:2; CLC 2, 4, 19, 64, 117; PC 19; WLCS**
  See also AAYA 22, 85; AITN 1; BW 2, 3; CA 29-32R; CAAS 6; CANR 18, 41, 60, 91, 130, 175; CDALBS; CLR 6, 73; CP 2, 3, 4, 5, 6, 7; CSW; CWP; CWRI 5; DA; DA3; DAB; DAC; DAM MST, MULT,

Grass, Gunter 1927- . **CLC 1, 2, 4, 6, 11, 15, 22, 32, 49, 88, 207; WLC 3**
See also BPFB 2; CA 13-16R; CANR 20, 75, 93, 133, 174, 229; CDWLB 2; CWW 2; DA; DA3; DAB; DAC; DAM MST, NOV; DLB 330; EW 13; EWL 3; MTCW 1, 2; MTFW 2005; RGHL; RGWL 2, 3; TWA

Grass, Gunter Wilhelm
See Grass, Gunter

Gratton, Thomas
See Hulme, T(homas) E(rnest)

Grau, Shirley Ann 1929- ...... **CLC 4, 9, 146; SSC 15**
See also CA 89-92; CANR 22, 69; CN 1, 2, 3, 4, 5, 6, 7; CSW; DLB 2, 218; INT CA-89-92; CANR-22; MTCW 1

Gravel, Fern
See Hall, James Norman

Graver, Elizabeth 1964- .... **CLC 70**
See also CA 135; CANR 71, 129

Graves, Richard Perceval 1895-1985 ... **CLC 44**
See also CA 65-68; CANR 9, 26, 51

Graves, Robert 1895-1985 . **CLC 1, 2, 6, 11, 39, 44, 45; PC 6**
See also BPFB 2; BRW 7; BYA 4; CA 5-8R; 117; CANR 5, 36; CDBLB 1914-1945; CN 1, 2, 3; CP 1, 2, 3, 4; DA3; DAB; DAC; DAM MST, POET; DLB 20, 100, 191; DLBD 18; DLBY 1985; EWL 3; LATS 1:1; MTCW 1, 2; MTFW 2005; NCFS 2; NFS 21; RGEL 2; RHW; SATA 45; TEA

Graves, Robert von Ranke
See Graves, Robert

Graves, Valerie
See Bradley, Marion Zimmer

Gray, Alasdair 1934- .... **CLC 41, 275**
See also BRWS 9; CA 126; CANR 47, 69, 106, 140; CN 4, 5, 6, 7; DLB 194, 261, 319; HGG; INT CA-126; MTCW 1, 2; MTFW 2005; RGSF 2; SUFW 2

Gray, Amlin 1946- .... **CLC 29**
See also CA 138

Gray, Francine du Plessix 1930- .... **CLC 22, 153**
See also BEST 90:3; CA 61-64; CAAS 2; CANR 11, 33, 75, 81, 197; DAM NOV; INT CANR-11; MTCW 1, 2; MTFW 2005

Gray, John (Henry) 1866-1934 ..... **TCLC 19**
See also CA 119; 162; RGEL 2

Gray, John Lee
See Jakes, John

Gray, Simon 1936-2008 .... **CLC 9, 14, 36**
See also AITN 1; CA 21-24R; 275; CAAS 3; CANR 32, 69, 208; CBD; CD 5, 6; CN 1, 2, 3; DLB 13; EWL 3; MTCW 1; RGEL 2

Gray, Simon James Holliday
See Gray, Simon

Gray, Spalding 1941-2004 ...... **CLC 49, 112; DC 7**
See also AAYA 62; CA 128; 225; CAD; CANR 74, 138; CD 5, 6; CPW; DAM POP; MTCW 2; MTFW 2005

Gray, Thomas 1716-1771 ...... **LC 4, 40, 178; PC 2, 80; WLC 3**
See also BRW 3; CDBLB 1660-1789; DA; DA3; DAB; DAC; DAM MST; DLB 109; EXPP; PAB; PFS 9; RGEL 2; TEA; WP

Grayson, David
See Baker, Ray Stannard

Grayson, Richard (A.) 1951- .... **CLC 38**
See also CA 85-88, 210; CAAE 210; CANR 14, 31, 57; DLB 234

Greeley, Andrew M. 1928- .... **CLC 28**
See also BPFB 2; CA 5-8R; CAAS 7; CANR 7, 43, 69, 104, 136, 184; CMW 4; CPW; DA3; DAM POP; MTCW 1, 2; MTFW 2005

Green, Anna Katharine 1846-1935 ... **TCLC 63**
See also CA 112; 159; CMW 4; DLB 202, 221; MSW

Green, Brian
See Card, Orson Scott

Green, Hannah
See Greenberg, Joanne (Goldenberg)

Green, Hannah 1927(?)-1996 .... **CLC 3**
See also CA 73-76; CANR 59, 93; NFS 10

Green, Henry
See Yorke, Henry Vincent

Green, Julian
See Green, Julien

Green, Julien 1900-1998 .... **CLC 3, 11, 77**
See also CA 21-24R; 169; CANR 33, 87; CWW 2; DLB 4, 72; EWL 3; GFL 1789 to the Present; MTCW 2; MTFW 2005

Green, Julien Hartridge
See Green, Julien

Green, Paul (Eliot) 1894-1981 . **CLC 25; DC 37**
See also AITN 1; CA 5-8R; 103; CAD; CANR 3; DAM DRAM; DLB 7, 9, 249; DLBY 1981; MAL 5; RGAL 4

Greenaway, Peter 1942- .... **CLC 159**
See also CA 127

Greenberg, Ivan 1908-1973 .... **CLC 24**
See also CA 85-88; DLB 137; MAL 5

Greenberg, Joanne (Goldenberg) 1932- ...... **CLC 7, 30**
See also AAYA 12, 67; CA 5-8R; CANR 14, 32, 69; CN 6, 7; DLB 335; NFS 23; SATA 25; YAW

Greenberg, Richard 1959(?)- .... **CLC 57**
See also CA 138; CAD; CD 5, 6; DFS 24

Greenblatt, Stephen J. 1943- .... **CLC 70**
See also CA 49-52; CANR 115; LNFS 1

Greenblatt, Stephen Jay
See Greenblatt, Stephen J.

Greene, Bette 1934- .... **CLC 30**
See also AAYA 7, 69; BYA 3; CA 53-56; CANR 4, 146; CLR 2, 140; CWRI 5; JRDA; LAIT 4; MAICYA 1, 2; NFS 10; SAAS 16; SATA 8, 102, 161; WYA; YAW

Greene, Gael CLC 8
See also CA 13-16R; CANR 10, 166

Greene, Graham 1904-1991 . **CLC 1, 3, 6, 9, 14, 18, 27, 37, 70, 72, 125; DC 41; SSC 29, 121; WLC 3**
See also AAYA 61; AITN 2; BPFB 2; BRWR 2; BRWS 1; BYA 3; CA 13-16R; 133; CANR 35, 61, 131; CBD; CDBLB 1945-1960; CMW 4; CN 1, 2, 3, 4; DA; DA3; DAB; DAC; DAM MST, NOV; DLB 13, 15, 77, 100, 162, 201, 204; DLBY 1991; EWL 3; MSW; MTCW 1, 2; MTFW 2005; NFS 16, 31, 36; RGEL 2; SATA 20; SSFS 14, 35; TEA; WLIT 4

Greene, Graham Henry
See Greene, Graham

Greene, Robert 1558-1592 .... **LC 41, 185**
See also BRWS 8; DLB 62, 167; IDTP; RGEL 2; TEA

Greer, Germaine 1939- .... **CLC 131**
See also AITN 1; CA 81-84; CANR 33, 70, 115, 133, 190; FW; MTCW 1, 2; MTFW 2005

Greer, Richard
See Silverberg, Robert

Gregor, Arthur 1923- .... **CLC 9**
See also CA 25-28R; CAAS 10; CANR 11; CP 1, 2, 3, 4, 5, 6, 7; SATA 36

Gregor, Lee
See Pohl, Frederik

Gregory, Lady Isabella Augusta (Persse) 1852-1932 .... **TCLC 1, 176**
See also BRW 6; CA 104; 184; DLB 10; IDTP; RGEL 2

Gregory, J. Dennis
See Williams, John A(lfred)

Gregory of Nazianzus, St. 329-389 .. **CMLC 82**

Gregory of Nyssa c. 335-c. 394 . **CMLC 126**

Gregory of Rimini 1300(?)-1358 . **CMLC 109**
See also DLB 115

Gregory the Great c. 540-604 .... **CMLC 124**

Grekova, I.
See Ventsel, Elena Sergeevna

Grekova, Irina
See Ventsel, Elena Sergeevna

Grendon, Stephen
See Derleth, August (William)

Grenville, Kate 1950- .... **CLC 61**
See also CA 118; CANR 53, 93, 156, 220; CN 7; DLB 325

Grenville, Pelham
See Wodehouse, P. G.

Greve, Felix Paul (Berthold Friedrich) 1879-1948 .... **TCLC 4, 248**
See also CA 104; 141; 175; CANR 79; DAC; DAM MST; DLB 92; RGEL 2; TCWW 1, 2

Greville, Fulke 1554-1628 .... **LC 79**
See also BRWS 11; DLB 62, 172; RGEL 2

Grey, Lady Jane 1537-1554 .... **LC 93**
See also DLB 132

Grey, Zane 1872-1939 .... **TCLC 6**
See also BPFB 2; CA 104; 132; CANR 210; DA3; DAM POP; DLB 9, 212; MTCW 1, 2; MTFW 2005; RGAL 4; TCWW 1, 2; TUS

Griboedov, Aleksandr Sergeevich 1795(?)-1829 .... **NCLC 129**
See also DLB 205; RGWL 2, 3

Grieg, (Johan) Nordahl (Brun) 1902-1943 .. **TCLC 10**
See also CA 107; 189; EWL 3

Grieve, C. M. 1892-1978 .. **CLC 2, 4, 11, 19, 63; PC 9, 122**
See also BRWS 12; CA 5-8R; 85-88; CANR 33, 107; CDBLB 1945-1960; CP 1, 2; DAM POET; DLB 20; EWL 3; MTCW 1; RGEL 2

Grieve, Christopher Murray
See Grieve, C. M.

Griffin, Gerald 1803-1840 .... **NCLC 7**
See also DLB 159; RGEL 2

Griffin, John Howard 1920-1980 .... **CLC 68**
See also AITN 1; CA 1-4R; 101; CANR 2

Griffin, Peter 1942- .... **CLC 39**
See also CA 136

Griffith, David Lewelyn Wark
See Griffith, D.W.

Griffith, D.W. 1875(?)-1948 .... **TCLC 68**
See also AAYA 78; CA 119; 150; CANR 80

Griffith, Lawrence
See Griffith, D.W.

Griffiths, Trevor 1935- .... **CLC 13, 52**
See also CA 97-100; CANR 45; CBD; CD 5, 6; DLB 13, 245

Griggs, Sutton (Elbert) 1872-1930 .... **TCLC 77**
See also CA 123; 186; DLB 50

Grigson, Geoffrey (Edward Harvey) 1905-1985 .... **CLC 7, 39**
See also CA 25-28R; 118; CANR 20, 33; CP 1, 2, 3, 4; DLB 27; MTCW 1, 2

Grile, Dod
See Bierce, Ambrose

Gutierrez Najera, Manuel 1859-1895 . **HLCS 2; NCLC 133**
See also DLB 290; LAW

Guy, Rosa 1925- .... **CLC 26**
See also AAYA 4, 37; BW 2; CA 17-20R; CANR 14, 34, 83; CLR 13, 137; DLB 33; DNFS 1; JRDA; MAICYA 1, 2; SATA 14, 62, 122; YAW

Guy, Rosa Cuthbert
See Guy, Rosa

Gwendolyn
See Bennett, (Enoch) Arnold

H. D.
See Doolittle, Hilda

H. de V.
See Buchan, John

Haavikko, Paavo Juhani 1931- . **CLC 18, 34**
See also CA 106; CWW 2; EWL 3

Habbema, Koos
See Heijermans, Herman

Habermas, Juergen 1929- .... **CLC 104**
See also CA 109; CANR 85, 162; DLB 242

Habermas, Jurgen
See Habermas, Juergen

Hacker, Marilyn 1942- ..... **CLC 5, 9, 23, 72, 91; PC 47**
See also CA 77-80; CANR 68, 129; CP 3, 4, 5, 6, 7; CWP; DAM POET; DLB 120, 282; FW; GLL 2; MAL 5; PFS 19

Hadewijch of Antwerp fl. 1250- .. **CMLC 61**
See also RGWL 3

Hadrian 76-138 .... **CMLC 52**

Haeckel, Ernst Heinrich (Philipp August) 1834-1919 .... **TCLC 83**
See also CA 157

Hafiz c. 1326-1389(?) ..... **CMLC 34; PC 116**
See also RGWL 2, 3; WLIT 6

Hagedorn, Jessica T. 1949- .... **CLC 185**
See also CA 139; CANR 69, 231; CWP; DLB 312; RGAL 4

Hagedorn, Jessica Tarahata
See Hagedorn, Jessica T.

Haggard, H(enry) Rider 1856-1925 .. **TCLC 11**
See also AAYA 81; BRWS 3; BYA 4, 5; CA 108; 148; CANR 112; DLB 70, 156, 174, 178; FANT; LMFS 1; MTCW 2; NFS 40; RGEL 2; RHW; SATA 16; SCFW 1, 2; SFW 4; SUFW 1; WLIT 4

Hagiosy, L.
See Larbaud, Valery (Nicolas)

Hagiwara, Sakutaro 1886-1942 .... **PC 18; TCLC 60**
See also CA 154; EWL 3; RGWL 3

Hagiwara Sakutaro
See Hagiwara, Sakutaro

Haig, Fenil
See Ford, Ford Madox

Haig-Brown, Roderick (Langmere) 1908-1976 .... **CLC 21**
See also CA 5-8R; 69-72; CANR 4, 38, 83; CLR 31; CWRI 5; DLB 88; MAICYA 1, 2; SATA 12; TCWW 2

Haight, Rip
See Carpenter, John

Haij, Vera
See Jansson, Tove (Marika)

Hailey, Arthur 1920-2004 .... **CLC 5**
See also AITN 2; BEST 90:3; BPFB 2; CA 1-4R; 233; CANR 2, 36, 75; CCA 1; CN 1, 2, 3, 4, 5, 6, 7; CPW; DAM NOV, POP; DLB 88; DLBY 1982; MTCW 1, 2; MTFW 2005

Hailey, Elizabeth Forsythe 1938- .... **CLC 40**
See also CA 93-96; 188; CAAE 188; CAAS 1; CANR 15, 48; INT CANR-15

Haines, John 1924-2011 .... **CLC 58**
See also AMWS 12; CA 17-20R; CANR 13, 34; CP 1, 2, 3, 4, 5; CSW; DLB 5, 212; TCLE 1:1

Haines, John Meade
See Haines, John

Hakluyt, Richard 1552-1616 .... **LC 31**
See also DLB 136; RGEL 2

Haldeman, Joe 1943- .... **CLC 61**
See also AAYA 38; CA 53-56, 179; CAAE 179; CAAS 25; CANR 6, 70, 72, 130, 171, 224; DLB 8; INT CANR-6; SCFW 2; SFW 4

Haldeman, Joe William
See Haldeman, Joe

Hale, Janet Campbell 1947- .... **NNAL**
See also CA 49-52; CANR 45, 75; DAM MULT; DLB 175; MTCW 2; MTFW 2005

Hale, Sarah Josepha (Buell) 1788-1879 .... **NCLC 75**
See also DLB 1, 42, 73, 243

Halevy, Elie 1870-1937 .... **TCLC 104**

Haley, Alex 1921-1992 ...... **BLC 1:2; CLC 8, 12, 76; TCLC 147**
See also AAYA 26; BPFB 2; BW 2, 3; CA 77-80; 136; CANR 61; CDALBS; CPW; CSW; DA; DA3; DAB; DAC; DAM MST, MULT, POP; DLB 38; LAIT 5; MTCW 1, 2; NFS 9

Haley, Alexander Murray Palmer
See Haley, Alex

Haliburton, Thomas Chandler 1796-1865 ... **NCLC 15, 149**
See also DLB 11, 99; RGEL 2; RGSF 2

Hall, Donald 1928- . **CLC 1, 13, 37, 59, 151, 240; PC 70**
See also AAYA 63; CA 5-8R; CAAS 7; CANR 2, 44, 64, 106, 133, 196; CP 1, 2, 3, 4, 5, 6, 7; DAM POET; DLB 5, 342; MAL 5; MTCW 2; MTFW 2005; RGAL 4; SATA 23, 97

Hall, Donald Andrew, Jr.
See Hall, Donald

Hall, Frederic Sauser
See Sauser-Hall, Frederic

Hall, James
See Kuttner, Henry

Hall, James Norman 1887-1951 ... **TCLC 23**
See also CA 123; 173; LAIT 1; RHW 1; SATA 21

Hall, Joseph 1574-1656 .... **LC 91**
See also DLB 121, 151; RGEL 2

Hall, Marguerite Radclyffe
See Hall, Radclyffe

Hall, Radclyffe 1880-1943 ..... **TCLC 12, 215**
See also BRWS 6; CA 110; 150; CANR 83; DLB 191; MTCW 2; MTFW 2005; RGEL 2; RHW

Hall, Rodney 1935- .... **CLC 51**
See also CA 109; CANR 69; CN 6, 7; CP 1, 2, 3, 4, 5, 6, 7; DLB 289

Hallam, Arthur Henry 1811-1833 ..... **NCLC 110**
See also DLB 32

Halldor Laxness
See Gudjonsson, Halldor Kiljan

Halleck, Fitz-Greene 1790-1867 ... **NCLC 47**
See also DLB 3, 250; RGAL 4

Halliday, Michael
See Creasey, John

Halpern, Daniel 1945- .... **CLC 14**
See also CA 33-36R; CANR 93, 174; CP 3, 4, 5, 6, 7

Hamann, Johann Georg 1730-1788 . **LC 198**
See also DLB 97

Hamburger, Michael 1924-2007 . **CLC 5, 14**
See also CA 5-8R, 196; 261; CAAE 196; CAAS 4; CANR 2, 47; CP 1, 2, 3, 4, 5, 6, 7; DLB 27

Hamburger, Michael Peter Leopold
See Hamburger, Michael

Hamill, Pete 1935- .... **CLC 10, 261**
See also CA 25-28R; CANR 18, 71, 127, 180

Hamill, William Peter
See Hamill, Pete

Hamilton, Alexander 1712-1756 .... **LC 150**
See also DLB 31

Hamilton, Alexander 1755(?)-1804 .... **NCLC 49**
See also DLB 37

Hamilton, Clive
See Lewis, C. S.

Hamilton, Edmond 1904-1977 .... **CLC 1**
See also CA 1-4R; CANR 3, 84; DLB 8; SATA 118; SFW 4

Hamilton, Elizabeth 1758-1816 .. **NCLC 153**
See also DLB 116, 158

Hamilton, Eugene (Jacob) Lee
See Lee-Hamilton, Eugene (Jacob)

Hamilton, Franklin
See Silverberg, Robert

Hamilton, Gail
See Corcoran, Barbara (Asenath)

Hamilton, (Robert) Ian 1938-2001 . **CLC 191**
See also CA 106; 203; CANR 41, 67; CP 1, 2, 3, 4, 5, 6, 7; DLB 40, 155

Hamilton, Jane 1957- .... **CLC 179**
See also CA 147; CANR 85, 128, 214; CN 7; DLB 350; MTFW 2005

Hamilton, Mollie
See Kaye, M.M.

Hamilton, Patrick 1904-1962 .... **CLC 51**
See also BRWS 16; CA 176; 113; DLB 10, 191

Hamilton, Virginia 1936-2002 .... **CLC 26**
See also AAYA 2, 21; BW 2, 3; BYA 1, 2, 8; CA 25-28R; 206; CANR 20, 37, 73, 126; CLR 1, 11, 40, 127; DAM MULT; DLB 33, 52; DLBY 2001; INT CANR-20; JRDA; LAIT 5; MAICYA 1, 2; MAICYAS 1; MTCW 1, 2; MTFW 2005; SATA 4, 56, 79, 123; SATA-Obit 132; WYA; YAW

Hamilton, Virginia Esther
See Hamilton, Virginia

Hammett, Dashiell 1894-1961 . **CLC 3, 5, 10, 19, 47; SSC 17; TCLC 187**
See also AAYA 59; AITN 1; AMWS 4; BPFB 2; CA 81-84; CANR 42; CDALB 1929-1941; CMW 4; DA3; DLB 226, 280; DLBD 6; DLBY 1996; EWL 3; LAIT 3; MAL 5; MSW; MTCW 1, 2; MTFW 2005; NFS 21; RGAL 4; RGSF 2; TUS

Hammett, Samuel Dashiell
See Hammett, Dashiell

Hammon, Jupiter 1720(?)-1800(?) . **BLC 1:2; NCLC 5; PC 16**
See also DAM MULT, POET; DLB 31, 50

Hammond, Keith
See Kuttner, Henry

Hamner, Earl (Henry), Jr. 1923- .... **CLC 12**
See also AITN 2; CA 73-76; DLB 6

Hampton, Christopher 1946- .... **CLC 4**
See also CA 25-28R; CD 5, 6; DLB 13; MTCW 1

Hampton, Christopher James
See Hampton, Christopher

Hamsun, Knut
See Pedersen, Knut

Hamsund, Knut Pedersen
See Pedersen, Knut

Handke, Peter 1942- .. **CLC 5, 8, 10, 15, 38, 134; DC 17**
See also CA 77-80; CANR 33, 75, 104, 133, 180; CWW 2; DAM DRAM, NOV; DLB 85, 124; EWL 3; MTCW 1, 2; MTFW 2005; TWA

Harvey, Jack
See Rankin, Ian

Harwood, Ronald 1934- .... **CLC 32**
See also CA 1-4R; CANR 4, 55, 150; CBD; CD 5, 6; DAM DRAM, MST; DLB 13

Hasegawa Tatsunosuke
See Futabatei, Shimei

Hasek, Jaroslav 1883-1923 .. **SSC 69; TCLC 4, 261**
See also CA 104; 129; CDWLB 4; DLB 215; EW 9; EWL 3; MTCW 1, 2; RGSF 2; RGWL 2, 3

Hasek, Jaroslav Matej Frantisek
See Hasek, Jaroslav

Hass, Robert 1941- ..... **CLC 18, 39, 99, 287; PC 16**
See also AMWS 6; CA 111; CANR 30, 50, 71, 187; CP 3, 4, 5, 6, 7; DLB 105, 206; EWL 3; MAL 5; MTFW 2005; PFS 37; RGAL 4; SATA 94; TCLE 1:1

Hassler, Jon 1933-2008 .... **CLC 263**
See also CA 73-76; 270; CANR 21, 80, 161; CN 6, 7; INT CANR-21; SATA 19; SATA-Obit 191

Hassler, Jon Francis
See Hassler, Jon

Hastings, Hudson
See Kuttner, Henry

Hastings, Selina 1945- .... **CLC 44**
See also CA 257; CANR 225

Hastings, Selina Shirley
See Hastings, Selina

Hastings, Lady Selina Shirley
See Hastings, Selina

Hastings, Victor
See Disch, Thomas M.

Hathorne, John 1641-1717 .... **LC 38**

Hatteras, Amelia
See Mencken, H. L.

Hatteras, Owen
See Mencken, H. L.; Nathan, George Jean

Hauff, Wilhelm 1802-1827 .... **NCLC 185**
See also CLR 155; DLB 90; SUFW 1

Hauptmann, Gerhart 1862-1946 ...... **DC 34; SSC 37; TCLC 4**
See also CA 104; 153; CDWLB 2; DAM DRAM; DLB 66, 118, 330; EW 8; EWL 3; RGSF 2; RGWL 2, 3; TWA

Hauptmann, Gerhart Johann Robert
See Hauptmann, Gerhart

Havel, Vaclav 1936- .... **CLC 25, 58, 65, 123, 314; DC 6**
See also CA 104; CANR 36, 63, 124, 175; CDWLB 4; CWW 2; DA3; DAM DRAM; DFS 10; DLB 232; EWL 3; LMFS 2; MTCW 1, 2; MTFW 2005; RGWL 3

Haviaras, Stratis
See Chaviaras, Strates

Hawes, Stephen 1475(?)-1529(?) .... **LC 17**
See also DLB 132; RGEL 2

Hawk, Alex
See Kelton, Elmer

Hawkes, John 1925-1998 . **CLC 1, 2, 3, 4, 7, 9, 14, 15, 27, 49**
See also BPFB 2; CA 1-4R; 167; CANR 2, 47, 64; CN 1, 2, 3, 4, 5, 6; DLB 2, 7, 227; DLBY 1980, 1998; EWL 3; MAL 5; MTCW 1, 2; MTFW 2005; RGAL 4

Hawking, S. W.
See Hawking, Stephen W.

Hawking, Stephen W. 1942- .... **CLC 63, 105**
See also AAYA 13; BEST 89:1; CA 126; 129; CANR 48, 115; CPW; DA3; MTCW 2; MTFW 2005

Hawking, Stephen William
See Hawking, Stephen W.

Hawkins, Anthony Hope
See Hope, Anthony

Hawthorne, Julian 1846-1934 .... **TCLC 25**
See also CA 165; HGG

Hawthorne, Nathaniel 1804-1864 .. **NCLC 2, 10, 17, 23, 39, 79, 95, 158, 171, 191, 226; SSC 3, 29, 39, 89, 130; WLC 3**
See also AAYA 18; AMW; AMWC 1; AMWR 1; BPFB 2; BYA 3; CDALB 1640-1865; CLR 103, 163; DA; DA3; DAB; DAC; DAM MST, NOV; DLB 1, 74, 183, 223, 269; EXPN; EXPS; GL 2; HGG; LAIT 1; NFS 1, 20; RGAL 4; RGSF 2; SSFS 1, 7, 11, 15, 30, 35; SUFW 1; TUS; WCH; YABC 2

Hawthorne, Sophia Peabody 1809-1871 ...... **NCLC 150**
See also DLB 183, 239

Haxton, Josephine Ayres 1921- ....
See Douglas, Ellen

Hayaseca y Eizaguirre, Jorge
See Echegaray (y Eizaguirre), Jose (Maria Waldo)

Hayashi, Fumiko 1904-1951 .... **TCLC 27**
See also CA 161; DLB 180; EWL 3

Hayashi Fumiko
See Hayashi, Fumiko

Haycraft, Anna 1932-2005 .... **CLC 40**
See also CA 122; 237; CANR 90, 141; CN 4, 5, 6; DLB 194; MTCW 2; MTFW 2005

Haycraft, Anna Margaret
See Haycraft, Anna

Hayden, Robert
See Hayden, Robert Earl

Hayden, Robert E.
See Hayden, Robert Earl

Hayden, Robert Earl 1913-1980 ... **BLC 1:2; CLC 5, 9, 14, 37; PC 6, 123**
See also AFAW 1, 2; AMWS 2; BW 1, 3; CA 69-72; 97-100; CABS 2; CANR 24, 75, 82; CDALB 1941-1968; CP 1, 2, 3; DA; DAC; DAM MST, MULT, POET; DLB 5, 76; EWL 3; EXPP; MAL 5; MTCW 1, 2; PFS 1, 31; RGAL 4; SATA 19; SATA-Obit 26; WP

Haydon, Benjamin Robert 1786-1846 .... **NCLC 146**
See also DLB 110

Hayek, F(riedrich) A(ugust von) 1899-1992 .... **TCLC 109**
See also CA 93-96; 137; CANR 20; MTCW 1, 2

Hayford, J(oseph) E(phraim) Casely
See Casely-Hayford, J(oseph) E(phraim)

Hayman, Ronald 1932- .... **CLC 44**
See also CA 25-28R; CANR 18, 50, 88; CD 5, 6; DLB 155

Hayne, Paul Hamilton 1830-1886 . **NCLC 94**
See also DLB 3, 64, 79, 248; RGAL 4

Haynes, Todd 1961- .... **CLC 313**
See also CA 220

Hays, Mary 1760-1843 .... **NCLC 114**
See also DLB 142, 158; RGEL 2

Haywood, Eliza (Fowler) 1693(?)-1756 .. **LC 1, 44, 177**
See also BRWS 12; DLB 39; RGEL 2

Hazlitt, William 1778-1830 ..... **NCLC 29, 82**
See also BRW 4; DLB 110, 158; RGEL 2; TEA

Hazzard, Shirley 1931- .... **CLC 18, 218**
See also CA 9-12R; CANR 4, 70, 127, 212; CN 1, 2, 3, 4, 5, 6, 7; DLB 289; DLBY 1982; MTCW 1

Head, Bessie 1937-1986 . **BLC 1:2, 2:2; CLC 25, 67; SSC 52**
See also AFW; BW 2, 3; CA 29-32R; 119; CANR 25, 82; CDWLB 3; CN 1, 2, 3, 4; DA3; DAM MULT; DLB 117, 225; EWL

3; EXPS; FL 1:6; FW; MTCW 1, 2; MTFW 2005; NFS 31; RGSF 2; SSFS 5, 13, 30, 33; WLIT 2; WWE 1

Headley, Elizabeth
See Harrison, Elizabeth (Allen) Cavanna

Headon, (Nicky) Topper 1956(?)- ... **CLC 30**

Heaney, Seamus 1939- .... **CLC 5, 7, 14, 25, 37, 74, 91, 171, 225, 309; PC 18, 100; WLCS**
See also AAYA 61; BRWR 1; BRWS 2; CA 85-88; CANR 25, 48, 75, 91, 128, 184; CDBLB 1960 to Present; CP 1, 2, 3, 4, 5, 6, 7; DA3; DAB; DAM POET; DLB 40, 330; DLBY 1995; EWL 3; EXPP; MTCW 1, 2; MTFW 2005; PAB; PFS 2, 5, 8, 17, 30, 41; RGEL 2; TEA; WLIT 4

Heaney, Seamus Justin
See Heaney, Seamus

Hearn, Lafcadio 1850-1904 .... **SSC 158; TCLC 9, 263**
See also AAYA 79; CA 105; 166; DLB 12, 78, 189; HGG; MAL 5; RGAL 4

Hearn, Patricio Lafcadio Tessima Carlos
See Hearn, Lafcadio

Hearne, Samuel 1745-1792 .... **LC 95**
See also DLB 99

Hearne, Vicki 1946-2001 .... **CLC 56**
See also CA 139; 201

Hearon, Shelby 1931- .... **CLC 63**
See also AITN 2; AMWS 8; CA 25-28R; CAAS 11; CANR 18, 48, 103, 146; CSW

Heat-Moon, William Least 1939- .... **CLC 29**
See also AAYA 9, 66; ANW; CA 115; 119; CANR 47, 89, 206; CPW; INT CA-119

Hebbel, Friedrich 1813-1863 . **DC 21; NCLC 43**
See also CDWLB 2; DAM DRAM; DLB 129; EW 6; RGWL 2, 3

Hebert, Anne 1916-2000 .... **CLC 4, 13, 29, 246; PC 126**
See also CA 85-88; 187; CANR 69, 126; CCA 1; CWP; CWW 2; DA3; DAC; DAM MST, POET; DLB 68; EWL 3; GFL 1789 to the Present; MTCW 1, 2; MTFW 2005; PFS 20

Hebreo, Leon c. 1460-1520 .... **LC 193**
See also DLB 318

Hecht, Anthony (Evan) 1923-2004 ... **CLC 8, 13, 19; PC 70**
See also AMWS 10; CA 9-12R; 232; CANR 6, 108; CP 1, 2, 3, 4, 5, 6, 7; DAM POET; DLB 5, 169; EWL 3; PFS 6; WP

Hecht, Ben 1894-1964 ... **CLC 8; TCLC 101**
See also CA 85-88; DFS 9; DLB 7, 9, 25, 26, 28, 86; FANT; IDFW 3, 4; RGAL 4

Hedayat, Sadeq 1903-1951 . **SSC 131; TCLC 21**
See also CA 120; EWL 3; RGSF 2

Hegel, Georg Wilhelm Friedrich 1770-1831 .... **NCLC 46, 151**
See also DLB 90; TWA

Heidegger, Martin 1889-1976 .... **CLC 24**
See also CA 81-84; 65-68; CANR 34; DLB 296; MTCW 1, 2; MTFW 2005

Heidenstam, (Carl Gustaf) Verner von 1859-1940 .... **TCLC 5**
See also CA 104; DLB 330

Heidi Louise
See Erdrich, Louise

Heifner, Jack 1946- .... **CLC 11**
See also CA 105; CANR 47

Heijermans, Herman 1864-1924 ... **TCLC 24**
See also CA 123; EWL 3

Heilbrun, Carolyn G. 1926-2003 ... **CLC 25, 173, 303**
See also BPFB 1; CA 45-48; 220; CANR 1, 28, 58, 94; CMW; CPW; DLB 306; FW; MSW

Heilbrun, Carolyn Gold
See Heilbrun, Carolyn G.

Hein, Christoph 1944- .... **CLC 154**
See also CA 158; CANR 108, 210; CDWLB 2; CWW 2; DLB 124

Heine, Heinrich 1797-1856 ...... **NCLC 4, 54, 147, 249; PC 25**
See also CDWLB 2; DLB 90; EW 5; PFS 37; RGWL 2, 3; TWA

Heinemann, Larry 1944- .... **CLC 50**
See also CA 110; CAAS 21; CANR 31, 81, 156; DLBD 9; INT CANR-31

Heinemann, Larry Curtiss
See Heinemann, Larry

Heiney, Donald (William) 1921-1993 ... **CLC 9**
See also CA 1-4R; 142; CANR 3, 58; FANT

Heinlein, Robert A. 1907-1988 . **CLC 1, 3, 8, 14, 26, 55; SSC 55**
See also AAYA 17; BPFB 2; BYA 4, 13; CA 1-4R; 125; CANR 1, 20, 53; CLR 75; CN 1, 2, 3, 4; CPW; DA3; DAM POP; DLB 8; EXPS; JRDA; LAIT 5; LMFS 2; MAICYA 1, 2; MTCW 1, 2; MTFW 2005; NFS 40; RGAL 4; SATA 9, 69; SATA-Obit 56; SCFW 1, 2; SFW 4; SSFS 7; YAW

Heinrich von dem Tuerlin fl. c. 1230- .... **CMLC 133**
See also DLB 138

Hejinian, Lyn 1941- .... **PC 108**
See also CA 153; CANR 85, 214; CP 4, 5, 6, 7; CWP; DLB 165; PFS 27; RGAL 4

Held, Peter
See Vance, Jack

Heldris of Cornwall fl. 13th cent. - ... **CMLC 97**

Helforth, John
See Doolittle, Hilda

Heliodorus fl. 3rd cent. - .... **CMLC 52**
See also WLIT 8

Hellenhofferu, Vojtech Kapristian z
See Hasek, Jaroslav

Heller, Joseph 1923-1999 ..... **CLC 1, 3, 5, 8, 11, 36, 63; TCLC 131, 151; WLC 3**
See also AAYA 24; AITN 1; AMWS 4; BPFB 2; BYA 1; CA 5-8R; 187; CABS 1; CANR 8, 42, 66, 126; CN 1, 2, 3, 4, 5, 6; CPW; DA; DA3; DAB; DAC; DAM MST, NOV, POP; DLB 2, 28, 227; DLBY 1980, 2002; EWL 3; EXPN; INT CANR-8; LAIT 4; MAL 5; MTCW 1, 2; MTFW 2005; NFS 1; RGAL 4; TUS; YAW

Hellman, Lillian 1905-1984 ...... **CLC 2, 4, 8, 14, 18, 34, 44, 52; DC 1; TCLC 119**
See also AAYA 47; AITN 1, 2; AMWS 1; CA 13-16R; 112; CAD; CANR 33; CWD; DA3; DAM DRAM; DFS 1, 3, 14; DLB 7, 228; DLBY 1984; EWL 3; FL 1:6; FW; LAIT 3; MAL 5; MBL; MTCW 1, 2; MTFW 2005; RGAL 4; TUS

Hellman, Lillian Florence
See Hellman, Lillian

Heloise c. 1095-c. 1164 .... **CMLC 122**

Helprin, Mark 1947- .... **CLC 7, 10, 22, 32**
See also CA 81-84; CANR 47, 64, 124, 222; CDALBS; CN 7; CPW; DA3; DAM NOV, POP; DLB 335; DLBY 1985; FANT; MAL 5; MTCW 1, 2; MTFW 2005; SSFS 25; SUFW 2

Helvetius, Claude-Adrien 1715-1771 . **LC 26**
See also DLB 313

Helyar, Jane Penelope Josephine 1933- .... **CLC 17**
See also CA 21-24R; CANR 10, 26; CWRI 5; SAAS 2; SATA 5; SATA-Essay 138

Hemans, Felicia 1793-1835 ..... **NCLC 29, 71**
See also DLB 96; RGEL 2

Hemingway, Ernest 1899-1961 . **CLC 1, 3, 6, 8, 10, 13, 19, 30, 34, 39, 41, 44, 50, 61, 80; SSC 1, 25, 36, 40, 63, 117, 137; TCLC 115, 203; WLC 3**
See also AAYA 19; AMW; AMWC 1; AMWR 1; BPFB 2; BYA 2, 3, 13, 15; CA 77-80; CANR 34; CDALB 1917-1929; CLR 168; DA; DA3; DAB; DAC; DAM MST, NOV; DLB 4, 9, 102, 210, 308, 330; DLBD 1, 15, 16; DLBY 1981, 1987, 1996, 1998; EWL 3; EXPN; EXPS; LAIT 3, 4; LATS 1:1; MAL 5; MTCW 1, 2; MTFW 2005; NFS 1, 5, 6, 14; RGAL 4; RGSF 2; SSFS 17; TUS; WYA

Hemingway, Ernest Miller
See Hemingway, Ernest

Hempel, Amy 1951- .... **CLC 39**
See also AMWS 21; CA 118; 137; CANR 70, 166; DA3; DLB 218; EXPS; MTCW 2; MTFW 2005; SSFS 2

Henderson, F. C.
See Mencken, H. L.

Henderson, Mary
See Mavor, Osborne Henry

Henderson, Sylvia
See Ashton-Warner, Sylvia (Constance)

Henderson, Zenna (Chlarson) 1917-1983 .... **SSC 29**
See also CA 1-4R; 133; CANR 1, 84; DLB 8; SATA 5; SFW 4

Henkin, Joshua 1964- .... **CLC 119**
See also CA 161; CANR 186; DLB 350

Henley, Beth 1952- . **CLC 23, 255; DC 6, 14**
See also AAYA 70; CA 107; CABS 3; CAD; CANR 32, 73, 140; CD 5, 6; CSW; CWD; DA3; DAM DRAM, MST; DFS 2, 21, 26; DLBY 1986; FW; MTCW 1, 2; MTFW 2005

Henley, Elizabeth Becker
See Henley, Beth

Henley, William Ernest 1849-1903 . **PC 127; TCLC 8**
See also CA 105; 234; DLB 19; RGEL 2

Hennissart, Martha 1929- .... **CLC 2**
See also BPFB 2; CA 85-88; CANR 64; CMW 4; DLB 306

Henry VIII 1491-1547 .... **LC 10**
See also DLB 132

Henry, O. 1862-1910(?) . **SSC 5, 49, 117; TCLC 1, 19; WLC 3**
See also AAYA 41; AMWS 2; CA 104; 131; CDALB 1865-1917; DA; DA3; DAB; DAC; DAM MST; DLB 12, 78, 79; EXPS; MAL 5; MTCW 1, 2; MTFW 2005; RGAL 4; RGSF 2; SSFS 2, 18, 27, 31; TCWW 1, 2; TUS; YABC 2

Henry, Oliver
See Henry, O.

Henry, Patrick 1736-1799 .... **LC 25**
See also LAIT 1

Henryson, Robert 1430(?)-1506(?) .... **LC 20, 110; PC 65**
See also BRWS 7; DLB 146; RGEL 2

Henschke, Alfred
See Klabund

Henson, Lance 1944- .... **NNAL**
See also CA 146; DLB 175

Hentoff, Nat(han Irving) 1925- .... **CLC 26**
See also AAYA 4, 42; BYA 6; CA 1-4R; CAAS 6; CANR 5, 25, 77, 114; CLR 1, 52; DLB 345; INT CANR-25; JRDA; MAICYA 1, 2; SATA 42, 69, 133; SATA-Brief 27; WYA; YAW

Heppenstall, (John) Rayner 1911-1981 . **CLC 10**
See also CA 1-4R; 103; CANR 29; CN 1, 2; CP 1, 2, 3; EWL 3

Heraclitus c. 540B.C.-c. 450B.C. . **CMLC 22**
See also DLB 176

Herbert, Edward 1583-1648 .... **LC 177**
See also DLB 121, 151, 252; RGEL 2

Herbert, Frank 1920-1986 . **CLC 12, 23, 35, 44, 85**
See also AAYA 21; BPFB 2; BYA 4, 14; CA 53-56; 118; CANR 5, 43; CDALBS; CPW; DAM POP; DLB 8; INT CANR-5; LAIT 5; MTCW 1, 2; MTFW 2005; NFS 17, 31; SATA 9, 37; SATA-Obit 47; SCFW 1, 2; SFW 4; YAW

Herbert, George 1593-1633 . **LC 24, 121; PC 4**
See also BRW 2; BRWR 2; CDBLB Before 1660; DAB; DAM POET; DLB 126; EXPP; PFS 25; RGEL 2; TEA; WP

Herbert, Zbigniew 1924-1998 .... **CLC 9, 43; PC 50; TCLC 168**
See also CA 89-92; 169; CANR 36, 74, 177; CDWLB 4; CWW 2; DAM POET; DLB 232; EWL 3; MTCW 1; PFS 22

Herbert of Cherbury, Lord
See Herbert, Edward

Herbst, Josephine (Frey) 1897-1969 .... **CLC 34; TCLC 243**
See also CA 5-8R; 25-28R; DLB 9

Herder, Johann Gottfried von 1744-1803 .... **NCLC 8, 186**
See also DLB 97; EW 4; TWA

Heredia, Jose Maria 1803-1839 ..... **HLCS 2; NCLC 209**
See also LAW

Hergesheimer, Joseph 1880-1954 .. **TCLC 11**
See also CA 109; 194; DLB 102, 9; RGAL 4

Herlihy, James Leo 1927-1993 .... **CLC 6**
See also CA 1-4R; 143; CAD; CANR 2; CN 1, 2, 3, 4, 5

Herman, William
See Bierce, Ambrose

Hermogenes fl. c. 175- .... **CMLC 6**

Hernandez, Felisberto 1902-1964 ... **SSC 152**
See also CA 213; EWL 3; LAWS 1

Hernandez, Jose 1834-1886 .... **NCLC 17**
See also LAW; RGWL 2, 3; WLIT 1

Herodotus c. 484B.C.-c. 420B.C. . **CMLC 17**
See also AW 1; CDWLB 1; DLB 176; RGWL 2, 3; TWA; WLIT 8

Herr, Michael 1940(?)- .... **CLC 231**
See also CA 89-92; CANR 68, 142; DLB 185; MTCW 1

Herrick, Robert 1591-1674 . **LC 13, 145; PC 9**
See also BRW 2; BRWC 2; DA; DAB; DAC; DAM MST, POP; DLB 126; EXPP; PFS 13, 29, 39; RGAL 4; RGEL 2; TEA; WP

Herring, Guilles
See Somerville, Edith Oenone

Herriot, James 1916-1995 .... **CLC 12**
See also AAYA 1, 54; BPFB 2; CA 77-80; 148; CANR 40; CLR 80; CPW; DAM POP; LAIT 3; MAICYA 2; MAICYAS 1; MTCW 2; SATA 86, 135; SATA-Brief 44; TEA; YAW

Herris, Violet
See Hunt, Violet

Herrmann, Dorothy 1941- .... **CLC 44**
See also CA 107

Herrmann, Taffy
See Herrmann, Dorothy

Hersey, John 1914-1993 . **CLC 1, 2, 7, 9, 40, 81, 97**
See also AAYA 29; BPFB 2; CA 17-20R; 140; CANR 33; CDALBS; CN 1, 2, 3, 4, 5; CPW; DAM POP; DLB 6, 185, 278, 299, 364; MAL 5; MTCW 1, 2; MTFW 2005; RGHL; SATA 25; SATA-Obit 76; TUS

Hobson, Laura Z(ametkin) 1900-1986 . **CLC 7, 25**
See also BPFB 2; CA 17-20R; 118; CANR 55; CN 1, 2, 3, 4; DLB 28; SATA 52

Hoccleve, Thomas c. 1368-c. 1437 ..... **LC 75**
See also DLB 146; RGEL 2

Hoch, Edward D. 1930-2008 .... **SSC 119**
See also CA 29-32R; CANR 11, 27, 51, 97; CMW 4; DLB 306; SFW 4

Hoch, Edward Dentinger
See Hoch, Edward D.

Hochhuth, Rolf 1931- .... **CLC 4, 11, 18**
See also CA 5-8R; CANR 33, 75, 136; CWW 2; DAM DRAM; DLB 124; EWL 3; MTCW 1, 2; MTFW 2005; RGHL

Hochman, Sandra 1936- .... **CLC 3, 8**
See also CA 5-8R; CP 1, 2, 3, 4, 5; DLB 5

Hochwaelder, Fritz 1911-1986 .... **CLC 36**
See also CA 29-32R; 120; CANR 42; DAM DRAM; EWL 3; MTCW 1; RGWL 2, 3

Hochwalder, Fritz
See Hochwaelder, Fritz

Hocking, Mary 1921- .... **CLC 13**
See also CA 101; CANR 18, 40

Hocking, Mary Eunice
See Hocking, Mary

Hodge, Merle 1944- .... **BLC 2:2**
See also EWL 3

Hodgins, Jack 1938- .... **CLC 23; SSC 132**
See also CA 93-96; CN 4, 5, 6, 7; DLB 60

Hodgson, William Hope 1877(?)-1918 .... **TCLC 13**
See also CA 111; 164; CMW 4; DLB 70, 153, 156, 178; HGG; MTCW 2; SFW 4; SUFW 1

Hoeg, Peter
See Hoeg, Peter

Hoeg, Peter 1957- .... **CLC 95, 156**
See also CA 151; CANR 75, 202; CMW 4; DA3; DLB 214; EWL 3; MTCW 2; MTFW 2005; NFS 17; RGWL 3; SSFS 18

Hoffman, Alice 1952- .... **CLC 51**
See also AAYA 37; AMWS 10; CA 77-80; CANR 34, 66, 100, 138, 170; CN 4, 5, 6, 7; CPW; DAM NOV; DLB 292; MAL 5; MTCW 1, 2; MTFW 2005; TCLE 1:1

Hoffman, Daniel (Gerard) 1923- ...... **CLC 6, 13, 23**
See also CA 1-4R; CANR 4, 142; CP 1, 2, 3, 4, 5, 6, 7; DLB 5; TCLE 1:1

Hoffman, Eva 1945- .... **CLC 182**
See also AMWS 16; CA 132; CANR 146, 209

Hoffman, Stanley 1944- .... **CLC 5**
See also CA 77-80

Hoffman, William 1925-2009 .... **CLC 141**
See also AMWS 18; CA 21-24R; CANR 9, 103; CSW; DLB 234; TCLE 1:1

Hoffman, William M.
See Hoffman, William M(oses)

Hoffman, William M(oses) 1939- .... **CLC 40**
See also CA 57-60; CAD; CANR 11, 71; CD 5, 6

Hoffmann, E(rnst) T(heodor) A(madeus) 1776-1822 ... **NCLC 2, 183; SSC 13, 92**
See also CDWLB 2; CLR 133; DLB 90; EW 5; GL 2; RGSF 2; RGWL 2, 3; SATA 27; SUFW 1; WCH

Hofmann, Gert 1931-1993 .... **CLC 54**
See also CA 128; CANR 145; EWL 3; RGHL

Hofmannsthal, Hugo von 1874-1929 . **DC 4; TCLC 11**
See also CA 106; 153; CDWLB 2; DAM DRAM; DFS 17; DLB 81, 118; EW 9; EWL 3; RGWL 2, 3

Hogan, Linda 1947- .. **CLC 73, 290; NNAL; PC 35**
See also AMWS 4; ANW; BYA 12; CA 120, 226; CAAE 226; CANR 45, 73, 129, 196; CWP; DAM MULT; DLB 175; SATA 132; TCWW 2

Hogarth, Charles
See Creasey, John

Hogarth, Emmett
See Polonsky, Abraham (Lincoln)

Hogarth, William 1697-1764 .... **LC 112**
See also AAYA 56

Hogg, James 1770-1835 . **NCLC 4, 109; SSC 130**
See also BRWS 10; DLB 93, 116, 159; GL 2; HGG; RGEL 2; SUFW 1

Holbach, Paul-Henri Thiry 1723-1789 ... **LC 14**
See also DLB 313

Holberg, Ludvig 1684-1754 .... **LC 6**
See also DLB 300; RGWL 2, 3

Holbrook, John
See Vance, Jack

Holcroft, Thomas 1745-1809 .... **NCLC 85**
See also DLB 39, 89, 158; RGEL 2

Holden, Ursula 1921- .... **CLC 18**
See also CA 101; CAAS 8; CANR 22

Holderlin, (Johann Christian) Friedrich 1770-1843 .... **NCLC 16, 187; PC 4**
See also CDWLB 2; DLB 90; EW 5; RGWL 2, 3

Holdstock, Robert 1948-2009 .... **CLC 39**
See also CA 131; CANR 81, 207; DLB 261; FANT; HGG; SFW 4; SUFW 2

Holdstock, Robert P.
See Holdstock, Robert

Holinshed, Raphael fl. 1580- .... **LC 69**
See also DLB 167; RGEL 2

Holland, Isabelle (Christian) 1920-2002 ...... **CLC 21**
See also AAYA 11, 64; CA 21-24R; 205; CAAE 181; CANR 10, 25, 47; CLR 57; CWRI 5; JRDA; LAIT 4; MAICYA 1, 2; SATA 8, 70; SATA-Essay 103; SATA-Obit 132; WYA

Holland, Marcus
See Caldwell, (Janet Miriam) Taylor (Holland)

Hollander, John 1929- . **CLC 2, 5, 8, 14; PC 117**
See also CA 1-4R; CANR 1, 52, 136; CP 1, 2, 3, 4, 5, 6, 7; DLB 5; MAL 5; SATA 13

Hollander, Paul
See Silverberg, Robert

Holleran, Andrew 1943(?)- .... **CLC 38**
See also CA 144; CANR 89, 162; GLL 1

Holley, Marietta 1836(?)-1926 ...... **TCLC 99**
See also CA 118; DLB 11; FL 1:3

Hollinghurst, Alan 1954- .... **CLC 55, 91**
See also BRWS 10; CA 114; CN 5, 6, 7; DLB 207, 326; GLL 1

Hollis, Jim
See Summers, Hollis (Spurgeon, Jr.)

Holly, Buddy 1936-1959 .... **TCLC 65**
See also CA 213

Holmes, Gordon
See Shiel, M. P.

Holmes, John
See Souster, (Holmes) Raymond

Holmes, John Clellon 1926-1988 ..... **CLC 56**
See also BG 1:2; CA 9-12R; 125; CANR 4; CN 1, 2, 3, 4; DLB 16, 237

Holmes, Oliver Wendell, Jr. 1841-1935 .... **TCLC 77**
See also CA 114; 186

Holmes, Oliver Wendell 1809-1894 ... **NCLC 14, 81; PC 71**
See also AMWS 1; CDALB 1640-1865; DLB 1, 189, 235; EXPP; PFS 24; RGAL 4; SATA 34

Holmes, Raymond
See Souster, (Holmes) Raymond

Holt, Samuel
See Westlake, Donald E.

Holt, Victoria
See Hibbert, Eleanor Alice Burford

Holub, Miroslav 1923-1998 .... **CLC 4**
See also CA 21-24R; 169; CANR 10; CD-WLB 4; CWW 2; DLB 232; EWL 3; RGWL 3

Holz, Detlev
See Benjamin, Walter

Homer c. 8th cent. B.C.- ... **CMLC 1, 16, 61, 121; PC 23; WLCS**
See also AW 1; CDWLB 1; DA; DA3; DAB; DAC; DAM MST, POET; DLB 176; EFS 1:1, 2:1,2; LAIT 1; LMFS 1; RGWL 2, 3; TWA; WLIT 8; WP

Hong, Maxine Ting Ting
See Kingston, Maxine Hong

Hongo, Garrett Kaoru 1951- .... **PC 23**
See also CA 133; CAAS 22; CP 5, 6, 7; DLB 120, 312; EWL 3; EXPP; PFS 25, 33; RGAL 4

Honig, Edwin 1919-2011 .... **CLC 33**
See also CA 5-8R; CAAS 8; CANR 4, 45, 144; CP 1, 2, 3, 4, 5, 6, 7; DLB 5

Hood, Hugh (John Blagdon) 1928- ...... **CLC 15, 28, 273; SSC 42**
See also CA 49-52; CAAS 17; CANR 1, 33, 87; CN 1, 2, 3, 4, 5, 6, 7; DLB 53; RGSF 2

Hood, Thomas 1799-1845 .... **NCLC 16, 242; PC 93**
See also BRW 4; DLB 96; RGEL 2

Hooker, (Peter) Jeremy 1941- .... **CLC 43**
See also CA 77-80; CANR 22; CP 2, 3, 4, 5, 6, 7; DLB 40

Hooker, Richard 1554-1600 .... **LC 95**
See also BRW 1; DLB 132; RGEL 2

Hooker, Thomas 1586-1647 .... **LC 137**
See also DLB 24

hooks, bell 1952(?)- .... **BLCS; CLC 94**
See also BW 2; CA 143; CANR 87, 126, 211; DLB 246; MTCW 2; MTFW 2005; SATA 115, 170

Hooper, Johnson Jones 1815-1862 .... **NCLC 177**
See also DLB 3, 11, 248; RGAL 4

Hope, A(lec) D(erwent) 1907-2000 ... **CLC 3, 51; PC 56**
See also BRWS 7; CA 21-24R; 188; CANR 33, 74; CP 1, 2, 3, 4, 5; DLB 289; EWL 3; MTCW 1, 2; MTFW 2005; PFS 8; RGEL 2

Hope, Anthony 1863-1933 .... **TCLC 83**
See also CA 157; DLB 153, 156; RGEL 2; RHW

Hope, Brian
See Creasey, John

Hope, Christopher 1944- .... **CLC 52**
See also AFW; CA 106; CANR 47, 101, 177; CN 4, 5, 6, 7; DLB 225; SATA 62

Hope, Christopher David Tully
See Hope, Christopher

Hopkins, Gerard Manley 1844-1889 . **NCLC 17, 189; PC 15; WLC 3**
See also BRW 5; BRWR 2; CDBLB 1890-1914; DA; DA3; DAB; DAC; DAM MST, POET; DLB 35, 57; EXPP; PAB; PFS 26, 40; RGEL 2; TEA; WP

Hopkins, John (Richard) 1931-1998 . **CLC 4**
See also CA 85-88; 169; CBD; CD 5, 6

Jin Ha
See Jin, Ha
Jodelle, Etienne 1532-1573 .... **LC 119**
See also DLB 327; GFL Beginnings to 1789
Joel, Billy
See Joel, William Martin
Joel, William Martin 1949- .... **CLC 26**
See also CA 108
John, St.
See John of Damascus, St.
John of Damascus, St. c. 675-749 ..... **CMLC 27, 95**
John of Salisbury c. 1120-1180 .. **CMLC 63, 128**
John of the Cross, St. 1542-1591 ...... **LC 18, 146**
See also RGWL 2, 3
John Paul II, Pope 1920-2005 .... **CLC 128**
See also CA 106; 133; 238
Johnson, B(ryan) S(tanley William) 1933-1973 .... **CLC 6, 9**
See also CA 9-12R; 53-56; CANR 9; CN 1; CP 1, 2; DLB 14, 40; EWL 3; RGEL 2
Johnson, Benjamin F., of Boone
See Riley, James Whitcomb
Johnson, Charles (Richard) 1948- . **BLC 1:2, 2:2; CLC 7, 51, 65, 163; SSC 160**
See also AFAW 2; AMWS 6; BW 2, 3; CA 116; CAAS 18; CANR 42, 66, 82, 129; CN 5, 6, 7; DAM MULT; DLB 33, 278; MAL 5; MTCW 2; MTFW 2005; RGAL 4; SSFS 16
Johnson, Charles S(purgeon) 1893-1956 ..... **HR 1:3**
See also BW 1, 3; CA 125; CANR 82; DLB 51, 91
Johnson, Denis 1949- . **CLC 52, 160; SSC 56**
See also CA 117; 121; CANR 71, 99, 178; CN 4, 5, 6, 7; DLB 120
Johnson, Diane 1934- .... **CLC 5, 13, 48, 244**
See also BPFB 2; CA 41-44R; CANR 17, 40, 62, 95, 155, 198; CN 4, 5, 6, 7; DLB 350; DLBY 1980; INT CANR-17; MTCW 1
Johnson, E(mily) Pauline 1861-1913 . **NNAL**
See also CA 150; CCA 1; DAC; DAM MULT; DLB 92, 175; TCWW 2
Johnson, Eyvind (Olof Verner) 1900-1976 .. **CLC 14**
See also CA 73-76; 69-72; CANR 34, 101; DLB 259, 330; EW 12; EWL 3
Johnson, Fenton 1888-1958 .... **BLC 1:2**
See also BW 1; CA 118; 124; DAM MULT; DLB 45, 50
Johnson, Georgia Douglas (Camp) 1880-1966 .... **HR 1:3**
See also BW 1; CA 125; DLB 51, 249; WP
Johnson, Helene 1907-1995 .... **HR 1:3**
See also CA 181; DLB 51; WP
Johnson, J. R.
See James, C.L.R.
Johnson, James Weldon 1871-1938 ...... **BLC 1:2; HR 1:3; PC 24; TCLC 3, 19, 175**
See also AAYA 73; AFAW 1, 2; BW 1, 3; CA 104; 125; CANR 82; CDALB 1917-1929; CLR 32; DA3; DAM MULT, POET; DLB 51; EWL 3; EXPP; LMFS 2; MAL 5; MTCW 1, 2; MTFW 2005; NFS 22; PFS 1; RGAL 4; SATA 31; TUS
Johnson, Joyce 1935- .... **CLC 58**
See also BG 1:3; CA 125; 129; CANR 102
Johnson, Judith 1936- .... **CLC 7, 15**
See also CA 25-28R; 153; CANR 34, 85; CP 2, 3, 4, 5, 6, 7; CWP
Johnson, Judith Emlyn
See Johnson, Judith
Johnson, Lionel (Pigot) 1867-1902 .... **TCLC 19**
See also CA 117; 209; DLB 19; RGEL 2

Johnson, Marguerite Annie
See Angelou, Maya
Johnson, Mel
See Malzberg, Barry N(athaniel)
Johnson, Pamela Hansford 1912-1981 . **CLC 1, 7, 27**
See also CA 1-4R; 104; CANR 2, 28; CN 1, 2, 3; DLB 15; MTCW 1, 2; MTFW 2005; RGEL 2
Johnson, Paul 1928- .... **CLC 147**
See also BEST 89:4; CA 17-20R; CANR 34, 62, 100, 155, 197
Johnson, Paul Bede
See Johnson, Paul
Johnson, Robert CLC 70
Johnson, Robert 1911(?)-1938 ...... **TCLC 69**
See also BW 3; CA 174
Johnson, Samuel 1709-1784 . **LC 15, 52, 128; PC 81; WLC 3**
See also BRW 3; BRWR 1; CDBLB 1660-1789; DA; DAB; DAC; DAM MST; DLB 39, 95, 104, 142, 213; LMFS 1; RGEL 2; TEA
Johnson, Stacie
See Myers, Walter Dean
Johnson, Uwe 1934-1984 ...... **CLC 5, 10, 15, 40; TCLC 249**
See also CA 1-4R; 112; CANR 1, 39; CDWLB 2; DLB 75; EWL 3; MTCW 1; RGWL 2, 3
Johnston, Basil H. 1929- .... **NNAL**
See also CA 69-72; CANR 11, 28, 66; DAC; DAM MULT; DLB 60
Johnston, George (Benson) 1913- ... **CLC 51**
See also CA 1-4R; CANR 5, 20; CP 1, 2, 3, 4, 5, 6, 7; DLB 88
Johnston, Jennifer (Prudence) 1930- ... **CLC 7, 150, 228**
See also CA 85-88; CANR 92; CN 4, 5, 6, 7; DLB 14
Joinville, Jean de 1224(?)-1317 ... **CMLC 38**
Jolley, Elizabeth 1923-2007 .... **CLC 46, 256, 260; SSC 19**
See also CA 127; 257; CAAS 13; CANR 59; CN 4, 5, 6, 7; DLB 325; EWL 3; RGSF 2
Jolley, Monica Elizabeth
See Jolley, Elizabeth
Jones, Arthur Llewellyn 1863-1947 . **SSC 20; TCLC 4**
See also CA 104; 179; DLB 36; HGG; RGEL 2; SUFW 1
Jones, D(ouglas) G(ordon) 1929- .... **CLC 10**
See also CA 29-32R; CANR 13, 90; CP 1, 2, 3, 4, 5, 6, 7; DLB 53
Jones, David (Michael) 1895-1974 ... **CLC 2, 4, 7, 13, 42; PC 116**
See also BRW 6; BRWS 7; CA 9-12R; 53-56; CANR 28; CDBLB 1945-1960; CP 1, 2; DLB 20, 100; EWL 3; MTCW 1; PAB; RGEL 2
Jones, David Robert 1947- .... **CLC 17**
See also CA 103; CANR 104
Jones, Diana Wynne 1934-2011 ...... **CLC 26**
See also AAYA 12; BYA 6, 7, 9, 11, 13, 16; CA 49-52; CANR 4, 26, 56, 120, 167; CLR 23, 120; DLB 161; FANT; JRDA; MAICYA 1, 2; MTFW 2005; SAAS 7; SATA 9, 70, 108, 160, 234; SFW 4; SUFW 2; YAW
Jones, Edward P. 1950- . **BLC 2:2; CLC 76, 223**
See also AAYA 71; BW 2, 3; CA 142; CANR 79, 134, 190; CSW; LNFS 2; MTFW 2005; NFS 26
Jones, Edward Paul
See Jones, Edward P.

Jones, Ernest Charles 1819-1869 ...... **NCLC 222**
See also DLB 32
Jones, Everett LeRoi
See Baraka, Amiri
Jones, Gayl 1949- . **BLC 1:2; CLC 6, 9, 131, 270**
See also AFAW 1, 2; BW 2, 3; CA 77-80; CANR 27, 66, 122; CN 4, 5, 6, 7; CSW; DA3; DAM MULT; DLB 33, 278; MAL 5; MTCW 1, 2; MTFW 2005; RGAL 4
Jones, James 1921-1977 .... **CLC 1, 3, 10, 39**
See also AITN 1, 2; AMWS 11; BPFB 2; CA 1-4R; 69-72; CANR 6; CN 1, 2; DLB 2, 143; DLBD 17; DLBY 1998; EWL 3; MAL 5; MTCW 1; RGAL 4
Jones, John J.
See Lovecraft, H. P.
Jones, LeRoi
See Baraka, Amiri
Jones, Louis B. 1953- .... **CLC 65**
See also CA 141; CANR 73
Jones, Madison 1925- .... **CLC 4**
See also CA 13-16R; CAAS 11; CANR 7, 54, 83, 158; CN 1, 2, 3, 4, 5, 6, 7; CSW; DLB 152
Jones, Madison Percy, Jr.
See Jones, Madison
Jones, Mervyn 1922-2010 .... **CLC 10, 52**
See also CA 45-48; CAAS 5; CANR 1, 91; CN 1, 2, 3, 4, 5, 6, 7; MTCW 1
Jones, Mick 1956(?)- .... **CLC 30**
Jones, Nettie (Pearl) 1941- .... **CLC 34**
See also BW 2; CA 137; CAAS 20; CANR 88
Jones, Peter 1802-1856 .... **NNAL**
Jones, Preston 1936-1979 .... **CLC 10**
See also CA 73-76; 89-92; DLB 7
Jones, Robert F(rancis) 1934-2003 ... **CLC 7**
See also CA 49-52; CANR 2, 61, 118
Jones, Rod 1953- .... **CLC 50**
See also CA 128
Jones, Terence Graham Parry 1942- ... **CLC 21**
See also CA 112; 116; CANR 35, 93, 173; INT CA-116; SATA 67, 127; SATA-Brief 51
Jones, Terry
See Jones, Terence Graham Parry
Jones, Thom (Douglas) 1945(?)- .... **CLC 81; SSC 56**
See also CA 157; CANR 88; DLB 244; SSFS 23
Jones, Sir William 1746-1794 .... **LC 191**
See also DLB 109
Jong, Erica 1942- .... **CLC 4, 6, 8, 18, 83**
See also AITN 1; AMWS 5; BEST 90:2; BPFB 2; CA 73-76; CANR 26, 52, 75, 132, 166, 212; CN 3, 4, 5, 6, 7; CP 2, 3, 4, 5, 6, 7; CPW; DA3; DAM NOV, POP; DLB 2, 5, 28, 152; FW; INT CANR-26; MAL 5; MTCW 1, 2; MTFW 2005
Jonson, Ben 1572(?)-1637 .. **DC 4; LC 6, 33, 110, 158, 196; PC 17; WLC 3**
See also BRW 1; BRWC 1; BRWR 1; CDBLB Before 1660; DA; DAB; DAC; DAM DRAM, MST, POET; DFS 4, 10; DLB 62, 121; LMFS 1; PFS 23, 33; RGEL 2; TEA; WLIT 3
Jonson, Benjamin
See Jonson, Ben
Jordan, June 1936-2002 . **BLCS; CLC 5, 11, 23, 114, 230; PC 38**
See also AAYA 2, 66; AFAW 1, 2; BW 2, 3; CA 33-36R; 206; CANR 25, 70, 114, 154; CLR 10; CP 3, 4, 5, 6, 7; CWP; DAM MULT, POET; DLB 38; GLL 2; LAIT 5; MAICYA 1, 2; MTCW 1; SATA 4, 136; YAW

Kaufman, George S. 1889-1961 ..... **CLC 38; DC 17**
See also CA 108; 93-96; DAM DRAM; DFS 1, 10; DLB 7; INT CA-108; MTCW 2; MTFW 2005; RGAL 4; TUS

Kaufman, Moises 1963- .... **DC 26**
See also AAYA 85; CA 211; DFS 22; MTFW 2005

Kaufman, Sue
See Barondess, Sue K.

Kavafis, Konstantinos Petrov
See Cavafy, Constantine

Kavan, Anna 1901-1968 .... **CLC 5, 13, 82**
See also BRWS 7; CA 5-8R; CANR 6, 57; DLB 255; MTCW 1; RGEL 2; SFW 4

Kavanagh, Dan
See Barnes, Julian

Kavanagh, Julie 1952- .... **CLC 119**
See also CA 163; CANR 186

Kavanagh, Patrick (Joseph) 1904-1967 ....
CLC 22; PC 33, 105
See also BRWS 7; CA 123; 25-28R; DLB 15, 20; EWL 3; MTCW 1; RGEL 2

Kawabata, Yasunari 1899-1972 ... **CLC 2, 5, 9, 18, 107; SSC 17**
See also CA 93-96; 33-36R; CANR 88; DAM MULT; DLB 180, 330; EWL 3; MJW; MTCW 2; MTFW 2005; RGSF 2; RGWL 2, 3; SSFS 29

Kawabata Yasunari
See Kawabata, Yasunari

Kaye, Mary Margaret
See Kaye, M.M.

Kaye, M.M. 1908-2004 .... **CLC 28**
See also CA 89-92; 223; CANR 24, 60, 102, 142; MTCW 1, 2; MTFW 2005; RHW; SATA 62; SATA-Obit 152

Kaye, Mollie
See Kaye, M.M.

Kaye-Smith, Sheila 1887-1956 ...... **TCLC 20**
See also CA 118; 203; DLB 36

Kaymor, Patrice Maguilene
See Senghor, Leopold Sedar

Kazakov, Iurii Pavlovich
See Kazakov, Yuri Pavlovich

Kazakov, Yuri Pavlovich 1927-1982 . **SSC 43**
See also CA 5-8R; CANR 36; DLB 302; EWL 3; MTCW 1; RGSF 2

Kazakov, Yury
See Kazakov, Yuri Pavlovich

Kazan, Elia 1909-2003 .... **CLC 6, 16, 63**
See also AAYA 83; CA 21-24R; 220; CANR 32, 78

Kazanjoglou, Elia
See Kazan, Elia

Kazantzakis, Nikos 1883(?)-1957 .... **PC 126; TCLC 2, 5, 33, 181**
See also AAYA 83; BPFB 2; CA 105; 132; DA3; EW 9; EWL 3; MTCW 1, 2; MTFW 2005; RGWL 2, 3

Kazin, Alfred 1915-1998 .... **CLC 34, 38, 119**
See also AMWS 8; CA 1-4R; CAAS 7; CANR 1, 45, 79; DLB 67; EWL 3

Keane, Mary Nesta 1904-1996 .... **CLC 31**
See also CA 108; 114; 151; CN 5, 6; INT CA-114; RHW; TCLE 1:1

Keane, Mary Nesta Skrine
See Keane, Mary Nesta

Keane, Molly
See Keane, Mary Nesta

Keates, Jonathan 1946(?)- .... **CLC 34**
See also CA 163; CANR 126

Keaton, Buster 1895-1966 .... **CLC 20**
See also AAYA 79; CA 194

Keats, John 1795-1821 ..... **NCLC 8, 73, 121, 225; PC 1, 96; WLC 3**
See also AAYA 58; BRW 4; BRWR 1; CD-BLB 1789-1832; DA; DA3; DAB; DAC; DAM MST, POET; DLB 96, 110; EXPP;

LMFS 1; PAB; PFS 1, 2, 3, 9, 17, 32, 36; RGEL 2; TEA; WLIT 3; WP

Keble, John 1792-1866 .... **NCLC 87**
See also DLB 32, 55; RGEL 2

Keene, Donald 1922- .... **CLC 34**
See also CA 1-4R; CANR 5, 119, 190

Keillor, Garrison 1942- .... **CLC 40, 115, 222**
See also AAYA 2, 62; AMWS 16; BEST 89:3; BPFB 2; CA 111; 117; CANR 36, 59, 124, 180; CPW; DA3; DAM POP; DLBY 1987; EWL 3; MTCW 1, 2; MTFW 2005; SATA 58; TUS

Keillor, Gary Edward
See Keillor, Garrison

Keith, Carlos
See Lewton, Val

Keith, Michael
See Hubbard, L. Ron

Kell, Joseph
See Burgess, Anthony

Keller, Gottfried 1819-1890 .. **NCLC 2; SSC 26, 107**
See also CDWLB 2; DLB 129; EW; RGSF 2; RGWL 2, 3

Keller, Nora Okja 1965- .... **CLC 109, 281**
See also CA 187

Kellerman, Jonathan 1949- .... **CLC 44**
See also AAYA 35; BEST 90:1; CA 106; CANR 29, 51, 150, 183; CMW 4; CPW; DA3; DAM POP; INT CANR-29

Kelley, William Melvin 1937- .... **BLC 2:2; CLC 22**
See also BW 1; CA 77-80; CANR 27, 83; CN 1, 2, 3, 4, 5, 6, 7; DLB 33; EWL 3

Kellock, Archibald P.
See Mavor, Osborne Henry

Kellogg, Marjorie 1922-2005 .... **CLC 2**
See also CA 81-84; 246

Kellow, Kathleen
See Hibbert, Eleanor Alice Burford

Kelly, Lauren
See Oates, Joyce Carol

Kelly, M(ilton) T(errence) 1947- ..... **CLC 55**
See also CA 97-100; CAAS 22; CANR 19, 43, 84; CN 6

Kelly, Robert 1935- .... **SSC 50**
See also CA 17-20R; CAAS 19; CANR 47; CP 1, 2, 3, 4, 5, 6, 7; DLB 5, 130, 165

Kelman, James 1946- .... **CLC 58, 86, 292**
See also BRWS 5; CA 148; CANR 85, 130, 199; CN 5, 6, 7; DLB 194, 319, 326; RGSF 2; WLIT 4

Kelton, Elmer 1926-2009 .... **CLC 299**
See also AAYA 78; AITN 1; BYA 9; CA 21-24R; 289; CANR 12, 36, 85, 149, 173, 209; DLB 256; TCWW 1, 2

Kelton, Elmer Stephen
See Kelton, Elmer

Kemal, Yasar
See Kemal, Yashar

Kemal, Yashar 1923(?)- .... **CLC 14, 29**
See also CA 89-92; CANR 44; CWW 2; EWL 3; WLIT 6

Kemble, Fanny 1809-1893 .... **NCLC 18**
See also DLB 32

Kemelman, Harry 1908-1996 .... **CLC 2**
See also AITN 1; BPFB 2; CA 9-12R; 155; CANR 6, 71; CMW 4; DLB 28

Kempe, Margery 1373(?)-1440(?) ..**LC 6, 56**
See also BRWS 12; DLB 146; FL 1:1; RGEL 2

Kempis, Thomas a 1380-1471 .... **LC 11**

Kenan, Randall (G.) 1963- .... **BLC 2:2**
See also BW 2, 3; CA 142; CANR 86; CN 7; CSW; DLB 292; GLL 1

Kendall, Henry 1839-1882 .... **NCLC 12**
See also DLB 230

Keneally, Thomas 1935- ... **CLC 5, 8, 10, 14, 19, 27, 43, 117, 279**
See also BRWS 4; CA 85-88; CANR 10, 50, 74, 130, 165, 198; CN 1, 2, 3, 4, 5, 6, 7; CPW; DA3; DAM NOV; DLB 289, 299, 326; EWL 3; MTCW 1, 2; MTFW 2005; NFS 17, 38; RGEL 2; RGHL; RHW

Keneally, Thomas Michael
See Keneally, Thomas

Keneally, Tom
See Keneally, Thomas

Kennedy, A. L. 1965- .... **CLC 188**
See also CA 168, 213; CAAE 213; CANR 108, 193; CD 5, 6; CN 6, 7; DLB 271; RGSF 2

Kennedy, Adrienne (Lita) 1931- ... **BLC 1:2; CLC 66, 308; DC 5**
See also AFAW 2; BW 2, 3; CA 103; CAAS 20; CABS 3; CAD; CANR 26, 53, 82; CD 5, 6; DAM MULT; DFS 9, 28; DLB 38, 341; FW; MAL 5

Kennedy, Alison Louise
See Kennedy, A. L.

Kennedy, John Pendleton 1795-1870 . **NCLC 2**
See also DLB 3, 248, 254; RGAL 4

Kennedy, Joseph Charles
See Kennedy, X. J.

Kennedy, William 1928- . **CLC 6, 28, 34, 53, 239**
See also AAYA 1, 73; AMWS 7; BPFB 2; CA 85-88; CANR 14, 31, 76, 134; CN 4, 5, 6, 7; DA3; DAM NOV; DLB 143; DLBY 1985; EWL 3; INT CANR-31; MAL 5; MTCW 1, 2; MTFW 2005; SATA 57

Kennedy, William Joseph
See Kennedy, William

Kennedy, X. J. 1929- ...... **CLC 8, 42; PC 93**
See also AMWS 15; CA 1-4R, 201; CAAE 201; CANR 9; CANR 4, 30, 40, 214; CLR 27; CP 1, 2, 3, 4, 5, 6, 7; CWRI 5; DLB 5; MAICYA 2; MAICYAS 1; SAAS 22; SATA 14, 86, 130; SATA-Essay 130

Kenny, Maurice (Francis) 1929- .... **CLC 87; NNAL**
See also CA 144; CAAS 22; CANR 143; DAM MULT; DLB 175

Kent, Kathleen CLC 280
See also CA 288

Kent, Kelvin
See Kuttner, Henry

Kent, Klark
See Copeland, Stewart

Kenton, Maxwell
See Southern, Terry

Kenyon, Jane 1947-1995 .... **PC 57**
See also AAYA 63; AMWS 7; CA 118; 148; CANR 44, 69, 172; CP 6, 7; CWP; DLB 120; PFS 9, 17, 39; RGAL 4

Kenyon, Robert O.
See Kuttner, Henry

Kepler, Johannes 1571-1630 .... **LC 45**

Ker, Jill
See Conway, Jill K.

Kerkow, H. C.
See Lewton, Val

Kerouac, Jack 1922-1969 ..... **CLC 1, 2, 3, 5, 14, 61; TCLC 117; WLC**
See also AAYA 25; AITN 1; AMWC 1; AMWS 3; BG 3; BPFB 2; CA 5-8R; 25-28R; CANR 26, 54, 95, 184; CDALB 1941-1968; CP 1; CPW; DA; DA3; DAB; DAC; DAM MST, NOV, POET, POP; DLB 2, 16, 237; DLBY 1995; EWL 3; GLL 1; LATS 1:2; LMFS 2; MAL 5; MTCW 1, 2; MTFW 2005; NFS 8; RGAL 4; TUS; WP

Kerouac, Jean-Louis le Brisde
See Kerouac, Jack
Kerouac, John
See Kerouac, Jack
Kerr, (Bridget) Jean (Collins)
1923(?)-2003 .... **CLC 22**
See also CA 5-8R; 212; CANR 7; INT
CANR-7
Kerr, M. E.
See Meaker, Marijane
Kerr, Robert CLC 55
Kerrigan, (Thomas) Anthony 1918- . CLC 4, 6
See also CA 49-52; CAAS 11; CANR 4
Kerry, Lois
See Duncan, Lois
Kesey, Ken 1935-2001 .. CLC 1, 3, 6, 11, 46, 64, 184; WLC 3
See also AAYA 25; BG 1:3; BPFB 2; CA
1-4R; 204; CANR 22, 38, 66, 124;
CDALB 1968-1988; CLR 170; CN 1, 2,
3, 4, 5, 6, 7; CPW; DA; DA3; DAB;
DAC; DAM MST, NOV, POP; DLB 2,
16, 206; EWL 3; EXPN; LAIT 4; MAL 5;
MTCW 1, 2; MTFW 2005; NFS 2; RGAL
4; SATA 66; SATA-Obit 131; TUS; YAW
Kesselring, Joseph (Otto) 1902-1967 ... CLC 45
See also CA 150; DAM DRAM, MST; DFS
20
Kessler, Jascha (Frederick) 1929- ..... CLC 4
See also CA 17-20R; CANR 8, 48, 111; CP
1
Kettelkamp, Larry (Dale) 1933- ..... CLC 12
See also CA 29-32R; CANR 16; SAAS 3;
SATA 2
**Key, Ellen (Karolina Sofia) 1849-1926 ....
TCLC 65**
See also DLB 259
Keyber, Conny
See Fielding, Henry
Keyes, Daniel 1927- .... CLC 80
See also AAYA 23; BYA 11; CA 17-20R,
181; CAAE 181; CANR 10, 26, 54, 74;
DA; DA3; DAC; DAM MST, NOV;
EXPN; LAIT 4; MTCW 2; MTFW 2005;
NFS 2; SATA 37; SFW 4
Keynes, John Maynard 1883-1946 .... TCLC 64
See also CA 114; 162, 163; DLBD 10;
MTCW 2; MTFW 2005
Khanshendel, Chiron
See Rose, Wendy
Khayyam, Omar 1048-1131 . CMLC 11, 137; PC 8
See also DA3; DAM POET; RGWL 2, 3;
WLIT 6
Kherdian, David 1931- .... CLC 6, 9
See also AAYA 42; CA 21-24R, 192; CAAE
192; CAAS 2; CANR 39, 78; CLR 24;
JRDA; LAIT 3; MAICYA 1, 2; SATA 16,
74; SATA-Essay 125
Khlebnikov, Velimir
See Khlebnikov, Viktor Vladimirovich
Khlebnikov, Viktor Vladimirovich
1885-1922 .... **TCLC 20**
See also CA 117; 217; DLB 295; EW 10;
EWL 3; RGWL 2, 3
Khodasevich, V.F.
See Khodasevich, Vladislav
Khodasevich, Vladislav 1886-1939 .... TCLC 15
See also CA 115; DLB 317; EWL 3
Khodasevich, Vladislav Felitsianovich
See Khodasevich, Vladislav
Kiarostami, Abbas 1940- .... CLC 295
See also CA 204

Kidd, Sue Monk 1948- .... CLC 267
See also AAYA 72; CA 202; LNFS 1;
MTFW 2005; NFS 27
**Kielland, Alexander Lange 1849-1906 ....
TCLC 5**
See also CA 104; DLB 354
Kiely, Benedict 1919-2007 . CLC 23, 43; SSC 58
See also CA 1-4R; 257; CANR 2, 84; CN
1, 2, 3, 4, 5, 6, 7; DLB 15, 319; TCLE
1:1
Kienzle, William X. 1928-2001 .... CLC 25
See also CA 93-96; 203; CAAS 1; CANR
9, 31, 59, 111; CMW 4; DA3; DAM POP;
INT CANR-31; MSW; MTCW 1, 2;
MTFW 2005
Kierkegaard, Soren 1813-1855 .... NCLC 34, 78, 125
See also DLB 300; EW 6; LMFS 2; RGWL
3; TWA
Kieslowski, Krzysztof 1941-1996 .. CLC 120
See also CA 147; 151
Killens, John Oliver 1916-1987 .... BLC 2:2; CLC 10
See also BW 2; CA 77-80; 123; CAAS 2;
CANR 26; CN 1, 2, 3, 4; DLB 33; EWL
3
Killigrew, Anne 1660-1685 .... LC 4, 73
See also DLB 131
Killigrew, Thomas 1612-1683 .... LC 57
See also DLB 58; RGEL 2
Kim
See Simenon, Georges
Kincaid, Jamaica 1949- . BLC 1:2, 2:2; CLC 43, 68, 137, 234; SSC 72
See also AAYA 13, 56; AFAW 2; AMWS 7;
BRWS 7; BW 2, 3; CA 125; CANR 47,
59, 95, 133; CDALBS; CDWLB 3; CLR
63; CN 4, 5, 6, 7; DA3; DAM MULT,
NOV; DLB 157, 227; DNFS 1; EWL 3;
EXPS; FW; LAIT 1:2; LMFS 2; MAL 5;
MTCW 2; MTFW 2005; NCFS 1; NFS 3;
SSFS 5, 7; TUS; WWE 1; YAW
King, Francis 1923-2011 ...... CLC 8, 53, 145
See also CA 1-4R; CANR 1, 33, 86; CN 1,
2, 3, 4, 5, 6, 7; DAM NOV; DLB 15, 139;
MTCW 1
King, Francis Henry
See King, Francis
King, Kennedy
See Brown, George Douglas
King, Martin Luther, Jr. 1929-1968 ..... BLC 1:2; CLC 83; WLCS
See also BW 2, 3; CA 25-28; CANR 27,
44; CAP 2; DA; DA3; DAB; DAC; DAM
MST, MULT; LAIT 5; LATS 1:2; MTCW
1, 2; MTFW 2005; SATA 14
King, Stephen 1947- ..... CLC 12, 26, 37, 61, 113, 228, 244; SSC 17, 55
See also AAYA 1, 17, 82; AMWS 5; BEST
90:1; BPFB 2; CA 61-64; CANR 1, 30,
52, 76, 119, 134, 168, 227; CLR 124; CN
7; CPW; DA3; DAM NOV, POP; DLB
143, 350; DLBY 1980; HGG; JRDA;
LAIT 5; LNFS 1; MTCW 1, 2; MTFW
2005; RGAL 4; SATA 9, 55, 161; SSFS
30; SUFW 1, 2; WYAS 1; YAW
King, Stephen Edwin
See King, Stephen
King, Steve
See King, Stephen
King, Thomas 1943- .... CLC 89, 171, 276; NNAL
See also CA 144; CANR 95, 175; CCA 1;
CN 6, 7; DAC; DAM MULT; DLB 175,
334; SATA 96
King, Thomas Hunt
See King, Thomas

Kingman, Lee
See Natti, Lee
Kingsley, Charles 1819-1875 .... NCLC 35
See also BRWS 16; CLR 77, 167; DLB 21,
32, 163, 178, 190; FANT; MAICYA 2;
MAICYAS 1; RGEL 2; WCH; YABC 2
Kingsley, Henry 1830-1876 .... NCLC 107
See also DLB 21, 230; RGEL 2
Kingsley, Sidney 1906-1995 .... CLC 44
See also CA 85-88; 147; CAD; DFS 14, 19;
DLB 7; MAL 5; RGAL 4
Kingsolver, Barbara 1955- . CLC 55, 81, 130, 216, 269
See also AAYA 15; AMWS 7; CA 129; 134;
CANR 60, 96, 133, 179; CDALBS; CN
7; CPW; CSW; DA3; DAM POP; DLB
206; INT CA-134; LAIT 5; MTCW 2;
MTFW 2005; NFS 5, 10, 12, 24; RGAL
4; TCLE 1:1
Kingston, Maxine Hong 1940- ... AAL; CLC 12, 19, 58, 121, 271; SSC 136; WLCS
See also AAYA 8, 55; AMWS 5; BPFB 2;
CA 69-72; CANR 13, 38, 74, 87, 128;
CDALBS; CN 6, 7; DA3; DAM MULT,
NOV; DLB 173, 212, 312; DLBY 1980;
EWL 3; FL 1:6; FW; INT CANR-13;
LAIT 5; MAL 5; MBL; MTCW 1, 2;
MTFW 2005; NFS 6; RGAL 4; SATA 53;
SSFS 3; TCWW 2
Kingston, Maxine Ting Ting Hong
See Kingston, Maxine Hong
Kinnell, Galway 1927- ... CLC 1, 2, 3, 5, 13, 29, 129; PC 26
See also AMWS 3; CA 9-12R; CANR 10,
34, 66, 116, 138, 175; CP 1, 2, 3, 4, 5, 6,
7; DLB 5, 342; DLBY 1987; EWL 3; INT
CANR-34; MAL 5; MTCW 1, 2; MTFW
2005; PAB; PFS 9, 26, 35; RGAL 4;
TCLE 1:1; WP
Kinsella, Thomas 1928- ...... CLC 4, 19, 138, 274; PC 69
See also BRWS 5; CA 17-20R; CANR 15,
122; CP 1, 2, 3, 4, 5, 6, 7; DLB 27; EWL
3; MTCW 1, 2; MTFW 2005; RGEL 2;
TEA
Kinsella, William Patrick
See Kinsella, W.P.
Kinsella, W.P. 1935- .... CLC 27, 43, 166
See also AAYA 7, 60; BPFB 2; CA 97-100,
222; CAAE 222; CAAS 7; CANR 21, 35,
66, 75, 129; CN 4, 5, 6, 7; CPW; DAC;
DAM NOV, POP; DLB 362; FANT; INT
CANR-21; LAIT 5; MTCW 1, 2; MTFW
2005; NFS 15; RGSF 2; SSFS 30
Kinsey, Alfred C(harles) 1894-1956 .. TCLC 91
See also CA 115; 170; MTCW 2
Kipling, Joseph Rudyard
See Kipling, Rudyard
Kipling, Rudyard 1865-1936 . PC 3, 91; SSC 5, 54, 110; TCLC 8, 17, 167; WLC 3
See also AAYA 32; BRW 6; BRWC 1, 2;
BRWR 3; BYA 4; CA 105; 120; CANR
33; CDBLB 1890-1914; CLR 39, 65;
CWRI 5; DA; DA3; DAB; DAC; DAM
MST, POET; DLB 19, 34, 141, 156, 330;
EWL 3; EXPS; FANT; LAIT 3; LMFS 1;
MAICYA 1, 2; MTCW 1, 2; MTFW 2005;
NFS 21; PFS 22; RGEL 2; RGSF 2; SATA
100; SFW 4; SSFS 8, 21, 22, 32; SUFW
1; TEA; WCH; WLIT 4; YABC 2
Kircher, Athanasius 1602-1680 .... LC 121
See also DLB 164
Kirk, Richard
See Holdstock, Robert
Kirk, Russell (Amos) 1918-1994 . TCLC 119
See also AITN 1; CA 1-4R; 145; CAAS 9;
CANR 1, 20, 60; HGG; INT CANR-20;
MTCW 1, 2

Kirkham, Dinah
  See Card, Orson Scott
Kirkland, Caroline M. 1801-1864 ..... **NCLC 85**
  See also DLB 3, 73, 74, 250, 254; DLBD 13
Kirkup, James 1918-2009 .... **CLC 1**
  See also CA 1-4R; CAAS 4; CANR 2; CP 1, 2, 3, 4, 5, 6, 7; DLB 27; SATA 12
Kirkwood, James 1930(?)-1989 .... **CLC 9**
  See also AITN 2; CA 1-4R; 128; CANR 6, 40; GLL 2
Kirsch, Sarah 1935- .... **CLC 176**
  See also CA 178; CWW 2; DLB 75; EWL 3
Kirshner, Sidney
  See Kingsley, Sidney
Kis, Danilo 1935-1989 .... **CLC 57**
  See also CA 109; 118; 129; CANR 61; CD-WLB 4; DLB 181; EWL 3; MTCW 1; RGSF 2; RGWL 2, 3
Kissinger, Henry A. 1923- .... **CLC 137**
  See also CA 1-4R; CANR 2, 33, 66, 109; MTCW 1
Kissinger, Henry Alfred
  See Kissinger, Henry A.
Kittel, Frederick August
  See Wilson, August
Kivi, Aleksis 1834-1872 .... **NCLC 30**
Kizer, Carolyn 1925- .... **CLC 15, 39, 80; PC 66**
  See also CA 65-68; CAAS 5; CANR 24, 70, 134; CP 1, 2, 3, 4, 5, 6, 7; CWP; DAM POET; DLB 5, 169; EWL 3; MAL 5; MTCW 2; MTFW 2005; PFS 18; TCLE 1:1
Klabund 1890-1928 .... **TCLC 44**
  See also CA 162; DLB 66
Klappert, Peter 1942- .... **CLC 57**
  See also CA 33-36R; CSW; DLB 5
Klausner, Amos
  See Oz, Amos
Klein, A. M. 1909-1972 .... **CLC 19**
  See also CA 101; 37-40R; CP 1; DAB; DAC; DAM MST; DLB 68; EWL 3; RGEL 2; RGHL
Klein, Abraham Moses
  See Klein, A. M.
Klein, Joe
  See Klein, Joseph
Klein, Joseph 1946- .... **CLC 154**
  See also CA 85-88; CANR 55, 164
Klein, Norma 1938-1989 .... **CLC 30**
  See also AAYA 2, 35; BPFB 2; BYA 6, 7, 8; CA 41-44R; 128; CANR 15, 37; CLR 2, 19, 162; INT CANR-15; JRDA; MAICYA 1, 2; SAAS 1; SATA 7, 57; WYA; YAW
Klein, T.E.D. 1947- .... **CLC 34**
  See also CA 119; CANR 44, 75, 167; HGG
Klein, Theodore Eibon Donald
  See Klein, T.E.D.
Kleinzahler, August 1949- .... **CLC 320**
  See also CA 125; CANR 51, 101, 153, 210
Kleist, Heinrich von 1777-1811 .... **DC 29; NCLC 2, 37, 222; SSC 22**
  See also CDWLB 2; DAM DRAM; DLB 90; EW 5; RGSF 2; RGWL 2, 3
Klima, Ivan 1931- .... **CLC 56, 172**
  See also CA 25-28R; CANR 17, 50, 91; CDWLB 4; CWW 2; DAM NOV; DLB 232; EWL 3; RGWL 3
Klimentev, Andrei Platonovich
  See Klimentov, Andrei Platonovich
Klimentov, Andrei Platonovich 1899-1951 .. **SSC 42; TCLC 14**
  See also CA 108; 232; DLB 272; EWL 3

Klinger, Friedrich Maximilian von 1752-1831 .... **NCLC 1**
  See also DLB 94
Klingsor the Magician
  See Hartmann, Sadakichi
Klopstock, Friedrich Gottlieb 1724-1803 .... **NCLC 11, 225**
  See also DLB 97; EW 4; RGWL 2, 3
Kluge, Alexander 1932- .... **SSC 61**
  See also CA 81-84; CANR 163; DLB 75
Knapp, Caroline 1959-2002 .... **CLC 99, 309**
  See also CA 154; 207
Knebel, Fletcher 1911-1993 .... **CLC 14**
  See also AITN 1; CA 1-4R; 140; CAAS 3; CANR 1, 36; CN 1, 2, 3, 4, 5; SATA 36; SATA-Obit 75
Knickerbocker, Diedrich
  See Irving, Washington
Knight, Etheridge 1931-1991 .... **BLC 1:2; CLC 40; PC 14**
  See also BW 1, 3; CA 21-24R; 133; CANR 23, 82; CP 1, 2, 3, 4, 5; DAM POET; DLB 41; MTCW 2; MTFW 2005; PFS 36; RGAL 4; TCLE 1:1
Knight, Sarah Kemble 1666-1727 .... **LC 7**
  See also DLB 24, 200
Knister, Raymond 1899-1932 .... **TCLC 56**
  See also CA 186; DLB 68; RGEL 2
Knowles, John 1926-2001 . **CLC 1, 4, 10, 26**
  See also AAYA 10, 72; AMWS 12; BPFB 2; BYA 3; CA 17-20R; 203; CANR 40, 74, 76, 132; CDALB 1968-1988; CLR 98; CN 1, 2, 3, 4, 5, 6, 7; DA; DAC; DAM MST, NOV; DLB 6; EXPN; MTCW 1, 2; MTFW 2005; NFS 2; RGAL 4; SATA 8, 89; SATA-Obit 134; YAW
Knox, Calvin M.
  See Silverberg, Robert
Knox, John c. 1505-1572 .... **LC 37**
  See also DLB 132
Knye, Cassandra
  See Disch, Thomas M.
Koch, C(hristopher) J(ohn) 1932- .. **CLC 42**
  See also CA 127; CANR 84; CN 3, 4, 5, 6, 7; DLB 289
Koch, Christopher
  See Koch, C(hristopher) J(ohn)
Koch, Kenneth 1925-2002 ...... **CLC 5, 8, 44; PC 80**
  See also AMWS 15; CA 1-4R; 207; CAD; CANR 6, 36, 57, 97, 131; CD 5, 6; CP 1, 2, 3, 4, 5, 6, 7; DAM POET; DLB 5; INT CANR-36; MAL 5; MTCW 2; MTFW 2005; PFS 20; SATA 65; WP
Kochanowski, Jan 1530-1584 .... **LC 10**
  See also RGWL 2, 3
Kock, Charles Paul de 1794-1871 ..... **NCLC 16**
Koda Rohan
  See Koda Shigeyuki
Koda Rohan
  See Koda Shigeyuki
Koda Shigeyuki 1867-1947 .... **TCLC 22**
  See also CA 121; 183; DLB 180
Koestler, Arthur 1905-1983 . **CLC 1, 3, 6, 8, 15, 33**
  See also BRWS 1; CA 1-4R; 109; CANR 1, 33; CDBLB 1945-1960; CN 1, 2, 3; DLBY 1983; EWL 3; MTCW 1, 2; MTFW 2005; NFS 19; RGEL 2
Kogawa, Joy 1935- .. **CLC 78, 129, 262, 268**
  See also AAYA 47; CA 101; CANR 19, 62, 126; CN 6, 7; CP 1; CWP; DAC; DAM MST, MULT; DLB 334; FW; MTCW 2; MTFW 2005; NFS 3; SATA 99
Kogawa, Joy Nozomi
  See Kogawa, Joy
Kohout, Pavel 1928- .... **CLC 13**
  See also CA 45-48; CANR 3

Koizumi, Yakumo
  See Hearn, Lafcadio
Kolmar, Gertrud 1894-1943 .... **TCLC 40**
  See also CA 167; EWL 3; RGHL
Komunyakaa, Yusef 1947- . **BLC 2:2; BLCS; CLC 86, 94, 207, 299; PC 51**
  See also AFAW 2; AMWS 13; CA 147; CANR 83, 164, 211; CP 6, 7; CSW; DLB 120; EWL 3; PFS 5, 20, 30, 37; RGAL 4
Konigsberg, Alan Stewart
  See Allen, Woody
Konrad, George
  See Konrad, Gyorgy
Konrad, George
  See Konrad, Gyorgy
Konrad, Gyorgy 1933- .... **CLC 4, 10, 73**
  See also CA 85-88; CANR 97, 171; CD-WLB 4; CWW 2; DLB 232; EWL 3
Konwicki, Tadeusz 1926- ...... **CLC 8, 28, 54, 117**
  See also CA 101; CAAS 9; CANR 39, 59; CWW 2; DLB 232; EWL 3; IDFW 3; MTCW 1
Koontz, Dean 1945- .... **CLC 78, 206**
  See Koontz, Dean R.
  See also AAYA 9, 31; BEST 89:3, 90:2; CA 108; CANR 19, 36, 52, 95, 138, 176; CMW 4; CPW; DA3; DAM NOV, POP; DLB 292; HGG; MTCW 1; MTFW 2005; SATA 92, 165; SFW 4; SUFW 2; YAW
Koontz, Dean R.
  See Koontz, Dean
  See also SATA 225
Koontz, Dean Ray
  See Koontz, Dean
Kopernik, Mikolaj
  See Copernicus, Nicolaus
Kopit, Arthur 1937- . **CLC 1, 18, 33; DC 37**
  See also AITN 1; CA 81-84; CABS 3; CAD; CD 5, 6; DAM DRAM; DFS 7, 14, 24; DLB 7; MAL 5; MTCW 1; RGAL 4
Kopit, Arthur Lee
  See Kopit, Arthur
Kopitar, Jernej (Bartholomaus) 1780-1844 . **NCLC 117**
Kops, Bernard 1926- .... **CLC 4**
  See also CA 5-8R; CANR 84, 159; CBD; CN 1, 2, 3, 4, 5, 6, 7; CP 1, 2, 3, 4, 5, 6, 7; DLB 13; RGHL
Kornbluth, C(yril) M. 1923-1958 ... **TCLC 8**
  See also CA 105; 160; DLB 8; SCFW 1, 2; SFW 4
Korolenko, V.G.
  See Korolenko, Vladimir G.
Korolenko, Vladimir
  See Korolenko, Vladimir G.
Korolenko, Vladimir G. 1853-1921 ... **TCLC 22**
  See also CA 121; DLB 277
Korolenko, Vladimir Galaktionovich
  See Korolenko, Vladimir G.
Korzybski, Alfred (Habdank Skarbek) 1879-1950 .... **TCLC 61**
  See also CA 123; 160
Kosinski, Jerzy 1933-1991 ... **CLC 1, 2, 3, 6, 10, 15, 53, 70**
  See also AMWS 7; BPFB 2; CA 17-20R; 134; CANR 9, 46; CN 1, 2, 3, 4; DA3; DAM NOV; DLB 2, 299; DLBY 1982; EWL 3; HGG; MAL 5; MTCW 1, 2; MTFW 2005; NFS 12; RGAL 4; RGHL; TUS
Kostelanetz, Richard 1940- .... **CLC 28**
  See also CA 13-16R; CAAS 8; CANR 38, 77; CN 4, 5, 6; CP 2, 3, 4, 5, 6, 7
Kostelanetz, Richard Cory
  See Kostelanetz, Richard

Author Index

Lee, Stan 1922- .... **CLC 17**
See also AAYA 5, 49; CA 108; 111; CANR 129; INT CA-111; MTFW 2005

Lee, Tanith 1947- .... **CLC 46**
See also AAYA 15; CA 37-40R; CANR 53, 102, 145, 170; DLB 261; FANT; SATA 8, 88, 134, 185; SFW 4; SUFW 1, 2; YAW

Lee, Vernon
See Paget, Violet

Lee, William
See Burroughs, William S.

Lee, Willy
See Burroughs, William S.

Lee-Hamilton, Eugene (Jacob) 1845-1907 ... **TCLC 22**
See also CA 117; 234

Leet, Judith 1935- .... **CLC 11**
See also CA 187

Le Fanu, Joseph Sheridan 1814-1873 .... **NCLC 9, 58; SSC 14, 84**
See also CMW 4; DA3; DAM POP; DLB 21, 70, 159, 178; GL 3; HGG; RGEL 2; RGSF 2; SUFW 1

Leffland, Ella 1931- .... **CLC 19**
See also CA 29-32R; CANR 35, 78, 82; DLBY 1984; INT CANR-35; SATA 65; SSFS 24

Leger, Alexis
See Leger, Alexis Saint-Leger

Leger, Alexis Saint-Leger 1887-1975 ... **CLC 4, 11, 46; PC 23**
See also CA 13-16R; 61-64; CANR 43; DAM POET; DLB 258, 331; EW 10; EWL 3; GFL 1789 to the Present; MTCW 1; RGWL 2, 3

Leger, Marie-Rene Auguste Alexis Saint-Leger
See Leger, Alexis Saint-Leger

Leger, Saintleger
See Leger, Alexis Saint-Leger

Le Guin, Ursula K. 1929- .... **CLC 8, 13, 22, 45, 71, 136, 310; SSC 12, 69**
See also AAYA 9, 27, 84; AITN 1; BPFB 2; BYA 5, 8, 11, 14; CA 21-24R; CANR 9, 32, 52, 74, 132, 192; CDALB 1968-1988; CLR 3, 28, 91; CN 2, 3, 4, 5, 6, 7; CPW; DA3; DAB; DAC; DAM MST, POP; DLB 8, 52, 256, 275; EXPS; FANT; FW; INT CANR-32; JRDA; LAIT 5; MAICYA 1, 2; MAL 5; MTCW 1, 2; MTFW 2005; NFS 6, 9; SATA 4, 52, 99, 149, 194; SCFW 1, 2; SFW 4; SSFS 2; SUFW 1, 2; WYA; YAW

Le Guin, Ursula Kroeber
See Le Guin, Ursula K.

Lehane, Dennis 1965- .... **CLC 320**
See also AAYA 56; CA 154; CANR 72, 112, 136, 168, 219; LNFS 1; MTFW 2005

Lehmann, Rosamond (Nina) 1901-1990 ...... **CLC 5**
See also CA 77-80; 131; CANR 8, 73; CN 1, 2, 3, 4; DLB 15; MTCW 2; RGEL 2; RHW

Leiber, Fritz (Reuter, Jr.) 1910-1992 ... **CLC 25**
See also AAYA 65; BPFB 2; CA 45-48; 139; CANR 2, 40, 86; CN 2, 3, 4, 5; DLB 8; FANT; HGG; MTCW 1, 2; MTFW 2005; SATA 45; SATA-Obit 73; SCFW 1, 2; SFW 4; SUFW 1, 2

Leibniz, Gottfried Wilhelm von 1646-1716 . **LC 35, 196**
See also DLB 168

Leino, Eino
See Lonnbohm, Armas Eino Leopold

Leiris, Michel (Julien) 1901-1990 ... **CLC 61**
See also CA 119; 128; 132; EWL 3; GFL 1789 to the Present

Leithauser, Brad 1953- .... **CLC 27**
See also CA 107; CANR 27, 81, 171; CP 5, 6, 7; DLB 120, 282

le Jars de Gournay, Marie
See de Gournay, Marie le Jars

Lelchuk, Alan 1938- .... **CLC 5**
See also CA 45-48; CAAS 20; CANR 1, 70, 152; CN 3, 4, 5, 6, 7

Lem, Stanislaw 1921-2006 .... **CLC 8, 15, 40, 149**
See also AAYA 75; CA 105; 249; CAAS 1; CANR 32; CWW 2; MTCW 1; SCFW 1, 2; SFW 4

Lemann, Nancy (Elise) 1956- .... **CLC 39**
See also CA 118; 136; CANR 121

Lemonnier, (Antoine Louis) Camille 1844-1913 .... **TCLC 22**
See also CA 121

Lenau, Nikolaus 1802-1850 .... **NCLC 16**

L'Engle, Madeleine 1918-2007 .... **CLC 12**
See also AAYA 28; AITN 2; BPFB 2; BYA 2, 4, 5, 7; CA 1-4R; 264; CANR 3, 21, 39, 66, 107, 207; CLR 1, 14, 57, 172; CPW; CWRI 5; DA3; DAM POP; DLB 52; JRDA; MAICYA 1, 2; MTCW 1, 2; MTFW 2005; NFS 32; SAAS 15; SATA 1, 27, 75, 128; SATA-Obit 186; SFW 4; WYA; YAW

L'Engle, Madeleine Camp Franklin
See L'Engle, Madeleine

Lengyel, Jozsef 1896-1975 .... **CLC 7**
See also CA 85-88; 57-60; CANR 71; RGSF 2

Lenin 1870-1924 .... **TCLC 67**
See also CA 121; 168

Lenin, N.
See Lenin

Lenin, Nikolai
See Lenin

Lenin, V. I.
See Lenin

Lenin, Vladimir I.
See Lenin

Lenin, Vladimir Ilyich
See Lenin

Lennon, John 1940-1980 .... **CLC 12, 35**
See also CA 102; SATA 114

Lennon, John Ono
See Lennon, John

Lennox, Charlotte 1729(?)-1804 .. **NCLC 23, 134**
See also BRWS 17; DLB 39; RGEL 2

Lentricchia, Frank, Jr.
See Lentricchia, Frank

Lentricchia, Frank 1940- .... **CLC 34**
See also CA 25-28R; CANR 19, 106, 148; DLB 246

Lenz, Gunter CLC 65

Lenz, Jakob Michael Reinhold 1751-1792 .. **LC 100**
See also DLB 94; RGWL 2, 3

Lenz, Siegfried 1926- .... **CLC 27; SSC 33**
See also CA 89-92; CANR 80, 149; CWW 2; DLB 75; EWL 3; RGSF 2; RGWL 2, 3

Leon, David
See Jacob, (Cyprien-)Max

Leon, Luis de 1527-1591 .... **LC 182**
See also DLB 318

Leonard, Dutch
See Leonard, Elmore

Leonard, Elmore 1925- ...... **CLC 28, 34, 71, 120, 222**
See also AAYA 22, 59; AITN 1; BEST 89:1, 90:4; BPFB 2; CA 81-84; CANR 12, 28, 53, 76, 96, 133, 176, 219; CMW 4; CN 5, 6, 7; CPW; DA3; DAM POP; DLB 173, 226; INT CANR-28; MSW; MTCW 1, 2; MTFW 2005; RGAL 4; SATA 163; TCWW 1, 2

Leonard, Elmore John, Jr.
See Leonard, Elmore

Leonard, Hugh 1926-2009 .... **CLC 19**
See also CA 102; 283; CANR 78, 140; CBD; CD 5, 6; DFS 13, 24; DLB 13; INT CA-102

Leonard, Tom 1944- .... **CLC 289**
See also CA 77-80; CANR 13, 31; CP 2, 3, 4, 5, 6, 7

Leonov, Leonid 1899-1994 .... **CLC 92**
See also CA 129; CANR 76; DAM NOV; DLB 272; EWL 3; MTCW 1, 2; MTFW 2005

Leonov, Leonid Maksimovich
See Leonov, Leonid

Leonov, Leonid Maximovich
See Leonov, Leonid

Leopardi, (Conte) Giacomo 1798-1837 .... **NCLC 22, 129; PC 37**
See also EW 5; RGWL 2, 3; WLIT 7; WP

Le Reveler
See Artaud, Antonin

Lerman, Eleanor 1952- .... **CLC 9**
See also CA 85-88; CANR 69, 124, 184

Lerman, Rhoda 1936- .... **CLC 56**
See also CA 49-52; CANR 70

Lermontov, Mikhail Iur'evich
See Lermontov, Mikhail Yuryevich

Lermontov, Mikhail Yuryevich 1814-1841 .. **NCLC 5, 47, 126; PC 18**
See also DLB 205; EW 6; RGWL 2, 3; TWA

Leroux, Gaston 1868-1927 .... **TCLC 25**
See also CA 108; 136; CANR 69; CMW 4; MTFW 2005; NFS 20; SATA 65

Lesage, Alain-Rene 1668-1747 .... **LC 2, 28**
See also DLB 313; EW 3; GFL Beginnings to 1789; RGWL 2, 3

Leskov, N(ikolai) S(emenovich) 1831-1895 ..
See Leskov, Nikolai (Semyonovich)

Leskov, Nikolai (Semyonovich) 1831-1895 .. **NCLC 25, 174; SSC 34, 96**
See also DLB 238

Leskov, Nikolai Semenovich
See Leskov, Nikolai (Semyonovich)

Lesser, Milton
See Marlowe, Stephen

Lessing, Doris 1919- . **CLC 1, 2, 3, 6, 10, 15, 22, 40, 94, 170, 254; SSC 6, 61, 160; WLCS**
See also AAYA 57; AFW; BRWS 1; CA 9-12R; CAAS 14; CANR 33, 54, 76, 122, 179; CBD; CD 5, 6; CDBLB 1960 to Present; CN 1, 2, 3, 4, 5, 6, 7; CWD; DA; DA3; DAB; DAC; DAM MST, NOV; DFS 20; DLB 15, 139; DLBY 1985; EWL 3; EXPS; FL 1:6; FW; LAIT 4; MTCW 1, 2; MTFW 2005; NFS 27, 38; RGEL 2; RGSF 2; SFW 4; SSFS 1, 12, 20, 26, 30, 35; TEA; WLIT 2, 4

Lessing, Doris May
See Lessing, Doris

Lessing, Gotthold Ephraim 1729-1781 ... **DC 26; LC 8, 124, 162**
See also CDWLB 2; DLB 97; EW 4; RGWL 2, 3

Lester, Julius 1939- .... **BLC 2:2**
See also AAYA 12, 51; BW 2; BYA 3, 9, 11, 12; CA 17-20R; CANR 8, 23, 43, 129, 174; CLR 2, 41, 143; JRDA; MAICYA 1, 2; MAICYAS 1; MTFW 2005; SATA 12, 74, 112, 157; YAW

Lester, Richard 1932- .... **CLC 20**

Lethem, Jonathan 1964- .... **CLC 295**
See also AAYA 43; AMWS 18; CA 150; CANR 80, 138, 165; CN 7; MTFW 2005; SFW 4

Lindholm, Anna Margaret
See Haycraft, Anna
Lindsay, David 1878(?)-1945 .... **TCLC 15**
See also CA 113; 187; DLB 255; FANT;
SFW 4; SUFW 1
Lindsay, Nicholas Vachel
See Lindsay, Vachel
Lindsay, Vachel 1879-1931 .... **PC 23; TCLC 17; WLC 4**
See also AMWS 1; CA 114; 135; CANR
79; CDALB 1865-1917; DA; DA3; DAC;
DAM MST, POET; DLB 54; EWL 3;
EXPP; MAL 5; RGAL 4; SATA 40; WP
Linke-Poot
See Doeblin, Alfred
Linney, Romulus 1930-2011 .... **CLC 51**
See also CA 1-4R; CAD; CANR 40, 44,
79; CD 5, 6; CSW; RGAL 4
Linton, Eliza Lynn 1822-1898 ...... **NCLC 41**
See also DLB 18
Li Po 701-763 .... **CMLC 2, 86; PC 29**
See also PFS 20, 40; WP
Lippard, George 1822-1854 .... **NCLC 198**
See also DLB 202
Lipsius, Justus 1547-1606 .... **LC 16**
Lipsyte, Robert 1938- .... **CLC 21**
See also AAYA 7, 45; CA 17-20R; CANR
8, 57, 146, 189; CLR 23, 76; DA; DAC;
DAM MST, NOV; JRDA; LAIT 5; MAI-
CYA 1, 2; NFS 35; SATA 5, 68, 113, 161,
198; WYA; YAW
Lipsyte, Robert Michael
See Lipsyte, Robert
Lish, Gordon 1934- .... **CLC 45; SSC 18**
See also CA 113; 117; CANR 79, 151; DLB
130; INT CA-117
Lish, Gordon Jay
See Lish, Gordon
Lispector, Clarice 1925(?)-1977 ..... **CLC 43; HLCS 2; SSC 34, 96**
See also CA 139; 116; CANR 71; CDWLB
3; DLB 113, 307; DNFS 1; EWL 3; FW;
HW 2; LAW; RGSF 2; RGWL 2, 3; WLIT
1
Liszt, Franz 1811-1886 .... **NCLC 199**
Littell, Robert 1935(?)- .... **CLC 42**
See also CA 109; 112; CANR 64, 115, 162,
217; CMW 4
Little, Malcolm
See Malcolm X
Littlewit, Humphrey Gent.
See Lovecraft, H. P.
Litwos
See Sienkiewicz, Henryk (Adam Alexander
Pius)
Liu, E. 1857-1909 .... **TCLC 15**
See also CA 115; 190; DLB 328
Lively, Penelope 1933- .... **CLC 32, 50, 306**
See also BPFB 2; CA 41-44R; CANR 29,
67, 79, 131, 172, 222; CLR 7, 159; CN 5,
6, 7; CWRI 5; DAM NOV; DLB 14, 161,
207, 326; FANT; JRDA; MAICYA 1, 2;
MTCW 1, 2; MTFW 2005; SATA 7, 60,
101, 164; TEA
Lively, Penelope Margaret
See Lively, Penelope
Livesay, Dorothy (Kathleen) 1909-1996 ....
CLC 4, 15, 79
See also AITN 2; CA 25-28R; CAAS 8;
CANR 36, 67; CP 1, 2, 3, 4, 5; DAC;
DAM MST, POET; DLB 68; FW; MTCW
1; RGEL 2; TWA
Livius Andronicus c. 284B.C.-c. 204B.C. .....
CMLC 102
Livy c. 59B.C.-c. 12 .... **CMLC 11**
See also AW 2; CDWLB 1; DLB 211;
RGWL 2, 3; WLIT 8
Li Yaotang
See Jin, Ba

Li-Young, Lee
See Lee, Li-Young
Lizardi, Jose Joaquin Fernandez de
1776-1827 .... **NCLC 30**
See also LAW
Llewellyn, Richard
See Llewellyn Lloyd, Richard Dafydd Viv-
ian
Llewellyn Lloyd, Richard Dafydd Vivian
1906-1983 .... **CLC 7, 80**
See also CA 53-56; 111; CANR 7, 71; DLB
15; NFS 30; SATA 11; SATA-Obit 37
Llosa, Jorge Mario Pedro Vargas
See Vargas Llosa, Mario
Llosa, Mario Vargas
See Vargas Llosa, Mario
Lloyd, Manda
See Mander, (Mary) Jane
Lloyd Webber, Andrew 1948- .... **CLC 21**
See also AAYA 1, 38; CA 116; 149; DAM
DRAM; DFS 7; SATA 56
Llull, Ramon c. 1235-c. 1316 ...... **CMLC 12, 114**
Lobb, Ebenezer
See Upward, Allen
Lochhead, Liz 1947- .... **CLC 286**
See also BRWS 17; CA 81-84; CANR 79;
CBD; CD 5, 6; CP 2, 3, 4, 5, 6, 7; CWD;
CWP; DLB 310
Locke, Alain Leroy 1885-1954 ... **BLCS; HR 1:3; TCLC 43**
See also AMWS 14; BW 1, 3; CA 106; 124;
CANR 79; DLB 51; LMFS 2; MAL 5;
RGAL 4
Locke, John 1632-1704 .... **LC 7, 35, 135**
See also DLB 31, 101, 213, 252; RGEL 2;
WLIT 3
Locke-Elliott, Sumner
See Elliott, Sumner Locke
Lockhart, John Gibson 1794-1854 . **NCLC 6**
See also DLB 110, 116, 144
Lockridge, Ross (Franklin), Jr. 1914-1948 ..
TCLC 111
See also CA 108; 145; CANR 79; DLB 143;
DLBY 1980; MAL 5; RGAL 4; RHW
Lockwood, Robert
See Johnson, Robert
Lodge, David 1935- .... **CLC 36, 141, 293**
See also BEST 90:1; BRWS 4; CA 17-20R;
CANR 19, 53, 92, 139, 197; CN 1, 2, 3,
4, 5, 6, 7; CPW; DAM POP; DLB 14,
194; EWL 3; INT CANR-19; MTCW 1,
2; MTFW 2005
Lodge, David John
See Lodge, David
Lodge, Thomas 1558-1625 .... **LC 41**
See also DLB 172; RGEL 2
Loewinsohn, Ron(ald William) 1937- .. **CLC 52**
See also CA 25-28R; CANR 71; CP 1, 2, 3,
4
Logan, Jake
See Smith, Martin Cruz
Logan, John (Burton) 1923-1987 ...... **CLC 5**
See also CA 77-80; 124; CANR 45; CP 1,
2, 3, 4; DLB 5
Lo-Johansson, (Karl) Ivar 1901-1990 ....
TCLC 216
See also CA 102; 131; CANR 20, 79, 137;
DLB 259; EWL 3; RGWL 2, 3
Lo Kuan-chung 1330(?)-1400(?) .... **LC 12**
Lomax, Pearl
See Cleage, Pearl
Lomax, Pearl Cleage
See Cleage, Pearl
Lombard, Nap
See Johnson, Pamela Hansford
Lombard, Peter 1100(?)-1160(?) .. **CMLC 72**

Lombino, Salvatore
See Hunter, Evan
London, Jack 1876-1916 ..... **SSC 4, 49, 133; TCLC 9, 15, 39; WLC 4**
See also AAYA 13, 75; AITN 2; AMW;
BPFB 2; BYA 4, 13; CA 110; 119; CANR
73; CDALB 1865-1917; CLR 108; DA;
DA3; DAB; DAC; DAM MST, NOV;
DLB 8, 12, 78, 212; EWL 3; EXPS;
JRDA; LAIT 3; MAICYA 1, 2; MAL 5;
MTCW 1, 2; MTFW 2005; NFS 8, 19,
35; RGAL 4; RGSF 2; SATA 18; SFW 4;
SSFS 7, 35; TCWW 1, 2; TUS; WYA;
YAW
London, John Griffith
See London, Jack
Long, Emmett
See Leonard, Elmore
Longbaugh, Harry
See Goldman, William
Longfellow, Henry Wadsworth 1807-1882 ..
NCLC 2, 45, 101, 103, 235; PC 30; WLCS
See also AMW; AMWR 2; CDALB 1640-
1865; CLR 99; DA; DA3; DAB; DAC;
DAM MST, POET; DLB 1, 59, 235;
EXPP; PAB; PFS 2, 7, 17, 31, 39; RGAL
4; SATA 19; TUS; WP
Longinus c. 1st cent. - .... **CMLC 27**
See also AW 2; DLB 176
Longley, Michael 1939- ..... **CLC 29; PC 118**
See also BRWS 8; CA 102; CP 1, 2, 3, 4, 5,
6, 7; DLB 40
Longstreet, Augustus Baldwin 1790-1870 ...
NCLC 159
See also DLB 3, 11, 74, 248; RGAL 4
Longus fl. c. 2nd cent. - .... **CMLC 7**
Longway, A. Hugh
See Lang, Andrew
Lonnbohm, Armas Eino Leopold
See Lonnbohm, Armas Eino Leopold
Lonnbohm, Armas Eino Leopold
1878-1926 .... **TCLC 24**
See also CA 123; EWL 3
Lonnrot, Elias 1802-1884 .... **NCLC 53**
See also EFS 1:1, 2:1
Lonsdale, Roger CLC 65
Lopate, Phillip 1943- .... **CLC 29**
See also CA 97-100; CANR 88, 157, 196;
DLBY 1980; INT CA-97-100
Lopez, Barry 1945- .... **CLC 70**
See also AAYA 9, 63; ANW; CA 65-68;
CANR 7, 23, 47, 68, 92; DLB 256, 275,
335; INT CANR-7, CANR-23; MTCW 1;
RGAL 4; SATA 67
Lopez, Barry Holstun
See Lopez, Barry
Lopez de Mendoza, Inigo
See Santillana, Inigo Lopez de Mendoza,
Marques de
Lopez Portillo (y Pacheco), Jose
1920-2004 .... **CLC 46**
See also CA 129; 224; HW 1
Lopez y Fuentes, Gregorio 1897(?)-1966 .....
CLC 32
See also CA 131; EWL 3; HW 1
Lorca, Federico Garcia
See Garcia Lorca, Federico
Lord, Audre
See Lorde, Audre
Lord, Bette Bao 1938- .... **AAL; CLC 23**
See also BEST 90:3; BPFB 2; CA 107;
CANR 41, 79; CLR 151; INT CA-107;
SATA 58
Lord Auch
See Bataille, Georges
Lord Brooke
See Greville, Fulke

Lord Byron 1788-1824 ..... **DC 24; NCLC 2, 12, 109, 149, 256; PC 16, 95; WLC 1**
See also AAYA 64; BRW 4; BRWC 2; CD-BLB 1789-1832; DA; DA3; DAB; DAC; DAM MST, POET; DLB 96, 110; EXPP; LMFS 1; PAB; PFS 1, 14, 29, 35; RGEL 2; TEA; WLIT 3; WP

Lord Dunsany
See Dunsany, Edward John Moreton Drax Plunkett

Lorde, Audre 1934-1992 .... **BLC 1:2, 2:2; CLC 18, 71; PC 12; TCLC 173**
See also AFAW 1, 2; BW 1, 3; CA 25-28R; 142; CANR 16, 26, 46, 82; CP 2, 3, 4, 5; DA3; DAM MULT, POET; DLB 41; EWL 3; FW; GLL 1; MAL 5; MTCW 1, 2; MTFW 2005; PFS 16, 32; RGAL 4

Lorde, Audre Geraldine
See Lorde, Audre

Lord Houghton
See Milnes, Richard Monckton

Lord Jeffrey
See Jeffrey, Francis

Loreaux, Nichol CLC 65

Lorenzo, Heberto Padilla
See Padilla (Lorenzo), Heberto

Loris
See Hofmannsthal, Hugo von

Loti, Pierre
See Viaud, Julien

Lottie
See Grimke, Charlotte L. Forten

Lou, Henri
See Andreas-Salome, Lou

Louie, David Wong 1954- .... **CLC 70**
See also CA 139; CANR 120

Louis, Adrian C. NNAL
See also CA 223

Louis, Father M.
See Merton, Thomas

Louise, Heidi
See Erdrich, Louise

Lounsbury, Ruth Ozeki
See Ozeki, Ruth L.

Lovecraft, H. P. 1890-1937 . **SSC 3, 52, 165; TCLC 4, 22**
See also AAYA 14; BPFB 2; CA 104; 133; CANR 106; DA3; DAM POP; HGG; MTCW 1, 2; MTFW 2005; RGAL 4; SCFW 1, 2; SFW 4; SUFW

Lovecraft, Howard Phillips
See Lovecraft, H. P.

Lovelace, Earl 1935- .... **CLC 51; SSC 141**
See also BW 2; CA 77-80; CANR 41, 72, 114; CD 5, 6; CDWLB 3; CN 1, 2, 3, 4, 5, 6, 7; DLB 125; EWL 3; MTCW 1

Lovelace, Richard 1618-1658 .... **LC 24, 158; PC 69**
See also BRW 2; DLB 131; EXPP; PAB; PFS 32, 34; RGEL 2

Low, Penelope Margaret
See Lively, Penelope

Lowe, Pardee 1904- .... **AAL**

Lowell, Amy 1874-1925 . **PC 13; TCLC 1, 8, 259**
See also AAYA 57; AMW; CA 104; 151; DAM POET; DLB 54, 140; EWL 3; EXPP; LMFS 2; MAL 5; MBL; MTCW 2; MTFW 2005; PFS 30; RGAL 4; TUS

Lowell, James Russell 1819-1891 .. **NCLC 2, 90**
See also AMWS 1; CDALB 1640-1865; DLB 1, 11, 64, 79, 189, 235; RGAL 4

Lowell, Robert 1917-1977 . **CLC 1, 2, 3, 4, 5, 8, 9, 11, 15, 37, 124; PC 3; WLC 4**
See also AMW; AMWC 2; AMWR 2; CA 9-12R; 73-76; CABS 2; CAD; CANR 26, 60; CDALBS; CP 1, 2; DA; DA3; DAB;

DAC; DAM MST, NOV; DLB 5, 169; EWL 3; MAL 5; MTCW 1, 2; MTFW 2005; PAB; PFS 6, 7, 36; RGAL 4; WP

Lowell, Robert Trail Spence, Jr.
See Lowell, Robert

Lowenthal, Michael 1969- .... **CLC 119**
See also CA 150; CANR 115, 164

Lowenthal, Michael Francis
See Lowenthal, Michael

Lowndes, Marie Adelaide (Belloc) 1868-1947 .... **TCLC 12**
See also CA 107; CMW 4; DLB 70; RHW

Lowry, (Clarence) Malcolm 1909-1957 . **SSC 31; TCLC 6, 40**
See also BPFB 2; BRWS 3; CA 105; 131; CANR 62, 105; CDBLB 1945-1960; DLB 15; EWL 3; MTCW 1, 2; MTFW 2005; RGAL 2

Lowry, Mina Gertrude 1882-1966 . **CLC 28; PC 16**
See also CA 113; DAM POET; DLB 4, 54; PFS 20

Lowry, Sam
See Soderbergh, Steven

Loxsmith, John
See Brunner, John (Kilian Houston)

Loy, Mina
See Lowry, Mina Gertrude

Loyson-Bridet
See Schwob, Marcel (Mayer Andre)

Lucan 39-65 .... **CMLC 33, 112**
See also AW 2; DLB 211; EFS 1:2, 2:2; RGWL 2, 3

Lucas, Craig 1951- .... **CLC 64**
See also CA 137; CAD; CANR 71, 109, 142; CD 5, 6; GLL 2; MTFW 2005

Lucas, E(dward) V(errall) 1868-1938 .... **TCLC 73**
See also CA 176; DLB 98, 149, 153; SATA 20

Lucas, George 1944- .... **CLC 16, 252**
See also AAYA 1, 23; CA 77-80; CANR 30; SATA 56

Lucas, Hans
See Godard, Jean-Luc

Lucas, Victoria
See Plath, Sylvia

Lucian c. 125-c. 180 .... **CMLC 32**
See also AW 2; DLB 176; RGWL 2, 3

Lucilius c. 180B.C.-102B.C. .... **CMLC 82**
See also DLB 211

Lucretius c. 94B.C.-c. 49B.C. .... **CMLC 48**
See also AW 2; CDWLB 1; DLB 211; EFS 1:2, 2:2; RGWL 2, 3; WLIT 8

Ludlam, Charles 1943-1987 ...... **CLC 46, 50**
See also CA 85-88; 122; CAD; CANR 72, 86; DLB 266

Ludlum, Robert 1927-2001 .... **CLC 22, 43**
See also AAYA 10, 59; BEST 89:1, 90:3; BPFB 2; CA 33-36R; 195; CANR 25, 41, 68, 105, 131; CMW 4; CPW; DA3; DAM NOV, POP; DLBY 1982; MSW; MTCW 1, 2; MTFW 2005

Ludwig, Ken 1950- .... **CLC 60**
See also CA 195; CAD; CD 6

Ludwig, Otto 1813-1865 .... **NCLC 4**
See also DLB 129

Lugones, Leopoldo 1874-1938 .... **HLCS 2; TCLC 15**
See also CA 116; 131; CANR 104; DLB 283; EWL 3; HW 1; LAW

Lu Hsun
See Shu-Jen, Chou

Lu Hsun
See Lu Xun

Lukacs, George
See Lukacs, Gyorgy

Lukacs, Gyorgy 1885-1971 .... **CLC 24**
See also CA 101; 29-32R; CANR 62; CD-WLB 4; DLB 215, 242; EW 10; EWL 3; MTCW 1, 2

Lukacs, Gyorgy Szegeny von
See Lukacs, Gyorgy

Luke, Peter (Ambrose Cyprian) 1919-1995 .... **CLC 38**
See also CA 81-84; 147; CANR 72; CBD; CD 5, 6; DLB 13

Lunar, Dennis
See Mungo, Raymond

Lurie, Alison 1926- .... **CLC 4, 5, 18, 39, 175**
See also BPFB 2; CA 1-4R; CANR 2, 17, 50, 88; CN 1, 2, 3, 4, 5, 6, 7; DLB 2, 350; MAL 5; MTCW 1; NFS 24; SATA 46, 112; TCLE 1:1

Lustig, Arnost 1926-2011 .... **CLC 56**
See also AAYA 3; CA 69-72; CANR 47, 102; CWW 2; DLB 232, 299; EWL 3; RGHL; SATA 56

Luther, Martin 1483-1546 ...... **LC 9, 37, 150**
See also CDWLB 2; DLB 179; EW 2; RGWL 2, 3

Luxemburg, Rosa 1870(?)-1919 .... **TCLC 63**
See also CA 118

Lu Xun 1881-1936 .... **SSC 158**
See also CA 243; DLB 328; RGSF 2; RGWL 2, 3

Luzi, Mario (Egidio Vincenzo) 1914-2005 ... **CLC 13**
See also CA 61-64; 236; CANR 9, 70; CWW 2; DLB 128; EWL 3

L'vov, Arkady CLC 59

Lydgate, John c. 1370-1450(?) ... **LC 81, 175**
See also BRW 1; DLB 146; RGEL 2

Lyly, John 1554(?)-1606 .. **DC 7; LC 41, 187**
See also BRW 1; DAM DRAM; DLB 62, 167; RGEL 2

L'Ymagier
See Gourmont, Remy(-Marie-Charles) de

Lynch, B. Suarez
See Borges, Jorge Luis

Lynch, David 1946- .... **CLC 66, 162**
See also AAYA 55; CA 124; 129; CANR 111

Lynch, David Keith
See Lynch, David

Lynch, James
See Andreyev, Leonid

Lyndsay, Sir David 1485-1555 .... **LC 20**
See also RGEL 2

Lynn, Kenneth S(chuyler) 1923-2001 .. **CLC 50**
See also CA 1-4R; 196; CANR 3, 27, 65

Lynx
See West, Rebecca

Lyons, Marcus
See Blish, James

Lyotard, Jean-Francois 1924-1998 .... **TCLC 103**
See also DLB 242; EWL 3

Lyre, Pinchbeck
See Sassoon, Siegfried

Lytle, Andrew (Nelson) 1902-1995 .. **CLC 22**
See also CA 9-12R; 150; CANR 70; CN 1, 2, 3, 4, 5, 6; CSW; DLB 6; DLBY 1995; RGAL 4; RHW

Lyttelton, George 1709-1773 .... **LC 10**
See also RGEL 2

Lytton, Edward G.E.L. Bulwer-Lytton Baron
See Bulwer-Lytton, Edward

Mahfouz, Najib
See Mahfouz, Naguib

Mahfuz, Najib
See Mahfouz, Naguib

Mahon, Derek 1941- .... **CLC 27; PC 60**
See also BRWS 6; CA 113; 128; CANR 88;
CP 1, 2, 3, 4, 5, 6, 7; DLB 40; EWL 3

Maiakovskii, Vladimir
See Mayakovski, Vladimir

Mailer, Norman 1923-2007 .. **CLC 1, 2, 3, 4,**
5, 8, 11, 14, 28, 39, 74, 111, 234
See also AAYA 31; AITN 2; AMW; AMWC
2; AMWR 2; BPFB 2; CA 9-12R; 266;
CABS 1; CANR 28, 74, 77, 130, 196;
CDALB 1968-1988; CN 1, 2, 3, 4, 5, 6,
7; CPW; DA; DA3; DAB; DAC; DAM
MST, NOV, POP; DLB 2, 16, 28, 185,
278; DLBD 3; DLBY 1980, 1983; EWL
3; MAL 5; MTCW 1, 2; MTFW 2005;
NFS 10; RGAL 4; TUS

Mailer, Norman Kingsley
See Mailer, Norman

Maillet, Antonine 1929- .... **CLC 54, 118**
See also CA 115; 120; CANR 46, 74, 77,
134; CCA 1; CWW 2; DAC; DLB 60;
INT CA-120; MTCW 2; MTFW 2005

Maimonides, Moses 1135-1204 .... **CMLC 76**
See also DLB 115

Mais, Roger 1905-1955 .... **TCLC 8**
See also BW 1, 3; CA 105; 124; CANR 82;
CDWLB 3; DLB 125; EWL 3; MTCW 1;
RGEL 2

Maistre, Joseph 1753-1821 .... **NCLC 37**
See also GFL 1789 to the Present

Maitland, Frederic William 1850-1906 ....
TCLC 65

Maitland, Sara 1950- .... **CLC 49**
See also BRWS 11; CA 69-72; CANR 13,
59, 221; DLB 271; FW

Maitland, Sara Louise
See Maitland, Sara

Major, Clarence 1936- ..... **BLC 1:2; CLC 3,**
19, 48
See also AFAW 2; BW 2, 3; CA 21-24R;
CAAS 6; CANR 13, 25, 53, 82; CN 3, 4,
5, 6, 7; CP 2, 3, 4, 5, 6, 7; CSW; DAM
MULT; DLB 33; EWL 3; MAL 5; MSW

Major, Kevin (Gerald) 1949- .... **CLC 26**
See also AAYA 16; CA 97-100; CANR 21,
38, 112; CLR 11; DAC; DLB 60; INT
CANR-21; JRDA; MAICYA 1, 2; MAIC-
YAS 1; SATA 32, 82, 134; WYA; YAW

Maki, James
See Ozu, Yasujiro

Makin, Bathsua 1600-1675(?) .... **LC 137**

Makine, Andrei
See Makine, Andrei

Makine, Andrei 1957- .... **CLC 198**
See also CA 176; CANR 103, 162; MTFW
2005

Malabaila, Damiano
See Levi, Primo

Malamud, Bernard 1914-1986 . **CLC 1, 2, 3,**
5, 8, 9, 11, 18, 27, 44, 78, 85; SSC 15,
147; TCLC 129, 184; WLC 4
See also AAYA 16; AMWS 1; BPFB 2;
BYA 15; CA 5-8R; 118; CABS 1; CANR
28, 62, 114; CDALB 1941-1968; CN 1, 2,
3, 4; CPW; DA; DA3; DAB; DAC; DAM
MST, NOV, POP; DLB 2, 28, 152; DLBY
1980, 1986; EWL 3; EXPS; LAIT 4;
LATS 1:1; MAL 5; MTCW 1, 2; MTFW
2005; NFS 27; RGAL 4; RGHL; RGSF 2;
SSFS 8, 13, 16; TUS

Malan, Herman
See Bosman, Herman Charles; Bosman,
Herman Charles

Malaparte, Curzio 1898-1957 .... **TCLC 52**
See also DLB 264

Malcolm, Dan
See Silverberg, Robert

Malcolm, Janet 1934- .... **CLC 201**
See also CA 123; CANR 89, 199; NCFS 1

Malcolm X 1925-1965 .... **BLC 1:2; CLC 82,**
117; WLCS
See also BW 1, 3; CA 125; 111; CANR 82;
DA; DA3; DAB; DAC; DAM MST,
MULT; LAIT 5; MTCW 1, 2; MTFW
2005; NCFS 3

Malebranche, Nicolas 1638-1715 ..... **LC 133**
See also GFL Beginnings to 1789

Malherbe, Francois de 1555-1628 .... **LC 5**
See also DLB 327; GFL Beginnings to 1789

Mallarme, Stephane 1842-1898 ..... **NCLC 4,**
41, 210; PC 4, 102
See also DAM POET; DLB 217; EW 7;
GFL 1789 to the Present; LMFS 2; RGWL
2, 3; TWA

Mallet-Joris, Francoise 1930- .... **CLC 11**
See also CA 65-68; CANR 17; CWW 2;
DLB 83; EWL 3; GFL 1789 to the Present

Malley, Ern
See McAuley, James Phillip

Mallon, Thomas 1951- .... **CLC 172**
See also CA 110; CANR 29, 57, 92, 196;
DLB 350

Mallowan, Agatha Christie
See Christie, Agatha

Maloff, Saul 1922- .... **CLC 5**
See also CA 33-36R

Malone, Louis
See MacNeice, (Frederick) Louis

Malone, Michael 1942- .... **CLC 43**
See also CA 77-80; CANR 14, 32, 57, 114,
214

Malone, Michael Christopher
See Malone, Michael

Malory, Sir Thomas 1410(?)-1471(?) . **LC 11,**
88; WLCS
See also BRW 1; BRWR 2; CDBLB Before
1660; DA; DAB; DAC; DAM MST; DLB
146; EFS 1:2, 2:2; RGEL 2; SATA 59;
SATA-Brief 33; TEA; WLIT 3

Malouf, David 1934- .... **CLC 28, 86, 245**
See also BRWS 12; CA 124; CANR 50, 76,
180, 224; CN 3, 4, 5, 6, 7; CP 1, 3, 4, 5,
6, 7; DLB 289; EWL 3; MTCW 2; MTFW
2005; SSFS 24

Malouf, George Joseph David
See Malouf, David

Malraux, Andre 1901-1976 . **CLC 1, 4, 9, 13,**
15, 57; TCLC 209
See also BPFB 2; CA 21-22; 69-72; CANR
34, 58; CAP 2; DA3; DAM NOV; DLB
72; EW 12; EWL 3; GFL 1789 to the
Present; MTCW 1, 2; MTFW 2005;
RGWL 2, 3; TWA

Malraux, Georges-Andre
See Malraux, Andre

Malthus, Thomas Robert 1766-1834 . **NCLC**
145
See also DLB 107, 158; RGEL 2

Malzberg, Barry N(athaniel) 1939- .. **CLC 7**
See also CA 61-64; CAAS 4; CANR 16;
CMW 4; DLB 8; SFW 4

Mamet, David 1947- . **CLC 9, 15, 34, 46, 91,**
166; DC 4, 24
See also AAYA 3, 60; AMWS 14; CA 81-
84; CABS 3; CAD; CANR 15, 41, 67, 72,
129, 172; CD 5, 6; DA3; DAM DRAM;
DFS 2, 3, 6, 12, 15; DLB 7; EWL 3;
IDFW 4; MAL 5; MTCW 1, 2; MTFW
2005; RGAL 4

Mamet, David Alan
See Mamet, David

Mamoulian, Rouben (Zachary) 1897-1987 ..
CLC 16
See also CA 25-28R; 124; CANR 85

Mandelshtam, Osip
See Mandelstam, Osip

Mandel'shtam, Osip Emil'evich
See Mandelstam, Osip

Mandelstam, Osip 1891(?)-1943(?) ... **PC 14;**
TCLC 2, 6, 225
See also CA 104; 150; DLB 295; EW 10;
EWL 3; MTCW 2; RGWL 2, 3; TWA

Mandelstam, Osip Emilievich
See Mandelstam, Osip

Mander, (Mary) Jane 1877-1949 .. **TCLC 31**
See also CA 162; RGEL 2

Mandeville, Bernard 1670-1733 .... **LC 82**
See also DLB 101

Mandeville, Sir John fl. 1350- ..... **CMLC 19**
See also DLB 146

Mandiargues, Andre Pieyre de
See Pieyre de Mandiargues, Andre

Mandrake, Ethel Belle
See Thurman, Wallace (Henry)

Mangan, James Clarence 1803-1849 . **NCLC**
27
See also BRWS 13; RGEL 2

Maniere, J. E.
See Giraudoux, Jean

Mankell, Henning 1948- .... **CLC 292**
See also CA 187; CANR 163, 200

Mankiewicz, Herman (Jacob) 1897-1953 ....
TCLC 85
See also CA 120; 169; DLB 26; IDFW 3, 4

Manley, (Mary) Delariviere 1672(?)-1724 ...
LC 1, 42
See also DLB 39, 80; RGEL 2

Mann, Abel
See Creasey, John

Mann, Emily 1952- .... **DC 7**
See also CA 130; CAD; CANR 55; CD 5,
6; CWD; DFS 28; DLB 266

Mann, Erica
See Jong, Erica

Mann, (Luiz) Heinrich 1871-1950 .. **TCLC 9**
See also CA 106; 164, 181; DLB 66, 118;
EW 8; EWL 3; RGWL 2, 3

Mann, Paul Thomas
See Mann, Thomas

Mann, Thomas 1875-1955 ..... **SSC 5, 80, 82;**
TCLC 2, 8, 14, 21, 35, 44, 60, 168, 236;
WLC 4
See also BPFB 2; CA 104; 128; CANR 133;
CDWLB 2; DA; DA3; DAB; DAC; DAM
MST, NOV; DLB 66, 331; EW 9; EWL 3;
GLL 1; LATS 1:1; LMFS 1; MTCW 1, 2;
MTFW 2005; NFS 17; RGSF 2; RGWL
2, 3; SSFS 4, 9; TWA

Mannheim, Karl 1893-1947 .... **TCLC 65**
See also CA 204

Manning, David
See Faust, Frederick

Manning, Frederic 1882-1935 .... **TCLC 25**
See also CA 124; 216; DLB 260

Manning, Olivia 1915-1980 .... **CLC 5, 19**
See also CA 5-8R; 101; CANR 29; CN 1,
2; EWL 3; FW; MTCW 1; RGEL 2

Mannyng, Robert c. 1264-c. 1340 .... **CMLC**
83
See also DLB 146

Mano, D. Keith 1942- .... **CLC 2, 10**
See also CA 25-28R; CAAS 6; CANR 26,
57; DLB 6

Mansfield, Katherine 1888-1923 . **SSC 9, 23,**
38, 81; TCLC 2, 8, 39, 164; WLC 4
See also BPFB 2; BRW 7; CA 104; 134;
DA; DA3; DAB; DAC; DAM MST; DLB
162; EWL 3; EXPS; FW; GLL 1; MTCW
2; RGEL 2; RGSF 2; SSFS 2, 8, 10, 11,
29; TEA; WWE 1

Mansfield, Kathleen
  See Mansfield, Katherine
Manso, Peter 1940- .... **CLC 39**
  See also CA 29-32R; CANR 44, 156
Mantecon, Juan Jimenez
  See Jimenez, Juan Ramon
Mantel, Hilary 1952- .... **CLC 144, 309**
  See also CA 125; CANR 54, 101, 161, 207;
  CN 5, 6, 7; DLB 271; RHW
Mantel, Hilary Mary
  See Mantel, Hilary
Manton, Peter
  See Creasey, John
Man Without a Spleen, A
  See Chekhov, Anton
Manzano, Juan Franciso 1797(?)-1854 ....
  NCLC 155
Manzoni, Alessandro 1785-1873 .. **NCLC 29,
  98**
  See also EW 5; RGWL 2, 3; TWA; WLIT 7
Map, Walter 1140-1209 .... **CMLC 32**
Mapu, Abraham (ben Jekutiel) 1808-1867 ..
  NCLC 18
Mara, Sally
  See Queneau, Raymond
Maracle, Lee 1950- .... **NNAL**
  See also CA 149
Marat, Jean Paul 1743-1793 .... **LC 10**
Marcel, Gabriel Honore 1889-1973 . **CLC 15**
  See also CA 102; 45-48; EWL 3; MTCW 1,
  2
March, William 1893-1954 .... **TCLC 96**
  See also CA 108; 216; DLB 9, 86, 316;
  MAL 5
Marchbanks, Samuel
  See Davies, Robertson
Marchi, Giacomo
  See Bassani, Giorgio
Marcus Aurelius
  See Aurelius, Marcus
Marcuse, Herbert 1898-1979 ...... **TCLC 207**
  See also CA 188; 89-92; DLB 242
Marguerite
  See de Navarre, Marguerite
Marguerite d'Angouleme
  See de Navarre, Marguerite
Marguerite de Navarre
  See de Navarre, Marguerite
Margulies, Donald 1954- .... **CLC 76**
  See also AAYA 57; CA 200; CD 6; DFS 13;
  DLB 228
Marias, Javier 1951- .... **CLC 239**
  See also CA 167; CANR 109, 139; DLB
  322; HW 2; MTFW 2005
Marie de France c. 12th cent. - .... **CMLC 8,
  111; PC 22**
  See also DLB 208; FW; RGWL 2, 3
Marie de l'Incarnation 1599-1672 .... **LC 10,
  168**
Marier, Captain Victor
  See Griffith, D.W.
Mariner, Scott
  See Pohl, Frederik
Marinetti, Filippo Tommaso 1876-1944 ....
  TCLC 10
  See also CA 107; DLB 114, 264; EW 9;
  EWL 3; WLIT 7
Marino, Giambattista 1569-1625 ..... **LC 181**
  See also DLB 339; WLIT 7
Marivaux, Pierre Carlet de Chamblain de
  1688-1763 .... **DC 7; LC 4, 123**
  See also DLB 314; GFL Beginnings to
  1789; RGWL 2, 3; TWA
Markandaya, Kamala 1924-2004 ..... **CLC 8,
  38, 290**
  See also BYA 13; CA 77-80; 227; CN 1, 2,
  3, 4, 5, 6, 7; DLB 323; EWL 3; MTFW
  2005; NFS 13

Markfield, Wallace (Arthur) 1926-2002 ......
  CLC 8
  See also CA 69-72; 208; CAAS 3; CN 1, 2,
  3, 4, 5, 6, 7; DLB 2, 28; DLBY 2002
Markham, Edwin 1852-1940 .... **TCLC 47**
  See also CA 160; DLB 54, 186; MAL 5;
  RGAL 4
Markham, Robert
  See Amis, Kingsley
Marks, J.
  See Highwater, Jamake (Mamake)
Marks-Highwater, J.
  See Highwater, Jamake (Mamake)
Markson, David M. 1927-2010 .... **CLC 67**
  See also AMWS 17; CA 49-52; CANR 1,
  91, 158; CN 5, 6
Markson, David Merrill
  See Markson, David M.
Marlatt, Daphne (Buckle) 1942- ... **CLC 168**
  See also CA 25-28R; CANR 17, 39; CN 6,
  7; CP 4, 5, 6, 7; CWP; DLB 60; FW
Marley, Bob
  See Marley, Robert Nesta
Marley, Robert Nesta 1945-1981 .... **CLC 17**
  See also CA 107; 103
Marlowe, Christopher 1564-1593 . **DC 1; LC
  22, 47, 117, 201; PC 57; WLC 4**
  See also BRW 1; BRWR 1; CDBLB Before
  1660; DA; DA3; DAB; DAC; DAM
  DRAM, MST; DFS 1, 5, 13, 21; DLB 62;
  EXPP; LMFS 1; PFS 22; RGEL 2; TEA;
  WLIT 3
Marlowe, Stephen 1928-2008 .... **CLC 70**
  See also CA 13-16R; 269; CANR 6, 55;
  CMW 4; SFW 4
Marmion, Shakerley 1603-1639 .... **LC 89**
  See also DLB 58; RGEL 2
Marmontel, Jean-Francois 1723-1799 . **LC 2**
  See also DLB 314
Maron, Monika 1941- .... **CLC 165**
  See also CA 201
Marot, Clement c. 1496-1544 .... **LC 133**
  See also DLB 327; GFL Beginnings to 1789
Marquand, John P(hillips) 1893-1960 . **CLC
  2, 10**
  See also AMW; BPFB 2; CA 85-88; CANR
  73; CMW 4; DLB 9, 102; EWL 3; MAL
  5; MTCW 2; RGAL 4
Marques, Rene 1919-1979 . **CLC 96; HLC 2**
  See also CA 97-100; 85-88; CANR 78;
  DAM MULT; DLB 305; EWL 3; HW 1,
  2; LAW; RGSF 2
Marquez, Gabriel Garcia
  See Garcia Marquez, Gabriel
Marquez, Gabriel Garcia
  See Garcia Marquez, Gabriel
Marquis, Don(ald Robert Perry)
  1878-1937 .... **TCLC 7**
  See also CA 104; 166; DLB 11, 25; MAL
  5; RGAL 4
Marquis de Sade
  See Sade, Donatien Alphonse Francois
Marric, J. J.
  See Creasey, John
Marryat, Frederick 1792-1848 .... **NCLC 3**
  See also DLB 21, 163; RGEL 2; WCH
Marsden, James
  See Creasey, John
Marse, Juan 1933- .... **CLC 302**
  See also CA 254; DLB 322
Marsh, Edith Ngaio
  See Marsh, Ngaio
Marsh, Edward 1872-1953 .... **TCLC 99**
Marsh, Ngaio 1895-1982 .... **CLC 7, 53**
  See also CA 9-12R; CANR 6, 58; CMW 4;
  CN 1, 2, 3; CPW; DAM POP; DLB 77;
  MSW; MTCW 1, 2; RGEL 2; TEA

Marshall, Alan
  See Westlake, Donald E.
Marshall, Allen
  See Westlake, Donald E.
Marshall, Garry 1934- .... **CLC 17**
  See also AAYA 3; CA 111; SATA 60
Marshall, Paule 1929- .. **BLC 1:3, 2:3; CLC
  27, 72, 253; SSC 3**
  See also AFAW 1, 2; AMWS 11; BPFB 2;
  BW 2, 3; CA 77-80; CANR 25, 73, 129,
  209; CN 1, 2, 3, 4, 5, 6, 7; DA3; DAM
  MULT; DLB 33, 157, 227; EWL 3; LATS
  1:2; MAL 5; MTCW 1, 2; MTFW 2005;
  NFS 36; RGAL 4; SSFS 15
Marshallik
  See Zangwill, Israel
Marsilius of Inghen c. 1340-1396 ..... **CMLC
  106**
Marsten, Richard
  See Hunter, Evan
Marston, John 1576-1634 .... **DC 37; LC 33,
  172**
  See also BRW 2; DAM DRAM; DLB 58,
  172; RGEL 2
Martel, Yann 1963- .... **CLC 192, 315**
  See also AAYA 67; CA 146; CANR 114,
  226; DLB 326, 334; LNFS 2; MTFW
  2005; NFS 27
Martens, Adolphe-Adhemar
  See Ghelderode, Michel de
Martha, Henry
  See Harris, Mark
Marti, Jose 1853-1895 ... **HLC 2; NCLC 63;
  PC 76**
  See also DAM MULT; DLB 290; HW 2;
  LAW; RGWL 2, 3; WLIT 1
Martial c. 40-c. 104 .... **CMLC 35; PC 10**
  See also AW 2; CDWLB 1; DLB 211;
  RGWL 2, 3
Martin, Ken
  See Hubbard, L. Ron
Martin, Richard
  See Creasey, John
Martin, Steve 1945- .... **CLC 30, 217**
  See also AAYA 53; CA 97-100; CANR 30,
  100, 140, 195, 227; DFS 19; MTCW 1;
  MTFW 2005
Martin, Valerie 1948- .... **CLC 89**
  See also BEST 90:2; CA 85-88; CANR 49,
  89, 165, 200
Martin, Violet Florence 1862-1915 . **SSC 56;
  TCLC 51**
Martin, Webber
  See Silverberg, Robert
Martindale, Patrick Victor
  See White, Patrick
Martin du Gard, Roger 1881-1958 ... **TCLC
  24**
  See also CA 118; CANR 94; DLB 65, 331;
  EWL 3; GFL 1789 to the Present; RGWL
  2, 3
Martineau, Harriet 1802-1876 .... **NCLC 26,
  137**
  See also BRWS 15; DLB 21, 55, 159, 163,
  166, 190; FW; RGEL 2; YABC 2
Martines, Julia
  See O'Faolain, Julia
Martinez, Enrique Gonzalez
  See Gonzalez Martinez, Enrique
Martinez, Jacinto Benavente y
  See Benavente, Jacinto
Martinez de la Rosa, Francisco de Paula
  1787-1862 .... **NCLC 102**
  See also TWA
Martinez Ruiz, Jose 1873-1967 .... **CLC 11**
  See also CA 93-96; DLB 322; EW 3; EWL
  3; HW 1
Martinez Sierra, Gregorio
  See Martinez Sierra, Maria

Martinez Sierra, Gregorio 1881-1947 ....
TCLC 6
See also CA 115; EWL 3

Martinez Sierra, Maria 1874-1974 . TCLC 6
See also CA 250; 115; EWL 3

Martinez Sierra, Maria de la O'LeJarraga
See Martinez Sierra, Maria

Martinsen, Martin
See Follett, Ken

Martinson, Harry (Edmund) 1904-1978 ......
CLC 14
See also CA 77-80; CANR 34, 130; DLB
259, 331; EWL 3

Marti y Perez, Jose Julian
See Marti, Jose

Martyn, Edward 1859-1923 .... TCLC 131
See also CA 179; DLB 10; RGEL 2

Marut, Ret
See Traven, B.

Marut, Robert
See Traven, B.

Marvell, Andrew 1621-1678 . LC 4, 43, 179;
PC 10, 86; WLC 4
See also BRW 2; BRWR 2; CDBLB 1660-
1789; DA; DAB; DAC; DAM MST;
POET; DLB 131; EXPP; PFS 5; RGEL 2;
TEA; WP

Marx, Karl 1818-1883 .... NCLC 17, 114
See also DLB 129; LATS 1:1; TWA

Marx, Karl Heinrich
See Marx, Karl

Masaoka, Shiki -1902 ....
See Masaoka, Tsunenori

Masaoka, Tsunenori 1867-1902 .... TCLC 18
See also CA 117; 191; EWL 3; RGWL 3;
TWA

Masaoka Shiki
See Masaoka, Tsunenori

Masefield, John (Edward) 1878-1967 .. CLC
11, 47; PC 78
See also CA 19-20; 25-28R; CANR 33;
CAP 2; CDBLB 1890-1914; CLR 164;
DAM POET; DLB 10, 19, 153, 160; EWL
3; EXPP; FANT; MTCW 1, 2; PFS 5;
RGEL 2; SATA 19

Maso, Carole 1955(?)- .... CLC 44
See also CA 170; CANR 148; CN 7; GLL
2; RGAL 4

Mason, Bobbie Ann 1940- .. CLC 28, 43, 82,
154, 303; SSC 4, 101
See also AAYA 5, 42; AMWS 8; BPFB 2;
CA 53-56; CANR 11, 31, 58, 83, 125,
169; CDALBS; CN 5, 6, 7; CSW; DA3;
DLB 173; DLBY 1987; EWL 3; EXPS;
INT CANR-31; MAL 5; MTCW 1, 2;
MTFW 2005; NFS 4; RGAL 4; RGSF 2;
SSFS 3, 8, 20; TCLE 1:2; YAW

Mason, Ernst
See Pohl, Frederik

Mason, Hunni B.
See Sternheim, (William Adolf) Carl

Mason, Lee W.
See Malzberg, Barry N(athaniel)

Mason, Nick 1945- .... CLC 35

Mason, Tally
See Derleth, August (William)

Mass, Anna CLC 59

Mass, William
See Gibson, William

Massinger, Philip 1583-1640 . DC 39; LC 70
See also BRWS 11; DLB 58; RGEL 2

Master Lao
See Lao Tzu

Masters, Edgar Lee 1868-1950 ..... PC 1, 36;
TCLC 2, 25; WLCS
See also AMWS 1; CA 104; 133; CDALB
1865-1917; DA; DAC; DAM MST,
POET; DLB 54; EWL 3; EXPP; MAL 5;
MTCW 1, 2; MTFW 2005; PFS 37;
RGAL 4; TUS; WP

Masters, Hilary 1928- .... CLC 48
See also CA 25-28R, 217; CAAE 217;
CANR 13, 47, 97, 171, 221; CN 6, 7;
DLB 244

Masters, Hilary Thomas
See Masters, Hilary

Mastrosimone, William 1947- .... CLC 36
See also CA 186; CAD; CD 5, 6

Mathe, Albert
See Camus, Albert

Mather, Cotton 1663-1728 .... LC 38
See also AMWS 2; CDALB 1640-1865;
DLB 24, 30, 140; RGAL 4; TUS

Mather, Increase 1639-1723 .... LC 38, 161
See also DLB 24

Mathers, Marshall
See Eminem

Mathers, Marshall Bruce
See Eminem

Matheson, Richard 1926- .... CLC 37, 267
See also AAYA 31; CA 97-100; CANR 88,
99; DLB 8, 44; HGG; INT CA-97-100;
SCFW 1, 2; SFW 4; SUFW 2

Matheson, Richard Burton
See Matheson, Richard

Mathews, Harry 1930- .... CLC 6, 52
See also CA 21-24R; CAAS 6; CANR 18,
40, 98, 160; CN 5, 6, 7

Mathews, John Joseph 1894-1979 . CLC 84;
NNAL
See also CA 19-20; 142; CANR 45; CAP 2;
DAM MULT; DLB 175; TCWW 1, 2

Mathias, Roland 1915-2007 .... CLC 45
See also CA 97-100; 263; CANR 19, 41;
CP 1, 2, 3, 4, 5, 6, 7; DLB 27

Mathias, Roland Glyn
See Mathias, Roland

Matsuo Basho 1644(?)-1694 ... LC 62; PC 3,
125
See also DAM POET; PFS 2, 7, 18; RGWL
2, 3; WP

Mattheson, Rodney
See Creasey, John

Matthew, James
See Barrie, J. M.

Matthew of Vendome c. 1130-c. 1200 ....
CMLC 99
See also DLB 208

Matthews, (James) Brander 1852-1929 ....
TCLC 95
See also CA 181; DLB 71, 78; DLBD 13

Matthews, Greg 1949- .... CLC 45
See also CA 135

Matthews, William (Procter III)
1942-1997 .... CLC 40
See also AMWS 9; CA 29-32R; 162; CAAS
18; CANR 12, 57; CP 2, 3, 4, 5, 6; DLB
5

Matthias, John (Edward) 1941- .... CLC 9
See also CA 33-36R; CANR 56; CP 4, 5, 6,
7

Matthiessen, F(rancis) O(tto) 1902-1950 .....
TCLC 100
See also CA 185; DLB 63; MAL 5

Matthiessen, Francis Otto
See Matthiessen, F(rancis) O(tto)

Matthiessen, Peter 1927- .. CLC 5, 7, 11, 32,
64, 245
See also AAYA 6, 40; AMWS 5; ANW;
BEST 90:4; BPFB 2; CA 9-12R; CANR
21, 50, 73, 100, 138; CN 1, 2, 3, 4, 5, 6,
7; DA3; DAM NOV; DLB 6, 173, 275;
MAL 5; MTCW 1, 2; MTFW 2005; SATA
27

Maturin, Charles Robert 1780(?)-1824 ....
NCLC 6, 169
See also BRWS 8; DLB 178; GL 3; HGG;
LMFS 1; RGEL 2; SUFW

Matute (Ausejo), Ana Maria 1925- . CLC 11
See also CA 89-92; CANR 129; CWW 2;
DLB 322; EWL 3; MTCW 1; RGSF 2

Maugham, W. S.
See Maugham, W. Somerset

Maugham, W. Somerset 1874-1965 . CLC 1,
11, 15, 67, 93; SSC 8, 94, 164; TCLC
208; WLC 4
See also AAYA 55; BPFB 2; BRW 6; CA
5-8R; 25-28R; CANR 40, 127; CDBLB
1914-1945; CMW 4; DA; DA3; DAB;
DAC; DAM DRAM, MST, NOV; DFS
22; DLB 10, 36, 77, 100, 162, 195; EWL
3; LAIT 3; MTCW 1, 2; MTFW 2005;
NFS 23, 35; RGEL 2; RGSF 2; SATA 54;
SSFS 17

Maugham, William S.
See Maugham, W. Somerset

Maugham, William Somerset
See Maugham, W. Somerset

Maupassant, Guy de 1850-1893 .... NCLC 1,
42, 83, 234; SSC 1, 64, 132; WLC 4
See also BYA 14; DA; DA3; DAB; DAC;
DAM MST; DLB 123; EW 7; EXPS; GFL
1789 to the Present; LAIT 2; LMFS 1;
RGSF 2; RGWL 2, 3; SSFS 4, 21, 28, 31;
SUFW; TWA

Maupassant, Henri Rene Albert Guy de
See Maupassant, Guy de

Maupin, Armistead 1944- .... CLC 95
See also CA 125; 130; CANR 58, 101, 183;
CPW; DA3; DAM POP; DLB 278; GLL
1; INT CA-130; MTCW 2; MTFW 2005

Maupin, Armistead Jones, Jr.
See Maupin, Armistead

Maurhut, Richard
See Traven, B.

Mauriac, Claude 1914-1996 .... CLC 9
See also CA 89-92; 152; CWW 2; DLB 83;
EWL 3; GFL 1789 to the Present

Mauriac, Francois (Charles) 1885-1970 ......
CLC 4, 9, 56; SSC 24
See also CA 25-28; CAP 2; DLB 65, 331;
EW 10; EWL 3; GFL 1789 to the Present;
MTCW 1, 2; MTFW 2005; RGWL 2, 3;
TWA

Mavor, Osborne Henry 1888-1951 . TCLC 3
See also CA 104; DLB 10; EWL 3

Maxwell, Glyn 1962- .... CLC 238
See also CA 154; CANR 88, 183; CP 6, 7;
PFS 23

Maxwell, William (Keepers, Jr.)
1908-2000 .... CLC 19
See also AMWS 8; CA 93-96; 189; CANR
54, 95; CN 1, 2, 3, 4, 5, 6, 7; DLB 218,
278; DLBY 1980; INT CA-93-96; MAL
5; SATA-Obit 128

May, Elaine 1932- .... CLC 16
See also CA 124; 142; CAD; CWD; DLB
44

Mayakovski, Vladimir 1893-1930 . TCLC 4,
18
See also CA 104; 158; EW 11; EWL 3;
IDTP; MTCW 2; MTFW 2005; RGWL 2,
3; SFW 4; TWA; WP

Mayakovski, Vladimir Vladimirovich
See Mayakovski, Vladimir

Mayakovsky, Vladimir
See Mayakovski, Vladimir

Mayhew, Henry 1812-1887 .... NCLC 31
See also DLB 18, 55, 190

Mayle, Peter 1939(?)- .... CLC 89
See also CA 139; CANR 64, 109, 168, 218

Maynard, Joyce 1953- .... CLC 23
See also CA 111; 129; CANR 64, 169, 220

Mayne, William 1928-2010 .... CLC 12
See also AAYA 20; CA 9-12R; CANR 37,
80, 100; CLR 25, 123; FANT; JRDA;
MAICYA 1, 2; MAICYAS 1; SAAS 11;
SATA 6, 68, 122; SUFW 2; YAW

Merlin, Arthur
See Blish, James

Mernissi, Fatima 1940- .... **CLC 171**
See also CA 152; DLB 346; FW

Merrill, James 1926-1995 .... **CLC 2, 3, 6, 8, 13, 18, 34, 91; PC 28; TCLC 173**
See also AMWS 3; CA 13-16R; 147; CANR 10, 49, 63, 108; CP 1, 2, 3, 4; DA3; DAM POET; DLB 5, 165; DLBY 1985; EWL 3; INT CANR-10; MAL 5; MTCW 1, 2; MTFW 2005; PAB; PFS 23; RGAL 4

Merrill, James Ingram
See Merrill, James

Merriman, Alex
See Silverberg, Robert

Merriman, Brian 1747-1805 .... **NCLC 70**

Merritt, E. B.
See Waddington, Miriam

Merton, Thomas 1915-1968 ... **CLC 1, 3, 11, 34, 83; PC 10**
See also AAYA 61; AMWS 8; CA 5-8R; 25-28R; CANR 22, 53, 111, 131; DA3; DLB 48; DLBY 1981; MAL 5; MTCW 1, 2; MTFW 2005

Merton, Thomas James
See Merton, Thomas

Merwin, W. S. 1927- .. **CLC 1, 2, 3, 5, 8, 13, 18, 45, 88; PC 45**
See also AMWS 3; CA 13-16R; CANR 15, 51, 112, 140, 209; CP 1, 2, 3, 4, 5, 6, 7; DA3; DAM POET; DLB 5, 169, 342; EWL 3; INT CANR-15; MAL 5; MTCW 1, 2; MTFW 2005; PAB; PFS 5, 15; RGAL 4

Merwin, William Stanley
See Merwin, W. S.

Metastasio, Pietro 1698-1782 .... **LC 115**
See also RGWL 2, 3

Metcalf, John 1938- .... **CLC 37; SSC 43**
See also CA 113; CN 4, 5, 6, 7; DLB 60; RGSF 2; TWA

Metcalf, Suzanne
See Baum, L. Frank

Mew, Charlotte (Mary) 1870-1928 . **PC 107; TCLC 8**
See also CA 105; 189; DLB 19, 135; RGEL 2

Mewshaw, Michael 1943- .... **CLC 9**
See also CA 53-56; CANR 7, 47, 147, 213; DLBY 1980

Meyer, Conrad Ferdinand 1825-1898 .... **NCLC 81, 249; SSC 30**
See also DLB 129; EW; RGWL 2, 3

Meyer, Gustav 1868-1932 .... **TCLC 21**
See also CA 117; 190; DLB 81; EWL 3

Meyer, June
See Jordan, June

Meyer, Lynn
See Slavitt, David R.

Meyer, Stephenie 1973- .... **CLC 280**
See also AAYA 77; CA 253; CANR 192; CLR 142; SATA 193

Meyer-Meyrink, Gustav
See Meyer, Gustav

Meyers, Jeffrey 1939- .... **CLC 39**
See also CA 73-76, 186; CAAE 186; CANR 54, 102, 159; DLB 111

Meynell, Alice (Christina Gertrude Thompson) 1847-1922 . **PC 112; TCLC 6**
See also CA 104; 177; DLB 19, 98; RGEL 2

Meyrink, Gustav
See Meyer, Gustav

Mhlophe, Gcina 1960- .... **BLC 2:3**

Michaels, Leonard 1933-2003 .... **CLC 6, 25; SSC 16**
See also AMWS 16; CA 61-64; 216; CANR 21, 62, 119, 179; CN 3, 45, 6, 7; DLB 130; MTCW 1; TCLE 1:2

Michaux, Henri 1899-1984 .... **CLC 8, 19**
See also CA 85-88; 114; DLB 258; EWL 3; GFL 1789 to the Present; RGWL 2, 3

Micheaux, Oscar (Devereaux) 1884-1951 .... **TCLC 76**
See also BW 3; CA 174; DLB 50; TCWW 2

Michelangelo 1475-1564 .... **LC 12**
See also AAYA 43

Michelet, Jules 1798-1874 ..... **NCLC 31, 218**
See also EW 5; GFL 1789 to the Present

Michels, Robert 1876-1936 .... **TCLC 88**
See also CA 212

Michener, James A. 1907(?)-1997 . **CLC 1, 5, 11, 29, 60, 109**
See also AAYA 27; AITN 1; BEST 90:1; BPFB 2; CA 5-8R; 161; CANR 21, 45, 68; CN 1, 2, 3, 4, 5, 6; CPW; DA3; DAM NOV, POP; DLB 6; MAL 5; MTCW 1, 2; MTFW 2005; RHW; TCWW 1, 2

Michener, James Albert
See Michener, James A.

Mickiewicz, Adam 1798-1855 . **NCLC 3, 101; PC 38**
See also EW 5; RGWL 2, 3

Middleton, (John) Christopher 1926- .. **CLC 13**
See also CA 13-16R; CANR 29, 54, 117; CP 1, 2, 3, 4, 5, 6, 7; DLB 40

Middleton, Richard (Barham) 1882-1911 .... **TCLC 56**
See also CA 187; DLB 156; HGG

Middleton, Stanley 1919-2009 ..... **CLC 7, 38**
See also CA 25-28R; 288; CAAS 23; CANR 21, 46, 81, 157; CN 1, 2, 3, 4, 5, 6, 7; DLB 14, 326

Middleton, Thomas 1580-1627 ..... **DC 5, 40; LC 33, 123**
See also BRW 2; DAM DRAM, MST; DFS 18, 22; DLB 58; RGEL 2

Mieville, China 1972(?)- .... **CLC 235**
See also AAYA 52; CA 196; CANR 138, 214; MTFW 2005

Migueis, Jose Rodrigues 1901-1980 ..... **CLC 10**
See also DLB 287

Mihura, Miguel 1905-1977 .... **DC 34**
See also CA 214

Mikszath, Kalman 1847-1910 .... **TCLC 31**
See also CA 170

Miles, Jack **CLC 100**
See also CA 200

Miles, John Russiano
See Miles, Jack

Miles, Josephine (Louise) 1911-1985 ... **CLC 1, 2, 14, 34, 39**
See also CA 1-4R; 116; CANR 2, 55; CP 1, 2, 3, 4; DAM POET; DLB 48; MAL 5; TCLE 1:2

Militant
See Sandburg, Carl

Mill, Harriet (Hardy) Taylor 1807-1858 ...... **NCLC 102**
See also FW

Mill, John Stuart 1806-1873 .. **NCLC 11, 58, 179, 223**
See also CDBLB 1832-1890; DLB 55, 190, 262; FW 1; RGEL 2; TEA

Millar, Kenneth 1915-1983 . **CLC 1, 2, 3, 14, 34, 41**
See also AAYA 81; AMWS 4; BPFB 2; CA 9-12R; 110; CANR 16, 63, 107; CMW 4; CN 1, 2, 3; CPW; DA3; DAM POP; DLB

2, 226; DLBD 6; DLBY 1983; MAL 5; MSW; MTCW 1, 2; MTFW 2005; RGAL 4

Millay, E. Vincent
See Millay, Edna St. Vincent

Millay, Edna St. Vincent 1892-1950 ... **PC 6, 61; TCLC 4, 49, 169; WLCS**
See also AMW; CA 104; 130; CDALB 1917-1929; DA; DA3; DAB; DAC; DAM MST, POET; DFS 27; DLB 45, 249; EWL 3; EXPP; FL 1:6; GLL 1; MAL 5; MBL; MTCW 1, 2; MTFW 2005; PAB; PFS 3, 17, 31, 34, 41; RGAL 4; TUS; WP

Miller, Arthur 1915-2005 ... **CLC 1, 2, 6, 10, 15, 26, 47, 78, 179; DC 1, 31; WLC 4**
See also AAYA 15; AITN 1; AMW; AMWC 1; CA 1-4R; 236; CABS 3; CAD; CANR 2, 30, 54, 76, 132; CD 5, 6; CDALB 1941-1968; DA; DA3; DAB; DAC; DAM DRAM, MST; DFS 1, 3, 8, 27; DLB 7, 266; EWL 3; LAIT 1, 4; LATS 1:2; MAL 5; MTCW 1, 2; MTFW 2005; RGAL 4; RGHL; TUS; WYAS 1

Miller, Frank 1957- .... **CLC 278**
See also AAYA 45; CA 224

Miller, Henry (Valentine) 1891-1980 ... **CLC 1, 2, 4, 9, 14, 43, 84; TCLC 213; WLC 4**
See also AMW; BPFB 2; CA 9-12R; 97-100; CANR 33, 64; CDALB 1929-1941; CN 1, 2; DA; DA3; DAB; DAC; DAM MST, NOV; DLB 4, 9; DLBY 1980; EWL 3; MAL 5; MTCW 1, 2; MTFW 2005; RGAL 4; TUS

Miller, Hugh 1802-1856 .... **NCLC 143**
See also DLB 190

Miller, Jason 1939(?)-2001 .... **CLC 2**
See also AITN 1; CA 73-76; 197; CAD; CANR 130; DFS 12; DLB 7

Miller, Sue 1943- .... **CLC 44**
See also AMWS 12; BEST 90:3; CA 139; CANR 59, 91, 128, 194, 231; DA3; DAM POP; DLB 143

Miller, Walter M(ichael, Jr.) 1923-1996 .... **CLC 4, 30**
See also BPFB 2; CA 85-88; CANR 108; DLB 8; SCFW 1, 2; SFW 4

Millett, Kate 1934- .... **CLC 67**
See also AITN 1; CA 73-76; CANR 32, 53, 76, 110; DA3; DLB 246; FW; GLL 1; MTCW 1, 2; MTFW 2005

Millhauser, Steven 1943- .. **CLC 21, 54, 109, 300; SSC 57**
See also AAYA 76; CA 110; 111; CANR 63, 114, 133, 189; CN 6, 7; DA3; DLB 2, 350; FANT; INT CA-111; MAL 5; MTCW 2; MTFW 2005

Millhauser, Steven Lewis
See Millhauser, Steven

Millin, Sarah Gertrude 1889-1968 . **CLC 49**
See also CA 102; 93-96; DLB 225; EWL 3

Milne, A. A. 1882-1956 .... **TCLC 6, 88**
See also BRWS 5; CA 104; 133; CLR 1, 26, 108; CMW 4; CWRI 5; DA3; DAB; DAC; DAM MST; DLB 10, 77, 100, 160, 352; FANT; MAICYA 1, 2; MTCW 1, 2; MTFW 2005; RGEL 2; SATA 100; WCH; YABC 1

Milne, Alan Alexander
See Milne, A. A.

Milner, Ron(ald) 1938-2004 . **BLC 1:3; CLC 56**
See also AITN 1; BW 1; CA 73-76; 230; CAD; CANR 24, 81; CD 5, 6; DAM MULT; DLB 38; MAL 5; MTCW 1

Milnes, Richard Monckton 1809-1885 .... **NCLC 61**
See also DLB 32, 184

Milosz, Czeslaw 1911-2004 ... **CLC 5, 11, 22, 31, 56, 82, 253; PC 8; WLCS**
See also AAYA 62; CA 81-84; 230; CANR 23, 51, 91, 126; CDWLB 4; CWW 2; DA3; DAM MST, POET; DLB 215, 331; EW 13; EWL 3; MTCW 1, 2; MTFW 2005; PFS 16, 29, 35; RGHL; RGWL 2, 3

Milton, John 1608-1674 .... **LC 9, 43, 92; PC 19, 29; WLC 4**
See also AAYA 65; BRW 2; BRWR 2; CDBLB 1660-1789; DA; DA3; DAB; DAC; DAM MST, POET; DLB 131, 151, 281; EFS 1:1, 2:2; EXPP; LAIT 1; PAB; PFS 3, 17, 37; RGEL 2; TEA; WLIT 3; WP

Min, Anchee 1957- .... **CLC 86, 291**
See also CA 146; CANR 94, 137, 222; MTFW 2005

Minehaha, Cornelius
See Wedekind, Frank

Miner, Valerie 1947- .... **CLC 40**
See also CA 97-100; CANR 59, 177; FW; GLL 2

Minimo, Duca
See D'Annunzio, Gabriele

Minot, Susan (Anderson) 1956- ..... **CLC 44, 159**
See also AMWS 6; CA 134; CANR 118; CN 6, 7

Minus, Ed 1938- .... **CLC 39**
See also CA 185

Mirabai 1498(?)-1550(?) ...... **LC 143; PC 48**
See also PFS 24

Miranda, Javier
See Bioy Casares, Adolfo

Mirbeau, Octave 1848-1917 .... **TCLC 55**
See also CA 216; DLB 123, 192; GFL 1789 to the Present

Mirikitani, Janice 1942- .... **AAL**
See also CA 211; DLB 312; RGAL 4

Mirk, John (?)-c. 1414 .... **LC 105**
See also DLB 146

Miro (Ferrer), Gabriel (Francisco Victor) 1879-1930 .... **TCLC 5**
See also CA 104; 185; DLB 322; EWL 3

Misharin, Alexandr CLC 59

Mishima, Yukio
See Hiraoka, Kimitake

Mishima Yukio
See Hiraoka, Kimitake

Miss C. L. F.
See Grimke, Charlotte L. Forten

Mister X
See Hoch, Edward D.

Mistral, Frederic 1830-1914 .... **TCLC 51**
See also CA 122; 213; DLB 331; GFL 1789 to the Present

Mistral, Gabriela 1899-1957 ..... **HLC 2; PC 32; TCLC 2**
See also BW 2; CA 104; 131; CANR 81; DAM MULT; DLB 283, 331; DNFS; EWL 3; HW 1, 2; LAW; MTCW 1, 2; MTFW 2005; PFS 37; RGWL 2, 3; WP

Mistry, Rohinton 1952- .. **CLC 71, 196, 281; SSC 73**
See also BRWS 10; CA 141; CANR 86, 114; CCA 1; CN 6, 7; DAC; DLB 334; SSFS 6

Mitchell, Clyde
See Ellison, Harlan; Silverberg, Robert

Mitchell, David 1969- .... **CLC 311**
See also BRWS 14; CA 210; CANR 159, 224

Mitchell, Emerson Blackhorse Barney 1945- .... **NNAL**
See also CA 45-48

Mitchell, James Leslie 1901-1935 ... **TCLC 4**
See also BRWS 14; CA 104; 188; DLB 15; RGEL 2

Mitchell, Joni 1943- .... **CLC 12**
See also CA 112; CCA 1

Mitchell, Joseph (Quincy) 1908-1996 .. **CLC 98**
See also CA 77-80; 152; CANR 69; CN 1, 2, 3, 4, 5, 6; CSW; DLB 185; DLBY 1996

Mitchell, Margaret 1900-1949 ..... **TCLC 11, 170**
See also AAYA 23; BPFB 2; BYA 1; CA 109; 125; CANR 55, 94; CDALBS; DA3; DAM NOV, POP; DLB 9; LAIT 2; MAL 5; MTCW 1, 2; MTFW 2005; NFS 9, 38; RGAL 4; RHW; TUS; WYAS 1; YAW

Mitchell, Margaret Munnerlyn
See Mitchell, Margaret

Mitchell, Peggy
See Mitchell, Margaret

Mitchell, S(ilas) Weir 1829-1914 .. **TCLC 36**
See also CA 165; DLB 202; RGAL 4

Mitchell, W(illiam) O(rmond) 1914-1998 .... **CLC 25**
See also CA 77-80; 165; CANR 15, 43; CN 1, 2, 3, 4, 5, 6; DAC; DAM MST; DLB 88; TCLE 1:2

Mitchell, William (Lendrum) 1879-1936 ..... **TCLC 81**
See also CA 213

Mitford, Mary Russell 1787-1855 .. **NCLC 4**
See also DLB 110, 116; RGEL 2

Mitford, Nancy 1904-1973 .... **CLC 44**
See also BRWS 10; CA 9-12R; CN 1; DLB 191; RGEL 2

Miyamoto, (Chujo) Yuriko 1899-1951 .... **TCLC 37**
See also CA 170, 174; DLB 180

Miyamoto Yuriko
See Miyamoto, (Chujo) Yuriko

Miyazawa, Kenji 1896-1933 .... **TCLC 76**
See also CA 157; EWL 3; RGWL 3

Miyazawa Kenji
See Miyazawa, Kenji

Mizoguchi, Kenji 1898-1956 .... **TCLC 72**
See also CA 167

Mo, Timothy (Peter) 1950- ...... **CLC 46, 134**
See also CA 117; CANR 128; CN 5, 6, 7; DLB 194; MTCW 1; WLIT 4; WWE 1

Mo, Yan
See Yan, Mo

Moberg, Carl Arthur
See Moberg, Vilhelm

Moberg, Vilhelm 1898-1973 .... **TCLC 224**
See also CA 97-100; 45-48; CANR 135; DLB 259; EW 11; EWL 3

Modarressi, Taghi (M.) 1931-1997 .. **CLC 44**
See also CA 121; 134; INT CA-134

Modiano, Patrick (Jean) 1945- ...... **CLC 18, 218**
See also CA 85-88; CANR 17, 40, 115; CWW 2; DLB 83, 299; EWL 3; RGHL

Mofolo, Thomas 1875(?)-1948 .... **BLC 1:3; TCLC 22**
See also AFW; CA 121; 153; CANR 83; DAM MULT; DLB 225; EWL 3; MTCW 2; MTFW 2005; WLIT 2

Mofolo, Thomas Mokopu
See Mofolo, Thomas

Mohr, Nicholasa 1938- .... **CLC 12; HLC 2**
See also AAYA 8, 46; CA 49-52; CANR 1, 32, 64; CLR 22; DAM MULT; DLB 145; HW 1, 2; JRDA; LAIT 5; LLW; MAICYA 2; MAICYAS 1; RGAL 4; SAAS 8; SATA 8, 97; SATA-Essay 113; WYA; YAW

Moi, Toril 1953- .... **CLC 172**
See also CA 154; CANR 102; FW

Mojtabai, A(nn) G(race) 1938- .... **CLC 5, 9, 15, 29**
See also CA 85-88; CANR 88

Moliere 1622-1673 .... **DC 13; LC 10, 28, 64, 125, 127, 200; WLC 4**
See also DA; DA3; DAB; DAC; DAM DRAM, MST; DFS 13, 18, 20; DLB 268; EW 3; GFL Beginnings to 1789; LATS 1:1; RGWL 2, 3; TWA

Molin, Charles
See Mayne, William

Molina, Antonio Munoz 1956- ...... **CLC 289**
See also DLB 322

Molnar, Ferenc 1878-1952 .... **TCLC 20**
See also CA 109; 153; CANR 83; CDWLB 4; DAM DRAM; DLB 215; EWL 3; RGWL 2, 3

Momaday, N. Scott 1934- ..... **CLC 2, 19, 85, 95, 160; NNAL; PC 25; WLCS**
See also AAYA 11, 64; AMWS 4; ANW; BPFB 2; BYA 12; CA 25-28R; CANR 14, 34, 68, 134; CDALBS; CN 2, 3, 4, 5, 6, 7; CPW; DA; DA3; DAB; DAC; DAM MST, MULT, NOV, POP; DLB 143, 175, 256; EWL 3; EXPP; INT CANR-14; LAIT 4; LATS 1:2; MAL 5; MTCW 1, 2; MTFW 2005; NFS 10; PFS 2, 11, 37, 41; RGAL 4; SATA 48; SATA-Brief 30; TCWW 1, 2; WP; YAW

Momaday, Navarre Scott
See Momaday, N. Scott

Momala, Ville i
See Moberg, Vilhelm

Monette, Paul 1945-1995 .... **CLC 82**
See also AMWS 10; CA 139; 147; CN 6; DLB 350; GLL 1

Monroe, Harriet 1860-1936 .... **TCLC 12**
See also CA 109; 204; DLB 54, 91

Monroe, Lyle
See Heinlein, Robert A.

Montagu, Elizabeth 1720-1800 ...... **NCLC 7, 117**
See also DLB 356; FW

Montagu, Mary (Pierrepont) Wortley 1689-1762 .... **LC 9, 57, 204; PC 16**
See also DLB 95, 101; FL 1:1; RGEL 2

Montagu, W. H.
See Coleridge, Samuel Taylor

Montague, John (Patrick) 1929- .... **CLC 13, 46; PC 106**
See also BRWS 15; CA 9-12R; CANR 9, 69, 121; CP 1, 2, 3, 4, 5, 6, 7; DLB 40; EWL 3; MTCW 1; PFS 12; RGEL 2; TCLE 1:2

Montaigne, Michel de 1533-1592 . **LC 8, 105, 194; WLC 4**
See also DA; DAB; DAC; DAM MST; DLB 327; EW 2; GFL Beginnings to 1789; LMFS 1; RGWL 2, 3; TWA

Montaigne, Michel Eyquem de
See Montaigne, Michel de

Montale, Eugenio 1896-1981 . **CLC 7, 9, 18; PC 13**
See also CA 17-20R; 104; CANR 30; DLB 114, 331; EW 11; EWL 3; MTCW 1; PFS 22; RGWL 2, 3; TWA; WLIT 7

Montemayor, Jorge de 1521(?)-1561(?) .. **LC 185**
See also DLB 318

Montesquieu, Charles-Louis de Secondat 1689-1755 .... **LC 7, 69, 189**
See also DLB 314; EW 3; GFL Beginnings to 1789; TWA

Montessori, Maria 1870-1952 ..... **TCLC 103**
See also CA 115; 147

Montgomery, Bruce 1921(?)-1978 ... **CLC 22**
See also CA 179; 104; CMW 4; DLB 87; MSW

Montgomery, L. M. 1874-1942 .... **TCLC 51, 140**
See also AAYA 12; BYA 1; CA 108; 137; CLR 8, 91, 145; DA3; DAC; DAM MST;

DLB 92, 362; DLBD 14; JRDA; MAI-CYA 1, 2; MTCW 2; MTFW 2005; RGEL 2; SATA 100; TWA; WCH; WYA; YABC 1

Montgomery, Lucy Maud
See Montgomery, L. M.

Montgomery, Marion, Jr. 1925- .... **CLC 7**
See also AITN 1; CA 1-4R; CANR 3, 48, 162; CSW; DLB 6

Montgomery, Marion H. 1925- ....
See Montgomery, Marion, Jr.

Montgomery, Max
See Davenport, Guy (Mattison, Jr.)

Montgomery, Robert Bruce
See Montgomery, Bruce

Montherlant, Henry de 1896-1972 .. **CLC 8, 19**
See also CA 85-88; 37-40R; DAM DRAM; DLB 72, 321; EW 11; EWL 3; GFL 1789 to the Present; MTCW 1

Montherlant, Henry Milon de
See Montherlant, Henry de

Monty Python
See Chapman, Graham; Cleese, John (Marwood); Gilliam, Terry; Idle, Eric; Jones, Terence Graham Parry; Palin, Michael

Moodie, Susanna (Strickland) 1803-1885 .... **NCLC 14, 113**
See also DLB 99

Moody, Hiram
See Moody, Rick

Moody, Hiram F. III
See Moody, Rick

Moody, Minerva
See Alcott, Louisa May

Moody, Rick 1961- .... **CLC 147**
See also CA 138; CANR 64, 112, 179; MTFW 2005

Moody, William Vaughan 1869-1910 . **TCLC 105**
See also CA 110; 178; DLB 7, 54; MAL 5; RGAL 4

Mooney, Ted 1951- .... **CLC 25**
See also CA 130; CANR 229

Moorcock, Michael 1939- ..... **CLC 5, 27, 58, 236**
See also AAYA 26; CA 45-48; CAAS 5; CANR 2, 17, 38, 64, 122, 203; CN 5, 6, 7; DLB 14, 231, 261, 319; FANT; MTCW 1, 2; MTFW 2005; SATA 93, 166; SCFW 1, 2; SFW 4; SUFW 1, 2

Moorcock, Michael John
See Moorcock, Michael

Moorcock, Michael John
See Moorcock, Michael

Moore, Al
See Moore, Alan

Moore, Alan 1953- .... **CLC 230**
See also AAYA 51; CA 204; CANR 138, 184; DLB 261; MTFW 2005; SFW 4

Moore, Alice Ruth
See Nelson, Alice Ruth Moore Dunbar

Moore, Brian 1921-1999 .. **CLC 1, 3, 5, 7, 8, 19, 32, 90**
See also BRWS 9; CA 1-4R; 174; CANR 1, 25, 42, 63; CCA 1; CN 1, 2, 3, 4, 5, 6; DAB; DAC; DAM MST; DLB 251; EWL 3; FANT; MTCW 1, 2; MTFW 2005; RGEL 2

Moore, Edward
See Muir, Edwin

Moore, G. E. 1873-1958 .... **TCLC 89**
See also DLB 262

Moore, George Augustus 1852-1933 ..... **SSC 19, 134; TCLC 7, 265**
See also BRW 6; CA 104; 177; DLB 10, 18, 57, 135; EWL 3; RGEL 2; RGSF 2

Moore, Lorrie 1957- ... **CLC 39, 45, 68, 165, 315; SSC 147**
See also AMWS 10; CA 116; CANR 39, 83, 139, 221; CN 5, 6, 7; DLB 234; MTFW 2005; SSFS 19

Moore, Marianne 1887-1972 .... **CLC 1, 2, 4, 8, 10, 13, 19, 47; PC 4, 49; WLCS**
See also AMW; CA 1-4R; 33-36R; CANR 3, 61; CDALB 1929-1941; CP 1; DA; DA3; DAB; DAC; DAM MST, POET; DLB 45; DLBD 7; EWL 3; EXPP; FL 1:6; MAL 5; MBL; MTCW 1, 2; MTFW 2005; PAB; PFS 14, 17, 38; RGAL 4; SATA 20; TUS; WP

Moore, Marianne Craig
See Moore, Marianne

Moore, Marie Lorena
See Moore, Lorrie

Moore, Michael 1954- .... **CLC 218**
See also AAYA 53; CA 166; CANR 150

Moore, Thomas 1779-1852 ..... **NCLC 6, 110**
See also BRWS 17; DLB 96, 144; RGEL 2

Moorhouse, Frank 1938- .... **SSC 40**
See also CA 118; CANR 92; CN 3, 4, 5, 6, 7; DLB 289; RGSF 2

Mootoo, Shani 1958(?)- .... **CLC 294**
See also CA 174; CANR 156

Mora, Pat 1942- .... **HLC 2**
See also AMWS 13; CA 129; CANR 57, 81, 112, 171; CLR 58; DAM MULT; DLB 209; HW 1, 2; LLW; MAICYA 2; MTFW 2005; PFS 33, 35, 40; SATA 92, 134, 186, 232

Moraga, Cherrie 1952- .. **CLC 126, 250; DC 22**
See also CA 131; CANR 66, 154; DAM MULT; DLB 82, 249; FW; GLL 1; HW 1, 2; LLW

Moran, J.L.
See Whitaker, Rod

Morand, Paul 1888-1976 .. **CLC 41; SSC 22**
See also CA 184; 69-72; DLB 65; EWL 3

Morante, Elsa 1918-1985 .... **CLC 8, 47**
See also CA 85-88; 117; CANR 35; DLB 177; EWL 3; MTCW 1, 2; MTFW 2005; RGHL; RGWL 2, 3; WLIT 7

Moravia, Alberto
See Pincherle, Alberto

Morck, Paul
See Rolvaag, O.E.

More, Hannah 1745-1833 ..... **NCLC 27, 141**
See also DLB 107, 109, 116, 158; RGEL 2

More, Henry 1614-1687 .... **LC 9**
See also DLB 126, 252

More, Sir Thomas 1478(?)-1535 . **LC 10, 32, 140**
See also BRWC 1; BRWS 7; DLB 136, 281; LMFS 1; NFS 29; RGEL 2; TEA

Moreas, Jean
See Papadiamantopoulos, Johannes

Moreton, Andrew Esq.
See Defoe, Daniel

Moreton, Lee
See Boucicault, Dion

Morgan, Berry 1919-2002 .... **CLC 6**
See also CA 49-52; 208; DLB 6

Morgan, Claire
See Highsmith, Patricia

Morgan, Edwin 1920-2010 .... **CLC 31**
See also BRWS 9; CA 5-8R; CANR 3, 43, 90; CP 1, 2, 3, 4, 5, 6, 7; DLB 27

Morgan, Edwin George
See Morgan, Edwin

Morgan, (George) Frederick 1922-2004 ...... **CLC 23**
See also CA 17-20R; 224; CANR 21, 144; CP 2, 3, 4, 5, 6, 7

Morgan, Harriet
See Mencken, H. L.

Morgan, Jane
See Cooper, James Fenimore

Morgan, Janet 1945- .... **CLC 39**
See also CA 65-68

Morgan, Lady 1776(?)-1859 .... **NCLC 29**
See also DLB 116, 158; RGEL 2

Morgan, Robin (Evonne) 1941- .... **CLC 2**
See also CA 69-72; CANR 29, 68; FW; GLL 2; MTCW 1; SATA 80

Morgan, Scott
See Kuttner, Henry

Morgan, Seth 1949(?)-1990 .... **CLC 65**
See also CA 185; 132

Morgenstern, Christian (Otto Josef Wolfgang) 1871-1914 .... **TCLC 8**
See also CA 105; 191; EWL 3

Morgenstern, S.
See Goldman, William

Mori, Rintaro
See Mori Ogai

Mori, Toshio 1910-1980 . **AAL; SSC 83, 123**
See also CA 116; 244; DLB 312; RGSF 2

Moricz, Zsigmond 1879-1942 .... **TCLC 33**
See also CA 165; DLB 215; EWL 3

Morike, Eduard (Friedrich) 1804-1875 .... **NCLC 10, 201**
See also DLB 133; RGWL 2, 3

Morin, Jean-Paul
See Whitaker, Rod

Mori Ogai 1862-1922 .... **TCLC 14**
See also CA 110; 164; DLB 180; EWL 3; MJW; RGWL 3; TWA

Moritz, Karl Philipp 1756-1793 .. **LC 2, 162**
See also DLB 94

Morland, Peter Henry
See Faust, Frederick

Morley, Christopher (Darlington) 1890-1957 .... **TCLC 87**
See also CA 112; 213; DLB 9; MAL 5; RGAL 4

Morren, Theophil
See Hofmannsthal, Hugo von

Morris, Bill 1952- .... **CLC 76**
See also CA 225

Morris, Julian
See West, Morris L(anglo)

Morris, Steveland Judkins (?)- ....
See Wonder, Stevie

Morris, William 1834-1896 ... **NCLC 4, 233; PC 55**
See also BRW 5; CDBLB 1832-1890; DLB 18, 35, 57, 156, 178, 184; FANT; RGEL 2; SFW 4; SUFW

Morris, Wright (Marion) 1910-1998 .... **CLC 1, 3, 7, 18, 37; TCLC 107**
See also AMW; CA 9-12R; 167; CANR 21, 81; CN 1, 2, 3, 4, 5, 6; DLB 2, 206, 218; DLBY 1981; EWL 3; MAL 5; MTCW 1, 2; MTFW 2005; RGAL 4; TCWW 1, 2

Morrison, Arthur 1863-1945 .... **SSC 40; TCLC 72**
See also CA 120; 157; CMW 4; DLB 70, 135, 197; RGEL 2

Morrison, Chloe Anthony Wofford
See Morrison, Toni

Morrison, James Douglas 1943-1971 ... **CLC 17**
See also CA 73-76; CANR 40

Morrison, Jim
See Morrison, James Douglas

Morrison, John Gordon 1904-1998 . **SSC 93**
See also CA 103; CANR 92; DLB 260

Morrison, Toni 1931- .... **BLC 1:3, 2:3; CLC 4, 10, 22, 55, 81, 87, 173, 194; SSC 126; WLC 4**
See also AAYA 1, 22, 61; AFAW 1, 2; AMWC 1; AMWS 3; BPFB 2; BW 2, 3; CA 29-32R; CANR 27, 42, 67, 113, 124, 204; CDALB 1968-1988; CLR 99; CN 3,

4, 5, 6, 7; CPW; DA; DA3; DAB; DAC; DAM MST, MULT, NOV, POP; DLB 6, 33, 143, 331; DLBY 1981; EWL 3; EXPN; FL 1:6; FW; GL 3; LAIT 2, 4; LATS 1:2; LMFS 2; MAL 5; MBL; MTCW 1, 2; MTFW 2005; NFS 1, 6, 8, 14, 37, 40; RGAL 4; RHW; SATA 57, 144, 235; SSFS 5; TCLE 1:2; TUS; YAW

Morrison, Van 1945- .... **CLC 21**
See also CA 116; 168

Morrissy, Mary 1957- .... **CLC 99**
See also CA 205; DLB 267

Mortimer, John 1923-2009 .... **CLC 28, 43**
See Morton, Kate
See also CA 13-16R; 282; CANR 21, 69, 109, 172; CBD; CD 5, 6; CDBLB 1960 to Present; CMW 4; CN 5, 6, 7; CPW; DA3; DAM DRAM, POP; DLB 13, 245, 271; INT CANR-21; MSW; MTCW 1, 2; MTFW 2005; RGEL 2

Mortimer, John C.
See Mortimer, John

Mortimer, John Clifford
See Mortimer, John

Mortimer, Penelope (Ruth) 1918-1999 . **CLC 5**
See also CA 57-60; 187; CANR 45, 88; CN 1, 2, 3, 4, 5, 6

Mortimer, Sir John
See Mortimer, John

Morton, Anthony
See Creasey, John

Morton, Thomas 1579(?)-1647(?) .... **LC 72**
See also DLB 24; RGEL 2

Mosca, Gaetano 1858-1941 .... **TCLC 75**

Moses, Daniel David 1952- .... **NNAL**
See also CA 186; CANR 160; DLB 334

Mosher, Howard Frank 1943- .... **CLC 62**
See also CA 139; CANR 65, 115, 181

Mosley, Nicholas 1923- .... **CLC 43, 70**
See also CA 69-72; CANR 41, 60, 108, 158; CN 1, 2, 3, 4, 5, 6, 7; DLB 14, 207

Mosley, Walter 1952- . **BLCS; CLC 97, 184, 278**
See also AAYA 57; AMWS 13; BPFB 2; BW 2; CA 142; CANR 57, 92, 136, 172, 201; CMW 4; CN 7; CPW; DA3; DAM MULT, POP; DLB 306; MSW; MTCW 2; MTFW 2005

Moss, Howard 1922-1987 ..... **CLC 7, 14, 45, 50**
See also CA 1-4R; 123; CANR 1, 44; CP 1, 2, 3, 4; DAM POET; DLB 5

Mossgiel, Rab
See Burns, Robert

Motion, Andrew 1952- .... **CLC 47**
See also BRWS 7; CA 146; CANR 90, 142; CP 4, 5, 6, 7; DLB 40; MTFW 2005

Motion, Andrew Peter
See Motion, Andrew

Motley, Willard (Francis) 1909-1965 ... **CLC 18**
See also AMWS 17; BW 1; CA 117; 106; CANR 88; DLB 76, 143

Motoori, Norinaga 1730-1801 .... **NCLC 45**

Mott, Michael (Charles Alston) 1930- . **CLC 15, 34**
See also CA 5-8R; CAAS 7; CANR 7, 29

Moulsworth, Martha 1577-1646 ...... **LC 168**

Mountain Wolf Woman 1884-1960 . **CLC 92; NNAL**
See also CA 144; CANR 90

Moure, Erin 1955- .... **CLC 88**
See also CA 113; CP 5, 6, 7; CWP; DLB 60

Mourning Dove 1885(?)-1936 .... **NNAL**
See also CA 144; CANR 90; DAM MULT; DLB 175, 221

Mowat, Farley 1921- .... **CLC 26**
See also AAYA 1, 50; BYA 2; CA 1-4R; CANR 4, 24, 42, 68, 108; CLR 20; CPW; DAC; DAM MST; DLB 68; INT CANR-24; JRDA; MAICYA 1, 2; MTCW 1, 2; MTFW 2005; SATA 3, 55; YAW

Mowat, Farley McGill
See Mowat, Farley

Mowatt, Anna Cora 1819-1870 .... **NCLC 74**
See also RGAL 4

Moye, Guan
See Yan, Mo

Mo Yen
See Yan, Mo

Moyers, Bill 1934- .... **CLC 74**
See also AITN 2; CA 61-64; CANR 31, 52, 148

Mphahlele, Es'kia 1919-2008 .... **BLC 1:3; CLC 25, 133, 280**
See also AFW; BW 2, 3; CA 81-84; 278; CANR 26, 76; CDWLB 3; CN 4, 5, 6; DA3; DAM MULT; DLB 125, 225; EWL 3; MTCW 2; MTFW 2005; RGSF 2; SATA 119; SATA-Obit 198; SSFS 11

Mphahlele, Ezekiel
See Mphahlele, Es'kia

Mphahlele, Zeke
See Mphahlele, Es'kia

Mqhayi, S(amuel) E(dward) K(rune Loliwe) 1875-1945 .... **BLC 1:3; TCLC 25**
See also CA 153; CANR 87; DAM MULT

Mrozek, Slawomir 1930- .... **CLC 3, 13**
See also CA 13-16R; CAAS 10; CANR 29; CDWLB 4; CWW 2; DLB 232; EWL 3; MTCW 1

Mrs. Belloc-Lowndes
See Lowndes, Marie Adelaide (Belloc)

Mrs. Fairstar
See Horne, Richard Henry Hengist

M'Taggart, John M'Taggart Ellis
See McTaggart, John McTaggart Ellis

Mtwa, Percy (?)- .... **CLC 47**
See also CD 6

Mueenuddin, Daniyal 1963- .... **CLC 299**
See also CA 292

Mueller, Lisel 1924- ...... **CLC 13, 51; PC 33**
See also CA 93-96; CP 6, 7; DLB 105; PFS 9, 13

Muggeridge, Malcolm (Thomas) 1903-1990 .... **TCLC 120**
See also AITN 1; CA 101; CANR 33, 63; MTCW 1, 2

Muhammad 570-632 .... **WLCS**
See also DA; DAB; DAC; DAM MST; DLB 311

Muir, Edwin 1887-1959 ..... **PC 49; TCLC 2, 87**
See also BRWS 6; CA 104; 193; DLB 20, 100, 191; EWL 3; RGEL 2

Muir, John 1838-1914 .... **TCLC 28**
See also AMWS 9; ANW; CA 165; DLB 186, 275

Mujica Lainez, Manuel 1910-1984 . **CLC 31**
See also CA 81-84; 112; CANR 32; EWL 3; HW 1

Mukherjee, Bharati 1940- ... **AAL; CLC 53, 115, 235; SSC 38**
See also AAYA 46; BEST 89:2; CA 107, 232; CAAE 232; CANR 45, 72, 128, 231; CN 5, 6, 7; DAM NOV; DLB 60, 218, 323; DNFS 1, 2; EWL 3; FW; MAL 5; MTCW 1, 2; MTFW 2005; NFS 37; RGAL 4; RGSF 2; SSFS 7, 24, 32; TUS; WWE 1

Muldoon, Paul 1951- .... **CLC 32, 72, 166**
See also BRWS 4; CA 113; 129; CANR 52, 91, 176; CP 2, 3, 4, 5, 6, 7; DAM POET; DLB 40; INT CA-129; PFS 7, 22; TCLE 1:2

Mulisch, Harry 1927-2010 .... **CLC 42, 270**
See also CA 9-12R; CANR 6, 26, 56, 110; CWW 2; DLB 299; EWL 3

Mulisch, Harry Kurt Victor
See Mulisch, Harry

Mull, Martin 1943- .... **CLC 17**
See also CA 105

Mullen, Harryette 1953- .... **CLC 321**
See also CA 218; CP 7

Mullen, Harryette Romell
See Mullen, Harryette

Muller, Herta 1953- .... **CLC 299**
See also CA 175; CANR 147, 210

Muller, Wilhelm NCLC 73

Mulock, Dinah Maria
See Craik, Dinah Maria (Mulock)

Multatuli 1820-1881 .... **NCLC 165**
See also RGWL 2, 3

Munday, Anthony 1560-1633 .... **LC 87**
See also DLB 62, 172; RGEL 2

Munford, Robert 1737(?)-1783 .... **LC 5**
See also DLB 31

Mungo, Raymond 1946- .... **CLC 72**
See also CA 49-52; CANR 2

Munnings, Clare
See Conway, Jill K.

Munro, Alice 1931- ... **CLC 6, 10, 19, 50, 95, 222; SSC 3, 95; WLCS**
See also AAYA 82; AITN 2; BPFB 2; CA 33-36R; CANR 33, 53, 75, 114, 177; CCA 1; CN 1, 2, 3, 4, 5, 6, 7; DA3; DAC; DAM MST, NOV; DLB 53; EWL 3; LNFS 3; MTCW 1, 2; MTFW 2005; NFS 27; RGEL 2; RGSF 2; SATA 29; SSFS 5, 13, 19, 28; TCLE 1:2; WWE 1

Munro, Alice Anne
See Munro, Alice

Munro, H. H.
See Saki

Munro, Hector H.
See Saki

Munro, Hector Hugh
See Saki

Murakami, Haruki 1949- ...... **CLC 150, 274**
See also CA 165; CANR 102, 146, 212; CWW 2; DLB 182; EWL 3; LNFS 2; MJW; RGWL 3; SFW 4; SSFS 23

Murakami Haruki
See Murakami, Haruki

Murasaki, Lady
See Murasaki Shikibu

Murasaki Shikibu 978(?)-1026(?) . **CMLC 1, 79**
See also EFS 1:2, 2:2; LATS 1:1; RGWL 2, 3

Murdoch, Iris 1919-1999 . **CLC 1, 2, 3, 4, 6, 8, 11, 15, 22, 31, 51; TCLC 171**
See also BRWS 1; CA 13-16R; 179; CANR 8, 43, 68, 103, 142; CBD; CDBLB 1960 to Present; CN 1, 2, 3, 4, 5, 6; CWD; DA3; DAB; DAC; DAM MST, NOV; DLB 14, 194, 233, 326; EWL 3; INT CANR-8; MTCW 1, 2; MTFW 2005; NFS 18; RGEL 2; TCLE 1:2; TEA; WLIT 4

Murdoch, Jean Iris
See Murdoch, Iris

Murfree, Mary Noailles 1850-1922 . **SSC 22; TCLC 135**
See also CA 122; 176; DLB 12, 74; RGAL 4

Murglie
See Murnau, F.W.

Murnau, Friedrich Wilhelm
See Murnau, F.W.

Murnau, F.W. 1888-1931 .... **TCLC 53**
See also CA 112

Murphy, Arthur 1727-1805 .... **NCLC 229**
See also DLB 89, 142; RGEL 2

North, Andrew
See Norton, Andre
North, Anthony
See Koontz, Dean
North, Captain George
See Stevenson, Robert Louis
North, Captain George
See Stevenson, Robert Louis
North, Milou
See Erdrich, Louise
Northrup, B. A.
See Hubbard, L. Ron
North Staffs
See Hulme, T(homas) E(rnest)
Northup, Solomon 1808-1863 ..... **NCLC 105**
Norton, Alice Mary
See Norton, Andre
Norton, Andre 1912-2005 .... **CLC 12**
See also AAYA 83; BPFB 2; BYA 4, 10, 12; CA 1-4R; 237; CANR 2, 31, 68, 108, 149; CLR 50; DLB 8, 52; JRDA; MAI-CYA 1, 2; MTCW 1; SATA 1, 43, 91; SUFW 1, 2; YAW
Norton, Caroline 1808-1877 . **NCLC 47, 205**
See also DLB 21, 159, 199
Norway, Nevil Shute
See Shute, Nevil
Norwid, Cyprian Kamil 1821-1883 ... **NCLC 17**
See also RGWL 3
Nosille, Nabrah
See Ellison, Harlan
Nossack, Hans Erich 1901-1977 .... **CLC 6**
See also CA 93-96; 85-88; CANR 156; DLB 69; EWL 3
Nostradamus 1503-1566 .... **LC 27**
Nosu, Chuji
See Ozu, Yasujiro
Notenburg, Eleanora (Genrikhovna) von
See Guro, Elena (Genrikhovna)
Nova, Craig 1945- .... **CLC 7, 31**
See also CA 45-48; CANR 2, 53, 127, 223
Novak, Joseph
See Kosinski, Jerzy
Novalis 1772-1801 ... **NCLC 13, 178; PC 120**
See also CDWLB 2; DLB 90; EW 5; RGWL 2, 3
Novick, Peter 1934- .... **CLC 164**
See also CA 188
Novis, Emile
See Weil, Simone
Nowlan, Alden (Albert) 1933-1983 . **CLC 15**
See also CA 9-12R; CANR 5; CP 1, 2, 3; DAC; DAM MST; DLB 53; PFS 12
Noyes, Alfred 1880-1958 .... **PC 27; TCLC 7**
See also CA 104; 188; DLB 20; EXPP; FANT; PFS 4; RGEL 2
Nugent, Richard Bruce 1906(?)-1987 ..... **HR 1:3**
See also BW 1; CA 125; CANR 198; DLB 51; GLL 2
Nunez, Elizabeth 1944- .... **BLC 2:3**
See also CA 223; CANR 220
Nunn, Kem CLC 34
See also CA 159; CANR 204
Nussbaum, Martha Craven 1947- . **CLC 203**
See also CA 134; CANR 102, 176, 213
Nwapa, Flora (Nwanzuruaha) 1931-1993 .... **BLCS; CLC 133**
See also BW 2; CA 143; CANR 83; CD-WLB 3; CLR 162; CWRI 5; DLB 125; EWL 3; WLIT 2
Nye, Robert 1939- .... **CLC 13, 42**
See also BRWS 10; CA 33-36R; CANR 29, 67, 107; CN 1, 2, 3, 4, 5, 6, 7; CP 1, 2, 3, 4, 5, 6, 7; CWRI 5; DAM NOV; DLB 14, 271; FANT; HGG; MTCW 1; RHW; SATA 6

Nyro, Laura 1947-1997 .... **CLC 17**
See also CA 194
O. Henry
See Henry, O.
Oates, Joyce Carol 1938- . **CLC 1, 2, 3, 6, 9, 11, 15, 19, 33, 52, 108, 134, 228; SSC 6, 70, 121; WLC 4**
See also AAYA 15, 52; AITN 1; AMWS 2; BEST 89:2; BPFB 2; BYA 11; CA 5-8R; CANR 25, 45, 74, 113, 129, 165; CDALB 1968-1988; CN 1, 2, 3, 4, 5, 6, 7; CP 5, 6, 7; CPW; CWP; DA; DA3; DAB; DAC; DAM MST, NOV, POP; DLB 2, 5, 130; DLBY 1981; EWL 3; EXPS; FL 1:6; FW; GL 3; HGG; INT CANR-25; LAIT 4; MAL 5; MBL; MTCW 1, 2; MTFW 2005; NFS 8, 24; RGAL 4; RGSF 2; SATA 159; SSFS 1, 8, 17, 32; SUFW 2; TUS
Obradovic, Dositej 1740(?)-1811 . **NCLC 254**
See also DLB 147
O'Brian, E.G.
See Clarke, Arthur C.
O'Brian, Patrick 1914-2000 .... **CLC 152**
See also AAYA 55; BRWS 12; CA 144; 187; CANR 74, 201; CPW; MTCW 2; MTFW 2005; RHW
O'Brien, Darcy 1939-1998 .... **CLC 11**
See also CA 21-24R; 167; CANR 8, 59
O'Brien, Edna 1932- .... **CLC 3, 5, 8, 13, 36, 65, 116, 237; SSC 10, 77**
See also BRWS 5; CA 1-4R; CANR 6, 41, 65, 102, 169, 213; CDBLB 1960 to Present; CN 1, 2, 3, 4, 5, 6, 7; DA3; DAM NOV; DLB 14, 231, 319; EWL 3; FW; MTCW 1, 2; MTFW 2005; RGSF 2; WLIT 4
O'Brien, E.G.
See Clarke, Arthur C.
O'Brien, Fitz-James 1828-1862 .... **NCLC 21**
See also DLB 74; RGAL 4; SUFW
O'Brien, Flann
See O Nuallain, Brian
O'Brien, Richard 1942- .... **CLC 17**
See also CA 124
O'Brien, Tim 1946- ...... **CLC 7, 19, 40, 103, 211, 305; SSC 74, 123**
See also AAYA 16; AMWS 5; CA 85-88; CANR 40, 58, 133; CDALBS; CN 5, 6, 7; CPW; DA3; DAM POP; DLB 152; DLBD 9; DLBY 1980; LATS 1:2; MAL 5; MTCW 2; MTFW 2005; NFS 37; RGAL 4; SSFS 5, 15, 29, 32; TCLE 1:2
O'Brien, William Timothy
See O'Brien, Tim
Obstfelder, Sigbjorn 1866-1900 .... **TCLC 23**
See also CA 123; DLB 354
O'Casey, Brenda
See Haycraft, Anna
O'Casey, Sean 1880-1964 ... **CLC 1, 5, 9, 11, 15, 88; DC 12; WLCS**
See also BRW 7; CA 89-92; CANR 62; CBD; CDBLB 1914-1945; DA3; DAB; DAC; DAM DRAM, MST; DFS 19; DLB 10; EWL 3; MTCW 1, 2; MTFW 2005; RGEL 2; TEA; WLIT 4
O'Cathasaigh, Sean
See O'Casey, Sean
Occom, Samson 1723-1792 ... **LC 60; NNAL**
See also DLB 175
Occomy, Marita (Odette) Bonner 1899(?)-1971 .... **HR 1:2; PC 72; TCLC 179**
See also BW 2; CA 142; DFS 13; DLB 51, 228
Ochs, Phil(ip David) 1940-1976 ...... **CLC 17**
See also CA 185; 65-68
O'Connor, Edwin (Greene) 1918-1968 . **CLC 14**
See also CA 93-96; 25-28R; MAL 5

O'Connor, Flannery 1925-1964 ... **CLC 1, 2, 3, 6, 10, 13, 15, 21, 66, 104; SSC 1, 23, 61, 82, 111; TCLC 132; WLC 4**
See also AAYA 7; AMW; AMWR 2; BPFB 3; BYA 16; CA 1-4R; CANR 3, 41; CDALB 1941-1968; DA; DA3; DAB; DAC; DAM MST, NOV; DLB 2, 152; DLBD 12; DLBY 1980; EWL 3; EXPS; LAIT 5; MAL 5; MBL; MTCW 1, 2; MTFW 2005; NFS 3, 21; RGAL 4; RGSF 2; SSFS 2, 7, 10, 19, 34; TUS
O'Connor, Frank 1903-1966 ....
See O'Donovan, Michael Francis
O'Connor, Mary Flannery
See O'Connor, Flannery
O'Dell, Scott 1898-1989 .... **CLC 30**
See also AAYA 3, 44; BPFB 3; BYA 1, 2, 3, 5; CA 61-64; 129; CANR 12, 30, 112; CLR 1, 16, 126; DLB 52; JRDA; MAI-CYA 1, 2; SATA 12, 60, 134; WYA; YAW
Odets, Clifford 1906-1963 .... **CLC 2, 28, 98; DC 6; TCLC 244**
See also AMWS 2; CA 85-88; CAD; CANR 62; DAM DRAM; DFS 3, 17, 20; DLB 7, 26, 341; EWL 3; MAL 5; MTCW 1, 2; MTFW 2005; RGAL 4; TUS
O'Doherty, Brian 1928- .... **CLC 76**
See also CA 105; CANR 108
O'Donnell, K. M.
See Malzberg, Barry N(athaniel)
O'Donnell, Lawrence
See Kuttner, Henry
O'Donovan, Michael Francis 1903-1966 ..... **CLC 14, 23; SSC 5, 109**
See also BRWS 14; CA 93-96; CANR 84; DLB 162; EWL 3; RGSF 2; SSFS 5, 34
Oe, Kenzaburo 1935- . **CLC 10, 36, 86, 187, 303; SSC 20**
See also CA 97-100; CANR 36, 50, 74, 126; CWW 2; DA3; DAM NOV; DLB 182, 331; DLBY 1994; EWL 3; LATS 1:2; MJW; MTCW 1, 2; MTFW 2005; RGSF 2; RGWL 2, 3
Oe Kenzaburo
See Oe, Kenzaburo
O'Faolain, Julia 1932- ... **CLC 6, 19, 47, 108**
See also CA 81-84; CAAS 2; CANR 12, 61; CN 2, 3, 4, 5, 6, 7; DLB 14, 231, 319; FW; MTCW 1; RHW
O'Faolain, Sean 1900-1991 .... **CLC 1, 7, 14, 32, 70; SSC 13; TCLC 143**
See also CA 61-64; 134; CANR 12, 66; CN 1, 2, 3, 4; DLB 15, 162; MTCW 1, 2; MTFW 2005; RGEL 2; RGSF 2
O'Flaherty, Liam 1896-1984 ...... **CLC 5, 34; SSC 6, 116**
See also CA 101; 113; CANR 35; CN 1, 2, 3; DLB 36, 162; DLBY 1984; MTCW 1, 2; MTFW 2005; RGEL 2; RGSF 2; SSFS 5, 20
Ogai
See Mori Ogai
Ogilvy, Gavin
See Barrie, J. M.
O'Grady, Standish (James) 1846-1928 .... **TCLC 5**
See also CA 104; 157
O'Grady, Timothy 1951- .... **CLC 59**
See also CA 138
O'Hara, Frank 1926-1966 ...... **CLC 2, 5, 13, 78; PC 45**
See also CA 9-12R; 25-28R; CANR 33; DA3; DAM POET; DLB 5, 16, 193; EWL 3; MAL 5; MTCW 1, 2; MTFW 2005; PFS 8, 12, 34, 38; RGAL 4; WP
O'Hara, John 1905-1970 . **CLC 1, 2, 3, 6, 11, 42; SSC 15**
See also AMW; BPFB 3; CA 5-8R; 25-28R; CANR 31, 60; CDALB 1929-1941; DAM NOV; DLB 9, 86, 324; DLBD 2; EWL 3;

Osofisan, Femi 1946- .... **CLC 307**
See also AFW; BW 2; CA 142; CANR 84;
CD 5, 6; CDWLB 3; DLB 125; EWL 3

Ossian c. 3rd cent. - ....
See Macpherson, James

Ossoli, Sarah Margaret
See Fuller, Margaret

Ossoli, Sarah Margaret Fuller
See Fuller, Margaret

Ostriker, Alicia 1937- .... **CLC 132**
See also CA 25-28R; CAAS 24; CANR 10,
30, 62, 99, 167; CWP; DLB 120; EXPP;
PFS 19, 26

Ostriker, Alicia Suskin
See Ostriker, Alicia

Ostrovsky, Aleksandr Nikolaevich
See Ostrovsky, Alexander

Ostrovsky, Alexander 1823-1886 . **NCLC 30,
57**
See also DLB 277

Osundare, Niyi 1947- .... **BLC 2:3**
See also AFW; BW 3; CA 176; CDWLB 3;
CP 7; DLB 157

Otero, Blas de 1916-1979 .... **CLC 11**
See also CA 89-92; DLB 134; EWL 3

O'Trigger, Sir Lucius
See Horne, Richard Henry Hengist

Otto, Rudolf 1869-1937 .... **TCLC 85**

Otto, Whitney 1955- .... **CLC 70**
See also CA 140; CANR 120

Otway, Thomas 1652-1685 . **DC 24; LC 106,
170**
See also DAM DRAM; DLB 80; RGEL 2

Ouida
See De La Ramee, Marie Louise

Ouologuem, Yambo 1940- ..... **CLC 146, 293**
See also CA 111; 176

Ousmane, Sembene 1923-2007 ...... **BLC 1:3,
2:3; CLC 66**
See also AFW; BW 1, 3; CA 117; 125; 261;
CANR 81; CWW 2; DLB 360; EWL 3;
MTCW 1; WLIT 2

Ovid 43B.C.-17 .... **CMLC 7, 108; PC 2**
See also AW 2; CDWLB 1; DA3; DAM
POET; DLB 211; PFS 22; RGWL 2, 3;
WLIT 8; WP

Owen, Hugh
See Faust, Frederick

Owen, Wilfred (Edward Salter) 1893-1918 .
PC 19, 102; TCLC 5, 27; WLC 4
See also BRW 6; CA 104; 141; CDBLB
1914-1945; DA; DAB; DAC; DAM MST;
POET; DLB 20; EWL 3; EXPP; MTCW
2; MTFW 2005; PFS 10, 37; RGEL 2;
WLIT 4

Owens, Louis (Dean) 1948-2002 .. **CLC 321;
NNAL**
See also CA 137, 179; 207; CAAE 179;
CAAS 24; CANR 71

Owens, Rochelle 1936- .... **CLC 8**
See also CA 17-20R; CAAS 2; CAD;
CANR 39; CD 5, 6; CP 1, 2, 3, 4, 5, 6, 7;
CWD; CWP

Oz, Amos 1939- .... **CLC 5, 8, 11, 27, 33, 54;
SSC 66**
See also AAYA 84; CA 53-56; CANR 27,
47, 65, 113, 138, 175, 219; CWW 2;
DAM NOV; EWL 3; MTCW 1, 2; MTFW
2005; RGHL; RGSF 2; RGWL 3; WLIT
6

Ozeki, Ruth L. 1956- .... **CLC 307**
See also CA 181

Ozick, Cynthia 1928- . **CLC 3, 7, 28, 62, 155,
262; SSC 15, 60, 123**
See also AMWS 5; BEST 90:1; CA 17-20R;
CANR 23, 58, 116, 160, 187; CN 3, 4, 5,
6, 7; CPW; DA3; DAM NOV, POP; DLB

28, 152, 299; DLBY 1982; EWL 3; EXPS;
INT CANR-23; MAL 5; MTCW 1, 2;
MTFW 2005; RGAL 4; RGHL; RGSF 2;
SSFS 3, 12, 22

Ozu, Yasujiro 1903-1963 .... **CLC 16**
See also CA 112

Pabst, G. W. 1885-1967 .... **TCLC 127**

Pacheco, C.
See Pessoa, Fernando

Pacheco, Jose Emilio 1939- .... **HLC 2**
See also CA 111; 131; CANR 65; CWW 2;
DAM MULT; DLB 290; EWL 3; HW 1,
2; RGSF 2

Pa Chin
See Jin, Ba

Pack, Robert 1929- .... **CLC 13**
See also CA 1-4R; CANR 3, 44, 82; CP 1,
2, 3, 4, 5, 6, 7; DLB 5; SATA 118

Packer, Vin
See Meaker, Marijane

Padgett, Lewis
See Kuttner, Henry

Padilla (Lorenzo), Heberto 1932-2000 . **CLC
38**
See also AITN 1; CA 123; 131; 189; CWW
2; EWL 3; HW 1

Paerdurabo, Frater
See Crowley, Edward Alexander

Page, James Patrick 1944- .... **CLC 12**
See also CA 204

Page, Jimmy 1944- ....
See Page, James Patrick

Page, Louise 1955- .... **CLC 40**
See also CA 140; CANR 76; CBD; CD 5,
6; CWD; DLB 233

Page, Patricia Kathleen
See Page, P.K.

Page, P.K. 1916-2010 ...... **CLC 7, 18; PC 12**
See also CA 53-56; CANR 4, 22, 65; CCA
1; CP 1, 2, 3, 4, 5, 6, 7; DAC; DAM MST;
DLB 68; MTCW 1; RGEL 2

Page, Stanton
See Fuller, Henry Blake

Page, Thomas Nelson 1853-1922 ...... **SSC 23**
See also CA 118; 177; DLB 12, 78; DLBD
13; RGAL 4

Pagels, Elaine
See Pagels, Elaine Hiesey

Pagels, Elaine Hiesey 1943- .... **CLC 104**
See also CA 45-48; CANR 2, 24, 51, 151;
FW; NCFS 4

Paget, Violet 1856-1935 . **SSC 33, 98; TCLC
5**
See also CA 104; 166; DLB 57, 153, 156,
174, 178; GLL 1; HGG; SUFW 1

Paget-Lowe, Henry
See Lovecraft, H. P.

Paglia, Camille 1947- .... **CLC 68**
See also CA 140; CANR 72, 139; CPW;
FW; GLL 1; MTCW 2; MTFW 2005

Pagnol, Marcel (Paul) 1895-1974 ...... **TCLC
208**
See also CA 128; 49-52; DLB 321; EWL 3;
GFL 1789 to the Present; MTCW 1;
RGWL 2, 3

Paige, Richard
See Koontz, Dean

Paine, Thomas 1737-1809 ..... **NCLC 62, 248**
See also AMWS 1; CDALB 1640-1865;
DLB 31, 43, 73, 158; LAIT 1; RGAL 4;
RGEL 2; TUS

Pakenham, Antonia
See Fraser, Antonia

Palamas, Costis
See Palamas, Kostes

Palamas, Kostes 1859-1943 .... **TCLC 5**
See also CA 105; 190; EWL 3; RGWL 2, 3

Palamas, Kostis
See Palamas, Kostes

Palazzeschi, Aldo 1885-1974 .... **CLC 11**
See also CA 89-92; 53-56; DLB 114, 264;
EWL 3

Pales Matos, Luis 1898-1959 .... **HLCS 2**
See Pales Matos, Luis
See also DLB 290; HW 1; LAW

Paley, Grace 1922-2007 .. **CLC 4, 6, 37, 140,
272; SSC 8, 165**
See also AMWS 6; CA 25-28R; 263; CANR
13, 46, 74, 118; CN 2, 3, 4, 5, 6, 7; CPW;
DA3; DAM POP; DLB 28, 218; EWL 3;
EXPS; FW; INT CANR-13; MAL 5;
MBL; MTCW 1, 2; MTFW 2005; RGAL
4; RGSF 2; SSFS 3, 20, 27

Paley, Grace Goodside
See Paley, Grace

Palin, Michael 1943- .... **CLC 21**
See also CA 107; CANR 35, 109, 179, 229;
DLB 352; SATA 67

Palin, Michael Edward
See Palin, Michael

Palliser, Charles 1947- .... **CLC 65**
See also CA 136; CANR 76; CN 5, 6, 7

Palma, Ricardo 1833-1919 .... **TCLC 29**
See also CA 168; LAW

Pamuk, Orhan 1952- .... **CLC 185, 288**
See also AAYA 82; CA 142; CANR 75, 127,
172, 208; CWW 2; NFS 27; WLIT 6

Pancake, Breece Dexter 1952-1979 ...... **CLC
29; SSC 61**
See also CA 123; 109; DLB 130

Pancake, Breece D'J
See Pancake, Breece Dexter

Panchenko, Nikolai CLC 59

Pankhurst, Emmeline (Goulden)
1858-1928 .... **TCLC 100**
See also CA 116; FW

Panko, Rudy
See Gogol, Nikolai

Papadiamantis, Alexandros 1851-1911 ....
TCLC 29
See also CA 168; EWL 3

Papadiamantopoulos, Johannes 1856-1910 .
TCLC 18
See also CA 117; 242; GFL 1789 to the
Present

Papadiamantopoulos, Yannis
See Papadiamantopoulos, Johannes

Papini, Giovanni 1881-1956 .... **TCLC 22**
See also CA 121; 180; DLB 264

Paracelsus 1493-1541 .... **LC 14**
See also DLB 179

Parasol, Peter
See Stevens, Wallace

Pardo Bazan, Emilia 1851-1921 ...... **SSC 30,
158; TCLC 189**
See also EWL 3; FW; RGSF 2; RGWL 2, 3

Paredes, Americo 1915-1999 .... **PC 83**
See also CA 37-40R; 179; DLB 209; EXPP;
HW 1

Pareto, Vilfredo 1848-1923 .... **TCLC 69**
See also CA 175

Paretsky, Sara 1947- .... **CLC 135**
See also AAYA 30; BEST 90:3; CA 125;
129; CANR 59, 95, 184, 218; CMW 4;
CPW; DA3; DAM POP; DLB 306; INT
CA-129; MSW; RGAL 4

Paretsky, Sara N.
See Paretsky, Sara

Parfenie, Maria
See Codrescu, Andrei

Parini, Jay 1948- .... **CLC 54, 133**
See also CA 97-100, 229; CAAE 229;
CAAS 16; CANR 32, 87, 198, 230

Parini, Jay Lee
See Parini, Jay

Plumpe, Friedrich Wilhelm
See Murnau, F.W.

Plutarch c. 46-c. 120 .... **CMLC 60**
See also AW 2; CDWLB 1; DLB 176; RGWL 2, 3; TWA; WLIT 8

Po Chu-i 772-846 .... **CMLC 24**

Podhoretz, Norman 1930- .... **CLC 189**
See also AMWS 8; CA 9-12R; CANR 7, 78, 135, 179

Poe, Edgar Allan 1809-1849 .... **NCLC 1, 16, 55, 78, 94, 97, 117, 211; PC 1, 54; SSC 1, 22, 34, 35, 54, 88, 111, 156; WLC 4**
See also AAYA 14; AMW; AMWC 1; AMWR 2; BPFB 3; BYA 5, 11; CDALB 1640-1865; CMW 4; DA; DA3; DAB; DAC; DAM MST, POET; DLB 3, 59, 73, 74, 248, 254; EXPP; EXPS; GL 3; HGG; LAIT 2; LATS 1:1; LMFS 1; MSW; PAB; PFS 1, 3, 9; RGAL 4; RGSF 2; SATA 23; SCFW 1, 2; SFW 4; SSFS 2, 4, 7, 8, 16, 26, 29, 34; SUFW; TUS; WP; WYA

Poet of Titchfield Street, The
See Pound, Ezra

Poggio Bracciolini, Gian Francesco 1380-1459 .... **LC 125**

Pohl, Frederik 1919- .... **CLC 18; SSC 25**
See also AAYA 24; CA 61-64, 188; CAAE 188; CAAS 1; CANR 11, 37, 81, 140; CN 1, 2, 3, 4, 5, 6; DLB 8; INT CANR-11; MTCW 1, 2; MTFW 2005; SATA 24; SCFW 1, 2; SFW 4

Poirier, Louis
See Gracq, Julien

Poitier, Sidney 1927- .... **CLC 26**
See also AAYA 60; BW 1; CA 117; CANR 94

Pokagon, Simon 1830-1899 .... **NNAL**
See also DAM MULT

Polanski, Roman 1933- .... **CLC 16, 178**
See also CA 77-80

Poliakoff, Stephen 1952- .... **CLC 38**
See also CA 106; CANR 116; CBD; CD 5, 6; DLB 13

Police, The
See Copeland, Stewart; Sting; Summers, Andy

Polidori, John William 1795-1821 ..... **NCLC 51; SSC 97**
See also DLB 116; HGG

Poliziano, Angelo 1454-1494 .... **LC 120**
See also WLIT 7

Pollitt, Katha 1949- .... **CLC 28, 122**
See also CA 120; 122; CANR 66, 108, 164, 200, 229; MTCW 1, 2; MTFW 2005

Pollock, (Mary) Sharon 1936- .... **CLC 50**
See also CA 141; CANR 132; CD 5; CWD; DAC; DAM DRAM, MST; DFS 3; DLB 60; FW

Pollock, Sharon 1936- .... **DC 20**
See also CD 6

Polo, Marco 1254-1324 .... **CMLC 15**
See also WLIT 7

Polonsky, Abraham (Lincoln) 1910-1999 ..... **CLC 92**
See also CA 104; 187; DLB 26; INT CA-104

Polybius c. 200B.C.-c. 118B.C. ..... **CMLC 17**
See also AW 1; DLB 176; RGWL 2, 3

Pomerance, Bernard 1940- .... **CLC 13**
See also CA 101; CAD; CANR 49, 134; CD 5, 6; DAM DRAM; DFS 9; LAIT 2

Ponge, Francis 1899-1988 .... **CLC 6, 18; PC 107**
See also CA 85-88; 126; CANR 40, 86; DAM POET; DLBY 2002; EWL 3; GFL 1789 to the Present; RGWL 2, 3

Poniatowska, Elena 1932- ... **CLC 140; HLC 2**
See also CA 101; CANR 32, 66, 107, 156; CDWLB 3; CWW 2; DAM MULT; DLB 113; EWL 3; HW 1, 2; LAWS 1; WLIT 1

Pontoppidan, Henrik 1857-1943 ... **TCLC 29**
See also CA 170; DLB 300, 331

Ponty, Maurice Merleau
See Merleau-Ponty, Maurice

Poole, (Jane Penelope) Josephine
See Helyar, Jane Penelope Josephine

Poole, Josephine
See Helyar, Jane Penelope Josephine

Popa, Vasko 1922-1991 . **CLC 19; TCLC 167**
See also CA 112; 148; CDWLB 4; DLB 181; EWL 3; RGWL 2, 3

Pope, Alexander 1688-1744 ..... **LC 3, 58, 60, 64, 164; PC 26; WLC 5**
See also BRW 3; BRWC 1; BRWR 1; CD-BLB 1660-1789; DA; DA3; DAB; DAC; DAM MST, POET; DLB 95, 101, 213; EXPP; PAB; PFS 12; RGEL 2; WLIT 3; WP

Popov, Evgenii Anatol'evich
See Popov, Yevgeny

Popov, Yevgeny **CLC 59**
See also DLB 285

Poquelin, Jean-Baptiste
See Moliere

Porete, Marguerite (?)-1310 .... **CMLC 73**
See also DLB 208

Porphyry c. 233-c. 305 .... **CMLC 71**

Porter, Connie (Rose) 1959(?)- .... **CLC 70**
See also AAYA 65; BW 2, 3; CA 142; CANR 90, 109; SATA 81, 129

Porter, Gene Stratton
See Stratton-Porter, Gene

Porter, Geneva Grace
See Stratton-Porter, Gene

Porter, Katherine Anne 1890-1980 .. **CLC 1, 3, 7, 10, 13, 15, 27, 101; SSC 4, 31, 43, 108; TCLC 233**
See also AAYA 42; AITN 2; AMW; BPFB 3; CA 1-4R; 101; CANR 1, 65; CDALBS; CN 1, 2; DA; DA3; DAB; DAC; DAM MST, NOV; DLB 4, 9, 102; DLBD 12; DLBY 1980; EWL 3; EXPS; LAIT 3; MAL 5; MBL; MTCW 1, 2; MTFW 2005; NFS 14; RGAL 4; RGSF 2; SATA 39; SATA-Obit 23; SSFS 1, 8, 11, 16, 23; TCWW 2; TUS

Porter, Peter 1929-2010 .... **CLC 5, 13, 33**
See also CA 85-88; CP 1, 2, 3, 4, 5, 6, 7; DLB 40, 289; WWE 1

Porter, Peter Neville Frederick
See Porter, Peter

Porter, R. E.
See Hoch, Edward D.

Porter, William Sydney
See Henry, O.

Portillo (y Pacheco), Jose Lopez
See Lopez Portillo (y Pacheco), Jose

Portillo Trambley, Estela 1927-1998 .... **HLC 2; TCLC 163**
See also CA 77-80; CANR 32; DAM MULT; DLB 209; HW 1; RGAL 4

Posey, Alexander (Lawrence) 1873-1908 ..... **NNAL**
See also CA 144; CANR 80; DAM MULT; DLB 175

Posse, Abel **CLC 70, 273**
See also CA 252

Post, Melville Davisson 1869-1930 .... **TCLC 39**
See also CA 110; 202; CMW 4

Postl, Carl
See Sealsfield, Charles

Postman, Neil 1931(?)-2003 .... **CLC 244**
See also CA 102; 221

Potocki, Jan 1761-1815 .... **NCLC 229**

Potok, Chaim 1929-2002 .. **CLC 2, 7, 14, 26, 112**
See also AAYA 15, 50; AITN 1, 2; BPFB 3; BYA 1; CA 17-20R; 208; CANR 19, 35, 64, 98; CLR 92; CN 4, 5, 6; DA3; DAM NOV; DLB 28, 152; EXPN; INT CANR-19; LAIT 4; MTCW 1, 2; MTFW 2005; NFS 4, 34, 38; RGHL; SATA 33, 106; SATA-Obit 134; TUS; YAW

Potok, Herbert Harold
See Potok, Chaim

Potok, Herman Harold
See Potok, Chaim

Potter, Dennis (Christopher George) 1935-1994 .... **CLC 58, 86, 123**
See also BRWS 10; CA 107; 145; CANR 33, 61; CBD; DLB 233; MTCW 1

Pound, Ezra 1885-1972 . **CLC 1, 2, 3, 4, 5, 7, 10, 13, 18, 34, 48, 50, 112; PC 4, 95; WLC 5**
See also AAYA 47; AMW; AMWR 1; CA 5-8R; 37-40R; CANR 40; CDALB 1917-1929; CP 1; DA; DA3; DAB; DAC; DAM MST, POET; DLB 4, 45, 63; DLBD 15; EFS 1:2, 2:1; EWL 3; EXPP; LMFS 2; MAL 5; MTCW 1, 2; MTFW 2005; PAB; PFS 2, 8, 16; RGAL 4; TUS; WP

Pound, Ezra Weston Loomis
See Pound, Ezra

Povod, Reinaldo 1959-1994 .... **CLC 44**
See also CA 136; 146; CANR 83

Powell, Adam Clayton, Jr. 1908-1972 .. **BLC 1:3; CLC 89**
See also BW 1, 3; CA 102; 33-36R; CANR 86; DAM MULT; DLB 345

Powell, Anthony 1905-2000 . **CLC 1, 3, 7, 9, 10, 31**
See also BRW 7; CA 1-4R; 189; CANR 1, 32, 62, 107; CDBLB 1945-1960; CN 1, 2, 3, 4, 5, 6; DLB 15; EWL 3; MTCW 1, 2; MTFW 2005; RGEL 2; TEA

Powell, Dawn 1896(?)-1965 .... **CLC 66**
See also CA 5-8R; CANR 121; DLBY 1997

Powell, Padgett 1952- .... **CLC 34**
See also CA 126; CANR 63, 101, 215; CSW; DLB 234; DLBY 01; SSFS 25

Power, Susan 1961- .... **CLC 91**
See also BYA 14; CA 160; CANR 135; NFS 11

Powers, J(ames) F(arl) 1917-1999 ... **CLC 1, 4, 8, 57; SSC 4**
See also CA 1-4R; 181; CANR 2, 61; CN 1, 2, 3, 4, 5, 6; DLB 130; MTCW 1; RGAL 4; RGSF 2

Powers, John
See Powers, John R.

Powers, John R. 1945- .... **CLC 66**
See also CA 69-72

Powers, Richard 1957- .... **CLC 93, 292**
See also AMWS 9; BPFB 3; CA 148; CANR 80, 180, 221; CN 6, 7; DLB 350; MTFW 2005; TCLE 1:2

Powers, Richard S.
See Powers, Richard

Pownall, David 1938- .... **CLC 10**
See also CA 89-92, 180; CAAS 18; CANR 49, 101; CBD; CD 5, 6; CN 4, 5, 6, 7; DLB 14

Powys, John Cowper 1872-1963 .. **CLC 7, 9, 15, 46, 125**
See also CA 85-88; CANR 106; DLB 15, 255; EWL 3; FANT; MTCW 1, 2; MTFW 2005; RGEL 2; SUFW

Powys, T(heodore) F(rancis) 1875-1953 ...... **TCLC 9**
See also BRWS 8; CA 106; 189; DLB 36, 162; EWL 3; FANT; RGEL 2; SUFW

Pyle, Howard 1853-1911 .... **TCLC 81**
See also AAYA 57; BYA 2, 4; CA 109; 137;
CLR 22, 117; DLB 42, 188; DLBD 13;
LAIT 1; MAICYA 1, 2; SATA 16, 100;
WCH; YAW

Pym, Barbara (Mary Crampton)
1913-1980 .... **CLC 13, 19, 37, 111**
See also BPFB 3; BRWS 2; CA 13-14; 97-
100; CANR 13, 34; CAP 1; DLB 14, 207;
DLBY 1987; EWL 3; MTCW 1, 2; MTFW
2005; RGEL 2; TEA

Pynchon, Thomas 1937- . **CLC 2, 3, 6, 9, 11,
18, 33, 62, 72, 123, 192, 213; SSC 14,
84; WLC 5**
See also AMWS 2; BEST 90:2; BPFB 3;
CA 17-20R; CANR 22, 46, 73, 142, 198;
CN 1, 2, 3, 4, 5, 6, 7; CPW 1; DA; DA3;
DAB; DAC; DAM MST, NOV, POP;
DLB 2, 173; EWL 3; MAL 5; MTCW 1,
2; MTFW 2005; NFS 23, 36; RGAL 4;
SFW 4; TCLE 1:2; TUS

Pynchon, Thomas Ruggels, Jr.
See Pynchon, Thomas

Pynchon, Thomas Ruggles
See Pynchon, Thomas

Pythagoras c. 582B.C.-c. 507B.C. ..... **CMLC
22**
See also DLB 176

Q
See Quiller-Couch, Sir Arthur (Thomas)

Qian, Chongzhu
See Qian, Zhongshu

Qian, Sima 145B.C.-c. 89B.C. ...... **CMLC 72**
See also DLB 358

Qian, Zhongshu 1910-1998 .... **CLC 22**
See also CA 130; CANR 73, 216; CWW 2;
DLB 328; MTCW 1, 2

Qroll
See Dagerman, Stig (Halvard)

Quarles, Francis 1592-1644 .... **LC 117**
See also DLB 126; RGEL 2

Quarrington, Paul 1953-2010 .... **CLC 65**
See also CA 129; CANR 62, 95, 228

Quarrington, Paul Lewis
See Quarrington, Paul

Quasimodo, Salvatore 1901-1968 .. **CLC 10;
PC 47**
See also CA 13-16; 25-28R; CAP 1; DLB
114, 332; EW 12; EWL 3; MTCW 1;
RGWL 2, 3

Quatermass, Martin
See Carpenter, John

Quay, Stephen 1947- .... **CLC 95**
See also CA 189

Quay, Timothy 1947- .... **CLC 95**
See also CA 189

Queen, Ellery
See Dannay, Frederic; Hoch, Edward D.;
Lee, Manfred B.; Marlowe, Stephen;
Sturgeon, Theodore (Hamilton); Vance,
Jack

Queneau, Raymond 1903-1976 .... **CLC 2, 5,
10, 42; TCLC 233**
See also CA 77-80; 69-72; CANR 32; DLB
72, 258; EW 12; EWL 3; GFL 1789 to
the Present; MTCW 1, 2; RGWL 2, 3

Quevedo, Francisco de 1580-1645 .... **LC 23,
160**

Quiller-Couch, Sir Arthur (Thomas)
1863-1944 .... **TCLC 53**
See also CA 118; 166; DLB 135, 153, 190;
HGG; RGEL 2; SUFW 1

Quin, Ann 1936-1973 .... **CLC 6**
See also CA 9-12R; 45-48; CANR 148; CN
1; DLB 14, 231

Quin, Ann Marie
See Quin, Ann

Quincey, Thomas de
See De Quincey, Thomas

Quindlen, Anna 1953- .... **CLC 191**
See also AAYA 35; AMWS 17; CA 138;
CANR 73, 126; DA3; DLB 292; MTCW
2; MTFW 2005

Quinn, Martin
See Smith, Martin Cruz

Quinn, Peter 1947- .... **CLC 91**
See also CA 197; CANR 147

Quinn, Peter A.
See Quinn, Peter

Quinn, Simon
See Smith, Martin Cruz

Quintana, Leroy V. 1944- ..... **HLC 2; PC 36**
See also CA 131; CANR 65, 139; DAM
MULT; DLB 82; HW 1, 2

Quintilian c. 40-c. 100 .... **CMLC 77**
See also AW 2; DLB 211; RGWL 2, 3

Quiroga, Horacio (Sylvestre) 1878-1937 ......
HLC 2; SSC 89; TCLC 20
See also CA 117; 131; DAM MULT; EWL
3; HW 1; LAW; MTCW 1; RGSF 2;
WLIT 1

Quoirez, Francoise
See Sagan, Francoise

Raabe, Wilhelm (Karl) 1831-1910 ..... **TCLC
45**
See also CA 167; DLB 129

Rabe, David 1940- ... **CLC 4, 8, 33, 200; DC
16**
See also CA 85-88; CABS 3; CAD; CANR
59, 129, 218; CD 5, 6; DAM DRAM;
DFS 3, 8, 13; DLB 7, 228; EWL 3; MAL
5

Rabe, David William
See Rabe, David

Rabelais, Francois 1494-1553 .... **LC 5, 60,
186; WLC 5**
See also DA; DAB; DAC; DAM MST;
DLB 327; EW 2; GFL Beginnings to
1789; LMFS 1; RGWL 2, 3; TWA

Rabi'a al-'Adawiyya c. 717-c. 801 ... **CMLC
83**
See also DLB 311

Rabinovitch, Sholem 1859-1916 ...... **SSC 33,
125; TCLC 1, 35**
See also CA 104; DLB 333; TWA

Rabinovitsh, Sholem Yankev
See Rabinovitch, Sholem

Rabinowitz, Sholem Yakov
See Rabinovitch, Sholem

Rabinowitz, Solomon
See Rabinovitch, Sholem

Rabinyan, Dorit 1972- .... **CLC 119**
See also CA 170; CANR 147

Rachilde
See Vallette, Marguerite Eymery; Vallette,
Marguerite Eymery

Racine, Jean 1639-1699 . **DC 32; LC 28, 113**
See also DA3; DAB; DAM MST; DFS 28;
DLB 268; EW 3; GFL Beginnings to
1789; LMFS 1; RGWL 2, 3; TWA

Radcliffe, Ann 1764-1823 . **NCLC 6, 55, 106,
223**
See also BRWR 3; DLB 39, 178; GL 3;
HGG; LMFS 1; RGEL 2; SUFW; WLIT
3

Radclyffe-Hall, Marguerite
See Hall, Radclyffe

Radiguet, Raymond 1903-1923 ..... **TCLC 29**
See also CA 162; DLB 65; EWL 3; GFL
1789 to the Present; RGWL 2, 3

Radishchev, Aleksandr Nikolaevich
1749-1802 .... **NCLC 190**
See also DLB 150

Radishchev, Alexander
See Radishchev, Aleksandr Nikolaevich

Radnoti, Miklos 1909-1944 .... **TCLC 16**
See also CA 118; 212; CDWLB 4; DLB
215; EWL 3; RGHL; RGWL 2, 3

Rado, James 1939- .... **CLC 17**
See also CA 105

Radvanyi, Netty 1900-1983 .... **CLC 7**
See also CA 85-88; 110; CANR 82; CD-
WLB 2; DLB 69; EWL 3

Rae, Ben
See Griffiths, Trevor

Raeburn, John (Hay) 1941- .... **CLC 34**
See also CA 57-60

Ragni, Gerome 1942-1991 .... **CLC 17**
See also CA 105; 134

Rahv, Philip
See Greenberg, Ivan

Rai, Navab
See Srivastava, Dhanpat Rai

Raimund, Ferdinand Jakob 1790-1836 ....
NCLC 69
See also DLB 90

Raine, Craig 1944- .... **CLC 32, 103**
See also BRWS 13; CA 108; CANR 29, 51,
103, 171; CP 3, 4, 5, 6, 7; DLB 40; PFS 7

Raine, Craig Anthony
See Raine, Craig

Raine, Kathleen (Jessie) 1908-2003 . **CLC 7,
45**
See also CA 85-88; 218; CANR 46, 109;
CP 1, 2, 3, 4, 5, 6, 7; DLB 20; EWL 3;
MTCW 1; RGEL 2

Rainis, Janis 1865-1929 .... **TCLC 29**
See also CA 170; CDWLB 4; DLB 220;
EWL 3

Rakosi, Carl
See Rawley, Callman

Ralegh, Sir Walter
See Raleigh, Sir Walter

Raleigh, Richard
See Lovecraft, H. P.

Raleigh, Sir Walter 1554(?)-1618 ...... **LC 31,
39; PC 31**
See also BRW 1; CDBLB Before 1660;
DLB 172; EXPP; PFS 14; RGEL 2; TEA;
WP

Rallentando, H. P.
See Sayers, Dorothy L(eigh)

Ramal, Walter
See de la Mare, Walter (John)

Ramana Maharshi 1879-1950 .... **TCLC 84**

Ramoacn y Cajal, Santiago 1852-1934 ....
TCLC 93

Ramon, Juan
See Jimenez, Juan Ramon

Ramos, Graciliano 1892-1953 .... **TCLC 32**
See also CA 167; DLB 307; EWL 3; HW 2;
LAW; WLIT 1

Rampersad, Arnold 1941- .... **CLC 44**
See also BW 2, 3; CA 127; 133; CANR 81;
DLB 111; INT CA-133

Rampling, Anne
See Rice, Anne

Ramsay, Allan 1686(?)-1758 .... **LC 29**
See also DLB 95; RGEL 2

Ramsay, Jay
See Campbell, Ramsey

Ramus, Peter
See La Ramee, Pierre de

Ramus, Petrus
See La Ramee, Pierre de

Ramuz, Charles-Ferdinand 1878-1947 ....
TCLC 33
See also CA 165; EWL 3

Reverend Mandju
See Su, Chien

Rexroth, Kenneth 1905-1982 ... **CLC 1, 2, 6, 11, 22, 49, 112; PC 20, 95**
See also BG 1:3; CA 5-8R; 107; CANR 14, 34, 63; CDALB 1941-1968; CP 1, 2, 3; DAM POET; DLB 16, 48, 165, 212; DLBY 1982; EWL 3; INT CANR-14; MAL 5; MTCW 1, 2; MTFW 2005; RGAL 4

Reyes, Alfonso 1889-1959 .. **HLCS 2; TCLC 33**
See also CA 131; EWL 3; HW 1; LAW

Reyes y Basoalto, Ricardo Eliecer Neftali
See Neruda, Pablo

Reymont, Wladyslaw (Stanislaw) 1868(?)-1925 .... **TCLC 5**
See also CA 104; DLB 332; EWL 3

Reynolds, John Hamilton 1794-1852 . **NCLC 146**
See also DLB 96

Reynolds, Jonathan 1942- .... **CLC 6, 38**
See also CA 65-68; CANR 28, 176

Reynolds, Joshua 1723-1792 .... **LC 15**
See also DLB 104

Reynolds, Michael S(hane) 1937-2000 . **CLC 44**
See also CA 65-68; 189; CANR 9, 89, 97

Reza, Yasmina 1959- .... **CLC 299; DC 34**
See also AAYA 69; CA 171; CANR 145; DFS 19; DLB 321

Reznikoff, Charles 1894-1976 .... **CLC 9; PC 124**
See also AMWS 14; CA 33-36; 61-64; CAP 2; CP 1, 2; DLB 28, 45; RGHL; WP

Rezzori, Gregor von
See Rezzori d'Arezzo, Gregor von

Rezzori d'Arezzo, Gregor von 1914-1998 ... **CLC 25**
See also CA 122; 136; 167

Rhine, Richard
See Silverstein, Alvin; Silverstein, Virginia B.

Rhodes, Eugene Manlove 1869-1934 . **TCLC 53**
See also CA 198; DLB 256; TCWW 1, 2

R'hoone, Lord
See Balzac, Honore de

Rhys, Jean 1890-1979 .. **CLC 2, 4, 6, 14, 19, 51, 124; SSC 21, 76**
See also BRWS 2; CA 25-28R; 85-88; CANR 35, 62; CDBLB 1945-1960; CD-WLB 3; CN 1, 2; DA3; DAM NOV; DLB 36, 117, 162; DNFS 2; EWL 3; LATS 1:1; MTCW 1, 2; MTFW 2005; NFS 19; RGEL 2; RGSF 2; RHW; TEA; WWE 1

Ribeiro, Darcy 1922-1997 .... **CLC 34**
See also CA 33-36R; 156; EWL 3

Ribeiro, Joao Ubaldo (Osorio Pimentel) 1941- .... **CLC 10, 67**
See also CA 81-84; CWW 2; EWL 3

Ribman, Ronald (Burt) 1932- .... **CLC 7**
See also CA 21-24R; CAD; CANR 46, 80; CD 5, 6

Ricci, Nino 1959- .... **CLC 70**
See also CA 137; CANR 130; CCA 1

Ricci, Nino Pio
See Ricci, Nino

Rice, Anne 1941- .... **CLC 41, 128**
See also AAYA 9, 53; AMWS 7; BEST 89:2; BPFB 3; CA 65-68; CANR 12, 36, 53, 74, 100, 133, 190; CN 6, 7; CPW; CSW; DA3; DAM POP; DLB 292; GL 3; GLL 2; HGG; MTCW 2; MTFW 2005; SUFW 2; YAW

Rice, Elmer (Leopold) 1892-1967 .... **CLC 7, 49; DC 44; TCLC 221**
See also CA 21-22; 25-28R; CAP 2; DAM DRAM; DFS 12; DLB 4, 7; EWL 3; IDTP; MAL 5; MTCW 1, 2; RGAL 4

Rice, Tim 1944- .... **CLC 21**
See also CA 103; CANR 46; DFS 7

Rice, Timothy Miles Bindon
See Rice, Tim

Rich, Adrienne 1929- .... **CLC 3, 6, 7, 11, 18, 36, 73, 76, 125; PC 5**
See also AAYA 69; AMWR 2; AMWS 1; CA 9-12R; CANR 20, 53, 74, 128, 199; CDALBS; CP 1, 2, 3, 4, 5, 6, 7; CSW; CWP; DA3; DAM POET; DLB 5, 67; EWL 3; EXPP; FL 1:6; FW; MAL 5; MBL; MTCW 1, 2; MTFW 2005; PAB; PFS 15, 29, 39; RGAL 4; RGHL; WP

Rich, Adrienne Cecile
See Rich, Adrienne

Rich, Barbara
See Graves, Robert

Rich, Robert
See Trumbo, Dalton

Richard, Keith
See Richards, Keith

Richards, David Adams 1950- .... **CLC 59**
See also CA 93-96; CANR 60, 110, 156; CN 7; DAC; DLB 53; TCLE 1:2

Richards, I(vor) A(rmstrong) 1893-1979 ..... **CLC 14, 24**
See also BRWS 2; CA 41-44R; 89-92; CANR 34, 74; CP 1, 2; DLB 27; EWL 3; MTCW 2; RGEL 2

Richards, Keith 1943- .... **CLC 17**
See also CA 107; CANR 77

Richardson, Anne
See Roiphe, Anne

Richardson, Dorothy Miller 1873-1957 .... **TCLC 3, 203**
See also BRWS 13; CA 104; 192; DLB 36; EWL 3; FW; RGEL 2

Richardson, Ethel Florence Lindesay 1870-1946 .... **TCLC 4**
See also CA 105; 190; DLB 197, 230; EWL 3; RGEL 2; RGSF 2; RHW

Richardson, Henrietta
See Richardson, Ethel Florence Lindesay

Richardson, Henry Handel
See Richardson, Ethel Florence Lindesay

Richardson, John 1796-1852 .... **NCLC 55**
See also CCA 1; DAC; DLB 99

Richardson, Samuel 1689-1761 ..... **LC 1, 44, 138, 204; WLC 5**
See also BRW 3; CDBLB 1660-1789; DA; DAB; DAC; DAM MST, NOV; DLB 154; RGEL 2; TEA; WLIT 3

Richardson, Willis 1889-1977 .... **HR 1:3**
See also BW 1; CA 124; DLB 51; SATA 60

Richardson Robertson, Ethel Florence Lindesay
See Richardson, Ethel Florence Lindesay

Richler, Mordecai 1931-2001 ... **CLC 3, 5, 9, 13, 18, 46, 70, 185, 271**
See also AITN 1; CA 65-68; 201; CANR 31, 62, 111; CCA 1; CLR 17; CN 1, 2, 3, 4, 5, 7; CWRI 5; DAC; DAM MST, NOV; DLB 53; EWL 3; MAICYA 1, 2; MTCW 1, 2; MTFW 2005; RGEL 2; RGHL; SATA 44, 98; SATA-Brief 27; TWA

Richter, Conrad (Michael) 1890-1968 . **CLC 30**
See also AAYA 21; AMWS 18; BYA 2; CA 5-8R; 25-28R; CANR 23; DLB 9, 212; LAIT 1; MAL 5; MTCW 1, 2; MTFW 2005; RGAL 4; SATA 3; TCWW 1, 2; TUS; YAW

Ricostranza, Tom
See Ellis, Trey

Riddell, Charlotte 1832-1906 .... **TCLC 40**
See also CA 165; DLB 156; HGG; SUFW

Riddell, Mrs. J. H.
See Riddell, Charlotte

Ridge, John Rollin 1827-1867 ..... **NCLC 82; NNAL**
See also CA 144; DAM MULT; DLB 175

Ridgeway, Jason
See Marlowe, Stephen

Ridgway, Keith 1965- .... **CLC 119**
See also CA 172; CANR 144

Riding, Laura
See Jackson, Laura

Riefenstahl, Berta Helene Amalia 1902-2003 .... **CLC 16, 190**
See also CA 108; 220

Riefenstahl, Leni
See Riefenstahl, Berta Helene Amalia

Riffe, Ernest
See Bergman, Ingmar

Riffe, Ernest Ingmar
See Bergman, Ingmar

Riggs, (Rolla) Lynn 1899-1954 .... **NNAL; TCLC 56**
See also CA 144; DAM MULT; DLB 175

Riis, Jacob A(ugust) 1849-1914 .... **TCLC 80**
See also CA 113; 168; DLB 23

Rikki
See Ducornet, Erica

Riley, James Whitcomb 1849-1916 ... **PC 48; TCLC 51**
See also CA 118; 137; DAM POET; MAICYA 1, 2; RGAL 4; SATA 17

Riley, Tex
See Creasey, John

Rilke, Rainer Maria 1875-1926 .... **PC 2; TCLC 1, 6, 19, 195**
See also CA 104; 132; CANR 62, 99; CD-WLB 2; DA3; DAM POET; DLB 81; EW 9; EWL 3; MTCW 1, 2; MTFW 2005; PFS 19, 27; RGWL 2, 3; TWA; WP

Rimbaud, Arthur 1854-1891 ... **NCLC 4, 35, 82, 227; PC 3, 57; WLC 5**
See also DA; DA3; DAB; DAC; DAM MST, POET; DLB 217; EW 7; GFL 1789 to the Present; LMFS 2; PFS 28; RGWL 2, 3; TWA; WP

Rimbaud, Jean Nicholas Arthur
See Rimbaud, Arthur

Rinehart, Mary Roberts 1876-1958 .. **TCLC 52**
See also BPFB 3; CA 108; 166; RGAL 4; RHW

Ringmaster, The
See Mencken, H. L.

Ringwood, Gwen(dolyn Margaret) Pharis 1910-1984 .... **CLC 48**
See also CA 148; 112; DLB 88

Rio, Michel 1945(?)- .... **CLC 43**
See also CA 201

Rios, Alberto 1952- .... **PC 57**
See also AAYA 66; AMWS 4; CA 113; CANR 34, 79, 137; CP 6, 7; DLB 122; HW 2; MTFW 2005; PFS 11

Rios, Alberto Alvaro
See Rios, Alberto

Ritsos, Giannes
See Ritsos, Yannis

Ritsos, Yannis 1909-1990 .... **CLC 6, 13, 31**
See also CA 77-80; 133; CANR 39, 61; EW 12; EWL 3; MTCW 1; RGWL 2, 3

Ritter, Erika 1948- .... **CLC 52**
See also CA 318; CD 5, 6; CWD; DLB 362

Rivera, Jose Eustasio 1889-1928 .. **TCLC 35**
See also CA 162; EWL 3; HW 1, 2; LAW

Rivera, Tomas 1935-1984 . **HLCS 2; SSC 160**
See also CA 49-52; CANR 32; DLB 82; HW 1; LLW; RGAL 4; SSFS 15; TCWW 2; WLIT 1

Rivers, Conrad Kent 1933-1968 .... **CLC 1**
See also BW 1; CA 85-88; DLB 41

Rivers, Elfrida
See Bradley, Marion Zimmer

Roquelaure, A. N.
See Rice, Anne
Rosa, Joao Guimaraes
See Guimaraes Rosa, Joao
Rose, Wendy 1948- . **CLC 85; NNAL; PC 13**
See also CA 53-56; CANR 5, 51; CWP;
DAM MULT; DLB 175; PFS 13; RGAL
4; SATA 12
Rosen, R.D. 1949- .... **CLC 39**
See also CA 77-80; CANR 62, 120, 175;
CMW 4; INT CANR-30
Rosen, Richard
See Rosen, R.D.
Rosen, Richard Dean
See Rosen, R.D.
Rosenberg, Isaac 1890-1918 .... **TCLC 12**
See also BRW 6; CA 107; 188; DLB 20,
216; EWL 3; PAB; RGEL 2
Rosenblatt, Joe
See Rosenblatt, Joseph
Rosenblatt, Joseph 1933- .... **CLC 15**
See also CA 89-92; CP 3, 4, 5, 6, 7; INT
CA-89-92
Rosenfeld, Samuel
See Tzara, Tristan
Rosenstock, Sami
See Tzara, Tristan
Rosenstock, Samuel
See Tzara, Tristan
Rosenthal, M(acha) L(ouis) 1917-1996 . **CLC 28**
See also CA 1-4R; 152; CAAS 6; CANR 4,
51; CP 1, 2, 3, 4, 5, 6; DLB 5; SATA 59
Ross, Barnaby
See Dannay, Frederic; Lee, Manfred B.
Ross, Bernard L.
See Follett, Ken
Ross, J. H.
See Lawrence, T. E.
Ross, John Hume
See Lawrence, T. E.
Ross, Martin 1862-1915 ....
See Martin, Violet Florence
See also DLB 135; GLL 2; RGEL 2; RGSF
2
Ross, (James) Sinclair 1908-1996 .. **CLC 13; SSC 24**
See also CA 73-76; CANR 81; CN 1, 2, 3,
4, 5, 6; DAC; DAM MST; DLB 88;
RGEL 2; RGSF 2; TCWW 1, 2
Rossetti, Christina 1830-1894 . **NCLC 2, 50, 66, 186; PC 7, 119; WLC 5**
See also AAYA 51; BRW 5; BRWR 3; BYA
4; CLR 115; DA; DA3; DAB; DAC;
DAM MST, POET; DLB 35, 163, 240;
EXPP; FL 1:3; LATS 1:1; MAICYA 1, 2;
PFS 10, 14, 27, 34; RGEL 2; SATA 20;
TEA; WCH
Rossetti, Christina Georgina
See Rossetti, Christina
Rossetti, Dante Gabriel 1828-1882 .... **NCLC 4, 77; PC 44; WLC 5**
See also AAYA 51; BRW 5; CDBLB 1832-
1890; DA; DAB; DAC; DAM MST,
POET; DLB 35; EXPP; RGEL 2; TEA
Rossi, Cristina Peri
See Peri Rossi, Cristina
Rossi, Jean-Baptiste 1931-2003 .... **CLC 90**
See also CA 201; 215; CMW 4; NFS 18
Rossner, Judith 1935-2005 ...... **CLC 6, 9, 29**
See also AITN 2; BEST 90:3; BPFB 3; CA
17-20R; 242; CANR 18, 51, 73; CN 4, 5,
6, 7; DLB 6; INT CANR-18; MAL 5;
MTCW 1, 2; MTFW 2005
Rossner, Judith Perelman
See Rossner, Judith

Rostand, Edmond 1868-1918 . **DC 10; TCLC 6, 37**
See also CA 104; 126; DA; DA3; DAB;
DAC; DAM DRAM, MST; DFS 1; DLB
192; LAIT 1; MTCW 1; RGWL 2, 3;
TWA
Rostand, Edmond Eugene Alexis
See Rostand, Edmond
Roth, Henry 1906-1995 .. **CLC 2, 6, 11, 104; SSC 134**
See also AMWS 9; CA 11-12; 149; CANR
38, 63; CAP 1; CN 1, 2, 3, 4, 5, 6; DA3;
DLB 28; EWL 3; MAL 5; MTCW 1, 2;
MTFW 2005; RGAL 4
Roth, (Moses) Joseph 1894-1939 .. **TCLC 33**
See also CA 160; DLB 85; EWL 3; RGWL
2, 3
Roth, Philip 1933- .. **CLC 1, 2, 3, 4, 6, 9, 15, 22, 31, 47, 66, 86, 119, 201; SSC 26, 102; WLC 5**
See also AAYA 67; AMWR 2; AMWS 3;
BEST 90:3; BPFB 3; CA 1-4R; CANR 1,
22, 36, 55, 89, 132, 170; CDALB 1968-
1988; CN 3, 4, 5, 6, 7; CPW 1; DA; DA3;
DAB; DAC; DAM MST, NOV, POP;
DLB 2, 28, 173; DLBY 1982; EWL 3;
MAL 5; MTCW 1, 2; MTFW 2005; NFS
25; RGAL 4; RGHL; RGSF 2; SSFS 12,
18; TUS
Roth, Philip Milton
See Roth, Philip
Rothenberg, Jerome 1931- .... **CLC 6, 57**
See also CA 45-48; CANR 1, 106; CP 1, 2,
3, 4, 5, 6, 7; DLB 5, 193
Rotter, Pat CLC 65
Roumain, Jacques 1907-1944 .... **BLC 1:3; TCLC 19**
See also BW 1; CA 117; 125; DAM MULT;
EWL 3
Roumain, Jacques Jean Baptiste
See Roumain, Jacques
Rourke, Constance Mayfield 1885-1941 ...... **TCLC 12**
See also CA 107; 200; MAL 5; YABC 1
Rousseau, Jean-Baptiste 1671-1741 ..... **LC 9**
Rousseau, Jean-Jacques 1712-1778 .. **LC 14, 36, 122, 198; WLC 5**
See also DA; DA3; DAB; DAC; DAM
MST; DLB 314; EW 4; GFL Beginnings
to 1789; LMFS 1; RGWL 2, 3; TWA
Roussel, Raymond 1877-1933 .... **TCLC 20**
See also CA 117; 201; EWL 3; GFL 1789
to the Present
Rovit, Earl (Herbert) 1927- .... **CLC 7**
See also CA 5-8R; CANR 12
Rowe, Elizabeth Singer 1674-1737 .... **LC 44**
See also DLB 39, 95
Rowe, Nicholas 1674-1718 .... **LC 8**
See also DLB 84; RGEL 2
Rowlandson, Mary 1637(?)-1678 .... **LC 66**
See also DLB 24, 200; RGAL 4
Rowley, Ames Dorrance
See Lovecraft, H. P.
Rowley, William 1585(?)-1626 ... **DC 43; LC 100, 123**
See also DFS 22; DLB 58; RGEL 2
Rowling, J.K. 1965- .... **CLC 137, 217**
See also AAYA 34, 82; BRWS 16; BYA 11,
13, 14; CA 173; CANR 128, 157; CLR
66, 80, 112; LNFS 1, 2, 3; MAICYA 2;
MTFW 2005; SATA 109, 174; SUFW 2
Rowling, Joanne Kathleen
See Rowling, J.K.
Rowson, Susanna Haswell 1762(?)-1824 ......
NCLC 5, 69, 182
See also AMWS 15; DLB 37, 200; RGAL 4

Roy, Arundhati 1961- .... **CLC 109, 210**
See also CA 163; CANR 90, 126, 217; CN
7; DLB 323, 326; DLBY 1997; EWL 3;
LATS 1:2; MTFW 2005; NFS 22; WWE
1
Roy, Gabrielle 1909-1983 .... **CLC 10, 14; TCLC 256**
See also CA 53-56; 110; CANR 5, 61; CCA
1; DAB; DAC; DAM MST; DLB 68;
EWL 3; MTCW 1; RGWL 2, 3; SATA
104; TCLE 1:2
Roy, Suzanna Arundhati
See Roy, Arundhati
Royko, Mike 1932-1997 .... **CLC 109**
See also CA 89-92; 157; CANR 26, 111;
CPW
Rozanov, Vasilii Vasil'evich
See Rozanov, Vassili
Rozanov, Vasily Vasilyevich
See Rozanov, Vassili
Rozanov, Vassili 1856-1919 .... **TCLC 104**
See also DLB 295; EWL 3
Rozewicz, Tadeusz 1921- ..... **CLC 9, 23, 139**
See also CA 108; CANR 36, 66; CWW 2;
DA3; DAM POET; DLB 232; EWL 3;
MTCW 1, 2; MTFW 2005; RGHL;
RGWL 3
Ruark, Gibbons 1941- .... **CLC 3**
See also CA 33-36R; CAAS 23; CANR 14,
31, 57; DLB 120
Rubens, Bernice (Ruth) 1923-2004 ...... **CLC 19, 31**
See also CA 25-28R; 232; CANR 33, 65,
128; CN 1, 2, 3, 4, 5, 6, 7; DLB 14, 207,
326; MTCW 1
Rubin, Harold
See Robbins, Harold
Rudkin, (James) David 1936- .... **CLC 14**
See also CA 89-92; CBD; CD 5, 6; DLB 13
Rudnik, Raphael 1933- .... **CLC 7**
See also CA 29-32R
Ruffian, M.
See Hasek, Jaroslav
Rufinus c. 345-410 .... **CMLC 111**
Ruiz, Jose Martinez
See Martinez Ruiz, Jose
Ruiz, Juan c. 1283-c. 1350 .... **CMLC 66**
Rukeyser, Muriel 1913-1980 . **CLC 6, 10, 15, 27; PC 12**
See also AMWS 6; CA 5-8R; 93-96; CANR
26, 60; CP 1, 2, 3; DA3; DAM POET;
DLB 48; EWL 3; FW; GLL 2; MAL 5;
MTCW 1, 2; PFS 10, 29; RGAL 4; SATA-
Obit 22
Rule, Jane 1931-2007 .... **CLC 27, 265**
See also CA 25-28R; 266; CAAS 18; CANR
12, 87; CN 4, 5, 6, 7; DLB 60; FW
Rule, Jane Vance
See Rule, Jane
Rulfo, Juan 1918-1986 . **CLC 8, 80; HLC 2; SSC 25**
See also CA 85-88; 118; CANR 26; CD-
WLB 3; DAM MULT; DLB 113; EWL 3;
HW 1, 2; LAW; MTCW 1, 2; RGSF 2;
RGWL 2, 3; WLIT 1
Rumi
See Rumi, Jalal al-Din
Rumi, Jalal al-Din 1207-1273 ..... **CMLC 20; PC 45, 123**
See also AAYA 64; RGWL 2, 3; WLIT 6;
WP
Runeberg, Johan 1804-1877 .... **NCLC 41**
Runyon, (Alfred) Damon 1884(?)-1946 ....
TCLC 10
See also CA 107; 165; DLB 11, 86, 171;
MAL 5; MTCW 2; RGAL 4
Rush, Benjamin 1746-1813 .... **NCLC 251**
See also DLB 37

Sale, John Kirkpatrick
See Sale, Kirkpatrick

Sale, Kirkpatrick 1937- .... **CLC 68**
See also CA 13-16R; CANR 10, 147

Salernitano, Masuccio c. 1420-c. 1475 .. **SSC 152**

Salinas, Luis Omar 1937- . **CLC 90; HLC 2**
See also AMWS 13; CA 131; CANR 81, 153; DAM MULT; DLB 82; HW 1, 2

Salinas (y Serrano), Pedro 1891(?)-1951 ..... **TCLC 17, 212**
See also CA 117; DLB 134; EWL 3

Salinger, J.D. 1919-2010 ..... **CLC 1, 3, 8, 12, 55, 56, 138, 243, 318; SSC 2, 28, 65, 146; WLC 5**
See also AAYA 2, 36; AMW; AMWC 1; BPFB 3; CA 5-8R; CANR 39, 129; CDALB 1941-1968; CLR 18; CN 1, 2, 3, 4, 5, 6, 7; CPW 1; DA; DA3; DAB; DAC; DAM MST, NOV, POP; DLB 2, 102, 173; EWL 3; EXPN; LAIT 4; MAICYA 1, 2; MAL 5; MTCW 1, 2; MTFW 2005; NFS 1, 30; RGAL 4; RGSF 2; SATA 67; SSFS 17; TUS; WYA; YAW

Salinger, Jerome David
See Salinger, J.D.

Salisbury, John
See Caute, (John) David

Sallust c. 86B.C.-35B.C. .... **CMLC 68**
See also AW 2; CDWLB 1; DLB 211; RGWL 2, 3

Salter, James 1925- .... **CLC 7, 52, 59, 275; SSC 58**
See also AMWS 9; CA 73-76; CANR 107, 160; DLB 130; SSFS 25

Saltus, Edgar (Everton) 1855-1921 . **TCLC 8**
See also CA 105; DLB 202; RGAL 4

Saltykov, Mikhail Evgrafovich 1826-1889 ... **NCLC 16**
See also DLB 238:

Saltykov-Shchedrin, N.
See Saltykov, Mikhail Evgrafovich

Samarakis, Andonis
See Samarakis, Antonis

Samarakis, Antonis 1919-2003 .... **CLC 5**
See also CA 25-28R; 224; CAAS 16; CANR 36; EWL 3

Samigli, E.
See Schmitz, Aron Hector

Sanchez, Florencio 1875-1910 .... **TCLC 37**
See also CA 153; DLB 305; EWL 3; HW 1; LAW

Sanchez, Luis Rafael 1936- .... **CLC 23**
See also CA 128; DLB 305; EWL 3; HW 1; WLIT 1

Sanchez, Sonia 1934- . **BLC 1:3, 2:3; CLC 5, 116, 215; PC 9**
See also BW 2, 3; CA 33-36R; CANR 24, 49, 74, 115; CLR 18; CP 2, 3, 4, 5, 6, 7; CSW; CWP; DA3; DAM MULT; DLB 41; DLBD 8; EWL 3; MAICYA 1, 2; MAL 5; MTCW 1, 2; MTFW 2005; PFS 26; SATA 22, 136; WP

Sancho, Ignatius 1729-1780 .... **LC 84**

Sand, George 1804-1876 ... **DC 29; NCLC 2, 42, 57, 174, 234; WLC 5**
See also DA; DA3; DAB; DAC; DAM MST, NOV; DLB 119, 192; EW 6; FL 1:3; FW; GFL 1789 to the Present; RGWL 2, 3; TWA

Sandburg, Carl 1878-1967 ..... **CLC 1, 4, 10, 15, 35; PC 2, 41; WLC 5**
See also AAYA 24; AMW; BYA 1, 3; CA 5-8R; 25-28R; CANR 35; CDALB 1865-1917; CLR 67; DA; DA3; DAB; DAC; DAM MST, POET; DLB 17, 54, 284; EWL 3; EXPP; LAIT 2; MAICYA 1, 2;

MAL 5; MTCW 1, 2; MTFW 2005; PAB; PFS 3, 6, 12, 33, 36; RGAL 4; SATA 8; TUS; WCH; WP; WYA

Sandburg, Carl August
See Sandburg, Carl

Sandburg, Charles
See Sandburg, Carl

Sandburg, Charles A.
See Sandburg, Carl

Sanders, Ed 1939- .... **CLC 53**
See also BG 1:3; CA 13-16R; CAAS 21; CANR 13, 44, 78; CP 1, 2, 3, 4, 5, 6, 7; DAM POET; DLB 16, 244

Sanders, Edward
See Sanders, Ed

Sanders, James Edward
See Sanders, Ed

Sanders, Lawrence 1920-1998 .... **CLC 41**
See also BEST 89:4; BPFB 3; CA 81-84; 165; CANR 33, 62; CMW 4; CPW; DA3; DAM POP; MTCW 1

Sanders, Noah
See Blount, Roy, Jr.

Sanders, Winston P.
See Anderson, Poul

Sandoz, Mari(e Susette) 1900-1966 . **CLC 28**
See also CA 1-4R; 25-28R; CANR 17, 64; DLB 9, 212; LAIT 2; MTCW 1, 2; SATA 5; TCWW 1, 2

Sandys, George 1578-1644 .... **LC 80**
See also DLB 24, 121

Saner, Reg(inald Anthony) 1931- ...... **CLC 9**
See also CA 65-68; CP 3, 4, 5, 6, 7

Sankara 788-820 .... **CMLC 32**

Sannazaro, Jacopo 1456(?)-1530 .... **LC 8**
See also RGWL 2, 3; WLIT 7

Sansom, William 1912-1976 . **CLC 2, 6; SSC 21**
See also CA 5-8R; 65-68; CANR 42; CN 1, 2; DAM NOV; DLB 139; EWL 3; MTCW 1; RGEL 2; RGSF 2

Santayana, George 1863-1952 ...... **TCLC 40**
See also AMW; CA 115; 194; DLB 54, 71, 246, 270; DLBD 13; EWL 3; MAL 5; RGAL 4; TUS

Santiago, Danny
See James, Daniel (Lewis)

Santillana, Inigo Lopez de Mendoza, Marques de 1398-1458 .... **LC 111**
See also DLB 286

Santmyer, Helen Hooven 1895-1986 .... **CLC 33; TCLC 133**
See also CA 1-4R; 118; CANR 15, 33; DLBY 1984; MTCW 1; RHW

Santoka, Taneda 1882-1940 .... **TCLC 72**

Santos, Bienvenido N(uqui) 1911-1996 .... **AAL; CLC 22; TCLC 156**
See also CA 101; 151; CANR 19, 46; CP 1; DAM MULT; DLB 312, 348; EWL; RGAL 4; SSFS 19

Santos, Miguel
See Mihura, Miguel

Sapir, Edward 1884-1939 .... **TCLC 108**
See also CA 211; DLB 92

Sapper
See McNeile, Herman Cyril

Sapphire 1950- .... **CLC 99**
See also CA 262

Sapphire, Brenda
See Sapphire

Sappho fl. 6th cent. B.C.- . **CMLC 3, 67; PC 5, 117**
See also CDWLB 1; DA3; DAM POET; DLB 176; FL 1:1; PFS 20, 31, 38; RGWL 2, 3; WLIT 8; WP

Saramago, Jose 1922-2010 ... **CLC 119, 275; HLCS 1**
See also CA 153; CANR 96, 164, 210; CWW 2; DLB 287, 332; EWL 3; LATS 1:2; NFS 27; SSFS 23

Sarduy, Severo 1937-1993 .... **CLC 6, 97; HLCS 2; TCLC 167**
See also CA 89-92; 142; CANR 58, 81; CWW 2; DLB 113; EWL 3; HW 1, 2; LAW

Sargeson, Frank 1903-1982 ... **CLC 31; SSC 99**
See also CA 25-28R; 106; CANR 38, 79; CN 1, 2, 3; EWL 3; GLL 2; RGEL 2; RGSF 2; SSFS 20

Sarmiento, Domingo Faustino 1811-1888 .... **HLCS 2; NCLC 123**
See also LAW; WLIT 1

Sarmiento, Felix Ruben Garcia
See Dario, Ruben

Saro-Wiwa, Ken(ule Beeson) 1941-1995 ...... **CLC 114; TCLC 200**
See also BW 2; CA 142; 150; CANR 60; DLB 157, 360

Saroyan, William 1908-1981 .. **CLC 1, 8, 10, 29, 34, 56; DC 28; SSC 21; TCLC 137; WLC 5**
See also AAYA 66; CA 5-8R; 103; CAD; CANR 30; CDALBS; CN 1, 2; DA; DA3; DAB; DAC; DAM DRAM, MST, NOV; DFS 17; DLB 7, 9, 86; DLBY 1981; EWL 3; LAIT 4; MAL 5; MTCW 1, 2; MTFW 2005; NFS 39; RGAL 4; RGSF 2; SATA 23; SATA-Obit 24; SSFS 14; TUS

Sarraute, Nathalie 1900-1999 .. **CLC 1, 2, 4, 8, 10, 31, 80; TCLC 145**
See also BPFB 3; CA 9-12R; 187; CANR 23, 66, 134; CWW 2; DLB 83, 321; EW 12; EWL 3; GFL 1789 to the Present; MTCW 1, 2; MTFW 2005; RGWL 2, 3

Sarton, May 1912-1995 .. **CLC 4, 14, 49, 91; PC 39; TCLC 120**
See also AMWS 8; CA 1-4R; 149; CANR 1, 34, 55, 116; CN 1, 2, 3, 4, 5, 6; CP 1, 2, 3, 4, 5, 6; DAM POET; DLB 48; DLBY 1981; EWL 3; FW; INT CANR-34; MAL 5; MTCW 1, 2; MTFW 2005; RGAL 4; SATA 36; SATA-Obit 86; TUS

Sartre, Jean-Paul 1905-1980 .... **CLC 1, 4, 7, 9, 13, 18, 24, 44, 50, 52; DC 3; SSC 32; WLC 5**
See also AAYA 62; CA 9-12R; 97-100; CANR 21; DA; DA3; DAB; DAC; DAM DRAM, MST, NOV; DFS 5, 26; DLB 72, 296, 321, 332; EW 12; EWL 3; GFL 1789 to the Present; LMFS 2; MTCW 1, 2; MTFW 2005; NFS 21; RGHL; RGSF 2; RGWL 2, 3; SSFS 9; TWA

Sassoon, Siegfried 1886-1967 . **CLC 36, 130; PC 12**
See also BRW 6; CA 104; 25-28R; CANR 36; DAB; DAM MST, NOV, POET; DLB 20, 191; DLBD 18; EWL 3; MTCW 1, 2; MTFW 2005; PAB; PFS 28; RGEL 2; TEA

Sassoon, Siegfried Lorraine
See Sassoon, Siegfried

Satterfield, Charles
See Pohl, Frederik

Satyremont
See Peret, Benjamin

Saul, John 1942- .... **CLC 46**
See also AAYA 10, 62; BEST 90:4; CA 81-84; CANR 16, 40, 81, 176, 221; CPW; DAM NOV, POP; HGG; SATA 98

Saul, John W.
See Saul, John

Saul, John Woodruff III
See Saul, John

Saunders, Caleb
See Heinlein, Robert A.

Saura (Atares), Carlos 1932-1998 ... **CLC 20**
See also CA 114; 131; CANR 79; HW 1

Sauser, Frederic Louis
See Sauser-Hall, Frederic

Sauser-Hall, Frederic 1887-1961 .... **CLC 18,
106**
See also CA 102; 93-96; CANR 36, 62;
DLB 258; EWL 3; GFL 1789 to the
Present; MTCW 1; WP

Saussure, Ferdinand de 1857-1913 ... **TCLC
49**
See also DLB 242

Savage, Catharine
See Brosman, Catharine Savage

Savage, Richard 1697(?)-1743 .... **LC 96**
See also DLB 95; RGEL 2

Savage, Thomas 1915-2003 .... **CLC 40**
See also CA 126; 132; 218; CAAS 15; CN
6, 7; INT CA-132; SATA-Obit 147;
TCWW 2

Savan, Glenn 1953-2003 .... **CLC 50**
See also CA 225

Savonarola, Girolamo 1452-1498 ..... **LC 152**
See also LMFS 1

Sax, Robert
See Johnson, Robert

Saxo Grammaticus c. 1150-c. 1222 .. **CMLC
58**

Saxton, Robert
See Johnson, Robert

Sayers, Dorothy L(eigh) 1893-1957 . **SSC 71;
TCLC 2, 15, 237**
See also BPFB 3; BRWS 3; CA 104; 119;
CANR 60; CDBLB 1914-1945; CMW 4;
DAM POP; DLB 10, 36, 77, 100; MSW;
MTCW 1, 2; MTFW 2005; RGEL 2;
SSFS 12; TEA

Sayers, Valerie 1952- .... **CLC 50, 122**
See also CA 134; CANR 61; CSW

Sayles, John 1950- .... **CLC 7, 10, 14, 198**
See also CA 57-60; CANR 41, 84; DLB 44

Sayles, John Thomas
See Sayles, John

Scalapino, Leslie 1947-2010 .... **PC 114**
See also CA 123; CANR 67, 103; CP 5, 6,
7; CWP; DLB 193

Scamander, Newt
See Rowling, J.K.

Scammell, Michael 1935- .... **CLC 34**
See also CA 156; CANR 222

Scannel, John Vernon
See Scannell, Vernon

Scannell, Vernon 1922-2007 .... **CLC 49**
See also CA 5-8R; 266; CANR 8, 24, 57,
143; CN 1, 2; CP 1, 2, 3, 4, 5, 6, 7; CWRI
5; DLB 27; SATA 59; SATA-Obit 188

Scarlett, Susan
See Streatfeild, Noel

Scarron 1847-1910 ....
See Mikszath, Kalman

Scarron, Paul 1610-1660 .... **LC 116**
See also GFL Beginnings to 1789; RGWL
2, 3

Sceve, Maurice c. 1500-c. 1564 . **LC 180; PC
111**
See also DLB 327; GFL Beginnings to 1789

Schaeffer, Susan Fromberg 1940-2011 . **CLC
6, 11, 22**
See also CA 49-52; CANR 18, 65, 160; CN
4, 5, 6, 7; DLB 28, 299; MTCW 1, 2;
MTFW 2005; SATA 22

Schama, Simon 1945- .... **CLC 150**
See also BEST 89:4; CA 105; CANR 39,
91, 168, 207

Schama, Simon Michael
See Schama, Simon

Schary, Jill
See Robinson, Jill

Schell, Jonathan 1943- .... **CLC 35**
See also CA 73-76; CANR 12, 117, 187

Schelling, Friedrich Wilhelm Joseph von
1775-1854 .... **NCLC 30**
See also DLB 90

Scherer, Jean-Marie Maurice
See Rohmer, Eric

Schevill, James (Erwin) 1920- .... **CLC 7**
See also CA 5-8R; CAAS 12; CAD; CD 5,
6; CP 1, 2, 3, 4, 5

Schiller, Friedrich von 1759-1805 .... **DC 12;
NCLC 39, 69, 166**
See also CDWLB 2; DAM DRAM; DLB
94; EW 5; RGWL 2, 3; TWA

Schisgal, Murray (Joseph) 1926- ...... **CLC 6**
See also CA 21-24R; CAD; CANR 48, 86;
CD 5, 6; MAL 5

Schlee, Ann 1934- .... **CLC 35**
See also CA 101; CANR 29, 88; SATA 44;
SATA-Brief 36

Schlegel, August Wilhelm von 1767-1845 ....
NCLC 15, 142
See also DLB 94; RGWL 2, 3

Schlegel, Friedrich 1772-1829 ..... **NCLC 45,
226**
See also DLB 90; EW 5; RGWL 2, 3; TWA

Schlegel, Johann Elias (von) 1719(?)-1749 ..
LC 5

Schleiermacher, Friedrich 1768-1834 ....
NCLC 107
See also DLB 90

Schlesinger, Arthur M., Jr. 1917-2007 . **CLC
84**
See Schlesinger, Arthur Meier
See also AITN 1; CA 1-4R; 257; CANR 1,
28, 58, 105, 187; DLB 17; INT CANR-
28; MTCW 1, 2; SATA 61; SATA-Obit
181

Schlink, Bernhard 1944- .... **CLC 174**
See also CA 163; CANR 116, 175, 217;
RGHL

Schmidt, Arno (Otto) 1914-1979 ..... **CLC 56**
See also CA 128; 109; DLB 69; EWL 3

Schmitz, Aron Hector 1861-1928 .... **SSC 25;
TCLC 2, 35, 244**
See also CA 104; 122; DLB 264; EW 8;
EWL 3; MTCW 1; RGWL 2, 3; WLIT 7

Schnackenberg, Gjertrud 1953- .... **CLC 40;
PC 45**
See also AMWS 15; CA 116; CANR 100;
CP 5, 6, 7; CWP; DLB 120, 282; PFS 13,
25

Schnackenberg, Gjertrud Cecelia
See Schnackenberg, Gjertrud

Schneider, Leonard Alfred 1925-1966 . **CLC
21**
See also CA 89-92

Schnitzler, Arthur 1862-1931 ... **DC 17; SSC
15, 61; TCLC 4**
See also CA 104; CDWLB 2; DLB 81, 118;
EW 8; EWL 3; RGSF 2; RGWL 2, 3

Schoenberg, Arnold Franz Walter
1874-1951 .... **TCLC 75**
See also CA 109; 188

Schonberg, Arnold
See Schoenberg, Arnold Franz Walter

Schopenhauer, Arthur 1788-1860 ...... **NCLC
51, 157**
See also DLB 90; EW 5

Schor, Sandra (M.) 1932(?)-1990 .... **CLC 65**
See also CA 132

Schorer, Mark 1908-1977 .... **CLC 9**
See also CA 5-8R; 73-76; CANR 7; CN 1,
2; DLB 103

Schrader, Paul (Joseph) 1946- . **CLC 26, 212**
See also CA 37-40R; CANR 41; DLB 44

Schreber, Daniel 1842-1911 .... **TCLC 123**

Schreiner, Olive 1855-1920 ..... **TCLC 9, 235**
See also AFW; BRWS 2; CA 105; 154;
DLB 18, 156, 190, 225; EWL 3; FW;
RGEL 2; TWA; WLIT 2; WWE 1

Schreiner, Olive Emilie Albertina
See Schreiner, Olive

Schulberg, Budd 1914-2009 .... **CLC 7, 48**
See also AMWS 18; BPFB 3; CA 25-28R;
289; CANR 19, 87, 178; CN 1, 2, 3, 4, 5,
6, 7; DLB 6, 26, 28; DLBY 1981, 2001;
MAL 5

Schulberg, Budd Wilson
See Schulberg, Budd

Schulberg, Seymour Wilson
See Schulberg, Budd

Schulman, Arnold
See Trumbo, Dalton

Schulz, Bruno 1892-1942 . **SSC 13; TCLC 5,
51**
See also CA 115; 123; CANR 86; CDWLB
4; DLB 215; EWL 3; MTCW 2; MTFW
2005; RGSF 2; RGWL 2, 3

Schulz, Charles M. 1922-2000 .... **CLC 12**
See also AAYA 39; CA 9-12R; 187; CANR
6, 132; INT CANR-6; MTFW 2005;
SATA 10; SATA-Obit 118

Schulz, Charles Monroe
See Schulz, Charles M.

Schumacher, E(rnst) F(riedrich)
1911-1977 .... **CLC 80**
See also CA 81-84; 73-76; CANR 34, 85

Schumann, Robert 1810-1856 .... **NCLC 143**

Schuyler, George Samuel 1895-1977 ...... **HR
1:3**
See also BW 2; CA 81-84; 73-76; CANR
42; DLB 29, 51

Schuyler, James Marcus 1923-1991 . **CLC 5,
23; PC 88**
See also CA 101; 134; CP 1, 2, 3, 4, 5;
DAM POET; DLB 5, 169; EWL 3; INT
CA-101; MAL 5; WP

Schwartz, Delmore (David) 1913-1966 . **CLC
2, 4, 10, 45, 87; PC 8; SSC 105**
See also AMWS 2; CA 17-18; 25-28R;
CANR 35; CAP 2; DLB 28, 48; EWL 3;
MAL 5; MTCW 1, 2; MTFW 2005; PAB;
RGAL 4; TUS

Schwartz, Ernst
See Ozu, Yasujiro

Schwartz, John Burnham 1965- ...... **CLC 59**
See also CA 132; CANR 116, 188

Schwartz, Lynne Sharon 1939- .... **CLC 31**
See also CA 103; CANR 44, 89, 160, 214;
DLB 218; MTCW 2; MTFW 2005

Schwartz, Muriel A.
See Eliot, T. S.

Schwartzman, Adam 1973- .... **CLC 318**
See also CA 307

Schwarz-Bart, Andre 1928-2006 ... **CLC 2, 4**
See also CA 89-92; 253; CANR 109; DLB
299; RGHL

Schwarz-Bart, Simone 1938- . **BLCS; CLC 7**
See also BW 2; CA 97-100; CANR 117;
EWL 3

Schwerner, Armand 1927-1999 .... **PC 42**
See also CA 9-12R; 179; CANR 50, 85; CP
2, 3, 4, 5, 6; DLB 165

**Schwitters, Kurt (Hermann Edward Karl
Julius)** 1887-1948 .... **TCLC 95**
See also CA 158

Schwob, Marcel (Mayer Andre) 1867-1905 .
TCLC 20
See also CA 117; 168; DLB 123; GFL 1789
to the Present

Sciascia, Leonardo 1921-1989 . **CLC 8, 9, 41**
See also CA 85-88; 130; CANR 35; DLB
177; EWL 3; MTCW 1; RGWL 2, 3

Scoppettone, Sandra 1936- .... **CLC 26**
See also AAYA 11, 65; BYA 8; CA 5-8R; CANR 41, 73, 157; GLL 1; MAICYA 2; MAICYAS 1; SATA 9, 92; WYA; YAW

Scorsese, Martin 1942- ...... **CLC 20, 89, 207**
See also AAYA 38; CA 110; 114; CANR 46, 85

Scotland, Jay
See Jakes, John

Scott, Duncan Campbell 1862-1947 .. **TCLC 6**
See also CA 104; 153; DAC; DLB 92; RGEL 2

Scott, Evelyn 1893-1963 .... **CLC 43**
See also CA 104; 112; CANR 64; DLB 9, 48; RHW

Scott, F(rancis) R(eginald) 1899-1985 . **CLC 22**
See also CA 101; 114; CANR 87; CP 1, 2, 3, 4; DLB 88; INT CA-101; RGEL 2

Scott, Frank
See Scott, F(rancis) R(eginald)

Scott, Joan
See Scott, Joan Wallach

Scott, Joan W.
See Scott, Joan Wallach

Scott, Joan Wallach 1941- .... **CLC 65**
See also CA 293

Scott, Joanna 1960- .... **CLC 50**
See also AMWS 17; CA 126; CANR 53, 92, 168, 219

Scott, Joanna Jeanne
See Scott, Joanna

Scott, Paul (Mark) 1920-1978 ..... **CLC 9, 60**
See also BRWS 1; CA 81-84; 77-80; CANR 33; CN 1, 2; DLB 14, 207, 326; EWL 3; MTCW 1; RGEL 2; RHW; WWE 1

Scott, Ridley 1937- .... **CLC 183**
See also AAYA 13, 43

Scott, Sarah 1723-1795 .... **LC 44**
See also DLB 39

Scott, Sir Walter 1771-1832 ... **NCLC 15, 69, 110, 209, 241; PC 13; SSC 32; WLC 5**
See also AAYA 22; BRW 4; BYA 2; CD-BLB 1789-1832; CLR 154; DA; DAB; DAC; DAM MST, NOV, POET; DLB 93, 107, 116, 144, 159; GL 3; HGG; LAIT 1; NFS 31; RGEL 2; RGSF 2; SSFS 10; SUFW 1; TEA; WLIT 3; YABC 2

Scotus, John Duns 1266(?)-1308 . **CMLC 59, 138**
See also DLB 115

Scribe, Augustin Eugene
See Scribe, (Augustin) Eugene

Scribe, (Augustin) Eugene 1791-1861 .... **DC 5; NCLC 16**
See also DAM DRAM; DLB 192; GFL 1789 to the Present; RGWL 2, 3

Scrum, R.
See Crumb, R.

Scudery, Georges de 1601-1667 .... **LC 75**
See also GFL Beginnings to 1789

Scudery, Madeleine de 1607-1701 . **LC 2, 58**
See also DLB 268; GFL Beginnings to 1789

Scum
See Crumb, R.

Scumbag, Little Bobby
See Crumb, R.

Seabrook, John
See Hubbard, L. Ron

Seacole, Mary Jane Grant 1805-1881 .... **NCLC 147**
See also DLB 166

Sealsfield, Charles 1793-1864 ..... **NCLC 233**
See also DLB 133, 186

Sealy, I(rwin) Allan 1951- .... **CLC 55**
See also CA 136; CN 6, 7

Search, Alexander
See Pessoa, Fernando

Seare, Nicholas
See Whitaker, Rod

Sebald, W(infried) G(eorg) 1944-2001 . **CLC 194, 296**
See also BRWS 8; CA 159; 202; CANR 98; MTFW 2005; RGHL

Sebastian, Lee
See Silverberg, Robert

Sebastian Owl
See Thompson, Hunter S.

Sebestyen, Igen
See Sebestyen, Ouida

Sebestyen, Ouida 1924- .... **CLC 30**
See also AAYA 8; BYA 7; CA 107; CANR 40, 114; CLR 17; JRDA; MAICYA 1, 2; SAAS 10; SATA 39, 140; WYA; YAW

Sebold, Alice 1963- .... **CLC 193**
See also AAYA 56; CA 203; CANR 181; LNFS 1; MTFW 2005

Second Duke of Buckingham
See Villiers, George

Secundus, H. Scriblerus
See Fielding, Henry

Sedges, John
See Buck, Pearl S.

Sedgwick, Catharine Maria 1789-1867 .... **NCLC 19, 98, 238**
See also DLB 1, 74, 183, 239, 243, 254; FL 1:3; RGAL 4

Sedley, Sir Charles 1639-1701 .... **LC 168**
See also BRW 2; DLB 131; RGEL 2

Sedulius Scottus 9th cent. -c. 874 . **CMLC 86**

Seebohm, Victoria
See Glendinning, Victoria

Seelye, John (Douglas) 1931- .... **CLC 7**
See also CA 97-100; CANR 70; INT CA-97-100; TCWW 1, 2

Seferiades, Giorgos Stylianou
See Seferis, George

Seferis, George 1900-1971 .... **CLC 5, 11; TCLC 213**
See also CA 5-8R; 33-36R; CANR 5, 36; DLB 332; EW 12; EWL 3; MTCW 1; RGWL 2, 3

Segal, Erich 1937-2010 .... **CLC 3, 10**
See also BEST 89:1; BPFB 3; CA 25-28R; CANR 20, 36, 65, 113; CPW; DAM POP; DLBY 1986; INT CANR-20; MTCW 1

Segal, Erich Wolf
See Segal, Erich

Seger, Bob 1945- .... **CLC 35**

Seghers
See Radvanyi, Netty

Seghers, Anna
See Radvanyi, Netty

Seidel, Frederick 1936- .... **CLC 18**
See also CA 13-16R; CANR 8, 99, 180; CP 1, 2, 3, 4, 5, 6, 7; DLBY 1984

Seidel, Frederick Lewis
See Seidel, Frederick

Seifert, Jaroslav 1901-1986 . **CLC 34, 44, 93; PC 47**
See also CA 127; CDWLB 4; DLB 215, 332; EWL 3; MTCW 1, 2

Sei Shonagon c. 966-1017(?) .... **CMLC 6, 89**

Sejour, Victor 1817-1874 .... **DC 10**
See also DLB 50

Sejour Marcou et Ferrand, Juan Victor
See Sejour, Victor

Selby, Hubert, Jr. 1928-2004 ... **CLC 1, 2, 4, 8; SSC 20**
See also CA 13-16R; 226; CANR 33, 85; CN 1, 2, 3, 4, 5, 6, 7; DLB 2, 227; MAL 5

Self, Will 1961- .... **CLC 282**
See also BRWS 5; CA 143; CANR 83, 126, 171, 201; CN 6, 7; DLB 207

Self, William
See Self, Will

Self, William Woodward
See Self, Will

Selzer, Richard 1928- .... **CLC 74**
See also CA 65-68; CANR 14, 106, 204

Sembene, Ousmane
See Ousmane, Sembene

Senancour, Etienne Pivert de 1770-1846 ..... **NCLC 16**
See also DLB 119; GFL 1789 to the Present

Sender, Ramon (Jose) 1902-1982 ..... **CLC 8; HLC 2; TCLC 136**
See also CA 5-8R; 105; CANR 8; DAM MULT; DLB 322; EWL 3; HW 1; MTCW 1; RGWL 2, 3

Seneca, Lucius Annaeus c. 4B.C.-c. 65 .... **CMLC 6, 107; DC 5**
See also AW 2; CDWLB 1; DAM DRAM; DLB 211; RGWL 2, 3; TWA; WLIT 8

Seneca the Younger
See Seneca, Lucius Annaeus

Senghor, Leopold Sedar 1906-2001 ...... **BLC 1:3; CLC 54, 130; PC 25**
See also AFW; BW 2; CA 116; 125; 203; CANR 47, 74, 134; CWW 2; DAM MULT, POET; DNFS 2; EWL 3; GFL 1789 to the Present; MTCW 1, 2; MTFW 2005; PFS 36; TWA

Senior, Olive (Marjorie) 1941- .... **SSC 78**
See also BW 3; CA 154; CANR 86, 126; CN 6; CP 6, 7; CWP; DLB 157; EWL 3; RGSF 2

Senna, Danzy 1970- .... **CLC 119**
See also CA 169; CANR 130, 184

Sepheriades, Georgios
See Seferis, George

Serling, (Edward) Rod(man) 1924-1975 ...... **CLC 30**
See also AAYA 14; AITN 1; CA 162; 57-60; DLB 26; SFW 4

Serna, Ramon Gomez de la
See Gomez de la Serna, Ramon

Serote, Mongane Wally 1944- .... **PC 113**
See also BW 2, 3; CA 142; CANR 81; CP 5, 6, 7; DLB 125, 225

Serpieres
See Guillevic, (Eugene)

Service, Robert
See Service, Robert W.

Service, Robert W. 1874(?)-1958 ...... **PC 70; TCLC 15; WLC 5**
See also BYA 4; CA 115; 140; CANR 84; DA; DAB; DAC; DAM MST, POET; DLB 92; PFS 10; RGEL 2; SATA 20

Service, Robert William
See Service, Robert W.

Servius c. 370-c. 431 .... **CMLC 120**

Seth, Vikram 1952- .... **CLC 43, 90, 277; PC 118**
See also BRWS 10; CA 121; 127; CANR 50, 74, 131; CN 6, 7; CP 5, 6, 7; DA3; DAM MULT; DLB 120, 271, 282, 323; EWL 3; INT CA-127; MTCW 2; MTFW 2005; WWE 1

Setien, Miguel Delibes
See Delibes Setien, Miguel

Seton, Cynthia Propper 1926-1982 . **CLC 27**
See also CA 5-8R; 108; CANR 7

Seton, Ernest (Evan) Thompson 1860-1946 .... **TCLC 31**
See also ANW; BYA 3; CA 109; 204; CLR 59; DLB 92; DLBD 13; JRDA; SATA 18

Seton-Thompson, Ernest
See Seton, Ernest (Evan) Thompson

Simmons, Richard
See Simmons, Dan
Simms, William Gilmore 1806-1870 . **NCLC 3, 241**
See also DLB 3, 30, 59, 73, 248, 254; RGAL 4
Simon, Carly 1945- .... **CLC 26**
See also CA 105
Simon, Claude 1913-2005 . **CLC 4, 9, 15, 39**
See also CA 89-92; 241; CANR 33, 117; CWW 2; DAM NOV; DLB 83, 332; EW 13; EWL 3; GFL 1789 to the Present; MTCW 1
Simon, Claude Eugene Henri
See Simon, Claude
Simon, Claude Henri Eugene
See Simon, Claude
Simon, Marvin Neil
See Simon, Neil
Simon, Myles
See Follett, Ken
Simon, Neil 1927- ...... **CLC 6, 11, 31, 39, 70, 233; DC 14**
See also AAYA 32; AITN 1; AMWS 4; CA 21-24R; CAD; CANR 26, 54, 87, 126; CD 5, 6; DA3; DAM DRAM; DFS 2, 6, 12, 18, 24, 27; DLB 7, 266; LAIT 4; MAL 5; MTCW 1, 2; MTFW 2005; RGAL 4; TUS
Simon, Paul 1941(?)- .... **CLC 17**
See also CA 116; 153; CANR 152
Simon, Paul Frederick
See Simon, Paul
Simonon, Paul 1956(?)- .... **CLC 30**
Simonson, Helen 1963- .... **CLC 318**
See also CA 307
Simonson, Rick CLC 70
Simpson, Harriette
See Arnow, Harriette (Louisa) Simpson
Simpson, Louis 1923- .. **CLC 4, 7, 9, 32, 149**
See also AMWS 9; CA 1-4R; CAAS 4; CANR 1, 61, 140; CP 1, 2, 3, 4, 5, 6, 7; DAM POET; DLB 5; MAL 5; MTCW 1, 2; MTFW 2005; PFS 7, 11, 14; RGAL 4
Simpson, Mona 1957- .... **CLC 44, 146**
See also CA 122; 135; CANR 68, 103, 227; CN 6, 7; EWL 3
Simpson, Mona Elizabeth
See Simpson, Mona
Simpson, N.F. 1919-2011 .... **CLC 29**
See also CA 13-16R; CBD; DLB 13; RGEL 2
Simpson, Norman Frederick
See Simpson, N.F.
Sinclair, Andrew (Annandale) 1935- .... **CLC 2, 14**
See also CA 9-12R; CAAS 5; CANR 14, 38, 91; CN 1, 2, 3, 4, 5, 6, 7; DLB 14; FANT; MTCW 1
Sinclair, Emil
See Hesse, Hermann
Sinclair, Iain 1943- .... **CLC 76**
See also BRWS 14; CA 132; CANR 81, 157; CP 5, 6, 7; HGG
Sinclair, Iain MacGregor
See Sinclair, Iain
Sinclair, Irene
See Griffith, D.W.
Sinclair, Julian
See Sinclair, May
Sinclair, Mary Amelia St. Clair (?)- ....
See Sinclair, May
Sinclair, May 1865-1946 .... **TCLC 3, 11**
See also CA 104; 166; DLB 36, 135; EWL 3; HGG; RGEL 2; RHW; SUFW
Sinclair, Roy
See Griffith, D.W.

Sinclair, Upton 1878-1968 .... **CLC 1, 11, 15, 63; TCLC 160; WLC 5**
See also AAYA 63; AMWS 5; BPFB 3; BYA 2; CA 5-8R; 25-28R; CANR 7; CDALB 1929-1941; DA; DA3; DAB; DAC; DAM MST, NOV; DLB 9; EWL 3; INT CANR-7; LAIT 3; MAL 5; MTCW 1, 2; MTFW 2005; NFS 6; RGAL 4; SATA 9; TUS; YAW
Sinclair, Upton Beall
See Sinclair, Upton
Singe, (Edmund) J(ohn) M(illington) 1871-1909 .... **WLC**
Singer, Isaac
See Singer, Isaac Bashevis
Singer, Isaac Bashevis 1904-1991 . **CLC 1, 3, 6, 9, 11, 15, 23, 38, 69, 111; SSC 3, 53, 80, 154; WLC 5**
See also AAYA 32; AITN 1, 2; AMW; AMWR 2; BPFB 3; BYA 1, 4; CA 1-4R; 134; CANR 1, 39, 106; CDALB 1941-1968; CLR 1; CN 1, 2, 3, 4; CWRI 5; DA; DA3; DAB; DAC; DAM MST, NOV; DLB 6, 28, 52, 278, 332, 333; DLBY 1991; EWL 3; EXPS; HGG; JRDA; LAIT 3; MAICYA 1, 2; MAL 5; MTCW 1, 2; MTFW 2005; RGAL 4; RGHL; RGSF 2; SATA 3, 27; SATA-Obit 68; SSFS 2, 12, 16, 27, 30; TUS; TWA
Singer, Israel Joshua 1893-1944 ... **TCLC 33**
See also CA 169; DLB 333; EWL 3
Singh, Khushwant 1915- .... **CLC 11**
See also CA 9-12R; CAAS 9; CANR 6, 84; CN 1, 2, 3, 4, 5, 6, 7; DLB 323; EWL 3; RGEL 2
Singleton, Ann
See Benedict, Ruth
Singleton, John 1968(?)- .... **CLC 156**
See also AAYA 50; BW 2, 3; CA 138; CANR 67, 82; DAM MULT
Siniavskii, Andrei
See Sinyavsky, Andrei (Donatevich)
Sinibaldi, Fosco
See Kacew, Romain
Sinjohn, John
See Galsworthy, John
Sinyavsky, Andrei (Donatevich) 1925-1997 . **CLC 8**
See also CA 85-88; 159; CWW 2; EWL 3; RGSF 2
Sinyavsky, Andrey Donatovich
See Sinyavsky, Andrei (Donatevich)
Sirin, V.
See Nabokov, Vladimir
Sissman, L(ouis) E(dward) 1928-1976 . **CLC 9, 18**
See also CA 21-24R; 65-68; CANR 13; CP 2; DLB 5
Sisson, C(harles) H(ubert) 1914-2003 .. **CLC 8**
See also BRWS 11; CA 1-4R; 220; CAAS 3; CANR 3, 48, 84; CP 1, 2, 3, 4, 5, 6, 7; DLB 27
Sitting Bull 1831(?)-1890 .... **NNAL**
See also DA3; DAM MULT
Sitwell, Dame Edith 1887-1964 .... **CLC 2, 9, 67; PC 3**
See also BRW 7; CA 9-12R; CANR 35; CDBLB 1945-1960; DAM POET; DLB 20; EWL 3; MTCW 1, 2; MTFW 2005; RGEL 2; TEA
Siwaarmill, H. P.
See Sharp, William
Sjoewall, Maj 1935- .... **CLC 7**
See also BPFB 3; CA 65-68; CANR 73; CMW 4; MSW
Sjowall, Maj
See Sjoewall, Maj
Skelton, John 1460(?)-1529 ... **LC 71; PC 25**
See also BRW 1; DLB 136; RGEL 2

Skelton, Robin 1925-1997 .... **CLC 13**
See also AITN 2; CA 5-8R; 160; CAAS 5; CANR 28, 89; CCA 1; CP 1, 2, 3, 4, 5, 6; DLB 27, 53
Skolimowski, Jerzy 1938- .... **CLC 20**
See also CA 128
Skram, Amalie (Bertha) 1846-1905 ... **TCLC 25**
See also CA 165; DLB 354
Skvorecky, Josef 1924- . **CLC 15, 39, 69, 152**
See also CA 61-64; CAAS 1; CANR 10, 34, 63, 108; CDWLB 4; CWW 2; DA3; DAC; DAM NOV; DLB 232; EWL 3; MTCW 1, 2; MTFW 2005
Skvorecky, Josef Vaclav
See Skvorecky, Josef
Slade, Bernard 1930- ....
See Newbound, Bernard Slade
Slaughter, Carolyn 1946- .... **CLC 56**
See also CA 85-88; CANR 85, 169; CN 5, 6, 7
Slaughter, Frank G(ill) 1908-2001 .. **CLC 29**
See also AITN 2; CA 5-8R; 197; CANR 5, 85; INT CANR-5; RHW
Slavitt, David R. 1935- .... **CLC 5, 14**
See also CA 21-24R; CAAS 3; CANR 41, 83, 166, 219; CN 1, 2; CP 1, 2, 3, 4, 5, 6, 7; DLB 5, 6
Slavitt, David Rytman
See Slavitt, David R.
Slesinger, Tess 1905-1945 .... **TCLC 10**
See also CA 107; 199; DLB 102
Slessor, Kenneth 1901-1971 .... **CLC 14**
See also CA 102; 89-92; DLB 260; RGEL 2
Slowacki, Juliusz 1809-1849 .... **NCLC 15**
See also RGWL 3
Small, David 1945- .... **CLC 299**
See also CLR 53; MAICYA 2; SATA 50, 95, 126, 183, 216; SATA-Brief 46
Smart, Christopher 1722-1771 ... **LC 3, 134; PC 13**
See also DAM POET; DLB 109; RGEL 2
Smart, Elizabeth 1913-1986 .... **CLC 54; TCLC 231**
See also CA 81-84; 118; CN 4; DLB 88
Smiley, Jane 1949- ..... **CLC 53, 76, 144, 236**
See also AAYA 66; AMWS 6; BPFB 3; CA 104; CANR 30, 50, 74, 96, 158, 196, 231; CN 6, 7; CPW 1; DA3; DAM POP; DLB 227, 234; EWL 3; INT CANR-30; MAL 5; MTFW 2005; NFS 32; SSFS 19
Smiley, Jane Graves
See Smiley, Jane
Smith, A(rthur) J(ames) M(arshall) 1902-1980 .... **CLC 15**
See also CA 1-4R; 102; CANR 4; CP 1, 2, 3; DAC; DLB 88; RGEL 2
Smith, Adam 1723(?)-1790 .... **LC 36**
See also DLB 104, 252, 336; RGEL 2
Smith, Alexander 1829-1867 .... **NCLC 59**
See also DLB 32, 55
Smith, Alexander McCall 1948- .... **CLC 268**
See also CA 215; CANR 154, 196; SATA 73, 179
Smith, Anna Deavere 1950- .... **CLC 86, 241**
See also CA 133; CANR 103; CD 5, 6; DFS 2, 22; DLB 341
Smith, Betty (Wehner) 1904-1972 ... **CLC 19**
See also AAYA 72; BPFB 3; BYA 3; CA 5-8R; 33-36R; DLBY 1982; LAIT 3; NFS 31; RGAL 4; SATA 6
Smith, Charlotte (Turner) 1749-1806 ....
NCLC 23, 115; PC 104
See also DLB 39, 109; RGEL 2; TEA
Smith, Clark Ashton 1893-1961 ...... **CLC 43**
See also AAYA 76; CA 143; CANR 81; FANT; HGG; MTCW 2; SCFW 1, 2; SFW 4; SUFW

Smith, Dave
    See Smith, David (Jeddie)
Smith, David (Jeddie) 1942- ...... **CLC 22, 42**
    See also CA 49-52; CAAS 7; CANR 1, 59,
    120; CP 3, 4, 5, 6, 7; CSW; DAM POET;
    DLB 5
Smith, Iain Crichton 1928-1998 ...... **CLC 64**
    See also BRWS 9; CA 21-24R; 171; CN 1,
    2, 3, 4, 5, 6; CP 1, 2, 3, 4, 5, 6; DLB 40,
    139, 319, 352; RGSF 2
Smith, John 1580(?)-1631 .... **LC 9**
    See also DLB 24, 30; TUS
Smith, Johnston
    See Crane, Stephen
Smith, Joseph, Jr. 1805-1844 .... **NCLC 53**
Smith, Kevin 1970- .... **CLC 223**
    See also AAYA 37; CA 166; CANR 131,
    201
Smith, Lee 1944- ...... **CLC 25, 73, 258; SSC
142**
    See also CA 114; 119; CANR 46, 118, 173,
    225; CN 7; CSW; DLB 143; DLBY 1983;
    EWL 3; INT CA-119; RGAL 4
Smith, Martin
    See Smith, Martin Cruz
Smith, Martin Cruz 1942- . **CLC 25; NNAL**
    See Smith, Martin Cruz
    See also BEST 89:4; BPFB 3; CA 85-88;
    CANR 6, 23, 43, 65, 119, 184; CMW 4;
    CPW; DAM MULT, POP; HGG; INT
    CANR-23; MTCW 2; MTFW 2005; RGAL
    4
Smith, Patti 1946- .... **CLC 12, 318**
    See also CA 93-96; CANR 63, 168
Smith, Pauline (Urmson) 1882-1959 . **TCLC
25**
    See also DLB 225; EWL 3
Smith, R. Alexander McCall
    See Smith, Alexander McCall
Smith, Rosamond
    See Oates, Joyce Carol
Smith, Seba 1792-1868 .... **NCLC 187**
    See also DLB 1, 11, 243
Smith, Sheila Kaye
    See Kaye-Smith, Sheila
Smith, Stevie 1902-1971 ... **CLC 3, 8, 25, 44;
PC 12**
    See also BRWR 3; BRWS 2; CA 17-18; 29-
    32R; CANR 35; CAP 2; CP 1; DAM
    POET; DLB 20; EWL 3; MTCW 1, 2;
    PAB; PFS 3; RGEL 2; TEA
Smith, Wilbur 1933- .... **CLC 33**
    See also CA 13-16R; CANR 7, 46, 66, 134,
    180; CPW; MTCW 1, 2; MTFW 2005
Smith, Wilbur Addison
    See Smith, Wilbur
Smith, William Jay 1918- .... **CLC 6**
    See also AMWS 13; CA 5-8R; CANR 44,
    106, 211; CP 1, 2, 3, 4, 5, 6, 7; CSW;
    CWRI 5; DLB 5; MAICYA 1, 2; SAAS
    22; SATA 2, 68, 154; SATA-Essay 154;
    TCLE 1:2
Smith, Woodrow Wilson
    See Kuttner, Henry
Smith, Zadie 1975- .... **CLC 158, 306**
    See also AAYA 50; CA 193; CANR 204;
    DLB 347; MTFW 2005; NFS 40
Smolenskin, Peretz 1842-1885 ...... **NCLC 30**
Smollett, Tobias (George) 1721-1771 .. **LC 2,
46, 188**
    See also BRW 3; CDBLB 1660-1789; DLB
    39, 104; RGEL 2; TEA
Snodgrass, Quentin Curtius
    See Twain, Mark
Snodgrass, Thomas Jefferson
    See Twain, Mark

Snodgrass, W. D. 1926-2009 .. **CLC 2, 6, 10,
18, 68; PC 74**
    See also AMWS 6; CA 1-4R; 282; CANR
    6, 36, 65, 85, 185; CP 1, 2, 3, 4, 5, 6, 7;
    DAM POET; DLB 5; MAL 5; MTCW 1,
    2; MTFW 2005; PFS 29; RGAL 4; TCLE
    1:2
Snodgrass, W. de Witt
    See Snodgrass, W. D.
Snodgrass, William de Witt
    See Snodgrass, W. D.
Snodgrass, William De Witt
    See Snodgrass, W. D.
Snorri Sturluson 1179-1241 . **CMLC 56, 134**
    See also RGWL 2, 3
Snow, C(harles) P(ercy) 1905-1980 .. **CLC 1,
4, 6, 9, 13, 19**
    See also BRW 7; CA 5-8R; 101; CANR 28;
    CDBLB 1945-1960; CN 1, 2; DAM NOV;
    DLB 15, 77; DLBD 17; EWL 3; MTCW
    1, 2; MTFW 2005; RGEL 2; TEA
Snow, Frances Compton
    See Adams, Henry
Snyder, Gary 1930- . **CLC 1, 2, 5, 9, 32, 120;
PC 21**
    See also AAYA 72; AMWS 8; ANW; BG
    1:3; CA 17-20R; CANR 30, 60, 125; CP
    1, 2, 3, 4, 5, 6, 7; DA3; DAM POET; DLB
    5, 16, 165, 212, 237, 275, 342; EWL 3;
    MAL 5; MTCW 2; MTFW 2005; PFS 9,
    19; RGAL 4; WP
Snyder, Gary Sherman
    See Snyder, Gary
Snyder, Zilpha Keatley 1927- .... **CLC 17**
    See also AAYA 15; BYA 1; CA 9-12R, 252;
    CAAE 252; CANR 38, 202; CLR 31, 121;
    JRDA; MAICYA 1, 2; SAAS 2; SATA 1,
    28, 75, 110, 163, 226; SATA-Essay 112,
    163; YAW
Soares, Bernardo
    See Pessoa, Fernando
Sobh, A.
    See Shamlu, Ahmad
Sobh, Alef
    See Shamlu, Ahmad
Sobol, Joshua 1939- .... **CLC 60**
    See also CA 200; CWW 2; RGHL
Sobol, Yehoshua 1939- ....
    See Sobol, Joshua
Socrates 470B.C.-399B.C. .... **CMLC 27**
Soderberg, Hjalmar 1869-1941 .... **TCLC 39**
    See also DLB 259; EWL 3; RGSF 2
Soderbergh, Steven 1963- .... **CLC 154**
    See also AAYA 43; CA 243
Soderbergh, Steven Andrew
    See Soderbergh, Steven
Sodergran, Edith 1892-1923 .... **TCLC 31**
    See also CA 202; DLB 259; EW 11; EWL
    3; RGWL 2, 3
Soedergran, Edith Irene
    See Sodergran, Edith
Softly, Edgar
    See Lovecraft, H. P.
Softly, Edward
    See Lovecraft, H. P.
Sokolov, Alexander V. 1943- .... **CLC 59**
    See also CA 73-76; CWW 2; DLB 285;
    EWL 3; RGWL 2, 3
Sokolov, Alexander Vsevolodovich
    See Sokolov, Alexander V.
Sokolov, Raymond 1941- .... **CLC 7**
    See also CA 85-88
Sokolov, Sasha
    See Sokolov, Alexander V.
Soli, Tatjana CLC 318
    See also CA 307
Solo, Jay
    See Ellison, Harlan

Sologub, Fedor
    See Teternikov, Fyodor Kuzmich
Sologub, Feodor
    See Teternikov, Fyodor Kuzmich
Sologub, Fyodor
    See Teternikov, Fyodor Kuzmich
Solomons, Ikey Esquir
    See Thackeray, William Makepeace
Solomos, Dionysios 1798-1857 ...... **NCLC 15**
Solwoska, Mara
    See French, Marilyn
Solzhenitsyn, Aleksandr 1918-2008 . **CLC 1,
2, 4, 7, 9, 10, 18, 26, 34, 78, 134, 235;
SSC 32, 105; WLC 5**
    See also AAYA 49; AITN 1; BPFB 3; CA
    69-72; CANR 40, 65, 116; CWW 2; DA;
    DA3; DAB; DAC; DAM MST; NOV;
    DLB 302, 332; EW 13; EWL 3; EXPS;
    LAIT 4; MTCW 1, 2; MTFW 2005; NFS
    6; PFS 38; RGSF 2; RGWL 2, 3; SSFS 9;
    TWA
Solzhenitsyn, Aleksandr I.
    See Solzhenitsyn, Aleksandr
Solzhenitsyn, Aleksandr Isayevich
    See Solzhenitsyn, Aleksandr
Somers, Jane
    See Lessing, Doris
Somerville, Edith Oenone 1858-1949 .... **SSC
56; TCLC 51**
    See also CA 196; DLB 135; RGEL 2; RGSF
    2
Somerville & Ross
    See Martin, Violet Florence; Somerville,
    Edith Oenone
Sommer, Scott 1951- .... **CLC 25**
    See also CA 106
Sommers, Christina Hoff 1950- .... **CLC 197**
    See also CA 153; CANR 95
Sondheim, Stephen 1930- . **CLC 30, 39, 147;
DC 22**
    See also AAYA 11, 66; CA 103; CANR 47,
    67, 125; DAM DRAM; DFS 25, 27, 28;
    LAIT 4
Sondheim, Stephen Joshua
    See Sondheim, Stephen
Sone, Monica 1919- .... **AAL**
    See also DLB 312
Song, Cathy 1955- .... **AAL; PC 21**
    See also CA 154; CANR 118; CWP; DLB
    169, 312; EXPP; FW; PFS 5
Sontag, Susan 1933-2004 . **CLC 1, 2, 10, 13,
31, 105, 195, 277**
    See also AMWS 3; CA 17-20R; 234; CANR
    25, 51, 74, 97, 184; CN 1, 2, 3, 4, 5, 6, 7;
    CPW; DA3; DAM POP; DLB 2, 67; EWL
    3; MAL 5; MBL; MTCW 1, 2; MTFW
    2005; RGAL 4; RHW; SSFS 10
Sophocles 496(?)B.C.-406(?)B.C. ... **CMLC 2,
47, 51, 86; DC 1; WLCS**
    See also AW 1; CDWLB 1; DA; DA3;
    DAB; DAC; DAM DRAM, MST; DFS 1,
    4, 8, 24; DLB 176; LAIT 1; LATS 1:1;
    LMFS 1; RGWL 2, 3; TWA; WLIT 8
Sordello 1189-1269 .... **CMLC 15**
Sorel, Georges 1847-1922 .... **TCLC 91**
    See also CA 118; 188
Sorel, Julia
    See Drexler, Rosalyn
Sorokin, Vladimir CLC 59
    See also CA 258; DLB 285
Sorokin, Vladimir Georgievich
    See Sorokin, Vladimir
Sorrentino, Gilbert 1929-2006 ..... **CLC 3, 7,
14, 22, 40, 247**
    See also AMWS 21; CA 77-80; 250; CANR
    14, 33, 115, 157; CN 3, 4, 5, 6, 7; CP 1,
    2, 3, 4, 5, 6, 7; DLB 5, 173; DLBY 1980;
    INT CANR-14

Tan, Amy Ruth
See Tan, Amy

Tandem, Carl Felix
See Spitteler, Carl

Tandem, Felix
See Spitteler, Carl

Tania B.
See Blixen, Karen

Tanizaki, Jun'ichiro 1886-1965 .. **CLC 8, 14, 28; SSC 21**
See also CA 93-96; 25-28R; DLB 180; EWL 3; MJW; MTCW 2; MTFW 2005; RGSF 2; RGWL 2

Tanizaki Jun'ichiro
See Tanizaki, Jun'ichiro

Tannen, Deborah 1945- .... **CLC 206**
See also CA 118; CANR 95

Tannen, Deborah Frances
See Tannen, Deborah

Tanner, William
See Amis, Kingsley

Tante, Dilly
See Kunitz, Stanley

Tao Lao
See Storni, Alfonsina

Tapahonso, Luci 1953- .... **NNAL; PC 65**
See also CA 145; CANR 72, 127, 214; DLB 175

Tarantino, Quentin 1963- ...... **CLC 125, 230**
See also AAYA 58; CA 171; CANR 125

Tarantino, Quentin Jerome
See Tarantino, Quentin

Tarassoff, Lev
See Troyat, Henri

Tarbell, Ida 1857-1944 .... **TCLC 40**
See also CA 122; 181; DLB 47

Tarbell, Ida Minerva
See Tarbell, Ida

Tarchetti, Ugo 1839(?)-1869 .... **SSC 119**

Tardieu d'Esclavelles,
Louise-Florence-Petronille
See Epinay, Louise d'

Tarkington, (Newton) Booth 1869-1946 .... **TCLC 9**
See also BPFB 3; BYA 3; CA 110; 143; CWRI 5; DLB 9, 102; MAL 5; MTCW 2; NFS 34; RGAL 4; SATA 17

Tarkovskii, Andrei Arsen'evich
See Tarkovsky, Andrei (Arsenyevich)

Tarkovsky, Andrei (Arsenyevich)
1932-1986 .... **CLC 75**
See also CA 127

Tartt, Donna 1964(?)- .... **CLC 76**
See also AAYA 56; CA 142; CANR 135; LNFS 2; MTFW 2005

Tasso, Torquato 1544-1595 .... **LC 5, 94**
See also EFS 1:2, 2:1; EW 2; RGWL 2, 3; WLIT 7

Tate, (John Orley) Allen 1899-1979 . **CLC 2, 4, 6, 9, 11, 14, 24; PC 50**
See also AMW; CA 5-8R; 85-88; CANR 32, 108; CN 1, 2; CP 1, 2; DLB 4, 45, 63; DLBD 17; EWL 3; MAL 5; MTCW 1, 2; MTFW 2005; RGAL 4; RHW

Tate, Ellalice
See Hibbert, Eleanor Alice Burford

Tate, James 1943- .... **CLC 2, 6, 25**
See also CA 21-24R; CANR 29, 57, 114, 224; CP 1, 2, 3, 4, 5, 6, 7; DLB 5, 169; EWL 3; PFS 10, 15; RGAL 4; WP

Tate, James Vincent
See Tate, James

Tate, Nahum 1652(?)-1715 .... **LC 109**
See also DLB 80; RGEL 2

Tauler, Johannes c. 1300-1361 ..... **CMLC 37**
See also DLB 179; LMFS 1

Tavel, Ronald 1936-2009 .... **CLC 6**
See also CA 21-24R; 284; CAD; CANR 33; CD 5, 6

Taviani, Paolo 1931- .... **CLC 70**
See also CA 153

Tawada, Yoko 1960- .... **CLC 310**
See also CA 296

Taylor, Bayard 1825-1878 .... **NCLC 89**
See also DLB 3, 189, 250, 254; RGAL 4

Taylor, C(ecil) P(hilip) 1929-1981 ... **CLC 27**
See also CA 25-28R; 105; CANR 47; CBD

Taylor, Charles 1931- .... **CLC 317**
See also CA 13-16R; CANR 11, 27, 164, 200

Taylor, Charles Margrave
See Taylor, Charles

Taylor, Edward 1642(?)-1729 .... **LC 11, 163; PC 63**
See also AMW; DA; DAB; DAC; DAM MST, POET; DLB 24; EXPP; PFS 31; RGAL 4; TUS

Taylor, Eleanor Ross 1920- .... **CLC 5**
See also CA 81-84; CANR 70

Taylor, Elizabeth 1912-1975 .. **CLC 2, 4, 29; SSC 100**
See also CA 13-16R; CANR 9, 70; CN 1, 2; DLB 139; MTCW 1; RGEL 2; SATA 13

Taylor, Frederick Winslow 1856-1915 .... **TCLC 76**
See also CA 188

Taylor, Henry 1942- .... **CLC 44**
See also CA 33-36R; CAAS 7; CANR 31, 178; CP 6, 7; DLB 5; PFS 10

Taylor, Henry Splawn
See Taylor, Henry

Taylor, Kamala
See Markandaya, Kamala

Taylor, Mildred D. 1943- .... **CLC 21**
See also AAYA 10, 47; BW 1; BYA 3, 8; CA 85-88; CANR 25, 115, 136; CLR 9, 59, 90, 144; CSW; DLB 52; JRDA; LAIT 3; MAICYA 1, 2; MTFW 2005; SAAS 5; SATA 135; WYA; YAW

Taylor, Peter (Hillsman) 1917-1994 . **CLC 1, 4, 18, 37, 44, 50, 71; SSC 10, 84**
See also AMWS 5; BPFB 3; CA 13-16R; 147; CANR 9, 50; CN 1, 2, 3, 4, 5; CSW; DLB 218, 278; DLBY 1981, 1994; EWL 3; EXPS; INT CANR-9; MAL 5; MTCW 1, 2; MTFW 2005; RGSF 2; SSFS 9; TUS

Taylor, Robert Lewis 1912-1998 ..... **CLC 14**
See also CA 1-4R; 170; CANR 3, 64; CN 1, 2; SATA 10; TCWW 1, 2

Tchekhov, Anton
See Chekhov, Anton

Tchicaya, Gerald Felix 1931-1988 . **CLC 101**
See also CA 129; 125; CANR 81; EWL 3

Tchicaya U Tam'si
See Tchicaya, Gerald Felix

Teasdale, Sara 1884-1933 ... **PC 31; TCLC 4**
See also CA 104; 163; DLB 45; GLL 1; PFS 14; RGAL 4; SATA 32; TUS

Tecumseh 1768-1813 .... **NNAL**
See also DAM MULT

Tegner, Esaias 1782-1846 .... **NCLC 2**

Teilhard de Chardin, (Marie Joseph) Pierre
1881-1955 .... **TCLC 9**
See also CA 105; 210; GFL 1789 to the Present

Temple, Ann
See Mortimer, Penelope (Ruth)

Tennant, Emma 1937- .... **CLC 13, 52**
See also BRWS 9; CA 65-68; CAAS 9; CANR 10, 38, 59, 88, 177; CN 3, 4, 5, 6, 7; DLB 14; EWL 3; SFW 4

Tenneshaw, S.M.
See Silverberg, Robert

Tenney, Tabitha Gilman 1762-1837 .. **NCLC 122, 248**
See also DLB 37, 200

Tennyson, Alfred 1809-1892 .. **NCLC 30, 65, 115, 202; PC 6, 101; WLC 6**
See also AAYA 50; BRW 4; BRWR 3; CD-BLB 1832-1890; DA; DA3; DAB; DAC; DAM MST, POET; DLB 32; EXPP; PAB; PFS 1, 2, 4, 11, 15, 19; RGEL 2; TEA; WLIT 4; WP

Teran, Lisa St. Aubin de
See St. Aubin de Teran, Lisa

Terence c. 184B.C.-c. 159B.C. ..... **CMLC 14, 132; DC 7**
See also AW 1; CDWLB 1; DLB 211; RGWL 2, 3; TWA; WLIT 8

Teresa de Jesus, St. 1515-1582 ... **LC 18, 149**

Teresa of Avila, St.
See Teresa de Jesus, St.

Terkel, Louis
See Terkel, Studs

Terkel, Studs 1912-2008 .... **CLC 38**
See also AAYA 32; AITN 1; CA 57-60; 278; CANR 18, 45, 67, 132, 195; DA3; MTCW 1, 2; MTFW 2005; TUS

Terkel, Studs Louis
See Terkel, Studs

Terry, C. V.
See Slaughter, Frank G(ill)

Terry, Megan 1932- .... **CLC 19; DC 13**
See also CA 77-80; CABS 3; CAD; CANR 43; CD 5, 6; CWD; DFS 18; DLB 7, 249; GLL 2

Tertullian c. 155-c. 245 .... **CMLC 29**

Tertz, Abram
See Sinyavsky, Andrei (Donatevich)

Tesich, Steve 1943(?)-1996 .... **CLC 40, 69**
See also CA 105; 152; CAD; DLBY 1983

Tesla, Nikola 1856-1943 .... **TCLC 88**
See also CA 157

Teternikov, Fyodor Kuzmich 1863-1927 ...... **TCLC 9, 259**
See also CA 104; DLB 295; EWL 3

Tevis, Walter 1928-1984 .... **CLC 42**
See also CA 113; SFW 4

Tey, Josephine
See Mackintosh, Elizabeth

Thackeray, William Makepeace 1811-1863 .
NCLC 5, 14, 22, 43, 169, 213; WLC 6
See also BRW 5; BRWC 2; CDBLB 1832-1890; DA; DA3; DAB; DAC; DAM MST, NOV; DLB 21, 55, 159, 163; NFS 13; RGEL 2; SATA 23; TEA; WLIT 3

Thakura, Ravindranatha
See Tagore, Rabindranath

Thames, C. H.
See Marlowe, Stephen

Tharoor, Shashi 1956- .... **CLC 70**
See also CA 141; CANR 91, 201; CN 6, 7

Thelwall, John 1764-1834 .... **NCLC 162**
See also DLB 93, 158

Thelwell, Michael Miles 1939- .... **CLC 22**
See also BW 2; CA 101

Theo, Ion
See Theodorescu, Ion N.

Theobald, Lewis, Jr.
See Lovecraft, H. P.

Theocritus c. 310B.C.- .... **CMLC 45**
See also AW 1; DLB 176; RGWL 2, 3

Theodorescu, Ion N. 1880-1967 ...... **CLC 80**
See also CA 167; 116; CDWLB 4; DLB 220; EWL 3

Theriault, Yves 1915-1983 .... **CLC 79**
See also CA 102; CANR 150; CCA 1; DAC; DAM MST; DLB 88; EWL 3

Therion, Master
  See Crowley, Edward Alexander
Theroux, Alexander 1939- .... **CLC 2, 25**
  See also CA 85-88; CANR 20, 63, 190; CN
  4, 5, 6, 7
Theroux, Alexander Louis
  See Theroux, Alexander
Theroux, Paul 1941- ... **CLC 5, 8, 11, 15, 28,
  46, 159, 303**
  See also AAYA 28; AMWS 8; BEST 89:4;
  BPFB 3; CA 33-36R; CANR 20, 45, 74,
  133, 179; CDALBS; CN 1, 2, 3, 4, 5, 6,
  7; CP 1; CPW 1; DA3; DAM POP; DLB
  2, 218; EWL 3; HGG; MAL 5; MTCW 1,
  2; MTFW 2005; RGAL 4; SATA 44, 109;
  TUS
Theroux, Paul Edward
  See Theroux, Paul
Thesen, Sharon 1946- .... **CLC 56**
  See also CA 163; CANR 125; CP 5, 6, 7;
  CWP
Thespis fl. 6th cent. B.C.- .... **CMLC 51**
  See also LMFS 1
Thevenin, Denis
  See Duhamel, Georges
Thibault, Jacques Anatole Francois
  See France, Anatole
Thiele, Colin 1920-2006 .... **CLC 17**
  See also CA 29-32R; CANR 12, 28, 53,
  105; CLR 27; CP 1, 2; DLB 289; MAI-
  CYA 1, 2; SAAS 2; SATA 14, 72, 125;
  YAW
Thiong'o, Ngugi Wa
  See Ngugi wa Thiong'o
Thistlethwaite, Bel
  See Wetherald, Agnes Ethelwyn
Thomas, Audrey (Callahan) 1935- .. **CLC 7,
  13, 37, 107, 289; SSC 20**
  See also AITN 2; CA 21-24R; 237; CAAE
  237; CAAS 19; CANR 36, 58; CN 2, 3,
  4, 5, 6, 7; DLB 60; MTCW 1; RGSF 2
Thomas, Augustus 1857-1934 .... **TCLC 97**
  See also MAL 5
Thomas, D.M. 1935- .... **CLC 13, 22, 31, 132**
  See also BPFB 3; BRWS 4; CA 61-64, 303;
  CAAE 303; CAAS 11; CANR 17, 45, 75;
  CDBLB 1960 to Present; CN 4, 5, 6, 7;
  CP 1, 2, 3, 4, 5, 6, 7; DA3; DLB 40, 207,
  299; HGG; INT CANR-17; MTCW 1, 2;
  MTFW 2005; RGHL; SFW 4
Thomas, Donald Michael
  See Thomas, D.M.
Thomas, Dylan 1914-1953 . **PC 2, 52; SSC 3,
  44; TCLC 1, 8, 45, 105; WLC 6**
  See also AAYA 45; BRWR 3; BRWS 1; CA
  104; 120; CANR 65; CDBLB 1945-1960;
  DA; DA3; DAB; DAC; DAM DRAM,
  MST, POET; DLB 13, 20, 139; EWL 3;
  EXPP; LAIT 3; MTCW 1, 2; MTFW
  2005; PAB; PFS 1, 3, 8; RGEL 2; RGSF
  2; SATA 60; TEA; WLIT 4; WP
Thomas, Dylan Marlais
  See Thomas, Dylan
Thomas, (Philip) Edward 1878-1917 ...... **PC
  53; TCLC 10**
  See also BRW 6; BRWS 3; CA 106; 153;
  DAM POET; DLB 19, 98, 156, 216; EWL
  3; PAB; RGEL 2
Thomas, J. F.
  See Fleming, Thomas
Thomas, Joyce Carol 1938- .... **CLC 35**
  See also AAYA 12, 54; BW 2, 3; CA 113;
  116; CANR 48, 114, 135, 206; CLR 19;
  DLB 33; INT CA-116; JRDA; MAICYA
  1, 2; MTCW 1, 2; MTFW 2005; SAAS 7;
  SATA 40, 78, 123, 137, 210; SATA-Essay
  137; WYA; YAW

Thomas, Lewis 1913-1993 .... **CLC 35**
  See also ANW; CA 85-88; 143; CANR 38,
  60; DLB 275; MTCW 1, 2
Thomas, M. Carey 1857-1935 ...... **TCLC 89**
  See also FW
Thomas, Paul
  See Mann, Thomas
Thomas, Piri 1928-2011 .. **CLC 17; HLCS 2**
  See also CA 73-76; HW 1; LLW; SSFS 28
Thomas, R(onald) S(tuart) 1913-2000 . **CLC
  6, 13, 48; PC 99**
  See also BRWS 12; CA 89-92; 189; CAAS
  4; CANR 30; CDBLB 1960 to Present;
  CP 1, 2, 3, 4, 5, 6, 7; DAB; DAM POET;
  DLB 27; EWL 3; MTCW 1; RGEL 2
Thomas, Ross (Elmore) 1926-1995 . **CLC 39**
  See also CA 33-36R; 150; CANR 22, 63;
  CMW 4
Thompson, Francis (Joseph) 1859-1907 ......
  TCLC 4
  See also BRW 5; CA 104; 189; CDBLB
  1890-1914; DLB 19; RGEL 2; TEA
Thompson, Francis Clegg
  See Mencken, H. L.
Thompson, Hunter S. 1937(?)-2005 . **CLC 9,
  17, 40, 104, 229**
  See also AAYA 45; BEST 89:1; BPFB 3;
  CA 17-20R; 236; CANR 23, 46, 74, 77,
  111, 133; CPW; CSW; DA3; DAM POP;
  DLB 185; MTCW 1, 2; MTFW 2005;
  TUS
Thompson, Hunter Stockton
  See Thompson, Hunter S.
Thompson, James Myers
  See Thompson, Jim
Thompson, Jim 1906-1977 .... **CLC 69**
  See also BPFB 3; CA 140; CMW 4; CPW;
  DLB 226; MSW
Thompson, Judith (Clare Francesca)
  1954- .... **CLC 39**
  See also CA 143; CD 5, 6; CWD; DFS 22;
  DLB 334
Thomson, James 1700-1748 ... **LC 16, 29, 40**
  See also BRWS 3; DAM POET; DLB 95;
  RGEL 2
Thomson, James 1834-1882 .... **NCLC 18**
  See also DAM POET; DLB 35; RGEL 2
Thoreau, Henry David 1817-1862 . **NCLC 7,
  21, 61, 138, 207; PC 30; WLC 6**
  See also AAYA 42; AMW; ANW; BYA 3;
  CDALB 1640-1865; DA; DA3; DAB;
  DAC; DAM MST; DLB 1, 183, 223, 270,
  298; LAIT 2; LMFS 1; NCFS 3; RGAL
  4; TUS
Thorndike, E. L.
  See Thorndike, Edward L(ee)
Thorndike, Edward L(ee) 1874-1949 . **TCLC
  107**
  See also CA 121
Thornton, Hall
  See Silverberg, Robert
Thorpe, Adam 1956- .... **CLC 176**
  See also CA 129; CANR 92, 160; DLB 231
Thorpe, Thomas Bangs 1815-1878 .... **NCLC
  183**
  See also DLB 3, 11, 248; RGAL 4
Thubron, Colin 1939- .... **CLC 163**
  See also CA 25-28R; CANR 12, 29, 59, 95,
  171; CN 5, 6, 7; DLB 204, 231
Thubron, Colin Gerald Dryden
  See Thubron, Colin
Thucydides c. 455B.C.-c. 399B.C. ..... **CMLC
  17, 117**
  See also AW 1; DLB 176; RGWL 2, 3;
  WLIT 8
Thumboo, Edwin Nadason 1933- .... **PC 30**
  See also CA 194; CP 1

Thurber, James 1894-1961 ... **CLC 5, 11, 25,
  125; SSC 1, 47, 137**
  See also AAYA 56; AMWS 1; BPFB 3;
  BYA 5; CA 73-76; CANR 17, 39; CDALB
  1929-1941; CWRI 5; DA; DA3; DAB;
  DAC; DAM DRAM, MST, NOV; DLB 4,
  11, 22, 102; EWL 3; EXPS; FANT; LAIT
  3; MAICYA 1, 2; MAL 5; MTCW 1, 2;
  MTFW 2005; RGAL 4; RGSF 2; SATA
  13; SSFS 1, 10, 19; SUFW; TUS
Thurber, James Grover
  See Thurber, James
Thurman, Wallace (Henry) 1902-1934 . **BLC
  1:3; HR 1:3; TCLC 6**
  See also BW 1, 3; CA 104; 124; CANR 81;
  DAM MULT; DLB 51
Tibullus c. 54B.C.-c. 18B.C. .... **CMLC 36**
  See also AW 2; DLB 211; RGWL 2, 3;
  WLIT 8
Ticheburn, Cheviot
  See Ainsworth, William Harrison
Ticknor, George 1791-1871 .... **NCLC 255**
  See also DLB 1, 59, 140, 235
Tieck, (Johann) Ludwig 1773-1853 ... **NCLC
  5, 46; SSC 31, 100**
  See also CDWLB 2; DLB 90; EW 5; IDTP;
  RGSF 2; RGWL 2, 3; SUFW
Tiger, Derry
  See Ellison, Harlan
Tilghman, Christopher 1946- .... **CLC 65**
  See also CA 159; CANR 135, 151; CSW;
  DLB 244
Tillich, Paul (Johannes) 1886-1965 ...... **CLC
  131**
  See also CA 5-8R; 25-28R; CANR 33;
  MTCW 1, 2
Tillinghast, Richard (Williford) 1940- . **CLC
  29**
  See also CA 29-32R; CAAS 23; CANR 26,
  51, 96; CP 2, 3, 4, 5, 6, 7; CSW
Tillman, Lynne (?)- .... **CLC 231, 312**
  See also CA 173; CANR 144, 172
Timrod, Henry 1828-1867 .... **NCLC 25**
  See also DLB 3, 248; RGAL 4
Tindall, Gillian (Elizabeth) 1938- ..... **CLC 7**
  See also CA 21-24R; CANR 11, 65, 107;
  CN 1, 2, 3, 4, 5, 6, 7
Ting Ling
  See Chiang, Pin-chin
Tiptree, James, Jr.
  See Sheldon, Alice Hastings Bradley
Tirone Smith, Mary-Ann 1944- ...... **CLC 39**
  See also CA 118; 136; CANR 113, 210;
  SATA 143
Tirso de Molina 1580(?)-1648 .... **DC 13;
  HLCS 2; LC 73**
  See also RGWL 2, 3
Titmarsh, Michael Angelo
  See Thackeray, William Makepeace
Tocqueville, Alexis (Charles Henri Maurice
  Clerel Comte) de 1805-1859 . **NCLC 7,
  63**
  See also EW 6; GFL 1789 to the Present;
  TWA
Toe, Tucker
  See Westlake, Donald E.
Toer, Pramoedya Ananta 1925-2006 .... **CLC
  186**
  See also CA 197; 251; CANR 170; DLB
  348; RGWL 3
Toffler, Alvin 1928- .... **CLC 168**
  See also CA 13-16R; CANR 15, 46, 67,
  183; CPW; DAM POP; MTCW 1, 2
Toibin, Colm 1955- .... **CLC 162, 285**
  See also CA 142; CANR 81, 149, 213; CN
  7; DLB 271

Literary Criticism Series
Cumulative Topic Index

This index lists all topic entries in Gale's *Children's Literature Review* (CLR), *Classical and Medieval Literature Criticism* (CMLC), *Contemporary Literary Criticism* (CLC), *Drama Criticism* (DC), *Literature Criticism from 1400 to 1800* (LC), *Nineteenth-Century Literature Criticism* (NCLC), *Short Story Criticism* (SSC), and *Twentieth-Century Literary Criticism* (TCLC). The index also lists topic entries in the Gale Critical Companion Collection, which includes the following publications: *The Beat Generation* (BG), *Feminism in Literature* (FL), *Gothic Literature* (GL), and *Harlem Renaissance* (HR).

Topic Index

Topic Index

Topic Index

DC Cumulative Nationality Index

ALGERIAN

Camus, Albert **2**

AMERICAN

Albee, Edward **11**
Anderson, Maxwell **43**
Baldwin, James **1**
Baraka, Amiri **6**
Brown, William Wells **1**
Bullins, Ed **6**
Chase, Mary Coyle **1**
Childress, Alice **4**
Chin, Frank **7**
Cleage, Pearl **32**
Edson, Margaret **24**
Elder, Lonne III **8**
Eliot, T. S. **28**
Foote, Horton **42**
Fornés, Mariá Irene **10**
Fuller, Charles H., Jr. **1**
Gale, Zona **30**
Glaspell, Susan **10**
Gordone, Charles **8**
Green, Paul **37**
Gray, Spalding **7**
Gremké, Angelina Weld **38**
Guare, John **20**
Hansberry, Lorraine **2**
Hellman, Lillian **1**
Henley, Beth **6, 14**
Howard, Sidney **42**
Howe, Tina **43**
Hughes, Langston **3**
Hurston, Zora Neale **12**
Hwang, David Henry **4, 23**
Inge, William **37**
James, Henry **41**
Kaufman, George S. **17**
Kaufman, Moises **26**
Kennedy, Adrienne **5**
Kopit, Arthur **37**
Kramer, Larry **8**
Kushner, Tony **10**
MacLeish, Archibald **43**
Mamet, David **4, 24**
Mann, Emily **7**
McCullers, Carson **35**
McNally, Terrence **27**
Miller, Arthur **1, 31**
Moraga, Cherríe **22**
Norman, Marsha **8**
Odets, Clifford **6**
O'Neill, Eugene **20**
Parker, Dorothy **40**
Parks, Suzan-Lori **23**
Rabe, David **16**

Rice, Elmer **44**
Saroyan, William **28**
Shange, Ntozake **3**
Shepard, Sam **5**
Sherwood, Robert E. **36**
Simon, Neil **14**
Sondheim, Stephen **22**
Stein, Gertrude **19**
Terry, Megan **13**
Uhry, Alfred **28**
Valdez, Luis **10**
Vogel, Paula **19**
Wasserstein, Wendy **4**
Wilder, Thornton **1, 24**
Williams, Tennessee **4**
Wilson, August **2, 31**
Wilson, Lanford **19**
Zindel, Paul **5**

AUSTRIAN

Bernhard, Thomas **14**
Grillparzer, Franz **14**
Handke, Peter **17**
Hofmannsthal, Hugo von **4**
Schnitzler, Arthur **17**

BARBADIAN

Kennedy, Adrienne **5**

BELGIAN

Ghelderode, Michel de **15**
Maeterlinck, Maurice **32**

CANADIAN

Highway, Tomson **33**
Pollock, Sharon **20**

CUBAN

Fornés, Mariá Irene **10**
Triana, José **39**

CZECH

Chapek, Karel **1**
Havel, Václav **6**

DUTCH

Bernhard, Thomas **14**

ENGLISH

Ayckbourn, Alan **13**
Beaumont, Francis **6**
Beddoes, Thomas Lovell **15**
Behn, Aphra **4**
Bond, Edward **45**
Byron, Lord **24**
Centlivre, Susanna **25**
Chapman, George **19**

Christie, Agatha **39**
Churchill, Caryl **5**
Congreve, William **2**
Coward, Noël **45**
Dekker, Thomas **12**
Delaney, Shelagh **45**
Dryden, John **3**
Edgar, David **44**
Eliot, T. S. **28**
Etherege, George **23**
Farquhar, George **38**
Fletcher, John **6**
Ford, John **8**
Frayn, Michael **27**
Fry, Christopher **36**
Gay, John **39**
Greene, Graham **41**
Hare, David **26**
Heywood, Thomas **29**
Jonson, Ben **4**
Kane, Sarah **31**
Kureishi, Hanif **26**
Kyd, Thomas **3**
Lawrence, D. H. **44**
Lyly, John **7**
Marlowe, Christopher **1**
Marston, John **37**
Massinger, Philip **39**
Middleton, Thomas **5, 40**
Orton, Joe **3**
Osborne, John **38**
Otway, Thomas **24**
Peele, George **27**
Pinter, Harold **15**
Rattigan, Terence **18**
Rowley, William **43**
Shaffer, Peter **7**
Shaw, George Bernard **23**
Sheridan, Richard Brinsley **1**
Shirley, James **25**
Stoppard, Tom **6, 30**
Storey, David **40**
Vanbrugh, John **40**
Webster, John **2**
Wilde, Oscar **17**
Wycherley, William **41**

FRENCH

Anouilh, Jean **8, 21**
Arrabal, Fernando **35**
Artaud, Antonin **14**
Beaumarchais, Pierre-Augustin Caron de **4**
Beckett, Samuel **22**
Becque, Henri **21**
Camus, Albert **2**
Cocteau, Jean **17**

Corneille, Pierre **21**
Dumas, Alexandre, fils **1**
Genet, Jean **25**
Giraudoux, Jean **36**
Hugo, Victor **38**
Ionesco, Eugène **12**
Joyce, James **16**
Marivaux, Pierre Carlet de Chamblain de **7**
Mérimée, Prosper **33**
Molière **13**
Musset, Alfred de **27**
Racine, Jean **32**
Reza, Yasmina **34**
Rostand, Edmond **10**
Sand, George **29**
Séjour, Victor **10**
Sartre, Jean-Paul **3**
Scribe, Eugène **5**
Triana, José **39**

GERMAN

Brecht, Bertolt **3**
Borchert, Wolfgang **42**
Georg Büchner **35**
Goethe, Johann Wolfgang von **20**
Hauptmann, Gerhart **34**
Hebbel, Friedrich **21**
Kleist, Heinrich von **29**
Lessing, G. E. **26**
Schiller, Friedrich von **12**
Weiss, Peter **36**

GREEK

Aeschylus **8**
Aristophanes **2**
Euripides **4**
Menander **3**
Sophocles **1**

IRISH

Farquhar, George **38**
Friel, Brian **8**
Goldsmith, Oliver **8**
O'Casey, Sean **12**
Sheridan, Richard Brinsley **1**
Synge, John Millington **2**
Yeats, William Butler **33**

ITALIAN

Fo, Dario **10**
Machiavelli, Niccolò **16**
Pirandello, Luigi **5**
Plautus **6**

JAPANESE

Mishima, Yukio **1**
Zeami **7**

MARTINICAN

Césaire, Aimé **22**

NIGERIAN

Clark Bekedermo, John Pepper **5**
Soyinka, Wole **2**

NORWEGIAN

Ibsen, Henrik **2, 30**

ROMAN

Plautus **6**
Seneca, Lucius Annaeus **5**
Terence **7**

ROMANIAN

Ionesco, Eugène **12**

RUSSIAN

Chekhov, Anton **9**
Gogol, Nikolai **1**
Turgenev, Ivan **7**

SOUTH AFRICAN

Fugard, Athol **3**

SPANISH

Arrabal, Fernando **35**
Benavente, Jacinto **26**
Buero Vallejo, Antonio **18**
Calderón de la Barca, Pedro **3**
Casona, Alejandro **32**
García Lorca, Federico **2**
Mihura, Miguel **34**
Molina, Tirso de **13**
Unamuno, Miguel de **45**
Vega, Lope de **44**

ST. LUCIAN

Walcott, Derek **7**

SWEDISH

Strindberg, August **18**
Weiss, Peter **36**

DC Cumulative Title Index

Title Index

Title Index

Title Index

"The Vision of Ben Jonson on the Muses of
His Friend M. Dayton" (Jonson) **4**:250
The Visioning (Glaspell) **10**:170, 172, 182
La visita del Angel (Triana) **39**:296
Une visite de Noces (Dumas) **1**:104-05, 108-09,
119
"Visitor from Forest Hills" (Simon) **14**:368
"Visitor from Hollywood" (Simon) **14**:367
"Visitor from Mamaroneck" (Simon) **14**:366
Visňevyi sad (Chekhov) **9**:8, 10-11, 14-17, 19-
21, 32, 37-8, 43-4, 46-50, 52-3, 55, 57-61,
63-4, 66, 72, 77-87, 90, 92-3, 95-6, 107-08,
111, 116-22, 127-30, 150-56, 158-59, 168,
172-73, 176, 180, 183-84, 188, 190, 217,
227-32, 241, 251, 259, 264, 268-69, 272,
280, 282-83, 290, 292, 196, 305, 318, 320,
329-72
La vita che ti diedi (Pirandello) **5**:195, 202-05
Vitoria (Vega) **44**:208, 213
La viuda valenciana (Vega) **44**:238
¡Viva lo imposible! (Mihura) **34**:120, 127-31,
139, 141-42, 144-45
Vließ (Grillparzer)
See *Das goldene Vließ*
La Voix humaine (Cocteau) **17**:34-7
Vole-moi un petit milliard (Arrabal) **35**:64
Les Volontaires de 1814 (Sejour) **10**:334, 339,
342
Volpone; or, the Foxe (Jonson) **4**:226-27, 236-
59, 261-62, 264-67, 269, 272, 276, 283, 291
Volunteers (Friel) **8**:212, 215-16, 251
The Volunteers of 1814 (Sejour)
See *Les Volontaires de 1814*
Vor dem Ruhestand (Bernhard) **14**:111, 114,
120, 128, 136, 145, 149, 155, 160-61, 165,
171, 200-08, 217
Vor Sonnenaufgang (Hauptmann) **34**:5, 12-16,
29-34, 36, 40-45, 47, 49-56, 58-59, 84, 88,
107-8, 110
*Vorrei morire anche adesso se sapessi che non
è servito a niente* (Fo) **10**:10, 18
The Vortex (Coward) **45**:134, 137-38, 161, 166-
72, 177, 183-86, 194, 213
The Voyage (Hwang) **23**:175
Voyage (Stoppard) **30**:263, 343, 345-47, 349-
52, 354, 358-64
Voyage to the Sonorous Land (Handke)
See *Das Spiel vom Fragen oder Die Reise
zum Sonoren Land*
Le voyageur sans bagage (Anouilh) **8**:71, 74-6,
78; **21**:3, 6, 14, 20-1, 23, 25-6
The Vultures (Becque)
See *Les corbeaux*
Waga tomo Hittōrā (Mishima) **1**:356
Wagatomo Hitler (Mishima)
See *Waga tomo Hittōrā*
Waiting for Godot (Beckett)
See *En attendant Godot*
Waiting for Lefty (Odets) **6**:205, 207-14, 219,
223, 230-34
Waiting in the Wings (Coward) **45**:182-83
The Wake (Henley)
See *The Wake of Jamey Foster*
The Wake of Jamey Foster (Henley) **6**:181, 183-
84, 189-90, 193; **14**:309, 318-21, 331
Wake Up, Jonathan (Rice) **44**:142, 162, 177
A Walk on the Water (Stoppard) **6**:298-99, 345
Walking through Walls (Terry) **13**:302
"The Wall" (Sartre)
See "Le Mur"
Wallenstein (Schiller) **12**:348-49, 351, 360, 369,
372-76, 378-81, 386, 390-92, 395-96, 398-
401, 406-15
Wallenstein's Camp (Schiller)
See *Wallenstein*
Wallenstein's Death (Schiller)
See *Wallenstein*
Wallenstein's Lager (Schiller)
See *Wallenstein*
Wallenstein's Tod (Schiller)
See *Wallenstein*

Walsh (Pollock) **20**:296-98, 301-03, 306-07,
310-11, 314-21, 325-26, 328, 330, 334, 338-
39, 343-44, 351
Waltz (Sondheim)
See *Do I Hear a Waltz?*
The Waltz of the Toreadors (Anouilh)
See *La valse des toréadors*
War Ceremonial (Triana)
See *Ceremonial de guerra*
The War Plays (Bond) **45**:119, 123, 125-26,
128
The Warder (Centlivre) **25**:8
The Wasps (Aristophanes)
See *Sphēkes*
Watch on the Rhine (Hellman) **1**:179-84, 188-
91, 193, 208
The Watch on the Rhine (Stein) **19**:219
The Water Engine: An American Fable
(Mamet) **4**:298-301, 306, 334
Waterloo Bridge (Sherwood) **36**:174, 178-79
Watsonville: Some Place Not Here (Moraga)
22:229, 232
The Way of Perfection (Stein) **19**:238
The Way of the World (Congreve) **2**:110-16,
120-23, 125-26, 130, 136-51
The Way to the Flower (Zeami)
See *Shikadō*
Way Upstream (Ayckbourn) **13**:23
We Can't Pay We Won't Pay! (Fo)
See *Non si paga non si paga*
We Come To The River (Bond) **45**:12, 42, 44,
50
We Do Not Know How (Pirandello)
See *Non si sa come*
We Righteous Bombers (Bullins) **6**:119, 133
We the People (Rice) **44**:142, 144, 146-48, 153,
172
We Won't Pay! We Won't Pay! (Fo)
See *Non si paga non si paga*
Wealth (Aristophanes)
See *Ploutos*
The Weaver of Dreams (Buero Vallejo)
See *La tejedora de sueños*
The Weavers (Hauptmann)
See *Die Weber*
Die Weber (Hauptmann) **34**:5, 29-30, 32-34,
58, 64, 66-69, 72, 75-80, 84-85, 87-88,
107-8, 110-11
The Wedding (Chekhov)
See *Svadba*
The Wedding (Shirley) **25**:214-15, 217, 220,
241, 249, 251, 255, 310-11
The Wedding at Cana (Fo)
See *Le nozze di Cana*
*Wedding Band: A Love/Hate Story in Black
and White* (Childress) **4**:68-70, 77, 81-8,
91
A Wedding Bouquet (Stein) **19**:252
The Wedding Feast of Canaan (Fo)
See *Le nozze di Cana*
The Wedding on the Eiffel Tower (Cocteau)
See *Les mariés de la Tour Eiffel*
The Weevil (Plautus)
See *Curculio*
Der Weg ins Freie (Schnitzler) **17**:202
Weh dem, der lügt! (Grillparzer) **14**:251, 254-
57, 295
The Weight of the World (Handke)
See *Das Gewicht der Welt*
Weihnachtseinkäufe (Schnitzler) **17**:184, 195,
197-200, 202-03, 210-13, 269
Weissagung (Handke) **17**:53-5
Welded (O'Neill) **20**:205, 207, 230, 248
The Well of Immortality (Yeats) **33**:133
The Well of the Saints (Synge) **2**:392-93, 395,
400, 407, 415
Der Weltverbesserer (Bernhard) **14**:111-12, 135,
144, 148, 155, 200
Werner (Byron) **24**:5-6, 9, 28-9
West Side Story (Sondheim) **22**:272-73, 279-81,
285, 287, 289, 292-96, 299-300, 307, 310-
11, 314, 317, 323, 325, 327, 331

Westward Ho (Dekker) **12**:7-8, 80
Wharton Dance (Foote) **42**:60, 64
The What D'Ye Call It (Gay) **39**:30-33, 36-42,
47, 50-53, 55, 58, 62, 71, 96, 104
What Happened: A Five Act Play (Stein)
19:183, 198-200, 205-06, 212
What Is Literature? (Sartre)
See *Qu'est-ce que la littérature?*
What Price Glory? (Anderson) **43**:5, 8, 12, 38-
39, 52
What the Butler Saw (Orton) **3**:393, 396-97,
399-400, 402-03, 405, 408, 412, 417,
419-25
"What the Twilight Says: An Overture"
(Walcott) **7**:310, 324
What Where (Beckett) **22**:46, 54-7, 63, 111
What You Will (Marston) **37**:214-15, 217, 227,
237-39, 251, 253, 255, 258, 320, 328, 359-
60, 363-67
When a Darkness Falls (Zindel) **5**:406-07
When Dinah Shore Ruled the Earth
(Wasserstein) **4**:346
When Five Years Pass (García Lorca)
See *Así que pasen cinco años*
When One Is Somebody (Pirandello)
See *Quando si è qualcuno*
When Someone is Somebody (Pirandello)
See *Quando si è qualcuno*
When the Jack Hollers (Hughes) **3**:275
When the Rattlesnake Sounds (Childress) **4**:78
When We Dead Awaken (Ibsen)
See *Når vi døde vågner*
Where Are They Now? (Stoppard) **30**:233, 238,
255
Where Has Tommy Flowers Gone? (McNally)
27:50
"Where It Is Thin, There It Breaks" (Turgenev
)
See "Gde tanko, tam i rvetsa"
"Where the Thread's Weakest, There It
Breaks" (Turgenev)
See "Gde tanko, tam i rvetsa"
Where There Is Nothing (Yeats) **33**:153-54, 167,
289, 307
Where's Daddy? (Inge) **37**:38, 40-41, 52-53,
65, 72-73
While the Sun Shines (Rattigan) **18**:103, 110,
114, 118, 141
Whiskey (McNally) **27**:48, 50
Whiskey Six Cadenza (Pollock) **20**:307, 311-12,
320-22, 324
White Desert (Anderson) **43**:5, 46-48
The White Devil (Webster) **2**:422-58
White Dresses (Green) **37**:21, 25, 27
"The White Liars" (Shaffer) **7**:203, 206
"White Lies" (Shaffer) **7**:184
The White Woman (Scribe)
See *La dame blanche*
Who Is Sylvia? (Rattigan) **18**:103, 108, 113-15,
128
Whom Do I Have the Honour of Addressing?
(Shaffer) **7**:184
Whore (Ford)
See *'Tis Pity She's a Whore*
The Whore of Babylon (Dekker) **12**:8, 10-2,
23-5, 35, 40-1
Who's Afraid of Virginia Woolf? (Albee) **11**:5-
12, 19-21, 23, 25-30, 32-3, 36-8, 40-1, 45-
50, 52-62, 67-76, 78-82, 84-6, 88, 90-7,
106-10, 113-15, 118-21, 125-26, 128-33,
135, 148, 150, 175-76, 179, 181-237, 240,
243, 245-49, 251-52, 259-60, 166-68, 274-
75, 277-78, 284-87, 289-94, 297, 299-301,
305, 309-12, 319, 326, 329, 336-37, 358,
362-63, 365, 370
Who's the Dupe? (Centlivre) **25**:16
Why She Would Not (Shaw) **23**:260
The Widow (Fornés) **10**:94, 116, 124
The Widow (Menander) **3**:346
The Widow (Middleton) **5**:140